MW00424193

THE EVANGELICAL DICTIONARY
of WORLD RELIGIONS

THE
EVANGELICAL
DICTIONARY
of WORLD
RELIGIONS

GENERAL EDITOR
H. WAYNE HOUSE

CONSULTING EDITORS
ROBERT M. BOWMAN JR.
IRVING HEXHAM

ASSOCIATE EDITORS	ASSISTANT EDITORS
ANTHONY W. BARBER	ALAN GOMES
JAMES BJORNSTAD	ROBERT PASSANTINO
WINFRIED CORDUAN	GRETCHEN PASSANTINO
ERIC PEMENT	STEPHEN ROST

BakerBooks
a division of Baker Publishing Group
Grand Rapids, Michigan

Library of Congress Cataloging-in-Publication Data
Names: House, H. Wayne, editor.
Title: The Evangelical dictionary of world religions / H. Wayne House, ed.
Description: Grand Rapids : Baker Publishing Group, 2018. | Includes bibliographical references and index.
Identifiers: LCCN 2017055472 | ISBN 9780801013232 (cloth : alk. paper)
Subjects: LCSH: Christianity and other religions—Dictionaries. | Religions—Dictionaries. |
    Christianity—Dictionaries.
Classification: LCC BR127 .E89 2018 | DDC 261.203—dc23
LC record available at https://lccn.loc.gov/2017055472

18 19 20 21 22 23 24   7 6 5 4 3 2 1

In memory of Bob and Gretchen Passantino,
who both passed away in the midst of this project.
They were dear friends,
and I cherished their friendship for many years.

And in memory of my late wife, Leta,
who gave me encouragement on this project from its beginning.

CONTENTS

LIST OF ENTRIES

CONTRIBUTORS

ABANES, RICHARD. Award-winning author/ journalist and actor who has written extensively on world religions. *Feng Shui; Holy Spirit, Misconceptions about; Native Americans, Mormon View of; Stigmata*

AECHTNER, REBECCA. PhD, University of Edinburgh. Assistant Curate, Lancaster Priority Church. *Rama, Swami; Shiva; Yogananda, Swami Paramahansa*

AECHTNER, THOMAS. PhD, University of Oxford. Senior Lecturer in Religion and Science, University of Queensland. *Sannyasa; Satori; Wahhabiyya Islam*

BARBER, ANTHONY W. PhD, University of Wisconsin, Madison. Director of Asian Studies and Associate Professor of Communication and Culture, University of Calgary. *Bardo; Book of the Dead, Tibetan; Buddha, Names of; Darshana; Kalacakra; Tantra; Li Chi / Liji; Nichiren Daishonin; Nichiren Shoshu; Sai Baba, Sathya; Shih Ching / Shijing; Taoism/Daoism*

BATES, TODD M. PhD, University of Texas, Arlington. Professor of Philosophy, California Baptist University. *Apostles, Belief in the Modern Existence of*

BECKWITH, FRANCIS J. PhD, Fordham University. Professor of Philosophy and Church-State Studies and Associate Director of Graduate Studies, Baylor University. *God, Mormon View of*

BJORNSTAD, JAMES. PhD, New York University. Executive Director, Institute of Contemporary Christianity. *Adonai-Shomo; Arhat; Beth el Shaddai Messianic Fellowship; Bodhi; Bodhicitta; Brahma; Butsu-dan; Chela; Da'wah; Fana (or Fanaa); Fiqh; Gathas; Ghanta; Gyatso, Geshe Kelsang; Ichinen Sanzen; Kami; Khalsa; Mandala Diagram; Namaste; Occult; Prasadam; Sankirtana; Smriti; Sutra; Tirthankara*

BORLAND, JAMES A. ThD, Grace Theological Seminary. Professor of Philosophy and Theology, Liberty University. *Shruti/Sruti*

BOWMAN, ROBERT M., JR. PhD, South African Theological Seminary. Executive Director, Institute for Religious Research. *Apostles, Belief in the Modern Existence of; Book of Abraham; Book of Mormon; Book of Moses; Christian, Use and Misuse of the Term; Church of Jesus Christ of Latter-day Saints; Doctrine and Covenants; False Prophecy; Heaven, Biblical Doctrine of; Jehovah's Witnesses (JW); Jesus, Mormon View of; John 1:1; New World Translation; Pearl of Great Price, The; Reformed Egyptian; Smith, Joseph, Jr.; Standard Works; Talmage, James; Telestial Kingdom; Terrestrial Kingdom; Tetragrammaton*

BRANCH, CRAIG. MRE. Researcher and Writer; Former Director of the Apologetics Resource Center. *Chakras*

CANER, EMIR. PhD, University of Texas at Arlington. President, Truett-McConnell University. *Muslim, Nation of Islam*

CANER, ERGUN. ThD, University of South Africa. Apologist, author, and minister. *Sikh Foundation; Zoroaster*

CARRIGAN, CKY J. PhD, Southeastern Baptist Theological Seminary. Executive Associate Pastor of Administration and Small Groups, Cornerstone Bible Church. *Book of Abraham; Cowdery, Oliver; Dark Skin Curse; Smith, Joseph, III; Talmage, James; Temples in Mormonism*

COLANTER, EDDIE N. MA, Faith and Culture, and MA, Bioethics, Trinity Graduate School, Trinity International University. Vice-Chair and Cofounder of the Intelligent Design and Evolution Awareness Center. Adjunct Professor, University of San Diego. *Ahura Mazda*

COOK, DAVID B. PhD, University of Chicago. Associate Professor of Religious Studies, Rice University. *Dhimmi; Islam, Basic Beliefs of; Islam, Eschatology of; Jihad; Jizya; Mevlevi Order; Muhammad; Qur'an; Shari'ah; Sufism*

CORDUAN, WINFRIED. PhD, Rice University. Professor Emeritus of Philosophy and Religion, Taylor University. *Ahmadiyya Islam; Avesta; Soka Gakkai; Yogi; Yoni; Zarathustra (Nietzsche); Zohar*

COWAN, STEVEN B. PhD, University of Arkansas. *Buddhist Scriptures; Jesus, Historical Evidence for; Providence of God; Revelation, General*

DEMY, TIMOTHY J. ThD, Dallas Theological Seminary; PhD, Salve Regina University. Professor of Leadership and Ethics, US Naval War College. *Ahmad, Mirza Ghulam; Bahá'u'lláh; Sankara; War and Peace in World Religions*

DEW, JAMES K., JR. PhD, Southeast Baptist Theological Seminary. Assistant Professor

of Philosophy of the History of Ideas and Philosophy, Southeastern Baptist Theological Seminary. *Adventist Movement; Unitarianism*

DROUHARD, ROBERT L. MA, Faith Evangelical Seminary. Independent Researcher. *Amesha Spentas; Avidya; Baptism, Christian; Baptism, Non-Christian; Bazm-e-Tolu-e-Islam; Bible, Canon of; Buddhist Churches of America; Day of Judgment, Islamic; Dhikr; Druze, The; Dualism; Eternal Life; Fravashi; Gassho; Guru; Guru Dev; Guru Nanak Dev; Hadith; Injil; Madhyamaka; Maharishi Mahesh Yogi; Martial Arts, East Asian; Maya; Miller, William; Millerite Movement; Nabuwwat; Nephites; P'u/Pu; Saoshyant; Seicho-No-Ie; Sema; Suluk; Sunnah; Sunyata; Swami; Ten Lost Tribes, Alternative Views of; Torii; Twelve Tribes; Tzaddik; Zoroastrianism*

EASTERLING, JOHN. DMin, DMiss, Trinity Evangelical Divinity School. Professor of Intercultural Studies, University of Northwestern, St. Paul. *Telestial Kingdom; Terrestrial Kingdom*

FATOVIC, DARIJA. MA, London School of Economics and Political Science. Director, Panacea First Aid Training, London (UK). *Rites of Passage; Rituals*

FRUCHTENBAUM, ARNOLD. PhD, New York University. Founder and Director, Ariel Ministries. *Bar/Bat Mitzvah; Halacha; Hanukkah (or Chanukah), Feast of; Hasidism; Judaism; Kosher (Kasher); Mikveh/Mikvaot; Pesach (Passover); Purim (the Feast of Lots); Rosh Hashanah (the Feast of Trumpets); Shabbat (the Sabbath), Jewish; Shavuot (the Feast of Weeks); Sukkoth (the Feast of Tabernacles); Synagogue; Talmud; Tanach; Torah; Yom Kippur (Day of Atonement)*

GEISLER, NORMAN L. PhD, Loyola University of Chicago. Chancellor, Distinguished Professor of Theology and Apologetics, and Norman L. Geisler Chair of Christian

Apologetics, Veritas International University. *Openness of God; Roman Catholicism*

GIBBS, JEREMIAH W. S. MTS, Garrett Evangelical Theological Seminary. Co-Chaplain and Director of the Lantz Center for Christian Vocations and Formation, University of Indianapolis. *Azusa Street Revival; Baptism in the Holy Spirit, Pentecostal View of*

GOMES, ALAN W. PhD, Fuller Theological Seminary. Professor of Historical Theology, Talbot School of Theology; Senior Research Fellow, Phoenix Seminary. *Arianism; Christianity, Protestant; Pelagianism*

GREGORY, S. L. *Kabbalah*

GROOTHUIS, DOUGLAS R. PhD, University of Oregon. Professor of Philosophy, Denver Seminary. *Christian; Monotheism; Religion*

HABERMAS, GARY R. PhD, Michigan State University. Distinguished Research Professor of Apologetics and Philosophy and Chairman of the Department of Philosophy and Theology, Liberty University. *Resurrection of Jesus*

HAUSAM, MARK C. PhD, University of Wales, Lampeter. *Arihant (Jainism); Báb; Jina*

HEXHAM, IRVING. PhD, University of Bristol. Professor, Department of Religious Studies, University of Calgary. *bin Laden, Osama bin Muhammad bin 'Awad; Liturgy; Myth; Mythology; Rama; Ramana Maharishi; Revelation; Sociology of Religion; Wisdom, Biblical View of; World Council of Churches*

HOLDEN, JOSEPH. PhD, University of Wales, Lampeter. President, Professor of Theology and Apologetics, Veritas International University. *Tawrat; Zabur*

HOLDING, JAMES PATRICK. MA, Library Science, Florida State University. President, Tekton Education and Apologetics Ministries. *Effendi, Shoghi; Nephites; Polygamy; Reformed Egyptian*

HOUSE, H. WAYNE. ThD, Concordia Seminary; JD, Regent University School of Law. Distinguished Research Professor of Theology, Law & Culture, Faith International University and Faith Seminary. *'Abdu'l-Bahá; Ahimsa; Ali, Maulana Muhammad; American Zen College; Analects, The; Anekantavada; Animism; Aurobindo, Sri; Auroville International; Avatar; Bhajan, Yogi; Book of Mencius (Meng-tzu); Book of the Dead, Egyptian; Caste; Chalcedonian Controversy; Chinmaya Mission; Chinmayananda, Swami; Chinmoy, Sri; Christian Zionism; Ch'un Ch'iu / Chunqiu; Dalai Lama XIV (Tenzin Gyatso); Eastern Orthodoxy; Evangelicalism; Gabriel the Archangel, Non-Christian Views of; Gabriel the Archangel in the Bible; Great Learning, The; Guru Granth Sahib; Heretic; Hsiao-ching/Xiaojing; Jainism; Jehovah; Juzu; Kalacakra; Knights Templar; Ko-ji-ki; Lieh-tzu/Liezi; Lingam; Logos; Maronite Christians; Muhammad, Elijah; Orthodoxy; Pratyeka Buddha; Quorum of the Seventy; Reincarnation; Ren/Jen; Sacraments; Sacred Fire; Shaykh/Sheikh; Sikh Dharma; Tao Te Ching / Dao de jing; Tawheed; Trikaya; Upanishads; Vedanta; Word of Wisdom; Xiao/Hsiao; Yidam; Zhuang-zi/Chuang-tzu; Zionism*

HUGGINS, RONALD V. ThD, University of Toronto, Wycliffe College, Toronto School of Theology. *Apostasy, Mormon View of; Articles of Faith, Mormon; Deification, Christian View of; Deification, Mormon View of; Gospel of Barnabas; Heresy, Definition of; Joseph Smith Translation of the Bible; Lost Books of the Bible, Mormon View of; Monophysitism; Monothelitism; Nibley, Hugh Winder; Origen on Preexistence*

HUX, CLETE. MDiv, Birmingham Theological Seminary. Director, Apologetics Resource Center. *Angels; Kundalini*

JOHNSON, ERIC. MDiv, Bethel Seminary. Researcher, Mormonism Research Ministry.

Confucianism; Golden Temple; Guru Nanak Dev; International Society for Krishna Consciousness (ISKCON); Karmi; Krishna Consciousness; Lamanites; Prabhupada, Abhay Charan de Bhaktivedanta Swami; Shinto; Sikhism; Young, Brigham; Zion, Mormon Beliefs about

JOHNSON, PHILIP. MTh, Australian College of Theology. Visiting Lecturer, Morling College. *Ananda Marga Yoga Society; Anandamurti, Shrii Shrii; Bhakti Yoga; Bhikkhu; Brahma Kumaris World Spiritual Organization; Divination in the Bible; Friends of the Western Buddhist Order; Fundamentalism, Christian; Japa Yoga; Paramahansa, Swami Muktananda; Raja Yoga; Siddha Yoga; Vipasyana; World's Parliament of Religions (1893 and 1993)*

JONES, ANDREW D. MDiv, Trinity Evangelical Divinity School. Pastor of Spiritual Formation, Christ Community Church. *Blood Transfusions*

JOWERS, DENNIS W. PhD, University of Edinburgh. Professor of Theology and Apologetics, Faith Evangelical College and Seminary. *Apologetics; Atonement; Christ, Natures and Attributes of; Conditional Immortality; Docetism; Justification, Biblical Doctrine of; Modalism; Monarchianism; Neo-orthodox Christianity; Polytheism; Socinianism; Trinitarian Controversies; Trinity, The*

KEMP, HUGH P. PhD, Victoria University of Wellington. *Bodhidharma; Bodhisattva; Buddha, Historical Person of; Dharma; Dharmakaya; Hinayana; Karma; Koan; Kumbha Mela; Kwan Yin; Lotus Sutra; Mahayana Buddhism; Maitreya; Mantra; Mudra; Nirvana; Nyingma; Pali Canon; Prana; Pranayama; Puja; Pure Land Buddhism; Samadhi; Sangha; Tantra; Tantric Yoga; Tibetan Buddhism; Tripitaka; Zen Buddhism*

KERNS, TRAVIS S. PhD, Southern Baptist Theological Seminary. Coordinator, SEND North America: Salt Lake City, North American Mission Board. *Danites; Mountain Meadows Massacre; Smith, Joseph F.; Smith, Joseph Fielding; Theological Method of the Church of Jesus Christ of Latter-day Saints*

KIM, CHANG HAN. PhD, University of Calgary. Sessional Instructor, Booth University College, Canada. *Sabbatarianism*

LOFTIN, R. KEITH. PhD, University of Aberdeen. Assistant Professor of Philosophy and Humanities and Assistant Dean, Southwestern Baptist Theological Seminary. *Materialism; Michael the Archangel*

LYONS, JANICE. RN. Director, Current Issues in Alternative Medicine. *Reiki*

MACGREGOR, KIRK R. PhD, University of Iowa. Assistant Professor of Philosophy and Religion, McPherson College. *Eightfold Path*

MANGES, ERNEST B. PhD, University of Edinburgh. Facilitator, EQUIP, Evangelical Free Church of America. *Mariolatry*

MCKEEVER, WILLIAM. Director, Mormonism Research Ministry. *Benson, Ezra Taft; Celestial Kingdom; Genealogies, Mormon; Harris, Martin; Heavenly Mother; Journal of Discourses; Lucifer, Mormon View of; Pratt, Orson; Pratt, Parley; Smith Bidamon, Emma; Snow, Lorenzo; Taylor, John; Urim and Thummim, Mormon Use of*

MEISTER, CHAD V. PhD, Marquette University. Professor of Philosophy, Bethel College, Indiana. *Four Noble Truths; Panentheism*

PEMENT, ERIC. MDiv, North Park Theological Seminary. Executive Director, Evangelical Ministries to New Religions; Research Associate, Centers for Apologetics Research. *Annihilationism; Community of Christ; Dark Skin Curse; Gohonzon; Lao Tzu / Laozi; Mahavira; Mahikari; Miracles in Non-Christian Religions; Muhammad, Elijah; Nation of Islam; Plural Marriage, Mormon Teaching and History of; Polygamy; Ramanuja;*

Religious Society of Friends (Quakers); Seicho-No-Ie; Shakti; Shree/Shri/Sri; Shruti/Sruti; Sikh Dharma; Speaking in Tongues; Swami; Twelve Tribes; Vedas; Watchtower, The; Yahwehism

PETTUS, DAVID. PhD, Baylor University. Associate Professor, School of Divinity, Liberty University. Torah

POEWE, KARLA. PhD, University of New Mexico. Professor Emerita, Department of Anthropology, University of Calgary; Adjunct Research Professor, Liverpool Hope University. Anthropology of Religion

POTTER, DOUG. DMin, Southern Evangelical Seminary. Director of Doctor of Ministry Program and Assistant Professor, Southern Evangelical Bible College. Council of the Seventy; Seer Stones

POWER, MATT. MA studies, University of Iowa. Al-Qadr; Bhagavan; Chan-khong/Zhenkong; Chen-jen/Zhenren; Dependent Origination; Devekuth; Dravya; Dukkha/Duhkha; Forty Immortals; Gongyo; Jiriki; Kabbalah; Kalpa Sutra; Moksha; Sadhana; Samsara; Sankirtan, The Hare Krishna Practice of; Shu-ching/Shujing; T'ien/Tian; Wu-wei

PRICE, RANDALL. PhD, University of Texas, Austin. Distinguished Research Professor and Curator of the Liberty Biblical Museum, Liberty University; President, World of the Bible Ministries, Inc. Temple in Judaism

PRICE, TIMOTHY SHAUN. PhD, University of Aberdeen. Associate Pastor of Families, Tabernacle Baptist Church. Confucius; Eucharist; Shi'a Islam; Soul Sleep; Sunni Islam

ROBERTS, R. PHILIP. PhD, Free University of Amsterdam. Former President, Midwestern Baptist Theological Seminary; Ministry Associate and Director of International Theological Education, Global Ministries Foundation. Baptism of the Dead, Christian;

Baptism of the Dead, Mormon; Enlightenment; Evangelism; Missiology; Pantheism; Virgin Birth; Ward

ROST, STEPHEN J. MDiv, Talbot Theological Seminary. Freelance researcher and author. Adam-God Theory; Albertus Magnus; Anitya; Anthropology in Christian Theology; Antinomianism; Antinomianism, Non-Christian; Apostasy, Biblical View of; Atman; Bahá'i; Bhagavad Gita; Blood Atonement; Book of the Dead, Egyptian; Brahmacharya; Brahmanism; Branch; Celestial Marriage; Demons and Demonization in the Bible; Doctrine of the Mean (Chung-yung/Zhongyong); Exaltation; First Vision; Hell, Orthodox and Unorthodox Christian Views of; Holy Spirit, Biblical View of; Mysticism; Orthodoxy; Plural Marriage, Mormon Teaching and History of; Preexistence, Mormon View of; Salvation, Evangelical View of; Scripture, Interpretation of; Theravada Buddhism; Trinity, Patristic Support for; Vajrayana Buddhism

SCOTT, BRAD. Advaita; Hinduism; Ramakrishna, Sri; Yoga

SHROPSHIRE, EVERETT. MA, Fuller Theological Seminary. President, TruthQuest. Eternal Life; Jehovah; Overseer; Watchtower, The

SPAULDING, MIKE. PhD, Trinity Theological Seminary. Pastor, Calvary Chapel of Lima, Ohio. Vishnu

STALLARD, MIKE. PhD, Dallas Theological Seminary. International Ministries Director, The Friends of Israel Gospel Ministry. Armageddon

STEWART, MARILYN. MDiv, Southwestern Baptist Theological Seminary. Liberal Christianity; Process Theology

STEWART, ROBERT B. PhD, Southwestern Baptist Theological Seminary. Professor of Philosophy and Theology and Chair, Greer-Heard Chair of Faith and Culture, New

Orleans Baptist Theological Seminary. *Testimony in Mormonism*

STREETT, DANIEL R. PhD, Southeastern Baptist Theological Seminary; PhD (ABD), Durham University. Associate Professor of Theology, Houston Baptist University. *Anointing; Dual Covenant Theory; Syncretism*

STREETT, R. ALAN. PhD, University of Wales; PhD, California Graduate School of Theology. Senior Research Professor of Biblical Theology, Criswell College. *I Ching / Yijing; Martial Arts, East Asian; Oneness Pentecostalism; Yin and Yang*

THUET, LANE. Coauthor of *What Every Mormon (and Non-Mormon) Should Know*. *Masonry (LDS)*

TINKER, COLLEEN. Cofounder, Former Adventist Fellowship; Editor, *Proclamation!* magazine. *Seventh-day Adventism*

WELLS, C. RICHARD. PhD, University of North Texas. Founding President and Professor of Humanities, John Witherspoon College. *Angra Mainyu; Asceticism; Avestan; Buddha, Nine Attributes of; Buddha, Three Bodies of; Buddhism; Idolatry; Legalism from a Christian Perspective; Pahlavi Texts; Shin Buddhism; Spirituality, Christian*

WELLUM, STEPHEN. PhD, Trinity Evangelical Divinity School. Professor of Christian Theology, Southern Baptist Theological Seminary; Editor, *The Southern Baptist Journal of Theology*. *Baptism, Christian; Baptism, Non-Christian; Bible, Canon of; Incarnation; Inerrancy*

WILSEY, JOHN D. PhD, Southeastern Baptist Theological Seminary. Associate Professor of Church History, The Southern Baptist Theological Seminary. *Chalcedonian Controversy; Krishna; Meditation; Sacraments*

WILSON, LUKE†. MTS, Calvin Theological Seminary. Former Executive Director, Institute for Religious Research. *Issa*

ACKNOWLEDGMENTS

Many people contributed to the completion of *The Evangelical Dictionary of World Religions*. First, I want to thank Baker Books for undertaking this book and for their unfailing support for this dictionary for a number of years. I want to thank Jim Weaver, my first editor with Baker, who encouraged me at the beginning and assisted in procuring a contract. Chad Allen worked with me for several years in keeping the project going, particularly during the years when I generally set the project aside due to the sickness and death of my late wife, Leta, and the difficult time that followed. Rob Bowman was especially helpful in revitalizing the dictionary and carefully reviewing the articles, and Eric Pement helped me over several weekends at his home in Florida by carefully examining each article and updating those that needed an update. In the final stages of the project, James Korsmo expertly led it to final publication; he was a pleasure to work with.

Irina, my wife of nearly three years, has been helpful in supporting me in my work. She took on tasks that freed up my time, making it possible for me to complete the project. I also want to thank all of the editors and authors of *The Evangelical Dictionary of World Religions*, who have made this volume on the study of the world religions possible. It is our hope that it will model an accurate and irenic approach to understanding other religions and be a witness to the gospel of Jesus, Messiah and Savior.

H. Wayne House
June 15, 2018

INTRODUCTION

The Evangelical Dictionary of World Religions recognizes that from its inception Christianity has been a world religion. This may surprise many people who identify Christianity with Western Europe and North America. Christianity was birthed in the Middle East, and it quickly traveled the world. Christian communities emerged in Europe, Africa, India, and China within a relatively short time.

This historically global character of Christianity has only been accentuated in our increasingly global world. People and ideas are spreading across the globe in new and unprecedented ways. This means that Christians (and those of all religions) are more likely than ever to interact with people of other faiths in their travels or on their street. So here we include information that will help Christians understand their own faith better in this context and information they will find useful in their encounters with members of other faiths.

This dictionary contains articles that describe Christianity, particularly in its evangelical form. This will help evangelicals understand their own beliefs and how they differ both from other Christian traditions and from other world religions. The other main focus is on the nature and beliefs of other major world religions. In the category of world religions, we have included Buddhism, the Hindu tradition, Islam, and Judaism, as well as a number of smaller groups. Here we followed a fairly common academic practice of classing any religious movement with around ten million members as a world religion. Therefore, in most cases, the groups chosen contain more than ten million members worldwide. They are also groups that have members scattered around the globe. Finally, they are groups with a history—that is, ones that have demonstrated staying power over several generations. At the same time, we also included some information about smaller or more localized groups that people are likely to encounter in their daily lives.

Some people may be surprised that we included the Mormons, or more correctly the Church of Jesus Christ of Latter-day Saints. Our reason for classifying them as a "world religion" is threefold. First, there are now well over ten million Mormons worldwide, making them a global religious movement. Second, while the Mormon Church claims to be Christian and many Mormons attempt to live "Christian lives," the core teachings of this new religion reject the Christian tradition and condemn all Christian groups as apostates. Third, when Mormon doctrines are examined closely (and even many Mormons do not realize this), they sharply differ from traditional Christianity and take the form of an entirely new religion.

We hope that *The Evangelical Dictionary of World Religions* will provide readers with a rich resource that will enable them to live as Christians in an increasingly complex world that reflects the religious confusion of the first century of the Christian era. In this way, we hope we have prepared Christians to understand the culture we now live in, their non-Christian colleagues and neighbors, and, in a possibly surprising way, the world of the New Testament.

All the contributors are Christians who hold to the core evangelical commitments. They are also scholars in the relevant fields, most in the academy, but others primarily in the field interacting with persons and groups of alternate faiths. So while much unites the contributors, there is certain to be a diversity in many areas, and we have not sought uniformity. Instead, scholarly differences will be seen in many matters, such as preferred dates for historical events and persons, preferred translations or transliterations of foreign-language terms, and the meaning or significance of various concepts.

ABBREVIATIONS

AD	*anno domini*, in the year of the Lord	Mt.	Mount
a.k.a.	also known as	NASB	New American Standard Bible
b.	born	NIV	New International Version
BC	before Christ	NKJV	New King James Version
BYU	Brigham Young University	NRSV	New Revised Standard Version
ca.	circa	NT	New Testament
cf.	confer, compare	NWT	New World Translation
chap(s).	chapter(s)	OT	Old Testament
d.	died	p(p).	page(s)
D&C	Doctrine and Covenants	par.	parallel
e.g.	*exempli gratia*, for example	r.	reigned
esp.	especially	RLDS	Reorganized Church of Jesus Christ of Latter Day Saints
ESV	English Standard Version		
fl.	flourished	RSV	Revised Standard Version
i.e.	*id est*, that is	sec.	section
JD	*Journal of Discourses*, edited by G. D. Watt et al., 26 vols. (1855–86)	SDA	Seventh-day Adventist
		UK	United Kingdom
JS-H	Joseph Smith—History	US	United States of America
JST	Joseph Smith Translation of the Bible	v(v).	verse(s)
JW(s)	Jehovah's Witnesses	WT	Watch Tower Bible and Tract Society
KJV	King James Version		
LDS	Latter-day Saints; the Church of Jesus Christ of Latter-day Saints		

A

'ABDU'L-BAHÁ. 'Abdu'l-Bahá (1844–1921; his name means "slave of the glory [of God]") was born 'Abbás Effendí in Tehran, Persia (now Iran). His father, Bahá'u'lláh (1817–92), founder of the Bahá'í Faith, believed himself to be the divine herald of all true religion about whom Siyyad Ali Muhammad (1819–50), the Bab (meaning "gate"), had prophesied. During his childhood, 'Abdu'l-Bahá witnessed intense persecution of his father as well as suffering some himself; when he was eight or nine years of age, his father was imprisoned for promoting and defending the Bahá'í Faith. After Bahá'u'lláh was released from prison and placed under house arrest in Akko, Israel, 'Abdu'l-Bahá traveled with him and became his father's most trusted ally as an adult. As a result of this strong alliance, Bahá'u'lláh appointed 'Abdu'l-Bahá (in his will and testament) to succeed him as the foremost leader and exponent of Bahá'í after his death. Yet, unlike his father, who believed himself to be a manifestation of God, 'Abdu'l-Bahá repeatedly stated that he was merely a servant of God.

As the authorized interpreter of Bahá'í, 'Abdu'l-Bahá proclaimed that "love is the greatest law" and that humankind's greatest need is international cooperation. His *Tablets of the Divine Plan* served to establish Bahá'í leadership in North America, and his *Will and Testament* set forth plans for a worldwide administrative order of the Bahá'í Faith. He began a world tour in 1912, during which he dedicated the grounds for the Bahá'í temple in Wilmette, Illinois. His major teachings included the fundamental oneness of the human race; condemnation of all forms of prejudice; the basic unity of all religions; advocacy of the independent quest for truth, unfettered by superstition or tradition; the essential harmony between science and religion; gender equality; the abolition of extreme wealth and poverty; universal compulsory education; and the institution of a world tribunal for adjudicating disputes between nations.

See also BAHÁ'Í; BAHÁ'U'LLÁH

Bibliography. Abdu'l-Bahá and Badi'u'llah, "Center of the Covenant: Tablet to Mason Remey, Interview with Badi'u'llah," https://www.bahai-library.com/abdulbaha_badiullah_remey_center-covenant; K. Beint, "The Bahá'í Faith," in *The Illustrated Encyclopedia of World Religions*, edited by Chris Richards; J. R. Lewis, *Peculiar Prophets: A Biographical Dictionary of New Religions*; C. Partridge, *Introduction to World Religions*; S. Scholl, ed., *Wisdom of the Master: The Spiritual Teachings of 'Abdu'l-Bahá*; P. Smith, *The Bahá'í Faith: A Short History*.

H. W. House

ADAM-GOD THEORY. The LDS doctrine of the plurality of Gods, coupled with the church's veneration of Adam, provided the ideal environment for the eventual development of the Adam-God theory. Because of Adam's elevated status in LDS theology, his fall in Eden is never said to be sin but is instead labeled a transgression. LDS authority Joseph Fielding Smith goes so far as to say that transgressing the law is not a sin in every instance. So Adam's transgression was

1

a legitimate and even honorable violation of the law since its purpose was for Adam to fall downward as a first step toward rising upward toward the goal of eventual godhood.

The controversial "Adam-God" doctrine originated with Brigham Young and was taught for the first time at the Salt Lake Tabernacle in 1852. In his sermon titled "Self-Government, Mysteries, Recreation and Amusements, Not in Themselves Sinful, Tithing, Adam, Our Father and Our God," Young declared, "When our father Adam came into the garden of Eden, he came into it with a celestial body, and brought Eve, one of his wives, with him. He helped to make and organize this world. He is Michael, the archangel, the Ancient of Days! about whom holy men have written and spoken—He is our Father and our God, and the only God with whom we have to do" (JD 1:50). Regarding the father of Jesus, Young stated, "Jesus, our elder brother, was begotten in the flesh by the same character that was in the garden of Eden, and who is our Father in Heaven" (JD 1:51). Regarding his Adam-God views and the response of his critics, Young wrote, "Some years ago, I advanced a doctrine with respect to Adam being our father and God. That will be a curse to many Elders of Israel because of their folly. With regard to it they yet grovel in darkness and will. It is one of the most glorious revealments of the economy of heaven" (Young, "A Few Words of Doctrine," quoted in Buerger, 29).

Young's Adam-God theory was new territory theologically, for nowhere in any LDS documents or "standard works" was the doctrine taught. Given that Young was president of the church, his teaching was seen as revelation from God and thus found support from numerous members. However, there were those who found the teaching not only strange but great cause for alarm, and it didn't take long for LDS reactions to Young's teaching on Adam to become a substantial controversy. While it has been argued that Young's statements have been taken out of context or misunderstood, the evidence from church documents shows that both supporters and opponents understood him to be teaching that Adam is God the Father, the father of Jesus Christ (which conflicts with the biblical record that Christ was conceived by the power of the Holy Spirit), and that he came to the earth in a celestial body, rather than a body created "from the dust of the earth" as is recorded in the book of Genesis. The most ardent opponent of Young's Adam-God doctrine was Orson Pratt, one of Mormonism's more capable theologians and a member of the Quorum of the Twelve Apostles. His vehement opposition to Young's doctrine presented another substantial problem for LDS leaders, the authority of the living prophet. Pratt's contention that Young's teaching was wrong raised an important question: Could a living prophet fall into doctrinal error? Pratt believed that the prophet was capable of error and that Young's Adam-God doctrine was evidence to that effect. However, the church authorities maintained that the living prophet could not err doctrinally, for to do so would undermine the belief that the prophet was God's mouthpiece. Logically, if Young was wrong, then either God was giving erroneous revelation, or Young was a false prophet.

Pratt recognized the seriousness of the Adam-God controversy by virtue of the fact that it contradicts the accounts of Adam's creation by God found in the King James Version and in the LDS scriptures called the Book of Moses and the Book of Abraham. As for Adam being the Father of Jesus Christ, according to Moses 6:51–62, Adam is conversing with God regarding Adam's need to repent in the name of God's Son, Jesus Christ. Pratt contended that Young's doctrine was clearly in contradiction with the scriptures and therefore a false doctrine. Not only did the Adam-God doctrine call into question the trustworthiness of the office of the living prophet as God's infallible mouthpiece; it put the prophet's teachings in direct contradiction with the standard works. Despite the magnitude of the controversy regarding his Adam-God teaching, Young continued to boldly assert the doctrine in stronger terms. In 1873 he stated, "How much unbelief exists in the minds of the Latter-day Saints in regard to one particular doctrine which I revealed to them, which God revealed to me—namely that Adam is our Father and God. . . . The Christian world read of, and think about, St. Paul, also St. Peter, the chief of the Apostles. These men were faithful to and magnified the priesthood while on the earth" (*Deseret News Weekly*).

Given that the Church of Jesus Christ of Latter-day Saints held the office of prophet in high regard and considered the prophet's revelatory teachings authoritative and trustworthy, Young was in no position to abandon his Adam-God doctrine. Furthermore, years earlier in the presence of Joseph Smith, Young stated that the living prophet was superior to the standard works. Wilford Woodruff recounts the incident:

> Brother Joseph turned to Brother Brigham Young and said, "Brother Brigham I want you to take the stand and tell us your views with regard to the living oracles and the written word of God." Brother Brigham took the stand, and he took the Bible, and laid it down; he took the Book of Mormon, and laid it down; and he took the Book of Doctrine and Covenants, and laid it down before him, and he said: "There is the written word of God to us, concerning the work of God from the beginning of the world, almost, to our day. And now . . . when compared with the living oracles those books are nothing to me; those books do not convey the word of God direct to us now, as do the words of a Prophet or a man bearing the Holy Priesthood in our day and generation. I would rather have the living oracles than all the writing in the books."

That was the course he pursued. When he was through, Brother Joseph said to the congregation: "Brother Brigham has told you the word of the Lord, and he has told you the truth." (Benson)

Eventually Pratt was relocated to the eastern US, but this didn't quell opposition to the Adam-God doctrine. Orson Pratt was not the only voice speaking out against the Adam-God doctrine of Brigham Young. The Reorganized Church of Jesus Christ of Latter Day Saints, which was committed to Smith's original teachings, also noted Young's error and published its opposition to his doctrine. In more recent times, LDS authorities such as former prophet Spencer Kimball and apostle Mark Petersen have condemned the doctrine (but without criticizing Young). Defenders of Brigham Young offer two lines of defense. First, they contend that the Adam-God doctrine, as interpreted by non-Mormons, is a distortion of Young's views. In his book *Mormon Doctrine*, Bruce McConkie says that Adam is a god, but not God the Father. However, in a letter to Eugene England dated February 19, 1981, McConkie acknowledges that Young did teach that God was the Father. He writes, "There are those who believe or say they believe that Adam is our father and our God, that he is the father of our spirits and our bodies, and that he is the one we worship. I, of course, indicated the utter absurdity of this doctrine and said it was totally false" (McConkie, "Letter to Eugene England"). Others contend Brigham Young was misquoted, and that his teachings found in the *Journal of Discourses* were poorly recorded. Yet there is no record of Young ever stating this to be the case. The historical evidence supports the fact that Mormons who attended Young's meetings understood him to be teaching the Adam-God doctrine. Harry Stout, Samuel Rogers, and Wilford Woodruff all recorded what Young taught, and their notes point out the particular elements in the Adam-God theory, namely, Adam came to the earth in a celestial body, he was the father of Jesus Christ, and he is the only God with whom we have any relationship.

The second line of defense has been to follow Pratt's position that the living prophet can and occasionally does teach things that are incorrect. McConkie says that Young taught this doctrine but also taught contrary to it, making it difficult to know which Young to believe. McConkie continues with a corrective: "The answer is we will believe the expressions that accord with the teachings of the Standard Works" ("Letter to Eugene England").

Having acknowledged that Young did teach the Adam-God doctrine, and that it was false, McConkie goes on to point out that God "permits false doctrine to be taught in and out of the Church and that such teaching is part of the sifting process of mortality" ("Letter to Eugene England").

McConkie's defense of Young doesn't solve the problem. The implications of the issue regarding the prophet's doctrinal integrity were best stated by Wilford Woodruff, who in 1890 wrote,

> The Lord will never permit me or any other man who stands as President of this Church, to lead you astray. It is not in the programme. It is not in the mind of God. (Woodruff, "Excerpts from Three Addresses")

The Adam-God doctrine continues to pose a substantial epistemological dilemma for the LDS Church. Differing streams of church authority and sources of knowledge were no longer unified but in conflict with each other. Given the fact that the president of the church was teaching a doctrine that conflicted with the standard works, what is now at issue is whether the standard works are doctrinally trustworthy, or is the living prophet the final word on matters of faith and practice? In this particular situation, to follow Brigham Young would have put the person in conflict with the standard works, and to follow the LDS canon of scripture would have conflicted with the living prophet, a dilemma that has yet to be resolved.

See also CHURCH OF JESUS CHRIST OF LATTER-DAY SAINTS

Bibliography. E. T. Benson, "Fourteen Fundamentals in Following the Prophet," presidential address given February 26, 1980, available at lds.org; D. Buerger, "The Adam-God Doctrine," *Dialogue: A Journal of Mormon Thought*; M. F. Cowley, *Wilford Woodruff: History of His Life and Labors as Recorded in His Daily Journals* (1909); B. R. McConkie, "Letter to Eugene England," February 19, 1981; McConkie, *Mormon Doctrine*; J. and S. Tanner, *LDS Apostle Confesses Brigham Young Taught Adam-God Doctrine: A Startling Letter Written by Apostle Bruce R. McConkie, and Other Important Documents*; R. Turner, "The Position of Adam in Latter-day Saint Scripture and Theology," MA thesis, Brigham Young University, 1953; C. Vlachos, "Adam Is God," *Journal of Pastoral Practice*; G. D. Watt, *Manuscript Addresses of Brigham Young* (1861); O. K. White, *Mormon Neo-Orthodoxy: A Crisis Theology*; W. Woodruff, "Excerpts from Three Addresses by President Wilford Woodruff Regarding the Manifesto" (addresses given in 1890, 1891, and 1893); Woodruff, "Living Oracles More Important than Written Word," quoted in R. Hulse, *When Salt Lake City Calls*; B. Young, *Deseret News Weekly*.

S. J. Rost

ADONAI-SHOMO. Adonai-Shomo (Hebrew, "The Lord is there") was a nineteenth-century religious society founded by Frederick I. Howland (ca. 1810–80) in 1861. A Quaker earlier in life, in 1843 Howland came to hold eschatological views similar to those of proto-Adventist preacher William Miller (1782–1849), largely as a result of Miller's preaching during the period prior to the Great Disappointment. Convinced that the "gift of inspiration" had been divinely bestowed on him in 1855, in 1861 Howland formed a group whose members shared a strong commitment to Howland's understanding of a number of Millerite theological distinctives. Many of these doctrines would later be appropriated by more influential groups such as the Seventh-day Adventists, the Advent Christian Church, the Bible Students (Russellites), and the Watch Tower Bible and Tract Society (Jehovah's Witnesses). The group eventually reached a peak membership of about thirty and established itself in Petersham, Massachusetts, where it was officially chartered in 1876. However, in 1896 the organization's charter was annulled by the Massachusetts State Supreme Court in light of the fact that only one member of the group was still living. By the twentieth century, the group was effectively defunct, a footnote in Seventh-day Adventist history.

The most basic teachings of Adonai-Shomo can be summarized as follows: As predicted by God's prophets, Jesus Christ will restore all things, at which time God's elect will be inducted into the everlasting priesthood of Melchizedek. Distinctive practices of the group included holding all possessions in common, observing the Sabbath on Saturday, and offering the Lord's Prayer as a morning and evening sacrifice.

See also JEHOVAH'S WITNESSES (JW); SEVENTH-DAY ADVENTISM; *WATCHTOWER, THE*

Bibliography. G. R. Knight, *Millennial Fever and the End of the World: A Study of Millerite Adventism*; L. A. Loetscher, ed., *New Schaff-Herzog Encyclopedia of Religious Knowledge*, vol. 3; E. Webber, *Escape to Utopia: The Communal Movement in America*.

J. Bjornstad

ADVAITA. Although in ancient Hinduism the terms were less connected, today Advaita (nondualism or monism) refers to a main school of Vedanta (the "supplement to the Vedas" or Upanishads), Advaita Vedanta, as first systematized by Sankara (AD 788–820), who is also known as Adi Sankara (the true or original Sankara) and, sometimes, as Shankaracharya, though the latter term is usually applied to his followers who became leaders in the movement he started. The Brahma Sutra, also known as Vedanta Sutra, epitomizes the philosophy or viewpoint (*darshana*) of Advaita Vedanta. Like all schools of Hinduism, it also claims the Bhagavad Gita as expressing its philosophy.

Unlike popular Hinduism, Advaita is sophisticated in theory and practice. At its core, however, are three main presuppositions: (1) that Brahma (God) alone exists as perfect existence, consciousness, and bliss; (2) that the Atman (self) and Brahma (God) are in *reality* one; and (3) that the goal of every soul universally is to achieve this eternal Oneness.

Unity of Existence. Because Brahma is the only reality, forming the warp and woof of existence, diversity and duality are merely appearances. Even the religionist's sense that he is worshiping a personal Creator (Isvara) is appearance rather than reality. When one obtains self-knowledge (*atmabodha*), this Creator himself disappears into the infinite, eternal ocean of Brahma, as an iceberg finally melts under the sun. Afterward, the liberated soul (*jivanmukta*) declares, "Aham Brahmasmi" (I am Brahma). Until then it is the appearance of duality and separateness (*maya*) that bars the way to this truth. One who sees the universe rather than Brahma, claims Sankara, is like one who encounters a rope at dusk and mistakes it for a snake.

Unity of Identity. The cause of this delusion is ignorance (*avidya*). One mistakenly identifies with his body, senses, mind, and ego rather than his "true self" (Atman). In time a person can overcome this ignorance by practicing spiritual disciplines. Employing discrimination (*viveka*), he separates reality from maya by repeating, "Neti, neti" (I am not this, not that), meditates on Brahma, renounces all desires, and often, too, practices yoga. After many incarnations, he eventually realizes his identity with Brahma, whereupon his illusory self disappears. According to one analogy, as water trapped within a jar in the ocean becomes one with the ocean when the jar breaks, so does the soul merge with Brahma when it ceases to identify with the body, senses, and so on.

Unity of Truth. The Rig Veda states, "Ekam sat vipra bahudha vadanti" (The truth is one, but sages call it by different names). For Advaitans that "truth" is nonduality: all is Brahma; Brahma, all. For them, then, Brahma is also behind all temporal truths, including those of the world's religions. Each believer must find his own way. In the famous words of Ramakrishna (a notable nineteenth-century guru), "As many faiths, so many paths." Advaita Vedanta, its proponents maintain, is compatible with all religions.

Today, groups that embrace religious syncretism—for example, Theosophy, The Fourth Way—incorporate advaitic concepts into their teachings. Traditional Advaita, nevertheless, remains a significant force inside and outside India, espoused in modern times by figures such as Ramakrishna, Ramana Maharishi, Swami Yogananda, and Swami Sivananda Saraswati.

As a rule, teachers whose names begin with "Swami" and end with "-ananda" are proponents of Advaita Vedanta—for example, Swami Vivekananda, Swami Satchidananda, Swami Kriyananda.

See also ATMAN; BHAGAVAD GITA; BRAHMA; HINDUISM; MAYA; RAMAKRISHNA, SRI; RAMANA MAHARISHI; SUTRA; SWAMI; UPANISHADS; VEDANTA; VEDAS

Bibliography. E. Deutsch, *The Advaita Vedanta: A Philosophical Reconstruction*; S. Radhakrishnan, *A Sourcebook in Indian Philosophy*; P. Vrajaprana, *Vedanta: A Simple Introduction*.

B. Scott

ADVENTIST MOVEMENT. Originating in the nineteenth century, the Adventist movement focuses on the imminent return of Christ, who will usher in his millennial reign. Therefore, Adventism has much in common with other historical forms of premillennial schools of thought. Though typically associated with Seventh-day Adventism, Adventism itself is actually much broader than this particular denomination. Moreover, while Seventh-day Adventism in some respects has turned more toward orthodoxy, Adventism in general is still seen to be more heterodox.

Beginning with a Baptist minister from New York named William Miller, the Adventist movement began to take form. After serving in the War of 1812, Miller began seriously studying both religious and nonreligious literature. Converting to Christianity shortly thereafter, he focused his readings on the Bible, carefully attending to the smallest details of Scripture, such as symbolism and numbers. He soon concluded that Christ would return between March 21, 1843, and March 21, 1844. The Millerite movement, however, based on the suggestion of Samuel Snow, subsequently also advocated for October 22, 1844.

By this point, Miller's teachings had been circulated widely by Joseph Himes, who printed over five million pieces of Miller's work. Thus, by October 22, 1844, thousands of devotees gathered in anticipation of Christ's return. When this prediction went unfulfilled, most members in the movement were devastated and returned to the denominations to which they previously belonged. Miller himself was no exception. When his first prediction failed, he responded with a revised prediction. Upon his second failed attempt, Miller abandoned this teaching altogether.

Nevertheless, the "Great Disappointment" of 1844 did not utterly destroy the Adventist movement. On October 23, 1844, just one day removed from the Great Disappointment, Hiram Edson, a staunch Millerite, went to pray with a friend about how to interpret the events of the preceding day. While walking through a field to pray, Edson claimed that he was stopped in the field and heaven was opened to him. According to Edson, he saw Christ enter into the holy of holies of the heavenly sanctuary to begin a new work of redemption on earth. With this the remaining Millerites reinterpreted and celebrated the Great Disappointment as a fulfillment of prophecy. In their view, Miller simply misidentified the location in which the prophecy would be fulfilled, but not the timing.

By December 1844, another staunch devotee of Miller, Ellen White, began having visions that were taken to confirm Adventist teaching. In one early vision, White claimed to have risen above the earth, where she could look down and see that Adventist believers were on the road to heaven, while those who turned back from their teachings fell back to the ways of the world. In a second vision, Christ appeared to her, revealing the Ten Commandments to her, with the fourth commandment in a small glowing halo of light. Though she had originally opposed certain Adventists who taught that the Sabbath should be the day of worship, this second vision caused White to change her view and accept the Sabbath as the proper day of worship in preparation for the Lord's return.

Critics have noted that this movement gave tremendous authority to White and her visions. Her influence was so strong at one point that when her husband began to have questions about the validity and authority of her visions, he was asked to resign as editor of the *Review and Herald*. Indeed, within the movement itself, White's visions seemed to rival the Bible in terms of authority. Yet this is not characteristic of all sectors of Adventist thinking. Even in White's day, moderate adherents viewed her and her followers as representatives from the fringes of Adventism. Today Seventh-day Adventists profess to hold the Bible as the sole authority for doctrine and practice while also upholding White as a prophetess through whom the Bible is illuminated.

See also MILLER, WILLIAM; SABBATARIANISM; SEVENTH-DAY ADVENTISM

Bibliography. W. Martin, *The Kingdom of the Cults*; M. A. Noll, *A History of Christianity in the United States and Canada*; R. A. Tucker, *Another Gospel*.

J. K. Dew

AHIMSA. Though many definitions of *ahimsa* (Sanskrit, "noninjury" or "the avoidance of violence") have been proposed, its advocates generally maintain that it involves the sincere effort to refrain from inflicting harm on (or from desiring the suffering of) any living creature. Ahimsa is closely linked with the belief that any type violence, whether manifested in thoughts, speech, or actions, results in the accumulation of bad karma in the one perpetrating the violence. However, most religions, sects, and cults that embrace the practice of ahimsa make exceptions to the rules regulating it, wherein at least some kinds of harm are allowed, or some classes of creatures are exempt from the demands of ahimsa, or various circumstances are recognized as mitigating the negative consequences of failing to adhere to ahimsa's dictates. Some practitioners of ahimsa claim that it is the most effective method of expunging the cruel, brutal, animalistic nature (*pasu-svabhava*) of human beings and that it is the only way to attain lasting peace. Others emphasize the importance of supplementing the habit of merely abstaining from violence with demonstrating love toward all sentient beings by doing kind things to them.

Hinduism. In many sects of Hinduism, ahimsa is said to be a means to the acquisition of mystical powers, protection from harm, and liberation from the cycle of death and rebirth. Notable Hindu religious authorities who have advocated the practice of ahimsa include Mahatma Gandhi (1869–1948), Sri Aurobindo (1872–1950), Ramana Maharishi (1879–1950), Swami Sivananda (1887–1963), and A. C. Bhaktivedanta Prabhupada

(1896–1977). Traditions within Hinduism that stress the importance of ahimsa include Hatha Yoga, Raja Yoga (the Patanjali school), and Bhakti Yoga (especially among devotees of Krishna and Vishnu).

Jainism. A prominent symbol of Jainism is a wheel on the palm of an open hand, which represents *dharmacakra*, the determination to employ ahimsa as the means of ending the cycle of death and rebirth. In Jainism the manner in which ahimsa is carried out is more meticulous and all-inclusive than in other Indian religions, such as Jain monks' practice of wearing face masks to avoid accidentally inhaling gnats, or sweeping the path with a broom as they walk in order to avoid stepping on ants. Jainists view ahimsa as a universal moral obligation, including either a lacto-vegetarian or a vegan diet.

Buddhism. Nearly all sects of Buddhism defend an understanding of ahimsa that is significantly less severe than the one proposed by Jain teachers and scholars. For example, Buddhist religious authorities generally do not demand that adherents eat a vegetarian diet. Instead, it is widely declared that the essence of ahimsa consists in making a reasonable attempt (during the various activities of ordinary human life) not to kill living creatures of any kind. Buddhists are advised to practice loving-kindness and compassion both in deed and in meditations.

See also BUDDHISM; HINDUISM; JAINISM

Bibliography. B. Balsys, *Ahimsa: Buddhism and the Vegetarian Ideal*; G. Kotturan, *Ahimsa: Gautama to Gandhi*; V. Moran, *Compassion the Ultimate Ethic: An Exploration of Veganism*, 4th ed.; V. A. Sangave, *The Jaina Path of Ahimsa*; U. Tähtinen, *Ahimsa: Non-Violence in Indian Tradition*.

H. W. House

AHMAD, MIRZA GHULAM. Founder of the Indian Ahmadiyya Islamic movement, also known as Qadiani or Ahmadi, Ahmad was born in 1835 to a wealthy, landowning family in the village of Qadian in the Punjab area of India. He was educated at home by tutors and became proficient in both Persian and Arabic. As a young man, he was drawn to religious thought and life and spent much time alone studying religious texts, praying in the local mosque, and debating with Christian missionaries.

In 1868, at age thirty-three, he claimed to receive a divine revelation telling him: "Thy God is well pleased with what thou hast done. He will bless thee greatly, so much so that Kings shall seek blessing from your garments" (quoted in Ahmad). In the ensuing years, he claimed at various times to have subsequent revelations, and in 1882 he claimed to have a definitive vision that commissioned him to alter the direction of orthodox Islam.

In his 1882 book *Barahin-i-Ahmadiyya* (The blessings of Ahmad), he wrote of his divine appointment as the Promised Messiah and Reformer (Mujaddid) of the era—in essence, the messiah of Islam. The book, which intimated that Ahmad was another prophet of Allah, created controversy among the ulama (scholars of Islam), especially as followers began to make pilgrimages to Qadian to listen to his teaching. During this era in India, many spiritual teachers had great followings, and the reported first visitor Ahmad received was Pir Sirajudin Haq Nomani, a renowned spiritual leader with many followers. Nomani quickly espoused Ahmad as the Islamic messiah, and Ahmad's following grew.

Other Indian spiritual leaders also visited Ahmad, which validated his claims. In 1886, his movement gained some social acceptance and regional prominence when two men, Munshi Zafar Ahmad, registrar of the High Court of Kapurthala, and Maulana Hakim Nooruddin of Bhera, royal physician to the Maharajah of Jammu and Kashmir, became followers, which further increased his popularity. He soon began to train other teachers in this new "dispensation" of Islam, including Bhai Abdur Rahman in 1895.

His movement, called Ahmadiyya, grew in both number of adherents and influence. Stories of Ahmad performing miracles became popular and were further enumerated in Ahmad's book, *Fateh Islam* (Victory of Islam). In 1891, Ahmad began to explicitly teach about his messianic nature. He issued a notice announcing his repeated revelations that Jesus of Nazareth had died a natural death of old age and that the second advent of Jesus, in which both Muslims and Christians believed, was not a second coming of Jesus but rather the appearing of another gifted individual. Ahmad claimed to be that person. The announcement caused enormous opposition from the orthodox Islamic community, which viewed Ahmadiyya as a *ghulat* (cult) and its teachings as heretical. Nonetheless, by the time of Ahmad's death in 1908, the Ahmadiyyas were firmly entrenched in India, with over two hundred thousand followers.

Among the other teachings of the Ahmadiyya are the hadithic prophecies of Ahmad as the final Prophet of Islam, the writings of Ahmad and others as equal to the Qur'an, the dissolution of the Christian teaching of the Trinity, and the prophetic unification of all religions under the leadership of Ahmad.

Bibliography. Amatul-Hadi Ahmad, "A Life Sketch of the Promised Messiah," *Review of Religions*, http://www.alislam.org/library/links/00000185.html.

T. J. Demy

AHMADIYYA ISLAM. Ahmadiyya Islam is a sect of Islam based on the nineteenth-century reformer Mirza Ghulam Ahmad (1835–1908), who proclaimed himself to be both messiah and mahdi ("guided one"; eschatological leader in Muslim thought). Even though most of the established mosques in the US today follow strict Middle Eastern interpretations of the Qur'an, the Pakistani Ahmadiyya sect makes itself felt with strong proselytizing efforts, such as on college campuses, by presenting Islam as a peaceful, rational religion. It must be added right at the outset that Ghulam Ahmad's teachings have been given two different interpretations, which have led to the formation of two different communities, known by the town names of Qadian and Lahore.

Mirza Ghulam Ahmad lived in the Punjab region, an area that straddles India and Pakistan. He was born in a small village called Qadian to a family of minor nobility (hence the title "Mirza") who were able to provide him with a modest education. Even though he was trained as a physician, it became obvious from his childhood on that his greatest passion was the spiritual disciplines of studying the Qur'an and of prayer. Ahmad first came to the attention of the greater Islamic world in 1880 with the publication of an exposition titled *Barahin-i-Ahmadiyya* (The blessings of Ahmad). It should be clarified that the name Ahmadiyya (and consequently the name of the movement) actually refers not to Ghulam Ahmad but to the prophet Muhammad, who carries the name Ahmad as a family name as well as a praise name.

A few years after his book was published, Ghulam Ahmad announced to the world that he was the long-awaited messiah. More specifically, he claimed that he was the mahdi—the messianic figure of Islam—as well as the second coming of Jesus Christ. There are many different understandings of the identity and nature of the mahdi in the world of Islam. He does not appear in the Qur'an, and the supplemental traditions (hadith) are not unambiguous. Nevertheless, there is a general consensus that shortly before the last judgment a great leader will appear who will establish Islamic peace and justice all over the world. Sometimes this belief is also associated with a second coming of Christ alongside the mahdi. Ghulam Ahmad professed that he was both.

We need to be careful to understand what Ghulam Ahmad probably meant with these assertions, particularly in light of his later, more radical statements. His claim to be the mahdi was unbending; he left no doubt about this position (though there would be disputes later on about what that position entailed). And there is no question that he saw himself as having fulfilled the prophecies of Christ's second coming. But this latter contention did not mean that he thought he was Jesus Christ as understood by Christians—that is to say, the incarnate Second Person of the Trinity; rather, it meant that he, the Islamic mahdi, also fulfilled Christians' anticipations of their future hope.

A few years before his death, Ahmad added to his claims by stating, "To the Hindus I am Krishna." But again did this declaration mean that he actually saw himself as an avatar of the Hindu god Vishnu, thereby endorsing an idolatrous and polytheistic religion, as is sometimes alleged? Probably not; again, what he most likely meant by that statement was simply that he fulfilled Hinduism's expectations of Krishna's return (or, a little more accurately, Hinduism's expectations of a future incarnation of Vishnu, as promised in the Bhagavad Gita).

Ghulam Ahmad attracted a sizable number of followers, who received a ceremony of initiation (baya) into his movement—something that is somewhat eccentric in Islam just by itself. The candidate would take a vow that encompassed an unyielding adherence to Islam as well as obedience to Ghulam Ahmad, which would take precedence over all other human relationships. He taught his disciples to be strict in their observances, to relate to one another with love, and to avoid violence at all costs. The Qur'an, as Ahmad and his subsequent movement interpret it, never permits physical violence, let alone a military jihad, no matter how dire the circumstances may be.

Soon after Ghulam Ahmad died, dissension among his followers surfaced, and in 1914, with the death of his immediate successor, a permanent split occurred. More than anything else, the focus of the dispute was on the identity of Ahmad himself. No one questioned whether he was the mahdi and messiah, but did that status make him a full prophet? If so he would be on a par with Muhammad, and all Muslims would be obliged to follow him. If not he would simply be a great reformer, and the movement could retain partnership with Muslims around the world.

One side took the more radical view that Ghulam Ahmad was, in fact, a prophet, and that his movement was the only true expression of Islam. This group has become known by Ahmad's town of birth as the Qadiyanis. Their leaders have followed Muhammad's successors in claiming the title of caliph; they believe that only those who recognize Ahmad are genuine Muslims. Everyone else is *kafir*, an unbeliever. Needless to say, this stance has not been popular with other Muslims, and Qadiyani Ahmadis are not permitted to identify themselves as Muslims in Pakistan.

The other group came to be known by the name of the city that houses its headquarters, Lahore, Pakistan. The Lahore group emphasizes the need for a pure, reformed Islam as taught by Ghulam Ahmad, but it identifies with mainstream Islam. It takes the view that Ahmad was a reformer and that Muhammad was the last genuine prophet.

Both groups of Ahmadis are very active in attempting to reach new converts. In the context of the early twenty-first century, when many Muslims are attempting to rationalize acts of terrorism that have been committed in the name of Islam, the Ahmadiyya movement can claim greater credibility because of its consistent renunciation of violence.

See also AHMAD, MIRZA GHULAM; ISLAM, BASIC BELIEFS OF

Bibliography. B. M. Ahmad, *Invitation to Ahmadiyya: Being a Statement of Beliefs, a Rationale of Claims, and an Invitation, on behalf of the Ahmadiyya Movement for the Propagation and Rejuvenation of Islam*; M. M. Ali, *True*

Conception of the Ahmadiyya Movement; M. M. Beg, *Christ Is Come: Prophecies about the Advent of the Promised Messiah*; Y. Friedmann, *Prophecy Continuous: Aspects of Ahmadi Religious Thought and Its Medieval Background.*

W. Corduan

AHURA MAZDA. Ahura Mazda is highest diety in Persian thought or Zoroastrianism, one of the sons of Zurvan, the god responsible for creation and the guardian of rulers and authorities along with those who are considered righteous.

The name Ahura Mazda is primarily identified with sources tied to Zoroastrianism. He is also known to be the father of the twins Spenta Mainyu, who is holy and just, and Angra Mainyu, who is evil.

In addition this deity, according to Zoroastrianism today, created not only this world but also all the variety of deities that followed. These deities are now sovereign over particular dimensions of the cosmos.

Zoroastrianism began as dualistic around 600 BC and evolved into a type of monotheism. Nonetheless, Ahura Mazda is the supreme deity of a pantheon of gods, the Amesha Spentas, and wages war against the evil spirit Angra Mainyu, who is also known as Ahriman, and those who follow in order to remove evil and deception. The winged disc symbolizes Ahura Mazda. He is also called by the names Ormazd, Ohrmazd, or Ormuzd.

See also AMESHA SPENTAS; SACRED FIRE; ZOROASTRIANISM

Bibliography. A. E. Smart, "Ahura Mazda," in *Encyclopedia Mythica*, rev. ed., http://www.pantheon.org/articles/a/ahura_mazda.html.

E. N. Colanter

ALBERTUS MAGNUS. Albertus Magnus was born around 1200 in Lauingen, Swabia, and died in 1280. A contemporary of Bonaventure and Thomas Aquinas, he is considered one of the great philosophers of the Middle Ages, at a time when scholasticism was reaching its apex. Roger Bacon, with whom Albert was occasionally in opposition, nevertheless held Albert in very high regard and considered him one of the greatest of medieval philosophers.

One of Albert's distinctions is that while a lecturer at the University of Paris, he became the mentor and teacher of Thomas Aquinas, scholasticism's greatest theologian and philosopher. Both men were Dominicans and learned students of Aristotle, together bringing the richness of Aristotelianism into the study of Christian theology.

Albert's interests were not limited to theology and philosophy but extended into the realm of the natural sciences. Along with his study of astronomy, Albert explored with great interest astrology, which for him entailed the study of how celestial bodies influence human affairs. Unlike modern astrology, which finds popular expression and practice among those engaged in esoteric religious practices, paganism, New Age thinking, and the occult in general, the study of astrology by the medieval philosophers such as Albert was grounded in an orthodox, theistic worldview.

Betsy Price, in her article "The Physical Astronomy and Astrology of Albertus Magnus," indicates that astrology provided the data by which Albert understood and explained observable effects on earth, such as rotation and the length of days or the moon's influence on tides. He believed that other natural phenomena not as readily observable nevertheless influenced births, chance occurrences, and so on. The four terrestrial elements—earth, air, fire, and water—coupled with qualities of hot-dry, hot-wet, cold-dry, and cold-wet, had corresponding relationships with the planets. Price notes that two works by Ptolemy, the *Quadripartitum* and *Centiloquium*, were very influential and described the relationship between the planets and the elements. Living things also possessed the corresponding qualities and were therefore linked to celestial bodies, each of which had unique attributes and exerted influence on life on earth.

In modern thought, alchemy is almost exclusively associated with occultism, sorcery, and witchcraft. Yet in the medieval period, alchemy was considered a science and was the forerunner of modern chemistry. Albert would have soundly condemned the use of alchemy in any way that would connect it with the black arts. Alchemists of the Middle Ages, including Albert, were predominantly focused on the study of metals and the possibility of altering their material makeup so as to change lesser metal into a higher material. This practice, the transmutation of metals, was an area of alchemy to which Albert devoted extensive study. Though he believed that the transmutation of metals was possible, he readily admitted that not only was it a difficult process, but it was questionable whether such a feat had been achieved. His interest in alchemy was limited to the academic side, the study of ancient texts, natural science relevant to alchemy, and the work of his contemporaries in meteorology. Albert's interest in alchemy as it relates to metals and his academic work dealing with the subject and practice were not unusual, given that he was not merely a theologian and a philosopher but also a naturalist. Today the academic community emphasizes specialization, whereas in the Middle Ages, intellectuals like Albert would endeavor to explore and become proficient in numerous disciplines. Thus it would not be unusual for men like Albert or Roger Bacon to delve deeply into metaphysics and the natural sciences.

Albert authored works on the natural sciences—namely, *Alchemy, Metals and Materials, Secrets of Chemistry, Origin of Metals,* and *Origins of Compounds*—and was the first to identify arsenic. Because of his extensive work in alchemy and encyclopedic knowledge of the natural sciences, he has been falsely associated with sorcery and occultism. In Mary Shelley's novel *Frankenstein,*

Dr. Frankenstein acknowledges his indebtedness to the writings of Agrippa and Albertus Magnus. In the footnotes, we are told that Agrippa was a reputed magician, and Albert moderately interested in the occult and supernatural. However, the historical evidence does not support any association of Albert Magnus with the practice of magic, sorcery, or occultism.

Bibliography. D. J. Kennedy, "Albertus Magnus," in *The Catholic Encyclopedia;* F. Kovach and R. Shahan, eds., *Albert the Great: Commemorative Essays;* J. Weisheipl, ed., *Albertus Magnus and the Sciences: Commemorative Essays.*

S. J. Rost

ALI, MAULANA MUHAMMAD. Maulana Muhammad Ali (1874–1951) was born in the state of Punjab (or Panjab) in the northwestern region of India (British region). In 1897 he became a member of the Ahmadiyya Islamic movement, which advocated Pan-Islamism and was known for promoting social justice in India. This involvement brought about his incarceration during World War I. Although Ali saw himself as helping to restore a pure form of Islam and did much to make available in translation works of Islam, many Muslim scholars considered Ahmadiyya, and Ali, heretical. He produced noteworthy translations of the Qur'an (*The Holy Qur'an: Arabic Text, English Translation and Commentary,* rev. ed.) and a theology of Islam (*The Religion of Islam: A Comprehensive Discussion of the Sources, Principles and Practices of Islam*) and *Muhammad the Prophet,* among other books. When Ahmadiyya experienced discord and then divided, Ali began another group, called Ahmadiyya Anjuman Isha'at-e-Islam Lahore (The Ahmadiyya Movement for the Propagation of Islam), with claims of holding to orthodox Islam. When he died, he was interred at Lahore, India.

See also AHMADIYYA ISLAM

Bibliography. M. Ahmad and M. A. Faruqui, *A Mighty Striving: Life Story of Maulana*

Muhammad Ali (trans. of *Mujahid-i Kabir*; English trans. Akhtar Aziz and Zahid Aziz); M. M. Ali, *The Holy Qur'an: Abrabic Text, English Translation and Commentary*, rev. ed.; Ali, *A Manual of Hadith*; Ali, *The Religion of Islam: A Comprehensive Discussion of the Sources, Principles and Practices of Islam*; Ahmadiyya Anjuman Isha'at Islam Lahore Inc. U.S.A., "Maulana Muhammad Ali (1874–1951)," http://www.muslim.org/m-ali/contents.htm.

H. W. House

AL-QADR. A fundamental doctrine of Islam, Al-Qadr refers to the eternal and unchangeable decree of Allah. This divine pronouncement is comprehensive, pertaining to everything: the creation and end of the world, the events of nature and history, and the actions and salvation (or damnation) of all persons. Al-Qadr is the ultimate determining cause of everything that occurs and implies that Allah possesses exhaustive foreknowledge (omniscience). Most Muslims stress that despite its immutability and severity, Al-Qadr is essentially gracious in character. The precise formulation and theological implications of this doctrine have been debated throughout the histories of both Sunni and Shi'ite Islam. The doctrine features less prominently within Sufism.

See also ISLAM, BASIC BELIEFS OF; ISLAM, ESCHATOLOGY OF

Bibliography. G. Endress, *An Introduction to Islam*; H. W. House, *Charts of World Religions*.

M. Power

AMERICAN ZEN COLLEGE. The American Zen College (AZC) was founded in 1978 by Go-sung Shin, a priest in the Chogye sect of Korean Buddhism and one-time pupil of Zen master Seo Kyung-bo Sunim (1914–96). Prior to establishing the AZC, Shin had studied at Harvard University and had founded three other Zen centers in the US (1970–77). Located in Germantown, Maryland, the AZC seeks to promote and reinforce the communal practice of Zen Buddhism. On the AZC campus, Shin lectures on subjects including the scriptures of Buddhism, Zen meditation and its attendant bodily positions, and the ways in which the practice of Zen impacts everyday life. Central teachings espoused by the AZC include the Threefold Refuge (taking refuge in the Buddha, the dharma, and the *sangha*) and the Four Vows (expunging desires, mastering the dharmas, working for the liberation of all sentient beings, and attaining the Way of the Buddha). The AZC publishes a newsletter, *Buddha World*, but does not disclose its enrollment figures to the public.

See also BUDDHISM; ZEN BUDDHISM

Bibliography. American Zen College website, http://www.americanzencollege.net; G. Shin, *Zen Teaching of Emptiness*.

H. W. House

AMESHA SPENTAS. In Zoroastrianism the Amesha Spentas (Persian, "holy immortals") are the six divine beings employed by Ahura Mazda (God) to fashion the physical universe. There are two main interpretations concerning the identity of these deities within the Zoroastrian religion. The first contends that these half-dozen creators are gods or angelic beings who are ontologically independent of Ahura Mazda. The second maintains that they are merely emanations of Ahura Mazda's divine nature; on this latter account, if Ahura Mazda is thought of as a cube, each Amesha Spenta may be thought of as a face of the cube. On both accounts, each Amesha Spenta has a name that distinguishes its role and function from those of the others. The names are (1) Ameretat (the spirit of immortality), (2) Asha Vahishta (the spirit of truth and justice), (3) Haurvatat Vairya (the spirit of wholeness and integrity), (4) Khshathra (the spirit of righteous power), (5) Spenta Armaiti (the spirit of holy serenity and devotion), and (6) Vohu Manah (the spirit of benevolent mind and intelligence). Each of the Amesha Spentas was responsible for an element of the creation: plants, fire, water, the sky and metals, the earth, human beings, and animals. They are also thought to permeate the essence of all things, in the guise of different aspects of our actions. They represent the law, the plan (or blueprint), action and dominion, love and faith, perfection, and immortality. Zoroastrians must adhere to these spirits to fulfill their purpose in the world. Failing to do so is wasteful and causes evil.

See also AHURA MAZDA; SACRED FIRE; ZOROASTRIANISM

Bibliography. M. Boyce, *Zoroastrians: Their Religious Beliefs and Practices*; S. A. Nigosian, *The Zoroastrian Faith: Tradition and Modern Research*; S. Shahriari, "Amesha Spentas and Chakras," http://www.zarathushtra.com/z/article/chakras.htm.

R. L. Drouhard

AMIDISM. *See* PURE LAND BUDDHISM

ANALECTS, THE. The Analects (Lun Yu, "discussion of the words") arguably has been one of the most influential books in human history, religious or otherwise. From the fourth century until the Communist takeover of China in 1950, a thorough familiarity with this text was considered an essential component of Chinese higher education. Without question the ideas espoused within its pages have had a deep and lasting influence on the culture and politics of China and other parts of East Asia. In a nutshell, the Analects is a compilation of the words (and an account of the life) of Confucius and his closest students. The near-consensus of modern scholarship is that initially the text was put together by several authors who drew upon both written and oral sources and that subsequently it was modified over the course of several centuries. Most scholars of Confucianism believe that the bulk of the text was composed over a period of about forty years during the Warring States period (ca. 480–221 BC). During the Han Dynasty (206 BC–AD 220) three versions of the Analects were in circulation: the Lu Analects, the Qi Analects, and the Ancient Text Analects; during the third century these various editions were combined into what is essentially the text consulted by the great majority of contemporary scholars. This standard text is divided into twenty chapters, each of which has a distinct theme. However, the arrangement of the material appears to be almost haphazard, in that no sustained argument unfolds when the chapters are read in sequence. At the same time, a number of key themes turn up regularly in the Analects. These include wisdom (*zhi*), righteousness (*yi*), trustworthiness or sincerity (*xin*), frugality (*lian*), loyalty (*zhong*), shame (*chi*), filial piety (*xiao*)—which regulates nearly every facet of human relationships—and (arguably) two of the highest moral qualities in Confucianism, propriety (*li*) and humaneness (*ren*). (The importance of proper education and the principles upon which government is to be founded and administered are also discussed.) These virtues are presented not as ethical innovations but as restatements of time-tested principles that apply to personal development, social conduct, and public ritual. Moreover, they are said to converge in the living paradigm of virtue, "the gentleman," a self-disciplined and gracious man who embodies and cultivates his good moral qualities in part by conveying them to others by means of meticulous Confucian rituals and character-building music. It is noteworthy that despite the text's clear indication that these virtues and the ethical framework in which they are fostered are objective, the Analects makes no attempt to ground them in a system of metaphysics or theology (though broadly religious issues, such as the significance of life and death, are addressed in various places).

See also CONFUCIANISM

Bibliography. R. T. Ames and H. Rosemont Jr., *The Analects of Confucius: A Philosophical Translation*; C. Huang, trans., *The Analects of Confucius: Lun Yu*; W. S. Morton and C. M. Lewis, *China: Its History and Culture*, 4th ed.; K. L. Ross, "*Confucius*," http://www.friesian.com/confuci.htm; A. Wright, *Confucianism and Chinese Civilization*.

H. W. House

ANANDA MARGA YOGA SOCIETY. The Ananda Marga Yoga Society was established in 1955 in Jamalpur, India, by Shrii Shrii Anandamurti (born Prabhat Ranjan Sarkar; 1921–90). Ananda Marga has centers in 160 countries, with its largest membership found in India and the Philippines. The teachings of Anandamurti emphasize self-realization and the praxis of love for all people, animals, and plant life. At the foundation of the group's teaching is the philosophy and practice of Tantric Yoga, which emphasizes the mystical liberation of the mind and the experience of eternal bliss. Tantric practice involves specific daily meditation exercises to eliminate personal addictions and to facilitate physical, mental, and spiritual growth. The group espouses a sociopolitical theory known as PROUT (Progressive Utilization Theory), which is meant to prevent social and material forces from gaining excessive political control. To overcome social inequities, a *sadvipra* (a philosopher-king) is needed to steer the world between the defects of both capitalism and Communism.

See also ANANDAMURTI, SHRII SHRII; TANTRA; TANTRIC YOGA

Bibliography. P. R. Sarkar, *Yoga Psychology*; A. Vijayananda, *The Life and Teachings of Shrii Shrii Anandamurti*.

P. Johnson

ANANDAMURTI, SHRII SHRII. Shrii Shrii Anandamurti (1921–90) founded the Ananda Marga Yoga Society. He was born in Jamalpur, India, to a Bengali family with the given name Prabhat Ranjan Sarkar. He was educated in Calcutta, and prior to Indian independence (1947) he worked as a subeditor for three English-language newspapers and then as an accountant at the Jamalpur Railway Workshop. During his student days in Calcutta, Sarkar studied tantra under the direction of his uncle Sarat Chandra Bose. Some critics have confused Sarkar's uncle with the revolutionary Indian nationalist Subhas Chandra Bose.

After engaging in the study of tantra, Sarkar then began to teach his own classes in 1955 and founded the Ananda Marga Pracaraka Samgha (Society for the Propagation of Ananda Marga). Ananda Marga means "path of bliss." Sarkar became known as Marga Guru Shrii Shrii Anandamurti, "he who attracts others as the embodiment of bliss," but he was affectionately known to his followers as Baba (Father).

Anandamurti wrote many books in which he developed the movement's complex spiritual and social teachings. He espoused a sociopolitical theory known as PROUT (Progressive Utilization Theory), which is meant to prevent social and material forces from gaining excessive political control. Only a *sadvipra* (a philosopher-king) can properly guide society on a middle course between the twin defects of capitalism and Communism, and such figures will emerge from Ananda Marga to run the world's affairs.

Within his teaching system, Anandamurti countenanced armed retaliation through a special "warrior" section. So Indian authorities suspected both him and the movement of being guilty of terrorism. In 1971 Anandamurti was arrested on a murder charge and served a prison sentence from 1977 to 1980. His case was retried and charges were quashed. The movement has established schools, orphanages, and hospitals, with meditation and social centers in 160 countries.

See also ANANDA MARGA YOGA SOCIETY

Bibliography. A. V. Avadhuta, *The Life and Teachings of Shrii Shrii Anandamurti*; P. R. Sarkar, *Yoga Psychology: Ancient and Mystical Order of the Rosa Crucis*.

P. Johnson

ANEKANTAVADA. Anekantavada (Sanskrit, "many descriptions of attributes"; "nononesidedness of reports") is a Jain philosophical theory of epistemic relativism regarding human perspectives on truth and the nature of existence. This theory maintains that reality has an infinite number of characteristics that ordinarily can be described only from the conditioned and limited perspective of the perceiver. According to anekantavada, people have mutually exclusive views of the world because during this life they are neither omniscient nor enlightened and therefore suffer from incomplete and imperfect perception. Anekantavada has two main aspects: (1) Syadvada, the doctrine that one can fully and accurately grasp the nature of things only if one is all-knowing (a Sarvajna), and (2) Nayavada, the doctrine that prior to one's liberation, the objects of human knowledge are so complex that they elude being comprehensively understood.

See also JAINISM

Bibliography. N. J. Shah, ed., *Jaina Theory of Multiple Facets of Reality and Truth*; N. Singh, ed., *Encyclopedia of Jainism*, vol. 1, *New Delhi*; R. Singh, "Non-Absolutism and Omniscience," http://www.jainworld.com/book/jainaphilosophy/jaina8.asp.

H. W. House

ANGELS. According to Christian belief, these are spiritual, immortal creatures that serve as intermediaries between God and humans. They live in heaven but can be sent to earth by God for special service. The word *angel* is derived from the Greek *angelos* and also translates the Hebrew *malak*. Both words mean "messenger." The Bible describes angels as making known and executing the purposes of God in the spiritual realm (Ps. 104:4; Matt. 4:6; Luke 1:11; Rev. 16:1).

Classification of Angels in Christianity. Even though the word *angel* appears nearly three hundred times in English translations of the Bible, other words also refer to these messengers. These words are used often to classify angels and delineate their duties.

Ministering Spirits. The word for minister in the Greek, *leitourgos*, and the Hebrew *mishrathim* both designate a priest or person with religious duties (1 Kings 8:11; 2 Kings 4:43; Rom. 15:16; Phil. 2:25 NRSV; Heb. 8:2 NRSV) and are used of angels (Ps. 104:4 NRSV) as those who minister for God in spiritual service.

Heavenly Host. The Hebrew *sava* is used for angels in connection with God's heavenly army. In Psalm 103:20–21, the *malakim* and *mishrathim* are called *sava* and are called upon to bless the Lord. The *sava* are an extension of God's power and providence, accomplishing his will and doing battle for him as a military force. God himself, Yahweh of Hosts, is the sovereign commander of this great heavenly army who does his will in both heaven and earth.

Watchers. This term designates angels employed by God to carry out his will in directing human government (Dan. 4:13, 17). As God is in sovereign control of his creation, he may use such watchers to effect decision making and execute his decrees in the world's affairs.

Sons of God. The Hebrew idiom *bene elohim* is used of angels as belonging to a class of powerful beings closely associated with God. As a family or class, they are "sons of *Elohim*," as in Job 1:6; 2:1; 38:7; possibly Genesis 6:2, 4. The term pictures angels as a supernatural class of beings similar in nature to God (i.e., beings of spirit) though inferior to him.

Chariots of God. These are part of God's heavenly host, or army. In Psalm 68:17, these intervened to enable victory for Israel when kings and armies opposed them. It is also used in 2 Kings 6:16–17, when Elisha and his servant were protected by an angelic force of horses and chariots. Zechariah described these as "four spirits of heaven, going out from standing in the presence of the Lord of the whole world" (Zech. 6:5).

Stars. "Stars" symbolizes the heavenly nature and abode of angels, comparing angels to stars as heavenly creations that reflect God's omniscience and power (Ps. 148:1–5). Both angels and stars are called the hosts of heaven (Deut. 4:19; 17:3; 1 Kings 22:19; Ps. 33:6). For angels to be called stars in Scripture is to speak symbolically of spirits created by God.

Holy Ones. A translation from the Hebrew *kadoshim,* meaning "set apart to God," as in Psalm 89:6–7. "Holy ones" is understood as referring to angels. Other passages using the same expression include Job 5:1; 15:15; Daniel 8:13; and Zechariah 14:5, reflecting the holy character and activities of angels devoted to God.

Cherubim. This is the plural form of the Hebrew *cherub,* describing special orders or classes of angels that have great power and beauty, beyond human imagination. After humanity was removed from the garden of Eden (Gen. 3:24), cherubim were placed by God at the garden's gate with flaming swords to protect the way to the tree of life, lest sinful human beings should partake of it. Figures of cherubim are associated with the tabernacle (Exod. 25:17–22; Heb. 9:5) and are important symbols of the Mosaic worship. They are represented with human features like faces and hands but also are seen as having wings. Though cherubim are considered a class of angels, they are never termed "angels," possibly because of the nonrevelatory nature of their duty. Instead of being messengers, they seem to be protectors of God's glorious presence, his sovereignty, and his holiness (Ps. 80:1; 99:1).

Seraphim. From the Hebrew word meaning "burning ones." It likely refers to their devotion to God rather than their outward appearance. They are represented as having human features such as faces, hands, and feet, as are the cherubim. They also have six wings, two of which cover their faces, indicating that no creature can look at God; two of which cover their feet, showing that the ground before God and his things is holy; and two of which allow them to fly, showing their readiness and speed to obey God's commands. In Isaiah 6:3, the seraphim cry, "Holy, holy, holy is the LORD Almighty; the whole earth is full of his glory." This passage appropriately displays the seraphim's devotion and desire to forever praise the perfect holiness of God. It represents a priestly service to God, which calls attention to his holy standard, which demands the holiness of anyone who approaches God, just as Isaiah's lips had to be cleansed before speaking God's word to human beings (Isa. 6:5–9).

Angels in Mormonism. The Church of Jesus Christ of Latter-day Saints (LDS Church), though it professes to be the only true Christian church, denies many of the essentials of the Christian faith. The angel Moroni supposedly showed Joseph Smith Jr., founder of the LDS Church, where gold plates could be found that contained the Book of Mormon. According to LDS theology, the term *angel* normally refers to a heavenly messenger who has a body of flesh and bones (either by having already been resurrected or by being "translated" to heaven without dying). Thus Moroni is identified as the final human author of the Book of Mormon, who lived in the Americas in the early fifth century AD. Joseph Smith also claimed that various biblical figures appeared to him as angels, such as John the Baptist, Peter, James, John, Moses, and Elijah.

Angels in the Jehovah's Witnesses. A notable doctrine of the Jehovah's Witnesses is that Jesus Christ is not the one true Jehovah

God but is instead a spirit creature known as Michael the Archangel. In false religions and pseudo-Christian groups where Christ is dethroned and the Bible is either disregarded or added to, there is evidence of doctrines of demons (1 Tim. 4:1–2) and deception that lead people away.

Angels in Other Religions. Just as there are angels in the Christian religion, they, or their functional equivalent, are also part of other religions. In many religions, there is no concept that is strictly identified with the Christian view of angels. Nevertheless, most religions have at least a belief in "spirit" beings that are analogous in some ways to the Christian idea of angels.

African Traditional Religion. On the surface, African traditional religion (ATR) is monotheistic, but many tribes recognize various gods subordinate to the one supreme God, who is known by different names in different tribes. For most ATR practitioners, the concept of God is vague or irrelevant to their daily lives. Their religious practice is more or less animistic. There are two types of spirits in animism: nature spirits and ancestor spirits. The latter receive the most attention in ATR. In some tribes, wayward nature spirits may actually be neglected ancestor spirits. Accordingly, such spirits can be responsible for illnesses, which may require the use of a medicine man or witch doctor for healing.

Native American Religion. Native American religion (NAR) is often viewed as monotheistic, referring to God as the Great Spirit. However, in traditional religious practice, NAR focused on nature spirits for the most part. Such were/are said to inhabit all things—objects, animals, and so on—and to be sacred. There are wind spirits, thunder spirits, and spirits for the bear, buffalo, and the moon. As with ATR, NAR uses shamans to appease different spirits if they present themselves as evil.

Hinduism. Hindu worship of gods, goddesses, and other spirit beings varies based on locale, provincial custom, and, to a lesser extent, caste tradition. Animistic spirit-worship is incorporated into religious life. Spirits of departed ones are often provided for and honored. However, demon spirits, which can cause disease and disasters, must be appeased to prevent them from causing harm.

Islam. The beliefs of orthodox Islam concerning angels are similar to those of Judaism and Christianity, and it is incumbent upon Muslims to believe in their existence. This similarity probably relates to Muhammad's borrowing of Jewish and Christian perspectives in forming Islam. Four archangels are acknowledged: Gabriel, the messenger of revelation who brought such to the Prophet Muhammad; Michael, guardian of the Jews; Israfil, the summoner to resurrection; and Izra'il, the messenger of death. Beyond these, Muslims also believe there are an indefinite number of ordinary angels. These include two recording angels for every person. One angel on the right of every person records the good deeds of that person, while the angel on the left of every person records the bad deeds. Animistic beliefs in Islam regarding *jinn* are common as well. These are good and bad spirits that make up this class of spirit creatures. It is believed that the good spirits help in the religious performance of Muslims. It is also believed that with the coming of Jesus and Muhammad, the bad jinn or disbelieving jinn have been cast out of the various levels of heaven, though they are believed to eavesdrop from time to time in the lowest levels of heaven. It is also believed that Muhammad allowed spells, using of the names of God and of good angels, to ward off evil jinn.

See also CHRISTIANITY, PROTESTANT; CHURCH OF JESUS CHRIST OF LATTER-DAY SAINTS; HINDUISM; ISLAM, BASIC BELIEFS OF; JEHOVAH'S WITNESSES (JW); LUCIFER, MORMON VIEW OF

Bibliography. J. Ankerberg and J. Weldon, *Encyclopedia of New Age Beliefs*; K. D. Boa and

R. M. Bowman Jr., *Sense and Nonsense about Angels and Demons*; G. W. Bromiley, "Angel," in *Baker's Dictionary of Theology*; J. Danielson and D. Heimann, *The Angels and Their Mission: According to the Fathers of the Church*; G. Davidson, *A Dictionary of Angels: Including Fallen Angels*; B. Graham, *Angels: God's Secret Agents*.

C. Hux

ANGRA MAINYU. Angra Mainyu is the evil spirit in the dualistic strain of Zoroastrianism (originally monotheistic but later dualistic in its representation of Ahriman). The implacable foe of Ahura Mazda (Ormazd), he resembles the biblical Satan but was uncreated and evil originally. As the source of all evil, including demons, he is destined for annihilation. Outside the small Zoroastrian community, Angra Mainyu has become a symbol for Satanist groups.

See also AHURA MAZDA; ZOROASTRIANISM

Bibliography. Huseyin Abiva and Noura Durkee, *A History of Muslim Civilization*; R. C. Zaehner, *The Teachings of the Magi: A Compendium of Zoroastrian Beliefs*.

C. R. Wells

ANIMISM. Animism is difficult to define with precision because it is a general concept that is applied to a great diversity of indigenous and tribal religions. Provisionally, animism can be said to be the view that many or most nonhuman objects in the world—both living and nonliving—are conscious or are inhabited by spirits of some kind. Broadly speaking, worldviews that incorporate animism maintain that the world is a place of continual (and in many cases sacred) interface between spirit and matter; hence such perspectives reject any proposed rigid dichotomy between spiritual reality and material reality. Some anthropologists and sociologists of religion maintain that animism functions primarily as a practical framework for negotiating concrete cultural, political, geographical, and ecological realities and only secondarily (if at all) as a metaphysical doctrine. In some cases, belief in animism is thought to manifest itself in hunting practices wherein hunter and prey mimic each other and possess identities that are not entirely distinct. Various understandings of animism are held by members of (some) African traditional religions, Native American tribes, indigenous Siberian people-groups, South Pacific island societies, northern European pagan clans, sects of Shinto, and many other religious communities.

See also SHINTO

Bibliography. E. E. Evans-Pritchard, *Theories of Primitive Religion*; G. W. Gilmore, *Animism; or, Thought Currents of Primitive Peoples*; G. Harvey, *Animism: Respecting the Living World*; E. B. Tylor, *Religion in Primitive Culture*; R. Willerslev, *Soul Hunters: Hunting, Animism, and Personhood among the Siberian Yukaghirs*.

H. W. House

ANITYA. *Anitya* (Sanskrit "impermanence"; also known in Pali as *anicca*) is a fundamental Buddhist doctrine, according to which all things in the world are in a state of continual change and thus cannot be relied upon to provide human beings with a basis for spiritual contentment. The source of human suffering is the attempt of unenlightened persons to find happiness in these fleeting objects of experience. When a person comes to grasp the nonenduring nature of all perceived entities, he no longer will crave these transitory phenomena and will not be harmed by their ontological instability. Part and parcel of real insight into the nature of existence is the realization that even the self is ultimately unreal (*anatta*).

See also BUDDHISM

Bibliography. P. Harvey, *An Introduction to Buddhism: Teachings, History and Practices*; J. S. Strong, *The Experience of Buddhism: Sources and Interpretations*, 2nd ed.

S. J. Rost

ANNIHILATIONISM. Annihilationism is the doctrine that the souls or spirits of the wicked will not suffer conscious torment for all eternity but be annihilated, permanently ceasing to exist. This view rejects the historic teaching of the church that Satan, the demons, and the "lost" will endure eternal punishment in the lake of fire (Rev. 21:8). Scriptures adduced to support the historic view include Matthew 3:12; 18:8; 25:41, 46; Mark 9:43–48; Luke 12:5; Revelation 14:10–11; 19:19–20; 20:10; and others.

The annihilationist view holds that at the final judgment, the lost will be punished in a way commensurate with their evil and then be annihilated. Some annihilationists hold that the lost will be annihilated immediately and not resurrected at all. The annihilationist argument rests on multiple grounds, such as the disparity between finite, temporal evil and infinite, eternal punishment; the lack of a redemptive purpose in eternal hell; the incongruity of God's final victory and universal reign requiring an eternal "torture chamber"; and various arguments from the New Testament that the wicked shall "perish" and be "destroyed" with the "second death." The language of fire and sulphur is necessarily figurative. Further, they argue that the doctrine of an eternal hell has often been used to justify torture in Christian history and is counterproductive to evangelism in modern times; holding to it creates difficult philosophical quandries for theodicy.

Many annihilationists *also* deny that there is any conscious existence between death and the resurrection for either the righteous or the wicked. Neither view logically entails the other. However, Seventh-day Adventists accept both doctrines, and movements influenced by Adventism generally inherit both views as well. People who accept both views are often called *conditionalists* because they advocate the view that the Bible teaches *conditional immortality* (immortality dependent on meeting God's conditions) as opposed to innate or natural immortality (immortality even in hell).

Adherents of annihilationism generally come from groups directly influenced by William Miller, including, in roughly chronological order, Seventh-day Adventists (1863); the General Conference of the Church of God, Seventh Day (1866); Jehovah's Witnesses and numerous Bible Student groups stemming from Charles Taze Russell (1875); Herbert Armstrong, founder of the Radio Church of God (1934) and the Worldwide Church of God (1968); and splinter groups, such as the Church of God, International (1978), founded by Garner Ted Armstrong.

A few religions accept annihilationism but lack a strong connection to Adventism. These include Christadelphianism (1848), The Way International (1950), and William Branham's teachings (1958).

In recent years, some well-known evangelical theologians have accepted annihilationism, or at least openly accepted it as a *possibility* without arguing that is clearly taught. Among these are John Wenham, John R. W. Stott, and F. F. Bruce. This is clearly a difficult issue, and it merits clear thinking, Christian charity, and theological understanding.

See also CONDITIONAL IMMORTALITY; HELL, ORTHODOX AND UNORTHODOX CHRISTIAN VIEWS OF; HERESY, DEFINITION OF

Bibliography. W. M. Branham, *An Exposition of the Seven Church Ages*; The General Conference of the Church of God, (Seventh Day), "What We Believe," https://cog7.org/about-us/what-we-believe/; J. I. Packer, "Evangelical Annihilationism in Review," *Reformation & Revival*; G. Peoples, "Fallacies in the Annihilationism Debate," and R. Peterson's response, *Journal of the Evangelical Theological Society*; J. Thomas, *Elpis Israel* (1848).

E. Pement

ANOINTING. Anointing is the act of pouring oil (usually olive oil) on someone or something, often for ritual purposes; the word *anointing* also refers to the effect of the act, so that one who has been anointed may be said to "have the anointing." In antiquity anointing oil was used primarily for hygiene (e.g., preventing dry skin) and medicine (e.g., healing wounds).

In the Old Testament (OT) tabernacle and temple system, vessels and altars were anointed to set them apart for sacral use (Exod. 29:36; 30:26; 40:10–11). In addition prophets (1 Kings 19:16), priests (Exod. 28:41), and kings (2 Sam. 5:3) were anointed to sanctify them for ministry. The link between anointing and kingship is crucial in the development of messianic expectation in the OT (Messiah is the English equivalent of the Hebrew for "anointed one," Christ being the Greek equivalent).

In the New Testament (NT), anointing is a picture of the outpouring of the Holy Spirit. Jesus fulfills Isaiah 61, which speaks of a prophet-messiah anointed with God's Spirit (Luke 4:18). Peter also describes Jesus as anointed by God with the Holy Spirit (Acts 10:38). As 1 John 2:27 makes clear, this anointing is not limited to the Messiah but extends universally to all believers (see also 2 Cor. 1:21–22).

Today Eastern Orthodox churches practice *chrismation*, anointing babies or new converts after baptism. In Roman Catholicism, anointing is a key part of the sacrament of extreme unction, for which scriptural support is adduced from James 5:14 and Mark 6:13.

Recent developments in the charismatic movement and Pentecostalism have greatly emphasized the concept of anointing. Many leaders and "prophets" (e.g., Benny Hinn, Rodney Howard Browne) in the movement claim a "special anointing" that brings with it healing power and authority to govern God's people.

See also ROMAN CATHOLICISM

Bibliography. M. Dudley, *The Oil of Gladness: Anointing in the Christian Tradition*; H. H. Hanegraaff, *Counterfeit Revival*.

D. R. Streett

ANTHROPOLOGY IN CHRISTIAN THEOLOGY. The biblical account of humanity's origin in Genesis 1–2 gives a detailed account of our race's point of origin and unique place in God's creation. Unlike all other living things, humanity was created in the image of God (Gen. 1:26–27). This does not mean that God is a physical, anthropomorphic being, since God is himself the Creator of all physical reality (Gen. 1:1) and is ontologically transcendent spirit (John 4:24). Humanity is not a physical copy of God but rather was made to be a physical representative of the invisible God—an intention fully realized in God incarnate, Jesus Christ (cf. Col. 1:15; 2:9), and in all those who by God's grace are being "conformed to the image of his Son" (Rom. 8:29).

The image of God is the expression in humankind of those qualities or attributes of God that he created human beings to have (often called God's "communicable" attributes). These include moral attributes (goodness, righteousness, holiness, love), mental attributes (intellect, the capacity to reason), and volition (a will, the capacity to make free, responsible choices). The first human beings, Adam and Eve, were created in a state of innocence that was without moral, spiritual, or physical flaws, but with the capacity to make good or bad choices.

In contrast to the biblical view, naturalistic evolution proposes that humanity is the accidental product of undirected, purely natural cause-and-effect processes. Contemporary intelligent design theory, particularly as it applies to the origin of humanity, claims to show that evolutionary explanations based on materialistic naturalism lack the necessary evidence to show that human origins are devoid of the work of a supreme intelligence. Advances in modern biology and even animal psychology have not erased the qualitative differences between humans and even the most intelligent and "social" animals.

Humankind's uniqueness is evident not only in its ontological distinction from all other created life forms but also in the dominion mandate of Genesis 1:28, where God tells human beings that they are to rule over and subdue the earth. As responsible stewards of the natural world, they are given authority to manage and use what God has made.

The Human Constitution. In general most nonbiblical anthropologies fall into two different extremes of *anthropological monism* (the idea that human nature is essentially of one substance). At one extreme is the belief, prevalent among atheists and other skeptics, that human beings are only material beings and that any mental or spiritual characteristics are purely functions of the physical body. The Jehovah's Witnesses also accept a form of this belief. At the other extreme is the belief, common in many forms of Eastern religion, that only spirit or mind is real and that the physical body is an expression or even an illusion of the mind/spirit. In contrast to these positions, the Bible teaches that human beings are a union of physical and spiritual parts or aspects (*anthropological dualism*). The physical aspect of human nature is typically called the body or flesh, while the spiritual aspect is typically called the soul or spirit (e.g., Matt. 10:28; 1 Cor. 5:3, 5; 2 Cor. 7:1; James 2:26). The apostle Paul also called these two aspects the outer being, which is seen, and the inner being, which is unseen (Rom. 7:22–25; 2 Cor. 4:16–18; Eph. 3:16).

The immaterial part of a human being consists of those qualities that constitute what in totality is identified as the heart. It is the seat of the mind (Prov. 2:10). The mind of a human being is of extraordinary importance, for it affects the whole person. No sharp or rigid distinction is made in Scripture with regard to such terms as *heart*, *mind*, or *soul*, all of which express with various nuances the inner person (e.g., Deut. 6:5; Matt. 22:37; Luke 10:27; Heb. 10:16). The heart also includes the affections (Jer. 15:16), will (Prov. 16:1), the religious or spiritual life (Deut. 6:5–6; 2 Cor. 5:2–3), and the center of affections (John 14:1, 27). Because the heart is the totality of our innermost being, Proverbs 4:23 warns us that it is to be guarded with diligence.

Humanity's Corruption. Genesis 3 describes the fall of humanity, which came about when Adam and Eve rebelled against God's specific instructions and succumbed to the temptation to be like God as autonomous beings instead of humbly serving as creatures in God's image. The result was spiritual and physical death, the corruption of all of creation, and the imputation of Adam's sin to all of his posterity (Rom. 5:12–14). Humanity now became morally corrupt (Rom. 3:10), lacked spiritual understanding (Rom. 3:11), and possessed a depraved will incapable of seeking after God and his righteousness. The effect of sin on humanity is internal, rising from the thoughts and inclinations of the heart; pervasive, affecting every inclination, so that our deeds are only evil; and continuous, operating at all times. The evidence of humanity's corruption is manifested universally, in every nation and culture, whether it be advanced or primitive.

Humanity's Redemption. Our fallen state and resultant spiritual depravity incurs the wrath of God (Rom. 1:18). However, God has made provision for our redemption and ultimate restoration not only to our prefall state but to a perfect condition of confirmed righteousness and glory. This is accomplished by the death of Christ as an atonement for sin. The salvation of every human being results in the transformation of that person's nature and the ongoing spiritual growth known as sanctification. Eventual physical and spiritual perfection will be realized at the resurrection, where the spiritual and physical aspects of the redeemed will be reunited and sealed in a state of immortality.

See also ANTHROPOLOGY OF RELIGION

Bibliography. J. G. Machen, *The Christian View of Man*; R. Machuga, *In Defense of the Soul: What It Means to Be Human*; H. D. McDonald, *The Christian View of Man*; J. P. Moreland and D. Ciocchi, eds., *Christian Perspectives on Being Human*; A. Pegis, *At the Origins of the Thomistic Notion of Man.*

S. J. Rost

ANTHROPOLOGY OF RELIGION. Anthropology is the study of human thought and behavior in societies worldwide. It is very similar to sociology. Traditionally the difference between anthropology and sociology was that anthropologists studied faraway, non-Western societies, while sociologists studied modern Western society. Over the years, this difference has broken down as anthropologists turned their attention to Western societies and sociologists applied their techniques worldwide. Today the main difference is in the preference for specific methods. Historically anthropologists concentrated on qualitative research, using such techniques as participant observation and life-history interviews, while sociologists relied on quantitative research, involving survey research and statistical analysis of the data. More recently scholars in both fields have tended to use similar methods, with anthropologists preferring qualitative methods while sociologists concentrate on quantitative methods.

Although the study of society by anthropologists remains wedded to the method of participant observation and to grassroots events, it has nevertheless become highly diversified. This is an adaptation to the fact that not only have societies changed, but with this change our analytical and theoretical approaches have multiplied.

Modern anthropology originated in the wake of the philosophical movement known as Romanticism. It has its origin primarily in the work of Johann Gottfried Herder (1744–1803), who encouraged the study of diverse cultures within an overall framework of universalism. In North America, Herder directly influenced the work of the founder of American anthropology, Franz Boas (1858–1942). In Britain, Herder's influence was felt through writers like Sir Walter Scott (1771–1832), who encouraged a new empathy for the past. Later British anthropology developed in close contact with German anthropological thinking through the influence of scholars like Bronislaw Malinowski (1884–1942) and Diedrich Westermann (1875–1956). The latter was a former missionary who, along with a missionary circle in London, founded the International Institute of African Languages and Culture (now the International African Institute). From 1926 to 1939, Westermann edited the influential journal *Africa.* He and both British and German colleagues worked with concepts of culture change and functionalism that showed great sympathy for non-Western peoples and societies as well as a solid appreciation of their history.

With the outbreak of war, Westermann's name was removed from the title page of the journal *Africa,* and all memory of the contribution of German scholars to British anthropology seems to have been eradicated. Instead, Malinowski, a Pole, was elevated as the "inventor of fieldwork," something he actually admitted learning from German scholars, especially Jan Stanislaw Kubary (1846–96), who was of mixed German and Slavic descent. Now a new school of British social anthropology that ignored history and decried "culture" as an American preoccupation emerged, with Alfred Radcliffe-Brown (1881–1955) at its head. Later the acknowledged leader of British social anthropology was E. E. Evans-Pritchard (1902–73), who, unlike Radcliffe-Brown, was an excellent fieldworker, social-structuralist, and historian. After laying a solid foundation, the British school of thought, with its heyday in the late 1950s and early 1960s, was superseded by new approaches developed in North

23

America and France. In America, anthropologists like Victor Turner (1920–86), Clifford Geertz (1926–2006), and Marshall Sahlins (1930–) developed what may be called symbolic approaches to religion. Turner elaborated the analysis of the semantic structure of dominant symbols with their emotive and cognitive poles. Geertz concentrated on the conceptual aspects of religion and is best known for his method of "thick description." Finally, Sahlins treated religion as part of a cultural design that gives order to practical experience, customary practices, and the relationship between the two.

The classic study of religion by an anthropologist is E. E. Evans-Pritchard's *Witchcraft, Oracles and Magic among the Azande* (1937). In this imaginative work based on solid fieldwork, he developed an understanding of the internal logic of Azande witchcraft beliefs. This work became the model for later studies by John Middleton (1921–2009), Mary Douglas (1921–2007), and others as they sharpened the contrasts among witchcraft, sorcery, and divination and attempted to correlate these with forms of social organization and kinship ties.

The idea that religion provides order and meaning was carried forward, almost to the point of obsession, by French structuralists like Claude Lévi-Strauss (1908–2009), and in the English world by Edmund Leach (1910–87). Leach's analysis of metaphor takes religion out of what he sees as its cognitive quagmire back into the world of ecstatic and charismatic religions. As societies changed and ideas of globalization replaced simpler views about the so-called third world, so also did the study of religion change. The analysis of processes became important, replacing earlier views of static, nonliterate societies. At the same time, interest in new religions in the West encouraged further study of millenarian or nativistic movements in the non-Western world. Here the work of Anthony F. C. Wallace (1923–2015) on revitalization

movements led the way. Wallace's study of the religion of the Seneca Nation provided a detailed picture of the forces that threaten to destroy a society and the stages of the subsequent revitalization process. More important, Wallace understood the often fragile boundaries between religion, politics, and the military.

More recently anthropologists have shown that modernization does not produce, as is so often assumed, "rational" individuals whose behavior loses symbolic dimensions. Actually the opposite is usually the case. Winston Davis (1939–), Irving Hexham (1943–), Karla Poewe (1941–), and others have argued that industrialization often furthers the growth of new religions and magical practices in urban settings. An exemplary study of religion is Kenelm Burridge's (1922–) *In the Way*. It is one of the few anthropological works on missionaries that also attempt to understand their Christianity.

Today anthropology provides a dynamic approach to the study of religion that frees scholars from the tyranny of armchair reflection and concentration on the publications of groups by challenging people to discover what others actually believe and how they practice their beliefs. In today's emerging multicultural world, where cross-cultural understanding is increasingly important, the anthropology of religions offers ways out of the impasse created by lack of contact between different groups. It also provides methods for approaching intercultural communication and vivid insights into how we understand others.

See also ANTHROPOLOGY IN CHRISTIAN THEOLOGY

Bibliography. R. N. Bellah, *Tokugawa Religion: The Values of Pre-Industrial Japan*; K. Burridge, *In the Way: A Study of Christian Missionary Endeavors*; Burridge, *New Heaven, New Earth*; M. L. Daneel, *The God of the Matopo Hills*; Daneel, *Old and New in Southern Shona Independent Churches*; W. Davis, *Dojo: Magic* and *Exorcism in Modern Japan*; Mary Douglas, *Explorations in Cosmology*; Douglas, *Natural Symbols*; Douglas, *Purity and Danger*; E. E. Evans-Pritchard, *Witchcraft, Oracles and Magic among the Azande*; C. Geertz, *The Interpretation of Cultures*; I. Hexham and K. Poewe, *New Religions as Global Culture*; Hexham and Poewe, *Understanding Cults and New Religions*; S. Kakar, *Shamans, Mystics and Doctors*; E. Leach, *Culture and Communication: The Logic by Which Symbols Are Connected*; C. Lévi-Strauss, *Structural Anthropology*; I. M. Lewis, *Ecstatic Religion*; G. C. Oosthuizen, *Pentecostal Penetration into the Indian Community in Metropolitan Durban, South Africa*; Oosthuizen, *Post-Christianity in Africa*; K. Poewe, *The Namibian Herero: A History of Their Psychosocial Disintegration and Survival*; M. Sahlins, *Culture and Practical Reason*; B. Sundkler, *Bantu Prophets in South Africa*; A. F. C. Wallace, *Religion: An Anthropological Approach*; F. B. Welbourn, *East African Rebels*.

K. Poewe

ANTINOMIANISM. *Definition*. *Antinomianism*, which means "against law" (from Greek, *anti* + *nomos*), refers to the belief that one is not obligated to adhere to moral laws in general. Klaus Bockmuehl defines antinomianism as "theoretical, conscious, intentional lawlessness" (85). Adherents of antinomianism, as well as philosophies and movements that engender antinomian thinking, are found in both Christian and secular contexts. Historically within the Christian community, the charge of antinomianism has been leveled against those who contend that believers are not obligated to adhere to the Old Testament (OT) moral law because they are under grace. It is argued that Christians live in accordance with the prompting and convicting work of the Holy Spirit, not the moral legal code.

In contradistinction to an antinomian approach to the moral law, OT scholars Walter Kaiser and Christopher Wright offer a balanced approach to the authority of the OT. In their writings, they argue that the OT law is, with qualification, applicable today. They appeal to 2 Timothy 3:16, which presents a serious challenge to antinomianism, stating explicitly that all Scripture is profitable for doctrinal and moral instruction. Scholars generally agree that this passage refers to the OT, which would include the law. Evangelicals such as Wright and Kaiser agree that Christ fulfilled the ceremonial law but insist that civil and moral prescriptions are still authoritative as moral guides even though they are not means of grace and do not facilitate justification. Jesus and Paul both used the OT in their preaching and teaching to advance moral principles, but also to demonstrate the sinfulness of humanity.

New Testament. The New Testament (NT) provides some of the earliest examples of antinomian thinking within the Christian community. The apostle Paul's writings indicate he encountered and responded to antinomian thinking and behavior. In 1 Corinthians 5:1–6, Paul addressed sexual immorality in the church, specifically incest. He was greatly troubled by both the presence of the kind of immorality being practiced (for even gentiles didn't engage in such behavior) and the church's toleration of it. It is possible the Corinthians were influenced by two converging streams of influence: an incipient gnosticism (see Yamauchi), which would incline them to view matter as evil, and an antinomian or libertine attitude toward the moral law. Thus a dualistic view of the material and spiritual world could lead one to conclude that the body, being material, was of no importance. So, logically, one could ignore moral restrictions on what one did with one's body. In Romans 5:20–21, Paul points out that where sin abounds, the grace of God equally abounds. Paul's point is that no sin can be great enough to elude the power of grace. However, in Romans 6:11 Paul anticipates that some will exploit his teaching on grace by embracing an antinomian application that advocates the unrestricted practice

25

of sin, thinking that in so doing they will cause grace to increase. Such antinomian thinking implicitly nullifies the moral law in favor of increasing grace by unrestrained sinful behavior.

The Early Church. In the early church, the rise of gnostic sects brought about a more definitive antinomianism. First, gnosticism considered the material world evil, so it made no difference spiritually what one did with the physical body. Some adherents of gnosticism took this view to its logical conclusion by indulging their physical passions. Second, gnosticism taught that the God of the OT was the Demiurge, an inferior god not to be equated with the true God. Furthermore, the Demiurge was the source of the OT Law. Since gnostics rejected the Demiurge as the true God, they took an antinomian approach to the OT law, thus rejecting the effect (law) by rejecting the cause (Demiurge).

Antinomian Controversies. During the Reformation, Martin Luther's teaching on justification by grace through faith alone eventually led to what would become the antinomian controversy. Luther taught that the law was essential for salvation in that it revealed the sinfulness of humans (Rom. 7:7). However, the law was not binding on Christians in either a judicial or ceremonial sense, given that civil authorities were responsible for overseeing and implementing laws for the welfare of society. Luther believed the law was of great spiritual value in that it elicited from people an understanding of their guilt before God. Johann Agricola, a former student and teaching colleague of Luther's, eventually proposed the antinomian thesis that the law played no role in justification. He believed it was the gospel, not the law, that should bring about an awareness of sin and the need for repentance. However, he didn't discount the law as a viable tool for civil stability. In response Luther published *Against the Antinomians.*

In seventeenth-century Massachusetts, an antinomian controversy erupted as a result of Puritan dissenter Anne Hutchinson, who took a critical stance against the teachings of other preachers, who were teaching that good works are an evidence of one's election. She contended that in no way can good works validate one's election; only by the internal witness of the Holy Spirit could one be assured of salvation. Thus believers are not bound to the law. Neither Agricola nor Hutchinson opposed the moral teachings of Scripture, but they did stand against the application of the law as a means by which conviction of sin or justification was in any way facilitated.

Around the same time, a vigorous division arose between preachers who taught that sanctification, or works of righteousness, gave evidence of one's true conversion. However, opponents of this teaching took Luther's understanding of imputed righteousness as the sole basis for assurance of salvation, viewing sanctification, or works of righteousness, as merely acts of thanksgiving. They argued that an emphasis on external works as evidence of one's justification minimized or ignored the promise that one's faith saves, and such faith is the sole source of assurance. Those preachers who taught this minimalist view of sanctification were accused of being antinomian.

See also LEGALISM FROM A CHRISTIAN PERSPECTIVE

Bibliography. K. Bockmuehl, "Keeping the Commandments," *Evangelical Review of Theology*; M. Brecht, *Martin Luther: The Preservation of the Church, 1532–1546*; J. F. Cooper, "Hutchinson, Anne Marbury," in *Dictionary of Christianity in America*; N. Geisler, "Antinomianism," in the *New Dictionary of Christian Ethics and Pastoral Theology*; E. Harrison, "Antinomianism," in *Baker's Dictionary of Christian Ethics*; W. Kaiser Jr., *Toward Old Testament Ethics*; R. Linder, "Antinomianism," in *Evangelical Dictionary of Theology*; A. H. Newman,

"Antinomianism," in the *The New Schaff-Herzog Encyclopedia of Religious Knowledge*; Simone Petrement, *A Separate God: The Origins and Teachings of Gnosticism*; C. J. H. Wright, *Walking in the Ways of the Lord*; Edwin Yamauchi, *Pre-Christian Gnosticism*.

S. J. Rost

ANTINOMIANISM, NON-CHRISTIAN. *Antinomianism*, which means "against law" (from Greek, *anti* + *nomos*), refers to the belief that one is not obligated to adhere to moral laws in general. In the non-Christian context, examples of antinomianism are found in existentialist philosophy such as that advocated by Jean-Paul Sartre, which taught, "Be true to yourself," which opens the door for self-expression and self-gratification. The thesis that God is dead, advocated by Friedrich Nietzsche, entailed the absence or demise of any absolute or final moral authority, a conclusion similar to Dostoyevsky's statement that if God doesn't exist, anything is permissible. Other expressions of antinomianism include hedonism, the love of pleasure without restraint; ethical relativism, popularized by Joseph Fletcher; and the rampant libertinism in France and Britain in the seventeenth through the nineteenth centuries, producing such notable practitioners as John Wilmot and Marquis de Sade.

See also LEGALISM FROM A CHRISTIAN PERSPECTIVE

Bibliography. A. H. Newman, "Antinomianism" in the *The New Schaff-Herzog Encyclopedia of Religious Knowledge*; Edwin Yamauchi, *Pre-Christian Gnosticism*.

S. J. Rost

APOLOGETICS. The term *apologetics* derives from the Greek word *apologia*, which originally signified a speech in someone's defense in a court of law. Christian apologetics constitutes the science and practice of arguing on behalf of historic Christianity's truthfulness and/or the advisability of accepting it, rebutting objections to historic Christianity, and arguing against systems of belief that are incompatible with historic Christianity.

This article first summarizes the reasons for cultivating Christian apologetics, then reviews common objections to Christian apologetics, and, finally, surveys apologetic methodologies.

Reasons for Cultivating Apologetics. That Scripture commands Christians to engage in apologetics, at least in a rudimentary sense of the term, constitutes by far the most important reason why Christians ought to employ apologetic reasoning in seeking to persuade others to embrace the historic Christian faith. Biblical Christians, after all, are committed to the propositions that one ought to love God with all one's heart, soul, mind, and strength (Mark 12:30; cf. parallel in Luke 10:27) and that "this is love for God: to keep his commands" (1 John 5:3). They ought, consequently, to require no further motive for cultivating Christian apologetics than the scriptural injunctions, "Always be ready to make your defense to anyone who demands from you an accounting for the hope that is in you" (1 Pet. 3:15 NRSV), and, "Contend for the faith that was once for all entrusted to the saints" (Jude 3 NRSV).

Nevertheless, at least three further considerations also warrant the study and practice of Christian apologetics. First, numerous persons refuse to consider the gospel seriously unless they are presented with evidence for its truthfulness. Simply in order to gain a hearing for the gospel, therefore, the Christian must frequently resort to apologetic reasoning. Like Paul, one must "become all things to all people," so that by all means one might win some (1 Cor. 9:22). Paul himself presented apologetic arguments in support of Christian faith, as in his famous speech in Athens, in which he reasoned in a manner that the Stoics and the Epicureans there could understand (Acts 17:16–34).

Second, responsible persons rightly weigh the evidence for and against beliefs proposed to them for acceptance, especially when those beliefs, if accepted, would necessitate a radical reorientation of their thought and lives. The Christian evangelist seeks, among other things, to awaken the unconverted to the enormity of the guilt they have incurred precisely by shirking their responsibilities to God and their neighbor. It behooves the Christian evangelist, therefore, above all other persons, to avoid the impression that he or she advocates shirking one's responsibility "not [to] believe every spirit, but [to] test the spirits to see whether they are from God" (1 John 4:1).

Third, numerous Christians find themselves weighed down by a burden of doubt, continually tempted to apostatize on account of specious objections to Christianity, which Christians properly trained in apologetics can answer convincingly. Those who pray that God would deliver them and other Christians from temptation and who seek to do good "especially to those who belong to the family of believers" (Gal. 6:10) thus possess ample reason to study apologetics and "build each other up" (1 Thess. 5:11) through apologetic reasoning. Even if Scripture did not command Christians to cultivate apologetics, therefore, zeal for the conversion of the lost, concern for the integrity of the gospel, and compassion for doubting saints would mandate its study and application, nonetheless.

Objections to Christian Apologetics. Nevertheless, some Christians do shun apologetics, even seriously objecting to its use in evangelism. Such persons argue, first, that "no one can say, 'Jesus is Lord,' except by the Holy Spirit" (1 Cor. 12:3). That is, if the Holy Spirit regenerates a hearer of the gospel, the person will necessarily believe, but if the Holy Spirit does not regenerate the hearer, the most compelling arguments will not suffice to persuade that person to accept Christ. Since only the Holy Spirit can move a person to faith—it seems to those who repudiate apologetics—arguments as to why one ought to believe are superfluous.

Second, Christian opponents of apologetics argue, apologetic reasoning appears positively irreverent inasmuch as it replaces the "demonstration of the Spirit's power" with "wise and persuasive words" (1 Cor. 2:4). Scripture explicitly states, such persons correctly observe, that "since in the wisdom of God the world through its wisdom did not know him, God was pleased through the foolishness of what was preached to save those who believe" (1 Cor. 1:21). In view of this, it seems to many that the employment of apologetic argumentation in evangelism brazenly usurps the Holy Spirit's prerogatives, empties the cross of Christ of its power (1 Cor. 1:17), and causes the faith of Christians to rest not in the power of God but in the wisdom of human beings (1 Cor. 2:4).

Indisputably, therefore, one can mount at least a superficially powerful case against apologetics on the basis of Scripture. Three considerations, nevertheless, suffice to dispel this case's patina of plausibility. First, applying the argument from 1 Corinthians 12:3 to the uselessness of apologetic reasoning, if pressed to its utmost implications, entails the absurd conclusion that gospel preaching itself is superfluous, for gospel preaching is no less impotent to save in the absence of the regenerating work of the Holy Spirit than apologetic argument. If the impotence of apologetic argument, minus the Holy Spirit, proves the enterprise of apologetics itself to be worthless, therefore, it proves the preaching of the gospel worthless as well.

Second, the verses cited above against the propriety of apologetics—namely, 1 Corinthians 1:17, 21; 2:4—need not imply that apologetic reasoning constitutes an intrinsically irreverent means of calling persons to obedience to the gospel. When Paul declares in 1 Corinthians 1:17, for example, that Christ sent him to preach "not with wisdom and eloquence, lest the cross of Christ be emptied of its power," he may mean merely that God commands him to forsake the elaborate artifices of Greek rhetoric in order to focus attention on Christ. When Paul avers, "My message and my preaching were not with wise and persuasive words, but with a demonstration of the Spirit's power, so that your faith might not rest on human wisdom, but on God's power" (1 Cor. 2:4–5), likewise, he may intend merely to disavow the kind of oratory that would inspire faith in the orator rather than God. Paul's statement that it pleased God to save not through wisdom but through the foolishness of the message preached, moreover, may indicate merely that God chose to save through faith in a supernatural revelation rather than through knowledge gained by philosophical inquiry into nature. Undoubtedly, Paul seeks to emphasize in these and kindred passages God's exaltation of the helpless over the mighty. "God has chosen the foolish things in the world," he writes, "to shame the wise; God chose what is weak in the world to shame the strong; God chose what is low and despised in the world, things that are not, to reduce to nothing things that are, so that no one might boast in the presence of God" (1 Cor. 1:27–29 NRSV).

None of this implies, however, that a humble and sincere appeal to facts, such as the evidence of design in nature or of fulfilled prophecy, can have no place in the faithful proclamation of the gospel. One may be assured, in fact, that God not merely allows but encourages such apologetic argumentation because in numerous instances God places apologetic arguments on the lips of prophets, apostles, various scriptural authors, and Jesus himself. In 2 Chronicles 25:15, for example, an unnamed prophet argues with Amaziah that he was foolish to take up the worship of the Edomites' gods because those gods had proved incapable of delivering the Edomites

from Amaziah's own hands. The author of Psalm 115, likewise, argues for the absurdity of idol worship on the basis of the idols' evident disabilities: having mouths, they speak not; having feet, they walk not; and so on (cf. vv. 4–8 and Ps. 135:15–18). Indeed, Isaiah portrays God as challenging the imaginary deities of the gentiles to an argument about the identity of the true God and proposing the ability to foretell the future as a criterion of true divinity (Isa. 41:21–23; cf. 44:7; 45:21; 46:10; 48:3, 5, 6).

In the New Testament (NT), moreover, one finds all the gospel writers appealing constantly to the argument from prophecy. Both Paul (Acts 13:31; 1 Cor. 15:5–8) and Peter (Acts 2:32; 3:15; 10:41) appeal to the evidence of eyewitness testimony for the bodily resurrection of Jesus. Paul, moreover, argues by analogy from the conceivability of a seed's rising from the earth as a plant to the conceivability of a physical resurrection of the dead; and Jesus himself appeals to the evidence of his miracles as proof of the message he preaches. "Do not believe me unless I do the works of my Father," he declares. "But if I do them, even though you do not believe me, believe the works, that you may know and understand that the Father is in me, and I in the Father" (John 10:37–38). Presumably, God would not employ an approach to persuading unbelievers that he himself condemns as ineffectual or worse. Christian critics of apologetics can hardly be correct, therefore, when they condemn apologetic argumentation as unscriptural.

Apologetic Methodologies. Christians, then, may and, in view of the rationale for Christian apologetics offered above, ought to employ apologetic reasoning in their efforts to win others to Christ. In order to do so consistently and systematically, it seems, they must adopt some apologetic methodology: some definite view, that is, as to what they can reasonably expect to prove by apologetic argument and what kinds of argument they ought to employ. The principle apologetic methodologies employed by Christians today are five: the classical, the exclusively historical, the pragmatic, the presuppositional, and the method associated with "Reformed epistemology."

Practitioners of classical apologetics typically distinguish between at least two stages in any thorough justification of the Christian faith. One must, classical apologists believe, establish, on the basis of natural revelation, God's existence and certain of his attributes, such as justice, honesty, and benevolence, before one can reasonably argue for the truthfulness of Scripture on the basis of the evidence of miracles and fulfilled prophecy. If God does not exist, advocates of this method reason, miracles cannot occur; if one cannot prove that God exists, therefore, one can never construct a compelling historical argument for a miracle's occurrence.

Naturally, classical apologists do not believe that the evangelist ought to expend hours discussing arguments for God's existence with someone who already believes in God. They do hold, however, that in order to construct an argument for Christianity that is sound in the abstract, one must, among other things, argue philosophically for the existence of God and his possession of certain attributes. In order, that is, to construct a science of Christian apologetics, whose task is to supply logically rigorous proofs of Christianity, on whose findings practical apologists/evangelists can draw in their efforts to engage particular unbelievers, one must, according to classical apologists, address both philosophical and historical questions.

Practitioners of the second widely employed apologetic methodology—that is, the exclusively historical approach—do not necessarily disagree with the convictions of classical apologists about the exigencies of apologetics as a science. They tend, rather, to view apologetics in exclusively practical terms and to hold, correctly, that contemporary persons tend to be neither patient with nor receptive of arguments founded on abstract, philosophical reasoning. Advocates of the exclusively historical approach conclude, accordingly, that effective, practical apologists/evangelists ought to confine themselves to historical arguments such as that from fulfilled prophecy or that from the empirical evidence for Christ's resurrection.

To the objection that no amount of argument for the occurrence of a miracle can establish that it occurred in the absence of evidence that God exists, exclusively historically minded apologists respond that the miracles themselves constitute sufficient evidence for God's existence. Just as one need not prove that Homer existed before one can reasonably establish, on the basis of the *Iliad* and the *Odyssey*, that he held certain views, adherents of this school argue, one need not establish that God exists before one can reasonably argue from God's causation of miracles to his endorsement of Scripture.

Proponents of the exclusively historical method, then, advocate a one-stage apologetic, which, to the extent that it is actually persuasive, does achieve its objectives more directly and efficiently than a thoroughly classical apologetic. However, whether in the long term the church can afford to do without the academic, scientific apologetics of the classical school and whether merely historical arguments can be widely persuasive in cultures saturated with atheism constitute serious questions for anyone who might advocate supplanting the classical method entirely with the exclusively historical approach to apologetics. Some apologists whose approach is methodologically akin to the historical method broaden their apologetic arsenal or repertoire to include philosophical, scientific, and other sorts of arguments, all of which the apologist treats as evidence for the Christian faith. Both the practitioners of the exclusively historical method and those who include other types of factual arguments are often called evidentialists.

Advocates of the third widely practiced apologetic method, the pragmatic, typically harbor deep skepticism about the ability of human beings to demonstrate rationally that God exists or that Christianity is true. Accordingly, eschewing the kind of arguments employed by the classical and exclusively historical schools, practitioners of the pragmatic method attempt to prove that, among all conceivable worldviews, only Christianity can consistently be lived. That is, non-Christian outlooks on life invariably contradict one or more of the presuppositions that human beings must adopt in order to lead happy, reasonable, and morally responsible lives.

The popularity of this approach surged in the 1960s, when rationality itself became widely suspect and when Christianity competed for the loyalty of youth with existentialism, Marxism, Eastern religions, and the drug culture—all of whose ideals, if consistently applied, lead to despair. As pragmatic apologists themselves would admit, their approach to apologetics supplies no means of securely establishing the conclusion for which they argue—namely, that only Christianity can be lived. For even if one could demonstrate that every existing worldview leads to hopelessness, one could not thereby prove that some livable alternative to Christianity might not emerge in the future. The pragmatic approach to apologetics presupposes, therefore, the indispensability of a nonrational element in a human being's decision to accept the gospel: the necessity of some kind of leap of faith. The question of whether one could responsibly adopt the pragmatic method as one's sole approach to apologetics hinges largely, it seems, on whether this is a reasonable assumption.

Enthusiasts for the fourth widely employed apologetic methodology, presuppositionalism, resemble adherents of the pragmatic school in that they consider demonstrative, noncircular proof of Christianity's truthfulness to be impossible. Presuppositionalists, however, do not generally follow pragmatic apologists in arguing for Christianity exclusively on the basis of other worldviews' putative unlivability. Rather, they argue that reality is ultimately intelligible only to one who presupposes the truthfulness of Christianity. In other words, whereas pragmatic apologists focus on the existential difficulties of worldviews that compete with Christianity, presuppositionalists highlight the logical inconsistencies of non-Christian outlooks with themselves and/or with intuitively obvious aspects of reality. The pragmatic and the presuppositional schools of apologetics, therefore, share fundamentally the same vision of the relation between the Christian faith and human reason. They differ strikingly, however, in how they apply that vision to the practice of Christian apologetics.

The fifth and newest widely endorsed method of Christian apologetics, finally, is the approach associated with so-called Reformed epistemology. Adherents of this school agree with the bulk of classical and exclusively historical apologists that non-Christian systems of belief need not be either internally inconsistent or flagrantly out of harmony with obvious truths. Proponents of Reformed epistemology differ from classical and exclusively historical apologists in that they consider proof that Christianity is at least probably true dispensable to reasonable Christian belief. According to Reformed epistemology, rather, one can responsibly consider Christian belief properly basic— that is, in no more need of justification than claims that are self-evident, evident from the senses, or incorrigible, claims such that one cannot help believing them.

One can reasonably ascribe proper basicality to Christian belief, in the view of Reformed epistemology's supporters, because such belief at least conceivably constitutes the product of a properly functioning human

31

faculty: the *sensus divinitatis*, or "sense of divinity." This term, borrowed from John Calvin, refers, in the literature of Reformed epistemology, to a faculty capable of apprehending the truthfulness of the Christian faith. When one's eyes, whose purpose it is to apprehend the visible, function properly, virtually all persons hold, one can reasonably believe that what one sees in front of one is actually there. The theorists of Reformed epistemology conclude, by parity of reasoning, that when a human being's *sensus divinitatis* functions properly, one can reasonably believe Christianity, which it apprehends as true, to be true as well. It is important to note, however, that Reformed epistemology's defenders do not profess to be capable of proving that human beings possess a *sensus divinitatis*.

Each of the five currently favored apologetic methodologies thus possesses its distinctive advantages and defects. The classical method, whose practitioners include Norman Geisler (1932–) and William Lane Craig (1949–), possesses the advantages of thoroughness and rigor. It suffers, however, from the defects of being cumbersome and, in a culture skeptical of abstract philosophizing, arguably outmoded. The exclusively historical method, employed, for example, by Gary Habermas (1950–) and John Warwick Montgomery (1931–), possesses the signal advantage of being direct and concrete. It suffers, however, from a corresponding lack of depth and comprehensiveness.

The pragmatic method, whose most distinguished practitioner was Edward John Carnell (1919–67), possesses the virtue of addressing non-Christians in terms of their own worldview in a way that is indubitably relevant to life. The pragmatic method, nevertheless, according to its own self-understanding, proves no distinctively Christian claims. Presuppositionalism, the apologetic methodology most closely associated with Cornelius Van Til (1895–1987), possesses the virtue of modesty

inasmuch as its practitioners do not claim to be capable of proving Christianity true by any noncircular argument. Yet it is correspondingly audacious in its assumption that all non-Christian worldviews are, more or less, absurd. Reformed epistemology, finally, whose foremost proponents include Alvin Plantinga (1932–) and Nicholas Wolterstorff (1932–), appears charitable in its allowance that non-Christian worldviews may be self-consistent, yet also presumptuous in its ascription to every human being of a *sensus divinitatis* capable of apprehending the truthfulness of Christian belief. None of the widely embraced apologetic methodologies, therefore, appears utterly unproblematic. Each, however, possesses notable assets, which a skillful apologist can exploit to great advantage in apologetic/evangelistic argument.

Conclusion. The discipline of Christian apologetics, then, constitutes the science and practice of warranting Christian belief, rebutting objections to it, and arguing for the falsehood of non-Christian religions and worldviews. Certain scriptural passages, especially in 1 Corinthians 1 and 2, have, admittedly, given rise to widespread doubt concerning the advisability and even the lawfulness of apologetic argument on Christianity's behalf. Inasmuch as God explicitly commands Christians to cultivate Christian apologetics in 1 Peter 3:15, however, and includes apologetic argumentation within the inspired text of Scripture, it seems certain that Scripture does not even implicitly proscribe the employment of apologetic reasoning.

Methodologies of Christian apologetics include the classical method, the exclusively historical approach, the appeal to pragmatic considerations, the presuppositionalist approach, and the apologetic method associated with Reformed epistemology. Notwithstanding the lack of consensus among contemporary Christian apologists about questions of methodology, their work remains highly relevant to the needs of the church in the context of a hostile culture and necessary to the progress of evangelism in a religiously and ideologically pluralistic world.

See also CHRISTIAN

Bibliography. K. D. Boa and R. M. Bowman Jr., *Faith Has Its Reasons: Integrative Approaches to Defending Christianity*; S. Cowan, ed., *Five Views on Apologetics*; A. Dulles, *A History of Apologetics*; N. L. Geisler, *Baker Encyclopedia of Christian Apologetics*; H. W. House and D. W. Jowers, *Reasons for Our Hope: An Introduction to Christian Apologetics*; A. Plantinga, *Warranted Christian Belief*; F. A. Schaeffer, *The God Who Is There*; R. C. Sproul, J. H. Gerstner, and A. W. Lindsley, *Classical Apologetics*; J. E. Taylor, *Introducing Apologetics: Cultivating Christian Commitment*; C. Van Til, *The Defense of the Faith*.

D. W. Jowers

APOSTASY, BIBLICAL VIEW OF. Apostasy is the act of abandoning or departing from a particular faith or belief system. Not only are individuals susceptible to falling away from the truth, but nations, churches, and denominations can fall into a state of total apostasy from God. An important distinction is to be made between apostasy and heresy. Whereas the act of apostasy entails a total departure from established beliefs, heresy is the corruption of an essential doctrine or a denial of orthodox teaching in exchange for that which is unorthodox, without necessarily denying the Christian faith.

The Old Testament records the first act of apostasy, which took place in the garden of Eden when Adam and Eve rebelled against God's authority (Gen. 3). The move away from God toward a self-serving belief was initiated by the serpent, who enticed Eve into abandoning God's specific instructions to follow her desire to know good and evil. Adam followed in her footsteps, and as a result both fell away and incurred the wrath and judgment of God.

The departure of Israel from its covenant relationship with God due to idolatry constituted a national apostasy that occurred on numerous occasions. The bull cult was common throughout the ancient world, finding expression in Israel in Exodus 32, which records the incident of the idolatrous worship of the golden calf. The children of Israel coerce Aaron into making a golden calf idol, to which the people ascribe divinity and offer worship. Leviticus 26:27–33 speaks of devastation that will come if Israel abandons God, and Israel did eventually become apostate, which led to severe judgment from God, Israel's division into two kingdoms, and its eventual dissolution as a nation. First Kings provides a record of evil kings who practiced idolatry and likewise led Israel astray into rebellion against God. In spite of Irael's apostasy, God did speak of restoration (2 Sam. 7:11–16), and Paul acknowledges the election and preservation of a remnant (Rom. 9).

Churches that embrace orthodox Christian beliefs can fall into apostasy if they abandon those beliefs due to the influence of liberal teaching and influences. Denominations that once held firmly to the historic Christian faith in time came under the influence of liberal theology and critical approaches to Scripture. The result was the demise of critical teachings on the doctrine of Christ—namely, his virgin birth and deity. The pull of secularism or popular culture also cripples denominations and draws them into a state of apostasy. The church of Laodicea (Rev. 3:14) exemplifies what can happen to both individual churches and entire denominations when they depart from their orthodox roots and become apostate due to the alluring nature of doctrinal error and moral compromise.

The New Testament (NT) has numerous warnings against apostasy. Hebrews 3:12 warns believers to beware of an unbelieving heart leading to a falling away from God. Paul addresses several situations where apostasy has occurred. In 2 Timothy 4:10, Paul tells Timothy that Demas, who loved the world, has deserted him. In 1 Timothy 1:10, Paul encourages Timothy to keep the faith, for some, namely Hymenaeus and Alexander (vv. 18–20), have abandoned, or apostatized from, the faith. Apostasy is implied in 2 Timothy 4:1–4, where Paul warns that some who once embraced sound doctrine will fall away due to false teachers. With respect to professing believers who fall away from the faith, apostasy poses serious implications for the doctrine of perseverance and how numerous warning passages in the NT (Heb. 6:4–12; 10:26–31, 35–39) are to be interpreted. According to Arminian theology, true believers can apostatize and lose their salvation. Calvinistic theology, however, would argue that no true believer can apostatize, and those who do were never true regenerated believers.

Peter warns his readers that false teachers will appear among the brethren and propagate destructive heresies and engage in ungodly behavior (2 Pet. 2). In 2 Peter 2:15, false teachers have not only corrupted the truth but abandoned or forsaken the right way, thus apostatizing.

In 2 Thessalonians 2:3, Paul mentions the apostasy, or a general falling in connection with the coming day of the Lord. This apostasy will precede the revealing of the man of lawlessness, or antichrist, who will aggressively exalt himself and not only repudiate all other gods but declare himself to be God. First John 2:18–19 warns about the coming of antichrist and the current work of many antichrists. These deceivers are described as having once been a part of the Christian community but having departed from it. John's appraisal of this situation is instructive, for it is clear that those who go the way of apostasy were never truly aligned theologically and spiritually with true believers in the first place. Eschatologically, Scripture speaks of a coming apostasy that will encompass the entire earth (Matt. 24:10–24) during the great tribulation period. So severe will this tendency be that even the elect, if possible, would be led astray.

See also Apostasy, Mormon View of

Bibliography. J. M. Gundry-Volf, "Apostasy, Falling Away, Perseverance," in *Dictionary of Paul and His Letters*; P. E. Hughes, "Hebrews 6:4–6 and the Peril of Apostasy," *Westminster Theological Journal*; I. H. Marshall, *Jesus the Saviour: Studies in New Testament Theology*; R. Peterson, "Apostasy," *Presbyterion*; C. Ryrie, "Apostasy in the Church," *Bibliotheca Sacra*.

S. J. Rost

APOSTASY, MORMON VIEW OF. In some religious groups, including the Church of Jesus Christ of Latter-day Saints (LDS Church, or Mormonism), any degree of defection by an individual member from total spiritual and intellectual surrender to the leadership is often considered apostasy. The group's authority, whether exercised by an individual prophet or a prophetic organization, is rooted in the assumption (often explicitly expressed) that the voice of the leadership is the voice of God. Thus the voice of the leadership and its official teachings replace the voice of the Bible and the guidance of the Holy Spirit in the life of members. Members may honestly believe they are taking their cues from the Bible and the Holy Spirit, but in reality they are not. Radical commitment to such a group subsists in a voluntary readiness to personally embrace and believe everything the "inspired" leadership sets forth as authoritative. "When our leaders speak," said one famous 1945 LDS statement, "the thinking has been done" (Church of Jesus Christ of Latter-day Saints, 5). This statement expresses well the mind-set of the LDS Church. What a particular teaching or practice is in itself (whether good or bad, true or false) becomes less important, in the LDS context, than how that teaching or practice becomes a litmus text of unquestioning allegiance and obedience to cultic leadership.

Today the LDS Church watchdogs its members through periodic "worthiness interviews," during which members are asked if they "sustain" their leaders. To "sustain" is to embrace leadership decisions unquestioningly as God's will for one's life. A successful worthiness interview is necessary for gaining access to the LDS Temple, a prerequisite to entering the celestial kingdom. For many years, when Mormons have voted at the General Conference, they have done so unanimously, "sustaining" whatever the LDS Church leadership has proposed.

The LDS Church also provides a striking example of how successful a prophetic organization can be in insulating its members from information that might undermine their confidence in its leadership. By actively cultivating the idea that Mormons are and always have been a persecuted people, the LDS leadership has been able to perpetuate a "myth of persecuted innocence" and so to plausibly characterize all dissent as persecution (this despite the many notorious instances of crimes, including holy murder, perpetrated by early LDS leaders).

Joining a group with this view of apostasy sometimes involves an affirmation by the would-be member that he or she has already received direct revelatory assurance from God that the teaching of the group is true and that its leaders have been divinely appointed. People joining the Love Family, for example, used to be asked whether it had been revealed to them (1) that they *already* belonged to the group and (2) that the group's leader, Love Israel, was the head of the new family of God. Similarly, the first Mormon missionary lesson presses new investigators to "read from the Book of Mormon and pray to know that it is true." In this way, any doubts that might crop up later are easily blamed on the member's slide into apostasy since the doubts contradict the doubter's earlier self-declared assurance that God had endorsed the group. This assigning of blame by the leadership for doubts, including those inspired by its own corrupt actions, can even

have a witness in doubting members' own heavily manipulated consciences, making it difficult for them to leave without carrying with them a false but very real sense of personal failure and divine displeasure.

See also CHURCH OF JESUS CHRIST OF LATTER-DAY SAINTS

Bibliography. Church of Jesus Christ of Latter-day Saints, "Ward Teachers Message," *Deseret News* (1945); R. M. Enroth, *Churches That Abuse*; S. Hassan, *Combatting Cultic Mind Control*.

R. V. Huggins

APOSTLES, BELIEF IN THE MODERN EXISTENCE OF. Various groups of modern origin that are regarded by orthodox Christians as heretical, most notably the Church of Jesus Christ of Latter-day Saints (LDS, or Mormons), the New Apostolic Church, and the Word-Faith movement, claim to have apostles today. Such groups typically view apostles as an element in the supposed "restoration" of full or true Christianity to the earth in the last days before Christ's return.

The LDS Church claims to have "the same organization that existed in the Primitive Church, namely, apostles, prophets, pastors, teachers, evangelists, and so forth" (Sixth Article of Faith, alluding to Eph. 4:11). These offices were missing during "the Great Apostasy," a period of spiritual darkness that overcame the world from the second century in the Old World, with the apostasy becoming complete in the New World in AD 421 (McConkie, 4:397) until the creation of the LDS Church in 1830. The loss of apostles and prophets meant the cessation of continuing revelation (including new Scriptures)—which Mormons believe is essential to the church—and of "the priesthood," the ecclesiastical authority to preach the gospel and administer ordinances such as baptism.

The New Apostolic Church traces its origins to the Catholic Apostolic Church (CAC), a movement that in the 1830s claimed to have twelve apostles whose evangelistic ministry would prepare for the imminent Second Coming. When the apostles began dying off, some factions of the CAC began appointing new apostles; one of these factions became known as the *Neuapostolische Kirche* (New Apostolic Church), or NAK. The NAK views its apostles as akin to the New Testament apostles such as Peter and Paul and maintains that there was and is no forgiveness of sins and no valid baptism, and there are no Christians, apart from the ministries of the living apostles (New Apostolic Church, 2–3; Kraus).

Word-Faith teachers do not deny the existence of a bona fide church on the earth before their arrival, but they do claim that the church was missing vital elements of the full Christian experience. One of these elements is the so-called fivefold ministry of apostles, prophets, evangelists, pastors, and teachers, based again on Ephesians 4:11. Kenneth E. Hagin, the movement's acknowledged "father," conceded that apostles like the Twelve or Paul do not function in the church today and thus agreed (unlike the Mormons) that no modern "apostle" can write Scripture or exercise ecclesiastical authority over the whole church. On the other hand, Hagin taught that God does raise up "nonfoundational" apostles today who perform signs and wonders and bring special messages to the church pertaining to neglected biblical truths.

In the New Testament, the Greek word *apostolos* (literally, "sent one") is used in four senses. One text calls Jesus "the Apostle and High Priest," meaning that he was sent from *God* (Heb. 3:1). Twice Paul speaks of certain men as "apostles" or emissaries of churches, meaning that they were sent from and spoke on behalf of *their church* (2 Cor. 8:23; Phil. 2:25). Two texts speaks of certain men as false apostles (2 Cor. 11:13; Rev. 2:2). All the other seventy-six occurrences refer to apostles of Christ, that is, men chosen by and sent *from Christ* as his emissaries.

According to Paul, "the apostles and prophets" who spoke for Christ were the "foundation" of the church (Eph. 2:20). Their function was to guide Christ's followers through the transition from a Jewish movement to the church as the body of Jewish and gentile believers united in Christ (Eph. 3:3–7). The offices of apostle and prophet, then, are not continuing offices like those of evangelist, pastor, and teacher (Eph. 4:11). Later New Testament writers, as the generation of the apostles was passing, urged Christians to remember what the apostles had taught (2 Pet. 3:2; Jude 17), not to look for new apostles. We find the teachings of the apostles in the New Testament.

See also CHURCH OF JESUS CHRIST OF LATTER-DAY SAINTS

Bibliography. R. M. Bowman Jr., *The New Apostolic Church (Centers for Apologetics Research)*; K. E. Hagin, *He Gave Gifts unto Men: A Biblical Perspective of Apostles, Prophets, and Pastors*; M. Kraus, *Completion Work in the New Apostolic Church*; B. R. McConkie, *Mortal Messiah*; W. O. Nelson, "Quorum of the Twelve Apostles," in *Encyclopedia of Mormonism*, edited by D. H. Ludlow, 4 vols.; New Apostolic Church, *House Rules and Creed for the Members of the New Apostolic Church*.

R. M. Bowman Jr. and T. M. Bates

ARHAT. In the *sramanic* traditions of ancient India, to which both Mahavira and Gautama Buddha can trace their religious heritage, an arhat (a term possibly meaning "worthy one" or "foe destroyer") is one who has removed all the causes for rebirth after physical death into any samsaric realm. In Jainism arhats are more commonly called *jinas* (conquerors) than *tirthankaras* (ford makers). In Buddhism an arhat (also known as a Sravaka Buddha) is a practitioner who reaches nirvana with the help of the teaching of a bodhisattva (or a Samyaksam Buddha). Such a person is not misled by the illusory nature of transitory phenomena and has no trace of anger or worldly attachment. According to the Mahayana tradition, arhats are able to assist unenlightened beings on the path toward enlightenment, but they do not have the capability to instruct others at times or in places wherein the teachings of Buddhism are unknown. In Theravada Buddhism, the word *arhat* usually denotes a Buddhist (a monk, not a layperson) who has attained full enlightenment. Though arhats are highly esteemed by Buddhists of all kinds, they are viewed as inferior to bodhisattvas by adherents of Mahayana.

See also BUDDHISM; JAINISM; MAHAYANA BUDDHISM; THERAVADA BUDDHISM

Bibliography. M. P. Hall, *The Adepts in the Eastern Esoteric Tradition*, part 2, *The Arhats of Buddhism*; P. Harvey, *An Introduction to Buddhism: Teachings, History and Practices*; P. Williams, *Mahayana Buddhism: The Doctrinal Foundations.*

J. Bjornstad

ARIANISM. The Arian heresy absorbed the church's attention particularly during the tumultuous fourth century and has presented itself as a continuing challenge in variegated forms ever since. It derives its name from Arius (b. AD 256 in Egypt), a presbyter in the church of Alexandria in 313. Arius charged that those who ascribed true deity to Christ undermined either monotheism (i.e., by teaching that Jesus and the Father are two gods) or Christ's independent being (i.e., by teaching that Jesus is God but as such is the same person as the Father—a teaching also known as "modalism").

Although this particular controversy involves some highly technical theological and philosophical argumentation, which is examined below, we must observe at the outset that a fundamentally religious motive drove this debate. That is, the worry underlying these often bitter and at the same time highly nuanced fourth-century disputes is that the church must have a Savior who can truly save, with the underlying recognition that a mere creature, however holy, could not accomplish this.

From its inception, the church recognized the deity of Christ, not only in its theology but also in its praxis. The church prayed to Jesus, preached Jesus, and worshiped Jesus. Christians baptized in his name and staked their eternal destiny on him as God in the flesh. In light of these practices, if Jesus were a creature, however exalted, the Christian faith would be but a species of idolatry or paganism. The teaching of Arius thus attacked the church's faith and practice at its root. Therefore, interpreters such as Adolph Harnack, who see philosophical speculation as the primary motive for the controversy, have failed to do justice to the profound religious issues undergirding this debate.

Though the church has always believed Jesus to be God—for the New Testament in particular states this explicitly (e.g., John 1:1, 14)—it took some time to work out a theologically adequate statement of the doctrine that took into account all the terms of the problem, namely, Christ's true deity, his distinction from the Father, and the fact of biblical monotheism. The issues stirred up in the Arian controversy thus spurred the church toward a more precise statement that would do justice to the issues involved.

According to Arius, there is only one unbegotten God. In agreement with trinitarians, Arius called the Son the "Logos" (*logos* means "Word"; cf. John 1:1), but unlike trinitarians, he said that this Son Logos was a creature of the Father, created before anything else. The Son's creation was captured in the pithy saying, "There was once when he was not."

As to the nature of this Son Logos, he was created a disembodied spiritual being. In some places, Arius identifies the Son Logos as an angelic being, though greater than all other creatures. This Son Logos served as the agent through whom the Father created everything else.

At this point, we should distinguish two senses in which Arius spoke of the Logos. In general, the word *logos* can be translated as "word" or "reason." It can refer both to a spoken word and to reason in the sense of a person's mind or rationality. Arius distinguished between the logos as immanent in God and the Son Logos as a creature of the Father. The two relate as follows. God himself, being rational, has logos in the sense of rationality as abiding or immanent within him; it is another name for the divine mind. At the same time, we can speak of the created Son as the Logos because he shares in the Father's wisdom or immanent logos. In other words, the appellation Son Logos may be applied to Christ because he participates in and is inspired by the divine mind—that is, God's immanent logos. The Son, therefore, is the Logos by participation and inspiration, not by nature.

In the incarnation, this inspired Son Logos creature took on a tangible human body. Thus the historical Jesus of Nazareth is in fact the preexistent Son Logos, inspired by the divine mind (God's immanent logos) and operating in and through a human body. Accordingly, Jesus of Nazareth does not have a human soul; the ego or person of Jesus is the Son Logos, now operating through a body of tangible flesh.

In the same way that Christ is called the Logos by gracious participation in the divine wisdom, he can also receive the names "God" and "Son of God." These titles are applied only relatively and figuratively. The Son Logos, being a creature of the Father, cannot be God in the full sense of the word. Metaphysically speaking, the Son and the Father are "utterly unlike from each other in essence and glory, unto infinity" (Arius, *Thalia*, cited in Athanasius, *Four Discourses against the Arians* 1.6). His oneness with the Father is only a oneness or unity of purpose.

Exegetically, Arius drew particularly on those texts that described the son as "begotten" (e.g., John 3:16), which he took to mean "created." He also leaned heavily on Proverbs 8:22–31, which he, together with the orthodox, took as a reference to the Son. Unlike the orthodox, he saw the descriptions of Wisdom as "set up," "brought forth," and so on as proofs of the Son's antemundane creation.

Arianism's greatest and tireless foe was Athanasius of Alexandria (ca. 296–373), deacon and ultimately bishop of Alexandria. He was the major leader on the orthodox side at the watershed Council of Nicaea in AD 325. Through his influence, a creed was drawn up with language that explicitly declared Christ to be eternal and uncreated, affirming also that he was "of the same substance" (*homoousios*) as the Father. Although the word *homoousios* had been used earlier by Origen and in Greek philosophy "to indicate a generic equality or sameness of substance," it was used at Nicaea to affirm "the substantial equality of the Father and the Son" (Muller, 139). In other words, *homoousios* was employed here to convey the idea that there is only one God and that the Father and the Son are one and the same God, numerically speaking.

The Arian heresy is found in quite a few of modern heterodox groups. The Jehovah's Witnesses probably approximate it the most closely, teaching that Jesus before the incarnation was an angel (Michael)—though, unlike Arius, they do claim to hold to his full humanity in the incarnation. The specific exegetical arguments against Christ's deity offered by the Jehovah's Witnesses are also very similar to those of Arius. Historically, some Unitarians also held an Arian Christology (though some opted for a dynamic monarchian position).

See also MODALISM; MONARCHIANISM; TRINITARIAN CONTROVERSIES; TRINITY, THE

Bibliography. E. Fortman, *The Triune God*; J. N. D. Kelly, *Early Christian Doctrines*; R. A.

Muller, *Dictionary of Greek and Latin*; R. See-berg, *The History of Doctrines*, vol. 1.

A. W. Gomes

ARIHANT (JAINISM). An *arihant* is one who has overcome the first four types of karma (*ghati*) that bind the soul (*jiva*) and who has attained *keval-jnan*, a state wherein the natural qualities of the soul have been restored, with the result that they have attained divinity while still in the body. There are two types of arihants: ordinary *kevalis* and *tirthankaras*.

See also JAINISM

Bibliography. J. P. Jain, *Religion and Culture of the Jains*.

M. C. Hausam

ARMAGEDDON. Armageddon, meaning "Mount of Megiddo," refers to a location southeast of Mt. Carmel (near modern Haifa) and on the southwestern edge of the Plain of Jezreel. The term refers in the context of Revelation 16:15 to the focal point for the gathering of world leaders and their armies in the final battle before Christ returns to earth. This final battle is often associated with a personal antichrist figure. Many interpretations exist in the Christian tradition for Armageddon, but the term also has special meaning to various heterodox groups and world religions outside orthodox Christian faith.

End-of-the-world, doomsday scenarios have often been proclaimed by various astrologers down through the centuries based on the projected conjunction of various planets. For example, astrologer John of Toledo in 1179 predicted the end of the world in 1186. Similarly, the German astrologer Johannes Stoeffler in 1499 proclaimed the specific day of February 20, 1544, to bring the end of the world via a giant flood based on planetary alignment. The use of celestial events to mark some form of the end of the present time is represented in modern times by groups such as Heaven's Gate. In its particular scheme,

the group's members had to leave this planet (which many did by mass suicide) to avoid the catastrophic recycling or wiping clean of the earth that was about to take place in light of the celestial marker of the Hale-Bopp comet in 1997.

Another astrological source for current cultlike fascination with Armageddon is the writing of the sixteenth-century French doctor and astrologer Nostradamus. Modern authors such as Michael Rathford tried to use Nostradamus's enigmatic and vague predictions as fodder to teach the coming of World War III near the end of the first decade of the twenty-first century. Such end-of-the-world thinking, as mentioned above, even when it does not focus on prophecies using fire and war imagery, is within the orbit of how the word Armageddon has come to be used. The astrological connection of these particular examples highlights the occultic experience that drives many such doomsday predictions.

An example of a rather tame heterodox interpretation of Armageddon can be found in the Jehovah's Witnesses, who do not see Armageddon as referring to a definite place and battle that involves a personal antichrist. Instead, they teach that Armageddon as a symbol refers to a global war between all nations and God himself. Jehovah will destroy his enemies before the world is ruined through war.

In an entirely different scheme, Seventh-day Adventists generally teach that the battle of Armageddon occurs at the end of the thousand-year reign of Christ and not prior to and in conjunction with the second coming of Christ. Following the earthly millennium, God will raise the wicked dead, whom Satan will lead in battle against God.

A more radical view was taken by the Branch Davidians in the 1990s under the leadership of David Koresh. Armageddon, from Revelation 16:16, is related to the seals in Revelation 6. Of special note is the fifth seal, which was interpreted as the time when God's people would be martyred. The Branch Davidians viewed themselves as the people of God who were about to die. They thought that the cause of their death would be a conflagration and battle with the forces of unbelief. Unfortunately, their expectations were realized in the tragedy at Waco, Texas, on April 19, 1993, when the Davidian compound at Mt. Carmel caught fire during a confrontation with authorities. Seventy-six Branch Davidians (tweny-one were children) lost their lives in this battle of Armageddon.

Several other examples of heretical fascination with Armageddon could be given. The sources and motivations of such schemes relative to Armageddon are numerous and complicated. Sometimes millennial overkill is at work. At other times, occultic astrology or some form of mysticism can be seen. In many cases, the particular group's self-identity is partly based on its understanding of the end of the world and an Armageddon scenario.

See also JEHOVAH'S WITNESSES (JW); OCCULT; SEVENTH-DAY ADVENTISM

Bibliography. R. Abanes, *End-Time Visions: The Doomsday Obsession*; P. Boyer, *When Time Shall Be No More: Prophecy Belief in Modern American Culture*; H. W. House, *Charts of Cults, Sects, and Religious Movements*; W. Martin, *Kingdom of the Cults*; B. McGinn, *Antichrist: Two Thousand Years of Fascination with Evil*; M. Rathford, *The Nostradamus Code: World War III*; D. Shantz, "Millennialism and Apocalypticism in Recent Historical Scholarship," in *Prisoners of Hope*, edited by C. Gribben and T. C. F. Stunt; T. P. Weber, *On the Road to Armageddon*; S. A. Wright, ed., *Armageddon in Waco: Critical Perspectives on the Branch Davidian Conflict*.

M. Stallard

ARTICLES OF FAITH, MORMON. The Articles of Faith are thirteen brief statements of doctrine drawn up by Joseph Smith Jr. in 1842 at the request of John Wentworth, editor of the *Chicago Democrat*. The Articles of Faith were first published in March 1842 in the early Mormon periodical *Times and Seasons* and are currently included in the portion of LDS Scripture called the Pearl of Great Price. Because the articles were carefully worded to make Mormon teaching sound more mainstream than it actually was, they continue to be useful in communicating Mormon beliefs to outsiders. Consequently, it has always been necessary to inquire into the meanings that lie behind the words of the Articles of Faith.

Article 1 affirms belief "in God, the Eternal Father, and in His Son, Jesus Christ, and in the Holy Ghost." Mormons, however, reject the Christian doctrine of the Trinity. "We hear the voice of false Christs," wrote apostle Bruce R. McConkie, "when we hear the Athanasian Creed proclaim . . . a Trinity of equals, who are not three Gods but one God" (*Millennial Messiah*). "And these three," said Joseph Smith on June 16, 1844, "constitute three distinct personages and three Gods." Nor is the Father really any more or less "eternal" than the rest of us. As former LDS president Lorenzo Snow put it in his famous couplet: "As man now is, God once was; as God now is, man may be." The present "Eternal Father" is an exalted man, has a body of flesh and bone, and is only one link in an eternal chain of gods.

Article 2 takes the side of the New England theology against traditional Calvinism by saying we are not punished for Adam's sin.

Article 3 underscores works-based participation in the atonement of Christ through "obedience to the laws and ordinances of the Gospel."

Article 4 identifies the "laws and ordinances" as faith, repentance, baptism, and the laying on of hands.

Article 5 asserts that "a man must be called of God" and ordained by a man with prophetic "authority" to be authorized to preach the gospel or administer its ordinances. This means that all baptisms and all missions outside the Mormon religion are invalid.

Article 6 affirms belief in the "same organization that existed in the Primitive Church," and it lists several New Testament offices. Conspicuously absent, however, are the two most important to Mormons, the Aaronic and Melchizedek priesthoods.

Article 7 affirms "the gift of tongues, prophecy, revelation, visions, healing, interpretation of tongues, and so forth." The early Mormons put forth the presence of restored New Testament gifts among them as evidence that they were the restored true church.

Article 8 affirms belief in the Bible "as far as it is translated correctly," meaning really insofar as it has escaped corruption at the hands of the "Great and Abominable Church," which, according to the Book of Mormon, removed many "plain and precious things" from it (1 Nephi 13:28).

Article 10 affirms the "literal gathering of Israel and . . . the restoration of the Ten Tribes" and that the New Jerusalem "will be built upon the American continent." Mormons believe that at his second coming Christ will establish the New Jerusalem at Independence, Missouri (D&C 57), and that the old Jerusalem will be restored as well (D&C 57 and 133).

The remaining articles affirm popular American ideals of good behavior and citizenship.

See also CHURCH OF JESUS CHRIST OF LATTER-DAY SAINTS; SMITH, JOSEPH, JR.; SNOW, LORENZO

Bibliography. B. R. McConkie, The Millennial Messiah; McConkie, A New Witness for the Articles of Faith; J. Talmage, The Articles of Faith; D. J. Whittaker, "Articles of Faith," in Encyclopedia of Mormonism, edited by D. H. Ludlow, 4 vols.

R. V. Huggins

ASCETICISM. The term *asceticism* (from Greek *askein*, "to exercise or practice") denotes training for some higher purpose (e.g., practice for athletic competition). Both Plato

(*Republic* 7) and Aristotle (*Nicomachean Ethics* 9) admired habits of self-mortification, while the theologies of Orpheus, Pythagorus, the Cynics, and especially the Stoics advocated negation of the body for the sake of the soul. Roman asceticism, which largely adapted Greek or Eastern practices, typically expressed the belief either that the gods demand suffering or that virtue demands painful exertion.

In the sense that asceticism involves training for a higher purpose, Scripture often extols spiritual discipline (1 Cor. 9:27). By the second century, however, Christians began to idealize ascetic privations. Desert monastics were seen as especially spiritual and were held up as models of piety. The *Shepherd of Hermas* (bk. 3), for example, advocated self-mortification as a spiritual exercise, and Athanasius celebrated the hermit Antony for his "piety toward God" (*Vita S. Antony*). Origen, Jerome, Chrysostom, Gregory of Nazianzus, Gregory of Nyssa, Cyprian, Lactantius, Methodius, and other early theologians prized ascetic practices, especially celibacy. Origen even had himself emasculated and praised sexual abstinence, even for married persons, as a "God-pleasing sacrifice" (*Contra Celsus*; *Commentary on Romans*). Early Christian asceticism had its own identity but often reflected pagan (especially Greek) ideals. Up through the medieval period, asceticism (sometimes radical) was seen as a spiritual virtue, and famous ascetics were sainted and venerated. St. Catherine of Sienna, for example, probably died of starvation, believing the eucharistic host was sufficient to sustain her. To this day, she is considered a model for the adoration and worship of the Eucharist in the Roman Catholic Church.

Even within Protestantism, some in the pietistic and Holiness traditions believe they are being pious by refraining from certain things—"worldly amusements," as they are called. Since these self-denials are seen as a way to sanctification, if not required for salvation, it can be argued that they are acts of asceticism.

Genuine asceticism differs from a number of superficially similar practices. Amish primitivism, for example, represents a merely *traditional* practice. Other practices are *symbolic* (e.g., shaving the head by Hare Krishnas) or *disciplinary* (e.g., regular worship, abstinence from coffee and tea by Mormons, the Islamic Ramadan). By contrast, authentic asceticism is both *punitive* and *durative*, involving self-denial to the point of suffering, as a means of salvation, atonement, liberation, enhanced piety, or expanded consciousness.

Eastern religions—Hinduism, Buddhism, and especially Jainism—offer the best examples of genuine asceticism today, though it is also known in fringe religious groups, for example, the Shakers and Islamic Sufism. Some nonreligious practices, such as extreme fitness training, may also be considered ascetic in nature.

See also BUDDHISM; HINDUISM; JAINISM

Bibliography. O. Chadwick, *Western Asceticism*; *Shepherd of Hermas*; V. L. Wimbush and R. Valantasis, eds., *Asceticism*.

C. R. Wells

ATMAN. In Hinduism, Atman is the eternal, unchanging self (or soul) associated with each empirical person. The vehicle for reincarnation, Atman leaves the body at death to undergo rebirth (or, in the case of enlightened persons, to attain liberation). Monistic schools of Hinduism claim that Atman is ontologically identical with Brahma and that this fact is fully realized and experienced when enlightenment is attained. Dualistic schools of Hinduism maintain that Atman is an aspect of Brahma and that the liberated Atman (which only appears to be entirely separate from Brahma) merges with Brahma at death. Theistic schools of Hinduism contend that Atman is metaphysically distinct from God and that its liberation consists in being in the presence of God. In many schools of Hindu epistemology, one cannot know Atman via ordinary conscious states. Enlightened ones alone know that their existence ultimately is beyond the duality of the knower and the known; apart from this realization, the experience of Atman cannot be achieved. Such accounts assert that one comes to the knowledge of Atman only by properly understanding oneself, directly grasping the reality that one is not to be identified with the provisional, phenomenal reality of worldly existence, but is none other than the permanent, imperishable Atman.

Buddhists declare that belief in Atman is the result of ignorance of one's true nature, usually involving the erroneous conviction that persons are distinct, individuated substances that persist over time, when in fact "persons" are but an aggregate of properties undergoing continual change. According to nearly all sects of Buddhism, this false belief—that personal identity is grounded in a particular enduring substance—along with a lack of awareness that persons actually consist of a fluctuating bundle of attributes, is the most fundamental impediment to enlightenment (and thus to the attainment of nirvana). On the Buddhist view of things, then, Atman is merely a concept.

See also BRAHMA; BUDDHISM; HINDUISM; REINCARNATION

Bibliography. S. Hamilton, *Indian Philosophy: A Very Short Introduction*; P. Harvey, *An Introduction to Buddhism: Teachings, History and Practices*; W. G. Oxtoby, ed., *World Religions: Eastern Traditions*, 2nd ed.; T. S. Rukmani, "Self, Indian Theories of" in *Routledge Encyclopedia of Philosophy*, edited by Edward Craig, vol. 8.

S. J. Rost

ATONEMENT. The term *atonement* refers to an act or process that makes amends, or atones, for offenses committed by one party against another and, by so doing, reconciles the two parties. Theologians of all stripes commonly acknowledge that Christ atoned for the sins of his people and thus reconciled his people to God. Controversy has raged for centuries, however, over the question of precisely wherein Christ's atonement consists. Most participants in this controversy conceive of the atonement as one of the following: (1) a vicarious punishment; (2) a conquest of powers that enslave human beings; (3) the elevation of human nature; (4) an example of loving sacrifice; or (5) a demonstration of God's wrath against sin.

Vicarious Punishment. According to the first of these conceptions, Christ's work of atonement consists primarily in his bearing the punishment his people deserve on account of their sins so that God can forgive them and admit them to heavenly blessings without compromising his justice, which requires that every sin receive a condign punishment. Advocates of this theory of the atonement typically admit that Christ does more for human beings by suffering in his life and death than merely paying the debt of punishment they owe for their sins. Christ also enacted throughout his life a righteousness that God imputes to believers, purchased the believers' actual forgiveness and heavenly blessings, annulled the ritual requirements of the Old Testament, and so on. Nevertheless, proponents of this theory insist, Christ's suffering divine punishment in his people's stead constitutes an integral aspect of his atoning work.

This conception of Christ's atonement possesses ample scriptural support. Scripture indicates, for instance, that Christ suffered on his people's behalf (Isa. 53:5; Matt. 26:28; John 10:11, 15; Rom. 4:25; 5:8; 8:32; Eph. 5:25; Titus 2:14; 1 Pet. 4:1) and, indeed, in their stead (Isa. 53:6, 11–12; Matt. 20:28; Mark 10:45; 1 Tim. 2:6; 1 Pet. 2:24; 3:18). Scripture identifies this suffering, moreover, as a sacrifice (1 Cor. 5:7; Eph. 5:2) offered for his people's sins (Heb. 7:27; 9:11–15, 26, 28; 10:12; 1 Pet. 1:18–19), which consists, at least in part, in enduring the punishment his people

merited by their sins. "All who rely on the works of the law are under a curse," writes Paul, "as it is written: 'Cursed is everyone who does not continue to do everything written in the Book of the Law.' . . . Christ [however] redeemed us from the curse of the law by becoming a curse for us, for it is written: 'Cursed is everyone who is hung on a pole'" (Gal. 3:10, 13). By suffering this curse, Christ propitiates God's righteous wrath against his people's sins (Rom. 3:25; Heb. 2:17; 1 John 2:2; 4:10) and reconciles the requirements of God's justice with his desire to show compassion to sinners. Christ suffers, Paul teaches, in order that God "be just and the one who justifies those who have faith in Jesus" (Rom. 3:26b).

Scripture appears, therefore, to warrant the conclusion that Christ's atonement consists, at least in part, in his vicarious suffering of the punishment due for his people's sins. Those who object to this view of the atonement, nevertheless, lodge two weighty criticisms against it. First, such persons argue, only a bloodthirsty, vindictive God would exact Jesus's suffering and death as the price of forgiving sinners. In response to this objection, one might observe that it presupposes a radical underestimation of the severity of human sin. The gravity of sins, it seems, varies in direct proportion to the dignity of the party against whom one offends. Sins committed against one's brother are, other things being equal, less heinous than those committed against one's father, which, other things being equal, are less heinous than those committed against the president of one's country, and so on. Every sin, however, offends against God, whose dignity is infinite. Even the slightest sins, therefore, merit infinite punishment.

If such a thing as retributive justice exists, moreover, it must belong among the virtues of a comprehensively perfect God. The divine perfection thus seems to require God to exact a condign punishment for every offense.

Mercifully, however, God the Son assumes a human nature so that, in that nature, he may suffer the penalty God's people deserve for their sins. Since Christ, notwithstanding the incarnation, is a divine person of infinite value, his suffering in the human nature assumed is infinitely meritorious and thus adequate to cover his people's infinite debt of punishment. God hardly acts in a blood-thirsty manner, therefore, in effecting his people's salvation through the incarnation and suffering of Christ. Rather, in Christ he takes upon himself the punishment his people deserve so that he might be "a righteous God and a Savior" (Isa. 45:21)—that is, so that, without compromising the requirements of justice, he might bestow compassion on those whom he loves.

Critics of the notion of atonement as vicarious punishment, nonetheless, object, second, that, since justice requires all persons to suffer for their own sins, Christ could not have satisfied justice's demands by vicarious suffering. It is true, one may respond, that Christ could not have satisfied the requirements of justice merely by suffering his people's punishment. Rather, Christ must also have purchased with the infinite merit of his suffering the transference of responsibility for his people's sins from them to himself. That such a transference actually occurred is presumably what Paul means when he writes, "God made him who had no sin to be sin for us" (2 Cor. 5:21a; cf. Calvin's comments on this verse).

The supposition that Christ purchased with his suffering this transference of responsibility seems to resolve the difficulty posed by God's apparently relaxing the demands of justice by failing to punish Christ's people in their own persons. For if Christ did indeed purchase this transference, then God could not have punished believers in their own persons without defrauding Christ of benefits he earned. Since God's justice toward Christ demands that he show mercy toward Christ's

people, one cannot credibly argue that he acted unjustly in accepting Christ's sacrifice as a substitute for the eternal punishment of those whom Christ represents.

The gravest objections to the notion of atonement as vicarious punishment, accordingly, appear misguided. Although the Reformers and their evangelical heirs have emphasized this conception to a virtually unprecedented extent, furthermore, it is noteworthy that the idea that Christ paid his people's debt of punishment by his suffering and death has never lacked influential supporters. From Tertullian and Cyprian in the West to Athanasius and Gregory of Nazianzus in the East, numerous church fathers acknowledged that vicarious suffering constituted a central aspect of Christ's saving work. Likewise, figures such as Anselm of Canterbury (*Cur Deus Homo*), Hugh of St. Victor, Thomas Aquinas, and Gregory of Rimini taught throughout the medieval period that Christ suffered vicariously for his people's sins. Although numerous post-Enlightenment theologians have censured the notion of atonement as vicarious punishment, moreover, this conception remains the most commonly held view of the atonement among Western Christians.

Conquest of Powers That Enslave Human Beings. A second conception of the atonement, according to which it consists principally in Christ's conquest of Satan, sin, hell, and death, enjoyed enormous support in the patristic and early medieval periods. The great strength of this theory is that it underscores Christ's triumph over humankind's enemies, a theme that pervades the New Testament (see, e.g., Matt. 12:29; Col. 2:15; 2 Tim. 1:10; Heb. 2:14–15; 1 John 3:8).

A key feature of this theory, moreover, is that it allows Christ's sacrifice to possess a dual reference—that is, not only to the Father but also to Satan. Numerous figures in the early church took biblical descriptions of Christ's atonement as a ransom (Matt. 20:28;

Mark 10:45; 1 Tim. 2:6) to mean that Christ offered himself not merely to God but also to Satan, who held God's people captive. Certain fathers, in fact, speak of Christ's flesh as the bait on a mousetrap or a fishhook with which God lures Satan to swallow the Son of God, whom Satan takes to be a mere man. When Satan swallows the Son of God, the narrative commonly goes, he finds it impossible to contain him who, being sinless, ought not to be trapped in Satan's prison and, being God, can overcome all demonic powers. The Son thus escapes from Satan's prison and brings with him human beings, whom Satan had previously held in thrall.

While this scenario possesses a certain dramatic flair, it also contains highly problematic elements. The notion that God sacrifices his Son to Satan, in particular, strikes many as grossly immoral, and the assertion that God saves human beings by tricking Satan appears to trivialize the atonement. The demerits of the idea that Christ paid satisfaction to Satan, however, ought not to blind one to the biblical evidence that Christ's death and resurrection did constitute a victory over Satan, hell, sin, and death. Without denying the indispensability of vicarious punishment to Christ's atonement, therefore, one ought to incorporate this theme of victory into one's understanding of Christ's atoning work.

The Elevation of Human Nature. A third conception of the atonement, which surfaces in the writings of certain Eastern fathers and modern theologians, is that it consists essentially in Christ's enabling of human beings to achieve immortality and incorruptibility. According to this understanding, Christ's incarnation fundamentally accomplishes the atonement by bridging the gap between God and humanity and rendering the "deification" of human beings—that is, their ascent to a godlike status—possible. While this theory possesses the merit of portraying Christ's incarnation, in addition to his death, as central to his atoning work, it fails

to explain why Christ died and possesses scant scriptural warrant.

Example of Loving Sacrifice. According to a fourth conception of the atonement, championed by Peter Abelard (1079–1142) and endorsed by many modern theologians, Christ reconciles human beings to God by demonstrating God's love for sinners and setting an inspiring example of Christian conduct. This theory, it seems, is correct in what it affirms and incorrect in what it denies. For although Scripture unmistakably describes Christ's sacrifice as both a demonstration of divine love (John 15:13; Rom. 5:8; 8:32; 1 John 4:10) and an example to be imitated (Luke 9:23; Phil. 2:5–11; Heb. 12:2–3; 1 Pet. 2:21; 4:1; 1 John 3:16), one cannot confine Christ's work to demonstrating God's love and furnishing a righteous example without denying, ignoring, or gravely misconstruing those passages that portray Christ's suffering and death as instrumental in the forgiveness of his people's sins (e.g., Rom. 8:3; 1 Cor. 15:3; Gal. 1:4; 2:20; Eph. 1:7; Col. 1:14; 1 John 1:7b; Rev. 1:5; 7:14). Any account of Christ's atoning work that makes it consist exclusively, or even primarily, in setting an example and manifesting divine love, therefore, profoundly distorts Scripture's testimony to Christ's atonement.

Demonstration of God's Wrath against Sin. A fifth conception of the atonement, pioneered by Hugo Grotius (1583–1645) and promoted by Jonathan Edwards Jr. (1745–1801) and Charles Finney (1792–1875), consists in the notion that Christ's suffering and death serve principally to convey to human beings the intensity of God's hatred of sin. This theory has proven popular because it allows one to hold that Christ died for all human beings without implying that, since Christ has already suffered the punishment due for all human beings' sins, God cannot justly subject anyone to eternal punishment.

The theory, nonetheless, suffers from two principal flaws. First, it does not adequately account for those scriptural passages which suggest that Christ suffered the punishment his people deserve for their sins. Second, it portrays God as forgiving sins without exacting punishment and thus implicitly denies God's retributive justice. Admittedly, Christ's suffering and death testify powerfully to the depth of God's wrath against sin. The notion that this testimony, rather than the propitiation of God's wrath against sin, is the primary purpose of Christ's suffering, however, seems difficult, if not impossible, to reconcile with Scripture's express teaching.

Conclusion. Each of the theories depicted above, admittedly, contains significant elements of truth. By his atonement, Christ did conquer sin, death, hell, and Satan. He did supply his people with the hope of an incorruptible body in the postresurrection state. He did embody God's love for humanity and model how human beings ought lovingly to obey God; and he vividly manifested God's righteous wrath against sin. Nevertheless, the conception of Christ's atonement as vicarious punishment, as suffering his people's punishment in their stead, ought to take precedence over all other conceptions of the atonement. For it rightly focuses on the work whereby Christ made peace between his people and God, without which Christ's other accomplishments on his people's behalf would be either meaningless or impossible.

See also CHRIST, NATURES AND ATTRIBUTES OF; RESURRECTION OF JESUS

Bibliography. G. Aulén, *Christus Victor: A Historical Study of the Three Main Types of the Idea of the Atonement,* trans. A. G. Hebert; John Calvin, *Commentary on the Epistles of Paul the Apostle to the Corinthians,* 2 vols.; J. M. Campbell, *The Nature of the Atonement and Its Relation to Remission of Sins and Eternal Life,* 2nd ed.; T. J. Crawford, *The Doctrine of Scripture respecting the Atonement,* 4th ed.; R. W. Dale, *The Atonement: The Congregational Union Lecture for 1875,* 7th ed.; C. E. Hill and F. A. James III, eds., *The Glory of the Atonement: Biblical, Historical, and Practical Perspectives*; S. Jeffrey, M. Ovey, and A. Sach, *Pierced for Our Transgressions: Rediscovering the Glory of Penal Substitution*; H. D. McDonald, *The Atonement of the Death of Christ: In Faith, Revelation and History*; L. Morris, *The Apostolic Preaching of the Cross,* 3rd ed.; J. Owen, *The Death of Death in the Death of Christ.*

D. W. Jowers

AUROBINDO, SRI. Sri Aurobindo (born Arvinda Ackroyd Ghose; 1872–1950) was an Indian-born scholar, mystic, and guru who popularized a distinctive form of Advaita Vedanta Hinduism (known as Integral Yoga) in the US. Aurobindo was taught by Irish nuns in Calcutta during his early childhood, and when he was seven years old, he and his two older brothers were sent to England to be formally educated; Aurobindo completed his collegiate studies in the early 1890s at King's College, Cambridge. In 1893 he returned to India, initially working in the city of Baroda. During the next fifteen years, he was involved in various nationalistic political activities, mainly in association with the Swadeshi Movement. In 1906 he moved to Calcutta to serve as principal of the recently founded Bengal National College; the following year he was prosecuted for sedition and acquitted. In 1908 Aurobindo became head of the Bengal National Party—a political group seeking Bengali national independence from Great Britain—and was arrested and incarcerated for his activities that same year. While in prison, he spent considerable time reading the Hindu scriptures, especially the Bhagavad Gita, and engaging in yogic exercises. (He later claimed that while meditating in his jail cell, he was visited by the spirit of Swami Vivekananda and had visions of Vishnu.) He was released in May 1909 and relocated to Pondicherry province in February 1910. There, in 1914 Aurobindo met Mira Richard (1878–1973; a.k.a. The Mother), a

Frenchwoman who convinced him that her earlier vision of Krishna actually had been a vision of him. That same year Aurobindo began publishing the *Arya*, a monthly journal of Hindu philosophy, which discussed subjects such as the meaning of the Vedas and the unification of the human race. The *Arya* ceased publication in 1921, at which time Aurobindo sequestered himself with several close disciples. Eventually there formed a fairly large group of people desiring to follow Aurobindo's spiritual path; Mira Richard organized it into a community that came to be known as the Ashram. In November 1926, Aurobindo proclaimed that Krishna had manifested himself in the material realm. Shortly after this announcement, he went into seclusion, whereupon spiritual charge of the Ashram was taken up by Richard. Under her guidance, the Ashram grew to nearly twelve hundred members. Aurobindo died in December 1950, and his work was continued by Richard until her death in November 1973. Several centers that promote Aurobindo's teachings have been established in the US; the two most significant are the Atmaniketan Ashram in Pomona, California, and the Matagiri in Mt. Tremper, New York.

Aurobindo repudiated those sects of Hinduism which insist that viewing the world primarily or exclusively as an illusion (*maya*) and at the same time committing oneself to asceticism and social withdrawal are prerequisites to attaining liberation (*moksha*). Instead, he advocated what he termed Integral Yoga, a general and flexible prescription of spiritual disciplines that presuppose and affirm the derived, phenomenal reality of the world and allow for active engagement with culture while one pursues enlightenment. Aurobindo permitted his followers to choose from among four main approaches to their spiritual evolution: the yoga of works, the yoga of knowledge, the yoga of love and devotion, and the yoga of self-perfection. Though Aurobindo held that ultimately there exists only one Eternal Consciousness (Brahma), which has manifested itself as a three-faceted reality of infinite existence, consciousness, and bliss (*sachchidananda*), he also believed that all finite creatures are ontologically unified in Brahma, though they are ignorant of this fact. (Aurobindo also taught that a fourth aspect of the divine, the supermind, mediates between *sachchidananda* and the phenomenal world.) Integral Yoga provides a means of escaping from this ignorance and its detrimental effects, aiding its practitioners in their evolution to a higher state of consciousness ("supramental" existence) in which they realize their inherent divinity and (corporately) have a transforming effect on global culture.

See also ADVAITA; BHAGAVAD GITA; BRAHMA; HINDUISM; MAYA; MOKSHA; YOGA

Bibliography. S. Aurobindo, *Integral Yoga: Sri Aurobindo's Teaching and Method of Practice*; Aurobindo, *The Life Divine*, 7th ed.; Aurobindo, *The Mind of Light*; P. Heehs, *Sri Aurobindo: A Brief Biography*; R. A. McDermott, *The Essential Aurobindo: Writings of Sri Aurobindo*; M. P. Pandit, *Sri Aurobindo and His Yoga*.

H. W. House

AUROVILLE INTERNATIONAL. Auroville International (AVI) is a worldwide network whose purpose is to support the development of the Auroville International Township (AIT), all of which is located in or near the state of Tamil Nadu in southern India. Its legal headquarters is located in the Netherlands; member associations and liaisons have been established in thirty-one countries. AVI provides financial, logistical, and other support to its affiliates, facilitates the formation of additional AIT-supporting organizations, spearheads fund-raising efforts for critical AIT projects, and supplies information to people interested in visiting AIT. Bill Leon is the current president of AVI-USA, whose headquarters is located in Santa Cruz, California.

Mira Richard (1878–1973) conceived of the Auroville community in the 1930s, though the concepts involved in its formation were not introduced to the Indian government until the mid-1960s. In 1966 the United Nations Educational, Scientific and Cultural Organization (UNESCO) passed a unanimous resolution commending AIT as a project important to the future of humanity. On February 28, 1968, approximately five thousand people participated in an AIT inauguration ceremony attended by representatives of 124 nations, at which time a four-point Auroville charter was established.

The stated purpose of AIT is to be a progressive, universal township where men and women from every nation live together in peace and harmony above all political ideologies and creeds, thereby achieving a cooperative coexistence demonstrating human unity in diversity in the spirit of the teachings of Hindu philosopher and activist Sri Aurobindo (1872–1950). The residents of AIT strive for a communal transformation of consciousness, promote spiritual education and mutual understanding, practice sustainable living, and work to meet the environmental, social, and spiritual needs of humankind. Hailing from more than thirty-five countries, they represent a wide spectrum of age groups, social classes, and cultures. In May 2008, the township's population was about seventeen hundred. Geographically, AIT is divided into a "peace area," a "green belt," and four zones: industrial, international, cultural, and residential. Prominent features of the township include the Savitri Bhavan Study Center, Pitanga workshops, the Center for Scientific Research, a healing center, the Earth Institute, the Integral Studies Program, and the Laboratory in Evolution.

See also AUROBINDO, SRI; HINDUISM

Bibliography. Auroville International, Auroville International home page, http://www.aviusa.org/default.html; Auroville International, Auroville Universal Township home page, http://www.auroville.org/; R. N. Minor, *The Religious, the Spiritual, and the Secular: Auroville and Secular India.*

H. W. House

AVATAR. In theistic forms of Hinduism—especially those in which popular devotion plays a major role—an avatar is a personal manifestation of the Supreme Being, who purposefully "descends" from the realm of spirit into the phenomenal world for the purpose of preserving the Hindu dharma (the Hindu way) or the superiority of the gods (*devas*) over the titans and evil spirits (*asuras* and others). Though Hindu mythology describes a number of gods who undertake such journeys, the passages of Vishnu are typically deemed the most important. (Brahma does not descend into the world of appearances; Shiva, though he has offspring, such as Ganesh, and though his appearances are called "the avatars of Shiva," has no avatars per se.) It is said that these avatars have appeared intermittently throughout the ages, each displaying a different aspect or proportion of Vishnu's divine essence. Depending on the Hindu sect or tradition consulted, the total number of avatars (past, present, and future) ranges from ten to innumerable. The Ten (primary) Avatars (*dasavatara*) of Vishnu in the Garuda Purana are (1) Matsya (the Fish), (2) Kurma (the Tortoise), (3) Varaha (the Boar), (4) Narasimha (the Man-Lion), (5) Vamana (the Dwarf), (6) Parashurama (Ax-Wielding Rama), (7) Rama (King Ramachandra), (8) Krishna, (9) Balarama or Gautama Buddha, and (10) Kalki (the Destroyer of Foulness). According to the Matsya Purana, there are twelve avatars of Vishnu; according to the Bhagavata Purana, there are twenty-two (on some readings, twenty-five). Various branches of Hinduism assert additional (or other) avatars and/or basic types of avatars: the avatar Chaitanya Mahaprabhu in the Mahabharata Purana, *purusha* avatars (the original four avatars of Vishnu), and *guna* avatars

(avatars who control the three fundamental modes of nature) are but a few examples that demonstrate the diverse theological frameworks within Hinduism that include avatars.

The early Vedic hymns never mention avatars, and such beings have no place in the metaphysical monism of the Upanishads. However, in many ancient Indian epics, avatars are depicted as mediators between the Supreme Being and ordinary mortals. Though they have no obligation to help humanity, out of love for our race, avatars leave their abode of bliss and travel to the sphere of suffering in order to instruct and care for the unenlightened. They appear in the phenomenal world whenever human ignorance and evil have reached epidemic proportions or when the titans (asuras) have grasped more power than they should, always acting in accordance with the divine nature. Yet unlike the incarnation of Jesus Christ in orthodox Christian doctrine, which involves one of the persons of the divine Godhead taking on a human nature (in all its physicality), in Hindu theology the forms of God do not actually become flesh or assume a material body since in the final analysis God consists of a single, indivisible spiritual essence.

The idea of an avatar was unique to Hinduism. More recently, devotees of some Hindu-based cults and branches of the New Age movement use the term avatar more loosely to refer to nontraditional embodiments of the divine such as Zoroaster, Jesus Christ, and other famous religious leaders.

In modern popular parlance, avatar refers to a representation of a personality of a person on a website or in a web-based game. In such a context, an avatar often represents an alter ego or an idealized self-image of the person.

See also BRAHMA; HINDUISM; MAHAYANA BUDDHISM

Bibliography. D. R. Kinsley, Hinduism: A Cultural Perspective, 2nd ed.; K. K. Klostermaier, A Survey of Hinduism; K. Knott, Hinduism: A Very Short Introduction; V. Lal, "Avatars of Vishnu," https://www.sscnet.ucla.edu/southasia/Religions/Avatars/Vishnu.html.

H. W. House

AVESTA. The Avesta (also sometimes called the Zend-Avesta) is the scripture of the ancient Persian religion of Zoroastrianism, thought to have been founded by Zoroaster (Greek; Persian: Zarathustra). The word avesta is also the name of the ancient language (avestan) possibly spoken by Zoroaster, known only from this work, and for much of its history, the Avesta was only known orally. The Avesta is a fairly diverse collection of writings, spanning many centuries and manifesting drastic developments in style and language. Some of its oldest sections probably go back to the prophet Zoroaster in the sixth century BC. The recognized text that survives today is divided into Yasna (sacred liturgy and hymns of Zarathushtra), Khorda Avesta (prayers and hymns), Visperad (extentions to the liturgy), Vendidad (purity laws, myths, and medicinal texts), and "fragments" (various surviving writings over several subjects).

See also AHURA MAZDA; AMESHA SPENTAS; AVESTAN; SACRED FIRE; ZOROASTER; ZOROASTRIANISM

Bibliography. M. Boyce, Zoroastrians: Their Religious Beliefs and Practices.

W. Corduan

AVESTAN. The ancient Persian language possibly spoken by Zoroaster (Greek; Persian: Zarathustra), known only from the scriptures of Zoroastrianism, called the Avesta. Scholars have identified two periods of development of the language: the Gathas, older, oral, and close to Vedic Sanskrit; and later Standard Avestan, which used Pahlavi script. It is thought that the sacred scriptures of Zoroastrinaism were orally passed down through priests until the fourth through sixth centuries AD, when the accepted canon was being fixed. By that time, Avestan was a long-dead language, no longer spoken by the general populace.

See also GATHAS; ZOROASTER; ZOROAS-TRIANISM

Bibliography. H. Bailey et al., eds., *The Cambridge History of Iran.*

C. R. Wells

AVIDYA. In Hinduism, Indian Buddhism, and many Hindu and Buddhist-based cults, *avidya* (literally, "not knowledge" in Sanskrit) means ignorance, illusion, and lack of wisdom. At times the term is used interchangeably with *maya*. Avidya is said to be incorrect focus that clouds one's religious vision, thereby hindering enlightenment. In Advaita Vedanta Hinduism in particular, avidya causes its possessor to fail to grasp the true nature of reality (which is undifferentiated being), substituting a delusional experience of individuated phenomena in its place. This unfortunate handicap of normal human perception is the root of all suffering endured by human beings, and its removal is the ultimate goal of Advaita Vedanta practitioners. In the various schools of Indian Buddhism, avidya is the fundamental cause of human misery in the cycle of death and rebirth, insofar as it results in the craving of and clinging to transient objects. Avidya can be overcome by means of meditation, awareness, and endurance.

See also ADVAITA; BUDDHISM; HINDUISM; MAYA

Bibliography. S. K. Chattopadhyaya, *The Philosophy of Sankar's Advaita Vedanta*; S. Kempton, "Understand Avidya To See Yourself As You Are," *Yoga Journal*; D. S. Noss and J. B. Noss, *A History of the World's Religions*, 9th ed; S. Ramanasramam, "Avidya," *The Mountain Path.*

R. L. Drouhard

AZUSA STREET REVIVAL. The Azusa Street Revival generally refers to a three-year period

at the Apostolic Faith Mission in Los Angeles, California, that is widely regarded as the genesis of the modern Pentecostal movement. Charles Parham and the students of his Bible school in Topeka, Kansas, began teaching in late 1900 that baptism of the Holy Spirit was an experience of mission empowerment that was evidenced by speaking in unknown tongues. Parham started a school in January 1906 in Houston, where he met African American Holiness preacher William J. Seymour. Jim Crow laws prevented Seymour's full inclusion in the school, but Parham allowed him to listen to lectures from a chair in the hallway. Seymour accepted Parham's teaching on Spirit baptism and tongues but left for Los Angeles on an invitation to pastor there without having received his Spirit baptism. Seymour's message was not well received by the congregation that had invited him, so Seymour began holding prayer meetings at a home at 214 North Bonnie Brae Street.

Seymour and the prayer group started experiencing tongues speech, healings, and a variety of other miraculous manifestations, which attracted significant crowds. When the crowds spilled out of the house and caused the front porch to collapse, it was time for the nightly meetings to move to a dilapidated former African Methodist Episcopal church at 312 Azusa Street. April 1906 began a three-year revival at the new Azusa Street Mission (later Apostolic Faith Mission) with basically nonstop prayer meetings and worship services. Prophecy, tongues speech, miraculous healings, and physical manifestations, including shaking and "slaying in the Spirit," characterized the worship services. Often there was no plan for worship or preaching, with the time instead filled with spontaneous singing, testimonies, and long periods of "tarrying," waiting in prayer for the baptism of the Holy Spirit and tongues. Often worship was loud and ran late into the night, with frequent police involvement.

The mission was interracial and marked by relative gender equality at the beginning, with people praying for one another across race lines and those "under the power of the Spirit" lying upon one another across genders lines. This transgressing of boundaries was criticized. Theology in the mission was typical of radical evangelicals and Holiness preachers of the period, with the addition of the unique theology of Spirit baptism and tongues. The revival was popular among spiritualists, but Seymour suppressed their non-Christian doctrine and testimony when they tried to speak publicly. Estimating attendance over the three-year period is difficult, but hundreds were in attendance on any given night, and most were visitors from all over the country.

The revival was widely publicized in secular media and in the mission's own periodical, *The Apostolic Faith*. The paper gained international readership with an estimated fifty thousand copies per edition, consisting mostly of excerpts from sermons, testimonials, and reports of missions involvement. The paper did not charge for subscription, and the mission took no offerings, but donations were accepted through the paper's readership and a wooden box at the rear of the mission. The mission used its financial resources to send evangelists and missionaries all over the country and the world with the Pentecostal message; a large number of the early missionaries received their Spirit baptism experience at the Azusa revival. The revival was mostly over in 1909 after *The Apostolic Faith* editor Clara Lum took the paper and mailing list with her to Portland, Oregon. The mission continued in a smaller capacity with Seymour and his wife, Jennie Evans Seymour, as pastors until about 1936.

The impact of the Azusa Street Revival on Pentecostalism cannot be overstated. Today, every major Pentecostal denomination traces its roots to this revival, including the Church of God in Christ, the Assemblies of God, the Pentecostal Church of God, and the United Pentecostal Church. According to some sources, Pentecostals constitute the second-largest group within Christianity (behind only the Roman Catholic Church).

See also BAPTISM IN THE HOLY SPIRIT, PENTECOSTAL VIEW OF; ONENESS PENTECOSTALISM; SPEAKING IN TONGUES

Bibliography. F. Bartleman, *Azusa Street*; C. M. Robeck Jr., *Azusa Street Mission and Revival*; V. Synan, *The Holiness-Pentecostal Tradition*, 2nd ed.

J. W. S. Gibbs

B

BÁB. Siyyid 'Ali-Muhammad, who would come to be known as the Báb (Arabic for "gate"; pronounced "bob"), was born in 1819 in Iran. In 1844 and thereafter, he made a number of claims about himself, including the claim that he was the "point" of a new revelation from God, one that would supersede the revelation given to Muhammad. This claim brought the Báb into direct conflict with orthodox Islam since one of the central claims of historic Islam is that Muhammad was the final prophet, who would never be superseded. Due to the Báb's unorthodox claims, as well as to the Bábi (as the followers of the Báb had come to be called) tendency to militancy, intense opposition arose against the Báb and his followers from Shi'ite clergy and from government officials. In the end, the Báb himself was sentenced to death by firing squad by Iranian prime minister Mirza Taqi Khan, with the collaboration of Shi'ite leaders. The principal writing to come from the Báb was the Bayan, in which he delivered to his followers the revelations for doctrine and life that he claimed had been committed to him by God. The Bayan also contains predictions of a future prophet who would supersede the Báb and the Bayan itself, bringing in a new religious dispensation. This prophet is referred to as "he whom God will make manifest." Many followers of the Báb came to see the Bábi leader Bahá'u'lláh, who claimed the role, as this promised one. Though Bahá'u'lláh's claim did not go completely unrivaled, eventually the majority of the Báb's followers gave their allegiance to

him as the promised messenger foretold by the Báb, and these followers were known as Bahá'ís from that time on. Bahá'ís consider the Bábi religion to be a separate religion from Bahá'í, and the Báb is honored as one of the nine great manifestations, including Krishna, Zoroaster, and so on.

See also Bahá'u'lláh; Islam, Basic Beliefs of; Shi'a Islam

Bibliography. J. R. Gaver, *The Baha'i Faith: Dawn of a New Day*; W. S. Hatcher, *The Baha'i Faith: The Emerging Global Religion*; W. M. Miller, *The Baha'i Faith: Its History and Teachings*; P. Smith, *The Babi and Baha'i Religions: From Messianic Shi'ism to a World Religion*; Smith, *The Baha'i Religion: A Short Introduction to Its History and Teachings*.

M. C. Hausam

BAHÁ'Í. Bahá'í (from the Arabic *bahá'*, meaning "splendor"), most often referred to as "the Bahá'í Faith," is a monotheistic religion that emphasizes the unity of all religious faiths. It is officially known as the Bahá'í International Community and is overseen by the Universal House of Justice, though many splinter and subgroups also claim to represent the official Bahá'í Faith.

History. In 1844 in Persia (modern-day Iran), Mirza Ali Muhammad (1819–50) publicly announced that he was the Báb (gate) and a manifestation of God. He also proclaimed that his mission was to pave the way for a coming world teacher who would unite the nations of the world and lead humanity to a new era of global peace. When the government of Persia realized that the Báb was gathering to himself a sizable following, it denounced the fledgling movement, imprisoned him, and finally put him to death in 1850. In 1863, one of the Báb's most loyal disciples, Mirza Husayn Ali (1817–92), declared himself to be the divine manifestation of which the Báb had spoken and gave himself the title Bahá'u'lláh (the glory of God). Soon thereafter a large majority of the Báb's former followers pledged their allegiance to Bahá'u'lláh. Bahá'u'lláh spent much of his time writing a massive corpus expounding the teachings of the Bahá'í Faith. When he died in 1892, his eldest son, Abbas Effendi (1844–1921), also known as 'Abdu'l-Bahá (servant of Baha), became the new leader of Bahá'í. Unlike his predecessors, 'Abdu'l-Bahá never claimed to be a divine manifestation, but he did maintain that only he was authorized to interpret the writings of Bahá'u'lláh and that his writings had the same authority as Bahá'u'lláh's. He spent almost thirty years promoting the Bahá'í Faith in North America and Europe before his death in 1921. At this time, Shoghí Effendí (1897–1957)—the oldest grandson of 'Abdu'l-Bahá—assumed leadership of the organization, taking on a new position called the Guardianship. During his tenure, he focused mainly on administrative affairs. Shoghí Effendí died in 1957, and since then the Universal House of Justice has overseen all matters of importance to the Bahá'í International Community.

However, within a few years after Shoghí Effendí's death, the Bahá'í community splintered into seven sects (besides the mainstream, parent group, which remains by far the largest): the Orthodox Bahá'í Faith, Bahá'ís under the Provisions of the Covenant, The House of Mankind and the Universal Palace of Order, the Orthodox Bahá'í Faith under the Regency (Tarbiyat Bahá'í Community), the Charles Mason Remey Society, Bahá'ís Loyal to the Fourth Guardian, and Independent Bahá'ís (Unenrolled Bahá'ís). Each of these groups claims to be the only true successor

of Shoghí Effendí and thus the only true defender of the Bahá'í Faith. In turn some of these sects further split over disagreements about the succession of leadership and their own competing claims to succession. Over time some of these sects, such as the Charles Mason Remey Society, have ceased to exist as organized bodies, though they continue as informal groups or in the writings and figures of their leaders.

Official Bahá'í sources (those affiliated with the Universal House of Justice) indicate that presently there are about 6,000,000 members worldwide, including about 140,000 in the US. However, other sources estimate 1,000,000 worldwide and 28,000 in the US. Sizable Bahá'í groups have been established in approximately 235 different regions of the world. The organization's international headquarters is located in Haifa, Israel; the US headquarters is located in Wilmette, Illinois.

Basic Teachings. The three most fundamental doctrines of the Bahá'í Faith are the oneness of God, the oneness of religion, and the oneness of humanity. Ultimately, then, there is only one true religion: that which God has revealed to humanity through a series of divine manifestations. According to Bahá'í, each of these manifestations spoke truly concerning the will of God for the human race during the stage of history in which he taught. However, God's revelation is ongoing and progressive; thus later disclosures of the divine will supersede earlier ones. Bahá'u'lláh is the most recent divine manifestation, and Baha'i is the system of religion that currently pronounces the will of God to the world.

Scripture and Authority. The Bahá'í scriptures consist of the writings of the Báb, Bahá'u'lláh, and 'Abdu'l-Bahá. Included among these writings are The Most Holy Book, The Book of Certitude, and The Seven Valleys. Before he died, Bahá'u'lláh chose 'Abdu'l-Bahá to become the next authoritative interpreter of the Bahá'í scriptures. After the death of 'Abdu'l-Bahá, Shoghí Effendí assumed this role. Bahá'í teachers often cite the Bible as well, though giving it different meanings than orthodox Jewish or Christian interpreters. In what appears to be a paradox, adherents of Bahá'í assert the authority of the sacred texts mentioned above while at the same time holding to a strong doctrine of intellectual autonomy. On this view, genuine faith involves independently searching for truth, free from the shackles of superstition and religious tradition. Anyone who desires to become a member of the Bahá'í community, then, must be willing to forsake any reliance on previous prophets; one cannot see the truth of the Bahá'í Faith without doing so.

God and Creation. Bahá'í theology contains several uneasy tensions in its understanding of God and his created world. God is so utterly transcendent that his divine nature cannot be understood. Nevertheless, his attributes have been adequately revealed in his divine manifestations by means of a long line of religious leaders through the ages. These include Adam, Noah, Abraham, Salih ibn Tarif, Hud, the unnamed founder of the Sabaean religion, Moses, Zarathushtra, the Buddha, Jesus Christ, Krishna, Muhammad, the Báb, and Bahá'u'lláh. These various manifestations are given power and wisdom by the primal will, a special life force sent by God. Though God is the source of the universe, he did not create it out of nothing. Instead, from eternity past, the universe has emanated from God. Because God is inactive and unchanging, he is unable to relate personally to his creation. Moreover, his transcendence renders him incapable of manifesting himself fully. Yet his human manifestations express (in a limited way, in the created world) his attributes to his human creatures.

Humankind and Sin. The entire human race is one, which means no particular class of people is superior to any other human group. Ontologically speaking, all mankind is the same (human), which logically means

ontological equality. Prejudice in any form is evil and presents a major obstacle to ushering in global peace and justice. Women and men are moral and intellectual equals. This strong emphasis on equality among persons is seen in the fact that the Bahá'í Faith has no clergy, sacraments, or rituals. Each person possesses an immortal soul. There is a Pelagian element to the Bahá'í understanding of the nature of humans. Human beings are not sinful by nature, nor are they basically evil. Their various abilities are given to them by God to be used for the promotion of spiritual growth. Evil is the privation or absence of good or imperfection. The devil does not exist in the form of an evil spirit. Rather, the image of the devil symbolizes the lower nature of humans.

Salvation and Afterlife. Bahá'í soteriology is pluralistic. In every period of history, salvation is attained by believing in and obeying the divine manifestations that God has sent at that time. Only religions that have been revealed have the potential to save people from their imperfections. People are given the opportunity to be delivered from their bondage to the lower nature, achieve their spiritual potential, and be united with God through these divine manifestations. After death the soul detaches from the body and makes a journey through the "spirit world," a strange dimension of the universe that is without space or time. Jesus Christ never will return to earth. Bahá'u'lláh was the "return of Christ" in a spiritual sense. Heaven and hell are not literal places but rather symbolize nearness to God and distance from God, respectively. Heaven is the result of making spiritual progress, while hell is the consequence of failing to make spiritual progress.

Other Teachings. In addition to the beliefs and practices mentioned above, the Bahá'í Faith has a number of others that make it distinctive:

1. *The Universal House of Justice.* Though not established until 1963, such an institution

had been intended by Bahá'u'lláh to serve as the legislative authority of the worldwide Bahá'í community. Consisting of an elected nine-member tribunal of judges, its duties include the administration of international affairs and overseeing various Bahá'í properties and holy sites. Bahá'u'lláh vested it with the authority to make binding decisions concerning any important issue on which the Bahá'í scriptures are silent.

2. *A Global Commonwealth.* Central to the Bahá'í Faith is the hope of establishing a global commonwealth. This is envisioned as a fraternity of nations that would work together to resolve disputes among various countries and thereby achieve lasting world peace. In this scenario, international leaders would consult with one another regularly so as to bring about political stability on a global scale. Institutions critical to the success of this commonwealth would include an international executive power, a world legislature, and a world court. Its top priorities would be compulsory education for every citizen, establishing a universal language, and rectifying economic inequalities.

3. *The Unity of Science and Religion.* Because truth and reality are one, science and religion are in complete concord. Something that is true in the sphere of science must be true in the sphere of religion, and vice versa. The manner of discovering truth in these two spheres differs, however. Truths of science are discovered by means of empirical investigation, whereas the truths of religion are revealed by God through his manifestations. Alleged contradictions between science and religion stem either from human error or from closed-mindedness.

See also BÁB; BAHÁ'U'LLÁH; EFFENDÍ, SHOGHÍ

Bibliography. Bahá'í International Community, The Bahá'í Faith: The Website of the worldwide Bahá'í Community, http://www.bahai.org/; Bahá'u'lláh, *Gleanings from the Writings of Baha'u'llah*, trans. Shoghí Effendí, rev. ed.; J. R. I. Cole, *Modernity and the Millennium: The Genesis of the Baha'i Faith in the Nineteenth-Century Middle East*; J. E. Esslemont, *Baha'u'llah and the New Era: An Introduction to the Baha'i Faith*, 5th ed.; W. S. Hatcher and J. D. Martin, *The Baha'i Faith: The Emerging Global Religion*; M. Momen, *The Baha'i Faith: A Short Introduction.*

S. J. Rost

BAHÁ'U'LLÁH. Bahá'u'lláh (1817–92), born Mírzá Ḥusayn-'Alí Núrí (Persian), was the founder of the Bahá'í religion. The title Bahá'u'lláh means "the glory of God." Bahá'ís recognize Bahá'u'lláh as "the Judge, the Lawgiver and Redeemer of all mankind, as the Organizer of the entire planet, as the Unifier of the children of men, as the Inaugurator of the long-awaited millennium, as the Originator of a new 'Universal Cycle,' as the Establisher of the Most Great Peace, as the Fountain of the Most Great Justice, as the Proclaimer of the coming of age of the entire human race, as the Creator of a new World Order, and as the Inspirer and Founder of a world civilization" (Effendí, 93–94). They believe that he is the great unifier of all major world religions and was referenced by Jesus Christ as the "Comforter" who would come after him (John 14:26; 15:26 KJV).

Bahá'u'lláh was born in 1817 into one of the ruling families of Persia, a wealthy family that could be traced genealogically to the royal dynasties of Persia's imperial history. He rejected his privileged lineage and became a seeker of religious truth. Though some histories record that he was raised as a Muslim, Bahá'í teaches that his father was a political officer but not one of the Islamic *ulema* (scholars). He had distinct political influence but was not a particularly educated man.

In 1844, when Bahá'u'lláh was twenty-seven years old, a mystic named Báb made a startling declaration in Persia (modern Iran). He said that he was a forerunner for a coming messiah and was the "messenger of

God" who prepared the people for the coming of Bahá'u'lláh. The title "the Báb" means "the gate." His followers were called Bábís. He quickly garnered a following, which was persecuted by the indigenous Islamic leadership. After six years of persecution, Báb was killed, along with over twenty thousand of his followers.

Following Báb's death, Bahá'u'lláh assumed the leadership of the fledgling movement. In 1863, he began to spread the religion but was banished several times from cities and regions where he was proclaiming his religion. These banishments had the unforeseen consequence of aiding in the spread of the new religion. In Baghdad, he proclaimed himself to be the "One promised by the Báb." Exiled from Baghdad for heresy, he went to Constantinople, Adrianople, and Acre (in northern modern-day Israel). While in Acre, Bahá'u'lláh wrote a series of letters exhorting all national leaders of the period to lay down their weapons and pursue world peace. He also predicted a coming time of the unification of all humanity and the rise of a singular global society.

Bahá'u'lláh died in 1892 and is buried at Bahji, just north of Acre. By the time of his death his teachings had begun to spread throughout the region. Today the Shrine of Bahá'u'lláh is the center of Bahá'í worship, and the world headquarters of the Bahá'í Faith is located in nearby Haifa, Israel. Through Bahá'u'lláh, the Bahá'ís believe their religion and teachings have abrogated all other religious systems.

Bibliography. 'Abdu'l-Bahá, *Some Answered Questions* (1908); "Bahá'u'lláh (1817–1892)— Founder of the Bahá'í Faith," The Bahá'í Faith website, http://info.bahai.org/bahaullah.html; Shoghí Effendí, *God Passes By*.

T. J. Demy

BAPTISM, CHRISTIAN. Christian baptism is one of the two ordinances or sacraments that the Lord of the church has instituted

for the life and health of the church until the end of the age, and as such, it is to be practiced today in obedience to the Lord (Matt. 28:18–20). In the Great Commission and the rest of the New Testament, the purpose of baptism is at least twofold: a sign of initiation and entrance into the Messiah's community, the church, and a graphic declaration of faith and surrender to the lordship of Jesus Christ. The New Testament writers cannot conceive of a disciple who has repented of sin and believed in Christ who has not also been baptized into the name of the Triune God. In fact, this understanding is borne out by the book of Acts. From Pentecost on, all those who repented of their sins and believed the gospel were also baptized, thus publicly testifying to their faith in Jesus Christ (see Acts 2:41; 8:12–13, 36–39; 9:17–18; 10:47–48; 16:14–15, 31–33; 18:8; 19:5).

At the heart of the meaning and significance of Christian baptism, in contrast to Jewish proselyte baptism or even the baptism of John, is the fact that it signifies a believer's union with Christ in his death, burial, and resurrection (Rom. 6:3–7; Col. 2:11–12) and all the saving benefits that are entailed by that union. For this reason, throughout the New Testament baptism is regarded as an outward sign or symbol that signifies an inward reality—namely, that a believer has entered into the realities of the new covenant that Christ Jesus inaugurated and sealed with his own blood on the cross. Therefore, when received in faith, baptism signifies Spirit-wrought regeneration (Titus 3:5), inward cleansing, renewal, and forgiveness of sins (Acts 22:16; 1 Cor. 6:11; Eph. 5:25–27), as well as the abiding presence of the Holy Spirit as God's seal testifying and guaranteeing that the believer will permanently be kept secure in Christ (1 Cor. 12:13; Eph. 1:13–14). In fact, so close is the association between baptism and new covenant blessings in Christ that many have argued that in the New Testament, baptism functions as shorthand or by metonymy for the conversion experience as a whole. This is not to say that baptism effects regeneration or that baptism is necessary for salvation. Instead, the New Testament data assume that baptism always presupposes faith for its validity and that true saving faith leads to baptism even though faith and baptism do not enjoy the same logical status of necessity. It is therefore possible for a person to be savingly united to Christ apart from baptism, even though this is not the New Testament pattern (see Rom. 6:1–4; Gal. 3:26–27; Eph. 4:5; 1 Pet. 3:21).

While much of the biblical teaching outlined above would meet with the agreement of most evangelicals, debate still rages over the mode of baptism and whether infants, who are not capable of faith or who have not exercised faith, should be baptized. Ultimately the latter disagreement centers on larger issues over the relationship between the old and the new covenants and the amount of continuity and discontinuity between them. But even in the midst of these differences there is agreement that baptism testifies to the great gospel realities of union with Christ and all the glorious benefits of new covenant blessings.

See also BAPTISM, NON-CHRISTIAN; BAPTISM IN THE HOLY SPIRIT, PENTECOSTAL VIEW OF; BAPTISM OF THE DEAD, CHRISTIAN; BAPTISM OF THE DEAD, MORMON; CHRISTIANITY, PROTESTANT; CHURCH OF JESUS CHRIST OF LATTER-DAY SAINTS; EASTERN ORTHODOXY; KUMBHA MELA; ROMAN CATHOLICISM

Bibliography. N. Altman, *Sacred Water: The Spiritual Source of Life*; R. Arvigo and N. Epstein, *Spiritual Bathing: Healing Rituals and Traditions from around the World*; "Baptisms for the Dead," http://www.lds.org/; G. R. Beasley-Murray, *Baptism in the New Testament*; D. Bridge and D. Phypers, *The Water That Divides*; G. W. Bromiley, "Baptism," in *Evangelical Dictionary of Theology*, ed. W. A. Elwell.

S. Wellum and R. L. Drouhard

BAPTISM, NON-CHRISTIAN. Although baptism is usually associated with Christianity, numerous other religions practice ritual bathing or washing or use water for cleansing. In Judaism ritual bathing is prescribed as a means of purification. Before the destruction of the temple in Jerusalem, ritual bathing was required to enter the temple. Hindus believe bathing in the sacred rivers purifies the soul of sin (called Kumbha Mela). While Buddhism retains some tradition of ritual bathing, some Buddhists see it as unnecessary. Still others ritually bathe statues of the Buddha to purify them. In Islam the *farid al-wudu* is a ritual bathing required before prayer, and an immersion similar to the Jewish practice is prescribed in certain circumstances.

Some heretical sects of Christianity practice baptism as well. The Church of Jesus Christ of Latter-day Saints (LDS Church) teaches that baptism by an authorized individual holding the LDS priesthood is required for salvation. It teaches that such baptism is required for all people, no matter the time or place. Hence, LDS practices baptism for the dead. Those who have died without being baptized are given the chance to accept the "proxy" baptism in the afterlife. Jehovah's Witnesses (JW) also practice baptism. It differs from orthodox Christian baptism in that the person wishing to be baptized must answer a lengthy series of questions before a council of JW elders. Also, people are baptized to identify them as "one of Jehovah's Witnesses in association with God's spirit-directed organization" ("Go and Make Disciples, Baptizing Them," 21–25). Finally, baptisms are generally done at large conventions of JWs, which can mean someone waiting a long time to be baptized.

See also BAPTISM, CHRISTIAN; BAPTISM IN THE HOLY SPIRIT, PENTECOSTAL VIEW OF; BAPTISM OF THE DEAD, CHRISTIAN; BAPTISM OF THE DEAD, MORMON; CHRISTIANITY, PROTESTANT; CHURCH OF JESUS CHRIST OF LATTER-DAY

SAINTS; EASTERN ORTHODOXY; ISLAM, BASIC BELIEFS OF; JEHOVAH'S WITNESSES (JW); JUDAISM; KUMBHA MELA; ROMAN CATHOLICISM

Bibliography. N. Altman, *Sacred Water: The Spiritual Source of Life*; R. Arvigo and N. Epstein, *Spiritual Bathing: Healing Rituals and Traditions from around the World*; "Baptisms for the Dead," http://www.lds.org/; G. R. Beasley-Murray, *Baptism in the New Testament*; D. Bridge and D. Phypers, *The Water That Divides*; G. W. Bromiley, "Baptism," in *Evangelical Dictionary of Theology*, ed. W. A. Elwell; "Go and Make Disciples, Baptizing Them," *Watchtower*.

S. Wellum and R. L. Drouhard

BAPTISM IN THE HOLY SPIRIT, PENTECOSTAL VIEW OF.

Pentecostals believe that baptism in the Holy Spirit is an event that happens in the life of a believer, empowering that person for a life of service and ministry. This experience initiates charismatic ministry that may include Spirit-empowered preaching and the miraculous spiritual gifts listed in 1 Corinthians 12. It is also often referred to as Holy Spirit Baptism, Baptism with the Holy Spirit, and sometimes Baptism *of* the Holy Spirit.

Differing Views. Most Pentecostals believe that Spirit-baptized persons will exhibit one or more of the miraculous gifts at different times in their life according to the needs of the church's mission. A minority believe that a certain gift, such as miraculous healing, is given to an individual for the duration of the person's life. Nearly all agree that Spirit baptism is to be sought not as an end of a mature Christian life but as the beginning of a mission-oriented life. Some Wesleyan-Holiness Pentecostals (sometimes called "third blessing" Pentecostals) dissent from this position, regarding Spirit baptism as an event after entire sanctification. Even those Pentecostals who deny that Spirit baptism is primarily about sanctification usually claim that the experience increases desire for the sanctified life and sensitivity to the Spirit.

Subsequent Experience of the Baptism of the Holy Spirit. Traditional Protestants usually associate the term *baptism in the Holy Spirit* with the initial acceptance of the Spirit that occurs when a person commits himself or herself to Christ. Pentecostals do not deny that the new Christian receives the Spirit, but they distinguish between this experience and the baptism in the Spirit. Spirit baptism happens at some time subsequent to conversion logically, though the events may occasionally happen so close in time as to be indistinguishable. Spirit baptism is not part of conversion to Christ for Pentecostals. It is a subsequent experience that directs and empowers a believer's life toward Christian mission.

Initial Evidence. North American Pentecostals typically believe that the normal experience of baptism in the Holy Spirit will include the initial evidence of prayer in other tongues. The first Pentecostals believed that this was God's empowering converts with a language that they had not learned so that they could preach the gospel to the unconverted in foreign missions. Soon afterward, Pentecostals began to understand tongues speech as an unknown "heavenly" language intended to increase the Spirit-baptized person's faith that God can use him or her in miraculous ways. Usually North American Pentecostals, following several passages in the book of Acts (especially chapters 2, 10, and 19), believe that every Spirit-baptized person will speak in tongues. Pentecostals in Europe and the majority world often also speak in tongues, but they do not see the connection to Spirit baptism as essential.

Oneness Pentecostals. A minority of Pentecostals regard the Spirit baptism experience and tongues speech as essential to a person's new birth experience. Oneness Pentecostals do not believe in distinct persons of the Trinity. They therefore regard baptism in the Holy Spirit as identical with conversion because one cannot receive Christ without receiving the baptism in the Holy Spirit (and also water baptism). Trinitarian Pentecostals, which are a majority, claim this is a heretical doctrine of the Godhead and a misappropriation of Spirit baptism.

See also ONENESS PENTECOSTALISM; SPEAKING IN TONGUES

Bibliography. H. D. Hunter, *Spirit Baptism*; R. Menzies, *Empowered for Witness*; A. D. Palma, *The Holy Spirit*; R. Stronstad, *Charismatic Theology of St. Luke*.

J. W. S. Gibbs

BAPTISM OF THE DEAD, CHRISTIAN. This practice is mentioned in 1 Corinthians 15:29 (RSV): "Otherwise, what do people mean by being baptized on behalf of the dead? If the dead are not raised at all, why are people baptized on their behalf?" It is the only Scripture in the New Testament referring to the practice. While some interpret this passage as referring to vicarious baptism for dead persons, there is no other historical evidence of its use in New Testament times.

There is reference to this practice in the late second century. It appears, however, that its practice largely was limited to heretical groups (Reaume, 459).

While most New Testament interpreters have tended to interpret this verse as referring to vicarious baptism for the dead, it is not assumed that its advantages included postmortem salvation. Some commentators postulate rather that it might have been a memorial vicarious rite for deceased Christians who had not been baptized. Other plausible interpretations include the notion that people were baptized due to the influence of deceased believers. It is also even possible that persons were understood to be baptized to take the place of dead Christians or to be reunited with the deceased at the resurrection (Reaume, 475). Most probably, 1 Corinthians 15:29 is referring not to vicarious baptism for the dead in order to fulfill an insufficiency in their confession

and experience but to baptism of the living as the result of the witness and faithful testimony of now deceased or dead saints. If Paul is referring to vicarious baptism for the dead, he is not necessarily approving of the activity but rather questioning why they performed this baptism if they rejected the physical resurrection.

See also BAPTISM, CHRISTIAN; BAPTISM OF THE DEAD, MORMON

Bibliography. J. D. Reaume, "Another Look at 1 Corinthians 15:29, 'Baptized for the Dead,'" in *Bibliotheca Sacra*.

R. P. Roberts

BAPTISM OF THE DEAD, MORMON. Among new religious movements, the practice is found in the Church of Jesus Christ of Latter-day Saints and also the Church of Jesus Christ (Cutlerite), a breakaway Mormon group formed a few years after Joseph Smith's death. It was instituted due to the claimed revelation delivered to Joseph Smith. Consequently there are five references to its practice in the LDS scripture Doctrine and Covenants (124:29, 33; 127:5–10; 128; 138:33). The entire section 128 is dedicated to this theme, having been recorded as a revelation given to Joseph Smith on September 6, 1842, at Nauvoo, Illinois. Among the elements of the rite elucidated here are the claims that it delivers salvific benefits for the dead; that it is a restored ritual of the early church as intimated by the words of Jesus to Peter in Matthew 16:18–19; that its sealing and salvific effect and the recording of these baptisms in LDS temples correspond to the book of life in Revelation 20:12; and that the LDS practice corresponds to the words of 1 Corinthians 15:29.

LDS Church publications further guide church practice by maintaining that Jesus "provided for everyone to hear the gospel." He went, according to LDS interpretation of 1 Peter 3:18–20 and Doctrines and Covenants 138, to proclaim the LDS gospel to those in spirit prison. In like fashion, "righteous messengers" are empowered to "teach the gospel to all the spirits of people who have died." This proclamation gives the dead an "opportunity to accept the gospel," and once baptism is performed for them, they will be elevated to paradise with inevitable promotion to the celestial kingdom.

See also BAPTISM OF THE DEAD, CHRISTIAN; CHURCH OF JESUS CHRIST OF LATTER-DAY SAINTS

Bibliography. Smith, *Gospel Principles.*

R. P. Roberts

BAPTISM OF/WITH THE HOLY SPIRIT. *See* BAPTISM IN THE HOLY SPIRIT, PENTECOSTAL VIEW OF

BAR/BAT MITZVAH. The term *bar* (Aramaic) *mitzvah* (Hebrew) means "a son of the commandment." The term *bat* (Hebrew) *mitzvah* means "a daughter of the commandment." They are applied to a child when the child officially reaches puberty, which for a boy is assumed to be one day after his thirteenth birthday, for a girl one day after her twelfth birthday. The term *bar mitzvah* officially appears no earlier than the fifteenth century AD; however, the significance of that age was recognized from at least the second century. The ceremony of the bat mitzvah dates back only to the nineteenth century.

The ceremony is significant because at age thirteen the Jewish lad is officially considered an adult and is now responsible to fulfill the regulations of Judaism, which include both biblical and rabbinic law. Until the bar mitzvah (and later the bat mitzvah), the parents are thought to be responsible for the child's sins, but after the ceremony the boy or girl becomes responsible for his or her own sins. By rabbinic law a Jewish service cannot be conducted until ten adult males are present. Once a lad has undergone his bar mitzvah, he can be counted in this number. The ceremony

itself requires preparation. In traditional Orthodox Judaism, a boy undergoes four years of training before the bar mitzvah ceremony. Other forms of Judaism have much more limited time elements. The ceremony is also followed by a festival of celebration in the evening, which can be rather extensive. Since the Six-Day War in 1967, many bar mitzvahs occur at the Western (Wailing) Wall, and many American Jews even travel to Jerusalem for that purpose. It is with the bar mitzvah ceremony that the lad begins to wear the *tefillin* (phylacteries). The bat mitzvah is a more recent innovation, begun in the nineteenth century in France and Italy and later introduced to other countries, including the US. The ceremony tends to be less extensive, and in an Orthodox setting a girl is not allowed to stand up front to read the Law and the Prophets. Thus in many synagogues, at the time of a girl's bat mitzvah it is her father or brother who is called to read the Torah rather than the girl herself. One of them preaches a special sermon, and a gift is presented to the girl. In other traditions, such as Reform Judaism, these limitations are not observed, and the girl will also stand before the congregation and do her own reading in her own prayer shawl.

See also JUDAISM

Bibliography. C. Roth, "Bar/Bat Mitzvah," in *Encyclopedia Judaica*, edited by C. Roth; I. Singer, "Bar/Bat Mitzvah," in *The Jewish Encyclopedia.*

A. Fruchtenbaum

BARDO. *Bardo* is a Tibetan word meaning "intermediate state" and most commonly refers to the Buddhist idea of the time between death and rebirth. The maximum duration of this transition period is forty-nine days, but one can also gain nirvana immediately upon death if one didn't gain it during one's lifetime. The Theravada School is one of the schools that do not recognize the bardo. During this intermediate state, the mind stream of the individual who recently died has many experiences that are directly connected to his or her spiritual development. The karma produced is the driving force that propels one to seek rebirth in one of the states of existence: hells, ghost realm, animal realm, human realm, titans realm, heavens.

See also BUDDHISM; MAHAYANA BUDDHISM; NIRVANA

Bibliography. Gyurme Dorje, trans., *The Tibetan Book of the Dead*; S. Rinpoche, *The Tibetan Book of Living and Dying*.

A.W. Barber

BAZM-E-TOLU-E-ISLAM. Bazm-e-Tolu-e-Islam (Arabic, literally, "gathering/celebration of the resurgence/dawn of Islam") is a "Qur'an only" organization founded by Ghulam Ahmad Parwez (1903–85) in India during the 1930s. Parwez (also spelled Pervez) was involved in the emergence of Pakistan as a sovereign Muslim nation whose political institutions were regulated by the Qur'an. The primary aim of Tolu-e-Islam is to reestablish a pure form of Islam that relies solely on the text of the Qur'an for its beliefs, ethics, and blueprint for civil government. Unlike the Sunni and Shi'ite sects of Islam, which hold that Islamic tradition plays an important role in interpreting the Qur'an, members of BTI insist that any doctrines and practices that cannot be directly supported by texts from the Qur'an are fraudulent. Not surprisingly BTI is not recognized as an orthodox Muslim group by Sunnis and Shi'ites, though some Sufis regard it as a legitimate organization.

See also ISLAM, BASIC BELIEFS OF; MUSLIM; QUR'AN; SUFISM

Bibliography. G. A. Parwez, *Islam: A Challenge to Religion*; A. I. Qureshi, *The Economic and Social System of Islam*.

R. L. Drouhard

BENSON, EZRA TAFT. Ezra Taft Benson became the thirteenth president of the Church of Jesus Christ of Latter-day Saints (LDS Church, or Mormonism), following the death of Spencer W. Kimball in 1985. At eighty-six Benson became the second-oldest man to hold this office.

Named after his great grandfather, a former Mormon apostle, Ezra Taft Benson was born on August 4, 1899, in Whitney, Idaho, to George and Sarah Benson. George came from a long line of farmers, a trade that would help his son eventually become US secretary of agriculture under President Dwight D. Eisenhower in 1953. Ezra Taft Benson would be the first Mormon to hold a cabinet position, which he held throughout the Eisenhower administration.

In 1926 Benson graduated with honors from Brigham Young University. That same year he married Flora Amussen, the daughter of a Danish-immigrant jeweler and watchmaker. Together they had six children.

On October 7, 1943, LDS president Heber J. Grant ordained him an apostle. He held this position for forty-two years and, as an apostle, served under six LDS presidents.

Benson was a strong anti-Communist, and his outspoken criticism of elected officials he felt were "soft on Communism" met with public disapproval by Hugh B. Brown, a member of the LDS First Presidency. Benson also believed that Communists inspired the civil rights movement. His ultraconservative politics led to a very close relationship with the John Birch Society. Although his wife and sons were members of the society, he was never an official member.

A firm believer that not "all scripture is of equal value," he urged members to "flood the earth with the Book of Mormon."

Through much of his presidency, he was beleaguered with health problems, and many of his duties were taken over by Gordon Hinckley, his first counselor. Benson died at age ninety-four on May 30, 1994.

See also CHURCH OF JESUS CHRIST OF LATTER-DAY SAINTS

Bibliography. L. J. Arrington, *The Presidents of the Church*; E. R. West, *Latter-day Prophets*.

W. McKeever

BETH EL SHADDAI MESSIANIC FELLOWSHIP.

Unlike some Jewish groups that have unorthodox theology, though aligning with Christianity (e.g., Sacred Name groups such as the Aaronic Order, the House of Yahweh, and the Assembly of YHWH-HOSHUA), Beth El Shaddai Messianic Fellowship (BSMF) is a theologically orthodox group of self-described "Jewish and gentile believers" that meets in Torrance, California. (A similar congregation, Beth El Shaddai Messianic Synagogue, is located in Bessemer, Alabama.) The main purpose of BSMF is to provide a place of worship wherein salvation through Y'shua the Messiah (for both Jews and gentiles) is proclaimed, the entire message of the Bible is presented in light of its fundamentally Jewish character, and a strong sense of Jewish identity is endorsed and upheld. Central to BSMF teaching is the belief that Y'shua (Jesus) is the promised Messiah of the Old Testament Scriptures and that he has made atonement for sins. Representatives of the group also advocate their views on such matters as Israel's national security, anti-Semitism, and the Holocaust. BSMF offers theological degrees through its Shomer Yisrael School of Theology. The public worship of the assembly includes such distinctive features as the reciting of the Shema and an Aaronic benediction. BSMF members gather periodically to celebrate the cycle of Jewish Holy Days, including Purim, Passover, Rosh Hashanah, Yom Kippur, Sukkoth, and Hanukkah.

Bibliography. Beth El Shaddai Messianic Synagogue home page, http://www.shaddai.com; D. Cohn-Sherbok, ed., *Voices of Messianic Judaism: Confronting Critical Issues facing a Maturing Movement*.

J. Bjornstad

BHAGAVAD GITA.

The Bhagavad Gita (The Holy Song; Song of the Divine One) is arguably the most popular and accessible of the Hindu scriptures (sharing authority alongside the other Hindu scriptures—namely, the Vedas, the Upanishads, and the Puranas), used widely among Hindus for devotional purposes. It is commonly deemed part of the sixth book of the Mahabharata (and thus a *smrti* text) and has been assigned dates of authorship ranging from the fifth to the second century BC. Originally written in Sanskrit, the Gita has been translated into many languages and is composed of eighteen chapters and seven hundred verses. It is structured as a dialogue between the Hindu god Krishna and the Indian warrior-prince Arjuna on the battlefield of Kurukshetra, where Arjuna is confronted with a very difficult moral dilemma. The story centers on the sometimes tragic links between the performance of duty and its accompanying sorrow, purporting to inform the reader about how he can fulfill his obligations while avoiding such suffering. Although the fundamental issues with which the text deals are ethical, during their conversation Krishna and Arjuna discuss a variety of topics that intersect with the core doctrines of Hinduism, including the nature of the universe and the self, knowledge and ignorance, humankind's relationship to God (Ishvara), and Hindu piety. The Gita commends bhakti (devotion to a particular deity), Karma Yoga (selfless action), and Jnana Yoga (self-transcending knowledge) as effective means to attain liberation.

The Gita teaches that the world outside the self is unreal, not in the sense that it doesn't exist and thus is utterly illusory, but in the sense that it is in a state of constant flux and thus is unreliable as a source of truth. Because of this metaphysical fact, those who cling to the unstable and impermanent phenomena of the external world will necessarily endure distress and misery. However, there exists an unchanging, enduring reality that provides the foundation for meaning, purpose, and serenity in human life and that can be perceived by means of the Three Secrets: *guhya* (secret; performing one's duty in accord with one's true nature, or *swadharmacharana*), *guhyatara* (more secret; each person has a real but concealed self that differs from his unreal, outward self), and *guhyatma* (most secret; nothing truly exists except the ubiquitous Vasudeva).

See also HINDUISM; SMRITI; UPANISHADS; VEDAS

Bibliography. V. Jayaram, "The Bhagavadgita Homepage," http://www.hinduwebsite.com/gitaindex.asp; W. J. Johnson, trans., *The Bhagavad Gita*.

S. J. Rost

BHAGAVAN. Bhagavan (sometimes Bhagwan; "Blessed One") is a name or title denoting reverence and respect, variously translated as "divine," "holy," "venerable," and so on. In Hinduism, depending on the context in which it is used, it can serve as an appellation for the Lord Vishnu, Krishna, or Shiva. However, in India—especially when uttered by devout Hindus who do not worship any particular deity—the word expresses the idea of a personal but unnamed Supreme Being, functioning as a generic term for God. Some Hindus in contemporary India also use the term to address gurus whom they greatly admire. In Buddhism and Jainism, the epithet can refer variously to Gautama Buddha, any number of Buddhas and bodhisattvas, Mahavira, and any of the twenty-four *tirthankaras*.

See also BUDDHISM; HINDUISM; JAINISM; MAHAVIRA; SHIVA; TIRTHANKARA

Bibliography. A. L. Basham, *The Origins and Development of Classical Hinduism*; G. D. Flood, *An Introduction to Hinduism*; P. Harvey, *An Introduction to Buddhism: Teachings, History and Practices*.

M. Power

BHAJAN, YOGI. Yogi Bhajan (1929–2004) was born Harbhajan Singh Puri in an area of India that is now part of Pakistan. He demonstrated an affinity for Sikh Yoga as a teenager, earned a degree from Punjab University in 1954, and worked as a customs officer at Palim International Airport from 1954 to 1968. In early 1968, Bhajan was offered a position as a yoga instructor at Toronto University in Ontario, which he accepted. However, after he relocated to Canada, in September 1968 the offer fell through. Despite this setback, Bhajan decided to stay in North America and presented a series of lectures on yoga in Los Angeles in December 1968 and January 1969. In July 1969, Bhajan founded the Healthy, Happy, Holy Organization (3HO) and soon thereafter opened the first 3HO center in Washington, DC. In February 1972, he established the Kundalini Research Institute in Santa Cruz, New Mexico. Bhajan also was influenced by white Tantric Yoga, and he claimed that he was Mahan Tantrical, a title that was conveyed to him by the last Mahan Tantrical, Lama Lilan Po of Tibet.

Bhajan popularized Sikhism and his signature yogic practices, aiming to make Kundalini Yoga (and its accompanying "yogic technology") available to all interested parties. In doing so, he defied the traditional guru-disciple approach to Sikh spirituality. In 1994 Bhajan and his collaborators formed the International Kundalini Yoga Teachers Association, which now includes more than 360 centers in 42 countries. During his lifetime, Bhajan consulted with prominent religious figures such as Pope John Paul II, the archbishop of Canterbury, and the Dalai Lama, and served as president of the World's Parliament of Religions and chairperson of the World Fellowship of Religions. He also developed a very close (and favorable) political relationship with New Mexico governor Bill Richardson and counted among his devotees several famous Hollywood celebrities, including Madonna, Cindy Crawford, and David Duchovny. However, during the 1990s Bhajan and his organization were plagued with scandal.

Bhajan's fundamental teaching was that happiness and good health are the birthright of all human beings and that the practice of Kundalini Yoga is the most effective way to procure that birthright. His Kundalini Yoga (also known as Yoga of Awareness) consists of techniques including breathing (*pranayam*), yoga postures (*asanas*), chanting, and meditation. These yogic practices allegedly enable their practitioners to obtain union with God (the universal self). Bhajan also advocated a vegetarian diet that includes consumption of copious amounts of garlic, ginger, and onion.

See also SIKHISM

Bibliography. Y. Bhajan, *The Mind: Its Projections and Multiple Facets*; A. B. Clagett, *Yoga for Health and Healing: From the Teachings of Yogi Bhajan*; Harbhajan Singh Khalsa, *The Power of Prayer: The Inspired Words of Yogi Bhajan*; Healthy, Happy, Holy Organization website, https://www.3ho.org/yogi-bhajan; Kundalini Research Institute website, http://www.kriteachings.org/.

H. W. House

BHAKTI YOGA. The word *bhakti* is Sanskrit for "love" or "devotion." Bhakti Yoga denotes in the Hindu faith a disciplined way of life centered in devotion to God, as opposed to a pathway based on knowledge (Jnana Yoga) and works (Karma Yoga). Devotion is always centered on personal deities such as Vishnu and Krishna; female deities, such as Laksmi, Uma, and Parvati, are also revered. The origins of Bhakti Yoga are obscure, but it had certainly emerged as a widespread practice by the third and fourth centuries AD. The earliest writings to explicate bhakti beliefs are the twin epics the Mahabharata and the Ramayana, and then some of the later Puranas. Devotees engage in puja or acts of worship—with gifts offered to the

deity either in a temple or home shrine—as well as in pilgrimages to sacred sites, devotional songs, dances, and festivals. The International Society for Krishna Consciousness (Hare Krishna) represents one modern Hindu expression of Bhakti Yoga.

See also HINDUISM; INTERNATIONAL SOCIETY FOR KRISHNA CONSCIOUSNESS (ISKCON); YOGA

Bibliography. A. L. Basham, *The Wonder That Was India*; M. Eliade, *Yoga: Immortality and Freedom*.

P. Johnson

BHIKKHU. *Bikkhu* is the Pali-language word for a male Buddhist monk (*bhikshu* in Sanskrit). Monks take vows renouncing material attachments to the world in pursuit of nirvana. Their monastic life is governed by rules set out in the Vinaya Pitaka, which include meditation, poverty, celibacy, peacefulness, and daily begging for food.

See also BUDDHISM

Bibliography. D. Keown, *Buddhism: A Very Short Introduction*.

P. Johnson

BIBLE, CANON OF. The term *canon* derives from the Greek *kanōn*, which originally meant "measuring reed" but subsequently came to mean "rule" or "standard." Applied to Scripture, the term refers to the list of books the church considers to be God's Word written and thus the church's sole standard for all matters of faith and practice. Most Christian groups accept at least the sixty-six-book canon, while some include the Apocrypha. However, some heterodox groups require followers to use their writings to interpret Scripture (claiming these writings are themselves inspired by God), while others actually consider some of their writings part of the canon.

Two major issues surround any discussion of the canon. First, we must distinguish between the *nature* of the canon and the *recognition* of certain writings as canonical. Protestants and Roman Catholics agree that divine inspiration of a book is what makes it Scripture. However, Catholics believe that the church authoritatively determines which books belong in the canon, and thus they view the canon as the product of the church. Protestants, on the other hand, argue that while the church may recognize and accept books as canonical, it does not have authority over the canon. Rather than viewing the church as defining the canon, they view the canon as defining the church. Second, there is the historical question of how God's people came to recognize specific books *as Scripture*, or better, as God's own self-authenticating Word. Three points need to be stated in regard to this latter issue.

First, the Old Testament canon of first-century Palestinian Judaism, which was the canon of Jesus and the apostles, consisted of the same books as our present Old Testament canon (which is now numbered as thirty-nine books). This is the same canon accepted in Judaism today. Not only is there good evidence to think that the Old Testament canon was viewed as closed in the time of Jesus (e.g., Josephus, *Contra Apion* 1.37–42; 1 Macc. 9:23–27; Luke 24:44; Matt. 23:35); we also discover from the teaching and example of Jesus and the apostles that they received the Old Testament as fully authoritative. In fact, the New Testament quotes from every section of the Old Testament canon (Law, Prophets, and Writings), and most Old Testament books are quoted *as Scripture*, thus proving that Jesus and the apostles accepted without question the full canonical status of the Old Testament (see Rom. 15:3–6; 1 Cor. 10:11; 2 Tim. 3:14–17; 1 Pet. 1:10–12). Even more, in Jesus's interaction with the Jewish leaders, particularly the Pharisees, we have no record of any dispute between them over the extent of the canon. Many New Testament texts refute or correct traditional Jewish theology; nevertheless, Jesus and the religious leaders appeal to what both of them have in common, namely, the Old Testament Scriptures (e.g., Mark 7:6–7, 10–13; 11:17; 12:10–11, 24; Luke 4:16–21; John 6:45; 10:34–35; 15:25; cf. Acts 17:2–3, 11; 18:28; 24:14–15; 26:22; Rom. 3:1–2).

Second, even though Christians have disputed over the canonical status of the apocryphal writings (Roman Catholics and Eastern Orthodox have accepted some or all of them as canonical), there is little evidence to view them as Scripture. No doubt, as many have argued, copies of the Septuagint from the fourth and fifth centuries included most of these books alongside recognized Scripture. But this in no way demonstrates that the Jewish community in first-century Palestine, let alone Jesus and the apostles, accepted them as authoritative Scripture. In fact, it can be shown that (1) the Jewish community in first-century Palestine did not regard the Apocrypha as Scripture; (2) the Apocrypha was not considered to be Scripture by Jesus and the apostles since nowhere does the New Testament quote *any* of these books; (3) the earliest Christian Old Testament lists contain few or none of these books, and early Christian scholars such as Origen and Jerome explicitly reject these writings as Scripture; and (4) the Apocrypha contains teachings inconsistent with the rest of Scripture. For these reasons, the Apocryphal writings should not be considered canonical.

Third, the New Testament canon, composed of twenty-seven books, came from the same source as the Old Testament canon, the Holy Spirit, whom the risen and glorified Christ sent, who enabled the apostles to speak and write about the full self-disclosure centered on the Son (see Heb. 1:1–2; cf. John 14:26; 16:12–15). The *criteria* by which the early church recognized specific documents as Scripture were basically three: (1) apostolic authorship or authentication, (2) conformity to the rule of faith as taught by Jesus and the apostles (see Gal. 1:8–9; Col. 2:8–15;

1 Tim. 6:3), and (3) widespread and continuous usage by the churches. Obviously this last criterion required the passage of time, which helps explain why the official "closing" of the canon did not occur until AD 397 at the Council of Carthage. Nevertheless, despite any ecclesiastical hierarchy, the early church came to recognize the same twenty-seven books of the New Testament. Providentially led by the Spirit, the church not only came to confess the sufficiency and finality of the Word made flesh; it also came to recognize the documents that bore witness to him. In Jesus Christ, the God who is self-disclosing, speaking, and covenant-keeping has supremely revealed himself, which necessitated both a canon to testify of him and also its implicit closure in him.

Regarding heterodox Christian groups and the canon, most such groups accept the canon as Scripture but introduce writings designed to allow their members to "understand" the Bible. Mary Baker Eddy's *Science and Health with Key to the Scriptures* is an example. Although the Jehovah's Witnesses have distanced themselves from claiming their writings are inspired, an article in the *Watchtower* magazine from 1931 states, "This book [*Light* by Joseph Rutherford] within itself conclusively proves that God directed its presentation, and that its human author was not employing his own judgment and wisdom in its preparation" (Feb. 1, 1931, p. 47).

Perhaps the most famous group claiming to have added to the canon is the Church of Jesus Christ of Latter-day Saints, which claims that Joseph Smith received direct divine revelation from God. Smith's allegedly inspired writings include the Book of Mormon (which he claimed to translate from gold plates), nearly all of the Doctrine and Covenants, and the Pearl of Great Price. Mormons consider these writings equal to the Bible in authority, calling them along with the Bible "the Scriptures." Beyond this, Mormon teaching affirms that the LDS Church continues to receive revelation: "It's a literal fact that we have the gift and power of the Holy Ghost. We have the spirit of revelation, the spirit of testimony, the spirit of prophecy" (McConkie, 1978). Because of this view, the LDS Church holds to an "open canon." In an address, Jeffrey R. Holland (93–94) proclaimed,

> I testify that the heavens are open. I testify that Joseph Smith was and is a prophet of God, that the Book of Mormon is truly another testament of Jesus Christ. I testify that Thomas S. Monson [the president of the LDS Church from 2008 to 2018] is God's prophet, a modern apostle with the keys of the kingdom in his hands, a man upon whom I personally have seen the mantle fall. I testify that the presence of such authorized, prophetic voices and ongoing canonized revelations have been at the heart of the Christian message whenever the authorized ministry of Christ has been on the earth. I testify that such a ministry *is* on the earth again, and it is found in this, The Church of Jesus Christ of Latter-day Saints.

See also CHRISTIAN

Bibliography. R. T. Beckwith, *The Old Testament Canon of the New Testament Church and Its Background in Early Judaism*; F. F. Bruce, *The Canon of Scripture*; E. C. Gruss, *Jehovah's Witnesses: Their Claims, Doctrinal Changes and Prophetic Speculation—What Does the Record Show?*; J. R. Holland, "My Words . . . Never Cease," *Ensign*; B. R. McConkie, "Agency or Inspiration," *Liahona Magazine*; "Scriptures," website of the Church of Jesus Christ of Latter-day Saints, https://www.lds.org/scriptures?lang=eng&cid=rdscriptures; *Watchtower*; P. D. Wegner, *The Journey from Texts to Translations: The Origin and Development of the Bible*.

S. Wellum and R. L. Drouhard

BIN LADEN, OSAMA BIN MUHAMMAD BIN 'AWAD.

Known as Osama bin Laden (1957–2011), he was the son of a leading Saudi Arabian businessman from Yemen.

After completing his education, bin Laden fought against the Soviet occupation of Afghanistan, where he favored rule by the Taliban. Most observers believe that he founded al-Qaeda as a loose-knit organization to oppose Western dominance of the Muslim world around 1988, although the British Broadcasting Company (BBC) claims it was formed in 1989 and means "the base."

The primary aim of al-Qaeda is to drive the unbelievers, meaning non-Muslims, from Arabia and free the Islamic world from Western influences. It seeks to destroy both the State of Israel and the Saudi monarchy and overthrow pro-Western governments in Muslim countries, eventually establishing a unified Islamic empire ruled by a caliph. Among its lesser aims is the restoration of Islamic rule in any country once ruled by Muslims. Thus bin Laden called for the restoration of Muslim rule in Spain, which he sees as a "lost" Muslim land.

For over a decade, bin Laden was the world's most wanted man—the master terrorist who orchestrated the bombing of the USS Cole, the destruction of the US embassies in Kenya and Tanzania, the September 11, 2001, attacks on the US, and various other violent actions that he justified in terms of jihad, or holy war, against the West. Bin Laden was a devotee of the eighteenth-century Islamic revival movement known as Wahhabism, the official religion of Saudi Arabia. After years of hiding, bin Laden was killed in a mansion in Pakistan on May 6, 2011, in a US covert operation.

Often described as "fundamentalist," Wahhabism is perhaps more accurately seen as an extremist form of Islam that denounces idolatry, including visiting the tombs of saints; invoking prophets, saints, and angels and seeking their intercession; and making vows to anyone but God. It stresses fatalistic predestination and denounces allegorical interpretation of the Qur'an in favor of more literal readings. Demanding that faith should be proved by works, it makes attendance at public prayer obligatory, forbids the use of prayer beads (*misbaha*), and strips mosques of ornaments. Despite Wahhabism's call for a return to foundational Islam, the movement is modernizing and has no hesitation about using technology and Western science.

Within the Muslim world many, if not most, Muslims saw bin Laden as a traditional Muslim gentleman who was sacrificing his life to defend Islamic society against the corrupting influence of the West. Consequently, "Osama" is now a very popular boy's name in many Muslim countries, while shops sell toy soldiers with bin Laden's features. Although many Western academics, such as John L. Esposito, tend to deny or downplay this claim, there can be little doubt that in Muslim countries bin Laden was popular at the grassroots level and that his influence grew in places like Pakistan. Therefore, it is vital that people in the West take his message seriously and admit that it appeals to many people. To dismiss him merely as a "fanatic," as many try to do, is foolish, provides a false sense of security, and fails to understand popular Islam. Similarly, to say that his form of Islam is not "real Islam" is arrogant presumption on the part of Western scholars who attempt to speak for Muslims.

See also ISLAM, BASIC BELIEFS OF

Bibliography. P. L. Bergen, *Holy War, Inc.: Inside the Secret World of Osama bin Laden*; O. Bin Laden and B. B. Lawrence, *Messages to the World: The Statements of Osama Bin Laden*; J. Corbin, *Al Qaeda: In Search of the Terror Network That Shook the World*.

I. Hexham

BLOOD ATONEMENT. The LDS Church teaches that Jesus Christ atoned for the sins of human beings by means of the shedding of his blood during his agony in the garden of Gethsemane (Luke 22:43–44) and by his suffering and death on the cross. More specifically, Jesus's atoning sacrifice and resurrection assure all people of resurrection from the dead to immortality in one of three heavenly kingdoms. Those who accept the gospel, believe in Christ's atonement, and obey God's commandments will attain eternal life in the celestial kingdom with the possibility of exaltation to become gods.

What in the LDS context is commonly known as the doctrine of "blood atonement" is the teaching that because some sins are so heinous that the blood of Christ cannot be applied to them, those who commit such sins must have their own blood shed in order to atone for them. According to many prominent nineteenth-century Mormon leaders, such grave sins include murder, adultery, lying, stealing, counterfeiting, a white person marrying or having sexual relations with a black person, using God's name in vain, resisting the gospel, covenant breaking, and apostasy (Quinn, 246). Brigham Young publicly taught the doctrine of blood atonement in such statements as the following:

> There are sins that men commit for which they cannot receive forgiveness in this world, or in that which is to come, and if they had their eyes open to see their true condition, they would be perfectly willing to have their blood spilt upon the ground, that the smoke thereof might ascend to heaven as an offering for their sins; and the smoking incense would atone for their sins, whereas, if such is not the case, they will stick to them and remain upon them in the spirit world. . . . And furthermore, I know that there are transgressors, who, if they knew themselves, and the only condition upon which they can obtain forgiveness, would beg of their brethren to shed their blood, that the smoke thereof might ascend to God as an offering to appease the wrath that is kindled against them, and that the law might have its course. I will say further: I have had men come to me and offer their lives to atone for their sins. It is true that the blood of the Son of God was shed for

sins through the fall and those committed by men, yet men can commit sins which it can never remit. (*JD* 4:53–54 [1856])

I could refer you to plenty of instances where men have been righteously slain, in order to atone for their sins. I have seen scores and hundreds of people for whom there would have been a chance (in the last resurrection there will be) if their lives had been taken and their blood spilled on the ground as a smoking incense to the Almighty, but who are now angels to the devil, until our elder brother Jesus Christ raises them up—conquers death, hell, and the grave. I have known a great many men who have left this Church for whom there is no chance whatever for exaltation, but if their blood had been spilled, it would have been better for them. The wickedness and ignorance of the nations forbid this principle's being in full force, but the time will come when the law of God will be in full force. This is loving our neighbor as ourselves; if he needs help, help him; and if he wants salvation and it is necessary to spill his blood on the earth in order that he may be saved, spill it. (*JD* 4:220 [1857])

Other LDS leaders from the same period made similar statements, such as the following notorious statement by Jedediah M. Grant, a member of the First Presidency:

> I say, that there are men and women that I would advise to go to the President immediately, and ask him to appoint a committee to attend to their case; and then let a place be selected, and let that committee shed their blood. We have those amongst us that are full of all manner of abominations, those who need to have their blood shed, for water will not do, their sins are of too deep a dye. You may think that I am not teaching you Bible doctrine, but what says the apostle Paul? I would ask how many covenant breakers there are in this city and in this kingdom. I believe that there are a great many; and if they are covenant breakers we need a

place designated, where we can shed their blood. (*JD* 4:49–50 [1856])

The blood atonement doctrine was never made into a regular or systematic practice, and it is not entirely clear how widespread blood atonement–related activities were. Some leaders talked about the possibility of establishing the practice as part of a theocratic system of government that the Utah Mormons hoped to establish, but such a system never formed. The most likely cases of blood atonement killings for which there is documentation were those of Rosmos Anderson and Thomas Coleman. Anderson was a Danish man who, according to the testimony of John D. Lee (who was involved in the Mountain Meadows Massacre), voluntarily underwent a blood atonement–type execution for adultery in 1856. (The Mountain Meadows Massacre of 1857, in which approximately 120 non-Mormon men, women, and children were slaughtered by a band of Mormons and Paiute Indians, is itself sometimes associated with the blood atonement doctrine. However, it is better characterized as an act of retribution for the killing of Joseph Smith and other LDS leaders.) Thomas Coleman was a former black slave who was ritually murdered in 1866 for his romantic involvement with a white Mormon woman. In this case, there is debate as to whether Coleman was killed as a blood atonement or out of racist opposition to the mixing of the races—though the two motives are not necessarily mutually exclusive.

By the 1880s, the LDS Church and the territory of Utah were under intense scrutiny and pressure from the US federal government with regard to polygamy and other issues, including blood atonement. In a speech in 1884 addressing the issue of blood atonement, LDS apostle Charles W. Penrose commented: "After baptized persons have made sacred covenants with God and then commit deadly sins, the only atonement they can make is the shedding of their blood. At the same time, because of the laws of the land, and the prejudices of the nation, and the ignorance of the world, this law can not be carried out. But when the time comes that the law of God shall be in full force upon the earth, then this penalty will be inflicted for those crimes committed by persons under covenant not to commit them" (Penrose, 38–39).

In 1889 the LDS Church publicly and officially disavowed teaching or practicing blood atonement for apostasy or similar sins. Since then various leaders have acknowledged the basic doctrine of blood atonement while denying that the LDS Church has ever practiced it. For example, Joseph Fielding Smith, while denying that the LDS Church practiced the killing of apostates, affirmed: "But man may commit certain grievous sins—according to his light and knowledge—that will place him beyond the reach of the atoning blood of Christ. If then he would be saved he must make sacrifice of his own life to atone—so far as in his power lies—for that sin, for the blood of Christ alone under certain circumstances will not avail" (*Doctrines of Salvation*, 1954, 1:133).

Since 1978, when leading Mormon theologian Bruce McConkie denied the necessity of practicing blood atonement in the "current dispensation," there has been considerable heated debate over whether the doctrine ever was practiced within Mormonism. (The fact that some form of the doctrine was taught is not in dispute; even McConkie reaffirmed the core elements of the doctrine in his writings.) At best the LDS Church has been inconsistent in its claims regarding this teaching. In an article titled "Quintessential Mormonism: Literal-Mindedness as a Way of Life," University of Utah professor Richard J. Cummings explains:

> The doctrine asserts that those who commit certain grievous sins such as murder and covenant-breaking place themselves

beyond the atoning blood of Christ, and their only hope for salvation is to have their own blood shed as an atoning sacrifice. In his writings, Joseph Smith only hinted at the doctrine, Brigham Young successively denied and asserted it, Joseph F. Smith ardently defended it, and in more recent years, Hugh B. Brown repudiated it and Joseph Fielding Smith and Bruce R. McConkie both have vigorously defended it in principle while staunchly denying that the [LDS] Church has ever put it into actual practice, whereas most other General Authorities have prudently preferred to remain silent on the subject. (93)

Interestingly, until March 2004 the state of Utah routinely used firing squads composed of trained marksmen for government-sanctioned executions. This was, in part, because it was believed by some Mormons that this method of execution (provided that the prisoner is shot through the heart, thus spilling his blood onto the soil) functions as a form of blood atonement for the person executed. Also noteworthy is the fact that in recent years, a number of Mormon splinter groups have sought to put into practice the doctrine of blood atonement: most notably Ervil LeBaron's Church of the Lamb of God and the Fundamentalist Church of Jesus Christ of Latter Day Saints, led by Warren Jeffs. Before dying in prison, LeBaron compiled a list of people he deemed traitors to true Mormonism and worthy of death; some of his followers later murdered some of the people on the list. In the case of Jeffs, it has been reported by former members of his group that he discussed blood atonement in sermons and planned to build an incinerator in which to dispose of the bodies of those who had been killed according to the dictates of his interpretation of the doctrine.

See also CHURCH OF JESUS CHRIST OF LATTER-DAY SAINTS; MOUNTAIN MEADOWS MASSACRE

Bibliography. Associated Press, "Utah Kills Off Death-Row Firing Squads," *Toronto Star*; W. Bagley, *Blood of the Prophets: Brigham Young and the Massacre at Mountain Meadows*; "Blood Atonement," http://www.shields-research.org/General/blood_atonement.htm; G. J. Bergera, *Line upon Line: Essays on Mormon Doctrine*; E. E. Campbell, *Establishing Zion: The Mormon Church in the American West, 1847–1869*; R. J. Cummings, "Quintessential Mormonism: Literal-Mindedness as a Way of Life," *Dialogue*; Foundation for Apologetic Information and Research, "Blood Atonement," https://www.fairmormon.org/answers/Topical_Guide/Church_history/Blood_Atonement; J. Krakauer, *Under the Banner of Heaven: A Story of Violent Faith*; O. Kraut, *Blood Atonement*; B. R. McConkie, *Mormon Doctrine*, 2nd ed.; B. McKeever and E. Johnson, *Mormonism 101: Examining the Religion of the Latter-day Saints*; N. Najacht, "FLDS Reinstituting 'Blood Atonement,'" *Custer Country Chronicle*; C. W. Penrose, *Blood Atonement, as Taught by Leading Elders of the Church of Jesus Christ of Latter-day Saints*; D. M. Quinn, *The Mormon Hierarchy: Extensions of Power*; Joseph Fielding Smith, *Answers to Gospel Questions*; Joseph Fielding Smith, *Doctrines of Salvation*; P. F. Stack, "Concept of Blood Atonement Survives in Utah despite Repudiation," *Salt Lake Tribune*; J. Tanner and S. Tanner, *The Changing World of Mormonism*; Tanner and Tanner, *Mormonism: Shadow or Reality?*; S. Tanner, "Gethsemane and Christ's Blood in LDS References," https://www.jashow.org/articles/mormonism/mormonism-christianity-compared-2/mormon-view-of-jesus/gethsemane-and-christs-blood-in-lds-references/.

S. J. Rost

BLOOD TRANSFUSIONS. Blood transfusions have been a common treatment method in medicine since the 1940s. Without a doubt, their administration to sick patients has saved countless lives. Despite their success, however, the practice itself is considered a controversial one by various religious groups, most notably the Jehovah's Witnesses. Since blood transfusions were first used in civilian medicine, it has been the official stance of the Jehovah's Witnesses to completely abstain from receiving or donating blood, regardless of the circumstances. Though this is often a confusing view for most outside the religion, Witnesses cite several biblical references that command abstention from blood, some of the more notable ones being Genesis 9:4; Leviticus 17:12–14; Acts 15:29; and Acts 21:25. Although most orthodox Christian and Jewish groups interpret these passages as dietary laws prohibiting the consumption of meat containing blood, Witnesses believe they prohibit all blood consumption of any kind, including transfusions.

Traditionally, Witnesses have taken their mandate to abstain from blood very seriously. In fact, since 1945 all Witnesses who have willingly accepted a transfusion have been "disfellowshipped." When an individual is disfellowshipped, all remaining Witnesses are to completely ignore him or her except in the most extreme of circumstances.

Because of their unorthodox stance on transfusions and the extreme way in which dissenters are punished, those outside the religion often accuse Witnesses of upholding a mandate that has needlessly cost people their lives. Many patients have died after refusing a simple transfusion that might have saved their lives. In 2007 an English Jehovah's Witness died after refusing a blood transfusion. She had begun to hemorrhage after giving birth to twins, and she died of massive blood loss, coupled with anemia.

The issue has been brought up in court multiple times. In May 2002, a Florida circuit-court judge ordered doctors to give a blood transfusion to a premature baby despite her parents' objections. In 2006 a fifteen-year-old Canadian girl was taken from her parents and forced to undergo a blood transfusion that saved her life. In 2008 she sued the Winnipeg Child and Family Services, claiming her religious rights were violated (citing that as a Jehovah's Witness she is forbidden to receive blood transfusions), even though she was a minor.

Though outside pressure to change this Witness doctrine is considerable, pressures from within the religion have begun to emerge as well, most notably the Associated Jehovah's Witnesses for Reform on Blood (AJWRB). This organization has criticized Witness policy on transfusions along with outsiders, and all members have been officially disfellowshipped for disagreeing with Witness doctrine.

Though AJWRB and other organizations desire radical change in Witness doctrine, leaders of the religion have modified the doctrine slightly since it was established in 1945. The June 2000 issue of the *Watchtower* (an official Witness publication) informed Witnesses that the transfusion of fractions of blood components is permissible if the individual's conscience allows it. Only fractions are permissible, however; the transfusion of the components themselves (red cells, white cells, plasma, and platelets) is still forbidden. Also, in April 2000 transfusions were relegated to the list of "non-disfellowshipping events." This, however, is misleading. The official policy now states that any member who receives a transfusion of blood (or of its major components) has, by his or her own choice, left the religion and should be treated as a nonmember. The congregation no longer has the right to disfellowship, but the effect is the same.

See also JEHOVAH'S WITNESSES (JW)

Bibliography. Associated Jehovah's Witnesses for Reform on Blood, "New Light on Blood: Biblical Summary"; Center for Studies on New Religions [CESNUR], "Jehovah's Witnesses: Official Statement to the Media on Blood Transfusions," http://www.cesnur.org/testi/geova_junek2.htm; B. A. Robinson, "Jehovah's Witnesses: Opposition to Blood Transfusions," *Religious Tolerance*; Watchtower Information Service.

A. D. Jones

BODHI. The word *bodhi* (Sanskrit, "awakening"; often translated "enlightenment" in

English) is a Buddhist term denoting either the profound spiritual illumination of Siddhartha Gautama (ca. 563–483 BC)—which, according to Buddhist legend, occurred while he meditated under the Bodhi tree in the northeast Indian town of Bodhgaya—or the unblemished consciousness (pure, faultless insight) of a liberated practitioner of Buddhism. This experience is variously described as perfect sanity, perfect wisdom, and the awareness of the true nature of reality. At the moment of such enlightenment, all greed, aversion, ignorance, craving, self-centeredness, and illusion are said to be extinguished. Theravada Buddhists see bodhi as the attainment of full and final liberation from the cycle of birth, suffering, death, and rebirth (samsara); Mahayana Buddhists believe that bodhi has gradations: arhat bodhi, bodhisatta bodhi, and full buddhahood. In Theravada Buddhism, bodhi is attained by conformity to the Eightfold Path, the cultivation of moral virtues, and grasping the true nature of phenomena as dependently arising. In some understandings of Mahayana Buddhism, bodhi is continually present at some level of awareness but must be unveiled; this occurs when the corruptions of samsara and its accompanying flawed perceptions are expunged from the consciousness of the devotee. Mahayana Buddhists also sometimes use the term *bodhi* to refer to the wisdom (*prajna*) that is acquired from understanding that all phenomena are fundamentally characterized by emptiness (*sunyata*) and that all sentient creatures possess a Buddha nature.

See also BODHICITTA; BUDDHISM; MAHAYANA BUDDHISM; SAMSARA; SUNYATA; THERAVADA BUDDHISM

Bibliography. J. Evola and H. E. Musson, trans., *The Doctrine of Awakening: The Attainment of Self-Mastery according to the Earliest Buddhist Texts*; R. M. L. Gethin, *The Buddhist Path to Awakening: A Study of the Bodhi-Pakkhiya Dhamma*; H. Smith and P. Novak, *Buddhism: A Concise Introduction*; K. R. White, *The Role of Bodhicitta in Buddhist Enlightenment.*

J. Bjornstad

BODHICITTA. Bodhicitta (Sanskrit, usually translated as "mind of enlightenment") is the primary (if not exclusive) motive for selfless, compassionate action in Buddhism, particularly in the Mahayana and Vajrayana traditions, in which it plays a central role. The word *bodhicitta* is formed from two stems, *bodhi* (enlightenment) and *citta* (mind). The fundamental feature of bodhicitta is the altruistic resolve to work diligently to facilitate the enlightenment of all sentient beings rather than focusing solely on the spiritual betterment of oneself. Bodhicitta involves such virtues as compassion (*karuna*), affectionate love, and the resolve to overcome self-centeredness and repay the kindness of others. According to its practitioners, bodhicitta is useless if not accompanied by wisdom (*prajna*) since the latter is needed in order to direct one's motives so that they result in the proper sorts of actions. The possession of bodhicitta is necessary if enlightenment and buddhahood are to be attained, at which time the devotee will be liberated from the impediments of ignorance and illusory perceptions and hence able to toil unceasingly for the benefit of unenlightened creatures.

The Indian Buddhist scholar Santideva (ca. eighth century AD) maintained that bodhicitta consists of two primary aspects: the desire for enlightenment and engaging in the practices that lead to enlightenment. Santideva also taught that there are two basic types of bodhicitta: relative (that which involves the desire to assist others in attaining enlightenment) and absolute (that which is founded on the insight that all things are "empty").

See also BODHI; BUDDHISM; MAHAYANA BUDDHISM

Bibliography. F. Brassard, *The Concept of Bodhicitta in Santideva's Bodhicaryavatara*; V. L.

Gyatso, *Bodhicitta: Cultivating the Compassionate Mind of Enlightenment*; K. R. White, *The Role of Bodhicitta in Buddhist Enlightenment*.

J. Bjornstad

BODHIDHARMA. Chinese Ch'an (and Japanese Zen) Buddhism traces its lineage to Bodhidharma, who is known as Ta Mo in China and Daruma in Japan. Born an Indian prince of the Hindu Brahman caste in the fifth century AD, he renounced his inheritance to seek enlightenment. His teacher Prajnatara taught him mind training (*dhyana*) and sent him to China to revive Buddhism, by promoting a return to Buddha's original precepts. Upon arrival, Bodhidharma was granted an audience with the emperor Wu Di. It is said that when Bodhidharma was asked what the foundational teaching of Buddha was, he replied, "Vast emptiness." Legend states he spent nine years meditating in a cave near Shaolin Temple (Ho Nan province, China)—of martial-arts film fame. He taught Shaolin monks meditative techniques that balanced spiritual and physical attainments, which subsequently evolved into kung fu.

Legend suggests that Bodhidharma fell asleep once while meditating and cut off his eyelids to prevent it from happening again. Where his eyelids fell, the first tea plants grew—hence the use of tea by Zen monks to stay awake while meditating. The Bodhidharma doll was developed as a symbol of this dedication. In Japan, when people have a task to complete, they purchase a Bodhidharma doll that comes without pupils. At the outset of the task one pupil is colored in, and upon completion, the other pupil is painted. In Asian art, Bodhidharma is usually pictured with large, bulging eyes.

See also BUDDHISM; ZEN BUDDHISM

Bibliography. D. T. Sukuki, *An Introduction to Zen Buddhism*.

H. P. Kemp

BODHISATTVA. The word *bodhisattva*, which in Sanskrit means "one whose being is *bodhi* [enlightenment]," refers to the ideal state to aspire to in Mahayana Buddhism. A bodhisattva attains enlightenment (or aspires to enlightenment), then postpones entering into nirvana to remain in the cycle of births and deaths (samsara) in order to help all sentient beings to enlightenment. The bodhisattva does this by transferring his or her karmic merit onto others. A bodhisattva is therefore regarded as the ideal of compassion, love, and wisdom and is a source of motivation for the spread of the dharma.

In some interpretations, celestial bodhisattvas are manifestations of eternal Buddhas. The current Buddhist age is under the Bodhisattva Avalokiteshvara (associated with the eternal Buddha Amitabha), the bodhisattva of compassion—also known as Kwan Yin—whose earthly incarnation was the historical Siddhartha Gautama (the Buddha). The term is used loosely today, and since all people can potentially become Buddhas, there is an infinite possibility that all can become bodhisattvas. It is a title that has been used for scholars and kings, and some regard the Dalai Lama as an incarnation of the Bodhisattva Avalokiteshvara, although the Dalai Lama himself claims to be merely a "simple monk" who pursues the bodhisattva ideal.

See also BUDDHA, HISTORICAL PERSON OF; BUDDHISM

Bibliography. T. Gyatso, *Freedom in Exile: The Autobiography of the Dalai Lama of Tibet*; D. S. Lopez Jr., *Buddhism: An Introduction and Guide*.

H. P. Kemp

BOOK OF ABRAHAM. The Book of Abraham is the second and perhaps the most controversial book in the Pearl of Great Price, a collection of short texts regarded individually as scripture and collectively as one of the four "standard works" of the Church of Jesus Christ of Latter-day Saints.

The church represents the Book of Abraham as a translation by LDS founder Joseph Smith Jr. of Egyptian papyri purchased at Smith's urging in the early years of the church's history.

Contents. The introductory description to published editions of the Book of Abraham states that it is "a Translation of some ancient Records that have fallen into our hands from the catacombs of Egypt. The writings of Abraham while he was in Egypt, called the Book of Abraham, written by his own hand, upon papyrus."

The text, in which Abraham writes in the first person, consists of five chapters. The first chapter has no parallel in Genesis but is an account of when Abraham lived "in the land of the Chaldeans" (1:1). His people, including his own father, worshiped false gods, and "the priest of Pharaoh" tried to kill him on an altar, as depicted on "the representation at the commencement of this record" (1:7, 12). This "representation" is a drawing known as Facsimile 1, which appears at the beginning of published editions of the book. God's angel delivered Abraham from the priest of Pharaoh and destroyed the priest and the altar.

Chapter 2 corresponds to Genesis 11:27–12:13, the early part of the Abraham narrative. The most significant difference between the two narratives is that in the Book of Abraham, the Lord tells Abraham to lie to the Egyptians about Sarai being his wife (Abraham 2:22–24).

In chapter 3, Abraham learns by divine revelation about astronomy, the preexistent spirits of man, and God's plan. The star nearest God's throne is identified as Kolob. All spirits are eternal, but they differ from one another in intelligence, with the Lord being the most intelligent of all. Abraham was one of the noble "intelligences" present when one of the spirits who "was like unto God" (3:24) announced that he and those with him would make an earth where the spirits could be tested to see if they would obey God's commands.

Chapters 4 and 5 for the most part closely parallel Genesis 1–2 verse for verse. A striking difference, however, is that throughout Abraham 4–5 it is "the Gods" who "organized and formed the heavens and the earth" (4:1). Humans were therefore formed "in the image of the Gods" (4:27). The book ends with the Gods forming the animals and bringing them to Adam after, not before, the making of the woman (5:14–21).

Accompanying the text were three drawings copied from the papyri, called facsimiles. Joseph Smith's interpretations of the drawings are included in the published editions of the Book of Abraham. Facsimile 1 is interpreted as a depiction of the priest of Pharaoh standing with a knife raised over Abraham, who is lying on an altar, as the angel of the Lord hovers nearby in the form of a bird to rescue Abraham. Facsimile 2, a circular drawing with many Egyptian hieroglyphics, is interpreted as representing the cosmos as expounded in Abraham 3. Facsimile 3 is interpreted as depicting Abraham seated on Pharaoh's throne, with Pharaoh standing behind him and Abraham "reasoning upon the principles of Astronomy, in the king's court."

Origin, Translation, and Editions. In early July 1835, the LDS Church purchased four Egyptian mummies and accompanying Egyptian papyri from Michael Chandler in Kirtland, Ohio, for $2,400. The mummies and papyri were part of a small collection originally exhumed by Italian explorer Antonio Lebolo from an Egyptian tomb near ancient Thebes sometime between 1817 and 1821. The LDS Church purchased the mummies and papyri after Joseph Smith gave the papyri an initial examination and quickly announced that one of the scrolls was the writings of the biblical patriarch Abraham and that another was the writings of his great-grandson Joseph. Smith began translating one of the papyri that same month. Abraham 1–3 was evidently produced in 1835 and early 1836, and Abraham 4–5 in 1841.

As with the Book of Mormon, Smith dictated his translation to scribes. It is not clear whether Smith used a "seer stone" or any other device, as he reportedly did with the Book of Mormon. (A couple of later reports say he did use some such device, but the reliability of these reports is uncertain.) One interesting difference between the two translations concerns the handling of the original-language texts that the translations supposedly represented. Smith never looked at the Book of Mormon gold plates when he was dictating his translation of them, and he never allowed anyone to look at them during the entire period when he was producing the translation. By contrast, Smith and his associates spent hours poring over the papyri that he said contained the Book of Abraham, and he freely displayed the papyri and even showed them to strangers.

Although it is unclear exactly how Smith produced his translation, we do know that he and his associates were working on some kind of reference guide to the Egyptian language using the papyri. Several references to this project appear in Smith's journals during the second half of 1835. The best-known manuscript resulting from this project was *Grammar and Alphabet of the Egyptian Language* (*GAEL*; more popularly known as the *Egyptian Alphabet and Grammar*). This manuscript was first published in its entirety by Jerald and Sandra Tanner in April 1966, and several other manuscripts related to this project have later come to light. Most or all of these papers were produced in 1835, though work on the *GAEL* may have continued into 1836 or 1837. Because these documents and most of the Book of Abraham manuscripts originated while Smith and his associates were based in Kirtland, Ohio, the entire collection is commonly designated the Kirtland Egyptian Papers (KEP). The precise

relationship between the Egyptian-alphabet-and-grammar documents and the papyri is hotly disputed, but that they are related is beyond reasonable doubt.

The Book of Abraham was published in the LDS newspaper *Times and Seasons* in three installments in early 1842 and reprinted in a British LDS periodical, the *Millennial Star*, later that same year. In 1851 British LDS leader Franklin D. Richards published the Pearl of Great Price, an anthology consisting mostly of some of Joseph Smith's revelations, including the Book of Abraham. In 1878 the LDS Church published an American edition of the Pearl of Great Price prepared by Orson Pratt, which in 1880 became one of the standard works, or scriptures, of the LDS faith.

Joseph Smith Papyri. After Joseph Smith was killed in 1844, the mummies and papyri were left in the possession of his mother, Lucy Smith, in the Midwest while most of the Mormons followed Brigham Young west to Utah. Days after Lucy's death in May 1856, her surviving relatives sold the mummies and papyri to Abel Combs. Combs sold two mummies and some of the papyri to a museum in St. Louis, which in turn resold them to a museum in Chicago, where they were probably destroyed in the Chicago fire of 1871. The rest of Combs's collection passed to his nurse and later to her daughter's widower, who sold the remaining papyri to the Metropolitan Museum of Art in 1947. Little or none of this information was public knowledge throughout this period of more than a century. Without access to the papyri, discussions about the validity of Joseph Smith's translation focused primarily on his interpretation of the facsimiles, which Egyptologists uniformly rejected as complete misunderstanding of their meanings.

In May 1966, a non-Mormon scholar from the University of Utah named Aziz S. Atiya saw the papyri at the Metropolitan Museum of Art and brought them to the attention of the LDS Church. Atiya recognized one of the papyrus fragments because it had the very drawing represented in the Book of Abraham as facsimile 1. In November 1967, the museum gave the papyri to the LDS Church. In the meantime, LDS scholar Hugh Nibley had already begun studying photographs of the papyri and had an amateur Egyptologist in the church named Dee Jay Nelson working on a translation. In January 1968, Nibley began publishing a series of articles on the Book of Abraham that ran for over two years in the LDS magazine *Improvement Era*. Photographs of the papyri were published in the February 1968 issue.

Nibley had hardly gotten his series of articles started when Nelson reported to him that the papyrus with facsimile 1 was a common pagan Egyptian funeral text and had nothing whatsoever to do with Abraham. In the summer and autumn 1968 issues of the independent Mormon periodical *Dialogue*, articles by Richard A. Parker and Klaus Baer, Egyptologists at Brown University and the University of Chicago, respectively, provided translations confirming that the papyrus was an Egyptian text called *The Book of Breathings* or *The Breathing Permit of Hôr*. The essential accuracy of these translations has been repeatedly confirmed by both Mormon and non-Mormon scholars.

Book of Abraham Apologetics. In the years that followed the recovery of the papyri, Mormon apologists proposed several patently ad hoc explanations for the mismatch between the Book of Abraham and scholars' findings concerning the papyri. At various times, Nibley himself proposed or endorsed each of these theories. Perhaps the Egyptian language of the papyrus contains a nonliteral, hidden meaning, discernible only through supernatural means. Maybe the words of the funeral text were mnemonic devices in which each word functioned as a reminder of a portion of the story of Abraham. The text of the papyrus might have been a pagan

corruption of an earlier Abrahamic book that Joseph Smith miraculously restored, or the papyri may have been merely a catalyst for the revelatory process of translating the nonextant Book of Abraham.

More common now is the claim that the Book of Abraham appeared on papyrus that was not included in the collection of papyrus fragments recovered in 1967. Specifically, since the roll from which the fragments containing facsimile 1 and text of the *Breathing Permit* came has not been preserved in its entirety, the text of the Book of Abraham might have been written on the missing part of the roll. This explanation has been defended especially by John Gee, a Mormon Egyptologist at Brigham Young University with a PhD from Yale University. Gee has suggested that the roll might have been about ten or even forty feet long. Gee's former Yale professor Robert Ritner (now at the University of Chicago), however, estimates that the entire roll was no more than about five feet long, meaning that only about two feet of papyrus are missing from the roll.

Whatever the actual length of the missing papyrus, the text immediately following the drawing reproduced as facsimile 1 is not the Book of Abraham, even though Abraham 1:12 states explicitly that the drawing appears at the commencement of the record. In addition, Ritner and other Egyptologists agree that Joseph Smith's interpretation of that drawing as a depiction of an angel of the Lord saving Abraham from being sacrificed on an altar is wildly incorrect, as are his interpretations of the other two facsimiles. The drawing in facsimile 1 was actually a common representation of Anubis, the god of mummification, reanimating Osiris, who is lying on a funerary bier while his wife, Isis, hovers in the form of a bird.

The main Book of Abraham apologetic today is that the book's account of Abraham includes elements found in various ancient and medieval traditions—though Joseph

Smith could have known nothing about these. LDS scholars cite numerous sources from Jewish, Christian, and even Muslim literature containing possible parallels to the book. Thus one can find references to Abraham's father worshiping idols, Abraham refusing to worship idols and being threatened with death, and God or an angel rescuing Abraham, as well as Abraham teaching the Egyptians about astronomy. However, most or all of these ideas about Abraham could easily be known to Joseph Smith. For example, some of the parallels occur in the first-century Jewish writer Josephus's book *Jewish Antiquities*, and in 1835 Joseph Smith's associate Oliver Cowdery cited that very book when explaining the significance of the drawings on one of the papyri. The literature from which Mormon scholars cull their parallels generally dates from about one to two thousand years ago, far too late to provide factually reliable information about the historical Abraham.

Joseph Smith's claim to be "a seer, a revelator, a translator, and a prophet" (Doctrine and Covenants 107:92) is difficult to test directly in the case of the Book of Mormon, for which the original text Smith said he translated is unavailable for scholars to compare to his translation. With the recovery of the Joseph Smith Papyri, however, such a test became possible for the Book of Abraham and has been thoroughly performed. The result is that this text has become one of the most severe challenges to belief in Joseph Smith's claim to be an inspired translator and prophet. A 2011 survey of factors contributing to disbelief for former Mormons found that well over half of those surveyed reported that challenges to the authenticity of the Book of Abraham were a major factor leading to their loss of faith in the LDS religion. An unsigned article on the LDS Church's official website in 2014 reviewed the controversy over the Book of Abraham. It admitted that the text on the papyri bore no relationship to the Book of Abraham and suggested both the missing-papyri and catalyst theories as possible explanations of the problem. The article in effect offers no clear solution to the problem and reflects the current LDS prophet's lack of any inspired understanding of the matter.

See also CHURCH OF JESUS CHRIST OF LATTER-DAY SAINTS; FALSE PROPHECY; LOST BOOKS OF THE BIBLE, MORMON VIEW OF; PEARL OF GREAT PRICE, THE; SMITH, JOSEPH, JR.; STANDARD WORKS

Bibliography. Pro: Church of Jesus Christ of Latter-day Saints, "Translation and Historicity of the Book of Abraham," https://www.lds.org/topics/translation-and-historicity-of-the-book-of-abraham?lang=eng; R. D. Draper, S. K. Brown, and M. D. Rhodes, *The Pearl of Great Price: A Verse-by-Verse Commentary*; J. Gee, *A Guide to the Joseph Smith Papyri*; B. M. Hauglid, *A Textual History of the Book of Abraham: Manuscripts and Editions*; Tyler Livingston, director, *A Most Remarkable Book: Evidence for the Divine Authenticity of the Book of Abraham*, DVD; H. Nibley, *Abraham in Egypt*; Nibley, *An Approach to the Book of Abraham*; Nibley, *The Message of the Joseph Smith Papyri: An Egyptian Endowment*; Nibley, "A New Look at the Pearl of Great Price," *Improvement Era*; M. D. Rhodes, *The Hor Book of Breathings: A Translation and Commentary*; J. A. Tvedtnes, B. M. Hauglid, and J. Gee, eds., *Traditions about the Early Life of Abraham*. **Con:** K. Baer, "The Breathing Permit of Hôr: A Translation of the Apparent Source of the Book of Abraham," *Dialogue*; L. Bell, "The Ancient Egyptian 'Book of Breathing,' the Mormon 'Book of Abraham,' and the Development of Egyptology in America," in *Egypt and Beyond*; A. C. Cook and C. C. Smith, "The Original Length of the Scroll of Hôr," *Dialogue*; John Grooters, director, *The Lost Book of Abraham: Investigating a Remarkable Mormon Claim*, DVD; C. M. Larson, *By His Own Hand upon Papyrus: A New Look at the Joseph Smith Papyri*; J. A. Larson, "Joseph Smith and Egyptology: An Early Episode in the History of American Speculation about Ancient Egypt, 1835–1844," in *For His Ka: Essays Offered in Memory of Klaus Baer*, edited by D. P. Silverman; R. K. Ritner, *The Joseph Smith*

Egyptian Papyri: A Complete Edition; WhyMormonsQuestion.org, "Understanding Mormon Disbelief Survey."

C. J. Carrigan and R. M. Bowman Jr.

BOOK OF MENCIUS (MENG-TZU). The *Book of Mencius*, sometimes referred to simply as *Mencius*, is one of the *Shih Shu* (Four Books) of classical Chinese literature. As the title suggests, traditionally this work has been attributed to Mencius (ca. 372–289 BC), an ancient Chinese philosopher and authoritative interpreter of the writings of Confucius. Though there are good reasons to believe that Mencius himself was the author of the book, most scholars who are acquainted with the evidence do not consider it adequate to establish this claim beyond reasonable doubt. The *Book of Mencius* is divided into seven sections, though the entire work deals with various aspects of social ethics and the social arrangements that Mencius thought contributed to human flourishing. In his writings, Mencius consistently focused on the ways in which moral behavior by individuals brings about social harmony. Though Mencius maintained that the Confucian virtues were a unified ensemble, the two most prominent virtues in his teachings were *jen* ("humaneness" or "benevolence") and *yi* ("righteousness" or "duty"). Mencius sought to ground morality not in a transcendent source but in human nature itself, which he viewed as inherently good. He taught that people commit evil acts only when they have been led astray by a corrupt social environment. In particular he said government rulers could sway their subjects to do either good or evil. Mencius thus encouraged citizens to overthrow their rulers if those authorities were conducting themselves in such a manner as to foment social turmoil. Having been thoroughly educated in Confucianism, during his adult life Mencius propounded the ideals of Confucius as a means of achieving political stability in China, motivated by the social anarchy prevalent in his day. In the eighteenth century, Jesuit missionaries to China translated some of Mencius's writings into Latin.

See also CONFUCIANISM

Bibliography. P. Fu, "On Human Nature as Tending toward Goodness in Classical Confucianism," in *Chinese Foundations for Moral Education and Character Development*, edited by Tran Van Doan, Vincent Shen, and George F. McLean; A. C. Graham, *Disputers of the TAO: Philosophical Argument in Ancient China*; D. Hinton, trans., *Mencius*; D. C. Lau, trans., *Mencius*; A. Waley, *Three Ways of Thought in Ancient China*, repr. ed.

H. W. House

BOOK OF MORMON. The Book of Mormon is one of the four "standard works" of the Church of Jesus Christ of Latter-day Saints, which views it as a scriptural record translated by founder Joseph Smith Jr. from gold plates engraved by ancient prophets in the lands Europeans would later call the New World. In 1841 Smith stated, "I told the brethren that the Book of Mormon was the most correct of any book on earth, and the keystone of our religion, and a man would get nearer to God by abiding by its precepts, than by any other book" (quoted in the modern introduction to the Book of Mormon). That statement, implying that the Book of Mormon is more reliable than the Bible, is confirmed in the LDS scriptural text Articles of Faith, composed by Joseph Smith in 1843: "We believe the Bible to be the word of God as far as it is translated correctly; we also believe the Book of Mormon to be the word of God." In 2010 the number of copies of the Book of Mormon in print reached 150 million, including complete versions in eighty-two languages.

Contents. The front matter of the Book of Mormon includes, among other items, two affidavits to the existence of the gold plates called the Testimonies of Three Witnesses and of Eight Witnesses as well as excerpts from Smith's account of how he came to translate the Book of Mormon. The Book of Mormon, running about 275,000 words, is divided into fifteen books, all but two of which form a narrative running from about 600 BC to AD 421 (these dates appear at the bottom of nearly each page of the published Book of Mormon). This narrative recounts the history of two warring peoples, the Lamanites and the Nephites, who were descended from an Israelite family that left Jerusalem and sailed from Arabia to the Americas. The Book of Mormon also tells about two other migrations from the Middle East to the New World, one around the same time (the people of Mulek) and another many centuries earlier (the Jaredites).

The Book of Mormon divides into two groups of books, each group engraved on a different set of gold plates and written in the Americas after these Jewish refugees arrived there. The (small) Plates of Nephi include the first six books and have Nephi as their main author. The Plates of Mormon consist of the remaining nine books, of which Mormon is the primary author. These nine books begin with a short transitional book written by Mormon, followed by six books that (except for two closing chapters) are Mormon's abridgment from a longer narrative on the (large) Plates of Nephi. Mormon's son, Moroni, who appends two chapters to Mormon's abridgment, is the author of the last two books and the one who buried the plates; he is also the angel, or resurrected being, who gave the gold plates to Joseph Smith. Thus the whole work is attributed to three main authors: Nephi, Mormon, and Moroni. Since Mormon composed about two-thirds of it, the whole is called the Book of Mormon. Following is a brief summary of the fifteen books.

1 Nephi and 2 Nephi (600–545 BC). Lehi takes his family from Jerusalem to Arabia shortly before the Babylonian exile and from there sails to the Americas. He and his son Nephi are prophets; Nephi's brother Laman, however, rejects Nephi's revelations, establishing the precedent for the wars between the Nephites and the Lamanites.

Jacob, Enos, Jarom, and Omni (544–130 BC). Nephi passes the gold plates to his brother Jacob, and from there the plates are passed from father to son, with each man serving as a prophet and writing briefly on the plates.

Words of Mormon (ca. AD 385). This is a short transitional book, the first book on the Plates of Mormon. In it Mormon explains that he has abridged the records from Lehi to Benjamin but has also included a shorter, parallel account on other plates of Nephi that he found, "for a wise purpose" that only the Lord knew. It is this shorter account that appears in the first six books. The significance of this information will be made clear below.

Mosiah, Alma, and Helaman (200–1 BC). These three books and the next two are all attributed to Mormon as his abridgment from the (large) Plates of Nephi. The three books give a detailed narrative covering the last two centuries BC, with an annual countdown to the birth of Jesus Christ (who is repeatedly named).

3 Nephi (AD 1–35). Mormon tells about the birth, death, and resurrection of Christ from the Nephite viewpoint. Following Jesus's resurrection, he appears to the Nephites, preaches the Sermon on the Mount, chooses twelve Nephite apostles, and establishes the church in the Americas.

4 Nephi (AD 36–321). Mormon tells about the rise and fall of the Christian church in the Americas. The Nephites and the Lamanites all convert to faith in Christ, and the people enjoy three centuries of peace and prosperity, which end in an apostasy.

Book of Mormon (AD 322–421). This short book has the same title as the whole work. The Lamanites utterly defeat the Nephites at the hill Cumorah. Mormon hides plates on that hill, but to his son Moroni he leaves the plates containing the material summarized so far.

Ether (undated). Moroni abridges a set of twenty-four plates about the Jaredites, a people who left the tower of Babel and settled in the New World, where their civilization flourished and then disintegrated about the time that Lehi's party arrived.

Moroni (AD 400–421). Moroni provides some final teaching before he seals up his father's record, ending with a challenge to future readers to pray to know that the record is true.

Modern Discovery and Translation. According to Joseph Smith, an angel (whom he later identified as Moroni) appeared to him repeatedly from 1823 to 1827 to show him the gold plates and related materials buried in a stone box in a hill near Smith's home in Manchester (bordering Palmyra), New York. According to the traditional account (JS-H 1:27–59), on September 22, 1827, Moroni allowed Smith to take custody of the plates, along with an apparatus for translating the plates called the interpreters (and later, after the publication of the Book of Mormon, called the Urim and Thummim).

Recently married and quite poor, Smith persuaded an older friend named Martin Harris, a prosperous farmer, to finance the work of translating and publishing the book contained on the plates. To encourage his support, Smith gave Harris a piece of paper on which he had copied from the plates characters described as Egyptian hieroglyphs and sent him in February 1828 to New York City to show them to some scholars for their opinion. One such scholar was Charles Anthon, a reputable classicist. According to Smith's later account, Anthon declared that the characters were authentic and that a translation Smith had written underneath was accurate (JS-H 1:62–65). However, according to Anthon's own account, the paper contained no translation, and the characters,

though some of them resembled characters of various ancient languages, represented no coherent language or text. Nor could Anthon have verified a translation of a text that used Egyptian hieroglyphs since the Rosetta Stone had only recently been deciphered by European scholars and the knowledge derived from it had not yet reached the US. Although Anthon warned Harris that he was being defrauded, Anthon's comparison of some of the characters to those of unrelated ancient languages was apparently enough to satisfy Harris. Years later the paper (or a copy of it), commonly called the Anthon transcript, surfaced in the possession of the Reorganized Church of Jesus Christ of Latter Day Saints (now known as the Community of Christ). The paper shows no translation of the characters, and the characters themselves overall bear no discernible relation to Egyptian, Hebrew, or any other known language.

For about two months in the spring of 1828, Smith dictated a translation from the gold plates to Harris, with a curtain shielding him so that Harris could not see Smith or the plates. The two men produced a reported 116 pages of handwritten manuscript even as Harris's wife, Lucy, repeatedly demanded to see the plates or at least the manuscript. After several denials of these requests, on June 14 Smith said that God had given permission for Harris to take the manuscript pages home. Within two weeks, someone had stolen the pages; they were never recovered, and the thief never identified. A common theory is that Lucy destroyed the manuscript.

When Harris informed Smith on July 1 that the pages were gone, Smith was at first distraught, and he reported that the angel had taken the plates and interpreters away. A week later, though, he issued his first modern revelation (known now as D&C 3), in which the Lord severely castigated Smith for letting Harris take the pages (despite the earlier claim of divine permission) and asserted that the Lord's purposes would nevertheless be accomplished. In a follow-up revelation, Smith said that the Lord had foreseen that evil men would steal the pages in order to alter them so as to make Smith look like a fraud if he dictated a new translation of the same text from the gold plates. To circumvent this threatened deception, the Lord had inspired two parallel accounts of the same history: the longer narrative that Mormon had abridged and a shorter narrative that emphasized spiritual matters over historical details (D&C 10). This is the significance of the short book called the Words of Mormon: it forms a transition between the "spiritual" account from 1 Nephi through Omni on the (small) Plates of Nephi and Mormon's abridged account of the events that followed Omni, an account that begins with Mosiah. The "wise purpose" for the inclusion of two accounts of the same period among the plates was that Smith would have a replacement account to translate after his first manuscript was stolen!

On September 22, 1828, Smith reported that the gold plates had again been entrusted to him to translate. Over the next six months, Smith dictated a translation of the plates occasionally to his wife, Emma, though how much is unknown. Up to this point, no one besides Smith had seen the plates. In March 1829, Smith issued another revelation announcing that three men would be permitted to be witnesses to the gold plates and that Martin Harris might be one of them if he repented (D&C 5). On April 7 Smith began dictating anew with Oliver Cowdery, a schoolteacher and new friend (see JS-H 1:66–67; D&C 6, 8, 9). Although no record of each day's work was kept, what references exist to the contents of the translation on various days has led to general agreement among both LDS and non-LDS researchers as to the order of translation. It appears that Smith began the dictation approximately where the narrative of the 116 pages had left off, dictated

Mosiah through Moroni, and then dictated 1 Nephi through Words of Mormon.

Although the gold plates were said to be in Smith's possession again, the interpreters were not. According to reports from those who observed the translation work, Smith did not look at the plates while dictating the translation. Instead, he would place a "seer stone" (which he had used as a youth for treasure hunting) inside his hat, put his face into the hat to block all outside light, and dictate the text he claimed to "see" in this manner. The plates themselves were laid on the table or nearby wrapped in cloths, or kept in another part of the house, or even hidden outside the house somewhere. Smith would dictate a line of words at a time, wait for Cowdery to write those words and read them back, and move on if Cowdery's text was correct.

Smith and Cowdery's work on the translation proceeded much more rapidly than Smith's work with Martin Harris a year earlier. In less than three months (April 7 through late June), they apparently produced a handwritten manuscript for the entire Book of Mormon. Again, no daily record was kept of the progress on the manuscript, and we know that Smith had dictated at least some pages to Emma earlier. Mormons commonly argue that the extreme rapidity of the dictation (equivalent to six to eight pages of the modern printed edition a day) makes any naturalistic theory of the book's origin implausible. From an outsider's point of view, on the other hand, the fact that Smith was able to generate text about three times faster with Cowdery than with Harris suggests that Cowdery, an educated man, had a more active role in the work than the men admitted.

In June 1829, as the work of translation neared completion, Smith arranged for select witnesses to view the gold plates (see D&C 17). Harris, Cowdery, and David Whitmer (in whose home Smith stayed during much of the translation work) reported that Smith took them to a secluded location in the woods, where after some intense prayer they were permitted to see the angel, who showed them the plates. (Harris, though, reported having his vision of the angel and plates separately from the other two.) "The Testimony of Three Witnesses" is vague as to the nature of this experience. Smith also showed the gold plates (without the angel) to eight other men, whose "Testimony of Eight Witnesses" affirms that they examined and even held the plates to verify their physical reality. All eight of these witnesses were members of the Smith or Whitmer family. The evidential value of the eleven witnesses has been a contentious issue ever since the Book of Mormon was published. Once the translation work was complete, Smith reported, Moroni took the gold plates back into his custody. It is therefore impossible for anyone to examine the plates or to decipher whatever text, if any, may have been written on them.

According to Smith and some of the witnesses, the gold plates altogether weighed about fifty to sixty pounds. The flat surfaces of the plates measured about six by eight inches, and the stacked collection measured about six inches high. However, a stack of gold plates of that size should weigh close to two hundred pounds. Mormon apologists usually explain this discrepancy by arguing that the plates were only gold in color, not in composition. Even if the plates weighed only fifty or sixty pounds, however, the weight raises other difficulties. For example, most Mormon scholars argue that Mormon and Moroni lived in Central America and that Moroni walked from there to upstate New York, where he buried the plates before his death. This means that Moroni would have walked some three thousand miles carrying fifty or sixty pounds of gold plates. Such a scenario seems highly implausible and even pointless, especially considering the fact that Smith never actually looked at the gold plates while dictating his translation.

The various issues just discussed lead to the question of the reality of the gold plates. On one side are Smith's secretiveness about the plates, the controversial elements of the testimonies of the eleven men who claimed to have seen the plates, and the discrepancies concerning the plates' dimensions and composition. These facts favor the view that Smith did not have a set of ancient gold plates. On the other side are the testimonies of the eleven men, reports of the plates wrapped up and sitting on the table, and the reported subterfuges of Smith to hide the plates from those who might try to steal them, all of which support the existence of the plates. Perhaps Smith at some point did have metal plates of some sort, but they were not gold and were not ancient documents written with Egyptian characters.

Once the translation was complete, Smith had Oliver produce a second handwritten manuscript by copying the dictation manuscript. These two manuscripts have become known as the Original (O) and the Printer's (P) manuscripts. Only 28 percent of O is now extant, while P has survived essentially intact and is in the possession of the Community of Christ. According to LDS scholars, about one-sixth of the first printed edition of the Book of Mormon actually followed O rather than P. The first edition of the Book of Mormon was released on March 26, 1830, with an initial printing of five thousand copies. Eleven days later, Joseph Smith founded the Church of Christ (as he then called it) on April 6, 1830.

Editions. Two major new editions of the Book of Mormon were published during Joseph Smith's lifetime. The most significant of these was published in Kirtland, Ohio, in 1837. Hundreds of grammatical and spelling changes were made to the text as well as some theologically significant revisions. The most interesting of these changes were the revisions of four references to Jesus in the first edition that had identified him as God the

Father. For example, "the mother of God" was changed to "the mother of the Son of God" (1 Nephi 11:18); "the Lamb of God, yea, even the Eternal Father" was changed to say "even the Son of the Eternal Father" (1 Nephi 11:21; see also 1 Nephi 11:32; 13:40). These changes are known departures from the original manuscript (O) as well as the 1830 edition. In 1840, Smith published another edition with additional changes. While some of these changes represented corrections conforming the text to O, at least one famous change was a departure from it. In O as well as the 1830 and 1837 editions, 2 Nephi 30:6 said that a remnant of people descended from Lehi's family would someday convert to faith in Christ and would thereby become "a white and delightsome people." The 1840 edition changed these words to "a *pure* and delightsome people." Subsequent editions, however, reverted to "white" until the 1981 edition.

In 1879 the LDS Church published a new edition of the Book of Mormon edited by apostle Orson Pratt. This edition introduced the chapter-and-verse system still used today. Significant new editions were published in 1920, edited by James E. Talmage, and in 1981, edited by a committee of LDS apostles led by Bruce R. McConkie.

The Reorganized Church of Jesus Christ of Latter Day Saints, which arose in the 1850s among Mormons who did not follow Brigham Young to Utah, published its own editions of the Book of Mormon. Its main edition was published in 1908 and continued to serve as the official RLDS version of the Book of Mormon for the rest of the twentieth century. It follows a different chapter-and-verse system than the LDS Church's editions.

In the 1980s, Royal Skousen, an English-language scholar at Brigham Young University (BYU), began work on a comprehensive study of the "textual criticism" of the Book of Mormon, reviewing the O and P manuscripts and the printed editions from

Joseph Smith's lifetime in an effort to establish a more correct Book of Mormon text. His Critical Text Project culminated in *The Book of Mormon: The Earliest Text* (2009).

The Use of the Bible in the Book of Mormon. The most obvious source used in the Book of Mormon is the King James Version of the Bible (KJV), a point on which all non-Mormons and even some Mormons agree. Of the 239 chapters in the Book of Mormon, 27 duplicate most or all of 27 chapters in the Bible. These include the Ten Commandments (from Exod. 20), 21 chapters from Isaiah (Isa. 2–14; 29; 48–54), Malachi 3–4, and Matthew 5–7. Eighteen of these duplicated chapters appear in the first two books of the Book of Mormon, mostly in 2 Nephi. This means that two-thirds of the Bible chapters duplicated in the Book of Mormon happen to appear in the material Joseph Smith produced to replace the lost 116 pages.

A close comparison of these Book of Mormon chapters to the Bible confirms their dependence on the KJV. For example, of the 651 words in Isaiah 11–12 KJV, the Book of Mormon version differs in only two words (it omits "the" in 11:6 and changes "is" to "has" in 12:3). The Book of Mormon also retains most of the mistranslations in the KJV passages it quotes, such as "Lucifer" (Isa. 14:12 KJV; 2 Nephi 24:12).

Other Possible Sources. The most controversial view of the Book of Mormon's origins is the "Spalding theory," the hypothesis that it was based in large measure on a novel by an early-nineteenth-century writer, Solomon Spalding (also spelled Spaulding). According to this theory, Spalding (1761–1816) wrote an unpublished novel about the ancient inhabitants of America that was stolen by Sidney Rigdon and secretly passed to Smith, who then used it as the basis of the Book of Mormon. One common objection to this theory is that Rigdon did not even join the LDS Church until several months after it was founded and no hard evidence links Rigdon to

Joseph Smith prior to late 1830. The Spalding or "Spalding-Rigdon" theory gained traction from a number of testimonies by individuals who had known Spalding and who said that the Book of Mormon was very similar to Spalding's lost manuscript. However, a manuscript by Spalding discovered in 1884 turned out not to have any significant similarities to the Book of Mormon. Advocates of the theory since that discovery have argued that Spalding wrote a second unpublished novel that remains lost.

The dominant theory among non-Mormons today is that Joseph Smith was the true author of the Book of Mormon, perhaps with the help of Oliver Cowdery. Several considerations support this theory: Smith's reported abilities as a storyteller, his evident familiarity with the KJV even as a youth (as he himself claimed in his 1832 autobiographical account), his reported lack of notes or other materials used in the dictation process, and the consistency of Book of Mormon doctrine with Smith's earliest doctrinal views. Against this view, Mormons as well as some non-Mormons have objected that Smith did not have the ability to produce such a complex text. The force of this objection is at least somewhat blunted by the use of the KJV and other sources and by the possibility of an active role for Cowdery in the production of the text.

The most commonly cited possible source for the Book of Mormon other than the KJV Bible is *View of the Hebrews*, published in 1823 by a pastor named Ethan Smith (no relation) in Poultney, Vermont. Since Oliver Cowdery lived for several years of his childhood in Poultney, he may have been Joseph Smith's connection to the book, although there is no hard evidence of Cowdery and Smith meeting before 1829 (when the general subject matter of the Book of Mormon was already established). B. H. Roberts, a noted Mormon leader and scholar, wrote a manuscript in 1927 listing eighteen parallels between the Book of Mormon and *View of the Hebrews*. This manuscript was part of a larger project in which Roberts addressed with unusual frankness many difficulties with the Book of Mormon in the hope that these difficulties could be definitively resolved. Ironically, one of the main objections to the argument is that many of the ideas in *View of the Hebrews* (especially about American Indians being the descendants of Israelites) were circulating widely in Joseph Smith's day. Such an objection may weaken the case for direct dependence on Ethan Smith's book, but it strengthens the case for an early-nineteenth-century origin of the Book of Mormon. LDS scholars have also pointed out numerous ways in which the two books differ from one another—but such an objection is logically invalid since the claim is not that the two books are identical but that one is significantly indebted to the other or at least reflects the same milieu.

The best explanation for the Book of Mormon is probably a complex one. Joseph Smith evidently made use of several sources, either directly and purposefully (as in his use of the KJV) or indirectly (as in his drawing on ideas attested in various books of the era, even if he never personally read them). He also likely had some help, with Oliver Cowdery being the most likely source of such assistance.

Book of Mormon Apologetics. Throughout the LDS Church's history, Mormons have mounted arguments to defend the historicity of the Book of Mormon. The field of Book of Mormon scholarship is now far too complex (and LDS scholars far too prolific) to allow for a thorough review and assessment here. Instead, some key recent figures and issues will be briefly described, with only cursory critical responses. Book of Mormon scholarship and apologetics today derive especially if not primarily from the work of three BYU scholars: Hugh Nibley, John Sorenson, and John Welch.

Hugh W. Nibley (1910–2005) taught at BYU from 1946 until 1994 and produced an intimidating body of scholarship, mostly in defense of the Book of Mormon, the Book of Abraham, and LDS theology. Contemporary Book of Mormon apologetics really began with two lengthy series of articles by Nibley on the Book of Mormon published in 1952 as the book *Lehi in the Desert and the World of the Jaredites*. Nibley's method was essentially a comparative approach, ransacking ancient literature far and wide for parallels to the Book of Mormon.

John L. Sorenson (1924–) founded the department of anthropology at BYU and later taught as professor of anthropology there from 1971 to 1985. The year he retired, Sorenson published *An Ancient American Setting for the Book of Mormon*, which argued for a "limited geography" theory that the Book of Mormon lands were restricted to ancient Mesoamerica, in what is now Guatemala and southern Mexico. That model, which Sorenson continued to develop in retirement (culminating in the book *Mormon's Codex*), now dominates LDS academic scholarship and popular apologetics, although a minority of Mormons vigorously contend for other models.

One of the implications of Sorenson's Mesoamerican model is that the Book of Mormon peoples never amounted to more than a very small part of the population of the Americas. This implication has been radically reinforced in LDS apologetics by the controversy over DNA and the Book of Mormon. The traditional LDS belief based on Joseph Smith's teaching has been that Native Americans, especially those living in the US, are Lamanites. Modern advances in genetics have allowed scientists to confirm the conventional scientific view that Native Americans are descended from people who came from eastern Asia across the Bering Strait many thousands of years ago. Such a view is inconsistent with the idea that Native Americans are descended from Israelites. LDS scholars, however, argue that Israelite ancestry need not be expected to show up in DNA studies of Native Americans because the Lamanites were only a very small people restricted to the ancient Mesoamerican civilization. This apologetic salvages the plausibility of the Book of Mormon at the cost of abandoning Joseph Smith's own teaching on the subject.

John W. Welch (1946–) published an article in 1969 arguing that the Book of Mormon contains significant instances of chiasmus (a literary feature in which a text forms a pattern like A-B-B-A or A-B-C-B-A). Welch argues that chiasmus was common in ancient Hebrew literature but was unknown to Joseph Smith, so its presence in the Book of Mormon suggests its authenticity. Several questions of relevance to this claim have been debated: whether Smith could not have known about this literary device, whether he might have used it without even realizing it, and the extent to which it can be found in his nontranslated writings (such as his revelations in the Doctrine and Covenants). In 1980 Welch, an attorney by training, became a professor of law at BYU. A year earlier, Welch had established the Foundation for Ancient Research and Mormon Studies (FARMS), which later became subsumed as part of the Neal A. Maxwell Institute for Religious Scholarship.

Theology. Theologically, the Book of Mormon differs substantially from the later teachings of Joseph Smith reflected in later parts of Doctrine and Covenants as well as from the current official teachings of the LDS Church. For example, the Book of Mormon appears to affirm in very explicit terms a trinitarian theology, asserting repeatedly that the Father, the Son, and the Holy Ghost are "one God" (2 Nephi 31:21; Mormon 7:7). Some Book of Mormon statements even seem to err on the side of collapsing the personal distinctions within the Trinity, specifically several statements identifying Jesus as both the Father and the Son (Mosiah 15:1–5; Mormon 9:12; Ether 3:14). By contrast, toward the end of his life Smith was teaching that the Father, the Son, and the Holy Ghost were "three Gods" (in the "Sermon at the Grove" on June 16, 1844).

The Book of Mormon also explicitly teaches that God has always and eternally been God, "unchangeable from all eternity to all eternity" (Moroni 8:18; see also 7:22; Mosiah 3:5; Alma 13:7). In another 1844 sermon, the "King Follett Discourse," Smith claimed to refute this idea: "We have imagined and supposed that God was God from all eternity. I will refute that idea." These differences between Book of Mormon doctrine and Joseph Smith's later theology reflect a shift in Smith's thinking to an entirely different worldview in which Godhood is an open category into which our God himself entered and to which human beings may also aspire—another idea missing from the Book of Mormon.

Some distinctive elements of LDS theology appeared for the first time in the Book of Mormon. These include, perhaps most notably, the idea that Adam and Eve's transgression was a good and necessary thing that made it possible for them to have children and experience the full joy God intended (see especially 2 Nephi 2:22–25).

Importance of the Book of Mormon. The Book of Mormon plays a primary role in Mormon evangelistic efforts. LDS missionaries encourage prospects to read the Book of Mormon and pray to receive a spiritual witness or testimony that it is the word of God (based on a statement in Moroni 10:4–5). Because the Book of Mormon's doctrines differ in comparatively subtle ways from those of orthodox Christianity, people with Christian backgrounds are more likely to obtain a positive impression of Mormonism based on the Book of Mormon than if they were introduced first to Joseph Smith's

later doctrinal innovations. Once a person accepts the Book of Mormon as the word of God, however, it is a small step to accepting Joseph Smith as God's prophet and the LDS Church as God's only true and living church on the earth.

See also CHURCH OF JESUS CHRIST OF LATTER-DAY SAINTS; HARRIS, MARTIN; REFORMED EGYPTIAN; SEER STONES; SMITH, JOSEPH, JR.; STANDARD WORKS; TESTIMONY IN MORMONISM; URIM AND THUMMIM, MORMON USE OF

Bibliography. Pro: T. L. Givens, *The Book of Mormon: A Very Short Introduction*; G. Hardy, *Understanding the Book of Mormon: A Reader's Guide*; D. H. Ludlow, ed., *Encyclopedia of Mormonism*, 4 vols.; H. W. Nibley, *"Lehi in the Desert," "The World of the Jaredites," "There Were Jaredites"*; R. Skousen, *The Book of Mormon: The Earliest Text*; J. L. Sorenson, *An Ancient American Setting for the Book of Mormon*; Sorenson, *Mormon's Codex*; J. W. Welch, "Chiasmus in the Book of Mormon," *BYU Studies*. **Con:** B. L. Metcalfe, ed., *New Approaches to the Book of Mormon: Explorations in Critical Methodology*; G. H. Palmer, *An Insider's View of Mormon Origins*; D. Persuitte, *Joseph Smith and the Origins of the Book of Mormon*; D. M. Quinn, *Early Mormonism and the Magic World View*, rev. ed.; B. H. Roberts, *Studies of the Book of Mormon*, ed. B. D. Madsen; S. G. Southerton, *Losing a Lost Tribe: Native Americans, DNA, and the Mormon Church*; D. Vogel, *Indian Origins and the Book of Mormon*; E. M. Wunderli, *An Imperfect Book*.

R. M. Bowman Jr.

BOOK OF MOSES. The Book of Moses is the first book in the Pearl of Great Price, a collection of scriptural texts of the Church of Jesus Christ of Latter-day Saints. The full title as it appears in published editions today is Selections from the Book of Moses. It was produced by Joseph Smith as part of an inspired translation of the Bible and contains material understood to be restoration of lost portions of the early chapters of Genesis.

Origin and Editions. Shortly after publishing the Book of Mormon and forming the LDS Church in the spring of 1830, Joseph Smith Jr. began producing an inspired version, or "translation," of the Bible, essentially a revision of the King James Version. He worked on Genesis from June 1830 to February 1831, producing a revision of Genesis 1:1–6:13. John Whitmer made a copy of the manuscript during the next several weeks; the original is commonly called OT1, and the copy OT2. When Smith returned to the work of revising the Old Testament, OT2 was the main document used, though he dictated some additional changes to Oliver Cowdery that were entered on OT1 and not copied on OT2. Additional handwritten copies of the text based on both OT1 and OT2 were also made by some early Mormons.

Although some small portions of the translation appeared in LDS newspapers as early as 1832, the revisions of the opening chapters of Genesis became widely known when British LDS leader Franklin D. Richards published his book *The Pearl of Great Price* in 1851. It included two lengthy extracts from the revision of Genesis, though not in canonical order and not with the same wording known today. Orson Pratt published a new edition of *The Pearl of Great Price* in 1878 that used the "Inspired Version"— the edition of Joseph Smith's complete revision of the Bible published in 1869 by the Reorganized Church of Jesus Christ of Latter Day Saints—for the selections from Genesis. What is known today as the Book of Moses is Pratt's selection from the Inspired Version (commonly known among the Salt Lake City–based Mormons as the Joseph Smith Translation) with relatively minor changes.

Contents. The Book of Moses contains eight chapters, which repeat the text of Genesis 1:1–6:13 largely as it appears in the King James Version though with various types of revisions and additions.

Moses 1 is entirely new material with no parallel in the Bible. In it Moses tells of God revealing himself to Moses and speaking of his "Only Begotten," a title for Christ that appears twenty-five times in the book. After an encounter with Satan, who tries to persuade Moses to worship him, Moses hears again from God, who speaks to him about "worlds without number" beyond the earth and about his purpose "to bring to pass the immortality and eternal life of man" (1:33, 39).

Moses 2–4 for the most part closely parallels Genesis 1–3, with three notable exceptions. (1) Throughout Moses 2, God speaks in the first person (whereas in Genesis 1 God is spoken of in the third person), stating that he created everything by his Only Begotten, whom he addressed directly when saying, "Let us make man." (2) Moses 3:5–9 amplifies Genesis 2:5–9 to explain that God had created everything spiritually in heaven before he had created them physically. (3) Moses 4:1–4, material with no parallel in Genesis, recounts Satan's fall: he had offered to be God's son and proposed a plan in which he would redeem all mankind without exception by destroying their "agency"; when his plan was rejected, he rebelled, becoming Satan, the devil.

Moses 5:1–6:25 contains Genesis 4:1–5:21 with three substantial new passages. The first of these passages (5:1–16a) tells about Adam and Eve hearing the gospel of redemption through the Only Begotten; Eve rejoices that had they not transgressed in Eden they would not have had children or known the joy of redemption and eternal life. Although Adam and Eve believed the gospel, their children loved Satan more than God. The second passage (5:24–31) tells about one such child, Cain, who was condemned and called Perdition. The narrative reports that Cain married one of his nieces and that he made a secret pact with Satan to kill Abel. The third passage (5:49–59) tells a similar story about Lamech, who killed Irad for revealing secrets of the pact with Satan.

By far the longest additions to Genesis come in Moses 6:26–28 and 7:1–67, an account of Enoch's revelations and ministry that follows Genesis 5:21. God sent Enoch to call the wicked to repentance, preaching explicitly about "Jesus Christ" by name (6:52, 57; 7:50). Enoch explained that the gospel had first been preached to Adam, who was the first man to be baptized, and that baptism was to be done in the name of the Father, the Son, and the Holy Ghost (7:11). Enoch built a city named Zion that God took up to heaven to await the completion of the plan of salvation; he prophesied of the judgment of the flood, the coming of the Son of Man, and the future millennium.

The final section of the Book of Moses (7:68–69 and 8:1–25) parallels Genesis 5:22–6:13 and concerns the events leading up to the flood. One noticeable revision states that "it repented Noah" (Moses 8:25–26) that God had made the human race, rather than that God repented of having done so (Gen. 6:6–7). The text also includes additions in which Noah preached the gospel of "Jesus Christ, the Son of God" (see Moses 8:18–24).

Analysis. The Book of Moses may be described from a non-LDS perspective as a modern pseudepigraphic text—that is, a religious book attributed to a famous biblical figure but historically originating from many centuries after that figure. Like many ancient pseudepigraphic Jewish and Christian writings, the Book of Moses seeks to answer several questions raised by earlier Scriptures, in this case the opening chapters of Genesis. How was Moses able to write about creation when he wasn't there? What about other planets that God made besides the earth? Who is the "us" to whom God spoke about making humans in his image? Is the serpent really Satan? If God made everything, where did Satan the devil come from? Would Adam and Eve have had children if they had not disobeyed God? If Jesus Christ is the only Savior, how were people in

the Old Testament saved? Where did Cain get his wife? Why did Cain kill Abel? Who was Enoch and what was so special about him? Did God really repent of making the human race? These questions are the very ones that Christian readers in Joseph Smith's time were commonly asking and that they continue to ask today. While some of these questions may have been of perennial interest throughout Christian history, at least one—the question about other worlds—reflects a distinctly modern concern. On the other hand, the Book of Moses does *not* address questions about Genesis that became pressing in the second half of the nineteenth century: Is the universe really billions of years old, and if so, how does this square with the six days of Genesis 1? Did animals and plants evolve from earlier living things? Did humans evolve from nonhuman animals? Thus the questions that the book answers and those that it does not are conspicuously consistent with an origin in the first part of the nineteenth century.

Conservative LDS scholars regard the Book of Moses as having been written by Moses himself. However, they also have compared the Book of Moses to ancient Jewish pseudepigraphic writings, noting parallels to those texts that they think provide some evidence for its antiquity. "For example, Adam and Eve were to offer sacrifices to God after being driven from the Garden (Moses 5:5–7; cf. *Life of Adam and Eve*, 29.4), and Satan rebelled against God and was expelled from heaven (Moses 4:3–4; cf. *Life*, 12–16)" (Taylor, 1:217). However, *Life of Adam and Eve* dates from no more than two thousand years ago, and the "parallels" to this and other works in the Book of Moses are just as easily explained as issuing from common Jewish and Christian interpretations of Genesis easily known to Joseph Smith. Most Protestants, for example, in Smith's day as well as today, have believed that Satan rebelled against God and was expelled from heaven, and also that

Adam and Eve offered sacrifices to God after leaving Eden.

Hugh Nibley mined the pseudepigraphic literature, especially texts attributed to Enoch, for parallels to the Enoch preaching of the Book of Moses. Some of these parallels are unremarkable, such as the expression "among the children of men," while others in and of themselves seem more suggestive, such as a reference to Enoch weeping (Moses 1:41; 7:41; see Nibley, 149, 189). The sheer volume of parallels he adduced is overwhelming, but their quality is generally poor. Most importantly, the method of ransacking the wealth of ancient Jewish literature for scattered parallels is fallacious as a way of demonstrating the antiquity of a book known only since the nineteenth century. Given a large enough body of ancient writings that had some of the same kinds of purposes or interests as the Book of Moses, it is not surprising that an impressive list of parallels can be compiled. Such parallels can be good evidence that the Book of Moses fits the pattern of pseudepigraphic literature but not that it was written more than three thousand years before Joseph Smith.

The most striking parallels in the Book of Moses are not to such ancient pseudepigraphic works, which one may freely acknowledge Joseph Smith in 1830 and 1831 did not know, but to the New Testament, which he obviously did know. The Book of Moses contains explicit references to Jesus Christ, his atoning death, his resurrection, and baptism—and often expressed in language that clearly comes straight out of the New Testament. One verse nicely illustrates the point: "If thou wilt turn unto me, and hearken unto my voice, and believe, and repent of all thy transgressions, and be baptized, even in water, in the name of mine Only Begotten Son, who is full of grace and truth, which is Jesus Christ, the only name which shall be given under heaven, whereby salvation shall come unto the children of men, ye shall receive the gift of the Holy Ghost, asking all things in his name, and whatsoever ye shall ask, it shall be given you" (Moses 6:52). This one verse weaves together wording easily recognized as coming from several New Testament verses (Matt. 7:7; John 1:14; 16:23; Acts 2:38; 4:12). Thus the best explanation for the origin of the Book of Moses is that it was composed in the early nineteenth century by Joseph Smith himself.

See also CHURCH OF JESUS CHRIST OF LATTER-DAY SAINTS; JOSEPH SMITH TRANSLATION OF THE BIBLE; PEARL OF GREAT PRICE, THE; STANDARD WORKS

Bibliography. J. M. Bradshaw, *In God's Image and Likeness: Ancient and Modern Perspectives on the Book of Moses*; K. P. Jackson, *The Book of Moses and the Joseph Smith Translation Manuscripts*; R. J. Matthews, "How We Got the Book of Moses," *Ensign*; H. Nibley, *Enoch the Prophet*; B. T. Taylor, "Book of Moses," in *Encyclopedia of Mormonism*, edited by D. H. Ludlow, 4 vols. (See also the bibliography for The Pearl of Great Price.)

R. M. Bowman Jr.

BOOK OF THE DEAD, EGYPTIAN. An extensive compilation of funerary texts, commonly known as the Book of the Dead, was written by Egyptian priests to provide information for the living regarding the afterlife and how to prepare for it. The title Book of the Dead was assigned to this collection by early Egyptologists who were the first to work with these texts. The collection describes how the ancient Egyptians viewed death and the afterlife and how individual Egyptians prepared for their transition from this world into the next life. It contains incantations, hymns, prayers, and spells, among other things. John Taylor, curator of an exhibition on the Book of the Dead at the British Museum, explains, "The Book of the Dead isn't a finite text—it's not like the Bible, it's not a collection of doctrine or a statement of faith or anything like that—it's a practical guide to the next world, with spells that would help you on your journey" ("What Is a Book of the Dead?").

Egyptologist E. A. Wallis Budge states that "the Recensions of the great body of religious compositions, which were drawn up for the use of dead kings, nobles, priests, and others, and which form the Book of the Dead of the ancient Egyptians" (*Book of the Dead*, 1), consist of three recensions (critical editions of a text) of religious material. These recensions are the Heliopolitan Recension, the Theban Recension, and the Saite Recension.

The earliest recension, the Heliopolitan, was first used by priests (Fifth to the Twelfth Dynasties) who resided in the ancient Egyptian city of Heliopolis. In the Old Testament, Genesis 41:45 mentions Potiphera, priest of On, whose daughter Asenath became Joseph's wife. Heliopolis, also known as On, was the third-largest city in Egypt, behind Thebes and Memphis. It was also known as the city of Ra, the Sun god, and was the center of his worship.

A second recension, the Theban, was reproduced on papyri and coffins and used from the Eighteenth to the Twenty-Second Dynasties.

The third and final recension was the Saite, the primary text used from the Twenty-Sixth Dynasty through the Ptolemic period. Budge points out that the Book of the Dead "has been usually given by Egyptologists to the Theban and Saite Recensions" (*Book of the Dead*, 3). Budge, however, considers the Book of the Dead to comprise the "general body of religious texts which deal with the welfare of the dead and their new life in the world beyond the Grave" (*Book of the Dead*, 3).

Bibliography. E. A. W. Budge, trans., *The Book of the Dead: The Papyrus of Ani* (1913); Marie Parsons, "The Book of the Dead: An Introduction," Tour Egypt website, http://www.touregypt.net/boda.htm; J. Taylor, *Journey through the Afterlife: Ancient Egyptian Book of the Dead*; Taylor,

"What Is a Book of the Dead?" (blog), https://blog.britishmuseum.org/what-is-a-book-of-the-dead/.

S. J. Rost and H. W. House

BOOK OF THE DEAD, TIBETAN. Taken from the *Zab-chos zhi khro dgongs pa rang grol* (a.k.a. *Bar do thos grol*), the Tibetan Book of the Dead, as it is known in English, forms one part of a larger work. A revelation of the master Karma Lingpa (1326–86), the entire work presents a complete path to liberation. The Tibetan Book of the Dead section presents information on the dying process and instructions for the dying person. This acts as a guide through the *bardo* and also as one of the main sources on the bardo teachings. The whole of the text is closely associated with the Secret Matrix Tantra, translated in the early period of Tibetan Buddhism. However, the idea of the forty-nine-day bardo period is well attested in much earlier Buddhist texts.

See also BARDO; TANTRA; TIBETAN BUDDHISM

Bibliography. Gyurme Dorje, *The Tibetan Book of the Dead*.

A. W. Barber

BRAHMA. In popular Hinduism, Brahma is a god who exists as part of a divine triad and represents the creative force of the universe. (The other two gods in this ensemble are Shiva, who signifies destruction, and Vishnu, who symbolizes preservation.) His consort is the goddess of learning, Saraswati. Brahma has often been identified with Prajapati, a Vedic deity. The diversity of Hindu mythology offers many differing accounts of Brahma's origin. The Mahabharata depicts him being born from a lotus that protruded from the navel of Vishnu. According to the ancient Hindu legal text Manu Smriti, God manifested himself so as to dispel an encroaching, enveloping darkness, planting a divine seed that later became a golden egg from which Brahma was born. On another motif, Hindu mythology has it that Brahma originally had five heads, one of which was severed by Shiva to prevent his lustful gazes. Typical icons of Brahma display him with four heads, four faces, and four hands, either in a standing posture on a lotus or sitting on a swan. With each head, he continually recites one of the four Vedas. In other works of Hindu art, Brahma is portrayed riding a chariot drawn by seven swans. Although there are very few temples dedicated to Brahma as the main deity, he is prayed to in almost all Hindu rituals and is widely venerated. The best-known Brahma temple is in Pushbar, in Rajasthan.

See also HINDUISM; SHIVA; VISHNU

Bibliography. S. P. Basu, *The Concept of Brahma: Its Origin and Development*; P. Hemenway, *Hindu Gods: The Spirit of the Divine*; K. K. Klostermaier, *A Survey of Hinduism*; A. Michaels, *Hinduism: Past and Present*.

J. Bjornstad

BRAHMACHARYA. *Brahmacharya* is the pattern of austere conduct (*acarya*) or commitment that is essential to yoga. It is the practice by means of which a Hindu ascetic searches for and is said to attain the experience of Brahma. The term *brahmacharya* is the combination of Brahma (a Hindu deity) and *acarya* (orders from the master). According to some branches of Hinduism, the essence of brahmacharya is total freedom from anything sexual, whether it be actions, thoughts, or desires (Sri Swami Sivananda and Mahatma Gandhi held this view). Other schools within Hinduism, such as the tantric tradition, regard nonsensuality as a frequently profitable but not necessary component of brahmacharya. What they insist on is that the practitioner maintain his focus on God at all times, whatever activity he may be engaged in. Often it is claimed that a person practicing brahmacharya rigorously is completely free from passion, which is similar to a stoic approach to living, one of tremendous self-discipline. In a broad sense, brahmacharya consists in absolute control of all the senses as a way of harnessing evil, internal compulsions such as lust, anger, and greed. Some Hindu swamis contend that the practice of brahmacharya is the only way to open the *sushumna* (chief "astral tube" inside the human spinal column) and awaken the kundalini (primordial cosmic energy that resides within each person). Many maintain that brahmacharya is the most fundamental aspect of spirituality because in performing it, one transforms even mundane tasks into acts of worship (*sadhana*).

A person who takes up the rigors of brahmacharya is called a *brahmacarin*. For those born into certain Hindu castes, the period of following brahmacharya is merely the first of four stages of life (*ashramas*). The practice of classical yoga requires brahmacharya. In the area of managing passions, the practitioner exercises sexual self-discipline in marriage by being faithful, and if single, by practicing diligent celibacy. Human sexuality is one of several major areas where human appetites are to be managed if one desires to achieve success in brachmacharya. The consumption of foods is linked to either excess or disciplined restraint, so diligent abstinence from excess in diet is essential.

See also HINDUISM; YOGA

Bibliography. Website of Bombay Sarvodaya Mandal and the Gandhi Research Foundation, www.mkgandhi.org/main.htm; the Divine Life Society website, http://www.dlshq.org/home.html; G. Lochtefeld, *The Illustrated Encyclopedia of Hinduism*; Modern Seers Inc. home page, http://www.modernseers.org/; B. M. Sullivan, *The A to Z of Hinduism*.

S. J. Rost

BRAHMA KUMARIS WORLD SPIRITUAL ORGANIZATION. The origins of the Brahma Kumaris World Spiritual Organization may be traced to a series of visions that a wealthy jeweler named Dada Lekh Raj (1876–1969) experienced in 1936 in Hyderabad on the

Indian subcontinent. Lekh Raj, who is better known in the movement as Prajapita Brahma, encountered a spiritual presence that announced, "I am the Blissful Self. I am Shiva." Prajapita felt he had an important message to impart, so he closed his business and dedicated the rest of his life to this task. A small community, known as Om Mandali, was formed initially in Hyderabad and then relocated to Karachi for fourteen years. In 1950 the community moved once more and settled in its permanent international headquarters in Mt. Abu, Rajasthan, India. Prajapita reached *karmateet* (freedom from karmic accounts) on January 18, 1969. It is said that his soul departed to higher realms, where he is working on the transition toward the golden-aged new world.

Prajapita's message is that God is the Supreme Soul and dwells in light beyond the physical realm. God has disclosed that we live in an era of tremendous spiritual potential but that a time of degeneration is at hand and it is to be followed by a golden age. God is able to bestow peace and love and to satisfy our needs, but for this to happen, we must be prepared to shift from our body consciousness to soul consciousness. This involves a process of concentration called *raja yoga* meditation and uses various exercises of the mind and intellect. Bodily postures and mantras found in other forms of yoga, however, are not important in this process. The understanding is that the mind, intellect, and individual personality all form parts of the soul. The soul is separate from the physical body and the human brain, but the soul works through them. The goal is to control one's thoughts irrespective of external circumstances and to manifest calmness, love, kindness, and generosity.

At the heart of this is the role of women who are celibate, prepared to act unselfishly, and detached from material gain and who want to serve the world by expressing the loving qualities of Shiva's consort Shakti.

When Prajapita established the community, he did so with eleven women serving as its trustees, and women have continued to be in leadership. Those women who are prepared to serve undergo a period of fourteen years of training in meditation and the development of ethical qualities. So one of the distinctive features of the community is that Prajapita entrusted the spread of the message to women followers who are known as Brahma Kumaris, or the pure daughters of Brahma. The movement is co-led by several women such as Dadi Prakashmani and Dadi Janki and has several thousand centers located in 108 nations, with thirty centers in the US.

The Brahma Kumaris is recognized as a nongovernmental organization at the United Nations and has coordinated projects such as the Million Minutes for Peace (1986), Global Cooperation for a Better World (1988), and the Year of Interreligious Understanding and Cooperation (1993). It now sponsors Living Values: An Educational Program, which explores values-based education.

See also HINDUISM; RAJA YOGA

Bibliography. L. Hodginson, *Peace and Purity: The Story of the Brahma Kumaris; A Spiritual Revolution*; V. Skultans, "The Brahma Kumaris and the Role of Women," in *Women as Teachers and Disciples in Traditional and New Religions*; J. Walliss, *The Brahma Kumaris as a "Reflexive Tradition": Responding to Late Modernity*.

P. Johnson

BRAHMANISM. Brahmanism is an ancient form of Vedic religion that continues to be practiced in India today. In many ways an incipient Hinduism, Brahmanism's core teachings and practices can be traced to a group of texts that elaborate on the portion of the Vedic scriptures known as the Brahmanas (explanations for the Brahmins). Collectively, these commentaries function as a "user's manual" for the performance of religious ceremonies by priests (Brahmins); they also describe adherents' fundamental beliefs concerning Brahma, the world, the plight of human beings, and the means of liberation. However, adherents of Brahmanism hold to a spectrum of views concerning specific doctrines, making precise characterizations of "Brahmanism" elusive. This is further complicated by the fact that during the course of its historical development Brahmanism has often had a syncretistic relationship with other forms of Indian religion.

The worldview and worship practices that constitute Brahmanism began to form more than three thousand years ago. By about 600 BC, a highly inflexible caste system was in place in India that included a priestly caste of Brahmins. Brahmanism came into serious competition with various schools of Hinduism around AD 200, resulting in both polemical and constructive interactions that served to further shape Brahmanism's doctrinal and ritual contours. Siddhartha Gautama (563–483 BC), the founder of Buddhism, argued persuasively against Brahmanic religion, maintaining that the Vedic scriptures were not authoritative, that the rituals of Brahmanism lacked power, and that the Brahmanic clergy neither instructed wisely nor possessed any holy prerogatives. He also strenuously opposed the caste system at the time, which granted the Brahmins a privileged position in Indian society. As a result of Gautama's critiques and a number of concomitant cultural developments, the influence of Brahmanism swiftly declined and several competing sects of Hinduism flourished. During the twentieth century, British colonialism in India and the reinvigoration of Indian Buddhism spearheaded by B. R. Ambedkar (1891–1956) reduced the cultural impact of Brahmanism even further. In the late 1990s, a mere 12 percent of Hindus residing in the Upper Ganges considered themselves adherents of Brahmanism, and the percentages of Hindus identifying themselves in this way are even lower in

other areas of India, in several cases lower than 3 percent.

The central sacred texts of Brahmanism are the first three Vedas, the Brahmanas, and parts of the Upanishads. The religious authority to interpret the holy books of Brahmanism and to perform its sacred rituals is held by the Brahmins, who utter powerful hymns said to originate with Brahma, who revealed it to the *risis*. Brahma—who is variously conceived of in polytheistic, henotheistic, monotheistic, and pantheistic terms—is the ordering principle of the cosmos and its ontological ground. Brahmanism admits of various understandings of the making of the world, the primary two of which are a theistic view according to which Brahma fashions eternally existing matter into a universe of differentiated objects and a pantheistic view wherein the world emanates from Brahma's divine substance. In addition, some adherents subscribe to any of several creation myths. Popular notions of Brahma include a group of thirty-three gods (divided into three sets of eleven); a ruling triumvirate consisting of the deities Vayu (or Indra), Sirya, and Agni; and a pantheon of divine beings created by Brahma who are his personifications. More-philosophical concepts of Brahma often depict him as ubiquitous, transcendent, self-aware in such a way that all of reality is encompassed in his being, and surpassing the grasp of finite human intellect. Perhaps the most widely held view of Brahma is one according to which he is "embodied" variously as Brahma the Creator, Vishnu the Preserver, and Shiva the Destroyer. The relationship of human beings to Brahma also is not understood monolithically. Some views portray humans as creatures having the ability to become godlike; others describe the individual (Atman) and Brahma as being metaphysically discrete beings that nevertheless are capable of being fused in such a manner that their ordinary ontological dissimilarity is reduced. It is thought that an enduring self undergoes the cycle of death and rebirth and that distinguishing between finite persons and Brahma aids in the achievement of liberation, yet it is also (usually) maintained that Atman is ultimately identical with Brahma.

Escape from the cycle of death and rebirth has been the primary focus of Brahmanism in all but its earliest stages and forms. (Early Brahmanism featured an intricate structure of rituals that included sacrifices, prayers, and reading from the Vedic scriptures; here the priest was believed to be a conduit for mystical powers latent in the cosmos by his enactment of prescribed ceremonies, though the deceased were thought to remain within the realm of nature.) Later in the history of Brahmanism, the attainment of final release (*moksha* or *mukti*) from bondage to craving, ignorance, and illusion required possessing a flawless understanding of Brahma, which knowledge was obtainable by diverting the mind's attention from things in the world to the divine reality. In this system, liberation is achieved through the insight that the self is identical with Brahma. Much of contemporary Brahmanism emphasizes good and evil deeds that result in corresponding rewards or punishments via the operation of the law of karma; adherents seek to avoid the sufferings of reincarnation by performing morally upright actions that will procure for them everlasting delight after their death. The postmortem destination of the wicked is believed to vary in accordance with the type and extent of ethical failing. The worst such existence consists in tremendous suffering in hell; lesser fates involve successive rebirths as sentient creatures until the attainment of liberation.

Modern Brahmanism involves sixteen sacramental rites (*samskaras*) that pertain to different stages of life: (1) Garbhadhan (performed after impregnation), (2) Punsavanam (performed during the second or third month of pregnancy), (3) Simantonnayana (performed between the fifth and eighth month of pregnancy), (4) Jatakarma (performed during childbirth), (5) Namakarana (the naming of the child), (6) Niskramana (done when the three- or four-month-old infant is taken out of the home), (7) Annaprashana (the first feeding of cereal at six months), (8) Chudakarma (the child's first haircut, when he or she is at least a year old), (9) Karnavedha (the piercing of the child's ears at the age of three to five years), (10) Upanayana (the appointment of a religious instructor to an eight-year-old boy), (11) *Samavartana* (performed when the child's formal studies are completed), (12) Vivaha Samskara (the marriage ceremony), (13) Grihasthashrama (rites for overseers of households), (14) Vanprasthashrama (the renouncing of household life), (15) Sanyasashrama (ordination as a monk), and (16) Antyeshti (funeral ceremonies). Most practitioners of Brahmanism also engage in rituals concerning devotion to the fathers (*pitris*). These devotional acts—which prominently feature feast offerings known as *sraddhas*—are performed in the belief that they will enhance the happiness of deceased relatives and persuade those ancestors to support the flourishing and well-being of those still living. Finally, Brahmanic piety often includes vegetarianism (though the associated dietary restrictions vary in their severity).

See also ATMAN; BRAHMA; HINDUISM; KARMA; VEDAS

Bibliography. A. L. Basham and K. G. Zysk, *The Origins and Development of Classical Hinduism*; W. J. Coleville, *Oriental Theosophy: Brahmanism and Buddhism*, repr. ed.; J. C. Heesterman, "Vedism and Brahmanism," in *Encyclopedia of Religion*, edited by Lindsay Jones, 2nd ed., vol. 14; H. Wayne House, *Charts of World Religions*; M. Monier-Williams, *Brahmanism and Hinduism: Religious Thought and Life in India*, repr. ed.; M. W. Myers, *Brahman: A Comparative Theology*.

S. J. Rost

BRANCH. In the Church of Jesus Christ of Latter-day Saints (LDS Church), a branch (ordinarily) is the smallest organized group of church members, a congregation typically having fewer than two hundred members. Larger congregations are known as wards. Congregations are grouped into geographical units called either districts (for smaller groups) or stakes (for larger ones). LDS branches and wards generally fall under the jurisdiction of a district or stake president. Although the LDS Church does not require that branch presidents hold the office of high priest, a branch president must be an ordained elder in the Melchizedekian priesthood. Normally branches are formed primarily on the basis of geographical considerations, but demographic-based branches may be created for single adults, residents of nursing homes, those whose native language is not English, or prison inmates in cases where otherwise there would not be enough people to form a ward. For example, in the 1980s LDS Church authorities began organizing urban ethnic minorities into branches.

In 2000 there were nearly 26,000 LDS congregations (wards and branches) worldwide. By 2010 this number had increased to over 28,600 congregations, including more than 21,000 wards and about 7,600 branches.

See also CHURCH OF JESUS CHRIST OF LATTER-DAY SAINTS

Bibliography. Association of Statisticians of American Religious Bodies, *Religious Congregations and Membership in the United States: 2000*; B. P. Hales, "Statistical Report, 2010," *Ensign*; D. H. Ludlow, ed., *Encyclopedia of Mormonism*, 4 vols.; D. G. Stewart, *The Law of the Harvest: Practical Principles of Effective Missionary Work*, http://www.cumorah.com/index.php?target=law _harvest; Temples of the Church of Jesus Christ of Latter-day Saints website, "Statistics: Church Units," http://www.ldschurchtemples.com/statistics/units/; F. M. Watson, "Statistical Report, 2000," *Ensign*.

S. J. Rost

BUDDHA, HISTORICAL PERSON OF. Siddhartha Gautama, also known as Sakyamuni, was a historical person who became the Buddha (enlightened one) and the founder of Buddhism. He lived in northern India sometime between the sixth and the fifth centuries BC. The son of King Suddhodana and Queen Mahamaya, he was thus of the warrior ruling caste within Hinduism.

Fact and fiction blur when texts recall the life of the historical Buddha, but a core of tradition exists, common to all Buddhism. "Buddha" is a title; "the Buddha," when used without further qualifications, usually refers to the historical person of Siddhartha, the Buddha for this, the fourth aeon (*kalpa*). When Buddhists want to emphasize particularly that they are referring to that specific man in history, they refer to him as Sakyamuni, the "wise man of the Shakya tribe." Innumerable Buddhas both past and future exist within a vast cosmology; hence Siddhartha Gautama is understood as "a Buddha" born into this world, after many previous lives, as recorded in the popular Jatakas. His life on earth is recorded in the Tripitaka (Pali, "three baskets"; the three sections of the Buddhist canon) and later commentaries.

Queen Mahamaya dreamed one night of a silver elephant entering her womb from the side. Hindu Brahman priests foretold a son who would become either a king or a Buddha. Passing through the village of Lumbini ten lunar months later, she gave birth on the full moon of Vesakha (May). The Buddhist patron-king Asoka in the third century BC commemorated this event by the erection of a pillar in Lumbini, which still stands. The boy was given the name Siddhartha, meaning "goal accomplished." At sixteen Siddhartha married his cousin Yasodhara. Another tradition is that the wise sage Asita told the king that his son would be a great king if he remained in the palace but that if not, he would become a Buddha.

At twenty-nine Siddhartha was exposed to the "Four Sights." When driving with his charioteer, he saw an old man, a sick man, and a corpse. His charioteer explained that all people were subject to old age, sickness, and death. On a fourth occasion, he encountered a Hindu ascetic and was impressed by his peaceful composure. Siddhartha decided to leave home and adopt this ascetic's lifestyle in hope of finding serenity among all the instances of suffering he had observed.

Siddhartha left his sleeping wife and son one night to take up the life of a wandering Hindu ascetic—this was "The Great Renunciation." He wandered throughout northern India, learning from various Hindu sages and always looking for truth. Unsatisfied with the attainments of these Hindu sages, Siddhartha flagellated himself with severe austerities that first alarmed and later impressed his band of five disciples. After doing this for some time without becoming convinced that self-mortification would lead to truth, he returned to a balanced diet.

He resolved then to sit beneath a pipal tree (known later as the Bodhi tree) one night until he experienced enlightenment. In deep meditation, he fought off Mara, the evil tempter, by his practice of the ten great virtues (*paramitas*) that he had perfected in previous lives (charity, morality, renunciation, wisdom, effort, patience, truth, determination, universal love, and equanimity). Continuing in meditation, Siddhartha gained knowledge of his previous lives, and then he attained the power to see the passing away of the rebirth of beings. Finally he realized the path to the end of suffering, namely, the Four Noble Truths: (1) existence is *dukkha* (or *duhkha*)—suffering; (2) *dukkha* is caused by *tanha*—desire/craving; (3) nirvana—liberation from *dukkha* and *tanha*—is possible; (3) the Eightfold Path is the means to this release—right view (or right understanding), right thought, right speech, right action, right living, right endeavor, right mindfulness, and right concentration.

Siddhartha experienced this enlightenment (or awakening) at age thirty-five, on the night of the full moon of Vesakha (the same date he had been born) at Bodhgaya, India. He then reassembled his original five ascetic disciples near Varanasi, a sacred city in Hindu culture; after some skepticism, they recognized him as a Buddha. Their skepticism was due to Siddhartha's failure to attain enlightenment while an ascetic. How, they thought, could he have attained it without that rigor? Siddhartha argued that the Eightfold Path was a "middle way" between the extremes of Hindu asceticism and princely indulgence. This first sermon, called "Setting in Motion the Wheel of Truth," occured at the deer park in Sarnath, where today a stupa commemorates the occasion.

Following this first sermon, the group of disciples continued to grow. The Buddha organized these disciples into a *sangha*, or community: one entered a sangha by taking refuge in the Buddha, the dharma (the Buddha's "teaching" or "body of knowledge"), and the sangha. Eventually included in the sangha were a variety of relatives, princes, and laypeople, including the Buddha's wife, Yasodhara. The Buddha eschewed the Hindu caste system and promoted a democratic ideal under the authority of the *vinaya*, or discipline, later canonized in the Tripitaka.

At eighty the Buddha predicted his own death within three months. His disciple Ananda requested instructions concerning the transfer of leadership. The Buddha replied that only the dharma would be authoritative, and the vinaya would regulate monastic life. Assembling various monks together at Kushinagar, the Buddha lay on his right side, and, on the full moon of Vasakha (the same night on which he had been born and on which he had attained enlightenment), experienced *parinirvana*, or death. According to some traditions, his devotees gathered his relics, mixed his ashes with flour paste, and distributed them widely; they are still used allegedly to empower stupas today.

The Buddha's chronological life is a template for all Buddhists. They renounce worldly indulgence for a time (often later in life) of meditation and service. Alternatively, one family member (usually the oldest male) is given for a time to the sangha. Refuge-taking in the Three Jewels (Buddha, dharma, and sangha) remains the ceremony of initiation, and pilgrimages to the holy sites of the Buddha's life are regarded as meritorious: Lumbini (birth), Bodhgaya (enlightenment), Sarnath (first sermon), and Kushinagar (death). Wesak (Vesakha) is the main Buddhist festival, celebrating birth, enlightenment, and parinirvana on the full moon in May.

The Buddha's innovations include meditative innovations and equanimity. He built a lineage of teacher and disciple founded on affection and efficacy of teaching. Although some miracles are attributed to the Buddha, he continued to prioritize the teaching of the dharma. The life of Buddha was popularized in the West through Sir Edwin Arnold's epic poem *The Light of Asia* (1908). Conrad Rook's 1972 film version of *Siddhartha* was rereleased in 2002.

See also BUDDHA, NAMES OF; BUDDHA, NINE ATTRIBUTES OF; BUDDHA, THREE BODIES OF; BUDDHISM

Bibliography. E. Arnold, *The Light of Asia*; S. Bercholz and S. Chodzin Kohn, eds., *Entering the Stream: An Introduction to the Buddha and His Teachings*; D. Burnett, *The Spirit of Buddhism: A Christian Perspective on Buddhist Thought*; D. S. Lopez Jr., *Buddhism: An Introduction and Guide*; J. Toula-Breysse, *The Paths of Buddhism*.

H. P. Kemp

BUDDHA, NAMES OF. There are many Buddhas in the Buddhist cosmology. The Indian prince Siddhartha Gautama Sakya, commonly called the Buddha in English, was a historic individual who received the epithet Buddha (awakened one / enlightened one).

However, Buddhas have many other epithets. Siddhartha is also called Sakyamuni (Sage of Sakyas), but other Buddhas do not receive this title. A common list of ten epithets is often provided in texts. In addition to the above two, one reads Tathagata, a term that can be analyzed in two ways: "the thus gone one" (i.e., one who went to nirvana) or "the thus come one" (i.e., one who came out of compassion). Closely related to this is Sugata (well gone one). Arhat (worthy one), Anuttara (unsurpassed), and Anuttara Samyaksambuddha (unsurpassed complete awakened) are frequently encountered. Vidyacaranasampanna (one perfect in wisdom and good conduct), Lokavid (knower of the world), Purusadamyasarathi (charioteer of humans that need to be tamed), Sastradevamanusyanam (teacher of gods and humans), and Buddha Bhagavat (victorious Buddha) are also used.

Most Buddhist traditions provide a list of names of Buddhas who taught on earth, predated Sakyamuni, were prehistoric, but are generally considered by modern scholars as mythic. The Bhadrakalpika Sutra lists Krakucchanda, Kanakamuni, and Kasyapa. Other texts include Vipasyin, Dipamkara, and more. A "perfect complete Buddha" is one who reintroduces the eternal teachings by expressing them so as to fit them to the era, but only after the teachings of the previous Buddha are no longer accessible. Thus Sakyamuni taught only after humanity was once again lost in darkness. Further, all traditions claim that there will be a future Buddha, referred to as Maitreya or Ajita, who now is a bodhisattva teaching in the heavens and who will be born on earth, go through the practices to become a perfect complete Buddha, and reintroduce the teachings once Sakyamuni's dispensation is lost. He once manifested himself in China and was called Budai, the "Happy Buddha" seen in Chinese restaurants.

The Mahayana tradition knows of many other Buddhas not recognized by the

Theravada school, some of whom have become extremely popular over the centuries. It is held that by arduously engaging in the correct practices one can have visions of these Buddhas. Also, for those who are spiritually less developed, by making a karmic connection with one or another of these Buddhas, one can be reborn in their realm (somewhere in the universe) upon death and from there achieve one's own nirvana. These realms, called "Buddha fields" in Sanskrit, were given the more poetic phrase "Pure Lands" in Chinese, and it is by this term that they are generally referred to in English.

Second only to Sakyamuni in popularity is Amitabha (Chinese, Omitofo; Japanese, Amida). This is no mere accident of history, as the Chinese emperors highly encouraged the rituals and teachings associated with this Buddha. Further, in East Asia, Amitabha became associated with ancestor worship, which guaranteed widespread appeal in China, Korea, Japan, and Vietnam. He also has a following in Nepal and Tibet, but in these traditions there is no ancestor worship.

The Buddha most popular after Sakyamuni in Nepal and Tibet is Aksobhya, who also has a Pure Land and is closely associated with the moment of enlightenment. His Pure Land is different in important ways from that of Amitabha, but in both excellent practice is possible and will lead to liberation from rebirth. Aksobhya is often confused with Sakyamuni, particularly in statue ware, although in paintings different colors are used to help distinguish them.

Another important Buddha recognized from Nepal to Japan is Vairocana. One of the great stone Buddha statues just outside the ancient capital of China is this Buddha. So, too, in the ancient capital of Japan, Nara, the giant bronze Buddha statue is Vairocana. In fact, that statue was a technological wonder, as it was the largest cast made for many centuries. The Shingon sect of Buddhism in Japan has Vairocana as its main focus. This Buddha is also significant in the massive Buddhist monument on Java called Borobudur. He also appears in numerous texts in Nepal and Tibet.

See also BUDDHA, HISTORICAL PERSON OF; BUDDHA, NINE ATTRIBUTES OF; BUDDHA, THREE BODIES OF; BUDDHISM

Bibliography. Paul Williams, *Mahayana Buddhism: The Doctrinal Foundations.*

A. W. Barber

BUDDHA, NINE ATTRIBUTES OF. Most basically, a Buddhist is one who believes in the so-called Triple Gem, expressed in the confession: "I take refuge in the Buddha; I take refuge in the dharma [Buddhist teaching of the right way of living]; I take refuge in the *sangha* [Buddhist community, which is understood slightly differently in each tradition]." The Triple Gem, in turn, is thought to consist in twenty-four "attributes": nine associated with the Buddha, six with the dharma, and nine with the sangha.

Recitation of the attributes, along with the Triple Gem and the Five Precepts (abstaining from killing, from what is not given, from sexual misconduct, from telling lies, and from intoxicating drinks and drugs), make up the core of both home and (especially) temple devotional exercises (*vandanas*). Contemplating the attributes is supposed to free the mind of defilements (at least temporarily) and thus help prepare for understanding, while chanting the attributes is supposed to protect from danger or provide needed insight. Buddhists also typically regard the statue of Buddha as a symbol of the "nine attributes" and pay homage to the statue as a sign of respect for his being. Devotees often recite the attributes, creed-like, as a formula:

> [The Buddha] is worthy of honor [*araham*], as free of all defilement;

he is the fully enlightened one [*samma-sambuddho*], having discovered all ultimate realities;

he is perfect in knowledge and conduct [*vijjacaranasampanno*], possessing the three (or eight) types of knowledge and fifteen types of virtue;

he is the blessed one [*sugato*], the "perfect speaker" for the welfare of the world;

he knows the worlds [*lokavidu*], is omniscient;

he is the tamer of unruly men [*anuttavo purisadamasirathi*], as well as nonhuman beings;

he is the teacher of gods and men [*sattha devamanussanam*], leading them on the path of nirvana;

he is the enlightened one [*buddho*], especially regarding the "Four Noble Truths";

he is the exalted one [*bhagava*]—that is, glorious.

Explanations of the nine attributes are drawn from the Theravada "scripture" known as the Tripitaka (Pali, Tipitaka), or the "three baskets." Although the attributes differ notably from teacher to teacher or sect to sect, elaborations on the attributes often serve as a combination of catechism, ethics handbook, and guide to the veneration of the Buddha.

Such veneration characterizes the Buddhist tradition known as Theravada (doctrine of the elders) rather than the Mahayana (great vehicle) tradition. While Mahayana recognized other Buddhas in addition to the historical Buddha (Siddhartha Gautama), Theravada focuses on Sakyamuni, his manner, and a renunciative approach to his teachings, including the first eight attributes and his excellence of person (i.e., the ninth attribute, *bhagavan*, takes special note of his noble birth and incomparable physical appearance).

All the attributes are said to guide the faithful in right living (dharma). Contemplation of bhagavan, for example, will show the importance of proper dress, speech, and behavior for gaining respect from others. The attributes are sometimes divided into three groups: (1) the Buddha's character qualities (attributes 1–3), (2) the Buddha's teaching qualities (4–6), and (3) the Buddha's leadership qualities (7–9).

In daily devotion, recitation of the nine attributes is usually preceded by the Triple Gem, followed by the threefold repetition of a Pali verse expressing qualities of the Buddha's enlightenment: *Namo tassa bhagavato arahato sammasambuddhassa* (Reverence to the blessed one, the exalted one, the fully self-enlightened one). Devotions may also include recitation of the Five Precepts and homage to benefactors (notably the three "refuges," parents, and teachers).

See also BUDDHA, HISTORICAL PERSON OF; BUDDHA, NAMES OF; BUDDHA, THREE BODIES OF; BUDDHISM; SANGHA

Bibliography. J. R. Carter and G. D. Bond, *The Threefold Refuge in the Theravāda Buddhist Tradition.*

C. R. Wells

BUDDHA, THREE BODIES OF. The "three body" (*trikaya*) doctrine of Mahayana Buddhism is usually associated with Asanga, the fourth-century founder of the Yogacara (ideas only) school, who attempted to reconcile the Buddha's physical existence with his enlightenment. As the enlightened one, the Buddha is presumed to embody dharma (the right way of living). His essential Buddha nature, the "body of essence," is therefore termed *dharma-kaya* (dharma body), which forms the basis for the other "bodies." In some traditions, notably in Tibetan Buddhism, the dharma-kaya represents the primordial Buddha, beyond words or even intellectual conceptualization. (Some traditions add a fourth "body," the *svabhava-kaya*, i.e., absolute reality.) As Siddhartha Gautama, the Buddha also lived historically as "body in the world" (*nirmana-kaya*)—that is, as "created body." Finally, the Buddha nature (dharma-kaya) manifests itself in spiritual realms as the *sambhoga-kaya* (enjoyment body), invisible to the physical senses but accessible through meditation. This "body of bliss" varies according to spiritual location.

In contrast to the older, Theravada tradition, which recognizes only one earthly Buddha (nirmana-kaya) at a time and in which the term *dharmakaya* means the sum total of the dharma, Mahayana recognizes numerous Buddhas and Buddhas-to-be (bodhisattvas), experienced by way of the sambhoga-kaya and conceived as presiding over "buddha-fields" (*Buddha-ksetra*), or mystical realms of influence.

The triple body doctrine has its roots in the *darshanic* ideas and practices noted in some of the earliest Buddhist scriptures (i.e., ideas by which one enters into the spiritual power). The Mahayana tradition added new emphasis and further developed visionary meditational techniques to this approach to spirituality.

See also BUDDHA, HISTORICAL PERSON OF; BUDDHA, NAMES OF; BUDDHA, NINE ATTRIBUTES OF; BUDDHISM; DARSHANA.

Bibliography. P. Harvey, *An Introduction to Buddhism: Teachings, History and Practices*; D. S. Noss, "The Trikaya or Triple Body," in *A History of the World's Religions*.

C. R. Wells

BUDDHISM. Buddhism is one of the world's major religions, a development of the *sramanic* tradition, founded by Siddhartha Gautama Sakya. Gautama is said to have become enlightened and thus a Buddha. Buddhism is markedly different in beliefs and practice from Hinduism and is much more diversified. Followers of Buddhism range from atheists to polytheists, but all share the core beliefs Buddha taught, known as the Four Noble Truths and the Eightfold Path.

Buddhist Origins. In May 1956, Buddhists celebrated the twenty-five-hundredth anniversary of their founder's birth, but the date is merely an estimate since biographies of the Buddha—mostly legendary and lacking historical points of reference—do not appear in writing earlier than about five hundred years after his death. The following details seem reasonably well-established:

1. The Buddha (born Siddhartha Gautama) was born about 566 BC into a noble family (his father was a "senator" in a democratic chiefdom called Kapilavastu, near the present Indian-Nepalese border, but is often depicted as being the king).

2. At the age of twenty-nine, he renounced his station and family (the "Great Renunciation"), which included a wife and a son to become a wandering ascetic.

3. He afterward experienced a radical religious transformation.

4. He spent the last forty-five years of his life teaching his new religion before he died at the age of eighty in Kushinagata, near his birthplace in northern India.

The traditional explanation for his religious transformation begins with the legend of the "Four Sights." Although Siddhartha's father attempted to shield him from suffering and sorrow, the gods intervened, assuming human shapes in order to awaken the prince to his destiny. On a certain day, Siddhartha saw a decrepit old man, a diseased man, and a corpse—"sights" that introduced him to decay, suffering, and death. Greatly disturbed, he saw the fourth "sight"—an ascetic wearing the yellow robe of a monk. Siddhartha resolved to pursue the ascetic path, believing he had found the answer to suffering. Six years after the Great Renunciation, however, Gautama determined that deliverance must come some other way. Tradition has it that he sat under a fig tree (now known as the Bodhi tree or Bo tree; in Sanskrit, *bodhi* means "knowledge" or "enlightenment"), determined not to arise until he attained enlightenment. Resisting the temptations of the god Mara, Siddhartha spent an entire night passing through stages of meditation, emerging at sunrise as the "enlightened [or 'awakened'] one," the Buddha, having grasped the Four Noble Truths.

At this point, according to tradition, Mara tempted the Buddha to enter immediately into *pari* (complete)-*nirvana* without proclaiming his newfound faith, but he refused. Instead, he made his way to the now-famous deer park and preached to five former colleagues. Now known as the first "turning of the wheel of the dharma" (teaching of the right way to live), this sermon set forth the Four Noble Truths and produced the first Buddhist converts. For the rest of his life, Gautama traveled throughout northern India, preaching and gathering followers into communities called *sanghas*.

Classic Buddhist doctrine is summarized by the Four Noble Truths: (1) "the noble truth of suffering" holds that suffering (*dukkha/ duhkha*) is the inevitable condition of existence; (2) "the noble truth of the cause of suffering" holds that suffering results from desire, culminating in the desire for individual existence; (3) "the noble truth of the cessation of suffering" holds that suffering ends when this craving for existence ends, along with desires and appetites; and (4) "the noble truth of the path" comprehends the Noble Eightfold Path, which makes possible escape from the craving for existence, and thus enlightenment.

The Noble Eightfold Path consists in (1) right belief (of the Four Noble Truths, but including rejection of erroneous philosophies and unworthy attitudes), (2) right aspiration (indicated by firm resolve to seek liberation), (3) right speech (avoiding lying and other forms of hurtful speech), (4) right conduct (avoiding harmful practices, while rooting out harmful motivations and perfecting virtue), (5) right livelihood (living so as not to violate right speech or conduct); (6) right effort; (7) right attention; and (8) right concentration. These last three involve the practice of meditation (*dhyana*), deemed most helpful in the quest for enlightenment. The Eightfold Path thus actually reduces to three essentials: (1) wisdom (rules 1 and 2); (2) ethics (3–5); and (3) mental discipline (6–8).

Basic Concepts in Buddhism. Buddhism is best characterized as a religious tradition sharing in the Indian spiritual dialogue: it shares with the Hindu yogic tradition, Jainism, and other now nonexistent religions a preoccupation with suffering, and it places a similar high value on meditation and the role of wise teachers. Buddhism is actually less a "religion" than "a vast and complex religious and philosophical tradition" (Gethin, 1), loosely connected to certain basic concepts rooted in the Indian spiritual dialogue.

Buddhism shares the fundamental Indian religious belief in *karma*, the inexorable law of cause and effect, extended from the physical to the spiritual realm. Karma is inextricably bound to the law of rebirth (*samsara*) since it passes on for good or ill through successive generations. The goal is liberation (*moksha*) from this cycle.

Strictly speaking, however, because it rejects the soul theory, Buddhism denies the transmigration of souls. "Rebirth" is rather continuation of pure karma (by its sheer force) from one life into another—as in the Buddha's traditional explanation that the light, but not the flame, of one candle passes to another. Further, in Buddhism the karma cycle can be broken by enlightenment. While Hinduism recognizes several paths of deliverance from karma/samsara, Buddhism emphasizes realization and detachment as the key.

Theistic Worship. Whereas Hinduism freely worships a vast assortment of gods, in Buddhism the gods are seen in a different light. In general, Buddhists recognize gods as existing and having extremely pleasurable lives that last for millennia but that also end; thus that particular being must be reborn. In India, the gods mentioned in Buddhist texts originate in the Indo-European pantheon. In China or Japan, for example, Buddhism also incorporates local gods. As the gods are also trapped in samsara, they need liberation as found in the Buddha's teachings. The gods may help followers with mundane things, but they cannot help with the goal of nirvana; the Buddha's teachings will guide one in those endeavors, but one must undertake the path oneself.

Dharma and Scripture. Like Socrates, Gautama purportedly wrote nothing; rather, it is said, he set in motion "the wheel of dharma." *Dharma*, a term familiar in the religions of India, denotes the underlying reality of things. It is roughly equivalent to "philosophy" in the ancient sense of life ordered by right reason, but with emphasis on ways of guiding *experience*, rather than thought, or even action.

The "wheel of dharma" helps explain the fact that Buddhism has no concept of canonical scripture equivalent to that of Christianity, Judaism, or Islam. The nearest candidate is the Tripitaka (three baskets). Buddhists do not, however, regard the scriptures as revelatory, so teachings that agree with the Buddha's dharma are deemed Buddha's teachings whether they actually came from Sakyamuni or not. The scriptures are thought to illuminate the path of dharma. Not surprisingly, the vast Buddhist writings have undergone numerous changes (including additions, editing, variations) even up to the twentieth century—for example, because of massive troves of forgotten scriptures—making standardization across all traditions all but impossible; and different Buddhist schools in different regions regard different writings as authoritative.

Impermanence. According to one *udana* (inspired utterance), a disciple asked about conscious existence in nirvana. The Buddha answered that "there is . . . a domain where there is no earth, no water, no fire, no wind, no sphere of infinite space, no sphere of infinite consciousness, no sphere of either awareness or nonawareness; there is not this world, there is not another world, there is no sun or moon. I do not call this coming or going, nor standing, nor lying, nor being reborn; it is without support, without occurrence, without object. Just this is the end of suffering" (*Udana* 80). This text illustrates two distinctive Buddhist concepts—"no soul" (*anatta*) and "impermanence" (*anicca*). Buddhist philosophy is fundamentally pragmatic (the cessation of suffering), rather than positivistic (e.g., "paradise oriented"). This way of seeing the world is viewed by many outside observers as negative, but Buddhists see it otherwise. In the Buddhist view, suffering results from desire, and desire in turn results, by way of ignorance (*avidya*) and delusion (*moha*), from "attachment" (*upadana*), especially attachment to the self (Atman). The absolutized "self" grasps for material goods, privileges, experiences, identity, and the like, in order to give reality to itself. The delusion of *self*hood, in other words, creates *self*ishness.

This delusion of selfhood is twofold: first, that the self as such exists; second, that objects of craving themselves possess permanence. Classical Buddhist thought resolves the first problem by denying real existence to the self (anatta). Words like "self," "person," "ego," and "I" are thus merely conventional. The realization of impermanence (anicca) resolves the second problem. The "cessation of suffering" (nirvana) consists in the actualization of anatta and anicca; this is enlightenment.

Nirvana/Parinirvana. Enlightenment makes possible entrance into nirvana, or, more commonly, pari (complete)-nirvana, which denotes a "blowing out" or "extinguishing" (of suffering). Unlike English translations such as "he/she enters nirvana," Buddhist texts generally employ a verbal idiom (e.g., "he/she *parinirvana*-s") to emphasize the *process* of extinguishing the delusions and cravings of the self more than a resultant state (Gethin, 75). So while nirvana/parinirvana does imply an *eternal state*, it is also an event (the moment of enlightenment) and an experience (cessation of desire and suffering).

As in the udana, or inspired utterance, above, nirvana can be described only by way of negation; it lacks any moral content whatsoever. Nirvana constitutes the Buddhist answer to suffering, not moral evil. The Buddhist goal generally has no place for creation, fall, sin, atonement, judgment, or re-creation.

The Sangha. Buddhism has no counterpart to church, synagogue, or mosque. The Buddhist ideal is the sangha, or community, purportedly inaugurated by the Buddha himself to carry on the teaching of dharma. What constitutes the sangha differs by tradition. Theravadins include the monks primarily (there is no extant nun tradition in Theravada). The Mahayana Buddhists include Buddhas, bodhisattvas, monks, nuns, laymen, and laywomen in the greater community and distinguish each subgroup as necessary—for example, the monastic sangha and the bodhisattva sangha.

The rules of the monastic sangha and the model for the lay sangha are drawn largely from the Tripitaka's Vinaya section, specifically two broad categories of ordination and four classes of monastics. Many Buddhist traditions also recognize ordination for specific, even brief periods; monks and nuns are generally free to leave at any time. *Novice* monks (samanera) or nuns (samaneri) keep the Ten Precepts, vowing to refrain from harming living creatures, taking what is not given, engaging in sexual activity, speaking falsely, using intoxicants, eating after noon, attending entertainments, wearing jewelry or perfumes, sleeping on luxurious beds, and

handling gold and silver. Familiar to Westerners because of their shaved head and robe, *fully ordained* monks and nuns (who must be at least twenty years of age) take vows for more than two hundred rules. Except for the novice, the Tripitaka provides no criteria for establishing levels of progress.

Monks and nuns are expected to depend entirely on lay support for material needs (although in East Asia there are exceptions). Correspondingly, lay support of monks, nuns, and monasteries constitutes meritorious action, and the sanghas are considered beneficial to laypersons both as centers of religious teaching and as possible sources of merit.

The Traditions of Buddhism. Soon after Gautama's death, according to tradition, five hundred monks convened the first Buddhist Council to establish the teaching of their master. (Three other councils followed in the next 250 years.) Meanwhile, the sanghas codified Gautama's teachings and applied them to monastic life. These teachings, with many elaborations, circulated as separate oral "texts" until the first century BC, when they began to be written and collected. The collection is the Tripitaka (three baskets), consisting of (1) the Sutras ("discourses" of the Buddha), (2) the Vinaya ("[monastic] discipline"), and (3) the Abhidharma ("higher teaching," or metaphysical theology).

Early Buddhism was more than doctrine and monastic rules; it also included such aspects as stupa worship. According to tradition, the Buddha himself authorized the building of mounds (stupas) over the relics or remains of holy persons, himself included. Often the center of a monastery, the stupa was supposed to radiate the merits of the person. In time earth-mound stupas gave way to the elaborate structures familiar in Buddhist lands today, and stupa worship includes music, incense burning, votive offerings, circumambulation (thought to produce merit), and other rituals.

Buddhism remained confined to the Ganges Valley of eastern India until the middle of the third century BC, when an Indian emperor named Ashoka embraced the new religion and sent missionaries (including his own son and daughter) across India and to Ceylon (Sri Lanka)—where Buddhism soon became the state religion—and as far away as Alexandria. From northern India, Buddhism spread across Central Asia into China, then into Korea, from which missionaries took Buddhism to Japan in the sixth century. Also from northern India and Nepal, it entered Tibet in the seventh century. And from eastern India, it spread into Southeast Asia before the modern era.

Buddhism today consists of three principal streams. Theravada (or "Southern") Buddhism, with over one hundred million adherents, predominates in Sri Lanka and Southeast Asia. East Asia claims the greatest number of Buddhists by far—estimates range from five hundred million to more than a billion—most of whom follow some form of the Mahayana (great vehicle). Tibetan (also known as Tantric) Buddhism, the third stream, numbers some twenty million adherents. Mahayana Buddhism has fragmented into numerous schools, sects, and subsects, sometimes differing as much from one another as Christian denominations do. The forms of Buddhism known to most Westerners are derived from Mahayana.

Theravada Buddhism. Theravada, the "way of the *theras*" (elders), is the conservative wing of Buddhism. Disparagingly labeled the "narrow path" or "little vehicle" (*Hinayana*) by Mahayana Buddhists, Theravada embraces the goal of individual liberation, or arhatship (an arhat being one who achieves *parinirvana*). Arhatship is open only to monks, who accumulate merit and wisdom through rigorous discipline. Monks cannot, however, as in Mahayana, dedicate merit to others. Laypersons instead earn merit by supporting monks (and monasteries) and

by other religious practices in order to attain rebirth to a higher order.

Theravada relies on the Tripitaka for authority, the 1956 Pali text (Tipitaka) being the most widely recognized version. There are also many commentaries on various texts in the Tripitaka, the most famous being the works of the fifth-century monk Buddhaghosa.

Most everyday Theravadins accept core Buddhist beliefs but freely incorporate non-Buddhist ideas, especially about the spirit world. Similarly, while the teaching denies the Buddha's divinity, lay attitudes vary greatly.

For monks and laypersons, the Theravada path begins with a confession, the formula of the three "refuges": (1) "I take refuge in the Buddha"; (2) "I take refuge in the dharma"; and (3) "I take refuge in the sangha." Most laypersons would also vow to keep the first five of the Ten Precepts vowed by novice monks.

Mahayana Buddhism. From its beginnings (first century BC), Mahayana self-consciously distinguished itself from earlier establishments, and several differences may be observed. First, as to authority, Theravada acknowledges the Tripitaka, while Mahayana recognizes no codified "scripture"; rather, the sects choose which texts from the Tripitaka they will utilize.

In its teaching of the "Triple Body," Mahayana postulates numerous cosmic Buddhas (*sambhoga-kaya*), teaching dharma in mystical realms called "Buddha-fields." Many of these cosmic ("celestial") Buddhas, as well as "Buddhas-to-be" (bodhisattvas), serve as objects of devotion. These beings form a pantheon characterized by numerous hierarchies and associations. In most Mahayana sects, the absolute (*dharma-kaya*) can have any number of historical manifestations; in principle, therefore, every person is a potential Buddha.

The bodhisattva concept in particular distinguishes Mahayana from Theravada. Whereas Theravadins idealize the arhat,

Mahayana idealizes the being (*sattva*) who delays nirvana to aid others seeking enlightenment (*bodhi*). The bodhisattva path is in principle open to anyone; it begins with an aspiration for enlightenment, through meditation and acts of compassion. As aspiration grows to firm commitment, the disciple takes the vow of a bodhisattva, ideally in the presence of one thought to be spiritually advanced, who complements the vow with a "prediction" of future enlightenment. The bodhisattva then sets out on a career to realize the six primary and four secondary "perfections" (*paramita*), leading through ten stages of attainment (*bhumis*), marked by ever-increasing insight into reality and ever more earnest work on others' behalf. At the tenth stage, the path of the bodhisattva melds into buddhahood.

However, whereas the Theravadin arhat escapes samsara, enters nirvana, and effectively disappears forever, the Mahayana bodhisattva/Buddha remain accessible. In Theravada nirvana opposes samsara, but in Mahayana they share the same ultimate reality, called *sunyata* (universal emptiness). Sunyata doctrine distinguishes between "conventional" truth, which includes such familiar ideas as karma, samsara, and nirvana, and "ultimate" truth, which comprehends the true nature of all things—sunyata. The bodhisattva transcends conventional truth and may be said, therefore, both to *escape* samsara and to *utilize* samsara for the sake of others ("in the world but not of the world" provides a rough analogy).

Mahayana Sects. The Theravada tradition is the only surviving sect out of more than eighteen related sects in ancient times, whereas Mahayana has given rise to numerous existing, divergent sects, beginning in India, developing in China, and many acquiring final form in Japan. The earliest Mahayana school is traced to the Indian monk Nagarjuna (second century AD), who systematized the doctrine of sunyata (see above)

and founded the Madhyamaka (the school of "the middle path"), seeking to resolve the tension between "conventional" and "ultimate" truth. A century later, two brothers, Asanga and Vasubandhu, founded the Yogacara ("Mind [Yoga] Practice," also known as *vijnapti-matra*, "ideas only") school, which explained reality as stores of ideas in the mind (similar to Freud's "unconscious").

As a highly developed culture, with other religions already well established, China gave a distinctive cast to Buddhism, which Japanese culture developed still further. From the sixth century onward, several indigenous sects arose based on Indian teachings, notably Ch'an (Japanese, Zen), T'ien-t'ai (Japanese, Tendai), Chen-jen/Zhenren (Japanese, Shingon), Ching-t'u (Japanese, Jodo), and the native Japanese sect Nichiren.

Westerners are probably most familiar with Zen, the way of enlightenment by means of contemplation. Rinzai, the best known Zen school, uses puzzle statements, called koans (e.g., "what is the sound of one hand clapping?"), to break habitual patterns of thought and bring enlightenment suddenly. Soto Zen, by contrast, emphasizes "just sitting," to empty the mind and open up enlightenment.

The founder of T'ien-t'ai (Tendai), Chih-i (AD 538–97), sought to harmonize the seeming diversity of Mahayana by claiming the Lotus Sutra as the Buddha's final teaching. This "scripture" sets forth the principle of "skillful means," according to which the Buddha employed apparently contradictory "ways" of teaching in order to rescue persons from illusion. The entire universe is conceived as participating in the Buddha nature; consequently, one may seek liberation by any number of means. Medieval Tendai exercised enormous influence on the development of all branches of Buddhism in Japan.

Chen-jen/Zhenren (Shingon) has roots in Indian tantrism (Chen-jen translates the Sanskrit word *mantra*), offering initiates a "shortcut" to enlightenment by way of esoteric prayers, rituals, symbols, and practices. Chen-jen established itself in Japan as Shingon-shu (true word sect) by adapting elements of traditional Shinto, especially linking Shinto deities with manifestations of the Buddha. (Shingon identifies the universe itself with the body of the Supreme Buddha, Vairocana.)

The most popular form of Buddhism in East Asia—and for Christians, the most fascinating, by far—is that of Ching-t'u (Jodo, or "pure land") centered on the Buddha Amitabha (Japanese: Amida, "infinite light"), also known as Amitayus (infinite life). According to tradition, Amida was originally a king (later the bodhisattva dharmakara), who renounced his kingdom to pursue buddhahood. Over eons of time (*kalpas*) spent in practice, he was enabled to integrate all the excellences he had seen into a single "pure land" called *sukhavati* over which he presides. Owing to his extraordinary merit, he now provides rebirth into the pure land for those who make a karmic connection to him, primarily through ritual recitation of his name (*nembutsu*). Despite parallels with Christian faith, Jodo notably lacks any doctrine of sin or atonement.

An uncharacteristically exclusivist Mahayana tradition is Nichiren, named for its founder, a thirteenth-century Japanese priest with the power of a prophet. Trained in Tendai, Nichiren nevertheless severely restricted worship forms and insisted on repetition of the sacred formula (*daimoku*)—"Hail to the Lotus Sutra!"—as the means of actualizing unity with the Buddha. Through its lay-led subsect, Soka Gakkai, Nichiren Buddhism has exercised enormous political influence in Japan since the 1960s.

Tibetan Buddhism. Though patronized by kings and defined intellectually by Mahayana scholars, Tibetan Buddhism emerged as a distinctive Buddhist tradition under the influence of a Indian tantric adept named Padmasambhava in the eighth century ("first diffusion"). Like Chen-jen Tibetan tantrism encompasses a wide range of esoteric practices, including divination, magic, shamanism, radical yogic exercises, and eroticism, typically drawn from tantric texts and calculated to bring about moksha (liberation). The Tibetan Tripitaka consists of most of the same text found in the Pali Tripitaka, Mahayana sutras, tantras, and a large collection of commentaries, laudatory verses, and ritual texts. Tibetan Buddhism emphasizes the guru, who instructs pupils in the practice (*sadhana*) of tantras, many of which incorporate visualizations for gaining wisdom and power. Visualizations range from "seeing" certain Buddhas or bodhisattvas to "becoming" the body of a Buddha to experiencing primordial bliss through sexual union or profound insight. The diversity of the tantras and the special role of the master have produced countless tantric traditions.

Tibetan Buddhism remains formally tied to Mahayana through the use of sutras and the philosophy of the Madhyamaka and Yogacara schools. After the thirteenth century ("second diffusion" of Buddhism in Tibet), these orders developed doctrines of internal succession through a *tulku*, considered the reincarnation of a previous teacher. With the ascendancy of Gluk-pa, a *tulku* of that order, known as the Dalai Lama (ocean of wisdom), has served since 1612 as head of state in Tibet. Following the Chinese invasion of 1950 and the subsequent repression of Buddhist culture, the Dalai Lama has "ruled" in exile from India since 1959.

Buddhism in the West. In the wake of Alexander the Great, Greeks became aware of Buddhism, and at least one famously converted, and Marco Polo directly knew of it; however, Buddhism as a whole remained largely isolated from (and unknown in) the West until the nineteenth century. The effects of these contacts may be observed in the emergence of new religious groups (e.g.,

Theosophy), in literature (e.g., Emerson, Thoreau, the Transcendentalists) and psychology (e.g., Jung), in the study of "comparative religion," in the translation of Buddhist texts, and in the transplantation of Buddhism itself to the West, especially after World War II.

The American Religious Identity Survey (ARIS) places the number of Buddhists in 2004 at about 1.5 million, or 0.5 percent of the US population (roughly the same as for Muslims), an increase of about 170 percent since 1960. The BuddhaNet website (sponsored by the Buddha Dharma Education Association) lists Buddhist centers in every state and every Canadian province. The appeal of Buddhism to Westerners doubtless has much to do with its generally tolerant, inclusive culture, its emphasis on moral achievement over doctrinal adherence, and its promise of psychological wholeness. The political plight of Tibet and the notoriety of the Dalai Lama (who won the Nobel Peace Prize in 1989) have also helped create a favorable climate for Buddhism.

While most major traditions have migrated to the West, Zen Buddhism and Tibetan Buddhism certainly enjoy the widest currencies. First introduced by the Japanese *roshi* (master) Soyen Shaku at the World's Parliament of Religions in Chicago (1893), Zen gained widespread popularity through the writings of D. T. Suzuki (1870–1966). Several Tibetan lamas representing different sects were teaching in the West in the 1960s and 1970s.

Another prominent version of Western Buddhism is Soka Gakkai, introduced to the US in 1960 as Nichiren Shoshu, although Soka Gakkai International (SGI) broke with the priest-controlled sect in 1991. SGI claims almost ninety US centers and twelve million adherents worldwide, but does not publish US membership statistics.

Organized in 1914, Pure Land Buddhism, known in the US as the Buddhist Churches of America (BCA), observes Sunday congregational worship and has adopted other "Christian" practices. The BCA claims over one hundred "temples, branch temples, fellowships and groups" and operates a ministry school in Berkeley, California, but membership (mostly ethnic Japanese) has declined precipitously in recent years.

See also BUDDHA, HISTORICAL PERSON OF; BUDDHA, NAMES OF; BUDDHA, NINE ATTRIBUTES OF; BUDDHA, THREE BODIES OF; CHEN-JEN/ZHENREN; MAHAYANA BUDDHISM; NICHIREN SHOSHU; SHIN BUDDHISM; SOKA GAKKAI; THERAVADA BUDDHISM; TIBETAN BUDDHISM; ZEN BUDDHISM

Bibliography. D. Bentley-Taylor and C. B. Offner, "Buddhism," in *The World's Religions*, edited by Norman Anderson; D. Burnett, *The Spirit of Buddhism: A Christian Perspective on Buddhist Thought*; S. Collins, *Selfless Persons: Imagery and Thought in Theravada Buddhism*; E. Conze, *Buddhist Wisdom Books*; M. Eliade, *A History of Religious Ideas*; R. Gethin, *The Foundations of Buddhism*; D. Keown, *Buddhism: A Very Short Introduction*; R. C. Lester, "Buddhism: The Path to Nirvana," in *Religious Traditions of the World*, edited by H. B. Earhart; J. B. Noss, *Man's Religions*; R. N. Robinson, W. L. Johnson, and T. Bhikku, *Buddhist Religions*; D. T. Suzuki, *Introduction to Zen Buddhism*; J. I. Yamamoto, *Buddhism, Taoism & Other Far Eastern Religions*; R. Zacharias, *The Lotus and the Cross: Jesus Talks with Buddha*.

C. R. Wells

BUDDHIST CHURCHES OF AMERICA. The Buddhist Churches of America (BCA) is a Shin Buddhist organization (i.e., Jodo Shinshu) affiliated with the Nishi Hongwan-ji sect in Japan. The BCA claims to be the oldest Buddhist organization in America. It is headquartered in San Francisco, having been organized to serve the religious needs of the Japanese immigrants who congregated in the city during the 1800s. It was originally called the Buddhist Missions of North America but changed to its current name in 1944 in an effort to curb hostility and gain acceptance in

American society. The BCA fought for and gained the right to ordain Buddhist chaplains in the US military in 1987.

See also BUDDHISM; SHIN BUDDHISM

Bibliography. Buddhist Churches of America home page, http://buddhistchurchesofamerica.org/home/.

R. L. Drouhard

BUDDHIST SCRIPTURES. Buddhist scriptures are extensive and complex and vary according to different schools of Buddhism. The earliest collection of scriptures, and the only one considered canonical by the Theravada school, is the Pali Canon, or Tripitaka, a body of literature many times larger than the Bible. Passed down orally for four hundred years, it was committed to writing in the first century BC. The term Tripitaka means "three baskets," and the collection is so called because of its three major divisions: Vinaya Pitaka, Sutra Pitaka, and Abhidharma Pitaka. The Vinaya (Book of Discipline) contains the rules that regulate the lives of the monks and nuns. The Sutra (Book of Discourses) contains the sermons and dialogues of the Buddha, the subject matter of which focuses primarily on key Buddhist doctrines such as the Four Noble Truths and the Eightfold Path. In addition, the Sutra contains the Jataka, stories of the Buddha's previous lives. The Abhidharma (Book of Higher Teachings) is a collection of seven philosophical treatises explaining, analyzing, and defending Buddhist metaphysics and psychology.

Mahayana Buddhists have adopted many other writings in addition to the Pali Canon that are considered equally authoritative. The earliest and most widely accepted Mahayana works are the Prajna Paramita Sutras (Teachings on perfect wisdom), composed between 100 BC and AD 500. The main subject of these sutras is the concept of *sunyata* (emptiness), the idea that the phenomenal world of our experience is empty or unreal. Summaries of the teachings in these lengthy works are found in the famous Diamond Sutra and Heart Sutra.

One of the most popular and important of Mahayana scriptures is the Lotus Sutra (ca. AD 200). This sutra teaches the possibility of universal liberation. Depending on each person's individual capacities and station in life, he or she may have access to a path that leads to nirvana. Such paths include traditional means such as meditation but also include works of charity, the cultivation of virtues like patience, the worship of Buddha, memorizing scripture, and so on. The Lotus Sutra also teaches that the Buddha is eternal and omniscient, and it expounds the key Mahayana doctrine of the bodhisattva.

Another popular Mahayana text is the Vimalakirti-nirdesa Sutra (Teachings of Vimalakirti), which recounts the story of the Mahayana layman Vimalakirti, who shames Theravada monks with his superior wisdom. This sutra had substantial influence on the development of Zen Buddhism. Pure Land Buddhism, a Mahayana school dedicated to the Buddha Amitabha, produced the two Pure Land Sutras (ca. AD 200), which describe the "pure land" or paradise promised to the faithful. The Lankavatara Sutra (ca. AD 300) teaches that everything that exists is the manifestation of mind. The Vajrayana or Tantric school added to the Mahayana collections with tantras and accompanying scriptures, for example, as well as the well-known Tibetan Book of the Dead.

See also BUDDHISM; LOTUS SUTRA; MAHAYANA BUDDHISM; PALI CANON; THERAVADA BUDDHISM; TRIPITAKA

Bibliography. K. K. S. Ch'en, *Buddhism: The Light of Asia*; C. Ericker, *Buddhism*; C. S. Prebish, ed., *Buddhism: A Modern Perspective*.

S. B. Cowan

BUTSU-DAN. A *butsu-dan* is a shrine or altar that is a central feature of many Buddhist monasteries, temples, and homes in Japan. Structurally, a butsu-dan consists of a wooden cabinet with doors that are alternately closed (to safeguard the cabinet's contents) and opened (to display the ritual objects during religious ceremonies). Items commonly found in a butsu-dan include iconic images (typically pictures or statues of Buddhas or bodhisattvas), memorial tablets for deceased ancestors (*ihai*), a register of family memorials, scrolls, offering cups or trays for water, rice (*buppan*), fruit, cakes, other food items, platforms on which the offering vessels are placed, flowers, candles, an incense burner, and bells (often rung while reciting).

Use of a butsu-dan was not always a part of Buddhist ceremonial practice. In the early ninth century, many Japanese families converted rooms in their homes into private Buddhist sanctuaries; it was at this time that the word *butsu-dan* (*butsu* = Buddha; *dan* = elevated pedestal) became common currency in Japan. During the Tokugawa Shogunate (1603–1868), the spread of Christianity was curbed in part by requiring every Japanese family to possess a butsu-dan. Household butsu-dans remain fairly common in Japanese society.

See also BUDDHISM; NICHIREN SHOSHU; PURE LAND BUDDHISM

Bibliography. R. Causton, *The Buddha in Daily Life: An Introduction to the Buddhism of Nichiren Daishonin*; J. Powers, *A Concise Encyclopedia of Buddhism*; H. Yun, *The Lion's Roar: Actualizing Buddhism in Daily Life and Building the Pure Land in Our Midst.*

J. Bjornstad

CASTE. Derived from the Portuguese word *casta* (meaning "color" or "race"), the English term *caste* was coined by British colonizers to designate the various social classes they observed in India. Yet the origin and function of the caste system is a matter of extensive debate among scholars of Indian religion and culture. Some such scholars believe that the Indo-Iranian (Aryan) conquerors of northwest India (who invaded ca. 1500 BC) structured their social life in accordance with a hierarchy of three people-groups—the Brahmins (priests), the Ksatriya (warriors), and the Vaisya (artisans and farmers)—and that the non-Aryan peoples of this then-occupied region were deemed a fourth social class, the Shudra. In any event, something akin to the Aryan system of social organization is found in the "Purusha Hymn" of the Rig Veda, wherein these four classes of persons are portrayed as having their divinely ordained genesis in the primeval sacrifice of the Cosmic Man. In light of the presumed authority of this narrative for patterning social order, many devout Hindus were permitted to engage only in those activities that were (allegedly) fitting for members of their particular class. In this scheme of things, each class (*varna*) was thought to have its own set of social-religious obligations (*dharma*) that must be fulfilled by its members. The widespread acceptance of the doctrine that people are reborn in accordance with the karma of their social group—and thus are suited to carry out the unique functions of that class—has served to reinforce the caste system. Brahmins are thought to possess the capacity of sacred knowledge and instruction; Ksatriyas, to possess skill in weaponry and governance; Vaisyas, to have aptitute for agriculture and commerce; and Sudras, to be suited for serving the other three classes. A fifth social group, the outcastes (untouchables), emerged later in India's history and was regarded as existing outside the caste system altogether; its members were consigned to performing ritually polluting tasks like disposing of corpses and were not allowed to live close to people of other castes.

Even though since its establishment in 1950 India's constitution has made it illegal to discriminate based on caste, many Hindus continue to identify themselves as members of a particular caste. In many cases, this is because they are still informally compelled to abide by the rules of their caste-related birth group (*jati*), which is confined to a certain geographical region and maintains distinctive traditions. The fact that the concept of caste still strongly influences the attitudes and practices of many Hindus in contemporary India is not difficult to demonstrate. Many traditional and/or rural communities still forbid their members to marry someone of a different caste. The widespread existence of caste-based organizations perpetuates the political ramifications of the caste system. Caste continues to play an important role during elections, when people frequently vote based wholly or in part on considerations of caste. Most people in higher castes are displeased by government measures that have undermined the social advantages they enjoyed previously. Students in educational institutions and workplace environments often still associate with others primarily on the basis of caste. Persisting conflicts between members of different castes continue to engender deep hostility and in some cases have resulted in violence and killings.

See also BRAHMA; DHARMA; HINDUISM

Bibliography. J. N. Bhattacharya, *Hindu Castes and Sects: An Exposition of the Origin of the Hindu Caste System*; N. B. Dirks, *Castes of Mind: Colonialism and the Making of Modern India*; L. Dumont, *Homo Hierarchicus: The Caste System and Its Implications*, rev. ed.; D. Gupta, *Interrogating Caste: Understanding Hierarchy and Difference in Indian Society*; B. K. Smith, *Classifying the Universe: The Ancient Indian Varna System and the Origins of Caste*.

H. W. House

CELESTIAL KINGDOM. The celestial kingdom is the highest of the three heavenly kingdoms according to the doctrine of the Church of Jesus Christ of Latter-day Saints (LDS Church, or Mormonism). Within the celestial kingdom are three more "degrees," the highest of which is called the "church of the firstborn." According to the Doctrine and Covenants, married couples who have been sealed for time and eternity in a Mormon temple and who achieve this degree in the afterlife receive exaltation or godhood. "Then shall they be gods, because they have no end; therefore shall they be from everlasting to everlasting, because they continue; then shall they be above all, because all things are subject unto them. Then shall they be gods, because they have all power, and the angels are subject unto them" (D&C 132:20).

Inhabitants of this kingdom will dwell with God the Father and Jesus Christ and will inherit "thrones, kingdoms, principalities, and powers." With exaltation comes the "power of eternal increase," which is the ability to procreate throughout eternity.

Joseph Smith Jr. claimed, "Except a man and his wife enter into an everlasting covenant and be married for eternity, while in this probation, by the power and authority of the Holy Priesthood, they will cease to increase when they die; that is, they will not have any children after the resurrection" (300–301).

According to Mormon apostle Bruce McConkie, "An inheritance in this glorious kingdom is gained by complete obedience to gospel or celestial law. . . . By devotion and faithfulness, by enduring to the end in righteousness and obedience, it is then possible to merit a celestial reward" (116).

Sixteenth LDS president Thomas S. Monson stated earlier in his career, "It is the celestial glory which we seek. It is in the presence of God we desire to dwell. It is a forever family in which we want membership. Such blessings must be earned" (53).

See also CHURCH OF JESUS CHRIST OF LATTER-DAY SAINTS

Bibliography. D. H. Ludlow, ed., *Encyclopedia of Mormonism*, 4 vols; B. R. McConkie, *Mormon Doctrine*; Thomas S. Monson, "An Invitation to Exaltation," *Ensign*; Joseph Smith Jr., *Teachings of the Prophet Joseph Smith*, edited by Joseph Fielding Smith.

W. McKeever

CELESTIAL MARRIAGE. A key belief and practice in the Church of Jesus Christ of Latter-day Saints (LDS Church, or Mormonism) is celestial marriage, which is entered into by means of a sacred wedding ceremony that is said to unite a Mormon husband and wife in a potentially eternal covenant bond. It involves a solemn promise the man and the woman make to each other and to God and is thought to be witnessed by angels. According to the LDS Church, in order for a wedding ceremony to result in a valid celestial marriage, it must be performed by an LDS official who possesses the priestly authority to invoke covenants, and it must take place in an LDS temple. When all the prerequisite conditions are met, such marriages are said to be sealed by the Holy Spirit, such that if the couple persevere in fulfilling their wedding vows, they will inherit the celestial kingdom after the resurrection. Thus celestial wedding ceremonies omit the traditional phrase "till death do us part," since this expression presupposes (erroneously, in the LDS view) that physical death dissolves the covenant of marriage. The divorce rate among Mormon couples who have undergone celestial marriage is very low. Good Mormons who, through no fault of their own, fail to get married in an LDS temple in this life are told that they will be given a postmortem opportunity for celestial marriage.

In addition to the blessings the spouses are thought to obtain, celestial marriage provides an LDS Church–sanctioned means of procreation, allegedly providing "mortal bodies" that function as vessels for preexisting, disembodied spirit children. LDS eschatology asserts that after death, worthy Mormons will be reunited with their "heavenly parents," forming one eternal, glorified, extended family. Moreover, the doctrine of celestial marriage plays a central role in the soteriology of the LDS Church.

Whereas to contemporary Mormons celestial marriage merely means being sealed in eternal marriage in an LDS temple, to nineteenth-century Mormons celestial marriage was virtually synonymous with plural marriage. Even many Mormon historians concede that celestial marriage and plural marriage were inseparable concepts in the minds of Utah Mormons during the late 1800s. According to numerous prominent Mormons such as Heber C. Kimball and Orson Pratt, the doctrine of plural marriage was considered equivalent to Mormonism, and to do away with it constituted a direct blow to the very core of Mormon restorationist theology. It is beyond dispute that Joseph Smith Jr. endorsed and practiced plural marriage long before he received the revelation on it from God that eventually became chapter 132 in the Doctrine and Covenants.

Because plural marriage was illegal in the US, the Utah Territory was barred from applying for statehood. Furthermore, in 1862 the Morrill Act made polygamy illegal in US territories, pitting the Church of Jesus Christ of Latter-day Saints against the federal government. After several confrontations with federal authorities (particularly a series of defeats at the US Supreme Court), the Mormon church was all but forced to change its stance on polygamy. In 1890 Wilford Woodruff (the fourth president of the LDS Church) announced the termination of plural marriage and stated that practitioners would be excommunicated. The announcement was made formally in a 510-word document, eventually reduced to 356 words, known as "the Manifesto." However, plural marriages continued to be performed, and in 1904 the church banned the practice once and for all. In response to the doctrinal shift on marriage, LDS leaders had to redefine celestial marriage. Evidence of this switch can be seen in the way later statements contrasted with the declarations of Brigham Young (1801–77). He considered the rejection of the doctrine of polygamy tantamount to apostasy and considered plural marriage a requirement for exaltation to godhood. This is considerably different from the statement of LDS president Heber J. Grant (1856–1945) that *celestial marriage* and *plural marriage* are not synonymous terms. Today several LDS splinter groups—most prominently, the Fundamentalist Church of Jesus Christ of Latter-day Saints—maintain that Young taught correctly on this issue. Consequently they practice polygamy illegally.

The problem the LDS Church faces today regarding the demise of polygamy is the historical theology of the practice. There is no doubt that the early Mormon leaders considered it to be a nonnegotiable doctrine, a significant part of the restored gospel that had been lost in the Great Apostasy. If the doctrine was to be abandoned, then the church would essentially be compromising the very principles it was allegedly restored to reinstitute.

See also CHURCH OF JESUS CHRIST OF LATTER-DAY SAINTS; PLURAL MARRIAGE, MORMON TEACHING AND HISTORY OF

Bibliography. *Achieving a Celestial Marriage*; D. E. Brinley, *Together Forever: Gospel Perspectives for Marriage and Family*; H. B. Brown, *You and Your Marriage*; T. M. Burton, *God's Greatest Gift*; B. R. McConkie, "The Eternal Family Concept," in *Genealogical Devotional Addresses of the Second Annual Priesthood Genealogical Research Seminar*; Mormonism Research Ministry, "Redefining Celestial Marriage," http://www.mrm.org/redefining-celestial-marriage; G. G. Taylor, *Sacred Union: Scriptural Keys to a Celestial Marriage*.

S. J. Rost

CHAKRAS. Chakra is a Sanskrit word that means "wheel" or "circle." Chakras are alleged to be centers or concentrations of life energy (*prana, kundalini*) in the human energy body and are said to integrate physical, emotional, psychological, and spiritual (psychic) facts of the human into a coherent whole. There are said to be seven major chakras running from the genital area (root chakra) up along the center of the body, to the top of the head (crown chakra).

The theory was developed within Hinduism, but it also plays a role in Buddhism, especially Vajrayana Buddhism; in various practices of yoga, including hatha and kundalini; and in various expressions of New Age alternative "medical" techniques (having to do with the flow of *chi* energy).

Some practitioners correlate chakras to physical body parts such as the belly, solar plexus, heart, and throat, which regulate all physiological functions. Also, they claim that the third-eye chakra and the crown chakra not only regulate the eyes, brain, and pituitary gland but also, especially, can awaken and control the psychic functions.

Another dimension of belief is that the imprint of every emotionally significant event in this life and past lives is energetically recorded in the chakras. One current "medical intuitive" (i.e., psychic), Carolyn Myss, claims to be able to read people's auras and chakras and can pick up past trauma events and experiences that affect a person's physical health.

Various spiritual techniques are said to produce effects ranging from physical healing to spiritual enlightenment. The techniques range from meditation to yoga postures to massage to even a practice of therapeutic touch, where the practitioner merely passes his or her hands five inches above the physical body.

There is no scientific basis for this subjective human energy field and chakra deposits.

See also BUDDHISM; HINDUISM; KUNDALINI

Bibliography. J. Ankerberg and J. Weldon, *Encyclopedia of New Age Beliefs*; "Shambhala," in *The Encyclopedia of Eastern Philosophy and Religion*, edited by S. Schumacher and G. Woerner.

C. Branch

CHALCEDONIAN CONTROVERSY. The Chalcedonian controversy, opening with the statements of Apollinaris of Laodicea (ca. AD 310–90) and formally closing at the Council of Chalcedon in 451, arose from this question: How does Christ's divine nature, which is immutable and eternal, relate to his human nature? The controversy involved three parties: in the East, the bishoprics of Alexandria (Egypt) and Antioch (in modern Turkey), and the Western church seated in Rome.

Background to the Controversy. For several decades, due to political and ecclesiastical rivalries, the theological schools in Alexandria and Antioch disputed over the person and nature of Christ. The Alexandrians, such as Apollinaris, Cyril, Eutyches, and Dioscorus, sought to emphasize Christ's divinity, often

113

at the expense of his humanity. Apollinaris's position was that Christ had a human body, but in place of a human soul, Christ possessed the divine Logos. Thus Christ had a divine intelligence and soul with enough of a human nature to communicate with humanity comprehensibly. The Antiochenes, such as Theodore of Mopsuestia, Nestorius, and Flavian, maintained that Christ was fully divine but was also fully human. They attempted to distinguish very clearly between the divine and the human nature of Christ. This is seen in Theodore's position, which was that Christ had two natures, a human one and a divine one.

In an attempt to clarify this position, Nestorius critiqued the notion of Mary as *theotokos*, or "bearer of God," advocating that she instead be called *christotokos*, or "bearer of Christ." Mary gave birth not to God but rather to the incarnate Christ. Further, some aspects of Christ may be taken to emphasize his humanity, and others, his divinity. The effort here was to avoid the temptation to overcorrect Arianism by shifting too heavily from Christ's humanity toward his divinity. Nestorius was charged with affirming that there were two persons and two natures in Christ, though he contended that he believed that Jesus was one person (*prosōpon*) but not one *hypostasis* (because he understood *hypostasis* to mean "nature").

A Failed Effort to Come Together. An ecumenical council was called by Emperors Valentinian III and Theodosius II and was held at Ephesus in 431. This council was convened in order to bring the Alexandrians and the Antiochenes together, but it drove them further apart. The two sides were unwilling to meet in the same location, and each group excommunicated the other. Theodosius sided with the Alexandrians and banished Nestorius.

Not long after Ephesus, Eutyches of Constantinople (ca. 378–ca. 452) sought to underscore the Alexandrian position by affirming that Christ possessed one nature, which was neither human nor divine but a *tertium quid*, a third thing. As a result, Eutyches was condemned by the patriarch of Constantinople, Flavian. However, due to Eutyches's popularity and influence, Theodosius, as well as the bishop of Alexandria, refused to enforce Flavian's decision.

The controversy entered into a new phase when Flavian appealed to Leo I of Rome for support. Leo's response, known as his *Tome*, became the heart of the resolution to the controversy. He wrote that Christ was a single person who had two natures. In other words, Jesus was God the Word, one person. Still, on taking flesh, he took on all that defines humanity, save sin, without leaving aside who he was as God. As Mark Noll has observed, "Leo kept together distinctiveness of natures along with unity of person" (75). Despite Leo's considerable influence being thrown into the controversy, the arguments over Christ's makeup threatened to tear the church apart.

In 449 Theodosius called the Second Council of Ephesus, which was attended by 130 bishops, notably excepting Leo, who sent a delegation with his *Tome*. The emperor decided to deny the vote to any bishop who had banished Eutyches earlier. Because of this, the embattled bishop received almost unanimous support. In fact, Flavian and a number of other prominent bishops were themselves deposed. Instead of bringing the church together, the decisions of the Second Council of Ephesus not only failed to bring unity but brought condemnation from Leo, who dubbed the council "Latrocinium" (council of robbers).

The Council of Chalcedon's Decision. Pope Leo called for another council, but the emperor refused, considering the matter decided. However, Theodosius died after being thrown from his horse in 450. His successor, Marcian, was a supporter of both Leo and Flavian (who had subsequently died) and called together another council at Chalcedon, this time to resolve the controversy decisively. The council was attended by about 370 bishops, although Leo again did not attend but sent delegates and his *Tome*. Although Marcian wanted the council to formulate a new creed, the bishops argued that Leo's *Tome* was sufficient to end the debate. Marican then asked the bishops to sign their agreement with Leo's statement, but 13 Egyptian bishops refused. As a result the council decided to compose a new confession.

The Chalcedonian Formulation, given in October 451, was meant to answer the heresies of Arianism, Apollinarianism, Nestorianism, and Eutychianism. That is, we find in Christ one person and two natures, divine and human, indivisible and comprehensible. The Western church was entirely satisfied with the formulation, but some elements in Eastern Christianity continue to reject it to this day.

Their concern centers on the statements that the Son "is to be acknowledged in two natures" and that "the distinction between natures was never abolished by their union, but rather the character proper to each of the two natures was preserved as they came together in one person and one hypostasis." Non-Chalcedonians argue that these statements went against Cyril's position and that they in fact embrace Nestorianism. Further, they object to Leo's assertion of primacy and authority over the council.

See also ARIANISM; CHRIST, NATURES AND ATTRIBUTES OF; EASTERN ORTHODOXY; ROMAN CATHOLICISM

Bibliography. J. L. Gonzalez, *The Story of Christianity*, vol. 1, *The Early Church to the Dawn of the Reformation*; T. Lane, *A Concise History of Christian Thought*, rev. ed.; M. A. Noll, *Turning Points: Decisive Moments in the History of Christianity*; W. Walker et al., *A History of the Christian Church*, 4th ed.

J. D. Wilsey and H. W. House

CHAN-KHONG/ZHENKONG. *Chan-khong* means "true emptiness" or "nothingness" and refers to the central concept within Zen Buddhist metaphysics. According to this doctrine, all phenomenal things are ultimately "empty" or unreal because every seemingly individual thing originated along with everything else as "part" of an ontologically indissoluble, unified reality. Because all things arose interdependently, it is futile for people to attempt to define or conceive of things as independent entities; purported distinctions between objects in the world result from erroneous perception and a lack of knowledge concerning their true nature.

See also ZEN BUDDHISM

Bibliography. M. H. Kohn, *The Shambhala Dictionary of Buddhism and Zen*; D. T. Suzuki, *Manual of Zen Buddhism*.

M. Power

CHANUKAH. *See* HANUKKAH (or CHANUKAH), FEAST OF

CHELA. A *chela* (Sanskrit, "student" or "disciple") is a person who enters into a long-term, formal relationship with a guru in order to achieve enlightenment and liberation. In many Eastern religions and Western esoteric traditions, the relationship between the guru and the chela is considered essential for properly transmitting sacred teaching and developing spiritual insight. In various forms, this arrangement is found in many schools of Hinduism (including Advaita Vedanta, bhakti, and tantra), sects of Buddhism (including Theravada, Vajrayana, and Zen), Sikhism, Theosophy, and Niscience. The degree of submission (to the authority of the guru) expected of the chela varies considerably from one tradition to another, ranging from fanatical devotion and unquestioning obedience to merely exhibiting great (but not uncritical) respect. Always the chela is expected to demonstrate appropriate humility and a firm commitment to undertaking a rigorous spiritual path. It has been increasingly recognized that the nature of the guru-chela relationship lends itself to the potential for abuse by the guru. Over the past several decades, numerous high-profile cases have emerged in which fraudulent gurus have used their position of power and influence to abuse their chelas, physically, emotionally, sexually, and/or financially. Prominent gurus such as the Dalai Lama have condemned such behavior and called for greater transparency and mutuality in guru-chela relationships.

See also ADVAITA; BHAKTI YOGA; BUDDHISM; GURU; HINDUISM; SIKHISM; TANTRA; THERAVADA BUDDHISM; VAJRAYANA BUDDHISM; VEDANTA; ZEN BUDDHISM

Bibliography. Swami Bhaskarananda, *The Essentials of Hinduism: A Comprehensive Overview of the World's Oldest Religion*, 2nd ed.; A. R. Colton and J. Murro, *The Pelican and the Chela: The Teacher-Student Relationship in the Spiritual Life*; H. Graat, "The Chela Path," *Theosophy World*; S. McLeod, "The Benefits and Pitfalls of the Teacher-Meditator Relationship," *Contemporary Buddhism*; El Morya, *The Chela and the Path: Meeting the Challenge of Life in the Twentieth Century*.

J. Bjornstad

CHEN-JEN/ZHENREN. In Taoism, a *chen-jen* (Chinese, "realized man") is a spiritual master whose attunement to the Tao is so perfect that he has become immortal, attaining a godlike status. Such a man is thought to possess an inexhaustible reservoir of spiritual power and a (nonmoral) purity that is likened to that of gold. Although in philosophical Taoism a chen-jen is viewed primarily as someone who has achieved mystical union with the Tao by means of contemplation, in popular, religious Taoism it is commonly believed that such persons are powerful sorcerers with abilities such as the power to levitate, heal, and transform common metals into precious stones.

See also TAOISM/DAOISM

Bibliography. L. Kohn, *Cosmos and Community: The Ethical Dimension of Daoism*; F. Pregadio, *Great Clarity: Daoism and Alchemy in Early Medieval China*; H. Welch, *Taoism: The Parting of the Way*.

M. Power

CHINMAYA MISSION. Chinmaya Mission is a Hindu religious organization that advocates the doctrines and practices of Advaita Vedanta. Administered by the Central Chinmaya Mission Trust, based in Mumbai, India, Chinmaya Mission was founded in India in 1953 by devotees of Swami Chinmayananda (1916–93). Prior to his work with Chinmaya Mission, Chinmayananda was a disciple of Swami Sivananda Saraswati (1887–1963) and Swami Tapovan Maharaj (1889–1957) and was instrumental in the establishment (in 1964) of Vishva Hindu Parishad, an international organization for the advancement of Hinduism. In the late 1960s, Chinmayananda came to the US, and by 1975 Chinmaya Mission West was established in Langhorne, Pennsylvania. Chinmaya Mission offers printed and online publications, audio and video materials, courses, lectures, seminars, and workshops relating to the study and practice of Chinmayananda's version of Advaita Vedanta, claiming that those who follow its precepts will achieve increased efficiency, personal growth and contentment, and the ability to live in harmony with others. The group also seeks to reinvigorate Indian culture by means of an array of institutes, projects, and social services, including schools, camps, medical clinics, homeless shelters, soup kitchens, disaster relief teams, a rural development center, and programs instructing in subjects ranging from Sanskrit to business management to classical Indian dance and music. Chinmaya Mission also boasts fifteen ashrams (fourteen in India and one in California) and a network of fifty-five Vedanta temples, twenty-nine of which are located in India and the remainder of which can be found in Canada, France, Hong Kong, Indonesia, Mauritius, Singapore, and several other locations worldwide. Currently Chinmaya Mission is led by Swami Tejomayananda (b. 1950), the spiritual head of more than three hundred Chinmaya Mission centers globally, including locations in the US, India, Sri Lanka, Great Britain, Australia, and Kenya. The doctrine espoused by Chinmaya Mission essentially is that of historic Advaita Vedanta, though in a somewhat modified and popularized form. In particular, the organization's literature emphasizes that truth lies within and that there is only one infinite reality, which transcends race, class, gender, nationality, and creed. The nature of this infinite reality is said to be pure consciousness; it is conceived as being both the universe and the immortal self (Atman).

See also ADVAITA; CHINMAYANANDA, SWAMI; HINDUISM; VEDANTA

Bibliography. Central Chinmaya Mission Trust home page, http://www.chinmayamission.com/; Chinmaya Mission, Chinmaya Mission West home page, http://chinmayamissionwest.com/; S. Chinmayananda, *Meditation and Life*; Chinmayananda, *Self-Unfoldment*; N. Patchen, *Journey of a Master: Swami Chinmayananda, the Man, the Path, the Teaching*.

H. W. House

CHINMAYANANDA, SWAMI. Swami Chinmayananda (born Balakrishna Menon on May 8, 1916) was raised in an aristocratic family in Ernakulam, India. After studying at Madras University and Lucknow University, in 1942 he joined the Indian independence movement and subsequently was imprisoned. During his time in prison, he contracted typhus fever and was released. In 1945, he moved to Delhi, where he wrote for the *National Herald* newspaper. Discontented with his life, Balakrishna began an investigation of Advaita Vedanta that culminated in his initiation, in February 1949, into the order of *sannyasa* under Sivananda

Saraswati Mahaaraj (1887–1963). It was at this time that he took the spiritual name Swami Chinmayananda. Then in 1951, while meditating on the banks of the Ganges River, Chinmayananda became convinced that his mission in life was to promote the philosophy and spirituality of Advaita Vedanta on a global scale. During the 1950s, he founded the Sandeepany Sadhanalaya (Academy of Knowledge) in Bombay and founded Tapovan Kuti (a training and meditation center) in the Himalayas. By the late 1950s, Chinmayananda was considered (in India) to be a leading authority on the Bhagavad Gita and the Upanishads. He began giving lectures outside India during the 1960s, and by 1985 numerous Chinmaya Mission centers had been established worldwide. When he began giving public lectures about the Vedas, many traditional Hindu teachers greatly resented that he was instructing the masses on such topics, viewing him as a distasteful popularizer. In 1992 Chinmayananda addressed the United Nations on the subject "planet in crisis." The following year he was chosen to represent Hinduism at the Centennial Conference of the Parliament of World Religions in Chicago and was honored at a major conference of religious leaders in Washington, DC, for his service to humanity. Chinmayananda died in San Diego on August 3, 1993.

Chinmayananda taught that there exists a Supreme Consciousness that created and sustains the world yet is the sole ultimate reality. This Supreme Consciousness is said to be ubiquitous, within every created thing, the ground of all phenomena, and the source from which have emerged every type of appearance and every name given to phenomenal things. The Supreme Consciousness can be recognized in and through all the various forms of the created world, though it is acknowledged that some created things provide a clearer reflection of the Supreme Consciousness than others. In this way, Chinmayananda attempted to steer a course between unqualified monism and metaphysical dualism. This "middle way" ontology was important in Chinmayananda's teaching because it allowed him to espouse a view of reality that was in keeping with the mainstream of historical Hinduism while addressing many of the practical concerns foremost in the minds of American consumers of Eastern religion. Indeed, the doctrines and practices promoted by Chinmayananda, though in a few cases slightly modified by his successors, continue to appeal to many Western practitioners of Hindu-based spirituality: as of early 2009 the organization Chinmaya Mission West had established forty-four active centers across North America.

See also CHINMAYA MISSION; HINDUISM; SANNYASA; VEDANTA

Bibliography. Chinmaya Mission, Chinmaya Mission West home page, http://chinmayamission west.com/; R. Krishnakumar, *Ageless Guru: The Inspirational Life of Swami Chinmayananda*; J. Masih, *The Role of Swami Chinmayananda in Revitalization of Hinduism and Reinterpretation of Christianity*; N. Patchen, *Journey of a Master: Swami Chinmayananda, the Man, the Path, the Teaching.*

H. W. House

CHINMOY, SRI. Sri Chinmoy (1931–2007) was born Chinmoy Kumar Ghose in East Bengal (now Bangladesh), the youngest of seven children. Orphaned at age twelve, he, with his siblings, joined the Sri Aurobindo Ashram, a spiritual community near Pondicherry, India. There he spent the next twenty years engaged in meditation, athletic training, and the writing of essays, poetry, and songs. In 1964 Chinmoy allegedly received a divine call to go to New York City, where he lectured, established meditation centers, and began publishing AUM Magazine. In 1967 he founded the first Sri Chinmoy Center, and within another year he had opened additional centers in upstate New York, Florida, and Puerto Rico. During the late 1960s,

Chinmoy's fame grew rapidly; he spoke at several Ivy League universities and in 1970 was appointed director of the United Nations Meditation Group by Secretary-General U Thant. In the mid-1970s, Chinmoy set up headquarters in Jamaica, New York, and began actively promoting his teachings as a means to the achievement of world peace. He subsequently met with several notable world leaders and dignitaries, including Pope Paul VI, Pope John Paul II, Mother Teresa, Mikhail Gorbachev, Nelson Mandela, and King Birendra of Nepal. Known for his showmanship, he pursued his mission by means of relatively innocuous forms such as poetry readings, musical concerts, and artistic displays but often engaged in well-orchestrated and much-hyped publicity events to garner media attention.

Beginning in 2001, he was plagued by repeated allegations of sexual misconduct and serious abuse of several former female disciples. These charges continued unabated for several years. They were particularly embarrassing for Chinmoy in that he publicly preached the necessity of strict celibacy for the attainment of spiritual maturity. Chinmoy died possessing an estate and assets exceeding $2 million.

Chinmoy's writings advocate a combination of yoga techniques, meditation, vegetarianism, celibacy, and civic involvement as means to union with God, whom he described as "Ever-Transcending Beyond" and "Inner Truth." Chinmoy believed aspiration to be the spiritual force behind all great achievements in history, asserting that by aspiring to transcend self-imposed limitations people can surpass their ordinary abilities and obtain genuine satisfaction. The Sri Chinmoy Center in New York City continues to serve as a meeting place for followers of Chinmoy's teachings and supports the efforts of the Sri Chinmoy Marathon Team. Chinmoy's disciples, who are said to number over three thousand worldwide, have established branch locations in more than forty countries.

See also AUROBINDO, SRI

Bibliography. J. T. Areddy, "Guru Thrills Devotees by Lifting Heavy Objects, Playing 25 Instruments," *Wall Street Journal*; Sri Chinmoy, *Beyond Within: A Philosophy for the Inner Life*; Chinmoy, *God Is . . .: Selected Writings of Sri Chinmoy*; Chinmoy, *The Wisdom of Sri Chinmoy*; Sri Chinmoy Centre, life of Sri Chinmoy home page, http://www.srichinmoy.org; Sri Chinmoy Centre, Sri Chinmoy Library website, http://www.sri chinmoylibrary.com.

H. W. House

CHRIST, NATURES AND ATTRIBUTES OF. Mainstream Christianity has progressed in its comprehension of Christ's natures and attributes not so much through private, theological speculation as through communal rejection of errors that at least appeared to threaten the substance of the Christian faith. It seems advisable, therefore, to present the Christian consensus on these subjects in the form of a chronological survey of the church's response to christological errors. This article, therefore, consists of an overview of orthodox Christianity's responses to the following errors: Arianism, Nestorianism, Monophysitism, and Monothelitism.

Arianism. Arius (ca. 250–336), a priest of Alexandria, rendered himself notorious in the early fourth century by denying the full deity of Jesus Christ. According to Arius, Christ was not God but a demigod of sorts: the greatest of God's creatures and yet merely a creature. In defense of Arius, one might note that a multitude of biblical texts, at first glance, appear to support the conclusion that Jesus Christ was not God. One reads in Psalm 121:4, for example, that "he who watches over Israel will neither slumber nor sleep," yet according to Mark 4:38 (par Matt. 8:24), Jesus was, at one point, "sleeping on a cushion." Again, according to Malachi 3:6 and James 1:17, God never

changes, yet one reads in Luke 2:52, "Jesus grew in wisdom and stature." Scripture describes God as omnipresent (1 Kings 8:27; Ps. 139:7–10; Jer. 23:24), yet Jesus did not arrive in Bethany until Lazarus had been dead for four days (John 11:17). According to James 1:13, "God cannot be tempted by evil," yet Jesus was "tempted in every way, just as we are" (Heb. 4:15). God, according to 1 Timothy 1:17, is both immortal and invisible, yet Jesus's enemies both saw him and slew him on the cross.

Considerations such as these, which one could multiply ad nauseam, by no means prove that Scripture unambiguously portrays Jesus as subdivine. Indeed, the mainstream church of the fourth century considered the scriptural evidence in favor of Jesus's deity so overwhelming that, at the Council of Nicaea in AD 325, it decreed that Jesus was *homoousios*—that is, of the same substance—with the Father and anathematized anyone who thought otherwise. The church reached this conclusion through reflection on biblical texts such as John 1:1, 18; 20:28; Acts 20:28; Romans 9:5; Titus 2:13; Hebrews 1:8; and 2 Peter 1:1, in which Scripture explicitly refers to Jesus as God. Verses that ascribe divine attributes such as omniscience (John 16:30; 21:17; Col. 2:3), omnipresence (Eph. 1:23; Col. 1:17), existence before creation (John 1:1; 17:5; Col. 1:15–17; Heb. 1:10; Rev. 1:8, 17; 2:8), equality with God (John 5:18; Phil. 2:6), and even deity itself (Col. 2:9) likewise powerfully confirm the church's position. Scriptural texts that attribute divine functions such as creation (John 1:3, 10; Eph. 2:9; Col. 1:16; Heb. 1:2, 10), the conservation of the universe (Col. 1:17; Heb. 1:3), salvation (Matt. 1:21; Acts 5:31; Phil. 3:20; 2 Tim. 1:10; Titus 1:4; 2:13; 2 Pet. 1:11; 2:20; 1 John 4:14; cf. Isa. 43:11), the forgiveness of sins (Matt. 9:2; par Luke 7:48; Acts 5:31; Col. 3:13), and, indeed, all functions of the Father (John 5:19) to Jesus similarly corroborate the church's confession that Christ was God.

The authors of the New Testament substantiated the church's position, moreover, by applying to Christ Old Testament passages that in their original contexts unmistakably refer to God; compare, for example, Deuteronomy 6:4 with 1 Corinthians 8:6; Psalm 68:18 with Ephesians 4:8; Isaiah 8:14 with Romans 9:33a; Isaiah 28:16 with Romans 9:33b and 10:11; Isaiah 45:23 with Romans 14:11 and Philippians 2:10; and Joel 2:32 with Romans 10:13. Indeed, the apostle Paul frequently employs the terms God and Christ interchangeably; the gospel of God (Rom. 15:16; 1 Tim. 1:11), for example, is, in Paul's usage, the gospel of Christ (1 Cor. 9:18; 2 Cor. 4:4). The judgment seat of God (Rom. 14:10), according to Paul, is the judgment seat of Christ (2 Cor. 5:10). The churches of God (1 Cor. 11:16; 1 Thess. 2:14), in Paul's language, are the churches of Christ (Rom. 16:16); and the Spirit of God (Rom. 8:9a), in Paul's judgment, is none other than the Spirit of Christ (Rom. 8:9b). The church thus possessed abundant scriptural warrant for its decree at the Council of Nicaea that Jesus was fully God. This scriptural warrant, nonetheless, hardly sufficed to resolve the dilemma engendered by the passages described above, which characterize Jesus as other than God and gave rise to the heresy of Arianism.

Nestorianism. A proposed solution to this dilemma, which the church overwhelmingly rejected as heretical, was Nestorianism, the brainchild of the sometime patriarch of Constantinople Nestorius (ca. 386–ca. 451). This heresy consisted essentially in the view that there were two Christs. The first of these, who has existed from all eternity, according to Nestorius, is the divine Son to whom Scripture attributes deity and all its prerogatives. The second, however, Nestorius depicted as a merely human person, Jesus, who suffered and died on the cross, slept on a pillow, and so on. Scripture frequently speaks of the human Christ as if he were the eternal Son, Nestorius taught, only because the divine

Logos dwells in the person of Jesus in an especially intimate way.

The church officially rejected this view at the Council of Ephesus (431) for at least two reasons. First, Nestorianism reduced the difference between Christ and other human beings to one of degree rather than one of kind. The Father, the Son, and the Holy Spirit, according to the teaching of Scripture, all dwell within the Christian (John 14:23; Rom. 8:9). If Nestorius was correct, therefore, and Jesus's dignity and authority flowed simply from the Son's indwelling in him, then it seems that the Christian could become Jesus's equal if only he enjoyed a fuller measure of the divine indwelling. Indeed, if Nestorius was correct, it seems that every Christian will become Jesus's equal in heaven when the divine indwelling in every believer is perfected. In the conceptual world of Nestorianism, consequently, the superiority of Jesus qua human to those for whom he suffered diminishes almost to the vanishing point.

Second, this Nestorian diminution of the difference between sinners and the crucified Christ wreaked havoc on the Christian doctrine of the atonement, for the macabre spectacle of the Son of God agonizing on the cross seems conceivable only if human beings could not otherwise obtain salvation. The Protestant tradition of mainstream Christianity, accordingly, holds that Christ's sacrifice was, in fact, indispensable to human salvation because the slightest sin against an infinitely benevolent God merits infinite punishment. That is, God, who is infinitely just, cannot, without forsaking his own perfection, leave any sin without its condign punishment; and the condign punishment for even a single human sin is infinite.

The sufferings of a finite, human being, it seems, could never fully compensate for this infinite debt of punishment; this is why, among other reasons, sinners must suffer for their sins eternally. Only a divine person's sacrifice, rather, would possess a value that is infinite and consequently sufficient to atone for the infinite guilt of sin. Such a divine sacrifice, therefore, at least appears to constitute a prerequisite sine qua non to God's forgiveness of human beings. God, however, being unchangeable, cannot suffer in and of himself. For a divine sacrifice to occur, consequently, a divine person must unite to himself a human nature in such a way that this human nature's suffering, although it in no way impinges on the divine nature's immutability, constitutes, nevertheless, the suffering of the divine person himself.

Inasmuch as Nestorianism posited that a mere human being, and not a person who is truly and fully God, suffered on the cross, it was, therefore, unacceptable. By depriving human beings of a divine sacrifice for their sins, Nestorianism deprived them of their salvation; for this reason as well, mainstream Christianity rejected Nestorianism as heretical at the Council of Ephesus. Regrettably, however, the church failed at the Council of Ephesus to resolve the dilemma engendered by scriptural texts that ascribe to the one Christ both attributes possessed only by the divine nature and attributes that cannot pertain to the divine nature—a dilemma to which Nestorianism constituted a well-meant, but misguided, solution.

Monophysitism. The church issued its first official answer to the question of how Christ could sleep although he was sleepless, change although he was changeless, suffer although he was impassible, and so on at the Council of Chalcedon in 451. The church formulated this answer in the process of countering the heresy of Monophysitism (from *monos physis,* "a lone nature")—the heresy, that is, according to which the incarnate Christ possessed only one nature, neither quite human nor quite divine, but rather a mongrel of the two. No actual human being ever seems to have adhered to Monophysitism, which is a caricature of the position—frequently designated miaphysitism (from *mia physis,* i.e., "one nature")—actually held by the Council of Chalcedon's opponents.

Nevertheless, the patently absurd phantom heresy of Monophysitism does appear to constitute the error that the church actually intended to condemn at Chalcedon. Over against the notion that Christ's divine nature and his human nature coalesced into a hybrid of both, the church declared at the Council of Chalcedon:

> With one accord, we confess one and the same Son to be our Lord Jesus Christ. The same one . . . is truly God, and the same one is truly man with a rational soul and body. He is of the same substance as the Father in deity, and of the same substance as we are in humanity, like us in all things except sin. He was, indeed, born of the Father before the ages according to the divine nature; but in the last days the same one was born of the virgin Mary, mother of God in human nature, for us and our deliverance. He is one and the same Christ, the only begotten Son, our Lord, acknowledged in two natures without confusion, without change, without division, without separation, the distinction of the natures being nowhere removed on account of the union, but rather the peculiarity of each nature being kept, and uniting in one person and subsistence. He is not divided or separated into two persons, but is one and the same Son, the only begotten God, the Word, the Lord Jesus Christ.

In this confession, the church did not repudiate the Council of Ephesus's teaching that there is only one Christ. The church at Chalcedon, rather, complemented the teaching of Ephesus by distinguishing between (1) the one divine person, or subject, in Christ, and (2) the two natures, one divine and one human, through which this one divine subject acted.

How precisely two entirely distinct natures could subsist in a single subject, or person, the church at Chalcedon did not explain; nor, perhaps, can one explain this with any precision. At Chalcedon, however, the church elaborated a conceptual framework within which one can do justice both to Scripture's attribution of divinity and to its attribution of humanity to one and the same Christ without contradicting oneself. One and the same Christ could be both visible and invisible, both mutable and immutable, both passible and impassible, and so on, the Council of Chalcedon taught because Christ possessed two natures, each of which exemplified properties that the other lacked. The one person of Jesus Christ could be both passible and impassible, therefore, because Christ's human nature was passible and his divine nature was impassible. The one Christ could be both visible and invisible, likewise, because his divine nature was invisible and his human nature was visible.

One ought not regard this doctrine as an innovation. It appears at least in embryonic form, for example, in Philippians 2:6–7. In this passage, Paul speaks of Christ as the one "who, being in the form [i.e., the nature] of God, did not consider it robbery to be equal with God, but made himself of no reputation, taking the form [i.e., the nature] of a bondservant, and coming in the likeness of men" (Phil. 2:6–7 NKJV). Certain earlier Christians, moreover, were unquestionably aware of the pith of this doctrine and assured of its truthfulness. Compare, for example, Augustine's *On the Trinity* 1.11.22 and Gregory of Nazianzus's *Oration* 29.17. The Council of Chalcedon, nevertheless, constitutes a milestone in the history of Christianity in that it offered the first official, ecclesiastical statement of the doctrine that Christ was one person in two natures.

We must still address the concerns of the many persons who rejected the Council of Chalcedon and insisted that Christ possessed *mia physis*—that is, one nature. As we have already noted, these dissenters from

Chalcedon, or miaphysites, did not imagine that Christ's divine nature and his human nature merged in the incarnation to form a third sort of being. Instead, they conceived of the distinction between Christ's divinity and his humanity as analogous to that between the human soul and the human body, which, although they are distinct from each other, form only one, individual, human nature. The miaphysites, moreover, did not deny the legitimacy of the distinction between person and nature. They themselves employed this distinction, in fact, when they affirmed the doctrine of the Trinity, according to which God consists in three divine persons who share a single, divine nature.

The miaphysites rejected the Chalcedonian formula, rather, because they considered it crypto-Nestorian. No nature actually exists, they reasoned, without hypostasis, or subsistence, the mode of being whereby an entity exists as a concrete whole distinguished from other beings. If there is no nature without hypostasis, the miaphysites concluded, then a Christ who possessed two natures must also possess two hypostases, and therefore two persons.

This miaphysite argument would be sound, it seems, if every nature required its own distinctive hypostasis to exist. As John of Scythopolis, Leontius of Byzantium (*Against the Nestorians and the Eutychians*), and Leontius of Jerusalem (*Against the Monophysites*) (all flourished in the early sixth century), among others, famously observed, however, this is not evidently the case. There is nothing self-contradictory, these theologians contended, about the notion that two entirely distinct natures might share a single hypostasis by virtue of which, their distinction notwithstanding, they constitute only one concrete whole.

For example, an ax's wooden handle and its iron head unquestionably possess two radically distinct natures. As long as they are separate, moreover, each possesses its own hypostasis by which it constitutes a concrete whole that is distinct from all other entities. When one attaches the ax's head to its handle, however, one incorporates them both into a single ax—that is, one concretely existing being. In the process of attaching the ax's handle and its head, one does not compromise the distinctness of the ax's two natures—iron and wood—in the slightest.

Just as the iron of the ax's head and the wood of the ax's handle can exist by virtue of only one hypostasis without compromising the distinction between iron and wood, Chalcedon's defenders reasoned, so Christ's human nature and his divine nature could exist by virtue of the one hypostasis of the eternal Logos without forming a single, divine-human nature. Chalcedon's proponents concluded, therefore, that one can affirm that Christ possessed two natures without tacitly endorsing Nestorianism.

Monothelitism. Tragically, the argument just rehearsed persuaded few miaphysites of the orthodoxy of Chalcedon. When the Byzantine emperor Heraclius (575–641) attempted to bring religious unity to his empire, therefore, he proposed a Christology of compromise, which, he believed, miaphysites would find more acceptable than unvarnished Chalcedonianism. Historians traditionally refer to the mediating position that Heraclius developed as Monothelitism, a term derived from the Greek words *monos* and *thelēma*, meaning "lone" and "will," respectively. The doctrine represented by this term consisted fundamentally in following two claims: (1) that Christ possessed only one will, and (2) that he possessed only one activity, or *energeia.* The appeal of this doctrine to miaphysites is obvious; it approximated the miaphysite position that Christ, notwithstanding the distinctness of his divinity and his humanity, constituted a single nature.

Nevertheless, the first plank of Monothelitism, that Christ possessed only one will, appears to face at least two insuperable difficulties. First, one cannot deny the presence in Christ's human nature of a human will that existed alongside the divine will that the Logos possessed from all eternity, without portraying Christ as incapable of fulfilling the moral law and suffering its penalty on human beings' behalf; possession of a specifically human will appears to constitute an essential property of human nature, and the moral law demanded the obedience and suffering of a human being— that is, one who possessed all the essential properties of human nature. Second, one cannot deny the presence of a distinctively human will in Christ without portraying his human nature as profoundly dissimilar to that of other human beings and thus running afoul of Hebrews 2:17 (NKJV): "In all things he had to be made like His brethren, that He might be a merciful and faithful High Priest." Either of these considerations, it seems, suffices to render Monothelitism's ascription of only one will to Christ untenable.

The other plank of Monothelitism, that Christ possessed no distinctively human activity, appears liable to precisely the same objections, for one cannot deny a distinctively human activity to Christ's human nature without rendering it a lifeless, subhuman instrument. Such an entity, it seems, would neither conform to the requirements of Hebrews 2:17 nor suffice to render the Logos capable of obeying those divine laws that apply specifically to human beings. Both the requirements of the orthodox doctrine of the atonement and the explicit statements of Scripture, therefore, seem to demand that one posit distinctively human activity in Christ alongside his strictly divine acts.

The orthodox believer, consequently, cannot reasonably endorse Monothelitism. The notion that a being can have two wills without having two subjects of those wills—that is, two persons—might, admittedly, appear counterintuitive. In order to prove the combination of two wills in a single person conceivable, however, it seems that one need merely distinguish between ontological subjects and psychological subjectivities. An ontological subject is a subject to which one attributes acts. A psychological subjectivity is, essentially, a mind. In order for an entity to possess two wills, it seems, it requires two psychological subjectivities but not two ontological subjects.

In order to confirm empirically the possibility that a single ontological subject might possess two psychological subjectivities, one need merely consider the case of split-brain patients. A split-brain patient is a person whose corpus callosum, the tissue that connects the right and the left hemispheres of the human brain, has been severed by a physician. As late as the 1960s, physicians actually performed this procedure on patients with severe epilepsy for the purpose of preventing epileptic seizures from spreading from one hemisphere of the brain to the other. Such persons, as the Nobel laureate Roger Sperry verified in a famous series of experiments on split-brain patients, have, in effect, two psychological subjectivities that can learn, will, and so on quite independently of each other. Evidently, a split-brain patient constitutes a concretely existing whole of a rational nature—that is, a single person in the theological sense of the term.

In order to establish the coherence of the doctrine that Christ possessed two fundamentally different activities, it seems, one need merely clarify what those who affirmed this doctrine meant to claim. Proponents of the "two *energeiai*" doctrine intended by this doctrine merely to assert that the one Christ performed two fundamentally different kinds of activity through two radically different instruments: his divine nature and his human nature. Just as a single pencil can both write through its graphite component and erase through its rubber head, the partisans of two *energeiai* claimed, one and the same subject, Christ, could and did perform distinctively human actions through his humanity and distinctively divine actions through his divinity.

The doctrine that Christ possessed two wills and two activities, therefore, the only reasonable alternative to Monothelitism, appears at least prima facie plausible. Given the compelling objections to Monothelitism outlined above, the mainstream church seems thoroughly justified, consequently, in its decisions at the Third Council of Constantinople (680–81): to condemn Monothelitism and to acknowledge the existence of two wills and two activities in Christ.

Conclusion. Through its struggles with the heresies of Arianism, Nestorianism, Monophysitism, and Monothelitism, then, the church reached the following consensus about the natures and attributes of Christ. Christ was one person, fully God and fully human, who existed in two unconfused natures, a divine and a human. Christ's human nature did not possess a distinctively human hypostasis but rather subsisted through the hypostasis of the eternal Word. However, notwithstanding its lack of a distinctively human hypostasis, Christ's human nature possessed both a distinctively human will and a distinctively human activity, which existed harmoniously alongside his divine nature's eternal activity and will.

See also JESUS, HISTORICAL EVIDENCE FOR; RESURRECTION OF JESUS; TRINITY, THE

Bibliography. Athanasius, *Orations against the Arians*; Cyril of Alexandria, *Letters to Nestorius*; M. J. Erickson, *The Word Became Flesh: A Contemporary Incarnational Christology*; G. D. Fee, *Pauline Christology: An Exegetical-Theological Study*; A. Grillmeier, *Christ in Christian Tradition*; R. P. C. Hanson, *The Search for the Christian Doctrine of God: The Arian Controversy, 318–381*; Thomas Aquinas, *Summa Theologica*, part III, questions 1–26; J. Meyendorff, *Christ in Eastern Christian Thought*.

D. W. Jowers

CHRISTIAN. A Christian is one whose identity and purpose are defined by being a believer in and follower of Jesus Christ. Since many members of groups who hold heretical doctrines claim to believe in "Jesus Christ" and to be "Christians," it is paramount to remember that apostolic Christianity was greatly concerned that people believe in the genuine Jesus rather than a counterfeit (2 Cor. 11:1–4). The apostle John stipulates that true and saving belief affirms that "Jesus is the Christ" (the divine Messiah), that he "has come in the flesh," which refers to his true humanity (1 John 2:22; 4:1–3), and that Jesus is the incarnate Word who is himself God (John 1:1–3, 14, 18; 20:28; see also Col. 2:9). Moreover, belief in Christ requires a monotheistic worldview, which Jesus himself affirmed (Mark 12:29). These christological stipulations rule out any religious groups that deny the true deity of Christ (e.g., nontrinitarian Jehovah's Witnesses) or teach that Jesus is one god among many (polytheistic Mormons) or claim that Jesus tapped into a universal "Christ Consciousness" available to anyone sufficiently enlightened (New Age adherents), and so on. Christological errors are many (2 Cor. 11:3–4), as the path of destruction is wide (Matt. 7:13–14).

A Christian has repented of his or her sinful ways (Acts 17:30) and has embraced the finished work of Christ's earthly life, death, and resurrection for the forgiveness of sin, justification before God, and the gracious gift of eternal life (John 3:16; Eph. 2:1–10). A Christian's saving faith is proven true by an ongoing confession of the gospel and by Spirit-led works that display the sincerity and genuineness of that faith (James 2:14–26). The works themselves, however, do not contribute to one's status as justified before God

through the work of Christ alone by God's grace alone (Eph. 2:8).

A Christian belongs to Christ (Mark 9:41; 1 Cor. 15:23) and confesses Jesus as Lord (Rom. 10:9). The term *Christian* was first used at Antioch to describe disciples taught by Barnabas and Saul (Acts 11:26). The term is used two other times in the New Testament: by Agrippa, when he accuses Paul of wanting to make him a Christian (Acts 26:28), and by Peter, who challenges believers not to be ashamed when they "suffer as a Christian" because they "bear that name" (1 Pet. 4:16). The term is taken from *christos*, which is Greek for the Hebrew *messiah*, the promised deliverer and anointed one. The term *Christ* is a title and office that exclusively refers to Jesus of Nazareth. Christian refers to countless people worldwide throughout the centuries who have entrusted their lives to Christ because other Christians have been faithful in making Christ known (Matt. 28:18–20; Acts 1:8). The book of Revelation declares that the redeemed will include "a great multitude that no one could count, from every nation, tribe, people and language" (Rev. 7:9).

Although Christian has become the term most commonly used for followers of Christ, the New Testament employs a wealth of other descriptions, only a few of which we can address. The book of Acts reveals that Christians are often called "disciples" of Christ (Acts 14:21), as were the first disciples in the Gospels. This involves more than being a student or a religious consumer because Jesus stipulates, "Whoever does not carry their cross and follow me cannot be my disciple" (Luke 14:27). Acts also refers to Christians as "followers of the Way" (9:2; 19:9, 23; 22:4; 24:14, 22), meaning the way of Jesus himself (John 14:6), the way of life instead of death (Matt. 7:13–14), the way of heaven instead of hell (Matt. 25:46: John 11:25–26).

Christians of both genders, at times, are referred to as "brothers" in Christ. This expresses the bond of divine love that all believers share (Rom. 12:10; 1 Pet. 3:8) through their friendship with Christ himself (Matt. 28:10; John 20:17; Rom. 8:29; Heb. 2:11–12). Every Christian is a part of the body of Christ (1 Cor. 12:27). In the New Testament church, this brotherhood revolutionized the relationship between a Christian master and his slave. Paul tells Philemon to receive Onesimus "no longer as a slave, but . . . as a dear brother" (Philem. 16).

Because the gospel claims that a person becomes a Christian through saving faith in Christ, those who have partaken of God's redeeming grace are sometimes simply called "believers," as opposed to "unbelievers" (2 Cor. 6:15; 1 Tim. 4:10, 12). The New Testament repeatedly warns of those who profess Christian faith but whose lives and/or beliefs belie their profession (Matt. 7:15–23; Gal. 1:6–9; 1 John 2:19).

All Christians are also called "saints" because they are made holy or set apart by God (Eph. 1:1) and because they become more holy (or sanctified) over time through the work of the Holy Spirit (Eph. 5:3). Their sainthood is completed when they are glorified in the presence of Christ after their earthly deaths (1 John 3:2). At the glorious second coming of Christ for his bride, Christians will be given resurrected and imperishable bodies (Phil. 3:20–21) and will dwell with God in a restored cosmos forever (Rev. 21–22).

Bibliography. R. C. Sproul, *Faith Alone: The Evangelical Doctrine of Justification*; J. Stott, *Basic Christianity*.

D. R. Groothuis

CHRISTIAN, USE AND MISUSE OF THE TERM. The word *Christian* was first used as a description of believers in Christ in Antioch, about ten years or so after Jesus's resurrection (Acts 11:26). The Greek word *Christianos* means "slave or follower of Christ." First Peter 4:16 suggests that the word was originally a term of abuse, though one Jesus's followers were glad to bear (see also Acts 26:28–29). No formal definition or exposition of the term is given in the New Testament.

It did not take long for religious groups to arise that professed to be Christian but that departed from the teachings of Christ and the apostles in radical ways. The New Testament writers themselves took note of this problem, and much of their writings sought to correct and refute the teachings of false prophets or false teachers. Paul warned the Galatian believers that if they sought to be right with God by their observance of the Mosaic law, then Christ would be of no benefit to them and they would find themselves severed from Christ (Gal. 5:2–4). Peter warned that many would follow false teachers who taught "destructive heresies" (2 Pet. 2:1–2). John described as "antichrists" those people who professed to follow Christ but who denied the truth about the Father and the Son, creating rival religious groups (1 John 2:18–23). Thus the idea that some groups of professing Christians were not authentic followers of Christ was clearly articulated in various ways in the New Testament.

In the mid-second century, Justin Martyr warned that "some who are called Christians, but are godless, impious heretics, teach doctrines that are in every way blasphemous, atheistical, and foolish." Regarding the resurrection of the dead, Justin asserted, "If you have fallen in with some who are called Christians, but who do not admit this [truth] . . . do not imagine that they are Christians" (*Dialogue with Trypho* 80). Justin, then, denied the designation *Christian* to groups denying a basic belief of the Christian faith as taught by the apostles.

While the principle of restricting the name Christian to groups and individuals who are faithful to the essential truths of the Christian faith is a time-honored one, uninspired Christian teachers are not infallible in their application of this principle in practice. Justin is himself a good example since in the same passage quoted above, he goes on to assert that he and others "who are right-minded Christians on all points" affirm not only the resurrection of the dead (which he had ample grounds for regarding as an essential; cf. 1 Cor. 15) but also a literal millennium during which Jerusalem would become a magnificent city. Even many "right-minded Christians" who hold to this view today doubt it is one of the essential truths of the faith. Such questions are answered far more reliably (though still not infallibly) through a process of corporate reflection and discussion within the church. In the early church, this process resulted in several creeds—notably the Apostles' Creed, the Nicene Creed, and the Definition of Chalcedon—that have stood the test of time and are recognized worldwide as reliable expressions of essential Christian doctrine.

In general we may distinguish two senses or uses of the terms *Christian* and *Christianity*. In the broad sense, any individual or group that identifies Jesus Christ as its primary religious figure is "Christian" and is part of the world religion known as Christianity. In this sense, really any group that identifies itself as Christian is defined as such for the purposes of religious classification. Roman Catholics, Orthodox, Protestants, Jehovah's Witnesses, Christian Science, the Unification Church, and a host of other religious groups can all be called Christian in this sense. No spiritual, moral, or doctrinal evaluation or approval attaches to the term as used in this religious-classification sense.

In a narrower sense, an individual or group is said to be "Christian" if its doctrine and behavior are considered adequately representative of what Christ's followers should believe and do. Inevitably different groups will disagree as to who are Christians in this more profound, evaluative sense. Even here it is best not to use the term as if it were a definitive judgment about who genuinely follows Christ and who does not (a judgment beyond our competency). Rather, the term in this narrower sense describes those individuals and groups whose outward profession (orthodoxy) and behavior (orthopraxy) are such that they appear to be upholding the essential standards of Christian faith and practice.

From an evangelical perspective, there are many individuals in most professing Christian denominations and independent churches who are Christians in this narrower sense. True Christianity is defined not institutionally but relationally, as adherence to "the faith that was once for all entrusted to God's holy people" (Jude 3) out of fidelity to Christ. Christians in this narrow sense accept in substance the doctrines of the early creeds and accept one another across institutional lines. Church bodies that uphold those creedal doctrines as well as minimal, traditional standards of right conduct (cf. 1 Cor. 5:9–13) are to be regarded as Christian churches. (This includes nonevangelical church bodies, though evangelicals generally view such denominations as in varying degrees theologically weak or corrupt.) Religious bodies that profess to be Christian but do not uphold these minimal doctrinal and practical standards cannot be accepted as authentically Christian.

One such group that expresses strong objections to evangelicals denying that it should be regarded as Christian is the Church of Jesus Christ of Latter-day Saints. In recent years, the LDS Church has mounted a campaign to change the perception that it is not Christian in the evangelical sense. The LDS Church does not (usually) deny that evangelicals or other orthodox believers are Christians; it simply wishes to be accepted as also being a legitimate Christian body. Its concerns in the main can be answered simply by agreeing that the LDS Church is "Christian" in the broad, world-religions classification sense, but explaining that from an orthodox perspective it is not "Christian" in the narrower theological sense.

See also CHRISTIANITY, PROTESTANT; CHURCH OF JESUS CHRIST OF LATTER-DAY SAINTS; EASTERN ORTHODOXY; JEHOVAH'S WITNESSES (JW); ROMAN CATHOLICISM

Bibliography. C. L. Blomberg, "Is Mormonism Christian?," in *The New Mormon Challenge*, ed. F. Beckwith, C. Mosser, and P. Owen; J. Gresham Machen, *What Is Christianity?*

R. M. Bowman Jr.

CHRISTIANITY, PROTESTANT. *Origin and Meaning of the Term*. Historically, the word *Protestant* is derived from the "protest" lodged by the German Lutheran rulers at the Diet of Speyer in 1529. Three years earlier, that same body agreed unanimously to allow each territorial ruler to regulate the religious affairs within his land, pending the convening of a general council by the pope to effect a final solution to the religious disputes agitating the empire. Contrary to this earlier decree, the council of 1529 rescinded this liberty by a majority vote, requiring the rulers of whatever territory to enforce the Edict of Worms against the Lutherans and to uphold the rights of the papal churches, including, where necessary, the restoration of property and of the Roman mass. In response to this, the princes of five territories and fourteen south German cities issued their protest, arguing that the earlier unanimous decision of the diet could not justly be overthrown by a mere majority, especially in such a matter of conscience.

It should be observed that the Latin verb *protestari*, used at Speyer, was not fundamentally an oppositional term but carried the sense of a public testimony or confession. While the minority party at Speyer certainly was registering its objections to the majority decision, its "protestation" was at least as much a positive declaration of its commitment to maintain the pure gospel as it was a negative protest. These observations apply equally to the English word *protest* derived from it, which only in later usage came to have an exclusively negative sense. Consequently, the word's modern connotations should not be injected into an earlier time, nor should we see in it, as some do, an expression of hostility to Rome.

It is also true that *protestari* was employed in formal juridical and political proceedings such as at Speyer. The word does not have a fundamentally religious provenance or coloring but was suited to the political context in which it first arose.

Defining Protestantism. Some have defined *Protestantism* exclusively or at least largely in terms of opposition to Roman Catholicism. This tendency is seen especially (though not exclusively) in Roman Catholic authors; for example, Rahner and Vorgrimler say, "What chiefly unites them is that they all protest against the Catholic Church" (420). However, such definitions focus inordinately on what Protestantism is not rather than on what it affirms. Furthermore, definitions of this class are too porous to be useful. They do not—sometimes by design—distinguish the magisterial reform of Luther and Calvin from the radical reformers of the sixteenth and seventeenth centuries, including those who denied orthodox credenda such as the doctrine of the Trinity and the two natures in Christ. Those who classify as Protestant modern heterodox groups, such as the Jehovah's Witnesses, Mormons, Christian Scientists, and Unitarian Universalists, perpetuate this lack of distinction. Nor is it adequate to classify such groups as "marginal Protestants," as some have suggested; those in the mainstream have never identified these groups as Protestant, marginal or otherwise. From the opposite angle, the radical wing of the sixteenth-century Reformation generally did not see itself as organically related to the magisterial reform, and in the case of the modern heterodox groups, its disavowal of Protestant status is more emphatic, if anything. (Indeed, the Unitarian Universalists, who are sometimes classified as Protestant, do not even allow themselves to be characterized as a "Christian" body, much less as a Protestant one.) Consequently, it is difficult to see the propriety of applying to such groups a title that the mainstream Protestant bodies disallow and that the groups themselves eschew.

Minimally, in order for a body to be considered Protestant there must be some connection to the magisterial Reformation of the sixteenth century—if not historically then at least ideologically. The historical lineage of many modern denominations—such as Presbyterians, Lutherans, and Methodists—is clear enough. Presumably, though, one could start a body de novo that might adopt, for example, the confessions of a historic Protestant denomination and might therefore reasonably be classified as a "Protestant" church.

This, of course, leads to the consideration of what theological elements are required in order for an individual or group to be considered generically "Protestant."

Theological Characteristics of Protestantism. Protestantism has significant continuities with the historic church. The early Protestants saw themselves as "catholic" in acknowledging the historic, core credenda of orthodox Christian faith, such as the doctrine of the Trinity, the two natures in Christ, and the bodily resurrection. On the other hand, they also believed that the institutional church needed reformation in certain key areas, particularly concerning the issues of *religious authority* and *the appropriation of salvation for the believer*. The Protestant position has been expressed in terms of the "solas" of the Reformation—that is, *sola Scriptura* (the Bible alone as the infallible source of religious authority, and not the church's tradition as interpreted by the magisterium), *sola gratia* (salvation is solely by God's grace, apart from human merit), and *sola fide* (salvation is appropriated through faith alone, again apart from human works). To these might also be added *solo Christo* (or

solus Christus)—that is, that we are saved by Christ alone, apart from the intercession and merits of human mediators, such as Mary and the saints.

The aforementioned doctrines were the common possession of Protestantism generically. At the same time, the discontinuities between the different Protestant factions ought not to be ignored. In its historical development, the issue of greatest moment that restrained the fledgling Protestant movement from uniting against a common Roman Catholic opponent was the question of the Eucharist, specifically the nature of Christ's presence in it. Zwingli and his followers took a *symbolic* view, while Luther's position was closer to (though not identical with) the Roman Catholic view, asserting that Christ's literal body and literal blood were truly present in, with, and under the elements of bread and wine. Calvin's doctrine was seen by some as a mediating position, arguing that Christ is really present in the Lord's Supper but in a spiritual way only. Numerous other theological differences of varying degrees of magnitude and importance between the different Protestant groups could be cited as well. Nevertheless, despite these and other variations, at least in the broadest sense a common view of religious authority and a similar soteriology provide a helpful starting point for distilling a common Protestant identity.

"Old" versus "New" Protestantism. A distinction is commonly made between "old" and "new" Protestantism. The new Protestantism arises from the tectonic shift in intellectual thought patterns emerging during the eighteenth-century Enlightenment. In its attempt to maintain the relevance of the Christian faith to a culture that had emphasized the greatness of human reason and accomplishment, the rationalizing tendencies of the new Protestantism appeared in several areas, most notably in the nineteenth-century rise of liberal biblical criticism and in an acceptance of Darwinian evolution. Liberal Protestants also tended to deny other doctrines of classic orthodoxy as no longer tenable to modern sensibilities, such as the deity of Christ, his miracles and virgin birth, and the bodily resurrection. The movement away from historic orthodoxy in liberal Protestantism was so great that, as Meinhold states, the "ancient Protestant traits [of liberal Protestantism had] little vitality or appear simply as rudiments owing their survival to a lack of resolution" (113–14). Others, however, regard the movement toward liberalism as the natural outgrowth of the germinal principles latent in Protestantism's essence from the start, specifically those of individualism, autonomy, and freedom of thought.

It seems most plausible to regard the development of a liberal theology within Protestantism as a deviation from its core principles rather than as their natural development. Indeed, as has been argued persuasively, the Enlightenment was more properly the child of Renaissance humanism, focusing, as it did, on human potential. But the reform movement of the sixteenth century stood in opposition to this humanism in many crucial respects, notably in its more robust, biblical doctrine of human moral inability and dependence on divine grace.

In light of Meinhold's observation, one might be tempted to ask whether the expression *liberal Protestant* is a contradiction in terms. Regardless, the term is well established and usefully classifies the liberal wing within the historic denominations deriving from the Reformation. It is significant that even those denominations viewed as "liberal" in their orientation have not abrogated their official doctrinal standards, even if strict and literal subscription by individual ministers and members is no longer required as in the past. It is also true that a conservative remnant is found within these denominations, which urges their respective bodies to return to those confessions and standards already

in place rather than to formulate fundamentally new ones.

Note also that the liberal and conservative wings of a given Protestant denomination typically have more in common with their ideological counterparts in other Protestant denominations than they do with the opposing faction found in their own denominational home. Much of the ecumenical, transdenominational cooperation among Protestants is predicated on this fact.

Major Protestant Denominations, Statistics, and Current Trends. Among the most common groups receiving the classification of "Protestant" are the various species of Lutherans, Baptists, Reformed (including Presbyterians), Congregationalists, Methodists, and mainstream Pentecostals. Anglicans/Episcopalians are sometimes classed as Protestants, though many Anglicans prefer to think of themselves as (non-Roman) "catholic."

Estimates vary as to the number of Protestants worldwide. In 2015 the Center for the Study of Global Christianity at Gordon-Conwell Theological Seminary estimated the global total for the number of Protestants (including Anglicans) at more than 543 million. Adding independent groups brings the total number to over 950 million.

As for current trends, Roof observes, "The geographic center for Protestantism, once located in northwestern Europe prior to its shift to North America, is now shifting to Latin America, sub-Saharan Africa, and the Pacific Rim. Here, amidst largely nonwhite indigenous populations, evangelical Protestant zeal and growth currently is at its greatest" (623). At the same time, the vitality of mainstream Protestantism in the West may be waning. Wright believes that "without a firm doctrinal backbone, Protestantism [in the West] faces continuing dissipation," with conversion to Roman Catholicism and Eastern Orthodoxy as "newly appealing" (964). Nevertheless, as Protestant churches continue to experience significant growth in other parts of the world, "whatever happens in the Old World, Protestantism promises to continue to be of major significance" (Gunton, 573).

See also CHRISTIAN

Bibliography. C. Gunton, *The Oxford Companion to Christian Thought*; T. M. Johnson, G. A. Zurlo, A. W. Hickman, and P. F. Crossing, "Christianity 2015: Religious Diversity and Personal Contact," *International Bulletin of Missionary Research*; P. Meinhold, "Protestantism (Self-Understanding)," in *Sacramentum Mundi: An Encyclopedia of Theology*; K. Rahner and H. Vorgrimler, *Dictionary of Theology*; W. C. Roof, "Protestantism," in *Encyclopedia of Politics and Religion*, edited by R. Wuthnow; D. F. Wright, *Evangelical Dictionary of Theology*.

A. W. Gomes

CHRISTIAN ZIONISM. Zionism has been defined as "an international movement originally for the establishment of a Jewish national or religious community in Palestine and later for the support of modern Israel" (*Merriam-Webster's Collegiate Dictionary*). In the broadest sense, then, Christian Zionism is support for a Jewish national and religious community in the land of Israel by Christians who view it as the historic, and therefore legitimate, Jewish homeland. Christian Zionists who are dispensationalists believe that the establishment of a Jewish state in Israel is either preparation for the fulfillment of end-times prophecies concerning the regathering of the Jews to their land or the actual fulfillment of predictive biblical prophecy. Christian Zionists believe that the Jewish people have a unique place in the history of the world and support their right to once again dwell in their ancient homeland. Israel has been occupied by Romans, Byzantine Christians, and Muslims for most of the last two thousand years. The Romans expelled the Jews from Jerusalem in AD 135 and renamed the Jewish homeland "Philistia," in Latin "Palestine," after the Jews' ancient enemies, the Philistines. Many Jews were subsequently scattered by the Byzantines, with yet others leaving the land under Muslim subjugation. Christian Zionists believe that this was an injustice that needs to be reversed so that the Jews can dwell peaceably in their ancient homeland and with their original capital, Jerusalem, restored to them.

Those who have supported this Jewish return to their home have included a diversity of individuals, including famed theologian Reinhold Niebuhr, civil rights leader Martin Luther King Jr., evangelists Dwight L. Moody and Billy Graham, prominent Christian personalities Jerry Falwell and Pat Robertson, and even preeminent biblical scholar and archaeologist W. F. Albright. The UK supported this view in the early twentieth century, especially with the Balfour Declaration (1917), and the US has promoted this view (in part) in the twentieth century and into the twenty-first century.

Christian Zionists do not believe one should support every action of the Jewish state, whether military or political, but they do assert that the Jewish people, because of biblical promises and matters of justice, should have a nation-state in their ancient home to call their own.

See also ZIONISM

Bibliography. M. Bard, "Zionism: Could the Zionists Have Chosen Another Country?," http://www.jewishvirtuallibrary.org/jsource/Zionism/palalt.html; H. W. House, ed., *Israel: The Land and the People*; W. Kaiser, *Jewish Christianity: Why Believing Jews and Gentiles Parted Ways in the Early Church*; *Merriam-Webster's Collegiate Dictionary*, 11th ed.; S. Sizer, *Christian Zionism: Road-map to Armageddon?*

H. W. House

CHRISTOLOGICAL CONTROVERSIES. *See* ARIANISM; CHALCEDONIAN CONTROVERSY; CHRIST, NATURES AND ATTRIBUTES OF;

DOCETISM; MONARCHIANISM; SOCINIANISM; TRINITARIAN CONTROVERSIES; TRINITY, THE

CHUANG-TZU. *See* ZHUANG-ZI/CHUANG-TZU

CH'UN CH'IU / CHUNQIU. One of the Five Classics (Wu-ching) of Confucianism, the *Ch'un Ch'iu* (annals of spring and autumn) provides a record of noteworthy events that took place during the reigns of twelve rulers of the ancient Chinese province of Lu during the period 722–481 BC. (Confucius died in 479 BC, was born in Lu, and is thought to have been one of the text's editors.) The title of this historical account reflects the common practice in ancient China of assigning political events to the season and year in which they occurred. The received text was organized into its final form by Lu Buwei (ca. third century BC), a servant of the imperial court of the Qin Dynasty. During the Han Dynasty, the Confucian scholar Tung Chung-shu (ca. 179–104 BC) elaborated on the *Ch'un Ch'iu*, contending that it was a repository of profound philosophical teaching that ought to be used to construct a normative model of government. Later, major commentaries on the *Ch'un Ch'iu* included *Tso-chuan*, *Kung-yang-chuan*, and *Ku-liang-chuan*.

See also CONFUCIANISM

Bibliography. S. A. Queen, *From Chronicle to Canon: The Hermeneutics of the Spring and Autumn Annals according to Tung Chung-shu*; J. D. Sellmann, *Timing and Rulership in Master Lu's Spring and Autumn Annals (Lushi Chunqiu)*; X. Yao, *An Introduction to Confucianism*.

H. W. House

CHURCH OF JESUS CHRIST OF LATTER-DAY SAINTS. The Church of Jesus Christ of Latter-day Saints (LDS Church) is the religion whose members are known as Mormons.

History. Origins: Joseph Smith (1827–44). In 1827 Joseph Smith claimed that an angel had directed him to a hill near his family's farm in Manchester, New York, where he dug up some gold plates on which was written a history of the Nephites and Lamanites, Israelite ancestors of the American Indians. After some setbacks, in 1829 Smith dictated what he claimed was an inspired translation of a portion of the gold plates titled the Book of Mormon. Near the time the translation was complete, Smith's chief scribe, Oliver Cowdery, his friend David Whitmer, and his chief financial backer, Martin Harris, attested that they saw both the gold plates and the angel. Shortly thereafter eight men from the Smith and Whitmer families signed an affidavit claiming they also had seen the plates. The first printing of the Book of Mormon was released on March 26, 1830, and on April 6 Smith formally organized the Church of Christ. He immediately began revising the King James Version of the Bible; the first part of his "inspired translation," a revision of the early chapters of Genesis, was later published as the Book of Moses.

A key element of the new church's agenda was evangelizing the Indians, or "Lamanites," a mandate articulated in the Book of Mormon. Smith commissioned a group of men led by Cowdery to travel west on a mission to the Lamanites. Along the way, the men made numerous converts in Kirtland, Ohio, so that by the end of 1830 there were about three hundred members in the area, almost triple the number in upstate New York. In December, Smith issued a revelation calling for the church to relocate to Ohio. Meanwhile, missionaries continued to Missouri, the state farthest west at the time. Many of Smith's revelations in 1831 concerned establishing a center and a temple in Independence, Missouri. As Mormons began to settle there, tensions with the non-Mormon population soon turned violent. In July 1833, a mob attacked Mormons in the town and destroyed their publishing company. By November, the Missouri Mormons had been forced to relocate north to Clay County. In the spring of 1834, shortly after changing the name of the religion to the Church of the Latter-day Saints, Smith led a contingent of Mormons to Missouri and set up an organization with David Whitmer as its president. Thus for several years the movement had two major centers with separate leadership structures. Many Missourians continued to be hostile toward Mormons for various reasons, including their growing numbers, their religious claims, and their favorable disposition toward abolitionism. In late 1836, the Missouri Mormons relocated again still farther north and built a city they called Far West.

Recognizing that it might be a long time before the Independence temple was built, in 1833 Smith had begun work on a temple in Kirtland. At great cost to the Ohio Mormons, the temple was built and dedicated in 1836. The Mormons' financial troubles were compounded in 1837 when they created a quasi-banking institution, the Kirtland Safety Society, only to have it fail in the wake of a nationwide economic panic. Martin Harris and more than two dozen other Mormons who faulted Smith were excommunicated by the end of the year, and many more Mormons simply abandoned the movement. In March 1838, Smith, facing arrest for bank fraud, moved with a few other Mormons to Far West; most of the nearly two thousand Ohio Mormons followed them over the next four months. Conflict with the leaders Smith had installed in Missouri led to more excommunications, notably those of Cowdery and Whitmer in April. Smith also issued a revelation at the time changing the religion's name again to the Church of Jesus Christ of Latter Day Saints (the hyphenated form "Latter-day" was adopted much later).

The arrival of Smith and the influx of more Mormons into Missouri intensified conflict there. Mormon leader Sidney Rigdon gave a speech on July 4 warning non-Mormons of a "war of extermination" in which one side or the other would be destroyed if mobs disturbed the Mormons again. Predictably, the disturbance came, and a three-month war ensued. On October 27, 1838, Governor Lilburn Boggs issued an executive order calling for the Mormons to "be exterminated or driven from the State if necessary." Four days later, Smith and other Mormons were arrested and eventually imprisoned for about six months in Liberty Jail in Clay County.

In April 1839, Smith escaped and traveled to Quincy, Illinois, where most of the Missouri Mormons had fled. They quickly began buying up property in Commerce, Illinois, which they renamed Nauvoo (beautiful). The Mormons obtained a strong city charter for Nauvoo that gave them a relatively free hand there, and Smith was emboldened to initiate radical changes. In 1841, construction began on a temple in Nauvoo, which was to have functions very different from what had been envisioned earlier in Kirtland. In 1840, Smith had already introduced the concept of baptism for the dead, which was to become one of the two main functions of the new temple. The other main function was a new "endowment" ceremony that was first conducted in the Nauvoo temple in May 1842. The endowment drew many of its ritual elements from the Freemasons, which Smith had joined two months earlier.

In April 1841, Smith began secretly practicing plural marriage, "sealing" to himself through November 1843 at least thirty wives in addition to his legal wife, Emma. About ten of these were married at the time of sealing, including two sisters and a mother and daughter. The wives also included three other pairs of sisters and (although Smith was thirty-seven at the time) two girls about fourteen years of age. Smith did not issue a written revelation about plural marriage until July 1843, and even then it was shared covertly with select individuals.

During this same period, Smith also radically reformulated Mormon doctrine. In March 1842, he published the Book of

Abraham, a book he claimed was an inspired translation of one of the ancient Egyptian papyri that the Mormons had purchased from a traveling salesman in 1835. It revealed an elaborate cosmology in which the spirits of human beings preexisted in heaven and contained an alternate version of the creation account of Genesis 1–2 with a plurality of Gods who organized, rather than created, the world. At the same time, Smith published an account he had written in 1838 of the origins of the LDS movement. In this account, Smith claimed that the Father and the Son had appeared to him as separate personages. Decades after Smith's death, this "First Vision" came to be viewed as the foundational event of the Restoration. In April 1843, Smith went even further, teaching that God the Father has a body of flesh and bones. In April 1844, Smith's "King Follett Discourse" taught that God was once a mortal man who progressed to becoming a God and that human beings should do the same.

Meanwhile, earlier in 1844 Smith announced his candidacy for US president. Many Mormons were provoked to open dissent by these developments. A group led by William Law obtained indictments against Joseph Smith in nearby Carthage, and on June 7 the group published an exposé about him titled the *Nauvoo Expositor*. Three days later, the Nauvoo city council had the press destroyed. Responding to the threat of arrest, Smith declared martial law, but on June 25, facing a potentially disastrous response from the state militia, Smith and his brother Hyrum surrendered and were jailed in the neighboring town of Carthage, where they were charged by the state with treason. Two days later, a mob of about two hundred men stormed the jail. Hyrum and Joseph Smith were both shot and killed. Despite Joseph Smith's use of a pepper-box pistol in self-defense, Mormons regard him as a martyr, sealing his testimony with his own blood.

Establishment: Brigham Young (1844–77). The Mormon movement, already strained by dissensions during Joseph Smith's lifetime, splintered following his death. The two most notable splinter sects were the Strangites, who accepted James J. Strang's claim of succession, and a group that eventually became known as the Reorganized Church of Jesus Christ of Latter Day Saints, which accepted Smith's son Joseph Smith III as the true successor. Most Mormons, however, accepted Brigham Young as the new leader. In 1846 Young led a large contingent of Mormons on a westward trek. The following year they reached the Salt Lake Valley, where they decided to settle. At the end of the year, Young was formally ordained as the president of the LDS Church. In 1850 the US designated Utah as a territory and appointed Young as its governor. As both religious and political head in Utah, Young asserted his authority freely. In 1852 he formally announced the exclusion of blacks from the LDS priesthood, based on statements in the Book of Moses and the Book of Abraham indicating that black skin was a curse from God. That same year, Young gave a notorious sermon stating that Adam was God, and in another address he openly acknowledged that Mormons in Utah practiced polygamy. Young himself eventually had fifty-five wives and fathered fifty-four children by sixteen of them. By 1857 tensions between the territory and the federal government were so high that the US Army was sent to Utah. During the short-lived Utah War, on September 11, 1857, at Mountain Meadows, Mormons massacred 120 Arkansans who were traveling through Utah on their way to California. Although a peace treaty was signed in 1858, the issue of polygamy remained unresolved for almost fifty years. When Young died in 1877, the LDS Church had grown to about one hundred thousand members.

Transition: Settling the Polygamy Issue (1877–1907). During the tenure of Young's successor, John Taylor, the US Congress enacted the Edmunds-Tucker Act in 1887, which disincorporated the LDS Church and called for the confiscation of its properties. Taylor passed away later that year and was succeeded by Wilford Woodruff, who spent the next three years in hiding while the church challenged Edmunds-Tucker. When the Supreme Court upheld the act, Woodruff faced an imminent threat of the government confiscating church properties and imprisoning him and other leaders. A "manifesto" disavowing polygamy, published in the LDS scriptures as Official Declaration 1, was drawn up and accepted in 1890. The government ceased proceedings against the LDS Church and permitted Utah to become a state in 1896—with a provision in the state constitution forever prohibiting polygamy. Despite these events, new polygamous unions were privately sanctioned by the church in the US and more openly in other countries. Such was the case during Lorenzo Snow's brief time as church president (1898–1901), and the practice continued into the presidency of Joseph F. Smith (son of Hyrum). When Mormon apostle Reed Smoot was elected to the US Senate in 1902, hearings were held from 1904 to 1907 in which Smoot's right to the office was challenged. The Reed Smoot hearings forced President Smith to issue a second "manifesto" in 1904, more explicitly repudiating polygamy and mandating excommunication for anyone entering into new polygamous unions. When Smoot prevailed and retained his seat, the polygamy issue was considered settled, although various so-called Fundamentalist Mormon sects arose later that practiced polygamy and viewed the LDS Church as having apostatized from the teachings of the first Joseph Smith by its repudiation of the practice.

Stabilization: The New Synthesis (1908–45). With the polygamy issue behind it, the LDS Church turned its attention to developing a coherent, stable belief system. During the last years of Joseph F. Smith's presidency, the church leadership issued two important statements. The first, *The Origin of Man* (1909), on the basis of Joseph Smith's revelations, denied that human beings evolved from lower animals and asserted that humans were "born of heavenly parents," that God himself was "an exalted man," and that each person is capable "of evolving into a God." The second, *The Father and the Son: A Doctrinal Exposition* (1916), sought to harmonize the teachings of the Mormon scriptures and to some extent later teaching. The Book of Mormon had taught an overly simplistic form of the Trinity that often sounded modalist—with verses asserting that Jesus was the Father and the Son. Joseph Smith had moved away from that idea fairly quickly, so that the 1835 *Lectures on Faith*, which were included in the LDS scripture Doctrine and Covenants, explained that the Father and the Son were two separate personages and the Holy Spirit was the Mind they shared. At the end of his life, Joseph Smith taught that the Father, the Son, and the Holy Ghost were three Gods. The 1916 statement harmonized these disparate doctrines by explaining that the divine title Father had four different meanings. Elohim is God the Father, the literal parent of all our spirits. Jesus Christ is Jehovah, the Son of Elohim, and can be called Father because he is the coorganizer of the world, the Savior, and the representative of God the Father. Literally, though, Jesus is not our Father but rather our elder spirit Brother. (Brigham Young's teaching about Adam as God was simply ignored.) As problematic as many of these distinctions are, they have functioned successfully for a century as an interpretive grid through which Mormons read the Bible and the LDS scriptures. The greatest difficulty remaining was *Lectures on Faith*, which explicitly taught that the Father was a personage of Spirit rather than having a body of flesh and bones as Joseph Smith had later taught. After Joseph F. Smith died in 1918 and was succeeded by Heber J. Grant, the church issued a new edition of the Mormon scriptures with *Lectures on Faith* removed (1921). By the end of Grant's tenure in 1945, the LDS Church had grown to nearly a million members worldwide.

Legitimation: Cultural and Apologetic Challenges (1945–Present). The postwar LDS Church was first led by George Albert Smith. As the first LDS Church president not to practice plural marriage, Smith represented the beginning of the cultural mainstreaming of Mormonism. Also in 1945 historian Fawn M. Brodie published *No Man Knows My History*, a biography of Joseph Smith that inaugurated serious historical scholarship into the origins of Mormonism. The challenges that such scholarship posed would intensify over the next several decades. George Albert Smith was succeeded in 1951 by David O. McKay. That same year, Hugh Nibley began publishing a series of articles titled *The World of the Jaredites*, typifying Nibley's career-long project of developing sophisticated defenses of the antiquity of the Book of Mormon and the Book of Abraham. The 1960s, however, produced several shock waves to traditional views of Mormon origins. In 1961 two former Mormons, Jerald and Sandra Tanner, published a reproduction of the Book of Commandments, the precursor to the Doctrine and Covenants, which showed that Joseph Smith had altered many of his earlier revelations to buttress his authority. The Tanners' *Mormonism—Shadow or Reality?* (1963), later published as *The Changing World of Mormonism*, was a massive work of documentary reproductions and commentary exposing problems in traditional views of Mormon origins and doctrine. In 1965, Paul Cheesman, a Mormon student at Brigham Young University, submitted a thesis that included a previously unpublished account by Joseph Smith in 1832 of his First Vision that contradicted the official account in the LDS scriptures. The Tanners published this

account as well. Mormon scholars dismissed the Tanners as unsophisticated critics, but they were bringing to light facts about Mormon origins that the scholars could not explain away. The biggest bombshell fell in late 1967, when the LDS Church acquired fragments of the Egyptian papyri from which Joseph Smith had supposedly translated the Book of Abraham. Thought to have been destroyed, these papyri turned out to contain not writings of Abraham but pagan Egyptian funerary texts.

At the same time as these apologetic challenges were mounting, the LDS Church struggled to address the cultural challenge posed by the civil rights movement in America. Under criticism for its exclusion of blacks from the priesthood, the church issued official statements affirming the exclusion in 1949 and again in 1969. LDS presidents Joseph Fielding Smith (1970–72) and Harold B. Lee (1972–73) made no changes to the policy, but Spencer W. Kimball (1973–85) did. In a way, Kimball helped to force the issue by his 1974 revelation summoning all worthy young Mormon men to serve two years as full-time missionaries; the increasingly global church was unsustainable without permitting men of all races to hold offices. In 1978 he announced a revelation rescinding the exclusion of blacks from the priesthood (Official Declaration 2), though without repudiating the doctrine of the curse on which that policy had been based.

The mainstreaming of Mormonism continued under Presidents Ezra Taft Benson (1985–95), who had been Dwight Eisenhower's secretary of agriculture; Howard W. Hunter (1995–96); and especially Gordon B. Hinckley (1995–2008). Hinckley set the tone for his presidency in the 1995 official statement *The Family: A Proclamation to the World*, emphasizing the strong family values of the Mormon faith. The Mormon evangelistic "pitch" became that it brings families together both in this life and, through its temple ceremonies, in the next. In a famous *Time* magazine interview in 1997, Hinckley downplayed the Mormon doctrine that God was once a human like us, a defensive strategy often seen to this day, although official sources still teach the doctrine. That same year InterVarsity Press published *How Wide the Divide?*, in which Mormon scholar Stephen Robinson and evangelical scholar Craig Blomberg discussed doctrine. Although admirably irenic, the book at various places understates the theological differences. Also in 1997, the number of Mormons was reported as ten million, more than half of them outside the US. Hinckley instituted an accelerated program of building temples worldwide even as the church's missionary force was cresting at over fifty thousand a year. In 2000, the church built its one hundredth temple and had printed one hundred million copies of the Book of Mormon. When Hinckley died in 2008, there were more than a million Mormons in Mexico alone, and the number of Mormons in Africa had swelled from almost none before the 1978 revelation to more than a quarter of a million (although statisticians have shown that these membership figures are somewhat inflated because they ignore the large number of members who drop out).

Under President Thomas S. Monson (2008–18), the LDS Church struggled to come to terms with the information explosion created by the internet during his predecessor's tenure and the intensified media focus on Mormonism due to the candidacy of Mitt Romney for US president in 2012. While Hinckley was still alive, the Church Historian's Office had recognized the impossibility of suppressing documentation of LDS Church origins and history, and it began publishing such documents, many of which had formerly been available only from dissidents and former Mormons such as the Tanners. The problem reached a boiling point in 2013, when a group of European Mormons represented by Hans Mattson went public with unanswered questions he had presented to church leadership in 2010. In response to this and other negative publicity, the church's official website published a series of articles addressing (if not satisfactorily answering) questions about the Book of Mormon and the Book of Abraham, Joseph Smith's plural wives, the exclusion of blacks from the priesthood prior to 1978, and the like. What long-term effects these issues will have on Mormonism remains to be seen. Although growth has slowed, as of 2013 the LDS Church reported fifteen million members.

Beliefs. God. The LDS Church teaches that Heavenly Father is an exalted, immortal Man, possessing a body of flesh and bones. He has a wife, our heavenly mother, and these heavenly parents gave birth in heaven to billions of spirit children. Heavenly Father, with the participation of some of his children, organized this universe and formed the earth so that they would have a place to become physical, mortal beings, as a stage on the way to becoming (potentially) gods like their heavenly parents. Life on earth was to be a testing ground in which each person would have to exercise his or her free will by choosing to follow the Father's plan. One of those spirit children, Lucifer, rejected Heavenly Father's plan and led a large group of spirit children in heaven in rebellion. Another of God's children, his firstborn son, Jesus, led the other spirits in accepting the Father's plan. Heavenly Father, Jesus, and the Holy Ghost (perhaps another spirit son of the heavenly parents) are three separate Gods who together rule over this world as the Godhead.

Humans and the Church. Essential to this plan was the need for human beings to fall from innocence in order to become mortal. Mormons regard the fall of Adam as a blessing in disguise—a necessary step downward on the way to stepping up to higher glory through resurrection to immortality with the potential for godhood. To pave the way, Jesus agreed to be born on the earth as Heavenly Father's only begotten son in the flesh, suffer and die, and then be resurrected. After his resurrection, Jesus commissioned apostles—both in Jerusalem and in the Americas—to be the leaders of the church in their hemispheres, each with two ongoing priesthoods through which members would perform temple rituals necessary for people to return to the celestial kingdom.

Apostasy and Restoration. Unfortunately, the church that Christ founded in the Americas perished, and the church that he started in Jerusalem became corrupt, eventually having no living apostles to lead it, no priesthood authority, no valid baptism or temple rituals, scriptures with important content removed, and a distorted understanding of Christian doctrine. Mormons call this disappearance of true Christianity the Great Apostasy; its return they call the Restoration. This Restoration began to take place when the Father and Jesus Christ appeared to Joseph Smith in 1820, told him that all the churches were wrong, and chose him to become the prophet through whom true Christianity would be restored. The Restoration is based on the scriptures of both ancient churches (the Bible and the Book of Mormon) and on other scriptures containing revelations received almost entirely by Smith—the Doctrine and Covenants and the Pearl of Great Price. The latter is a hodgepodge of supposed ancient texts (Book of Moses, Book of Abraham) and other writings by Joseph Smith (notably the 1838 *Joseph Smith—History*, the account of the First Vision and the finding of the Book of Mormon and a brief list of LDS doctrines called the Articles of Faith). Just as important as these scriptures is the authority of the "living prophet" and of the male church hierarchy grounded in the restored priesthood orders.

Salvation and Eschatology. Since Mormonism teaches that all mortal humans were good spirits in heaven, "salvation" in effect means the opportunity to advance spiritually through sin and mortality in order to attain exaltation to Godhood. Jesus Christ's suffering in Gethsemane and his death on the cross provided the atonement, which guarantees physical immortality to everyone (though a very small number of people, the "sons of perdition," can deliberately throw it away by knowingly rejecting the Mormon gospel). Salvation in the narrow sense refers to attaining life in the celestial kingdom, which requires lifelong repentance (overcoming sin), faith in Christ as revealed in LDS teaching, baptism into the LDS faith, reception of the Holy Ghost by the laying-on of hands, and obedience to Mormon moral standards and religious commitments—tithing, drink and substance taboos, marriage in the temple, and regular participation in temple proxy baptisms for the dead. Those who do these things are on track to becoming exalted beings, or "gods," like Heavenly Father and Jesus Christ. Those who do not may still be saved in a lesser heavenly realm, either the terrestrial kingdom for decent people or the telestial kingdom for the wicked, who must first suffer and accept the gospel in the spirit world. Those who died without a chance to accept the Mormon gospel may still reach the celestial kingdom. They will be given that chance in the spirit world, where faithful souls will preach the gospel to them and inform them of the proxy baptism and other rituals performed in the temples on their behalf.

Mormonism and Christianity. The relationship of the LDS faith to Christianity has been a bone of contention since the rise of the evangelical Christian "countercult" movement in the 1960s, pioneered by Walter Martin. In the interests of blunting criticisms of the church, Mormons commonly appeal to a minimalist definition of the term *Christian* that would apply to any individual or group that professed belief in Christ. Martin and many other evangelicals refer to Mormonism as a "cult," generally meaning that the LDS religion is a heretical offshoot of Christianity that has denied essential doctrines of the faith. More sociological uses of the term *cult* complicated the discussion, especially after Jonestown (1978), since the term came to connote a socially or even criminally deviant sect—a meaning that might fairly be applied to nineteenth-century Mormonism but not to the contemporary LDS Church. Some scholars, including a few evangelicals, have resorted to labeling Mormonism a new world religion. Theologically, the LDS Church is best characterized as a heretical form of Christianity since it has Christ as its central religious figure but teaches a worldview and theology that clearly fall well outside the parameters of biblical, orthodox Christian faith.

See also ADAM-GOD THEORY; APOSTASY, MORMON VIEW OF; ARTICLES OF FAITH, MORMON; BLOOD ATONEMENT; BOOK OF ABRAHAM; BOOK OF MORMON; BOOK OF MOSES; CELESTIAL KINGDOM; CELESTIAL MARRIAGE; COMMUNITY OF CHRIST; COWDERY, OLIVER; DARK SKIN CURSE; DEIFICATION, MORMON VIEW OF; DOCTRINE AND COVENANTS; EXALTATION; FIRST VISION; GENEALOGIES, MORMON; GOD, MORMON VIEW OF; HARRIS, MARTIN; HEAVENLY MOTHER; JESUS, MORMON VIEW OF; JOSEPH SMITH TRANSLATION OF THE BIBLE; *JOURNAL OF DISCOURSES*; LAMANITES; LOST BOOKS OF THE BIBLE, MORMON VIEW OF; LUCIFER, MORMON VIEW OF; MASONRY (LDS); MOUNTAIN MEADOWS MASSACRE; NATIVE AMERICANS, MORMON VIEW OF; NEPHITES; NIBLEY, HUGH WINDER; PEARL OF GREAT PRICE, THE; PLURAL MARRIAGE, MORMON TEACHING AND HISTORY OF; PREEXISTENCE, MORMON VIEW OF; QUORUM OF THE SEVENTY; REFORMED EGYPTIAN; SMITH, JOSEPH, III; SMITH, JOSEPH, JR.; SMITH BIDAMON, EMMA; STANDARD WORKS; TALMAGE, JAMES; TELESTIAL KINGDOM; TEMPLES IN MORMONISM; TERRESTRIAL KINGDOM; TESTIMONY IN MORMONISM; THEOLOGICAL METHOD OF THE CHURCH OF JESUS CHRIST OF LATTER-DAY SAINTS; WORD OF WISDOM; YOUNG, BRIGHAM; ZION, MORMON BELIEFS ABOUT

Bibliography. *Official Publications of the LDS Church:* Church Almanac (annual); *Church History in the Fulness of Times: Religion*, 341–43; *Gospel Principles*; *"Preach My Gospel": A Guide to Missionary Service*. **Other Sources:** R. Abanes, *One Nation under Gods: A History of the Mormon Church*; L. J. Arrington, *Brigham Young: American Moses*; P. Barlow, *Mormons and the Bible: The Place of the Latter-day Saints in American Religion*; F. J. Beckwith, C. Mosser, and P. Owen, eds., *The New Mormon Challenge*; C. L. Blomberg and S. E. Robinson, *How Wide the Divide? A Mormon and an Evangelical in Conversation*; R. M. Bowman Jr., *What Mormons Believe*; N. G. Bringhurst and J. Hamer, eds., *Scattering of the Saints: Schism within Mormonism*; R. L. Bushman, *Mormonism: A Very Short Introduction*; W. R. Cross, *The Burned-Over District*; D. J. Davies, *An Introduction to Mormonism*; J. S. Dinger, ed., *The Nauvoo City and High Council Minutes*; T. Givens, *People of Paradox: A History of Mormon Culture*; C. R. Harrell, *"This Is My Doctrine": The Development of Mormon Theology*; E. D. Howe, *Mormonism Unvailed* (1834); D. H. Ludlow, ed., *Encyclopedia of Mormonism*, 4 vols.; H. M. Marquardt, *The Rise of Mormonism, 1816–1844*; W. Martin, *The Maze of Mormonism*; B. M. McConkie, *Mormon Doctrine*; B. McKeever and E. Johnson, *Answering Mormons' Questions*; R. L. Millet et al., *LDS Beliefs: A Doctrinal Reference*; H. Nibley, *The Collected Works of Hugh Nibley*, 19 vols.; R. N. Ostling and J. K. Ostling, *Mormon America*; G. H. Palmer, *An Insider's View of Mormon Origins*; B. S. Plewe, ed., *Mapping Mormonism: An Atlas of Latter-day Saint History*; D. M. Quinn, *The Mormon Hierarchy: Origins of Power*; B. H. Roberts, ed., *History of the Church of Jesus Christ of Latter-day Saints*, 7 vols.; J. Shipps, *Sojourner in the Promised Land: Forty Years among the Mormons*; J. Talmage, *The Articles of Faith*; J. and S. Tanner, *The Changing World of Mormonism*; G. Underwood, *The Millenarian World of Early Mormonism*; R. S. Van Wagoner, *Mormon Polygamy: A History*; D. Vogel, ed., *Early Mormon Documents*, 5 vols.; L. K. Wilder, *Unveiling Grace:*

The Story of How We Found Our Way out of the Mormon Church.

R. M. Bowman Jr.

COMMUNITY OF CHRIST. Formerly called the Reorganized Church of Jesus Christ of Latter Day Saints (or RLDS Church), the Community of Christ is the second-largest group to spring from the teachings of Joseph Smith Jr. The largest is the Church of Jesus Christ of Latter-day Saints (or LDS Church), commonly called the Mormon Church. The new name, Community of Christ, was adopted in 2001.

The church headquarters in Independence, Missouri, boasts a landmark spiral-shaped temple, where no sacred ordinances or private rituals occur (unlike the temple of the LDS Church). The temple is used for public teaching and the promotion of world peace. The church publishes the *Saints Herald*, read by most members, and owns Graceland University (Lamoni, Iowa), a liberal arts school where it trains many of its prospective clergy. Clergy roles (pastor, elder, etc.) are open to both men and women and are unpaid. The Community of Christ has about 250,000 members in forty countries. Only 60 percent of its members are Americans or Canadians; most of the church growth occurs overseas. Unlike the LDS Church, the Community of Christ does not have an organized, socially mandated missionary program.

History and Origins. When Joseph Smith Jr. was assassinated in 1844, no plans for a successor to his office were in place. Smith had blessed his son, Joseph Smith III, to follow him as prophet but did not expect to die so soon. At the time of Smith's death, his son was twelve years old.

A majority of the LDS Church's members followed Brigham Young when he left Nauvoo, Illinois, in 1846, but Joseph Smith's widow Emma stayed behind. Several other leaders vied for the prophetic mantle after Smith's death. In 1853 a handful of people met in Beloit, Wisconsin, to establish a "New Organization" of the original church, opposed to several doctrines taught in Utah or by other rival churches. They solicited Joseph Smith III to be the prophet and president. Emma Smith encouraged her son to accept the role, and he accepted in 1860.

The Reorganized Church was initially defined in contrast with the much larger church in Utah. Both churches then accepted the doctrine of "one true church," which had fallen into apostasy after the first century and was restored in the latter days of the nineteenth century. God had provided a unique and restored gospel, priesthood, authority, teachings, and scriptures. This is the essence of the restorationist message, promoted in other movements besides Mormonism.

Doctrinal Distinctives. The RLDS Church distinctives focused on a few items: opposition to polygamy, different sets of scripture, opposition to LDS temple rituals, and belief that the "true successor" to the prophet must be a direct descendant of Joseph Smith Jr. The RLDS Church denies being "Mormon" since the term is typically used to indicate the LDS Church, with its unique theology and praxis.

The founders of the New Organization believed Joseph Smith had practiced polygamy (or been misled by others), but Emma Smith denied it and Joseph Smith III never believed it. For most of its history, the RLDS Church asserted that not only was polygamy a false doctrine but it was never practiced by Joseph Smith Jr. in Nauvoo.

In 1867 the RLDS Church issued "an inspired revision of the Authorized Version, by Joseph Smith, Jr." (title page), which it now commonly calls the Inspired Version, based on manuscripts donated by Emma Smith. The result was a book superficially like the King James Version, with many differences. The book of Genesis was revised the most: after Adam's fall, he "blessed God" and "began to prophesy" for the joy that would follow;

Adam and Eve were baptized by immersion "in the name of Jesus Christ," were "born again," and received the gift of the Holy Ghost; the mark on Cain (son of Adam) and on Canaan (son of Ham) was black skin; not just Enoch but the city of Enoch was translated to heaven; and several passages were added or changed to predict the coming of Joseph Smith and the Book of Mormon. The Song of Solomon was deleted entirely because it is "not inspired writing." Smith attempted to reconcile perceived contradictions in the Bible; the church now rewords the Lord's Prayer from "lead us not into temptation" to "suffer us not to be led into temptation."

The RLDS and the LDS Churches followed two different trajectories regarding the Book of Mormon, which was originally published with chapter divisions but no versification. The two churches introduced versification independently, and the LDS Church increased the number of chapters in its edition. In 1966 the RLDS Church introduced a modern English version of the Book of Mormon, eliminating archaic forms of speech.

The churches also followed different paths with the Doctrine and Covenants (D&C). The RLDS version has fewer revelations from Joseph Smith. It excised the revelation on plural marriage (sec. 132), baptism for the dead, and other esoteric topics. On the other hand, the RLDS version regularly added a new inspired revelation to its D&C with each biennial world conference. Since the death of Joseph Smith Jr., the Utah church has added sections to its D&C extremely rarely.

The RLDS Church did not accept the Pearl of Great Price used by the Utah church, though much of the Book of Moses (Smith's revision of Genesis) emerged in the Inspired Version. Taken together, the Bible, the Book of Mormon, and the Doctrine and Covenants make up the standard works of the church. (The Inspired Version is rarely used today.)

In terms of liturgy and ritual, the RLDS founders believed that the ordinances introduced in Nauvoo were partially responsible for Joseph Smith Jr.'s premature death. The RLDS rejected in toto the building of temples and the LDS ordinances of baptism for the dead, plural marriage, celestial marriage (marriage "for time and eternity"), sealings, receiving the keys to the Melchizedek priesthood, and the wearing of the garments of the holy priesthood. The sole exception was the expectation that some day in the future, the true temple would be rebuilt in Independence, Missouri, on a spot designated by Joseph Smith Jr. as the "temple lot," after which spiritual manifestations would flourish.

Together with rejecting the temple ordinances, the RLDS Church also rejected much of the underlying theology, including the LDS principles of a plurality of Gods, human exaltation to deity (through sacred temple rituals), the belief that God the Father has a tangible body of flesh and bones, and the belief in a Heavenly Mother.

A final distinctive in the early days of the reorganization was the belief that the "true successor" of Joseph Smith Jr. must be a direct, male descendant. The church capitalized on the fact that Joseph Smith Jr. had given a prophetic blessing to his son, asserting that this pronouncement must be fulfilled in establishing the lawful guidance of the true church.

Social and Cultural Values. Since the RLDS Church has often been confused with the LDS Church by a generally undiscerning public, the RLDS Church has received criticism, rejection, and even persecution for its faith. The RLDS / Community of Christ family can recall episodes of religious persecution into twentieth-century America. Consequently, their driving social consciousness is one of peace. Their corporate emblem for many years was a picture of a young child standing over a lion and a lamb, a picture of the messianic age of peace. The temple in Independence is built as a "place for peace," and a core offering today is the Peacebuilding

141

Ministries department for reconciliation and conflict resolution.

Another core concept in the RLDS / Community of Christ is that of Zion, which they understand not in a biblical fashion (Zion is the name of the hill Jerusalem sits on, often synonymous with the city of Jerusalem) but in a prophetic and millennial context. Zion, to them, is a metaphor for a peaceful community, both social and religious, which ideally should go forth beginning at the Center Place (i.e., Independence) but should represent a vision of a life and world transformed and brought into the love of God.

The Community of Christ today has much of the feel of a liberal Protestant church, including a strong commitment to social action, a denial of religious exclusivism, and an emphasis on peace and meditation. Homosexuality is tolerated within the Community of Christ, and the next issue to rise in the future will be the ordination of practicing homosexuals. A recent revelation in the Doctrine and Covenants (section 163) seems to make room for this, and the topic has been open for discussion for some time.

Developments since 1960. The RLDS Church went through massive shifts in the 1960s, possibly beginning with the installation of W. Wallace Smith as prophet/president in 1958. Believing that "the glory of God is intelligence" (D&C 90:6a), the church emphasized academic training. Church leaders in Independence were sent to St. Paul School of Theology in Kansas City, where they were immersed in the theological liberalism and neo-orthodoxy prevalent at the school. The effect was to bring the leadership much closer to the classical ecclesiology, while at the same time undercutting their views on scriptural reliability.

In 1967–68 a series of private meetings in the Department of Religious Education resulted in a collection called the *Position Papers*, raising questions going to the core of the Restoration message. The papers were restricted from public circulation. They gave evidence why the Book of Mormon was a product of the nineteenth century. They suggested that Smith's changes in the Inspired Version had no textual basis and did not "restore" anything originally lost. The Bible itself was deemed unreliable. *Position Papers* also questioned the notion of Apostasy and Restoration.

The publication of *Restoration Scriptures* in 1969 by church historian Richard P. Howard revealed that Joseph Smith Jr. had used a "divining rod" in obtaining some revelations for the Doctrine and Covenants but had changed the revelations to hide this in later printings. Sunday school lesson materials indicated that Joseph Smith Jr. himself taught the plurality of Gods and that God was once a man.

In 1970 the RLDS Church moved three revelations by Joseph Smith Jr. pertaining to baptism for the dead from the main body of its Doctrine and Covenants to the appendix. Twenty years later, the world conference voted to remove the appendix. In 1979 another summit conference under the First Presidency of the RLDS Church resulted in *The Presidential Papers*, a set of documents that promoted classic Christian teaching while rejecting the belief in "one true church."

The Bible and the Book of Mormon were now deemed human compositions. The touchstone for revolt was the revelation permitting the ordination of women (1984) since the foundational priesthood revelations did not allow it. The members holding traditional views were marginalized, and although congregations were supposed to be locally governed, legal measures were taken to force the dissenters out of the mainline RLDS Church. They now survive as various independent congregations, usually with the word Restored or Restoration prefixed to their title.

The 1984 revelation on the ordination of women also gave permission to build the temple in Independence, without regard to the previously designated "temple lot." The temple was constructed and dedicated in 1994. The doctrine of "close communion" was revoked in 1994 by a policy change (not a revelation). Historically, only baptized members had been permitted to partake of the communion emblems. Now any visitors who wished to partake were free to do so.

In 1996 the RLDS distinctive of presidential succession was given up when Wallace B. Smith, who had no heirs, presented a revelation naming W. Grant McMurray to the presidency. The RLDS Church changed its name to the Community of Christ in stages between 2000 and 2001, though the corporate name persisted for legal reasons.

In 2004 Grant McMurray stepped down and was replaced by Stephen M. Veazey as the president of the Community of Christ.

See also CHURCH OF JESUS CHRIST OF LATTER-DAY SAINTS

Bibliography. Community of Christ, "Community of Christ: Core Values," pamphlet; Community of Christ, "Community of Christ: Faith and Beliefs," pamphlet; Community of Christ, "Community of Christ: Sacraments," pamphlet; Community of Christ, "A Journey People: The Community of Christ Story," http://www.cofchrist .org/history/; Department of Religious Education, Reorganized Church of Jesus Christ of Latter Day Saints, *Position Papers* (1968); First Presidency, Reorganized Church of Jesus Christ of Latter Day Saints, *Presidential Papers* (1979); C. Hansen, *Reorganized Latter Day Saint Church: Is It Christian?*; R. P. Howard, *Restoration Scriptures: A Study of Their Textual Development*; P. A. Judd, *Who Are the Saints? An Introduction to the Reorganized Church of Jesus Christ of Latter Day Saints*; P. T. Trask, *Part-Way to Utah: The Forgotten Mormons.*

E. Pement

CONDITIONAL IMMORTALITY. According to the doctrine of conditional immortality, commonly referred to as conditionalism or annihilationism, human immortality is conditional on salvation by God. In the view of this doctrine's proponents, who include Jehovah's Witnesses, Christadelphians, all stripes of Adventists, and a number of well-known evangelical theologians, God eternally preserves in existence only those human beings whom he eternally saves. Everyone else he simply annihilates. Four principal arguments undergird the conditionalist position.

Eternal Torment Is Unjust. First, apologists for conditionalism argue, it would be unjust of God to consign any human being to eternal torment because, as finite creatures, human beings cannot incur the infinite guilt that alone could merit eternal punishment. Christians who retain historic orthodoxy, by contrast, maintain that the gravity of an offense increases proportionally with the dignity of the party offended. A sin against a parent thus incurs more guilt than a sin against a sibling; a sin against a high-ranking public official incurs more guilt than a sin against a parent; and so on.

God is of infinite dignity, the orthodox argue, and every sin constitutes an offense against him. Even one sin by a human being thus incurs infinite guilt and merits infinite punishment. The suffering of a finite creature over a finite time, however long, cannot constitute an infinite punishment. According to the historic Christian view, therefore, God's justice not only permits but also requires him to inflict eternal misery on all human beings whose debt of punishment Christ does not pay by his sacrifice on the cross. God does unsaved sinners no injustice, therefore, when he condemns them to eternal, conscious affliction.

Christ's Death Is Sufficient Penalty. Second, annihilationists argue that since Scripture identifies death as the penalty Christ paid for human sins, mere human beings cannot deserve a punishment graver than death, for if they did, Christ's death would not suffice to pay their debt of punishment. This argument reflects a gross underestimate of the value of Christ's sacrifice on the cross. Although Christ suffered only in his human nature, the orthodox hold, he suffered as a divine person, whose infinite value makes his sacrifice infinitely meritorious and consequently sufficient to satisfy the debt of punishment that all human beings owe God.

God's Promise to Adam Contradicts Eternal Punishment. Third, conditionalists argue, those who identify the punishment divinely ordained for sin as eternal torment thereby impugn the honesty of God, for God promised Adam that if he ate of the forbidden fruit, he would merely die (Gen. 2:17). He said nothing about eternal torment. To counter this argument, it seems, one need merely note that in Genesis 2:17 God also promised Adam that he would die on the day in which he tasted the forbidden fruit. If divine honesty requires that God fulfill this promise in the most crudely literal sense, then Scripture itself convicts God of dishonesty by reporting that Adam lived 930 years (Gen. 5:5). One who regards Scripture as the word of him who "does not lie" (Titus 1:2), it seems, would do better to interpret God's promise by its fulfillment than to impose on the text a prima facie plausible sense that Scripture as a whole falsifies.

Eternal Punishment Does Not Mean Eternal Existence. Fourth, annihilationists typically argue, the orthodox stance on the eternal punishment of the wicked effaces the difference between life and death. To equate the eternal destruction that Scripture promises the wicked with everlasting existence, however painful, they argue, is to empty biblical language of its obvious meaning. To this, perhaps the most powerful of conditionalist arguments, the orthodox response is fourfold.

First, certain texts of Scripture seem to indicate that those subject to eternal destruction and death endure ceaseless pain in consequence of sins committed before their natural death. In Isaiah 66:24 (NRSV), for instance, one reads that "they [i.e., the

godly] shall go out and look at the dead bodies of the people who have rebelled against me; for their worm shall not die, their fire shall not be quenched." By the last sentence in this passage, Isaiah cannot mean merely that the worms and the flames do not expire until they have consumed their victims, for he utters the sentence precisely in order to explain why the corpses are not consumed but rather remain for the godly to behold. Likewise, in Revelation 14:11, one reads that for those who "worship the beast and its image" "the smoke of their torment will rise forever and ever. There will be no rest day or night [for them]." See also especially Matthew 18:8; 25:41; Mark 9:43, 48.

Second, to persons in extreme distress, cessation of existence constitutes not a curse but a blessing. Moses (Num. 11:15), Samson (Judg. 16:30), Elijah (1 Kings 19:4), and Jonah (Jon. 4:3) pray that God would slay them. Saul (1 Sam. 31:4), his armor bearer (1 Sam. 31:5), Ahithophel (2 Sam. 17:23), and Zimri (1 Kings 16:18) slay themselves. The wicked will say to the mountains, "Fall on us" (Hos. 10:8; Luke 23:30; Rev. 6:16); they "will seek death but will not find it" (Rev. 9:6; cf. Jer. 8:3). Countless human beings in dire circumstances have felt with Agag: "Surely the bitterness of death is past" (1 Sam. 15:32). If the ultimate punishment of the wicked is to constitute a penalty and not a reprieve, then, it must consist in something harsher than annihilation.

Third, death and destruction constitute apt metaphors for that "living death," that condition so miserable that it would have been better for those in it not to have been born (Matt. 26:24; Mark 14:21), which Scripture identifies as the final destiny of the impenitent. Fourth and finally, the eternal life God promises the redeemed consists not merely in an infinitely prolonged existence but in indescribable bliss. When the orthodox construe the eternal destruction ordained for the wicked as never-ending agony, therefore, they do not obliterate the antithesis between eternal life and eternal death. Rather, they sharpen it.

See also ADVENTIST MOVEMENT; ANNI-HILATIONISM; JEHOVAH'S WITNESSES (JW); ORTHODOXY

Bibliography. K. D. Boa and R. M. Bowman Jr., *Sense and Nonsense about Heaven and Hell*; L. E. Froom, *The Conditionalist Faith of Our Fathers*, 2 vols.; E. W. Fudge, *The Fire That Consumes: The Biblical Case for Conditional Immortality*, 3rd ed.; E. W. Fudge and R. A. Peterson, *Two Views of Hell: A Biblical and Theological Dialogue*; M. J. Harris, *Raised Immortal: Resurrection and Immortality in the New Testament*; R. W. Landis, *The Immortality of the Soul and the Final Condition of the Wicked Carefully Considered*; R. Morey, *Death and the Afterlife*; C. W. Morgan and Robert A. Peterson, *Hell under Fire: Modern Scholarship Reinvents Eternal Punishment*; R. A. Peterson, *Hell on Trial: The Case for Eternal Punishment*.

D. W. Jowers

CONFUCIANISM. Not a formal religion in the traditional sense, Confucianism is a humanistic philosophical system responsible for forming some of the most common aspects of what is sometimes called "the Asian mind-set." Although it is impossible to determine how many are strict followers of Confucianism, certainly the Confucian way of thinking continues to dominate Asian culture. As Thomas Leung notes, if 90 percent of the 1.3 billion Chinese, 126 million Japanese, 26 million Koreans, and 74 million Vietnamese are influenced by Confucianism, this would equal approximately 1.5 billion people (Halverson, 70).

The name Confucius (551–479 BC) is the Latin version of the Chinese name Kung Fu-tzu, meaning "Grand Master Kong." Confucius was born of an aristocratic family in the ancient province of Lu, which is currently the Shandong province. Confucius's father died when he was very young, so his mother raised him with a special awareness of education.

Having grown up during a time of social disorder in Chinese history, Confucius decided at a young age to become a scholar in poetry and historical Chinese tradition. He believed the path to peace and order was tied to the ancients. When his mother died, the twenty-three-year-old Confucius mourned her death for three years by living in isolation.

Tradition says that Confucius held different government positions, including service as the prime minister of his province. However, he was a failure in politics. At age fifty-six, Confucius left home and wandered the country for thirteen years with some of his disciples. His goal was to restore the cultural-political order of his day by emphasizing the ritual-music culture, a humanistic system introduced during the Zhou Dynasty (1122–770 BC) and intended to create harmony in human relationships. However, his quest to establish peace and security failed, so he returned home at age sixty-eight to teach and write. He died five years later, apparently convinced that his life had been a failure.

Confucius was an extraordinary ethical teacher who stressed individual responsibility and living virtuously with proper personal reflection. He believed that a person who strove for good character while revering his elders and following moral guides of conduct was to be emulated. Claiming to be only a transmitter, not the originator, of his teachings, Confucius held that humankind was naturally good. He listed five cardinal virtues: *jen* (the greatest virtue, which is to seek the good of others), *yi* (righteousness by justice), *li* (religious and moral ways of acting), *chih* (wisdom), and *hsin* (faithfulness). Confucius denied the existence of a personal God who would be interested in the mundane happenings of humankind. Rather, an impersonal heaven (*t'ien*) can be attained through *jen* by seeking the common good of all people.

The current Asian way of thinking certainly has roots in Confucian ideas. As Huston

Smith has written, "Though Confucius did not author Chinese culture, he remains its supreme editor" (160). For instance, Confucius believed in the importance of family loyalty and maintaining a hierarchical line. Filial piety (*hsiao*) gives special reverence to age, with elders receiving full respect since they are said to possess wisdom. The viability of the family structure is also emphasized. A young man is expected to obey his father in all things until the father dies; at that time, the eldest brother is considered the authority. The one at the top of the hierarchical ladder has a tremendous responsibility to lead by example. The goal in Confucianism is to pass one's influence to one's descendants. Confucius endorsed ancestor worship, although he intended to promote respectfulness in regard to one's forebears rather than the literal worshiping of spirits. Today ancestor worship with the hope of obtaining good fortune is a common practice in many Asian homes.

Mencius (ca. 372–289 BC) is considered the second-greatest Confucian teacher. He further developed the concept of jen, teaching that the word *hsin* (which can mean "heart-mind" as well as "faithfulness") and the term *hsin-hsing* (heart-mind nature) are references to the good that all people have in their inner beings. Self-reflection and self-cultivation are ways to fully realize one's potential, as people are evil only when they forget that they are good. These ideas of innate righteousness were later contradicted by Xunzi, a Confucian leader who lived during the mid-200s BC. He taught that a right education and legislation of good conduct were necessary to lead people to correct action. Without a strong law, he said, nations falter. Although Mencius and Xunzi disagreed, they did agree about humankind's inherent potential for goodness.

Confucianism became China's state religion during the Han Dynasty (206 BC–AD 220), to the exclusion of other religions. The Confucian Code of Conduct dominated the Chinese landscape as the literate elite who entered the monarchy were educated in this system. Confucianism's influence waned when Buddhism dominated China between 500 and 850. However, Confucianism was revived during the Song Dynasty (960–1280). Chinese philosophers who were known as Neo-Confucianists combined Buddhist ideas with Confucian thought. The teachings of Confucius were emphasized, while Mencius was touted as the Second Sage. Confucianism remained the dominant Chinese philosophy until the Republic of China was founded in 1911.

Because Confucianism was blamed for China's lack of modernization, many eagerly accepted Mao's introduction of Communistic philosophy. The 1949 revolution and the birth of the People's Republic of China saw Communism overtake Confucianism as the official ideology. Confucianism was rekindled in the 1980s.

Confucianism's canon contains thirteen scriptures, including nine scriptures compiled in the Five Classics. They are the Book of Changes (I Ching), the Book of Poetry and Songs (Shih Ching), the Book of Documents (Shu Ching), the Book of Rites (Li Chi), and the Book of Spring and Autumn (Chun Chiu). The last two works contain a total of three scriptures each. In addition, the Four Books were more influential than the Five Classics, becoming the official standard for educators after the fourteenth century AD. The Four Books are composed of the Analects (Lun Yu, a collection of famous Confucian sayings—which were not written by Confucius but rather were compiled by his disciples—considered the most important source of material on Confucius), the Great Learning (Ta Hsueh), the Doctrine of the Mean (Chung Yung), and the Book of Mencius.

See also BOOK OF MENCIUS (MENG-TZU); DOCTRINE OF THE MEAN (CHUNG-YUNG/ ZHONGYONG); I CHING / YIJING; LI CHI / LIJI

Bibliography. D. L. Carmody and T. L. Brink, *Ways to the Center: An Introduction to World Religions*, 4th ed.; A. M. Frazier, *Readings in Eastern Religious Thought: Chinese and Japanese Religions*, vol. 3; D. C. Halverson, *The Compact Guide to World Religions*; D. S. and J. B. Noss, *A History of the World's Religions*, 8th ed.; H. Smith, *The Religions of Man*.

E. Johnson

CONFUCIUS. Confucius (551–479 BC) was a Chinese thinker and social philosopher whose ideas influenced the developing religious thoughts of Eastern people-groups. At age fifty-three, he was appointed head of the Department of Justice in the state of Lu, but he left because of corruption within the state (Chenglie, 100). He then began a long journey in northeast and central China expounding his political philosophy until age sixty-eight. Confucius died at seventy-three and was buried at Sishang, north of the capital of Lu (Chenglie, 266). The most famous writings about Confucius are the Analects, which record the words and acts of both Confucius and his disciples. This book is thought to be the most reliable source for thoughts on his philosophy (Ni, 6).

See also ANALECTS, THE; CONFUCIANISM

Bibliography. L. Chenglie, *The Story of Confucius*; Confucius, *The Analects of Confucius*; D. L. Hall and R. T. Ames, *Thinking through Confucius*; P. Ni, *On Confucius*.

T. S. Price

COUNCIL OF THE SEVENTY. In 1835 Joseph Smith Jr., founder of the Church of Jesus Christ of Latter-day Saints, organized a special group of seventy ministers, loosely alluding to biblical groups of seventy (see Luke 10:1). The men were chosen due to their extreme loyalty to Smith. He gave them missionary and church-organizational duties. Over time Smith chose several other councils in addition to the original. These groups are sometimes referred to as "quorums."

Quorums of seventies have been dispensed with and revived throughout the history of the LDS Church. They are usually given responsibilities within the church including oversight of stakes.

See also CHURCH OF JESUS CHRIST OF LATTER-DAY SAINTS

Bibliography. S. D. Young, "The Seventies: A Historical Perspective," *Ensign*.

D. Potter

COWDERY, OLIVER. Scribe of the Book of Mormon, early associate of Joseph Smith Jr., and second witness to the LDS Restoration, Oliver Cowdery (1806–50) met Joseph Smith, founder of the Church of Jesus Christ of Latter-day Saints (LDS Church), while a boarder in the New York home of Smith's parents. During the spring of 1829, Smith is said to have dictated the Book of Mormon to Cowdery from the golden plates. Cowdery was among the party of three witnesses with Smith who allegedly were shown the golden plates in June 1829. His name is on the list of "Three Witnesses" to the plates that is prepended to all current editions of the Book of Mormon. He also was Smith's scribe for the Joseph Smith Translation of the Bible in 1830. According to Mormon sources, Cowdery was alone with Smith on the occasion of several foundational Restoration events in 1829. He was alone with Smith when John the Baptist reportedly appeared bodily to them and conferred the Aaronic priesthood on them. Cowdery also baptized Smith in the Susquehanna River that year. The two were alone together when Peter, James, and John allegedly appeared bodily to them and endowed them with the Melchizedek priesthood. Cowdery was with Smith during several other important events during the early years of the Mormon Church. He was one of several persons present when the LDS Church was formally organized on April 6, 1830, and he was the lone witness with Smith when Jesus Christ, Moses, Elias, and Elijah reportedly appeared to them in the Kirtland Temple on April 3, 1836. Cowdery was the associate president and second-ranking priest of the early LDS Church.

As the second witness of the Restoration, he was very active in all aspects of the early church. Cowdery was the first recording secretary, he was either the editor or associate editor of the first publications of the church, and he was the leader of the first major Mormon mission. Cowdery also assisted Smith as they corrected and published the alleged revelations for the Doctrine and Covenants in 1835. Despite Cowdery's close association with Smith, their relationship became strained in early 1838 because of disagreements over Smith's economic program, his autocratic leadership, and his practice of plural marriage. This estrangement from Smith finally led to Cowdery's excommunication later that year. The historical facts about Cowdery's life after 1838 are puzzling and disputed. Mormon historians insist that after his excommunication Cowdery never recanted his testimony authenticating the Book of Mormon; his testimony about the encounters with John the Baptist, Peter, James, and John; or his affirmation of the basic tenets of Mormonism. But the historical record demonstrates that he joined the Methodist Church of Tiffin, Ohio, sometime after 1840 and may have rejected Mormonism at that time. However, Mormon historians claim that Cowdery moved to Iowa, reaffirmed his support of Mormonism, and rejoined the LDS Church in 1848.

See also BOOK OF MORMON; CHURCH OF JESUS CHRIST OF LATTER-DAY SAINTS

Bibliography. R. L. Anderson, *Investigating the Book of Mormon Witnesses*; A. L. Baugh, *Days Never to Be Forgotten: Olivery Cowdery*; J. B. Groat, "Facts on the Book of Mormon Witnesses—Part 1," http://mit.irr.org/facts-on-book-of-mormon-witnesses-part-1; Groat, "Facts on the Book of Mormon Witnesses—Part 2," http://mit.irr.org/facts-on-book-of-mormon-witnesses-part-2; S. R. Gunn, *Oliver Cowdery, Second Elder and Scribe*; G. H. Palmer, *An Insider's View of Mormon Origins*; D. M. Quinn, *The Mormon Hierarchy—Origins of Power*; J. W. Welch and L. E. Morris, eds., *Oliver Cowdery: Scribe, Elder, Witness*.

C. J. Carrigan

D

Dalai Lama XIV (Tenzin Gyatso).
Tenzin Gyatso (b. 1935) is the current Dalai Lama, the fourteenth in a lineage of Buddhist masters that began in Tibet in 1391. In the Gelugpa sect of Tibetan Buddhism, each Dalai Lama is thought to be an incarnation of the compassionate Bodhisattva Avalokiteshvara. From the late fourteenth century until the 1960s, each successive Dalai Lama held the dual position of Tibet's highest-ranking government ruler and its most influential spiritual leader. Tibetans typically refer to the 14th Dalai Lama as Yeshin Norbu (wish-fulfilling gem) or Kundun (the presence).

History. Tenzin Gyatso was born Lhamo Thondup on July 6, 1935, to a farming family in northeast Tibet. When Lhamo was two years old, it was determined by a group of Tibetan Buddhist monks that he was a likely candidate to be the reincarnation of the recently deceased 13th Dalai Lama, Thubten Gyatso (1876–1933). At six years of age, Lhamo began to study Tibetan Buddhism formally. In November 1950, at age sixteen, Lhamo was installed as Tibet's top political leader, though he was soon deposed by the Communist government of neighboring China. At twenty-two, Lhamo was officially pronounced to be the reincarnation of the 13th Dalai Lama and took the spiritual name Geshe Tenzin Gyatso. In March 1959, not long after Tenzin had received a high-level degree in Buddhist philosophy from the Jokhang Temple in Lhasa, Tibet, Chinese troops invaded Tibet. Tenzin had little choice but to flee. He relocated in Dharamsala, India.

Subsequently he has worked in exile in various capacities as part of an attempt to end human rights abuses in Tibet by the Chinese military and to restore the political autonomy and culture of Tibet. This work has included meetings with dozens of prominent world leaders, including Pope John Paul II (1920–2005) and former US president George W. Bush (b. 1946), and was the basis for his receiving the Nobel Peace Prize in 1989 and a Congressional Gold Medal in 2007. On July 5, 2005, the day before his seventieth birthday, the Chinese government refused Tenzin's request to return to Tibet before his death. Despite discussion of his retirement in 2007 and undergoing gallstone surgery in October 2008, the Dalai Lama continues to promote Buddhism (especially its Mahayana form) in the US and Europe and is unquestionably the leading figure associated with Buddhism in the West. This was evidenced by his participation in a World Religions Dialogue interfaith conference in Gujarat, India, in January 2009.

Teachings. Though displaying many of the distinctive emphases found in the Vajrayana-Tibetan Buddhist tradition, most of the Dalai Lama's teachings focus on the basics of Buddhism, especially the Four Noble Truths. Tenzin identifies these four truths as the nature of suffering, the origin of suffering, the cessation of suffering, and the path to the eradication of suffering. Other key instructions of the Dalai Lama concern how to awaken to the illusory nature of normal human perception and how to attain happiness by grasping the emptiness of things in the phenomenal world. Tenzin propounds a system of ethics that includes a strong commitment to nonviolence (though he allows for abortion in a number of cases) and the avoidance of war, striving for world peace, eschewing all forms of hatred, and broad religious tolerance, though he also is reported to endorse homosexual rights (despite holding a generally negative view of human sexuality). In recent years, the Dalai Lama has been at the forefront of academic discussions concerning the relationship of religion (especially Buddhism) and modern science.

See also TIBETAN BUDDHISM

Bibliography. J. F. Avedon, *In Exile from the Land of Snows: The Definitive Account of the Dalai Lama and Tibet since the Chinese Conquest*; Dalai Lama XIV, *Freedom in Exile: The Autobiography of the Dalai Lama*; Dalai Lama XIV, *A Simple Path: Basic Buddhist Teachings by the Dalai Lama*; G. T. Jinpa, ed., *Essence of the Heart Sutra: The Dalai Lama's Heart of Wisdom Teachings*; D. H. Strober and G. S. Strober, *His Holiness the Dalai Lama: The Oral Biography.*

H. W. House

DANITES. Organized in June 1838 by Latter-day Saints member Sampson Avard, the Danites were a secret group of men united around the common purpose of silencing dissent both inside and outside the LDS Church. There is considerable debate about who actually led the Danites; it seems, however, that Avard, not Joseph Smith Jr., was in command (Bushman and Lyman, 349–52). Many historians think the Danites played a central role in the 1838 "Mormon war" in Daviess County, Missouri, and were used to intimidate dissenters from the Mormon Church. Although the organization was officially disbanded, many claim that the Danites, rather, assumed other positions and formed other groups within the Mormon Church, such as Brigham Young's Destroying Angels. These groups are said by many to have been involved in notorious "blood atonement" killings and the Mountain Meadows Massacre.

See also BLOOD ATONEMENT; CHURCH OF JESUS CHRIST OF LATTER-DAY SAINTS; MOUNTAIN MEADOWS MASSACRE

Bibliography. L. J. Arrington and D. Britton, *The Mormon Experience: A History of the Latter-day Saints*; R. L. Bushman and Richard Lyman, *Joseph Smith: Rough Stone Rolling.*

T. S. Kerns

DARK SKIN CURSE. For most of its history, the Church of Jesus Christ of Latter-day Saints held that dark-skinned people were descendants of Ham and that their dark skin was the mark indicating the denial of priesthood blessings. Theologically, the church explained that at the rebellion of Lucifer before the creation of the earth, some spirits fought "valiantly" against Lucifer, while others were not as "valiant" in their premortal estate. As a consequence, Heavenly Father cursed them by denying them the priesthood in their second (earthly) estate. These children were destined to be born of the lineage of Ham, whose offspring populated Africa; the mark of the curse would be their skin of darkness. In LDS vocabulary, the seed of Ham were not yet entitled to the full blessings of the gospel.

On June 9, 1978, the First Presidency of the LDS Church announced that President Spencer W. Kimball had received a revelation from God permitting all worthy males to hold the priesthood. This alleged revelation was sustained by a general conference of the LDS Church in October of the same year, and the modified doctrine was appended to the Doctrine and Covenants as Official Declaration 2. While this declaration removed the prohibition against dark-skinned people of African descent receiving the priesthood, it did not repudiate the doctrine of the curse itself. The doctrine has not been taught since the 1978 modification and is generally ignored.

The Book of Abraham 1:26–27 in the Pearl of Great Price was the source of the LDS teaching that black Africans, descendants of Ham, were "cursed . . . pertaining to the priesthood." This teaching was held by the first twelve Mormon presidents, with the possible exception of David O. McKay (in office 1951–70). Brigham Young (1847–77) and Joseph Fielding Smith (1970–72) were very fierce protectors of this doctrine. Young taught that interracial marriage between a white Mormon and a black African would result in a decreased number of racially qualified men for the priesthood and ordered "death on the spot" for doing so (*JD* 10:110). Young did teach that African people would be permitted to receive the priesthood after the general resurrection of all earth-born men, but not before ("Speech"). Joseph Fielding Smith agreed with Joseph Smith Jr., Brigham Young, and many others and identified descendants of Cain as an "inferior race" that must be "denied the priesthood" (Smith, 101).

The 1978 revision of the Mormon doctrine on Africans and the priesthood modified Mormon missionary strategy, increased rates of growth in membership, and increased the number of Mormon temples. Before 1978 there were almost no missionary activities on the continent of Africa except among whites in South Africa, and there was very little missionary interest in Afro-Caribbean peoples of Central and South America. But since 1978, missionary activities in these locations have increased dramatically. Dozens of temples have been built in these regions, and church membership increased by about 60 percent over a period of ten years immediately after 1978.

See also CHURCH OF JESUS CHRIST OF LATTER-DAY SAINTS

Bibliography. J. L. Lund, *The Church and the Negro*; Joseph Fielding Smith, *The Way to Perfection*; J. J. Stewart and W. E. Berrett, *Mormonism and the Negro: An Explanation and Defense of the Doctrine of the Church of Jesus Christ of Latter-day Saints in Regard to Negroes and Others of Negroid Blood*; J. and S. Tanner, *Mormonism: Shadow or Reality?*; Brigham Young, "Speech by Brigham Young in Joint Session of the Legislature," http://mit.irr.org/brigham-young-we-must -believe-in-slavery-23-january-1852.

C. J. Carrigan and E. Pement

DARSHANA. *Darshana* is an important Indian concept that has several meanings. In general, different schools of thought in India are termed *darshana*, or "views." Thus this term covers the Western concept of philosophy. Moreover, the term can also mean "auspicious view"; with this connotation, the term is used when a person goes to a temple or to meet his guru. It is a seeing and being seen by the god or guru. In the case of the god, the temple icon acts as the focal point of the activity.

In Buddhism darshana can be understood as the entering into the nirvanic power of a Buddha, bodhisattva, or arhat. This entering into the field of the awakened helps one to gain enlightenment. There are stories from the Pali sutras up through the tantras wherein Buddhists engage in this activity.

See also BUDDHISM; HINDUISM; TANTRA

Bibliography. A. W. Barber, "Darshanic Buddhism: The Origins of Pure Land Practice," in *The Pure Land: The Journal of Pure Land Buddhism*; D. L. Eck, *Darsan: Seeing the Divine Image in India*.

A. W. Barber

DA'WAH. The term *da'wah* (Arabic, "call," "issuing a summons") often denotes an appeal made by Muslims to non-Muslims, urging them to convert to Islam. (In the Qur'an the word sometimes refers to Allah's beckoning people to embrace Islam; the word also can mean to invoke Allah and place one's faith in him.) In contemporary, Westernized Islam, this summons takes place in the context of missionary activity rather than by means of jihad. Militant Islamic sects view da'wah as the call for compromised Muslims to return to the uncorrupted, monotheistic religion proclaimed by Muhammad and practiced by the early Islamic communities.

During much of Islam's history, missionary da'wah took place in conjunction with trade and commerce and in many cases served as a follow-up to successful battles for control of previously non-Muslim territory. Da'wah also was undertaken by Islamic caliphs who sought to exercise authority over Muslims living in non-Islamic regions and to promote unity among members of various Islamic sects. In the twentieth century, da'wah was commonly employed as a way of helping to achieve various Islamic cultural and political endeavors, as a justification for overthrowing secular colonizers, as a means of legitimating Islamic governments, and as a call to membership in orthodox Islamic communities. In some Islamic countries such as Libya and Saudi Arabia, the carrying out of da'wah is considered a responsibility of the government. In more moderate Islamic nations, da'wah usually is thought to be an activity reserved for individual Muslims or Islamic organizations not directly sponsored by the government.

See also ISLAM, BASIC BELIEFS OF

Bibliography. I. al-Faruqi, "On the Nature of Islamic Da'wah," *International Review of Mission*; J. L. Esposito, ed., *The Oxford History of Islam*; C. T. R. Hewer, *Understanding Islam: An Introduction*; L. Poston, *Islamic Da'wah in the West: Muslim Missionary Activity and the Dynamics of Conversion to Islam.*

J. Bjornstad

DAY OF JUDGMENT, ISLAMIC. The day of judgment (Arabic, *yawm al-qiyamah*) is the day on which, according to Islamic eschatology, the universe will be destroyed and all human beings who have ever lived will be bodily resurrected and judged by Allah. Those whose deeds are pleasing to Allah will be rewarded with entry to Paradise (Qur'an 2:82). Those who are rejected by Allah will be

cast into eternal torment (Qur'an 3:85). The topic of al-Qiyamah is second only to that of strict monotheism in importance in Islam. Belief in the day of judgment is the fifth of the Pillars of Faith in Islam (see Quran 2:62; 54:52–53), belief in which is considered a test of Islamic orthodoxy by nearly all Muslims. No one except Allah knows the timing of Qiyamat, the magnitude and extent of which will be so enormous and all-encompassing that it will result in the obliteration of the entire world. An unimaginably loud and deafening trumpet blast (produced by the angel Hazrat Israfeel) will indicate that Qiyamat is under way, knocking the entire population of the earth into a state of unconsciousness. Just after this blast, Allah will unleash the devastating series of cosmic cataclysms that precede the resurrection and judgment.

See also ISLAM, BASIC BELIEFS OF; ISLAM, ESCHATOLOGY OF

Bibliography. Vincent J. Cornell, *Voices of Islam*; S. Q. M. M. Kamoonpuri, *Basic Beliefs of Islam for Secondary Schools*; J. I. Smith and Y. Y. Haddad, *The Islamic Understanding of Death and Resurrection.*

R. L. Drouhard

DEIFICATION, CHRISTIAN VIEW OF. Also called *theosis* and *divinization*, deification is "the central theme, chief aim, basic purpose, or primary religious ideal" of Eastern Orthodox Christianity (Clendenin, 120). The classic formulation of the teaching comes from section 54 of *On the Incarnation of the Divine Word*, by the fourth-century Christian writer Athanasius of Alexandria (d. 373): "The Word of God Himself . . . assumed humanity that we might become God." Early Christians did not have trouble describing their future hope in terms of "becoming gods" because they took Jesus's quote of Psalm 82:6, "I said, 'You are "gods,"'" at John 10:34, to be a reference to "those . . . who have received the grace of the 'adoption, by which we cry, Abba Father [Rom. 8:15]'"

(Irenaeus, *Against Heresies* 3.6.1; cf. Justin Martyr, *Dialogue with Trypho* 124). The explicit use of deification language begins to appear already in the mid-second century. Its earliest occurrences are in Justin Martyr, *Dialogue with Trypho* 124 (after 135 and before 164); Theophilus of Antioch, *To Autoclycus* 2.27 (ca. 180); Clement of Alexandria (d. 215), in *Exhortation to the Greeks 1* and elsewhere; and Irenaeus of Lyons (d. ca. 202), *Against Heresies* 4.38.1–4. Clement's deification language is heavily colored by contact with the conceptual world of Platonism, so it is ultimately Irenaeus who will contribute most directly to the development of the Orthodox doctrine. Some, however, of what is later made explicit in the Orthodox doctrine is still only implicit in Irenaeus. This is important to remember, especially since scholarly discussion of the doctrine's history has been skewed in recent decades by a widely circulated misquotation of the preface to book 5 of *Against Heresies* that has Irenaeus saying, in language very close to what we see more than a century later in Athanasius, "If the word has been made man, it was so men may become gods." Actually the passage in question says nothing about becoming gods, only about becoming "what He [Jesus] is Himself" (*quod est ipse*). The misquotation in the present literature appears to have originated in the linking of a loosely phrased statement of the traditional formula to Irenaeus by the prominent Orthodox theologian Vladimir Lossky (e.g., *The Vision of God*, 35; see Clendenin, 117, 127; Lash, 147).

Irenaeus does, however, use deification language when giving reasons for not blaming God that "we have not been made gods from the beginning, but at first merely men, and at length gods" (*Against Heresies* 4.38.4). But again in the context he finds justification for the language in his "Christian" reading of Psalm 82:6. In Irenaeus's mind, deification parallels Paul's concept of our adoption in

Christ (Rom. 8:15–17), an understanding that has continued in Orthodox theology down to the present time: "The meaning of theosis in the New Testament is the adoption of man" (Stavropoulos, 185).

To the ears of Western Christians, who have tended to view the work of Christ more from the perspective of how it leads to the forgiveness and rescue of sinners, rather than how it restores the divine image and/or likeness lost in the fall, the language of deification can come across as jarring or even blasphemous when initially encountered. Such alarm, however, wanes when it is understood that the doctrine has always been carefully qualified so as to make it absolutely clear that the language implies no real ultimate confusion between mortal humans and the eternal, unbegotten God: "Although 'engodded' or 'deified' the saints do not become additional members of the Trinity. God remains God, and man remains man. Man becomes god by grace but not God in essence" (Ware, 125).

Another way this infinite distinction has been expressed is by saying that when 2 Peter 1:4 says we "participate in the divine nature," it refers to participating in the divine *energies* (cf. Col. 1:29), but not in the divine *essence* or *being*. In terms more familiar to Western ears, it might be said that the deified come to share in God's *communicable* attributes but not his *incommunicable* ones. Being united with Jesus in his death, we come to share in his own divine life. But it is all of him and none of us. And this distinction was perfectly understood from the beginning. Irenaeus, indeed, finds it expressed in the very passage he uses to justify calling Christians gods in the first place. For even though Psalm 82:6 says, "You are 'gods,'" Irenaeus goes on to point out that, "since we could not sustain the power of divinity, He adds, 'But ye shall die like men,' setting forth both truths—the kindness of His free gift, and our weakness" (*Against Heresies* 4.38.4). The same point was made by Athanasius; we partake of Christ's divine life only because Jesus first partook of our mortal flesh: "But if death was within the body, woven into its very substance . . . the need was for Life to be woven in instead. . . . The Saviour assumed a body for Himself, in order that the body [i.e., our bodies], being interwoven as it were with life, should no longer remain a mortal thing, in thrall to death, but as endued with immortality and risen from death, should therefore remain immortal. For once having put on corruption, it could not rise, unless it put on life instead" (*On the Incarnation of the Divine Word* 44).

When properly understood, then, the Orthodox doctrine of deification is perfectly biblical. The Western church is used to speaking of Christians as becoming sons of God by grace without ever imagining that, in doing so, it might lead some to view these Christians as claiming equal status in the Godhead with Jesus. The same is true of the Eastern church when it speaks of becoming gods by grace. In addition to the famous passage in 2 Peter already cited, there is also much in the writings of the Bible that can be seen as supporting the language or at least the conceptual framework of the doctrine of deification. It is declared in 1 John 3:2 that "when Christ appears, we shall be like him" (NRSV), and in 2 Corinthians 5:21 that "God made him who had no sin to be sin for us, so that in him we might become the righteousness of God." In John's Gospel, Jesus prays that believers will be one as he and the Father are one (17:21; cf. 10:30), yet it is without in any way losing sight of Jesus's unique relationship with God as both preexistent Word and only begotten of the Father (1:1 and 18). The Son has divine life in himself (5:26). We have it only through the Son (3:36; 6:53–54, 68; 10:28), and only as we abide in him (15:1–7). In addition to this, there is the larger teaching on humanity as creatures made in the image and likeness of God (Gen. 1–2)

and on Christ as the second Adam (1 Cor. 15:45–49). The principal objection against using the language of deification, therefore, is only that it is based on a misapplication of Psalm 82:6 and John 10:34. Contrary to the opinion of early Christian writers who contributed to development of deification terminology, those passages simply do not refer to Christians.

Unlike in the Eastern church, where the doctrine of deification has always been regarded as a controlling concept in the doctrine of salvation, in the Western church it is scarcely known. Still we do occasionally find it, as, for example, in the eighth-century Celtic theologian John Scotus Eriugena (d. ca. 877), who declares: "He [Jesus] came down alone but ascends with many. He who made of God a human being makes gods of men and women" (*Prologue to the Gospel of John* 21). The great Western father Augustine of Hippo (d. 430) also uses the language of deification: "For God wishes to make thee a god; not by nature, as He is whom He has begotten, but by his gift and adoption" (*Sermon* 166.4). Deification language has even been preserved as part of the Roman Catholic Mass, where it currently appears as part of the Liturgy of the Eucharist: "By the mystery of this water and wine may we come to share in the divinity of Christ, who humbled himself to share in our humanity." On the Protestant side, we find it, for example, in the lyrics of the great Methodist hymnologist Charles Wesley (d. 1788): "He deigns in flesh to appear, / Widest extremes to join; / To bring our vileness near, / And make us all divine" ("Let Heaven and Earth Combine"). Or again, speaking more broadly of trinitarians as such, Ralph Waldo Emerson writes in his journal entry for February 14, 1827: "The Trinitarian urges a natural & sublime deduction from his creed when he says of the Saviour that as he became a partaker in our humanity so we also shall become partakers in his divinity."

See also CHRISTIAN; DEIFICATION, MOR-MON VIEW OF; EASTERN ORTHODOXY; ROMAN CATHOLICISM

Bibliography. D. B. Clendenin, *Eastern Orthodox Christianity: A Western Perspective*; S. Lash, "Deification," in *The Westminster Dictionary of Christian Theology*; V. Lossky, *The Mystical Theology of the Eastern Church*; Lossky, *The Vision of God*; D. V. Meconi, SJ, and Carl E. Olson, eds., *Called to Be the Children of God: The Catholic Theology of Human Deification*; N. Russell, *The Doctrine of Deification in the Greek Patristic Tradition*; C. Stavropoulos, "Partakers of Divine Nature," in *Eastern Orthodox Theology: A Contemporary Reader*; J. Vajda, "Partakers of the Divine Nature": A Comparative Analysis of Patristic and Mormon Doctrines of Divinization*; K. Ware, *The Orthodox Way*, rev. ed.

R. V. Huggins

DEIFICATION, MORMON VIEW OF. The doctrine of deification, with its language of "becoming gods," appears in the arena of Mormon apologetics. Although we do find occasional earlier references to the similarity between the Mormon and the Orthodox teaching on deification (e.g., Hunter), the current interest did not arise until the 1970s and 1980s, after two Mormon scholars, Philip L. Barlow and Keith E. Norman, became interested in the subject while pursuing advanced degrees. Interestingly, both seem to have made the discovery independent of each other and both while studying at Harvard. Barlow would receive his doctorate from Harvard, but Norman would go on to get his from Duke, where he would write a dissertation titled "Deification: The Content of Athanasian Soteriology" in 1980. Already by 1975, Norman had placed some of the results of his research on deification before the LDS community in an article appearing in the first issue of *Sunstone* magazine. Barlow would also contribute an article on the subject to *Sunstone* in 1983. Even though both Norman and Barlow are of a more scholarly than apologetic temper, these two articles (supplemented more recently by Norman's dissertation, which was published in 2000—without Norman's participation and much to his surprise upon seeing it in print—by the Mormon apologetic organization Foundation for Ancient Research and Mormon Studies [FARMS]) would serve as the basis and source for the Mormon apologetic that would afterward develop.

The primary supporter of the new deification apologetic is another LDS writer who was also at Duke while Norman was there and who has since become one of Mormonism's most popular writers and apologists: Stephen E. Robinson. Robinson develops his apologetic around the famous couplet of the fifth president of the LDS Church, Lorenzo Snow: "As man now is, God once was; As God now is, man may become." "Latter-day Saints," Robinson writes, "share the ancient biblical doctrine of deification (*apotheosis*) with Eastern Orthodoxy. Several of early Christianity's theologians said essentially the same thing as Lorenzo Snow" ("God the Father," 2:401). Robinson sees particular significance in the similarity between Snow's couplet and the traditional formula as commonly misquoted from Irenaeus: "If the word became a man, it was so men may become gods." More recently Mormon apostle Dallin Oaks similarly asserted that the LDS understanding of the future life "should be familiar to all who have studied the ancient Christian doctrine of deification or apotheosis" ("Apostasy," 86).

In reality, of course, any similarity that seems to exist between Lorenzo Snow's couplet and the traditional formula is only apparent and has to do only with a similar structuring and the use of similar words. The underlying concepts being described in the two cases, however, are infinitely different. In the traditional formula, it was the Son who became human; in Snow's couplet it was the Father. In the traditional formula, Jesus became human in order that by joining his nature with ours he might enable us to become what we never had the potential to be—it was only because Jesus had divine life within himself that we could partake of divine life through him. In Snow's couplet, God the Father had been a man and had trodden the same path on his journey to godhood that we must each now tread on our own journeys to godhood. In the traditional formula, we share in the attributes of God in some limited sense by virtue of the fact that we were created (and re-created) in the image of God, becoming "gods" by grace only because we have been united with Christ, who is God by nature. In Snow's couplet, we do not so much become gods as grow up into the gods we already are by nature, being part of the same "species" or "race" as God: "Gods and humans," writes Stephen E. Robinson, "represent a single divine lineage, the same species of being, although they and he are at different stages of progress" ("God the Father," 2:549). We are the literal spirit children of our heavenly parents: "[We are] formed in the divine image and endowed with divine attributes, and even as the infant son of an earthly father and mother is capable in due time of becoming a man, so the undeveloped offspring of celestial parentage is capable . . . of evolving into a God" (Smith, Winder, and Lund, 30). Ultimately, then, "all the personal attributes which are ascribed to God by inspired men, we find in ourselves" (Charles W. Penrose, quoted in Hunter, *Gospel*, 107).

One of the difficulties related to this discussion is the fact that the deification apologetic was growing in popularity among LDS apologists at the same time that the LDS leadership was taking steps to suppress the memory of the traditional Mormon account of the history of the Mormon God, that is, of why and how the Father came to be human in the first place. In this process, LDS president Gordon B. Hinckley has even gone so far as to publicly deny knowledge of this traditional Mormon teaching (Ostling

and Ostling, 296). The apparent goal of this effort is to transform the LDS God into something more like the traditional idea of God as an ultimate being. The traditional LDS God was only one in an apparently endless sequence of Gods in which each new generation of Gods was not essentially different from the ones that went before. As humans now both have a God and have the potential of becoming Gods themselves, so the present God, when he was "as man is," had a God *and* had the potential of becoming God himself. This teaching indeed goes back to Joseph Smith: "If Jesus Christ was the Son of God, and . . . God, the Father of Jesus Christ, had a Father, you may suppose that *he* had a Father also. Where was there ever a son without a father?" (*Millennial Star*, 24:109–10). The most recent work actually published by the LDS Church that speaks plainly about the history of God is an institute manual titled *Achieving a Celestial Marriage* (1992), which was finally taken out of circulation in 2002: "Our heavenly Father and mother [*sic*] live in an exalted state because they achieved a celestial marriage. As we achieve a like marriage we shall become as they are and begin the creation of our own spirit children" (p. 1). Some observers see this shift away from the traditional view as a positive thing, hoping that perhaps the LDS Church is quietly dropping the older view and looking to the doctrine of deification as a pattern for establishing a new and more Orthodox view of God. Others, however, have been more skeptical, noting that although official LDS Church publications and public-relations materials are very careful to exclude any discussion of the history of God, less official works still contain very explicit statements about it. As recently as 1998, for example, the following passage from nineteenth-century LDS apostle Orson Pratt was approvingly quoted in a book published by the LDS Church–owned Deseret Book Company: "The Father of our spirits has only been doing what his progenitors did before him. . . . The same plan of redemption is carried out by which more ancient worlds have been redeemed" (Matthews, 115).

Where differences are admitted to exist between the LDS and the Eastern Orthodox doctrines of deification, or theosis, they are normally explained away on the LDS side by an appeal to the Great Apostasy, the time when, according to Mormon theology, the ancient church was supposed to have lost its authority and fallen away from the teachings of Christ. The general methodology used by many Mormon writers for sifting the evidence is well stated by LDS apologists Daniel C. Peterson and Stephen D. Ricks in the context of discussing the doctrine of deification. Mormons, they tell us, "are in an enviable position here. Given our belief in the apostasy, we fully expect there to be differences, even vast differences, between the beliefs and the teachings of the Early Church Fathers and Mormon doctrine. Any similarities that exist, however, are potentially understandable as survivals from before that apostasy. When any similarities, even partial ones, exist between Latter-day Saints beliefs and the teachings of the Fathers *but are absent between contemporary mainstream Christendom and the Fathers*, they can be viewed as deeply important" (76; italics original). It is curious that the authors miss the fact that the use of this formula turns all early evidence, no matter what it is, into proof of Mormonism—either proof of Mormon doctrine or proof of the Mormon doctrine of the Great Apostasy. Any similarities between the current LDS doctrine about becoming Gods and the ancient doctrine of deification, no matter how superficial, are interpreted as fragmentary remnants of the original teachings of Jesus and the apostles. Any differences, no matter how significant, are credited to the corrupting influence of the Great Apostasy. The final determiner of what constitutes the influence of the Great

Apostasy is alleged to be current Mormon teaching. Naturally, so fallacious a methodology tends to blind its users to the real import of the ancient evidence.

See also CHRISTIAN; CHRISTIAN, USE AND MISUSE OF THE TERM; EASTERN ORTHODOXY; ROMAN CATHOLICISM

Bibliography. *Achieving a Celestial Marriage*; P. L. Barlow, "Unorthodox Orthodoxy: The Idea of Deification in Christian History," *Sunstone*; D. B. Clendenin, *Eastern Orthodox Christianity: A Western Perspective*; M. R. Hunter, *The Gospel through the Ages*; S. Lash, "Deification," in *The Westminster Dictionary of Christian Theology*, edited by A. Richardson and J. Bowden; V. Lossky, *The Mystical Theology of the Eastern Church*; Lossky, *The Vision of God*; R. J. Matthews, "The Doctrine of the Atonement: The Revelation of the Gospel to Adam," in *Studies in Scripture*, vol. 2; *Millennial Star* (LDS periodical); R. L. Millet, N. B. Reynolds, and L. E. Dahl, *Latter-day Christianity: 10 Basic Issues*; K. E. Norman, "Deification, Early Christian," in *Encyclopedia of Mormonism*, edited by D. H. Ludlow, 4 vols.; Norman, *Deification: The Content of Athanasian Soteriology*; D. Oaks, "Apostasy and Restoration," *Ensign*; R. N. Ostling and J. K. Ostling, *Mormon America: The Power and the Promise*; D. C. Peterson and S. D. Ricks, *Offenders for a Word: How Anti-Mormons Play Word Games to Attack the Latter-day Saints*; S. E. Robinson, *Are Mormons Christians?*; Robinson, "God the Father," in Ludlow, *Encyclopedia of Mormonism*, 4 vols.; J. F. Smith, J. R. Winder, and A. H. Lund, "The Origin of Man," *Ensign*; C. Stavropoulos, "Partakers of Divine Nature," in *Eastern Orthodox Theology: A Contemporary Reader*, edited by D. B. Clendenin; J. Vajda, *"Partakers of the Divine Nature": A Comparative Analysis of Patristic and Mormon Doctrines of Divinization*; K. Ware, *The Orthodox Way*.

R. V. Huggins

DEMONS AND DEMONIZATION IN THE BIBLE.

The term *demon* comes from the Greek words *daimōn* and *daimonion* and refers to supernatural beings with extraordinary powers and functions. In biblical literature, demons, including Satan, are described as fallen angels who are waging an aggressive war against God and humankind.

Demonology in the Old Testament. The Old Testament discusses demonic beings and their activity very little. The best-known encounter between humans and a demonic being is first mentioned in Genesis 3, where Eve is tempted by a creature identified as the serpent, whose identity according to Revelation 12:9 is Satan, the master of deception and corrupter of humankind. The Genesis 3 account of the fall is paradigmatic with respect to the modus operandi of demonic forces. The temptation demonstrates a well-organized, directed approach to luring human beings into ultimate rebellion against God.

First Chronicles 21:1 records the incident when David was influenced by Satan to take a census, which displeased God and brought about judgment against Israel. Job 1 and 2 describes Satan's challenge that Job's loyalty to God is due to God's benevolence toward Job. Through the ages, many have interpreted Ezekiel 28 and Isaiah 14 as describing the original state and fall of Satan (or Lucifer, which is the Latin translation of "star of the morning" in Isa. 14:12), though biblical scholars generally question this interpretation. Satan and fallen angels were originally created equal with respect to moral consistency. They were created not evil or good but with the freedom to bring about whatever moral differences would occur in their personal existence. The fall of Satan and angels shows that even with unblemished reasoning powers, a person can be led by temptation to destructive decisions. Angels with an acute awareness of God's omnipotence still succumbed to folly by their own choice.

In Zechariah 3:1, Satan comes before God to accuse Joshua. Other references to malevolent spiritual beings include Daniel 10:13, where Daniel is hindered by the prince of Persia, against whom Michael the archangel is dispatched. Saul is tormented by an evil spirit (1 Sam. 16:14). Leviticus 17:7, Deuteronomy 32:17, and Psalm 106:37 refer to sacrifices offered to demons.

Classical Greek Writers and Demons. Demons and demonic activity as understood in pre–New Testament classical Greek sources differ substantially from what is attested in the New Testament. Platonic writings describe a threefold division of all animals endowed with a rational soul: gods, demons, and human beings. Gods occupy the highest region (heaven), humanity the lowest (earth), and demons serve in the intermediate (air). Demons are superior to human beings and possess immortality but have the same passions as human beings. Plato's *Cratylus*, *Laws*, and *Symposium* provide insights into the classical Greek world's understanding of demonic beings and their activity. In *Cratylus* 397 and 398, Plato engages Socrates and Hermogenes in a discussion about names. It is argued that a name is nothing more than a word used to describe an object. Socrates asks Hermogenes what follows the name and concept of "gods," to which the reply is demons, heroes, humans. Socrates, quoting Hesiod, states that demons are guardians of mortals. Socrates goes on to state that demons are good and noble. In the *Symposium* 202, demons (*daimōn*) are great spirits who act as intermediaries between the gods and human beings. Later Platonism also taught this view of demonic activity. The *Laws* 4.713 states that demons were appointed by Cronos (a benevolent ruler of the primeval world) to ensure the peace and tranquility of mankind. Augustine challenged the Platonic view of demons and found the mediatorial concept in Platonic demonology to be devastating to the coherency of the Platonic system. The gods relied on demons for mediatorial work because their abode was so far away. Therefore, the aerial demons supplied the gods with information on the affairs of human beings, but this presents several problems. First, if the gods are superior to demons, it seems useless to depend on them for relaying information. Demons would use methods that are inferior to the gods' abilities to gather the same things. Second, the problem of distance is equally flawed, for it shows that the gods are incapable of overcoming distance, which is a sign of weakness. The gods, then, are less than competent in ruling over human beings because they cannot escape their dependence on subordinate beings for information.

Platonism, in teaching the three levels of animal forms (gods, demons, and humans), relegated humanity to the very least of the three beings. Yet humanity is superior to animals in reason and understanding and superior to demons in that human beings live virtuous and good lives. Furthermore, those who are God's elect will someday acquire immortal bodies, but demons will suffer punishment.

Demons and the Intertestamental Period. In the intertestamental literature, demons are malevolent beings that afflict humankind and are associated with various sins. An evil demon named Asmodeus is mentioned in Tobit 3:8, 17. Scholars note that *The Testaments of the Twelve Patriarchs* contains an extensive demonology. Demons, or evil spirits, are deceitful and cause error (*Testament of Reuben* 2.1; 3.2–3; *Testament of Judah* 20.1; 23.1).

New Testament Demonology. The New Testament presents a more fully developed understanding of demons, one that is consistent with the demonology presented in the Old Testament and intertestamental literature. Demons are incorporeal beings that oppose God and seek the destruction of humanity. Numerous incidents of demon possession and deliverance are recorded in the Gospels (Matt. 4:24; 8:16, 33; 9:33; 17:18; Mark 7:26; Luke 4:33; 8:29; 11:14) and Acts (16:16–18). Scripture indicates demons are intelligent and knowledgeable, but they are not omniscient. They have a clear understanding of the person and nature of God. Demons are monotheistic according to James 2:19, which states demons believe that God is one, or is the true God, and fear him. They also know who Jesus is and recognize his authority over them according to Luke 4:33–35, 41 and Acts 19:15–16. They specifically call Christ the Holy One of God, which identifies Jesus Christ as the Messiah (cf. Luke 1:31–34). The confession of demons regarding Christ's messianic status is explicitly stated in Luke 4:41, according to which demons acknowledge Jesus to be the Christ. Demons also understand the gospel (Acts 16:16–18). The slave girl follows Paul around and proclaims he is preaching the way of salvation. Based on the biblical record, demons are orthodox in their understanding of who God and Christ are and of the means of salvation. Thus they aggressively seek to distort and misrepresent these truths.

Satan in particular is well versed in the use of Scripture, which he quotes in Matthew 4. In 1 Timothy 4:1, demons are described as both deceitful and the authors of false doctrine. The existence of complex doctrinal systems contrary to orthodox Christianity indicates demons' exceptional ability to reason. Augustine says that demonic beings are fully capable of decision making and have acute reasoning powers. The demonic realm also apparently lacks hierarchy or authority structure. In Ephesians 2:2, Satan is identified as the ruler of the air (according to Plato's threefold division of animals, demons occupy the air) and as being in authority over demons (Matt. 9:34; Luke 11:15).

Post–New Testament Demonology. The church has historically played an important role in combating spiritual evil by carrying out exorcisms and requiring believers to renounce the devil as a condition for baptism. However, in its dealing with demonic forces, the early church did resort to extraordinary practices that have little or no scriptural support. Exorcism, the practice of expelling demons from the possessed, is attested in the New Testament. Jesus cast out demons, as did Paul. However, exsufflation, the act of breathing against the evil spirits, has no biblical support but was a common practice with the early church fathers.

The early church used baptism as a time for renouncing the devil and his demonic cohorts. This is known as the baptismal renunciation. Origen and Augustine characterized the devil as the ruler of this world, and they considered it essential that during the ceremony of baptism the candidate for baptism publicly renounce the devil wholeheartedly.

Demonization. Demonization is a complex and controversial issue that continues to be debated frequently among theologians and biblical scholars. By definition *demonization* describes the condition of one who is demon possessed. Some theologians argue that the translation "demon possession" is incorrect, for demons do not technically own anyone. The preferred translation would be "demonization" or "demonized," for these terms convey the idea that, at worst, demons control or invade individuals, but they don't possess.

One particular question about demonization that has caused considerable controversy is whether Christians can be demonized (invaded). In 1971 Old Testament scholar Merrill F. Unger published *Demons in the World Today*, in which he took the position that Christians could be "invaded" (or possessed, according to some reviews of the book) by demonic beings. This was a significant shift for Unger, who in a much earlier work, *Biblical Demonology* (a revision of Unger's 1945 ThD dissertation), held that Christians could not be invaded by demonic beings but were subject to attacks from without by means of pressure, suggestion, and temptation. In a later work, *What Demons Can Do to Saints*, Unger addressed in much more detail the relationship between demons and true believers, arguing that Christians can be invaded. His research was significantly influenced by

case studies, which prompted him to change his position. It is this application of what some describe as experiential theology that raises concern.

C. Fred Dickason has written extensively on demonology and the influence of demons on people. He contends that the idea of demon possession is incorrect, for demons do not possess people but are mere squatters. From the standpoint of biblical theology, which is theology derived directly from the clear statements of Scripture, there are no passages that conclusively support the demonization of believers. New Testament descriptions of alleged believers who seem to be victims of demonization include Ananias and Sapphira (Acts 5:1–3) and Simon Magus (Acts 8). However, these instances are inconclusive and cannot be used to substantiate the belief that Christians can be invaded.

Whether Christians can be demonized is debated from the standpoint of systematic theology. The fact that Scripture is inconclusive on this issue does not preclude, it is argued, the possibility of believers being inhabited by demonic beings. A number of theological arguments are used to support the belief that demons can inhabit believers. It is argued that believers can lose their salvation if they sin continuously and repudiate Christ. This leads to the loss of salvation and eventual invasion by demonic beings. Some contend that Satan has the power to exert his will over people, including believers who are entrenched in sin (2 Tim. 2:26). Some, citing King Saul as evidence, argue that God may chastise believers for repeated sin by using demons as instruments of correction. Other ways in which believers can open themselves up to demonic invasion include seeking sign gifts, which can open one up to a deceiving spirit. Inappropriate participation in occult activities such as the Ouija board, divination, or necromancy (seeking contact with the dead) provides opportunities for demonization.

Opponents of the view that believers can be demonized contend that spatial constraints prevent the concurrent presence of both demons and the Holy Spirit. Salvation in Christ means we are no longer our own but bought with a price. Therefore, demonic beings cannot possess believers, for demons do not have the authority to take over those who belong to Christ. One common argument contends that demons and the Spirit of God cannot dwell in the same body because God is holy and evil spirits unholy, making close proximity impossible.

Both biblical and theological support for and opposition to the demonization of believers are inconclusive. What has contributed to the view that Christians can be inhabited by demonic beings and poses strong evidence for such a view is the existence of case studies by Christian counselors and those who have dealt with allegedly demonized Christians in varied ministries. The clinical evidence that has been amassed includes specific case studies by competent Christian counselors and theologians who have dealt with people who claim to be believers yet are afflicted by the presence of demonic forces within them.

Though the evidence from clinical sources for the demonization of believers seems irrefutable, it remains circumstantial. On the other hand, the biblical and theological evidence against such demonization is inconclusive.

Bibliography. C. Arnold, *Powers of Darkness*; M. Bubeck, *The Adversary*; Bubeck, *Overcoming the Adversary*; C. F. Dickason, *Demon Possession and the Christian: A New Perspective*; H. A. Kelly, *The Devil at Baptism*; S. Noll, *Angels of Light, Powers of Darkness*; S. Page, *Powers of Evil: A Biblical Study of Satan and Demons*; G. Riley, "Demon," in *Dictionary of Deities and Demons in the Bible*; M. Unger, *Biblical Demonology*; Unger, *Demons in the World Today*; Unger, *What Demons Can Do to Saints*.

S. J. Rost

DEPENDENT ORIGINATION. At the heart of Buddhist metaphysics, the doctrine of dependent origination (Sanskrit, *pratityasamutpada*), also known as dependent arising, states that all the phenomena experienced by human beings make up a mutually interdependent system of entities that ultimately is an undifferentiated unity of existence. On this view, any given phenomenon can be said to exist (in a provisional sense) only because of its interrelationship with every other phenomenon; nothing has a genuine, substantive identity independently of everything else. Because all things are so conditioned and transient in nature, they are, in the final analysis, "empty." The Buddha's spiritual awakening was fundamentally a receiving of profound insight into the real nature of the world as dependently originating.

See also BUDDHISM

Bibliography. C. Feldman, "Dependent Origination," *Insight Journal*, https://www.bcbsdharma.org/article/dependent-origination/; M. Sayadaw, *A Discourse on Dependent Origination*.

M. Power

DEVEKUTH. In Hasidic Judaism, *devekuth* is a communion between God and human beings that takes the form of continual awareness of the presence of God and unceasing devotion to him. Although devekuth is supposed to be cultivated in all areas and stages of life, Hasidic Jews especially focus on this "cleaving to God" during times of prayer—which often are passionate to the point of being ecstatic—and when performing their religious duties. Hasidic Jews believe that there is a reciprocal relationship between God and human beings: God exerts an influence on human affairs, and human beings can likewise persuade God to act in certain ways.

See also BUDDHISM; HASIDISM; HINDUISM; JUDAISM; MYSTICISM; ZOHAR

Bibliography. L. Jacobs, *The Jewish Religion: A Companion.*

M. Power

DHAMMA. *See* DHARMA

DHARMA. *Dharma* (Pali, *dhamma*) is a word derived from a Sanskrit root with a broad semantic field but generally understood to mean "teaching" or "body of knowledge." Thus *dharma* can refer to canonical texts and their commentaries, or knowable phenomena, or the path to realization.

In Hinduism dharma is a religious or moral law related to one's caste. In Buddhism, dharma is the teaching of the Buddha, namely, the Four Noble Truths: all is suffering, the cause of suffering is ignorance that gives rise to desire/attachment, there is an end to suffering, and the means to this is through the Eightfold Path. Dharma is one of the Three Jewels in which a Buddhist takes refuge: the Buddha, the dharma, and the *sangha.* The dharma is transmitted through lineages from master to pupil and is symbolized by the eight-spoked wheel.

Dharma also refers metaphysically to mind and matter, and consequently to eternal law and truth. Hence it is nuanced to mean moral virtue or the eternal substance that animates life.

Used in compound nouns, dharma can refer to any number of things—dharma center (a teaching center), dharma name (a name given to a devotee), dharma practice (the praxis of Buddhism), dharma bum (a drifter between lineages in Buddhism).

See also BUDDHISM; HINDUISM

Bibliography. C. S. Prebish and M. Baumann, *Westward Dharma: Buddhism beyond Asia.*

H. P. Kemp

DHARMAKAYA. *Dharmakaya* (Sanskrit, "dharma body") is one of the "three bodies" (*trikaya*) or modes of being of the Buddha, specifically, the transcendent. In Mahayana Buddhism, the dharmakaya is understood as the ultimate reality from which other forms of the Buddha derive. Hence the three bodies are dharmakaya (body of essence—the unmanifested, absolute mode), *sambhogakaya* (body of enjoyment—the heavenly mode), and *nirmanakaya* (body of transformation—the earthly manifested mode). In their simplest form, the three bodies can be understood as the abstract, the mythic, and the human realms.

Dharmakaya is the absolute and the source of everything; therefore the word *dharmakaya* is synonymous with *emptiness.* Dharmakaya lacks personality and therefore is not usually prayed to, although it is honored and praised. It can only be experienced by fully realized beings.

See also BUDDHISM; MAHAYANA BUDDHISM

Bibliography. D. S. Lopez Jr., *Buddhism: An Introduction and Guide.*

H. P. Kemp

DHIKR. *Dhikr* (Arabic, "invocation" or "remembrance") is a fundamental Sufi devotional exercise that frequently involves the repetitive utterance of various names and attributes of God, though some practitioners also petition God and read aloud from the Qur'an and portions of the hadith (sayings of Muhammad). In some cases, dhikr is performed inaudibly. The aim of dhikr is to produce an intense awareness of God in the devotee. Often dhikr is performed by groups of Sufis (in which case it is called *hadrah*), though it also is done by individuals. The details of this practice and its accompanying rituals vary from one Sufi order to the next. Elements of such ceremonies include singing, dancing, playing musical instruments, burning incense, and trance meditation. In a more general sense, dhikr refers to any activity that cultivates an awareness of God in the practitioner.

See also SUFISM

Bibliography. W. C. Chittick, *The Sufi Path of Knowledge*; M. R. B. Muhaiyaddeen, *Dhikr: The Remembrance of God*.

R. L. Drouhard

DHIMMI. The word *dhimmi* means "protected" and is the name accorded to Jews, Christians, the Sabeans (Qur'an 22:17), and sometimes the Zoroastrians when they live submissively under Islamic rule. The identity of the Jews and the Christians, usually called "people of the book" in Muslim literature, is not in doubt, but the Sabeans remained a mystery to early Muslims. Several groups, most notably the star worshipers of the city of Harran (today in southeastern Turkey), claimed this title and the protection that went along with it. In general the protection was accorded to those groups that, according to the sacred history of Islam, had received revelations that were genuine but were superseded by the coming of Islam. Each one of them had received a "book" (revelation) from God; for the most part they had corrupted the message of the book but still deserved some residual respect as a result of this historical revelation. The Zoroastrians also were accorded the title of "people of the book," although there was some disagreement about whether Zoroaster was a prophet of God. Since most Zoroastrians converted to Islam during the first three hundred years of Islam, this problem was not a major one. However, as Muslims conquered territories that contained adherents to religions not mentioned in the Qur'an or without an obvious prophet or book, it became problematic to know how to deal with them from a religious point of view. This issue was far from academic since if a religious group was not classified as one of the "peoples of the book," then it would be incumbent upon Muslims to fight and kill them until the only survivors were those who had converted to Islam. The problem was particularly acute in India, where both Buddhists and Hindus

were nonmonotheists and too numerous to be fought or killed. Eventually both were given the status of "people of the book."

The basic agreement of what constitutes the *dhimma* was worked out in the document known as the Pact of 'Umar. The pact is ascribed to the second caliph, 'Umar b. al-Khattab (r. 634–44), but more probably dates from the eighth or perhaps even the ninth century. Its terms include the payment of a tax called the *jizya* tax and the agreement not to aid enemies of the Muslims, not to carry any weapons, not to build any new churches or synagogues or renovate them, and to wear distinctive clothing (so Muslims could distinguish the dhimmi from themselves).

It seems that the Pact of 'Umar was first applied during the period of the caliph al-Mutawakkil (847–61), and its application was rather intermittent until the period of the Crusades except in areas such as Spain and North Africa where there were hostilities between Muslims and Christians. However, during the period of the Crusades and afterward, the Pact of 'Umar became much more important and normative, and a number of its terms were part of Mamluk (1250–1517) and Ottoman (1517–1924) law. Under the pressure of Europeans, the Ottomans revoked discriminatory aspects of the Pact of 'Umar by an edict called the Hatt-i Sharif of the Gülhane in 1839. Despite this edict, the Pact of 'Umar continues to this day to be influential in deciding what are the social limits of non-Muslims within a majority-Muslim society, though it does not have the force of law.

See also ISLAM, BASIC BELIEFS OF; JIZYA; ZOROASTRIANISM

Bibliography. S. al-Din Ibn Qayyim al-Jawziyya, *Ahkam ahl al-dhimma*; S. Goitein, *A Mediterranean Society*.

D. B. Cook

DIVINATION IN THE BIBLE. The Bible condemns divination in several polemical passages (e.g., Lev. 19:26, 31; 20:27; Deut. 18:9–14; 2 Kings 17:17) because of idolatry. Some techniques are specifically prohibited, such as contacting the dead via a medium (Lev. 20:6; 1 Sam. 28:3–25; 1 Chron. 10:13). However, the listing of prohibited activities is of secondary importance, as the biblical writers compel the reader to meditate on the question, "Which God are you dealing with here—Yahweh or a false god?" The primary lesson is about trusting God because it is spiritually fatal to enter into relations with other deities.

However, the Bible approves of some divinatory practices, as being based on belief in God's sovereignty over human history. Laban admits that through an unspecified form of divination God has shown him that Jacob is blessed (Gen. 30:27). Abimelech receives a revelatory dream from God concerning the true marital status of Abraham and Sarah (Gen. 20:1–13). God is revealed to Jacob in a dream (Gen. 28:12–17). Joseph is an interpreter of dreams (Gen. 37:5–10; 40:5–23; 41:1–36), and two principal episodes occur in Egypt, where, as was noted earlier, dreams had a pivotal role in the religion of the pharaohs. Joseph also used a cup for divination (Gen. 44:5).

Like Joseph, Daniel is renowned as an interpreter of dreams (Dan. 1:17; 2:1–19). Dreams and night visions are often the mode through which prophecies are given (Num. 12:6; Deut. 13:1–5; Isa. 29:7; Jer. 23:25–32). In some cases, either God or an angel sent from God speaks through a dream (Gen. 31:10–13; 1 Kings 3:5–15; Matt. 1:20; 2:13, 19; Acts 16:9). An angel may be sent to clarify the meaning of a dream (Dan. 7:16; 9:21–26; Zech. 4:1–6:8; Rev. 7:13–17).

The casting of lots is justified in that the will of God is made known through it (Prov. 16:33). Lots were cast to discover a guilty person (1 Sam. 14:41; Jonah 1:7), divide up the tribal lands (Num. 26:55; 33:54; 34:13; 36:2; Josh. 15:1; 16:1; 17:1), choose the goat on the Day of Atonement (Lev. 16:7–10), and select someone for a task or role (1 Sam. 10:20; 1 Chron. 24:5, 7–19; Neh. 10:34; Luke 1:9; Acts 1:26). The use of the Urim and Thummim by the high priest (Exod. 28:30; Num. 27:21; 1 Sam. 23:9–12) involved a form of stone or stick throwing to obtain a yes or no answer. The use of a sign as confirming a predetermined action is attested in Gideon's testing with the fleece (Judg. 6:36–40) and in his selecting a raiding force on the basis of which way his soldiers drank water (Judg. 7:4–7). The prophet Elisha instructed Joash (2 Kings 13:14–19) to strike the ground with arrows for a sign of a victory over Aram. Finally, God uses the celestial bodies as signs (Rev. 6:12–14), and even to woo the Magi astrologers of Persia to find the Christ child (Matt. 2:1–12).

Current Debate on Prophecy. Prophecy has been traditionally regarded as a divinatory practice because it involves foretelling events and discerning the will of a deity. However, modern scholarly opinion has been divided over divination and prophecy. Nineteenth-century scholars such as Julius Wellhausen and James Frazer interpreted religious phenomena using a unilinear evolutionary model that artificially dictated how religions must develop from magic and animism through to polytheism and then monotheism. These scholars separated prophecy out from divination, and they argued that religions in Mesopotamia and Canaan were characterized by magic and divination, while the religion of Israel was characterized by prophecy.

Recently scholars such as Frederick Cryer, Lester Grabbe, Ann Jeffers, and Ben Witherington have called into question the position adopted by Wellhausen and Frazer. There is a growing realization that Israel shared much in common with its ancient Near Eastern neighbors. As a phenomenon, prophecy was not unique to Israel and is attested in neighboring cultures. So in terms of cultural anthropology and religious phenomenology, there was some overlap between prophecy and divination, both in terms of a cosmology of divine guidance and even in terms of techniques. What primarily differentiated Israel from its neighbors was the theological content of biblical religion. The biblical texts reiterate the need to distinguish between "which deity" is being manifested and whom you believe and trust in. While God condemned specific divinatory techniques in order to prevent idolatry, he did not reject divination altogether.

See also KABBALAH

Bibliography. R. Buckland, *The Fortune-Telling Book: The Encyclopedia of Divination and Soothsaying*; F. H. Cryer, *Divination in Ancient Israel and Its Near Eastern Environment*; L. L. Grabbe, *Priests, Prophets, Diviners, Sages*; P. G. Hiebert, R. D. Shaw, and T. Tiénou, *Understanding Folk Religion: A Christian Response to Popular Beliefs and Practices*; A. Jeffers, *Magic and Divination in Ancient Palestine and Syria*; B. Witherington, *Jesus the Seer: The Progress of Prophecy*.

P. Johnson

DOCETISM. The term *Docetism* refers to the heresy according to which Christ's body, birth, suffering, and/or death were in some sense unreal; they only "seemed" real. Docetism was widespread in the second and third centuries. John, for instance, appears to attack it in 2 John 7. Ignatius of Antioch (d. ca. 110) criticizes it (cf., e.g., *To the Trallians* 10). Irenaeus (d. ca. 202) charges a wide array of gnostic sects with Docetism (cf., e.g., *Against Heresies* 1.23.2; 1.26.1; 2.24.4; 3.11.3; 4.33.3), and Tertullian devotes his treatise *On the Flesh of Christ* to its refutation. Docetism's prevalence notwithstanding, few groups actually called themselves "docetists" (cf. Hippolytus, *Refutation of All Heresies* 8.1–4; Clement of Alexandria, *Stromateis* 7.17), and patristic authors rarely applied the term to others (cf., however, Eusebius, *Ecclesiastical History* 6.12; Theodoret, *Epistle* 82). Docetist sentiments appear in several apocryphal works (e.g., *Acts of John* 88–104; *Apocalypse of Peter* 81–83). Docetism survived gnosticism's demise in heresies such as Manichaeism and Catharism and in Christian Science and modern esotericism.

See also HERESY, DEFINITION OF

Bibliography. P. L. Gavrilyuk, *The Suffering of the Impassible God: The Dialectics of Patristic Thought*; L. Hurtado, *Lord Jesus Christ: Devotion to Jesus in Earliest Christianity*.

D. W. Jowers

DOCTRINE AND COVENANTS. One of the four standard works, or scriptural collections, of the Church of Jesus Christ of Latter-day Saints, and the only one acknowledged to be of completely modern origin rather than including inspired translations of ancient texts. The introduction to the Doctrine and Covenants (D&C) describes it as "a collection of divine revelations and inspired declarations given for the establishment and regulation of the kingdom of God on the earth in the last days." It is divided into 138 "sections" (not chapters), each of which is subdivided into verses, and all but five of which were authored solely by Joseph Smith Jr. Two "Official Declarations" are also appended to the D&C. The sections are generally arranged in the chronological order in which they were produced (out-of-order sections include 1, 10, 99, 133, 134, and 137).

Origin and Editions. On November 1, 1831, the LDS Church convened a priesthood conference in Hiram, Ohio. By this time, Joseph Smith had already produced some sixty-five revelations, and a decision was made at the conference to publish Smith's revelations. The first edition of this collection was titled *A Book of Commandments, for the Government of the Church of Christ* (the official name of the LDS Church at the time). Between the time of the conference and the scheduled date of first publication of the Book of Commandments in 1833, Smith produced thirty-four more revelations, and a large print run was expected. However, both the number of copies and the number of revelations included were cut short by a fire set at the printers by a mob on July 20, 1833. Section 1 of this first edition was Smith's revelation that was issued on the date when he had officially organized the church (April 6, 1830) and that had circulated independently as "The Articles and Covenants of the Church."

In the winter of 1834–35, a series of seven "lectures on theology" were presented to the School of the Elders in Kirtland, Ohio. Although no name is explicitly attached to the lectures, it is generally agreed that Sidney Rigdon, an early leader of the movement, was the principal author and that Joseph Smith was both involved in crafting the lectures and responsible for "preparing the lectures on theology for publication" (Smith, *History of the Church*, 2:180). Thus Joseph Smith clearly endorsed the theology of these lectures. The lectures covered the meaning of faith; ancient history of God's revelation; God's attributes; the Father, the Son, and the Holy Ghost; salvation; and the effects of faith. According to these lectures, the Father is a personage of spirit, the Son is a personage of tabernacle (i.e., he has a physical body), and the Holy Ghost is the mind shared by those two personages.

In 1835 the LDS Church published a collection that included both the seven lectures and a larger, edited corpus of Smith's revelations. The lectures were titled "On the Doctrine of the Church of the Latter Day Saints" (as the church was at that time called) and are better known today as the *Lectures on Faith*. The title of the edited compilation of revelations was "Covenants and Commandments." The whole collection was published in August 1835 with the title *Doctrine and Covenants of the Church of the Latter Day Saints: Carefully Selected from the Revelations of God*. This edition contained 103 sections (including two accidentally given

the same number, 66), all but the last two of which were written by Joseph Smith. The sections then numbered 101 and 102 were written by Oliver Cowdery, and section 101 later proved especially controversial, as it permitted Mormons to marry non-Mormons and explicitly rejected the practice of polygamy. The order and enumeration of the sections in the D&C differed from the first edition (e.g., Book of Commandments 1 became D&C 20).

Several other editions of the D&C have appeared over the years, but four contained especially significant changes. The 1876 edition divided the sections into verses, added twenty-six new sections (including one from Brigham Young, sec. 136), and dropped Cowdery's old section 101 because Mormons were at the time openly practicing polygamy. Printings from 1908 and later included Official Declaration 1, announcing that polygamous unions would no longer be performed. The most dramatically different edition was that of 1921, when the *Lectures on Faith* were dropped from the D&C. The usual explanation is that the lectures were never recognized as scripture, but such a claim is strained in view of their inclusion for eighty-six years in the D&C, which has been consistently treated as scripture. The real reason is no doubt that the lectures' theology was no longer compatible with LDS teaching and had not been since at least 1843, when Smith began teaching that the Father had a body of flesh and bones. The 1981 edition added visions from Joseph Smith in 1838 (sec. 137) and from Joseph F. Smith in 1918 (sec. 138) as well as Official Declaration 2 (extending the priesthood to men of all races).

Contents. The sections in the current edition of the D&C can be grouped chronologically and geographically into five periods, reflecting the physical relocations of the LDS movement during its formative years.

(1) Prior to Ohio (1828–January 1831). Thirty-nine sections of the D&C (3–40, 133)

date from these early years preceding the founding of the LDS Church and the first ten months or so after its founding. (The LDS Church dates D&C 2, a brief statement based on Mal. 4:5–6 from the angel Moroni in his first visit to Smith, to the year of that visitation in 1823, but it was not written until 1839.) These sections originated from revelations given in Harmony, Pennsylvania, and the towns of Manchester and Fayette in New York. Typical subjects of these earliest sections include matters pertaining to the translation of the Book of Mormon, the establishment of the new church, and the commissioning of the movement's first missionaries.

(2) The Saints in Kirtland (1831–37). Seventy-five sections (1, 41–112, 134, 137) were delivered when Kirtland, Ohio, was the primary location of the gathering Saints. Most of these sections originated in Kirtland and nearby Hiram. Notable subjects of these sections include Smith's work on an inspired translation of the Bible and some theological matters arising from that work, prophecies and teachings pertaining to establishing a new gathering place in Missouri, and the building of a temple in Kirtland. Important concepts introduced during this period include the three heavenly kingdoms (D&C 76), humanity's preexistence with God before creation (D&C 90), and the two priesthood orders named for Aaron and Melchizedek (D&C 107).

(3) Far West (1838–39). Twelve sections (2, 113–23) originated at Far West, Missouri, a city north of the Kansas City/Independence area to which the Saints had gathered during this stormy period of their history. The last three of these sections were originally revelations that Joseph Smith gave from the nearby Liberty Jail (121–23).

(4) Nauvoo (1841–43). Nine sections (124–32) consisting of some of Smith's last revelations, were given either at Nauvoo, a city in Illinois just across the eastern Missouri border where the Saints had settled after being driven out of Missouri, or in the nearby town known then as Ramus. These sections include Smith's most theologically radical revelations found anywhere in LDS scripture, revelations that decisively marked Mormonism as religiously distinct from orthodox Christianity, including teachings about baptisms for the dead (127–28), God the Father as a being of flesh and bones (130), and the doctrines of celestial marriage, polygamy, and becoming gods (131–32).

(5) After Joseph Smith (1844–1978). During this period, three sections (135, 136, and 138) dated 1844, 1847, and 1918, respectively, and the two Official Declarations dated 1890 and 1978 were added. D&C 135, by John Taylor, pronounces Smith a martyr and affirms that he did more for the salvation of the world than anyone besides Jesus Christ. D&C 136, by Brigham Young, instructed the Saints about how they should organize and behave for the journey west. D&C 138, by Joseph F. Smith, was a vision concerning the preaching of the gospel to the spirits of the departed. Official Declaration 1 was Wilford Woodruff's statement that the LDS was no longer sanctioning plural marriages, while Official Declaration 2 was Spencer W. Kimball's directive that the priesthood orders were now to be open to men of all races.

Analysis. Several considerations raise difficult questions concerning the claim that the D&C is a collection of inspired texts. As has already been noted, materials have been removed and other materials added to the D&C by the LDS Church in ways that imply that its contents are something other than the unchanging word of God. At different times, the D&C rejected, then affirmed, and then disavowed the practice of polygamy. Although numerous other significant changes were made, the removal of the *Lectures on Faith* after it had been part of the collection for eighty-six years is perhaps the most dramatic example of the malleability of scripture in LDS religion. Another consideration is the fact that the D&C contains predictive prophecies that did not and cannot come to pass, most notably its 1832 prediction that a temple would be built in Jackson County, Missouri, before that generation had all passed away (D&C 84:1–5). Finally, for orthodox Christians the most telling evidence against the inspiration of the D&C is its lack of theological coherence with the Bible. The problems include its doctrine that God the Father has a body of flesh and bones, its turning polygamy into part of a path to godhood, its recasting of the Aaronic priesthood and Melchizedek's typological priesthood into a two-tier Christian sacerdotal system, and its view that virtually all human beings will enjoy immortality in one of three separate heavenly kingdoms.

See also CHURCH OF JESUS CHRIST OF LATTER-DAY SAINTS; STANDARD WORKS

Bibliography. T. G. Alexander, "The Reconstruction of Mormon Doctrine," *Sunstone*; L. H. Dahl and C. D. Tate Jr., *The Lectures on Faith in Historical Perspective*; R. W. Doxey et al., "Doctrine and Covenants," in *Encyclopedia of Mormonism*, edited by D. H. Ludlow, 4 vols.; R. S. Jensen et al., eds., *The Joseph Smith Papers: Revelations and Translations*, 2 vols.; H. M. Marquardt, *The Joseph Smith Revelations: Text & Commentary*; N. Reynolds, "Case for Sidney Rigdon as Author of the Lectures on Faith," *Journal of Mormon History*; H. Smith and J. Sjodahl, *Doctrine and Covenants Commentary*; Joseph Smith Jr., *History of the Church of Jesus Christ of Latter-day Saints*, 7 vols.; R. S. Van Wagoner, S. C. Walker, and A. D. Roberts, "The 'Lectures on Faith': A Case Study in Decanonization," *Dialogue: A Journal of Mormon Thought*; R. J. Woodford, "The Historical Development of Doctrine and Covenants," 3 vols., PhD diss., BYU.

R. M. Bowman Jr.

DOCTRINE OF THE MEAN (CHUNG-YUNG/ZHONGYONG). Contained in a larger work titled Record of Rites (Li chi), the Doctrine of the Mean is a short composition traditionally attributed to Kung-chi (ca. mid-fifth century BC), a grandson of Confucius. The title of this work has been translated variously as "the constant mean," "the middle way," "the common centrality," and "the unwobbling pivot." Its central purpose is to explicate how to follow a prescribed path of virtue. The Doctrine of the Mean is divided into twenty-three brief chapters that describe the "mandate of heaven" that is applicable to rulers and subjects alike. According to the text, heaven (*t'ien*) has established a way to achieve the Confucian virtues that can be followed by everyone, though this way does not consist in legalistic rule-keeping. Instead, it involves developing a moral sense that unwaveringly gravitates toward the proper balance between extremes of human conduct. Adhering to this path of equilibrium is said to bring about personal and corporate tranquility and prosperity.

See also CONFUCIANISM

Bibliography. J. H. and E. N. Berthrong, *Confucianism*; W. T. De Bary and I. Bloom, *Sources of Chinese Tradition*, 2nd ed., vol. 1; J. Legge, ed., *The Analects of Confucius, The Great Learning, Doctrine of the Mean*.

S. J. Rost

DRAVYA. *Dravya* (substance) is an important category in Jain metaphysics. Jainism asserts that the world in which we live is merely one of seven layers of the cosmos. This portion of the universe consists of two basic types of things, living beings (*jiva*) and nonliving entities (*ajiva*), which together make up the Six Universal Substances. Though these half-dozen substances (*dravyas*) are continually changing with regard to their ephemeral (*anitya*) exterior form, their underlying essence is indestructible and eternal (*nitya*). Thus the *dravya* and fundamental qualities (*gunas*) of each object remain immutable, in static permanence (*dhrauvya*), notwithstanding the innumerable outward alterations that are perceived to occur in them.

See also JAINISM

Bibliography. H. W. House, *Charts of World Religions*; P. S. Jain, *Essentials of Jainism*; P. S. Jaini, *The Jaina Path of Purification*.

M. Power

DRUZE, THE. The Druze are an Islamic-like sect mostly located in Syria, Israel, Lebanon, and Jordan, though there are Druze in Australia, Canada, the US, Africa, and Europe. It is thought that there are as many as one million Druze worldwide, with as many as half living in Syria. The sect is considered heretical by mainstream Muslims.

The Name of the Group. The origin of the term *Druze* is unknown. The Druze refer to themselves as Ahl al-Tawhid (people of unitarianism or monotheism) or al-Muwahhidun (unitarians or monotheists). The majority of opinion is that the name Druze comes from one of the early leaders of the movement, Anushtakin ad-Darazi. However, the Druze regard ad-Darazi as a heretic. Others see the term as a derisive, ironic use of an Arabic term: *derasa* (those who read) or *derrisa* (those in possession of the truth) or *drugs* (the clever, initiated). The first historical use of the name Druze is in the accounts of a Jewish traveler to Lebanon around 1165.

History. The Druze trace their founding to Abu Ali al-Mansur al Aziz Billah, the sixth Fatimid caliph and the sixteenth Isma'ili imam, also known as al-Hakim. He lived during the eleventh century AD. Al-Hakim began life in the Isma'ili branch of Shi'a Islam. Shi'a Islam by this time had diverged from Sunni Islam to the extent that their adherents violently persecuted each other over theological disputes. Shi'ites hold that there is a succession of divinely inspired leaders, descended from Muhammad through various imams. These imams are considered infallible in matters of Islamic interpretation.

Isma'ili was the largest of the many branches of Shi'a at the time of al-Hakim's rule in Egypt. Isma'ili Islam became focused on the mystical aspects of Islam and the nature of Allah and taught that the imams were the manifestation of the truth and reality of Allah. There was a strong element of messianic expectation within Isma'ili, with many expecting one of the Fatimids to usher in a universal Islamic kingdom. Al-Hakim was seen by many to be this deliverer figure, known in Islam as the mahdi. One of al-Hakim's followers, Hamza ibn Ali, began to propagate the idea that al-Hakim was a divine manifestation of the Creator and the expected mahdi. This idea was embraced by al-Hakim himself, who in 1017 issued an official decree that he was the manifestation of Allah and that his subjects should embrace this belief and worship him accordingly. Hamza was tasked with spreading this new proclamation throughout the Fatimid Empire. Hamza spread the message that al-Hakim had come to introduce a new paradigm and that people should abandon all previous religious systems and worship "the one" as revealed in al-Hakim.

Al-Hakim disappeared in 1021 under mysterious circumstances. Immediately after his disappearance, proclamations were posted in mosques announcing that al-Hakim was disappointed with the lack of success he had in correcting "religious divisions, social disparities, and moral ills of his time" (Betts, 11). Historians are divided over why al-Hakim disappeared. Some say he was assassinated on orders from his sister, whom he had accused of immoral acts. Other stories include that he left Cairo to become a Christian monk (his mother was a Christian from an important Orthodox family), or that he traveled east to Persia and continued to teach there for many years.

Hamza disappeared shortly after al-Hakim, probably fleeing the intense persecution of al-Hakim's successor, al-Zahir, who made it his personal mission to completely destroy the Druze in the Fatimid Empire, which he almost succeeded in doing. After six years the persecutions eased, so Hamza and other Druze leaders came out of hiding and once again began to preach the message. Al-Hakim had promised he would return to the faithful at any moment within their generation, fueling missionary zeal. After al-Hakim failed to return immediately, the Druze began to preach that he would come at the end of time to usher in an eternal kingdom.

By the late fifteenth century, the Druze had been all but pushed out of Egypt and most of the Middle East. However, their stronghold of Lebanon, northern Palestine, and southern Syria had achieved a somewhat autonomous rule, under prominent Druze families. They took advantage of the power vacuum between the decline of the Mamelukes and ascendency of the Ottomans. Their autonomous kingdom culminated in the rule of Fakhr al-Din al-Ma'ni II, whom the Druze hold in special regard due to his religious tolerance, fair rule, and political acumen. The Ottomans, fearing his rising power, had him assassinated in 1635.

Over the next three centuries the Druze were persecuted externally and fought a series of internal wars over leadership. These conflicts resulted in a gradual decline in the autonomy of the Druze as well as in their actual numbers. After World War II, the Druze participated in the political changes occurring all over the Middle East, and they gained a measure of political influence in the newly created nations of Lebanon and Syria.

Since the creation of Israel, the Druze have had an uneasy but generally positive relationship with the nation of Israel. Due to several attacks on Druze villages by Arab militants, the Druze mostly chose to support Israel in its war of independence. Since then, the Druze have enjoyed tentative toleration from Israel, although the taking of the Golan Heights by Israel in the Six Day War has caused a strain in this relationship since many Druze families are now divided between Syria and Israel, and many Golan Druze consider themselves Syrian, not Israeli.

Beliefs. Although Druze are most often classified as a Muslim sect, they do not consider themselves Muslim or Islamic, and a study of their beliefs reveals they have only superficial and cultural ties to Islam.

God and His Prophets. The foundational belief in the Druze faith is "the revelation of God in the form of a human being" (Dānā, 15). Druze theologians argue that God thought it necessary to manifest himself in physical form because human beings would have difficulty believing in his existence otherwise. According to Druze belief, al-Hakim was the final revelation of God, and Hamza "is granted senior status as the connecting link between divinity and humanity" (Dānā, 15). Druze believe God is one, thus their self-designation as unitarians or monotheists. They also hold that there were seven great prophets: Adam, Noah, Abraham, Moses, Jesus, Muhammad, and Muhammad ibn Isma'il (the founder of the Isma'ili sect). Each of these prophets was given only a partial, progressive revelation. However, throughout history a select number of men have been granted special access to secretly study the true faith. The first, and therefore most important, such man was Jethro, Moses's father-in-law, whose tomb in the Golan the Druze venerate and believe to be a place of blessing.

Evangelism. Druze teach that there was a limited period of preaching when new believers were to be sought. This period ended in 1043, when Druze disciple Baha al-Din died and the "gates were locked." From that time to the present, except in very rare circumstances, a person is not considered a Druze unless he or she was born to a Druze father and mother, and intermarriage outside the Druze faith is considered a serious sin.

Scriptures. Druze writings reflect the insular character of the faith. Druze consider the letters of correspondence between Hamza and al-Din to be holy writings, and they keep them hidden from anyone who is not a Druze in good standing. They consist of wisdom writings, codes of ethics (including condemnation for those who leave the faith), and defenses of the faith. They consist of 111 letters, divided into six books. Commentaries on the letters written in the fifteenth century are also considered holy and are not allowed to be seen by non-Druze. Due to their secrecy, Druze scriptures are not allowed to be printed but must be hand-copied by special calligraphers.

Ethical Requirements. The Druze have seven ethical requirements:

1. Hold your tongue. Druze are required to show care in what they say. They are not to lie and are supposed to keep promises, admit mistakes, refrain from gossip, and "be pleasant in conversation" (Dānā, 19).

2. Watch over your brothers. Druze are expected to uphold the unity of the faith by protecting one another's person and honor. Druze use the picture of a copper plate for illustration—hit one part of the plate, and the sound will reverberate through the whole plate.

3. Abandon worship of the occult, idols, and vanity. Idols include graven images and pictures.

4. Flee the devil and reject acts of evil. Druze, by acting kindly to strangers, being hospitable, and upholding justice, separate themselves from the devil and his evil deeds.

5. Acknowledge the uniqueness of God in all times and all places. Although this is not the first requirement listed by the Druze, it is probably the most important since the uniqueness of God is what al-Hakim is said to have revealed.

6. Willingly accept God's deeds, whatever they are. This concept means that the Druze accept that the deeds of God transcend human understanding, so good or ill events must be accepted as coming from God.

7. Understand and accept both the revealed and the concealed decrees of God. The Druze faith is fatalistic and requires blind faith. God has decreed the exact fate of all people, so no one can change it. "He determines all and is omniscient" (Dānā, 19–20).

Human Nature. Druze believe in a form of Neoplatonic reincarnation, teaching that the number of souls is constant, each one having been created at the beginning of the universe. Each soul was created a believer or a nonbeliever. Thus the soul of an old Druze person leaves the body immediately upon death and is transferred to a newly conceived Druze infant. Druze society is divided into two groups. The clergy as well as the very religious and pious (including women) are called *'uqqal* (knowers) and are granted full access to the secrets of Druze faith. The large majority of Druze are in the second group, called *juhhal* (ignorant), and are not permitted access to Druze scripture or special religious services.

Druze men are expected to have a shaved head and a mustache, and many do not shave their beards. Druze are forbidden to smoke, drink alcohol, or eat pork, *mulukhiyya* (a mint-like herb), or *jarjir* (arugula). Druze reject polygamy, in contrast to the majority of Muslims. Anyone who commits adultery or murder is excluded from religious gatherings for life and is excommunicated from the faith.

Pious Druze go to the *khalwa*, the Druze version of the mosque, every evening, but all

171

Druze are required to go on Sunday and especially on Thursday. The khalwa are simple, lacking any decoration or ornamentation. The only furniture are stands and cabinets for the scriptures and the most basic seating, which consists of rugs or mats. The khalwa are divided so that men and women are separate; those who are 'uqqal are also separated from those who are excluded for breaking one of the commandments or because they are among the juhhal. Worship consists of reading in Druze scripture, interpretation and teaching, and the singing of *mawa'iz*, which are poems of doctrine and ethics set to music.

Druze have one official holiday, the Festival of Sacrifice. The festival lasts ten days and consists of fasting, singing special songs, reading special scriptures, and a feast on the tenth day. Reconciliation of acrimonious parties is encouraged during this time.

The American radio personality and voice actor Casey Kasem (1932–2014) was a Druze.

See also ISLAM, BASIC BELIEFS OF

Bibliography. R. B. Betts, *The Druze*; N. Dānā, *The Druze in the Middle East: Their Faith, Leadership, Identity and Status.*

R. L. Drouhard

DUAL COVENANT THEORY. Dual covenant theory is the belief that God has a special, redemptive path (German, *Sonderweg*) for the Jewish people that is separate from that for gentile believers. According to the theory, God's covenant with Abraham guarantees the salvation of Jews, regardless of whether they accept Jesus as Messiah. Thus evangelism of Jews is unnecessary and perhaps even harmful.

While the theory had some supporters in early Christianity (such as *Pseudo-Clementine* 8.6–7, written in the third century), the medieval church almost uniformly held to *supersessionism* (the belief that the church had replaced Israel as the people of God). In the late nineteenth century, some dispensationalists tended toward a dual covenant theory, as did several sects (Seventh-day Adventists, Christadelphians; Vendyl Jones is a contemporary example). Though they may differ on the question of Israel's future and place in God's plan, evangelicals today universally affirm the need for Jews to be saved by faith in Christ.

Spurred on by the atrocities of the Holocaust and the rising popularity of religious pluralism, many liberal theologians (e.g., Rosemary Radford Ruether) embraced the theory in the latter half of the twentieth century. Among biblical scholars, the works of Krister Stendahl, Stanley K. Stowers, and John G. Gager, among others, advocate a pluralistic reading of the New Testament, usually employing Romans 9–11 as an interpretive key.

Most evangelicals would posit that the dual covenant theory is correct to point to the fundamental Jewishness of Christianity as well as to the possibility of a future for national Israel but would believe that Scripture leaves no doubt that Jews must accept Jesus as Messiah to be saved (cf. John 1:12–13; 14:6; Acts 4:12; Rom. 3:22–30; 10:1). God's covenant with Abraham includes both Jews and gentiles and operates on the principle of faith rather than physical descent (cf. Matt. 3:9; Rom. 4; Gal. 3:7).

See also SEVENTH-DAY ADVENTISM

Bibliography. John G. Gager, *The Origins of Anti-Semitism*; D. Holwerda, *Jesus and Israel: One Covenant or Two?*; H. K. Larondelle, *The Israel of God in Prophecy: Principles of Prophetic Interpretation*; O. P. Robertson, *The Christ of the Covenants*; R. Ruether, *Faith and Fratricide*; K. Stendahl, *Paul among Jews and Gentiles.*

D. R. Streett

DUALISM. The philosophy that sees real (not illusory) distinctions between two categories is known as dualism. It stands in contrast to monism, which teaches that there are no real distinctions, and pluralism, which teaches that there can be more than two categories.

Dualism is expressed in several different ways: ethical (good versus evil) dualism, Greek and gnostic ontological dualism, and Judeo-Christian ontological dualism.

Ethical Dualism. As opposed to monism, ethical dualism sees a real distinction between good and evil. Often, this dualistic philosophy takes the form of good being locked in a struggle against evil. Zoroastrianism in particular emphasizes this struggle, pitting the good god Ahura Mazda against the evil spirit Angra Mainyu. Humans participate in this struggle, either supporting Ahura Mazda by good thoughts, words, and deeds or promoting Angra Mainyu's chaotic activities by doing evil. At times some Christians have embraced this kind of dualism, seeing God and Satan fighting over the souls of human beings or seeing "good angels" warring with demons. Although orthodox Christian theology acknowledges that Satan's activities are meant to thwart God, it nonetheless teaches that Satan cannot do anything that God does not allow.

Greek and Gnostic Ontological Dualism. Greek dualism probably originated with Plato. He saw a distinction between perfect, eternal "forms" and temporal, imperfect copies of these forms. A person's body was a copy of the form, but the mind was not because the mind grasps and desires to dwell in the realm of the form. Plato believed souls were eternal, coming into and leaving physical bodies, but always striving to return to the eternal. Aristotle rejected Plato's idea of eternal souls, believing instead that particular souls were the forms of physical bodies. He saw forms as natures and properties of things, which attached themselves to those things. However, he argued that the soul could not be the same kind of thing as the physical body because the soul could perceive things beyond the physical, while the physical body can only perceive the physical. Thus there is a distinction between the physical body and the soul. This view developed into seeing an ontological distinction between the material universe and the immaterial.

The gnostics amalgamated the Greek, ontological dualism and the ethical dualism of Zoroastrianism (among other religions). They saw material as essentially evil, emanating from an either imperfect or evil god (often said to be Yahweh of the Old Testament). They saw the spiritual as essentially good, connected with the divine source they often called the Pleroma (Greek, "fullness"). According to gnostic theology, there are many "emanations" from this source, each one less perfect than the last. Yahweh is seen to be an emanation far removed from the original divine source. Salvation, for the gnostics, was escaping this evil, material world and returning to the perfect Pleroma. Within gnosticism this thought took two extremes. Gnostics either sought to deny physical pleasures and therefore engaged in radical asceticism or (to a lesser extent) believed that what was done in the physical realm had little import for the spiritual and therefore engaged in radical antinomianism and libertinism.

Judeo-Christian Ontological Dualism. Judeo-Christian theology has historically rejected monism. Instead it sees a real distinction between God and his creation. In this way, Judeo-Christian theology embraces dualism. However, Judeo-Christian theology rejects gnostic dualism. Creation is not a part of God, nor did it emanate from within God himself; rather, it is an actual, distinct creation by God. Since God created the material, it can be used for evil (since it is corrupted by sin), but it cannot be said to be essentially evil.

See also ANTINOMIANISM; JUDAISM; ORTHODOXY

Bibliography. K. L. King, *What Is Gnosticism?*; Arthur O. Lovejoy, *The Revolt against Dualism*; H. Robinson, "Dualism," in *Stanford Encyclopedia of Philosophy*, edited by E. N. Zalta, http://plato.stanford.edu/archives/fall2009/entries/dualism/.

R. L. Drouhard

DUKKHA/DUHKHA. A concept fundamental to Buddhism, *dukkha* encompasses the notions of human suffering, dissatisfaction, and aversion. The Buddha taught his disciples concerning three major kinds of *dukkha*: (1) *dukkha-dukkha*, suffering caused by bodily pain, sickness, aging, and the death of loved ones; (2) *viparinama-dukkha*, suffering caused by changes, especially unexpected or unwanted ones; (3) *sankhara-dukkha*, suffering that resides in the conditioned and impermanent nature of existence. The Four Noble Truths of Buddhism address the problem of dukkha, revealing its universality, its source, the necessary conditions for its elimination, and the way to eliminate it. The Buddha taught that striving to expunge dukkha from one's experience of reality is the most important component of Buddhist practice.

See also BUDDHISM

Bibliography. M. V. R. K. Ratnam and D. B. Rao, *Dukkha: Suffering in Early Buddhism.*

M. Power

EASTERN ORTHODOXY. Eastern Orthodoxy is made up of fourteen regional churches but is largely in unison in matters of theology and acceptance of the ecumenical patriarch of Constantinople. The Orthodox Church is the second-largest Christian church, estimated at more than 225 million members. Within this communion are eight major ecclesiastical jurisdictions—Alexandria, Antioch, Bulgaria, Constantinople, Jerusalem, Moscow, Romania, and Serbia—and the independent churches of Albania, Cyprus, Czechoslovakia, Georgia, Greece, and Poland. Additionally, some communions that are related to Eastern Orthodoxy are the Oriental Orthodox Church and the Russian Orthodox Church, which exists outside Russia but is not in communion with Constantinople. The bishops of the Eastern Orthodox trace themselves back to the apostles through the apostolic succession.

Early History. The Eastern Orthodox Church is able to trace its origins back to the beginning of Christianity, and the church claims ancestry to the apostles themselves through apostolic succession, which is said to begin with the apostle Peter. The church was unified throughout the Roman Empire until the time of the emperor Constantine (AD 272–337) in areas of doctrine, liturgy, and government. The entire church was the "one holy catholic [Greek *katholikē*, meaning "universal"] and apostolic church." After the divisions of the church over the centuries, different elements of the church, such as

the Roman Catholic Church or the Oriental Orthodox Church, have claimed this title.

Strictly speaking, the growth of the church began in the eastern portion of the Roman Empire. The earliest fathers of the church and the great theological documents, councils, and creeds were in the East. For example, only two bishops of more than four hundred at the Council of Nicaea in AD 325 were from the West. Theologians of the East included men like Origen (ca. 185–ca. 254), Gregory Nazianzus (ca. 330–ca. 389), Athanasius (c. 293–373), Basil of Caesarea (329–79), Gregory of Nyssa (ca. 335–ca. 394), Jerome (ca. 347–420), and John Chrysostom (347–407). Most of the apostolic fathers, such as Justin Martyr (100–165) and Ignatius of Antioch (d. ca. 110), were of the East, and the first theologian of the church, Irenaeus (early second century; d. 202), was from the East, though eventually he was connected with Gaul (France). The major seven councils of early Christianity, between the fourth and eighth centuries, were located in the East. These include the Council of Nicaea (325), the First Council of Constantinople (381, called Nicaea II), the Council of Ephesus (431), the Council of Chalcedon (451), the Second Council of Constantinople (553), the Third Council of Constantinople (680–81), and the Second Nicaean Council (787).

In the next seven hundred years, there were three major schisms involving the Eastern church. The first was in 451, in which churches that are now known as the Oriental Orthodox separated from the Orthodox Church (East and West) because of disagreement with the conclusions at the Council of Chalcedon over the person and natures of Christ. The second schism occurred in the ninth century due to the conflict between Patriarch Photius of Constantinople (ca. 820–91) and Pope Nicholas I (birth date unknown; d. 867). Nicholas opposed the promotion of Photius to his position in Constantinople and supported the deposed Ignatius, though Photius was lawfully promoted. Nicholas attempted to assert the authority of Roman papacy over the entire church rather than accepting his position as the first among equals. Third, in 1054, what is known as the Great Schism occurred. At this time, the Eastern and Western churches developed a serious disagreement regarding the doctrine of the procession of the Holy Spirit, whether he proceeds only from the Father or from both the Father and the Son, the latter doctrine being articulated in the *filioque* clause of the Nicene Creed: "and [from] the Son."

With the defeat of Constantinople in 1453 by the Ottoman Turks, matters grew worse for the church of the East. Islamic leaders began to persecute the Orthodox Christians. Because of this, the Orthodox Church began to make alliances with various European countries that blurred the line between the church and the civil authority, so that the church was the most important element within the culture. Also, the Russian Orthodox Church was founded as autonomous from Constantinople in 1448. Later, in the nineteenth century, additional Orthodox churches were established in Greece (1833), Romania (1859), Bulgaria (1870), and Serbia (1879). In view of the fact that these latter Orthodox churches were not the direct result of the efforts of Constantinople, the see of Constantinople has exercised little power over them.

Summary of Beliefs. When one speaks of Eastern Orthodoxy, the reference is to those churches, with their traditions, liturgy, and theology, that date to the Byzantine Empire (ca. 395–1453). As stated earlier, many groups claim to trace their roots and traditions to the earliest beginnings of Christianity and to the apostles, and the Eastern Orthodox Church does similarly. It claims to be the one holy catholic and apostolic church and believes it has a duty to protect the same doctrines and practices that were present in earliest Christianity. The distinction between Eastern Orthodoxy and other branches of Christianity may be defined by four major controversies: First, the Eastern church declares that the insertion of the filioque clause ("and the Son") into the Nicene Creed by the Council of Toledo in Spain (447) was an error. The Western church affirms that the Holy Spirit proceeds from the Father and the Son, while the Eastern Church has maintained that the Holy Spirit proceeds from the Father only. Second, the Eastern Orthodox Church says that the Roman pope does not have authority over the entire church, and even if accorded highest honor, he is yet one among equals. Third, the Eastern church considers the Roman Catholic doctrine of the immaculate conception of the Virgin Mary to be a heresy. Last, the Eastern Orthodox Church and the Roman Catholic Church have many differences on the matter of church liturgy.

Eastern Orthodox Theology. Creation. According to Orthodox belief, God is independent of the universe, free to create it or not. It is simply the act of his free will. His ex nihilo act of creation is due to his love and is the act of all three persons of the Trinity, with the Logos giving to each creature its existence and divine energy. By means of what is called "double movement," God desires to spiritually join (not in substance) with his creation. Creation at its inception was in harmony with God but, because of the fall, moved away from him. He desires to bring the creation back into participation with him, called deification.

Revelation and Authority. The Eastern Orthodox Church has within it two different approaches to revelation and authority. In the two-source theory, God's revelation to the church is in two forms, the Scriptures and tradition. Divine revelation in the early church was in the form of oral tradition, which became the basis of the New Testament text. According to Orthodox teaching, neither the New Testament nor the oral tradition is the complete revelation of God, so the church was the custodian of the Word of God, written and unwritten, and both sources are consistent with each other and are legitimate sources of the revelation of God. In contrast, the one-source theory says that the Holy Scriptures are only a part of the larger tradition of the church, so consequently the Bible is not the ultimate authority for church doctrines and practices. In view of this, the church alone is the God-determined interpreter of Holy Scripture, and its teachings are the infallible truth. Through the bishops of the church, both in councils and individually, this truth is disseminated.

According to the Orthodox faith, the doctrine of *sola Scriptura* is a dangerous teaching because the truth of Scripture cannot be alienated from the traditions of the church that gave rise to them. Also, the Scripture is not for private interpretation but must be within the tradition of the church that created it. The Eastern Orthodox Church considers the Greek Old Testament and the Greek New Testament to be sacred text and also includes Deuterocanonical books rejected by Protestants, but these are not considered to be on the same level with the other books of the Bible.

God. Eastern Orthodoxy believes that God is both three persons and one being, in concert with the historical position of Christianity and the creeds of the church. The divine being is uncreated, immaterial, and eternal, and all of God's attributes are infinite and shared in common with each of the three equal and distinct persons. God's absolute nature is only approximately understood by humans through analogy and by his express revelation. God's being may be seen in three aspects: First is his essence (*ousia*). Second, the three distinct persons (*hypostases*) share indivisibly the one divine essence without any overlapping of their persons or modes of being. Third, the uncreated energies (*energeiai*) of God are used to communicate with his creatures. Regarding the distinct persons, the Father is the fount of the Godhead, with the Son begotten from the Father from all eternity ("God of very God" in the Nicene Creed), and the Holy Spirit proceeds from the Father eternally. This Triune God alone has self-existence (*aseity*), and all other beings depend on God for their existence.

Humanity. The intent of God from eternity was that humans would participate in the divine nature (*theosis*, or deification). Thus God created humans in his image, which consists of rationality and moral freedom, in a quality and degree different from the rationality and freedom given to animals. Humans are therefore like God in that they have the ability to develop and express moral virtue and thereby to be deified. Deification allows humans to have relationship with an infinite but transcendent God. Originally Adam and Eve had a perfect nature but also the capacity to achieve moral and spiritual deification through obedience to, and communion with, God. In view of this, Eastern Orthodox theologians believe that the fall "broke the harmony of God's good creation" and was a "cosmic catastrophe" (Payton, 98).

Sin. Humans fell into sin because of human limitations, and the current condition of the world, along with humanity's alienation from God, makes the commission of sin expected. Since the fall, humans are more inclined toward sin than they were before the fall, when all of Adam's and Eve's needs were met by God. God had intended for our first parents to gradually move to perfection, but through the work of Satan they chose to disobey God's commandment and thus became disposed toward sickness and death. Instead of following God, humans began to follow their own perspective, resulting in three basic sins, namely, spiritual ignorance, self-love, and hatred of other people. In contrast with the view of other Christian traditions, in the Eastern view the natural world was largely unaffected by the fall of humanity.

Deification. Because of Adam's sin, a mortal barricade was built between humans and God. Since humans cannot reconcile with God by themselves, God's Son entered human existence to make it possible for humans to establish a mystical union with God. Unlike the Protestant view of forensic justification, substitutionary atonement, or redemption, Eastern Orthodox theology focuses on the incarnation as the key to salvation. In the incarnation, God took upon himself, in the person of the Son, our humanity to unite the essence of humanity to the divine nature. To quote a famous Eastern theologian, Athanasius: "For the Son of God became man so that we might become God" (*On the Incarnation of the Word* 54). In saying this, Athanasius was asserting not that humans actually become the same being as God but that humans are able to share aspects of God's divine nature that are communicable to humans. The mystical union of God with humanity comes from God giving divine energies through the sacraments of the church, the major channel through which these energies are given. In order to receive these energies, human beings must participate in the process of salvation. In addition to these sacraments, humans must also perform good works, pray, and contemplate God in achieving this mystical union with God.

The Church. The Eastern Orthodox Church believes itself to be the one and only true church that was founded by Christ and his apostles. It remains such by unbroken apostolic succession. Eastern Orthodox Christians are fervent in arguing that they alone have faithfully preserved the faith reflected in their theology and practices.

Future Things. Eastern Orthodoxy believes that Jesus will return to the earth in great power at the end of history to begin the final judgment and refurbish creation to a new heaven and new earth. Those who are righteous—have achieved or sought mystical union—will receive an eternal reward, and the unrighteous will be separated from God in hell by their own choice by repudiation of God. This torture is not divine retribution but a result of human rejection of the love and goodness of God.

Liturgical Worship. The Eastern Orthodox Church has significant liturgy, with the inside of the church full of colorful pictures and stained-glass windows, all based on religious themes. The typical Orthodox religious service includes the burning of incense and candles, priests wearing elaborate clothing, and worshipers venerating icons. One has a complete religious experience in Orthodox worship, with the worshipers having all their senses involved. Worshipers carry the smell of incense on their bodies, their eyes take in beautiful religious imagery, their ears hear the sound of preaching and chanting, their mouths praise God, their hands perform the sign of the cross, and they prostrate their bodies before the icons. Each part of the liturgy has its own meaning and symbolism, and Eastern Orthodox Christians believe that every part of the liturgy is essential. Eastern Orthodox liturgy may be traced to that given by St. John Chrysostom (ca. 347–407).

Icons. The use of icons is very important in Eastern Orthodox theology and worship. They are venerated (not worshiped), and the priests use them in the performance of their rituals. They are viewed not as idols but as a manifestation of God expressed in his incarnation in Christ. Eastern Orthodox churches celebrate the triumph of orthodoxy, an event commemorating the acceptance of icons by the church on March 11, 843, and a rebuke of the iconoclasts who opposed this. Included with this ceremony is a denunciation of all who forbid the use of icons. Interestingly, the Eastern Orthodox, in concert with the Second Council of Nicaea in 787, believe that the gospel can be communicated through the use of icons as well as by reading the Bible.

See also CHALCEDONIAN CONTROVERSY; DEIFICATION, CHRISTIAN VIEW OF; DEIFICATION, MORMON VIEW OF; ROMAN CATHOLICISM; SACRAMENTS

Bibliography. J. Binns, *An Introduction to the Christian Orthodox Churches*; V. Lossky, *Orthodox Theology: An Introduction*; J. M. Neale, *A History of the Holy Eastern Church: The Patriarchate of Antioch*, repr. ed.; J. R. Payton, *Light from the Christian East: An Introduction to the Orthodox Tradition*; J. Pelikan, *The Spirit of Eastern Christendom*; K. Ware, *The Orthodox Way*, rev. ed.

H. W. House

EFFENDÍ, SHOGHÍ. Shoghí Effendí Rabbání (1897–1957, known simply as Shoghi Effendi) was the spiritual leader of the Bahá'í Faith, and the great-grandson of the Bahá'í founder, Bahá'u'lláh. Effendi assumed headship of the Bahá'í Faith in 1921 at the age of twenty-four, after the death of his grandfather, 'Abdu'l-Baha, who had instructed in his will that Effendi should assume the role of "Guardian of the Cause of God." Educated at Oxford, Effendi established himself as an effective communicator and organizer, and under his watch, the Bahá'í Faith rose to international prominence. He focused heavily on evangelism, and one of his primary accomplishments was a translation of the teachings of Bahá'u'lláh into English. Effendi also played a significant role in defining and interpreting Bahá'í doctrines. Various contradictory decrees by Effendi have caused controversy and schism within the Bahá'í Faith, from which it has not recovered. The controversy stems from at least two different named successors, each of whom has followers claiming legitimate authority within Bahá'í and each of whom disparages the other's claims. This disunity is ironic since the central goal of Bahá'í is unity among all religious belief.

See also BAHÁ'Í; BAHÁ'U'LLÁH

Bibliography. K. Bowers, *God Speaks Again: An Introduction to the Baha'i Faith*; P. Smith, *An Introduction to the Baha'i Faith*.

J. P. Holding

EIGHTFOLD PATH. The Eightfold Path is the process formulated by Siddhartha Gautama the Buddha (ca. sixth to fifth century BC) through which he taught that an individual may obtain enlightenment possibly during this life and pass into nirvana at death. The last of the Four Noble Truths proclaimed by the Buddha in his famous deer park sermon (ca. 528 BC), the Eightfold Path constitutes the practical implementation of the Buddha's theoretical solution to the human condition. The human condition, according to the First Noble Truth, is characterized by *dukkha*, or the suffering that arises when impermanent things cease to exist. Since the Second Noble Truth diagnoses craving as the cause of dukkha, the Third Noble Truth deductively infers that the way to liberate oneself from dukkha (and hence overcome the human condition) is by eliminating craving. This can be done by following the Eightfold Path, which seeks to transform a person in the successive realms of wisdom, morality, and mental discipline.

Steps One and Two. The cultivation of wisdom comprises the first two steps of the Eightfold Path. Step one, right understanding, designates cognizance of and intellectual assent to the Four Noble Truths. Here a person gains deeper insight into the law of karma, or the cause-and-effect relationship between thoughts, words, and deeds of a

179

certain quality and the generation of karma of this same quality, which if left unchecked will produce situations of that quality in either this or a future life.

In step two, right thought, adherents come to view themselves according to the Buddha's anthropology of *anatman* (literally, "no-soul" or "no-self"), where the immaterial entity we perceive as the ego is not a changeless center of self-consciousness but rather an amalgamation of five conditioned and changing spiritual forces known as *skandhas*, held together by the glue of karma. These skandhas include form (the faculty that attaches to a physical body), sensation (the ability to receive sensory stimuli from the body), reason, volition, and memory. Hence it is these five skandhas, not a soul (Atman) as in Hinduism, that transmigrate from life to life; however, in nirvana the karmic bonds are dissolved, and the skandhas disperse forever.

Steps Three through Five. Steps three through five of the Eightfold Path promote the acquisition of morality. Through step three, right speech, one learns, in recognition of one's lack of any permanent self, how to speak about others from a selfless perspective, thereby only saying things that would support the well-being and advance the flourishing of other persons. Consequently, one must refrain from gossip, lying, obscenity, and harsh words.

Step four, right actions, entails that individuals keep the five *sila* (basic moral prohibitions), which forbid, respectively, killing any sentient (conscious) being, deception, sexual misconduct, theft, and the consumption of intoxicants.

Concerning step five, right livelihood, persons take up occupations consistent with the sila. It should be emphasized that occupations where individuals do not themselves violate the sila but cause or pressure others to do so are just as forbidden as occupations where individuals themselves break the sila.

Steps Six through Eight. In steps six through eight of the Eightfold Path, practitioners obtain the necessary mental discipline to make the final break with any remaining desire for impermanent things. While the first five steps of the Eightfold Path can obviously be accomplished by laypeople and religious (i.e., monks or nuns) alike, the last three steps are possible but extremely difficult to perform while living amid job, family, and social obligations. Hence the Theravada insistence on completion of the Eightfold Path for nirvana virtually requires adherents to at least temporarily enter the *sangha*, or monastic community, whereas Mahayana Buddhism, though promoting the monastic approach, was more accepting to a lay approach.

Step six, right effort, impresses on individuals how precious their time as humans is, for it is only as a human being that one may gain the path; lower forms of life lack the intellectual resources to distance themselves from craving. Because there is no guarantee that an individual will be reincarnated as a human being quickly, right effort insists that this life may be one's best chance at nirvana for a long time. Therefore, persons must commit to do everything in their power and make whatever sacrifices are necessary for completing the Eightfold Path.

With step seven, right awareness, one realizes that the mind contains two levels: the surface mind, or the stimulus-response level, which perceives all sensory data and constantly devises responses to those data, and the deep mind, which exists in a state of equanimity, unperturbed by the external world. Upon this realization, one learns to tap into the peace afforded by the deep mind by ignoring, rather than fighting against or fleeing from, the distractions generated by the surface mind.

Regarding the eighth and final step, right concentration, the practitioner masters two forms of meditation, *dhyana* and *samadhi*. Dhyana occurs when one finds an object (any object suffices) and concentrates on the object to such a degree that one loses consciousness of one's consciousness of the object. In other words, dhyana is completed when the individual no longer thinks, "I am meditating on the object" but rather simply thinks, "Object." At this juncture, the individual can advance to samadhi, a state of pure consciousness that has no object. When such independence from the phenomenal world obtains, craving for all objects is destroyed, and the person experiences enlightenment and becomes an arhat (a perfected one who has apprehended the true nature of existence). All nonphysical karmic ties are broken, so that the only thing holding the five skandhas together is the body. Unless one desires rebirth (as does a bodhisattva), at death the skandhas are said to disperse, causing the person to enter into the ineffable state of nirvana, or liberation from all suffering.

See also ATMAN; BUDDHA, HISTORICAL PERSON OF; BUDDHISM; DUKKHA/DUHKHA; FOUR NOBLE TRUTHS; KARMA; MAHAYANA BUDDHISM; SAMADHI; SANGHA; THERAVADA BUDDHISM; VAJRAYANA BUDDHISM

Bibliography. R. C. Bush, gen. ed., *The Religious World*, 3rd ed.; C. Humphreys, *Buddhism*; D. S. Lopez Jr., *The Story of Buddhism*; T. A. Robinson and H. Rodrigues, eds., *World Religions*; Sangharakshita, *The Buddha's Noble Eightfold Path*, 2nd ed.

K. R. MacGregor

ENLIGHTENMENT. This term defines the acquisition of spiritual knowledge, insight, and/or spiritual experience, generally leading to a sense of peace, self-improvement, and control. It is assumed to provide complete insight into the nature of reality, particularly within Buddhism.

While Buddhism depends historically, ideologically, and experientially on the phenomenon of enlightenment, other religions embracing the concept include Hinduism, Sufism, New Age, and Sikhism, as well as many expressions of occultism, although each understands the concept differently.

The archetypical experience of enlightenment is that of the Buddha's, occurring, as traditionally believed, under the Bodhi tree around 530 BC. During this event, Buddha supposedly transitioned through five stages, including (1) the confrontation and defeat of various temptations; (2) the experience of intense meditation leading to self-awareness and a sense of peace; (3) self-analysis of all past actions; (4) insight into other people's predicaments and complexities; and (5) a realization of the Four Noble Truths of Buddhism as well as a realization of the Eightfold Path to end suffering. Final and full enlightenment provides for the passing into nirvana, releasing the mind stream from the cycle of birth and rebirth. Hinduism embraces meditation and other forms of devotion to provide enlightenment, as do, in some form or fashion, other religions. This experience is often identified as being made aware of oneness with the divine.

In New Age thought, enlightenment takes on a different meaning. Enlightenment for a practitioner of New Age spirituality means achieving the realization of oneness with the universe. This is done through various spiritual techniques and may take several lifetimes through reincarnation. Sikhism is similar to New Age spirituality in its view of enlightenment, the difference being that Sikhs attempt to achieve oneness with the one God rather than with an ethereal "force" or "energy," as with New Age spirituality.

See also BUDDHISM; HINDUISM; SIKHISM; SUFISM

Bibliography. M. Banarsiass, *Joyful Path of Good Fortune*; J. Davenport, *The New Age Movement and the Biblical Worldview: Conflict and Dialogue*; J. Singh, "My Thirteen Reasons for Sikhism," http://www.sikhs.org/art4.htm.

R. P. Roberts

ETERNAL LIFE. Many of the world's religions believe in eternal life in some form—that is, in a life that continues in some way after physical death. Among these faiths are some forms of Hinduism and Buddhism, Islam, Judaism, and Christianity. However, the teachings within these groups vary greatly. Some sects of Hinduism and Buddhism teach that once a person escapes the cycle of reincarnation, he or she will reside for eternity either as one with Brahma or as a kind of spirit. Islam, Judaism, and Christianity hold that a person who gains eternal life will reside in heaven. Within these three traditions, the idea of heaven varies as well.

In the Bible, eternal life is a gift God gives to those who receive Jesus Christ as Savior (John 3:16–18). Eternal life is not simply an unending existence but the best of all possible existences. Those who receive the gift of eternal life will dwell with God forever (1 Pet. 1:4; Rev. 21:1–4). They possess that eternal life now and also in the future, according to the New Testament.

A number of heterodox groups reinterpret the Bible's teaching on this subject. Christian Science teaches that life and death are illusory, so that "eternal life" is simply the awakening of a soul from the "dream" of reality. This teaching reflects an Eastern philosophy rather than the biblical portrayal of eternal life. In many cases, it seems, "eternal life" in Christian Science is at least partially a reward for adherence to the teaching of Christian Science. This nullifies the concept of the grace of God (Rom. 11:6).

The Watch Tower Bible and Tract Society (the governing body of the Jehovah's Witness organization) teaches that Jesus Christ died on the cross to make it possible for people to prove their own worthiness for eternal life. However, to actually obtain eternal life, one must meet Watch Tower requirements, including at least these four: growing in Bible knowledge, obeying God's laws (as spelled out by the Watch Tower—including such things as avoidance of blood transfusions and not smoking), being associated with God's organization (exclusively the Watch Tower), and advocating God's kingdom to others (spreading the Watch Tower's message). This conflicts with the Bible's teaching that human effort is not sufficient to gain eternal life.

The Church of Jesus Christ of Latter-day Saints (LDS Church, the Mormons) teaches that Christ's atonement (accomplished by his suffering in the garden of Gethsemane and his death on the cross) secures resurrection to immortality ("general salvation") for all humanity but that full or "individual" salvation requires human effort. The LDS Church believes that all people (with a few exceptions, such as apostate Mormons) will have an eternal existence in one of three heavenly kingdoms. Most of the world's people will go to the "telestial" (bottom) kingdom after a period of chastisement for their sins. Good people (including many Mormons) will go to the next level up, the terrestrial kingdom. However, the highest level, the only one in which fellowship with God the Father can be experienced, will be the celestial kingdom. Faithful Mormons hope to achieve this level on the basis of a combination of faith, repentance, and good deeds. The LDS Church also teaches that those who are completely obedient may attain "eternal life," the kind of life God has, and actually become gods in eternity and rule over their own worlds. This highly complex and stratified version of eternal life is totally absent from the Bible.

In New Age philosophy, eternal life is held to be the possession of every person, though the definition of that "life" is alien to the biblical teaching of eternal life. Most in the New Age movement hold to reincarnation and a belief that when people die they become one with the impersonal life force they believe in, if they have become sufficiently "enlightened" with whatever knowledge the particular New Age adherent believes is necessary.

See also BUDDHISM; CHRISTIAN; CHURCH OF JESUS CHRIST OF LATTER-DAY SAINTS; EXALTATION; HINDUISM; ISLAM, BASIC BELIEFS OF; JEHOVAH'S WITNESSES (JW); JUDAISM

Bibliography. L. Berkhof, *Systematic Theology*; W. Grudem, *Systematic Theology*; G. Mather and Larry Nichols, "Jehovah's Witnesses," in *Dictionary of Cults, Sects, Religions and the Occult*.

E. Shropshire and R. L. Drouhard

EUCHARIST. The Eucharist, also referred to as Holy Communion or the Lord's Supper, is a Christian sacrament celebrating and commemorating the Last Supper, at which Jesus Christ shared a final meal with his disciples before his eventual arrest and crucifixion. The term *Eucharist* is taken from the Greek noun *eucharistia*, from *eu*, meaning "good" or "well," and *charis*, meaning "favor" or "grace." More often in the New Testament and the Septuagint, the verb *eucharisteō* is used, which means "to thank." The institution of the Eucharist is contained in all three of the Synoptic Gospels. Matthew 26:26–29 states,

> While they were eating, Jesus took bread, and when he had given thanks, he broke it and gave it to his disciples, saying, "Take and eat; this is my body."
> Then he took a cup, and when he had given thanks, he gave it to them, saying, "Drink from it, all of you. This is my blood of the covenant, which is poured out for many for the forgiveness of sins. I tell you, I will not drink from this fruit of the vine from now on until that day when I drink it new with you in my Father's kingdom."

To this instruction from Jesus, Paul adds the following statement from the tradition that he received as a quotation of Jesus: "This cup is the new covenant in my blood; do this, whenever you drink it, in remembrance of me" (1 Cor. 11:25). There is therefore a tradition early in the New Testament period in which the Eucharist is something that should be practiced by the church. The belief in the Eucharist as being instituted by Christ is a uniting factor practiced by virtually all branches of Christianity (see Erickson, chap. 53).

The Eucharist is referred to as a "sacrament" (means of grace) by Roman Catholics, but many Protestants prefer the term *ordinance*, referring to the rite as a channel of grace expressing faith. With this in mind, there are three primary views of the presence of Christ in the Eucharist. First, there is the Roman Catholic view, called transubstantiation. This takes a very literal view of Christ's presence in the bread and wine when he said, "This is my body," and, "This is my blood." This view is called transubstantiation because it regards the bread and wine as literally changing substance, although all that is accessible to the senses remains the same. Catholic priest and missionary Lawrence Lovasik writes, "The Eucharist is the sacrament which contains the true body and blood of Jesus Christ, together with His soul and divinity, the entire living and glorified Christ, under the appearances of bread and wine" (8). In this view, grace is given to those present *ex opere operato*, meaning "by the work performed." Therefore, the measure of grace dispensed is in proportion to the subjective disposition of the recipient of grace. In addition, whenever the Mass is celebrated, the sacrifice of Christ is in some sense repeated. The Catholic Church affirms that the sacrifice of the Eucharist is a real sacrifice, the same sacrifice paid on the cross, having the same Priest and Victim (Jesus Christ), except that the sacrifice of the Mass is offered in an "unbloody manner" (Denzinger, §§938–39). Another aspect of the Roman Catholic view of the Eucharist is sacerdotalism, the idea than an ordained priest must be present in order to consecrate the bread and wine.

There are two primary objections to the Roman Catholic view. First, Jesus often spoke in symbolic terms when referring to himself. For instance, in the book of John, Jesus states, "I am the door" (John 10:9) and "I am the true vine" (John 15:1). Even at the Last Supper, it is doubtful that Jesus's disciples thought that the bread in Jesus's hand was actually Jesus's physical body. Second, this tends to undermine the finality of the completed work of Christ on the cross. The book of Hebrews especially makes it clear that Christ's atonement for sin on the cross was completed once and need not be repeated (Heb. 1:3; 9:25–28; 10:3, 12).

A second view is the Lutheran view, often called consubstantiation. Luther rejected the Catholic view of transubstantiation but maintained that in some sense Christ's statement, "This is my body" should be taken literally. *Con* means "in, with, and under"; and Christ's presence is therefore in, with, and under the physical bread and wine of the Eucharist. In his *Large Catechism*, Luther states, "Now what is the Sacrament of the Altar? Answer: It is the true body and blood of the Lord Christ in and under the bread and wine, which Christ's Word commands us to eat and drink" (111). A foundational text from which Luther formed this doctrine is 1 Corinthians 10:16, which states, "Is not the cup of thanksgiving for which we give thanks a participation in the blood of Christ? And is not the bread that we break a participation in the body of Christ?" The primary objection to this view lies in how Christ's physical body and human nature could be everywhere present. If Christ ascended to the Father and stated he would no longer be in the world, how could his physical presence remain on the earth? In answer to this, Luther taught the ubiquity of Christ's nature, in which his humanity could be present everywhere. The ubiquity of Christ's nature has been challenged since Luther's time as an extrabiblical explanation in order to show consubstantiation as true (Grudem, 994).

A third view is the symbolic view in which Christ's presence in the Eucharist is a spiritual presence. Although there were differences between them, John Calvin and other Reformers such as Huldrych Zwingli and Heinrich Bullinger argued that the bread and wine are not, nor do they somehow contain, the body and blood of Christ. In a famous debate between Luther and Zwingli, Zwingli referenced numerous scriptural texts in which "this is" more likely means "this signifies" (Blount and Wooddell, 77). Essentially this position affirms that although the body and blood are symbolized by bread and wine, Christ is spiritually present at the Eucharist. An example of this type of presence would be Matthew 18:20, in which Jesus states, "For where two or three gather in my name, there am I with them." The symbolic view does not wish to understate the importance of the Eucharist; in fact, John Calvin stated, "Communion (Eucharist) was the culmination of one's life as a Christian" (Wandel, 140). The primary objection to this view, as explained above, is in the literal understanding of Christ's statements, when he instituted the Eucharist, that the bread was his body and the wine was his blood.

See also CHRISTIANITY, PROTESTANT; ROMAN CATHOLICISM

Bibliography. D. K. Blount and J. D. Wooddell, eds., *Baptist Faith and Message 2000: Critical Issues in America's Largest Denomination*; H. Denzinger, *Sources of Catholic Dogma*; M. Erickson, *Christian Theology*, 3rd ed.; W. Grudem, *Systematic Theology*; L. Lovasik, *The Eucharist in Catholic Life*; M. Luther, *Luther's Large Catechism*, translated by F. S. Janzow; G. T. Smith, ed., *The Lord's Supper: Five Views*; L. P. Wandel, *The Eucharist in the Reformation*.

T. S. Price

EVANGELICALISM. Within the broader Christian communion is an element of Protestantism known as evangelicalism, a term used of many Protestants, coming from the Greek term *euangelion*, meaning "good news." Whereas mainline Protestant churches have decreased in numbers during the last several decades, evangelicals have grown remarkably. This growth in the United States has been studied by the Pew Research Center, comparing the progress of evangelicals from 2007 through 2014 (see Zylstra). The study came to five conclusions. First, the number of evangelicals has remained fairly stable in comparison to other Christian groups in America (evangelicals remained the largest religious group in the US and made up just over 25% of the US population in 2014). Second, approximately half of those who say they are Christians also claim the label of evangelical, in contrast to 44 percent in 2007; over 70 percent of those in historically black Protestant denominations identify themselves as evangelical.

Third, evangelicals have increased their numbers through evangelism and "religious switching" and also retained more of their children than most other Christian groups. It is true that evangelicals have lost individuals from their ranks, but at the same time they have had much growth, for a net gain from 2007 to 2014 of 1.5 percent. Evangelicals retain two-thirds of their children, while Protestants in general retain less than half. Fourth, an interesting finding of the Pew study is that evangelicalism is an increasingly diverse group, with more than one-third of evangelical adults being nonwhite. This feature is also true in non-evangelical Christian denominations in the United States. Fifth, evangelicals tend to marry other evangelicals (75% do so). And in contrast to the national birthrate (2.1 children per couple), and among Christians in general, evangelicals have many more children (2.3 children per couple).

What Does It Mean to Be an Evangelical?
The term *evangelical* is used in at least three different ways. First, it may refer to Christians who share in common four theological perspectives: conversionism, activism, biblicism, and crucicentrism. *Conversionism* is the belief that a person does not become a Christian due to his ethnic or family background, church association, or belief system. In order to become a Christian, one must be justified before God, which occurs by a change brought about by the work of the Holy Spirit and a person's belief in the truth of the gospel. The purpose of gospel proclamation is to move those who hear it to believe in the person of Jesus the Messiah and his salvific acts for humanity. The essence of practical teaching relates to spiritual growth that comes from a relationship to Jesus. *Activism*, in evangelical perspective, is a handmaiden to the spread of the gospel; it means engaging the culture from a Christian worldview and in order to live out the social implications of the gospel. Activism includes a variety of areas, such as the arts, business, economics, law, medicine (including bioethics), philosophy, and politics. The third perspective, *biblicism*, is that the Bible is the sole Christian authority for faith and practice, setting forth God's special revelation of himself to humanity, and the infallible standard for the conduct of one's life. Consequently evangelicals have great respect for the teachings of the Bible and attempt to obey its norms. Last of all is *crucicentrism*. At the center of evangelical theology are the death, burial, and resurrection of the Messiah. This is true both for its theology and its devotion. Apart from these central truths, there can be neither gospel nor hope of salvation.

Second, *evangelical* refers to "an organic group of movements and religious traditions" (Institute for the Study of American Evangelicals). Used in this manner, the term speaks of style as much as beliefs, and many Christian groups that are dissimilar in many areas of theology and divergent in manner of worship fit under this umbrella. They include groups as diverse as African American "Baptists, Dutch Reformed Churches, Mennonites and Pentecostals, Catholic charismatics and

Southern Baptists" (Institute for the Study of American Evangelicals).

The third meaning of *evangelical* is as a label that arose after World War II referring to a coalition of Christians. This coalition arose due to the concerns of many Christians about the fundamentalist movement in America. Though there was largely agreement with the theology of fundamentalism, which in turn arose out of the modernist-fundamentalist controversy in the immediately preceding years regarding fundamentals of the Christian faith such as the virgin birth of Jesus and the necessity of the atonement of Christ, there was concern about issues such as anti-intellectualism and separatism. From this coalition arose many prominent Christians in America such as Harold J. Ockenga and Billy Graham, schools such as Moody Bible Institute and Wheaton College, and the National Association of Evangelicals.

Early History. Possibly the term *evangelical* originated with Martin Luther (1483–1546), who called his embryonic movement the "evangelical church" (*evangelische kirche*), that is, one that preaches the good news. The more normal use of the term is to refer to those Christian groups in the revival movement of the eighteenth and nineteenth centuries in the United Kingdom and North America. Important preachers led this movement, namely, Jonathan Edwards (1703–58), John Wesley (1703–91), and George Whitefield (1714–70). The movement as a whole, and the preachers in particular, were committed to the Bible alone as the basis of their methods and the content of their sermons. The long-lasting nature of the revivals in America caused evangelical Protestantism to gain a secure place within the dominant Protestant movement. The focus of the revivalism was an emotional experience (especially with the influence of revivalist Charles Finney and, later, Billy Sunday) and a social and personal change in the converts. In many respects, the social concern of evangelicals influenced important movements of the nineteenth century such as charitable organizations, abolition, women's suffrage, and prohibition. The influence of evangelism began to wane in the early twentieth century for a number of reasons, including the influx of Roman Catholic immigrants and the confusion in the minds of many between evangelicalism and fundamentalism. Beginning in the 1940s, the distinction between these two became clearer with the prominence of various evangelical leaders, particularly Billy Graham, and important institutions and groups, such as Wheaton College and the National Association of Evangelicals.

Summary of Beliefs. One may recognize evangelical churches by their stress on the preaching of Scripture, personal study of the Bible, and engaging the contemporary culture, in contradistinction to other Christian communions that emphasize sacraments and liturgy. Evangelicals agree that conversion is necessary for being saved and often use the terms *born again* or *born from above* to identify this conversion. Moreover, those who wear the name *evangelical* believe that the Bible gives God's will to humans and is the sole basis for determining truth and ethics. Additionally, an evangelical embraces the need to share the gospel of Jesus Christ rather than this being only the task of the clergy. Last of all, evangelicals believe that the death of Jesus on the cross was necessary for salvation. In addition, they accept the historical fact of Christ's miracles; his virgin birth; his crucifixion, burial, and resurrection; and his second coming. In summary, evangelicals hold to the cornerstones of the Reformation, the four solas: *sola Scriptura* (Scripture alone), *sola fide* (faith alone), *sola gratia* (grace alone), and *soli Christi* (Christ alone). Regarding cultural matters, evangelicals tend to be conservative in their social perspective, to believe that homosexual behavior and same-sex marriage are sinful, and to hold that abortion is murder, though there is a liberal minority within evangelism who differ with the broader movement in these matters.

Evangelical Theology. Creation. Belief in the act of creation out of nothing (*creatio ex nihilo*) by an omnipotent deity—the God of the Bible—is a standard belief among evangelicals. They differ, however, regarding the manner of this creation. Some hold to six contiguous days of creation several thousand years ago, some believe in a universe of billions of years with the days of creation being long periods of time, while others believe in progressive creation, the days in Genesis being actual solar days but separated by aeons of time in which created living beings developed. And increasing number are advocates of intelligent design. A minority accept the theory of evolution to some degree. Most evangelicals also accept the Noahic flood as literal history, with many and perhaps most holding to a universal flood. Evangelicals believe that knowledge of truth, and God specifically, may be acquired in empirical science and history, as well as in the Bible.

Revelation. Unlike liberal Protestants who believe the Bible has error, and some fundamentalists who believe that the King James Version is uniquely the Word of God, evangelicals believe that the sixty-six books of the Protestant Bible are inspired by God, without error (for most) in the original manuscripts, and the final authority for faith, practice, and all matters that it teaches. Though the Bible is verbally and plenarily inspired, so that every word of the original writings is the very word of God, the authors of Scripture write within the limitations of their vocabulary, setting, education, and personality.

God. The God of the Bible is a Trinity; that is, three persons—Father, Son, and Holy Spirit—share one indivisible essence. As one God, each distinct but not separate person has all of the attributes of God, though they differ in the manner in which they act in reference to each other—the Father begets, the Son is begotten, and the Spirit proceeds—and to creation. The Father is primarily seen as the sovereign over creation and history, the Son as the one who took upon himself true human nature as the Messiah Jesus, and the Spirit of God as the person who generally works as the unseen expression of God in individuals specifically and in the church in general.

Humanity and Sin. Evangelicals also generally believe that Adam and Eve were historical persons, the first parents of all humanity. Adam was created as both a physical and a spiritual being, with Eve receiving her full humanity from Adam, as does the remainder of the human race. Those first humans were created without sin, but when they sinned, their fall brought them and all their posterity into sin and its effects, bringing all humans under the judgment of God, with the result that all need salvation. Evangelicals differ as to whether humans are incapable in themselves of responding to the grace of God, or whether they have partial ability to respond, divided between Calvinist and Arminian camps.

Salvation. Few among evangelicals differ regarding the absolute necessity of Christ's death and resurrection to redeem human beings and also the absolute necessity that one has to believe in Christ's work for personal salvation. There is general agreement that the death of Jesus provided both expiation (forgiveness of human sins) and substitution (taking the wrath of God for humans). Upon believing in Jesus and his work, the believer receives the benefits of expiation and substitution. The resurrection of Jesus is the capstone of the accomplishment of salvation. The Holy Spirit regenerates the individual who believes in Jesus in response to the preaching of the gospel. There are differences among evangelicals regarding the basis of God's election of humans, the extent of Christ's atonement, exactly how God's grace works in bringing about salvation, and whether salvation can be forfeited.

The Church. Differing theories of the polity of the church exist among evangelicals. One may find episcopal, presbyterian, and congregational models, and sometimes a hybrid of these. Evangelicals also differ as to whether the church is a replacement for physical Israel or whether these two are distinguishable in the plan of God, though both are only saved by grace through faith.

Future Things. Evangelicals believe, in agreement with the church of all ages, in the physical resurrection of all humans, the saved to life eternal and the unsaved to everlasting separation from God. Most believe in eternal punishment of the unsaved, but a minority believe in temporal punishment or annihilationism. A variety of views are held in regard to the events of the last days, such as the nature, length, and timing of the return of Christ and of the millennium, and how we should approach the book of Revelation.

See also CHRISTIANITY, PROTESTANT

Bibliography. R. H. Balmer, *Blessed Assurance: A History of Evangelicalism in America*; D. W. Bebbington, *The Dominance of Evangelicalism: The Age of Spurgeon and Moody*; K. S. Kantzer and C. F. H. Henry, *Evangelical Affirmations*; M. A. Noll, *American Evangelical Christianity: An Introduction*; Noll, *The Rise of Evangelicalism: The Age of Edwards, Whitefield and the Wesleys*; S. E. Zylstra, "Pew: Evangelicals Stay Strong as Christianity Crumbles in America," *Christianity Today*, http://www.christianitytoday.com/news/2015/may/pew-evangelicals-stay-strong-us-religious-landscape-study.html.

H. W. House

EVANGELISM. The word *evangelism* is a transliteration of the Koine Greek *euangelizomai*, which means "to proclaim/declare/announce good news." Outside the Bible, the term was understood in purely secular terms and possessed no religious significance. It does occur in religious contexts in a few places in the Septuagint (the Greek translation of the Old Testament), notably in Isaiah,

referring to the redemption of Zion and the coming of the Messiah (Isa. 40:9; 52:7; 61:1). This usage becomes prominent in the writings of the New Testament and in first-century Christian parlance in reference to the ministry and work of Jesus Christ (e.g., Mark 1:1). Such usage focused especially on the saving work of Jesus as fulfilled in his atoning and vicarious sacrifice for sin on the cross, his burial, and his subsequent triumphant resurrection from the tomb and death itself (e.g., 1 Cor. 15:1–4). The event of Jesus's return from the dead was interpreted as a victory over sin, death, and the grave.

In union with the events of Jesus's passion, there was proclaimed the offer of forgiveness of sin, the gift of the Holy Spirit, and the promise of eternal life for all people who would repent of sin, believe in the Lord Jesus Christ, and confess him as Lord and Savior. These truths, together with the promises offered to those who meet the condition of faith and thereby gain the promise of salvation, constitute for the Christian community "good news" or the gospel. The evangel forms the contents of the one who evangelizes. *Evangelism* is the noun describing the task. New religious movements do not usually refer to the task of evangelism. *Proselytizing*, or the attempt to gain adherents to a particular group or church movement, is most often identified as the missionary activity of heterodox Christian groups. *Evangelism*, referring to the declaration of the good news of the life and work of Jesus, is the term used to identify the central activity of mainstream Christianity, including especially evangelicals.

With the emergence of evangelicals over the course of the last three-hundred-plus years, the term *evangelical* has been used more and more often. The responsibility of evangelism, preaching and sharing the gospel, is considered by evangelicals themselves as critical to the central mission of the church (sometimes even becoming the organizing principle of the church itself). Perhaps in reaction to Protestant efforts, both the Roman Catholic Church and Eastern Orthodoxy have increased their evangelism efforts.

See also CHRISTIANITY, PROTESTANT; CHURCH OF JESUS CHRIST OF LATTER-DAY SAINTS; EASTERN ORTHODOXY; EVANGELICALISM; JEHOVAH'S WITNESSES (JW); ROMAN CATHOLICISM

Bibliography. P. W. Chilcote and L. C. Warner, eds., *The Study of Evangelism: Exploring a Missional Practice of the Church*; M. Green, *Evangelism in the Early Church*.

R. P. Roberts

EXALTATION. Exaltation is a complex teaching of the Church of Jesus Christ of Latter-day Saints regarding the attainment of eternal life; the teaching falls under the doctrine of eternal progression. According to Mormon theology, eternal progression is the process by which one strives for perfection, which extends well beyond the grave. Exaltation, which is the final result of eternal progression, is synonymous with full or individual salvation and is the means by which individuals become like God.

Progress is made by exercising what is called free agency, the ability to choose between good and evil. Evangelical writer Ron Rhodes identifies three states of existence in LDS doctrine that are involved in eternal progression and lead to final exaltation. The first is premortality, or preexistence, a state in which the spirit children of God exist with the seeds of potential godhood. Even in the premortal state, these spirit children must exercise agency carefully, and by doing so they advance to the next stage, mortality.

Having attained mortality, the premortal spirit children take on human bodies and now must persevere in their mortal existence, using their free agency to make wise choices regarding good and evil. They must strictly adhere to Mormon teachings, including obedience to the Word of Wisdom (strictures against use of "strong drinks," tobacco, and "hot drinks"), baptism, membership in the LDS Church, marriage in an LDS temple, and the diligent practice of various rituals mandated by the church.

The final state is the return to the spirit world at death, but here there are three potential destinations. The first is the telestial kingdom, reserved for those who never repented of their sins in the mortal life. The second is the terrestrial kingdom, which is inhabited by people who, in this life, never fully accepted the full gospel of Christ but nevertheless lived good lives. The final destination is the highest and most desired, the celestial kingdom. It is reserved for faithful members of the LDS Church and for some who accept the LDS gospel in the spirit world. Within the celestial kingdom, some will attain the highest degree of glory by demonstrating total compliance with the fullness of the gospel, notably the practice of church rituals, especially celestial marriage. Celestial marriage, which is performed in the temple and seals the couple for eternity, is the gate to achieving exaltation (eternal life), which also entails continuing the family in eternity.

See also CELESTIAL KINGDOM; CHURCH OF JESUS CHRIST OF LATTER-DAY SAINTS; TELESTIAL KINGDOM; TERRESTRIAL KINGDOM

Bibliography. Church of Jesus Christ of Latter-day Saints, *"Preach My Gospel": A Guide to Missionary Service*; R. Rhodes, *Reasoning from the Scriptures with the Mormons*; Joseph Fielding Smith, *Doctrines of Salvation*, vol. 2.

S. J. Rost

FALSE PROPHECY. In the Bible, a prophet is someone who speaks authoritatively for God, so anyone who falsely claims to speak authoritatively for God, or who speaks on behalf of a false god, is a false prophet. A prophet who performs miracles is not to be followed if he represents other gods or seeks to sway God's people from obeying his word (Deut. 13:1–5). Anyone who claims to speak for God, or for other gods, and who in that capacity utters false predictions concerning the future is also to be rejected (Deut. 18:20–22). Thus "false prophecy" in the narrower sense of a false prediction on divine authority is one indication, but not a necessary condition, that an individual is a false prophet. Even a prophet who claims to represent the Lord Jesus and who performs miracles in his name must be deemed a false prophet if his or her life and ministry are not faithful to Jesus's teaching (Matt. 7:15–27). False teachers who arise within the church are also akin to false prophets (2 Pet. 2:1). Their false teachings deny the full deity or humanity of Christ or in some other way misrepresent Christ or his teachings (1 John 4:1–3; 2 John 7, 9; cf. 2 Cor. 11:2–4).

A wide variety of religious teachings meet these criteria of false prophecy. The claim of the Unification Church that the Messiah would come from Korea (generally understood to mean that the Unification Church's founder, Sun Myung Moon, may himself be the Messiah) is an example of false prophecy in both the broad and the narrow senses. Mary Baker Eddy, the founder of Christian

Science, was a false prophet, and her book *Science and Health with Key to the Scriptures* (1875) is in its entirety a work of false prophecy.

Joseph Smith, the founder of the Church of Jesus Christ of Latter-day Saints, actually claimed to be a prophet of God. His doctrines that are contradictory to the Bible, such as Smith's assertion that God was once a man like us and became a God, mark him as a false prophet according to the Bible (Smith, *Teachings of the Prophet Joseph Smith*, 345–47). His erroneous predictions found in LDS scriptures also show him to be a false prophet in the narrow sense. These include his 1832 predictions that a temple would be built in Jackson County, Missouri, before the generation of his day passed away (there is still no temple there) and that a war between the northern and southern states (which did occur) would become a world war, which did not occur (Doctrine & Covenants 82:1–5; 87).

The Adventist tradition originated with false predictions of the second coming in 1843 and 1844, though these were presented not as authoritative prophecies but as earnest interpretations of the Bible. In the aftermath of that failed prediction, an Adventist visionary named Ellen G. White came to be regarded as a prophetess in the Seventh-day Adventist Church. White's aberrant interpretations of the Bible, her extensive plagiarism, and other errors mark her as a false prophet.

Originally an Adventist sect, the Jehovah's Witnesses have published numerous speculations concerning the date of the end of the present age, as well as concerning events having to do with the "last days." Their founder, Charles Taze Russell, taught that Jesus had become invisibly present in 1874 and would bring a final end to wickedness by 1914. After extending the deadline to 1918 and later to 1925, Russell's followers revised the chronology so that 1914 was the date of Christ's invisible return and the final end of wickedness was imminent. This is still the position of the Jehovah's Witnesses, who have been taught these erroneous dates as part of the "food at the proper time" that God's servant organization was serving and that the faithful were required to accept without question. The Jehovah's Witnesses, then, meet the criterion of claiming to speak authoritatively for God; thus their teachings and speculative predictions are false prophecy.

See also ADVENTIST MOVEMENT; BOOK OF ABRAHAM; JEHOVAH'S WITNESSES (JW); SEVENTH-DAY ADVENTISM; SMITH, JOSEPH, JR.

Bibliography. R. Abanes, *End-Time Visions: The Doomsday Obsessions*; W. M. Alnor, *Soothsayers of the Second Advent*; E. C. Gruss, *Jehovah's Witnesses: Their Claims, Doctrinal Changes and Prophetic Speculation; What Does the Record Show?*; J. R. Lewis, *Doomsday Prophecies: A Complete Guide to the End of the World*; Joseph Smith Jr., *Teachings of the Prophet Joseph Smith*, edited by Joseph Fielding Smith.

R. M. Bowman Jr.

FANA (OR FANAA). *Fana* (Arabic, "to pass away" or "to cease to exist"), in Sufi Islamic theology, refers to the annihilation of the contingent aspects of the self that occurs when a person is united with the being of Allah in a higher mode of existence. The concept is derived from the Qur'an, sura 55:26–27.

The mystical state in which the Divine absorbs the personal identity of the devotee is called *fana fi Allah* (extinction of the self in God). Devotees attain this state by means of a demanding regimen of spiritual disciplines, including focused meditation, contemplation

of the divine attributes, and the renunciation of all human (and thus contingent) qualities.

There are three types of fana in Sufism: of actions, of attributes, and of essence. Most versions of the doctrine maintain that fana consists not in the utter annihilation of the self but only in the obliteration of those aspects of the self that are contingent, of everything that is not God. This is often interpreted to mean that even after fana fi Allah, the person continues to exist as an aspect of Allah (since only Allah exists in an ultimate sense).

The doctrine of fana is sufficiently complex that it is difficult to determine whether it consists primarily of an epistemological claim (the devotees' knowledge of their fundamental identity with Allah) or of a metaphysical teaching (that the devotees undergo a substantial ontological change at the time of absorption into the divine being). In either case, fana fi Allah results in an eternal union with God known as *baqa billah*, wherein the devotees experience endless joy because of their intimate knowledge of (and participation in) the Divine.

See also SUFISM

Bibliography. J. Baldick, *Mystical Islam: An Introduction to Sufism*; J. Renard, trans., *Knowledge of God in Classical Sufism: Foundations of Islamic Mystical Theology*.

J. Bjornstad

FENG SHUI. Feng Shui is a Chinese philosophy of construction and interior design dating back, at least in a primitive form, to perhaps three thousand years ago. It seems to have been well developed by AD 220. Astrology, numerology, the *I-Ching*, and other forms of divination also contributed to its maturation. Some feng shui consultants, in fact, still couple their practices with these divination techniques. Also known as "Chinese geomancy," it is based on the belief that a universal energy, or life force, permeates and sustains all that exists. Many Eastern religions hold such a belief. In Taoism, for instance, this life force is called *chi*. In Hinduism it is referred to as *prana*.

In Chinese, the term *feng shui* means "wind, water," and the concept comes directly from the idea that chi moves like the wind but can be trapped like water. It also can have its path interrupted or diverted in wrong directions. Trapped chi, if allowed to stagnate, supposedly will have negative ramifications not only for nearby structures but also for persons. Likewise, misdirected chi can cause all manner of unpleasant consequences. Unwanted results might range from minor inconveniences such as simple irritability and substandard work performance to far more serious fallouts such as physical injury or even death.

Feng shui consultants claim to guide their clients toward building a healthy and harmonious environment, whether it be by properly positioning flowers in a garden or arranging furniture in an office. Their task is to ensure the presence of a clear pathway through which chi can flow unhindered. This in turn will properly balance the *yin* and *yang* (negative and positive) aspects of the life force in the immediate area. According to feng shui proponents, good fortune, increased energy, emotional satisfaction, and mental wellness will surely follow.

Within feng shui, there are many theories and approaches, including Black Hat, Four Pillars, Flying Stars, and Nine Star Ki. All these techniques emphasize one or more of several variables. The basics of feng shui, however, primarily deal with four aspects of any given area: building, environment, time, and people. Their harmony with chi is evaluated through study of their interaction with nature's five elemental energies: fire, wood, water, metal, and earth. Corrective measures are based on nine Eastern forms of traditional curing techniques adapted for modern use in the Western world: light, sound, life, movement, stability, electricity, symbolism, color, and transcendental solutions.

The twenty-first-century popularity of feng shui in major cities (e.g., New York, Los Angeles, and Washington, DC) cannot be overstated. Especially fashionable has been the use of elite consultants by multimillion-dollar businesses (e.g., Merrill Lynch) and high-powered investors (e.g., Donald Trump), usually at exorbitant costs.

See also I CHING / YIJING; TAOISM / DAOISM

Bibliography. K. R. Carter, *Move Your Stuff, Change Your Life: How to Use Feng Shui to Get Love, Money, Respect, and Happiness*; S. Post, *The Modern Book of Feng Shui*.

R. Abanes

FIQH. *Fiqh* (Arabic, "deep understanding" or "full comprehention"), the word for Islamic jurisprudence, refers to (1) the methods of legal reasoning used by Muslim legal scholars (*faqihs*) and (2) the legal rulings (*fatwas*) arrived at by those jurists. The purpose of fiqh is to derive binding precepts from authoritative Islamic sources such as the Qur'an, the Sunnah (practices of the Prophet Muhammad), and the hadith (traditions about the life of Muhammad). These derived statutes are intended to assist Muslims in obeying Allah and to guide them in the particular social contexts in which they find themselves. In Sunni Islam it is acknowledged that the decrees of the faqihs, though generally reliable, may be in error; in Shi'ite Islam such edicts are deemed infallible. Sunni and Shi'ite views of fiqh differ regarding the degree of authority vested in jurists and the perspicuity of the Qur'an. The four major schools of Sunni jurisprudence are Hanafi, Maliki, Shafi'i, and Hanbali. The Ja'fari school of legal theory is prominent within Shi'ism. Rashid Khalifa (1935–90) was the leading proponent of the "Qur'an alone" approach to jurisprudence until his assassination in January 1990.

See also HADITH; ISLAM, BASIC BELIEFS OF; QUR'AN; SHARI'AH

Bibliography. W. B. Hallaq, *A History of Islamic Legal Theories: An Introduction to Sunni usul al-fiqh*; A. A. Sachedina, *The Just Ruler in Shi'ite Islam: The Comprehensive Authority of the Jurist in Imamite Jurisprudence*; D. Waines, *An Introduction to Islam*, 2nd ed.

J. Bjornstad

FIRST VISION. According to the official account of Joseph Smith Jr.'s first vision in Joseph Smith—History (part of the LDS scripture Pearl of Great Price), in 1820 Smith witnessed spiritual renewal taking place in various denominational churches. Given their differing doctrinal views and varied practices, Smith struggled to understand which church had the truth. Upon reading James 1:5, which promises wisdom to anyone who asks, Smith went into the woods and asked God to show him the true church. According to Smith, two personages appeared to him in a vision, God the Father and Jesus Christ. They told him to join none of the churches because they were all wrong and their creeds were all an abomination.

The First Vision is considered one of the fundamental truths that missionaries present to prospects, and to which faithful Mormons give assent. An important theological point that Mormons derive from the First Vision is that God the Father is a personage who possesses a physical body, in contradistinction to the position of historic Christianity, which has a strictly immaterial understanding of the Godhead. Furthermore, the theology of the Godhead presented in the First Vision as understood in LDS teaching is not monotheistic but polytheistic, given Smith's later explicit claim that the Father, the Son, and the Holy Ghost are three distinct deities. The official account does not, however, make these points clear, and it was not until long after Joseph Smith's death that Mormons began assigning fundamental importance to the First Vision.

The First Vision has come under careful scrutiny by evangelical apologists. They note that the vision, which was allegedly received in 1820, appears to have been completely unknown in the 1820s or through much of the 1830s, even years after the LDS Church was founded. A second significant issue that has been raised concerns the discrepancies in the various early accounts of the First Vision. The official account was written in 1838 (dictated by Joseph Smith). As noted, it claims that Smith did not know which church was right, asked God in 1820 which church to join, and was answered with a vision of the Father and the Son. The earliest account, which was written in 1832 in Smith's own handwriting but did not come to light until 1965, indicates that Smith was in his "sixteenth year" (i.e., the year 1821) and was already fully convinced that all the churches were wrong before he prayed. Smith's prayer in this account was not to know which church to join but an appeal for forgiveness of his sins. He was answered by a vision in which "the Lord" Jesus appeared to him—with no mention of the Father. In late 1834 and 1835, Oliver Cowdery recorded an account in three installments in which there is some confusion. Cowdery first states that Smith was in his fifteenth year, then corrects himself and says Smith was in his seventeenth year, but then says the event took place in 1823, when Smith was actually eighteen years of age. According to Cowdery, Smith was not sure if God existed but sought forgiveness of sins and was visited by a single messenger from the Lord. In late 1835, Smith gave a different account to "Joshua the Jewish minister." In this account, Smith was not sure which church was right and which was wrong, and he saw one personage and then another who told him that his sins were forgiven and that Jesus was the Son of God; these personages were evidently angels, not the Father or the Son. Several other versions were told during Smith's lifetime, but these are the most notable. They show confusion over the date and contradict one another as to Smith's purpose in praying and who appeared to him in the vision.

Mormon explanations of the various versions of the First Vision vary. Milton Backman Jr. claims that Smith dictated to different scribes for differing purposes and perspectives. In his article titled "Eight Contemporary Accounts of Joseph Smith's First Vision," LDS historian James Allen describes eight of the accounts (1831–32; 1835; 1838–39; Orson Pratt account of 1840; Orson Hyde account of 1842; Wentworth Letter of 1842; *New York Spectator* version published in 1843; Alexander Neibaur's personal diary entry dated 1844) and contends that the discrepancies are not as substantial as some have made them. When it comes to the details, he concludes, there is general agreement.

See also CHURCH OF JESUS CHRIST OF LATTER-DAY SAINTS; SMITH, JOSEPH, JR.

Bibliography. J. Allen, "Eight Contemporary Accounts of Joseph Smith's First Vision," *Era*; Allen, "The Significance of Joseph Smith's 'First Vision' in Mormon Thought," in *The New Mormon History: Revisionist Essays on the Past*, edited by D. M. Quinn; R. M. Bowman Jr., "How Mormons Are Defending Joseph Smith," *Christian Research Journal*; B. McKeever, "The First Vision's Slow Entrance into the LDS Story," *Mormonism Researched*; J. and S. Tanner, *Mormonism—Shadow or Reality?*; K. Van Gorden, *Mormonism*.

S. J. Rost

FORTY IMMORTALS. The Forty Immortals (known among Sikhs as the Chali Mukte) are a group of forty Sikh warriors who are thought to have attained liberation as a result of their bravery in dying as martyrs during a lopsided battle against a Mughal army in the Muktsar region of northwestern India in December 1705. These forty men previously had abandoned Guru Gobind Singh (1666–1708) but had a change of heart and proved their loyalty to him by their willingness to sacrifice their lives for his safety. Today devoted Sikhs keep alive the memory of these fighting men by singing sacred hymns (*kirtan*) and offering petitions (*ardas*) during religious ceremonies at Sikh temples (*gurdwaras*).

See also SIKHISM

Bibliography. All about Sikhs, "Introduction to Sikhism: Khalsa Saint and Soldier," https://www.allaboutsikhs.com/introduction/introduction-to-sikhismkhalsa-saint-a-soldier; A. S. Madra and P. Singh, *Warrior Saints: Three Centuries of the Sikh Military Tradition*; K. Singh, *The Illustrated History of the Sikhs*.

M. Power

FOUR NOBLE TRUTHS. The Four Noble Truths are the doctrinal core of Buddhist teaching and were allegedly the subject of the Buddha's first sermon, known in Buddhism as the "Setting in Motion of the Wheel of the Law (Dharma)."

Within Buddhism a fundamental notion is nirvana. While the nirvanic state cannot be adequately expressed in words, Buddhists claim that it can be experienced with the consequence of release from *dukkha*—a term typically translated as "suffering." *Dukkha* has various meanings, but the general idea is that life is commonly experienced as unfulfilling, unsatisfactory, and painful. The term was used in early Buddhism to refer to bones that had slipped from their sockets. Buddhists recognize that, though one can experience joy and pleasure, most of life is not lived this way, and even when it is, upon deeper reflection one recognizes that all is not right; something is deeply wrong with the human condition.

The First Noble Truth is that of the existence of dukkha/suffering—a truth that is especially evident at birth, during sickness, and at death. Life, as is common to the human experience, is alienated from ultimate reality and needs to be made right.

In order for things to be made right, we must know the cause of the problem. This leads to the Second Noble Truth, which identifies the cause of suffering as *tanha*, translated as "desire" or "craving," an attachment to the pleasures of possessions, others, or even one's own life.

The Third Noble Truth is that, since suffering has a cause, the cessation (*nirodha*) of suffering can be achieved by removing the cause. If the cause is desire or craving, the solution can be found in overcoming such desire or craving.

The Fourth Noble Truth is the way (*marga*) leading to the cessation of suffering. This way, referred to as the Noble Eightfold Path, is a lifestyle that one must follow to remove dukkha. It consists of right views, right intent, right speech, right conduct, right livelihood, right effort, right mindfulness, and right concentration. The Buddhist traditions spell out what each of these "rights" entails, and conscientiously following this path leads to the cessation of suffering—to ultimate reality and bliss (nirvana).

For Buddhists the doctrine of the Four Noble Truths is both fundamental and provisional teaching. It is like a portable bridge used to cross a gully; having reached the other side, one discards the bridge.

See also BUDDHISM; DUKKHA/DUHKHA; EIGHTFOLD PATH; NIRVANA

Bibliography. Buddha Dharma Education Association, Inc. home page, http://www.buddhanet.net/; J. S. Strong, *The Experience of Buddhism: Sources and Interpretations*; R. Walpola, *What the Buddha Taught*; P. Williams, *Mahayana Buddhism: The Doctrinal Foundations*; K. Yandell and H. Netland. *Buddhism: A Christian Exploration and Appraisal*.

C. V. Meister

FRAVASHI. In Zoroastrianism a *fravashi* is a higher soul or self that exists within every human being. Each fravashi embodies the divine nature of Ahura Mazda (the supreme deity of Zoroastrianism) and hence is immune to ontological (though not moral) corruption. A person's fravashi serves as that person's protector and guide during his or her earthly life. All fravashis existed in an eternal, disembodied state prior to the creation of human beings. A great company of them chose to descend into the created order as warriors of Ahura Mazda in the battle against the forces of evil, and all of them will be resurrected by Ahura Mazda on the day of judgment. Zoroastrians believe that the good fravashis of deceased persons return to the land of the living just prior to the Persian New Year, at which time practitioners demonstrate their respect for these spirits by performing special rituals.

See also AHURA MAZDA; ZOROASTRIANISM

Bibliography. S. A. Nigosian, *The Zoroastrian Faith: Tradition and Modern Research*; Farrokh Vajifdar, "The Descent of the Fravashis," http://www.cais-soas.com/CAIS/Religions/iranian/Zarathushtrian/decent_fravashis.htm.

R. L. Drouhard

FRIENDS OF THE WESTERN BUDDHIST ORDER. Dennis Lingwood (1925–) is an English-born Buddhist monk who is best known today as Urgyen Sangharakshita (meaning "protected by the spiritual community"). In 1967 he created the Friends of the Western Buddhist Order (FWBO) in London, a movement that now has sixty-five centers worldwide, with eleven centers in the US. At the age of fifteen, Lingwood read the Diamond Sutra, or Vajracchedika, which is a fourth-century AD text of the Buddhist Mahayana tradition, and he felt an immediate affinity with Buddhism. During the Second World War, he served in India, and in 1946 he traveled through Sri Lanka and Singapore. In 1949 he went to Kusinagara in India, where he became a *samanera*, or novice, in the Theravadin tradition and was ordained a monk the following year. His first teacher was Jagadish Kashyap in Benares, who then requested that Sangharakshita establish a Buddhist monastery in Kalimpong in the eastern Himalayas.

Kalimpong became Sangharakshita's home base and remained so for fourteen years, and from there he established a magazine, began writing books, and served as an itinerant teacher of Buddhism in every state of India except Kashmir. Much of his work was centered on spreading Buddhism among the *dalits*, or "untouchables" of India. He also spent time learning about other Buddhist traditions, such as the Chinese tradition of Cha'an, and received training from seven Tibetan Buddhist lamas, including Jamyang Khyentse Rimpoche and Dudjom Rimpoche. These experiences enabled Sangharakshita to develop a very broad and nonsectarian attitude concerning the various traditions and schools of thought in Buddhism. In 1964 he returned to England, where he began to adapt the unifying essence of Buddhist practice and teaching found in all the various traditions. He felt that there are universal elements to Buddhism but that it has been expressed in different cultural forms through history. According to Sangharakshita, the principal teachings and precepts of Buddhism must be distinguished from its cultural forms, and these teachings must be suitably contextualized for living in the modern Western world.

The FWBO is the tangible outworking of that project of the adaptation of Buddhism. Those who belong to the FWBO are women and men for whom the Buddhist path is their central spiritual commitment. That commitment is grounded in the "Three Jewels" of Buddhism: taking refuge in the Buddha, the teachings (dharma), and the community (*sangha*).

In the FWBO, there is no belief in a creator god, and hence there are no divinely revealed laws to be obeyed. However, there are traditional ethical precepts that are incumbent on ordained members and must be applied in the body, in the mind, and in speech. Members are taught two basic forms of meditation: the Theravadan approach to mindfulness in breathing and loving-kindness and the insight into the emptiness of the self and reality, leading to the death of self/ego and a rebirth. The FWBO is responsible for operating the movement's city centers, retreat centers, residential communities, and team-based forms of ethical businesses. In 2000 Sangharakshita retired from the leadership of the FWBO. He has written over fifty books on various aspects of Buddhism and maintains an interest in the fine arts and classical music.

See also BUDDHISM; MAHAYANA BUDDHISM; THERAVADA BUDDHISM; TIBETAN BUDDHISM; ZEN BUDDHISM

Bibliography. Sangharakshita, *A Survey of Buddhism: Its Doctrines and Methods through the Ages*; Sangharakshita, *Who Is the Buddha?*; Subhuti, *Sangharakshita: A New Voice in the Buddhist Tradition*.

P. Johnson

FUNDAMENTALISM, CHRISTIAN. The term *fundamentalism* was originally coined in 1919 by Curtis Lee Laws to denote a theologically conservative standpoint taken by orthodox Christian Protestant believers. That conservative standpoint was initially expressed in the twelve-volume series titled The Fundamentals (1910–15). This series of booklets written by prominent academics such as James Orr (1844–1913) presented scholarly arguments in popular language against the growing influence of German theology that denied many traditional Christian doctrines. An early study of the fundamentalist movement was James Barr's *Fundamentalism* (1977), which is marred by his disparaging of well-respected Christian scholars such as the archaeologist Kenneth Kitchen. A more balanced study is George M. Marsden's *Fundamentalism and American Culture* (2006).

The term has subsequently been occasionally applied to traditional Roman Catholic believers who disapprove of the church's theological stances taken since Vatican II (especially the stance of the Pious Brotherhood). It denotes a reiteration of orthodox doctrine in reaction to secular and liberal theological views.

Bibliography. J. Barr, *Fundamentalism*; George M. Marsden, *Fundamentalism and American Culture*; Marsden, *Reforming Fundamentalism*; E. R. Sandeen, *The Roots of Fundamentalism*.

P. Johnson

G

GABRIEL THE ARCHANGEL, NON-CHRISTIAN VIEWS OF. References to the angel Gabriel are prominent in noncanonical Jewish writings such as the Dead Sea Scrolls and the books of *Enoch* (*1 Enoch* 9:1, 9–10; 40:3, 6; 54:6; *2 Enoch* 24:1), and various Targums refer to the angel.

In Islam he is said to be the angel who dictated the Qur'an to Muhammad. Heterodox Christian groups and alternative religions also include Gabriel in their sacred literature and teachings.

The Urantia movement considers him an important intermediary, and the Church of Jesus Christ of Latter-day Saints (Mormons) believes that he first was Noah, next to Adam in the priesthood, and only later was the angel who appeared to Zechariah and the virgin Mary. Contemporary New Agers have also said that they have channeled Gabriel.

See also CHURCH OF JESUS CHRIST OF LATTER-DAY SAINTS

Bibliography. J. Howard-Johnston and P. A. Hayward, *The Cult of Saints in Late Antiquity and the Middle Ages: Essays on the Contribution of Peter Brown*; M. Smith and J. Neusner, *Christianity, Judaism and Other Greco-Roman Cults: Studies for Morton Smith at Sixty*, vol. 12, part 4.

H. W. House

GABRIEL THE ARCHANGEL IN THE BIBLE. The Bible gives the names of only two angels, Michael and Gabriel. The latter is never called an archangel but is mentioned in three different verses; his name means "God is powerful." In Daniel 8:16, he provides Daniel with understanding of a vision. In Daniel 9:21, he comes to Daniel the prophet in response to Daniel's prayer regarding Israel. In Luke 1:19, he is recorded as coming to the priest Zechariah, and afterward in Luke 1:26 he appears to the young virgin Mary, announcing the conception and subsequent birth of Jesus.

Bibliography. J. Howard-Johnston and P. A. Hayward, *The Cult of Saints in Late Antiquity and the Middle Ages: Essays on the Contribution of Peter Brown*; M. Smith and J. Neusner, *Christianity, Judaism and other Greco-Roman Cults: Studies for Morton Smith at Sixty*, vol. 12, part 4.

H. W. House

GASSHO. Though its origin is in ancient India, the *gassho* (Japanese, "to place the two palms together") is a *mudra* (a symbolic hand gesture) used by nearly all Buddhist sects and has a particularly prominent role within Zen Buddhism. Buddhist tradition says the practice was started when the Buddha's five companions encountered him for the first time after he was enlightened. They were so struck by his serenity and radiance that they "spontaneously placed their palms together and greeted him with deep bows" (Maezumi and Glassman, 53). Gassho is the most fundamental of Buddhist mudras, for it is associated with the attainment of enlightenment. The precise manner of placing the hands together and the placement of the arms relative to the face and body vary depending on the particular type of gassho. Often it is done in conjunction with a deep bow. Gasshos are used by their practitioners to display respect, focus the mind, unify spiritual polarities, and express the complete unity of reality. The most formal of the gasshos, the firm gassho, is thought to assist the practitioner in establishing an alert and reverential state of mind. The gassho of no-mind is said to deepen one's state of mental concentration (*samadhi*). The lotus gassho and diamond gassho are primarily used by Buddhist priests during various Buddhist ceremonies.

See also BUDDHISM; MUDRA; SAMADHI; ZEN BUDDHISM

Bibliography. P. Harvey, *An Introduction to Buddhism: Teachings, History and Practices*; T. Maezumi and B. Glassman, *On Zen Practice: Body, Breath, and Mind*; J. Maguire, *Essential Buddhism: A Complete Guide to Beliefs and Practices*.

R. L. Drouhard

GATHAS. The Gathas ("sublime songs" in Persian) are the seventeen hymns of the Persian poet and philosopher Zoroaster (his Greek name; Persian name: Zarathushtra; ca. 1300 BC) found in the seventy-two-chapter Yasna (a section of the Avesta), the oldest extant Zoroastrian holy book. The poetic dialect of the Gathas, sometimes referred to as Old Avestan, stems from an ancient Indo-Iranian language group (about which little is known) and is characterized by a rich and complex literary style. Because of this, and because relatively few commentaries on the Gathas survive, translating the text is difficult. The Gathas are divided into five groups, each consisting of songs (originally intended to be recited) with the same Vedic-like meter: (1) Ahunavaiti Gatha (principle of choice; chaps. 28–34), (2) Ushtavaiti Gatha (having happiness; chaps. 43–46), (3) Spentamainyush Gatha (bounteous spirit; chaps. 47–50), (4) Vohukhshathra Gatha (good dominion; chap. 51), and (5) Vahishtoishti Gatha (best beloved; chap. 53). The 241 stanzas of the Gathas are at the heart of Zoroastrian devotion, though they are the only portion of the Zoroastrian scriptures thought to have been written by Zoroaster himself. Most scholars of Zoroastrianism believe that Zoroaster composed the Gathas not as a means of systematic religious instruction—though theological teachings are dispersed throughout—but rather as a way of invoking and praising the omniscient creator Ahura Mazda and exhorting others to govern their lives in accordance with his commands.

See also AVESTA; ZOROASTRIANISM

Bibliography. M. Boyce, *Zoroastrians: Their Religious Beliefs and Practices*; P. Clark, *Zoroastrianism: An Introduction to an Ancient Faith*; P. Nanavutty, trans., *The Gathas of Zarathushtra: Hymns in Praise of Wisdom*; S. A. Nigosian, *The Zoroastrian Faith: Tradition and Modern Research*; J. H. Peterson, "Avesta: Zoroastrian Archives," http://www.avesta.org/.

J. Bjornstad

GENEALOGIES, MORMON. The compilation of family histories is considered a sacred responsibility among members of the Church of Jesus Christ of Latter-day Saints (Mormons). The Family History Library (located across the street from Temple Square in Salt Lake City, Utah, the headquarters city of the LDS Church) is the largest of its kind, with millions of names being added to its database each year. Hundreds of satellite libraries have also been built all over the world. Access is available to all; membership in the LDS Church is not a requirement for using the library resources.

In 1894 the Genealogical Society of Utah was organized under the authority of the LDS First Presidency. Its purpose was to train individuals in how to trace their ancestry as well as to encourage LDS members to perform temple ordinances on their ancestors' behalf. According to LDS teaching, members have the ability to become "saviors on Mount Zion" by vicariously performing sacred ordinances in LDS temples for their deceased relatives and friends. In the words of Mormon apostle Dallin Oaks, "We are not hobbyists in genealogy work. We do family history work in order to provide the ordinances of salvation for the living and the dead."

The most common ritual performed in LDS temples is baptism for the dead. Since Mormonism makes water baptism a requirement for salvation, living members may be baptized as proxies for "those who would have accepted the gospel in this life, had they been permitted to hear it." Since it is believed that the deceased have a choice whether to accept the baptism, proxies have no way of knowing in this life whether their efforts have had a positive result. LDS folklore is replete with stories of dead ancestors appearing to members asking for work to be done on their behalf.

Mormonism's founder, Joseph Smith Jr., said: "The greatest responsibility in this world that God has laid upon us is to seek after our dead" (356). He also warned, "Those Saints who neglect it in behalf of their deceased relatives, do it at the peril of their own salvation" (193).

See also BAPTISM OF THE DEAD, MORMON; CHURCH OF JESUS CHRIST OF LATTER-DAY SAINTS

Bibliography. D. H. Ludlow, ed., *Encyclopedia of Mormonism*, 4 vols.; D. H. Oakes, "Family History: 'In Wisdom and in Order,'" *Ensign*; Joseph Smith Jr., *Teachings of the Prophet Joseph Smith*; Joseph Fielding Smith, *Doctrines of Salvation.*

W. McKeever

GHANTA. A *ghanta* (Sanskrit, "bell") is a wood or metal instrument used in Asia in a religious setting. Monasteries frequently have large ghantas, like the wooden ones used in Bali, but smaller ones can be for personal use. They have a special meaning in Vajrayana Buddhism, where the bell is also known, in Tibetan, as a *drilbu*, a carved metal handbell employed during Tibetan Buddhist ceremonies. As one of the key ritual implements of the Vajrayana tradition, it symbolizes the feminine principle (wisdom) and instruction

in dharma (key Buddhist doctrines). The ghanta is thought to be a propitious object capable of producing many favorable results if used properly. These include the visualization of tantric Buddhas, bodhisattvas, and gods; the safety provided by benevolent deities; and the warding off of evil deities. During rituals the ghanta is paired with the *dorje* (Sanskrit, *vajra*), a short metal scepter that symbolizes the masculine principle (compassion-based skillful means). The ghanta is held in the left hand, and the dorje is held in the right hand; in some cases the ritual performer crosses his wrists and holds both hands against his or her chest. The ghanta represents the body of the Buddha, the dorje represents the mind of the Buddha, and the sound of the bell represents the Buddha's voice instructing his pupils. Together the ghanta and the dorje signify the seamless, synergistic union of wisdom and compassion that results in indestructible enlightenment.

See also DHARMA; TANTRA; TIBETAN BUDDHISM; VAJRAYANA BUDDHISM

Bibliography. C. B. Levenson, *Symbols of Tibetan Buddhism*; R. A. Ray, *Secret of the Vajra World: The Tantric Buddhism of Tibet.*

J. Bjornstad

GLOSSOLALIA. *See* SPEAKING IN TONGUES

GOD, MORMON VIEW OF. The doctrine of God held by the Church of Jesus Christ of Latter-day Saints (LDS Church) is unique among groups having their origin in the Judeo-Christian tradition. Many within the LDS community express this doctrine as a form of finite theism, stating that God is a radically contingent, embodied deity who, like each of us, is a creature of a universe he did not create and is subject to and not the source of its laws and principles. Some Mormons, however, maintain that the LDS church is not necessarily committed to this radical formulation, that there are resources within Mormon writings by which the church may affirm a doctrine of God closer to that which has been held by traditional Christians.

Sources. According to the LDS Church, its doctrine of God is derived primarily from five groups of sources, the first four being the most important. (1) The first is the Protestant Christian Bible, "as far as it is translated correctly" (The Articles of Faith, 1:8). (2) The second group consists of works regarded by the Mormon church as inspired scripture: The Book of Mormon (BM), the Doctrine and Covenants (D&C), and the Pearl of Great Price (PGP). (3) The Mormon concept of God is also shaped by the extrascriptural statements and doctrinal commentaries of Joseph Smith Jr., founding prophet of the LDS Church. Although not regarded as scripture per se, Smith's extracanonical pronouncements on doctrine are accepted by the Mormon laity and leadership as authoritative for Mormon theology. (4) The statements and writings of the church's ecclesiastical leaders—especially its presidents, who are considered divinely inspired prophets—contain authoritative presentations of the LDS doctrine of God. (5) The insights of LDS scholars, such as B. H. Roberts, David L. Paulsen, Blake Ostler, Robert Millet, and Stephen Robinson, though not authoritative, have helped systematize and clarify the Mormon concept of God.

Because there are so many doctrinal sources, it may appear (with some justification) that it is difficult to determine precisely what the LDS Church teaches about God. For example, BM (first published in 1830) seems to teach a strongly Christian monotheism with modalistic overtones (see Alma 11:26–31, 38; Moroni 8:18; Mosiah 3:5–8; 7:27; 15:1–5), while the equally authoritative PGP (first published in 1851) clearly teaches that more than one God made the world (see Abraham 4–5) and that these gods are finite. This finite view of God reached its apex in the theology of Smith's successor, Brigham Young, who in public sermons taught the doctrine that Adam, the first man, is God of this world. It is explicitly rejected by LDS authorities today. As in the Catholic understanding of the papacy, not everything taught or preached by an LDS president is thought by the church to be infallible or even a doctrine to which all Mormons must assent.

Nevertheless, it is clear that the LDS doctrine of God—as a number of scholars, including Mormon writers, have argued (see Alexander; Allen; Kirkland; Widmer)—developed from a fairly conventional monotheism to a full-blown plurality-of-gods theology. This is why Kirkland writes that "Mormons who are aware of the various teachings of the LDS scriptures and prophets over the years are faced with a number of doctrinal possibilities." For example, "they can choose to accept Book of Mormon theology, but this varies from biblical theology as well as from Joseph Smith's later plurality-of-gods theology. . . . While most Mormons are unaware of the diversity that abounds in the history of Mormon doctrine, many Latter-day Saints . . . have, despite the risk of heresy, continued to believe or promote publicly many of the alternative Godhead theologies from Mormonism's past" (Kirkland, "Development," 48).

The Attributes of the LDS God. Because of the diversity of sources, there is disagreement among LDS scholars concerning how best to understand the nature of the Mormon God. Nevertheless, given the dominant reading of the documents the church presently considers authoritative, certain core LDS convictions about God seem unassailable. Since the Mormon Church rejects the traditional Christian doctrine of the Trinity—and embraces the view that Father, Son, and Holy Ghost are three separate Gods who are one in purpose but not being—the best way to understand the LDS doctrine of deity is to begin with God the Father. According to the church, God the Father is (1) a contingent being, who was at one time not God; (2) perhaps finite in knowledge (contemporary LDS teaching is unclear on this; see below); (3) one of many gods; (4) a corporeal (bodily) being, who physically dwells at a particular spatiotemporal location and is therefore not omnipresent like the classical God; and (5) a being who is subject to the laws and principles of a beginningless universe with an infinite number of entities in it.

This concept of God can be better grasped by seeing its place in the overall Mormon worldview and how the deity fits into it. Mormonism teaches that God the Father is a resurrected, "exalted" man named Elohim who was at one time *not* God. He was once a mortal man on another planet who, through obedience to the precepts of *his* God, eventually attained exaltation, or godhood, through "eternal progression." The Mormon God, located in time and space, has a body of flesh and bone (D&C 130:22); thus he is neither spirit nor omnipresent as understood in their traditional meanings within orthodox Christianity. Joseph Smith asserts in his famous "King Follet Discourse" (1844):

God himself was once as we are now, and is an exalted man, and sits enthroned in yonder heavens! . . . I am going to tell you how God came to be God. *We have imagined and supposed that God was God from all eternity. I will refute this idea*, and take away the veil, so that you may see. . . . It is the first principle of the gospel to know for a certainty the character of God, and to know that we may converse with him as one man converses with another, and that He was once a man like us; yea, that God himself, the Father of us all, dwelt on an earth, the same as Jesus Christ himself did; and I will show it from the Bible. . . . Here, then, is eternal life—to know the only wise and true God; and you have got to learn how to be gods yourselves, and be kings and priests to God, *the same as all* gods have done before you, namely, by going from one small degree to another,

and from a small capacity to a great one; from grace to grace, from exaltation to exaltation, until you attain to the resurrection of the dead, and are able to dwell in everlasting burnings, and sit in glory, as do those who sit enthroned in everlasting power. (Smith, *History*, 6:305–6)

Some LDS intellectuals, however, have raised questions about aspects of this exaltation narrative that they maintain are not explicitly affirmed anywhere in the Mormon canon of scripture. For example, Millet writes: "It is true that Presidents Joseph Smith and Lorenzo Snow both spoke of God once being a man, but we know very little if anything beyond the idea itself. I am not aware of any official statement or declaration of doctrine that goes beyond what I have just stated. Anything you may hear or read beyond that is speculative" (Millet and Johnson, 58).

Omniscience, according to LDS thought, is one of the attributes God the Father attained as a result of his progression to godhood. Mormon thinkers, however, appear to be divided on the meaning of *omniscience*. Some seem to hold that omniscience means that God knows all true propositions about the past, present, and future, a view consistent with the traditional Christian view (Blomberg and Robinson, 92). On the other hand, others maintain that God does not know the future (Ostler, 76–78). This view affirms that only the present and the past can be known by God since the former is occurring and the latter has already occurred. Consequently, since the future is not yet a "thing" and has not become actual (and hence cannot possibly be known), God cannot know the future. Therefore, the Mormon God is "omniscient" in the sense that he knows everything that can possibly be known, but he nevertheless increases in knowledge as the future unfolds and becomes the present. Although a more traditional view of omniscience seems to be the dominant position among contemporary

Mormons, the view that denies God's knowledge of the future is still embraced by some within the church, especially among academics who maintain that LDS finitism is philosophically superior to classical theism (Ostler; Paulsen). However, the embracing of the openness view of God—a view that denies God's knowledge of the future—among some evangelical thinkers has provided LDS finitists with unexpected allies on the issue of divine omniscience (Blomberg and Robinson, 109).

According to LDS thought, Elohim created this present world by "organizing" both eternally preexistent, inorganic matter and the preexistent primal intelligences from which human spirits are made (PGP, Abraham 3:22). For this reason, Joseph Smith Jr. writes that "man was also in the beginning with God. Intelligence, or the light of truth, was not created or made, neither indeed can be" (D&C 93:29). In other words, humans' basic essence or primal intelligence is as eternal as God's since God and humans are members of the same species of being, a species whose members by nature have the potential to achieve godhood. Nevertheless, by "organizing" these intelligences (what some in the LDS Church have called "spirit birth"), God the Father plays a necessary creative role in their preparation for corporeal existence.

The Mormon God, by creating this world out of preexistent matter, has granted these organized spirits the opportunity to receive physical bodies, pass through mortality, and eventually progress to godhood—just as this opportunity was given to him by his Father God. Consequently, if human persons on earth faithfully obey the precepts of Mormonism, they, too, can attain godhood like Elohim before them. And the purpose of attaining godhood is so that "we would become heavenly parents and have spirit children just as [Elohim] does" (Church of Jesus Christ of Latter-day Saints, 11).

Comparing the Mormon concept with the traditional Christian concept of God, Mormon philosopher Blake Ostler writes that in contrast to the self-sufficient God who creates the universe

> ex nihilo (out of nothing), the Mormon God did not bring into being the ultimate constituents of the cosmos—neither its fundamental matter nor the space/time matrix which defines it. Hence, unlike the Necessary Being of classical theology who alone could not not exist and on which all else is contingent for existence, the personal God of Mormonism confronts uncreated realities which exist of metaphysical necessity. Such realities include inherently self-directing selves (intelligences), primordial elements (mass/energy), the natural laws which structure reality, and moral principles grounded in the intrinsic value of selves and the requirements for growth and happiness. (67)

Mormonism, therefore, teaches that certain basic realities have always existed and are indestructible even by God. According to Mormon thought, God, like each human being, is merely another eternal being in the universe. In the Mormon universe, God is not responsible for creating or sustaining matter, energy, natural laws, personhood, moral principles, the process of salvation (or exaltation), or much of anything. Instead of the universe being subject to him, the Mormon God is subject to the universe. One should keep in mind that when traditional Christians say that God is Creator, they mean that God is the source of all contingent reality, that he brought the entire universe into existence out of nothing (*creatio ex nihilo*). In this sense, no creature—that is, anything that is not God—can ever literally be a creator since creatures can only make new things from things that already exist. God, on the other hand, requires no such preexisting materials. For this reason, under traditional Christianity, the LDS God is not technically a creator.

Unlike the God of traditional Christianity, who is omnipresent in being, the God of Mormonism is only omnipresent insofar as he is aware of everything in the universe. Since the Mormon God is a physical body and hence is limited by time and space, his being cannot be present everywhere. Although according to LDS doctrine God's influence, power, and knowledge are all-pervasive, the focal point of God's being (his body) exists at a particular place in time and space. Because Mormon theology does not teach that the universe is contingent upon God either to bring it into being or to sustain its existence, there is no need for Mormon theology to hold to the traditional Christian view of omnipresence.

The Trinity. Although the LDS Church affirms the doctrine of the Trinity, its definition of the Trinity is radically different from the traditional Christian understanding of that doctrine. Founding prophet Smith asserts: "Many men say there is one God; the Father, the Son, and the Ghost are only one God! I say that is a strange God anyhow—three in one, and one in three! . . . He would be a wonderfully big God—he would be a giant or a monster" (Smith, *History*, 6:476). Mormon theology affirms tritheism, the belief that there exist three gods with whom this world should be concerned (though Mormon theology teaches that there exist many other gods as well): Elohim (the Father), Jehovah (the Son), and the Holy Ghost. Writes Smith: "The Father has a body of flesh and bone as tangible as man's; the Son also; but the Holy Ghost has not a body of flesh and bones, but is a personage of spirit. Were it not so, the Holy Spirit could not dwell in us" (D&C 130:22). The Father, the Son, and the Holy Ghost are "three separate individuals, physically distinct from each other," forming "the great presiding council of the universe" (Talmage, 237). And even the Holy Ghost is not really what traditional Christian theology means by a spirit since, according to Smith, there is no such thing as a nonphysical reality: "There is no such thing as immaterial matter. All spirit is matter, but is more fine or pure, and can only be discerned by purer eyes" (D&C 131:7–8).

According to Mormon thought, the pre-incarnate Jesus, Jehovah (or Yahweh), does not have a body of flesh and bone. Although McConkie writes that "Christ is *Jehovah*; they are one and the same Person" (392), some Mormon scholars admit that it is not always clear in Mormon literature whom the name Jehovah refers to (see Kirkland, "Elohim and Jehovah").

Development of LDS Theology. Stephen Parrish points out that one can find in contemporary Mormonism two identifiable views of deity: (1) the plurality-of-finite-gods theology, the view expounded above, and (2) monarchotheism, a view that there is one eternally existing though corporeal (perhaps finite) God who is above all the other gods (Beckwith, Mosser, and Owen). Although the plurality-of-gods tradition seems to be the most dominant, the latter view has been gaining ground among some Mormon intellectuals since the mid-1990s. Robinson, for example, writes: "Evangelicals often accuse Latter-day Saints of believing in a limited, finite, changeable god, but there is absolutely nothing in LDS Scriptures or beliefs to justify such a charge" (Blomberg and Robinson, 92). He also seems to claim that humans may become "gods" but not in the sense of being truly independent, a status reserved exclusively to God (Blomberg and Robinson, 86). Yet in other places Robinson seems to affirm doctrines that appear inconsistent with this notion, such as God's corporeality and that he *may have* once been finite (Blomberg and Robinson, 85–93). Nevertheless, Robinson's theological reflections (along with those of Millet) reveal a sincere and sophisticated effort to move Mormonism in the direction of more traditional theological categories without compromising LDS distinctives.

Conclusion. LDS theology seems presently committed to some form of finite theism. It has, however, within its body of authoritative literature resources by which the Mormon church may shift to a more traditional orthodox doctrine of God and eventually embrace something closer to classical theism (White).

See also CHURCH OF JESUS CHRIST OF LATTER-DAY SAINTS

Bibliography. T. G. Alexander, "The Reconstruction of Mormon Doctrine: From Joseph Smith to Progression Theology," *Sunstone*; J. B. Allen, "Emergence of a Fundamental: The Expanding Role of Joseph Smith's First Vision in Mormon Religious Thought," *Journal of Mormon History*; F. Beckwith, C. Mosser, and P. Owen, eds., *The New Mormon Challenge: Responding to the Latest Defenses of a Fast-Growing Movement*; C. Blomberg and S. Robinson, *How Wide the Divide? An Evangelical and a Mormon in Conversation*; Church of Jesus Christ of Latter-day Saints, *Gospel Principles*, rev. ed.; B. Kirkland, "The Development of the Mormon Doctrine of God," in *Line upon Line: Essays on Mormon Doctrine*, edited by G. J. Bergera; Kirkland, "Elohim and Jehovah in Mormonism and the Bible," *Dialogue: A Journal of Mormon Thought*; B. R. McConkie, *Mormon Doctrine*, 2nd ed.; R. L. Millet and G. C. V. Johnson, *Bridging the Divide: The Continuing Conversation between a Mormon and an Evangelical*; B. Ostler, "The Mormon Concept of God," *Dialogue: A Journal of Mormon Thought*; D. L. Paulsen, *The Comparative Coherency of Mormon (Finitistic) and Classical Theism*; Joseph Smith Jr., *Articles of Faith*; Joseph Smith Jr., *History of the Church of Jesus Christ of Latter-day Saints*, 2nd rev. ed., 7 vols.; Joseph Smith Jr., *The King Follet Discourse: The Being and Kind of Being God Is, The Immortality of the Intelligence of Man*; J. Talmage, *A Study of the Articles of Faith*; O. K. White Jr., *Mormon Neo-orthodoxy: A Crisis Theology*; K. Widmer, *Mormonism and the Nature of God: A Theological Evolution, 1813–1915*.

F. J. Beckwith

GOHONZON. The word *gohonzon* (Chinese, "religious object") is a parchment that is inscribed with Chinese characters from the Lotus Sutra and serves as an object of worship in Nichiren Shoshu Buddhism. The gohonzon, about ten inches wide and twenty inches long, is placed in a *butsu-dan* (shrine) in one's home. Devotees direct their chanting, prayers, and worship to the gohonzon and believe that speaking evil of it can result in poverty, blindness, disease, or other ill effects.

See also BUTSU-DAN; LOTUS SUTRA; NICHIREN SHOSHU

Bibliography. D. Ikeda, "The Sin of Slandering the Gohonozon," in *Lectures on Buddhism*, vol. 1, translated by T. Kamio; G. M. Williams, *New Members' Handbook: The Basics of Nichiren Shoshu Buddhism*.

E. Pement

GOLDEN TEMPLE. The Golden Temple, also known as Darbar Sahib, is the most sacred site in the religion of Sikhism. Located in Amritsar in the state of Punjab (northern India), the Golden Temple was established in 1577 by fourth Sikh guru Ram Das (1534–81). Surrounded by a 250,000-square-foot lake, the temple got its name when a thin coat of gold plate was applied to the exterior in 1802. It has housed the original holy Sikh scripture, the Guru Granth Sahib, since 1604. Temple priests read from the Granth twenty-four hours a day.

The three-story domed temple is surrounded by a fortified wall with eighteen gates and a white marble bridge leading up to it. Those who enter must remove their shoes and cover their heads. There are four doors on each side, figuratively offering entrance to the four castes in India. The north entrance has a Victorian clock tower. A Jubi tree planted 450 years ago by the religion's first high priest is located in the northwest of the compound and is said to contain special powers. Special marble, mirror, and inlay work took place during the nineteenth century.

The temple was desecrated in June 1984 when it was invaded by the Indian Army at the command of Prime Minister Indira Gandhi. Militant Sikhs were using the temple as a refuge and storing weapons there. More than one thousand Sikhs were killed, and the temple suffered significant damage. Scripture reading was interrupted for the first time in hundreds of years.

See also GURU GRANTH SAHIB; SIKHISM

Bibliography. M. P. Fisher, *Living Religions*; J. B. Noss, *Man's Religions*; R. Schmidt et al., *Patterns of Religion*.

E. Johnson

GONGYO. *Gongyo* (diligent practice) refers to a variety of central daily rituals performed by adherents of several Buddhist sects, especially those of Japanese origin. Although admitting of many particular forms, typically gongyo involves reciting a Buddhist text or hymn while facing an object of veneration; a ceremonial offering is also given. Depending on the particular school of Buddhism regulating gongyo, it can be performed at a Buddhist temple or at a nonsacred site. Gongyo is an essential aspect of Nichiren Shoshu Buddhism, wherein it consists of reading from the Lotus Sutra and chanting the mantra "*Namu myoho renge kyo*" (called the *daimoku*) next to the gohonzon (a religious object).

See also BUDDHISM; GOHONZON; LOTUS SUTRA; NICHIREN SHOSHU

Bibliography. E. Andreasen, *Popular Buddhism in Japan: Shin Buddhist Religion and Culture*; Y. Kirimura, *Buddhism and the Nichiren Shoshu Tradition*.

M. Power

GOSPEL OF BARNABAS. The Gospel of Barnabas (GB) is a late-medieval gospel forgery by an Islamic propagandist writing in the name of Paul's companion Barnabas (portrayed as one of the twelve apostles) and presenting Muhammad as the true Messiah. One sixteenth-century Italian manuscript and one seventeenth-century copy of a partial Spanish manuscript exist. It was originally written in Italian by a convert to Islam who was still more familiar with the Latin Bible than with the Qur'an. For example, the Qur'an refers to Jesus, not Muhammad, as Messiah (al Masih). But the GB does the reverse: Muhammad is the Messiah, not Jesus. Interestingly, Jesus *is* called *christos*, or "anointed one" (Christ being a transliteration of the Greek word) in the GB, even though he is made to explicitly deny he is the *Messiah* (the transliteration of the Hebrew word for "anointed one").

The purported author wants to refute those "preaching most impious doctrine, calling Jesus son of God, repudiating the circumcision ordained of God for ever, and permitting every unclean meat: among whom also Paul hath been deceived." When Peter confesses, "You are Christ, son of God," Jesus responds: "Be gone and depart from me, because you are the devil." The offense is calling Jesus the *son of God*: "The impious believe that I am God and son of God."

The forger's "supreme ignorance" of the historical setting of the New Testament is seen, for example, in his assertion that Nazareth can be reached by boat, that Pilate was governor when Jesus was born (more than a quarter century too early), and that Jubilee Years happened once a century (rather than once every fifty years).

Echoing the Qur'an's teaching that "they did not kill [Jesus] nor did they crucify him, but he was made to resemble another" (sura 4:157), the GB has Judas crucified in Jesus's place after having been miraculously transformed, at the very moment of his attempted betrayal, to look just like Jesus.

Some Muslim apologists claim that the GB was used and accepted in the early church. They assert that the churches in Alexandria considered it canonical until AD 325, that Irenaeus (d. ca. AD 200) quoted it against

Paul, and that Jerome used it in the production of his Latin translation of the scriptures (the Vulgate). The Muslim apologists have confused the *Gospel* of Barnabas with the apocryphal *Epistle* of Barnabas, which was well known in the early church and which we still have copies of. The *Epistle of Barnabas* contradicts the GB by speaking of Jesus as crucified and of circumcision as abolished in Christ. The first citation regarding an apocryphal *Gospel of Barnabas* comes from the Decree of Gelasius in the sixth century. There is no evidence to suggest that the one mentioned in the sixth century is related in any way to the present GB.

Despite the charge that Christendom suppressed the GB, it was from Christendom that the Muslim world learned of its existence, mainly from the Raggs' 1907 English translation. All translations of the GB into Middle Eastern languages appear to derive from that same edition as well.

See also ISLAM, BASIC BELIEFS OF

Bibliography. P. Bescow, *Strange Tales about Jesus: A Survey of Unfamiliar Gospels*; L. and L. Ragg, *The Gospel of Barnabas: Edited and Translated from the Italian MS*; D. Sox, *The Gospel of Barnabas*.

R. V. Huggins

GREAT LEARNING, THE. The Great Learning (Ta Hsueh) is a Confucian treatise presenting information on personal cultivation and instruction for the people. It was also used for the advanced education of persons pursuing careers in civil service. It is composed of a main body of text followed by nine commentaries. Its authorship is uncertain, though all present-day scholars of Confucianism believe it to be the work of multiple authors. In addition to Confucius himself—to whom the basic concepts therein almost certainly may be traced—portions of the Great Learning have been attributed to figures such as Confucius's grandson Tzu-szu (483–402 BC) and Confucius's pupil Tseng-tzu (505–436 BC),

though an increasing number of scholars date it as late as the late third century BC. During the Song Dynasty (AD 960–1279), the Confucian scholar Zhu Xi (1130–1200) selected the Great Learning as one of several texts to be used as an introduction to the fundamentals of Confucianism. It was an integral part of China's civil service examination system until 1950, when the Communist government of Mao Zedong (Mao Tse-tung; 1893–1976) came to power.

The Great Learning sets forth an understanding of moral and political philosophy in which the example of ancient emperors, rather than the will of a transcendent deity, provides an authoritative standard for human cultural institutions and social interaction. It advances the thesis that the key to properly ordering society consists in knowing the logical order in which things must be set right and resolving to act accordingly. This process begins with the investigation of the proper subjects of inquiry. Having done this, the investigators have complete knowledge, which then results in a positive "chain reaction" of subsequent events: sincerity of thoughts, the rectification of hearts, the cultivation of virtue in individuals, the proper regulation of family life, and the right governance of provinces, culminating in kingdom-wide peace and contentment.

See also CONFUCIANISM

Bibliography. J. H. Berthrong and E. N. Berthrong, *Confucianism*; R. Eno, "The Great Learning and the Doctrine of the Mean," http://www.indiana.edu/~p374/Daxue-Zhongyong.pdf; J. Legge, ed. and trans., *Confucian Analects, The Great Learning & The Doctrine of the Mean*; K. Thompson, "Zhu Xi," in *The Stanford Encyclopedia of Philosophy*, https://plato.stanford.edu/archives/sum2017/entries/zhu-xi/.

H. W. House

GURU. *Guru* (Sanskrit, literally "destroyer of darkness," now "teacher") is a term used to describe a teacher of enlightenment in

Hinduism, Sikhism, Buddhism, and the New Age movement. Within Hinduism the term most often speaks of one who is a spiritual guide and mentor. Gurus are thought of in roughly the same way as saints in Christianity—examples to be looked up to and emulated, or as the apostles or great teachers of the Christian faith.

The term has also become a title used by those who espouse Eastern religious beliefs, such as Guru Ram Das, Ramakrishna, Sri Aurobindo, Sathya Sai Baba, and Swami Prabhupada.

In popular Western culture, the term has come to mean anyone considered an authority on a given subject. Thus there are "gurus" for almost any topic: fitness gurus, computer programming gurus, economic gurus, photography gurus, music gurus, and so on.

See also AUROBINDO, SRI; BUDDHISM; HINDUISM; PRABHUPADA, ABHAY CHARAN DE BHAKTIVEDANTA SWAMI; SAI BABA, SATHYA; SIKHISM

Bibliography. T. Forsthoefel and C. A. Humes, eds., *Gurus in America*; V. Mangalwadi, *World of Gurus*.

R. L. Drouhard

GURU DEV. Guru Dev (1870–1953) is one of the most revered Vedic teachers and gurus of Maharishi Mahesh Yogi, the founder of Transcendental Meditation (TM). Swami Brahmananda Saraswati, known to his followers as Guru Dev (greatest teacher), was born to a family of Brahmins in northern India. According to his followers, he left home at age nine, dissatisfied with the futility of the worldly pursuits that his caste required of him. After a time of wandering, he became the disciple of Swami Krishnanand, who taught him Vedic philosophy. Eventually, Guru Dev's teacher sent him to a cave, where Dev became enlightened by the revelation of the "self-luminous truth." At age thirty-six, he participated in the Kumbha Mela and was formally ordained. In 1941 he was joined by

Maharishi Mahesh Yogi, who would go on to push Transcendental Meditation to wild popularity. Allegedly Guru Dev appointed Maharishi to spread the message of TM to the rest of the world.

See also HINDUISM; YOGA

R. L. Drouhard

GURU GRANTH SAHIB. The only text afforded sacred status in Sikhism, the Guru Granth Sahib is a collection of more than five thousand theological-devotional songs (*shabhads*), containing nearly thirty thousand rhymed verses. Faithful Sikhs rely on these words for spiritual guidance as well as for general rules for living. In the year of his death, the tenth and final living Sikh guru, Gobind Singh (1666–1708), installed the Granth Sahib as his permanent successor. Since then copies of the Granth Sahib have been venerated by Sikh devotees and are treated with the utmost respect and care, including an extensive protocol for handling and reading them. Copies kept in Sikh temples (*gurdwaras*) are displayed prominently on a special raised area and covered with a beautiful canopy (*chandoa*). It is mandatory among Sikhs that adherents who own a personal copy of the Granth Sahib store it in a specially constructed room in their residence upon an altar (*manji*) of holy pillows.

Gobind Singh compiled the Granth Sahib in 1705, arranging its hymns according to the thirty-one musical forms (*ragas*) of their composition. However, many of these hymns were written by six other Sikh gurus: Nanak Dev (1469–1539), Angad Dev (1504–52), Amar Das (1479–1574), Ram Das (1534–81), Arjan Dev (1563–1606), and Teg Bahadur (1621–75). A minority of practitioners maintain that the Adi Granth, compiled in 1604 by the fifth guru, Arjan Dev, is the sole authoritative scripture of Sikhism. (The Adi Granth is not a separate book but rather a portion of the Granth Sahib.) Several different languages are found in the pages of the Granth Sahib, including Punjabi, Arabic, Persian, Sanskrit, Hindi, Multani, Marathi, and Prakrit. The *Khalsa Consensus Translation* is regarded by many scholars as an authoritative rendering of the text. A printed edition runs about 1,430 pages.

Major doctrines and practices expounded in the Granth Sahib include devotion to God (True Name), a dual-natured, panentheistic deity; pursuing righteousness (*dharmsal*) and avoiding vice by following an elaborate moral code known as Rahit Maryada; and meditation as a means to attain the soul's liberation from the cycle of death and rebirth (*awagaun*) and merge with God. The Granth Sahib is unique among holy books of major world religions in that it contains the teachings of devotees of other faiths.

See also GOLDEN TEMPLE; SIKHISM

Bibliography. P. Singh, *The Guru Granth Sahib: Canon, Meaning and Authority*; Singh, *The Sikhs*; G. S. Talib, *Introduction to Sri Guru Granth Sahib*; Gurumustuk Singh Khalsa et al., "About the Siri Guru Granth Sahib," http://www.sikhnet.com/s /GuruGranthSahib.

H. W. House

GURU NANAK DEV. Guru Nanak Dev (1469–1539) was the founder of Sikhism. Growing up in the Indian province of Punjab, Nanak was educated in Hinduism, then Islam. Later, however, Nanak rejected both in their original forms. When he was thirty-six, he allegedly disappeared while bathing in a river. The local villagers searched for him, thinking him to be drowned, but he reappeared three days later where he had last been seen. He claimed he had become enlightened in the river. Nanak was a fervent missionary who spread the Sikh gospel throughout India. According to Sikh teaching, near the end of his life, Hindus and Muslims argued over what would be done with his body. Nanak ordered that flowers be placed around his body at death, Hindu on one side, Muslim on the other. Those flowers that did not wilt would signify which group had the true teaching. When he died, allegedly nothing was found under his death sheet except fresh flowers.

See also SIKHISM

Bibliography. S. S. Brar, "The First Master: Guru Nanak Dev," http://www.sikhs.org/guru1 .htm; M. P. Fisher, *Living Religions*; J. B. Noss, *Man's Religions*.

E. Johnson and R. L. Drouhard

GYATSO, GESHE KELSANG. Geshe Kelsang Gyatso (1931–) is an internationally renowned teacher and scholar of Tibetan Buddhism and the founder and director of the New Kadampa Tradition organization. Born as Lobsang Chuponpa, in Tibet, he was given the name Kelsang (ocean of good fortune) when he was ordained as a monk at age eight. Gyatso studied in the monastic universities of Tibet under the tutelage of Kyabje Trijang Rinpoche (1901–81). After leaving Tibet in 1959, Gyatso spent the next eighteen years in Nepal and northern India practicing Buddhist meditation. In 1977 he accepted an invitation to take up residence and give classes at the Manjushri Kadampa Buddhist Meditation Center in Ulverston, England, where for many years he taught students about the scriptures of Mahayana Buddhism. Since 1982 Gyatso has published many books on various aspects of Kadampa Buddhism, established programs of study in more than eight hundred centers worldwide, trained Buddhist teachers and monks, and spearheaded a project whose goal is to build a Buddhist temple in every major city in the world. Gyatso presently divides his time between Europe and the US, where he instructs and councils thousands of his disciples.

Gyatso's teachings emphasize the methods and benefits of Buddhist meditation and its application in daily life. He also provides instruction about cultivating compassion, how to cherish other people, how to manage anger, accepting suffering, achieving *bodhichitta* (mind of enlightenment), the Four Noble Truths, death, reincarnation, and nirvana.

See also BUDDHISM; NIRVANA; TIBETAN BUDDHISM

Bibliography. K. Gyatso, *Eight Steps to Happiness: The Buddhist Way of Loving Kindness*; Gyatso, *How to Solve Our Human Problems: The Four Noble Truths*; Gyatso, *Joyful Path of Good Fortune: The Complete Guide to the Buddhist Path to Enlightenment*, 2nd ed.; Gyatso, *Meaningful to Behold: The Bodhisattva's Way of Life*, 4th ed; Gyatso, *The New Meditation Handbook: Meditations to Make Our Life Happy and Meaningful*, 5th ed.; Gyatso, *Transform Your Life: A Blissful Journey*, 4th ed.; New Kadampa Tradition–International Kadampa Buddhist Union, "Venerable Geshe Kelsang Gyatso," http://kadampa.org/buddhism/venerable-geshe-kelsang-gyatso.

J. Bjornstad

H

HADITH. Hadith (Arabic, "narrative") is the body of oral tradition pertaining to the teachings and actions of the Prophet Muhammad. Although the Qur'an contains Allah's revelations, Muslims believe the hadith contains all that Muhammad approved of, disapproved of, forbade, or did not forbid. Muslims believe that nearly all the hadith is merely the esteemed words of Muhammad, though a small portion (Qudsi) is sometimes said to be divine revelation, and Muslim theologians often ascribe the same authority to the hadith that they give to the Qur'an. They argue that Allah acted through Muhammad; therefore all of Muhammad's words and actions were Allah working through him. In this way, Muslims have an authoritative pattern for all situations in life. In much of Islam, various collections of hadith are considered crucial for ascertaining the correct interpretation of obscure passages in the Qur'an and for deciding certain matters of Muslim conduct. The three major classifications of hadith are what Muhammad taught (*qawl*), the behavior of Muhammad (*fi'l*), and that of which Muhammad approved (*taqrir*). The vast majority of Muslims believe that the Qur'an directs them to obey all parts of hadith that have been shown to be authentic. The six-part hadith of Sunni Islam includes Sahih al-Bukhari, Sahih Muslim, Sunan al-Sughra, Sunan al-Tirmidhi, Sunan Abi Da'ud, and Sunan Ibn Maja (in some cases Sunan Muwatta replaces Sunan Ibn Maja). In Shi'ite Islam, it is held that hadith transmitted by those who were loyal to Ali ibn Abi Talib (599–661) are more reliable than hadith lacking this pedigree.

See also ISLAM, BASIC BELIEFS OF; MUHAMMAD; QUR'AN

Bibliography. G. Endress, *An Introduction to Islam*; R. Swarup, *Understanding the Hadith: The Sacred Traditions of Islam*; Thesaurus Islamicus Foundation, "International Hadith Study Association Network."

R. L. Drouhard

HALACHA. The term *halacha* is a noun derived from the Hebrew root *halach*, meaning "to go" or "to walk." Thus the derived meaning of *halacha* refers to a way of acting, a way of living, but living a life in conformity to specific standards. In Judaism the term is actually applied to all legal matters, not only to biblical requirements but also to rabbinic laws. *Halacha* should be distinguished from *haggadah*, a term for all the nonlegal material found in rabbinic literature. But halacha consists of the absolute rules that Jews must conform themselves to throughout daily life and practice.

One of the elements that differentiate the branches of Judaism from one another is their attitude and view of the halacha. For Orthodox Judaism, the halacha is absolutely binding and mandatory, and according to rabbinic teaching even rabbinic laws were not innovated by rabbis; rather, they came from Moses. Therefore, Moses is the originator of both the written law and the oral law that became known as the rabbinic law. Reform Judaism does not recognize halacha to be binding at all, believing that the halacha is a set of rules from the past, offering guiding principles that individuals and Jews may choose to follow or not. Conservative Judaism recognizes the halacha to be binding but follows a free form of interpretation and application of the halacha, less strict than the interpretation of Orthodoxy.

See also JUDAISM; TALMUD

Bibliography. N. T. L. Cardozo, *The Written and Oral Torah: A Comprehensive Introduction*; A. Cohen, *Everyman's Talmud*; Y. Galas, *Halacha*; S. Hermann, *Introduction to the Talmud and Midrash*; E. J. Lipman, *The Mishnah: Oral Traditions of Judaism*; J. Neusner, *Invitation to the Talmud: A Teaching Book*; J. Neusner, *Scriptures of the Oral Torah: Sanctification and Salvation in the Sacred Books of Judaism*; C. Roth, "Halakha," in *Encyclopedia Judaica*; I. Singer, "Halakha," in *The Jewish Encyclopedia*.

A. Fruchtenbaum

HANUKKAH (OR CHANUKAH), FEAST OF. Hanukkah is a feast that arose during the time between the end of the Old Testament and the beginning of the New Testament. Although it is not found in the Bible, the events that brought about the Feast of Hanukkah were predicted in the book of Daniel (the desecration of the temple by Antiochus IV Ephiphanes in Dan. 8:9–14 and 11:21–35). Jesus also authenticated this particular feast in that he went to Jerusalem to observe it (John 10:22).

The Hebrew Names for the Feast. Hanukkah is the Hebrew word that means "dedication." The feast is called the Feast of Dedication because it marks the occasion when the Jewish temple was rededicated after it had been desecrated by the Greeks.

Another name for the festival is Hag Ha-Orim, which means "the feast of lights." This name is found in the writings of Josephus, a first-century-AD Jewish historian. This second name is based on a legend. According to the legend, when the Jews rededicated the temple and wished to rekindle the lampstand, they found enough oil for only one day. It would take eight days to make a new supply, but they decided to kindle and burn up the one-day supply of oil anyway. By a miracle, the legend states, the oil lasted for the eight days. So the festival became known as Hag Ha-Orim, the Feast of Lights. The historical books that speak of the Maccabean Revolt, such as I and II Maccabees, make no mention of any such miracle. It is found only in later rabbinic tradition. Because of that legend, however, the most common English name for this feast today is the Feast of Lights.

The Laws of Hanukkah. The rabbis developed twenty-four laws concerning the proper observance of the Feast of Hanukkah. The laws cover everything from the proper motivation for celebrating, to where the lights should be placed, to what kind of lamp should be used (what it should look like and how big it should be), to when the lights should be lit and what things should be done on each day of the festival.

The Liturgy of Hanukkah. The specific lampstand used on this occasion is called the *channukiyyah* (also known as the menorah). This is a special type of lampstand that has eight places for eight candles in a row, with a ninth candle either above it or over to the side, as the servant candle. With the actual service of the kindling of the lights, specific prayers must be recited. Before actually kindling the candles, the Jewish male must say: "Blessed are you, O Lord, our God, king of the universe, who have sanctified us by your commandments and commanded us to kindle the light of Hanukkah. Blessed are you, O Lord, our God, king of the universe, who did miracles for our fathers in those days and that time."

On the first night only, an additional blessing, known as the Shechecheyanu, is recited: "Blessed are you, O Lord, our God, king of the universe, who have kept us alive and caused us and enabled us to reach this season."

The Blessing after the Kindling Ceremony. After the candles are kindled, on all eight nights, the blessing, known as Haneirot Halalu, is said: "These lights we kindle on account of the deliverance, miracles, and wonders, which you did for our fathers in those days and that time by means of your holy priests. During all the eight nights of Hanukkah, these lights are sacred, and it is not permitted for us to make any use of them, but only to look at them in order that we may give thanks and praise for your wonders and your deliverance."

The Singing of a Special Song. These blessings are followed with a special song known as Maoz Tzur, which means "rock of ages." It was written in the thirteenth century by a Jew named Mordecai. It has six stanzas, which express the messianic hope in the reestablishment of the ancient temple worship, praise to God for the deliverance of Israel from Egypt and Babylon, praise for deliverance from the hands of Haman, a summary of the miracles of Hanukkah, and a reference to the German emperor Frederick Barbarossa and to the Jewish deliverance from that wicked emperor.

Prayers. Three specific prayers are recited on this occasion. The first is called Al Ha-nisim, which means "concerning the miracles." It is a special prayer recited on each of the eight days. The content is a thanksgiving to God for his miracles, and the prayer declares that heroism is not to be found in the many but in the few who are mighty. The prayer emphasizes the battles and not the lights. The second prayer is the Hallel, which consists of Psalms 113–18. This is also recited on each day. The third prayer is Ana Bechoach (which means "in strength"), a mystical, kabbalistic prayer.

Scripture Readings. Scriptures are read from the Law, the Prophets, and the Writings. From the Law, Exodus 40 is read, which concerns the dedication of the tabernacle. Hanukkah is not a feast found in the Mosaic law, but this passage carries the concept of dedication of the altar of God. From the Prophets, the book of Zechariah is read on the first Sabbath of Hanukkah, along with 1 Kings. From the Writings, Psalms 33, 67, 90, 91, and 133 are read.

Other Readings. Other readings include 2 Maccabees 7 (the story of Hannah and her seven sons) and the book of Judith from the Apocrypha.

Hanukkah Customs. Several customs are often associated with Hanukkah. These include the giving of gifts, especially to teachers; the giving of small sums of money (known as *gelt*) to children; special foods eaten on this occasion such as pastries and potatoes fried in oil as a reminder of the miracle of the oil; and special games. The most popular game involves the *dreidel*, which is a Yiddish term. The Hebrew term is *sevivon*. The dreidel is a spinning top that has four sides. On each side is a Hebrew letter, and each letter stands for a Hebrew word, making the sentence, "A great miracle happened there." Again, it is a reference to the miracle of the oil. In Israel the last letter is changed to stand for "here."

See also JUDAISM

Bibliography. Rabbi H. Golwurm, Rabbi M. Zlotowitz, and Rabbi N. Scherman, *Chanukah—Its History, Observance, and Significance*; R. Posner, *Minor and Modern Festivals*; C. Roth, "Hanukkah," in *Encyclopedia Judaica*, edited by C. Roth; H. Schauss, *The Jewish Festivals: History & Observance*; I. Singer, "Hanukkah," in *The Jewish Encyclopedia*; M. Strassfeld, *The Jewish Holidays: A Guide & Commentary*.

A. Fruchtenbaum

HARE KRISHNA. *See* INTERNATIONAL SOCIETY FOR KRISHNA CONSCIOUSNESS (ISKCON)

HARRIS, MARTIN. Born in Washington County, New York, Martin Harris (1783–1875) played an important role in the early years of the Church of Jesus Christ of Latter-day Saints. Harris moved to Palmyra, New

York, and became an affluent and much-respected landowner. In 1808 he married Lucy Harris, his first cousin.

It was in Palmyra that Harris became acquainted with Joseph Smith, a self-proclaimed prophet who insisted he had discovered some gold plates that spoke of ancient American inhabitants. Harris was not totally convinced of Smith's claims until Smith copied some of the characters from the plates and told him to have them evaluated. Harris took copied characters to Professor Charles Anthon of Columbia University. The details surrounding this meeting are confusing, but apparently it was enough to persuade Harris to become the first of Smith's many scribes. According to Harris, Anthon endorsed the writings as authentic, while Anthon himself later said this was false and that he thought the characters were done to defraud Harris. Harris's involvement in this project would result in irreconcilable problems with his wife, Lucy.

Although both Harrises were initially interested in Smith's "revelations," Lucy also became suspicious that Smith was going to defraud her husband. In an attempt to cure his wife of her skepticism, Harris persuaded Smith to let him take 116 pages of the completed manuscript (the book of "Lehi") home with him. Smith relented after Harris swore an oath that he would show the manuscript only to his wife and four others. However, Harris apparently showed the papers to several other people. Then, to Smith's anguish, these pages disappeared. To this day no one knows what exactly happened to the manuscript, although some suspect that perhaps Lucy was responsible. She is claimed to have said to Martin, "If this be a divine communication, the same being who revealed it to you can easily replace it" (Brodie, 54).

In the preface to the first edition of the Book of Mormon (no longer published), Smith provided an awkward explanation for the loss of the manuscript. An exact duplicate of the lost pages could not be made (as might be expected of a divine translation) because God was punishing him for showing it to Harris, and also because God knew the thief would "alter" the manuscript pages if God *did* provide a duplicate translation. So to thwart the plans of his enemies (i.e., Harris's wife), God would enable Smith to translate a different history in the shorter book of Nephi. This story would be even better than the one stolen from the farm.

The futility of this explantion is obvious. Forged changes to a handwritten, inked manuscript from 1828 would be patently obvious. Smith replaced Harris with Oliver Cowdery and called Harris a "wicked man" (Phelps).

However, when money was needed to print the first edition, Harris used his farm as collateral to supply Smith with $3,000, which apparently was enough to bring Harris back into the good graces of Smith. Harris lost his farm when the Book of Mormon failed to sell. Lucy was outraged and unsuccessfully sued Smith for defrauding her husband. Lucy finally divorced Martin in 1831. In 1837 he married Caroline Young, the niece of Mormon prophet Brigham Young.

Harris was convinced that the voice of God told him that the finished translation of the Book of Mormon was true. His name, along with those of David Whitmer and Oliver Cowdery, appears in this book under "The Testimony of Three Witnesses." The testimony claims, "We beheld and saw the plates." In 1859 Harris was asked in an interview with *Tiffany Monthly* magazine how the Lord showed him these things. He replied, "I am forbidden to say anything [about] how the Lord showed them to me, except that by the power of God I have seen them." When John Gilbert, the primary typesetter for the original edition of the Book of Mormon, asked Harris if he had seen the plates with his "naked eyes," Harris replied, "No, I saw them with a spiritual eye."

Harris always believed that Joseph Smith was a prophet of God, but Harris was also a man whose spiritual loyalties were often divided. He stayed behind when most Latter-day Saints traveled to Utah with Brigham Young and was known to support men who had been excommunicated from the LDS Church. Historian Richard Van Wagoner has noted that Harris was also reported to be a "firm believer in Shakerism, a Strangite, and a member of the Church of Christ." Harris eventually moved to Utah. He died on July 10, 1875, at the age of ninety-two.

See also BOOK OF MORMON; CHURCH OF JESUS CHRIST OF LATTER-DAY SAINTS; SMITH, JOSEPH, JR.

Bibliography. F. Brodie, *No Man Knows My History: The Life of Joseph Smith the Mormon Prophet*; R. L. Bushman, *Joseph Smith: Rough Stone Rolling*; M. H. Marquardt and W. P. Walters, *Inventing Mormonism*; W. W. Phelps, ed., *A Book of Commandments, for the Government of the Church of Christ*; R. S. Van Wagoner and S. C. Walker, *A Book of Mormons*.

W. McKeever

HASIDISM. Hasidism first appeared in Podolia (part of modern Ukraine and Moldova) and Volhynia (in modern Poland and Ukraine). It arose at a time when Rabbinic Judaism was trying to regain control of and protect people in Jewish ghettos from further mass delusions after the events surrounding Shabbetai Tzvi, one of the more famous false messiahs of the seventeenth century. Hasidism focuses on God, the universe, Israel, corporate worship, and enthusiastic prayer. It introduced the doctrine of joy, optimism, and enthusiastic worship styles. Although it began as a revolt against the strict rules of the rabbis, it eventually also incorporated them.

By the mid-1800s, in the third generation of Hasidism, different factions were formed with different dynasties and traditions. Today there are nine major Hasidic groups, thirty small groups, and hundreds of minor groups; some Hasidic groups have disappeared. Historically, serious conflicts have arisen between Hasidic groups, sometimes leading to violent clashes.

The Founder of the Movement. The Hasidic movement was founded by Israel ben Eliezer, who became known as the Baal Shem Tov (the master of the good name) or simply the Besht (an acronym of the first letter of each of the three words). Born in Podolia in 1700, ben Eliezer entered rabbinic study and spent many years preparing for a career as a worker of miracles. In 1740, after a long period of mystical introspection and visions of earthly perfection, he abandoned his vocation as a faith healer in order to go forth to preach a message imparted to him by heavenly forces. Jews by the thousands flocked to him to receive his blessing and join him in frenzied prayer. He died in 1760.

Rise in Popularity and the Tzaddikim. The teachings of the Besht were spread by Rabbi Dov Baer the Maggid, who emphasized a living relationship with God over ritual and law and focused on the emotions over the intellect. Though condemned as heresy by traditional and Rabbinic Judaism, the Hasidic movement spread to every corner of Poland, gaining hundreds of thousands of adherents until it was embraced by virtually the majority of Eastern European Jews.

Following the death of the Besht, the Hasidic movement developed into different Hasidic dynasties. The head of each dynasty is the *tzaddik*, and his authority is passed down dynastically from father to son. The tzaddik is the just, perfect man in whom immortality found mortal incarnation. His words are beyond question, and his actions are beyond criticism. He holds absolute authority over his segment of the Hasidic movement. The authority of the tzaddik is based on the conviction of his followers that he has direct contact with God and that he can perform miracles. Much more attention is given to the life of the tzaddik than to his teachings, so the tzaddik's personality, habits, and even idiosyncrasies all tend to become part of the follower's adoration of the leader. As a result, Hasidic groups have often deteriorated into personality cults.

Opposition to the Movement. The Hasidic movement faced extreme opposition from Rabbinic Judaism. It was banned in Lithuania, and one of the more famous opponents of the Hasidic movement was Elijah Gaon of Vilna. As a result, two different camps developed in East Europe: the Hasidim and the Mitnagdim (opponents). By the 1830s, Hasidism was the Judaism of the majority of the Jews of Eastern Europe.

Only after the Russian conquest of Volhynia and the Podolia parts of Poland did the squabbles finally cease with a final compromise: The Hasidim recognized the traditional order of things, and the Mitnagdim recognized the need for intensity of faith. The author of the compromise was Rabbi Shneor Zalmon of Lodi. Both a Talmudist and a Hasid, he taught that both Talmudism and Hasidism were necessary, and he developed the three essentials known as Chabad (ChaBad), an acronym of the three key Hebrew words *chochmah* (wisdom), *binah* (understanding), and *deah* (knowledge). After 1881 the movement spread to Western Europe and the US but remained a minority in these areas.

See also JUDAISM; KABBALAH; TEMPLE IN JUDAISM; ZOHAR

Bibliography. R. A. Foxbrunner, *Habad: The Hasidism of R. Shneur Zalman of Lyady*; Rabbi Yehudah HeChasid, *Seder Chasidim: The Book of the Pious*; R. Posner, *Hasidism*; C. Roth, "Hasidim," in *Encyclopedia Judaica*, edited by C. Roth; I. Singer, "Hasidim," in *The New Jewish Encyclopedia*.

A. Fruchtenbaum

HEAVEN, BIBLICAL DOCTRINE OF.

The biblical words for "heaven" (Hebrew, *shamayim*; Greek, *ouranos*) can refer to the atmospheric heaven or sky occupied by the birds (Gen. 1:20; Matt. 6:26) or to the celestial heaven of outer space occupied by the sun, the moon, and the stars (Gen. 1:14–17; Heb. 11:12). The Hebrew *shamayim*, like many other Hebrew nouns in the Old Testament, is dual in form (Hebrew has dual in addition to singular and plural forms) but is commonly singular in meaning. There is no singular form of the word in the Old Testament. The Greek New Testament often uses the plural form with a singular meaning. These words can also be used to refer to the spiritual heaven occupied by God and the angels (1 Kings 8:30; Matt. 18:10). That this "third heaven," as Paul once calls it (2 Cor. 12:2), is a spiritual realm is indicated by the fact that both God (John 4:24) and the angels (Heb. 1:7) are spiritual, invisible beings (Col. 1:15–16).

When human beings die, their physical life ends, but they continue to exist as personal but disembodied souls or spirits awaiting the resurrection from the dead and the final judgment (Dan. 12:2–3; Matt. 10:28; Luke 16:19–31; John 5:28–29; Heb. 12:9, 23; Rev. 6:9–11). Very little is said about this intermediate state, especially as it applied to believers before Christ's first coming. Those who are saved through faith in Christ are promised that when they die they will be with Christ (Luke 23:43; 2 Cor. 5:6–9; Phil. 1:2–23), that is, in heaven (also called paradise).

Although Christians often refer to the final abode of the righteous as heaven, a more complete term for it biblically would be the new heavens and the new earth (Isa. 65:17; 66:22; 2 Pet. 3:13; Rev. 21:1). At the end of the age, Christ will raise the dead and glorify the redeemed by perfecting them in the image of God and giving them immortal bodies like Christ's own resurrected body (Rom. 8:23, 29–30; 1 Cor. 15:42–57; Phil. 3:21). This means that the repose of the righteous in heaven after death is only the penultimate state of blessedness. The final state is one of embodied life as glorified human beings with the capacity for physical interaction on earth (though they will no longer have marital relations [Luke 22:34–36]) as well as direct spiritual or heavenly communion with God (cf. Matt. 5:5, 8).

The precise relationship between the present earth and the new earth is a matter of some controversy. Some orthodox Christian theologians, appealing especially to 2 Peter 3:10–13, maintain that the present physical universe will be annihilated and replaced with a completely new one with radically different properties. Others, appealing especially to Romans 8:18–23, hold that the universe, primarily the earth, will be cleansed and glorified along with glorified humanity. What is clear is that the new heaven and new earth will be a domain of unimpeachable righteousness and joy in which all redeemed humans and all of God's holy angels will enjoy eternal life forever in God's presence (Rev. 21:1–22:5).

See also ORTHODOXY

Bibliography. K. D. Boa and R. M. Bowman Jr., *Sense and Nonsense about Heaven and Hell*; A. A. Hoekema, *The Bible and the Future*; A. E. McGrath, *A Brief History of Heaven*.

R. M. Bowman Jr.

HEAVENLY MOTHER. In the teachings of the Church of Jesus Christ of Latter-day Saints (LDS Church, or Mormonism), the existence of a heavenly mother was described by apostle Bruce McConkie as "an unspoken truth" (516). It is "unspoken" in that she is not mentioned in the Bible or in any of the LDS scriptures (nor did Joseph Smith ever refer to her). The LDS idea that there is a "mother in heaven" is considered a logical conclusion based on the Mormon teaching that all human beings are born as spirit children of a heavenly Father before inhabiting the earthly bodies prepared for them by their earthly parents. Said McConkie, "The begetting of children makes a man a father and a woman a mother whether we are dealing with man in his mortal or immortal state" (516).

Twelfth LDS president Spencer Kimball wrote that men and women are made in the image of heavenly parents. "God made man in his own image and certainly he made woman in the image of his wife-partner" (25). According to Mormon apostle Neal A. Maxwell, "In other dispensations, the truths given to us through modern prophets about a Heavenly Mother were not stressed, so far as surviving records show, but in this dispensation the Lord gave us this doctrinal truth through a prophet, Lorenzo Snow, whose sister, Eliza R. Snow, expressed it in her hymn 'O My Father'" (67). Snow's hymn states, "In the heav'ns are parents single? / No, the thought makes reason stare! / Truth is reason; truth eternal / Tells me I've a Mother there."

This notion was the basis of a controversy within the LDS Church in the early 1990s when Mormon feminists began to address their prayers to Heavenly Mother. In response leaders said such a practice was inappropriate, insisting that prayers must be directed only to "Heavenly Father." Gordon B. Hinckley, while affirming the existence of "Heavenly Mother," reasoned that since Jesus taught his followers to pray only to "Our *Father*," Mormon women should follow his practice (97; emphasis original). It was an argument from silence.

See also CHURCH OF JESUS CHRIST OF LATTER-DAY SAINTS; EXALTATION; GOD, MORMON VIEW OF; SNOW, LORENZO

Bibliography. G. B. Hinckley, "Daughters of God," *Ensign*; S. Kimball, *The Teachings of Spencer W. Kimball*; N. A. Maxwell, *Things As They Really Are*; B. R. McConkie, *Mormon Doctrine*; L. Wilcox, "The Mormon Concept of a Mother in Heaven," *Sunstone*.

W. McKeever

HELL, ORTHODOX AND UNORTHODOX CHRISTIAN VIEWS OF. *Five Main Views.* The doctrine of everlasting punishment, or hell, is a subdivision of systematic theology that falls under the general heading of eschatology, or the study of last things. In all of Christian theology, no issue generates more difficulty and controversy for Christians and non-Christians alike than theodicy, or the problem of evil. In particular the idea that a good, loving God would consign human beings to a fate of endless torment is considered by opponents to be both unjust and morally indefensible. In order to deal with the tremendous difficulty posed by the doctrine of endless punishment, people adopt one of five different viewpoints regarding the afterlife, four that are unorthodox and one that is orthodox: (1) there is no afterlife, (2) everyone will eventually make it to heaven (universalism), (3) unbelievers will get a second chance after death, (4) all unregenerate souls are destroyed at some point following death (annihilationism), and (5) hell is a place of eternal suffering (the orthodox view).

There is no afterlife. Two distinct worldviews embrace either the position that there is no clear evidence for an afterlife or that it does not exist. Agnostics claim that one cannot know with certainty whether there is life after death, a heaven or a hell. Atheists, on the other hand, contend that there is no life after death. They hold to a strict materialist view of existence.

Everyone will eventually make it to heaven (universalism). According to the doctrine of universalism, hell does not exist and all humanity will eventually be received into the kingdom of God. One of the issues that compel many to embrace universalism is the problem of evil. The fact that evil exists is self-evident, and a good God will defeat it eventually. However, the existence of hell, to which the unregenerate will be consigned for eternity, is the ultimate expression of evil and incompatible with the goodness of God.

This position is not new to Christianity but was embraced by the early church theologian Origen, who went so far as to say that even the devil will eventually be saved.

Universalism is particularly common within the theologically liberal tradition, which embraces a pluralistic view of the world's religions, arguing that the many faiths that exist contain truth and that God works through them to effectively bring adherents to himself. A more conservative form of universalism maintains that Christ's death atones for everyone's sins in such a way as to free all people from any punishment whether or not they hear or accept the gospel.

Universalism in general and pluralism in particular pose a serious challenge to the major doctrines of Christianity. The doctrine of original sin and its consequences and the need for redemption is unique to Christianity. If other religions are legitimate sources of truth that enable adherents to have a relationship with God for eternity, then the issue of original sin is irrelevant and salvation becomes just one of many concepts within the religious scheme of things. Christology is affected because only Christianity emphasizes the need for salvation in Christ before anyone can be reconciled to God.

Unbelievers will get a second chance after death. Clark Pinnock is a major proponent of the postmortem-second-chance position. His radical Arminianism is strongly opposed to the limitations of God's mercy taught by Calvinists. God's mercy is "wide," and his love extends to all humankind, so much so that even in death the unregenerate are given a second chance to repent. Pinnock qualifies his position by stating that those who have heard the gospel and rejected it prior to death will be annihilated without the opportunity for a second chance. His approach makes allowances for those who have never heard or who have embraced a religious system that knows nothing of God's redeeming work. Mormons espouse an elaborate doctrine of postmortem salvation in which virtually all people will receive their opportunity to hear the gospel in the spirit world. Eventually nearly everyone will be given immortality and will be saved in one of three heavenly kingdoms.

All unregenerate souls are destroyed at some point following death (annihilationism). Annihilationism is the view that at the final judgment the unregenerate will be utterly destroyed, ceasing to exist. Annihilationists agree that there must be punishment for sin, but they contend that the duration of the punishment is not eternal, for if it were, such a judgment on the wicked would be a flagrant violation of any reasonable understanding of justice and disproportionate to the nature and severity of the offense. Eternal punishment is also inhumane and cannot be reconciled with the notion of a morally good God. Annihilationists are not in agreement as to the immediacy of such destruction. Some believe the soul is immediately destroyed, while others believe there must be a period of suffering for sin before annihilation occurs.

Evangelical theologian John R. W. Stott is a major proponent of annihilationism. He believes the term "destroy" or "perish," as used in Matthew 10:28 and John 3:16, is to be taken literally. In other passages where hell is referred to as fire (Matt. 3:12; 5:22; 18:9; Luke 3:17), eternal fire (Matt. 18:8; 25:41), or the lake of fire (Rev. 20:14–15), fire is not the cause of pain but the means by which the soul is destroyed, goes out of existence. The reference to smoke in Revelation 14:11 and 19:3 is evidence that destruction has taken place. Stott believes the concept of God's justice militates against the doctrine of eternal punishment. Other annihilationists contend that the duration of the punishment of the wicked is based on their deeds. This ensures that justice is served in direct proportion to crimes committed.

Another aspect of annihilationism is conditional immortality, which denies the inherent immortality of mankind. Immortality is a gift of God that is granted only to those who have been redeemed. The exclusion of the unregenerate from immortality logically results in their annihilation—thus conditional immortality's affinity with annihilationism. Seventh-day Adventists and Jehovah's Witnesses are two well-known heterodox groups that adhere to the conditional immortality or annihilationist position.

Hell is a place of eternal suffering (the orthodox view). Annihilationism, universalism, postmortem second chance, and the denial that there is life after death are all alternatives to the orthodox view of hell, which states that at death the unregenerate will be consigned to everlasting torment as a consequence of their rejection of Christ. This has been the position of the church from apostolic times until the nineteenth century. Though there have been theologians who did not accept the traditional view (notably Origen and Arnobius), they were a very small minority. With the rise of nineteenth-century theological and biblical liberalism, alternative positions to the traditional view have steadily increased. A growing number of evangelicals find annihilationism and the possibility of postmortem regeneration more persuasive and emotionally, morally, and judicially defensible.

Hell in the Bible and Ancient Literature. *Old Testament.* The Old Testament does not present a well-developed doctrine of everlasting punishment. The most common Hebrew term used to describe the abode of the dead is *sheol.* It is used sixty-five times and can also be translated "grave," "pit," or "hell." In the ancient Near East, both Israelite and non-Israelite cultures divided the universe into three distinct realms: heaven, where deity dwells; earth, the abode of the living; and sheol, where the dead reside. Some scholars embrace what is known as the compartmental view of sheol. The Old Testament saints went into limbo at death, awaiting the resurrection of Christ, and the wicked went into a separate place until final judgment.

Daniel 12:1–3 presents one of the most explicit descriptions of the postmortem state of the righteous and wicked. Their respective destinies are described thus: the righteous awaken to everlasting life, whereas the wicked to shame and everlasting contempt. There is no indication that the wicked will eventually be destroyed (annihilated) or eventually be saved (universalism). The key term is "everlasting," which may or may not refer to endless existence. It can mean long duration, implying there is eventually an end. In Psalm 90:2, it refers to God's eternality, and Daniel uses it to describe the final state of both the righteous and the wicked. Logically, if the righteous live eternally, then the term must also refer to the eternal shame or contempt of the wicked.

"Hell" in Intertestamental Literature. The four hundred years between the Old and the New Testaments, known as the intertestamental period, witnessed the development of a rich body of Jewish literature, such as the Apocrypha, apocalyptic material, and most of the Jewish pseudepigrapha. Though not inspired material, these writings are of tremendous importance to understanding the historical development of rabbinic theology. Both the Apocrypha and pseudepigrapha provide clear teaching regarding the eternal state of the wicked.

Apocrypha. The apocryphal book of Judith describes the everlasting suffering of the wicked (16:17). Second Maccabees 7 refers to those who will be resurrected to everlasting life, whereas the wicked will be denied life. Ecclesiasticus 7:16–17 says the wicked will suffer fire and worms, a clear reference to ongoing torment in the afterlife. In 4 Maccabees 10:15; 13:17; 17:18; 18:23, the righteous will inherit eternal life and tranquility, but the wicked are cast into everlasting torment (9:9, 32; 10:11, 15; 12:18; 13:15; 18:5, 22. Second Esdras 7:32–36 gives another graphic description of the everlasting torment of the wicked.

Pseudepigrapha. Jubilees 36:9–11 says the wicked will go into eternal torment. In *2 Baruch* 30:4; 44:12–15; 51:5–6; 59:2; 64:7–10;

83:8, evildoers are tormented forever by fire (44:13–15). *Psalms of Solomon* 3:11 reads, "The perdition of the sinners shall be forever." The *Ascension of Isaiah* 1:3 says the wicked will be subject to "eternal judgments and the torments of Gehenna."

New Testament. The New Testament has a more detailed, well-developed doctrine of hell. The four Gospels of Matthew, Mark, Luke, and John record Jesus's teaching on hell and pending judgment. First, Jesus taught that hell is a literal place. In Matthew 5:21–30, Jesus addresses the problem of anger and immorality and their consequences. The issue here is the application of the law. Those who believed they were in compliance with the law by not literally killing another person or committing immorality outwardly were not vindicated from being murderers or adulterers. Jesus makes it clear that seething anger against another person or immoral desires constitute a violation of the law as if the actions were literally committed, and he warns that those who engage in such practices are in danger of being cast into hell. In 5:21–22 Jesus uses the word *gehenna*, which is the English rendering of the Greek word derived from the Hebrew *Ge Hinnon*, the Valley of Hinnon. This valley was a place where human sacrifices were offered to the false god Molech. Jesus uses it as a powerful metaphor to describe the terrible judgment of hell.

Clearly Jesus understood hell to be a real place; otherwise his warning is without merit (cf. also Matt. 23:15, 33). In Matthew 10:28, he warns his listeners about who should be truly feared. Those who are capable of killing the body are not to be feared; rather, it is God who is able to destroy both body and soul in hell.

Hell is a place of pain. In the parables of the weeds and of the dragnet (Matt. 13:40–43, 49–50), Jesus indicates the wicked will be judged with fire and then suffer greatly. He gives the same warning about people who cause children (little ones) to stumble, for they shall be cast into the fire that is eternal (18:1–9).

In contrast to the belief that the wicked are destroyed (annihilated at death), Jesus indicates hell is eternal in duration (Mark 9:42–48). One of the most graphic examples of the eternality of hell found in the Gospels is the parable of the rich man and Lazarus (Luke 16:19–31). Though some debate whether the story refers to real people, it does convey the idea that there will be eternal torment for the wicked.

In the writings of the apostle Paul, the doctrine of hell does not receive much attention, but Paul does say the wicked will be judged. In Romans 1:18 and 2:5, he speaks of the wrath of God, which is and will be revealed against the wicked. However, he does not address the specific nature of that wrath. In 2 Thessalonians 1:9, Paul does say that those who reject Christ will suffer eternal destruction, which is consistent with the teachings of Christ.

In Hebrews 6:1–3, the writer addresses the need to move beyond what are identified as elementary or beginning doctrines. He refers to both doctrinal issues and practices within the believing community. It is evident from this text that these teachings were considered basic to the Christian faith. One of the doctrines mentioned is eternal judgment, which indicates its importance to the collective body of doctrinal instruction.

No book of the Bible describes hell and eternal suffering more graphically than Revelation. In Revelation 14:9–11, John describes the fate of those who follow the beast and receive his mark. They will incur the judgment of God, which is torment with fire for all eternity. Those who are judged will never rest from their punishment. In Revelation 20:10, John says the devil, deceivers, the beast, and the false prophet will be cast into the lake of fire to be tormented eternally. In verses 14 and 15, death, Hades, and those

not included in the book of life are also cast into the lake of fire.

The evidence presented in the Gospels, Paul's Letters, the general epistles, and the book of Revelation shows that the wicked, along with the devil and demonic spirits, will suffer eternally.

With few exceptions, the writings of the church fathers on the doctrine of hell show that they agreed with what the Scriptures teach. They believed in the eternality of hell, that those who reject Christ will suffer forever, and that hell is permanent separation from God. The *Epistle of Barnabas* speaks of eternal punishment, as does *Second Clement* 5.5. In his *First Apology*, Justin Martyr says the wicked will be punished for eternity by means of an eternal fire. *The Martyrdom of Polycarp* refers to the fire that is eternal into which those who tortured the righteous will be cast. Tatian writes that the wicked will be given immortality in order to suffer eternal pain. In *To Autolycus*, Athenagoras refers to eternal punishments and those wicked people who will be consigned to everlasting fire. Irenaeus says the wicked will be damned forever in everlasting fire. In *On the Resurrection of the Flesh*, Tertullian describes hell as a place of eternal suffering. He rejects annihilationism as unreasonable, arguing that heaven and hell are equally eternal. Hippolytus describes hell as eternal, unquenchable suffering, where the worm continuously torments the body. Cyprian of Carthage says the souls and bodies of the wicked will be preserved for all eternity, suffering in unlimited agonies. Cyril of Jerusalem speaks of bodies of the wicked that will be fit for eternal suffering for their sins.

The most influential theologians in church history, such as Augustine, Aquinas, Calvin, and Luther, all taught that the final judgment of the wicked would be eternal suffering by fire. In *The City of God*, Augustine defends the doctrine of eternal punishment against those who would repudiate it. He also argues that Origen's position on the universal salvation of humanity is to be rejected. Aquinas, like Augustine, rejects the argument that the suffering of the wicked is temporary or in any way intended to be a purifying process. Regarding the magnitude of sin and its proper punishment, Aquinas observes, "Quantity of punishment corresponds to quantity of fault, according to Deuteronomy 25:2. Now a sin which is committed against God, is infinite: because the gravity of a sin increases according to the greatness of the person sinned against (thus it is a more grievous sin to strike the sovereign than a private individual), and God's greatness is infinite. Therefore an infinite punishment is due for a sin committed against God" (*Summa Theologica* I-II, question 87).

Luther firmly believed in both the present and the future punishment of the wicked. He considered hell a reason to praise God, for it represented God's ultimate exercise of justice against the wicked. The reality of hell and the eternal suffering of the wicked indicate the magnitude of humankind's sin, the holiness of God, the seriousness and severity of Christ's atoning work on the cross, and the great grace God bestows on those who are redeemed. In his *Institutes of the Christian Religion*, Calvin says the doctrine of hell is so severe that human language cannot do justice to it. At best metaphors such as fire, weeping, gnashing of teeth, and darkness are used to give human beings a glimpse into the terrible consequences that befall those against whom the wrath of God is exercised.

In the modern period, Jonathan Edwards's sermon "Sinners in the Hands of an Angry God" has become a classic. His depiction of hell and the awful conditions that befall those who reject Christ so terrified those who heard it that people began falling to their knees seeking the mercy of God. Following in the tradition of Edwards, William G. T. Shedd wrote what has become a standard work on the doctrine of hell. His book *The Doctrine of Endless Punishment* presents a thorough biblical, historical, theological, and rational argument for the eternal suffering of the wicked.

The most striking criticism against the doctrine of endless punishment is that the doctrine is morally unacceptable and is inconsistent with a good, loving God. A number of arguments are offered in response to the moral objection. God's holiness and goodness cannot be in conflict with each other, and both are who he is. God's holiness defines his greatness and moral nature, and as Aquinas points out, sin against God is an offense against a being of infinite greatness, necessitating the greatest degree of punishment. God's propositional revelation teaches that the wicked will suffer eternally. God is also perfect in his goodness, which means his goodness cannot contradict what he has revealed about the fate of the unregenerate in Scripture. It logically follows that the eternal suffering of the wicked is consistent with the goodness of God. Given the fact that human beings are finite and therefore morally imperfect and limited in understanding, they do not have the capacity to make perfect moral judgments regarding the ways God chooses to deal with the wicked either in this life or eternity.

See also ANNIHILATIONISM; CONDITIONAL IMMORTALITY; ORTHODOXY

Bibliography. K. D. Boa and R. M. Bowman Jr., *Sense and Nonsense about Heaven and Hell*; R. H. Charles, *The Old Testament Apocrypha and Pseudepigrapha*, vol. 2, *Pseudepigrapha*; W. Crockett, ed., *Four Views of Hell*; E. Fudge and R. Peterson, *Two Views on Hell: A Biblical and Theological Debate*; P. Johnson, *Shades of Sheol: Death and Afterlife in the Old Testament*; R. Morey, *Death and the Afterlife*; C. Morgan and R. Peterson, *Hell under Fire*; W. G. T. Shedd, *The Doctrine of Endless Punishment*; P. Toon, *Heaven and Hell: A Biblical and Theological Overview*; J. Walls, *Hell: The Logic of Damnation*.

S. J. Rost

HERESY, DEFINITION OF. Traditionally, heresy is adherence to false and soul-destroying opinions about primary Christian doctrines, having a wrong doctrine about God, Christ, or salvation. Not only is it wrong but to such a degree that it fundamentally undermines the essential orthodoxy of core articles of the faith. The Greek word of which "heresy" is a translation (*hairesis*) occurs nine times in the New Testament, with the related adjective *hairetikos* (from which we get "heretical") occurring once. *Hairesis* originally had no negative connotation. It was used to refer very simply to a school of opinion or thought, and in particular to one or another of the schools of Greek philosophy. The same neutral meaning appears in reference to the major Jewish sects in the first-century Jewish writers Philo (*On the Contemplative Life* 29) and Josephus (*Jewish War* 2.118). The six occurrences of the word in the Acts of the Apostles (5:17; 15:5; 24:5, 14; 26:5; 28:22) refer to the different sects within Judaism: Pharisees, Sadducees, and the new sect, Christianity, and carry this same older nonpejorative sense. It is only in the remaining three uses of *hairesis* (1 Cor. 11:19 [NIV "factions"]; Gal. 5:20 [NIV "factions"]; 2 Pet. 2:1 [NIV "opinions"]) and the one use of the adjective *hairetikos* (Titus 3:10 [NIV "divisive"]) that we begin to see a more specialized meaning. Paul rebukes the Corinthians for being divisive when they say: "I belong to Paul," "I belong to Apollos," "I belong to Cephas," "I belong to Christ" (1 Cor. 1:12). Later in the same epistle, he says, "I hear that when you come together as a church, there are divisions among you, and to some extent I believe it. No doubt there have to be differences among you to show which of you have God's approval" (1 Cor. 11:18–19). The word translated "faction" here is *hairesis*. So far as Paul is concerned, the identification of the church with the body of Christ rules out all "parties" within the church. In the first chapter, he has countered with a question:

"Is Christ divided?" Here in the eleventh, he follows with a discussion of the body of Christ and its essential unity. For Paul in this context *hairesis* parallels the English word *divisions* (*schismata*, schisms), which has appeared earlier in the same passage. The heresy Paul is concerned about involves not a specific false teaching but the factious or divisive propensity—with the sinful tendency, that is—to work at undermining the "unity of the Spirit through the bond of peace" (Eph. 4:3). The same idea is present in Titus 3:10, where Paul commands us: "Warn a *divisive person* [a *hairetikos anthrōpos*] once, and then warn them a second time. After that, have nothing to do with them." Again the focus is not on false teaching but on divisiveness. In Galatians 5:20, *hairesis* is listed as one of the works of the flesh. Although the New King James Version translates the word as "heresies" there, the focus of Paul's other uses of the term on factiousness and divisiveness rather than false teaching makes it better to translate the word as "factions," following the New American Standard Bible.

Only in 2 Peter 2:1 do we encounter *hairesis* used in a way that clearly involves false teaching. Peter warns of "false teachers . . . [who] will secretly introduce destructive heresies, even denying the sovereign Lord who bought them, bringing swift destruction on themselves." Here, as one standard New Testament Greek lexicon informs us, *hairesis* must mean something like "opinion," hence "destructive opinions." Yet even here we should not overlook the fact that the negative connotation resides not in the word *hairesis* but in the accompanying adjective that is translated "destructive."

Strictly speaking then, *heresy* is not used in the New Testament in the same way that it later came to be understood in the church. This is to say not that the New Testament does not speak against false teaching but only that it does not use the term *heresy* standing by itself to describe it. That being said, there is a dimension to the New Testament usage, and especially Paul's, that the church needs to recapture—namely, the relation of the word to the idea of sinful factiousness or divisiveness. The factious person (the *hairetikos*) often causes divisions in the church by means of an unhealthy appeal to some teaching or teacher. The teaching/teacher in question may be good or bad. The main thing is that the appeal results in an interruption of the unity of the body of Christ. In the case of the Corinthian church, for example, the appeal was to several teachers who were perfectly orthodox in themselves and who were in fellowship with one another (Paul, Apollos, and Cephas). It was only their self-appointed champions who were promoting factions. We are probably right in saying that the reason the term *heresy* quickly came in the post–New Testament period to refer to adherence to false teaching was that the earliest heretics (docetists and gnostics) were not only factious but were also false teachers. This in turn made it difficult for the church later on to know how to cope with internal strife based on differences in policy rather than doctrine (e.g., splits that began to occur in the third century over whether Christians who denied the Lord during persecutions ought to be let back into the church afterward). Using the term *schism* to refer to divisions over nonessentials and *heresy* for divisions over essentials has been a helpful distinction, though, again, not one directly sanctioned by the Bible. From a pastoral perspective, it is important to remember that one can sometimes be as heretical in the biblical sense by holding doctrines wrongly (i.e., using them to draw away a following after oneself) as by holding wrong doctrines. This is especially so when we're evaluating groups that are basically orthodox in doctrine but have dominant charismatic leaders who exercise unhealthy and unbiblical types of control over their followers' lives and consciences. The other side of this coin is dealing with people in the church who may believe false things but have no tendency toward divisiveness. Given the biblical emphasis, one should be careful not to rush to judgment in such cases since it is clearly one thing to believe something false but quite another to actively promote it.

Bibliography. H. O. J. Brown, *Heresies*; R. M. Enroth, *Churches That Abuse*; H. W. House, "With an Apology to Arius: When and How Should We Deal with Heresies and Heretics?," *Journal of Christian Apologetics*; H. Schlier, "αἵρεσις," in *Theological Dictionary of the New Testament.*

R. V. Huggins

HERETIC. The word *heretic* comes from the Greek word *hairesis*, meaning "sect" or "party," originally without negative connotations. However, in the New Testament, the word took on the meaning of someone who caused division, often by teaching false doctrine (Titus 3:10; 2 Pet. 2:1). As the history of the church progressed, *heretic* came to mean someone who denied an essential doctrine of Christian theology (and often taught those views), the definition that the word has had ever since.

Due to the interconnected nature of theology, for one to deny just one essential orthodox teaching is to become a heretic. For example, denying the Trinity means denying at least one essential attribute of Christ, God the Father, or the Holy Spirit.

True to the New Testament meaning of the word *heresy*, heretics often lead movements focused on moving their followers away from orthodox teaching, in this way promoting division. Throughout church history, heretics have been known as charismatic leaders with strong personal characteristics who are commonly able to persuade others to follow them. Arius, perhaps the most famous heretic, gathered so much support that his teachings threatened to become the official teachings of the church. To this day, there remain those loyal to Nestorianism, despite the teachings having been declared heresy over fifteen hundred years ago.

While the Protestant Reformation, in large part, led to a return to biblical doctrine, it also led to the resurgence of heretics. Those who would stray from orthodox theology became free to publicly teach their heresies, and people who wished to follow these heretics became free to do so. This has led to a rapid rise in the number of heretical groups. Following the ancient pattern, several large, contemporary groups holding heretical theology trace their founding to single personalities. Among these are Jehovah's Witnesses, founded by Charles Taze Russell, and the Church of Jesus Christ of Latter-day Saints, founded by Joseph Smith. These two heretics account for over thirty million followers (as reported by their official publications), nearly 1.5 percent of all "Christians" worldwide (as defined as those who self-identify as Christians).

See also ARIANISM; CHRISTIANITY, PROTESTANT; CHURCH OF JESUS CHRIST OF LATTER-DAY SAINTS; HERESY, DEFINITION OF; JEHOVAH'S WITNESSES (JW)

Bibliography. H. O. J. Brown, *Heresies*; The Church of Jesus Christ of Latter-day Saints, "Statistical Information: Official 2007 Statistics about The Church of Jesus Christ of Latter-day Saints"; H. Wayne House, "With an Apology to Arius: When and How Should We Deal with Heresies and Heretics?," *Journal of Christian Apologetics*; P. Hunter, "Major Religions of the World Ranked by Number of Adherents"; Watch Tower Bible and Tract Society of Pennsylvania, "Membership and Publishing Statistics."

H. W. House

HINAYANA. Hinayana ("lower or lesser vehicle" in Sanskrit) is a disparaging term used by Mahayana Buddhists to describe anyone who doesn't accept Mahayana scriptures that elevate the bodhisattva ideal of universality and compassion as the path to "buddhahood." The ideal in Hinayana Buddhism is the arhat, the enlightened disciple or perfected saint, who has attained enlightenment solely by his own efforts.

The only surviving Hinayana tradition is Theravada Buddhism—that is, the Buddhism of Sri Lanka, Myanmar, Thailand, Laos, Cambodia, and of some Buddhists in Vietnam. Hinayana/Theravada is one of the three main divisions of Buddhism, along with Mahayana (the greater vehicle), and Vajrayana (the diamond vehicle). Hinayana Buddhism recognizes the authority of the Pali Canon and therefore is conservative, accepting the historical Buddha as the perfected master and rejecting the celestial metaphysics of Mahayana and the tantrism of Vajrayana.

See also BUDDHISM; MAHAYANA BUDDHISM; PALI CANON; THERAVADA BUDDHISM

Bibliography. J. Toula-Breysse, *The Paths of Buddhism*.

H. P. Kemp

HINDUISM. Among the five major world religions, Hinduism is perhaps the most ancient, multifaceted, and mysterious. The word *Hindu* derives from Old Persian *Hindū*, "Indian," and from Sanskrit *sindhu*, "river," specifically "the Indus River region." The term *Hinduism* itself refers to the sum of the philosophical, religious, and cultural traditions, doctrines, and practices that have developed in India over millennia. It also implies that these varied streams sprang from a common source of authority: the Vedas, an expression of Indo-European religiosity.

The "polytheism" of Hinduism—with its "thirty million gods"—often leads to hasty conclusions about its beliefs and practices. It would be unfair to judge Hinduism solely by its early primitive beliefs. Over millennia Hinduism developed many different trends and major movements. The earliest documentable level is Vedic Hinduism, based on the traditions of the Indo-European people who migrated to India more than three thousand years ago. However, other sources of spirituality developed based on the Vedas, such as the Upanishads, wherein notions of karma, reincarnation, and yoga become prominent. Connected with the Upanishads, six classic schools of thought developed. Later, devotional forms became popular. Folk religion is widespread, and in some of the remote regions tribal religions still survive. In addition some Hindu thinkers have been influenced by the thousand years of contact with Islam and several hundred years' contact with Christianity, particularly during the period of British rule. While no single universal creed is professed by all Hindus, Hinduism can be understood as a collective or umbrella term for the many forms of spirituality of Indian origin. The objectives of human life—moral living, prosperity, pleasure/love, and liberation—are seen as prominent themes, wherein the concepts of samsara (cycle of rebirth), karma, and the possibility of liberation play out. The concept of divinity is varied and extremely complex. Nearly every way of understanding god/gods and humans' relation to the divine is found within Hinduism. Some modern Hindus believe that when worshiping their preferred deity (Ishta-devata), they are really worshiping the supreme deity or principle, whether in a henotheistic, polytheistic, or monistic (pantheistic) sense, but not all agree with such a view.

Ultimately, Hinduism can best be understood when it is examined historically and developmentally. Over centuries early observations and reflections gradually coalesced into complex systems of philosophy, practice, and ways of living.

Historical Context. In recent years, the study of Indian history has provoked controversies and reinterpretations. Archaeological discoveries at Mohenjo-daro, Harappa, and Saurashtra have resulted in fresh insights and revisions. One increasingly questioned interpretation is the Aryan invasion theory.

It held that a people called Aryans invaded northern India in about 1500 BC, destroying a more sophisticated, ancient Indus civilization and forcing their warlike rule and religion on the indigenous peoples. The current theory, however, places the Aryans first in Persia and then in India as early as 4000–2500 BC.

Even with such a revision, the history of Hinduism may still be roughly divided into four epochs. Nevertheless, it is important to keep in mind that the history of India is inexact (see Schmitthenner). To begin with, India as a political entity did not exist before the eighteenth century. Prior to that, the subcontinent was a mosaic of states and nomadic territories. Further, we lack extant historical documents earlier than the sixteenth century, and there are few archaeological remains before the fifth century AD. Therefore, caution is needed in reconstructing Indian history or the history of Indian literature and religion.

Conservatively speaking, the Vedic period was the earliest in Indian history. It extended from 2500 to 200 BC. During this era, the Vedas were composed (the Rig Veda, the oldest, at the beginning of the period; these were composed as oral texts and were not written down until the sixteenth century AD). Of the earliest Hindu scriptures, the four Vedas that we know today are the Rig, Yajur, Sama, and Atharva. Each book consists of four sections: Mantras (which are like hymns), Brahmanas (ritualistic and sacrificial duties), Aranyakas (advice on meditation for hermits), and Upanishads (the philosophical and spiritual discourses of forest-dwelling seers and sages). Hindus regard the Vedas as *shruti* (revealed scriptures).

During the second era, the epic period (approximately 200 BC–AD 500), several *smritis* (traditional texts) were composed. Philosophical doctrines were transmitted nonsystematically through imaginative literature, called epics: the Ramayana and the Mahabharata (probably the most popular of all Indian texts, the Bhagavad Gita, was composed in this period as part of the Mahabharata). Also written during this period, however, were treatises on ethical conduct and social philosophy (known as the Dharmashastras).

In the third era, the Sutra period (often dated AD 320–650 but with roots from around AD 100 and thus overlapping with the epic period), various schools of thought produced systematic treatises to establish their positions. Proponents set forth their doctrines coherently and logically through brief but often obscure aphorisms (*sutras*). Among these were the Yoga Sutras of Patanjali (ca. AD 150–200) and the Vedanta Sutra of Badarayana (ca. AD 200), also called the Brahma Sutra. During this time, the six basic systems of Hindu thought were organized and detailed, so much so that they contained sophisticated polemics against other systems. Note, however, that throughout the first millennium AD many of the Puranas, the legendary stories—part narrative, part theological—were also written.

Finally, during the scholastic period (approximately AD 650–1100), numerous commentaries on the original sutras were written. Layers upon layers of commentaries followed, each promising to elucidate an earlier commentary. Through some of them, subsystems were even devised. For the purposes of this article, the most prominent philosophers of this period were Sankara, Ramanuja, and Madhva. The scholastic period is said to have declined after the Hindus became the subjects of Muslim and English invaders.

A more positive view, however, finds in the postconquest era a reform period and a renaissance period. During the former, reformers like Kabir, Nanak, and Chaitanya composed a large body of devotional literature. The first two attempted to harmonize Islam and Hinduism, with Guru Nanak eventually founding Sikhism. Chaitanya founded a devotional movement, one branch of which is today's ISKCON (International Society for Krishna Consciousness). In the renaissance period, from the eighteenth century on, certain teachers tried to synthesize the best of East and West, Hinduism and Christianity, in the face of mounting European and Christian influence. Notable figures included Raja Ram Mohun Roy, Debendranath Tagore, and Keshab Chandra Sen, all leaders of the Brahmo Samaj Movement. Later, with similar goals, came Sri Ramakrishna, Swami Vivekananda, Sri Aurobindo, and Mahatma Gandhi.

Finally, an overview of Indian history would be incomplete if it failed to mention some other achievements. Contemporaries of the ancient Greeks, Hindus excelled in several fields: mathematics, music theory, physics (atomism), anatomy, and medicine. The mathematics of the Hindus was superior to that of the Greeks, except in geometry, and they developed algebra independently of the Greeks. The Hindus also used the decimal system and invented zero. In medicine, as early as 600–500 BC, physicians precisely described ligaments and muscles; the lymphatic, nervous, and vascular systems; digestion; fetal development; membranes and tissues; even sutures. Around this time, Atreya concluded that the parent's seed contains in miniature the whole parental organism. And Sushruta, who described numerous surgical procedures and instruments, performed the first skin graft and nose reconstruction.

Six Basic Viewpoints (Darshanas). Philosophy and spirituality have had a higher priority in the intellectual life of the Hindus than even science. These disciplines acquired still greater importance when the old Vedic religion was threatened by the non-Vedic-based philosophies that emerged from within India itself. The Charvakas, a strict materialistic school, arose briefly but soon retreated into obscurity. In the first millennium BC, the more serious threats came from Jainism and Buddhism. In response to these formidable challengers, Hindu philosophers quickly developed into excellent critical thinkers and organized their theories into defensible systems. Dogmatism alone, they realized, would no longer suffice; sound reasons were necessary. Out of this intellectual ferment, the "brahmanical systems" were born. In all, six basic systems, called "viewpoints" (*darshanas*), have been most influential in Hinduism. Although their chronologies remain uncertain, they provide a useful framework for understanding Hinduism further.

Nyaya. This system is noted for its logical realism. The word *nyaya* means "argument," the way the mind is led to a conclusion. Now it has come to mean the science of right reasoning or proof of right knowledge. The first Hindu work to elucidate the principles of logic and rhetoric was the Nyaya Sutra, ascribed to Akshapada Gautama (300–200 BC). Across twenty centuries, this system produced a significant body of thought and literature. The other systems generally accept its rules of logic and proof.

Nyaya holds that the logical examination of the objects of experience is the surest way to secure right knowledge and pursue legitimate goals. It identifies four factors that assist or impede this effort: subject, object, consequent cognition, and means of knowledge. Through the means of knowledge, if they are logical, one apprehends accurately, grasps the truth that an infinite self (or subject) is the agent behind the mind, and obtains liberation from the grip of desire and ignorance. Thus Nyaya combines epistemology and metaphysics. Before Gautama, its exponents tended to be atheists; after him, theists.

More importantly, much like Aristotle, Gautama constructed a framework of logic within which thought and knowledge became pragmatic tools. He explained inductive and deductive inferences. He created a five-part syllogism consisting of proposition, reason, example, application, and conclusion. Moreover, not only did he set forth the principles of argument; he also dealt with propaganda devices and logical fallacies.

This framework of investigation, along with its rich philosophical vocabulary, represents the chief contribution of the Nyaya system.

Vaisheshika. This system is referred to as "realistic pluralism" or "atomic realism." Like Nyaya it is analytical. Because the word *vishesha* means "particularity," the system is also called "distinctionism" because it focuses on the distinctions among really existent things. Its primary text, the Vaisheshika Sutra (600–300 BC), was written by Kanada, its founder. Similar in approach and metaphysics to Nyaya, Vaisheshika later embraced the Nyaya conception of God.

Vaisheshika—atomic realism and pluralism—acknowledges multiplicity in the world but concludes from it that all "things" consist merely of combinations of atoms. Forms are changeable and destructible; atoms are indestructible. Nothing exists but "atoms and the void," nor are the movements of the atoms determined by the will of an intelligent deity. They are directed by impersonal force, "the invisible" (Adrishta). Later exponents located a world of minute souls alongside the world of atoms, with both being supervised by an intelligent Deity—an idea somewhat akin to the "preestablished harmony" of German philosopher Gottfried Wilhelm Leibniz. The Vaisheshika system is all but extinct today.

Samkhya. Perhaps the oldest of these systems, Samkhya has been accepted, at least in part, by most other systems. The creation of Samkhya is attributed to the realist Kapila (700–600 BC), but the earliest extant text on the subject, the Samkhya-karika, is dated about the third century AD. This system is termed "evolutionary dualism" because it claims that the universe consists only of *purusha* (the knowing subject) and *prakriti* (the known object). The evolution of the universe unfolds from prakriti in a descent through layers of materiality. Because prakriti is unconscious, this evolution can only occur in the presence of the ever-conscious purusha. Because this system claims that there are multitudinous selves, in a state of either bondage or release, it has been said that reference to a supreme deity is unnecessary to Samkhya.

Samkhya posits several components to prakriti, although the system consists of far fewer categories than either Nyaya or Vaisheshika. Twenty-four sheaths (*koshas*) exist—for example, the intellect, "I-sense," lower mind—descending from the subtle to the gross, from Mahat (the great one) through the mind and senses to the five elements: ether, air, fire, water, and earth. There are also three interplaying energetic qualities (*gunas*) that compose the created universe: purity (*sattwa*), activity (*rajas*), and inactivity (*tamas*). Everything in prakriti, including the empirical self (*jiva*), is bound; only purusha, the animating spirit, is free.

The goal is to search out and destroy all false identification with prakriti. A seeker effects his liberation by balancing in himself the three *gunas* and discriminating between prakriti (false self) and purusha (true self). The practices of virtue and yoga are essential to the process. Because self-restraint and self-mastery clarify and steady the mind, they are prerequisites for liberation. Properly understood, then, prakriti—assisted by the deluded "I-sense" (*ahamkara*)—prevents the soul from realizing the truth about itself. Ultimately, however, the release that is effected through discriminative knowledge is phenomenal only. The soul merely discovers that which it had always been from the beginning: purusha—pure, free, eternal. Thence follows, claims Kapila, "the complete cessation of pain."

The Samkhya system was intended to help the bound one not so much to understand the world as to transcend it. Second only to Vedanta, this system has most deeply affected the Hindu mind. Later, Samkhya met its fiercest critic in Sankara (AD 788–820).

Yoga. Patanjali, who was influenced by Samkhya, first systematized yoga. Like Samkhya yoga requires discrimination between the subject and the object, witness and witnessed, purusha and prakriti. Although Patanjali composed the Yoga Sutras sometime before AD 400, yoga had already been mentioned as early as the Upanishads (between 800 and 300 BC). Apparently it even fascinated Alexander the Great, who was interested in the way the ascetic yogis bore up silently under pain. Today yoga is an essential part of the teachings of almost every sect in India.

Special features of yoga are that it is nonsectarian, practical, and experiential. In the system of Patanjali, the aspiring yogi is told that the goal is simply the liberation of the soul from the bondage of prakriti and karma. He is not urged to seek God, Ishvara, because Ishvara is merely one object on which the yogi may meditate to effect his liberation. Patanjali provides the method and leaves the role of God to others.

Most important to this system is the step-by-step practice of yoga as both means and method. By practicing the eight limbs of yoga (*ashtanga*), claims Patanjali, a yogi disassociates himself gradually from the body-mind and other material obstructions that prevent his liberation. After meeting certain ethical requirements (*yama* and *niyama*), the yogi attempts to master the disciplines of various positions but most importantly sitting still (*hatha*) and controlling his breath (*pranayama*), for hours if necessary. Next he practices withdrawing his five senses from sense objects (*pratayahara*) to gain control of his thoughts. Then, focusing his mind longer and longer on a single object, he learns to retrieve his mind when it wanders and restrain it when it resists, until his focus is unbroken. From concentration (*dharana*), the yogi progresses to meditation (*dhyana*), and from meditation to transcendental insight (*samadhi*), at which point he realizes that he is nothing but pure consciousness. In this way, the yogi secures his own liberation from worldly and bodily attachments and sorrows.

The image of the yogi in the Hindu mind holds not only an idealistic but also a romantic appeal, even for householder yogis. Ascetic wanderers (*sadhus*) and seers on dusty roads, under tamarind trees, and in quiet forest retreats have been common sights in India for centuries. They are symbols of freedom from bondage and care. They are mystics and experimenters par excellence, committed to abstinence, austerities, and ceaseless meditation, who doggedly seek firsthand experiences of the spiritual. In the end, whatever the yogi's goal—self-knowledge, union with God, or supernatural powers (*siddhis*)—he believes that yoga can help him sever the root of ignorance, help him overcome his karma, and convey him to his destination.

Purva Mimamsa. This system is based on interpretative investigations of the early portions of the Vedas: the Mantras and the Brahmanas. Least important of the six systems, it is more religion than philosophy because it focuses solely on right conduct (dharma). In the main, it is an orthodox response to the excesses of philosophers who seemed to flout the authority of the Vedas. In particular Jaimini in his Mimamsa Sutra (ca. 400 BC) inveighs against the hypocrisy of Kapila and Kanada for granting the authority of the Vedas and then proceeding to ignore it. The human mind, to Jaimini, is too feeble to master the complexities of metaphysics. Reason deceives because it rationalizes its own desires and pride. Thus wisdom is to be found not in the mazes of logic but in the humble performance of the duties prescribed by scripture and tradition.

The Mimamsa Sutra thus concerns itself exclusively with moral duties and sacrificial rituals. To establish the validity of the Vedic injunctions and their promised rewards, Jaimini also investigates sounds, words, and semantics. In Mimamsa moral action itself is regarded as a powerful, invisible force (*apurva*) capable of shaping the world and human destiny. Action alone determines the quality of human life in the present incarnation, the afterlife, and future incarnations. Free will, ensuring the best results and rewards, assists in the accumulation of good results and nullification of bad ones. Therefore, the wise man, faithful to the injunctions of the Vedas, performs only prescribed actions and abstains from prohibited ones.

Liberation for the Mimamsaka is life in heaven, the ultimate fruit of moral action. Thus performance of dharma is considered sufficient to effect the detachment of the soul from the body-mind and its liberation. Jaimini acknowledges the reality of the Vedic deities but does not refer to a supreme Deity. In light of the power of the enjoined actions of the Vedas to secure liberation, Jaimini apparently saw no need to include God in his system. Although Purva Mimamsa made notable contributions in logic, dialectics, and epistemology, it is remembered mainly for its emphasis on dharma for dharma's sake.

Uttara Mimamsa. In contrast to Purva Mimamsa, this system is based on interpretative investigations of the later portions of the Vedas, especially the Upanishads. Thus this school of thought is also called Vedanta because it interprets the religious and philosophical material at the end (*-anta*) of the Vedas. Badarayana (who lived sometime between 500 and 200 BC) wrote the earliest authoritative commentaries on the Upanishads: the Vedanta Sutra (or Brahma Sutra) and Sariraka Sutra. The former deals with the nature of Brahma (the creative force of the universe); the latter with the Atman (unconditioned self). In both Badarayana attempted to systematize and synthesize the often-contradictory teachings of the Upanishads. Because these works consisted of over 555 sutras of no more than two to three words each, subsequent interpretations were bound to vary and controversies to arise. Within the span of a thousand years, this system had subdivided into three main branches that continue to this day.

The first to gain ascendancy was Advaita Vedanta (nondualism). In the first millennium after Christ, this view was expounded by various commentaries and teachers, until the mantle came to rest on Sankara (AD 788–820). The greatest philosopher of Advaita, Sankara carried this system to its pinnacle. In this nondualistic Vedanta, the distinctive belief is that God (Brahma), who is "one without a second," and the soul (Atman) are one. Realization of this truth is called self-knowledge (*atmajnana*).

Sankara developed his discussion around two categories, variously referred to as the one and the many, subject and object, and self (Atman) and not-self (*anatma*). Although the phenomenal universe is *in a sense* real, it is not, Sankara asserted, ultimate reality (Brahma). In fact, everything in it, including intellect and ego, is dependent on that ultimate reality. The truth, however, is that the embodied soul, the little separate self (*jiva*), is really that one eternal, undivided reality. Ignorance of this truth (*avidya*) persists as long as the ego sense (*ahamkara*) falsely identifies with the delusion of separateness and multiplicity. Because the jiva mistakenly superimposes the not-self onto the self, it suffers endlessly. The solution, according to Sankara, is the practice of discrimination (*viveka*). Once the soul fully identifies with Atman, with its true nature instead of with the not-self, Atman alone will then shine forth eternally. The liberated soul then declares, "I am Brahma" (*aham brahmasmi*), existing forever after as pure existence-consciousness-bliss (*satchitananda*).

Later, in reaction to the cold austerity of the Advaita school, Ramanuja (AD 1017–1137) established the Vishishtadvaita branch of Vedanta (qualified nondualism). Of course, Ramanuja had to refute Sankara. To this end, he delineated three, rather than two, main categories: God (Brahma), world, and selves. To Ramanuja these are real, forming a unity: God eternal, personal; the world of unconscious matter created, vitalized by God; each self eternally dependent on and subordinate to God. Ramanuja qualified Advaita by assigning to Brahma two forms—selves and matter—which nevertheless remained in essence and nature different from Brahma.

The three categories help to explain the beliefs and practices at the core of qualified nondualism. First of all, Brahma is the controlling self and power behind the world and selves. There is, however, no undifferentiated, nondual Brahma. God is personal, *saguna* (with qualities), rather than impersonal, *nirguna* (without qualities), as is the Brahma of Sankara. The world, according to Ramanuja, is not phenomenal. He rejects the notion that the world is merely an ignorance-born superimposition of the unreal on the real. Moreover, both before and after the soul is released through the grace of God from bondage, he or she persists eternally as a unique individual. Although the barriers to the truth are removed, the self is not dissolved into God. After liberation the self possesses an everlasting intuition of God. Both before and after liberation, the soul obtains true knowledge of God not by practicing some theory but rather by loving and worshiping God.

Then later, reacting to Sankara, especially, but also to Ramanuja, Madhva (1197–1276) established the *dvaita* branch of Vedanta (dualism). This branch differs from the other two in that it recognizes four basic dualities: between God and self, between selves, between selves and matter, between materials and substances.

With the background on the previous branches in mind, *dvaita* may be understood in summary form. God, identified with Vishnu, exists in perfection. Although he has a supernatural body, he transcends it, even while he is also immanent in the world and in the heart of every soul as its ruler. Each self, by nature, is blissful but suffers because past karma binds it to a material body. By becoming freed from impurities through the grace of God, the self ceases to incarnate. After liberation it exists as an individual who delights perpetually in the presence of God, always worshiping and adoring him. In any event, the divine will is always supreme. God determines who will be liberated into his presence and who will continue in bondage.

Modern Hinduism. Hinduism continues to flourish worldwide. The estimated number of Hindus in the world today is seven hundred million. Among Hindus throughout the world, and particularly in the West, Vedanta and Yoga remain ever popular, especially the modified, synthetic versions of Sri Ramakrishna and others who have attempted to harmonize and validate all "paths" to God. This broad-minded Vedanta has left its mark on nearly every form of Hinduism today.

Despite the rural Hindus who still worship local deities, three main sects seem to predominate wherever Hinduism is found— from India to Indonesia, South Africa to Fiji, Europe to America. Each is based on the preferred deity (Ishta-devata) of that sect. Less numerous are the Shaktas (devotees of the multiformed divine mother), whose origin may be traced to the tantra of the Middle Ages. More numerous are the Shaivites (devotees of Shiva)—often associated with the Shaktas—who have closer ties to the nondualists and qualified nondualists of Vedanta. Even more numerous are the Vaishnaivites (devotees of Vishnu), whose origin may be traced to Madhva. In the West, Vaishnaivites are recognized as the Hare Krishnas. Vaishnaivites and other Vedantins have been most responsible, too, for introducing the idea of the avatar to the West.

Decades of Indian immigrants, not only Hindus but Sikhs, have been settling and thriving in Western countries. Scores of Hindu temples exist in the US—one or more in almost every state—and the UK. General interest in hatha yoga and Ayurvedic medicine remains high. Drawing Hindus together, the internet is now serving as an effective form of communication for those of the "diaspora," as they term it. Currently many impressive websites addressing Hindu interests appear on the internet, with their numbers growing. Finally, among Hindu scholars, a renewed interest in Indo-Aryan archaeology and Sanskrit studies has been increasing. Hindus seem to be trying to reclaim their history and philosophy, for so long defined and managed by Western interpreters.

In India, meanwhile, the brightly colored *pujas* and *melas*, religious services and festivals, continue unchanged, with an Ishta-devata to suit every taste.

See also INTERNATIONAL SOCIETY FOR KRISHNA CONSCIOUSNESS (ISKCON); JAINISM; SIKHISM; UPANISHADS; VEDANTA

Bibliography. W. Durant, *The Story of Civilization*, part 1, *Our Oriental Heritage*; G. Feuerstein, *The Yoga Tradition: Its History, Literature, Philosophy and Practice*; D. Frawley, *From the River of Heaven: Hindu and Vedic Knowledge for the Modern Age*; J. J. Lipner, *Hindus: Their Religious Beliefs and Practices*; K. H. Potter, *Presuppositions of India's Philosophers*; Swami Prabhavananda, *The Spiritual Heritage of India: A Clear Summary of Indian Philosophy and Religion*; S. Radhakrishnan and C. A. Moore, *A Sourcebook in Indian Philosophy*; Walter Schmitthenner, "India and Rome," *Journal of Roman Studies*; Ninian Smart, *Doctrine and Argument in Indian Philosophy*; S. B. Veylanswami, "In a World Where Men Are Labeled Good or Evil, the Hindu Vision Helps," *Hinduism Today*, http://www.hinduismtoday.com/; H. Zimmer, *Philosophies of India*, edited by Joseph Campbell.

B. Scott

HOLY SPIRIT BAPTISM. *See* BAPTISM IN THE HOLY SPIRIT, PENTECOSTAL VIEW OF

HOLY SPIRIT, BIBLICAL VIEW OF. Orthodox Christianity teaches that the Holy Spirit is the third member of the Trinity, fully God and coeternal with the Father and the Son. "The attributes of God are ascribed to him, such as life, truth, love, holiness, eternity, omnipresence, omniscience, omnipotence; he does the works of God, such as creation, regeneration, resurrection; he receives honor due only to God; he is associated with God on a footing of equality, both in formula of baptism and in the apostolic benedictions" (Strong, 315).

The Holy Spirit in the Old Testament. The Old Testament does not present the Holy Spirit in an explicit, theologically developed way. His presence throughout the Old Testament speaks mostly of his power and influence. This does not mean that the person of the Holy Spirit is absent. Old Testament references to the Holy Spirit are quite sufficient for developing a working understanding of his person and work. When these are coupled with New Testament references, it is clear that the totality of Scripture supports the view that the Spirit is the Third Person of the Trinity.

In Genesis 1:2, the Holy Spirit is actively involved in creation. Further references that give more detail about his work in creation include Job 26:13 (NIV "breath"), which describes the Spirit's role in creating the heavens, and 33:4, where Job acknowledges that his existence is by the work of the Spirit of God. The word used for breath in Psalm 33:6 is also used in Genesis 1:2 for Spirit. When God speaks to Moses regarding the plan to build the tabernacle, he informs Moses that the master craftsman Bezalel is going to be empowered by the Spirit to accomplish the task. This will include filling Bezalel with wisdom, understanding, and knowledge in all areas of craftsmanship. In Numbers 11:16–17, God tells Moses to gather together seventy key men who will be called to assist him with the people of Israel. God will provide his Spirit for both Moses and the seventy, and the Spirit will provide divine assistance and guidance. Judges 3:10; 6:34; 11:29; 13:25

describe instances where the Holy Spirit filled specific leaders (Othniel, Gideon, Jephthah, Samson) to enable them to accomplish important tasks. In Isaiah 63:10, 11, reference is made to the sins of Israel and how its behavior toward God grieved the Holy Spirit. The response of the Spirit to the sins of the people indicates that he is a person, not merely a force or power.

The Holy Spirit in the New Testament. The New Testament treats the person and work of the Holy Spirit far more extensively, which seems to fit the theological understanding of the procession of the Son from the Father, and the Spirit from the Son. In the Old Testament, God the Father is the primary member of the Trinity who is described. As we move into the New Testament, the Gospel accounts focus on the person and work of God the Son, revealing his interactions with both the Father and the Holy Spirit. In John 14–16, Jesus promises to send the Spirit, who will continue where Jesus leaves off. The book of Acts inaugurates the arrival of the Spirit and describes the work of the Spirit in the growth and development of the church, fulfilling the words of Christ when he indicated that a comforter would follow his ascension.

The Gospels present important information on the person and work of the Holy Spirit. The birth narrative in Matthew 1:18, 20 indicates that Jesus Christ is conceived in Mary's womb by the Holy Spirit. This work of the Holy Spirit in the incarnation fulfills the Old Testament prophecy regarding the virgin birth of Christ, and he is born with a sinless nature. Luke 1:35 explains that the Holy Spirit will overshadow Mary, and she will give birth to the Son of God. Later, at Christ's baptism, the Holy Spirit comes upon him and confirms his relationship with God the Father. Here we see a glimpse of the Trinity together: the Spirit coming upon Christ and the Father declaring his love for and pleasure in the Son. The Spirit leads Christ into the wilderness to be tempted by Satan (Matt. 4:1; Mark 1:12). Luke 4:1 points out that the Lord was full of the Holy Spirit and that upon his return from Jordan he was led by the Spirit into the desert to face temptation.

The Holy Spirit is very active in the ministry of Jesus. In Luke 4:14, 18, the power of the Spirit is with Christ, and he is anointed to preach the gospel. Matthew 12:18 says the Spirit will be upon Christ, who will proclaim justice to all the peoples of the earth. Jesus drives out demonic beings by the power of the Holy Spirit (Matt. 12:28). Matthew 12:31–32 describes the seriousness of blasphemy against the Holy Spirit. Much debate surrounds the exact nature of what is commonly called the unpardonable sin. Some say it has to do with accusing Christ of casting out demons by the power of Satan, equating the Spirit with the devil. Others believe the blasphemy is repeated rejection of the Spirit's convicting work on behalf of the unregenerate. Blasphemy against the Holy Spirit is serious enough that it will not be forgiven (Matt. 12:31–32; Luke 12:10). Jesus indicates that the Holy Spirit is actively involved in the work of salvation. John 3:5–6, 8 states one must be born of the Spirit, and John 6:63 says the Spirit gives life. He also convicts the world of sin, righteousness, and judgment (John 16:8–11). John 14 describes the impending departure of Christ, which causes the disciples grave concern. Christ has been their support, teacher, guide, and comfort. He promises them that they will receive another comforter (Paraclete), the Holy Spirit, who will be with them forever, the Spirit of truth. He will be both their helper and teacher and will enable them to remember the things Jesus taught them as well. The Spirit plays an important role in the evangelistic work of the disciples. He will clothe them with power (Luke 24:48–49) and testify about Christ.

In his postresurrection appearance to the disciples in Acts 1, Jesus is asked if the kingdom is going to be restored. He responds by telling them that the time of the restoration is not for them to know. In the meantime, the Holy Spirit will come upon them in due time and empower them to go and proclaim the gospel throughout Jerusalem, Judea, and Samaria and to the ends of the earth. On the day of Pentecost, the Holy Spirit comes upon the disciples, empowering them with the ability to speak in tongues (languages of numerous nations). Peter preaches to the crowd, proclaiming the fulfillment of Joel 2:28–32 and the good news of Jesus Christ (Acts 2). The work of the Spirit in the beginning stages of the church in Jerusalem is evidenced by the conversion of three thousand souls who receive the gift of the Holy Spirit (Acts 2:37–41). The new congregation continues to be empowered by the Spirit, and the apostles perform many signs and wonders. The new congregation is deeply enriched by the Spirit's work, and God adds more souls each day. The case of Ananias and Sapphira in Acts 5:1–11 reveals the severity of lying to the Holy Spirit. Their deaths as a result of their deception instill much fear in those who witness the incident, and it moves people to show respect for the ministry of the apostles.

The Deity of the Holy Spirit. The deity of the Holy Spirit is attested in a number of passages. In Matthew 28:19, Jesus commands his disciples to baptize new converts in the name of the Father, the Son, and the Holy Spirit. This is early evidence of the Spirit's equality with the Father and the Son, as set forth in a trinitarian formula. Ephesians 1:1–14 reveals a similar tight association between the persons of the Trinity. The Father elects/chooses us, the Son atones for sin, and the Holy Spirit seals us. In Acts 5:3–4, lying to the Holy Spirit and the severe consequences that follow reveal that both Ananias and Sapphira lied to God (v. 4). We are God's temple and the dwelling place of God's Spirit (1 Cor. 3:16), which equates the Holy Spirit with God. First Corinthians 2:10–11 says the Spirit searches the depths of God. To accomplish this, the Spirit would have to be omniscient and therefore equal with God.

Several passages attest that the act of regeneration is a work of the Holy Spirit. In John 3:3–7, Jesus explains to Nicodemus that he must be born again, specifically by the Spirit. Titus 3:5 is more explicit, stating that the Spirit both regenerates and renews us. The Spirit is actively involved in providing spiritual discernment so that the things of God can be accepted. In 1 Corinthians 2:14, Paul says the natural human being does not understand or comprehend the things of the Spirit of God, implying that the Spirit must first enable the unregenerate to apprehend the things of God before they can embrace them. The Westminster Shorter Catechism says the Spirit applies redemption, and the effectual calling unto salvation is the work of the Holy Spirit. The fact that the Spirit regenerates and renews indicates that he has a distinct role in bringing about the entire process of salvation, from the work of conviction of sin (John 16:8–11) to regeneration and justification. Second Thessalonians 2:13 says we have been chosen for salvation through the sanctification of the Holy Spirit. The Spirit separates us from the world and brings us into newness of life. Once the saving work is accomplished, the Spirit indwells us (Rom. 8:9; 1 Cor. 3:16; 6:19).

The Old Testament Scriptures are inspired by God, specifically, the Holy Spirit. Second Peter 1:20–21 says prophecy came not by human will but directly from the Holy Spirit, who inspired the words of human beings. Also 2 Timothy 3:16 says all Scripture is given by inspiration of God. The extent of the Spirit's work in propositional revelation is total. The Scriptures' accuracy and power are the work of the Holy Spirit. Illumination of the truths of God's revelation comes by means of the Holy Spirit's work in us.

The empowering work of the Holy Spirit on behalf of the universal church is manifested in the various gifts he gives to all believers. In 1 Corinthians 12, Paul describes the various gifts of the Spirit, noting that they are given for the purpose of building up the body. The gifts include wisdom, word of knowledge, faith, healing, miracles, prophecy, discernment of spirits, tongues, and the interpretation of tongues. These gifts are given not for personal benefit but for the edification of the body, into which the Spirit places the believer by means of Spirit baptism.

Early Controversies regarding the Holy Spirit. In an effort to protect Christianity's monotheistic understanding of God, Monarchians taught a radical view of monotheism that diminished the identity of the distinct persons of the Godhead. Out of Monarchianism two related heresies developed: modalism (Sabellianism) and dynamic monarchianism (Adoptionism). Modalism taught that God was not three distinct persons who shared equally all of the essence of God, but rather that he manifested himself in three distinct modes. Thus in the Old Testament, God was the Father. In the New Testament, he manifested himself as the Son and then finally as the Holy Spirit. The early modalist heretic Sabellius expressed it in this manner: God is the Father in creation, the Son in redemption, and the Holy Spirit in sanctification and regeneration.

The earliest direct attack on the deity and person of the Holy Spirit came from Arius, who also repudiated the deity of Christ in favor of a strict, nontrinitarian, monotheistic view of God. He argued that the Holy Spirit is a force, power, or energy that comes from God. The Council of Nicaea (AD 325) addressed Arius's heretical view of the Trinity, not only rejecting his denial of Christ's deity but also acknowledging the Holy Spirit. Given that the deity of Christ was the main issue, the Nicene Creed did not give explicit attention to the deity of the Holy Spirit but rather implied it. This weakness was addressed at the Council of Constantinople

(AD 381), which settled the issue regarding the Spirit's deity. Out of that council came the Constantinopolitan Creed, which states the following regarding the Holy Spirit: "And in the Holy Spirit, the Lord and life-giver, Who proceeds from the Father, Who is worshipped and glorified together with the Father and Son, Who spoke through the prophets." This creed effectively established a thoroughgoing orthodox view of the Trinity that left no doubt what the church believed regarding the three persons of the Trinity, thus effectively repudiating once again the Arian heresy and also other errors such as Monarchianism and its offshoots.

Controversies during the Reformation. Around the time of the Reformation, Faustus Socinus (Fausto Sozzini, 1539–1604), nephew of Laelius Socinus (Lelio Sozzini, 1525–62, the orthodox reformer), promoted antitrinitarian views. Regarding the Holy Spirit, the Socinians taught that the Spirit was merely a power or operation of God.

Conclusion. In spite of the aggressive efforts by heretical teachers to diminish the person and work of the Holy Spirit, the major branches of the church have historically maintained a firm grasp on the deity of the Spirit and his coeternal, coequal status as the third member of the Trinity. Orthodox teaching on the Spirit is derived from both the Old and the New Testaments.

See also HOLY SPIRIT, MISCONCEPTIONS ABOUT

Bibliography. G. Burge, *The Anointed Community: The Holy Spirit in the Johannine Tradition*; G. Fee, *God's Empowering Presence*; W. Grudem, *Systematic Theology*; J. I. Packer, *Keep in Step with the Spirit*; "Sabellius," in *New World Encyclopedia*, http://www.newworldencyclopedia.org/entry/Sabellius?oldid=687583; A. H. Strong, *Systematic Theology: A Compendium Designed for the Use of Theological Students*; J. Walvoord, *The Holy Spirit*; L. Wood, *The Holy Spirit in the Old Testament*.

S. J. Rost

HOLY SPIRIT, MISCONCEPTIONS ABOUT.

The doctrine of the Holy Trinity, which articulates the orthodox Christian understanding of God's nature, may be stated as follows: There is only one true God, who within his eternal nature exists as three distinct persons—Father, Son, and Holy Spirit—all of whom are coequal and coeternal. These persons *are* the one God. Hence all three persons may properly be called "God" either collectively or individually.

Obviously, the soundness of the trinitarian formula rests, at least in part, on whether the personality and deity of the Holy Spirit can be demonstrated from Scripture. In other words, for trinitarianism to be valid, the Bible must indicate that the Holy Spirit is not only personal but also deity. According to most heterodox groups, however, Scripture does not provide such information, or it provides information to the contrary.

Some groups, especially those influenced by Eastern philosophy, do not even recognize God as a personal being. Although they might mention a "Spirit" or "One Soul," such references only allude to a kind of universal consciousness through which all life is united as one. This belief, called monism, asserts that all reality is reducible to a single unifying substance. Individuality is nothing but an illusion. Everything is part of a great cosmic One, which is variously referred to as the Reality, All, Mind, or Force. Such a notion, of course, excludes the possibility of any Holy Spirit existing separate from humanity.

Yet Scripture teaches that there is indeed a Holy Spirit utterly distinct from humanity. In the Old Testament, this Spirit is commonly spoken of as the "Spirit of God" (Gen. 1:2; Num. 11:26; 1 Sam. 10:10; 2 Chron. 24:20) or the "Holy Spirit" of God (Ps. 51:11; Isa. 63:10–11). The New Testament also mentions a "Holy Spirit" (Acts 19:6; Rom. 15:16; 1 Cor. 12:3; 2 Cor. 13:14; Eph. 1:13; 1 Thess. 4:8).

Other heterodox groups, though they may accept the existence of the Holy Spirit, hold widely varying opinions on the subject. To Jehovah's Witnesses, the Holy Spirit is "an invisible active force" by which Jehovah God accomplishes his will (Watch Tower Bible and Tract Society, 11); to Christadelphians, "the energy or power of God" (Mansfield, 15); to members of Freemasonry, a "Life-Principle" (Pike, 734); to Eckankar followers, God's "Light and Sound" (1); to Church Universal and Triumphant adherents, the "seventh-ray aspect of the sacred fire [which] transmutes the cause, effect, record, and memory of negative karma" (Prophet, 9). But Scripture repeatedly paints the Holy Spirit in a radically different way.

First, many Old and New Testament passages ascribe to the Holy Spirit characteristics consistent with personhood—for example, feeling emotion (Isa. 63:10; Rom. 15:30; Eph. 4:30), possessing knowledge (1 Cor. 2:11), and having a mind (Rom. 8:27). Second, the Holy Spirit acts in ways that indicate personhood—for example, he teaches (Neh. 9:20; Luke 12:12; John 14:26), bears witness (John 15:26; Acts 5:32; Rom. 8:16), leads and guides (John 16:13), glorifies Christ (John 16:14), convicts hearts (John 16:8), intercedes for believers (Rom. 8:27), speaks and gives commands (Acts 8:29; 10:19–20; 11:12; Rev. 22:17), calls Christians into service (Acts 13:2), makes decisions (Acts 15:28), and exhibits self-control by not acting "on his own initiative" when doing so would conflict with the will of the Father and the Son (John 16:13).

Concerning the deity of the Holy Spirit, this too is clearly discerned in various ways from a number of biblical passages. Acts 5, for instance, tells the story of Ananias and his wife, Sapphira, who sell their property but are dishonest about how much they have profited from the transaction. Peter confronts the couple, saying: "Ananias, how is it that Satan has so filled your heart that you have

lied to the Holy Spirit?" (v. 3). Peter goes on to tell Ananias that in lying to the Holy Spirit, he actually had lied "to God" (v. 4). Additionally, it must be remembered that someone can only lie to another person. This passage, therefore, not only presents the Holy Spirit as God but also offers yet more proof that the Holy Spirit is not an impersonal force.

The Church of Jesus Christ of Latter-day Saints (LDS), unlike the aforementioned groups, actually does recognize both the personality and the deity of the Holy Spirit. However, LDS Church members, also known as Mormons, still err by identifying the Holy Spirit as an altogether different god existing in the cosmos. This places Mormonism in the category of polytheistic religions (belief in many gods), whereas Christianity is a monotheistic faith (belief in one God). Biblical passages militating against multiple gods include Isaiah 42:8; 43:10; 48:10–11. Even the demons readily concede there is only one God (James 2:19). A unique view found within some Mormon writings is a distinction between Holy Spirit and Holy Ghost, though there is no such distinction in the original texts of Scripture.

Another common misconception about the Holy Spirit involves the misdefinition of the term *Holy Spirit* as nothing more than an alternate expression for God the Father—that is, God is "holy" and God is "spirit." Victor Paul Wierwille, founder of The Way International, advocated this belief despite verses like Isaiah 48:16 and 63:9–10, wherein God the Father is mentioned in conjunction with the Holy Spirit. Such passages show a clear distinction between the Father and the Spirit.

Finally, some within modalist groups (e.g., the United Pentecostal Church) claim that the Holy Spirit is simply a "mode" of operation that is assumed by God the Father in order to interact with humanity. According to modalism, a heresy traceable to Sabellius (third century AD), God is not three persons but only appears as such in order to manifest different aspects of his character. In other words, the Father became the Son, who became the Holy Spirit. But numerous biblical passages distinguish between all three persons, proving also that all three exist simultaneously (e.g., Matt. 3:16–17; John 15:26).

See also HOLY SPIRIT, BIBLICAL VIEW OF

Bibliography. R. Abanes, *Defending the Faith: A Beginner's Guide to Cults and New Religions*; L. Berkhof, *Systematic Theology*; Eckankar, *What You Need to Know about the Light and Sound of God*; M. Erickson, *God in Three Persons*; W. Grudem, *Systematic Theology*; H. W. House, *Charts of Cults, Sects, & Religious Movements*; H. P. Mansfield, ed., *God Is One, Not Three*; A. Pike, *Morals and Dogma*; E. C. Prophet, *Profile: Elizabeth Clare Prophet*; P. Toon, *Our Triune God: A Portrayal of the Trinity*; Watch Tower Bible and Tract Society, *Holy Spirit*.

R. Abanes

HSIAO-CHING/XIAOJING. The Hsiao-ching (Chinese, "classic of filial piety") is one of the shortest of the thirteen classic texts of Confucianism, consisting of less than two thousand Chinese characters. Although of unknown authorship, it has exerted considerable authority over the development of Chinese culture for more than two millennia. According to the Hsiao-ching, filial piety is the most foundational moral virtue for guiding personal conduct, "the root of (all) virtue." It provides a vital and necessary condition for social order and ought to be cultivated by people of every station in society, whether they be rulers, sages, or commoners. Forsaking the duties involved in filial piety is the worst possible offense and leads to social anarchy if practiced on a wide scale. Essentially, filial piety is the display of love, devotion, obedience, and respect toward one's parents, grandparents, and deceased ancestors. It involves such acts as heeding parental advice, not rebelling against parental authority, concealing the faults of one's parents, maintaining good relations with one's brothers, caring for one's parents when they become sick or elderly, mourning the death of one's parents, and performing prescribed sacrifices when a parent dies.

See also CONFUCIANISM

Bibliography. C. Chai and W. Chai, eds. and trans., *The Humanist Way in Ancient China: Essential Works of Confucianism*; A. K. Chan and Sor-hoon Tan, eds., *Filial Piety in Chinese Thought and History*; M. E. Wiesner et al., *Discovering the Global Past: A Look at the Evidence*.

H. W. House

I

ICHINEN SANZEN. The Nichiren Buddhist doctrine of *ichinen sanzen* (all worlds contained in one thought) describes the reality wherein every act of human thinking encompasses all existing worlds. These are the ten spheres: Perfect Buddhas, bodhisattva state, Solitary Buddhas, Hinayana state, heaven, human, titans, animals, ghosts, hell. Each of these is multiplied by the ten factors: appearance, nature, entity, power, influence, internal cause, relation, latent effect, manifest effect, consistence. And these are multiplied by the three realms, which are the five-aggregates realm, the living-being realm, and the environmental realm. In this way, each thought is said to contain within itself the entire cosmos. According to this doctrine, there is a continual, reciprocal interface between the world of phenomena and the most fundamental reality. It is also taught that every momentary experience a person has is one of ten states, or worlds (*jikkai*). The basic content of the doctrine of ichinen sanzen is taken from the Lotus Sutra and was developed by the Buddhist scholar Zhi-yi (538–97), the founder of T'ien Tai Buddhism (a Chinese Mahayana school); later it was modified by Nichiren (1222–82), the founder of the Japanese sect Nichiren Shoshu.

See also BUDDHISM; LOTUS SUTRA; NICHIREN SHOSU

Bibliography. P. B. Yampolsky, ed., *Letters of Nichiren.*

J. Bjornstad

I CHING / YIJING. The I Ching, or Yijing, is an ancient book of Chinese wisdom and divination. Also known as the Book of Changes, the I Ching (pronounced "ee-ching") consists of sixty-four hexagrams of solid and broken lines. Solid lines represent the force of yang. Broken lines represent the force of yin. Each hexagram is associated with a particular social, psychological, or spiritual symbol, similar to the drawings on tarot cards. One consults I Ching to receive wise counsel.

The Origin of the I Ching. According to Chinese legend, Emperor Fu Hsi (2953–2838 BC) invented an eight-trigram form of I Ching as a tool of divination. Around 1150 BC, Wen Wang, an imprisoned political leader during the Shang Dynasty, revised the system into sixty-four hexagrams. His son Wu Wang and a nephew added commentary on each symbol. Researcher Cyril Javary contends that the real inventor of I Ching is Confucius, who attributed its evolution to important historical figures so that it might receive wide acceptance.

In the early 1840s, James Legge, a well-known missionary to China, translated the I Ching into English. Richard Wilhelm, another missionary, wrote the most popular translation in 1882. It received wide acceptance in the West.

The Underlying Philosophy behind I Ching. Yin/yang describes the dualistic nature and movement of the universe. This essence is bipolar in design, composed of light and dark, male and female, positive and negative, and so forth. Yin/yang is not two separate entities but merely two aspects of the same essential motion that permeates all. An analogy might be that of riding a bicycle. To move one must push one pedal while releasing the other. Pushing and releasing are part of one movement. They cannot be separated. Pushing only one pedal will lead nowhere, and so will pushing both pedals at the same time. The Chinese view the universe as perpetual motion. There are sixty-four movements in the universe, each represented by the hexagrams.

Use of the I Ching. Each hexagram has a name, a commentary, and six lines, some solid and others broken. In the solid lines, energy is understood to flow outward from the center of the hexagram. In broken lines, energy flows from the outer edge toward the center, where the gap appears. The solid and broken lines and the direction of the energy symbolize the need for balance in one's life between ex-tension and in-tension. Through an elaborate process one reads the chosen hexagram to determine how to balance one's life and bring everything into harmony, thus producing the desired results. The process involves asking a question concerning some life situation, then tossing specially designed coins three times or dividing sticks into small random bundles. The random results point to a corresponding hexagram in the I Ching, which, when interpreted correctly, offers advice, predicts the future, or helps one figure out a solution to the problem. The ultimate goal of the exercise is to help one reach a state of harmony with yin/yang, which produces health, happiness, and peace.

See also CONFUCIANISM; YIN AND YANG

Bibliography. C. Javary, *Understanding the I Ching*; E. Shaughnessy, *I Ching: The Classic Book of Changes.*

R. A. Streett

IDOLATRY. Idolatry is usually defined as veneration of material objects believed to represent or embody sacred power, especially that of a god or goddess. "Idolatry" may be said, however, to include a range of practices involving a variety of objects that together constitute a hierarchy of meaning-symbols. At the most basic level, many religions, including Christianity (especially the Roman Catholic and Eastern traditions), use statues or images simply as symbolic representations of personages (e.g., saints, the devil, or the Buddha) or ideals (e.g., the Assyrian winged lion or the Hindu lotus-flower). A biblical example might be Aaron's "golden calf" (Exod. 32:4), which, in violation of the second commandment, visually represented Yahweh. At another level, an object may be thought to possess magical or supernatural powers via some external power or rite (a talisman) or because it embodies a spirit (a fetish). Laban's "household idols" (*teraphim*), which Rachel took and hid (Gen. 31:19), probably fall into this category. The true idol takes the meaning-symbol a step further by embodying the actual *form* of a spirit or power. Even here the relation between "idol" and deity is variously understood. The image of Artemis, for example, supposedly "fell from heaven" (Acts 19:35), perhaps indicating it was produced in an ecstatic state, or that it was fashioned from some material object that bore a striking resemblance to the goddess, or that it was a meteorite that came to be regarded as a divinely sent image, but not that Artemis *was* the image. Isaiah, on the other hand, ridicules those who fashion gods and end up worshiping blocks of wood (Isa. 44:18–19)!

Behind all forms of idolatry is the desire to have continual access to, relationship with, and/or control over sacred powers believed to affect the courses of nature and life. Idolatry also sets limits on the "power" represented, however, which helps to explain the categorical prohibition of images and idols in Scripture (Exod. 20:4).

C. R. Wells

INCARNATION. The word *incarnation* is derived from a Latin word developed from *in* + *caro* (flesh), which literally means "in the flesh." In Christian theology, the term refers to the supernatural act of God, effected by the Holy Spirit, whereby the eternal Son of God, the second person of the Triune Godhead, in the fullness of time, took into union with himself a complete human nature apart from sin and thus, as a result of that action, has now become the God-man forever, the Word made flesh (John 1:1, 14; cf. Rom. 1:3; 8:3; Gal. 4:4; Phil. 2:7–8; 1 Tim. 3:16; 1 John 4:2).

The means whereby the incarnation came about is the virgin conception, commonly known as the virgin birth—the miraculous action of the Holy Spirit in the womb of Mary—so that what was conceived was nothing less than the Lord Jesus, who is fully God and fully man in one person forever (Matt. 1:18–25; Luke 1:26–38). He did this in order to become the Redeemer of the church, our prophet, priest, and king, and thus to "save his people from their sins" (Matt. 1:21). By becoming one with us, the Lord of Glory is not only able to share our sorrows and burdens but was also able to secure our redemption by bearing our sin on the cross as our substitute and being raised for our justification (see Rom. 4:25; Heb. 2:17–18; 4:14–16; 1 Pet. 3:18).

In later church reflection on the biblical data that present Jesus as simultaneously God and man, the Council of Chalcedon (AD 451) affirmed that in the incarnation God the Son gave personal identity to the human nature that he had assumed without losing or compromising his divine nature; hence the affirmation that the Lord Jesus now exists forever as one person in two natures and that the properties of each nature are preserved without confusion, change, division, and separation. This entails that *the man* Jesus from the moment of conception was personal by virtue of the union of the human nature with the divine Son. As a result of this affirmation, a significant part of the church was split from the official church. To this day, several groups (including the Copts of Egypt and the Syrian Orthodox Church) continue to be out of communion with both the Roman Catholic and the Eastern Orthodox churches over the issue of the incarnated Jesus, although in recent years efforts have been made to reconcile divergent Orthodox groups.

See also CHALCEDONIAN CONTROVERSY; CHRIST, NATURES AND ATTRIBUTES OF

Bibliography. M. Erickson, *The Word Became Flesh*; D. Macleod, *The Person of Christ*; R. L. Reymond, "Incarnation," in *Evangelical Dictionary of Theology*, edited by W. Elwell; D. F. Wells, *The Person of Christ*.

S. Wellum

INERRANCY. The inerrancy of Scripture is a consequence of its verbal-plenary inspiration. Scripture, in the original autographs (i.e., the original manuscripts) and correctly interpreted, is free from error, or better, entirely true and never false in all that it teaches and affirms precisely because it is the product of a sovereign-personal, omniscient God who cannot err (2 Tim. 3:15–17; 2 Pet. 1:20–21; cf. Num. 23:19; Ps. 119:89, 160; Prov. 30:5; John 17:17; Heb. 6:16–18). Recently, inerrancy has been the hallmark of evangelical Christianity. Even though the term was used in the past, it was introduced into the contemporary discussion to emphasize what the church has always held—namely, that Scripture, in its entirety, is the authoritative, infallible Word of God. As such it alone is the sufficient, certain, and authoritative rule of all saving knowledge, faith, and obedience.

At least three important points need to be emphasized in regard to inerrancy. First, inerrancy applies equally to all parts of Scripture as originally written. The emphasis in such texts as 2 Timothy 3:16 is on the *origin* of Scripture and thus its autographic form.

There is no biblical evidence that inspiration and inerrancy pertain to copies or translations of the biblical text except insofar as those texts accurately reflect what was originally given. That is why Scripture repeatedly warns not to alter the text either by addition or subtraction (see Deut. 4:2; 12:32; Prov. 30:6; Rev. 22:18–19). Second, inerrancy is limited not merely to matters of faith and practice but to all areas of knowledge that Scripture addresses. It is impossible to create a neat dichotomy between the theological and the factual given the fact that God acts to bring about redemption in history. Third, Scripture is inerrant even though it speaks in ordinary, phenomenological language and various literary forms. The amount of precision demanded of the biblical text must be consistent with the standards of the time when it was written.

The warrant for affirming inerrancy is Scripture itself. Given what the Bible claims for itself—namely, that it is God's Word written, that the biblical tests for a prophet demand total and complete truthfulness of his message in order for it to be viewed as from God (see Deut. 13:1–5; 18:20–22), and that Scripture uses Scripture to build its arguments, sometimes on a single word or even a tense of a verb (see Matt. 22:32, 43–45; John 10:34–35; Gal. 3:16)—it is difficult not to affirm the full authority and inerrancy of Scripture.

Bibliography. D. A. Carson and J. Woodbridge, eds., *Hermeneutics, Authority and Canon*; P. D. Feinberg, "Bible, Inerrancy and Infallibility of," in *Evangelical Dictionary of Theology*, 141–45; N. L. Geisler, ed., *Inerrancy*.

S. Wellum

INJIL. Mentioned several times in the Qur'an, the Injil (whose title is an Arabic transliteration for the Greek *evangelion*, "gospel") is an alleged protogospel that describes the life and ministry of Jesus Christ. It is considered one of the five Holy Books of Islam, along with the Qur'an, the Suhuf Ibrahim (scrolls of Abraham), the Zabur (hymns or songs), and the Tawrat (the Arabic word for Torah). Some Muslims use the term Injil to refer to the four canonical Gospels, while others use it for the entire New Testament. Islamic apologists maintain that the information once contained in the (no longer extant) Injil accords with everything taught in the Qur'an. According to the Islamic doctrine of Tahrif (corruption), the original gospel writings were distorted by Jewish and Christian editors, resulting in the disparity between the texts of the four Christian gospels and the message of the Qur'an. In particular Muslims dispute the Gospels' reports of Jesus being called the Son of God and their accounts of his death and resurrection.

See also ISLAM, BASIC BELIEFS OF; QUR'AN

Bibliography. G. Adelphi and E. Hahn, "The Integrity of the Bible according to the Qur'an and the Hadith"; J. L. Esposito, *The Oxford Dictionary of Islam*; D. A. Madigan, *The Qur'an's Self-Image: Writing and Authority in Islam's Scripture*.

R. L. Drouhard

INTERNATIONAL SOCIETY FOR KRISHNA CONSCIOUSNESS (ISKCON). ISKCON was founded in 1966 by A. C. Bhaktivedanta Swami Prabhupada (1896–1977). Adherents of ISKCON are commonly known as Hare Krishnas, although within the organization they are called "devotees." There are approximately three hundred Hare Krishna temples throughout the world.

ISKCON theology is based in pantheistic thought and incorporates major Hinduistic tenets such as reincarnation, karma, and yoga. Many unique doctrinal aspects to this religion come from Prabhupada's interpretation of the Hindu scripture the Bhagavad Gita. He taught that Krishna, whose name in India's Sanskrit language means "all-attractive," is the supreme personality of God. Krishna is said to have first appeared on earth about five thousand years ago and proved his divinity by performing superhuman feats. It is believed that, since his initial appearance, Krishna has been transformed into different humans known as avatars, with his last incarnation coming in the body of Caitanya Mahaprabhu (1486–1534) from India. Prabhupada taught that God has a number of names, including Jesus; in fact, he claimed that the Greek Christos and the Sanskrit Krishna are the same word.

Devotees adopt Sanskrit names and practice devotional Bhakti Yoga to rid their souls of bad karma. Many Hare Krishna males don orange robes and shave their heads except for a single lock of hair in the back of the head; the women wear Indian dresses. Devotees commonly apply a V-shaped yellow clay symbol on their foreheads known as a *tilak*. A major part of Hare Krishna worship is the daily recitation of a three-word devotional chant: "Hare Krishna, Hare Krishna, Krishna Krishna, Hare Hare, Hare Rama, Hare Rama, Rama Rama, Hare Hare." Devotees are required to repeat this mantra a total of 1,728 times a day, either individually or in groups. They often use Indian instruments such as drums, hand cymbals, and hand organs to dance to the melodic expression, sometimes publicly in parks or universities. They also sell literature, including the ISKCON *Back to Godhead* magazine. Instructed to abstain from drugs, tobacco, alcohol, caffeine drinks, and gambling, devotees practice strict vegetarianism; in fact, they equate the killing of animals with killing one's brother or sister. Sex is allowed only for procreation within marriage, and then only once per month. Any sexual act not performed for the procreation of children is considered illicit sex.

See also KARMI; KRISHNA CONSCIOUSNESS; PRABHUPADA, ABHAY CHARAN DE BHAKTIVEDANTA SWAMI

Bibliography. S. J. Gelberg, *Hare Krishna, Hare Krishna*; J. Hubner et al., *Monkey on a Stick:* *Murder, Madness, and the Hare Krishnas*; J. S. Judah, *Hare Krishna and the Counterculture.*

E. Johnson

ISLAM, BASIC BELIEFS OF. Islam (from Arabic, "submission") is a belief system that encompasses at least 1.5 billion people throughout every corner of the globe. The basis for Islam is the revelations (purportedly) given to Muhammad (ca. 570–632) during a twenty-two-year ministry in the cities of Mecca and Medina (both in present-day Saudi Arabia), which are gathered in the text of the Qur'an. From the Arabian Peninsula, Islam spread through conquest over the Middle East, the Iranian plateau, and Central Asia initially. Over a period of centuries, sometimes through conquest, sometimes through trading links and the ministry of Sufi holy men, adjacent areas in Anatolia and southeastern Europe, West and East Africa, India, and Southeast Asia were converted.

The basic teachings of Islam are that God (Allah) has no partners and that the message of his divine unity has been imparted continually to a series of messengers (or prophets) through human history. In general humanity has systematically rejected this message, causing God to punish nations with destruction as a sign to others. Most of the important messengers—Adam, Noah, Moses, Aaron, Solomon, John the Baptist, and Jesus—are taken from the Bible, although the stories told about them in the Qur'an sometimes diverge considerably from the biblical accounts. All are said to have preached the message of Islam in the form of progressive revelation—valid for its time until the next messenger appeared—which culminated in the appearance of Muhammad. Islamic doctrine holds that there will be no further prophets after Muhammad and that all prior revelations are void after the proclamation of Islam.

Islam is expressed in daily life by the five pillars of Islam: the *shahada* (confession of faith), the five daily prayers, the giving of charity (usually 2.5 percent of one's income), fasting during the month of Ramadan, and a pilgrimage (*hajj*) to Mecca once during one's lifetime. Beyond these basics, Sunni Islam is practiced by emulating the actions of Muhammad as closely as possible. Approximately 85 percent of the world's Muslims are Sunni. This type of Islam is named for the *sunna*, or way that Muhammad acted, and is based on the massive number of traditions (hadith) that purport to detail every aspect of his life for the benefit of future generations. Legal scholars then converted the principles contained within the hadith literature into law codes (the shari'ah). Sunni Muslims recognize four legal schools: the Hanafi (predominating in the Middle East, Turkey, Central Asia, India, Pakistan, and Bangladesh), the Maliki (in North and West Africa), the Shafi`i (in parts of Egypt, East Africa, Indonesia, and Malaysia), and the Hanbali (in Saudi Arabia). In most cases, each school has recognized the legitimacy of the other schools.

Politically, Sunnis are differentiated from the minority Shi'ite group by their adherence to the idea that Muhammad's successor, given the title of caliph (meaning "deputy"), should be elected by the community. This election would manifest God's will and give the caliph much of the spiritual and temporal authority that Muhammad had (but not his prophetic office) in theory. However, in practice, although the first caliphs were elected, the later ones were dynastic and quickly lost both their temporal and their spiritual authority. Most of the spiritual authority was taken up by the religious scholars (the ulama), who effectively since the ninth century have constituted the leadership of Sunni Islam.

Shi'ism, comprising most of the remaining 15 percent of Muslims, is another interpretation based on the idea that both spiritual and temporal authority come from the descendants of Muhammad (venerated by Sunnis but not accorded the right to rule).

Because of the numerous branches of Muhammad's family, there are many different Shi'ite groups, each one claiming authority for a certain family or individual. The two largest Shi'ite groups are the Twelver Shi'ites (Ithna'ashariyya) and the Seveners, also called the Isma'ilis. Twelver Shi'ites ascribe authority to twelve imams (leaders), including 'Ali, Muhammad's son-in-law; Muhammad's two grandsons, Hasan and Husayn; and nine of Husayn's descendants down to 874.

For Shi'ites the most important early event was the murder of Husayn in 680 at the site of Karbala (today in southern Iraq). This event is given cosmic importance, and the blood of Husayn continues (according to Shi'ites) to stain their opponents for all time, while the guilt of not having succored him continues to burden Shi'ites, who mourn his death on the tenth of Muharram each year. Both Twelvers and Seveners descend from Husayn, but the Seveners break off from the seventh imam after 'Ali (the fourth after Husayn), while the Twelvers continue through another line. In 874 the last of the Twelve imams is said to have gone into occultation (disappeared from human eyes) for his own protection. According to Twelvers, God has elongated his lifetime down to the present, and he will be revealed at the end of the world and establish a messianic kingdom. Unlike the Twelvers, the Sevener Isma'ilis have never been without the physical presence of an imam (today the Agha Khan). Their theology relies on an eternal cycle of divine revelation in the pattern of seven; as each heptad comes to an end, God opens up another cycle, sometimes with a considerably different message (usually based on Neoplatonic beliefs).

There are smaller, breakaway Shi'ite groups that have usually formed trinitarian systems based on the divinity of 'Ali (Muhammad's son-in-law). The major representative of this tendency is the Nusayri-'Alawites (in Syria). Because of the nonmonotheistic teachings of these groups, their existence within the fold of Islam is problematic. The Druze (in Lebanon, Syria, and Israel), who divinized one of the Isma'ili imams (the caliph al-Hakim; d. 1021), are also a breakaway group that no longer claims to be Muslim. Later breakaway groups from Islam include the Bahá'ís (Iran) and the Ahmadis (Pakistan and India), both of which claim to have prophetic revelation after the time of Muhammad.

A third grouping of Muslims, Sufis, overlaps with both Sunnis and Shi'ites. Sufism is the mystical interpretation of Islam and has its roots in the common ascetic tradition of the Middle East. Early Sufis, up until the tenth and eleventh centuries, were ecstatic in their pronouncements and often made exaggerated claims concerning their identity with God that enraged the ulama. Starting with the eleventh century, Sufism became more mainstream, and from this period until the end of the nineteenth century most major Muslim personalities practiced Sufism. In its essence, Sufism is a path leading to union with God that involves self-denial (but not chastity), spiritual exercises, and ultimately annihilation of the self. For the most part, since the fourteenth century it has been practiced as part of extensive brotherhoods (tariqas), the most prevalent of which are the Qadiriyya (pan-Islamic), the Naqshbandiyya (Central Asia, South Asia, Indonesia), the Mevleviyya (Turkey and Central Asia), the Tijaniyya (North and West Africa), the Shadhiliyya (North Africa), and the Rifa'iyya (Middle East). Each one of the brotherhoods is characterized by a different interpretation of the path; in practice some can be highly militant and involved in society, while others can practice withdrawal and be almost pacificist.

Contemporary Islam has all the above currents present but also has produced a synthesis known as radical Islam. Radical Islam is a protest against the removal of Islamic norms from Muslim societies, and it demands a reimposition of the Shari'ah (usually not defined) and the establishment of a pan-Islamic state. Radical Muslims often aggressively confront the ulama, which they characterize as being a tool of secular governments; often label Sufis or other Muslims with whom they disagree non-Muslims (takfir); and use calls for jihad as a cover to proclaim their message.

Islam is a vital and growing missionary religion that seeks and gains converts from every walk of life in the entire world. It has a global and totalizing message that does not permit its followers to compromise the absolute monotheism it preaches. However, it should be noted that large numbers of Muslims, especially in Africa, South Asia (India, Pakistan, and Bangladesh), and Southeast Asia (Indonesia) are essentially syncretistic in their belief system, having adopted Islam through the medium of Sufism. This syncretism has allowed these large numbers of Muslims to engage many practices and beliefs that are not necessarily compatible with normative Islam. Vis-à-vis Judaism and Christianity, Islam is supersessionist and has appropriated the sacred history of the Bible and modified the stories of the important biblical figures (usually called prophets in Islam but not necessarily identical to those referred to as prophets in the Bible) so that in the Qur'anic narratives they are made to preach the message of Islam. The principal differences between Islam and Christianity focus first on the figure of Jesus, who in Islam is merely a prophet who heralds the coming of Muhammad. Additionally, Jesus is believed to have not been crucified but lifted into heaven. Other key differences include the rejection of the doctrine of original sin in Islam and the role of the law (Shari'ah) in the process of salvation (as opposed to grace).

See also DRUZE, THE; ISLAM, ESCHATOLOGY OF; SHI'A ISLAM; SUNNI ISLAM; WAHHABIYYA ISLAM

Bibliography. D. Brown, *A New Introduction to Islam*; F. Denny, *An Introduction to Islam*; J. Esposito, *Islam: The Straight Path*; I. Goldziher, *Introduction to Islamic Theology and Law*; F. Rahman, *Islam*; Rahman, *Major Themes of the Qur'an*; A. Rippin, *Muslims: Their Religious Beliefs and Practices*; D. Waines, *An Introduction to Islam*.

D. B. Cook

ISLAM, ESCHATOLOGY OF. Islamic eschatology is divided into two very distinct types: that which is concerned with this world (*malahim* and *fitan*) and that which is concerned with the next (e.g., the day of resurrection, the day of judgment, heaven and hell). The eschatological sense of the Qur'an is very well developed, with themes implying that the end of the world will be cataclysmic and is imminent. However, the events on earth leading up to this cataclysm are not very well developed in the Qur'an, and one has to rely on the tradition literature (hadith) for most of the basic themes.

Historical Background. Apocalyptic historical traditions revolve around the battles that the Muslims fought with the Byzantine Empire (seventh through ninth centuries) and stem from the frustration felt by Muslims at their inability to conquer Constantinople, the empire's capital. These traditions also reflect the fears of the Syrian Muslims that the Byzantines would be able to reconquer the region of Syria. Concurrent with these traditions are historical traditions about the numerous civil wars (*fitan*) that wracked the Muslim world for its first two hundred years. It is from this period that we find the various competing groups using messianic propaganda for their political ends.

The Mahdi. The messianic figure is called the mahdi (the rightly guided one). Traditions concerning his identity can be divided into two strands: an Arab strand, which emphasizes his Arab heritage and descent from Muhammad (usually directly but sometimes from his tribe, the Quraysh), and a universalist strand, which emphasizes that he can be from any ethnicity or genealogy but must be the best possible Muslim at his time. The first, Arab, strand is promoted by Shi'ites, who hold their Twelfth Imam (occulted in 874) to be the mahdi and look for his future revelation, as well as by many Sunnis who look to the descendants of Muhammad's elder grandson, al-Hasan, to provide a candidate descended from him (today the royal families of Jordan and Morocco). The second strand is held only by Sunnis who embrace a universalist interpretation of Islam and has contributed to the appearance of a wide range of mahdi claimants throughout Muslim history.

Jesus in Islamic Eschatology. Jesus's role in the messianic future is controversial. As Jesus is held to have been lifted bodily into heaven from the cross (Qur'an 4:157), there is a concurrent tradition (not Qur'anic) that he will return. Frequently the tradition literature holds him to be a messianic figure and can even identify him as the mahdi in early materials. But in general Jesus's reappearance is more closely connected to fighting the antichrist (the dajjal), who will appear either during the reign of the mahdi or slightly before it. The dajjal is usually said to be a monstrous figure, with one eye, and with the word *infidel* (*kafir*) written on his forehead. He will attempt to lead the entire world astray, using miracles that are parodies of those of Jesus (healing the sick, supplying food, raising the dead, etc.). Only a few Muslims will be able to withstand this temptation. At the last extremity, Jesus will appear, descending on either Jerusalem or Damascus, fight the dajjal and kill him, and then live out the rest of his life as a Muslim (while inducing Jews and Christians to convert to Islam).

The Islamic Messianic Age. The messianic age in Islam is characterized as a repeat of the ideal age of the conquests, when wealth was plentiful and there was a constant influx of people and territories into the world of Islam. Messianic citations such as Isaiah 11:6–8 are common within the literature. The mahdi is usually described as a man who will "fill the earth with justice and righteousness just as it had been filled with injustice and unrighteousness" (Wensinck). However, the messianic age in Islam is extremely short, usually said to last between three and nine years, when Gog and Magog (Yajuj wa-Majuj) come from the east to destroy the entire world. These tribes, usually said to be subhuman creatures dwelling in Central Asia, kill everyone in their path and destroy everything. God will kill them using a worm that devours their bodies.

Islamic Day of Judgment. It is difficult to find an apocalypse that takes one beyond these events. There is a break between earthly apocalyptic events and heavenly judgment events. However, it is clear that after the destruction of Gog and Magog, God destroys the earth and causes all humanity to be raised for judgment. This day is frequently described in the Qur'an as the day of judgment or the day of resurrection. Until that point, people who had died would be held preparatory to their judgment, with only a few able to go straight to heaven prior to everyone's judgment (this category includes prophets, righteous people, and martyrs). On that day, humanity would be resurrected and brought before the throne.

The Role of Jerusalem. In some Islamic literature, this eschatological future would be given the earthly landscape of the city of Jerusalem, in which humanity would be raised in the desert area to the east of the city, brought up to the Mount of Olives, and made to walk on a narrow bridge over the Valley of Kidron (where hell was said to be located in a chasm) to the Haram al-Sharif (Temple Mount) on the other side. The blessed would be able to make this crossing in haste, while the damned would fall off into hell. Art in the Dome of the Rock (also on the Temple Mount) dating from the early Muslim period emphasizes its close connection with paradise, and according to tradition, under the Mosque of Al-Aqsa (located on the south end of the Haram platform) there is a well that gives entrance into paradise.

Stratified Heaven and Hell. Both heaven and hell are divided into several levels, with rewards and punishments accorded to believers and unbelievers on the basis of the level to which they are sent. It is possible for believers to have to suffer for a time in hell in order to expiate their sins, and certain theologians made provisions for unbelieving innocents (children, people who could not have converted to Islam, etc.) to spend eternity in hell while not suffering any punishment.

Conclusion. Much of the eschatological material in Islam is closely related to biblical materials or is in reaction to it. Contemporary interpretations of apocalyptic predictions have been popular throughout the Muslim world and frequently portray contemporary events as having been predicted by classical material, but most of the material covering heaven and hell has not been changed since medieval times.

See also HADITH; ISLAM, BASIC BELIEFS OF

Bibliography. D. Cook, *Contemporary Muslim Apocalyptic Literature*; Cook, *Studies in Muslim Apocalyptic*; M. Fakhry, *The Qur'an: A Modern English Version*; al-Maqdisi, al-Musharraf b. al-Murajja', *Fada'il Bayt al-Maqdis wa-l-Khalil wa-fada'il al-Sham*, edited by O. Livne-Kafri; J. I. Smith and Y. Y. Haddad, *The Islamic Understanding of Death and Resurrection*; A. J. Wensinck, ed., *Concordance et indices de la tradition musulmane*.

D. B. Cook

ISSA. Issa (also spelled "Isa") is the true name of Jesus, according to the Qur'an. Beginning in the late nineteenth century, the name also became a common designation for Jesus among Theosophists and authors of related esoteric religious works—one example is

Nicholas Notovitch, author of *The Lost Years of Jesus: The Life of St. Issa* (1894).

In Islam Issa is given an exalted status among the succession of prophets of Allah. The Qur'an describes him as the virgin-born son of Mary (Maryam) and a miracle worker, and Islamic tradition (hadith) assigns him a unique role in striking down an end-time antichrist figure. But Jesus only appeared to die on the cross, according to the Qur'an; in reality God took him alive up to heaven: "They slew him not, . . . but it appeared so unto them. But God took him up to Himself" (4:157–58). Islam also denies the cardinal Christian doctrines of Jesus's deity and the atoning value of his death.

Modern Western Theosophical and New Age teachers commonly reject these same central New Testament teachings (except that they do not accept Islam's semidocetic view that the crucifixion of Jesus was really an illusion) and view Jesus as simply one of many great religious teachers.

See also JESUS, HISTORICAL EVIDENCE FOR; QUR'AN

Bibliography. C. Glassé, "Jesus," in *The Concise Encyclopedia of Islam*; E. C. Prophet, *The Lost Years of Jesus: On the Discoveries of Notovitch, Abhedananda, Roerich, and Caspari*.

L. Wilson

JAINISM. Jainism is one of the *sramanic* traditions, like Buddhism, founded in India. Today it is estimated to have between three million and eight million members, most living in central and southern India. Its two primary sects are Svetambara and Digambara, with prominent organizations in North America including the Federation of Jain Associations in North America, Young Jains of America, the Jain Meditation International Center in New York City, and the Anekant Education Foundation.

According to Jainism, its history began 8.4 million years ago with a *jina* who was a giant, but historians trace its origins to the sixth century BC and believe it was founded by Vardhamana (559–527 BC), also known as Mahavira. He was raised in a royal family and left his home at approximately thirty years of age to become a religious ascetic. During this period, it is claimed, he attained perfect enlightenment, developing ideas quite different at points from traditional Hinduism. He began to amass many followers and organized them into orders of monks and nuns. When Mahavira was seventy-two years old, he entered into a religious fast until death. By the first century AD, Jainism had begun to diversify, forming moderate and strict elements. The moderate order was known as Svetambara, "white-clad," while the stricter was called Digambara, "unclothed," because they repudiated all material possessions, even their clothes. Starting in the seventh century, the Svetambaras split into more than eighty subsects. By the thirteenth century, Muslims had invaded India far enough that the Jains suffered persecution and destruction of their temples. South of this invasion, rulers of the Hindu Vijayanagar Empire (1136–1660) protected the Jains who were displaced by the Muslim invasion. During the twentieth century, many Jains migrated to East Africa, the UK, and the US.

Jains believe that all sentient beings are in bondage spiritually and are not aware of their inherent perfection. Due to this unawareness, humans are trapped in their bodies and not able to experience their true selves. One can achieve progress toward liberation through the Three Jewels: correct conception of reality, correct knowledge, and proper conduct.

Jainism believes in an eternally self-existent universe that operates according to intrinsic laws. The universe has cosmic layers: the Supreme Abode (abode of liberated souls), the Upper World (where celestial beings live), the Middle World (earth and the remainder of the universe), the Nether World (levels of different kinds of punishment), Nigoda (abode of lowest forms of life), and Space Beyond (a void where nothing exists). The universe is composed of living beings and nonliving objects.

One of the important scriptures of Jainism is known as the Kalpa Sutra (a collection of twenty-four accounts of Jain tirthankaras). Further, it has forty-five sacred texts, divided into six major groups: Angas, Upangas, Pakinnakas, Chedas, Mulasutras, and Sutras. Originally these were part of an oral tradition, but finally they were written down in the early fourth century BC.

Jainism holds to polytheism, believing in countless gods, but belief in a god or gods is not important for liberation. Mahavira is generally considered the last tirthankara. Each of the tirthankaras, or perfect souls, was a human but attained perfection.

Jains hold that every embodied soul is covered with karma particles and is trapped in the cycle of birth-death-rebirth. Humans are made up of an intrinsically pure soul imbedded in matter, time, space, condition of motion, and condition of stillness. Jains believe that all human life is of great value but that all living beings are equal and should be treated with respect. Additionally, Jainism believes in the accumulation of negative karma, which is counteracted by following specific ethical standards, including vows and certain actions.

Liberation, in Jainism, is attained through three key elements that are performed simultaneously: correct concept of reality, correct knowledge, and correct conduct. This process destroys eight types of karma: illusion, knowledge, vision, natural qualities, body, life span, social status, and bodily pleasures and pains. All persons can attain liberation, which is an existence of pure consciousness and bliss. If one has not attained liberation by the time of physical death, the karma that accompanies one's soul fashions a new body to inhabit. If one has eliminated all the bad karma, then one's soul is liberated from the world forever.

See also HINDUISM; KARMA; POLYTHEISM

Bibliography. A. K. Chatterjee, *Comprehensive History of Jainism*, 2nd ed., 2 vols; P. Dundas, *The Jains*; ; H. W. House, *Charts of Cults, Sects & Religious Movements*; Y. K. Malaiya "An Outline of Jain History," Computer Science Department of Colorado State University, http://www.cs.colostate.edu/~malaiya/jainhout1.html; N. Shah, *Jainism: The World of Conquerors*; V. K. Sharma, *History of Jainism*.

H. W. House

JAPA YOGA. Japa Yoga is the discipline of meditation in which an aspirant recites a mantra either audibly or inaudibly. In the early Hindu traditions, a mantra consisted of a Vedic hymn in temple worship to praise various deities such as Indra, Agni, and Varuna. It could also be used in sacrificial rites to ward off evil and promote blessings. In later times, the concept of mantras expanded to include abstract ideas and more.

The theory of Japa Yoga rests on a metaphysical belief found in the tantric traditions concerning the power of sounds and vibrations in the cosmos. Divine syllables or verbal phrases must be recited and repeated in order to transform the reciter's consciousness. Mantras can include repeated divine syllables, such as Om, which are believed to have secret meanings or powers because they correspond to divine names or divine forms.

The neo-Hindu International Society for Krishna Consciousness teaches devotees how to chant or repeat various mantras to aid meditation and worship of Lord Krishna. Transcendental Meditation introduced the use of murmured mantras to the Western world in the 1960s. The practice of Japa Yoga is also present in some Buddhist schools of meditation like Pure Land Buddhism, where the mantra "*Namu-amida-butsu*" is recited.

See also HINDUISM; INTERNATIONAL SOCIETY FOR KRISHNA CONSCIOUSNESS (ISKCON); PURE LAND BUDDHISM; TANTRIC YOGA; YOGA

Bibliography. H. G. Coward and D. J. Goa, *Mantra: Hearing the Divine in India and America*; M. Eliade, *Yoga: Immortality and Freedom*; S. Strauss, *Positioning Yoga: Balancing Acts across Cultures*.

P. Johnson

JEHOVAH. The word *Jehovah* is used in some English translations of the Old Testament—notably, the King James Version (7 instances) and the American Standard Version (6,889 instances)—to refer to the name of God, but the word does not properly reflect the pronunciation of the Hebrew word for God found about seven thousand times in the Old Testament. Several hundred years ago, the Hebrew consonants for YHWH and the vowels for 'Adonai (meaning Lord) were combined to form Jehovah, creating an English representation of the personal name of God in the Old Testament.

In Exodus 3:13, Moses asks God for his name, signifying his identity. God's response (in v. 14) has been transliterated as either YHWH or JHVH, sometimes referred to as the Tetragrammaton, meaning "the four letters." At the time the Hebrew Bible was written, the Hebrew alphabet contained no written vowels. The vowel sounds were understood by native speakers as they read the text, but the actual written text contained only consonants. The ancient Jewish people knew how the words were pronounced in daily communication, so they were able to fill in the proper pronunciation as they wrote the biblical manuscripts.

The difficulty faced today regarding the correct pronunciation of the divine name of God is related to the fact that Hebrew people considered the name of God to be too sacred to speak. This created two difficulties. First, when the Scriptures were read publicly, the speaker had to use a substitute word, often either Adonai, normally translated as "Lord," or Elohim, normally translated as "God." This Hebrew tradition was carried on by translators of English-language Bibles to the present day for different reasons. One is that there is no absolute certainty regarding the pronunciation of the divine name, though Yahweh is most likely. Moreover, since the generally accepted pronunciation among scholars of the divine name, Yahweh, is not well known among nonscholars, there is concern that use of the Hebrew name for God—Yahweh—may injure Bible sales. More recently the Holman Christian Standard Bible is an example of an English version (produced by evangelical scholars) that uses the name Yahweh numerous times in the Old Testament.

For the English-speaking reader to know whether the word Adonai or Yahweh was behind the word Lord, a convention was adopted of writing LORD, using small capital letters, when the name Yahweh was being translated and using Lord in the conventional way when Adonai was being translated.

The second difficulty, mentioned earlier, was created by the tradition among postexilic Jews of not speaking the divine name. Instead of saying, most likely, Yahweh, they would use an alternate name for God, Adonai, whenever reading the sacred text aloud. In translating the divine name into English, translators preferred JHVH to YHWH, as is common in English Bible translations (for example, instead of Yeshua, they use Joshua, or Elijah instead of Eliyah). Combining JHVH with Adonai, translators came up with JeHoVaH.

Some religious groups, notably the Watch Tower Bible and Tract Society (Jehovah's Witnesses), insist that God must be addressed as Jehovah. This, of course, does not square with the biblical record since the New Testament authors did not use Jehovah or Yahweh but rather used *kurios*, or "Lord," when quoting the Old Testament texts that contained the divine name. Some church fathers, in their writings, did attempt to approximate the Hebrew Yahweh by means of the Greek Iae, with iota for *y*, but this is a rough pronunciation of the divine name. Further, YHWH (or JHVH, Jehovah) does not appear in any of the nearly six thousand Greek manuscripts of the New Testament, although the shortened form Jah appears in the expression "Hallelujah" in Revelation 19:1–6. In fact, Jesus characteristically referred to God in prayer as "Father" but never as "Jehovah."

See also TETRAGRAMMATON

Bibliography. K. S. Hemphill, *The Names of God*; R. Rhodes, *Reasoning*.

E. Shropshire and H. W. House

JEHOVAH'S WITNESSES (JW). The Jehovah's Witnesses are a heretical Christian group best known for their door-to-door and street-corner proselytizing and many religious and social taboos.

History. The JWs were founded by Charles Taze Russell (1852–1916). Russell grew up in Pittsburgh; he was raised nominally as a Presbyterian but had abandoned orthodox Christianity by his teen years. As a young adult, Russell discovered the teachings of a nontrinitarian Adventist group. Their use of the Bible to dispute the doctrine of eternal punishment and to construct a chronology pointing to their own day as the end times rekindled Russell's faith and interest in the Bible.

Following some initial publishing efforts with his Adventist associates, Russell went his own way and in 1879 launched the magazine *Zion's Watch Tower and Herald of Christ's Presence.* The title reflected Russell's teaching that Christ had become invisibly "present" in 1874 and within one generation's time—by 1914—would reconstitute Zion in the Holy Land. In 1881 Russell and his fellow "Bible Students" incorporated the Watch Tower Bible and Tract Society in Brooklyn, which was to evolve from a publishing house to the headquarters (known as Bethel) of an international religious body.

Russell died in 1916 at the height of World War I, believing that the war would prove to be Armageddon and would usher in the millennium. For three years, the organization was rocked by conflict from both within and without. Various factions sought to gain control of the corporation; meanwhile, the society's vocal criticism of the US government's role in the war led to serious legal troubles for the organization. When it was all over, the society's chief legal counsel, J. F. Rutherford (1869–1942), was its second president. "Judge" Rutherford ousted several members of the Watch Tower's board and led the society, and the religion as a whole, in an autocratic fashion.

A top item on Rutherford's teaching agenda was handling the crisis of the apparent failure of Russell's prophetic speculations. At first the 1914 prophetic deadline was "extended" to 1918, and later, most notoriously, to 1925, when Rutherford predicted the patriarchs would be resurrected and the New World would finally begin to appear. When these predictions failed, Rutherford quietly revised the society's chronology to make 1914 the *beginning* of Christ's invisible "presence" and of the final generation before Armageddon—and left the ending date unspecified.

Later Rutherford lived for a number of years in a mansion in San Diego, called Beth Sarim (Hebrew for "house of the princes"), that had been purchased for the patriarchs. In 1931 Rutherford gave the religion's advocates a new name, Jehovah's Witnesses, to distinguish them from the other "Bible Students" groups that had broken ties with the society in the wake of Rutherford's seizing control. The largest of these groups are the Laymen's Home Missionary Movement and the Dawn Bible Students Association. In 1939 he also changed the name of the flagship magazine to *The Watchtower announcing Jehovah's Kingdom.* This name change further distanced the JWs from Russell's teaching that "Christ's presence" had begun in 1874; the change also reinforced the importance of the name Jehovah for the religion.

Rutherford died in 1942 and was succeeded by Nathan Knorr (1905–77). More of an organization man than a personality leader, Knorr made the Brooklyn corporation's board of directors the collective Governing Body for the religion. Watch Tower books were now published anonymously, and programs were developed to train all faithful members to be able to explain and defend the religion's teachings. The society published its own version of the Bible, the New World Translation (NWT), which reflected its specific and sometimes unique doctrinal positions. In addition the society published such traditional Bible study tools as a concordance, a two-volume Bible dictionary (*Aid to Bible Understanding*—later revised as *Insight on the Scriptures*), and a Greek-English interlinear (*The Kingdom Interlinear Translation of the Greek Scriptures*).

Knorr's efforts to make rank-and-file members of the religion biblically literate had a double-edged effect. On the one hand, practically every JW in good standing became a formidable advocate for their doctrines, citing biblical texts on a wide array of subjects and prepared with seemingly knockdown responses to proof texts and arguments for orthodox Christian beliefs. On the other hand, the heavy exposure to biblical texts and the training in religious argumentation gave JWs the tools to become genuinely thoughtful students of the Bible. As a result, many JWs were ready to turn their critical argumentative habits of mind on their own organization's teachings; they needed only something to set them off.

Less than two years before Knorr passed away, the religion suffered a setback that led to widespread questioning of the organization's teachings. In the late 1960s, under Knorr's leadership, the society's publications began speculating that 1975 would mark the end of six thousand years of human history—and that Armageddon should happen immediately, with a paradisiacal thousand years to follow. Many JWs sold their homes, quit their jobs, and put off college, marriage, or having children in order to devote themselves to "the preaching work" in the short time they thought was left. Not surprisingly, when 1975 came and went, a good number of JWs became disillusioned and left the religion.

Over the next several years, many JWs quietly reexamined the society's teachings on biblical chronology and other doctrinal matters. Knorr was succeeded by Frederick W. Franz (1893–1992), a longtime member of the Governing Body and its chief theologian for

decades. Franz had headed up the committee that produced the NWT and, though not professionally trained, was by far the most theologically knowledgeable president the religion has ever had. In 1980 the Knorr-Franz legacy of encouraging members to be biblically knowledgeable and doctrinally critical caught up with the organization. Several leading JWs in the headquarters at Bethel questioned JW teachings on certain subjects and were "disfellowshipped" (the JW term for excommunication). Raymond Franz, a nephew of President Franz, questioned some doctrines and was forced off the Governing Body.

One of the doctrines that JWs at the highest levels were questioning was the division of believers into two classes, an uncountable number of "other sheep" that will "live forever in paradise on Earth" and an "anointed class" of 144,000 Christians destined for life in heaven (see discussion of this teaching below). The doctrine originated during Rutherford's tenure as president when it became evident that the number of JWs was going to exceed 144,000. In principle, all available openings for this anointed class were filled by 1935; since then newer members were understood to be added to its ranks only by the apostasy of older anointed members. Moreover, the spiritual leadership of the religion was supposed to be drawn entirely from the anointed class. As the number of living members of the anointed class dwindled, some JWs began to question the doctrine.

Fred Franz passed away in 1992 and was succeeded by Milton G. Henschel. Under Henschel the Governing Body made further adjustments to the organization's end-times doctrine to accommodate the lengthening years since 1914. The most important of these adjustments was a series of articles in the 1995 *Watchtower* in which the organization abandoned Rutherford's claim that the generation that had seen the events of 1914 would not all die before Armageddon.

For the first time, JWs no longer lived under an eschatological cloud: the "apocalypse delayed" was now only potentially imminent. That same year, 1995, the number of persons considered members of the anointed class reached its lowest figure, about 8,500 (see the table). Since that time, the number has been increasing.

Meanwhile, though, another cloud threatened the organization's integrity. One of the religion's most controversial and infamous teachings was its ban on giving or receiving blood transfusions. Throughout the second half of the twentieth century, the society weathered a variety of legal challenges to this taboo. In the 1990s, though, it became evident that the society itself was vulnerable to litigation against it because of the many members, including children, who died as a result of adhering to the prohibition. Various articles in the religion's magazines detailed certain qualifications but stopped short of retracting the doctrine. Late in the year 2000, Henschel stepped down as the head of the Governing Body and was replaced by Don Adams. The Governing Body members also vacated their positions as the administrative board of directors for the Brooklyn corporation, which was reorganized into separate corporations of more limited scope. The Governing Body in theory became the spiritual and moral authority over the religion but not the administrative and financial officers of its corporate assets. These changes not only made it less likely that the corporations would be targeted for expensive litigation but also placed them in the hands of men who were not all of the "anointed class." (Meanwhile, the number of the "anointed" mysteriously leveled off and even increased slightly.) Thus the likely prospect of that class entirely dying off no longer poses a problem for the administration of the religious corporations.

Statistics. JWs count not attendees but rather active members (whom they call "publishers"), who are not only baptized but are involved in the preaching and literature-distribution work. The number of JWs worldwide exceeded one million in 1965, when almost one in three JWs lived in the US. Already by this time, the JWs were growing faster outside the US, especially in Latin America and the Pacific Rim. Over the next ten years, the worldwide JW population doubled under the urgent expectation that the end would likely come in 1975. Not surprisingly, growth of the religion slowed in the years following the 1975 disappointment, but it picked up under Franz's tenure. The JWs added more than two million new members between 1985 and 1995—with seven of every eight new members coming from outside the US. The religion grew quickly in the former Soviet republics after the fall of the USSR in 1989, with Russia and Ukraine exceeding one hundred thousand members each in about ten years (the growth there has since slowed to a crawl). In 2002 the religion reported over a million members in the US for the first time and over six million worldwide. The largest JW populations outside the US continue to be found in Mexico and Brazil, with sizable followings also in Nigeria, Italy, and Japan. The most dramatic growth of JWs is taking place in Africa (notably in Angola, the Democratic Republic of Congo, Rwanda, and Madagascar).

The broadening influence of the JW religion can be seen from the number of people attending its annual Memorial. This observance is the JW version of Communion and is held on or about Passover. Earlier in the history of the JW, the number of people attending the Memorial was roughly double the number of active members. In the 1980s and 1990s, that number was close to triple the active membership, with the trend reversing in the new century. According to the official Jehovah's Witnesses' website, in 2013 over nineteen million people attended the Memorial worldwide.

Jehovah's Witnesses Statistics, 1965–2013

	1965	1975	1985	1995	2005	2013
Brazil Peak Publishers	36K	103K	178K	417K	638K	767K
Mexico Peak Publishers	33K	80K	173K	444K	594K	807K
Former USSR Peak Publishers	*	*	*	123K	356K	407K
US Peak Publishers	330K	567K	730K	967K	1.04M	1.22M
World Peak Publishers	1.1M	2.2M	3.0M	5.2M	6.6M	8.0M
Memorial Attendees	2M	5M	8M	13M	16M	19M
"Anointed" Participants	11,550	10,550	9,051	8,645	8,524	13,204
Hours Preaching	171M	382M	591M	1,200M	1,278M	1,841M

Notes: "Publishers" are members active in preaching and proclaiming. K = thousand, M = million.

* Information unavailable.

It is interesting to note that only members of the anointed class are permitted to participate by taking of the elements (these are the "anointed" participants shown in the table). In 1965 this meant that about 1 of every 100 members partook of the elements—roughly 1 of every 200 attendees. By 2005 only 1 of every 774 members—and only 1 of every 1,877 persons attending—partook of the elements. Even with the number of attendees per participant falling in recent years to about 1,400, one can only infer that in many JW congregations around the world, no one partakes of the elements at all.

The Watch Tower Society is renowned for the sheer volume of its publication efforts. In 2014 the twice-monthly *Watchtower* magazine was being published in 210 languages and averaging forty-five million copies per issue. (Compare this to *Reader's Digest*, which at its peak sold about sixteen million copies monthly and by 2004 was selling about twelve million.) Of its introductory book *What Does the Bible Really Teach?*, used to instruct prospective converts, 214 million copies have been published in 240 languages since it was first published in 2005. The society had also published, between 1950 and 2014, 184 million NWT Bibles in 121 languages. The organization boasts on its website, jw.org, that it "is the world's most translated website," with some 500 languages represented.

Culture. The JW religion forms a kind of subculture wherever it is found. Its distinctiveness is the result of both the insular nature of JW life and the long, stringent list of activities of the general culture that JWs consider pagan. They spend far more time in weekly meetings (and in preparation for those meetings) with their congregations—in modest buildings called Kingdom Halls—and in small home study groups than the vast majority of churchgoers. They also tend to derive many of their perspectives on the world from their own literature. In addition to the *Watchtower*, the society also publishes *Awake!*—a twice-monthly general-interest magazine that functions as a kind of *Time* magazine for JWs, who are broadly suspicious of the media. JWs are discouraged from participating in civic affairs; they are not permitted to hold government office, serve in the military (even as noncombatants), join a political party, or even vote. They view birthday celebrations, religious holidays such as Christmas and Easter, national holidays such as Thanksgiving in the US, and cultural holidays such as Mother's Day or the New Year as pagan and forbidden.

Until recently the society's publications discouraged but did not forbid outright the pursuit of higher education; although they have not yet begun actively encouraging JWs to seek university degrees, an increasing number appear to be doing so. Unfortunately for the religion, JWs who attain some scholarly proficiency are also more likely to question some of what they were taught at the Kingdom Hall. One of the best examples was the Canadian JW historian James Penton, whose earlier work on the history of JWs in Canada was lauded within the religion. When Penton researched a book on the general history of the JW religion, his discoveries eventually led to his being disfellowshipped.

The practice of disfellowshipping is one of the more onerous elements of JW religion and culture. The JWs take the apostle Paul's teaching on church discipline in 1 Corinthians 5:9–13 to mean that family and friends should have little or no dealings with ex-members. The practice approaches the severity of shunning associated with Amish communities. Moreover, a JW can be disfellowshipped for a wide array of infractions, many of which are unlike anything mentioned by Paul. While Paul did discourage Christians from carrying on friendships with persons claiming to be believers but living unrepentantly in gross sin, he did not say that those who got too friendly with such persons would also be subject to removal from the church. Nor, of course, did he advocate church discipline for those who questioned speculative teachings on arcane doctrinal matters. A JW can be disfellowshipped for questioning doctrines in Watch Tower publications on such matters as biblical chronology and end-times speculations (which happened, for example, to the Swedish JW writer Carl Olof Jonsson) or for eating with an ex-JW (which happened to Raymond Franz, whose employer and landlord was an ex-JW). Naturally, this overly strict form of discipline makes it difficult for members to contemplate leaving the religion or even to question the organization's teachings.

Theology. JWs believe that God is a single person, Jehovah, the Almighty God, who is the Father. They reject the doctrine of the Trinity. God has always existed and is all-powerful, holy, and loving. JWs do not accept the doctrine of divine omnipresence, at least as understood in orthodox theology; in their view, Jehovah God has a "spirit body" and is in some sense localized, though he can make his power and will known anywhere. JWs also deny that God possesses exhaustive foreknowledge of the free acts of his creatures; they argue that God could know such acts but chooses not to exercise that power (a position similar to open theism).

The divine name YHWH is God's name forever, and therefore, according to JWs, a mark of true Christians is their use of this name. Following what was English convention until the mid-twentieth century, JWs use the form Jehovah (which was used, for example, in the American Standard Version [ASV] of 1901). The substitution of LORD or other surrogates for the divine name in Old Testament translations, and its alleged removal from the New Testament, are cited as evidence of apostasy in early Christianity.

According to JWs, God's first creation—and the only creation for which he was directly and immediately responsible—was the Logos, or Word, his only-begotten Son. This Logos, also called Michael the archangel, was a pre-human spirit later known as Jesus. The Logos was "a god," not Almighty God. After making this created Son, Jehovah commissioned him to make the rest of creation, including the angels and the physical universe. JW publications are not clear on whether creation was performed ex nihilo. Jehovah does all his works utilizing what they call "holy spirit," which JWs define as God's invisible active force. This force seems to emanate from Jehovah's spirit body, though no explanation of how this works seems to have been published.

Human beings, in the view of JWs, do not have a soul or spirit distinct from the body.

The soul is the life of the body, and the spirit is the life force that energizes that bodily life. Thus there is no intermediate state between death and resurrection. Physical death is the consequence of Adam's sin. Had Christ not come, that physical death would have been the end of the matter.

In order to make it possible for human beings to live forever, Jehovah sent the Son to live as a human being, Jesus Christ. JWs agree that Jesus was conceived and born of the virgin Mary. He lived a sinless life as a perfect human being—no more and no less. He was neither God incarnate nor even a powerful spirit incarnate, but could only be a perfect man in order to serve as a "corresponding ransom" (1 Tim. 2:6 NWT), laying down an equivalent perfect human life for the one Adam forfeited when he sinned. (This interpretation overreaches the significance of the prefix *anti-* in the Greek *antilutron*, which simply emphasizes the substitutionary purpose of the ransom; and Paul states that Christ died as a ransom "for all," not as a ransom corresponding to Adam.) And in order for the ransom to be effective, JWs argue, Jesus could not have received human life back in the resurrection since to do so would be to take back the "ransom price." Thus Jesus was instead raised (*re-created* would be a better word) as a glorious spirit creature, essentially as he was before, though with more authority. The physical body (or bodies, according to the JWs) in which Jesus appeared to his disciples after the resurrection was a temporary materialized form, not Jesus's own body (which is, again, a "spirit body" akin to those of Jehovah and the angels).

As a result of Christ's ransom sacrifice, all or nearly all people will be resurrected from the dead with an opportunity to prove themselves faithful and worthy of everlasting life. Thus, although JWs attribute salvation to God's "unmerited favor" (i.e., grace), this favor only affords human beings a kind of second chance. In order to be saved, one must believe in Jehovah God and his arrangement for salvation (which includes Jesus's ransom sacrifice). Beyond that belief, one must "take in knowledge" of Jehovah and his purposes (through Bible study using Watch Tower publications), obey God's laws (which include not only legitimate moral standards but also the JWs' distinctive taboos), associate with God's organization (found in the JW religion as represented by the Watch Tower Bible and Tract Society), and participate in the "preaching work" of spreading the message of the kingdom (that Christ's invisible presence began in 1914 and will culminate in the inauguration of a Paradise Earth).

As has already been mentioned, JWs divide the ransomed into the "other sheep" of uncounted millions of believers and the "anointed class" of 144,000 believers, mostly from the first and twentieth centuries. The other sheep are destined for life on Paradise Earth, which will gradually come about when they recondition this earth during the millennium. The anointed class will live in heaven with Jehovah, Jesus, and the angels. This bifurcation distorts not only biblical eschatology but also the biblical teaching on salvation and the church. In JW teaching, the anointed gain final assurance of salvation only at death, while the other sheep must await the end of the millennium—during which their salvation will continue to be provisional—for such complete assurance.

The JW doctrine that Christ became invisibly present in 1914 also bears further elaboration. According to JWs, the Greek word *parousia*, commonly translated "coming" in English versions of the New Testament, should be translated "presence" and can refer to an invisible presence. The question of invisibility is moot since the actual JW view is that Christ will never literally be present on earth at all; his "presence" is strictly figurative, mediated by the work of invisible angels and of the anointed class. However one translates *parousia*, that Christ will visibly and literally return to earth to consummate salvation and judgment is the clear teaching of the New Testament (e.g., Acts 3:20–21; 1 Thess. 4:16; Heb. 9:26–28).

The 1914 date depends on a complicated interpretation of biblical prophecy correlated with an idiosyncratic system of biblical chronology. JWs interpret the seven years of Nebuchadnezzar's madness in Daniel 4 as referring to a period of 2,520 years (since 7 x 360 = 2,520) during which gentile powers supplanted God's kingdom on earth. This period is said to have begun when Nebuchadnezzar destroyed Jerusalem in 607 BC, according to JWs, despite the fact that all biblical scholars date the event to 587–586 BC. (Russell actually dated this event 606 BC; he arrived at the 1914 date by failing to take into account that there is no year zero between 1 BC and AD 1.) The outbreak of World War I in 1914 is claimed as vindication of the chronology, even though gentile powers seem no less entrenched a century later. The emergence of the Watch Tower as a religion sharply separated from "Christendom" in the period 1914–18 is thought to mark the beginning of the reestablishment of Jehovah's kingdom on earth. Not surprisingly, many JWs have therefore viewed advancement in the JW religion as the best "career move" they could make.

JWs hold that the "presence" of Christ will culminate in Armageddon, a war in which the angels will bring destruction on the governments and other institutions of the unbelieving world. Only the "theocratic" government of the JW organization will be left standing. The millennium will then commence—a period of peace and fruitful labor in which JWs and other faithful ones of old will clean up the earth and remake it into a paradise. At the end of the millennium, those who do not remain faithful will be destroyed. The rest of the wicked will be resurrected to face the final judgment, at which they will be destroyed again (what JWs understand to be "the second death" of Revelation 20). Since death is extinction of the person, there will be no unending punishment or torment of the wicked. The Bible "hell" is Sheol, the grave, not a place of torment. The JW doctrine here capitalizes on the confusion engendered by the KJV use of "hell" in the New Testament to translate both *hades* (the Greek word used to translate the Old Testament Hebrew word *sheol*) and *gehenna*. In New Testament usage, hades sometimes refers to death and sometimes to the intermediate state of the dead, whereas Jesus used gehenna to refer to the final state of horrific punishment for the wicked. The real basis for the JWs' rejection of eternal punishment is their belief that it is incompatible with God's love—an understandable objection but one that is not biblically grounded. For JWs today, as for their founder Russell, the reasonableness of Christianity depends on a rejection of the doctrine of eternal punishment.

See also HEAVEN, BIBLICAL DOCTRINE OF; JOHN 1:1; NEW WORLD TRANSLATION; WATCHTOWER, THE

Bibliography. *Official Publications (All of the Watch Tower Bible and Tract Society):* Awake! (periodical); Jehovah's Witnesses website, jw.org.; *Jehovah's Witnesses: Proclaimers of God's Kingdom; Reasoning from the Scriptures; The Watchtower announcing Jehovah's Kingdom* (periodical); *What Does the Bible Really Teach? Other:* J. Bergman, *Jehovah's Witnesses: A Comprehensive and Selectively Annotated Bibliography;* R. M. Bowman Jr., *Jehovah's Witnesses;* R. Franz, *Crisis of Conscience;* H. W. House, *Charts of Cults, Sects, & Religious Movements;* C. O. Jonsson, *The Gentile Times Reconsidered: Chronology and Christ's Return;* M. J. Penton, *Apocalypse Delayed: The Story of Jehovah's Witnesses.*

R. M. Bowman Jr.

JESUS, HISTORICAL EVIDENCE FOR. *The Four Gospels.* By far the most extensive sources we have for the life of Jesus are the four canonical Gospels: Matthew, Mark,

Luke, and John. Some biblical critics doubt the historical reliability of these sources, believing that the four evangelists so embellished the story of Jesus that very little accurate history remains. Nevertheless, evangelicals accept their testimony at face value. In rough outline, the Gospels tell us that Jesus (1) was born of a virgin in Bethlehem near the end of the life of Herod the Great, (2) was raised in Nazareth, (3) was baptized by John the Baptist, (4) conducted a ministry of teaching and healing in Galilee and Judea, (5) gathered a large following of disciples, twelve of whom he appointed as apostles, (6) taught that the kingdom of God was present in his ministry, (7) proclaimed that he was in fact the Son of God, (8) engaged in a controversy with the Jewish leaders in Jerusalem, who accused him of blasphemy, (9) was crucified on the authority of Pontius Pilate and buried in a tomb owned by Joseph of Arimathea, and (10) rose from the dead three days later. Liberal and skeptical scholars typically deny that Jesus was born of a virgin, that he claimed to be divine, and that he rose from the dead, but generally accept the rest of the above summary as historical. Recent studies by such scholars as Richard Burridge and Richard Bauckham have done much to rehabilitate the Gospels as biographical accounts of Jesus.

Roman Sources. Several ancient Roman documents mention Jesus. Three in particular deserve attention. Suetonius, in his *De vita Caesarum*, remarks that Emperor Claudius "expelled the Jews from Rome on account of the riots in which they were constantly indulging at the instigation of Chrestus" (cf. Acts 18:2). Most scholars agree that the reference to "Chrestus" is actually a reference to "Christ" and that Suetonius is alluding to conflicts between non-Christian and Christian Jews in Rome around AD 49.

The historian Tacitus, writing about 115, describing Nero's persecution of Christians fifty years earlier, explained that "Christ, during the reign of Tiberius, had been executed

by the procurator Pontius Pilate." Here we have excellent confirmation of one of the key events in the Gospels, the crucifixion of Jesus.

Pliny the Younger, governor of Pontus and Bithynia from 111 to 112, wrote a letter to Emperor Trajan asking advice on how to treat Christians, by that time an illegal sect. In part of the letter, he had this to say about Christians: "It was their habit on a fixed day to assemble before daylight and recite by turns a form of words to Christ as a god." Though not saying anything about Jesus's life, Pliny does tell us that Jesus was worshiped by his followers and that the Christian movement had spread not only to Rome but to northern Asia Minor as well.

Rabbinic Sources. The Babylonian Talmud appears to refer to Jesus twice. In *b. Sanhedrin* 43a, we read: "On the eve of Passover Yeshua [Jesus] was hanged." It goes on to say that he was executed "because he . . . practiced sorcery and enticed Israel to apostasy." The second reference is *b. Sanhedrin* 107b, which records an alleged meeting between Jesus and Rabbi Joshua that concludes with the accusation: "Jesus the Nazarene practiced magic and led Israel astray." Those texts are of limited value historically because of their late date (ca. 500). Nevertheless, they are possible echoes of the early Jewish reaction against Jesus that we find in the Gospels (cf. Matt. 12:24; Luke 23:2). It is also clear that the Jews did not deny what the Gospels affirm—that Jesus was a healer and miracle worker—but simply attributed his powers to magic.

Josephus. Without doubt the best extrabiblical evidence for Jesus is found in the works of Josephus, the first-century Jewish historian. In his *Antiquities* (20.200), he mentions the execution of James, Jesus's brother: "He convened a judicial session of the Sanhedrin and brought before it the brother of Jesus, the one called Christ . . . —James by name." Few doubt the authenticity of this text, and the indirect way in which Josephus refers to

Jesus as "the one called Christ" indicates that he has mentioned him before. And indeed there is an earlier reference to Jesus known as the *Testimonium Flavianum* (*Antiquities* 18.63–64), which reads:

Now, there was about this time Jesus, a wise man, *if it be lawful to call him a man*, for he was a doer of surprising works, a teacher of such men as receive the truth with pleasure. He drew over to him both many of the Jews, and many of the Gentiles. *He was the Christ.* And when Pilate, at the suggestion of principal men among us, had condemned him to the cross, those that loved him at the first did not forsake him; *for he appeared to them alive again the third day, as the divine prophets had foretold these and ten thousand other wonderful things concerning him.* And the tribe of Christians, so named for him, are not extinct to this day.

Some scholars dismiss this entire text as a later Christian interpolation, but the later reference regarding James makes it virtually certain that at least part of the *Testimonium* is authentic. The italicized portions are clearly Christian additions, but read without those lines, we probably have what Josephus wrote. This means that Josephus knew that Jesus was a religious teacher and a worker of miracles, that the Jewish leaders conspired to have him crucified by Pilate, and that his followers persisted into Josephus's own day.

Other Gospels? Other written accounts of the life and teaching of Jesus have also appeared in history and been appealed to for historical information about Jesus. Such works include the *Gospel of Thomas*, a second-century work, which some view as gnostic; the *Gospel of Peter*, which portrays a docetic, nonhuman Jesus; various "infancy" gospels that fill in the gaps of Jesus's early years; the Muslim-inspired (or edited) *Gospel of Barnabas*, which claims that Judas replaced Jesus on the cross; and

other stories that have Jesus traveling to India or living with the Essenes. However, none of these documents have any claim to historical reliability, all having been written very late (many in the Middle Ages) and obviously attempting to supplement or "correct" the New Testament Gospels.

See also CHRIST, NATURES AND ATTRIBUTES OF; DOCETISM; JESUS, MORMON VIEW OF; RESURRECTION OF JESUS

Bibliography. P. W. Barnett, *Jesus and the Logic of History*; R. Bauckham, *Jesus and the Eyewitnesses*; C. L. Blomberg, *The Historical Reliability of the Gospels*; D. L. Bock, *Studying the Historical Jesus*; F. F. Bruce, *Jesus and Christian Origins outside the New Testament*; R. Burridge, *What Are the Gospels?*; P. R. Eddy and G. A. Boyd, *The Jesus Legend*; C. S. Evans, *Fabricating Jesus: How Modern Scholars Distort the Gospels*; C. S. Keener, *The Historical Jesus of the Gospels*; E. M. Yamauchi, "Jesus outside the New Testament: What Is the Evidence?," in *Jesus under Fire*, edited by Michael J. Wilkins and J. P. Moreland; R. E. Van Voorst, *Jesus outside the New Testament*.

S. B. Cowan

JESUS, MORMON VIEW OF. Mormons insist that their belief in Jesus Christ eminently qualifies them as Christians. His name is part of the official name of their religion (the Church of Jesus Christ of Latter-day Saints). Their keystone scripture, the Book of Mormon, goes so far as to represent the faithful living even before Christ's earthly life as explicitly Christ-centered: "We talk of Christ, we rejoice in Christ, we preach of Christ, we prophesy of Christ" (2 Nephi 25:23). Joseph Smith once said, "The fundamental principles of our religion is the testimony of the apostles and prophets concerning Jesus Christ, 'that he died, was buried, and rose again the third day, and ascended up into heaven'; and all other things are only appendages to these, which pertain to our religion" (*Elders' Journal* 1, July 1838, 44). While there is no disputing that Mormons are sincere in their profession of faith in Jesus Christ, it is nevertheless appropriate to ask what Mormons believe about him.

Traditional Beliefs about Jesus Christ Affirmed in Mormonism. LDS doctrine agrees with traditional Christian beliefs about Jesus in some very important respects. Most notably, Mormons accept the historical statements of the New Testament Gospels regarding the birth, life, teachings, miracles, death, burial, resurrection, and ascension of Jesus. Mormons affirm that Jesus was born of Mary in Bethlehem; that he lived a sinless life; that he performed such miracles as healings, exorcisms, and raising people from the dead; that he was crucified; and that he rose physically from the grave with an immortal human body. Mormon leaders and theologians, such as James Talmage and Bruce McConkie, have written voluminously and at times passionately about the life, death, and resurrection of Jesus.

Mormon beliefs about Christ prior to and subsequent to his mortal life on earth also coincide in some significant ways with traditional Christian belief. Mormon doctrine identifies the premortal Jesus Christ as Jehovah, the God of the Old Testament. LDS scripture affirms, "We believe in God, the Eternal Father, and in His Son, Jesus Christ, and in the Holy Ghost" (Article of Faith 1). Admittedly, some important differences, to be addressed below, underlie these apparent agreements. Mormons also affirm "that Christ will reign personally upon the earth" in a literal second coming (Article of Faith 10).

Finally, Mormons share important beliefs with historic Christianity regarding the essential role of Jesus Christ in salvation; in fact, Mormons quite often refer to him simply as "the Savior." Mormonism teaches that salvation comes only through "the Atonement of Christ" and that "faith in the Lord Jesus Christ" is the first principle of the gospel (Articles of Faith 3, 4). Again, there are important differences as well with regard to these points of agreement.

Mormon Approach to Knowledge of Jesus Christ. Mormonism does not base its views of Jesus Christ on the Bible alone. The LDS view of Christ is based on the four standard works, or Mormon scriptures, which include the Bible (with textual changes made by Joseph Smith), the Book of Mormon, the Doctrine and Covenants (D&C), and the Pearl of Great Price. Mormons accept what these four scriptural canons say about Christ as interpreted by their living prophet (the current LDS Church president) and other living authorities. The statement of Robert J. Matthews is representative: "I do not believe any person can know enough about the real Jesus without knowing what the Book of Mormon, the Doctrine and Covenants, the Pearl of Great Price, and the Joseph Smith Translation have to say" (viii). Joseph Fielding McConkie has warned that "there is no salvation in the worship of a false Christ" and that the LDS Church exists on the premise "that a true knowledge of Christ, the purity of his doctrines, and the authority to act in his name were restored to the earth through the instrumentality of the Prophet Joseph Smith" (3).

Mormonism's Novel Teachings about Jesus Christ. On the basis of its expanded canon and the authoritative pronouncements of its prophets and apostles, the LDS Church holds to a view of Christ that differs in dramatic ways from the traditional (and biblical) doctrine. Gordon B. Hinckley, former president of the LDS Church, admitted as much: "As a Church we have critics, many of them. They say we do not believe in the traditional Christ of Christianity. There is some substance to what they say" ("We Look to Christ," 90).

Mormon beliefs about Jesus differ radically most specifically with regard to his divine nature and identity. To understand how this is so, one must understand the larger picture of Mormon theology. The LDS Church teaches that God the Father and Heavenly Mother are the literal heavenly parents of billions of spirit children. Their firstborn spirit son, Jesus Christ, was also the first of their children to become a God. The Mormon "Godhead" is not one God but a ruling council of three Gods. This means that when Mormonism affirms that Jesus Christ was "Jehovah," it is actually saying that Jesus was one of at least three Gods (four, if one counts Heavenly Mother) that existed before the world was made.

One regrettable consequence of this faulty theology is that Mormons do not pray to Jesus Christ. The Old Testament constantly represents Jehovah as the *only* God to whom people should pray (e.g., Deut. 9:26; 1 Kings 8:22–30; Ps. 5:1–3). The New Testament teaches believers to pray both to the Father (e.g., Matt. 6:6–13; Luke 11:1–3; Eph. 3:14–16) and to Jesus (John 14:14; Acts 1:24–25; 7:59–60; Rom. 10:12–13; etc.). Yet Mormons refuse prayer to Jesus Christ. This fact, in the broader context of the LDS worldview, calls into question the validity of concessions by some evangelical scholars that Mormons affirm "the full divinity of Jesus Christ" (Blomberg and Robinson, 142) or "that Jesus was fully God" (Millet and McDermott, 16). To affirm that Jesus is fully divine or fully God while redefining divinity and God in unbiblical ways is unacceptable.

In Mormon theology, Jesus is our "elder brother," the first of our spirit brethren to become a God. The natural implication, of course, is that we can do the same. Hence Mormonism flatly rejects any permanent or essential qualitative difference between Jesus Christ and the rest of the human race. All human beings, all angels, and all Gods are members of the same species, beings of the same kind, with the same divine potential. Jesus Christ is simply further than we are along the path of what Mormons traditionally have called "eternal progression."

There is no room in Mormon theology for the traditional Christian doctrine of the two natures of Christ, according to which Jesus Christ is like us with respect to his human nature but unlike us with respect to his divine nature. Mormonism recognizes only one nature in Christ, the divine-human nature inherited from our common heavenly parents, who are themselves glorified physical beings. Lucifer himself was our spirit brother and therefore had the same potential, but he failed to make the right choices as Jesus did (Christensen). This is the context in which Mormonism's doctrine that Jesus and Lucifer were "spirit brothers" should be understood.

The belief that Jesus was our elder spirit brother in heaven and is one of God's billions of spirit children leads to some other doctrinal problems. For example, Mormons believe that Jesus's conception and birth on earth were unique, but they explain it in a rather different way. Jesus was unique in that he was "the only person on earth to be born of a mortal mother and an immortal father," so that God the Father was "the literal father of Jesus Christ" in the flesh (Church of Jesus Christ of Latter-day Saints, 64). Although Mormons say that Mary was a "virgin," this affirmation is at least in tension with the claim that the Father, who is supposed to be an exalted man with a literal body of flesh and bones, is the "literal" father of Jesus's human body. The logical implication is that Jesus was conceived through a procreative act of God and Mary, a conclusion that Mormons often dismiss as an anti-Mormon slur. If so, though, it is odd that the LDS Church has never officially repudiated the idea, and in fact several Mormon leaders over the years from Brigham Young to Bruce McConkie have apparently embraced it. By contrast, in orthodox Christian theology such an idea is adamantly and consistently rejected. God is incorporeal Spirit, and Jesus Christ was conceived in the Virgin Mary through the supernatural agency of the Holy Spirit (Matt. 1:18–25; Luke 1:35).

Mormon doctrine also presents a rather different understanding of Christ's work of salvation. The basic facts are the same—Jesus lived a sinless life, died on the cross, and rose from the dead—but the way they are interpreted differs. The LDS Church teaches that Jesus accomplished the atonement primarily (though not exclusively) in Gethsemane by literally bleeding "from every pore" (Mosiah 3:7; D&C 19:18) during the ordeal. This idea is based on a misreading of Luke 22:44, which reports that "his sweat was as it were great drops of blood falling down to the ground" (KJV). Luke actually says that the beads of sweat falling from Jesus's face were *like* large drops of blood, not that they *were* blood. In any case, the New Testament consistently teaches that Jesus atoned for our sins specifically by his death on the cross (Matt. 20:28; Rom. 5:6–10; 1 Cor. 1:18; 2:2; 15:3; Eph. 2:16; Col. 1:20; 1 Pet. 2:24).

Finally, Mormonism teaches that Jesus's atonement and resurrection guarantee resurrection to immortal life for practically everybody—Christian or not, moral, immoral, and heinously criminal—in one of three heavenly kingdoms (D&C 76). (The only exceptions are the "sons of perdition," incorrigibly evil people, including some ex-Mormons.) Even the lowest and least glorious of these kingdoms is far more wonderful than this present mortality on earth. This resurrection to immortality is sometimes called unconditional salvation, and everyone except the sons of perdition will receive it eventually by repentance and faith in Jesus Christ, though for most people their conversion will come only in the spirit world after death. Ironically, for the vast majority of the human race how they live and whether they come to faith in this life has no ultimate bearing on their eternal future since they will be given an opportunity for salvation in the next life. Thus Mormonism teaches a form of near-universalism in which repentance and faith in this life are not necessary.

On the other hand, entrance into the highest of the heavenly realms, the celestial kingdom, where Heavenly Father lives, requires far more than repentance and faith in Christ. It requires baptism and reception of the "gift of the Holy Ghost" administered by a Mormon with the proper priesthood authority; obedience to the laws and ordinances of the LDS Church, including tithing and certain food and drink taboos (called the Word of Wisdom); and regular participation in the secret ceremonies of the LDS temples. This "conditional salvation" is obtained by grace and works, not by grace alone.

The Bible, contrary to LDS doctrine, consistently teaches that human beings face two possible futures. The wicked or unredeemed will be resurrected only to face, in their bodies, their condemnation to eternal punishment (Dan. 12:2; Matt. 10:28; 25:46; John 5:28–29; Acts 24:15). They derive no benefit from Christ's atoning death. The righteous "in Christ"—those who belong to Christ—will be made alive and given immortality (1 Cor. 15:22–23, 53–54), eternal life in God's presence as a free gift in Christ (Rom. 6:23; see also John 3:16–18; 5:24). They become like Christ in his glorified humanity, but they do not become gods or beings of the same divine essence and powers as Christ. Jesus Christ remains forever unique as the one and only God-man (John 1:1, 14–18; Col. 2:9; Heb. 1:8–12; 13:8).

See also ARTICLES OF FAITH, MORMON; BOOK OF MORMON; CHURCH OF JESUS CHRIST OF LATTER-DAY SAINTS; FIRST VISION; JOSEPH SMITH TRANSLATION OF THE BIBLE; MASONRY (LDS); THEOLOGICAL METHOD OF THE CHURCH OF JESUS CHRIST OF LATTER-DAY SAINTS

Bibliography. C. L. Blomberg and S. E. Robinson, *How Wide the Divide? A Mormon and an Evangelical in Conversation*; J. Christensen, "I Have a Question," *Ensign*; Church of Jesus Christ of Latter-day Saints, *Gospel Principles*; *Elders' Journal* (LDS periodical); C. R. Harrell, *"This Is My Doctrine": The Development of Mormon Theology*; G. B. Hinckley, "We Look to Christ," https://www.lds.org/general-conference/2002/04/we-look-to-christ?lang=eng; G. B. Hinckley et al., "The Living Christ: The Testimony of the Apostles," *Ensign*; D. H. Ludlow, ed., *Encyclopedia of Mormonism*, 4 vols.; R. J. Matthews, *Behold the Messiah*; B. L. McConkie, *The Millennial Messiah*; McConkie, *The Mortal Messiah*, 4 vols.; McConkie, *The Promised Messiah*; J. F. McConkie, *Here We Stand*; R. L. Millet, *A Different Jesus? The Christ of the Latter-day Saints*; R. L. Millet and G. R. McDermott, *Claiming Christ: A Mormon–Evangelical Debate*; J. F. Smith et al., "The Father and the Son: A Doctrinal Exposition by the First Presidency and the Quorum of the Twelve Apostles"; J. E. Talmage, *Jesus the Christ*; C. Volluz, "Jesus Christ as Elder Brother," *BYU Studies*.

R. M. Bowman Jr.

JIHAD. *Jihad* is the term used in Islam for divinely sanctioned warfare—whether against an external human enemy or against one's internal evil inclination. Linguistically, the root of *jihad* means "to struggle, to exert oneself," and in the Qur'an many references to jihad and its cognates are not military in nature. For this reason, the standard verses describing warfare and martyrdom in the Qur'an use mostly the term *qital* (fighting) for Muslim warfare. However, in the later verses of the Qur'an (e.g., sura 8:72; 9:19) and especially the hadith (tradition) literature that spans the first three centuries of Islam, jihad, usually accompanied by the phrase "in the way of God [Allah]," came to signify fighting.

The standard verse used to describe jihad is Qur'an 9:111: "Allah has bought from the believers their lives and their wealth in return for Paradise; they fight in the way of Allah, kill and are killed. That is a true promise from Him . . . and who fulfils His promises better than Allah? Rejoice then in the bargain you have made with him; for that is the great triumph." Most of the Qur'anic teachings concerning jihad are to be found in suras 3, 8–9, 33, and 61, all of which are closely related to battles that Muhammad fought.

Later Muslim teaching on the subject of jihad is fleshed out in the hadith literature, in which jihad is described as the pinnacle of Islam, with unique salvational qualities being accorded both to fighters and to martyrs. Muslim legal scholars (*fuqaha*) developed the doctrine of jihad in order to delineate the type of warfare that had the spiritual rank of jihad. The warfare had to take place between Muslims and infidels, to be proclaimed by a legitimate leader (either a caliph or an imam), and to be accompanied by an invitation either to convert to Islam, submit, and pay the *jizya* tax, or to fight. Those who could participate in a jihad had to be Muslim, male, free, sane, mature, and able bodied. The tactics used in (offensive) jihad were limited: indiscriminate killing was forbidden, and the killing of women, children, the elderly, and monks was also prohibited. However, in cases when Muslim countries were attacked by infidels, some of these prohibitions lapsed.

Jihad also involves personal struggle against the lower self (*nafs*, "soul"). This aspect of jihad is particularly popular among Sufi mystics, who taught that the lower self was more dangerous than human enemies and more difficult to overcome. Much of the Qur'anic terminology referring to Muhammad's temporal battles was reinterpreted by Sufis in terms of this struggle.

Contemporary Muslim teaching concerning jihad either is very apologetic, avoiding (or in some cases denying) the military meaning of the term, or, if associated with radical Muslims, is very aggressive and expansive in defining the boundaries of legitimate warfare. Today the term *jihad* is very freely used throughout the Muslim world, and it is difficult to say whether the classical definitions of the term have much contemporary relevance.

See also HADITH; ISLAM, BASIC BELIEFS OF; JIZYA; MUHAMMAD; QUR'AN

Bibliography. D. Cook, *Understanding Jihad*; M. Fakhry, trans., *The Qur'an: A Modern English Version*; M. K. Haykal, *al-Jihad wa-l-qital fi al-siyasa al-shara'iyya*; A. Morabia, *Le Ğihad dans l'Islam medieval*; R. Peters, *Islam and Colonialism*.

D. B. Cook

JINA. In Jainism *jinas*, or tirthankaras, are persons who, upon liberation from the four karmas that obscure the original state of the soul, revive the teaching and practice of Jainism. Twenty-four jinas arise during each time cycle of the universe, the last jina in our current cycle being Mahavira (599–527 BC).

See also JAINISM

Bibliography. J. P. Jain, *Religion and Culture of the Jains*.

M. C. Hausam

JIRIKI. *Jiriki* (Japanese, "own-power") is a term used in Japanese Buddhism to refer to the inward spirituality of self-effort as a means of attaining enlightenment. Jiriki is contrasted with *tariki* (other power), or reliance on external powers such as Buddhas and bodhisattvas in the quest for liberation. The jiriki approach focuses on the power of the devotee's virtuous actions and meditation practices to facilitate sudden enlightenment, rather than looking to the favor or gracious power of a higher being to attain release from ignorance and illusion. Historically, this contrast between religious self-empowerment and relying on the assistance of Buddhas and bodhisattvas manifested itself in twelfth-century Japan when Myoan Eisai (1141–1215) worked to establish the Rinzai school of Zen (a form of jiriki), whereas Shinran Shonin (1173–1263) advocated Pure Land Buddhism (a tariki sect). The practices of most schools of Buddhism (outside of Zen and Pure Land) fall within a spectrum somewhere between the extremes of pure jiriki and pure tariki.

See also PURE LAND BUDDHISM; ZEN BUDDHISM

Bibliography. B. Faure, *Visions of Power: Imagining Medieval Japanese Buddhism*; J. D. Loori, *The Heart of Being: Moral and Ethical Teachings of Zen Buddhism*; D. S. Wright, *Philosophical Meditations on Zen Buddhism*.

M. Power

JIZYA. The *jizya* is the tax, usually called a "poll-tax," levied on non-Muslims under Muslim political control. It is based on Qur'an 9:29: "Fight those among the People of the Book [Jews and Christians] who do not believe in Allah and the Last Day, do not forbid what Allah and His Apostle have forbidden and do not profess the true religion until they pay the poll-tax out of hand and submissively." Payment of the jizya tax therefore is an integral part of the *dhimmi* system (whereby the "people of the book" were protected under certain conditions). Payment of the tax and the desire to avoid payment contributed significantly to conversion to Islam in a number of areas (Iraq, Iran, and North Africa, especially).

During the early period of Islam, there were different types of jizya: it could be levied on individuals, it could be a land tax (the vast majority of the land-working peasant population of the Middle East were non-Muslim), or it could be levied on a community as a whole. In early Muslim Iraq, the tax was generally a dinar per person per year, whereas in Syria and Egypt the payment tended to be in kind or levied on whole communities. In most cases, monks and the disabled were exempt, but this exemption led (especially in Egypt) to a growth of the monastic community and an eventual removal of the exemption.

Conversion to Islam has been linked to the poll tax, probably not because of the economic burden it imposed on the non-Muslim population—which was considerable, but not different from the many other taxes imposed during the pre-Islamic period—but because of the humiliation that accompanied the payment of the jizya. Certainly by the middle Islamic period (twelfth to fourteenth centuries), in many areas the payment of the jizya was part of a number of humiliating rites that non-Muslims had to go through according to the Pact of 'Umar (document stating the terms under which "people of the book" could be "protected").

The Ottomans in the Middle East and the Mughals in India for the most part did not distinguish the jizya tax from other land taxes; however, certain zealous rulers such as Aurangzeb (r. 1658–1707), the last of the great Mughals, did attempt to impose the jizya with all of its religious connotations on the Hindu population. This led directly to numerous revolts and ultimately to the overthrow of Muslim rule. By the middle of the nineteenth century, the jizya tax was mostly abolished throughout the Muslim world.

See also DHIMMI; ISLAM, BASIC BELIEFS OF

Bibliography. M. Fakhry, trans., *The Qur'an: A Modern English Version*; S. Goitein, *A Mediterranean Society*; M. Khadduri, trans., *The Islamic Law of Nations: Shaybani's Siyar*; Khadduri, *War and Peace in the Law of Islam*.

D. B. Cook

JOHN 1:1. One of the most influential—and in modern times controversial—verses in the Bible, John 1:1 is a crucial text in debates about the person of Christ. Orthodox Christianity understands the verse to affirm that Christ, prior to becoming a human being, was existing eternally, personally distinct from God (that is, the Father), and yet was himself no less than God.

Liberal theology generally views John 1:1 as a transitional form marking Christianity's development from an original Jewish messianism into a Hellenistic philosophical system. In the Joseph Smith Translation

(an "inspired" version used by Mormons), the verse is rewritten: "In the beginning was the gospel preached through the Son. And the gospel was the word, and the word was with the Son, and the Son was with God, and the Son was of God." Mary Baker Eddy, the founder of Christian Science, understood the verse to mean that "the Christ-healing . . . was practiced even before the Christian era" (29). Various Oneness Pentecostal writers (who hold that Jesus is the Father manifested in the flesh) have argued that the middle clause should be translated "and the Word was pertaining to God," meaning that Christ was in God's mind as a plan to manifest himself as a human being. The best-known alternative view of the text, though, is that of the Jehovah's Witnesses (JWs). They (along with a smattering of other antitrinitarians of the past two centuries) render the last part of the verse "and the Word was a god" and understand this to mean that the prehuman Christ was a mighty, divine spirit created by God before everything else.

It is customary in the exegesis of John 1:1 to divide it into three clauses, shown below in an interlinear translation:

In [the] beginning was the Word
En archē ēn ho logos (A)

And the Word was with God
Kai ho logos ēn pros ton theon (B)

And God was the Word
Kai theos ēn ho logos (C)

The meaning of all three clauses is contested.

Clause A: The Word was "in the beginning." Most interpreters, orthodox or not, have understood this clause to affirm that the Word's existence was without beginning because the Word already "was" when creation began (cf. the opening words, *en archē*, with the same opening words in the ancient Greek versions of Gen. 1:1). Thus Oneness Pentecostals and many Unitarians have acknowledged that the Word existed eternally but as something in God's mind, not as a concrete person. The Arian approach, however, represented today especially by JWs, denies that this clause implies the eternal preexistence of Christ. Historically, JWs have claimed that the word "beginning" here (*archē*) actually means that Christ was the beginning or first creature. Though some JWs continue to make this claim, more recently others have argued that John's statement implies only that Christ existed before the physical creation (Stafford, 315–20). Such a claim appears moot in light of the fact that even JWs acknowledge that all things, including all spiritual creatures such as angels and those that became demons, were created through Christ. Moreover, in John 1:1–3 the created things antedated by the Word are spoken of in the most general and universal terms, and the confession parallels Colossians 1:16–17, where the "all things" that were created in and through the Son explicitly include spiritual, supernatural powers.

Clause A, then, speaks of the Word as existing already before anything, whether material or spiritual, was created. But who or what is this Word? The succeeding clauses address this question.

Clause B: The Word was "with God." Orthodox Christians understand this clause to affirm that the preexistent Christ existed in relationship with the Father, here called God. Unorthodox views of this middle clause are quite varied.

As noted earlier, those who deny that Christ existed before his human conception argue that the Word was not the person later known as Jesus Christ but rather God's plan or intention to reveal or manifest himself in Christ. Two points are often made in support of this interpretation.

First, the term *Word* (Greek, *logos*) is said to prove this understanding. *Logos* had many denotations (word, saying, message, account, reason, etc.), but its application to a person would have been very unusual indeed. Those who deny that the Logos was a person, though, have difficulty specifying a denotation for the term that falls within ancient Greek usage. The concept of "plan" does not seem to have been one of the meanings conveyed by the ancient word *logos*. The orthodox view embraces one or two of the most common meanings of *logos*—"word" and "reason"—and sees both as applied in a special way to the preexistent Son. This application of an abstract noun to a divine person has precedent: Paul, for example, calls the incarnate Christ God's "wisdom" (1 Cor. 1:30).

Second, those who deny the personhood of the Logos sometimes argue that clause B should be translated "the Word was pertaining to God." The basis for this claim is that the expression *pros ton theon* (here usually translated "with God") is rendered "pertaining to God" in a few places. However, in all such texts the actual phrase is "things pertaining to God" and is fronted by the neuter plural article (*ta pros ton theon*, Rom. 15:17; Heb. 2:17; 5:1; see also Exod. 4:16; 18:19; Deut. 31:27 in the Septuagint). This idiom is not in use in John 1:1.

In biblical Greek, the phrase *pros ton theon* is almost always used in contexts of persons speaking "to God" (very common), of persons coming to or before God literally or in worship (e.g., Exod. 19:21, 24; 24:2; Hos. 5:4; Zeph. 3:2 in the Septuagint; 1 Thess. 1:9; Rev. 12:5), or of persons existing in some positive relationship with God (Acts 24:16; Rom. 5:1; 1 John 3:21). In John 13:3, John states that Jesus had come from God and was returning "to God" (*pros ton theon*). This is the only other occurrence of the phrase in the Gospel besides John 1:1–2 and strongly supports the orthodox understanding that Jesus was the Word existing in personal relationship with God before coming to the earth as a man.

JWs raise a rather different perspective on clause B. They agree that it speaks of Christ as a preexistent (though not eternal) person coexisting with God. But this affirmation, they argue, flatly contradicts the orthodox claim that the preexistent Christ was God. That is, they find it contradictory to affirm both that the Word was *with* God and that the Word *was* God.

Orthodox scholars have always been aware of this apparent contradiction and have addressed it from a couple of different perspectives. The best explanation begins with the observation that the two occurrences of "God" (*ton theon* and *theos*) have the same denotation (God, the Divine Being) but refer to two distinct persons (*ton theon* referring here to the Father, *theos* referring here to the Son). This explanation certainly has contextual support since no denotative difference can be shown between the two uses (see below on clause C) and since the Son clearly was with the Father (cf. 1 John 1:1–3). The weakness of this explanation as stated is that it does not address the difficulty logically of the two occurrences of "God" having different referents without implying two Gods. Distinguishing the two occurrences as expressing personal identity (*ton theon* = the Father) in contrast to nature (*theos* = God by nature, Deity) may be reading more into the anarthrous *theos* (i.e., *theos* lacking the definite article) than is warranted (see below) and in any case doesn't really resolve the logical question.

It may be best to recognize these opening lines of the Gospel of John as intentionally paradoxical: somehow this Word who was with God was also himself God. The biblical descriptions of the Son frankly challenge human categories and language of identity and referent. Somehow Christ is both Lord and God (John 1:1, 18, 23; 12:37–41; 20:28), yet he is also the Son of God, the One sent by God the Father (John 1:14, 18; 5:17–26; 20:17; etc.). Neither John nor the other New Testament writers attempt to offer any logical or philosophical explanation for the paradox

since their focus is on confessing who Jesus is and what he did. The later orthodox distinction between the relation of the three persons *ad intra* (within the Divine Being) and *ad extra* (to those outside the Divine Being) may be as far as we can or should go: God (the Father) and the Word are distinct referents ("persons") *ad intra* but are one and the same referent ("God") *ad extra*.

Clause C: The Word was "God." The last clause of John 1:1 is the most often discussed, and even its translation is a matter of never-ending debate. John 1:1c has been cited to prove two opposite heresies. Oneness Pentecostals, like the ancient Monarchians, take the clause to mean that the Word was the one person known as God, namely, the Father, simply in another mode or role. Their interpretation gives the third clause full weight but at the cost of directly contradicting the second clause. The JWs, like the ancient Arians, take the clause to mean that the Word was a second deity subordinate to the absolute God. Their interpretation avoids a contradiction between the second and third clauses but at the expense of weakening the import of the third clause. The truth is to be found between these two extremes, in affirming both that the Word was God and that he was personally distinct from God the Father.

The New World Translation (NWT), the Bible version published for the JWs, renders John 1:1c "and the Word was a god." The NWT was not the first to use this rendering: it was used in several Unitarian versions in the late 1700s and early 1800s and in Benjamin Wilson's Emphatic Diaglott (1864), which the JWs also have published and from which they probably derived the rendering.

The basic rationale for the rendering "a god" is that the grammar allows it (because *theos* does not have the article) and the context supposedly requires it (because the Word cannot be God if he is "with God"). We have already addressed the contextual argument above in our discussion of clause

B. The argument from context only has force if one assumes that the trinitarian position or something like it is impossible. Moreover, the argument from context cuts another way: in context John makes no such distinction between "God" (*ho theos*) and "a god" (*theos*). In fact, after verse 2 (which repeats the point made in verse 1b) the rest of the prologue consistently uses *theos* without the article (vv. 6, 12, 13, 18a, 18b). The last two are especially noteworthy because verse 18, like verse 1, uses the words *theon* and *theos* to refer, respectively, to God the Father and to Jesus Christ, yet both are anarthrous. One would have expected *theon* to have the article if, as the JWs maintain, in verse 1 John was carefully distinguishing "the God" from an inferior, subordinate "god." This is one of several indications that the presence or absence of the article simply is not that significant.

It is a mistake to argue that the JW argument is flawed because the NWT does not render all anarthrous occurrences of *theos* as "a god." Their claim is that the absence of the article makes the rendering "a god" possible, not that it makes it certain. In this respect, they are partially correct. An anarthrous *theos* could, in certain contexts, be construed as "a god." Their error is not so much grammatical as it is semantic—selecting a connotation for *theos* that is alien to the literary, religious, and theological context in which it appears. In biblical Greek, the singular *theos* is never used in an affirmative sense to refer to or describe anyone other than the Lord God (Jehovah). The notion of the supreme God having a second deity under his command simply has no biblical precedent or support.

It is also a mistake to argue that the rendering "a god" is grammatically impossible. What is commonly called "Colwell's rule" is almost just as commonly misunderstood. E. C. Colwell's widely cited article argues that definite predicate nouns were likely to have the article if they followed the verb but likely not to have the article if they preceded the verb. (By a "predicate noun" is meant a noun that is part of the predicate part of the sentence and describes or identifies the subject. For example, in the sentence "George was the king," "king" is a predicate noun; in the sentence, "The king was George," "George" is the predicate noun.) But this generalization cannot tell us whether a particular noun is definite in the first place.

Another grammatical approach to the matter that is now widely held is to characterize the anarthrous *theos* in John 1:1c as "qualitative," meaning that it expresses the nature of the Logos rather than his identity (e.g., Philip Harner, Daniel Wallace). This distinction may be valid, but it may also be overly subtle—and does not really settle the issue of how the noun is to be interpreted. It is especially doubtful if taken as the basis for such alternate translations as "the Word had the same nature as God" (Harner, 87) or "what God was, the Word was" (as in the New English Bible). *Theos* occurs as an anarthrous predicate noun in other places in the New Testament, and in all English versions it is translated simply as "God" (Luke 20:38; Phil. 2:13; see also Mark 12:27; John 8:54; Heb. 11:16). Other titles used as anarthrous predicate nouns likewise are routinely translated as simple titles, such as "Lord" (*kurios*, Matt. 12:8; Mark 2:28), "King" (*basileus*, Matt. 27:42), and "Son of God" (*theou huios*, Matt. 14:33; Mark 15:39).

Rather than trying to settle the meaning of *theos* in John 1:1c on the basis of grammar, then, it would be better to focus attention on the semantic range of the affirmative use of the singular *theos* in biblical Greek and on the context of the passage. That semantic evidence and the fact that in John 1 the Word is said to antedate creation and to be the source of life and illumination vindicate the orthodox interpretation as the best explanation of this controversial text.

See also JEHOVAH'S WITNESSES (JW)

Bibliography. R. M. Bowman Jr., *Jehovah's Witnesses, Jesus Christ, and the Gospel of John* [see esp. pp. 17–84]; E. C. Colwell, "A Definite Rule for the Use of the Article in the Greek New Testament," *Journal of Biblical Literature*; Mary Baker Eddy, *Miscellaneous Writings, 1883–1896*; P. B. Harner, "Qualitative Anarthrous Predicate Nouns: Mark 15:39 and John 1:1," *Journal of Biblical Literature*; M. J. Harris, *Jesus as God: The New Testament Use of* Theos *in Reference to Jesus* [see esp. pp. 55–71]; G. Stafford, *Jehovah's Witnesses Defended: An Answer to Scholars and Critics*, 2nd ed. [see esp. pp. 305–66]; D. B. Wallace, *Greek Grammar beyond the Basics: An Exegetical Syntax of the New Testament* [see esp. pp. 206–70].

R. M. Bowman Jr.

JOSEPH SMITH TRANSLATION OF THE BIBLE. Also known as the Inspired Version, the JST followed from the Book of Mormon teaching that the Bible had gone forth "from the Jews in purity, unto the Gentiles," but afterward was corrupted by the "Great and Abominable Church" (i.e., apostate Christendom and especially Roman Catholicism), which took "many plain and precious things" out of it (1 Nephi 13:25–28). It now fell to Joseph Smith as prophet of the great latter-day restoration to return the Bible to its original purity via revelation. The stage set for the JST in a June 1830 prophecy in which God tells Moses that "in a day when the children of men shall esteem my words as naught and take many of them from the book which thou shalt write, behold, I will raise up another like unto thee; and they shall be had again among the children of men" (Pearl of Great Price, Moses 1:41). The reference was obviously to Smith himself, and the prophecy is printed as a prophetic introduction to the JST.

As his base text, Smith used a King James Version pulpit-style Bible published in 1828 by H. & E. Phinney, Cooperstown, New York, that he and Oliver Cowdery purchased from Palmyra printer and bookseller Egbert B. Grandin on October 8, 1829. Smaller corrections were marked in this Bible and then written out in separate manuscripts. Larger sections were simply written out in the manuscripts. Smith was aided in the project by a number of scribes, including Oliver Cowdery, John Whitmer, and especially the former Campbellite minister Sidney Rigdon. Work on the JST was completed on July 2, 1833. On that day Rigdon, writing on behalf of the First Presidency, declared: "We this day finished the translating of the Scriptures, for which we returned gratitude to our Heavenly Father." We also find at the end of the manuscript for the book of Malachi the words: "Finished on the 2d day of July 1833." Joseph Smith considered the JST an important "branch of [his] calling" and tried several times to see it through to publication, but without success. After his death it remained in the hands of his widow, Emma, from whence it passed into the possession of the Reorganized Church of Jesus Christ of Latter Day Saints (RLDS) of Independence, Missouri (now the Community of Christ), which published it for the first time in 1867. Since then the JST has passed through several editions as the canonical Bible of the RLDS Church.

In contrast, the LDS Church of Salt Lake City, Utah, the largest group of Mormons, has never officially accepted the JST as a whole. Two excerpts from it did, however, become canonical as a result of their inclusion in the 1851 Pearl of Great Price. These are the Book of Moses, paralleling Genesis 1:1–8:18 in the JST, and Joseph Smith—Matthew, paralleling Matthew 24 in the JST. From the beginning, the LDS Church viewed the remainder of the JST with deep suspicion, and it was only during the second half of the twentieth century that serious moves were made to rehabilitate it. The earlier suspicion was partly due to the more general atmosphere of distrust that existed between the LDS Church and the RLDS Church as the two main claimants to the prophetic legacy of Joseph Smith, and partly to the fact that it was not until the late 1960s that LDS scholars were granted access to the JST manuscript materials.

Long before that time, however, the King James Version had already established itself as the canonical Bible of the LDS Church. Its position was further enhanced when, after the publication of the Revised Standard Version in the 1950s, J. Reuben Clark Jr., a member of the First Presidency, adopted the arguments of the anti-RSV King-James-only advocates and vigorously defended them before a Mormon audience in his book *Why the King James Version?* (1956). So influential was Clark's book that even as recently as 2002 a book by a professor at Brigham Young University credited the heretic Arius with producing the Alexandrian family of New Testament manuscripts (Marsh, 17).

A significant step for the authority and acceptance of the JST among Utah Mormons was taken with the production in 1979 by the LDS Church of its own edition of the KJV with short excerpts from the JST in footnotes and longer ones in an appendix in the back.

LDS apologists have attempted to sidestep problems associated with trying to treat the JST seriously as a restoration of the Bible to its original purity by insisting that Joseph Smith never revealed exactly what his intent was in producing it. In the very month of the JST's completion, however, the official Mormon newspaper the *Evening and Morning Star* published an article intended to whet the appetite of the faithful for its appearance: "Both the old and new testaments are filled with errors," the article declared, "obscurities, italics and contradictions, which must be the work of men." Fortunately, however, "the Church of Christ will soon have the scriptures, in their original purity." "The bible," it goes on to say, "must be PURIFIED! . . . O what a blessing, that the Lord will bestow the gift of the Holy Spirit, upon the meek and humble, whereby they can know of a

surety, his words from the words of men!" But it is not only from such statements as these that we may gather what Smith's intentions were. They were also clear from his actual procedures in entering changes in the JST. In a revelation dated February 16, 1832 (now D&C 76), Smith reported: "I resumed the translation of the Scriptures. . . . It was apparent that many important points touching the salvation of man had been taken from the Bible, or lost before it was compiled."

Consistent with this assessment, the changes made in the JST consist almost entirely of additions to the King James Version rather than deletions from it. An important exception to this is the way Smith treats the italicized words he found in the King James Version. "Throughout the Bible," writes Robert J. Matthews, "many italics are crossed out, even when it does violence to the sense" (59). Since the 1833 article referred to the italicized words in the Bible as the "works of men," it is not surprising that Smith often marked them out. Yet he often did not stop there. He regularly went on to replace the one or two italicized words he had marked out with whole phrases of many more words. This seems to imply that he incorrectly assumed that the presence of italics in English represented gaps in the original Greek and Hebrew texts—that is, places where "plain and precious things" had been taken out.

Of the many thousands of changes introduced by Joseph Smith in the JST, very few can claim support from biblical manuscripts ancient or modern. Moreover, in those places where Smith should have corrected well-known textual corruptions, he failed to do so. The JST evidences no familiarity with issues relating to texts that were disputed in Smith's day, such as the inclusion of the longer ending of Mark (16:9–20), the placement of the story of the woman taken in adultery (John 8:1–11), the replacement of "tree" with "book" (Rev. 22:19), and—by far the most debated biblical verse at the time—1 John 5:7, the so-called Johannine Comma.

There are, however, two changes among the thousands Smith made that LDS apologists still single out as evidence of the miraculous character of the JST. The first is the phrase "without a cause," present in the KJV of Matthew 5:22 but absent from the best early manuscripts and from the JST. The second is Isaiah 2:16, where they want to see in the JST a combination of the readings of the Greek Septuagint and the Hebrew text. However, Smith could have easily derived both variants from popular Methodist works available at the time. To mention only one example, John Wesley's edition of the New Testament did not include the phrase "without a cause" at Matthew 5:22. And in his *Explanatory Notes on the New Testament*, which was one of the Doctrinal Standards of the Methodist Church and part of the standard kit of every Methodist preacher, Wesley condemned the inclusion of the reading as "utterly foreign to the whole scope and tenor of our Lord's discourse." Smith's wife, Emma, was from a prominent Methodist family. Smith himself also repeatedly expressed sympathy with the Methodists and even attempted to join them in 1828.

Another reason the JST cannot be a restoration of the ancient text of Scripture is the regular transfer of distinctive language from one part of the Bible to other parts where it clearly does not belong. For example, we find Smith repeatedly introducing favorite phrases from the New Testament into his restorations of the Old. To mention only one example among many, we find language borrowed from John 1:14 in JST Genesis 4:7 ("the Only Begotten of the Father, which is full of grace and truth") and 6:53 ("mine Only Begotten Son, who is full of grace and truth"). John 1:14 is one of many biblical passages that regularly came to Joseph Smith's mind when he was engaged in prophesying, translating, or restoring. We find its phraseology also

in the Book of Mormon (Alma 5:48; 9:16; 13:9) and in Doctrine and Covenants (93:11).

Although RLDS scholars have long since come to terms with the fact that the JST is not a restoration of the ancient biblical text, many LDS scholars still insist that it is. The main problem with this assertion, as we have already seen, is that the ancient evidence in no way supports it. Consequently, a number of ingenious arguments have to be developed by LDS apologists to get around this.

The first argument is that all extant biblical manuscripts are already corrupted. This is refuted, however, by the fact that (1) the JST retains corrupt readings of the text that clearly entered the manuscript tradition very late, (2) there was not a Great and Abominable Church powerful enough and early enough to accomplish the needed universal corruption of the New Testament evidence, and (3) too much Old Testament textual evidence exists (e.g., Dead Sea Scrolls, Samaritan Pentateuch) to admit both Joseph Smith's biblical corrections *and* his claim in the Book of Mormon that the Bible went forth "from the Jews in purity."

The second argument is that Smith never finished the JST because he kept on modifying the manuscript after 1833 and supposedly later told certain early leaders he wanted to work through its translation again. Some have speculated that the kinds of changes Smith would have made in such a second run through would have served the radical changes that were taking place in his doctrinal views (see, e.g., his shift from modalistic monotheism to belief in a plurality of gods), not the restoration of the original biblical text. Such updates could only move the JST further away from the original text and sense of Scripture. That this is so may be seen, for example, in the changes made in the creation story of the Book of Abraham published in 1842, which, despite claims to the contrary, represents yet another reworking of the KJV of Genesis 1. The most basic problem with this argument, however, is that it acts as if the JST was a partial restoration of the ancient text of Scripture that only needed to be finished, which is simply not true.

The third argument is that the "plain and precious things" taken out had to do with so-called missing books, such as the Book of Jasher and Enoch, not with textual variants. Although Smith was interested in the "lost books" of the Bible, his main purpose was to restore the ones that were not lost. This is clear from both the kinds of changes he actually made in the JST and the 1833 article already mentioned, which explicitly spoke of purifying the existing biblical text.

See also CHURCH OF JESUS CHRIST OF LATTER-DAY SAINTS

Bibliography. P. L. Barlow, *Mormons and the Bible: The Place of the Latter-day Saints in American Religion*; R. P. Howard, *Restoration Scriptures: A Study of Their Textual Development*; R. V. Huggins, "Joseph Smith's 'Inspired Translation' of Romans 7," *Dialogue: A Journal of Mormon Thought*; S. Larson, "The Historicity of the Matthean Sermon on the Mount in 3 Nephi," in *New Approaches to the Book of Mormon: Explorations in Critical Methodology*, edited by B. L. Metcalfe; W. J. Marsh, *The Joseph Smith Translation: Precious Truths Restored*; R. J. Matthews, *"A Plainer Translation": Joseph Smith's Translation of the Bible; A History and Commentary*; R. L. Millet and R. J. Matthews, eds., *Plain and Precious Truths Restored: The Doctrinal and Historical Significance of the Joseph Smith Translation*; M. S. Nyman et al., *The Joseph Smith Translation: The Restoration of Plain and Precious Things*; D. P. Wright, "Isaiah in the Book of Mormon: Or Joseph Smith in Isaiah," in *American Apocrypha: Essays on the Book of Mormon*, edited by D. Vogel and B. L. Metcalfe.

R. V. Huggins

JOURNAL OF DISCOURSES. The *Journal of Discourses* consists of twenty-six volumes of selected sermons from leaders of the Church of Jesus Christ of Latter-day Saints (LDS Church or Mormonism) covering a period of about twenty-six years during the nineteenth century. It includes a compilation of 1,438 messages from fifty-five different people, most of whom were church general authorities. Brigham Young gave nearly 400 of these recorded messages.

Compiling the sermons of Mormonism's general authorities was the innovation of George D. Watt, an English convert who also served as a clerk for second LDS president Brigham Young. Watt was commissioned by the LDS Church to record the words of LDS leaders during church conferences. These, in turn, were published in the church-owned *Deseret News*. However, Watt wanted the messages of LDS leaders to go far beyond the limited subscribers to the *Deseret News*. His desire was given the blessing of the First Presidency, who issued the following statement on June 1, 1853:

Dear Brethren.—It is well known to many of you that Elder George D. Watt, by our counsel, spent much time in the midst of poverty and hardships to acquire the art of reporting in Phonography which he has faithfully and fully accomplished; and he has been reporting the public sermons, discourses, lectures, &c., delivered by the Presidency, the Twelve and others in this city, for nearly two years, almost without fee or reward.

"Elder Watt now proposes to publish a Journal of these reports, in England for the benefit of the Saints at large, and to obtain means to enable him to sustain his highly useful position of Reporter. You will perceive at once that this will be a work of mutual benefit, and we cheerfully and warmly request your co-operation in the purchase and sale of the above-named Journal, and wish all the profits arising therefrom to be under the control of Elder Watt." [signed] BRIGHAM YOUNG, HEBER C. KIMBALL, WILLARD RICHARDS." (Clark, 2:119; this message is also found in the beginning of vol. 1 of the *Journal of Discourses*)

The *Journal* began as a sixteen-page semi-monthly publication. Although it was considered a private operation, it was produced in the LDS Church printing office in Liverpool, England. When Watt first produced the *Journal*, there seemed to be no question that the actual words and beliefs of Mormonism's latter-day prophets were faithfully recorded. In his introduction to the first issue, Watt proclaimed, "It affords me great pleasure in being able to put in your possession the words of the Apostles and Prophets, as they were spoken in assemblies of the Saints in Zion, the value of which cannot be estimated by man, not so much for any great display of worldly learning and eloquence, as for the purity of doctrine, simplicity of style, and extensive amount of theological truth which they develop."

Most of the volumes of the *Journal* were edited and published under the direct auspices of men who either were currently serving as general authorities in the LDS Church or would later do so. The names are a veritable Who's Who list of Mormon leaders and include such men as Franklin Richards, Orson Pratt, George Q. Cannon, Amasa Lyman, Daniel H. Wells, Brigham Young Jr., Joseph F. Smith, and Albert Carrington.

The *Encyclopedia of Mormonism* notes that a total of "twelve people reported sermons for the Journal of Discourses." These included David W. Evans, an associate editor of the *Deseret News* who succeeded Watt as the main reporter for the *JD* from 1867 to 1876. Another was George F. Gibbs, who served as secretary to the First Presidency of the Church for fifty-six years. Even one of Brigham Young's daughters, Julia, is credited with recording one of her father's sermons (Ludlow, 2:769–70).

Speaking in Conference in 1905, Mormon apostle Hyrum Mack Smith, son of sixth LDS president Joseph F. Smith, told members of the church that they "should be firmly rounded in the knowledge of the truth." Said apostle Smith, "They [the Latter-day Saints] have the Holy Scriptures, the Bible, which contains the word of God; the Book of Mormon, the D&C, and the Pearl of Great Price; they have the *Journal of Discourses*; also periodicals, books and papers which are published from time to time, containing the discourses and inspired words of the servants of the Lord."

It is doubtful that many modern Mormons would want to include the *Journal* in the aforementioned list. Ironically, some of the *Journal*'s biggest critics today are Mormons themselves. Since the *Journal* is one of the few nineteenth-century LDS publications that have not seen revision or tampering, many of the teachings it contains are out of step with the "Christian" image the current LDS Church is trying to project. Some Latter-day Saints are quick to downplay embarrassing comments by insisting that the *Journal* is not "official doctrine" or that much of its contents are nothing more than the mere opinions of the speakers. The fact that the LDS Church has often cited the *Journal* in its many manuals and other publications certainly seems to send a mixed message regarding its authority.

Mormon apostle John Widtsoe used the *Journal* as a primary source for his 1925 book titled *Discourses of Brigham Young*. In his preface, Widtsoe makes no effort to hide the fact that it played a significant role in his book. There he writes:

This book was made possible because Brigham Young secured stenographic reports of his addresses. As he traveled among the people, reporters accompanied him. All that he said was recorded. Practically all of these discourses (from December 16, 1851 to August 19, 1877) were published in the Journal of Discourses, which was widely distributed. The public utterances of few great historical figures have been so faithfully and fully preserved. Clearly, this mass of material, covering nearly thirty years of incessant public speaking could not be presented with any hope of serving the general reader, save in the form of selections of essential doctrines. (vi)

A 1997 priesthood manual titled *Teachings of Presidents of the Church: Brigham Young* cites literally hundreds of quotations from Widtsoe's work. In essence the LDS Church is still endorsing the *Journal* since the great majority of Widtsoe's compilation was taken from it.

See also CHURCH OF JESUS CHRIST OF LATTER-DAY SAINTS

Bibliography. The Church of Jesus Christ of Latter-day Saints, *Teachings of Presidents of the Church: Brigham Young*; J. R. Clark, ed., *Messages of the First Presidency*, 2 vols; D. H. Ludlow, ed., *Encyclopedia of Mormonism*, 4 vols.; J. Widtsoe, *Discourses of Brigham Young*.

W. McKeever

JUDAISM. *Definition.* In Hebrew the terms that are translated "Jew" (*yehudi*), "Judah" (*yehudah*), and "Judaism" (*yahadut*) all come from the same Hebrew root meaning "to praise." The distinction between "Jewishness" and "Judaism" is that the former is an ethnic identity into which one is born but says nothing about one's beliefs, while the latter term refers to a religion or religious beliefs to which one can either be born or converted. Whereas in postbiblical Judaism, rabbis would apply the term Jew to gentile converts to Judaism, the Bible never does so and refers to them as "proselytes."

The essence of Judaism is that this is the religion of most Jews. But one can reject Judaism and still be a Jew, as often happened in Jewish history when Jewish people fell into different forms of idolatry. Judaism had a valid phase when it was based on Scripture, but it became invalid when it was revamped in the course of Jewish history. The essence is that while Judaism is the religion of most Jews, historically Judaism has not always been the same.

The Development of Orthodox Judaism.
Biblical Judaism. Biblical Judaism is the Judaism revealed through Scripture, primarily through Moses and the Prophets. This was a divinely revealed religion spelling out various requirements that included sacrificial laws, dietary laws, clothing laws, sexual laws, agricultural laws, and farming laws, among many others. The essence of biblical Judaism is that salvation was by grace through faith, just as Abraham believed God and it was reckoned to him for righteousness (Gen. 15:6). But the rule of life began with the Abrahamic covenant and continued through the Mosaic covenant, containing the 613 commandments of the law of Moses.

Post–Old Testament Judaism. When the Jews first returned from Babylonian captivity (only a minority of the Jewish population in Babylon chose to return), Ezra began a process of explaining and teaching the commandments of the Mosaic law with the goal that the people should understand what was involved in keeping it and what was involved in breaking it—to give the Jewish people a knowledge of what the Mosaic law required. If they had this knowledge, they would faithfully keep the law and thus avoid another divine judgment like the Babylonian captivity. This was still within the bounds of biblical Judaism.

The Period of the Sopherim (400–30 BC). Things began to change within a generation or so after the close of the Old Testament. While the rabbis see the first period as extending from Ezra to Hillel, the period actually begins before the time of Ezra and before the time of Malachi, when Judaism was still strictly a biblical Judaism. But around 400 BC began the period of the Sopherim, a Hebrew word meaning "scribes." The principle they initiated, which went beyond what Ezra was doing, was that it was no longer enough to merely explain the law; it was now necessary to build a fence around the law. This fence would consist of new rules and regulations that could be logically derived from the original 613 commandments, and their thinking was that Jews might break the laws of the fence—break rabbinic law—but that might keep them from breaking *through* the fence, breaking the Mosaic law, and thus bringing divine discipline down on themselves again. In making these new rules and regulations, the scribes followed a specific principle: a Sopher may disagree with a Sopher, but he cannot disagree with the Torah. The Torah (the law of Moses) was given by God to Moses on Mt. Sinai, it was sacrosanct, and therefore there was no valid basis for debating the validity of what God gave to Moses. But in making new rules and regulations, they could disagree among themselves until a decision was made by majority vote. Once the majority of rabbis voted on a new rule and regulation, it became mandatory for all Jews in the world to follow.

It was during this period that the scribes separated from the priests, with the result that the priestly class developed into Sadducean Judaism and the scribes developed into Pharisaic Judaism.

The Period of the Tannaim (30 BC–AD 220). With Hillel a transition in Judaism occurred, the period of the Sopherim ended, and there arose a new school of rabbis known as the Tannaim (i.e., "repeaters," "teachers"). Rabbinically, this is viewed as the period from Hillel to Yehudah HaNasi (Judah the Prince). As they considered the rules and regulations passed down by tradition from the Sopherim, the Tannaim concluded there were still too many holes in the fence around the law, and they continued the process of establishing new rules for the next two and a half centuries. However, they changed their principle of operation to be as follows: a Tana can disagree with a Tana, but he cannot disagree with a Sopher. At this point, all the rules and regulations of the Sopherim became sacrosanct, equal with Scripture.

But then in order to validate their claim that the laws of the Sopherim were equal with the laws of the Torah, the Tannaim developed a teaching still taught in Orthodox Jewish schools to this day, which is that on Mt. Sinai God gave to Moses two separate laws. The first law is the written law, which contains the 613 commandments that were actually written down in the books of Exodus, Leviticus, Numbers, and Deuteronomy. But God also gave Moses the oral law, comprising hundreds of thousands of new laws. Moses memorized them and then passed them down to Joshua, who passed them down to the judges, who passed them down to the prophets, who passed them down to the Sopherim. Therefore, the Sopherim did not innovate all these new rules and regulations; they simply got them from the prophets, who got them from the judges, who got them from Joshua, who got them from Moses, who got them from God.

Indeed, from 400 BC until AD 220, these laws were not written down, but they became part of the oral law passed down by tradition, and they were memorized by certain key men who would maintain their remembrance. In fact, it was forbidden to write out the commandments of the oral law for a long time. Yehudah HaNasi finally permitted the oral law to be written down, which ended the period of the Tannaim.

The kind of Messiah that the Tannaim expected would be a fellow Pharisee, who would submit himself to both the written law and the oral law and join them in the work of plugging the holes in the fence. Jesus affirmed that he would submit himself to the written law, but he rejected the authority of the oral law and therefore the authority of the Pharisees, which in turn would lead to their rejection of his messianic claims (Matt. 12–13).

The product of the Sopherim and the Tannaim is the Mishnah, which became the bone of contention between Jesus and the Pharisees. In the New Testament this product is referred to as the tradition of the elders (Mark 7:5).

The Period of the Amoraim (AD 220–500). Once the oral law was written down in the body of the Mishnah, the period of the Tannaim ended, and thus began a new set of rabbinic scholars known as the Amoraim. They observed the work of the Sopherim and the Tannaim, determined there were still too many holes in the fence, and continued the process for the next three centuries, concluding with the production of the Gemara. However, they also changed their principle of operation: an Amora may disagree with an Amora, but he cannot disagree with a Tana. Thus all the rules and regulations of the Tannaim also became sacrosanct and equal with Scripture.

The Period of the Seboraim (Sixth and Seventh Centuries). The rabbis of the next age, the Seboraim, began a process of enlarging the rabbinic writings to make them more understandable, committing everything to written form, unifying both the Mishnah and the Gemara, and producing what is now called the Talmud, which incorporates both the Mishnah and the Gemara. The additions of the Amoraim also became sacrosanct, equal with Scripture. This ended the long development of Talmudic Judaism from 400 BC until the seventh century AD.

Denominations of Judaism in the First Century. *Pharisaic Judaism.* Pharisaic Judaism was the Judaism developed through the Sopherim and the Tannaim, which held to both the written law and the oral law. The Pharisees required the application of both the Mosaic (written) law and the oral law and were strongly inclined to impose duties on all Jews. The mass of the nation inclined toward Pharisaic Judaism, though they were not necessarily members of the guild. Pharisees did not reject the temple but claimed that much more than temple observance was required, and the new laws of the Pharisees were accepted as authoritative. They dominated the Judaism of Israel, Babylonia, and Diaspora Jewry.

Key points of Pharisaic Judaism that appear in the New Testament are belief in both angels and demons, belief in the resurrection of the dead, and the belief that doctrine can be derived from any part of Scripture, be it the Law, the Prophets, or the Writings.

By the end of the Hasmonean period, the Pharisees had the loyalty of the masses, and this would be the only Judaism that would survive after AD 70.

Sadducean Judaism. Sadducean Judaism was composed primarily of the priestly class and the aristocracy, and its adherents supported Hellenizing Judaism. While they did adhere to the Mosaic law, they rejected the authority of the oral law. They were always a minority Judaism but had great political power because of their tendency to cooperate with Rome up to a specific point. They controlled the temple services, and their religious practices focused on and around the sacrifice. The Judaism of the Sadducees was largely restricted to the land of Israel and had virtually no influence outside the land. It firmly rejected the doctrines of angels, demons, and the resurrection of the dead. Sadducean Judaism did not survive after AD 70.

Zealot Judaism. While mainline Pharisaic Judaism held to passive resistance to Roman rule, Zealot Judaism was a faction within Pharisaism that was active in guerrilla warfare against Rome and considered armed uprising as a divine command. Their policy of active resistance was denounced by mainline Pharisaism. Zealot Judaism and mainline Pharisaic Judaism, however, differed not in what they believed doctrinally but in their policy concerning resistance to Rome. Zealot Judaism was responsible for sparking the First Jewish Revolt (AD 66–70) and did not survive after AD 70.

Essene Judaism. Mainline Pharisaism recognized that Sadducees were in control of the temple compound and sacrifices; nevertheless, they thought it was still necessary to follow the sacrificial system. Essene Judaism was part of Pharisaic Judaism that believed continuing the sacrifices at the time of Sadducean control would be sacrilegious, and therefore they chose to live in segregated communities, whether within the city or outside the city, as in the wilderness of Judah. They were very concerned with ethics and social justice, and they abandoned the world to devote themselves to religious observance. They bathed frequently, and they dressed in white as a symbol of their purity. This Judaism did not survive after AD 70 either.

Development of Rabbinic Judaism (AD 70–90). The year AD 70, the year that the temple was destroyed and the practice of sacrifices ceased, Judaism underwent a change from Pharisaic Judaism to rabbinic Judaism.

During the Roman siege of Jerusalem, a key Pharisaic rabbi of that period named Yohanan ben Zakkai escaped in a coffin and arranged to be brought before the Roman general Vespasian. He requested that he be allowed to set up a school on the coastal city of Yavne, and his request was granted. He gathered around him the Pharisaic rabbis who had survived the Roman destruction of the city and the land and began to adapt Judaism to the new, changing situation. All the historical national institutions had to be replaced by a new focus of loyalty, but at the same time the temple must continue to be remembered. As a result, prayer was substituted for sacrifice, and the synagogue replaced the temple as the center of Jewish life. The rabbis adopted rituals to reinforce a symbolic link between synagogue and temple, and they attempted to establish a spiritual control over the Jews of the diaspora. They did two things: first, they formed a new central institution that would contain all the authority of the temple; and second, they enacted new laws to affirm the authority of the new center. The result of the rabbis' work in Yavne was essentially a new Judaism

that became known as rabbinic Judaism and continued through what is now known as Orthodox Judaism. It resembles biblical Judaism very little.

Denominations of Modern Judaism. *Orthodox Judaism.* Traditional mainline Orthodox Judaism stands in a continuous line from Pharisaic Judaism to rabbinic Judaism through talmudic Judaism to the present. Like those earlier forms of Judaism, it believes in the fundamentals of Judaism and the doctrines it considers pure. The essence of Orthodox Judaism is the Thirteen Articles of Faith that were formulated by Maimonides. They are as follows: (1) God created all things; (2) God is one; (3) God is incorporeal; (4) God is eternal; (5) God alone must be worshiped; (6) the prophets are true; (7) Moses was the greatest of all prophets; (8) the entire Torah was divinely given to Moses; (9) the Torah is immutable; (10) God knows all the acts and thoughts of human beings; (11) God rewards and punishes; (12) the Messiah will come; and (13) there will be resurrection. In addition to Scriptures and the Talmud, the extensive writings of posttalmudic rabbis, known as the Gaonim, play an important role in Orthodox Judaism, though they are never elevated to Talmudic authority. While not always comfortable with Zionism in its early days because Zionism was a secular movement, Orthodox Judaism now fully supports the State of Israel.

Hasidic/Chasidic Judaism. Hasidic Judaism is an extreme form of Orthodox Judaism. It originated with Israel ben Eliezer, known as the Baal Shem Tov and sometimes referred to as the Besht (vocalizing the initials "B.Sh.T."). He was born in 1700 in Podolia (today parts of Ukraine and Moldova) at a time when rabbinic Judaism was attempting to consolidate power because of certain pseudomessianic movements. He proclaimed a doctrine of joy, optimism, and enthusiastic worship. Hasidism actually began as a revolt against the strict rules of the rabbis, and Jews by the thousands flocked to the Besht, receiving blessing and joining in a frenzied prayer. He died in 1760.

His teachings spread to every corner of Poland, and various Hasidic dynasties were formed. Although considered a heresy by mainline Orthodox Judaism, Hasidism gained hundreds of thousands of adherents. Eventually the division between Hasidics and Orthodox was overcome by Rabbi Shneur Zalmon of Lodi, who was both a Talmudist and a Hasidic. Zalmon taught that both Talmudism and Hasidism were necessary. Hasidism thus continued its fervent type of joyful practice but also became more zealous in its application of the Talmud.

While mainline Orthodox Judaism recognizes the role of the modern State of Israel, Hasidic Judaism is divided over the issue. Some segments are opposed, believing there can be no Jewish state until the Messiah comes; others tolerate it but hold to a view that a distinction between the religious and the secular should apply.

Modern Orthodoxy. This is an American innovated orthodoxy that practices Judaism in an Orthodox manner up to a point but has removed many elements, such as a continuous head-covering and the wearing of tassels. It is as far left of Orthodox Judaism as it can be while still claiming to be Orthodox.

Reform Judaism. Following their emancipation from the restrictions and confinement of European ghettos, Jewish people began to adopt more and more of modern culture and education and began establishing secular Jewish schools over against religious Jewish schools. This development began the Reform movement. The first Reform synagogue was established in Germany in 1818 by Eduard Klay. Israel Jacobson initiated new forms of worship in Berlin, introducing into the service some things that were normally forbidden in Orthodox Judaism, such as the use of the organ and a choir. In place of Hebrew prayer books, Reform Jews produced German prayer books and prayer books that were less religious. They moved away from belief in the future Messiah and instead held to the messianic mission of Israel in the world. Not believing that any future temple would be rebuilt, they called their places of worship "temples" rather than "synagogues." They did not, and do not, wear any distinctive Jewish clothing or keep kosher.

By 1850 Reform Judaism was firmly established in Europe, and it soon spread to the US; it is still the predominant form of Judaism in America today. Reform Judaism made some radical changes to traditional Judaism in its Orthodox format. It is very modernistic and does not share the religious focus of Orthodox Judaism. In its early years, it gave up the hope of a national Jewish homeland and discarded the vast majority of Jewish traditions. However, following the Holocaust, it became (and still is) a strong supporter of the State of Israel and in more recent years has returned to the practice of some Jewish traditions, though not to the extent of either Orthodox or Conservative Judaism.

Conservative Judaism. Conservative Judaism is an American-innovated Judaism founded by Zechariah Frankel. In essence it follows many of the principles of Orthodox Judaism but adopts some of the changes introduced by Reform Judaism. It teaches that changes must come, but they must come slowly and naturally, not radically. Conservative Jews wear the head covering during religious services but not all day or every day. They have also discarded the wearing of distinctive clothes such as the tassels. The Talmud plays an important role but is not viewed as authoritative as it is in Orthodoxy; Conservative Jews keep kosher but not to the same degree of strictness as Orthodox Jews.

Conservative Judaism was once a very strong movement among American Jews, but in recent decades it has become smaller and is losing much ground.

Reconstructionist Judaism. Reconstructionist Judaism takes a much more radical approach than Reform Judaism, allowing for both belief in a God and atheism. It essentially teaches that every generation of Jews must reconstruct Judaism to meet the needs of a new generation.

Humanistic Judaism. Humanistic Judaism is simply atheistic Judaism, and its services and prayer books leave out any reference to God whatsoever.

Messianic Judaism. Messianic Judaism is a term favored by many Jewish believers in the messiahship of Jesus. It is a broad term and does not always explain what individual Messianic Jewish congregations may believe or disbelieve. The essence of agreement among all Messianic Jews is that Yeshua (Jesus) is indeed the Messiah, and most Messianic Jews hold to the basic fundamentals of the Christian faith that fundamentalist and conservative Christians would believe. However, it also includes radical elements that have moved it into heretical territory such denying the Trinity and the deity of the Messiah and believing that a person can be saved apart from faith in Yeshua. Others have adopted cultic elements similar to those that characterize British Israelism, though with a Jewish twist such as teaching that all gentile believers are really members of the lost tribes of Israel and therefore need to return to the law of Moses.

The Messianic movement has attracted many gentiles, and, in fact, the majority of Messianic congregations are composed mostly of gentiles, some even exclusively so.

A Summary of the Essential Beliefs of Orthodox Judaism. Orthodox Judaism is the only Judaism that has continuity from the postbiblical to modern times. The following is the essence of Orthodoxy but not necessarily the view of non-Orthodox Judaism.

God. Orthodox Judaism holds to an absolute unity of God, an absolute oneness, and therefore, God exists as only one person, not three persons. Judaism rejects any concept of plurality in the Godhead.

Inspiration. Orthodox Judaism holds to a dictation theory of the inspiration of Scriptures but does not assign the same degree of inspiration to all parts. The Torah (Law) is the most inspired; the Neviim (Prophets) less so; and the Ketuvim (Writings) even less.

The Torah. On one hand, Orthodox Judaism holds that God revealed the Torah to Moses on Mt. Sinai, but on the other it also holds that the Torah preexisted Moses, so even the patriarchs followed the Torah. The Torah has become the essential of Orthodoxy; thus it has become the focus of rabbinic Judaism, which continually studies what the Torah says. Further, once the Torah was given to Israel, it was no longer God who determined the meaning of the Torah; rather, the rabbis signify its meaning by majority vote. Note that the term *Torah* is not strictly limited to the five books of Moses, nor even the written law, but sometimes includes the oral law as well.

Israel. The name Israel is used to refer to the Jewish people as a people and not merely to the State of Israel as such. God has an eternal covenant with the Jewish people, though in Orthodox Judaism the focus is more on the Mosaic covenant than on the Abrahamic covenant. It was God who dispersed the Jews around the world, but the purpose of the dispersion was to spread the knowledge of the one true God among the gentiles. While gentiles need not convert to Judaism, to be able to enter into God's kingdom they must adhere to the one-God principle (i.e., monotheism) and keep the seven laws of the Noahic covenant. As for the State of Israel, it is supported by mainline Orthodoxy, though elements in Ultra-Orthodoxy and Hasidism oppose it, saying Israel does not have a right to exist until the Messiah comes.

In the State of Israel, only Orthodoxy is recognized, and while non-Orthodox Jews are recognized as Jews ethnically, their Judaism is rejected as invalid. Within Israel only Orthodoxy applies to issues such as marriage, divorce, remarriage, circumcision, and burial. Thus Israelis who wish to marry non-Jews or wish to have a non-Orthodox wedding must leave the country to do so. While husbands can divorce wives, wives cannot divorce their husbands. In Israel today, there are many *agunot* women, separated from their husbands but unable to remarry for lack of a bill of divorcement. The vast majority of Israelis are secular, not Orthodox, but they must follow the Orthodox law on these issues.

Messiah. The Messiah is a very high figure in Orthodox Judaism, perhaps the highest, but less than God. For Orthodox Jews the Messiah is not God nor a God-man. When he comes, he will defeat the enemies of Israel, bring all Jews back into the promised land, rebuild the temple, and set up the messianic kingdom, finally bringing in world peace and prosperity. Before Rashi crafted a new interpretation of Isaiah 53 in the eleventh century, the passage was viewed as messianic. To rectify the contradictions between a suffering messiah and a ruling messiah, the rabbis innovated two possibilities. The minority view is that if Israel is unrighteous, he will come as the suffering messiah riding on the donkey; if Israel is righteous, then he will come as a ruling messiah in the clouds of heaven. But the majority view was simply to innovate two separate Messiahs, each coming one time. The first Messiah was called Mashiach ben Yosef, or Messiah the son of Joseph, and he would fulfill the prophecies of suffering and be killed in the Gog and Magog war. Then would come the second Messiah, Mashiach ben David, or Messiah the son of David, the conquering Messiah, who would raise the first Messiah back to life, establish the messianic kingdom, and bring all Jews back into the promised land. In modern Orthodox Judaism, there is little talk of the first Messiah but much talk of the second.

The Sabbath. Before AD 70 the temple was the real center of Judaism, but that was replaced by Sabbath observance once the temple was destroyed. Many of the rituals of the Orthodox service on the Sabbath are intended to imitate the rituals formerly practiced in the temple, such as the morning and evening sacrifice, although prayer has replaced the actual blood sacrifice. To the one commandment that Moses gave to remember the Sabbath and keep it holy, the rabbis added about fifteen hundred Sabbath regulations, teaching that Israel was made for the purpose of honoring the Sabbath. In Israel, in hotels and high-rise buildings, one elevator is designated as the Sabbath elevator and preprogrammed to stop on every floor so that an Orthodox Jew does not need to kindle a light by pushing the button. For the same reason, hotels that use keycards to open doors provide Orthodox Jews with regular keys for the Sabbath. Public transportation is not used on the Sabbath, and Orthodox Jews will neither ride nor drive in cars.

The Jewish Festivals. The Mosaic festivals are still observed, with many rabbinic traditions and additions but not in their biblical format, due to the absence of the temple. Passover, Weeks, and Tabernacles are now observed in the home and local synagogue but are no longer pilgrimage festivals to be observed in Jerusalem. The Day of Atonement (Yom Kippur) is now a day of a twenty-six-hour fast from both liquids and solids. While mainline Orthodoxy today does not practice blood sacrifice, in Ultra-Orthodoxy it is still practiced on this occasion. However, in place of a goat, a chicken is sacrificed—a rooster for a male or a hen for a female. In addition to the Mosaic festivals, other festivals include Purim (the Feast of Lots) and Hanukkah (the Feast of Dedication). The last was normally a minor Jewish holy festival, but in North America it has become a major one, to offset Christmas, which falls around the same time of year. While Yom Kippur is now the most important fast, second to it is Tisha be-Av, "the ninth of [the month of] Av" (July/August on the Gregorian calendar), marking the date when both temples were destroyed.

Other Practices. The Mosaic law and its rabbinic interpretation are applied in all areas of life. That includes the dietary laws, which are not merely the Mosaic, such as abstention from certain kinds of meat, fish, or bird life, but also rabbinic innovations such as separating milk and meat products and wearing distinctive clothing such as a head covering (in most cases it is a simple skullcap), tassels, and other distinctive items. The whole daily life of an Orthodox Jew is influenced by both biblical and rabbinic laws to point out how Jews are different from all other people.

See also HASIDISM; PURIM (THE FEAST OF LOTS); TALMUD; YOM KIPPUR (DAY OF ATONEMENT)

Bibliography. L Baeck, *The Essence of Judaism*; W. Dosick, *Living Judaism: The Complete Guide to Jewish Belief, Tradition, & Practice*; E. Feldman, *On Judaism*; M. M. Friedlander, *Guide of the Perplexed*; G. F. Moore, *Judaism in the First Centuries of the Christian Era: The Age of Tannaim*, 3 vols.; F. J. Murphy, *Early Judaism*; J. Neusner, *Judaism: The Evidence of the Mishnah*; Neusner, *Transformations in Ancient Judaism*; J. Neusner, A. Avery-Peck, and B. Chilton, eds., *Judaism in Late Antiquity*, 3 vols.; E. P. Sanders, *Judaism: Practice & Belief, 63 BCE–66 CE*; J. D. Sarna, *American Judaism*; S. Schechter, *Aspects of Rabbinic Theology*; P. Sigal, *Judaism: The Evolution of a Faith*; J. C. VanderKam, *An Introduction to Early Judaism*; M. Weber, *Ancient Judaism*; H. Wouk, *This Is My God*.

A. Fruchtenbaum

JUSTIFICATION, BIBLICAL DOCTRINE OF.

The term *justify* (Greek, *dikaioō*), as the New Testament authors employ it, means simply "declare righteous." One reads, accordingly, of human beings justifying God (Matt. 11:19; Luke 7:29, 35; Rom. 3:4), the Spirit justifying Christ (1 Tim. 3:16), and

self-righteous persons justifying themselves (Luke 10:29; 16:15). One also reads, more importantly, of God justifying human beings in three distinct ways. First, God justifies human beings, or declares them righteous, by imputing, or crediting, the righteousness of Christ to them. This first kind of justification occurs when God unites a sinner to Christ by faith and effects his reconciliation with God (Rom. 5:1). Second, God would justify persons by declaring them flawless if they merited eternal life by rendering God lifelong perfect obedience. Mere human beings cannot attain this second kind of justification because inherited corruption renders them naturally incapable of pleasing God (8:7–8). Third, God justifies all persons to whom he has imputed Christ's righteousness when he acknowledges that these persons manifest the sincerity of their faith by good works (2:7–10, 13).

Paul writes of God's justifying human beings primarily in the first and second of these manners. Over against those who claim that fallen human beings can merit God's favor by obeying him, Paul insists that "by the works of the Law no flesh will be justified in His sight; for through the Law *comes* the knowledge of sin" (Rom. 3:20; all quotations in this entry are NASB). Human sin, according to Paul, thus eliminates the possibility that a human being might receive the second kind of justification. Justification of the first kind, Paul asserts, is nonetheless possible. For "now apart from the Law *the* righteousness of God has been manifested, being witnessed by the Law and the Prophets, even *the* righteousness through faith in Jesus Christ for all those who believe" (3:21–22).

That God imputes this righteousness to those who believe in Jesus is seen in 2 Corinthians 5:21: "He [God] made Him who knew no sin [Christ] *to be* sin on our behalf, so that we might become the righteousness of God in Him." Christ, who became like other human beings in every respect except sin

(Heb. 4:15), naturally, does not become substantially sin; and Christians manifestly do not become substantially the righteousness of God. Rather, when God unites the Christian to Jesus by faith so that the Christian becomes a member of Christ's body (Rom. 12:5; 1 Cor. 12:13, 27), God imputes the Christian's sins to Christ so that Christ might suffer the penalty for those sins. Likewise, just as God imputes Christ's death, resurrection, and ascension to the Christian (Rom. 6:6–8; Eph. 2:5–6; Col. 2:12–13), so God imputes the righteousness of the God-man, Jesus Christ (1 Cor. 1:30), to the Christian so that the Christian might be accounted righteous notwithstanding his or her ungodliness (Rom. 4:5).

Moses refers to this imputation of Christ's righteousness to the believer, Paul explains, when he writes, "Abraham believed God, and it was credited to him as righteousness" (Rom. 4:3; Gen. 15:6). Abraham received this divine imputation of righteousness, Paul insists, not through performing righteous works but through faith. "To the one who does not work, but believes in Him who justifies the ungodly, his faith is credited as righteousness" (Rom. 4:5). God imputes Christ's righteousness to human beings through faith without any consideration of works, Paul asserts, in order to preserve the gracious character of this imputation; "*it is* by faith, in order that *it may be* in accordance with grace" (4:16). Those who gain divine favor by faith, Paul apparently reasons, unlike those who earn divine favor by works, do not rely on meritorious actions of their own but look away from themselves to another on whom they rely entirely for their salvation. By teaching that "man is justified by faith apart from works of the Law" (3:28), accordingly, Paul exalts the grace of God and removes all ground of boasting from human beings (3:27).

By thus teaching, however, Paul by no means denies that God also justifies persons in the third manner indicated above—namely, by

acknowledging that persons justified by faith manifest the sincerity of their faith through good works. Everyone who savingly believes in Jesus, Paul maintains, is a "new creature" (2 Cor. 5:17), "created in Christ Jesus for good works" (Eph. 2:10). Paul holds, accordingly, that those to whom God imputes the alien righteousness of Christ will ultimately excel the unsaved in inherent righteousness, which manifests itself in good works. In his words, "God . . . WILL RENDER TO EACH PERSON ACCORDING TO HIS DEEDS: to those who by perseverance in doing good seek for glory and honor and immortality, eternal life; but to those who are selfishly ambitious and do not obey the truth, but obey unrighteousness, wrath and indignation" (Rom. 2:6–8). For, explains Paul, "*it is* not the hearers of the Law *who* are just before God, but the doers of the Law will be justified" (2:13). In other words, Paul holds that, notwithstanding the impotence of human works for procuring God's favor, those who are justified by faith and thereby saved will receive, in addition to this paramount blessing, God's declaration that, relative to the ungodly, they are inherently righteous.

It is of this species of justification, the third type enumerated above, that James appears to write when he asserts that Abraham and Rahab were justified by works (James 2:21, 24–25). Admittedly, James declares faith without works dead (2:17, 26) and useless (2:14, 20). He describes Abraham and Rahab as justified by works (2:21, 25), moreover, and asserts that "a man is justified by works and not by faith alone" (2:24). Nevertheless, James declares only a fruitless faith useless, not the "faith working through love" (Gal. 5:6) preached by Paul. He also acknowledges the orthodoxy of the gospel Paul preaches during the latter's visit to Jerusalem recorded in Galatians 2:1–10 (see especially vv. 6–9). It seems highly improbable, therefore, that James denies Paul's doctrine of justification by faith alone.

Bibliography. J. Buchanan, *The Doctrine of Justification*; D. A. Carson, P. T. O'Brien, and M. A. Seifrid, eds., *Justification and Variegated Nomism*; J. Davenant, *A Treatise on Justification*, trans. J. Allport, 2 vols.; J. Edwards, *Justification by Faith Alone*, in *Works of Jonathan Edwards*, ed. M. X. Lesser, vol. 19; S. Gathercole, *Where Is Boasting? Early Jewish Soteriology and Paul's Response in Romans 1–5*; J. Owen, *The Doctrine of Justification by Faith*, in *Works of John Owen*, ed. William H. Goold, vol. 5; J. Piper, *The Future of Justification: A Response to N. T. Wright*; B. Vickers, *Jesus' Blood and Righteousness: Paul's Theology of Imputation*; G. P. Waters, *Justification and the New Perspectives on Paul: A Review and Response*; J. R. White, *The God Who Justifies*.

D. W. Jowers

JUZU. *Juzu* (Japanese, "counting beads") refers to a string of prayer beads used by most sects of Japanese Buddhism. Originally called *nenju* (contemplating Buddha beads), these beads were introduced in Japan by Chinese Buddhists during the seventh century, though they did not become popular there until the eighth century, when the Indian monk Bodaisenna presented a nenju to Emperor Shomu (r. 724–49). A common juzu's central string is threaded through 108 identically sized beads (*koshu*), which represent the number of earthly desires (*bonnou*) had by unenlightened mortals. There are exactly 108 beads because of the formula used to arrive at that number: 6 senses (5 ordinary ones + that of the mind) x 3 aspects of time (past, present, and future) = 18; 18 x 2 characteristics of the human heart (pure or impure) = 36; 36 x 3 attitudes (like, dislike, or indifference) a person may have toward something = 108. Representing the Buddha, 2 larger beads (*boshu*) are set at either end of the 108. One of them, the Father's Bead, has two strings of 10 beads each hanging from it (these symbolize the Ten Worlds and their mutual possession); the other, the Mother's Bead, is attached to three hanging strings of beads (which jointly symbolize *ichinen sanzen*: "three thousand worlds in a single thought"). Next to the Father's Bead is a medium-size bead that represents the eternal, absolute truth of Buddhism. These hanging beads are strung with white braided cord having white pompom tassels at the end. There are also 4 smaller beads (*shitendama*) that represent four bodhisattvas (Jogyo, Muhengyo, Jyogyo, and Anryugyo) and the Buddha's four virtues: eternity, happiness, true self, and purity. The string as a whole represents the eternal mystical law by means of which all Buddhas attain enlightenment. The roundness of the beads signifies the benefits of the mystic law and the true nature of all phenomena.

In Nichiren Shoshu, juzu function as a means of communicating the Three Treasures (the Buddha, the law, and the priesthood) to the people of *mappo* (the current age in which the Buddha's teachings are said to be obscured) as an aid to counting the number of times practitioners have chanted the *daimoku* (the mantra "nam-myoho-renge-kyo") as an aid to focusing the mind and, less commonly, as a protective charm against evil spirits. It is thought that during prayer juzu must be held in a very particular way in order to ensure that they possess maximum efficacy. Among other things, this proper holding of juzu involves placing one of the two *boshu* beads over the middle finger of each hand—holding the entire juzu in a figure-eight position—and placing the palm and fingers of each hand against the palm and fingers of the other. Practitioners believe that if they rub juzu together while facing the gohonzon (a ritual object of devotion) and chanting daimoku, their earthly desires, bad karma, and suffering will be transformed into enlightenment and nirvana. Moreover, practitioners are instructed to carry properly sanctified juzu with them wherever they go and always to handle them carefully and with respect, for the beads are considered to be one of the Three Robes that are essential to orthodox Buddhist practice. In fact, juzu are held in such high esteem by adherents of Nichiren Shoshu that, before being sold, they must be purified in front of a gohonzon by a Nichiren Shoshu priest in an event called the Eye-Opening ceremony. It is believed that during this ritual the beads are transformed into the very body and mind of the Buddha.

The other sects of Japanese Buddhism have different understandings even while using the juzu in a similar manner. For example, for Jodo-Shinshu, the whole of the string is understood as representing the Buddha's teachings, and when it is wrapped around the hands in *gassho* (prayer hands), it is a symbol of oneness. Members of the Shingon sect, while using the beads on different occasions, also rub them together for purification.

See also BUDDHISM; NICHIREN SHOSHU

Bibliography. R. Causton, *Nichiren Shoshu Buddhism*; Nichiren Shoshu Temple, *An Introduction to True Buddhism: Answers to Frequently Asked Questions*; "The Prayer Beads," *Nichiren Shoshu Monthly*.

H. W. House

KABBALAH. Kabbalah is a form of Jewish mysticism, based on allegorical interpretations of the Bible and dependent on the Talmud, that seeks to bring devotees into union with God. For three hundred years (approximately between 1500 and 1800), kabbalah was considered part of mainstream Jewish theology, but it lost much of its appeal with the emergence of the antisupernatural Enlightenment period. With the rise of postmodernism, kabbalah has made a comeback. It gained worldwide notoriety when pop divas Madonna and Barbra Streisand announced they had become followers of kabbalah.

The word *kabbalah* comes from a Hebrew root meaning "tradition" or "that which is received." Properly understood kabbalah is not a book that one can reference but rather a set of mystical traditions that have been developed and passed down orally over the centuries from teacher to pupil. Tracing its origin to early forms of Jewish gnosticism, kabbalah has much in common with other esoteric-based religions such as Theosophy and Rosicrucianism. The earliest form of kabbalistic teaching was Maaseh Merkavah, also known as the "Matter of the Chariot," based on Ezekiel's vision of the chariot (Ezek. 1). Adherents are encouraged to keep the law, observe ritual purity, and practice a variety of mystical exercises such as meditative travel, which will enable them to spiritually ascend through the seven heavenly halls to the throne of God, where they can encounter God in an ecstatic vision.

Another form of kabbalah, known as Maaseh Beresheet or the "Matter of Creation," speculates about the methods God used to create the various heavens and earths that make up the universe. The Sefer Yetzirah (Book of Formation), written between the third and sixth centuries and often attributed to Rabbi Akiva, deals with this topic and speaks of God creating the universe out of himself through ten emanations called *sefiroth* or *sephirot*, which represent his knowable attributes. These attributes are found in the various descriptive names for God: Keter (Crown), Hokhmah (Wisdom), Hesed (Mercy), Nezar (Eternal), Binah (Understanding), Din (Justice), Hod (Glory), Tiferet (Beauty), Yesod (Foundation), and Malkut (King). These are names ancient Jews often substituted for the unutterable name of God, and according to kabbalah, they form a mystical "tree of life" representing the descent of the divine in creation and the tenfold ascent one must traverse to reach God. In purist form, God is called En Sof and is infinite and unknowable. While he cannot be comprehended, he can be experienced through kabbalah.

Medieval Jewish mysticism of the eleventh and twelfth centuries saw the rise of the Hasidei Ashkenaz, or "the pious ones of Germany," who believed in the unity of several different forces within God, as opposed to the simple unity expressed in the Bible. During this period, many different collections of ethical teachings were formulated.

France and Spain became the geographical centers for the next era of kabbalah development, which spanned the thirteenth to sixteenth centuries. The Sefer ha-Bahir, or "Book of Brightness," is concerned with the hidden and secret meanings of the biblical text and the Hebrew letters. Rabbi Isaac the Blind is one of the key figures of this period. His followers focused on connecting with ten sefiroth through meditation. Kabbalah really began to grow in popularity when two of Isaac's students spread his teachings throughout Spain.

The Sefer ha-Zohar (Zohar, for short), or "Book of Splendor," a work largely attributed to thirteenth-century mystic Moses de León, is considered by many kabbalists to be the most important of their writings. It also reveals that the unknowable God can only be understood through the ten manifestations or emanations. But there is a twist. The third of these manifestations, known as Binah, brought forth creation. The next seven sefiroth constitute the seven days of creation. Hence there are two levels of emanations: upper and lower.

Joseph Gikatilla and Abraham Abulafia, who worked closely with Moses de León, spread Zohar kabbalism throughout Spain. They developed prophetic kabbalah by assigning numerical values to the twenty-two letters of the Hebrew alphabet and linking them to twenty-two paths of wisdom. Prophetic kabbalah flourished in Spain until the sixteenth century.

After the Jews were expelled from Spain in 1492, many found their way to Safed, Israel, a Galilean town, where Isaac Luria formed a new school of kabbalistic thought. While holding to the original beliefs about En Sof (infinite God) and the ten sefiroth, he expanded on the creation myth, the self-development of God, the origin of evil, and the solution for evil. He taught that the first emanation from God was a ray of light that brought forth Adam Kadmon (the first man).

Out of Adam's head, the light shone forth. God sent forth other emanations, which became vessels to contain the light. More emanations poured forth from God as one gigantic stream of light with such explosive force that the vessels were shattered. The light contained a hidden quality called *kelipot*, or evil. The light and evil mixed to produce demons. The salvation process, called *tikkun*, involves the restoration of the cosmos through prayer, obedience to the Torah, and arrival of the Messiah.

Between 1665 and 1666, Shabbetai Tzvi, a Turkish Jew, proclaimed himself to be this Messiah. This gave rise to the popular Shabbatean kabbalah movement. Many followers left their homes to travel with him to Israel, where, he claimed, he would reinstitute the Jewish commonwealth. As they traveled through Constantinople, Shabbetai was captured by a Muslim sultan, who gave him the option to either convert to Islam or face death. Shabbetai chose the former. His followers abandoned him, but their Shabbatean hope of a mystical messiah who brings salvation lived on. Many turned to a new form of mysticism called Hasidim.

Hasid comes from the Hebrew word meaning "pious." The Hasidic movement, based on the teachings of a Polish Jew, Israel ben Eliezer, also known as the Baal Shem Tov, or "Master of the Good Name," gained a following during the eighteenth century. Israel ben Eliezer did not emphasize Talmudic study or the sort of meditations taught by Isaac Luria but encouraged his followers to see God in everyday life and devote themselves to prayer, joyous singing, dancing, and storytelling. Many rabbis were attracted to his simple teachings and carried on his traditions for generations.

Over the years, Hasidic kabbalism faced many difficulties and adversaries. Many Jews considered the traditions to be little more than superstition and a corruption of Judaism. The rise of modernism, along with the horrors of the Holocaust, dealt massive blows to Jewish mysticism. In the late 1960s, with the Western world facing a spiritual vacuum, Hasidic mysticism made a comeback. Small, informal congregations were formed, called *havurot*, or "fellowships." The earliest was Havurot Shalom in Boston, which revived dancing, singing, meditation, and teachings on mysticism and was the first to allow women to participate equally with men. In 1979 Arthur Waskow founded the *New Menorah*, a quarterly journal featuring mystical articles. Rabbi Zalman founded another havurot in Philadelphia and introduced Buddhist and Sufi spiritual practices into the services.

Gershom Scholem founded the first academic program in Jewish mysticism at Hebrew University in Jerusalem in the 1920s and wrote many books on kabbalah. The Kabbalah Centre opened in 1922 in Jerusalem, with other centers opening around the world, many of which are still in operation. The Beverly Hills Kabbalah Centre, led by controversial New Age guru Philip Berg, attracts the rich and famous.

Occultic Kabbalah. In the mid-1800s, Frenchman Eliphas Levi combined the Jewish kabbalah with tarot and astrology to concoct an alternative occultic religion that he dubbed Qabalah. By the end of the century, other occult societies, such as the Order of the Golden Dawn, were inventing new hybrids of Jewish-based cults.

Christian Kabbalah. In the fifteenth century, Giovanni Pico della Mirandola of Florence, Italy, introduced a Christianized form of kabbalah, linking the first three sefiroth with the three persons of the Trinity: Keter (Father), Hokhmah (Son), and Binah (Holy Spirit). He developed an elaborate gnostic system of theology, which he called Cabala. Christian mysticism was given a big boost at the beginning of the twentieth century with the rise of the various theosophical and anthroposophical schools of thought, followed in midcentury by the birth of the New Age movement.

Regardless of the form it takes, kabbalah is essentially pantheistic in nature. Pantheism is the belief that God and his creation are one. This is contrary to the biblical record that God created all that exists from nothing.

See also MYSTICISM; PANTHEISM

Bibliography. M. Berg, *Becoming like God: Kabbalah and Our Ultimate Destiny*; D. A. Cooper, *God Is a Verb: Kabbalah and the Practice of Mystical Judaism.*

M. Power and S. L. Gregory

KALACAKRA. In Jainism, Kalacakra (or Kalachakra) is the endless "wheel of time" that provides the backdrop for the Jain understanding of the unfolding of history. Jain cosmology maintains that time itself is without beginning or end but is split into two epochs that are used to explain the eternal, cyclical pattern that allegedly governs the historical process (and in particular, the development of human civilization and religion). The Kalacakra is divided into two subcycles of equal length: one in which things ascend and become progressively better (*utsarpini*) and one in which things descend and become progressively worse (*avasarpini*). Each of these subcycles is further divided into six unequal periods of time called *aras*. By Jain reckoning, the universe is now going through the fifth *ara* of an *avasarpini* phase; it is believed that these series of cycles will continue to elapse forever. The six aras are as follows: (1) Sukham Sukham Kal, an era of great happiness in which people live extremely long lives, never suffer unfulfilled desire, and are perfectly virtuous; (2) Sukham Kal, an era in which people still experience considerable happiness, have all their needs met, and live fairly long lives, but which is not as wonderful as the era preceding it; (3) Sukham Dukham Kal, a marginally happy era that nevertheless contains a fair amount of misery and during which people learn basic survival skills like farming, the manufacturing of clothing, and political organization (in anticipation of the next, less-fortunate era); (4) Dukham Sukham Kal, an era in which there is more misery than happiness but things are nonetheless not terribly bad, inasmuch as there remains some measure of prosperity and enjoyment; (5) Dukham Kal, the present era of substantial misery—intermingled with some happiness—which will continue for another eighteen thousand to nineteen thousand years (by the end of this time period Jainism will have ceased to be practiced by anyone); and (6) Dukham Dukham Kal, an era of tremendous misery during which the knowledge of Jainism will be nonexistent and people will have very brief life spans, suffer constantly, and be so immoral that the social order will collapse into ruin.

See also JAINISM

Bibliography. J. E. Cort, *Jains in the World: Religious Values and Ideology in India*; P. Dundas, *The Jains*; N. Shah, *Jainism: The World of Conquerors*; K. L. Wiley, *Historical Dictionary of Jainism*.

H. W. House

KALACAKRA TANTRA. The Kalacakra (Sanskrit, "wheel of time") Tantra is one of the many texts that makes up the Buddhist canon and acts as the foundation for the Vajrayana form of Buddhism. This is one of the most important tantras still being widely followed today, the initiation for which has been repeatedly offered by the Dalai Lama. It is divided into two broad divisions of "outer" and "inner." The outer text contains history, prophecy, calendar calculations, cosmology, and so on. The inner section presents information on being human, including conception, development, functions of the body, and medical information. Following this, the text teaches a complicated ritual system with initiations, yogas, mandalas, worship, meditations, and the state of enlightenment.

Bibliography. Geshe Ngawang Dhargyey, *Kalacakra Tantra*; J. Hopkins, *The Kalacakra Tantra, Rite of Imitation*.

A. W. Barber

KALPA SUTRA. The Kalpa Sutra is an important book in Jainism that contains the authorized biography of each of the twenty-four Jain tirthankaras (beings who have attained liberation). The final and most prominent of these is Mahavira (559–527 BC). Adherents of Jainism do not view the Kalpa Sutra as having the same authority as the sacred texts that compose the Jain canon; however, it is deemed helpful as a source of inspiration in pursuing the rigorous path toward liberation enjoined in Jainism.

See also JAINISM

Bibliography. K. C. Lalwani, trans., *Kalpa Sutra*, 2nd ed.; B. S. Shah, *An Introduction to Jainism*.

M. Power

KAMI. *Kami*, a Japanese word used in the Shinto faith, refers to a divine consciousness that flows through all life, manifesting itself in different ways. For the most part, kami can be described roughly as spirits. In some cases, however, this characterization is misleading because there is such a great diversity of kami—sometimes it is claimed that there are more than eight million—not all of which are conceived of as personal. Types of kami include those related to objects in nature (such as the sun, mountains, rivers, trees, rocks, and rice paddies) and living animals (like foxes, tigers, raccoons, rabbits, and cats); kami can be forces of nature (such as wind, rain, thunder, and earthquakes), the occurrence of fertility and growth, the production of goods and services, guardian spirits (of individual clans, particular regions, and the islands of Japan as a whole), ancestral spirits (of the Japanese imperial family, deceased national leaders, and Japanese heroes and nobility), "straightening" kami who rectify problems, "bending" kami who cause disasters, and many deities, including the sun goddess Amaterasu-Omikami. According to the grand legend of Shinto recorded in a medieval chronicle known as the Kojiki, beginning in 660 BC with Emperor Jimmu, the emperors of Japan can trace their line of descent all the way back to Amaterasu Omikami. Japanese emperors were regarded as living kami by their subjects until January 1946, when Emperor Hirohito (1901–89) disavowed his divine status under intense pressure from the Allied forces of World War II.

See also SHINTO; SOKA GAKKAI

Bibliography. C. S. Littleton, *Understanding Shinto: Origins, Beliefs, Practices, Festivals, Spirits, Sacred Places*; S. Ono, *Shinto: The Kami Way*.

J. Bjornstad

KARMA. Karma (Sanskrit, "action") is a fundamental concept in Hinduism, Buddhism, Jainism, and the New Age movement. It was originally found in the Upanishads (written from the early 800s BC) and finds full expression in the Hindu classic the Bhagavad Gita.

The law of karma is a complex collection of variously nuanced ideas. In its simplest expression, it means doing good works, especially religious duties associated with caste. Hence it is one of the three Hindu ways of attaining salvation, along with gaining spiritual wisdom (*jnana*) and devotional worship (bhakti).

In its classic sense, karma is the law of cause and effect, where actions (intentional and nonintentional) of body, speech, and mind cause future results: virtuous actions result in happiness, and nonvirtuous actions result in suffering. The principle of karma assumes immortality of the soul and an eternal cycle of existence (samsara) within a monistic worldview (*advaita*). Karmic merit (or demerit) is accumulated over many lifetimes—karma in past lifetimes has consequences in this life, while actions in this life have consequences in future lives,

into which the conscious soul (in Hinduism) is reborn. Buddhist constructs vary on the idea of "soul," proposing five *skandhas*, or qualities of existence, constantly reforming at each new incarnation and in effect being manifestations of karmic law. Buddhism also rejects the idea of caste and emphasizes one's intention. Jainism also rejects caste but maintains that both intentional and unintentional actions have their karma.

The mechanism of transference of karmic debt is that actions leave imprints on the consciousness that transmigrate to the next lifetime and fructify as one's position in class or caste, one's nature or personality, or as the actual circumstances one experiences throughout that lifetime. The process is purely mechanical, with no intervention from a deity. To earn karmic merit, one must be active.

While some actions produce neither positive nor negative merit, bad karma leads to future births eventually in any number of hells, and good karma leads to births as human or in any number of heavens. In Mahayana Buddhism, a bodhisattva delays his own entrance to nirvana to assist other sentient beings into nirvana by transference of his excess karmic credit.

In this lifetime, one may earn karmic merit by doing good deeds (supporting monks, freeing animals from captivity, reading religious texts, going on pilgrimages, and the like) so that ultimately, over many lifetimes, one aspires to release from the bondage of karmic law and samsara, into oneness with Brahma (in Hinduism) or nirvana (in Buddhism), the extinction of individual consciousness and desire.

The law of karma is self-evident and non-changeable for those with an Eastern, monistic worldview and explains the inequalities among sentient beings in general and in human society in particular. Hence Hindu and Buddhist societies often appear fatalistic to the outsider.

Hinduism and Buddhism understand most if not all gods themselves to be bound by the law of karma.

In New Age thinking, karma is the context of all one's experiences and operates against the path to higher consciousness and personal or cosmic harmony. In the Divine Life Society, Karma Yoga is the consecration of all actions and their consequences in self-surrender to the divine. Self-realization is attained when an altruistic act of service is an act of worship.

The word Karma is sometimes incorporated into names of institutions and appears periodically as a personal feminine name.

See also BUDDHISM; HINDUISM; UPANISHADS

Bibliography. D. Burnett, *The Spirit of Hinduism: A Christian Perspective on Hindu Thought*; T. Gyatso, *Freedom in Exile: The Autobiography of the Dalai Lama of Tibet*; D. S. Lopez Jr., *Buddhism: An Introduction and Guide*; V. Mangalwadi, *The World of Gurus: A Critical Look at the Philosophies of India's Influential Gurus and Mystics*.

H. P. Kemp

KARMI. *Karmi* is a common term used by adherents of Krishna spirituality to refer to an outsider, one who is not a devotee of Krishna and who is therefore bound by karma. Known as a "fruitive actor" in the International Society for Krishna Consciousness (ISKCON), such a person is said to have wrong motives. On the other hand, a Hare Krishna devotee attempts to eliminate all impure worldly desires (*kaman*) by seeking spiritual enlightenment through the continual chanting of the Hare Krishna mantra, among other activities.

See also INTERNATIONAL SOCIETY FOR KRISHNA CONSCIOUSNESS (ISKCON); KRISHNA CONSCIOUSNESS; PRABHUPADA, ABHAY CHARAN DE BHAKTIVEDANTA SWAMI

Bibliography. S. Gelberg, *Hare Krishna, Hare Krishna*; J. Judah, *Hare Krishna and the Counterculture*.

E. Johnson

KHALSA. Khalsa (Punjabi, "pure") is the name given to a volunteer army of Sikhs who have devoted themselves to protecting and serving the Sikh people, especially the weak and defenseless. The Khalsa was formed in India during the seventeenth century by Guru Gobind Singh in response to the extreme and sustained maltreatment of Sikhs by Islamic rulers there. Each member of this military force is called upon to be both a soldier and a saint, emulating the religious ideal of *bhagti* (devotion to God). Every Khalsa Sikh vows to carry on his or her person, at all times, the five primary symbols of Sikhism. These are (1) a short sword (*kirpan*), which symbolizes dignity and bravery, (2) uncut hair (*kesh*), indicating the submission of the warrior to God's will, (3) a wooden comb (*kangha*)—worn beneath a turban—that represents purity, (4) a metal bracelet (*kara*) worn around the wrist as a sign of commitment and self-discipline, and (5) special underpants (*kacha*). To become a Khalsa member, initiates go through an elaborate ceremony known as Amritsanskar in which they vow to behave in accordance with high standards of Sikh purity. Each initiate is given a new surname; for males it is Singh (Punjabi, "lion"), for females it is Kaur (Punjabi, "princess").

See also SIKHISM

Bibliography. S. S. Kapoor, *Sikhism—An Introduction*; E. Nesbitt, *Sikhism: A Very Short Introduction*; P. Singh, *The Sikhs*.

J. Bjornstad

KNIGHTS TEMPLAR. The Knights Templar were medieval warrior-monks who were charged by the Roman pontiff with the task of defending Christians in the Holy Land against the persecution of Muslim warriors. At the Council of Troyes in AD 1128, the Knights embraced the Rule of St. Benedict, which was described by Jacques-Benigne Bossuet, a seventeenth-century Roman Catholic writer, as "an epitome of Christianity, a learned and mysterious abridgment of all the doctrines of the Gospel, all the institutions of the Fathers, and all the counsels of perfection" (quoted in "Rule of Benedict"). Philip Schaff called Boussuet's statement an "evident exaggeration" (n380). Alternate names for the order were Poor Knights of Christ and Poor Knights of the Temple of Solomon, though during the Crusades these orders acquired considerable wealth, prestige, and land.

A Knight was an odd mixture of spiritual leader and warrior. The men lived in monasteries that also served as barracks. They were fierce in battle but also committed to their monastic vows. They vehemently rejected anything offered in exchange for a denial of their faith, even when they faced torture and death. During the two hundred years of their history, approximately twenty thousand of them died in battle. Their dedication and courage served as a model for other military orders that arose during the periods of the Crusades to liberate the Holy Land (Israel) from the encroachment of Islam begun in the seventh century.

Though respected during the Crusades, after the failure of the Crusades to secure the Holy Land for Christians, the Knights became a liability, and because they had acquired so much land, many leaders in various countries began to oppose them. The secrecy of the Knights Templar worked against them, and they were even accused of heresy. Jacques de Molai, considered the Grand Master of the Templars around 1298, was condemned to be burned at the stake by Philip the Fair.

Finally, in 1312, Pope Clement V took away the property of the order and gave it to the Order of Hospitallers, another military order, but did allow the Knights Templar to either return to civil life or join another military order.

Bibliography. "Council of Troyes," in *Encyclopedia Britannica*, http://www.britannica.com/Ebchecked/topic/606920/Council-of-Troyes; "Jacques-Benigne Bossuet," in *The Catholic En-*cyclopedia, http://www.newadvent.org/cathen/02698b.htm; "Jacques de Molai," in *The Catholic Encyclopedia*, http://www.newdvent.org/cathen/10433a.htm; "The Rule of Benedict," Order of Saint Benedict website, http://www.osb.org/rb/index.html#English; "Rule of St. Benedict," in *The Catholic Encyclopedia*, http://www.newadvent.org/cathen/02436a.htm; P. Schaff, *History of the Christian Church*, vol. 3, *Nicene and Post-Nicene Christianity, A.D. 311–600.*

H. W. House

KOAN. Etymologically *koan* (Japanese, from the Chinese *kung-an*) means "public case" in the context of a standard or judgment. Traditionally, koans are famous utterances of Chinese Ch'an masters. In modern Zen Buddhism, koans are short paradoxical statements—often a riddle that cannot be solved by pure reason—used as meditative tools to transcend or suddenly dissolve logical thought to achieve new insight (satori).

Using a koan clears the way, by transcending dualities, to direct seeing into the true nature of existence, specifically nonself. There are two types of koan: the breakthrough koan, used to "break through" the dualism of conceptual thought and awaken one to one's true nature, and subsequent koans, used to free one from the lingering bonds of delusion. One cannot study koans; they must be experienced, inasmuch as they allow one to enter into the mind of the original speaker but also go beyond this to experience the one mind from which the koan originated. Koans are compiled into various texts such as the *Mumonkan* and the *Blue Cliff Record*, which are used as manuals for Zen training.

Well-known koans include "What is the sound of one hand clapping?" and "All the peaks are covered with snow—why is this one bare?"

See also ZEN BUDDHISM

Bibliography. D. T. Suzuki, *An Introduction to Zen Buddhism.*

H. P. Kemp

KO-JI-KI. The Ko-ji-ki (Japanese, "record of ancient matters") is the most important of the sacred texts of Shinto and the oldest extant writing dealing with ancient Japanese history. It was commissioned by the Japanese emperor Temmu (r. ca. 672–86). Though said to have been dictated from memory by the esteemed scholar Hieda no Are (late seventh and early eighth centuries), it was compiled primarily by the Japanese scribe Ono Yasumaro (d. 723) and presented to Empress Genmei (r. 707–15) at the Imperial Court at Heijo-kyo (modern-day Nara) in AD 712. The Ko-ji-ki is arranged into three sections: the Kamitsumaki (upper roll), Nakatsumaki (middle roll), and Shimotsumaki (lower roll). The Kamitsumaki mainly concerns the creation of the islands of Japan and the origins of various Shinto gods. The Nakatsumaki relates the story of the first Japanese emperor, Jimmu—said to have ascended the throne in 660 BC—as well as the reigns of the next fourteen emperors, ending with Ojin (ca. AD 300). The Shimotsumaki chronicles the administrations of the sixteenth through thirty-third rulers of Japan, beginning with Emperor Nintoku (ca. 350) and ending with Empress Suiko (r. 593–628). The stories found in the Ko-ji-ki are variously myths, legends, history, or a blending of genres, though scholars who have examined these writings generally affirm that the first and second sections contain substantially less history than the third. The Ko-ji-ki also contains a number of patriotic songs. Most scholars who are conversant with the history of the Ko-ji-ki believe that several lines of oral tradition, many of which concerned the worship of ancestors, were brought together to form the document. Some such scholars maintain that the Ko-ji-ki is specifically an attempt by the rulers of the late Yamato period (ca. 250–715) to justify their claim to possess a divine mandate to rule the nation of Japan.

See also SHINTO

Bibliography. J. S. Brownlee, *Political Thought in Japanese Historical Writing from Kojiki (712) to Tokushi Yoron (1712)*; B. H. Chamberlain, trans., *Kojiki: Records of Ancient Matters*, repr. ed.; T. P. Kasulis, *Shinto: The Way Home*; D. L. Philippi, *Kojiki*.

H. W. House

KOSHER (KASHER). The basic meaning of the word *kosher* is something that is "fit" or "proper," but *kosher* became the key rabbinic term for anything that is ritually fit, proper, or permitted. This is in contrast to *terefah* (or simply *treif*), which refers to something that is nonkosher or something that is ritually unclean or unfit.

When applied to food, *kosher* covers foods permitted by the Mosaic law. Therefore, beef would be kosher but pork would be terefah. However, even permitted meats can be nonkosher if they were not ritually slaughtered in the proper way. The term is also applied to nonmeat food items such as "kosher pickles." This is often based on the way they are prepared and how they are stored. Since Mosaic law prohibits cooking a goat in its mother's milk, dairy and meat cannot be either cooked or stored together. While many dishes can be ritually cleaned to become kosher, others must be thrown away after becoming unkosher. Due to these minute restrictions, many Orthodox Jews have two complete kitchens. Less-affluent Jews have two sets of dishes and storage containers. So ritual stipulations concerning food by rabbinic theology go beyond Mosaic law. The term *kosher* is also applied to items that may be proper for certain days but not for other days. Thus *matzot* (unleavened bread) may be kosher for all other days of the year but marked as "not kosher for Passover" if, in the preparation of the matzot, the rules necessary to make sure that no leavening could occur were not followed. Also, wine is kosher for Passover, but beer and whiskey are not, since these are made from grain or vegetables that can contain leaven.

The term *kosher* is also applied to the *tzitzit*—the tassels on the corners of Orthodox Jewish garments—if they were properly spun, and to the *tefillin* (phylacteries) and *mezuzot* (small rectangular boxes nailed to the doorways of Jewish homes), which contain scrolls that have been properly written.

See also JUDAISM

Bibliography. Rabbi B. Forst, *The Laws of Kashrus: A Comprehensive Exposition of Their Underlying Concepts and Applications*; Rabbi Y. Lipschutz, *Kashruth: A Comprehensive Background and Reference Guide to the Principles of Kashruth*; C. Roth, "Kosher," in *Encyclopedia Judaica*, edited by C. Roth; I. Singer, "Kosher," in *The Jewish Encyclopedia*; I. Welfeld, *Why Kosher? An Anthology of Answers.*

A. Fruchtenbaum

KRISHNA. Krishna is a Hindu god of love and compassion and considered one of the eight incarnations (avatars) of the god Vishnu. He is worshiped as a supreme god by some and as a member of a group by others.

Krishna's iconography depicts him at different points in his growth. Sometimes he is shown as a child eating butter; a handsome young man playing a flute; alongside his wife, Radha; or in other stages of development. One popular form is Krishna as charioteer to the great warrior Arjuna. This depiction is directly related to the major Krishna narrative as given in the Bhagavad Gita (the midportion of the Mahabharata epic), where he appears as a teacher and as a victorious warrior over a demon king. He is also the god worshiped in the famous Jagannath, with its fantastic procession.

Krishna is preached as the supreme form of the godhead by the International Society for Krishna Consciousness (ISKCON), which is a form of Vaishnavite or devotional Hinduism known as bhakti. The branch of this tradition out of which ISKCON developed goes back to Sri Mahaprabhu Caitanya, a teacher in the sixteenth century. ISKCON was introduced in America in the mid-1960s by A. C. Bhaktivedanta Swami Prabhupada, a former pharmacist from Bengal. The form of ISKCON that took shape in America is known as Hare Krishna, which emphasizes devotion to Krishna, or God, and does not distinguish persons by caste.

Hare Krishna is based on a dualistic ontology. Adherents strive to escape the material world and be joined to God. They do this by escaping the cycle of birth/death/reincarnation, which, in turn, they achieve by strictly controlling the senses through Bhakti (a term meaning "devotion") Yoga. One aspect of this devotion is to chant the mantra, "Hare Krishna, Hare Krishna, Krishna Krishna, Hare Hare, Hare Rama, Hare Rama, Rama Rama, Hare Hare" (Newport, 70). Another aspect of Krishna spirituality is to devote one's life to service to Krishna and the spread of Krishna consciousness through preaching and chanting.

See also BHAKTI YOGA; BRAHMA; HINDUISM; INTERNATIONAL SOCIETY FOR KRISHNA CONSCIOUSNESS (ISKCON); MANTRA; PRABHUPADA, ABHAY CHARAN DE BHAKTIVEDANTA SWAMI; SHIVA

Bibliography. W. Corduan, *Neighboring Faiths: A Christian Introduction to World Religions*; Corduan, *A Tapestry of Faiths: The Common Threads between Christianity and World Religions*; D. Halverson, "Hinduism," in *The Illustrated Guide to World Religions*, edited by D. Halverson; J. P. Newport, *The New Age Movement and the Biblical Worldview: Conflict and Dialogue.*

J. D. Wilsey

KRISHNA CONSCIOUSNESS. A special realization that one is eternally related to God, as taught by the International Society for Krishna Consciousness (ISKCON), Krishna consciousness is achieved through the chanting of Krishna's name and the practice of devotional yoga. A person who is able to completely control his physical senses will then be able to return to a "natural, pure state of consciousness" and awaken his soul from the "dreamlike condition of material life." The understanding of one's godlike potentiality is vital in being delivered from the cycle of births and deaths that is involved in the reincarnation process. The Hare Krishna mantra—which followers, known as devotees, are supposed to chant 1,728 times per day—helps cleanse one's mind and free it from anxiety and material illusion. According to ISKCON founder A. C. Bhaktivedanta Swami Prabhupada (1896–1977): "Krishna consciousness is not an artificial imposition on the mind. . . . By chanting this *maha-mantra*, or the Great Chanting for Deliverance, one can at once feel a transcendental ecstasy coming through the spiritual stratum."

See also INTERNATIONAL SOCIETY FOR KRISHNA CONSCIOUSNESS (ISKCON); KARMI; PRABHUPADA, ABHAY CHARAN DE BHAKTIVEDANTA SWAMI

Bibliography. S. J. Gelberg, *Hare Krishna, Hare Krishna*; J. S. Judah, *Hare Krishna and the Counterculture*; A. C. B. Swami Prabhupada, *Bhagavad-Gita as It Is.*

E. Johnson

KUMBHA MELA. Kumbha (or Kumbh) Mela is the greatest Hindu festival, held every twelve years at Allahabad, India, at the confluence of the Ganges, Yamuna, and mythical Saraswati Rivers, attracting millions. Smaller Kumbh Melas occur every four years at three other holy river sites. Pilgrims bathe at the most auspicious time to gain merit and to cleanse body and soul.

See also HINDUISM

Bibliography. P. P. Bhalla, *Hindu Rites, Rituals, Customs, and Traditions.*

H. P. Kemp

KUNDALINI. Taken from the Sanskrit word *kundal* (coiled up), *kundalini* refers to the Hindu belief that a "serpent power" lies coiled like a snake in the root chakra (wheel of energy) at the base of the spine.

In Hindu mythology, it is the serpent goddess Kundalini who rests at the base of an individual's spine. It is said that she begins to evolve in a person's first incarnation (in the reincarnation cycle), being fed by the other six chakras on the spine and by the cosmic energy entering through the feet from the earth. Starting at the lowest chakra, she is aroused through yoga practice and travels up through the other chakras, finally reaching the crown chakra. In Tantric Yoga, which is more sexual than other forms of yoga, Kundalini is a part of Shakti, the divine female energy and consort of Shiva (male deity).

Though Eastern in origin, kundalini is certainly a part of the West's New Age movement, and as a yoga practice, it teaches that the mind and the body are ultimately "one." The basic goal in all yoga is the same: union with ultimate reality. In Hinduism it is to be "one" with the impersonal Brahma, the highest Hindu god; in Buddhism, it would be union with nirvana (state of bliss).

See also HINDUISM; TANTRA; TANTRIC YOGA

Bibliography. J. G. Bletzer, *The Donning International Encyclopedic Psychic Dictionary*; R. E. Guiley, *Harper's Encyclopedia of Mystical Paranormal Experience*; Swami S. Radha, *Kundalini: Yoga for the West.*

C. Hux

KWAN YIN. Also known as Kuan Yin, Guanyin, or Kannon, in Buddhism Kwan Yin is the feminine form of Avalokiteshvara, the Buddhist bodhisattva of compassion as found in East Asia. Kwan Yin is revered throughout China, Japan, and Korea in a variety of images. She is popular with women, being regarded as the bodhisattva of compassion, wealth, and fertility and the protector of children. In Taoism she is regarded as an immortal (from non-Buddhist sources)

295

and is the favorite goddess of Chinese rural dwellers and fishermen. Within the New Age movement and esoterica, Kwan Yin is associated with Mary, Sophia, and other goddess figures.

See also BODHISATTVA; BUDDHISM; TAOISM/ DAOISM

Bibliography. Paul Williams, *Mahayana Buddhism: The Doctrinal Foundations*.

H. P. Kemp

LAMANITES. The Lamanites are an alleged rebellious group of people who are the principal antagonists in the Book of Mormon. They are descended from the wicked Laman, who is said to have left Israel in order to sail to the American continent with his father, Lehi, in the sixth century BC. The Book of Mormon details how Laman plotted to kill his righteous brother the prophet Nephi and how the Lamanites eventually destroyed the Nephites in the fifth century AD. Controversially, the Book of Mormon also claims that the Lamanites were cursed with a "skin of darkness" due to their sinfulness, while the Nephites were "white and delightsome." Recent editions of the Book of Mormon have been changed to say "pure" instead of "white." The Mormons generally believe that American Indians are Lamanite descendants (while certain Mormon leaders have called all indigenous peoples "Lamanites").

See also BOOK OF MORMON; CHURCH OF JESUS CHRIST OF LATTER-DAY SAINTS; SMITH, JOSEPH, JR.

Bibliography. R. Abanes, *One Nation under God: A History of the Mormon Church*; R. E. Lee, *What Do Mormons Believe?*

E. Johnson

LAO TZU / LAOZI. Lao Tzu is the common name of the acclaimed Chinese founder of Taoism. Lao Tzu or Lao-tse is an honorific title meaning "old man" or "old master"; the spelling Laozi is preferred academically.

Lao Tzu's earliest biography appears in the Shi-Chi (historical records), composed around 90 BC. It says he was born Li Erh or Li Dan in 605 BC in a village now called Honan. The account contains both credible narrative and miracle stories, such as his mother conceiving him after seeing a falling star and carrying him in her womb for sixty-two years until his birth.

According to tradition, Lao Tzu was keeper of the imperial archives at Zhou. There he met Confucius, who twice sought his counsel on certain rituals. In his old age, Lao Tzu left the kingdom when he recognized its imminent collapse. As he was traveling to the mountains, the keeper of the pass insisted that he write down his wisdom, which he did in five thousand Chinese characters. They became two books, the Tao Ching and the Te Ching, now joined as the Tao Te Ching (scholars believe these books were composed in the third century BC). Though he was never seen again, he supposedly lived a very long life. Over the centuries, an accretion of legend and hero worship grew around Lao Tzu, and by the third century AD he had been deified as a Buddha, one of the Three Heavenly Worthies, and the supreme being of some Taoist sects.

See also TAOISM/DAOISM; TAO TE CHING / DAO DE JING

Bibliography. J. M. Boltz, "Laozi," in *Encyclopedia of Religion*, 2nd ed., edited by L. Jones; M. J. O'Neal and J. S. Jones, "Laozi," in *World Religions: Biographies*, edited by N. Schlager and J. Weisblatt; J. F. Pas, *Historical Dictionary of Taoism*.

E. Pement

LEGALISM FROM A CHRISTIAN PERSPEC-TIVE. In general legalism (also "nomism," from Greek, *nomos*, law) denotes the belief that morality and/or salvation consist(s) in the observance of laws. Closer inspection, however, reveals at least four forms of legalism.

Biblical Legalism. First, *biblical legalism* stands as a corrective to antinomianism, the view that grace frees the believer from obligation to law (which in practice usually results in antinomians claiming they are under no behavioral or moral restrictions). Jesus declared that he came not to abolish but to "fulfill" the Law (Matt. 5:17). The "law is a transcript of the holiness of God" (Strong, 875) and, even in believers, still has the force of exhortation, so "that by teaching, admonishing, rebuking, and correcting, it may fit and prepare us for every good work" (Calvin, II. 7.14). Thus many psalms express delight in the law; for example, "Your word is a lamp for my feet, a light on my path" (Ps. 119:105). Some forms of early Christian asceticism, especially popular in the post-apostolic church, represent special applications of biblical legalism.

Theological or Ideal Legalism. Second, *theological* or *ideal legalism* advocates respect (even love) for law as the foundation of civilized society. In his *Republic*, for example, Plato defined the ideal state in terms of obedience to laws derived from the universal good. Similar sentiments can be traced throughout the cultures of ancient Greece and Rome. Immanuel Kant (1724–1804) conceived of morality as "conformity of actions to universal law as such," expressed in the famous categorical imperative: "I ought never to act except in such a way *that I can also will that my maxim should become a universal law*" (70).

Meritocratic Legalism. Third, Christians often embrace a kind of *meritocratic legalism*, even while holding intellectually to salvation by grace. Paul wrote Galatians to oppose this belief in the efficacy of law-keeping rather than (or in addition to) faith as a means to divine favor. "Having begun by the Spirit," Paul asks, "are you now being perfected by the flesh?" (Gal. 3:3 NASB). The fourth-century Donatists exemplify the meritocratic form of legalism. There are strains of this kind of legalism today in parts of evangelicalism. They assert that doing certain activities, while not resulting in the loss of salvation per se, is always sinful for Christians. Conversely, avoiding these activities results in sanctification. While it is true the New Testament does preclude certain activities (e.g., the eating of blood, fornication, lying), these modern legalists add activities not precluded in the New Testament (e.g., dancing, drinking alcohol, entertainment).

Salvific Legalism. Finally, there is *salvific legalism*, such as characterized Pharisaic Judaism and diverse religious movements both ancient and modern, ranging from the rigidly ascetical Ebionites to modern moral progressivists, such as the Mormons. Every non-Christian or sub-Christian doctrine of salvation is "legalistic" in the narrow sense that the only alternative to salvation by grace is works-based autosoterism. But the term is more accurately applied to religious systems that consider strict observance of individual laws as the substance of moral life and equate this moral life with salvation. Such movements are often highly *casuistic*—that is, they formulate systems of rules to define obedience in specific cases. Legalistic systems thus tend not only to disconnect moral laws from any underlying unity but to eliminate distinctions between the laws themselves by making the mere *act* of observance supreme. Hence Jesus rebuked the Pharisees for failing to grasp the theological basis for Moses's divorce legislation (Matt. 19:3–9). The "whole Law and the Prophets," Jesus declared, is summarized by love of God and neighbor (Matt. 22:35–40 NASB; also Luke 18:18–22).

Bibliography. J. Calvin, *Institutes of the Christian Religion*, translated by Henry Beveridge;

C. E. Ehrhardt, "Nomism," in *The Encyclopedia of Religion and Ethics*; I. Kant, *Groundwork of the Metaphysic of Morals*; M. Luther, *On Christian Liberty*; A. H. Strong, *Systematic Theology: A Compendium Designed for the Use of Theological Students*.

C. R. Wells

LIBERAL CHRISTIANITY. Born in nineteenth-century post-Enlightenment Germany, liberalism marked a dramatic shift in prominent Christian theology. The diverse range of beliefs liberalism encompasses defies a tightly drawn definition.

German theologian Friedrich Schleiermacher redefined Christian theology by emphasizing religious experience over doctrine and feeling over objective truth. The authority and inspiration of Scripture were questioned, and doctrine became subject to the tests of experience and reason. Rudolf Bultmann's "demythologization" of the New Testament contributed to the idea that the Bible was fallible and incapable of communicating with modern human beings. Through the years, liberalism has maintained one nonnegotiable, that of a nonliteral interpretation of Scripture.

Intent on relating faith through the confines of culture, liberalism modified or repressed the unique particulars of the Christian faith. Humanity's condition as sinners was dismissed, replaced with a fervent optimism about humankind's ability to imitate the moral and loving example of Jesus and attain perfection. Liberal thought abounded with hope that the kingdom of God could be established on earth through believers' efforts. Good works took precedence over confessions and creeds, and liberalism connected with a social gospel to effect social change.

The belief that God is present in the world and in the cultural movements of history is an important tenet of Christian liberalism. Evolution was heralded as validation that God works through natural law. This belief led liberalism to seek out "universal" elements common to all belief systems and to embrace them. Liberalism still persists today, though its heady optimism was dispelled by two world wars and a waning popularity.

Bibliography. A. E. McGrath, *A Passion for Truth: The Intellectual Coherence of Evangelicalism*; B. M. G. Reardon, ed., *Liberal Protestantism*.

M. Stewart

LI CHI / LIJI. The Li Chi (also spelled Liji) is one of the five Confucian classics. It explains ritualized life according to Confucian values. This includes institutional and social customs, home discipline, royal regulations, dress, the theory of ceremonies and rituals, utensils used, the lives of Confucius and his disciples, and more. Much of the material is indeed ancient, but scholars think it was compiled during the Han Dynasty.

See also CONFUCIANISM; CONFUCIUS

Bibliography. B. D. Kyokai, *The Teachings of Confucianism*.

A. W. Barber

LIEH-TZU/LIEZI. The Lieh-tzu (Chinese, scripture of the perfect emptiness) is one of the four major scriptures of Taoism, widely considered to be the most accessible and practical of this collection of texts. Until recently it was thought that Lieh-tzu (ca. fifth century BC) had written most (if not all) of the book, but the latest historical research has demonstrated that this hypothesis is highly unlikely. Instead, it is now generally believed by scholars of Taoism that the book was composed by multiple authors and was not arranged in its present form until sometime during the Qin Dynasty (221–206 BC). Some scholars see evidence of Buddhist influences in certain portions of the text. Containing eight chapters, the Lieh-tzu includes stories, speeches, dialogues, sayings, and didactic passages. Many of its chapter titles are names of well-known persons from the history or mythology of China. Prominently featured in the text is the Taoist concept of nondoing (*wu-wei*), as contrasted with the Confucian ideal of ongoing activity in the public sphere. Other topics covered in the volume include fatalism and human destiny, preparation for death, criticisms of Confucian epistemology, the metaphysics and epistemology of certain sects of Taoism, and the joys of human imagination and the natural world.

See also CONFUCIANISM; TAOISM/DAOISM; WU-WEI

Bibliography. A. C. Graham, *The Book of Lieh-Tzu: A Classic of Tao*, repr. ed.; A. McCarron, "Lieh Tzu," http://www.philtar.ac.uk/encyclopedia/taoism/lieh.html; J. Paper and L. G. Thompson, eds., *Chinese Way in Religion*, 2nd ed.; E. Wong, *Lieh-Tzu: A Taoist Guide to Practical Living*.

H. W. House

LINGAM. Lingam (Sanskrit, "mark" or "sign") is a symbol representing Shiva in Hinduism. It is depicted as a male sexual organ and often associated with the yoni (the female organ, representation of Shakti, Shiva's consort), with the lingam being placed in the yoni. Together they are said to bring fertility or to represent the creative power of the universe and union.

See also HINDUISM; SHAKTI; SHIVA; YONI

Bibliography. U. Becker and L. W. Garmer, *The Continuum Encyclopedia of Symbols*.

H. W. House

LITURGY. The word *liturgy* is from the Greek word *leitourgia*, which originally meant public duty and was used of the service to the state done by a citizen. It was the Greek word used in the Greek translation of the Hebrew Bible (the Septuagint, or LXX) to refer to the public service of priests in the temple. This religious meaning develops in New Testament times, and afterward, as the public service of the church. In this sense, the term comes to be used to describe the order or structure of worship. It deals with the way worship is conducted in different denominations. The oldest liturgies are those of the Coptic, the Eastern Orthodox, and the Roman Catholic Churches. In these churches, the priests play a key role, with the congregation as participants, in a divine act that brings them to God. The central act in these traditions is that of Communion or the Mass, which is performed by the priests with little input from the congregation. The Roman Catholic Church includes all of the public rites of the church as *liturgy*, while the Eastern Orthodox Church restricts the term to the Holy Eucharist.

Since the Reformation, Protestant Christians have developed their own unique forms of liturgy that stress the centrality of preaching and the role of the Bible in the service. Lutheran and Anglican churches have reformed the Roman Catholic liturgy largely on the basis of the works of the church fathers and other early liturgies. As they did so, their principle was to remove anything that they believed conflicted with a clear reading of Scripture but leave intact other practices that were supported by tradition. On the other hand, churches in the Calvinist and Baptist traditions reformed the liturgy in terms of only doing things that are clearly found in Scripture. In the nineteenth century, Roman Catholic–type liturgy was revived within the Anglican and some other Protestant churches. Today the Eastern Orthodox tradition appears to be influencing many evangelical Christians in their thoughts about liturgy.

One of the determining influences on the formation of traditional liturgies is the clear biblical injunction to remember what God has done (cf. Deut. 8:2) and the quest for spiritual roots (Josh. 4; Luke 11:29–32; Acts 7; Heb. 12). Consequently, Christians follow practices such as the observance of the church year, which is based on the life of Christ and celebrates things like Advent, the period leading up to the birth of Christ; Christmas, the birth of Christ; Lent, a time of personal reflection and repentance that remembers the temptations of Christ; and, of course, the central liturgical events of Holy Week and the death of Christ, followed by his triumphal resurrection and ascension. Following a regular pattern of Bible readings and recalling events from Scripture shape the worship of liturgical churches. This worship, they believe, develops a deep-seated piety and sense of the divine based on Scripture.

On the other hand, many evangelical churches of the Plymouth Brethren variety see such acts as "dead rituals" and reject them. Such churches claim to lack a ritual structure, although their liturgical critics argue that they have one that they simply fail to recognize.

Bibliography. W. K. Clark and C. Harris, *Liturgy and Worship*; D. G. Dix, *The Shape of the Liturgy*; C. Jones, G. Wainwright, and Edward Yarnold, *The Study of Liturgy*; C. Price and L. Weil, *Liturgy for Living*; P. Z. Strodach, *The Church Year.*

I. Hexham

LOGOS. This Greek word has a variety of meanings, including "word," "reason," "thought," and "speech." It is a significant theological term used by the apostle John, particularly in John 1:1 and 14 in reference to Jesus. Though John was using the Greek language, the idea of an intermediary between God and humans was well developed in Jewish thought. The term *memra*, found in Aramaic Jewish writings and meaning "word," was thought to be this intermediary. By Jesus's time, the Jewish philosopher Philo had linked the idea of the Jewish *memra* and the Greek *logos*. The Greeks thought of *logos* as an "abstract principle of reason exhibited by an orderly universe"(White, 2.2160). Philo saw the Jewish idea of this principle of reason as the mediator between God and man, though he did not personalize the term as John very clearly does. The early church fathers saw *logos* as conveying the idea of Jesus's divinity. Ignatius taught

"that there is one God, the Almighty, who has manifested Himself by Jesus Christ His Son, who is His Word, not spoken, but essential" (*Epistle to the Magnesians* 8). The "Word" then was "a substance begotten by divine power." This thought has continued to the present. The Word, Jesus, is the perfect revelation of the invisible God, the "utterance of God's mind," who declares God's purpose and mediates God's power—all functions of a word (White, 2.2160). In the first chapter of John's Gospel, the apostle speaks of Jesus as the expression of God, the *logos* (John 1:1, 14), and most translations use the term *Word* to translate *logos*. In the book of Revelation, the apostle John uses the term to speak of the triumphant judge and leader of heaven's armies as the "Word" of God whose robe drips blood, referring to Jesus's sacrifice (Rev. 19:13).

Many religions and heterodox groups deny that Jesus was *the* Word (believing him to be simply a prophet, a guru, an enlightened one, or some other spiritual person) or assert that his being the Word does not mean being divine. In this way, they depart from John's understanding of Jesus and orthodox teaching about Jesus.

See also TRINITY, THE

Bibliography. C. Brown, ed., *The New International Dictionary of New Testament Theology*; G. Kittel, ed., *Theological Dictionary of the New Testament*; R. E. O. White, "Word of God," in vol. 2 of *The Baker Encyclopedia of the Bible.*

H. W. House

LOST BOOKS OF THE BIBLE, MORMON VIEW OF. The Church of Jesus Christ of Latter-day Saints (LDS Church or Mormonism) claims that references in the Bible to works that are no longer extant "attest to the fact that our present Bible does not contain all of the word of the Lord." These so-called lost books contain "those documents that are mentioned in the Bible in such a way that it is evident they are considered authentic and valuable, but that are not found in the Bible today" (Church of Jesus Christ of Latter-day Saints). These books include the Wars of the Lord (Num. 21:14), the Book of Jashar (2 Sam. 1:18), the book of Nathan the Prophet (1 Chron. 29:29), the Book of Jehu (2 Chron. 20:34), Paul's lost Epistle to the Corinthians (previous to the letter we have today), and a letter to the Ephesians (also thought to be earlier than the one we have today). Also included are books mentioned but not found in the Book of Mormon, such as the writings of Zenock, Zenos, and Neum (Alma 33:3–17). Joseph Smith also argued that the supposed Book of Abraham and the Book of Moses were among the "lost books."

The Book of Moses. In 1830 Joseph Smith claimed that an angel had instructed him to produce a new translation of the Bible and include "many important points touching the salvation of men, [that] had been taken from the Bible, or lost before it was compiled" (*Teachings of the Prophet Joseph Smith*, 10–11). The Book of Moses is composed of some of these "lost" writings, and Smith placed them in his new version of Genesis. Unlike the Book of Mormon and the Book of Abraham, the Book of Moses did not come from an alleged or actual physical source but was simply a "revelation" from an angel. Although Smith completed the first draft of his "revelation" in 1831, over the next thirteen years he continued to edit, revise, and correct the Book of Moses. The new material Smith introduced included modifications to the stories of the creation, Adam and Eve, and the fall. Smith's writings also "wove Christian doctrine into the text" by expanding the text "far beyond the biblical version" (Bushman, 138). Since the Book of Moses was a "revelation" rather than a translation from "golden plates" or papyri, critics have not been able to judge the authenticity of the text.

The Book of Abraham. The Book of Abraham is allegedly "a Translation of some An-

cient Records that have fallen into our hands, from the Catacombs of Egypt, purporting to be the writings of Abraham, while he was in Egypt, called the Book of Abraham, written by his own hand upon papyrus" (Smith, *History of the Church*, 524). Smith bought the papyri from an antiquities dealer in 1835. When Michael Chandler came to Kirtland, Ohio, with his exhibit of mummies and papyri, Smith was given permission to view the papyri, and he declared that they "contained the writings of Abraham . . . another the writings of Joseph of Egypt" (Smith, *History of the Church*, 236). Under Smith's authority, the church bought the entire exhibit for $2,400. Smith "translated" the "Book of Abraham" but did not translate the writings of the biblical Joseph before his death. The papyri were later lost and were thought to have been destroyed in a fire in 1871. In 1880 the Book of Abraham, along with the rest of the Pearl of Great Price, was declared scripture. Smith copied several drawings contained in the papyri, along with explanations, and these were included in church publications.

In 1966 papyri were found in New York's Metropolitan Museum of Art. They had drawings of a temple and maps of the Kirtland area on the back. The papyri were passed down from Joseph's first wife, Emma, who sold them to Abel Combs, who gave them to his housekeeper, Charlotte, who gave them to her daughter, who gave them to the museum in 1918.

Hieroglyphics have only been translatable since the Rosetta Stone was fully deciphered in 1824. At the time Smith came into possession of the papyri, no one outside a select group of scholars would have even had a possibility of translating them. Consequently, during Smith's lifetime and again when the papyri were rediscovered, Smith's translation of the hieroglyphics was vehemently disputed. Today, scholars know that the papyri are actually excerpts from the Egyptian Book of the Dead and the Book of

Breathing. Smith's explanations of the drawings have been shown to be wholly wrong as well. Abraham's name is not mentioned, and the papyri have been dated to the late Ptolemaic or early Roman period, roughly fifteen hundred years after Abraham lived. This last point is important since Smith claimed the Book of Abraham was "written by his [Abraham's] own hand upon papyrus" (*History of the Church*, 524). Mormon apologists claim that, while the papyri known today may have been used by Smith, the papyri he used to compose the Book of Abraham are not among them.

Enoch. Mormons also claim, somewhat confusingly, that writings *within* the Book of Moses, the "extracts" from the prophesies of Enoch, are from another "lost book." They argue that their "Enoch" writings are the same as the pseudepigraphic books of *Enoch*, probably composed between 200 BC and AD 200. Gordon Hinckley has claimed, "There was once indeed an ancient book of Enoch, but it became lost and was not discovered until our own time, when it can be reliably reconstructed from some hundreds of manuscripts in a dozen different languages" (78). He argued that the church shunned *Enoch* and that even though "Enoch was treasured as a canonical book by the early Christians . . . they would have none of it" (78). In reality the books of *Enoch* were written in Aramaic, Greek, Ethiopic, and Slavonic; have been known since the early centuries of the church (they are cited in the book of Jude); and are known from three principal versions. The historical books of *Enoch* bear no resemblance to Smith's "Enoch" in either style or content and "appear to be independent productions" (Bushman, 138).

Conclusion. In the case of the lost Book of Moses, there is no physical evidence to compare with Smith's translation. However, modern textual criticism has shown that the materials used by Joseph Smith to "find" the lost Book of Abraham and the writings of Enoch bear no resemblance to Smith's writings, and thus the scholarship casts doubt on Smith's claim of supernatural ability to "translate" them.

See also BOOK OF ABRAHAM; CHURCH OF JESUS CHRIST OF LATTER-DAY SAINTS; STANDARD WORKS

Bibliography. R. L. Bushman, *Joseph Smith: Rough Stone Rolling*; Church of Jesus Christ of Latter-day Saints, "Lost Books," in *Bible Dictionary*, http://scriptures.lds.org/en/bd/l/40; G. B. Hinckley, "A Strange Thing in the Land: The Return of the Book of Enoch, Part 1," *Ensign*; Joseph Smith Jr., *History of the Church of Jesus Christ of Latter-day Saints*, vol. 2; Joseph Smith Jr., *Teachings of the Prophet Joseph Smith*, edited by Joseph Fielding Smith.

R. V. Huggins

LOTUS SUTRA. The Lotus Sutra is a Mahayana Buddhist text venerated throughout China and Japan, especially by Tendai and Nichiren Buddhist sects. It is regarded as containing the quintessential expression of truth.

The Lotus Sutra has twenty-eight chapters, in narrative, dialogue, and verse. The main character is the historic Buddha Sakyamuni, who is joined by another Buddha (Prabhutaratna) and a host of bodhisattvas, arhats, monks, gods, and others. The sutra describes a complex cosmology and emphasizes the power of the Buddha—for example, in his revealing myriads of worlds, each with its own Buddha. The text derides the Hinayana ideals of the arhat and claims that all people can become fully enlightened beings through the compassion of bodhisattvas. For example, in chapter 25, the bodhisattva of compassion, Avalokiteshvara, is especially glorified, and this chapter becomes an independent text. Out of profound compassion, this bodhisattva assumes thirty-three different forms and manifests himself anywhere in the world to save people from danger or suffering.

Nichiren Buddhism and Soka Gokkai International both elevate the Lotus Sutra as their core text and chant, as an act of worship, the mantra *Namu-myoho-renge-kyo* (Praise to the Lotus Sutra). The mere chanting of this mantra is believed to bring liberation.

See also Kwan Yin; Mahayana Buddhism; Nichiren Shoshu; Soka Gakkai

Bibliography. C. S. Prebish and K. K. Tanaka, eds., *The Faces of Buddhism in America*; Soka Gakkai International, *SGI-USA* home page, http://www.sgi-usa.org/; Soka Gakkai International, "Lotus Sutra," http://www.nichirenlibrary.org/en/lsoc/toc/.

H. P. Kemp

LUCIFER, MORMON VIEW OF. In Mormon thought, Lucifer is a literal son of Elohim (God the Father) and brother to the Mormon Jesus and all humankind. According to Mormon scripture, Lucifer disapproved of a salvation plan that featured his brother Jesus as humanity's savior, a plan that allowed human beings their "free agency" to choose. When Lucifer's alternate plan to compel people to believe was rejected, he led a rebellion in heaven and was ultimately "thrust down" along with "a third part of the host of heaven," thus becoming the "devil and his angels." By them all human beings are tempted and enticed to live in opposition to righteousness (Moses 4:1–4; 6:49; D&C 29:36–38).

As part of their punishment neither Lucifer nor the fallen angels will be able to gain mortal bodies, which means they will have no opportunity to progress throughout eternity. Their future includes being cast into outer darkness along with the sons of perdition, those who had a perfect knowledge of the Mormon gospel but chose to speak against it.

See also Angels; Church of Jesus Christ of Latter-day Saints

Bibliography. Joseph Smith Jr. et al., Pearl of Great Price; Smith et al., Doctrine and Covenants.

W. McKeever

M

MADHYAMAKA. Madhyamaka (Sanskrit, "of the middle") is a widely held philosophical school within Buddhism that was originally propounded during the second and third centuries AD in India by the Buddhist scholar Nagarjuna (ca. 150–250). Nagarjuna contended that each and every phenomenon of human experience is devoid of a "self-nature" (*svabhava*); that is, these phenomena do not have an ontological ground in themselves but arise only interdependently with all other phenomena. Moreover, he maintained that the very concept of an enduring essence is incoherent. Madhyamaka doctrine thus includes the concepts of the emptiness (*sunyata*) and non-self-existence (*nihsvabhavavada*) of all things. Madhyamaka rejects two "extreme" views: on the one hand, that all things exist eternally and never undergo change, and on the other, that all things have been annihilated. Nagarjuna believed that the erroneous convictions that stem from such extreme views are the fundamental reason that people are unable to attain enlightenment.

See also BUDDHISM

Bibliography. J. L. Garfield, trans., *The Fundamental Wisdom of the Middle Way: Nagarjuna's Mulamadhyamakakarika*; T. R. V. Murti, *The Central Philosophy of Buddhism: A Study of the Madhyamika System*, repr. ed.; R. C. Pandeya, *Nagarjuna's Philosophy of No-Identity*.

R. L. Drouhard

MAHADEVA. *See* SHIVA

MAHARISHI MAHESH YOGI. Maharishi Mahesh Yogi (1918–2008) was born to a Kayastha (scribal) caste family and earned a degree in physics from Allahabad University. In 1953 he became the disciple of Guru Dev. Two years later, he began traveling around India spreading the message of Transcendental Meditation (TM), which he had learned from his guru. In 1958 he decided to undertake a worldwide tour to introduce the West to Transcendental Meditation. He traveled first to Hawaii, then to California, and later to Europe and Africa. During the 1960s, Maharishi's popularity surged. Celebrities such as the Beach Boys, Andy Kaufman, and later Clint Eastwood, David Lynch, and Deepak Chopra embraced the Transcendental Meditation techniques of Maharishi.

However, it was Maharishi's association with the Beatles that caused his fame to skyrocket. The Beatles joined him in 1968, with a great deal of publicity. Much of their "White" album was written while studying TM, with references to Maharishi. A short time later, the Beatles and their entourage left a TM seminar amid charges of sexual impropriety by Maharishi. Although Maharishi denied anything improper had taken place and the charges were never proven, he refused to discuss the matter later in his life.

Also during this time, he began to conduct seminars for training TM teachers. Critics in the media labeled him the "Giggling Guru" due to his constant laughing, and they dismissed him as a hippie mystic. Maharishi Mahesh Yogi announced that his public ministry was concluded in January 2008, and he died in February of that year in Norway.

Maharishi Mahesh Yogi's contribution to the hippie, yoga, and New Age movements cannot be overstated. It is estimated that forty thousand people have been trained as teachers and that he gained five million adherents. He also founded thousands of schools, colleges, and universities. In the US alone, Maharishi's organization is estimated to be worth $300 million and includes Global Financial Capital, located in Manhattan.

See also GURU DEV; HINDUISM; YOGA

Bibliography. Global Good News, "Maharishi's Achievements, 1957–2008," http://www .maharishi-programmes.globalgoodnews.com /achievements/Maharishi-Achievements/02.html; L. Koppel, "Maharishi Mahesh Yogi, Spiritual Leader, Dies," *New York Times.*

R. L. Drouhard

MAHAVIRA. In Sanskrit Mahavira literally means "great hero" and is the popular name of the founder of Jainism, which takes its name from another title of the founder, *jina* (conqueror). He was born Vardhamana into a ruling caste in northern India around 550 BC. At the age of thirty, he renounced his privileged life, and he spent the remainder of his days in severe renunciation and deep meditation, eventually reaching nirvana. He established an order of monks as his followers. Jainism split into two sects after his death. The Jain scriptures or sermons attributed to Mahavira—the Agamas (precepts)—and his biography did not appear until one thousand years after his death, around AD 500.

See also JAINISM; TIRTHANKARA

Bibliography. B. S. Shah, *An Introduction to Jainism.*

E. Pement

MAHAYANA BUDDHISM. Mahayana, which in Sanskrit means the "greater vehicle," refers to one of the three major Buddhist traditions, the other two being Hinayana (a pejorative term meaning "lesser vehicle"; Theravada is the sole remaining representative of this branch) and Vajrayana (diamond vehicle; Tibetan Buddhism is one example of this branch, though some include Vajrayana within Mahayana). Mahayana is predominant in northern Asia—namely, China, Taiwan, Korea, Japan, Tibet, Mongolia, Buriatia, and Tuva, although it is also influential in Vietnam, Bhutan, Nepal, and the Tibetan diaspora. Mahayana Buddhism has become widespread and influential in the West, particularly in the traditions of Zen and Tibetan sects.

Theories about the rise of Mahayana are varied: it may have started as a lay movement after enthusiastic promulgation of the Buddhist dharma by King Ashoka (d. 232 BC) or after intersectarian maneuvering within Buddhist schools. Whatever the reasons, Mahayana emerged around the first century AD (approximately four hundred years after the Buddha's death) among Buddhists who embraced a collection of new noncanonical texts (sutras). Mahayanists believe these sutras contain further authoritative words of the Buddha, and they base their practice on them.

Many of the Mahayana sutras depict themselves as correctives to developments found in the earlier traditions, and these texts represent the transition of oral to written traditions: the Hinayana Tripitaka canon (a complete version was preserved in Pali and the Sanskrit version was preserved in Chinese and Tibetan translations) was probably closed around the end of the second century BC. This is regarded as a textual collection honored by all Buddhists. However, the innovative Mahayana texts were written in Sanskrit and include (among others) the popular Lotus Sutra, Diamond Sutra, Heart Sutra, and Pure Land Sutras. In embracing these latter sutras, Mahayanists moved to an innovative and liberal interpretation of Buddhism, away from the conservative tradition they called the Hinayana.

Mahayanists have core Buddhist teachings in common with Hinayanists: the Four Noble

Truths, karma, rebirth, enlightenment, nirvana, refuge in the Three Jewels. However, the rise of Mahayana gave Buddhism new vigor: innovations centered on the nature of the Buddha and the ideal goal of a Buddhist practitioner, coupled with *darshanic* allegiance and speculative cosmology. Narratives about Sakyamuni Buddha (the founder of Buddhism) are much enhanced, and he is frequently joined by bodhisattvas such as Avalokiteshvara (Chenresig in Tibet, Kwan Yin in China) or other Buddhas like Amitabha in the collection of texts. This new cosmic framework for the Buddha can be understood in terms of the doctrine of the Triple Body: the body of transformation was the physical body that the Buddha had on earth; the body of communal enjoyment is a nonmaterial body that teaches out of compassion and is accessible to humans through advance practice in visionary experiences; and the body of truth is the nondifferentiated reality in itself, and the very mind of the Buddha.

The Hinayana/Theravadan ideal of the arhat, or perfected saint, is replaced with the bodhisattva; Mahayanists considered the arhat path too self-consumed, whereas the bodhisattva ideal introduces the notion of compassion (*karuna*) in that the bodhisattva postpones his nirvana in order to work toward—or transfer his karmic credit toward—the liberation of all sentient beings. Hence compassion is elevated to equal value with wisdom; in fact, compassion is the active force of wisdom, with wisdom the mental attribute of compassion. The bodhisattva ideal is recognized in two examples: His Holiness 14th Dalai Lama of Tibet is regarded as a bodhisattva; and—frequently in art, for example—the cosmic Buddha Amitabha, popular in Pure Land Buddhism (the tradition followed in the Buddhist Churches of America), is flanked by two bodhisattvas.

Thus Mahayana offers the lay practitioner the possibility of enlightenment, contrary to the Hinayana/Theravadan doctrine, wherein this was open only to the monk through the denial of the world and practice of various austerities. Possibilities of enlightenment are now based on the notion that the historical Buddha had said he was concerned not only with his own enlightenment but, out of compassion, postponed his entrance into nirvana to teach the dharma to his disciples. Thus the *sangha* (the community of disciples) was now to engage with samsara (the cycle of being) rather than seek release from it, in order to practice compassion to others to aid in their release from samsara. Practicing compassion within samsara then became enlightenment in and of itself, and this notion, within Tibetan schools especially, is symbolized by the construction of mandalas, stupas, and other material objects. In other words, all sentient beings now have the possibility of becoming Buddha in this lifetime due to the large amount of merit being generated by compassionate bodhisattvas. Various levels in a darshanic relationship to a number of bodhisattvas and cosmic buddhas are characteristic of Mahayana, contrasted with the more conservative expressions of Hinayana/Theravada Buddhism.

It is tempting to identify bridging points between Mahayana and Christian doctrines (as theologian Marcus Borg has argued), but these are superficial. Mahayana Buddhism is essentially monistic: *anatta* (nonself) means that no being or thing exists in, of, or by itself, but they exist only as an ever-changing interrelationship of *skandhas* (aggregates), which are transitory and only give the allusion of existing phenomena, which may or may not have consciousness. "Compassion," then, does not appear to be altruistic in the Christian sense, as there is no metaphysical distinction between the one showing and the one receiving acts, prayers, or thoughts of compassion: self/ego only gives the illusion of existing. In a similar way, the doctrine of the Three Bodies cannot be equated in any sense to the doctrine of the Trinity. Defining terms becomes crucial in Christian-Mahayana conversations.

Major schools of Mahayana Buddhism include Zen Buddhism (Ch'an in China), Nichiren Buddhism, Tendai, Pure Land, and Tibetan (although some would classify Tibetan as Vajrayana due to its strong tantric roots). Mahayana texts also have had some influence in the Theosophical Society.

See also ARHAT; BODHISATTVA; BUDDHISM; DHARMA; HINAYANA; NIRVANA; SAMSARA; THERAVADA BUDDHISM; TIBETAN BUDDHISM

Bibliography. M. Baumann and C. Prebish, "Introduction: Paying Homage to the Buddha in the West," in *Westward Dharma*, edited by M. Baumann and C. Prebish; M. Borg, "Jesus and Buddhism: A Christian View," in *Buddhists Talk about Jesus, Christians Talk about the Buddha*, edited by R. M. Gross and T. C. Muck; D. Burnett, *The Spirit of Buddhism: A Christian Perspective on Buddhist Thought*; D. S. Lopez Jr., *Buddhism: An Introduction and Guide*.

H. P. Kemp

MAHIKARI. Mahikari (the name means "true light") is a Japanese religion founded in 1960 by Kotama Okada (1901–74) and now existing as two rival branches.

Okada had previously been a follower of the Church of World Messianity, a Japanese religion that provided much of the worldview later to become Mahikari. In 1959 Okada had a revelation that the earth was in danger of imminent destruction from the *kami* (divine spirits or forces of nature that flow through all of life), who would cleanse the world with fire. However, the kami also provided a way of escape through the effusion of the "true light," which was dispensed through the palm of Okada's hand. This light could be conveyed to his followers, who would retain it in a pendant worn around their neck. They, in turn, would learn how to dispense the light to other people. Okada's disciples referred to him as Sukuinushisama (Lord Savior).

After Okada's death in 1974, the movement split over succession in leadership and control of the group's property. A very powerful leader in place before Okada's death was Sekiguchi Sakae; his rival was Okada's adopted daughter, Keishu Okada. Following a lawsuit, the court awarded Sakae the headquarters property. He founded Sekai Mahikari Bunmei Kyodan, which today has about seventy-five thousand followers. Keishu reorganized as Sukyo Mahikari, and today this branch claims about two hundred thousand followers. Together, both groups claim to have about two dozen centers in the US.

See also KAMI; SHINTO

Bibliography. C. M. Cornille, "Mahikari," in *Encyclopedia of New Religious Movements*, edited by P. B. Clarke; J. G. Melton, "Mahikari of America," in *Encyclopedia of American Religions*, 6th ed.; D. Reid, "Mahikari Organizations," in *A New Dictionary of Religions*, rev. ed., edited by John R. Hinnells.

E. Pement

MAITREYA. Maitreya is the future Buddha who is to appear at the beginning of the fifth cosmic age and revive the dharma when the teachings of the Buddha of this age (Siddhartha Gautama) will have decayed. Maitreya is honored in all schools of Buddhism as a bodhisattva. Hence Maitreya's images are found throughout Asia. He is usually depicted sitting on a chair, attempting to convey a sense of expectancy and hope. The Foundation for the Preservation of the Mahayana Tradition (FPMT), plans to build a 152-meter (500-foot), $195 million image of Maitreya Buddha at Kushinagar, Uttar Pradesh, India, the site where Gautama Buddha is thought to have died.

In Western esoteric traditions, especially in Share International and the Tara Network, Maitreya is known as the World Teacher and is presented as the manifestation of Christ, Maitreya-Buddha, Messiah, Imam Mahdi, or another "master of wisdom." Benjamin Creme

(b. 1922) is the protagonist of this movement; he is well schooled in Theosophy, having been influenced by Helena Blavatsky and Alice Bailey. According to Creme, Maitreya the World Teacher first appeared in 1977, from his ancient Himalayan retreat and lives incognito among the Indian-Pakistani community of London. Choosing to reveal himself gradually to the world, Maitreya manifests himself periodically at different times and in different places (the most publicized being in Nairobi in 1988); empowered water for healing is often associated with his manifestations. According to Creme, Maitreya the World Teacher is accompanied by a group of wise teachers that has guided humanity from behind the scenes, inspiring us to create a "New Age of Synthesis and Brotherhood" based on sharing and justice. Creme travels internationally, teaching on Maitreya the World Teacher.

Various New Age groups, informed by Buddhism, use Maitreya as a title for their leader or for an expected messiah figure who fulfills messianic prophesies of all religions and will bring unity and utopia. Prophecies in Buddhist sutras and literature regarding the coming of Maitreya have been appropriated by some Christians messianically within a fulfillment eschatology paradigm and viewed as an antichrist with iconography drawn from the book of Revelation.

See also BODHISATTVA; BUDDHISM

Bibliography. D. S. Lopez Jr., *Buddhism: An Introduction and Guide*; Foundation for the Preservation of the Mahayana Tradition home page, http://www.fpmt.org; Share International home page, http://www.shareintl.org/.

H. P. Kemp

MANDALA DIAGRAM. In general terms, a mandala (Sanskrit, "circle") is any drawing, chart, map, figure, or geometric pattern intended to depict the universe in symbolic fashion, wherein the diagram functions as a microcosm of the whole of reality as interpreted by the advocate of a particular religion (often an Eastern one). Typically both intricate and colorful, mandalas are viewed as sacred objects that remind one of the true reality that permeates the mundane world of experience. Commonly, the center of the mandala focuses the minds of advocates while they meditate. The particulars of a mandala vary according to the religion in which it is employed. The mandala concept originated with Buddhists and Hindus. In Hinduism mandalas are frequently square, representing the four corners of the world in Hindu cosmology. The well-known Vastu Purusha Mandala is an example of such a diagram. In Buddhism mandalas often portray the Buddha as seen by enlightened persons, in conjunction with the geography of the pure lands in which he resides. In Tibetan Buddhism in particular, the famous Kalacakra mandala diagram is a highly detailed map of the cosmos (picturing hundreds of Vajrayana beings and multiple aspects of practice) that signifies the fleeting nature of existence. In many cases, the complex structure of Tibetan Buddhist mandalas incorporates the Five Wisdom Buddhas, known as Aksobhya, Amitabha, Amoghasiddhi, Ratnasambhava, and Vairocana. The mandala used in Nichiren Shoshu is a paper scroll (sometimes a wooden tablet) called a *moji-mandala*. Written in Sanskrit and Chinese, it contains a message that speaks of the spiritual awakening of the Buddha, Buddhist doctrines, guardian deities, and certain Buddhist concepts. Mandalas are also found in Jainism.

See also BUDDHISM; HINDUISM; JAINISM; NICHIREN SHOSHU; TIBETAN BUDDHISM

Bibliography. B. Bryant, *The Wheel of Time Sand Mandala: Visual Scripture of Tibetan Buddhism*; G. Bühnemann, ed., *Mandalas and Yantras in the Hindu Traditions*.

J. Bjornstad

MANTRA. A sound deemed to possess mystical power. Repetition of a mantra may induce a deep state of meditation; hence it is a tool for visualization, empowerment, and enlightenment in Hinduism, Vajrayana (Tibetan) Buddhism, and New Age streams. Mantras are often given from teacher to disciple at initiation rites as personal tools for meditation. The Tibetan *om mani padme hum* (Hail to the jewel in the lotus) is the mantra of compassion, associated with the Buddhist Bodhisattva Avalokiteshvara (of whom the 14th Dalai Lama is said to be an incarnation). The word *mantra* has worked its way into the English language to mean something continuously repeated or any goal or value that needs constant reviewing.

See also BODHISATTVA; BUDDHISM; HINDUISM; TIBETAN BUDDHISM

Bibliography. D. S. Lopez Jr., *Buddhism: An Introduction and Guide.*

H. P. Kemp

MARIOLATRY. The word *mariolatry* is derived from "Mary" and *latreia* (Greek, "worship"); thus mariolatry is the worship of Mary, the mother of Jesus. Mariolatry was a problem in the early church, eliciting warnings from both Eastern and Western church fathers. Epiphanius of Salamis (d. 403) described the Collyridians who offered cakes (Greek, *kolluris*) to Mary, possibly as an unorthodox revision of the Eucharist rite. Epiphanius made this distinction: "Now the body of Mary was indeed holy, but it was not God; the Virgin was indeed a virgin and revered, but she was not given us for worship, but herself worshipped him who was born in the flesh from her" (*Panarion* 79, in Graef, 1:73). In the West, Ambrose of Milan (d. 397) challenged devotees of the Great Mother (Latin, *Magna Mater*), who apparently had adopted Mary into their goddess worship. He wrote: "Without doubt the Holy Spirit too must be adored when we adore him who is born of the Spirit according to the flesh. But let none apply this to Mary: for Mary was the temple of God, not the God of the temple.

And therefore he alone is to be adored, who worked in the temple" (*On the Holy Spirit* 3.80, in O'Carroll).

Theological interest in Mary began early. Justin Martyr (d. ca. 165) sets her in parallel with Eve in one of the first known theological reflections concerning Mary (*Dialogue* 84, 100). However, the main theological use of Mary in the first three centuries of the church was in polemics against the gnostic docetists, who asserted that Christ only "seemed" to be human but was not really so. She is presented by the ante-Nicene fathers as proof of the genuine human nature of Christ. Simply put, he is truly human because he had a real human mother. This assertion is found already in Ignatius of Antioch, just after the year 100 (*To the Ephesians* 7.2; 18.1–2; 19.1; *Trallians* 9.1; *To the Smyrnaeans* 1.1). Later fathers followed the same line of argument: Irenaeus (d. ca. 202; *Against Heresies* 5.1.2; *Demonstration of the Apostolic Preaching* 37), Clement of Alexandria (d. ca. 215; *Miscellanies* 3.17.102), Tertullian (d. ca. 220; *Against Marcion* 3.11.2–3; 3.20.6–8; *On the Flesh of Christ* 17.2), Origen of Alexandria (d. 254; *Homilies on Genesis* 8.9; *Commentary on the Gospel of Matthew* 33; *Commentary on the Gospel of John* 10.263; *Homilies on Song of Songs* 2.12).

The *Infancy Gospel of James*, written much later than the four canonical Gospels (ca. 150), is an early witness to a rising tide of popular piety centered on Mary. While the overriding purpose of this work was to describe her exceptional holiness and purity, it does not present her either as divine or as someone who intercedes for others. In fact, this aprocryphon depicts her as rather passive, hardly speaking or acting.

The title Theotokos (Greek, literally, "one who bears God"), in its original context, does not connote divinity. Mary was granted this honorific at the Council of Ephesus in 431 to safeguard the unity of Christ's person by asserting that the child in the womb was fully

God. Nestorius (d. 451), who objected to this title, fearing it could lead to Mary worship, was disciplined by the council. While the intention of the council in approving this title was to further define the identity of Christ, the people in the streets, upon hearing the news, responded with direct cries of praise to the Theotokos. This contrast between formal theological discourse and popular piety still persists. The Greek term *Theotokos* was widely understood as "Mother of God," especially in the Latin title *Mater Dei*. This less accurate rendering of Theotokos may have aided some in moving from honor to worship.

Occasionally the idea appears that Mary commands obedience from God himself. In praise of Mary, Germanus, patriarch of Constantinople (d. ca. 733), writes, "But you, having maternal power with God, can obtain abundant forgiveness even for the greatest sinners. For he can never fail to hear you, because God obeys [Greek, *peitharchei*] you through and in all things, as his true Mother" (Homily 1 on the Dormition, in Graef, 1:146–47). Germanus cannot be dismissed as a dusty footnote since this same sermon is cited by recent official Roman Catholic Church documents on Mary, including the 1950 definition of Mary's assumption by Pope Pius XII, and twice in one of the most significant works issued by the Second Vatican Council (*Lumen Gentium* 56 and 59). Duns Scotus (d. 1308) rebuked such dangerous speculation: "The blessed Virgin has authority to intercede by prayer, not to command" (Graef, 1:302). But devotion to Mary continued to express itself in such terms, for instance, in Louis-Marie Grignion de Montfort (d. 1716), who made this claim for Mary: "The greatness of her power which she exercises even over God himself, is incomprehensible" (introduction to *True Devotion to the Blessed Virgin*, in Graef, 2:59).

Praying to Mary is an important component of Catholic piety and is defended as being analogous to sharing prayer concerns with a friend. Mary is considered the most effective pray-er of all. No explanation is offered for how she would be able to hear the plethora of prayers, not possessing omniscience. Praying to her (and to other saints) is based on the Catholic doctrine of the communion of the saints, which assumes the dead in Christ can hear our prayers. Prayers to Mary, it is said, are not idolatrous per se unless the one praying places more trust in Mary than in God. A small portion of church tradition portrays Mary as more merciful than her son. Eadmer (d. ca. 1128) writes, "Sometimes salvation is quicker if we remember Mary's name than if we invoke the name of the Lord Jesus." He adds, "Her Son is the Lord and Judge of all men, discerning the merits of the individuals, hence he does not at once answer anyone who invokes him, but does it only after just judgement. But if the name of his Mother be invoked, her merits intercede so that he is answered even if the merits of him who invokes her do not deserve it" (*Book on the Excellence of the Virgin Mary* 4 and 6, in Graef, 1:216). When church teaching emphasized Christ as the harsh judge, many sought out Mary, including Bernard of Clarvaux (d. 1153), who states, "Man needs a mediator with that Mediator, and there is no-one more efficacious than Mary" (*Sermon on the Twelve Stars* 1, in Graef, 1:239). Peter Damian (d. 1072) exalted her even more: "By the dignity of her excellent merits she transcends the very nature of mankind" (sermon 46, in O'Carroll).

Excessive statements such as these and devotion to Mary that at times overshadowed that offered to Jesus became issues during the Protestant Reformation. John Calvin (d. 1564) acknowledged Mary's unique role, writing: "It cannot be denied that by electing and destining Mary to be the mother of his Son, God gave her the highest honour" (*Harmony of Gospels* 1.27, in Graef, 2:13). Martin Luther (d. 1546), who affirmed Mary's perpetual virginity and allowed some measure of devotion to her, issued this caution: "When preaching [on the Annunciation] one should stick to the story, so that we may celebrate the incarnation of Christ, rejoice that we were made his brethren, and be glad that he who fills heaven and earth is in the womb of the maiden. . . . Bernard [of Clairvaux] filled a whole sermon with praise of the Virgin Mary and in so doing forgot to mention what happened; so highly did he and Anselm esteem Mary" (*Luther's Works* 54.84–85, in Wright, 177). Calvin strongly rejected praying to any saint, including Mary. He dismissed the difference between honor (Latin, *dulia*; from Greek) and worship (Latin, *latria*; from Greek), saying that in practice the common people are actually engaging in idolatry: "In fact, the distinction between *latria* and *dulia*, as they called them, was invented in order that divine honors might seem to be transferred with impunity to angels and the dead. For it is obvious that the honor the papists give to the saints really does not differ from the honoring of God. Indeed, they worship both God and the saints indiscriminately, except that, when they are pressed, they wriggle out with the excuse that they keep unimpaired for God what is due him because they leave *latria* to him" (*Institutes* 1.12.2). The Council of Trent (1545–63) responded to Protestant criticism with a careful defense of the veneration of Mary and other saints (session 25). Yet despite such caution, excesses still occasionally arose, even in writings of leading theologians.

Lawrence (or Laurence) of Brindisi (d. 1619) said that Mary is "the woman . . . who is united [Latin, *copulata*] to God" in "a divine marriage" (sermons 1.7 and 2.4, in Graef, 2:27). Lawrence depicted Mary the bride using her beauty to seduce God into the incarnation: "Great is the might and power a beautiful woman has over a man who is in love with her. . . . She causes him to rave [*insanire*], and causes the lover to go out of his mind [*amantem amentem reddit*] even with the mere glance of her eyes. But the Virgin could do this with God himself, hence he says, 'Avert thine eyes from me' (Cant. 4.4). She has caused God in some way to rave so that, having left his majesty behind, He took on the form of a servant" (*In Salut. Angel.* 5.5, in Graef, 2:28). *The Glories of Mary*, by Alphonsus Liguori (d. 1787), has appeared in numerous editions since 1750 and remains to this day a powerful influence on Catholic piety. While Liguori begins well, stating that Mary only possesses attributes given her by God ("Declaration of the Author"), he soon moves to less moderate views. He includes with approval a quote from Bonaventure: "Before Mary there was nobody who dared stay God's hand. But now, whenever God is angry with a sinner, and Mary takes him under her protection, she restrains her son's hand and withholds him from punishing" (*Glories of Mary* 1.3.2, p. 59). The significance is not whether this text is genuine to Bonaventure (d. 1274) but rather that Liguori cites it as correct doctrinal teaching on Mary. He relates a vision told to him portraying sinners attempting entry to heaven. They first climb the ladder leading to Jesus but soon fall back because of the difficulty. Then they turn to the ladder leading to Mary, who, as they ascend, extends her hand to help (*Glories of Mary* 1.8, p. 36).

Certain honorifics for Mary are sometimes misread as divine titles. "Queen of Heaven" is an expression of Mary's status as the most exalted of all the saints in heaven. It is usually said to have been bestowed on her at her assumption. The title Co-Redeemer is not officially recognized for Mary and has attracted some opposition among Catholic theologians who realize its negative impact on ecumenical dialogues. Yet it appears often in much devotional literature, and there is an active movement promoting its official adoption. Protestants sometimes balk at a phrase found often in Catholic writing: "the cult of Mary." From the Catholic perspective, this phrase refers to proper devotion to the greatest of saints, but it does not connote worship. Modern official Catholic teaching (the magisterium) clearly and repeatedly condemns worship of Mary. At the Second Vatican Council, adoration of Mary (Latin, *hyperdulia*) is differentiated from worship (*latria*) of God (*Lumen Gentium* 66–67). This is reiterated by the 1994 *Catechism of the Catholic Church* (paragraph 971).

While officially condemned, worship of Mary is a sad reality among some Catholics. A Latin American recently said, "In my country God is a woman." An airport in the Philippines provides a place for preflight prayers with an ornately carved seven-foot-tall shrine to Mary. On the wall nearby hangs a simple, much smaller framed print of the face of Jesus. When Mary is depicted with her son, she is often the dominant, active figure, and Jesus is in her arms either as an infant or dead from the cross (the pietà form).

Appearances (apparitions) of Mary have generated much popular devotion to Mary, some of it extravagant. Catholic authorities have been very careful in granting official recognition to these visitations. Most of the appearances do not enjoy such official approval, but among those that do, the best known are Guadalupe in Mexico, Lourdes in France, and Fatima in Portugal.

The Catholic magisterium has found it difficult to restrain elevated expressions about Mary since such are found among the most revered teachers of the church. Peter Damian, Anselm (d. 1109), Bernard of Clairvaux, Bonaventure, Lawrence of Brindisi, and Alphonse de Liguori are all "doctors of the church," a title that recognizes those with the deepest theological insight and that has been granted to only thirty-three individuals from two millennia of theology. It should be noted that some doctors are more restrained in their praises to Mary namely, Ambrose (d. 397), Augustine (d. 430), and Aquinas (d. 1274). Warnings against excessive Marian devotion in recent Catholic Church documents are a witness that this remains a perennial problem (*Lumen Gentium* 60, 66, 67; *Catechism of the Catholic Church* 971, 1676; *United States Catholic Catechism for Adults*, 297, 344, 347, 472).

See also CHRISTIANITY, PROTESTANT; ROMAN CATHOLICISM

Bibliography. J. Calvin, *Institutes of the Christian Religion*; H. Graef, *Mary: A History of Doctrine and Devotion*, 2 vols., 1st ed.; A. M. de Liguori, *The Glories of Mary: A New Translation from the Italian*; M. O'Carroll, *Theotokos: A Theological Encyclopedia of the Blessed Virgin Mary*; Pope Pius XII, *Munificentissimus Deus*; Joseph Ratzinger et al., eds., *Catechism of the Catholic Church, with Modifications from the Editio Typica*; Second Vatican Council, *Lumen Gentium*; United States Conference of Catholic Bishops, *United States Catholic Catechism for Adults*; University of Dayton, website of the International Marian Research Institute, https://udayton.edu/imri/; D. F. Wright, "Mary in the Reformers," in *Chosen by God: Mary in Evangelical Perspective*, edited by D. F. Wright.

E. B. Manges

MARONITE CHRISTIANS. Maronite Christians date back to the Syriac monk St. Maron (whose existence is denied by some) of the fifth century, who is said to have been a friend of St. John Chrysostom. Unlike most Eastern Christians, Maronites are in communion with the bishop of Rome. The Maronites are of Syrian origin but speak an Aramaic dialect. They inhabit Lebanon, Syria, Cyprus, and Egypt and number about 1.5 million people, with approximately 800,000 living in Lebanon, making up 25 percent of the population there. They hold considerable political power in Lebanon, to the extent that the constitution of Lebanon requires that the president of that country be a Maronite Christian. When the diaspora is included, they compose the majority of the Lebanese people. Though the country was conquered by Arab Muslims, the majority remained Christian, and the rites of the church are still in Syriac, a dialect of Aramaic. While many Syrian Christians rejected the creed of Chalcedon in AD 451, the Maronites embraced it. After the slaughter of 350 Maronite monks in 451 by the Monophysites of Antioch, the Maronites fled to Lebanon, where they have since remained.

Tensions that developed among various Christian groups in the East made Islamic conquest of the eastern Christian regions easier, and the Maronites came under Islamic rule. For this reason, they began to receive greater support from other eastern Christians, which helped them gain some independence from the Muslim conquerors. Only with the beginning of the Crusades in the tenth century did the Maronites come to the attention of the Roman Catholic Church. When the Maronites sided with the crusaders against Islam, they came under the protection of the Catholic Church, and they have remained in communion with the Roman Church since then. This connection gave them greater independence from Muslims in their area. Under Ottoman rule, they remained largely independent and exercised considerable political power, with many of them becoming aristocrats. In Lebanon their importance increased when the Syrian family of Benî Shibâb abandoned Islam to become Christian.

After the tenth-century Crusades, the Maronites came into conflict with a new Islamic sect, the Druze, whose members fled persecution by orthodox Muslims in Egypt and came to Lebanon. As the number of Druze in Lebanon increased, they oppressed the Maronite Christians. The country became divided, and two emirs were created in Lebanon, one Maronite and one Druze. Finally, in 1860 the Druze massacred Maronites at Damascus and then in Lebanon. With the Ottoman Empire merely observing, France intervened and brought the persecution to an end. Since then the Maronites in Lebanon have maintained considerable independence, surrounded by Muslims on the east and the west.

In the mountain areas, Maronites are primarily involved in farming, cattle grazing, or work in the silk industry, and in urban communities they are involved in commerce. The Maronites have migrated to countries in regions such as Europe, France, and, most of all, to the US.

See also DRUZE, THE

Bibliography. BBC News, "Who Are the Maronites?," http://news.bbc.co.uk/2/hi/middle_east/6932786.stm; D. Belt, "The Forgotten Faithful," *National Geographic Magazine*; P. Kenyon, "Maronite Christians Thrive in Lebanon," http://www.npr.org/templates/story/story.php?storyId=16067482; J. Labourt, "Maronites," in *The Catholic Encyclopedia*, http://www.newadvent.org/cathen/09683c.htm.

H. W. House

MARTIAL ARTS, EAST ASIAN. Martial arts are ancient Eastern forms of hand-to-hand combat that have become popular in the West and have come to be taught at health clubs, YMCAs, and privately owned martial arts studios. Early itinerant Buddhist monks, in order to protect themselves from highway robbers, marauding bandits, and thugs, mastered fighting techniques for defense. They developed hand-to-hand combat techniques—based on their religious understanding of reality—that employ both weapon and nonweapon forms.

Religious Basis of Martial Arts. The religious basis for all martial arts in Buddhism is the idea of emptiness, and in Taoism the basis is in the balance of yin and yang. Once people understand their true nature, they can learn to harness cosmic *chi* power (also referred to as *ki* or *qi*) and use it to advantage, including defeating foes. In Asia this is accomplished by aligning oneself with a dojo (a martial arts studio, originally a building in a Buddhist temple) and a *sensei* (a martial arts instructor), who teaches the philosophy and techniques of the art. A lifetime of self-discipline, obedience to the *sensei*, and meditation combine to turn the student into a master of the martial arts.

Some claim that by the power of *chi* (pronounced *chee*), they can crack five-hundred-pound blocks of ice in half with their bare hands. However, Bernie McPherson, the highest-ranking black belt in Texas, says, "I've whipped men who claim to have *chi* and some have whipped me, but there is no power of *chi*. It's all kinetics and discipline."

Various Types of Martial Arts. The five most popular martial arts traditions are the following:

1. Karate. The full name of karate is *karate-do*, a term that comes from three Japanese words: *kara*, "empty"; *te*, "hand"; and *do*, "way." Hence, karate-do is "the way of the empty hand," or simply empty-handed fighting. Karate involves quick and forceful hand and foot movements. Brought to America from Japan, karate may be the most popular of all the martial arts. Meditation, concentration, and a heightened self-awareness are the integral parts of the art. Zen Buddhism is the religious basis of karate. Movie star Chuck Norris, a world-class karate master, was a Zen disciple before professing faith in Jesus Christ.

2. Kung Fu. Kung fu (full name: *shaolin kung fu*) is the martial art tradition with the most diverse set of techniques, including weapon forms, bare-hand forms, wrestling, limb locks, and strikes at the vital points of the body that instantly kill the opponent. Many prominent people have hired kung fu specialists as bodyguards. Another school of kung fu is white eyebrow, a tradition known to very few. The term *kung fu* is a mispronunciation of the Chinese term *gongfu*, meaning "achievement through great effort." Its Japanese counterpart is called *shorinji kempo* (kung fu of shaolin).

3. Aikido. Developed in 1942 by Master Moribei Uyeshiba, aikido is a combination of several martial arts and Zen Buddhism. *Aikido* is a compound word derived from *ai*, "union"; *ki*, "universe"; and *do*, "way." Its etymology reveals its purpose: to be the road or way to experience oneness with the universe. Using circular motion and a series of acrobatic and tumbling moves, one can overcome an enemy. Movie star Steven Seagal is an aikido master.

4. Judo. Known as "the way of flexibility," judo was the first martial art to become a recognized Olympic sport (1964). Based on quickness, timing, balance, and throwing and falling techniques, judo evolved out of jujitsu ("art of softness" or "way of yielding"), a military form of deadly hand-to-hand combat.

5. Tae Kwon Do. Tae kwon do, whose name, in Korean, means literally "the way of the foot and fist," is a Korean form of karate, primarily involving high and sweeping kicks.

Western ingenuity has produced new forms of martial arts. Because of market competition, some instructors invent so-called superior techniques and offer students shortcuts to obtaining a desired black belt, the highest level of achievement.

Areas of Concern. Because most martial arts stress Eastern religious beliefs and practices, some Christians are concerned that learning martial arts might influence people with (if not lead them into) Eastern religion. They contend that the religious aspects of martial arts are inseparable from the physical skills and activities because they developed in conjunction. Some object to the violence inherent in martial arts, arguing that it is incompatible with Christian principles. Others counter that the physical skills can be separated from the spiritual because they are merely a form of physical training, like any other athletic activity. They say that Christians can practice their faith while learning and performing martial arts. Some, in fact, contend that martial arts can even be used in Christian ministry and evangelism (see the Gospel Martial Arts Union at http://www.gmau.org).

See also BUDDHISM; PANTHEISM; TAOISM/DAOISM; YIN AND YANG

Bibliography. Biblical Discernment Ministries, "Karate: Tool for Christian Evangelism or Zen Buddhism?," http://www.rapidnet.com/~jbeard/bdm/Psychology/karate.htm; C. and D. Engelhardt, "Martial Arts Ministry as Small Group Ministry," *Grace Martial Arts Fellowship Newsletter*; Gospel Martial Arts Union website, http://www.gmau.org; W. Williamson, *Martial Arts: The Christian Way.*

R. A. Streett and R. L. Drouhard

MASONRY (LDS). Freemasonry and the LDS Church (the Church of Jesus Christ of Latter-day Saints, or Mormonism) exist independently of each other, but Mormonism has been influenced by Masonry. The origins of Freemasonry are vague and shrouded in mystery. Some historians believe it began with the brick masons who built the European cathedrals. The fraternity itself teaches that it began in the early twelfth century AD with an oath taken by a Burgundian knight named Hugh de Payens and eight of his fellow knights in Jerusalem. Mormonism, on the other hand, was formally established by Joseph Smith Jr. in 1830. The two organizations have no direct ties to each other in origin.

When Joseph Smith organized his church, many Americans opposed Freemasonry, partly because of an exposé of the order (*Illustrations of Masonry*, 1827) published by William Morgan and his subsequent disappearance. This prevailing sentiment even made its way into the Book of Mormon, which is considered to be scripture by the LDS Church. It contains many remarks hostile to Masonry scattered throughout its pages. By 1842 the anti-Masonic opinions of the general public had settled, and Joseph Smith

had lost his own personal opposition to the order as well.

Several of Smith's close associates and followers were Masons. His brother Hyrum Smith and his uncle John Smith were both members of the fraternity. After successfully settling the city of Nauvoo in Illinois, Joseph Smith was approached by a few of these Masons about petitioning for a lodge in the new city. Smith gave his consent, so a formal request was sent to the Deputy Grand Master of the Illinois Masonic Order, Judge James Adams. The lodge was formally installed on March 15, 1842, but was considered "Under Dispensation" rather than formally chartered. Joseph Smith received the Masonic first-degree initiation on that same night, and the next night was uncharacteristically raised to the third degree (Brodie, 280).

Smith apparently was greatly impressed with the ritual of the Masonic Lodge, and his enthusiasm for the order extended to the followers of his church. Within just five months, there were 286 candidates in the Nauvoo Lodge. At that time, there were only 227 Masons in all of Illinois, so, understandably, the leadership of the Illinois fraternity became concerned. The Grand Lodge felt that the Nauvoo Lodge was not being very selective in its admission of candidates to the order. More importantly, they feared that the Nauvoo Lodge would seize control over the Springfield Grand Lodge if something was not done about the problem soon. The Grand Lodge began demanding the Nauvoo Lodge records for inspection, anxious to find a way to suspend or control the actions of the new lodge.

Joseph Smith had previously built a temple in Kirtland, Ohio, but his temple ceremony, called the "Endowment Ceremony," was never issued there. Rather, LDS members visiting that temple engaged in a largely emotional type of worship service closely resembling that of late twentieth-century Pentecostalism. Those present would swoon, speak in tongues, claim to see visions of angels, and even fall on the floor with fits of shaking. In 1841, when the original LDS Nauvoo temple was still under construction, Smith promised to reveal an elaborate ritual of ordinances that he claimed had been hidden for ages. Those permitted to receive these ordinances were told they would be endowed with power from on high. This new ceremony would be radically different from what his followers had previously understood as "temple worship."

Just six weeks after Smith experienced the first three degrees of the Masonic ritual, this new LDS temple ceremony was begun. At first only men were admitted to Smith's new temple ceremony. They were stripped, washed, and anointed, then dressed in a peculiar garment. The square and compass (obvious symbols borrowed from Freemasonry) were cut into the right and left breast of the garment, and a slash was cut into it just above the knee and even into the skin of the candidate, leaving a scar. As with the Masonic ritual, the men swore various oaths and had secret handshakes, secret words, new names, and even "executions of the penalties"— agreeing to keep the ritual secret or forfeit their lives in ghastly ways. Obviously, Smith borrowed many of these elements from the Masonic ritual, altered them, then instituted them into his own temple ritual. Brigham Young, second president of the Mormon Church, highlighted the similarities in the rituals, often referring to the Mormon temple ceremony as "Celestial Masonry" (Brodie, 280–81).

While several similarities do exist between the two rituals, there are important differences. The Masonic ritual centers on a story of the legendary Hiram Abiff, which was extrapolated from references to a minor Bible character who participated in the building of King Solomon's temple in Jerusalem (see 2 Chron. 2:13; 4:16). The Mormon ritual, on the other hand, centers on peculiar LDS beliefs about the creation of the world, the

fall of humanity, and the necessity of Mormon teachings to return to heaven and become a God.

Smith explained that similarities existed because the Masonic ritual had started with heavenly truths but had been corrupted by uninspired men. He simply restored the ceremony to its perfected state.

Rumors of the defilement of the Masonic rites eventually made their way to the Illinois Grand Lodge, which still feared the Mormon lodges. By 1844 the LDS Church controlled a total of five lodges—three in Nauvoo and two in Iowa. Meanwhile, it refused to send any of the lodge records for inspection, as requested. Finally, in the 1844 meeting of the Grand Lodge, the LDS lodge dispensations were revoked, and they were declared to be separate and renegade bodies.

Even after the permission to operate Mormon Masonic lodges was revoked, Masonic elements continued to be used in the new religion. Joseph Smith was killed in June 1844, but the surviving leaders continued to use the new and obviously Masonic components. The LDS temple ceremony kept the Masonic influence and also incorporated some Masonic symbolism into other religious aspects—particularly on LDS buildings (i.e., the symbols of the sun, the moon, stars, the handshake of fellowship, the all-seeing eye, Alpha and Omega, the beehive, the point within the circle, the square, the compass, the baphomet, and the inverted pentagram).

Due to the actions of Joseph Smith, a schism developed between the Freemasons and the LDS Church. Officially, Masonry lists the LDS concept of priesthood, polygamy, and the LDS condemnation of Masonry as their grounds for discord. The LDS Church holds that it alone possesses all truth, so involvement in Masonry is profitless for LDS Church members and would distract them from fulfilling church duties. Both bodies are antagonistic toward each other, and for a time each group refused to admit into membership anyone associated with the other group. These sentiments continued to exist in Utah in the late twentieth century, though not as dogmatically.

As time passed, the LDS temple ceremony was revised. The most notable revisions went into effect on April 10, 1990. Some of the more obvious Masonic elements (such as the executions of the penalties) were removed, while others remained—the garment markings, secret handshakes, arm signs, and token names. Masonic symbolism continues to be heavily used on LDS buildings, the most obvious examples being the Salt Lake City Temple and the rebuilt Nauvoo Temple.

See also BOOK OF MORMON; CHURCH OF JESUS CHRIST OF LATTER-DAY SAINTS; SMITH, JOSEPH, JR.

Bibliography. F. Brodie, *No Man Knows My History: The Life of Joseph Smith the Mormon Prophet*, 2nd ed.; D. J. Buerger, *The Mysteries of Godliness*; H. W. Coil, *Coil's Masonic Encyclopedia*; William Morgan, *Illustrations of Masonry*; *Proceedings of the Grand Lodge of Freemasons, Illinois, from Its Organization in 1840 to 1850 Inclusive*; J. C. Reynolds, *History of the M. W. Grand Lodge of Illinois, Ancient, Free & Accepted Masons*; Joseph Smith Jr., *History of the Church of Jesus Christ of Latter-day Saints*, 7 vols.

L. Thuet

MATERIALISM. Taken in the usual sense, materialism is the metaphysical doctrine that argues that whatever exists is properly studied by the hard sciences: all reality is material, that is, is composed only of (or is completely dependent on) matter. Thus, for materialists, the world can be exhaustively described in physical terms. This implies, for example, that all events are physical events. Materialists disagree on the status of abstract entities (e.g., numbers, sets, or universals). Philosophers have come to use the term *physicalism* interchangeably with *materialism*. The philosophical use of the term *materialism* has nothing to do with the

desire for wealth, possessions, or the pleasures of the body.

Versions of materialism/physicalism typically arise in response to the question of just what constitutes a person. Here materialism stands in opposition to any form of substance dualism (the idea that there are two types of substances in the world: material and nonmaterial). Strictly speaking, substance dualists hold that a person is a nonmaterial thing that has and is closely related to (but is not identical with) a body. Materialism, on the other hand, clearly denies the existence of souls, spirits, or immaterial minds, insisting rather that humans are identical with their brain, central nervous system, and body. There are two main versions of materialism: reductive and nonreductive.

Reductive materialists argue that those properties commonly believed to be mental (i.e., nonmaterial/physical) properties—such as a belief or a desire—are in fact identical with physical properties. In other words, mental states/properties can be reduced to material states/properties. Reductive attempts have come primarily in the form of philosophical behaviorism and type identity theory. The former is more than anything an attempt to make sense of mental talk. Statements such as "Bob is in pain" or "Sue believes she is hungry" refer not to a state of some immaterial mind or soul but rather are shorthand expressions for observable physical behavior. For example, "Bob is in pain" means he is grabbing his toe and hopping around wincing. Similarly, "Sue believes she is hungry" means Sue is rummaging around the pantry for a snack. Hence these statements may be expanded—without any loss of meaning—into complex physical statements about what behavior would occur as a result of a given stimulus. Type identity theories make an even stronger claim: mental states / properties are just physical (more specifically, neurological) states / properties; the two are identical. So "Bob believes grass is green" is identical to some type of physical state (such as certain neurons firing).

Reductive materialist accounts face serious difficulties. First, it seems the mental state called "being in pain" can (and sometimes does) occur without any observable behavior like shouting or hopping around. For that matter, we routinely have mental states with no corresponding behavior at all (e.g., my belief that 2 + 2 = 4). People can also pretend to be in severe pain (thus exhibiting painful behavior) yet have no corresponding mental state. Thus one cannot always be expressed in terms of the other. Regarding type identity theories, mental states clearly are not identical with physical states because they have quite different properties. For example, mental states have the property of being a first-person (private) experience, while physical states have the property of being third-person observable. Moreover, there is simply no evidence that each mental state is identical to a physical (neural) state. For these reasons and others, reductive materialism is widely rejected today.

Nonreductive materialists maintain that a person is purely physical (i.e., has no non-physical parts), while insisting that the mental is not reducible to or identifiable with the physical. Traditionally, the two main nonreductive accounts are eliminative materialism and functionalism. The former makes the quite radical claim that mental terms (i.e., terms referring to nonmaterial or nonphysical mental states) are simply useless and should be eliminated. Neurophysiology has moved us beyond them. Like the phlogiston theory of yesteryear, the incorrect folk psychology (the commonsense theory that refers to mental states—such as beliefs, desires, fears—in explaining human behavior) that promoted such terms is becoming obsolete, being progressively replaced by better and better neuroscience. Functionalists understand "the mind" in terms of physical inputs and outputs, that is, causal relationships.

"Mental" states are causal functions of physical states. What makes something a mental state is solely a question of its function in a person's cognitive system. This counts as a materialist/physicalist theory because functionalists agree that only neurophysiological states are needed to produce mental (functional) states.

Nonreductive materialists also face significant problems. First, we know from experience (e.g., first-person introspection) that we do have mental states. I am directly aware of my beliefs and desires, even when I'm not trying to explain some behavior. Such states, then, cannot simply be eliminated. Another problem for eliminativism is that it seems self-refuting. If one eliminates the mental states of folk psychology, such as beliefs, then on what grounds is eliminative materialism to be believed? If intentional stances are eliminated, then no one could even know if eliminative materialism were true! Functionalism is not without its own problems, including the problem of inverted qualia (qualia are specific experiential qualities, such as what it's like to experience pain or redness). Imagine that Joe perceives red when everyone else perceives blue (his color perception is inverted), yet he functions in the same way as everyone else (who all correctly perceive reds and blues). If functionalism is true, then mental states are explained solely by their input-output causal functions. Since Joe's function (output) is the same as everyone else's, functionalists have to say that Joe has the same mental states as everyone else. But clearly seeing red and seeing blue are different mental states, so functionalism fails as an account of mental states. Another problem involving qualia is that according to functionalism, many nonhuman physical systems (e.g., robots) could achieve "mental states." But this seems absurd, for even if a robot is programmed to yell and hop around on one foot (output) after kicking a brick (input), that robot is not genuinely experiencing the mental state of being in pain, but is simply performing a predetermined set of commands.

Bibliography. D. Armstrong, *A Materialist Theory of the Mind*; P. M. Churchland, *Matter and Consciousness*; A. Menuge, *Agents under Fire: Materialism and the Rationality of Science*; P. K. Moser and J. D. Trout, *Contemporary Materialism: A Reader*.

R. K. Loftin

MAYA.

In Hinduism *maya* (literally, "not that" in Sanskrit) is generally said to be the persistent illusion that things are ultimately real when in fact they are unreal (illusory). This illusion is endemic to the faculties of perception possessed by human beings. Depending on the school of Hinduism in question, maya can have many forms or aspects. In Advaita Vedanta, maya is the illusion that the world of persons and distinguishable entities is the sole existent realm, when in fact there are other dimensions of reality beyond that world. Most types of Hinduism agree that it is critical for devotees to realize that the distinction ordinarily made between oneself and the universe is an illusion imposed by one's deceptive sense organs. Thus devotees may break free of maya.

In more polytheistic strains of Hinduism, maya is personified as several different deities, depending on the tradition, and each tradition gives its version different characteristics and names. Thus, Maya can be anything from the "magician-architect" of the Asuras (titans) to a goddess who both keeps and frees people from delusion (named Mahayama) to the Mother Maya (Devi Mahatmyam), who is said to have been given the power of all the gods to defeat a titan army and who now upholds the universe.

See also HINDUISM

Bibliography. A. Danélou, *The Myths and Gods of India*; H. Torwesten, *Vedanta: Heart of Hinduism*, trans. J. Phillips.

R. L. Drouhard

MEDITATION.

Meditation is a religious discipline practiced in both Eastern and Western religious traditions. The purpose of meditation for all religions, generally speaking, is to separate oneself from the cares and pressures of the world and to experience peace, healing, and transcendence through communion with God; to focus on higher teachings; and sometimes both.

Eastern. Meditation as a practice in Eastern religion is associated with Buddhism. Siddhartha Gautama, who would later be known as the Buddha, had become so disciplined in meditation that he mastered all possible levels of it. As part of his teaching on the Noble Eightfold Path, Gautama taught his followers to have "the right mindfulness—meditating properly" (Corduan, *Neighboring Faiths*, 224) and to practice "right concentration"—that is, to attain deep meditational states. Zen Buddhism, of the Mahayana school of Buddhism, stresses meditation as one of the four ways to attain satori, which is the moment at which one accepts reality as it is rather than complicating it with trivial ideas that merely distract. The fifth- or sixth-century-AD founder of Zen Buddhism, Bodhidharma, according to legend, cut off his eyelids and meditated for three years in front of a bare wall. Zazen meditation, practiced in Zen Buddhism, is done sitting in a cross-legged, straight-backed position while one focuses on the breath.

Tibetan Mahayana Buddhism has two aspects of meditation: (1) the mastering of passion through its exercise and (2) becoming one with a buddha or bodhisattva. In this second aspect of meditation, one practices a discipline of repeating a mantra; the most famous mantra is *Om mani padme hum*, literally, "Om, the jewel is in the lotus, hum" (Corduan, *Neighboring Faiths*, 239).

Not all meditation arising from Eastern thought is alike, however. Transcendental meditation (TM) is practiced in order to relieve stress, improve health, foster creativity, and contribute to healthy relationships. Rather than being part of a particular religion or a philosophy, TM is done in order to bring health, balance, and serenity to an individual's life. While there are certain techniques for TM, as a practice it is differentiated from Zazen meditation by the fact that it is not necessary to sit with legs crossed, nor is it necessary to practice it for hours on end. Fifteen or twenty minutes, twice a day, is what is recommended by the TM Program.

Hinduism, too, has many teachings about meditation. In general the idea is to free the soul from its constraints in the material world. This can be accomplished by meditating on a deity or a *yantra*/mandala or by more abstract meditations. The classical exposition, Patanjali's yoga sutra, understands that morality, observances, positions, breath control, and withdrawing one's senses support one's meditation—often on a mantra, breath, or a concept—leading to deep contemplation. With repeated contemplations, one achieves oneness.

Western. Christian meditation is in contrast to Eastern forms of meditation. While the purpose of Tibetan Buddhist meditation is to rid oneself of distractions in order to attain nirvana (the breaking of the cycle of reincarnation and the achievement of nonexistence), meditation in the Christian experience is to commune with the personal God of the Bible. Brother Lawrence, Thomas à Kempis, Peter of Celles, St. John of the Cross, and a host of other medieval Christians, as well as many more modern authors such as Richard Foster and Watchman Nee, have written on meditation. According to Foster, for Christian meditation "detachment is not enough; we must go on to *attachment*" (21). Eastern forms of meditation stress the need for the individual to detach himself from the phenomenal world, which is illusory. Christian meditation seeks to detach from the world of fleshly pursuits but attach the person to

Christ. Christ desires a relationship with the individual. As Christ tells the church of Laodicea in Revelation 3:20, "Behold, I stand at the door and knock. If anyone hears my voice and opens the door, I will come in and eat with that person, and they with me." This word is directed to Christian people, and it emphasizes Christ's desire to commune with his people intimately.

Christian meditation is done through a focus on the words of Scripture. This is to be differentiated from the preparation of a teaching lesson or a sermon, where exegesis of a text is the goal. Meditation on Scripture is meant not to analyze the text but merely to allow the text to sink into the heart. It is also practiced through focusing on repentance for specific sins and seeking God's grace to overcome future temptation. Meditation on creation is also part of Christian meditation, as is meditation on the transcendent purposes of God in current events.

Thus Christian meditation is centered on the person and work of Jesus Christ. It is meant to draw the person away from the temptations that appeal to the flesh, but this is only the beginning. This is in contrast to Eastern forms of meditation, which focus mainly on detachment but do not point the person to God.

See also BODHIDHARMA; BUDDHA, HISTORICAL PERSON OF; BUDDHISM; MAHAYANA BUDDHISM; TIBETAN BUDDHISM; ZEN BUDDHISM

Bibliography. W. Corduan, *A Tapestry of Faiths: The Common Threads between Christianity and World Religions*; Corduan, *Neighboring Faiths: A Christian Introduction to World Religions*; R. J. Foster, *Celebration of Discipline: The Path to Spiritual Growth*, 20th anniv. ed.; National Center for Complementary and Alternative Medicine, "Meditation: An Introduction," http://nccam.nih.gov/health/meditation/overview.htm; Maharishi Vedic Education Development Corporation, The Transcendental Meditation Program Home Page, http://www.tm.org/.

J. D. Wilsey

MEVLEVI ORDER. The Sufi order called the Mevlevi Order (*mawlana* in Arabic, *mevlana* in Turkish) was founded by Jalal al-Din al-Rumi (d. 1273), is widespread in Turkey, and is best known for its colorful dance (the Whirling Dervishes) ceremony.

Al-Rumi was a refugee from the Mongol invasions who fled Central Asia and sought shelter in the Turkish Sultanate of Rum (central Anatolia), in the city of Konya, by approximately 1228. His most abiding passion was for a wandering Sufi called Shams al-Din Tibrizi, who was with him between 1244 and 1248, when the latter was most likely murdered by Rumi's followers. Most of Rumi's later works celebrate his relationship with Shams and focus on a universalistic love exemplified by Shams (as a type of divine figure). Today Rumi's mystical and sometimes romantic poems are gaining renewed popularity with Sufis and even the general public.

After his death, Rumi's followers commemorated him by their characteristic dance, during the course of which they performed their *dhikr* (remembrance of God) ceremony in an ecstatic state. The Qur'an and Rumi's "Mathnawi" poem are read, music is played, and then the actual dancing begins. Everything about the ceremony is symbolic, from each move of the dance to the type and color of their garments, to the colors and shape of their meeting halls, called *tikiyyas* ("hostels" in Persian).

The Mevlevis benefited from their close relationship with the Ottoman elite and spread throughout Anatolia and beyond. Eventually Mevlevis were found from the Balkans to Egypt. Since the establishment of the Turkish republic in 1925, they have frequently been banned there, but their whirling dance has been permitted for the sake of tourism. After the dance was outlawed in Turkey, the tikkiya in Cairo, Egypt, replaced Konya as the center of Mevlevi spiritual life. Until recent times, the tikkiya in Cairo was believed to be the only one that was fully functioning.

See also DHIKR; SUFISM

Bibliography. Z. Abul-Gheit, "Dance of the Soul: The Mevlavi Tikiyya Espouses Poetry in Motion, Structure and Spirit," *Horus*; A. Arberry, *Mystical Poems of Rumi*; Arberry, *Mystical Poems of Rumi II*; A. Hamarlund, T. Olson, and E. Ozdalga, eds., *Sufism, Music and Society in Turkey and the Middle East*; Mevlevi Order of America home page, http://www.hayatidede.org/; R. A. Nicholson, trans., *The Mathnawi of Jalal al-Din al-Rumi*; H. Paul, *Jalal al-Din al-Rumi and His Tasawwuf*; W. M. Thackston, trans., *Signs of the Unseen: The Discourses of Jalaluddin Rumi*.

D. B. Cook

MICHAEL THE ARCHANGEL. One of only two named angels in all of Scripture (the other is Gabriel, mentioned in Dan. 8:16, 9:21; Luke 1:19, 26), Michael is the solely named archangel (Jude 9). It should be noted at the outset that the scriptural data regarding archangels generally—and Michael the archangel specifically—are sparse, though there is considerable apocalyptic tradition regarding each.

The term *archangel* (Greek, *archangelos*, "chief angel") appears only twice in Scripture (Jude 9 and 1 Thess. 4:16), which prevents dogmatic responses to questions such as whether "archangel" is an office held by a single angel or an entire class of angels, or precisely what tasks an archangel performs. We can, however, say some things about archangels—and thus about Michael—with some degree of confidence. For example, there is good lexical evidence that an archangel has prominent status among angels. The semantic range of the prefix *arch-* includes "chief," "prominent," and "first." This same prefix is used in the words "chief priest" (*archiereus*; Matt. 26:57), "chief of the synagogue" (*archisunagogos*; Mark 5:22), and "chief tax collector" (*architelones*; Luke 19:2), among others. We also know that Christ's second coming will be marked by an archangel's shout (1 Thess. 4:16).

Scripture refers many other times to an angel named Michael, who scholars generally agree is in fact Michael the archangel—although there is no explicit biblical evidence for that conclusion. The angel visiting Daniel mentions "Michael, one of the chief princes" (Dan. 10:13; cf. *1 Enoch* 20:5), who combated the prince of Persia, and the angel later identifies Michael as Israel's prince (Dan. 10:21; 12:1; cf. Josh. 5:13–15). This is consonant with Michael's contending with the devil over the body of Moses in Jude 9. During the war in heaven, it is Michael and his angels who battle the dragon and his angels (Rev. 12:7).

Various sects teach unbiblical views concerning Michael the archangel. According to Joseph Smith Jr. in the LDS Church scripture Doctrine and Covenants, Adam was Michael as a preexistent spirit (D&C 27:11; 107:54; 128:21). Jehovah's Witnesses teach that Michael the archangel is another name for Jesus Christ, whom they view as the chief angel. Seventh-day Adventists traditionally agree that Michael is Jesus Christ but take the view that *archangel* means chief over the angels, thus making the identification compatible with the deity of Christ.

See also CHRISTIAN

Bibliography. K. D. Boa and R. M. Bowman Jr., *Sense and Nonsense about Angels and Demons*; C. F. Dickason, *Angels Elect and Evil*; D. Jeremiah, *What the Bible Says about Angels*.

R. K. Loftin

MIKVEH/MIKVAOT. *Mikveh* is a rabbinic Hebrew noun (pl., *mikvaot*) primarily used for a collection of water. In Judaism it has become a technical term for the place of ritual immersion. The Hebrew term for immersion itself is *tvilah* (in Greek, *baptismos*, or "baptism"), but the place where tvilah is performed is in the mikveh.

The purpose of the ritual is to undergo ritual cleansing from ritual uncleanness. It is also used for conversion purposes when a gentile converts to Judaism. One of the convert's three obligations is immersion (the other two are circumcision if the convert is male, and a donation to the temple).

For a mikveh to be acceptable, it must be large enough to allow for the total immersion of an average-size individual. Furthermore, it must contain at least 150 gallons of water. Further rabbinic rules include that the water of the mikveh must come from either a natural spring or a river that originates from a spring. A mikveh filled with rainwater is also permitted.

Many mikvaot have been uncovered through archaeology on the south wall of the Temple Mount in Jerusalem, which was the main entry point for pilgrims entering the temple compound. These were places where the majority of the population who were not wealthy could be ritually immersed for ritual uncleanness or prepare for special righteous duties. Members of the wealthy class also had their own private mikvaot in their homes for the necessary ritual immersions.

See also JUDAISM

Bibliography. C. Roth, "Mikveh/Mikvot," in *Encyclopedia Judaica*, edited by C. Roth; I. Singer, "Mikveh," in *The Jewish Encyclopedia*.

A. Fruchtenbaum

MILLER, WILLIAM. William Miller (1782–1849) founded the Millerite movement, a Christian millenarian movement, and in 1822 he predicted that Jesus Christ's second coming would occur in 1843 or 1844.

Miller had been raised by a Baptist mother but did not follow in her faith. He was a Deist for a time, being a voracious reader of popular Deists such as Voltaire, Hume, and Paine.

Miller's experience in the War of 1812 affected him deeply. A cannon round exploded only feet from him but left him uninjured. This event, coupled with the victory of the US despite the seemingly insurmountable odds it faced against the mighty British Empire, convinced Miller that God was not the uncaring and inactive god of Deism. After purchasing a farm in Low Hampton, New York, Miller began attending a Baptist church. Later, he was asked to read a sermon for the pastor, who was often absent. During the sermon, Miller was so moved by the story of Jesus's death that he embraced Christianity. This was during a time when northern New York was a hotbed of religious revival and fervor, especially Adventism.

After his conversion, and challenged by his Deist friends, Miller began studying the Bible intensely, starting with Genesis. When he encountered Daniel's revelations in 1822, Miller became convinced they contained the date on which Christ would return to earth. He settled on a time between 1843 and 1844 and began to spread his message.

Miller's message of the impending return of Jesus proved popular, and his fame spread as newspapers were set up in several northeastern cities to proclaim Miller's views. For the next twenty years, Miller wrote constantly and gained an estimated fifty thousand to five hundred thousand followers. As 1843 approached, Miller's followers began preparing for the coming kingdom. Some quit working and sold all their possessions. Although Miller was reluctant to set a specific date, he eventually proclaimed the period of March 21, 1843, to March 21, 1844, as the time frame for Christ's return. When the later date came and went, Miller and his followers were thrown into confusion. The majority of Millerites gave up their beliefs, while a small minority, including Miller, simply continued to expect Christ's return at any moment. Miller continued in this belief until his death.

See also ADVENTIST MOVEMENT; MILLER-ITE MOVEMENT; SEVENTH-DAY ADVENTISM; SMITH, JOSPEH, JR.

Bibliography. E. N. Dick, *William Miller and the Advent Crisis*; G. R. Knight, *Millennial Fever and the End of the World*.

R. L. Drouhard

MILLERITE MOVEMENT. The Millerite movement was a Christian millenarian movement founded by William Miller (1782–1849), who, in 1822, predicted that Jesus Christ's second coming would occur in 1843 or 1844.

Miller lived in northern New York, an area that became known as the "Burned-Over District" due to its many revivals and new religious movements. Joseph Smith Jr., Lily Dale, the Shakers, and several other religious figures and movements traced their roots to the area. Miller became interested in the millennium as a result of his study of the book of Daniel, after his conversion from Deism to Christianity.

Using a form of the "day-year" (considering each "day" as a literal year) interpretational method of Daniel's prophecies for the return of Jesus, Miller used 457 BC (the decree of Artexerxes to allow the rebuilding of Jerusalem) as the starting date for Daniel's prophecy that "unto two thousand and three hundred days; then shall the sanctuary be cleansed" (Dan. 8:14 KJV), which Miller interpreted as the purification of the earth and Christ's return. He added twenty-three hundred years and came up with AD 1843 or 1844 as the year when the prophecy would be fulfilled.

He published his findings in the *Vermont Telegraph*, a Baptist newspaper, and received so much interest in his views that he printed a pamphlet outlining his beliefs. In 1840 Joshua Vaughan Himes, a Boston pastor who embraced Miller's views, established the *Sign of the Times* newspaper to publicize his views (the Seventh-day Adventist Church continues to publish it). Eventually, Miller's views were published in forty-eight other periodicals in New York City, Philadelphia, Rochester, Cleveland, and Montreal, among others. Miller also personally funded the printing of materials for converts in England, and later two more Millerite newspapers were published there. Through the spreading of Millerite literature, the movement eventually had followers in Australia, Norway, Chile, and Hawaii.

As 1843 approached, Miller's followers urged him to set a specific date when Christ would return. Although reluctant to do so, Miller settled on the period between March 21, 1843, and March 21, 1844. When March 21, 1844, came and went, Miller simply began to preach that Christ could come at any moment, but the Millerites began to adjust his calculations. They set April 18, 1844, as the date, then when this passed, claimed they were in the "tarrying time" taken from Habakkuk 3:2–3 and Matthew 25:5. By August the Millerite movement was on the verge of crisis. Then a Millerite preacher named Samuel S. Snow presented what was to be called the "seven-month" message. Snow employed biblical typology to calculate that the twenty-three hundred years would actually fall on October 22, 1844. Although there is little indication that Miller himself accepted the date, the majority of rank-and-file Millerites embraced it and spread it with renewed fervor.

When nothing unusual happened on October 22, 1844, the Millerite movement was thrown into disarray. Some reset the date once more. Others began acting like children, citing Mark 10:15 as a requirement for entering the kingdom. However, most Millerites abandoned the movement altogether. October 22, 1844, has become known as the Great Disappointment.

Eventually three major groups vied for the remaining Millerite faithful. The first group appropriated Christ's parable of the ten virgins in Matthew 25:1–13 to true believers. The "shut door" of the house in the parable meant that there would be no more salvation to those outside. All who were inside (the Millerites) would be living in the kingdom, while all the others would be left out. Not surprisingly, the "shut door" movement lost popularity quickly. The second group rejected the "shut door" group and instead focused on preaching to the lost and looking for the return of Jesus. This group persuaded Miller himself to join them and became the foundation for the Advent Christian Church. The third group continued to believe that October 22, 1844, was the correct date, but they began to teach that Miller's interpretation of the "cleansing of the sanctuary" was not an earthly but a heavenly event. Hiram Edson, an early follower of Miller, claimed to have received a vision of Jesus entering the holy of holies in the temple in heaven. The Seventh-day Adventist Church was born from this group, and Edson's idea became the root of the doctrine of investigative judgment in Seventh-day Adventist theology.

It is also interesting to note that Charles Taze Russell, founder of the Jehovah's Witnesses, had connections to the Millerite movement, having studied the Bible and early Christianity with Millerites from 1870 to 1875.

See also ADVENTIST MOVEMENT; MILLER, WILLIAM; SEVENTH-DAY ADVENTISM

Bibliography. E. N. Dick, *William Miller and the Advent Crisis*; G. R. Knight, *Millennial Fever and the End of the World*; "The Exeter Camp-meeting," *Advent Herald*, August 21, 1844; R. E. Winkle, "Disappearing Act: Hiram Edson's Cornfield Experience," *Spectrum*.

R. L. Drouhard

MIRACLES IN NON-CHRISTIAN RELIGIONS. Miracles are events or acts of power that appear to violate the normal expectations of science, physics, medicine, or probability. Miracles are not simply scientific anomalies but function as *wonders* to draw attention to God and *signs* to confirm that one is on the right path.

In a Judeo-Christian context, miracles are construed as originating from a supernatural domain (*outside* nature) to confirm God's existence and authenticate his messengers. Other religions that believe in miracles may conceive of them not as interventions from outside nature but as the manipulation of a "higher law" *within* nature; thus "miracles" are a kind of science we have not yet discovered. A personal God who acts is not as necessary as a practitioner who understands the higher laws.

In Islam the miracles of the biblical prophets are called signs. Allah gave "nine clear signs" to Moses (sura 17:101) for Pharaoh, who did not listen. The Qur'an affirms the healings and virgin birth of Jesus (19:20) but includes extrabiblical miracle stories from apocryphal books (3:49; 19:29–34). Muhammad had no miraculous sign but the Qur'an itself (29:49–51), though certain miracles were later attributed to him in the hadith.

Aberrational forms of Christianity take diverging views. Mormonism was founded on the continuation of miracles (Mormon 9:7–20), particularly the discovery of the Book of Mormon. Jehovah's Witnesses believe miracles and divine healing ceased with the death of the apostles. Christian Science espouses the miracles-as-higher-law theory mentioned above and touts a 150-year record of healings as proof of Mrs. Eddy's claim that sickness is an illusion. Pentecostal healer William Branham used healing miracles and his own prophecies as one proof that his doctrines were correct (another proof was that they were taught in the Bible).

Hinduism has long had many gurus claiming *siddhi* powers, but the best-known is the late Sathya Sai Baba (d. 2011), who was worshiped by millions of people as the incarnation of Shiva for nearly fifty years. His popularity arose from his ability to materialize *vibhutti* (sacred ash), candy, flowers, and small idols allegedly out of thin air. Though his powers have convinced some scientists and government officials of his deity, videotape caught him using sleight-of-hand to perform the "materializations." Other gurus attempted to do the same, but with less popularity.

Outside a monotheistic context, such as among tribal religions or in occult circles, the notion of "miracle" is not relevant because there is no God behind it, only a display of raw power mediated through spirits or magic incantations. The function of wonder creates awe of the magician or shaman, and the function of sign points to the magician's power to bless, curse, heal, or control the unknown. Since Christians worship a supernatural God, some missionaries advocate a public *power encounter* with shamans or occultists, to openly confront and defeat the spirits believed to be behind the "demonic miracles" of pagan supernaturalism.

See also SAI BABA, SATHYA

Bibliography. H. Brant, "Power Encounter: Toward an SIM Position," *International Journal of Frontier Missions*; N. L. Geisler, *Baker Encyclopedia of Christian Apologetics*; G. Lindsay, *William Branham: A Man Sent from God*; V. Mangalwadi, "Sathya Sai Baba," in *World of Gurus*, rev. ed.; G. Milmine, *The Life of Mary Baker G. Eddy and the History of Christian Science*; Watch Tower Bible and Tract Society, *Reasoning from the Scriptures*, 2nd ed.

E. Pement

MISSIOLOGY. The word *missiology* is used to describe the study and practice of Christian missions. Included in its field of review are such varied topics as the history, theology, practice, and methodology of missions. Ancillary areas of study and practice are sociology, anthropology, and comparative religion. *Missio*, or "sent," is the Latin term transliterated into English as "mission." A missionary, hence, is one who is sent, in particular, one who is sent on a Christian ministry, usually focusing on the task of evangelism, church planting, or ministry to the poor or indigent.

The term *missiology* emerged in the late twentieth century. Prior to the emergence of the more refined science of missiology, much of the study of missions practice was subsumed into the disciplines of practical theology and missions. Numerous journals committed to the study of missiology also emerged in the 1900s. Academic programs developed, offering doctorates of missiology, among other degrees.

Missiology and missiologists in recent decades have focused particularly on the possibility of the fulfillment of the Great Commission (cf. Matt. 28:18–20). Some missiologists believe it is within the grasp of the Christian world to reach every person on the earth—seven billion by recent census—with the gospel of Jesus Christ, thus possibly completing the task of global evangelism.

Recent trends in missiology have led to the strategic focus of evangelistic and church-planting resources on people groups—that is, self-identified ethno-linguistic and social groupings within countries and cities—instead of on nations alone. Additionally, the more refined science of missiology has helped to direct Christian resources to the least evangelized or least reachable areas of the world. The emergence of the "10–40 window" concept, referring to the northern latitudes in the Eastern Hemisphere, stretching from northern Africa to the Pacific, is an emphasis developed and refined by missiology.

See also CHRISTIAN; CHRISTIANITY, PROTESTANT

Bibliography. F. A. Oborji, *Concepts of Mission: The Evolution of Contemporary Missiology*; E. C. Pentecost, *Issues in Missiology*.

R. P. Roberts

MODALISM. Modalism is the heresy according to which (1) there is only one divine person; (2) "Father," "Son," and "Holy Spirit" are merely different names for this one divine person; and (3) the Father, Son, and Holy Spirit, consequently, are identical with each other. The names "Father," "Son," and "Holy Spirit," modalists insist, signify not different persons but different *modes* in which God manifests himself to human beings.

One may hold, with orthodox theologians from Basil of Caesarea to Herman Bavinck, either that the divine persons are modes of the divine being or that they differ only in their modes of being, without committing oneself to the heresy of modalism. In order to avoid modalism, rather, one need merely affirm that the distinctions between the divine persons are (1) eternal, (2) unchangeable, and (3) real, and in particular, intrinsic to the divine being and not dependent for their existence on the activity of nondivine minds.

History of Modalism. One can trace five phases in the history of modalism. The first occurred in the patristic era, when Noetus of Smyrna (fl. ca. 200) reputedly originated the heresy and Sabellius (excommunicated for heresy in 220) organized its adherents into a distinct sect. Early opponents of the heresy such as Tertullian and Hippolytus designated its followers "Patripassians" to underscore one of its least palatable implications—namely, that the Father suffered (*pater passus est*) on the cross. To avoid this untoward consequence, Sabellius and most subsequent modalists tended to minimize the connection between Christ's human and divine natures and to affirm that, although the man Jesus suffered, neither the Father nor the Son, strictly speaking, suffered crucifixion.

Ironically, therefore, persons so passionately committed to the Father and the Son's consubstantiality that they denied all distinction between them came to deny that the man Jesus was God. Though they identified the Logos with the Father, they regarded Christ as a mere man. The synod of Constantinople (335), accordingly, condemned the Sabellian Marcellus of Ancyra as both a modalist and an adoptionist. His disciple Photinus suffered a similar fate at the synod of Sirmium (351). The only organized religious bodies that professed Sabellianism in the patristic period—that is, the ones founded by Sabellius and named after him and the Priscillianists—apparently perished shortly after their condemnation by the First Council of Constantinople (381) and the synod of Braga (561), respectively.

In its second, medieval phase, Sabellianism lay largely dormant in elite circles. Gottschalk of Orbais, admittedly, charged Hincmar of Rheims with modalism early in this period, and according to some reports, Peter Abelard suffered condemnation for Sabellianism. Otherwise, modalism surfaced primarily in popular movements such as Bogomilism and Patarinism. During the Reformation, the third phase of modalism's history, the heresy began to reemerge from obscurity. The Anabaptist Michael Servetus, this era's most vocal modalist, composed three works against orthodox trinitarianism and famously suffered capital punishment for his views in Calvin's Geneva. David Joris and Hans Denck, both Anabaptists like Servetus, also advocated Sabellianism in this period.

Modalism reached the summit of its popularity in the fourth phase of its history, which extends from the beginnings of the Enlightenment in the late seventeenth century until the collapse of old-fashioned theological liberalism in the aftermath of World War I. Most theologians, by the end of this period, denied that God had ever communicated information about himself in propositional form to human beings. In the majority's eyes, therefore, the doctrine of the Trinity constituted, at best, a speculative projection of threefold patterns in God's historical self-manifestation into his inner being. Since these theologians considered such speculation presumptuous, most of them denied that God had revealed himself as intrinsically tripersonal.

In the fifth period of modalism's history, which began after World War I and extends into the present, the doctrine of the Trinity has revived somewhat. Karl Barth influenced many to adopt the doctrine of the Trinity on the grounds that God's threefold historical self-manifestation must correspond to the realities of his inner being. So-called social trinitarians, furthermore, have portrayed the Trinity as a kind of egalitarian society that human beings can emulate. Outright modalism, nonetheless, persists among liberal thinkers, especially process theologians. "Jesus only" Pentecostal organizations like the United Pentecostal Church International, moreover, continue to preach Sabellianism to the masses.

Refuting Modalism. In order to refute modalism, one need observe merely (1) that Scripture testifies just as plainly to the distinctness of the divine persons as it does to their deity and the divine unity and (2) that two or more entities can be identical to the same substance and yet distinct from each other through the distinctness of their properties. As to the first point, Scripture states that the Father sends the Son (e.g., John 5:23, 30, 36–37; 6:39, 44, 57; 10:36; 12:49; 14:24; 20:21; 1 John 4:14), that the Father and the Son send the Spirit (John 14:26; 15:26; 16:7), and that the Spirit constitutes "another helper" besides the Son (John 14:16). None of this would be conceivable if the Father, the Son, and the Holy Spirit were not really distinct. Inasmuch as God is immutable, then, this real distinction between the divine persons must be not merely real but also eternal.

As to the possibility of two entities being identical to a single substance and yet really distinct from each other, examples of this exist among creatures. The ancient road from Thebes to Athens, for instance, was substantially identical to that from Athens to Thebes. Yet the two roads were really distinct in that one went upward and the other downward. Likewise, teaching, in the strict sense of the term, consists in the impartation of knowledge to a student's intellect: until the student learns, no teaching has occurred. This enrichment of the student's mind, in which teaching consists, when viewed from the student's perspective, constitutes learning.

Teaching and learning, therefore, are identical to the same process, yet few things differ more radically than teaching and learning. Creaturely entities, accordingly, can be identical to a third substance without being identical to each other. If mere creatures can accomplish this, it seems unreasonable to suppose that the divine persons cannot do so as well.

Conclusion. Modalists are simply wrong, therefore, when they assert that one cannot affirm both the deity of the divine persons and the singularity of the divine nature without implicitly identifying the divine persons with one another. Scripture testifies that the Father, the Son, and the Holy Spirit are really distinct from one another and that each is equally identical to the one God; and logic poses no obstacle to human acceptance of Scripture's verdict.

See also SOCINIANISM; TRINITARIAN CONTROVERSIES; TRINITY, THE

Bibliography. Aristotle, *Physics* 3.3; E. J. Fortman, *The Triune God: A Historical Study of the Doctrine of the Trinity*; Pseudo-Athanasius, *Against the Arians*, Oration 4; Tertullian, *Against Praxeas*.

D. W. Jowers

MOHAMMED. *See* MUHAMMAD

MOKSHA. In several Eastern religions, including Buddhism, Hinduism, Jainism, and Sikhism, *moksha* (or *mukti*) is defined as liberation from the cycle of death and rebirth. Fundamentally it is said to involve (1) the understanding that what we identify as the self is ultimately unreal and (2) the transformative experience of its dissolution. Some schools of thought claim that this happens only at death; others assert that persons can achieve moksha during this life. Some Hindu sects view moksha as the loss of all experience of space, causality, or time; nearly all insist that it involves the realization that Atman is the same as Brahma and that phenomenal things (the components of

the world of appearances as experienced by the unenlightened) are illusory. In Hinduism there are three main paths to the attainment of moksha: Brahmanism (the way of works), Advaita Vedanta (the way of knowledge), and Bhakti (the way of devotion). In Buddhism moksha is understood as realizing that there is no Atman. In Jainism it is the freeing from the weight of karma. Sikhs hold that moksha is the loss of individuality as one realizes the ultimate.

See also HINDUISM; JAINISM; SIKHISM

Bibliography. H. W. House, *Charts of World Religions*; K. Knott, *Hinduism: A Very Short Introduction*; W. G. Oxtoby, *World Religions: Eastern Traditions*, 2nd ed.

M. Power

MONARCHIANISM. Historians employ the term Monarchianism to designate two heresies that flourished in the late second and third centuries. The first is dynamic Monarchianism, whose proponents denied the deity of Christ. The second is modalistic Monarchianism, whose advocates denied any real distinction between the Father and the Word.

Dynamic Monarchianism first appeared in the teaching of Theodotus, a leather merchant, who gathered a school of adherents in Rome before the close of the second century. Theodotus and his followers taught that Jesus was a mere man whose exemplary virtue God rewarded, after his baptism, with a special endowment of the Holy Spirit. The Theodotians applied the term *Christ* exclusively to this gift of the Holy Spirit, not to the man Jesus himself. A synod in Antioch condemned dynamic Monarchianism and its most distinguished exponent, Paul of Samosata, in 272.

Modalistic Monarchianism originated near the end of the second century in the teaching of Noetus of Smyrna. This heresy, also known as Patripassianism because its tenets imply that the Father suffered in Jesus's crucifixion, entered Rome through the preaching of Noetus's pupil, Epigonus. Here it reached its most mature form in the speculations of Sabellius, who identified not only the Father and the Word but also the Spirit with a single, undifferentiated divine person, who manifests himself in three modes.

See also HERESY, DEFINITION OF; MODALISM

Bibliography. Eusebius of Caesarea, *Ecclesiastical History*; J. N. D. Kelly, *Early Christian Doctrines*, 5th ed.; Tertullian, *Against Praxeas*.

D. W. Jowers

MONOPHYSITISM. Monopysitism is the doctrine that the incarnate Christ had only one nature (Greek *mono*, "one," and *physis*, "nature"). The Council of Chalcedon (451) declared the view heretical, countering that if Jesus was both fully divine *and* fully human, he needed both a divine and a human soul, lest he be conceived of as God in the empty shell of a human body. The council's decision sparked controversy within the church, and several churches broke away, contending that the council had reverted to Nestorianism.

To this day, several traditions are often labeled Monophysite (such as the Armenian, Coptic, Ethiopian, and Syrian Orthodox churches), though they strenuously deny this characterization. They contend they are *miaphysite*; that is, they assert that the one person of Christ possesses one united nature, both human and divine, but unmixed and unconfused. Much of the controversy seems to stem from the difficulty describing the complex theological terms across several different languages used by the parties involved.

See also CHALCEDONIAN CONTROVERSY; CHRIST, NATURES AND ATTRIBUTES OF

Bibliography. J. Chapman, "Monophysites and Monophysitism," in *The Catholic Encyclopedia*, vol. 10, edited by Charles G. Herbermann et al.; A. E. McGrath, *Christian Theology: An Introduction*.

R. V. Huggins

MONOTHEISM. Monotheism (sometimes abbreviated as "theism") is the worldview that affirms the existence of one immaterial, omnipotent, omniscient, omnipresent, personal, and wholly good God, who is worthy of perfect worship and obedience. God created the universe out of nothing and is metaphysically distinct from the creation; yet God is active and immanent in the world through providence, miracles, and various modes of revelation. Scripture, nature, and conscience reveal that monotheism is true to reality (Rom. 1:18–20; 2:14–15). The Bible affirms, and some anthropological evidence indicates, that monotheism was the world's original religion (Gen. 1–2). Because of its uncompromising insistence on God's peerless power, majesty, and authority, monotheism has had a worldwide influence unmatched by any other religious worldview.

Monotheism is distinguished from polytheism or animism (there are many gods), pantheism (everything is God), panentheism (God is in the universe, like the soul is in the body), deism (God is transcendent but not active in the world he made), metaphysical dualism or gnosticism (God transcends an evil world of matter), and atheism (there is no God). The three great and categorically monotheistic religions are Judaism, Christianity, and Islam—although forms of Hinduism and Buddhism have monotheistic elements.

Christianity is unique among monotheistic religions in affirming the Trinity (one God eternally existing in three coequal persons: Father, Son, and Holy Spirit) and the incarnation (God the Son takes on a human nature in Jesus Christ for the redemption of the world).

See also ANIMISM; BUDDHISM; HINDUISM; ISLAM, BASIC BELIEFS OF; JUDAISM; PANENTHEISM; PANTHEISM; POLYTHEISM

Bibliography. N. Geisler, "Primitive Monotheism," in *Baker Encyclopedia of Christian*

Apologetics; H. P. Owen, "Theism," in *The Encyclopedia of Philosophy*, edited by P. Edwards; R. Stark, *One True God: Historical Consequences of Monotheism*.

D. R. Groothuis

MONOTHELITISM. Monothelitism is the doctrine that the incarnate Christ had only one will (Greek, *mono*, "one," and *thelein*, "to will"); the doctrine is closely associated with Monophysitism. It was condemned as heresy by the Third Council of Constantinople (680–81). The council insisted that if Jesus was both fully divine and fully human, he needed both a divine and a human will. Pope Honorius was excommunicated for his advocacy of Monothelitism in 680.

See also CHRIST, NATURES AND ATTRIBUTES OF; ROMAN CATHOLICISM

Bibliography. "Third Council of Constantinople" and "Monothelitism and Monothelites," in *The Catholic Encyclopedia*.

R. V. Huggins

MOSLEM. *See* MUSLIM

MOUNTAIN MEADOWS MASSACRE. The Mountain Meadows Massacre is the name given to an interaction in September 1857 between Latter-day Saints militiamen (possibly assisted by some Native Americans) and a group of emigrants traveling through Utah to California.

The group of emigrants, known as the Fancher-Baker company, was traveling to California during the fall of 1857. Rather than following a direct route through the Sierra Nevada, they chose to avoid the mountains by taking a more southern route through Utah. This route was heavily populated by Native Americans and Latter-day Saints. At the time, tensions were running high among the Mormon residents of Utah. The US Army had been sent to the region, and many Mormons were ready to retaliate against any non-Mormons who were involved in the persecutions in Missouri or in the murder of LDS founder Joseph Smith Jr. and his brother Hyrum.

When the emigrants arrived in southern Utah, they stopped in an area known as Mountain Meadows. On September 7, 1857, a Mormon militia dressed as Native Americans, who according to some accounts were assisted by a small group of actual Native Americans, attacked the encamped emigrants, and they continued attacking them throughout the remainder of the week. Finally, on September 11, 1857, after learning that the emigrants had discovered their true identity, and fearing reprisal, John D. Lee and a group of Latter-day Saints militiamen promised the emigrants safe passage for the rest of their trip in Utah. At a prearranged signal, the militiamen turned on the emigrants. They executed 1,120 men, women, and children that morning; only 17 young children (deemed too young to remember the event) survived. The emigrants' property was auctioned off, and the children were dispersed to Mormon families in the area. Due to the outbreak of the Civil War (and, according to some historians, efforts by Mormons to block criminal investigations), it was not until two decades later that John D. Lee was tried, convicted, and executed for his involvement in the massacre. Scholars debate to this day the extent to which Brigham Young, LDS Church president and Utah governor at the time, was complicit in the massacre or had contributed to the climate in which it occurred.

See also CHURCH OF JESUS CHRIST OF LATTER-DAY SAINTS

Bibliography. W. Bagley, *Blood of the Prophets*; J. Brooks, *The Mountain Meadows Massacre*; S. Denton, *American Massacre*; R. E. Turley Jr. and G. L. Leonard, *Massacre at Mountain Meadows*; R. W. Walker and R. E. Turley Jr., "The Mountain Meadows Massacre," *Ensign*.

T. S. Kerns

MUDRA. *Mudra* (Sanskrit, literally, "seal" or "mark") is a symbolic gesture of the entire body, but the word usually refers to the hands and fingers used in Hindu and Buddhist ceremonies and dance or in sculpture and painting. The mudra "seals" an utterance and is often used together with mantras. The hundreds of mudras used in Asian dances are illustrated in large technical manuals, as are the ones used in religious ceremonies.

An example of mudra is found in the statute of Buddha seen in many temples, sitting cross-legged with his left hand open on his lap and his right hand directed toward the earth (calling on earth to witness his buddhahood).

See also BUDDHISM; HINDUISM; MANTRA; NAMASTE

Bibliography. M. Schumacher, "Mudra: Hand Gestures with Religious Meaning," http://www.onmarkproductions.com/html/mudra-japan.shtml.

H. P. Kemp

MUHAMMAD. Muhammad (AD ca. 570–632) is the prophet and messenger of Islam and the founder of Islam. His teachings are found in the tradition (hadith) literature that is ascribed to him or to his close companions.

Muhammad was born into a minor branch of the tribe of Quraysh, which dominated the holy town of Mecca. During his youth and early adulthood, he is said to have participated in the merchant caravans that were the economic backbone of the town. In approximately 610, while meditating and seeking God's will on Mt. Hira (located outside Mecca), he claimed to have encountered the angel Gabriel and received revelations from God. These revelations were of a strongly monotheistic nature, and belief in their veracity set Muhammad and his first followers in opposition to the cult of Mecca that revolved around the cubical Ka'ba in the middle of the town and was devoted to pagan gods.

During this initial phase of Muhammad's ministry, he gained several dozen followers: some close relatives, others transients attracted to his message, and yet others who were slaves (mostly from Christian Ethiopia). Both Muhammad and his followers faced some persecution and social ostracism from their pagan relatives and neighbors, which eventually forced Muhammad to leave Mecca. He had earlier proclaimed his message to some of the tribesmen of the oasis town of Medina (about one hundred miles north of Mecca), and they had converted others to Islam, so in 622 Muhammad and the Meccan Muslims emigrated (in Arabic *hijra*) to Medina, where Muhammad was accepted by the population as a holy man and prophet who could arbitrate their disputes.

Medina was divided between two major Arab tribes, the Aws and the Khazraj, from whom Muhammad drew the majority of converts, and three smaller, Jewish tribes, the Banu Qaynuqa, the Banu al-Nadir, and the Banu Qurayza. Although the Jewish tribes were small, they held a good deal of economic power and occupied strategic positions in the oasis. Few of them, however, were willing to convert to Islam, and they occasionally ridiculed Muhammad's teachings.

Starting in 624, the Muslim community began a series of engagements with the Meccans, who depended on the trade routes going to Syria—which passed right by Medina—for their livelihood. The Battle of Badr, fought during that year, ended in an overwhelming Muslim victory; however, the Muslims were still too weak to follow it up. The following year the Meccans attacked the Muslims in Medina and won an equally overwhelming victory; likewise, they were too weak to totally destroy the Muslim community. During the following years, both sides fought skirmishes and tried to gain as many allies as they could from the Bedouin tribes around Mecca and Medina. All these conflicts were inconclusive or draws. But Muhammad used this period to consolidate his position within the oasis of Medina and progressively expelled the Jewish tribes and had one of them, the Banu Qurayza, slaughtered. Additionally, the numbers of his followers grew immensely, while the pagan Meccans lacked a charismatic leader to counter his influence. By 630 he had taken Mecca in a bloodless attack and purified the Ka'ba of all the idols hitherto contained within it.

During the final two years of Muhammad's life, he gained the submission of most of the tribes inhabiting the Arabian Peninsula and countered the influence of a number of other self-proclaimed prophets who had appeared as a result of his success. Heralding, during the final years of his life, the great Muslim conquests that were to follow his death, Muhammad sent troops to attack the Christian Byzantine Empire in present-day Jordan. These attacks failed, but they signaled the direction that Muslim leaders would take for expansion. Muhammad died in Medina in 632 and was succeeded by his oldest supporter, Abu Bakr.

The reasons for Muhammad's success are numerous. First, the message of Islam, that of absolute monotheism, was one that, while completely contradictory to the paganism of Arabia, offered a coherent belief system that answered a number of problems apparent in the society (what happens after death, social inequalities, etc.). Second, Muhammad's personal determination and consistency, even if one does not accept the hagiographic nature of the sources, was impressive. With a few brief exceptions, he held to his message against all opposition. Third, although Muhammad was by no means a military genius and lost almost as many battles as he won, he had the ability to consolidate his gains politically and to win people, especially key figures, over to Islam on a personal level. Finally, it was his fortune that he faced no organized and structured opposition.

Muhammad's first marriage, to a wealthy widow, Khadija, was the one that gained him financial stability and all but one of his children. However, of his (approximately) eight children, all four of the boys died young, and of his four daughters only one, Fatima—through marriage to his cousin, ward, and fourth successor, 'Ali—gave him male grandchildren (Hasan and Husayn). After Khadija's death, he married a total of thirteen other wives, for which he received a special dispensation (Qur'an 33:50). Most of these marriages were political alliances, and only the marriage to six-year-old 'A'isha, his only virgin bride and a daughter of Abu Bakr, is fully detailed in the sources; the marriage was consummated when she was nine. 'A'isha, however, bore him no children. Muhammad did have a son by Mariam (a Christian slave concubine) during his old age, but the child died in infancy.

The literary legacy of Muhammad is immense and of crucial importance for the development of Islam. Part of this legacy is the Qur'an, which Muslims believe is the revealed Word of God spoken by Muhammad. The Qur'an, as we know it today, was assembled about thirty years after the death of Muhammad by his third successor, 'Uthman. The suras, or chapters, into which it is divided are arranged in order of descending length, so the chronologically earlier materials appear to be located at the end, while the later materials are at the beginning. The Qur'an contains themes of eschatology, exhortations to the community and to its opponents, stories of the prophets (mainly biblical in origin but with some Arabian material), and laws for the Muslim community, as well as personal material concerning Muhammad and his family.

Another part of Muhammad's literary legacy is called the hadith literature, which Muslims believe describes the eyewitness accounts from Muhammad's companions of what he said and did. Muslim religious scholars use this material, especially in the case of Sunnis, to emulate the life of Muhammad as closely as possible. Both Muslim and non-Muslim scholars recognize that doubts exist about the authenticity of certain parts of the hadith literature. Consequently, the study of hadith and the verification of its authenticity form a large part of traditional Islamic scholarship and learning. Non-Muslim scholars often argue that the hadith literature is so vast and apparently contradictory that it probably represents the efforts of a large number of Muslims to influence the early development of Islam, especially in legal and political matters. Muslim scholars deny this and argue that through scholarship one can reach reliable conclusions about the life and teachings of Muhammad.

For non-Muslims many problems remain with the reconstruction of the life of Muhammad. The earliest Muslim sources date from at least 150 years after his life. The work of his biographer Ibn Ishaq (d. 767) has survived only in the later version of Ibn Hisham (d. 833). These sources contain a large amount of hagiographical material that appears to have grown through the centuries. There are no contemporary non-Muslim sources from the region of Arabia that can be used as a control (although a few outside sources mention the appearance of someone claiming to be a prophet, they give no details). Further, none of the words of Muhammad's opponents have survived in non-Muslim sources. In the end, all his opponents or their descendants converted to Islam, so it is very difficult to know to what degree the historical record of their words and actions can be trusted.

Since approximately the eighth century, the position of Muhammad within some branches of Islam has been greatly magnified. Although the Qur'an insists that Muhammad was only a human (Qur'an 18:110) who did not perform miracles, gradually a vast collection of hagiographic and miraculous tales has grown up around him. Today it is forbidden in most Muslim countries to make any denigrating characterizations of him or even criticize him because doing so is considered blasphemy. Thus his persona, while not divine, has achieved infallibility and a superhuman status. Within Islam overall, his influence is paramount, and his example is normative.

See also ISLAM, BASIC BELIEFS OF

Bibliography. M. Cook, *Muhammad*; A. Guillaume, trans., *The Life of Muhammad: A Translation of Ibn Ishaq's Sirat Rasul Allah*; Hisham Ibn, *al-Sira al-Nabawiyya*; M. J. Kister, "The Massacre of Banu Qurayza," *Jerusalem Studies in Arabic and Islam*; M. S. Lings, *Muhammad: His Life Based upon the Earliest Sources*; F. E. Peters, "The Quest for the Historical Muhammad," *International Journal of Middle Eastern Studies*; M. Rodinson, *Muhammad*; A. Schimmel, *And Muhammad Is His Messenger: The Veneration of the Prophet in Islamic Piety*; W. M. Watt, *Muhammad at Mecca*; Watt, *Muhammad at Medina*; Watt, *Muhammad: Prophet and Statesman*.

D. B. Cook

MUHAMMAD, ELIJAH. Born Elijah Poole, Elijah Muhammad (1897–1975) became the head of the Nation of Islam in 1934 and continued in that role until his death. Elijah was the seventh child and second son in a family of thirteen children, born and reared in Sandersville, Georgia.

Early Life. Elijah's parents were William and Mariah Poole. His father was a poor black sharecropper who on weekends pastored two Baptist churches. Elijah left school after the third grade to help in the fields, and by age sixteen he was working in factories in the area. Elijah joined the church, but because of the hypocrisy of others, he didn't fully believe what the church taught. At age ten, he witnessed a lynching that deeply affected him.

He married twenty-year-old Clara Evans in 1919, and in 1923, having "seen enough of the white man's brutality" (Clegg), he joined the exodus of blacks from the rural South to find work in northern industrial towns. The Pooles moved to Hamtramck, just north of Detroit. Despite having trouble finding work during the Great Depression, Elijah and his wife had eight children in the next decade. Poverty and alcohol became his regular companions for the next several years.

Conversion and Ascendency in the Nation of Islam. In 1931 Elijah attended a speech on Islam at the insistence of his wife. The speaker was Wallace Fard Muhammad, who called himself Master Fard (pronounced "Far-rod"), the leader of the Allah Temple of Islam. Fard sold clothes and household goods in the black neighborhoods. He said that he was born in Mecca, having a black father and a white mother (Muhammad, *Our Saviour*, 183). Fard provided hundreds of eager listeners with a new identity and a radically different vision of their origin and destiny. Elijah learned that the white man was the devil, the religion of black people was Islam, their book was the Qur'an, and God was black. Fard instructed students in a blend of Masonry, mathematics, and Islamic lore. Although Fard's message was presented as Islam, the beliefs he taught differed significantly from orthodox Islam. Moved by Fard's message of black empowerment, Elijah and two of his brothers joined the group; Fard gave each one a different Muslim name. Elijah's last name was changed to Karriem. New converts took lessons in the Lost-Found Nation of Islam, with secret papers they hand-copied and were required to memorize. Though there were many potential leaders for Allah Temple, Master Fard spontaneously named Elijah Karriem as the "Supreme Minister," second only to himself, and "helped him rouse support for the Nation of Islam" (Halasa, 81–82).

A small mosque was formed in Detroit. Elijah periodically traveled to Chicago to proclaim this new truth to the "so-called Negroes," who were really black Gods blinded by the "tricknology" of the dominant culture. Fard gave further lessons about UFOs, the myth of Yakub, the cycle of black Gods, and his true identity as Allah in person.

In November 1932, a member of Allah Temple committed a ritual murder. Fard was arrested because his hand-copied lessons declared "all Moslems will murder the devil." The police released Fard on the condition that he leave Detroit. Fard complied, moved to Chicago, and established "Temple no. 2," leaving Elijah in control of the original group.

Before Fard disappeared in 1934, he appointed Elijah to continue his work. Elijah took on the surname "Muhammad," and the group's name was changed to the Nation of Islam. Elijah carried on with vigor and success, creating a disciplined and powerful movement in cities with large black populations. His followers were called Black Muslims, although their version of the *shahada* (the Islamic creed, "There is no God but Allah, and Muhammad is his prophet") generally referred to Elijah Muhammad, not to the author of the Qur'an. His followers also distributed his newspaper, *Muhammad Speaks*, as well as books compiled from his regular columns.

Over the next three years, Muhammad faced a series of bitter internal battles over the leadership of the Nation. Eventually he was forced to leave Detroit for Chicago due to death threats. Continuing to fear for his safety, he moved from Chicago to Milwaukee, where he established Temple no. 3, and finally to Washington, DC, where he established Temple no. 4. In 1942 Muhammad was arrested for failing to register for the draft. On advice from his attorney (who feared a lynching), he fled Washington for Chicago. In Chicago he was arrested again and charged and found guilty of eight counts of sedition for teaching Nation of Islam members to refuse to register with the Selective Service or serve in the military. He served four years in prison.

Growth of the Nation of Islam.

After World War II, the Nation of Islam, under the now-firm control of Muhammad, experienced rapid growth. By 1959 there were fifty temples in twenty-two states. In the 1950s and 1960s, Elijah taught that "the whole Caucasian race is a race of devils" (*Supreme Wisdom*), requesting that separate states be given to black people as reparation for centuries of slavery.

Elijah's most famous converts were Malcolm Little and Cassius Clay: Little converted to the Nation of Islam while in prison in Massachusetts in 1948, becoming Malcolm X in 1950; Clay became the world heavyweight boxing champion in 1964 and then changed his name to Muhammad Ali. Most (but not all) new members of Nation of Islam replaced their "slave name" with the letter X, signifying their unknown African family name. Malcolm X experienced a significant conversion from a life of crime, quickly became a top leader in the movement, and for most of his life served as the foremost spokesman for "the Honorable Elijah Muhammad" (by far, his most common title). More than anyone else, Malcolm X is credited with increasing both the membership and the media exposure of the Nation.

Malcolm X would have been the heir apparent, even above Elijah's own sons, were it not for two turning points. First, on December 1, 1963, Malcolm suggested to the media that John F. Kennedy brought his assassination upon himself, and he wasn't even sorry—violating an order from Elijah Muhammad to say nothing at all about the assassination. Elijah silenced Malcolm from public speaking for ninety days and took steps against his prized lieutenant. Second, Malcolm discovered that Elijah had fathered children by several of his female disciples. Sexual infractions were treated severely in the Nation of Islam, and this discovery was crushing to Malcolm.

Malcolm made a pilgrimage to Mecca in 1964, converted to Sunni Islam, took steps to help Nation of Islam sisters who had been impregnated and abandoned by Elijah Muhammad, and tried to organize a new movement. He was killed by three renegade Nation members in Harlem in February 1965. If Malcolm's death was not directed by Elijah Muhammad, it was certainly expected to occur.

Elijah had groomed his seventh son, Wallace D. Muhammad, to take over the movement, but it was never publicly announced that Wallace was to be his successor. Wallace was named after Wallace D. Fard. It was well-known that Wallace (who later renamed himself Warith Deen) had been a very close friend of Malcolm X, aware of his father's infidelity, a skeptic of the Yakub myth, and favorable to orthodox Islam. He fell in and out of favor with Elijah over the next ten years.

Controversy.

In 1973 Muhammad was embroiled in controversy after seven Nation of Islam members invaded the home of Hanafi head Khalifa Hamaas Abdul Khaalis (Hanafi is one of the four schools of jurisprudence within Sunni Islam) and brutally murdered Khaalis's children, a grandchild, and one of his followers. Khaalis was not home at the time. Khaalis had been severely critical of the Nation in an open letter written several weeks prior to the murders. Five of the seven murderers were captured and convicted, and they received life sentences. Although it was never proven that Muhammad was directly involved, critics charge that Muhammad was directly or indirectly responsible.

On February 25, 1975, at the age of seventy-seven, Elijah Muhammad died of congestive heart failure caused by diabetes and asthma.

After his death, his son Warith tried to disband the Nation of Islam. He recast Fard's teaching as deep symbolism and persuaded some followers to accept traditional Islam. He even abandoned the name Nation of Islam. Warith died in 2008.

Louis Farrakhan, who joined the Nation of Islam in 1955 under Malcolm X, revived the discarded name in 1977 and returned the Nation of Islam to Elijah Muhammad's original teaching.

In recent years, some of Elijah's followers have sought to clear his memory by recasting his extramarital affairs as polygamous marriages, more acceptable to Islamic practice. However, bigamy was illegal throughout Elijah's lifetime, and none of these purported "marriages" were performed legally or publicly. Today there is little doubt about the extent of Elijah's infidelity. "Mother" Tynetta Muhammad, a regular columnist for the Nation of Islam newspaper, openly claims to have four children by Elijah Muhammad, and there is a long history of court proceedings involving over a dozen illegitimate children claiming millions of dollars in withheld inheritance from his multimillion dollar estate.

In additional to Farrakhan's movement, a small number of independent organizations and publishers continue to promote Elijah's teachings today.

See also ISLAM, BASIC BELIEFS OF; NATION OF ISLAM

Bibliography. C. A. Clegg III, *An Original Man: The Life and Times of Elijah Muhammad*; E. U. Essien-Udom, *Black Nationalism: A Search for an Identity in America*; K. Evanzz, *The Messenger: The Rise and Fall of Elijah Muhammad*; M. Gardell, *In the Name of Elijah Muhammad: Louis Farrakhan and the Nation of Islam*; M. Halasa, *Elijah Muhammad*; C. E. Lincoln, *The Black Muslims in America*, 3rd ed.; E. Muhammad, *The Fall of America*; E. Muhammad, *Message to the Blackman in America*; E. Muhammad, *Our Saviour Has Arrived*; E. Muhammad, *The Supreme Wisdom*; S. Tsoukalas, *The Nation of Islam: Understanding the "Black Muslims."*

E. Pement and H. W. House

MUKTANANDA. *See* PARAMAHANSA, SWAMI MUKTANANDA

MUSLIM. The term *Muslim* literally means "one who submits" (obsolete variant, Moslem). The term represents someone who believes in, belongs to, and performs Islam. A Muslim resigns himself to the divine will of Allah. As explained in the Qur'an (33:35), a Muslim is someone who is devout, patient, humble, and chaste. This, then, is demonstrated through the five pillars of Islam: creed (*shahada*), prayer (*salat*), tithes (*zakat*), fasting (*sawm*), and pilgrimage to Mecca (*hajj*).

A Muslim is also defined by his adherence to the six beliefs of Islam explained in the Qur'an (2:177): Allah (God is one), angels (invisible beings who execute God's will), prophets (conveying the message of Allah), sacred books (Qur'an and hadith), judgment ("last day"), and decree (paradise or hell).

A Muslim, therefore, is someone who follows this "straight path" while fearing Allah.

See also ISLAM, BASIC BELIEFS OF

Bibliography. G. Braswell, *Islam: Its Prophets, Peoples, Politics, and Power*; Ergun and Emir Caner, *Unveiling Islam*.

Emir Caner

MYSTICISM. It is difficult to define *mysticism* precisely. The term is used to describe the practice of seeking a personal, subjective experience with God. It has some affinity with existentialism in that both derive knowledge predominantly from the psychological/experiential realm. Mysticism appeals to, or emphasizes, the emotional side of human experience over cognitive activity.

Religious mysticism is closely aligned with the search for spirituality and centers not so much on what one believes as on the inner person. Non-Christian religious movements such as Hinduism, Buddhism, Krishna consciousness, New Age thought, and the occult have strong tendencies toward mysticism.

Within the Christian community, mysticism is manifested in numerous ways. Mystical elements have been a part of Christianity from its inception, although at times the mystical has been at odds with orthodox doctrine. Most forms of mysticism in ancient Christianity centered on devotion to some aspect of mystery within Christianity, such as the Eucharist or the Trinity. Traditionally, the Eastern church has emphasized the mystical more than the Western church.

The spread of aberrant mysticism within the Christian community is evident through some aspects of Pentecostalism, with its use of dreams, extrabiblical revelation, emotional/psychological manipulation, and visions.

See also BUDDHISM; HINDUISM; INTERNATIONAL SOCIETY FOR KRISHNA CONSCIOUSNESS (ISKCON)

Bibliography. W. Corduan, *Mysticism: An Evangelical Option?*; G. Friesen, *Decision Making and the Will of God*; A. Johnson, *Faith Misguided: Exposing the Dangers of Mysticism*; D. D. Martin, "Mysticism," in *Evangelical Dictionary of Theology*.

S. J. Rost

MYTH. A myth is a type of narrative that seeks to express in imaginative form a belief about humans, the world, and/or God or gods that cannot be expressed adequately in simple propositions. Since the word is used in contemporary scientific and theological literature in a variety of ways, any definition of it appears to be arbitrary. In common language, *myth* is used to denote a story that is untrue. Perhaps a better term for myth is, as Walter Fisher has suggested, a "narrative paradigm," since this term serves well to denote a story that directs individuals and communities.

Until recently *myth* was used in biblical studies to denote a mistaken worldview based on supernatural assumptions that stand in sharp contrast to the modern scientific worldview. It was this understanding of myth that inspired the biblical criticism of scholars like D. F. Strauss (1808–74) and Rudolf Bultmann (1884–1976), who sought to "demythologize" the New Testament.

The contrast between *myth* and *science* has been challenged by many philosophers, literary critics, religious studies scholars, and others who compare myths with legends, fairy tales, and the like and argue that myths are stories with some sort of inner or spiritual meaning. For such people, myths portray a "truer" or "deeper" version of reality than secular history, realistic description, or scientific explanation. This spiritualized view of myth ranges from outright irrationalism and post-Christian supernaturalism to more sophisticated accounts where myths are held to be fundamental expressions of certain psychological properties of the human mind. The work of Carl Gustav Jung (1875–1961) is a good example of this type of approach to myths and mythology.

The problem with these spiritualist ways of understanding myth is that the term eventually becomes so vague that it is virtually meaningless. Further, many contemporary definitions of *myth* have their origins in different forms of fascist thought and in the writings of men like Alfred Rosenberg (1893–1946), the official ideologue of the Nazi Party, where myths were deliberately promoted as a way of manipulating people to avoid rational analysis. The works of many popular writers on myth, such as Mircea Eliade (1907–86), Joseph Campbell (1904–87), and even Jung all reflect the influence of fascist thinking and open the door to irrationalism.

Probably the best definition of *myth* is based on the work of anthropologists like John Middleton, who defined a *myth* as "a statement about society and man's place in it and in the surrounding universe. . . . Myths and cosmological notions are concerned with the relationship of people with other people, with nature and with the supernatural" (x).

In social anthropology, what makes a story a myth is not its content, as the rationalists thought, or some "inner spiritual meaning," as the spiritualist interpreters argue, but the use to which the story is put. Once accepted a myth can be used to ennoble the past, explain the present, and hold out hope for the future. It gives individual and social life meaning and direction. This ability to guide action distinguishes myths from legends, folk tales, and other stories. In short myths have the power to change lives and shape societies. Probably the best definition of *myth* is "a story with culturally formative power."

See also MYTHOLOGY

Bibliography. W. Fisher, *Human Communication as Narration: Towards a Philosophy of Reason, Value and Action*; B. Malinowski, *Magic, Science and Religion*; J. Middleton, ed., *Myth and Cosmos*; R. Samuel and P. Thompson, *The Myths We Live By*.

I. Hexham

MYTHOLOGY. Strictly speaking, mythology is the study of myths. In ancient times shamans, oracles, priests, and other holy men learned and passed on the myths of their culture, most often through oral storytelling. The term may also refer to a series of stories that function as myths and hang together as a whole or coexist as isolated fragments in a person's consciousness without any need being felt to express their meaning propositionally. Today the term is often used for collections of stories with titles like *The Greek Myths*, without acknowledgment that in their original setting these stories were believed to be true and taken as a guide for daily living.

Once the exclusive arena of classical studies and literature, myths have begun to be studied by scholars in a new light, with the realization that important insight can be gained into a culture through the study of its myths. A culture's values, mores, influences, and other anthropological information can be revealed in its myths. Some scholars have even begun to study modern mythology and how it relates to modern culture.

Another modern phenomenon is the rise of "urban" myths. These are usually incredible stories that seem to defy nature. With the advent of the internet and email, many of these stories are widely dispersed. The popularity of urban mythology has given rise to groups seeking to verify these stories, and to at least one television show.

See also MYTH

Bibliography. P. Maranda, ed., *Mythology*.

I. Hexham

NABUWWAT. *Nabuwwat* is the word for the office of prophethood in Islam. Nabuwwat carry the authoritative revelation from Allah, so their words are binding for Muslims. Islamic teaching maintains that Allah desires for all people to be informed of his divine intentions and hence that throughout history he has sent holy prophets (*nabis*) to every human society. Beginning with the first created man, Hazrat Adam, and continuing until the time of Muhammad, Allah has sent prophets (124,000 in all) to proclaim the true religion of Islamic monotheism and guide humanity in its religious development. According to Islam, Allah has authorized and enabled every one of these prophets to relay his will in such a fashion that it is communicated with perfect accuracy. The core of this urgent message is the divine imperative of submission to the will of Allah. Of the twenty-five prophets specifically mentioned in the Qur'an, Islamic tradition regards five in particular as the most significant: Nuh (Noah), Ibrahim (Abraham), Musa (Moses), Issa (Jesus), and Muhammad, who is the final and most definitive of the prophets. A small number of prophets who were entrusted with the task of writing the sacred scriptures as Islam are called *rasul* (messengers).

See also ISLAM, BASIC BELIEFS OF

Bibliography. J. L. Esposito, *Islam: The Straight Path*, 3rd ed.; S. B. Noegel, *Historical Dictionary of Prophets in Islam and Judaism.*

R. L. Drouhard

NAMASTE. In traditional Indian culture, *namaste* (pronounced "na-ma-stay") is a Sanskrit word spoken in conjunction with a specific gesture of salutation and obeisance; typically it is uttered as a way of conveying the humble submission of one person to another, and when addressing another person it is accompanied by a bow. The term more literally is translated "I bow to you," but more loosely it can mean "The divine in me honors and blesses the divine in you." Namaste, then, reminds one of the ontological equality and sacredness of all persons (though social, political, and economic inequalities remain in much of India due to the lingering effects of caste-based culture). To perform namaste, a person places his hands together near his heart, closes his eyes, and bows his head. A way of demonstrating even greater homage is placing the hands together in front of the forehead, bowing the head, and then bringing the hands down to the heart. The reverence and deference expressed in namaste is essentially the same as the devotion (bhakti) many Hindus show to their chosen deities. The performance of namaste also draws attention to the penultimate dualities of this world while pointing to a higher metaphysical unity. Popular Hinduism views the spoken word *namaste* as a sacred sound with magical power that can be uttered as a way to put oneself in harmonious alignment with cosmic vibrations. The gesture is seen as a *mudra*, a well-recognized symbolic hand position. A number of Hindu sects and groups in the US endorse the practice of namaste—the concept being central to yoga and New Age in America—including Self-Realization Fellowship, the Ananda Marga Yoga Society, Siddha Meditation, and Shambhala International. It is also performed in East Asian Buddhism with the same gesture but with the Chinese or Japanese pronunciation as "*namo/namu.*"

See also ANANDA MARGA YOGA SOCIETY; BHAKTI YOGA; HINDUISM; MUDRA; YOGA

Bibliography. A. K. K. Nambiar, *Namaste: Its Philosophy and Significance in Indian Culture*; R. S. K. Rao, *Bharatiya Pranama Paddhati: Respectful Salutations in India*; P. Sudhi, *Symbols of Art, Religion and Philosophy.*

J. Bjornstad

NANAK. *See* GURU NANAK DEV

NATION OF ISLAM. Also known as "Black Muslims," this group, founded by the mysterious Wallace D. Fard and his disciple Elijah Muhammad, blended Christian principles, Islamic theology, and black nationalism that resonated throughout the oppressed communities of the US. Fard, influenced by the message of Noble Drew Ali (1886–1929) that Caucasians were the embodiment of evil, asserted that Christianity was the white man's religion, not the religion of the black man. Ali—like W. D. Fard, who came after him—taught that blacks were Asiatic, not African, and their religion was Islam. After Fard's disappearance in 1934, Muhammad took control of the movement and preached that the black man would one day rule the world after the battle of Armageddon.

Elijah Muhammad systematized the theology of the Nation of Islam. Nation members were required to believe in the traditional Islamic doctrines of one God (Allah) and reverence to the Qur'an and the hadith. He modified the doctrines of the resurrection (exclusively mental) and judgment (occurring first in America). Politically, Muhammad argued for the immediate separation of blacks and whites, while opposing fighting in the US Armed Forces. Yet what set Muhammad's theology apart was his acknowledgment of Fard as Allah in the flesh and the Muslim mahdi ("guided one"; an eschatological leader in Muslim tradition).

Since the black community had long been oppressed by Caucasians, the Nation campaigned for the release of all Muslims from prison, while promoting equal employment opportunities, tax exemption for blacks, and an end to the mixing of the races. In the end, Black Muslims believe that Allah will judge the inferior white race and reinstate the original black race to its rightful place. In order for this to come about, social reforms must take place in the black community. Nation leaders, therefore, advocate the abolition of alcohol, gambling, dancing, fornication, lying, and the eating of pork. In the 1950s and 1960s, Elijah Muhammad was typically represented before the media by Malcolm X, his personal spokesman. In 1964 both Malcolm X and Wallace Muhammad (one of Elijah Muhammad's sons) became convinced that the Nation of Islam was an aberrational form of traditional Islam.

After Muhammad's death in 1975, an internal struggle ensued between Muhammad's son Wallace and Louis Farrakhan. Wallace quickly rejected the theological tenets of God being black and Fard being God. He rejected the vilification of the white man, instead blaming the church as the agent of evil throughout the world.

By 1985 the Nation (now called the American Muslim Mission) was integrated into traditional Islam. In 1992 Wallace Muhammad (then known as Warith Muhammad) gave the invocation for the US Senate, praying to Allah, "the Most Merciful Benefactor, the Merciful Redeemer."

Farrakhan, desiring to reestablish the old Nation and salvage the reputation and vision of Elijah Muhammad, restored the Nation of Islam, with many disgruntled members joining his fold. Emphasizing the social aspects of his message, he cleaned up black neighborhoods while removing many drug lords through his Fruit of Islam security force. In 1995 the Nation once again came into national prominence through the Million Man March, a platform for black self-reliance and respect.

Today, through the leadership of Louis Farrakhan, the Nation of Islam is known as a black separatist group that assists in raising the morality of its own race while teaching anti-Semitism and hatred of others. It is still considered unorthodox and unacceptable by many traditional Muslims due to its theological heterodoxy and political militancy.

See also ISLAM, BASIC BELIEFS OF; MUHAMMAD, ELIJAH

Bibliography. G. Braswell, *Islam: Its Prophet, Peoples, Politics, and Power*; S. Tsoukalas, *The Nation of Islam: Understanding the "Black Muslims."*

Emir Caner and E. Pement

NATIVE AMERICANS, MORMON VIEW OF. The LDS Church has traditionally taught that Native Americans are predominantly descendants of Israelite emigrants who traveled to the Americas in two migrations around 600 BC (Lehi's family) and 588 BC (the Mulekites). Their history is detailed in the Book of Mormon, which, according to Mormonism's founder, Joseph Smith Jr., was translated by him into English from gold plates engraved with "Reformed Egyptian" characters.

According to the Book of Mormon, a sharp division among the Israelite colonists descending from Lehi's sons created two opposing factions: the "Nephites" (God's followers) and the "Lamanites" (wicked apostates). God responded by prohibiting intermarriage of the groups and cursing the Lamanites by giving them a "skin of blackness" instead of the white and delightful skin they had had (2 Nephi 5:21), so they would appear repulsive to the white Nephites (3 Nephi 2:15). God, however, mercifully added that repentant Lamanites would have their curse removed and become "white" again (3 Nephi 2:14–16).

In the Book of Mormon account, in the fifth century AD war ultimately destroyed every Nephite, but the Lamanites became the ancestors of Native Americans. The scattered remnants, whom Columbus would eventually refer to as Indians, forgot about God and lost all memory of their Israelite identity. They also forgot that their dark skin was a curse. According to classic Mormon doctrine of earlier generations, as Native Americans convert to Mormonism, they will gradually regain their white skin per Book of Mormon promises (2 Nephi 30:6, pre-1981 edition). Since the 1978 declaration opening the LDS priesthood to males of all colors, the LDS Church has backed away from its historic position on this subject.

Since the nineteenth century, critics of the Book of Mormon pointed out the incongruity of ascribing a Semitic ancestry to virtually all Native Americans. Ignoring the issue of skin color, there is no real comparison between these two cultures in terms of language, writing, military implements, animal husbandry, building construction, coinage, and known religion and mythology (e.g., see Lamb, *The Golden Bible*, published in 1887). One LDS response was to shift the arena of the Book of Mormon from the North Atlantic region to Central and South America, focusing on the more developed Incan and Mayan cultures. This was contradicted by Joseph Smith's own assertion of a midwestern and northern locale for events narrated in the Book of Mormon. More recently, DNA studies have confirmed that Native Americans in North, Central, and South America are descended from Asian ancestors, with no DNA markers of Israelites or ancient Hebrews. The evidence has been sufficiently compelling that the LDS Church's official website has issued a statement on DNA studies, denying its relevance to the historicity of the Book of Mormon.

See also BOOK OF MORMON; CHURCH OF JESUS CHRIST OF LATTER-DAY SAINTS; DARK SKIN CURSE; LAMANITES; NEPHITES

Bibliography. R. Abanes, *One Nation under Gods: A History of the Mormon Church*; M. Lamb, *The Golden Bible*; Living Hope Ministries, *DNA vs. the Book of Mormon*; T. Murphy, "Lamanite Genesis, Genealogy, and Genetics," in *American Apocrypha*, edited by D. Vogel and B. Metcalfe; D. Persuitte, *Joseph Smith and the Origins of the Book of Mormon*; D. Vogel, *Indian Origins and the Book of Mormon*.

R. Abanes

NEO-ORTHODOX CHRISTIANITY. Neo-orthodox Christianity, or neo-orthodoxy, constitutes a current of thought that dominated European and American theology from approximately 1930 until 1960. Over against the theological liberalism that dominated Protestant thought in the late nineteenth and early twentieth centuries, neo-orthodox theologians sought to combine acceptance of the results of post-Enlightenment biblical criticism with a renewed appreciation for the theology of the Reformation. Central themes of neo-orthodox theology include divine transcendence, human sinfulness, and the centrality of Scripture to a correct understanding of the Christian faith. Its leading thinkers are Karl Barth (1886–1968), Emil Brunner (1889–1966), and Reinhold Niebuhr (1892–1971).

Karl Barth. The brightest star in the firmament of neo-orthodox theologians is unquestionably Karl Barth. The child of a conservative evangelical theologian, Barth embraced liberalism during his theological studies. In his first pastorate, however, Barth found the liberal theology he had imbibed from his teachers unhelpful in preaching and turned for assistance in this area to the study of Scripture. Shocked by the brutality of World War I, moreover, Barth repudiated liberalism's optimistic view of human moral capacities.

Barth gave some voice to his disillusionment with liberalism in a commentary on Romans published in 1919. In the book's thoroughly revised edition of 1922, however, Barth condemned liberalism so harshly that he ignited a firestorm of controversy. Here he also sketched a third way of sorts between conservative evangelicalism and liberalism. Barth elaborated his third way in his *Church Dogmatics* (fourteen volumes), which he never completed. He also authored most of the Barmen Declaration, a manifesto of Germany's Confessing Churches, which opposed Adolph Hitler's ecclesiastical policies.

Among the most significant elements of Barth's theology are his opposition to natural theology, his concept of revelation, his doctrine of the Trinity, and his doctrine of election. As to the first, Barth denies that natural revelation exists. He maintains that all human knowledge of God must come through God's Word and that it is positively harmful to attempt to justify this Word on the basis of anything other than itself.

As to revelation, Barth maintains that God reveals himself, not doctrines about himself, and that, strictly speaking, only Christ Incarnate is the Word of God. Scripture and Christian proclamation constitute human witnesses to the Word of God, which can become the Word of God only when the Holy Spirit employs them as vehicles of God's self-communication.

As to the Trinity, Barth holds that God reveals himself in his self-communication as trinitarian: the Father, who reveals; the Son, who is the revelation; and the Spirit, who is the revealedness of, or the condition of human receptivity for, God's Word. Because God reveals himself as he is, Barth asserts, the trinitarian form in which God manifests himself to the world must correspond to the reality of his inner being. Hence, Barth concludes, God does not merely represent himself as trinitarian; he is trinitarian in his innermost, eternal being.

343

As to election, Barth contends that God predestines no human being to either salvation or damnation; the only object of election, God's choice of persons to be saved, and reprobation, God's choice of persons to be damned, is Christ. Christ is reprobate, according to Barth, inasmuch as he bears the judgment that all human beings deserve in their place. He is elect, however, inasmuch as God bestows his favor on him and, through him, the entire human race whom he represents.

Emil Brunner. Emil Brunner, the second most influential of the neo-orthodox theologians, authored numerous works, which tend to be more accessible to students and lay readers than the tomes of Barth. Among the most celebrated of Brunner's works are *Mysticism and the Word*, a critique of the theology of Friedrich Schleiermacher; *Man in Revolt*, an overview of theological anthropology; and *Truth as Encounter*, an introduction to Brunner's concept of revelation. Also significant is Brunner's three-volume dogmatics: *The Christian Doctrine of God*, *The Christian Doctrine of Creation and Redemption*, and *The Christian Doctrine of the Church, Faith, and Consummation*. Central themes of Brunner's theology include his understanding of revelation as personal encounter and his belief in the existence of a natural human awareness of God.

Brunner conceives of divine revelation as a personal encounter in which God communicates himself to the individual. Over against liberalism, Brunner maintains that this personal encounter constitutes a free and unpredictable gift of God; it is not merely the unfolding of human beings' religious consciousness. Over against more conservative theologians, however, Brunner insists that this revelation does not consist in or even contain propositions or information of any sort.

As to natural revelation, although Brunner shares Barth's aversion to natural theology,

he asserts that all human beings possess a natural awareness of God, which renders it possible for them to understand the gospel, even if they reject it. Barth famously denounced Brunner's stance on this issue in a booklet titled *Nein!* In Barth's view, Brunner's position amounted to a concession to the German Christians, who attempted to integrate elements of Nazi ideology with the Christian faith.

Reinhold Niebuhr. Reinhold Niebuhr, neo-orthodoxy's foremost American theologian, abandoned liberalism and adopted a pessimistic view of humanity while serving as a pastor to factory workers in Detroit. His theology's most remarkable feature is his endorsement of violations of the law of love. Violence as such, in Niebuhr's view, contravenes the law of love set forth in the Sermon on the Mount, which he considers the ultimate, albeit unattainable, moral standard. Nevertheless, Niebuhr maintains, in practical affairs one ought to seek "proximate justice": a realizable ideal whose attainment frequently requires the commission of intrinsically evil acts.

Conclusion. Neo-orthodoxy's popularity waned in the 1960s. It supplied scant assistance to those who wished to defend Christianity against secular trends of thought, and the old-fashioned liberalism it opposed was almost entirely dead. The theology of Karl Barth, nevertheless, remains a significant source of inspiration for postliberal theologians such as Hans Frei (1922–88), Stanley Hauerwas (1940–), Thomas F. Torrance (1913–2007), and Eberhard Jüngel (1934–).

See also LIBERAL CHRISTIANITY; ORTHODOXY

Bibliography. K. Barth, *Evangelical Theology: An Introduction*, trans. G. Foley; E. Brunner, *Our Faith*, trans. J. W. Rilling; G. Dorrien, *The Barthian Revolt in Modern Theology: Theology without Weapons*; D. J. Hall, *Remembered Voices: Reclaiming the Legacy of "Neo-Orthodoxy"*; C. F. H. Henry, ed., *Christian Faith and Modern*

Theology; R. Niebuhr, *The Nature and Destiny of Man: A Christian Interpretation.*

D. W. Jowers

NEPHITES. In the Book of Mormon, the Nephites are the descendants of the Jewish prophet Nephi, who took his family to the Western Hemisphere from Jerusalem shortly before the Babylonian invasion of 589 BC (1 Nephi 1). Nephi was one of the sons of Lehi and a younger brother of Laman. When Laman and other brothers plotted to kill Nephi, Nephi took his family and followers into the wilderness, where they supposedly established their own civilization.

The Nephites are portrayed in the Book of Mormon as obedient to God and are said to have been "white and delightsome" (2 Nephi 12:12, pre-1981 ed.). They were opposed by the Lamanites, who are described as "idle" and "full of mischief" and cursed with a "skin of blackness" (2 Nephi 5:24; 4:4).

The two groups warred for several hundred years, until Jesus Christ visited both after his resurrection and preached the gospel to them. The Book of Mormon says that after this event, "there were no robbers, nor murderers, neither were there Lamanites, nor any manner of -ites; but they were in one, the children of Christ, and heirs to the kingdom of God" (4 Nephi 1:17). This peace lasted for approximately two hundred years, until a few people revolted from "the church" and began to call themselves Lamanites again (4 Nephi 1:20). Eventually the Lamanites far outnumbered the Nephites, and the Nephites themselves became "exceedingly wicked" (4 Nephi 1:45). A series of wars decimated the Nephites, until they were completely destroyed around AD 400. Before their annihilation, the prophet Mormon finished the gold plates containing the entire record of the Book of Mormon and buried them in the "hill of Cumorah" (Mormon 8:2), where Joseph Smith would allegedly find them approximately fourteen hundred years later.

See also BOOK OF MORMON; CHURCH OF JESUS CHRIST OF LATTER-DAY SAINTS; LAMANITES; NATIVE AMERICANS, MORMON VIEW OF

Bibliography. T. L. Givens, *By the Hand of Mormon: The American Scripture That Launched a New World Religion*; D. Persuitte, *Joseph Smith and the Origins of the Book of Mormon.*

R. L. Drouhard and J. P. Holding

NEW WORLD TRANSLATION. The version of the Bible produced by the Watch Tower Bible and Tract Society is called the New World Translation (NWT). The New Testament portion, which Jehovah's Witnesses (JWs) call the Christian Greek Scriptures, was originally published in 1950 (*NWTCGS*). The Old Testament (JW: "Hebrew Scriptures") was published in installments throughout the 1950s, and a revised one-volume Bible was published in 1961. In 1969 the New Testament portion was published with an interlinear Greek text (produced by the society) based on the 1881 Westcott-Hort Greek text; the work (revised in 1985) was called the *Kingdom Interlinear Translation of the Christian Scriptures (KIT)*. Revised editions of the NWT appeared in 1970, 1971, 1984, and 2013. In August 2013, the society claimed that over 201 million copies of the New World Translation had been published "in whole or in part" in over 110 languages.

The New World Translation Committee, which was and remains officially anonymous, was headed by Frederick W. Franz, who went on to become the society's fourth president (1977–92). Neither Franz nor any of the other committee members held any academic qualifications relevant to Bible translation. Reviewers have noted its wooden, awkward style, the result of a tendency to overtranslate words (especially verbs) and to follow the original-language word order too closely. For example, the NWT renders Luke 19:7, "But when they saw [it], they all fell to muttering, saying: 'With a man that is a sinner he went in to lodge.'"

The NWT purports to be what is called a concordant translation, that is, one that renders each major original-language word as uniformly as possible by one English word and avoids rendering two different original-language words with the same English word (*NWTCGS*). In an independent work of some sophistication, Rolf Furuli, a Norwegian JW, argues that a concordant translation allows the reader to take a more active role in the interpretation of the text. With certain key words, the NWT does indeed follow this policy, even where it results in awkward wording. For example, it renders the Hebrew *nephesh* and the Greek *psychē* uniformly by the word "soul," which in some places required some creativity (e.g., Acts 14:2; Eph. 6:6).

On the other hand, where following a concordant policy would conflict with JW doctrine, a single Greek word may be rendered with a variety of English words or phrases. For example, the word *pneuma*, a noun normally translated "spirit" or "Spirit," is rendered as the adjective "spiritual," and "spiritual life" is changed to mean "[gift of the] spirit," and even "force" in passages where "spirit" might be taken to imply that humans have an immaterial spirit as an intrinsic aspect of their being (e.g., 1 Cor. 14:12–15, 32; Eph. 4:23; Heb. 12:9, 23). The same word is frequently rendered "inspired expression" or "inspired utterance" when the translation is contrasting the true, divine Spirit with the lying, demonic spirits (e.g., 1 Tim. 4:1; 1 John 4:1–6), evidently because such a contrast implies that the Spirit is a divine person. Similarly, the word *proskyneō* is routinely translated "worship" when the object of the action is God, but when the object is clearly Christ, it is consistently rendered "do obeisance," even in contexts implying his deity (e.g., Matt. 28:17; Heb. 1:6).

The most obvious difference between the NWT and other versions of the Bible is its use of the name Jehovah 237 times in the New Testament where Greek manuscripts read "Lord" (*kyrios*) or, occasionally, "God" (*theos*). The translators' justification for such usage is flawed. Moreover, it is evident in many passages that the NWT inconsistently renders *kyrios* as something besides "Jehovah" or "Lord" where a uniform rendering throughout the passage would all too clearly show the NT writings equating Jesus with the Lord God of the Old Testament. In Colossians 3:12–4:1, for example, a single passage focusing on relations among believers, *kyrios* is rendered "Jehovah" (3:13, 16, 22b, 23, 24a), "the Lord" or "[the] Lord" (3:17, 18, 20), and "master(s)" (3:22a, 24b; 4:1ab). There is no textual evidence to support such variations; they are based solely on the theological assumptions of the translators.

Besides its use of the name Jehovah in the New Testament, the NWT is best known for its controversial renderings of various texts that appear to call Jesus "God" (*theos*). Several of these are translated so that Jesus is not called God at all (Rom. 9:5; Titus 2:13; Heb. 1:8; 2 Pet. 1:1). In the NWT version of John's prologue, the Word (Jesus) is called "a god" and "the only begotten god" (John 1:18). (The textual and syntactical issues in John 1:18 are sufficiently vexed that dogmatic conclusions based on one interpretation are hazardous; see Harris.) The only New Testament text in the NWT where Jesus appears to be called God is John 20:28 ("My Lord and my God!"); here the JWs argue either that Thomas was calling Jesus his God in a secondary sense or that Thomas was addressing the Father as God.

Perhaps the most notorious rendering in the NWT, though, is its translation of Colossians 1:16–20. Four times in this passage the NWT inserts "other" to represent Paul as speaking of Christ as the one in whom "all [other] things" are created and reconciled. (The 1950 and 1951 editions generally did not use brackets to show that words had been inserted. Later editions of the NWT did so, evidently in response to criticism of its rendering of texts such as this one. However, the 2013 edition reverts to the unbracketed form.) A 1950 *Watchtower* article on the *NWTCGS* explained that the rendering "all other things" was used to "harmonize these verses" with other biblical texts thought to teach that Jesus was a creature made by Jehovah. The NWT thus makes Paul say that Jesus was "the firstborn of all creation, because by means of him all [other] things were created" (Col. 1:15–16a NWT); that is, that Jesus was the "firstborn" in relation to all creation because he was the creature through which all other creatures were created. What Paul actually says, though, is that Jesus was the "firstborn" in relation to all creation because he was the One in, through, and for whom all things were created.

For reasons such as those discussed here, most biblical scholars do not regard the NWT as a particularly respectable or credible version of the Bible. Old Testament scholar H. H. Rowley (whose review is titled "How Not to Translate the Bible") and New Testament scholar Bruce Metzger were among the reviewers to pan the NWT. Religion scholar Jason BeDuhn in his 2003 book, *Truth in Translation*, compared the way that nine English versions handled such controversial texts as John 1:1 and Philippians 2:6–7, concluding that the NWT was the least biased version. BeDuhn's method, however, seems designed more to repudiate the orthodox view of Christ than to vindicate the scholarship of the NWT (see Howe for a thorough critique of BeDuhn).

See also JEHOVAH'S WITNESSES (JW); JOHN 1:1; TETRAGRAMMATON; WATCHTOWER, THE

Bibliography. J. D. BeDuhn, *Truth in Translation*; R. M. Bowman Jr., *Understanding Jehovah's Witnesses*; R. H. Countess, *The Jehovah's Witnesses' New Testament: A Critical Analysis of the New World Translation of the Christian Greek Scriptures*; R. Furuli, *The Role of Theology and Bias in Bible Translation: With a Special Look at the New World Translation of Jehovah's Witnesses*; M. J. Harris, *Jesus as God: The New Testament Use of* Theos *in Reference to Jesus*; T. Howe, *The Truth about Truth in Translation*.

R. M. Bowman Jr.

NIBLEY, HUGH WINDER. Hugh Winder Nibley (1910–2005) was the most prolific and influential Mormon apologist of the last generation. Extensively educated and extremely gifted in languages, Nibley inspired generations of LDS students with his teaching at Brigham Young University and aroused interest among LDS scholars and apologists in the importance of studying ancient texts and languages. Negatively, Nibley had the reputation of burying the problems of Mormonism in erudition rather than answering them, an approach widely imitated among more recent Mormon apologists. In 2005 his daughter Martha shocked the LDS Church when she accused her father of fraud and ritualized sexual abuse, a charge her siblings and mother vehemently deny. Nibley died shortly after the publication of his daughter's book, *Leaving the Saints: How I Lost the Mormons and Found My Faith*.

See also CHURCH OF JESUS CHRIST OF LATTER-DAY SAINTS

Bibliography. M. Beck, *Leaving the Saints: How I Lost the Mormons and Found My Faith*; R. V. Huggins, "Hugh Nibley's Footnotes," *Salt Lake City Messenger*; L. Midgley, "A Mighty Kauri Has Fallen: Hugh Winder Nibley (1910–2005)," *FARMS Review*; Midgley, "H. W. Nibley: Bibliography and Register," in *By Study and Also by Faith: Essays in Honor of Hugh W. Nibley*, edited by John M. Lundquist and Stephen D. Ricks; H. Nibley, *The Collected Works of Hugh Nibley*; B. J. Peterson, *Hugh Nibley: A Consecrated Life*.

R. V. Huggins

NICHIREN DAISHONIN. The Japanese Buddhist Nichiren Daishonin (1222–82) was a highly educated monk of the Tendai School who originally tried Zen and Pure Land approaches to Buddhism. However, he lost faith in these approaches and after much study determined that the Lotus Sutra was the highest teaching (much in line with Tendai thought). After this insight, he chanted the Japanese title of the Lotus Sutra (*nam-myoho-renge-kyo*) as his practice. He was a prolific writer, and more than seven hundred of his compositions exist.

Nichiren's work gave birth to what became Nichiren Buddhism. His disciple Nikko (1246–1333) founded Nichiren Shoshu, which is one of the major subschools of Nichiren Buddhism in Japan, with a worldwide following. Nichiren Buddhism is the only major tradition that is Japanese in origin, as the others were imported from China and then made Japanese.

See also NICHIREN SHOSHU; PURE LAND BUDDHISM; ZEN BUDDHISM

A. W. Barber

NICHIREN SHOSHU. Nichiren Shoshu is a Mahayana Buddhist school headquartered at Mt. Fuji. Basing itself on the teachings in the Lotus Sutra, it fully accepts the theory that the current age is one of degeneration, when people's capacity to achieve enlightenment is limited, and therefore, specific practices must be relied on. With this school, the chief practice is chanting the Dai-muko, or title of the sutra (along with other traditional practices). This is accompanied by the Dai-Gohonzon, or object of worship, and the Dai Sekiji no Honmon Daidan, or the "Essential Teachings High Sanctuary." The main object used to represent the essence of the teachings is not a statue or painting, as with other schools, but the inscribed title of the sutra on a scroll. Nichiren Shoshu maintains that through its teachings one can gain enlightenment in this degenerate age regardless of gender, class, ethnicity, and so on. This subschool has birthed a number of important groups, including Soka Gakkai.

See also GOHONZON; LOTUS SUTRA; MAHAYANA BUDDHISM; SOKA GAKKAI

Bibliography. R. Tsunoda, W. T. De Bary, and D. Keene, *Sources of Japanese Tradition*.

A. W. Barber

NIRVANA. Literally, *nirvana* means "extinction" or "blowing out" or "state beyond sorrow" in Sanskrit. Nirvana is the ultimate goal of meditation schools born out of Hindu, Jain, and Buddhist roots.

Nirvana is transcendent in that one becomes free of samsara but is also, in some formulations, imminent, as it can be identified with the nondual ultimate reality. In Buddhism delusions of the existence of self bind a person to samsara, the cycle of rebirths of suffering (*dukkha*). Release from samsara is the state of nirvana. Hence nirvana is the ultimate goal of religious practitioners, as it promises the end of both the causes of suffering and the results of karma. The concept is variably nuanced: for Theravadans, nirvana is an ultimate peace; in Mahayana schools, nirvana is synonymous with emptiness (*sunyata*), ultimate reality (*darma dhatu*), and hence the unchanging nature of the Buddha (*dharma kaya*). In some Asian cultures, "becoming a Buddha" is a euphemism for physical death, implying entrance into the nature of Buddha—that is, nirvana. Nirvana is sometimes metaphorically expressed as a drop of water merging back into the ocean.

However, achievement of nirvana does not necessarily equate with physical death. A person who has achieved nirvana (usually a lama, an arhat, or other perfected being) experiences *parinirvana* on death, that is, the final physical departure of the body. In Mahayana Buddhism, a bodhisattva delays his *parinirvana* so as to aid other sentient beings into enlightenment and nirvana. Lay practitioners of Hinduism and Buddhism are often resolved that achievement of nirvana in this lifetime is unlikely.

The word *nirvana* has also found its way into popular language; capitalizing on the nuance of "ultimate bliss," it has been used to name anything from chocolate to clothing shops or (using the word in relation to a physical location rather than a state of being) drug outlets and beachfront hotels. The music band Nirvana (1987–94) was largely responsible for popularizing "grunge" in Western music culture.

See also BUDDHISM; DUKKHA/DUHKHA; HINDUISM; SAMSARA

Bibliography. D. S. Lopez Jr., *Buddhism: An Introduction and Guide*; J. Snelling, *The Buddhist Handbook: A Complete Guide to Buddhist Teaching and Practice*.

H. P. Kemp

NYINGMA. Recognized by their red hats, Nyingma (Tibetan, "ancient") is the oldest Tibetan Buddhist tradition (Gelug, Sakya, and Kagyu are the other three). Nyingma is the "old" tradition inasmuch as it achieved the first wave of major translation of Buddhist texts from Sanskrit into Tibetan in the eighth century AD. The Tibetan king Trisong Detsen (r. 742–97) had invited Santarakshita, the abbot of Nalanda Monastery in India, to build Tibet's first monastery, Samye. Tradition describes the difficulty of founding the monastery due to meddling malevolent spirits of the indigenous Bon religion. The greater tantric-occult powers of Padmasambhava subdued these Bon spirits. The combination of the political patronage of King Trisong Detsen, the monastic rigor of Abbot Santarakshita, and the tantric teachings of Padmasambhava combined to establish Buddhism in Tibet. Thus Nyingma played a significant role in the formation of a Tibetan identity and civilization in that it facilitated the establishment of a large and sophisticated literary and ritual tradition. Nyingma's supreme doctrine is *dzogchen*, or "great perfection," which holds that "original mind" is the foundation of all consciousness. Dzogchen teachings are perhaps the most accessible aspect of Nyingma in the West.

There are three streams of transmissions in Nyingma Buddhism. The first is the "distant canonical": Buddhist texts brought from India to Tibet. The second is the "close lineage," or *terma*: texts and religious objects concealed by Padmasambhava, who claimed they were the quintessence of the canonical Buddhist teachings. He concealed them in temples, images, the sky, rocks, and lakes. The idea was that his disciples would reincarnate and discover them (and become *tertons*, or "treasure masters") and then continue to propagate the dharma (teaching). The teachings can also be discovered as "mind treasures," rather than being physically discovered. The third transmission is the "profoundly pure visions" in which Padmasambhava appears to the terton and speaks to him in person.

Nyingma has nine teachings, six in common with other Buddhist schools, with an additional three unique tantric teachings. Those initiated into *upayoga* can attain enlightenment in five lifetimes and can attain *mahayoga* in the next lifetime and *atiyoga* in this present existence. Essential Nyingma doctrine stresses that the phenomena of the world are unsubstantial and that those who know the secret wisdom may be able to obtain sudden enlightenment and buddhahood in this lifetime. In tantric Buddhism, both ritual sexual intercourse and visualization of the wrathful aspect of Buddhas and bodhisattvas are means to this end. In Nyingma art, Padmasambhava and his consort Yeshe Tsogyal are often depicted in sitting copulation.

Shambhala International, Odiyan Retreat Center, Padmasambhava Centers, and Aroter Community are all informed by Nyingma. Siddhartha's Intent, an organization also informed by Nyingma, is in the process of placing *terma* (or "peace vases") throughout the world, promoting them as a contribution to global environmentalism. Chogyam Trungpa Rinpoche (1939–87), who was trained in both Kagyu and Nyingma traditions, established both Shambhala International and the Buddhist Naropa University in Boulder, Colorado. Both of these institutions have been influential in establishing Buddhism in America. Today the principal Nyingma monasteries are in India (Dehra Dun, Uttaranchal). The traditional head monastery of Nyingma Buddhism is Ngedon Gatsal Ling, known in English as Mindrolling Monastery, located about forty-three kilometers from Lhasa. Since the absorption of Tibet into China in 1950, a major branch of this sect led by Tibetan refugees has been located in India. This is the branch of the sect best known in the Western world. The monastery is led by the *tulku*. A tulku, in this and other Tibetan Buddhist sects, is chosen as a young child after a long search by the leaders of the sect. The chosen child is believed to be the reincarnation of the last tulku, who in turn was part of a long line of reincarnated tulkus going back to the sect's founder. After extensive training, the child eventually grows up to assume full authority and become the sect's sacred leader. The most recent head of the tradition, Mindrolling Trichong Rinpoche, died in February 2008, and a reincarnation has yet to be named.

See also BUDDHISM; TIBETAN BUDDHISM

Bibliography. G. Coleman, ed., *A Handbook of Tibetan Culture: A Guide to Tibetan Centres and Resources throughout the World*; L. Huaizhi, *Tibet*; the Office of Tibet, "The Nyingma Tradition."

H. P. Kemp

OCCULT. The term *occult* is from the Latin *occultus*, meaning "hidden," "secret," or "mysterious," referring to knowledge of what lies beyond. For many occultists, it is simply understood as the study of a deeper spiritual reality extending beyond reason and the physical sciences.

From this definition, it would seem that the whole of supernatural religion with its belief in God and reality beyond the physical should be the domain of the occult, but this is not the case. World religions, such as Christianity, Judaism, Hinduism, and Islam, which are supernatural in nature, are not generally considered to be part of the occult, yet some modified forms within these religions—for example, gnosticism in Christianity, some variants of kabbalah in Judaism, tantra in Hinduism, and the "folk religion" of Islam—are often connected with the occult. Such modifications are usually unacceptable to orthodox members of their religion.

Some have sought to show how various aspects of what have traditionally been considered occult, such as astrology, kabbalah, and tarot, are in fact scientific in the way that physics is scientific. Hypotheses are proposed to explain what underlies the practice and conceptually how it functions. Then the practice itself is examined, along with its effects, providing feedback for affirming or qualifying its theories. This systematic research of occult concepts has been referred to as occult science.

The term *occult* can apply to a broad and varied assortment of theories, practices, and rituals based on an alleged or esoteric knowledge of the world of unknown forces and spirits. It can include alchemy, a medieval "science" and speculative philosophy aimed at achieving the transmutation of base metals into gold and silver; divination, the practice of consulting beings (human or divine) or observing things (objects or actions) in an attempt to gain information about the future or discover hidden knowledge; magic or magick, the ritual performance or activity believed to influence human or natural events through access to an external mystical force or power beyond the ordinary human sphere; spiritualism, the belief that the human personality continues to exist after death and can communicate with the living through the agency of a medium (e.g., trance speaking, automatic writing) or a manifestation (e.g., poltergeist activity); and witchcraft, the human exercise of alleged supernatural or paranormal power(s) for helpful or harmful purposes. *Occult* can also be used to describe magical, mystical, and esoteric groups as well as a rather large body of literature classified as such. The broad usage of the word *occult* makes defining it more difficult than discussing aspects of it.

Theories of the Origin and Development of Occult Beliefs and Practices. Prominent in the study of the occult of the past has been the theory of an evolution of religion generated by Charles Darwin's postulations on biological evolution. This theory places the foundational beliefs of the occult, such as animism and spiritualism, and practices, such as divination, very early in the ascent of humanity. In general it assumes that humans evolved from a presimian ancestor and that as humans appeared on the scene and developed, so did religion and the occult. Since animals have no religion, there must have been a long ascent until human beings emerged and engaged their environment and the first form of religion developed. Animatism, as it has been called, has humanity perceiving the whole world outside filled with a vague force or power that was terrifying. As humans became familiar with the world around them, they noticed distinctions and movements. Some have thought that simple forms of divination, of what was later classified as aeromancy, were present later in this stage, in which cloud formations, comets, shooting and falling stars, and thunder and lightning were taken to be omens and signs of what was to come.

Later this vague force or power became alive to humans in the form of multiple spirits, and animism became their religion. They created more simple forms of divination. As they pondered these spiritual forces, they personalized the forces, first as ancestor spirits and later as nature spirits. Animism gave way to spiritualism. As humans lived with these spirits, they learned how to appease the spirits and communicate with them by various means—namely, the practice of necromancy.

Gradually, a transition occurred from venerating finite personal spirits to worshiping them as gods, and human beings became polytheistic. They came to see their present life as entirely under the gods. To discern the revealed will and mind of the gods, people developed many forms of divination, such as examining strange happenings and studying the entrails and other parts of sacrificed birds and animals. Of special interest was the liver, which early humans believed became identified with the god to which it was sacrificed.

Then, focusing on a particular deity who appeared more powerful or helpful, people elevated this god above others in a heavenly hierarchy resembling a human kingdom. This religion was appropriately called monarchianism. While acknowledging the existence of other gods, before long people were worshiping only one god. Monarchianism morphed into henotheism. When people focused on that one god as the only god, they forgot the others, and monotheism finally appeared.

During the long development of the occult, those more proficient became teachers. Others became priests, shamans, or mediums, standing between a person or the people and the divine. Many occult activities were approved and allowed; others were not. Those approved were usually those acceptable to the deity worshiped. Some were permitted or used simply because they were believed to work.

Support for the evolutionary development of religion has dwindled considerably. The prevailing view posits monotheism as the earliest religion. Thus religions and the occult should be seen as devolving from humanity's rejection of original monotheism. This is the view presented in the Bible, where God made everything, including the heavens and the earth and human beings (Gen. 1). He saw that all he had made "was very good" (Gen. 1:31). The goodness of human beings consisted in being what God wanted them to be. The tragedy is that humans did not stay as they were created. As Genesis 3 reports, the original pair, Adam and Eve, chose to disobey God. This act of rebellion affected Adam and Eve and all subsequent generations. Humanity became alienated from God, from others, from nature, and even from themselves.

When human beings rejected the true God, their understanding of the supernatural became corrupted and replaced by distortions of what they perceived to exist beyond. As Romans 1:21, 25 informs us, "Although they knew God, they neither glorified him as God nor gave thanks to him, but their thinking became futile and their foolish hearts were darkened. . . . They exchanged the truth about God for a lie, and worshiped and served created things rather than the Creator."

A re-creation of this degenerative process would begin after the fall with the descendants of Adam and Eve withdrawing more and more from worshiping the only true God and Creator. A decadent monotheism developed, followed by other degrading beliefs. Because of human evilness, God sent a flood to destroy humanity. The only survivors were Noah, his wife, his three sons, and their wives. When Noah emerged from the ark, he restored pure monotheism. With the introduction of different languages at the Tower of Babel, different language-names for God created something of a henotheistic religion. People worshiped God by the language-name they knew, while realizing that other language-names existed. With humanity spreading out into different parts of the world, different language-names became different gods, resulting in polytheism and polyidolatry. As people focused on the sky above, deification of the sky, of the sun, and of other heavenly bodies may have followed. Later, people deified animals (hunting societies) and plants and the earth (agricultural societies and empires). Finally, more degenerate forms appeared, such as animism, spiritualism, totemism, and fetishism.

Here beliefs and practices associated with the occult are postdiluvian formulations by fallen human beings, a result of their rejection of God. Therefore, the term *occult* should be defined as seeking knowledge and power from what lies beyond *apart from the one true God.* Since God forbids the pursuit of and service to any other god (see Exod. 20:3–5), it follows that he would also condemn the occult. In Deuteronomy 18:10–12 (NASB), God is recorded as saying to Israel: "There shall not be found among you . . . one who uses divination, one who practices witchcraft, or one who interprets omens, or a sorcerer, or one who casts a spell, or a medium, or a spiritist, or one who calls up the dead. For whoever does these things is detestable to the LORD." Furthermore, the occult would also be associated with the enemy of God, Satan.

Prehistoric Times. Determining what of an occult nature existed in prehistoric times is difficult. Discoveries of the remains of early cultures have provided little in the way of understanding their religious beliefs or interest in the occult. However, deductions from objects found by archaeologists and pictures in caves have often been used to provide glimpses of the beliefs and practices of the occult prehistoric humans may have had.

Some in their quest have viewed existing undeveloped or primitive cultures as reflective of what archaic human cultures must have been like. For example, sorcerers; witches; the use of magic; belief in demons, spirits, and ancestral spirits; and all kinds of rituals have been observed in Melanesia. Should these be taken as vestiges of the earliest occult practices simply because this culture is not as advanced as others? The studies of missionary scholars, anthropologists, and others indicate otherwise. They have found that occult activity changes over time. Sometimes practices are imported; other times they are discarded. In each generation, the occult is made to fit that culture's worldview and the present interests of those people.

Similarly, some have thought that what one sees in the present (or in recent times) is what existed in primitive times. For example, Margaret Murray, a British anthropologist, believed that the testimonies and evidence presented in witch trials were accurate. Thus, she concluded that the witchcraft of recent times was the remnant of a pre-Christian religion she called the Dianic cult. Despite criticism by several historians of witchcraft, she still became a popular authority on this subject.

Historic Times. In ancient Mesopotamia, the home of the Sumerians, the Assyrians, and the Babylonians, fascination with the occult grew. The earliest known records of human beings' astronomical observations were found here. To satisfy the demands of their developing religion, their agriculture, and their budding scientific interest, they constructed large astronomico-religious sites. Those who were astronomers became priests and gradually recorded not only the scientific data of the heavenly bodies and their movements but also the myths that grew up around their deities. As the original meanings of the myths were lost, the priests began to associate magical elements with the heavenly gods, and astronomy began to move in the direction of magic and divination. Future events were predicted for the people. Though most of the ingredients necessary for casting personal horoscopes existed centuries before the fall of Babylon, they were not organized and used until the time of the great Greco-Roman astronomer-astrologer Claudius Ptolemaeus (Ptolemy).

There was also great interest in the practice of divination. The interpretation of dreams became a sophisticated art, and reading omens was particularly important since every event was thought to have a personal meaning to the observer. A special class of priests was created just to interpret omens. Tablets have been found describing many of the omens observable in the heavens, in human events, in the flight of birds, and in the organs of animals. All kinds of phenomena were included, such as the murmuring of springs, the cracking of furniture, and the "speech" of animals and even of trees. The Old Testament prophet Nahum referred to Nineveh as "the charming one, the mistress of sorceries" (Nah. 3:4 NASB). Back then, omens were understood not by causality but as communication from the gods.

In ancient Egypt, magic was taught in temple schools and by devoted priests. The early focus seems to be on the association of magic with health-related areas and the afterlife. There were also wonder-workers known as magicians. Evidence of their existence and some of their success has survived in Egyptian records. The Old Testament also records an encounter between Moses and Aaron and the magicians of Pharaoh. The magicians of Pharaoh worked their wonders, but whatever power they had (and they had some power) was limited and no match for the power of God displayed in the miracles of Moses and Aaron (Exod. 7:1–11:10).

Dreams were thought to convey divine messages, so their interpretations were important. Interpreters were not only sought by common people; they were prominent in the courts of ancient kings, including the pharaohs. The Old Testament tells of a time when Pharaoh had an unusual dream to which he attached great significance. He called for his interpreters, but none could interpret it. Hearing about Joseph's ability with a previous dream, he called on him to give the meaning. Joseph said, "I cannot do it, . . . but God will give Pharaoh the answer he desires," and he did (see Gen. 41:1–32, esp. vv. 8, 16).

Amulets, small objects worn or carried that were believed to magically bestow a power, were popular in the Egyptian culture. They were placed among a mummy's wrappings to ensure a safe, healthy, and productive afterlife. Egyptians carried them for several reasons, including protection, health, and success. Small representations of animals appear to be the earliest forms, but later recognizable deities were used as charms.

Biblical Times. Surrounding Israel were nations with different beliefs and practices, including the occult. Though God's people were to be holy and separate, the temptation to be like these nations was ever present.

When Moses addressed the people prior to crossing the Jordan River to enter the promised land and drive out the pagan nations, he warned them about any acceptance or compromise with the occult practices of those peoples. He specifically mentioned nine activities: child sacrifice, divination, soothsaying, augury, sorcery, use of charms, mediums, wizards, and necromancy (Deut. 18:9–13).

God communicated to people by several means—for example, by dreams (Num. 12:6) and by prophets. Other nations also believed in dreams as a communication from their god and had prophets proclaiming his message. So the children of the true God were instructed to use discernment (see Deut. 13:1–5; 1 John 4:1–3). Dreams and prophets were not to be placed above the commandments of God. In the New Testament, the teachings of Jesus were added.

Elsewhere in the Bible, several occult activities are mentioned, such as necromancy and mediums (Lev. 19:31; 20:6), witches and sorcerers (Isa. 8:19–20; Ezek. 13:18; Acts 8:9–13; 13:8–10), magicians or wonder-workers (Exod. 7–11), and diviners and fortune-tellers (Acts 16:16–19). Doing what God forbids can lead to death, as when King Saul consulted with a medium at Endor (1 Sam. 28:7–19) and God took his life for this (1 Chron. 10:13–14).

More Recent Times. Sorcery, charms, and fortune-telling continued to be of interest after the first century. Babylonian astrology and the horoscope began to gain popularity in the third century, and after the fall of Rome, alchemy was introduced to Western Europe.

In the Middle Ages, witches were sought out for healing and divination. Grimoires offering formulas for theurgy and thaumaturgy were collected. Astrology was given a positive status in the Roman Catholic Church in the thirteenth century when Thomas Aquinas, in his *Summa Theologica*, recognized the influence of the stars on certain aspects of human affairs.

During the Renaissance, there was a renewed interest in occult practices and a recovery of older texts on magic, alchemy, and hermeticism. Alchemy became a serious science in the fourteenth to sixteenth centuries, with great interest in the transmutation of common metals into precious metals, such

as gold and silver. Alchemists often counterfeited their results to make it appear as though they had brought about transmutation. The posthumous reputation of Nicholas Flamel (1330–1418) claimed that he decoded enough of an ancient text, *Book of Abraham the Mage*, to be able to replicate its meaning and produce silver in 1382 and then gold. The birth of modern chemistry in the eighteenth century put an end to alchemical theories and practices.

Attempts to uncover practitioners of witchcraft and force them to recant were fairly common during the fifteenth, sixteenth, and seventeenth centuries in England. The most famous witch trial, however, took place in America, in Salem, Massachusetts, when more than 150 persons were accused of being witches and imprisoned. Ultimately, 19 were convicted and hanged; 1 was crushed to death.

In 1747 Emanuel Swedenborg, a Swedish seer, had his first interaction with the spirit world and became a great channel for the dispensing of spirit truth. Public interest in spiritualism did not begin until the Fox sisters, Kate and Margaret, made contact with the spirit of a murdered peddler in 1848. Spiritualists began meeting in homes for séances, in lecture halls for lectures by trance mediums, and at camp meetings. This movement grew in the nineteenth century but faded in the twentieth century due to the number of accusations of fraud.

The Theosophical Society, founded in 1875 by Madame Blavatsky and Colonel Olcott, and later perpetuated by Annie Besant, brought to the West the teaching of ascended masters—that is, spiritually enlightened teachers from the realms of spirit. An increase in the interest in astrology also developed around this time in America.

By the middle of the twentieth century, many different types of occult activities were practiced, much under the label of New Age. The occult could be found in books and magazines as well as on television and, later, on the internet. Under the guise of channeling, trance mediums have produced books by their controlling spirit (e.g., Jane Roberts, *Seth Speaks*; Helen Schucman, *A Course in Miracles*) and lectures, allowing their spirit to speak through them (e.g., Ramtha through J. Z. Knight and Lazaris through Jack Pursel). Television programs such as *Charmed*, *Ghost Whisperer*, and *Medium* have portrayed experiences of witches and spiritualist mediums, while books such as the Harry Potter series by J. K. Rowling have introduced the younger generation to many aspects of the occult.

See also ANIMISM; HINDUISM; ISLAM, BASIC BELIEFS OF; JUDAISM; KABBALAH; MONOTHE-ISM; TANTRA

Bibliography. J. M. Greer, *The New Encyclopedia of the Occult*; C. Hawkins, *Witchcraft: Exploring the World of Wicca*; W. Martin, J. Martin Rische, and K. Van Gorden, *The Kingdom of the Occult*; L. Shepherd, ed., *Encyclopedia of Occultism & Parapsychology*; C. Wilson, *The Occult: A History*.

J. Bjornstad

ONENESS PENTECOSTALISM. Oneness Pentecostals believe that speaking in tongues is the evidence of salvation and that Jesus is the only member of the Godhead. Classical Pentecostalism from its start denounced the Oneness movement as heretical.

Within a few years of the Azusa Street Revival (1906–9) and the birth of Pentecostalism, a major theological controversy split the movement. During the International Pentecostal Camp Meeting of April 1913 in Arroyo Seco, California, Robert Edwin McAlister, a well-known Canadian evangelist, preached a baptismal sermon. In commenting on the subject, he noted that the apostolic church did not use a trinitarian formula when baptizing new believers but rather baptized in the name of Jesus only (Acts 2:38; 8:16; 19:5).

One of the attendees, John G. Scheppe, an immigrant from Danzig, Germany, pondered McAlister's remarks late into the night. At dawn Scheppe claimed the light of God's revelation brilliantly burst forth to illuminate his mind. He jumped up and ran throughout the campground, shouting that the Lord had shown him the truth about baptism in Jesus's name. Relatively few people paid attention, but one who did listen was Australian-born Frank J. Ewart, a Baptist minister turned Pentecostal.

It was only a matter of time before the proponents of baptism in Jesus's name only stepped outside the bounds of orthodoxy to embrace heresy. On April 15, 1914, Frank Ewart, now a pastor in the newly formed Assemblies of God (AG) denomination, preached a sermon comparing Matthew 28:19 to Acts 2:38. He pointed out that the Lord commanded his disciples to baptize in the "name" (singular) of the Father, Son, and Holy Spirit (Matt. 28:19), and Ewart concluded that "Jesus" is that name (Acts 2:38). Hence, Jesus is the Father, the Son, and the Holy Spirit.

Glenn A. Cook, another Canadian-born evangelist convinced by Ewart's scriptural argument, submitted to rebaptism using the "apostolic" formula. In turn he rebaptized Ewart. The duo established a new periodical called *Meat in Due Season* and then embarked on a preaching tour to spread their message. The Oneness doctrine quickly spread throughout Pentecostalism, particularly among the Assemblies of God churches. By spring 1915, for example, all twelve Assemblies of God pastors in Louisiana converted to the Oneness position, or what had become known as the "New Issue."

To combat the inroads the movement was making within AG ranks, J. Roswell Flower, a respected leader of the denomination, called for a general council to be convened in St. Louis in October 1915. Here AG pastors on both sides of the New Issue could discuss the doctrinal controversies in a civil manner. After all was said and done, the council declared Ewart's and Cook's teachings to be unscriptural.

Since the AG had no standardized statement of faith at the time, the condemnation carried little weight. The problem persisted. In October 1916, another general council was held, where a "Statement of Fundamental Truths" was adopted and the classical doctrine of the Trinity was officially affirmed. This action culminated with 156 of the 585 ordained delegates withdrawing fellowship from the AG. They immediately formed the General Assembly of Apostolic Assemblies (GAAA). In 1918 the GAAA merged with the Pentecostal Assemblies of the World (PAW) and retained the PAW name.

The Heresy Explained. Modalism is a belief that God is one person only, although he manifests himself in three different roles or modes. He appears as the Father in creation and the giving of the law, as the Son in his humanity and redemption, as the Spirit in his activity in the church and the world—hence, one God in three modalities.

The first recorded modalist was Praxeas, who lived at the end of the second century in Asia Minor and later in Rome. He taught that Jesus not only revealed the Father but was the Father. Tertullian (ca. 155–ca. 220) responded to this teaching in *Against Praxeas* by saying that Praxeas had "put the Holy Spirit to flight and crucified the Father."

Noetus of Smyrna (fl. ca. 200) also carried the banner of modalism by saying that Jesus Christ was the Father, and thus the Father himself was born, suffered, and died. Known as Patripassianism, the heresy was condemned by the Synod of Smyrna in 200.

Sabellius, another teacher at the beginning of the third century, said that the Father, the Son, and the Holy Spirit are the one God, without distinction of person. To Sabellius God was merely called by different names, just as this author is called a husband by his wife, a father by his children, and a son by his mother—one person with three roles.

The Nicene and Athanasian Creeds both condemned Sabellianism.

Oneness Pentecostals believe that Jesus is the only true God. He manifests himself as the Father, the Son, and the Holy Spirit. This concept is entirely different from the scriptural doctrine of the Trinity, which teaches there is one God who subsists as three coeternal and coequal persons, of the same substance, but distinct in function.

The Apostolic Formula. Many Oneness Pentecostal groups have the word "Apostolic" in their title because they believe they alone teach salvation based on the apostolic formula as found in Acts 2:38: "Repent and be baptized, every one of you, in the name of Jesus Christ for the forgiveness of your sins. And you will receive the gift of the Holy Spirit." All Oneness groups believe that God is a unipersonal being and that one must follow the "Apostolic" formula to be saved. They reject the Trinity as unscriptural and believe Acts 2:38 to represent the true baptismal formula. Speaking in tongues is the evidence that one has scripturally repented and received the Holy Spirit.

The United Pentecostal Church International. With the growth of Pentecostalism many new Oneness groups sprang up. The two largest were the Pentecostal Church, Inc., and the Pentecostal Assemblies of Jesus Christ. In 1945 the two merged to form the United Pentecostal Church International (UPCI).

Headquartered in Hazelwood, Missouri, northwest of St. Louis, UPCI is the largest Oneness Pentecostal group in the world, with 4,400 churches in America and Canada and another 36,804 located in 203 other countries as of 2012. Each local church is autonomous and owns its own property. An estimated three million people regularly attend worship services. The UPCI operates six Bible colleges and one graduate school. It publishes seven magazines, including *Forward* and *Pentecostal Herald.* Over 850 foreign missionaries and national workers serve on the field in 100 countries. Its annual foreign missionary budget runs approximately $12 million. Over 31,000 licensed clergy serve the churches worldwide.

The church holds to traditional Oneness Pentecostal doctrines but also practices foot washing. Adhering to a strict code of holiness, members are admonished not to participate in mixed bathing or dancing. They must wear modest clothes (no sleeveless blouses for women) and refrain from patronizing movie theaters, joining secret societies, smoking tobacco, and drinking alcoholic beverages. Additionally, women must not cut their hair.

The Modern Oneness Revival. With many Oneness preachers gaining access to the airwaves, there has been a recent numerical explosion within the ranks of Oneness Pentecostalism. The most famous proponent of Oneness doctrine is T. D. Jakes, pastor of The Potter's House in Dallas, Texas, whom *Time* magazine proclaimed to be one of the most influential and innovative religious leaders in the US. Jakes serves as a bishop in the Higher Ground Always Abounding Assemblies, a black Oneness Pentecostal denomination. The first two points of his official doctrinal statement read (emphasis added):

We believe that there are *three dimensions* of one God. . . .

We believe in one God who is eternal in his existence, Triune in his *manifestation.*

Others with Oneness Pentecostal connections include Tommy Tenney, author of the best-selling book *The God Chasers*; songwriter Geron Davis, known for the praise choruses "In His Presence" and "Holy Ground"; and singing group Phillips, Craig and Dean. As Christian media outlets provide opportunities for modalists to espouse their views, many orthodox believers are exposed to the Oneness heresy.

Other Influential Groups. The following discussion includes only denominations with 25,000 members or more.

Pentecostal Assemblies of the World (PAW). PAW is the oldest of the Oneness groups. When whites withdrew en masse from its membership in 1924, PAW was reorganized with Garfield Thomas Haywood elected its first bishop. The group practices foot washing, uses wine for its communion meal, and stresses pacifism. Headquartered in Indiana, PAW has a worldwide membership of 500,000 in 1,400 churches scattered throughout the 50 states, plus Africa, Asia, the West Indies, and Europe. It operates Aenon Bible College and Pentecostal Publications, both in Indianapolis, and publishes *Christian Outlook* magazine. Missionaries serve in Africa, Jamaica, and England.

United Church of Jesus Christ (Apostolic) (UCJC). Randolph Carr left PAW in 1945 to start the UCJC. In 1957 Bishop Monroe Saunders Sr. succeeded him as presiding bishop, and he served in that office until 2004. He stepped down that year, and his oldest son, Monroe Saunders Jr., now serves as presiding bishop. Headquartered in Baltimore, Maryland, UCJC has seventy-five churches spread throughout the country with a total membership of one hundred thousand. The Center for More Abundant Life and the Institute of Biblical Studies sit on a large Baltimore campus offering nearby residents social and educational assistance.

Way of the Cross Church of Christ International (WCCC). Founded in Washington, DC, by Henry Brooks in 1927, as an independent "Jesus Only" church, the WCCC has grown to sixty-four congregations, mostly on the east coast of the US, with a total membership exceeding fifty thousand. Missionary efforts are conducted in western Africa. A presiding bishop leads the church, assisted by a bishopric of twelve other men.

Church of Our Lord Jesus Christ of the Apostolic Faith (CLJCAF). Robert C. Lawson, a former PAW pastor, started the CLJCAF in Columbus, Ohio. Through his outreach program and organizational skills, the congregation not only grew but reproduced itself. Today there are five hundred churches. Lawson opened a Bible school in New York City to train parishioners. The *Contender for the Faith* magazine keeps the worldwide membership of thirty thousand informed and inspired.

In 1933 the CLJCAF splintered over the liberalization of the moral code. Sherrod C. Johnson, a local pastor, was particularly upset over women wearing jewelry and makeup and over the observation of Christmas, Lent, and Easter. He took a group of followers and started the Church of Our Lord Jesus Christ of the Apostolic Faith (Philadelphia). The doctrines of the New York and Philadelphia sects are similar, except the latter does not allow remarriage after divorce, women preachers, or worldly dress.

The Bible Way Church of Our Lord Jesus Christ World-Wide. In 1957 another split occurred within the Church of Our Lord Jesus Christ of the Apostolic Faith (Brooklyn, NY). Members from seventy affiliated churches, concerned over the dictatorial rule of its leaders and desiring a more democratic church government, withdrew and asked Smallwood E. Williams of Washington, DC, to be their new bishop. Williams proved to be a worthy leader. The Bible Way Church has twenty-five thousand members and 250 congregations. *The Bible Way News Voice* serves as the primary periodical of the church.

After Williams passed away in 1991, the church sought a successor. Two leaders, Bishop Huie Rogers and Bishop Lawrence Campbell, were each given temporary assignments, but the governing boards could not decide, so the church split yet again in 1997. The larger group became the International Bible Way Church of Jesus Christ, Inc. (with headquarters in Baltimore, MD). It currently claims to have over 350 churches in the US and another 250 overseas. A smaller number of people stayed with the parent body, which retained its original name. The current presiding bishop of Bible Way (in Brooklyn) is apostle Huie Rogers.

Conclusion. Dozens of smaller denominations and thousands of independent churches make up the Oneness Pentecostal network. In a culture that views all forms of spirituality as equal and truth as less important than experience, Oneness Pentecostalism is finding acceptance among the masses. It is even gaining favor within the ranks of evangelicalism, as believers in orthodox denominations become less circumspect and discerning. Christian television makes even the absurd seem normal. Given the times in which we live, Oneness Pentecostalism may soon be looked upon as part of mainline Christianity, simply another variation from which to choose.

According to Dr. Gregory Boyd, a former Oneness advocate, approximately one in four Pentecostals embraces Oneness. Boyd also claims that Oneness Pentecostalism trails only behind the Mormons and Jehovah's Witnesses in size among groups that have nonorthodox teachings on the Trinity.

See also MODALISM

Bibliography. *References.* E. C. Beisner, *Jesus Only Churches*; G. A. Boyd, *Oneness Pentecostals and the Trinity*; J. L. Grady, "The Other Pentecostals," https://forerunner.com/orthodoxy/cu197123.htm; F. S. Mead, *Handbook of Denominations in the United States*; J. G. Melton, ed., *The Encyclopedia of American Religions*, vol. 1; D. Reed, "Oneness Pentecostalism," *Journal of Pentecostal Theology*; R. Riss, *A Survey of 20th Century Revival Movements in North America*. ***Organization Websites.*** Bible Way Church of Our Lord Jesus Christ World-Wide, http://www.biblewaychurch.org; International Bible Way Church of Jesus Christ, Inc., http://www.intlbibleway.com; Pentecostal Assemblies of the World, http://pawinc.org; United Church of Jesus Christ (Apostolic), http://www.unitedchurchjc.org; United Pentecostal Church International, http://www.upci.org; Way of the Cross Church of Christ International, http://wotcc.net.

R. A. Streett

OPENNESS OF GOD. The "openness of God view" has several names. From its starting point in the libertarian view of free will, it is called free will theism. In contrast to traditional theism, it is labeled neotheism. One noted proponent, Clark Pinnock, has described it as "between classical and process theism" in his article of the same title.

Proponents of the View. Those who embrace this view include Clark Pinnock, Richard Rice, John Sanders, William Hasker, David Basinger, and Gregory Boyd. Several authors collaborated on a volume titled *The Openness of God* (edited by Clark Pinnock). Many have written volumes of their own. These include William Hasker, *God, Time and Knowledge*; Stephen T. Davis, *Logic and the Nature of God*; Richard Rice, *God's Foreknowledge and Man's Free Will*; Greg Boyd, *Trinity and Process* and *God of the Possible*; J. R. Lucas, *The Freedom of the Will* and *The Future*. Perhaps the frankest and most radical presentations of open theism are found in Clark Pinnock's *The Most Moved Mover*. Others show affinities with the view, such as Peter Geach, *Providence and Evil*; Richard Swinburne, *The Coherence of Theism*; Thomas V. Morris, *Our Idea of God*; and Linda Zagzebski, *The Dilemma of Freedom and Foreknowledge*. A. N. Prior, Richard Purtill, and others have written articles defending open theism.

The Distinctives of Open Theism. Proponents of open theism list five characteristics of their position:

1. God not only created this world ex nihilo but can and at times does intervene unilaterally in earthly affairs.

2. God chose to create us with incompatibilistic (libertarian) freedom—freedom over which he cannot exercise total control.

3. God so values freedom—the moral integrity of free creatures and a world in which such integrity is possible—that he does not normally override such freedom, even if he sees that it is producing undesirable results.

4. God always desires our highest good, both individually and corporately, and thus is affected by what happens in our lives.

5. God does not possess exhaustive knowledge of exactly how we will utilize our freedom, although he may very well at times be able to predict with great accuracy the choices we will freely make. (Basinger, 156)

A Contrast with Theism and Panentheism. Theism contends that God created all. Pantheism affirms that God is all. Panentheism (process theology), which is a kind of halfway house between the two, asserts that God is in all in a way similar to how a soul is in a body. Open theism is positioned between panentheism and theism, leaning in the direction of the former.

Similarities with Traditional Theism. Like classical theism (as in Augustine, Anselm, Aquinas, Calvin, and Arminius), open theism believes God is uncaused, eternal, necessary, infinite, omnipotent, and even omniscient in a qualified sense. Likewise, open theists agree that God created the world ex nihilo (out of nothing), is sovereign over the world, and even supernaturally intervenes in the world. Indeed, Pinnock, Sanders, and Boyd all profess belief in the inerrancy of the Bible.

Similarities with Process Theology. Unlike traditional theism and like panentheism (process theology), open theism contends that God is not simple (without parts), not omniscient, not unchangeable, and not atemporal, but is in time. Indeed, Pinnock has confessed: "Maybe modern influences, which create a distorting tilt in the direction of divine immanence, are present in my work" (Pinnock, *Most Moved Mover*, 141). He frankly admits that

there are things about process theism that I find attractive and convictions that we hold in common. We: make the love of God a priority; hold to libertarian human freedom; are both critical of conventional [classical] theism; seek a more dynamic model of God; contend that God has real, and not merely rational, relationships with the world; believe that God is affected by what happens in the world; say that God knows what can be known, which does not amount to exhaustive foreknowledge; appreciate the value of philosophy in helping to share theological convictions; connect positively to Wesleyan/Arminian traditions. (Pinnock, *Most Moved Mover*, 142–43)

Pinnock, quoting Alfred North Whitehead, the father of radical liberal process theology, says, "Here is a theology that tries to work with modern science and has a dynamic metaphysic that doesn't equate God with everything superior and the world with everything inferior. I find the dialectic in its [process theology's] doctrine of God helpful, for example the idea that God is necessary and contingent, eternal and temporal, infinite and finite. I think it is right about God affecting everything and being affected by everything. I agree with it that God is temporally everlasting rather than timelessly eternal." Finally, he concludes: "Candidly, I believe that conventional theists are more influenced by Plato, who was a pagan, than I am by Whitehead, who was a Christian" (Pinnock, *Most Moved Mover*, 143–44).

Biblical Arguments Offered by Open Theism. Open theists offer several biblical arguments in support of their view. The following are the major ones.

God's Change of Mind. The Bible often speaks of God as "repenting" or changing his mind (cf. Gen. 6:6; 1 Sam. 15:11; Jon. 3:10). Open theists insist that this implies that God does not have infallible foreknowledge of human free choices.

However, since the Bible declares that God cannot change (1 Sam. 15:29; Mal. 3:6; Heb. 6:18; Titus 1:2; James 1:17), classical

theists respond by pointing out that these are anthropomorphisms: the representation of God (or more accurately, his actions) using human attributes or affections. Further, the Bible says God "forgets" our sins (Job 11:6) and has arms, legs, eyes (Deut. 7:19; Job 40:9; Gen. 3:8; Deut. 11:12; 2 Chron. 6:40), and even wings (Pss. 17:8; 36:7), yet open theists do not take these verses literally. Indeed, to do so would contradict the clear statement of Scripture that God is immaterial (Luke 24:39; John 4:24). Further, Genesis 6:6 does not use the same Hebrew word for "repenting" as does 1 Samuel 15:29. Samuel uses *shaqar*, which means that God will not cheat, lie, deceive, break a covenant, act falsely, or be untrue. But the Hebrew word (*nacham*) used in Genesis 6:6 is translated "sorry" (NRSV). It means to be "grieved" (NIV), to sigh, breathe strongly, groan, be sorry. It reflects God's feeling toward humankind's sin, not a change in his thinking. What is more, since the contrast in this text is between a state of innocence in which God created humans (cf. Gen. 3:5, 22) and their perverted state just before the flood (Gen. 6:5), it is speaking about God's feelings toward *different things*. Or, better yet, it is speaking not about different feelings God has about the same thing but about different feelings he has toward different things. God always has the same consistent feeling toward the same thing. As an unchangingly holy God, he always feels grieved about sin and unvaryingly good about his perfect creation (Gen. 1:31). So the change is not in God but in man. Thus this alleged proof text for open theism fails to accomplish its purpose.

Abraham Negotiated with God. According to Genesis 18, Abraham negotiated with God until God reduced the number of righteous persons required to save Sodom and Gomorrah from fifty to ten. This, open theists claim, reveals that God did not determine in advance what the outcome would be but entered into genuine negotiation with Abraham.

In response traditional theists point out that every good negotiator knows his bottom line before he begins the negotiation, and surely an all-knowing God knew how far he would go with Abraham. The Bible says clearly that God can declare "the end from the beginning" (Isa. 46:10) and even sometimes answers our prayers before we call on him (65:24). Indeed, God even chose the elect before the foundations of the world (Eph. 1:4; cf. 1 Pet. 1:2). So certainly God knew this bottom line with Abraham before he began the discussion.

The Allegation That God Learns. Open theism contends that the Bible sometimes describes God as learning through experience. For instance, God said to Abraham after he proved his willingness to offer Isaac: "Now I know that you fear God, because you have not withheld from me your son, your only son" (Gen. 22:12). According to open theism, this verse implies that God did not know how Abraham would respond to his command since it was only after Abraham obeyed that God said, "Now I know that you fear God."

However, the problem with this interpretation is twofold. First, look at the context. The passage begins by stating that "God tested Abraham" (v. 1). There is nothing here about God's desire to *learn* anything. Rather, God wanted to *prove* something (cf. 2 Chron. 32:31). What God knew by *cognition*, he desired to show by *demonstration*. After Abraham passed the test, he demonstrated what God always knew, namely, that he feared God. For example, a math teacher might say to her class, "Let's see if we can find the square root of 49," and then, after demonstrating it, declare, "Now we know that the square root of 49 is 7," even though she knew the answer from the beginning. Even so, God, who knows all things cognitively from the beginning, could appropriately say after Abraham had proved his faith, "now I know [demonstratively] that you fear God."

Second, since the Bible does not contradict itself, what might otherwise be a possible interpretation of this text is eliminated by the clear teaching of Scripture elsewhere. Namely, God's "understanding has no limit" (Ps. 147:5); he knows "the end from the beginning" (Isa. 46:10) and has foreknown and predestined us from the foundation of the world (Rom. 8:29–30). So in his omniscience God knew exactly what Abraham would do before he tested him since he knows all things (cf. Ps. 139:2–4; Jer. 17:10; Acts 1:24; Heb. 4:13).

Moses's Prayer Changed God's Mind. According to Exodus 32:7–14, God declared that he would destroy the children of Israel, and Moses interceded on their behalf and changed God's mind. Some open theists take this as proof that God has not determined the future completely but that it is open to change by our free actions, even to the point of changing God's mind. Open theists reason, "The fact is that God relents in direct response to Moses's plea, not as a consequence of the people's repentance of their apostasy." Thus "the repentance mentioned in this case clearly applies to a change that took place in God, not in his people" (Rice, "Biblical Support," 28). Further, they argue that "the assurance that God will not repent presupposes the general possibility that God can repent when he chooses" (Rice, "Biblical Support," 33).

This objection, however, falls short of its mark for a number of reasons. First of all, it is contorted logic to affirm, as they do, that God's unchangeableness implies that he could change. Does this mean that God's faithfulness to his nature and to his Word implies that he could be unfaithful to it? Does this mean that when the Scriptures affirm that "God never lies" (Titus 1:2 NRSV; cf. Heb. 6:18), it implies he can lie? What about when the Word of God declares that when "we are faithless, he remains faithful, for he cannot disown himself" (2 Tim. 2:13)? Does this mean God could be unfaithful?

Second, even open theists admit that "God's essential nature and his ultimate purpose did not change—Moses's appeal presupposes this" (Rice, "Biblical Support," 28). But if God's "essential nature" did not change (which is precisely what classical theists contend), then God did not change in his essence. For "essential nature" is precisely what classical theists mean by "essence." "Nonessential nature," whatever that may mean, is not part of the essence of God. Indeed, it would seem that the only sense in which God has what is nonessential to his nature is his acts. And classical theists readily admit that God engages in different and changing actions. But all these flow from his unchanging nature as occasioned by the changing conditions in his creation (see Pinnock, *Openness*, chaps. 5–6).

Third, open theists even acknowledge that God's "ultimate objectives" did not change. So neither God's nature nor purpose changed. Why, then, speak of a change in God? Ironically, they hint at the answer themselves when they add, "His [God's] ultimate objectives require him to change his immediate intentions" (Rice, "Biblical Support," 28). Had they used the word "tactics" instead of "intentions," no classical theist would object. With unchanging nature and unvarying ultimate intention, God uses various means to accomplish his immutable will. In this case, it was Moses's prayer that God ordained as the means by which he would accomplish his ultimate will to deliver his people. There is no need to say that God's essence changed to fully explain this (or any other) passage of Scripture. God has ordained that his mercy is released through those calling on him to help. Like any good parent, he wants to be asked. Suppose, for example, that a concerned mother knows in advance that her fevered child will awake later in the night crying for help. In anticipation she places water and aspirin by her bedside. But she does not administer the help until the child awakes and cries for it. Even so, our heavenly Father, who knows "the end from the beginning" (Isa. 46:10), often waits for us to call on him before he responds, whether it is for ourselves or for someone else.

Finally, even in the case of Moses's intercession there is evidence of God's unchanging will. For Moses reminded God of his promise to Israel, saying, "Remember your servants Abraham, Isaac and Israel, to whom you swore by your own self: 'I will make your descendants as numerous as the stars in the sky and I will give your descendants all this land I promised them, and it will be their inheritance forever'" (Exod. 32:13). No conditions were attached to this promise. Indeed, Abraham was not even conscious when God's promise was unilaterally ratified by God (Gen. 15). So Moses was simply praying the promise of God, reminding God of what he had promised to do. Effective prayer is, as Jesus said, asking in God's will (John 15:7). Prayer is not a means by which we get our will done in heaven. Rather, it is a means by which God gets his will done on earth. We do not change God by our prayers. Rather, our prayers are a means by which God changes others and us.

The Argument from Modern Linguists. Open theists appeal to current trends among linguists to interpret Exodus 3:14 as "I will be who I will be." This, they believe, supports their view that God can and does change.

However, this linguistic possibility must be rejected for many reasons.

1. The context opposes it since God is asked to give his "name" (which equates to his character or essence).

2. The history of both Jewish and Christian interpretation of this text is overwhelmingly in favor of the classical interpretation. Nearly all the great patristic, medieval, and Reformation theologians understood Exodus 3:14 as an affirmation of God's self-existence.

3. The Greek translation of the Old Testament (Septuagint, or LXX) translates the Hebrew "I Am Who I Am" (*ehyeh 'asher ehyeh*) as "he who is" (*ho on*).

4. The rendering "I will be who I will be," while grammatically possible, is contextually implausible and historically late, emerging in the wake of process theology.

5. The very name Yahweh (YHWH), usually translated LORD in the Old Testament, is probably a contraction of "I Am Who I Am." Old Testament commentator R. Alan Cole says, "This pithy clause is clearly a reference to the name YHWH. Probably 'Yahweh' is regarded as a shortening of the whole phrase, and a running together of the clause into one word" (69). Even *The Theological Dictionary of the Old Testament* acknowledges that "the name is generally thought to be a verbal form derived from the root *hwy* [*hayah*], 'be at hand, *exist*, come to pass'" (500). Joseph Pohle sums it up well: "The more general and more ancient opinion among theologians favors the view that aseity constitutes the metaphysical essence of God. Hence, we shall act prudently in adopting this theory, especially since it is well founded in Holy Scripture and Tradition, and can be defended with solid philosophical arguments. . . . Sacred Scripture defines [Yahweh] as [the One being, *ho on* in the Greek of the LXX], and it would seem, therefore, that this definition is entitled to universal acceptance" (172).

6. This process and open theist understanding is contrary to Jesus's use of Exodus 3:14 in John 8:58 (NRSV): "Before Abraham was, I am." Notice Jesus did not affirm: "Before Abraham was, I will be who I will be," as he should have if the process understanding of

this text is correct. For a follower of Christ, Jesus's understanding of this text should be definitive. Finally, even if it could be proven that Exodus 3:14 does not support the claim of God for self-existence, there are plenty of other texts and good arguments that do. The very concept of God as uncreated Creator (Gen. 1:1) who brought all other things into existence (John 1:2; Col. 1:15–16; Heb. 1:2) is sufficient to prove his self-existence. And even open theists claim to believe in ex nihilo creation, affirming that "the triune God is the Creator of the world out of nothing" (Pinnock, "Systematic Theology," 109). Reason demands that if God is Creator of all things, then he was uncreated. And if he did not get his existence from another, then he must exist in and of himself (aseity).

Philosophical Arguments Offered by Open Theism. The extrabiblical arguments for open theism are rooted in several assumptions. The primary one is their libertarian view of free will.

Truly Free Acts Eliminate Unqualified Omniscience. According to open theists, God cannot have infallible foreknowledge of truly free actions. According to the libertarian view, a genuinely free act is one that could have been otherwise. But if God has infallible foreknowledge of an event, then it cannot be otherwise. If it were, then God would have been wrong. But an omniscient mind cannot be wrong about what it knows. Hence, it would follow that even God cannot know for sure what free creatures will choose to do.

In response to this argument, classical theists from the earliest times have maintained that there is no contradiction in God knowing for sure (determining) what a person chooses to do (freely). One and the same act can be determined from the standpoint of God's foreknowledge and yet free from the vantage point of our choice. The law of noncontradiction is only violated when both are from the same vantage points, which they are not.

Indeed, the Bible gives examples of events that are both determined from all eternity yet freely chosen. The cross is an example. God determined it from eternity past (Acts 2:23; Rev. 13:8), yet Jesus said, "I lay down my life—only to take it up again. No one takes it from me, but I lay it down of my own accord" (John 10:17–18).

Further, God does not have to "look ahead" in order to see the future. From his lofty perch beyond time, he sees the whole course of time (past, present, and future) laid out for him in his eternal Now. Indeed, since all effects preexist in their cause, the entire course of history preexisted in him. Thus he knew it "in himself" as the Cause before it ever occurred.

God's Actions in Time Show That He Is Temporal. Open theists also reject the concept of a nontemporal God, which has been part of theism from the earliest times. This they do based on the fact that God is continually referred to in Scripture as acting in time. God's acts of creation were in time (Gen. 1–2), as were his acts of redemption (cf. Exod. 12:1–2 and John 1:10–14). But if God was in time at the exodus, then there was a time before that and a time after that. But whatever being has a before and after is a temporal being. What is more, the Bible sometimes refers to God as having a past, present, and future. He is "the one who is, and who was, and who is to come" (Rev. 1:8). Indeed, the very words used to describe God as being eternal (*aiōn*, *aiōnios*) can mean "age" or "ages." So, it would seem, God is "eternal" in the sense of being in endless time.

In response several comments are in order. First, these objections to God's timelessness are based on a confusion of his *actions* with his *attributes*. God's essence is beyond time, but his actions are in time. This should not

be difficult for open theists to understand since they believe God is infinite yet acts in the finite world. God is Creator yet acts in creation without being a creature. Why, then, cannot God act in time without being temporal? What is more, the origin of the world is not an instance of creation *in* time; it was the creation *of* time. For time did not begin until there was a changing world in which it could be measured. Further, this objection overlooks the fact that the Bible clearly affirms that the God who is the Creator of time is, by that very fact, beyond time. Hebrews 1:2 speaks of God "framing the ages," or time. But if he is Creator of time, then he cannot be in time. Jude 25 says Christ was "before all ages." But clearly he who was before the temporal world is not himself temporal. Jesus spoke of the glory he had with the Father "before the world began" (John 17:5). The Bible also uses parallel phrases such as "before the creation of the world" (Eph. 1:4). Paul spoke emphatically of grace "given us in Christ Jesus *before the beginning of time*" (2 Tim. 1:9, emphasis added). But if time began, then God is not part of it since admittedly he has no beginning or end.

Classical Theism Is Rooted in Greek Philosophy. Open theists often argue that traditional theism is rooted in Greek philosophy, not in the Bible. It is more Platonic than Christian. It follows from Greek ideas imported via the Greek translation of the Old Testament and early Christian philosophers who were steeped in Greek philosophy rather than from biblical exegesis. This is particularly evident, they claim, in the theist's understanding of God's statement in Exodus 3:14 ("I Am Who I Am") as referring to a self-existent being (aseity) (see Sanders, 99).

However, besides being a genetic fallacy, the charge is a double-edged sword. For as Pinnock has admitted (see above), open theism is based in philosophy as well—the process philosophy of Alfred North Whitehead, who was not a "Christian" (as Pinnock claimed) in any orthodox sense of the term. Whitehead denied every major attribute of God as held by orthodox theology down through the ages (see Geisler and House, 8–11, 90, 216, 268, 272, 319). Further, simply charging that something is wrong because it is Greek in origin will not do since even open theists accept many things taught by the Greeks—for example, the basic laws of logic. The question is not whether it is Hellenic but whether it is authentic.

An Evaluation of Open Theism. Open theism has many positive features. These include belief in (1) God's infinity, (2) his ontological independence from the world, (3) ex nihilo creation, (4) God's unchanging character, (5) God's intimate interaction with his creation, (6) God's ultimate victory over evil, (7) human free choice, and, for many, (8) the divine authority of the Bible.

However, in significant ways open theism falls short of the standard of orthodoxy in its view of God. For example, its denial of (1) God's complete sovereignty, (2) his absolute simplicity, (3) his immutability, (4) his nontemporality, (5) his pure actuality, (6) his impassibility, (7) his infallible foreknowledge of free choices, and (8) the inerrancy of the Bible. Whether measured by orthodox fathers or the creeds, confessions, and councils, a denial of any of these, to say nothing of all of them, is contrary to the historic orthodox view of God (see Geisler and House, chap. 11).

In addition to failing the historic test, open theism has many inconsistencies as illustrated in one of its chief proponents, Clark Pinnock. These are found in his book *The Most Moved Mover.* Insofar as other open theists hold to many of these same things, the critiques apply to them as well. First, Pinnock claims that God is "above time" (96) but not "outside of time" (98). But how can he be both?

Second, Pinnock claims that God's time and ours differ (*Most Moved Mover*, 99).

But how does God's being "beyond time" and having a "different time" than ours really differ from God's being eternal? To claim that God's time is uncreated does not help since an infinite number of moments is not possible, as the Kalām argument for God has shown (see Craig). How does an uncreated, eternal time that is "beyond time" in the created sense differ from saying God is not in time?

Third, Pinnock claims that God has limited "omniscience" (*Most Moved Mover*, 138). But how does this differ from saying God is not omniscient, since omniscience means unlimited knowledge, and a limited unlimited is contradictory?

Fourth, Pinnock affirms that "God is necessary and contingent, eternal and temporal, infinite and finite" (*Most Moved Mover*, 143). But how can opposites both be true? Positing a dipolar nature of God does not solve the problem, for two reasons. First of all, it is an admission that open theism is really a form of dipolar theism or process theology, which open theists deny it is. Further, even on the dipolar view, one nature is nontemporal and immutable—the very thing they deny to traditional theism. Finally, the other "pole"—being contingent, temporal, finite, and so on—is not really part of God but is the created universe. But if this is so, then open theists have backed into the very classical theistic view they are attempting to avoid.

Fifth, Pinnock decries the classical view of God's unchangeable nature, yet he holds that God is unchangeable in essence. He states that "God's essential nature remains the same" and that "nothing at all in His essential nature changes" (*Most Moved Mover*, 86). Why then is the traditional theist vilified for believing in an immutable God?

Sixth, Pinnock claims that God is "unchangeable in changeable ways" (*Most Moved Mover*, 86). "God is changeless in nature but ever changing in His experience." That is, "God changes in relation to creatures" (86).

But how can God change without changing in his nature? How can God be separated from his experience, which admittedly changes? And if it is posited that he has an unchanging part of his nature and a changing activity, then this reduces to the dreaded view of classical theism open theists wish to avoid.

Seventh, according to Pinnock God has an unchanging nature or essence in contrast to his relationships with creatures, yet "the essence of a thing now depends on its relationships with other things" (*Most Moved Mover*, 121). But if essence is determined by changing relationships, how can it remain unchanged? In fact, if essence is determined by changing relations, then there is no essence at all. But this is a denial of orthodox teaching affirmed in the ecumenical creeds that God has an "essence."

Eighth, open theists affirm that God is ontologically independent from the world. He is a necessary being, and the world is contingent (Pinnock, *Most Moved Mover*, 85–86). But if God is necessary, then he has no potentiality to be other than he is. But without potentiality one cannot change. Pinnock believes God can and does change, but how, if he has no potential for it?

Ninth, on the one hand, Pinnock condemns classical theism for its ancient influence from the Greeks (*Most Moved Mover*, chap. 2). On the other hand, he admits an influence from modern process theology on his view (141). He even acknowledges that a synthesis with philosophy can be good (7, 113). Apparently it is wrong for opponents of his view to be influenced by philosophy but right for proponents of his view.

Tenth, Pinnock claims to believe in inerrancy (signing the Evangelical Theological Society's statement annually). Yet he asserts that the Bible has errors in it and has affirmed that there were mistaken predictions in the Bible (*Most Moved Mover*, 50, 51). For example, the city of Tyre was not destroyed as Ezekiel said it would be (29:17–20), and

"the city continued to be inhabited right up until Jesus's own day." Pinnock declares flatly, "Nebuchadnezzar did *not* do to Tyre exactly what Ezekiel had predicted" (50, emphasis added). In a revealing footnote, Pinnock adds, "We may not want to admit it, but prophecies often go unfulfilled—Joseph's parents never bowed to him (Gen. 37:9–10); the Assyrians did not destroy Jerusalem in the eighth century (Mic. 3:9–12); despite Isaiah, Israel's return from exile did not usher in a golden age (Isa. 41:14–20)" (51). Shockingly, he adds, "Despite Jesus, in the destruction of the temple, some stones were left on the other (Matt. 24:2)" (51). In short Jesus was wrong in what he predicted! Under pressure of being expelled from the ETS, Pinnock changed the wording "in certain problematic language" regarding these predictions. However, no substantial change was made in his essential view that God does not have infallible knowledge of future free acts (see Geisler, "Did Clark Pinnock Recant?").

Open theists cannot avoid this criticism by redefining truth as intention and not correspondence. For on an intentionalist view of truth, almost any mistake could be true, thus undermining almost all Scripture. Further, Pinnock elsewhere claims to embrace a correspondence view of truth (*Most Moved Mover*). Indeed, such a view is both biblical (see Geisler, *Systematic Theology*) and undeniable since any denial of correspondence claims to correspond with reality.

Eleventh, Pinnock exhorts classical theists to avoid caricatures of others' views. Yet he repeatedly calls the opposing view "fatalistic" and "deterministic." He even dubs the classical God "a solitary narcissistic being" (*Most Moved Mover*, 6; quoting Walter Kasper)!

Twelfth, Pinnock claims that viewed from one vantage point (namely, process theology), his position is that of "Classical Theism" (*Most Moved Mover*, 145). Yes, and viewed from one vantage point, the pope is Protestant!

367

Finally, open theism claims that God is not simple (indivisible). Yet it affirms that God is infinite. But an infinite number of parts is impossible since no matter how many parts there are, there could always be one more, and more than an infinite is impossible. Further, many open theists agree with the Intelligent Design movement that whatever is irreducibly complex must have a cause. If God is irreducibly complex, then he must be caused.

Books Evaluating Open Theism. Numerous books critique open theism from across the theological spectrum, including various forms of Calvinism and Arminianism. These works include Millard Erickson, *God the Father Almighty*; John Feinberg, *No One like Him*; John Frame, *No Other God*; Norman L. Geisler, *Creating God in the Image of Man*; Norman L. Geisler and H. Wayne House, *The Battle for God*; Douglas Huffman and Eric L. Johnson (eds.), *God under Fire*; Robert Morey, *The Battle for the Gods*; John Piper, Justin Taylor, and Paul Kjoss Helseth (eds.), *Beyond the Bounds*; Bruce Ware, *God's Lesser Glory*; R. K. M. Wright, *No Place for Sovereignty*.

This is to say nothing of the untold number of books written in defense of classical theism, which are thereby indirect criticisms of crucial premises held by open theists. These include all relevant works by Augustine (e.g., *The City of God*), Anselm, and Aquinas (*Summa Theologica*), as well as those who follow in their tradition, such as Luther, Calvin (*Institutes of the Christian Religion*), Arminius, modern Thomists like Reginald Garrigou-Lagrange (*God: His Existence and Nature*), H. P. Owen (*Concepts of Deity*), James D. Collins (*God in Modern Philosophy*), and numerous others.

Summary and Conclusion. In summary open theism fails its own test for "coherence" and "internal consistency" (quotations in this paragraph are from Pinnock, *Most Moved Mover*; here, 22). It has constructed the gallows on which it has hanged itself. Some open theists, like Pinnock, have gone so far into process theology that they admit that God has a body and suggest evangelicals rethink the Mormon view of God. Pinnock wrote: "If he is with us in the world, if we are to take biblical metaphors seriously, is God in some way embodied?" (33). He answers positively, "I do not believe that the idea is as foreign to the Bible as we have assumed" (33). "Is there perhaps something in God that corresponds with embodiment? Having a body is certainly not a negative thing because it makes it possible for us to be agents. Perhaps God's agency would be easier to envisage *if he were in some way corporeal*" (33, emphasis added). He adds, "I do not feel obligated to assume that God is a purely spiritual being when *his self-revelation does not suggest it*" (34, emphasis added). Surely Pinnock has read John 4:24 ("God is spirit") and Luke 24:39, when Jesus said, "Touch me, and see. For a spirit does not have flesh and bones as you see that I have" (ESV). In view of Pinnock's startling and heretical view that God is corporeal, one must take more seriously the suggestion that there are possible similarities between Pinnock's view and that of the Mormons (35, 141).

See also CHRISTIAN; PANENTHEISM

Bibliography. D. Basinger, "Practical Implications," in Pinnock, *Openness*; G. Boyd, *God of the Possible: A Biblical Introduction to the Open View of God*; Boyd, *Trinity and Process*; R. A. Cole, *Exodus*; J. D. Collins, *God in Modern Philosophy* (1959); W. L. Craig, *The Kalām Cosmological Argument*; S. T. Davis, *Logic and the Nature of God*; M. Erickson, *God the Father Almighty*; J. Feinberg, *No One like Him*; J. Frame, *No Other God*; D. N. Freedman, "YHWH," in *The Theological Dictionary of the Old Testament*, vol. 5; R. Garrigou-Lagrange, *God, His Existence and His Nature*; P. Geach, *Providence and Evil*; N. L. Geisler, *Creating God in the Image of Man*; Geisler, "Did Clark Pinnock Recant His Errant Views?," http://normangeisler.com/pinnock -open-theists-and-inerrancy/; Geisler, *Systematic Theology*, vol. 1, *Introduction, Bible*; N. L. Geisler and H. W. House, with M. Herrera, *The Battle for God: Responding to the Challenge of Neotheism*; W. Hasker, *God, Time and Knowledge*; D. S. Huffman and E. L. Johnson, gen. eds., *God under Fire*; J. R. Lucas, *The Freedom of the Will*; Lucas, *The Future: An Essay on God, Temporality and Truth*; R. Morey, *The Battle for the Gods*; T. V. Morris, *Our Idea of God: An Introduction to Philosophical Theology*; R. Nash, ed., *Process Theology*; H. P. Owen, *Concepts of Deity*; C. Pinnock, "Between Classical and Process Theism," in Nash, *Process Theology*; Pinnock, *The Most Moved Mover: A Theology of God's Openness*; Pinnock, "Systematic Theology," in Pinnock, *Openness*; Pinnock, ed., *The Openness of God: A Biblical Challenge to the Traditional Understanding of God*; J. Piper, J. Taylor, and P. K. Helseth, eds., *Beyond the Bounds*; J. Pohle, *God: His Knowability, Essence, and Attributes*, translated by A. Preuss; R. Rice, "Biblical Support for a New Perspective," in Pinnock, *Openness*; J. Sanders, "Historical Considerations," in Pinnock, *Openness*; Rice, *God's Foreknowledge and Man's Free Will*; R. Swinburne, *The Coherence of Theism*; B. Ware, *God's Lesser Glory*; R. K. M. Wright, *No Place for Sovereignty*; L. Zagzebski, *The Dilemma of Freedom and Foreknowledge*.

N. L. Geisler

ORIGEN ON PREEXISTENCE. Origen's views on humanity are controversial and have never been universally accepted in the church. Platonism colors Origen's doctrine. His pagan teacher Ammonius Saccas also taught Plotinus, the founder of Middle Platonism.

Origen of Alexandria (d. ca. AD 251) taught that in the beginning God created a specific number of intelligences (souls), all equal (God being no respecter of persons) and all endowed with free will. As these intelligences sinned to greater or lesser degrees, their sin gave rise, according to what each deserved, to the different orders of beings in the universe: archangels, angels, demons, and Satan. Human souls, whose sin was greater than the angels' but lesser than the demons', were fettered in material bodies

both as punishment and as help in returning to God. According to Origen, the creation account of Genesis refers partly to the original creation of intelligences in the image of God and partly to material creation. The "garments of skin" made for Adam and Eve in Genesis 3:21 were material bodies. Origen echoes Philo in this interpretation and is in turn echoed by Joseph Smith Jr.'s Book of Moses. Origen's understanding of free will led him to posit repeated falls and returns, necessitating both a doctrine of reincarnation and one of the multiplication of material worlds. Many think Origen's views logically lead to universalism, that all will be saved, even Satan. It remains difficult to determine Origen's views on various topics because his surviving works are few and highly edited, mostly by those opposed to him.

Although the fourth-century church historian Eusebius of Caesarea and Pamphilus, his teacher, wrote favorably of Origen, and the Cappadocian fathers Basil of Caesarea and Gregory of Nazianzus (also in the fourth century) used his work, already by the late second and early third centuries Origen's views were increasingly seen as heretical. His works were finally condemned in 533 at the Fifth General Council in Constantinople, although Origen himself was never formally labeled as a heretic.

See also CHRISTIAN; ORTHODOXY

Bibliography. R. A. Greer, ed., *Origen: An Exhortation to Martyrdom, Prayer, and Selected Works*; J. N. D. Kelly, *Early Christian Doctrines*; J. B. Russell, *Satan: The Early Christian Tradition*; J. Stevenson, ed., *A New Eusebius: Documents Illustrating the History of the Church to AD 337*.

R. V. Huggins

ORTHODOXY. A term of Christian origin, *orthodoxy*, in contrast to *heresy*, is ascribed to those teachings that constitute the foundational doctrines of the historic Christian faith. Etymologically, the word is the English version of the Greek word *orthodoxia*, which combines *orthos* (right) and *doxa* (teaching). Essentially, orthodoxy is doctrine, but not just any doctrine. Care must be taken not to ascribe to orthodoxy those beliefs on which there can be more than one legitimate interpretation and application.

The importance of establishing and maintaining an orthodox body of doctrine is derived from one's worldview, the nature of truth, and epistemology. The logical starting point for establishing an orthodox body of truth is the Christian theistic worldview, which states that God exists and has revealed himself to us by means of general and special revelation. God's self-disclosure is the epistemological means by which truth both is made known and is knowable. Therefore, God, through propositional revelation, provides us with those doctrinal truths that constitute orthodoxy.

The New Testament amply instructs us in sound doctrine, beginning with the Gospels. In Luke 24:44–48, Jesus explains his atoning work to the disciples. John 1:1 explicitly teaches the orthodox doctrine of the deity of Jesus Christ. In John 14:6, Jesus Christ points out that he is the way, the truth, and the life exclusively.

According to Acts 2:42, the early church committed itself to a body of doctrine that originated with the apostles. In 1 Timothy 3:15, Paul states that the church is the pillar and support of the truth, undoubtedly apostolic doctrine.

In contrast to orthodoxy, there also exist heretical teachings. Second Corinthians 11 and Galatians 1 warn of false gospels and those who spread them. Bowman (78) identifies nine enemies of truth: false doctrines (Rom. 16:17; 1 Tim. 1:3), false miracles (Matt. 24:24; 2 Thess. 2:9), false deities (Deut. 13:2; 2 Thess. 2:4), false Christs (Matt. 24:24; 2 Cor. 11:4), false spirits (1 John 4:1–2), false prophets (Matt. 24:24; 2 Pet. 2:1), false apostles (2 Cor. 11:13; Rev. 2:2), false teachers (1 Tim. 1:7; 2 Pet. 2:1), and false gospels (Gal. 1:6–9).

Orthodoxy is that which was taught by the apostles and embraced by the church (Acts 2:42), entrusted to the church—which is to serve as a steward of truth (1 Tim. 3:15)—and defended by able overseers (Titus 1:9).

Those who are considered orthodox or unorthodox may vary among different religious bodies. Eastern Orthodox, Roman Catholic, and Protestant branches of Christianity may hold many points in common and declare those who differ or reject these to be unorthodox, but may differ among themselves as to the orthodoxy of one another's teaching. For example, all three major branches hold to the Nicene Creed and would declare those who reject the doctrine of the Trinity, in which all three eternal persons of the Trinity are indivisibly the one divine being, to be unorthodox. On the other hand, Roman Catholics would declare the rejection of transubstantiation regarding the Eucharist to be unorthodox, though Protestants would view the Roman Catholic doctrine as unorthodox; Eastern Orthodox would declare the acceptance of the phrase "and the Son" regarding the procession of the Holy Spirit to be unorthodox, but Roman Catholics consider the phrase required; Protestants would say that rejection of "faith alone" is unorthodox, while Roman Catholics believe that faith must be accompanied by works.

Doctrinal Categories. Doctrine is divided into two distinct categories: nonnegotiable and negotiable. An example of a negotiable doctrine is baptism. Scripture does not set forth a definitive procedure for administering baptism. Lutherans sprinkle, Baptists immerse, but neither practice can be labeled either orthodox or heretical. Regarding Communion, some Christian traditions believe it is a sacrament, while many traditions view it as simply an ordinance. Premillennialism, amillennialism, and postmillennialism are three distinct schools of eschatology, but none is considered orthodox or heretical.

Nonnegotiable doctrines are teachings that are properly identified as orthodox, that define the historic Christian faith, and to which there are no legitimate alternatives. In the history of the Christian church, trinitarianism, and by extension Christology, have been the litmus test for orthodoxy. Though Islam, Judaism, and Christianity are the three great monotheistic religions, Christianity holds to trinitarian monotheism, which asserts that the three persons of the Godhead form the Trinity, comprises a distinct Christology (that Jesus was both God and man), and establishes Christianity as exclusively the one true faith. Every aspect of Christian theology is impacted by Christology, so the doctrine of Christ is what Carl Braaten calls the "christological tripod," upon which the gospel rests (9).

Doctrinal categories are not established arbitrarily. Doctrinal truth is established on the basis of four sources that carry varying degrees of authority. They are the Scriptures, apostolic fathers, creeds, and catechisms.

The Scriptures. The Scriptures constitute foundational authority to which all other authorities are subject and upon which all other authorities are founded. This is not to discount that revelation from God is found in general revelation and in statements of God through the prophets, apostles, and Jesus, but that the written revelation of God is propositional, is equated in Scripture as the very words of God (e.g., Rom. 9:17; 1 Tim. 3:16), and is the truth (John 17:17)—it is accorded a unique status as the written and infallible Word of God. This is clearly because the Scriptures are propositional revelation from God. Scripture is not the product of human effort or collusion but is revealed truth by means of divine inspiration, recorded by human beings moved by the Holy Spirit. The Scriptures are therefore infallible and inerrant in all that they teach regarding doctrine, reproof, correction, and instruction in right behavior (2 Tim. 3:16) and never subject to revision.

The Church Fathers. The early church fathers were faithful to the apostolic faith (Acts 2:42), defended it against vigorous attacks, and propagated it throughout the known world. Given their close proximity to the apostolic era, from the standpoint of historiography the church fathers would undoubtedly be quite familiar with the work and teachings of the apostles. These leaders not only ministered to churches established by the apostles; some were contemporaries of and discipled by John.

The apostolic fathers distinguished themselves as leaders deeply committed to the fidelity of the apostolic faith, and their tireless efforts to articulate the truths of Christianity contributed greatly to the ongoing geographical spread and numerical growth of Christianity.

One contemporary heretical offshoot of Christianity, the Watch Tower Bible and Tract Society (Jehovah's Witnesses), appeals to the early church fathers in support of its teachings regarding Christ. What is particularly noteworthy about this is the Watch Tower's posture toward the early church fathers. In 1992 the organization's official periodical, the *Watchtower*, stated:

> "Apostolic fathers" is the designation used for churchmen who wrote about Christianity in the late first and early second centuries of our Common Era. Some of them were Clement of Rome, Ignatius, Polycarp, Hermas, and Papias. They were said to be contemporaries of some of the apostles. Thus, they should have been familiar with apostolic teachings. Regarding what those men wrote, *The New Encyclopedia Britannica* says: "taken as a whole the writings of the Apostolic Fathers are more valuable historically than any other Christian literature outside the New Testament." If the apostles taught the Trinity doctrine, then those Apostolic Fathers should have taught it too. It should have been prominent in their

teaching, since nothing was more important than telling people who God is. ("Trinity Doctrine," 19)

Ecumenical Creeds. These symbols, though not inspired, are the culmination of extensive theological debate and reflection that stand in congruence with one another, with biblical theology, and with the early church fathers. Philip Schaff points out that, to this day, Protestants, Roman Catholics, and the Orthodox Church embrace one or more of the major creeds. Creeds are important instruments in the service of orthodoxy in three areas: history, theology, and teaching. Their historical value resides in the fact that they testify to the church's commitment to specific doctrinal truths and the continuity of orthodox doctrine. Theologically, they represent careful theological and biblical reflection and encapsulate those doctrines deemed by the church to be consistent with apostolic doctrine. They also serve as valuable teaching tools, given their concise statements on those doctrines considered essential to orthodoxy.

Creeds reflect the core beliefs of the historic Christian faith and serve as a litmus test for orthodoxy. Heretical groups such as Mormons and Jehovah's Witnesses not only deny the legitimacy of the creeds but mistakenly assert that Christians put them on par with Scripture.

John Leith points out that the early orthodox statements (creeds) countering heretical views are to be understood as an attempt to articulate the Christian faith in an intelligent manner.

> The creed is simply the Church's understanding of the meaning of Scripture. The creed says, Here is how the Church reads and receives Scripture. . . .
>
> The rise of heresy was still another situation that created the need for creeds. . . . As was said long ago, creeds are signposts to heresies. The task of the creed was to defend the church against

heresy. The creed has the negative role of shutting the heretic out and setting the boundaries within which authentic Christian theology and life can take place. . . .

> Creeds are also a standard, a battle cry, a testimony and witness to the world. (Leith, 8–9)

The New Testament contains a number of basic statements that scholars consider to be early creeds. In 1 Corinthians 15:3–7, Paul reminds the Corinthian believers of their spiritual roots and of his ministry in their lives by reiterating a basic statement encapsulating the gospel of salvation on which they stand. Romans 1:1–4 is an introduction of Paul's letter to Roman Christians in which he explains in concise terms the gospel of God and its relationship to Christ. First Timothy 3:16 is an excellent example of the structure and content of an early creedal statement that was in circulation prior to Paul's ministry. It reveals the high Christology present in the apostolic church and its importance as a succinct statement of orthodoxy. Philippians 2:6–11 is the premier theological exposition of Christ's preexistence, incarnation, and eventual exaltation. Though considered a hymn, it nevertheless exhibits creedal qualities and is used as a creed. Matthew 28:19 presents an early trinitarian formula that Jesus Christ himself gave to his disciples as the basis for the baptismal event.

In the post–New Testament period, creeds continued to develop, and they served as definitive statements of orthodoxy that gave detailed and fresh expression to the apostolic tradition. Two important or chief creeds of the church embraced by Roman Catholicism, the Orthodox Church, and Protestantism are the Apostles' Creed and the Nicene Creed. They mainly deal with the orthodox doctrines of God and Christ or the dogmas of the Trinity and the incarnation. Schaff writes that these creeds (or symbols) are a brief statement of the fundamental tenets of the Christian faith, essential and sufficient for salvation. The Apostles' Creed, also known as the Old Roman Creed, is the earliest of the post–New Testament creeds. It was used in the Western church around the late second century into the early years of the third century. Though it has undergone numerous changes, the Apostles' Creed represents the early codification of the core beliefs of the early church. Regarding Jesus Christ, it states he is the Son of God, Lord, conceived by the power of the Holy Spirit, virgin born, who suffered and died, was resurrected on the third day, ascended into heaven, and is seated at the right hand of the Father. With the rise of heretical teachings repudiating the deity of Christ, the church was forced to articulate its Christology in a more sophisticated way, eventually producing the more refined, definitive Nicene Creed in response to the heresy of Arianism. Lesser known but of equal importance is the Athanasian Creed. There is no evidence that Athanasius penned the creed to which his name is attached, and since the seventeenth century, Catholic and Protestant authorities have not ascribed authorship to Athanasius. Nevertheless, this creed comprises the doctrinal conclusions of the four ecumenical councils and is explicitly trinitarian. Regarding the Trinity, it explicitly states that the Father, the Son, and the Holy Spirit are uncreated, incomprehensible, eternal, almighty, God, and Lord.

Challenges to Orthodoxy. Historically, the early church fathers, Roman Catholicism, Eastern Orthodoxy, and post-Reformation Protestantism agree that the doctrine of the person and work of Jesus Christ (Christology) constitutes a litmus test for orthodoxy. Specifically, to be orthodox on Christology one must acknowledge that Christ is God, is the second member of the Trinity, took on human flesh (incarnation), atoned for our sins, and was raised on the third day in a literal, physical body. Furthermore, the early church and later ecclesiastical traditions (Catholicism, Protestantism, Orthodoxy) agree that the deity of Christ is clearly presented in the New Testament. In John 1:1, Jesus is declared to be God. John 1:18, referring back to the prologue, refers to Jesus as the only-begotten God. Though this translation has been challenged on the basis of textual variants (some manuscripts read "only-begotten Son"), the best evidence supports "only-begotten God" (probably best translated "God the only Son," as in the NRSV). Thomas, who initially doubted the resurrection and declared he would accept it only if he could physically touch the resurrected Christ, was given the opportunity to touch Christ, to which he responded by declaring Christ to be his Lord and God (John 20:28). Paul declares Christ to be God in Romans 9:5 and Titus 2:13. The writer of Hebrews refers to Christ when he refers to the eternality of the throne of God (Heb. 1:8–9). Second Peter 1:1 speaks of Christ as both God and savior, and 1 John 5:20 speaks of Christ as God, which is consistent with John's Gospel, which explicitly affirms the deity of Christ.

In the centuries following the close of the New Testament period, christological and trinitarian heresies began to make inroads into the Christian community, questioning the deity of Christ and, by extension, the Trinity, thus constituting a pervasive challenge to orthodoxy.

Significant challenges to Christian orthodoxy came from numerous sources, the earliest being the gnostics, who taught that salvation is achieved by the acquisition of secret, special knowledge, that the supreme God is unknowable, and that all that is physical is evil and the spiritual realm is good (dualism). This had serious implications for Christology, given that in his incarnation Christ took on human flesh, which from a gnostic perspective would constitute corruption. Heresies such as Docetism denied the literal, physical suffering of Christ on the cross and, because of their dualism, rejected the doctrine of Christ's incarnation. Given its dualistic view of spirit and matter, Docetism has strong affinities with gnosticism. Apollinarianism, which gets its name from Apollinarius of Laodicea (ca. 310–ca. 390), was a heretical strain of Docetism that denied Jesus had a human mind and soul. The Second Ecumenical Council (381) condemned this teaching as unorthodox.

Ebionism taught that Jesus was the Messiah but not the Son of God. Furthermore, he overcame sin by exercise of his will, an ability Ebionites claimed was available to anyone willing to develop it. Though Jesus was not initially divine, he was adopted into divinity. The heresy of Adoptionism taught that Jesus was not the incarnation of the Son of God but was a great teacher who, at his baptism, was adopted by God. However, his adoption did not confer on him divinity.

Eutychianism, which denied that Jesus had two natures, gets its name from a monk named Eutyches (ca. 378–ca. 452). Given its denial of Christ's physical nature, Eutychianism manifested Docetic tendencies. The Fourth Ecumenical Council, held in 451, declared that Jesus was one person who possessed both a divine nature and a human nature, rendering Eutychianism heretical.

One of the most pervasive challenges to the doctrine of Christ in history is Arianism, a christological heresy that originated with Arius (ca. 256–336). He rejected the divinity of Jesus Christ and taught that Jesus was a created being, not fully God or fully human. In 325 the Council of Nicaea was convened to address this serious problem. The outcome of Nicaea's position on Christ revolved around two important terms, *homoousios* (of the same substance), proposed by Athanasius, and *homoiousios* (of like or similar substance), preferred by Arius. The Council of Nicaea dealt a blow to Arianism

by declaring its view of Jesus Christ to be heretical. Arianism is quite prevalent today, finding its most vigorous expression in the teachings of the Watch Tower Bible and Tract Society (Jehovah's Witnesses).

With the aid of Greek philosophy and a more technical terminology, the person of Christ and his relationship to the Trinity were developed with greater clarity and reasoned logical constructs. In its confrontation with heretical challenges to the deity of Christ and the Trinity, the church universal came to a consensus on what constituted true orthodoxy and codified doctrinal orthodoxy in the ecumenical creeds.

See also CHALCEDONIAN CONTROVERSY; CHRIST, NATURES AND ATTRIBUTES OF; CHRISTIAN; CHRISTIANITY, PROTESTANT; EASTERN ORTHODOXY; JEHOVAH'S WITNESSES (JW); ROMAN CATHOLICISM; TRINITARIAN CONTROVERSIES

Bibliography. C. L. Blomberg, "The New Testament Definition of Heresy," *Journal of the Evangelical Theological Society*; R. M. Bowman Jr., *Orthodoxy and Heresy*; C. Braaten, "The Gospel for a Neopagan Culture," in *Either/Or: The Gospel or Neopaganism*, edited by C. Braaten and R. W. Jenson; G. Bray, *Creeds, Councils and Christ*; H. O. J. Brown, *Heresies*; J. H. Leith, ed., *Creeds of the Churches*; "Trinity Doctrine," *Watchtower*, February 1, 1992.

S. J. Rost and H. W. House

OVERSEER. The term *overseer* often translates the Greek word *episkopos*, rendered as "bishop" in some translations. Several Christian denominations, such as Eastern Orthodox, Roman Catholic, Anglican/Episcopalian, Methodist, and so on, use the latter term, while some other Protestant groups also use the former. *Overseer* is used also by heterodox organizations such as Jehovah's Witnesses (JWs), who use the term to designate those who are appointed to supervise various activities in their organization. A local congregation of JWs may have a number of overseers directing the affairs of that congregation, while circuit overseers are those who have authority over several congregations in a geographical region.

See also EASTERN ORTHODOXY; JEHOVAH'S WITNESSES (JW); ROMAN CATHOLICISM

Bibliography. C. Brown, ed., *New International Dictionary of New Testament Theology*; G. Kittel, ed., *Theological Dictionary of the New Testament*.

E. Shropshire

PACIFISM. *See* WAR AND PEACE IN WORLD RELIGIONS

PAHLAVI TEXTS. These texts make up an extensive literature supplementing the Zoroastrian Avesta in the Pahlavi (Middle Persian) language—properly Zend-Avesta (Interpretation of the Avesta). They include translations of the Avesta (the Denkard contains lost fragments) and original works, notably the Bundahishn (Original creation) and Arda Viraf Namak (Visit to heaven and hell), a Parsi eschatology.

See also AVESTA; ZOROASTRIANISM

Bibliography. M. Boyce, *Zoroastrians: Their Religious Beliefs and Practices.*

C. R. Wells

PALI CANON. Pali is one of the Prakrits, or vernacular languages, used in ancient India that are closely related to Sanskrit (used by the educated classes). The Pali Canon (Tipitaka; Sanskrit, Tripitaka) is the Buddhist scriptures in three main sections or "baskets." These texts are regarded by Theravadan Buddhists as the original, pure, and authoritative accounts and teachings of the Buddha. The Pali Text Society was established in 1881 by Thomas Rhys-Davids to translate the Pali Canon into European languages. Only a portion of the Sanskrit Buddhist canon is still extant; however, translations of the whole are found in the Chinese and Tibetan Buddhist canons.

See also BUDDHIST SCRIPTURES; THERAVADA BUDDHISM; TRIPITAKA

Bibliography. Hajime Nakamura, *Indian Buddhism: A Survey with Bibliographical Notes.*

H. P. Kemp

PANENTHEISM. Panentheism is a system of beliefs about God that attempts to integrate strengths of classical theism and pantheism. The term is derived from three Greek words: *pan,* "all"; *en,* "in"; and *theos,* "God." Unlike pantheism, in which God is identical to all reality, and unlike theism, in which God is separate from the created world, in panentheism all reality—including the created world—is a part of the being of God; that is, God contains the whole universe within Godself but is not completely exhausted by it.

While the term *panentheism* was first coined in the eighteenth century by Karl Krause (1781–1832) in an attempt to integrate monotheism and pantheism, both proponents and detractors claim that insipient forms date back much earlier, possibly as early as 1300 BC in the poetic description of Ikhnaton (1375–1358 BC), the Egyptian pharaoh often considered to be the first monotheist. Other prominent historical figures who allegedly anticipated some form of panentheism include the authors of the Hindu Upanishads (ca. 800–400 BC), Lao-Tse (fourth century BC), Plato (427–347 BC), Plotinus (AD 204–70), Proclus (AD 412–85), Pseudo-Dionysus (late fifth to early sixth centuries AD), Meister Eckhart (1260–1328), Nicholas of Cusa (1401–64), Baruch Spinoza (1632–77), Friedrich Schleiermacher (1768–1834), and G. W. F. Hegel (1770–1831).

In the twentieth century, Alfred North Whitehead (1861–1947), Charles Hartshorne (1897–2000; pronounced "Harts-horne"), and John B. Cobb Jr. (1925–) developed a philosophical theology called "process theology," which is rooted in a panentheistic worldview. These philosopher/theologians saw problems in classical or traditional theism that they maintained could be solved by bringing together various aspects of theistic and pantheistic ontologies. They developed a process metaphysics in an attempt to solve them. More recently, process thinkers including Arthur Peacocke and Philip Clayton have advanced process ideas by combining contemporary, evolutionary understandings of the world with panentheistic theological concepts.

According to the process panentheistic view, while God is not identical to the world, God *participates* in the world—God and the world are in process together. God not only acts on the world but also is acted upon. All things, including God, are in the process of *becoming* rather than statically *being*. In this process of becoming, entities (people, animals, and so on) respond to each moment by making choices, and these choices are real and significant; they are never lost but are continually added to God's overall experience. God learns from such experiences, ever growing in knowledge and understanding.

This view of God's *knowledge* is clearly in contrast to traditional theology, in which God's omniscience is eternally complete and exhaustive, and this view of God's *nature* also contrasts with the traditional attribute of divine immutability. For process thinkers, while the abstract qualities of God, such as goodness and wisdom, are stable, God is changeable and evolves as the world does. God grows in experiencing new joys, in acquiring new knowledge of real events, and in experiencing the values created over time by free agents in the world. So in this sense God is mutable.

Also, according to the process panentheistic view, the traditional understanding of God's omnipotence is rejected. God's power is not infinite but limited, as other free entities, such as human persons, have the power to make their own free choices and decisions. Furthermore, God's power is persuasive rather than coercive; God does not force creatures to do good but attempts to lure them in the right direction. Unfortunately, they cannot always be so lured, and sometimes they make the wrong choices; sometimes they do evil things. But all entities, including God, continue to evolve, and the hope is that eventually all evil will be eradicated as free creatures learn from prior experiences (their own and those of history) what is ultimately good and right. Thus together God and the world—as dynamic processes rather than static substances—are moving toward ultimate perfection.

Forms of panentheism today can be found in Hinduism, Judaism, Christianity, Islam, and New Age thought.

See also HINDUISM; ISLAM, BASIC BELIEFS OF; JUDAISM; LAO TSU / LAOZI; PANTHEISM; PROCESS THEOLOGY; UPANISHADS

Bibliography. Center for Process Studies, home page, http://www.ctr4process.org; P. Clayton and A. Peacocke, eds., *In Whom We Live and Move and Have Our Being: Panentheistic Reflections on God's Presence in a Scientific World*; J. B. Cobb Jr. and D. R. Griffin, *Process Theology: An Introductory Exposition*; J. W. Cooper, *From Plato to the Present*; Cooper, *Panentheism: The Other God of the Philosophers*; W. L. Craig, "Pantheists in Spite of Themselves," in *For Faith and Clarity*, edited by J. K. Beilby; R. G. Gruenler, *Inexhaustible God: Biblical Faith and the Challenge of Process Theism*; C. Hartshorne and W. L. Reese, eds., *Philosophers Speak of God*.

C. V. Meister

PANTHEISM. Pantheism expresses the view that all things, persons, and matter are God. The word stems from the Greek *pan*, "all," and *theos*, "God." Pantheism advocates the concept that all that exists is identical with deity, because either the cosmos in all its essence is deity or the cosmos is derived from the being of God. Creation ex nihilo therefore is denied. Creation, on both its physical and spiritual plane, is an emanation from and of God. In some forms of pantheism (see below), the world is an illusion because there is only one reality—Brahman.

A number of religions and philosophies embrace pantheism, including forms of Hinduism, New Age thought, Mahayana Buddhism, and other Eastern perspectives. Sufism (within Islam) and some expressions of Judaism express pantheistic concepts. The early Greek thinker Parmenides taught an "absolute pantheism," maintaining that there is only one being in and of the universe. Later Plotinus advocated "emanational pantheism"—the view that everything flows from God as a flower from a seed. "Developmental pantheism" such as G. W. F. Hegel's (1770–1831) argues that God is unfolded in an evolutionary or historical process. Baruch Spinoza (1632–77) advocated "modal pantheism," proposing that all finite things are modes or moments in one infinite substance, while forms of Hinduism embrace "manifestational or multilevel pantheism" (Geisler, 173, paraphrased).

The Hindu or Eastern mode of "pantheism" is the dominant position for most contemporary pantheistic religious thought, embracing the possibility of millions of gods. Hinduism does evidence two basic pantheistic positions, which may be described as either qualified nondualist or complete nondualist. Qualified nondualists perceive themselves and the universe to be qualitatively one with God though not completely identical with God. One teacher of this system, A. C. Bhaktivedanta Swami Prabhupada, explains,

> We are all qualitatively one with God.
> . . . Whatever we have as spirit souls,

God also has. There is no difference in quality. For example, suppose you take a drop of water from the vast Atlantic Ocean and you chemically analyze the ingredients. The composition of the drop of water is the same as the composition of the vast Atlantic Ocean. . . . Similarly, you are a spirit soul, a spark of the supreme spirit soul, God. You have all the spiritual qualities that God has. But God is great, you are minute. He is infinite, you are infinitesimal. So you and God are qualitatively one but quantitatively different. (15)

Eastern apologist Ramanuja compares the world to God's body. The world is one with God, inseparable from the Divine, but God transcends the world like a soul transcends the body. The world is made out of God, creation *ex deo* as opposed to the Judeo-Christian concept of creation *ex nihilo*.

Qualified nondualists such as Ramanuja maintain that the cosmos and individual souls are identical with God in their fundamental being but different in their properties. In this sense, the world is not the absolutely real but rather an echo of the real—or the Divine—God.

Complete nondualists perceive themselves as one with God. This oneness, however, is not recognized because of human preoccupation with the material world, which is only an illusion. The eighth-century Hindu philosopher Sankara, the founder of Advaita Vedanta Hinduism, maintained that there is only one reality: Brahman, the absolute ground of all being, pure, distinctionless consciousness. Ignorance of Brahman, therefore, produces the illusion of a material world. Robin Collins aptly describes this position as "cosmic illusionism" (see Murray, 188).

The Upanishads seemingly agree with this view when they state, "I am Brahman," and the self is the Brahman (Brihadaranyaka Upanishad 1.4.10 and 2.5.19). Modern Western yoga gurus such as Sharon Gannon and David Life concur when they comment that liberation "is when the jiva (soul) realizes that it is not individual but Absolute" (xvii). They continue, "The realized soul is Atman. It is a pure consciousness, in a state of absolute joy. . . . It is unchangeable and eternal and is not destroyed when the body is destroyed. Atman is I-Am" (29).

Pantheistic Eastern thought may be seen in many modern religious thinkers and movements. Hegel viewed history as the manifestation of Absolute Spirit. Spinoza argued that there is only one reality, which could be named "God" or "Nature," and all things are modifications of this phenomenon (Ferguson, 656). Christian Science and the Unity School of Christianity clearly demonstrate elements of pantheistic thought.

The New Age movement is obviously pantheistic. Contemporary diva Shirley MacLaine writes, the "tragedy of the human race was that we had forgotten that we were each divine." Additionally, "You are everything. Everything you want to know is inside of you. You are the universe" (347).

In summary pantheism's position on theological issues is as follows:

1. *Epistemology*. Truth is discovered by enlightenment to the concept of monism, all in oneness, the idea that God is a part of everything and that everything is one with the Divine. Meditation, enlightenment, and reading and reflection on the Upanishads, among other pantheistic writings, are various avenues to this truth.

2. *Theology*. God is impersonal. God is spirit and a force, not a person. "Ground of being," "life force," "universal soul consciousness," and "It" are various ways to express the Divine. Immanence is "God's" key characteristic, either as the spiritual or exact essence of all things.

3. *Cosmology*. All matter is seen as one with God—monism. This position can be interpreted either literally—that is, material essence is a part of the divine "It"—or spiritually, as asserting that material itself is an illusion, and hence all is one.

Pantheism is in reality a challenge to the Christian worldview and seriously departs in key areas from Christian thinking. As a system, it has inherent weaknesses. First, it is logically self-contradictory. While it maintains that God is all that exists and is by nature immanent and not distinct from the material order, nonetheless, it seemingly does make distinctions about God. While God is reputedly nondescript, pantheists often assert descriptions—such as that God is nondescript. Second, pantheism is consistently counterintuitive. If humans are divine, what accounts for this universal and general lack of awareness of the divine internal essence? Perhaps most concerning is the question of theodicy. If God is all, then either God is evil, or God is at least the author of evil, or evil does not exist. Notably, some Eastern expressions of pantheism attempt to dismiss or redefine evil so as to argue for its nonexistence, which in the world of human experience is a glaring shortfall.

See also ADVAITA; ATMAN; BRAHMA; DUALISM; HINDUISM; ISLAM, BASIC BELIEFS OF; JUDAISM; MAHAYANA BUDDHISM; PRABHUPADA, ABHAY CHARAN DE BHAKTIVEDANTA SWAMI; SUFISM; YOGA

Bibliography. D. C. Clark and N. L. Geisler, *Apologetics in the New Age: A Christian Critique of Pantheism*; S. Ferguson, ed., *New Dictionary of Theology*; S. Gannon and D. Life, *JivaMukti Yoga: Practices for Liberating Body and Soul*; N. L. Geisler, *Christian Apologetics*; S. MacLaine, *Out on a Limb*; Swami Madhavananda, trans., *Brihadaranyaka Upanishad*; M. Murray, ed., *Reason for the Hope Within*; A. C. B. Swami Prabhupada, *The Quest for Enlightenment*.

R. P. Roberts

PARAMAHANSA, SWAMI MUKTANANDA.
Swami Muktananda Paramahansa (1908–82,
known as Muktananda) was an Indian guru
of the Kashmir Shaivite tradition known as
Siddha Yoga. He was born in Mangalore with
the given name of Krishna, the only son of
a wealthy family. At age fifteen, he became
a renunciant (one who forsakes all for devotion to God), left home, and spent the next
twenty-five years as a wandering devotee. During that period, he encountered some sixty
different ascetic saints, such as Zipruanna,
Hari Giri Baba, and Siddharuda. The last,
who taught him Vedanta, bestowed on him
the name Muktananda, which means "love
of bliss." In 1947 he came under the tutelage of Bhagawan Sri Nityananda (d. 1961).
Over the next nine years, Muktananda progressed in his spiritual development under
Nityananda's guidance. He is said to have
attained the state of being beyond body consciousness and, in the Siddha tradition, to
have become spiritually perfect.

After Nityananda's death, Muktananda
established the Shree Gurudev Siddha Yoga
Ashram in Ganeshpuri (an ashram is the
dwelling of a Hindu teacher). In 1968 an
American-born Lithuanian named Franklin
Jones (Da John) came to Ganeshpuri for a
brief time of study, and he returned again
the following year. Jones led the Johannine
Daist Communion. By 1969 at least three
Western devotees had taken up residence at
the ashram. In 1970 Muktananda visited the
US and Australia in a three-month tour coordinated by Werner Erhard, Baba Ram Dass,
and Michael Graham. Meditation centers
and ashrams were established in the wake
of this tour. Muktananda made more extensive visits to the West in 1974 and 1978.
Various celebrities were attracted to Muktananda, such as Jerry Brown, John Denver,
Olivia Hussey, Marsha Mason, Raoul Julia,
Diana Ross, and Buckminster Fuller, though
not all of them necessarily became serious
aspirants. The movement has now spread to
some forty-six nations and has gained more
than a quarter of a million aspirants.

Muktananda taught that the purpose of
life is to know the "true Self" and that the
guru facilitates "Self-realization." The Siddha Guru is the physical expression of ultimate reality, and the guru spiritually awakens
aspirants. The conduit for this awakening
entails a transmission of power from the
guru called *shaktipat*. Shaktipat may be
accompanied by ecstatic phenomena such
as spontaneous yogic movements (*kriyas*),
dancing, laughter, tears, mimic animal calls,
and utterances in tongues. In this experience, the aspirant's false ego "dies," and
the phenomenal experience of the world
as a duality ceases. The Siddha Guru is the
sacred center of devotion.

Muktananda developed a heart condition, and in May 1982 he passed on the Siddha lineage to two young people in a public
ceremony. His nominated successors were
a sister and brother then known as Swami
Chidvilasananda and Swami Nityananda.
Muktananda died on October 2, 1982. In
the wake of both his death and a subsequent
rift between Chidvilasananda (now known
as Gurumayi) and her brother Nityananda,
several Western female devotees came forth
with allegations that Muktananda had been
guilty of sexual misconduct. These allegations were popularly reported in the *CoEvo-
lution Quarterly* (Winter 1983) and again
in the *New Yorker* (November 14, 1994).
Gurumayi denied their validity, but the allegations are repeated on an internet website
for ex-members.

See also SIDDHA YOGA

Bibliography. Leaving Siddha Yoga website,
http://www.leavingsiddhayoga.net; Swami M.
Paramahansa, *Meditate*; Paramahansa, *Play of
Consciousness*; G. R. Thursby, "Siddha Yoga:
Swami Muktananda and the Seat of Power," in
When Prophets Die.

P. Johnson

PEARL OF GREAT PRICE, THE. The Pearl of Great Price is the shortest of the four standard works of the Church of Jesus Christ of Latter-day Saints (LDS Church, or Mormonism), consisting of five distinct works—none of which is complete. Two of these are excerpts from the Joseph Smith Translation (JST), the supposedly inspired revision of the King James Version of the Bible made by LDS founder Joseph Smith Jr.: Selections from the Book of Moses (an excerpt from the JST of Genesis) and Joseph Smith—Matthew (an excerpt from the JST of Matthew). One of the works is presented as Smith's inspired translation of part of a hitherto unknown ancient work, the Book of Abraham. The final two works are Joseph Smith—History, an excerpt from the official history of the LDS Church, and the Articles of Faith, an excerpt from a letter written by Smith. Thus Joseph Smith is credited as the author or translator of all five works in the Pearl of Great Price.

Selections from the Book of Moses. This material is described in current published editions as "an extract from the translation of the Bible as revealed to Joseph Smith the Prophet, June 1830–February 1831." Its eight chapters consist of a revision of Genesis 1:1–6:13 with new introductory material and an extensive addition concerning Enoch.

The Book of Abraham. This book of five chapters purports to be Joseph Smith's inspired translation from papyri he obtained in 1835. It presents an alternate version of Genesis 1–2, 11–12, supposedly penned by Abraham himself, in which Abraham learns that a plurality of Gods organized the world. The book also contains material with no parallel in Genesis, recounting an attempt by false priests to kill him and of his later revelations concerning astronomy, the preexistence of human spirits, and the plan of salvation. The papyri were long thought to be lost, but large portions were recovered in 1966–67 and turned out to have nothing to do with Abraham.

Joseph Smith—Matthew. This short book consists of an extract from the JST of Matthew 24, produced in 1831. Joseph Smith's version of Matthew 24 (part of the Olivet Discourse containing Jesus's prophecy of the destruction of Jerusalem) is essentially the same as the KJV, with just a couple of minor changes.

Joseph Smith—History. This short autobiographical account was written by Smith in 1838 and was originally published as part of *History of the Church*. In it Smith tells about his First Vision, which he says took place in 1820, and about early events concerning his obtaining the gold plates containing the Book of Mormon.

In the first part of the narrative, Smith recounts his discouragement as a teenager over the apparent confusion among the various denominations regarding the truths of God. He presents the details surrounding his First Vision, in which he was visited by what he calls two personages, one of whom identified the other as "My beloved Son." The message Smith says he received was that all churches are corrupt and doctrinally in error. Smith then describes the persecution he received from religious leaders when they heard his testimony (1:1–26).

The next section of the history (1:27–54) describes Smith's contact with the angel Moroni (the son of Mormon), who tells Smith about the Book of Mormon and the hiding place of the gold plates from which the Book of Mormon will be translated. In verses 55–65, Smith explains how he came to acquire the plates and began the translation process with the aid of Martin Harris. The remaining verses, 66–75, include details regarding Cowdery's assistance with the translation of the Book of Mormon and John the Baptist's bestowal of the Aaronic priesthood on Smith and Cowdery.

Articles of Faith. The last part of the Pearl of Great Price is the Articles of Faith, a thirteen-point list of basic beliefs of the

LDS Church, written by Joseph Smith as part of a letter in 1842 and published in *History of the Church*.

Editions of the Pearl of Great Price. In 1851 a British leader of the LDS Church named Franklin D. Richards published in Liverpool *The Pearl of Great Price: Being a Choice Selection from the Revelations, Translations, and Narrations of Joseph Smith*. The contents included the material mentioned above plus several revelations of Joseph Smith that are now part of the Doctrine and Covenants (D&C 20, 27, 77, 87, and 107) and a poem: "Truth," by John Jaques, later made into a hymn titled "Oh Say, What Is Truth?" The first American edition of the Pearl of Great Price was published in Salt Lake City in 1878 and included what is now D&C 132, with the title "A Revelation on the Eternity of the Marriage Covenant, including Plurality of Wives." In 1880 the LDS Church officially adopted the Pearl of Great Price as one of the standard works of the church. In 1902 the LDS Church published a new edition, edited by James Talmage, that omitted the materials that are in D&C. Two additional revelations (from Joseph Smith Jr. and from Joseph F. Smith) were added to the Pearl of Great Price in 1976 and three years later moved to become D&C 137 and 138.

See also ARTICLES OF FAITH, MORMON; BOOK OF ABRAHAM; BOOK OF MOSES; CHURCH OF JESUS CHRIST OF LATTER-DAY SAINTS; JOSEPH SMITH TRANSLATION OF THE BIBLE; SMITH, JOSEPH, JR.; STANDARD WORKS

Bibliography. K. W. Baldridge, "Pearl of Great Price: Contents and Publication," in *Encyclopedia of Mormonism*, edited by D. H. Ludlow, 4 vols.; J. R. Clark, *The Story of the Pearl of Great Price*; R. S. Draper, S. K. Brown, and M. D. Rhodes, *The Pearl of Great Price: A Verse-by-Verse Commentary*; O. G. Hunsaker, "Pearl of Great Price: Literature," in *Encyclopedia of Mormonism*, edited by D. H. Ludlow, 4 vols.; R. L. Millet and K. P. Jackson, eds., *Studies in Scripture*, vol. 2, *The Pearl of Great Price*; H. D. Peterson, *The Pearl of Great Price: A History and Commentary*; H. D. Peterson and C. D. Tate Jr., eds., *The Pearl of Great Price: Revelations from God*; G. Reynolds and J. M. Sjodahl, *Commentary on the Pearl of Great Price*.

R. M. Bowman Jr.

PELAGIANISM. Pelagianism derives its name from the late fourth-/early fifth-century lay monk Pelagius (AD 354–ca. 420). Possibly of British origin, Pelagius developed his teaching in Rome and then traveled to North Africa and Palestine, spreading his views on the nature of man, sin, and moral ability and responsibility.

Pelagius held that people are not born morally corrupt nor in a state of guilt. Adam's sin served only as a bad example that we as his offspring sometimes choose to imitate. Human beings have completely free will, which he understood as the full moral ability to keep all of God's commands. This power to choose good or evil is essential to free moral agency. All sin is a deliberate, willful choice to break God's commandments, just as holiness is a willful choice to obey. In essence Pelagius taught that people can save themselves through their own obedience to God's moral commands.

Pelagius also taught that humans were created mortal, denying that physical death is a punishment for Adam's sin. His position required this because in Pelagius's view people are punished only for their own personal sins. Since infants, who are unable to commit sins, nevertheless die physically, Pelagius was forced to conclude that physical death could not be the punishment for sin and, consequently, that Adam (and his offspring) would have died regardless. Accordingly, when Romans 5:12 states that death spread to all human beings because all sinned, Pelagius claimed that the death mentioned here was spiritual death only, thus linking the death to actual and not to original sin. Because infants cannot commit actual sins, they do not die spiritually even though, being naturally mortal, they sometimes do die physically in infancy. Adults, on the other hand, can sin, and when they do, then death—spiritual death—spreads to them.

Against the charge that his optimistic view of human ability obviated any need for grace, Pelagius responded by identifying two kinds of grace. First, there is a grace of nature, meaning that God graciously created us in such a way that we are fully able to keep his commandments—that is, he created us with free will. Pelagius also acknowledged special grace, which makes right action *easier* than it otherwise would be. Included in the category of special grace are Christ's example, the sacraments, and the Bible.

Pelagius's teaching was opposed most strenuously by St. Augustine (AD 354–430), who taught the doctrine of original sin. As a result of Adam's defection from God, his offspring are born morally corrupt and in a state of guilt. Human beings are unable to attain salvation through their own moral efforts and are saved solely by God's grace.

Pelagianism was condemned officially at the Council of Ephesus in AD 431. In modern times, a Pelagian anthropology is taught in many and perhaps even most heterodox Christian groups, at least implicitly. Some modern groups that espouse an overtly Pelagian anthropology, including a denial of original sin, are Mormonism, Unitarian Universalism, and moral government theology.

See also ORTHODOXY

Bibliography. R. W. Battenhouse, ed., *A Companion to the Study of St. Augustine*; P. Schaff, *History of the Christian Church*, vol. 3, *Nicene and Post-Nicene Christianity, AD 311–600*; B. B. Warfield, *Calvin and Augustine*.

A. W. Gomes

PENTATEUCH. *See* TORAH

PESACH (PASSOVER). The Feast of Passover is the most frequently mentioned festival of all the feasts of Israel in both Testaments. It is mentioned over fifty times in the Old Testament and twenty-seven times in the New Testament. Within the framework of Judaism, this is the most important festival of the entire Jewish religious calendar.

Names. Two different names are given for this feast. The first, *pesach*, comes from a Hebrew root meaning "to pass over, to exempt," originating from the motif of "the destroyer" passing over the people of Israel in Exodus 12. The Jews were commanded to take a lamb, slay it, then take the blood of the lamb and sprinkle it on the lintel and doorposts of each home. That night the Lord and the destroyer passed through the land of Egypt (Exod. 12:23, 29). When the Lord came to a Jewish home and saw the blood on the lintel and doorposts, he would *pass over* that Jewish home. But when he came to an Egyptian home and did not see the blood on the lintel and doorposts, instead of "passing over," he would "pass through" and slay the firstborn son of that Egyptian family.

The second Hebrew name for this festival is *zman cheruteinu*, which means the "season of our emancipation." This name emphasizes the result of the first Passover: freedom from Egyptian slavery.

The Biblical Practice. The biblical practice of Passover included two key elements: killing the lamb and eating the lamb.

1. *Killing the Lamb.* The lamb for the paschal meal was to be set aside on the tenth day of the first month, Aviv (Hebrew) or Nissan (Aramaic). From the tenth day to the fourteenth day, the lamb was to be tested to make sure it was without spot and without blemish. If it proved acceptable, the lamb for the Passover meal was killed by each Jewish family on the first night of Passover, the evening of the fourteenth. Another key point concerning the paschal lamb was that not a bone of the lamb was to be

broken (Exod. 12:46). On the following morning, the first day of the Passover, a special, sacrificial lamb would be killed on the altar by the priesthood.

2. *Eating the Lamb.* The second main element was the paschal meal (Exod. 12:8), which was eaten on the first night of passover. The paschal meal included the eating of the lamb with two other items: unleavened bread and bitter herbs.

The Jewish Observance. The Jewish observance of the Passover or paschal meal includes two key elements: unleavened bread and wine.

1. *The Unleavened Bread.* By rabbinic law, the bread qualified for the Passover must be unleavened. Because leaven is often a symbol of sin in the Bible, God would not permit even the symbol of sin to be in the Jewish home. In modern Israel, a ceremony is held symbolically ridding the country of all leaven.

2. *The Wine.* Each person will drink four cups of wine during the paschal meal, and each cup has its own name. The first cup at the beginning of the ceremony is called "the cup of blessing" or "the cup of thanksgiving." The second cup, called "the cup of plagues," symbolizes the ten plagues that fell on Egypt. The third cup, "the cup of redemption," symbolizes the physical redemption of the firstborn of Israel from the tenth plague by the shedding of the blood of the paschal lamb. The fourth cup is "the cup of praise," with which the Jewish people sing Psalms 113–18 and with which the ceremony officially ends.

The Messianic Significance. Within the framework of the Old Testament, the messianic significance is found in Isaiah 52:13–53:12. The coming Messiah is pictured in terms of a lamb in that statements made of the Servant of the Lord in Isaiah 53 are similar to statements used of the paschal lamb. In this passage, Isaiah teaches that the Messiah will be the final Passover lamb.

1. *The Passover Lamb.* The New Testament sees the death of the Messiah as the fulfillment of the Passover motif: the slaying of the lamb. For example, four New Testament passages clearly connect the Messiah with the Passover lamb (John 1:29, 35–36; 1 Cor. 5:7; 1 Pet. 1:18–19; Rev. 5:12).

2. *The Last Supper.* Some of the Jewish observances of the Passover discussed earlier are reflected in the gospel accounts of the last Passover or the first Lord's Supper. The passage that gives the most details is Luke 22:14–20.

Jesus referred to the Passover bread as representing his body in Luke 22:19. Furthermore, Luke mentions the first and third cups of wine noted above. The first cup is in Luke 22:17–18. The third cup is mentioned in Luke 22:20. The third cup symbolizes a physical redemption brought about in the land of Egypt by the blood of the Paschal lamb. Now it becomes a symbol of a spiritual redemption from enslavement to sin. Jesus clearly identified himself in terms of the Jewish observance of the Passover; therefore, the Passover is fulfilled by the death of the Messiah.

See also JUDAISM

Bibliography. Rabbi S. Finkelman, Rabbi M. D. Stein Lieber, Rabbi S. Moshe, and Rabbi Nosson, *Pesach, Passover—Its Observance, Laws, and Significance*; R. Posner, *Passover*; C. Roth, "Pesach/Passover," *Encyclopedia Judaica*, edited by C. Roth; I. Singer, "Pesach," in *The Jewish Encyclopedia*.

A. Fruchtenbaum

PLURAL MARRIAGE, MORMON TEACHING AND HISTORY OF. Plural marriage, or polygamy, has been a contentious doctrine within the Church of Jesus Christ of Latter-day Saints. Even though the church officially declared that plural marriage would no longer be practiced or tolerated, there are currently over one hundred splinter groups of polygamous Mormons.

Historical Background. In the early years of Mormonism, monogamy was declared to be the only acceptable expression of marriage. In the 1835 edition of the Doctrine and Covenants (D&C), monogamy was set forth in the Article on Marriage (then sec. 101), which stated that "one man should have one wife; and one woman, but one husband, except in case of death, when either is at liberty to marry again."

Though the young church was formally monogamous, Robert Woodford states that when the Saints gathered at Kirtland, Ohio, in August 1835 to approve the D&C as scripture, a curious objection occurred. Two articles written by Oliver Cowdery were read and ordered to be placed in D&C by a vote of the church. One article was a statement on governments and laws that now appears as section 134 of D&C. The other article was read by William W. Phelps as shown in the following minutes: "President Wm. W. Phelps read the material dealing with the stated rules for marriage among the saints, and the whole church voted to receive it. Joseph Smith was not in attendance in this meeting and, therefore, was not able to voice his opinion concerning these statements; however, he evidently let it be known that at least this one did not meet with his approval" (Woodford, 3:1834).

Robert J. Woodford points out that given Smith's opposition to the Article on Marriage, it is noteworthy that he did not remove it from later editions of D&C. However, throughout the 1830s most church members were not ready to receive a revelation endorsing polygamy since polygamy was strongly condemned in the Book of Mormon.

The 1876 edition of the D&C replaced the Article on Marriage with Smith's 1843 revelation on polygamy (sec. 132). This change is quite significant, for the D&C now declared that the "new and everlasting covenant" included both celestial marriage (marriage for time and eternity) and earthly plural marriage. Mormon historian D. Michael Quinn explains that polygamy then became a critical part of Mormon doctrine and the church's mission. Church authorities went so far as to say that plural marriage was so important to Mormonism that to do away with it would be the destruction of the Church of Jesus Christ of Latter-day Saints.

However, Utah was seeking statehood in the 1870s, a status that would grant it more liberty than would persistence as a territory, and the practice of polygamy was a severe obstacle to statehood. The US Congress passed laws addressing bigamy and polygamy in 1862, 1874, and 1882, making it a criminal behavior. The Edmunds-Tucker Act of 1887 was passed for the purpose of disincorporating the church and receiving its assets because it sanctioned plural marriage. In September 1890, President Wilford Woodruff issued "the Manifesto" (Official Declaration 1 in current editions of the D&C), immediately and solemnly prohibiting any further practice of plural marriage, either as a ritual in the temples or as a practice throughout the territory. Woodruff's revelation undoubtedly arose from political expediency, and it took a good twenty years or more for the "official" declaration of 1890 to become established in practice.

Although abandonment of plural marriage was not immediate, eventually the principle of monogamy became universal throughout the church, notwithstanding objections of "fundamentalists" and others who pointed to endorsement of plural marriage by previous prophets and apostles.

Theological Considerations. Polygamy has consistently been a controversial issue for the

Mormon church, especially given that Joseph Smith advocated it, declaring the practice to be the most important doctrine ever given to man and essential to one's exaltation in the celestial kingdom. The later theology of Joseph Smith and Brigham Young ties plural marriage directly to salvation.

Mormon documents present a changing perspective on plural marriage. The church's earliest and foundational scripture, the Book of Mormon (1830), condemns polygamy in multiple locations. It is a "wicked practice" (Jacob 1:15), a "crime" committed by those who "seek to excuse themselves in committing whoredoms" (Jacob 2:23). The polygamy of David and Solomon "was abominable before me, saith the Lord" (Jacob 2:24), who demands monogamy (Jacob 2:27). In Mosiah 11:1–2, polygamy is associated with sin, abomination, "whoredoms and all manner of wickedness." Wicked king Riplakish had "many wives and concubines," which was evil "in the sight of the Lord" (Ether 10:5), and "he did afflict the people with his whoredoms" (10:7).

A scant five years later, Oliver Cowdery's disputed section 101 became part of the D&C. Though the text endorses monogamy, the introduction admits that "this church of Christ has been reproached with the crime of fornication, and polygamy," suggesting that the problem was not restricted to a few errant members. In truth there was an unpublished revelation in 1831 for already-married men to "take unto [them] wives of the Lamanites and Nephites" in their missionary work, but this revelation was not disclosed to most of the Saints.

Smith's revelation on plural marriage (D&C 132) became public knowledge another fifteen years or so later (ca. 1850–52), but section 132 did not become scripture until 1876, as noted earlier. Fourteen years later, the church evolved again, with the Manifesto of 1890 abrogating the commands of section 132.

A distinct feature of Mormonism is its claim to be the restored church. In this schema, not long after the completion of the New Testament, the church succumbed to false teaching, lost the true gospel, and fell into apostasy. This lasted until the nineteenth century, when God raised up Joseph Smith Jr. as his servant, the recipient of the restored gospel. So in the early 1830s and beyond, the Mormon Church considered itself to be the restoration of God's truth. Brigham Young taught that plural marriage was part of the restored gospel. In a revealing message printed in the *Journal of Discourses*, he states that according to the word of the Lord,

> if you desire with all your hearts to obtain the blessings which Abraham obtained, you will be polygamists at least in your faith, or you will come short of enjoying the salvation and the glory which Abraham has obtained. This is as true as that God lives. You who wish that there were no such thing in existence, if you have in your hearts to say: "we will pass along in the Church without obeying or submitting to it in our faith or believing this order, because, for aught that we know, this community may be broken up yet, and we may have lucrative offices offered to us; we will not, therefore, be polygamists lest we should fail in obtaining some earthly honor, character and office, etc."—the man that has that in his heart, and will continue to persist in pursuing that policy, will come short of dwelling in the presence of the Father and the Son, in celestial glory. The only men who become Gods, even the Sons of God, are those who enter into polygamy. (*JD* 11:268–69)

No less emphatic regarding the importance of plural marriage, Heber Kimball declared that opponents of plural marriage are listening to demons, condemned, and subject to God's curse. To repudiate plural marriage is to deny Mormonism. Polygamy is a holy principle and the means of salvation for mankind (*JD* 5:203–4).

Orson Pratt, considered one of Mormonism's greatest intellectuals and defenders, heartily defended polygamy in his sermon "God's Ancient People Polygamists." According to Pratt, Mormons stand to be condemned if they fail to accept plural marriage. He rebuked those who refused to enter into the principle, and he made this important observation: it is irrational to believe in the authority of the living prophet and yet refuse to abide by the prophet's authority.

If one portion of the doctrines of the Church is true, the whole of them are true. If the doctrine of polygamy, as revealed to the Latter-day Saints, is not true, I would not give a fig for all your other revelations that came through Joseph Smith the Prophet; I would renounce the whole of them, because it is utterly impossible, according to the revelations that are contained in these books, to believe a part of them to be divine—from God—and part of them to be from the devil; that is foolishness in the extreme; it is an absurdity that exists because of the ignorance of some people. I have been astonished at it. I did hope there was more intelligence among Latter-day Saints, and a greater understanding of principle than to suppose that any one can be a member of this Church in good standing, and yet reject polygamy. The Lord has said, that those who reject this principle reject their salvation, they shall be damned, saith the Lord; those to whom I reveal this law and they do not receive it, shall be damned. Now here comes in our consciences. We have either to renounce Mormonism, Joseph Smith, Book of Mormon, Book of Covenants, and the whole system of things as taught by the Latter-day Saints, and say that God has not raised up a church, has not raised up a prophet, has not begun to restore all things as he promised, we are obliged to do this, or else to say, with all our hearts,

"Yes, we are polygamists, we believe in the principle, and we are willing to practice it, because God has spoken from the heavens." (*JD* 17:224)

Pratt understood plural marriage to be a binding principle that was not optional for members of the Mormon Church. If it was indeed revealed to the church by God—and he firmly believed such to be the case—then plural marriage was to be practiced.

In the decades preceding 1890, Wilford Woodruff stated that the demise of polygamy meant the end of Mormonism. He made it clear that by God's command Mormons were to bear testimony to the revealed truth of plural marriage, regardless of the consequences. However, in 1890 Woodruff presented his revelation regarding polygamy known as the Manifesto, which brought to an end the practice of plural marriage.

The records of the leaders of the Church of Jesus Christ of Latter-day Saints make it clear that these men were unmistakably committed to the practice of plural marriage, considering it a nonnegotiable, doctrinal truth. They understood it to be essential to the very salvation of humankind and the only means by which one could enter into the celestial kingdom.

Given the obvious importance plural marriage was given in Mormonism prior to the manifesto of 1890, what do contemporary Mormons say about the practice? Modern Mormons do not agree that polygamy was of any great importance. Richard Winwood claims that according to Mormon doctrine, "plural marriage is not an essential principle of the gospel, nor is it preferable to monogamy. . . . Today, because God forbids the practice, all who engage in plural marriage are guilty of great wickedness and are subject to excommunication from the Church" (30, 31). Stephen Robinson, one of Mormonism's more popular and widely read theologians, essentially teaches that plural marriage is neither a universally binding practice nor an important gospel principle (92).

The demise of polygamy within the Church of Jesus Christ of Latter-day Saints poses several significant challenges to the church. First, the continuity of doctrinal truth is called into question. If leaders such as Wilford Woodruff, Orson Pratt, Brigham Young, Joseph Smith, and Heber Kimball were convinced that plural marriage was not only part of the restored gospel but essential to the very identity of and foundational to Mormonism, then why would it be terminated? Such changes not only bring discontinuity but also leave the church wide open to theological relativism, which means there are no doctrines in Mormonism that cannot change in the due course of time.

Second, there is discontinuity between church authorities. Though Mormons embrace both the standard works and the living prophet, the problem they face is, Which authority is to be followed? The historical theology or doctrinal development of plural marriage appears to be fraught with difficulty. It is part of the authoritative D&C yet condemned in the Book of Mormon. Early Mormon theologians such as Orson Pratt understood it to be foundational to the very integrity of Mormonism, as did Brigham Young, yet in 1890 it would be done away with, and anyone practicing it would be subject to excommunication. Though today it is considered relatively unimportant by modern Mormon scholars, their position on polygamy contradicts the teachings of respected Mormon leaders and theologians of the nineteenth century.

Third, if the doctrine of plural marriage was revealed to Joseph Smith Jr. and considered by other Mormon leaders and authorities to be part of the restored gospel, then it would be reasonable to conclude that the abandonment of plural marriage in 1890 constituted an apostasy from the fullness of the gospel. To get around this problem, one explanation is that plural marriage is reserved for those who make it to the celestial kingdom. But early Mormon teaching indicates plural marriage to be the very means by which one is granted access to the celestial kingdom.

See also CHURCH OF JESUS CHRIST OF LATTER-DAY SAINTS; POLYGAMY; SMITH, JOSEPH, JR.

Bibliography. T. Compton, "A Trajectory of Plurality: An Overview of Joseph Smith's Thirty-Three Plural Wives," *Dialogue*; Compton, *In Sacred Loneliness: The Plural Wives of Joseph Smith*; H. Kimball, "Reformation—Satisfaction Should Be Made to Parties Aggrieved—Practical Religion, &c," in *JD* 5; C. Miles, "Polygamy and the Economics of Salvation," *Sunstone*; O. Pratt, "God's Ancient People Polygamists [. . .]," in *JD* 17; D. M. Quinn, *The Mormon Hierarchy: Extensions of Power*; Quinn, *The New Mormon History*; S. Robinson, *Are Mormons Christians?*; R. S. Van Wagoner, *Mormon Polygamy: A History*; R. Winwood, *Take Heed That Ye Be Not Deceived*; R. Woodford, *The Historical Development of the Doctrine and Covenants*.

S. J. Rost and E. Pement

POLYGAMY. Polygamy is the practice of taking multiple marriage partners (from the Greek term meaning "many marriages") and has been accepted throughout human history. Polygamy was widely practiced in the ancient world and continues to be practiced in a few nations to this day. Several figures of the Old Testament, such as Abraham, David, and Solomon, had multiple wives, but by the time of the New Testament, monogamy was the generally accepted custom among Jews and later Christians. Interestingly, according to W. Luck, "When Henry VIII sought the counsel of [Martin] Luther on the morality of divorcing Catherine, he was told that it would be a lesser evil to simply marry Anne Boleyn as well! This is not considered the best advice of the German reformer" (228).

Among contemporary world religions, only Islam is still commonly associated with polygamy. This practice is often justified by the fact that Muhammad, the founder of Islam, reportedly had as many as twelve wives, and the Qur'an permits men to marry as many as four (sura 4:3), though most Muslims are monogamous. In Hinduism, Krishna, a leading diety, is said to have had over sixteen thousand wives, and polygamy was originally a part of the culture in which Hinduism grew, but modern Hinduism has largely abandoned the practice.

Few groups that desire to identify with Christianity would embrace the practice of polygamy. The Church of Jesus Christ of Latter-day Saints (Mormons) did practice polygamy in its early history but has not advocated it since the late nineteenth century, when the viewpoint ran afoul of an act of Congress and US Supreme Court rulings. Only small breakaway organizations from Mormonism support polygamy today. Other than Mormonism, there are a few independent advocates of polygamy who are not associated with any cult or religious organization but defend the practice on religious grounds. For example, a group calling itself an "Organization for Christian Polygamy," founded by Mark Henkel, maintains a website at truthbearer.org in defense of polygamy, based on biblical teachings. The group otherwise identifies itself with evangelical teachings.

See also CHURCH OF JESUS CHRIST OF LATTER-DAY SAINTS; HINDUISM; ISLAM, BASIC BELIEFS OF; KRISHNA; PLURAL MARRIAGE, MORMON TEACHING AND HISTORY OF

Bibliography. W. Luck, *Divorce and Remarriage: Recovering the Biblical View*; M. Zietzen, *Polygamy: A Cross-Cultural Analysis*.

J. P. Holding and E. Pement

POLYTHEISM. The worship or acknowledgment of multiple deities constitutes polytheism. First, I will provide an overview of the varieties of gods worshiped or acknowledged by polytheists. Second, I will classify polytheists by their attitudes toward these gods. Third, I will outline the roots of polytheism's contemporary popularity. Finally, I will provide an overview of Christian responses to polytheism now and in former periods.

Varieties of Gods. Jordan Paper distinguishes five categories of deities acknowledged or worshiped by polytheists today (14–15). The first is that of cosmic deities, such as the sun, the moon, the stars, and forces that govern weather. The second consists in spirits of animals, plants, and minerals, which figure prominently in shamanism. The third is that of ancestral spirits, usually honored only within extended families. The fourth comprises nonancestral ghosts (usually contacted through mediums) revered throughout a community or culture. The fifth is that of culture heroes such as Heracles and Prometheus, whom human beings rarely venerate but who play central roles in myths. To Paper's categories, one may reasonably add two: avatars or other manifestations of a single deity, frequently identified with the substance of the universe, and professedly mythological hypostatizations of elementary principles or impulses. Deities of the last category loom especially large in the forms of polytheism popular in Western societies today.

Most polytheists of all times have worshiped or acknowledged deities from several of the categories just enumerated. Shamans, for instance, besides performing acts with the aid of animal and plant spirits, frequently serve as mediums through whom one attempts to contact both ancestral and nonancestral ghosts. Countless persons who worship the sun, the moon, and the stars, moreover, delight in relating tales of culture heroes to young people in order to imbue them with the ethos of their community. Those who regard their narratives about gods as transparent fictions, similarly, often invoke a kaleidoscopic variety of deities.

Varieties of Polytheists. Less permeable boundaries seem to separate what one might call literal and figurative polytheists, the latter being persons who naively assent to tales about gods and goddesses and those who treat them as useful fictions. One ought not to distinguish too sharply between these groups, however, for two reasons. First, contemporary persons attracted to paganism, who belong to the second class initially, frequently slide at least functionally into the first as their religious practice grows more serious. Second, persons who belong at least functionally in the literal camp frequently respond to criticism of their faith by disputing the importance or meaningfulness of questions about its truth or falsehood. Polytheists and their spiritualities, to say the least, defy easy classification.

Sources of Contemporary Polytheism. The contemporary vogue for polytheism, it seems, derives from at least six sources. The first is Jungian psychology. Carl Jung and his followers teach that human beings require powerful symbols to divert their psychic energy from mundane tasks to higher cultural pursuits. The mythologies of polytheistic civilizations contain symbols of enormous power to move the human spirit. Predictably, therefore, Jungians commonly regard polytheistic mythology as a fruitful resource for the elevation of human consciousness.

The second root of polytheism's contemporary popularity lies in many persons' disillusionment with Christianity. Something must fill the vacuum left by the erosion of Christian faith in Western culture, and polytheistic spiritualities, to a certain extent, are fulfilling this role. Third, polytheism appeals to anti-Semites in Europe and North America. In order to liberate themselves from Jewish-influenced Christianity and its antiracist morals, neo-Nazi groups frequently seek to revive some form of ancient European paganism. Indeed, anti-Semitic neo-paganism played a central role in shaping the ideology of the original Nazi movement.

Fourth, ironically, polytheism seems conducive to religious tolerance. Especially in the wake of the events of September 11, 2001, many persons have come to view polytheism, according to which multiple gods can be equally real and legitimate, as preferable to monotheistic faiths, which cannot consistently acknowledge other religions' gods. Fifth, many contemporary persons are hostile toward authority. Whereas monotheistic religions typically portray human beings as automatically obliged to worship and obey God, certain polytheistic traditions regard devotion to particular gods as optional. Persons who harbor antiauthoritarian sentiments, naturally, find the latter approach to human-divine relations more congenial than the former.

A sixth root of contemporary enthusiasm for polytheism lies in its consonance with the ethical pluralism characteristic of today's world. Contemporary persons tend, in practice at least, to acknowledge several ultimate goods and to adjudicate conflicts between them on an ad hoc basis. Monotheistic religions, by contrast, typically recognize only one ultimate good—namely, God—and demand that human beings subordinate all else to him. One can reasonably trace polytheism's contemporary attractiveness, therefore, to six principal roots: Jungian psychology, mass disaffection from Christianity, the mutual affinity of Nazism and neo-paganism, polytheism's seeming conduciveness to tolerance, widespread hostility to authority, and ethical pluralism, the polytheism of values.

Christian Responses to Polytheism. Historically, Christians have responded to polytheism in at least three ways. First, they have sought to demythologize pagan gods. Ancient Christian authors, for instance, sought to falsify claims that pagan gods brought benefits to those who worshiped them and to expose myths about these gods as palpable frauds. Indeed, early Christian missionaries frequently destroyed sacred oaks and other monuments to pagan deities and then employed these deities' failure to avenge themselves as arguments against their existence or power (cf. Judg. 6:31). Present-day Christians might fruitfully supplement these efforts by observing that contemporary neo-pagan cults bear little genuine resemblance to the ancient polytheistic religions from which they claim descent.

Second, ancient Christians frequently called attention to the ethical failures of the gods of Greek myth and the atrocities, such as the sacrifice of infants, these gods sometimes demanded of their devotees. A tribe as prone to incest, murder, deceit, and petty quarreling as the Greek gods were, they argued, merited censure rather than praise from decent human beings. In a contemporary setting, likewise, one might call attention to the role of paganism in fostering murderous hatred in the Nazi era and today. One might also note that even the most benign forms of polytheism tend to encourage a relativism that weakens human beings' resolve to combat encroachments on human dignity.

Third, Christians of all ages have argued on philosophical grounds that polytheistic theologies are either incoherent or flatly contradictory to the data of human experience. Contemporary scientists, for instance, have good reason to believe that precisely the same physical laws operate in every sector of the universe. This is precisely what one would expect if the universe derived from a single Creator. It would seem highly counterintuitive, however, if the universe derived from a heterogeneous medley of deities.

Conclusion. Contemporary polytheism, therefore, seems especially liable to criticism on the grounds of its historical inauthenticity, its record of fostering hatred, and its discordance with the uniformity of the laws of nature. An effective apologetic against polytheistic religions, however, must combine criticisms of neuralgic points such as these with responses to the roots of polytheism's resurgence and with appreciation of the extraordinary diversity of polytheistic beliefs and practices.

See also MONOTHEISM

Bibliography. J. Campbell, *The Hero with a Thousand Faces*, 2nd ed.; N. Goodrick-Clarke, *Black Sun: Aryan Cults, Esoteric Nazism, and the Politics of Identity*; Goodrick-Clarke, *The Occult Roots of Nazism: Secret Aryan Cults and Their Influence on Nazi Ideology*; J. Hillman, *Re-Visioning Psychology*; W. James, *The Varieties of Religious Experience: A Study in Human Nature*; C. G. Jung, *Psychology and Religion: West and East*, ed. and trans. G. A. Hull and R. F. C. Hull, vol. 11 in *Collected Works of C. G. Jung*; D. L. Miller, *The New Polytheism: Rebirth of the Gods and Goddesses*; H. R. Niebuhr, *Radical Monotheism and Western Culture*; R. Noll, *The Jung Cult: Origins of a Charismatic Movement*; J. D. Paper, *The Deities Are Many*.

D. W. Jowers

PRABHUPADA, ABHAY CHARAN DE BHAKTIVEDANTA SWAMI. Abhay Charan de Bhaktivedanta Swami Prabhupada (1896–1977) is the founder of the International Society for Krishna Consciousness (known as ISKCON or Hare Krishna) religion. When he was twenty-six, Prabhupada was challenged by his guru to tell the English world about Caitanya Mahaprabhu (1486–1534), who, he believed, was the last incarnation of God known as Krishna. Prabhupada later founded a successful pharmaceutical company from which he retired in 1954 at the age of fifty-eight.

Prabhupada renounced worldly pleasures in 1959. He first came to the US from India in 1965, when he was seventy, having begged passage on a cargo ship and endured thirty-five days of an excruciating journey in which he suffered two separate heart attacks. Within six months after his arrival, Prabhupada had rented a small storefront in a shady neighborhood in New York City's Lower East Side. After he had recruited some followers, many of them hippies, ISKCON was incorporated in July 1966. Prabhupada regularly gave lectures and hosted chanting sessions at the New York storefront. Later he traveled to San Francisco to establish his religion on the West Coast. The Hare Krishna movement quickly grew, allowing Prabhupada to send disciples throughout the US and the world.

Prabhupada was a prolific writer, compiling more than fifty books in only eleven years while in the US (though much of his writing was transcribed from audiotapes). It is said that Prabhupada slept just three hours a day and ate little. He traveled around the world eight different times and initiated five thousand disciples. Prabhupada died in 1977 at the age of eighty-one.

See also INTERNATIONAL SOCIETY FOR KRISHNA CONSCIOUSNESS (ISKCON); KARMI; KRISHNA CONSCIOUSNESS

Bibliography. S. J. Gelberg, ed., *Hare Krishna, Hare Krishna*; Hare Krishna Home Page, http://www.harekrishna.com/; J. S. Judah, *Hare Krishna and the Counterculture*.

E. Johnson

PRANA. In Sanskrit *prana* means "breath." Originating from the Upanishads, the term is used widely in Indian philosophy. In Hinduism, at a cosmic level, prana is the impersonal all-pervading vital energy of the universe, synonymous with the Chinese *chi*. At an individual level, prana is the body's airs or energies, hence vitality. As the life force of an individual, prana is identified by some as "self."

In the New Age movement, prana is understood as the life force that affects energy centers (chakras) in the body. Hence Prana Yoga seeks to control prana (breath/breathing) so that the practitioner can meditate. *Pranayama* is one of the limbs of yoga as taught by Patanjali. Pranic healing includes a number of therapeutic practices that claim to manipulate prana flowing through the chakras, aiming to restore balance and flow in the body.

Prana is sometimes misunderstood as synonymous with the biblical *ruah* (Hebrew,

OT) and *pneuma* (Greek, NT). Prana assumes a monistic worldview, whereas *ruah* and *pneuma* are the breath/spirit of the living God who exists outside creation and actively animates organisms within creation.

See also CHAKRAS; HINDUISM; UPANISHADS

Bibliography. J. Mascaro, trans., *The Upanishads*.

H. P. Kemp

PRANAYAMA. *Pranayama* is the combination of two Sanskrit words: *prana* (life force, cosmic energy) and *yama* (self control), and refers to a breath-control meditation technique in yoga that seeks to control the life force in order to quiet it and balance it within one's body. Pranayama is achieved through inhalation, retention, and exhalation modulations and, in yoga, is a necessary step to deeper meditation. It is thought that through pranayama one can control one's mind because the prana "moves" the mind.

See also PRANA; YOGA

Bibliography. Sri Swami Sivananda, *The Science of Pranayama*.

H. P. Kemp

PRASADAM. In Sanskrit *prasadam* means "the Lord's mercy." Prasadam is ritually prepared food or drink that has been offered to a Hindu deity by devotees during worship. Persons who handle prasadam believe that when it is properly prepared and offered, the deity to whom it is presented "consumes" a portion of it, leaving his divine mark on the remains. These sacred leftovers are later distributed to worshipers of the deity as a token of his favor and as a means of their spiritual development. Since it is thought to have holy qualities, devotees cannot refuse prasadam when it is offered to them, and they are forbidden to dispose of it under any circumstances. Foods mentioned in the Bhagavad Gita as being appropriate for prasadam include grains, nuts, legumes, fruits, vegetables, and milk. Meat, fish, eggs, mushrooms, onions, garlic, coffee, and alcohol all are considered unfit for prasadam. The International Society for Krishna Consciousness (ISKCON) requires its members to consult a detailed set of instructions that regulate the preparation of food offered to Krishna. In contemporary Hindu practice in India, the desire to get prasadam and have *darshana* (i.e., a vision of, or being in the presence of, the divine) are the two major motivations of pilgrimages and temple visits.

See also BHAGAVAD GITA; HINDUISM; INTERNATIONAL SOCIETY FOR KRISHNA CONSCIOUSNESS (ISKCON)

Bibliography. S. R. Dasa, *Devotional Practice*; R. S. Khare, *The Eternal Food: Gastronomic Ideas and Experiences of Hindus and Buddhists*; N. Rajan, *Prasadam: Food of the Hindu Gods.*

J. Bjornstad

PRATT, ORSON. Born to Jared and Charity Pratt on September 19, 1811, in Washington County, New York, Orson Pratt was probably the most influential apologist for the Church of Jesus Christ of Latter-day Saints (LDS Church) during its early years, despite his very limited formal education. Not only did he write several works on topics relating to Mormonism; he also wrote on subjects pertaining to mathematics and astronomy. Many of his theories regarding astronomy were printed in LDS periodicals, though modern science has found several of his ideas to be flawed.

He joined Joseph Smith Jr.'s new movement shortly after it was formed in 1830. Baptized on his nineteenth birthday by his older brother Parley P. Pratt in 1830, he became an apostle in the church in 1835.

A very strong proponent of polygamy, he had seven wives and forty-five children. In August 1852, Pratt was asked by LDS president Brigham Young to publicly announce the practice of plural marriage at a special missionary conference. Pratt's ardent defense

of polygamy would lead to his appointment by Young to publish a periodical called the *Seer.* Its purpose was to make clear "the doctrines of the Church of Jesus Christ of Latter-day Saints, as revealed in both ancient and modern Revelations" (1). In this work, Pratt argued that God the Father and Jesus Christ were both practicing polygamists (172) and that God the Father personally "begat Jesus" through the Virgin Mary (158). He also maintained that God the Father "was begotten on a previous heavenly world by His Father" (132).

Pratt also carried Mormon doctrine to its logical conclusions by expounding on the teaching that Mormon men who eventually became Gods would also receive worship just as mortals now worship God the Father (*Seer*, 37). The *Seer* ran from January 1853 to August 1854.

Recognized as a fearless debater, Pratt was also a man who was known to speak his mind, even when it contradicted his ecclesiastical colleagues. At times this got him into trouble with both Joseph Smith and Brigham Young. His firm belief that God was always omniscient ran counter to Young's teachings that God was progressing in knowledge. Pratt also believed that Adam was made from the dust of *this* earth, whereas Young held that both Adam and Eve had earned their exaltation elsewhere. Said Young, "Adam was made from the dust of an earth, but not from the dust of this earth" (3:319). Pratt also vehemently disagreed with Young's Adam-God doctrine, which was first introduced by the Mormon prophet at a general conference in April 1852. Ultimately time has vindicated apostle Pratt's opposition to Young on these issues. Modern Mormonism denounces the idea that God is progressing in knowledge or that Adam is God, even though Mormonism's second president stubbornly defended both of these doctrines.

Defying the leadership of the church brought consequences. On April 10, 1875,

Brigham Young rearranged the order of seniority in the Quorum of the Twelve, thus placing three others ahead of Pratt. Had it not been for this realignment, Pratt would have succeeded Young as Mormonism's third president.

Diabetes took the life of Orson Pratt on October 3, 1881, at the age of seventy.

See also ADAM-GOD THEORY; CHURCH OF JESUS CHRIST OF LATTER-DAY SAINTS; PLURAL MARRIAGE, MORMON TEACHING AND HISTORY OF; POLYGAMY; PRATT, PARLEY; SMITH, JOSEPH, JR.; YOUNG, BRIGHAM

Bibliography. O. Pratt, *The Essential Orson Pratt*; Pratt, *The Seer*; R. S. Van Wagoner and S. C. Walker, *A Book of Mormons*; Brigham Young, "Disinclination of Men to Learn [. . .]," in *JD* 3.

W. McKeever

PRATT, PARLEY. Born in Burlington, New York, Parley Pratt (1807–57) converted to the Church of Jesus Christ of Latter-day Saints (LDS Church) on September 1, 1830, and was baptized by Oliver Cowdery, a close associate of LDS founder Joseph Smith Jr. On the same day, he was ordained an elder. On his first missionary journey, he baptized his former minister, Sidney Rigdon, as well as his younger brother Orson. On June 6, 1831, Joseph Smith ordained Parley to the high priesthood. Both Parley and Orson would later become apostles in Joseph Smith's church.

Parley Pratt is credited with writing several Mormon hymns and, like his brother Orson, was also involved in publishing books and periodicals that defended the Mormon faith.

A practicing polygamist, he had a total of twelve wives, the most controversial of whom was Eleanor J. McComb McLean. McLean was not yet divorced from her husband, Hector, when Brigham Young sealed her to Parley in marriage. Hector vowed to kill Pratt and did so on May 13, 1857.

See also CHURCH OF JESUS CHRIST OF LATTER-DAY SAINTS; PLURAL MARRIAGE, MORMON TEACHING AND HISTORY OF; POLYGAMY; PRATT, ORSON; SMITH, JOSEPH, JR.; YOUNG, BRIGHAM

Bibliography. R. S. Van Wagoner and S. C. Walker, *A Book of Mormons*.

W. McKeever

PRATYEKA BUDDHA. A (Sanskrit) Pratyeka (Pali, Pacceka) Buddha is a solitary person who attains perfect insight into the interdependent origination of all things by means of his own rigorous spiritual practices, apart from having been taught by an enlightened instructor. Such Buddhas are thought to exist only during those periods of history in which the dharma (Buddhist teachings) have been lost. They are neither willing nor able to teach other devotees about the doctrines of Buddhism but speak (occasionally) only concerning matters of ethics and ritual practice. Unlike bodhisattvas, who return to the world of illusion after attaining enlightenment so as to help unenlightened beings in their quest for liberation, Pratyeka Buddhas enter nirvana at the first opportunity, leaving all other beings behind. Differing schools of Buddhism debate whether the choice of a Pratyeka Buddha not to aid his fellow beings is selfish and whether Pratyeka Buddhas are all-knowing. Pratyeka Buddhas are esteemed more highly in Theravada Buddhism than in Mahayana Buddhism.

See also BODHISATTVAS; BUDDHISM; DHARMA; MAHAYANA BUDDHISM; THERAVADA BUDDHISM

Bibliography. R. Gethin, *The Foundations of Buddhism*; P. Harvey, *An Introduction to Buddhism: Teachings, History and Practices*; M. Wijayaratna, *Buddhist Monastic Life: According to the Texts of the Theravada Tradition*.

H. W. House

PREEXISTENCE, MORMON VIEW OF. Preexistence in Mormon theology is the pre-earth life of the spirit children of God. These spirit children of God are both male and female, possessing spirit bodies composed of a pure, refined substance. As with all spirit children, Jesus Christ and Lucifer (who were also preexistent spirit children) were born through the procreative act of heavenly parents. According to Heavenly Father's plan, Jesus was selected to be the savior of the world, but Lucifer desired this role as well. In response Lucifer offered to come to earth and exercise dominion over humankind by imposing salvation on even the unwilling. Lucifer's proposal was in direct conflict with free agency, so his offer was rejected. In response Lucifer rebelled against his father and influenced one-third of the spirit children to follow him. As a result of this rebellion, Lucifer became Satan and the spirit children who followed him in his rebellion became demons.

The preexistent state is the first stage in the overall eternal progression of the spirit child toward final exaltation. In the preexistent state, spirit children exercise agency, which is the ability to choose between good and evil. If, in the preexistent state, spirit children exercise their free agency wisely, they are sent to earth to receive mortal bodies, which is the second phase of eternal progression.

During the earthly sojourn, individuals are put through what Joseph Fielding Smith describes as mortal probation. Through this process, each person must make choices, either good or evil. The wise use of agency is membership in the Church of Jesus Christ of Latter-day Saints, baptism, temple marriage, adherence to temple rituals, and overall obedience to the fullness of the gospel. At death those who have persevered in their commitment to the fullness of the gospel enter into the celestial kingdom and, through ongoing wise use of agency, eventually achieve exaltation.

See also CHURCH OF JESUS CHRIST OF LATTER-DAY SAINTS; EXALTATION; LUCIFER, MORMON VIEW OF

Bibliography. B. McConkie, *Mormon Doctrine*; B. Ostler, "The Idea of Preexistence in Mormon Thought," in *Line upon Line: Essays on Mormon Doctrine*; R. Rhodes, *Reasoning from the Scriptures with the Mormons.*

S. J. Rost

PROCESS THEOLOGY. Process thought can be traced as far back as the Greek philosopher Heraclitus in 500 BC, with its present form originating in the early twentieth century with mathematician and philosopher Alfred North Whitehead. Only after being sufficiently developed by philosopher Charles Hartshorne, a student of the Whiteheadian system, did process theology gain prominence in its challenge to classical and biblical theism. A natural theology with an appeal to scientific verification and experiential accessibility, process theology has been highly influential in the theological scholarship of the second half of the twentieth century, particularly among non-evangelicals. Noted process theologians include John B. Cobb Jr., David Ray Griffin, Norman Pittenger, Schubert Ogden, Daniel Day Williams, Ewert Cousins, and others.

Process theology departs from historical Christian tenets on the doctrines of the nature of God, the nature and work of Jesus, and the sin nature of humans, particularly as it is defined by classical or Thomistic theism. Process, or *becoming*, rather than *being*, is fundamental to its views of creation, reality, and God. To be *actual* is to be in process. Whereas human existence is understood to be in process "for a time," God is understood to be always in process, continually surpassing himself as he changes through experience.

God and the world are thought to be inseparable. Process theologians distinguish their system of belief from pantheism (all is God), preferring instead the term *panentheism* (all is in God). God and the world are not identical, but the events and experiences of the world are encompassed within the life of God. Human freedom is paramount, and God's actions are limited to persuasion, rather than intervention, in luring creation toward more creative and more satisfying aesthetic goals.

Alfred North Whitehead (1861–1947), the son of an Anglican vicar, had an early interest in theology that faded in adulthood. After a full academic career in mathematics and in philosophy of science at Cambridge, Whitehead accepted a chair of philosophy at Harvard, where his interest in metaphysics and philosophical theism developed.

Whitehead was not unaffected by the revolution taking place within the scientific world during his lifetime. On the heels of the advent of Darwin's *Origin of the Species* came Einstein's theories of relativity and the reexamination of long-held tenets of physics. Within this atmosphere, Whitehead took upon himself an investigation into a philosophy of nature, a study that later played a part in his process theism. Whitehead developed his metaphysical system based on process in his work *Process and Reality*.

Whitehead's distinctive view of reality utilized the atomic theory: actual events are made up of smaller, atomic events of extremely short duration. Time also is not continuous but comes into being in small bundles, perishing immediately and giving rise to the next bundle, or event. In a reversal of the ordinary understanding of a cause producing an effect, Whitehead understood the lapse of time between these atomic events, or "actual occasions," to mean that an occasion actively produces itself out of past, perished events. Whitehead fashioned the word *prehension* to refer to the way in which each event spontaneously and creatively takes account of past data, unifies those data, and produces itself. Personal human existence is seen as a "society of occasions," a series of ordered individual occasions of experience.

Creatio ex nihilo, the biblical doctrine that God created the world out of nothing, is rejected by process theology. Instead, process theology views the world as fashioned from preexistent matter in a process that allows for the creative self-determination of each occasion. Hartshorne held the view that this universe was created out of an earlier universe, which was created from an earlier one, ad infinitum.

Relatedness is essential to the process view of reality and ties the world's significance to its ability to affect God and enrich his experience. The immutable God of classical theism is understood by process theologians to be static and unable to respond to human experience and suffering. Completeness or perfection as an attribute of God is unacceptable to the process thinker, who understands it to mean that God would be incapable of existing in relationship. In process theology, God does not exist substantively apart from his relatedness to other events and occasions and therefore must have a world to which he can relate. Hartshorne reasoned that whereas God was free to create a world different from this one, he was never free not to create.

Whitehead fashioned a dipolar system in which he described God as having two poles or natures, a primordial nature and a consequent nature. Hartshorne identifies the two poles as an abstract (transcendent) pole and a concrete (contingent) pole. Regarding God's consequent/concrete pole, Whitehead and Hartshorne are largely in agreement, understanding the pole to be the world and the actualization of God's potentialities. In this pole, God is temporal, relative, finite, and constantly changing as he responds in empathy to worldly beings. God's knowledge is limited to what is knowable up to that moment. He knows the events as they happen, and he responds to them as the "fellow sufferer who understands." Open theism bears a likeness to process thought on this point.

Hartshorne's view of the other pole is distinguishable from Whitehead's, in that Hartshorne interprets the primordial/abstract pole to be what God is eternally, at every moment in his life, and Hartshorne refers to this pole as absolute, transcendent, necessary, eternal, or immutable. Whitehead represents this pole as the creative activity that persuasively nudges the universe to new and novel achievements by providing an "initial aim" to which every actuality can aspire. As such the primordial/abstract pole is a limitless reservoir of possibilities and is persuasive, adventurous, creative, and focused on promoting the enjoyment of each actuality. Process thinkers will refer to the abstract pole as the "mind" or "soul" of God and to the world as the "body" of God, what he is as an actualized entity.

John B. Cobb Jr. and David Ray Griffin, in their work *Process Theology: An Introductory Exposition*, present the dipolar nature of God as a wholly integrated unit. Therefore, they recognize a point of affinity with the Taoist notion of the Tao, in which the two dimensions of the power that moves the universe, the "feminine and masculine (yin and yang)," are in perfect harmony, an element they deem to be worthy of inclusion in the Christian view of God.

Logos is identified with the primordial nature and is seen as the "initial aim" provided to help an actuality or on occasion produce itself in a way that will be novel and enjoyable. The incarnate Logos is called Christ and is not uniquely identified with Jesus but is seen as a creative transformation available to all. Jesus is viewed as a man more fully open to the Logos than any other human, rather than as the absolutely unique, second member of the Godhead in human flesh. In this sense, process theologians will speak of the Christ presence in Jesus. Different in degree rather than in kind, Jesus is seen as completely and fully human and divine only in the sense that he was a special instrument of God's presence and activity.

Process theology rejects the orthodox Christian doctrine of the Trinity, a Godhead of three persons consisting of Father, Son, and Holy Spirit. Rather, the trinitarian language used in process theology is used in a modalistic manner, referring to a "tri-unity" of principles representing the manner in which God acts or to different aspects of the creative process.

The existence of evil in the world is not seen as the outgrowth of a fallen human nature in process theology. A dipolar God can only hope to persuade creation to move toward loftier goals but cannot control the choices made by earthly creatures. Evil, then, over which he has no control and no power to stop, exists. Although God feels for his creatures in their suffering, he is not culpable for their suffering. All experiences, both good and bad, are taken up into the life and memory of God and harmonized, thus making right the wrongs of the world.

Critics of process theology point out that a forced dichotomous choice between classical theism and process theology is unnecessary and sets up a "straw man" argument. Without embracing panentheism, one can still affirm a biblically sound doctrine of a God who is unchanging in attributes, character, and purposes and who, at the same time, lovingly interacts with his creation.

Process thought draws criticism for failing to adequately address the most fundamental of metaphysical questions: Why is there anything at all? What is the ultimate source of the universe? Critics also propose that process theology fails to explain how God's infinite potentialities become actualized in a concrete world since potentiality cannot actualize itself. The appeal to "creativity" that is often made in process thought does not satisfactorily answer these questions but instead brings into the discussion another, ill-defined entity with a status seemingly above God.

Essentially anthropocentric in approach, process theology sees the actualization of human potential in the service of a better world as its goal. Biblical theists are theocentric and place ultimate value on service to the glory of God and his kingdom rather than on personal enrichment.

See also CHRISTIAN; CHRISTIAN, USE AND MISUSE OF THE TERM; MODALISM; ORTHODOXY

Bibliography. J. B. Cobb Jr., *A Christian Natural Theology based on the Thought of Alfred North Whitehead*; J. B. Cobb Jr. and D. R. Griffin, *Process Theology: An Introductory Exposition*; L. S. Ford, *The Lure of God: A Biblical Background for Process Theism*; R. Gruenler, *The Inexhaustible God: Biblical Faith and the Challenge of Process Theism*; C. Hartshorne, *The Divine Relativity: A Social Conception of God*; R. Nash, ed., *Process Theology*; A. N. Whitehead, *Process and Reality: An Essay in Cosmology*.

M. Stewart

PROVIDENCE OF GOD. The word *providence* refers to God's control over his creation. It concerns God's superintendence of history and his working to fulfill his good purposes in the world. Christians have traditionally held that God's providential control is *meticulous*. God guides the events in his creation so that nothing happens that is outside his plan and over which he has no control. This is a "no risk" view of providence according to which there are no accidents in God's creation. God leaves nothing to chance.

Several Christian confessions articulate the view of meticulous providence. For example, the Westminster Confession of Faith says that "God, from all eternity, did, by the most wise and holy counsel of His own will, freely and unchangeably ordain whatsoever comes to pass" (chap. 3) and that "God . . . doth uphold, direct, dispose, and govern all creatures, actions, and things, from the greatest even unto the least, by His most wise and holy providence" (chap. 5).

There is much biblical support for God's meticulous providence over his creation. One key text is Daniel 4:35, in which King Nebuchadnezzar declares of God: "All the inhabitants of the earth are accounted as nothing, and he does what he wills with the host of heaven and the inhabitants of the earth. There is no one can stay his hand or say to him, 'What are you doing?'" We are told that God does *his* will in his creation, even when it comes to the lives of human beings. Paul also tells us that God "accomplishes all things according to his counsel and will" (Eph. 1:11). Further evidence of God's meticulous providence includes Jesus's teaching that the hairs of our heads are numbered and that creatures as insignificant as sparrows do not fall to the ground without God's knowledge (Matt. 10:29–30). Further, Christians are assured that "all things work together for good for those who love God" (Rom. 8:28). And David expressed his confidence that God had ordained the course of his life before he was born (Ps. 139:16).

Biblical support for meticulous providence is also found in the covenantal structure of Scripture. In 2 Timothy 1:9, we read that God gave us the grace to be found in Christ "before the ages began" (cf. Titus 1:2). This appears to indicate that the fall and God's subsequent plan of redemption (cf. Gen. 3:15) were not an ad hoc "Plan B" after an original experiment in the garden failed. Rather, God intended to redeem fallen sinners from all eternity, which means that the fall and the historical unfolding of the covenant of grace leading to the first advent of Christ were God's one and only plan—a plan that he meticulously guided to its completion, as Peter declared at Pentecost (Acts 2:23).

The "no risk" view of providence is not without its problems, however. At first glance, it would seem to conflict with human freedom and responsibility. In fact, an argument may be constructed to attempt to prove that God's meticulous providence is incompatible with human freedom and responsibility:

1. If God exercises meticulous providence, then no human being could do other

than he or she does (i.e., no human being has free will).

2. If no human being could do other than he does, then no human being is morally responsible for his actions.

3. Hence, if God exercises meticulous providence, then no human being is morally responsible for his actions.

The upshot of this argument is that it would force a choice between human freedom and God's meticulous providence. That is, assuming the argument is sound, we would have to either give up on human freedom and responsibility or weaken our view of divine providence.

Christian thinkers have attempted to address this problem in several ways. Perhaps the simplest is to accept the conclusion of the above argument and reject the "no risk" view of providence. This is the strategy of those who hold the view known as open theism. On this view, God exercises not meticulous providence but only a general providence. God establishes certain structures or boundaries that delimit what free creatures are able to do, but within those boundaries free creatures are free to make choices that are not controlled, intended, or planned by God. That is, God allows human beings to make free choices within the general framework he has created. Many of the events that take place in creation have no specific, God-ordained purpose. Indeed, in this view, many things may happen in creation that God does not want to happen. Though God does have a general plan for his creation, many of the details of that plan are determined by the choices of human beings. Of course, as open theists admit, this view of providence introduces significant risk into God's plan, with the result that things may not turn out exactly as God would have them.

The "risk" view of providence has difficulty, however, reconciling itself with the biblical data outlined above that seem to indicate that God exercises meticulous control over his creation. Moreover, when we introduce risk into God's plan, it is difficult to see how we can have any confidence that God will be able to fulfill his promises to his redeemed people. Many aspects of God's plan of redemption as revealed in Scripture require the cooperation of human beings (e.g., Abraham's obedience to God's call and Pilate's complicity in Jesus's crucifixion). But if God exercises no control over the choices of human beings, then it is possible that his plan of redemption could fail. Because of these and other significant problems associated with open theism (especially its denial of God's foreknowledge of future human choices), most evangelicals do not see this approach to the puzzle of providence and freedom as a viable option.

Among those who take a "no risk" view of providence, we may distinguish three different approaches to resolving the problem. One is called Ockhamism (after the medieval philosopher William of Ockham). According to this view, God controls the future by utilizing his foreknowledge of what human beings will freely choose. That is, since God knows what each person will do at every point in the future, he may, like a grand chess master, act in history so as to guide events toward his desired goals without violating human freedom. For example, suppose God knew ahead of time that terrorists would destroy the World Trade Center on September 11, 2001. He also knows that a businessman named Jack plans to be in the WTC on that day, but God does not want Jack to be killed. So God causes a truck to blow a tire and block the freeway, preventing Jack from making it to the WTC that day. The Ockhamist, then, denies premise 1 of the above argument, claiming that God's exercising meticulous providence does not imply that human beings cannot do other than they do. It only implies that God, using his foresight, intervenes in human affairs when necessary to influence (and sometimes prevent) certain events.

The problem for the Ockhamist, though, is that it is unclear how God's foreknowledge gives him the kind of providential control described in the above scenario. For what God foreknows is not simply what might happen but what *will* happen. That is, every event that he foreknows *will inevitably take place*. Prior to any intervention on God's part, he already knows whether the truck blows a tire, whether Jack makes it to the WTC, and whether he is killed in the explosion. How then can God use his foreknowledge of what will take place to intervene and *alter* any course of events? Since God infallibly knows everything that *will* occur, the future is already set in exhaustive detail. God cannot utilize his foreknowledge, then, to alter what he foresees; otherwise he would not have foreseen it in the first place.

Another "no risk" view of providence is called Molinism (after the Jesuit philosopher Luis de Molina). Like Ockhamism, Molinism denies premise 1 of the argument against the compatibility of freedom and providence. According to Molinism, God has a type of knowledge known as "middle knowledge," which refers to God's knowledge not simply of what will or might happen but of what free agents *would* do in hypothetical or counterfactual circumstances. This means that God knows a particular class of statements called *counterfactuals of freedom*, statements about free agents that take the form, "If person *S* were placed in circumstance *C*, then *S* would do action *x*." God is alleged to know these kinds of statements even if person *S* never actually exists or circumstance *C* never actually occurs, and he knows them prior to his creation of the world.

If God were to have such middle knowledge, he would be able to meticulously control the course of history by creating that possible world (i.e., maximal set of circumstances) where free creatures freely choose to do those things that God wants them to do. So before creating the world, God observes all the possible worlds that he might create, and he creates that world in which the choices of human beings most closely approximate his plan for history. And once he creates that world, the course of history will unfold as God intends in every detail. God thus has strong control over his creation without endangering human freedom or responsibility.

One potential difficulty for Molinism, however, has to do with whether there could be any true counterfactuals of freedom. If human beings have free will, so that nothing determines their actions, then arguably there is no means to know what a free agent would do in a hypothetical situation. If not, then God cannot have middle knowledge.

Perhaps a more serious problem is the apparent weakening of divine providence in the Molinist view. It is not up to God but to free creatures to determine which counterfactuals of freedom are true. Thus, if God (before he creates) has a particular plan for how he would like history to turn out, his ability to fulfill that plan is entirely consequent on what the free creatures he might create would do. This entails the notion that God is able to create a world that closely matches his plan *only if he is lucky*! Despite its allowance for the meticulous unfolding of God's plan after creation, Molinism does seem to diminish God's sovereignty in this way.

All of the first three solutions to the providence-freedom puzzle assume a view of freedom known as *libertarianism*. According to libertarianism, a person has free will (and moral responsibility) just in case he has the "ability to do otherwise," which means that when an agent chooses to do some action *x*, in the very same circumstances, he could have refrained from doing *x*. It is the assumption of libertarianism that motivates both the Ockhamist and the Molinist to reject premise 1 of the argument for the incompatibility of providence and freedom.

A third "no risk" view, however, rejects libertarianism and grants the truth of premise 1: providence *does* imply that people cannot do other than what they do. This view, known as compatibilism, rejects the second premise instead. The compatibilist argues that not having the ability to do otherwise does not undermine moral responsibility. As long as an agent does what she *wants* to do in a given situation, she is morally responsible for her actions even if she does not have free will in the libertarian sense.

Compatibilism has the advantage of preserving the strongest possible view of divine providence. It is also consistent with the biblical data that speak of human actions being under God's control (Exod. 7:3; Prov. 16:4, 9; 21:1; Dan. 4:35; etc.). Of course, it is no easy matter to explain how human beings can be responsible for actions that they could not avoid. Compatibilism also has a more difficult problem than the other views with exonerating God from being the author of evil.

None of the proposed solutions to the providence-freedom puzzle is without problems. Yet any of the "no risk" views is a viable option for evangelicals, with none of their apparent problems being insuperable obstacles from a biblical point of view.

See also OPENNESS OF GOD

Bibliography. D. Basinger and R. Basinger, eds., *Predestination and Free Will*; J. K. Beilby and P. R. Eddy, eds., *Divine Foreknowledge: Four Views*; G. C. Berkouwer, *General Revelation*; Center for Reformed Theology and Apologetics, Westminster Confession of Faith, http://www.reformed .org/documents/wcf_with_proofs/; W. L. Craig, *The Only Wise God: The Compatibility of Divine Foreknowledge and Human Freedom*; B. A. Demarest, *General Revelation*; J. M. Fischer, ed., *God, Foreknowledge and Freedom*; P. Helm, *The Providence of God*; J. Sanders, *The God Who Risks*; T. R. Schreiner and B. A. Ware, eds., *The Grace of God, the Bondage of the Will*, 2 vols.; R. C Sproul, J. Gerstner, and A. Lindsley, *Classical Apologetics*.

S. B. Cowan

P'U/PU. A fundamental feature of Taoism, *p'u* ("uncut wood" in Chinese) is a state of moral and epistemic purity in which a person views the world without being affected by corrupting desires and presuppositions, analogous to an uncarved block of wood. It carries the idea of not obstructing nature's "flow." Taoism maintains that the most basic reality of the universe and human existence— the Tao—is simple and uncomplicated, yet people persist in imposing complexities on nature, culture, and their relationships with all things. These unnecessarily complicated ways of engaging the world burden people with a tendency toward being arrogant and pretentious rather than humble and unassuming and consequently impede their ability to flow with the Tao. Much of the problem stems from the innumerable ways in which societies "carve" their members, such that the government and larger community benefit materially at the expense of their individual members' spiritual flourishing.

See also TAOISM/DAOISM

Bibliography. J. Oldstone-Moore, *Understanding Taoism*; H. Welch, *Taoism: The Parting of the Way*.

R. L. Drouhard

PUJA. In Sanskrit *puja* literally means "adoration." The term is used generically to mean "worship" in both Hinduism and Buddhism. *Puja* may also refer to specific ritual acts of worship to a deity, Buddha, or a bodhisattva and ceremonial acts within a community. The word was originally used with connotations of animal sacrifice but has been modified to refer to both public and private ceremonies that involve offerings of flowers, pastes, incense, water, fruit, and/or money.

See also BUDDHISM; HINDUISM

Bibliography. A. Michaels and B. Harshav, *Hinduism, Past and Present.*

H. P. Kemp

PURE LAND BUDDHISM. Pure Land Buddhism, or Amidism, is the most popular Buddhist sect in East Asia. It claims that since the dharma (the Buddha's teaching) is decaying, enlightenment cannot be attained by traditional Buddhist means of self-effort, austerity, insight, or accumulation of merit and, therefore, an intermediate state is needed. The authoritative texts are the Pure Land Sutras (pre–second century AD), which describe a monk named Dharmakara (not to be confused with *dharmakaya*), who made a number of vows—the eighteenth vow was to assist all who called on his name; these would then enjoy peace, happiness, long life, and freedom from want and pain in his Pure Land, named (Sanskrit) Sukhavati (literally, "decorated with bliss," and wrongly called in English "western paradise"), which he would create when he became Amitabha Buddha.

Amitabha now sits in his Pure Land, assisting peoples' entrance. He is flanked by two attendant bodhisattvas: Avalokiteshvara (the bodhisattva of compassion—Chenrezig in Tibet and Kwan Yin in China) and Mahasthamaprapta (the bodhisattva of wisdom and strength—Seishi in Japanese). Technically, rebirth into the Pure Land is a means to the ultimate goal of nirvana, but in reality, for those who understand the Pure Land as a metaphor, it is a symbol for nirvana, and thus residence in the Pure Land is perceived as the primary goal. Hence, liberation is through personal *darshanic* relation with Amitabha, sometimes referred to as by "faith"; by invoking his name, especially if near death, one relies on Amitabha's compassion and merit so that one can be conveyed to the Pure Land.

The Pure Land sect was founded in China in 402 by Hui-Yuan. Pure Land spread throughout China, often by the preaching of the contrast of the torments of hell with the future paradise-like Pure Land. Monks of the Tendai school took Pure Land to Japan, where it was further developed by Honen (1133–1212), who encouraged people to renounce the sophisticated philosophies of Mahayana Buddhism and recite only the formula *Namu amida butsu* ("praise to Amitabha Buddha"—known as the *nembutsu*) with a pure heart.

Honen's disciple Shinran (1173–1262) took this to its logical conclusion by discarding austerities and especially monasticism, declaring that any reliance on one's own efforts for enlightenment other than the recitation of the nembutsu portrayed a lack of trust in Amitabha. Shinran proposed that saying the nembutsu was required only once for liberation (rather than continuously, according to Honen), and subsequently all further recitations of the nembutsu were an expression of gratitude for the liberation that was assured from the moment that trust was expressed. Hence, exclusive trust in Amitabha (rather than the efficacy of the nembutsu or other deities) is characteristic. Shinran's innovations, known as *shin*, or the "true" sect, became the dominant sect in Japan.

Shin Buddhism (a.k.a. Jodo Shinshu) remains the largest Pure Land sect and continues to play a significant role in Japanese cultural life through the arts and educational and social welfare programs. In 1899 two Shin missionaries arrived in the US. Since then, accompanied by Japanese immigration, the Jodo Shinshu movement has grown into the Buddhist Churches of America, headquartered in San Francisco. Membership peaked in 1977 at 21,600 members (mainly Japanese), and by 1997 claimed sixty temples with sixty-one priests.

See also BODHISATTVA; BUDDHIST CHURCHES OF AMERICA; DARSHANA; DHARMA; MAHAYANA BUDDHISM; SHIN BUDDHISM

Bibliography. T. Kashima, *Buddhism in America*, Contributions in Sociology 26; C. S.

Prebish and K. K. Tanaka, *The Faces of Buddhism in America*; D. R. Williams and C. S. Queen, *American Buddhism: Methods and Findings in Recent Scholarship*.

H. P. Kemp

PURIM (THE FEAST OF LOTS). Today there are nine major feasts or holy seasons of Israel. One is the Feast of Purim, or the Feast of Lots, a feast inaugurated in the book of Esther. *Purim* is the plural form of the singular word *pur*, meaning "lot," so Purim means "lots." The reason this name was given to the feast is explained in Esther 9:24: because Haman had cast pur, the lot, to decide which day to destroy the Jews (Esther 3:7; 9:24). The feast is celebrated on the fourteenth of Adar, which corresponds to sometime in February or March. It celebrates the salvation of the people of Israel from the evil Haman, through the valiant efforts of Queen Esther. In modern Israel, on the night of Purim thousands congregate in streets closed off to vehicles. It is a raucous celebration involving impromptu music and dancing, special foods (especially a sweet triangular pastry known as *hamantashen*),

face painting, plays, and the reading of the Meghillah (the scroll of Esther). Traditional rabbinic mores about public drunkenness are relaxed during Purim, and rabbinic law concerning personal injury restitution due to drunkenness is suspended.

Another tradition is the noisemaker known as a "grogger." It is used whenever Haman's name comes up during the reading of the book of Esther. When the listeners sound the grogger, they stamp their feet. Haman's name is mentioned fifty-four times, so the audience gives this response that many times. They also do it when the ten sons of Haman are named, for a total of sixty-four times.

See also JUDAISM

Bibliography. Rabbi A. Gold and Rabbi N. Scherman, *Purim—Its Observance and Significance*; R. Posner, *Minor and Modern Festivals*; C. Roth, "Purim," in *Encyclopedia Judaica*; H. Schauss, *The Jewish Festivals: History & Observance*; I. Singer, "Purim," in *The Jewish Encyclopedia*; M. Strassfeld, *The Jewish Holidays: A Guide & Commentary*; Y. Vainstein, *The Cycle of the Jewish Year: A Study of the Festivals and of Selections from the Liturgy*.

A. Fruchtenbaum

QUAKERS. *See* RELIGIOUS SOCIETY OF
FRIENDS (QUAKERS)

QUORUM OF THE SEVENTY. A Quorum of
the Seventy is a group of male leaders of the
Church of Jesus Christ of Latter-day Saints
(LDS Church) who have been set apart for
the purpose of proclaiming the Mormon
gospel to non-Mormons. Each Quorum of
the Seventy is overseen by seven presidents,
each of whom is a member of that same
quorum and corporately manages that quorum's affairs; moreover, each subgroup of
seven presidents is governed by a presiding
president. Though under the direct super-
vision of the Quorum of the Twelve Apostles and indirectly accountable to the First
Presidency, members of these quorums are
invested with the same authority as that
of the Twelve Apostles appointed by LDS
Church founder Joseph Smith Jr. (1805–44).
As of November 2013, the LDS Church had
eight seventy-member quorums: two (the
first and second) that are general authorities
with global jurisdiction and six (the third
through eighth) that are area authorities
with distinct regional jurisdictions.

The First Quorum of the Seventy met in
1835 and counted Joseph Young (1797–1881)
and Levi Ward Hancock (1803–82) among
its seven presidents. By 1845 there were ten
quorums of seventy, geographically unrestricted and dispersed worldwide. In 1883
LDS president John Taylor (1808–87) gave
each seventy-member quorum authority over
a particular LDS stake. This arrangement

continued until 1975–76, when LDS president Spencer W. Kimball (1895–1985) reorganized the LDS Church, merging the First
Quorum of the Seventy, the First Council of
the Seventy, and the Assistants to the Twelve
into a new First Quorum of the Seventy. In
1989 the Second Quorum of the Seventy was
formed. In 1997 LDS president Gordon B.
Hinckley (1910–2008) announced the formation of the Third, Fourth, and Fifth Quorums of the Seventy, which were assembled
to replace the former regional representatives
of the Quorum of the Twelve. In 2004 the
Fifth Quorum of the Seventy was divided to
create the Sixth Quorum of the Seventy; the
Seventh and Eighth Quorums of the Seventy
were formed in 2005.

See also CHURCH OF JESUS CHRIST OF
LATTER-DAY SAINTS

Bibliography. S. Fidel, "President Hinckley
Announces New Quorums of the Seventy and
Other New Officers," *Deseret News*; D. L. Larson, "Seventy: Quorums of Seventy," in *Encyclopedia of Mormonism*, edited by D. H. Ludlow,
4 vols.; A. K. Parrish, "Seventy: Overview," in
Encyclopedia of Mormonism, edited by D. H.
Ludlow, 4 vols.; L. A. Porter, "A History of the
Latter-Day Seventy," *Ensign*; "Quorums of the
Seventy," https://www.lds.org/church/leaders
/quorums-of-the-seventy; R. C. Roberts, "Seventy: First Council of the Seventy," in *Encyclopedia of Mormonism*, edited by D. H. Ludlow,
4 vols.; Joseph Smith Jr. et al., *The Doctrine
and Covenants of the Church of Jesus Christ
of Latter-day Saints*; J. Young, *History of the
Organization of the Seventies*.

H. W. House

QUORUM OF THE TWELVE APOSTLES. *See* QUORUM OF THE SEVENTY

QUR'AN. The holy book of Islam believed by Muslims to be the words of God given to the Prophet Muhammad (d. 632) over the period of his twenty-two years of ministry is called the Qur'an. The word Qur'an appears seventy-three times inside the book and appears to mean "recitation" (from the Syriac *qeryana*), but only in 9:111, where the word is placed opposite the Torah and the Gospels, does it appear to refer to the Qur'an as an actual book of revelation.

Organization. In form the Qur'an is divided into 114 suras (conventionally, chapters), which are arranged roughly in order of descending length, with the exception of the opening sura, al-Fatiha (That which opens), which has seven verses. The reasons for this arrangement are unclear. Each sura has a title (some have several competing titles), but the title bears no necessary relation to the content of the sura. Instead, the title is usually a catchword taken from within the sura, apparently designed for easy memorization. Some of the shorter suras, however, such as 112, al-Ikhlas (Devotion), do roughly accord with their titles. The size of the suras varies widely, from sura 2, which has 286 verses, to sura 108, which has 3 verses. The final two suras, the Mu'awwidhatan (Suras of taking refuge) are, like the Fatiha, slightly out of place in terms of their verse number but have been placed at the end because they are amulets.

Chronology. The arrangement of the Qur'an bears no necessary relationship to the chronological revelation of the suras; indeed, the shorter suras at the end of the Qur'an are more likely to have been the earlier ones.

There is some disagreement about the first revelation given to Muhammad. In general Muslim consensus has stated that sura 96:1–5, "Recite in the name of your Lord," was the first revelation (approximately 610; see Fakhry). In general the form of the early revelations is a dramatic one, invoking the natural and cosmic world by means of oaths (e.g., "by the sun and its forenoon brightness"; sura 91) and continuing on to explicit descriptions of the imminent end of the world and the coming day of judgment. Often Muhammad is spoken to directly and told to "say" something (sometimes as a response to outside events), which is then cited indirectly as a quotation in the text.

Themes. The themes of the Qur'an are varied. The basic theme is a bedrock monotheism, summarized by sura 112: "Say: He is Allah, the only One, Allah the everlasting. He did not beget and is not begotten. And none is His equal." This monotheism is said to have been proclaimed by numerous messengers and prophets throughout history (mostly found in the biblical tradition) in a series of progressive revelations culminating in that given to Muhammad. Stories of the prophets (although the term *prophet* in Islam does not necessarily correspond to that in the Bible) are a major component of the Qur'an. For the most part, their experiences are monochromatic: God sends a prophet (or a messenger) to a sinful people, usually with signs; the people reject the prophet, sometimes killing him; and then God sends some form of punishment on the people. The stories of the prophets are sometimes related to those in the Bible (e.g., the story of Abraham's sacrifice of one of his sons, 37:102, or the story of Joseph, sura 12) but in many cases are more closely related to Jewish midrashic or Christian apocryphal materials. Most of the stories concerning Jesus, said to be the last prophet prior to Muhammad, are closely related to noncanonical gospel stories.

Other major themes of the Qur'an are apocalyptic visions of the end of the world and threats against disbelievers and the heedless, who live their lives in willful ignorance of the coming day of judgment. Teachings about Allah (God) describe him as a merciful and compassionate god and one who supplies humanity with knowledge but who is also completely unconnected with his creation other than through the sending of messengers and the punishment of sinners. In the Qur'an, the Muslim social order is detailed, including frequent admonishments to pray, do acts of charity, fast for Ramadan, and follow other standard Muslim ordinances. A high percentage of the long first suras detail the founding of the Muslim community in Medina (622–32), the theological controversies Muhammad had with the Jewish population of the oasis town, and his wars with both the Jews and his polytheist neighbors that culminated in his conquest of Mecca (630). Descriptions of fighting and the theological justifications for it and rewards stemming from it are frequent inside these suras.

The Qur'an and Muhammad. Muhammad is addressed personally in the Qur'an. In general the revelation of the Qur'an is said to have been through the agency of the angel Gabriel (Jibril) to Muhammad personally, after which the latter then recited the content to the believers. Many of the suras deal with Muhammad's personal life, his doubts and depression, his conflicts with his polytheist and Jewish foes, and his struggles to bind the Muslim community together. The Qur'an speaks of several different groups: the believers who accepted Muhammad's leadership completely; the polytheists, who rejected it completely; the Jews, who should have been allies of Muhammad but instead rejected him out of spite; and the "hypocrites," who sometimes accepted Muhammad but sometimes proved to be unreliable (e.g., sura 33). Beyond the building of the community, Muhammad's personal life focused on his wives, who, although they held a special place (33:32), were also unruly and the focus of a great many restrictions that were later imposed on Muslim women as a whole.

The Qur'an's Impact on Culture. The attraction of the Qur'an from the time of Muhammad has been centered on the fact that it is an "Arabic" revelation (e.g., 12:2), especially for Arabic-speaking people but later for all humanity. Through the Qur'an, Arabic was standardized and popularized throughout the Muslim world, and it continues to be the portal through which most Muslims experience the Qur'an. In general, since the first revelations, that experience has been an auditory one, where the sonorous nature of the recitation has a hypnotic and captivating quality about it.

Textual Criticism and Interpretations. Because the Qur'an was recited during the early period of Islam, its collection was delayed somewhat—to the period of the caliph 'Uthman (644–56), according to the traditional accounts. Although the text established by 'Uthman has been authoritative among Muslims (with some disagreements by Shi'ites, who claimed that sections were suppressed), there are numerous variant readings (*qira'at*). This fact is due to the unvocalized and unpointed nature of the Arabic script during this early period, which means that Arabic words can be read in a number of different ways. These variant readings exist in seven (or fourteen) separate reading traditions descending from the early reciters of the Qur'an; however, in practice only two of those are in wide currency today.

Variant readings were one of the contributing factors to the appearance of exegetical literature (*ta'wil* or *tafsir*) about the Qur'an. Early commentators like Muqatil b. Sulayman (d. 767) interworked their interpretation with the text, supplying explanations, glosses, or additional detail as needed. Major medieval commentators such as al-Tabari (d. 923) took each verse separately and explained it by means of traditions, grammatical comments, and their own opinions. This exegesis is summarized in the most popular commentary by al-Suyuti (d. 1505), the Tafsir al-Jalalayn, which is portable. Many exegetes used the Qur'an as a mine for legal rulings and arranged their commentaries according to the law that could be derived from the Qur'an. For this purpose, the Qur'an was rearranged into chronological order, where certain verses that were chronologically said to be later abrogated earlier verses (as there are numerous apparent contradictions inside the text). Sufi mystics interpreted the Qur'an allegorically, radically rereading many of the themes described above and searching out hidden and symbolic meanings. In this they were joined by Shi'ites, who were in many cases dissatisfied because the content of the Qur'an does not explicitly affirm the rights of the Prophet's family to rule. In some cases, such as Isma'ili Shi'ite exegesis, the exegesis is completely divorced from or even in opposition to the plain meaning of the text. In general contemporary exegetes of the Qur'an have favored the idea that the Qur'an is its own exegesis and have avoided using the traditional materials or have sought to "prove" that science is in accord with or is prophesied by the text.

Scholarly critique of the Qur'an has focused on establishing a scientific text that would include the best possible readings from all the variants, examining the sources on which the Qur'an is based, or in some cases its parallels in other classical religious literature, and the foreign vocabulary of the Qur'an. However, the Qur'an has been particularly resistant to any type of source criticism or absolute chronology, and there is no consensus even as to the likely sources of its ideas or imagery.

Issues of Translation. Traditionally the Qur'an has been read in Arabic, and in contradistinction to the Bible there has never been a massive Muslim effort to translate it. Usually the paradigm has been to bring people to the Qur'an, to surround it with an aura of holiness that is both physical (in terms of ensuring that it is not desecrated

or dishonored in any way) and linguistic in nature. Muslims who are not Arabic speaking will have to learn some of the Qur'an (usually the Fatiha) for the purpose of prayers, but frequently this learning will be nothing more than memorization without any comprehension. Very conservative Muslims still maintain that the Qur'an should not be translated and are sometimes reluctant to give the Arabic text to a nonbeliever for fear it would be desecrated.

However, numerous translations are available. The oldest standard one is that of George Sale (d. 1736), which was in use during the nineteenth century. During the early twentieth century, the two major Muslim translations, that of 'Abdallah Yusuf 'Ali (1934), *The Qur'an* (favored by South Asian Muslims), and that of Muhammad Marmaduke Pickthall (1930), *The Meaning of the Glorious Qur'an* (favored by the Saudi Arabian government), were completed. Standard non-Muslim translations by Arthur Arberry (*The Koran Interpreted*, 1955), as well as Ahmed Ali (*al-Qur'an*), Majid Fakhry (*The Qur'an: A Modern English Version*), and Tarif Khalidi (*The Qur'an*), have avoided the King James style utilized by the two Muslim translations. Others such as Richard Bell (*The Qur'an*) and N. J. Dawood (*The Koran with Parallel Arabic Text*) have radically rearranged the text with either chronology or readability in mind.

The Meaning of the Qur'an for Muslims. For Muslims the Qur'an is the very words of God, and reverence for the Qur'an and belief in its power, its eternal relevance, and its abrogation of any other possible revelation have been central to Islam. As Wilfred Cantwell Smith said a half century ago, the Qur'an is to Islam what Jesus is to Christianity. Criticism of it, denigration of it (real or perceived), or interpretation of it in an allegorical or nonliteral manner has been met in the recent past with hostility and sometimes violence. Its presentation of the cosmos, of history (especially salvation history), and of humanity continues to be fundamental to Islam.

See also ISLAM, BASIC BELIEFS OF; MUHAMMAD

Bibliography. A. Ali, *al-Qur'an*; A. Y. Ali, *The Qur'an*; A. Arberry, *The Koran Interpreted*; R. Bell, *The Qur'an*; C. E. Bosworth et al., eds., *Encyclopedia of Islam*; N. J. Dawood, *The Koran with Parallel Arabic Text*; M. Fakhry, *The Qur'an: A Modern English Version*; H. Gatje, trans., *The Qur'an and Its Exegesis*; T. Khalidi, *The Qur'an*; J. MacAuliffe, ed., *The Encyclopedia of the Qur'an*; M. M. Pickthall, *The Meaning of the Glorious Qur'an*; Quran and Science website, http://www.quranandscience.com/; W. C. Smith, *Islam in Modern History*; M. b. Sulayman, *Tafsir*, edited by A. M. Shihata; J. a. al-Suyuti, *Tafsir al-Jalalayn*; M. b. J. al-Tabari, *Jami' al-bayan fi ta'wil ayy al-Qur'an*.

D. B. Cook

R

RAJA YOGA. Raja Yoga is a term that has been used in modern times by Hindu commentators, such as Vivekananda (1863–1902), when referring to the meditative techniques described in the second-century-AD Yoga Sutras of Patanjali. Although the term does not appear in Patanjali's sutras, for these modern commentators Raja Yoga denotes the path of "royal yoga" or the "king of all yoga," as it constitutes the pinnacle of meditative practice. Some advocates concentrate more attention on the meditative attainments while deemphasizing the bodily postures that many Westerners associate with yoga generally. In Raja Yoga, several techniques are used to distinguish between human awareness and pure consciousness. The goal is to disentangle pure consciousness from human awareness so as to attain yogic liberation from the cycle of rebirth and attachment to the material creation. The Brahma Kumaris World Spiritual Organization is one of several modern neo-Hindu movements that promote Raja Yoga meditation.

See also BRAHMA KUMARIS WORLD SPIRITUAL ORGANIZATION; HINDUISM; YOGA

Bibliography. M. Eliade, *Yoga: Immortality and Freedom*; S. Strauss, *Positioning Yoga: Balancing Acts across Cultures*.

P. Johnson

RAMA. Next to Krishna, Rama is the most important Hindu God and the seventh avatar of Vishnu. In Indian religious thought, he is the supreme example of patience, faithfulness, and justice. The epic Ramayana describes his exploits through a gripping adventure story.

See also AVATAR; HINDUISM; KRISHNA

Bibliography. "Lord Rama," The Hindu Universe website, http://www.hindunet.org/god/Gods/rama/index.htm.

I. Hexham

RAMA, SWAMI. Swami Rama (1925–96), a yogi and charismatic leader, attempted to reconcile Western science with Eastern philosophy and religiosity.

Born as Brij Kishore Dhasmana, he grew up in the Indian state of Uttar Pradesh in northern India. He spent his early years traveling through the Himalayas under the spiritual guidance of Bengali Baba. Between 1949 and 1952, he was the Shankaracharya of Karvirpitham in South India, a distinguished spiritual position. In 1966 he built the Sadhana Mandir ashram (an ashram is the dwelling of a Hindu teacher) in Rishikesh, India. In 1969 he traveled to the US, where he consented to scientific observation at the Menninger Foundation in Topeka, Kansas. The control of his automatic bodily processes (such as heartbeat, body temperature, respiration, and brain waves) was studied and recorded using psycho-physiological equipment. In 1971 he continued to couple science with his spiritual teachings, opening the Himalayan Institute of Yoga Science and Philosophy in Honesdale, Pennsylvania.

Swami Rama published numerous books, including *Meditation and Its Practice, Enlightenment without God (Mandukya*

Upanishad), and *Living with the Himalayan Masters*, in which he promoted his belief in the benefits of yoga, meditation, and self-control (what he popularized as "knowing oneself"). In 1989 he started work on the Himalayan Institute Hospital Trust in the Garhwal Himalayas.

Controversy stained his reputation when in December 1990 the *Yoga Journal* published an exposé of his alleged sexual misconduct toward and abuse of women; in 1997 the Himalayan Institute was fined $1.6 million in punitive damages. In 1993 he returned to India, where he spent the remainder of his life.

See also ENLIGHTENMENT; MEDITATION; YOGA

Bibliography. S. Rama, *Living with the Himalayan Masters*; R. Tigunait, *At the Eleventh Hour: The Biography of Swami Rama.*

R. Aechtner

RAMAKRISHNA, SRI. Sri Ramakrishna (1836–86) is an East-Indian saint and was a guru of Swami Vivekananda, who first carried his master's teachings to the West in 1893. Ramakrishna's life and message inspired the modern Vedanta movement. Ramakrishna is considered an avatar (an incarnation of God) by his followers.

Ramakrishna was born to a poor Brahmin family in rural Bengal. Reportedly, he experienced his first spiritual ecstasy at age six. At sixteen he relocated to Calcutta, where up until his final illness he served as priest of the Kali Temple in Dakshineswar, in the suburbs. There he practiced many spiritual "paths": tantra, Vedanta, Islam, and Christianity. With each he experienced numerous visions and ecstasies. Once he envisioned Jesus striding toward him, then merging into his body.

The Gospel of Sri Ramakrishna provides a firsthand account of Ramakrishna's daily visits with people of all ranks. Ramakrishna met with people in his quarters, where he taught, sang, and fell into ecstasies. From these people he selected the young men who were eventually to form his inner circle and establish his religious order. He taught that all religions are true paths to God, that sincere dedication to God will lead to God-realization, and that all who call on God sincerely, even once, will come to him.

Among the religious orders of India, the Ramakrishna Order is among the most respected. In the West, many prominent thinkers have felt Ramakrishna's influence, including Aldous Huxley, Christopher Isherwood, and Huston Smith. Sri Ramakrishna has had a major influence on the growing religious syncretism of our day.

See also AVATAR; VEDANTA

Bibliography. C. Isherwood, *Ramakrishna and His Disciples*; Swami Nikhilananda, trans., *The Gospel of Sri Ramakrishna*, with foreword by A. Huxley.

B. Scott

RAMANA MAHARISHI. Maharishi Ramana (1879–1950) was educated at the American school in Madurai, South India. He claimed to have renounced his Western education to rely on Indian spiritual knowledge, which he further claimed to have learned in past lives. It appears that at the age of seventeen he experienced a form of conversion that drew him to the Indian classics and through meditation he embraced a doctrine of self-inquiry. Over the years, he gathered a band of devoted followers as he became a leading guru of the twentieth-century Hindu renaissance.

See also HINDUISM; MEDITATION; REINCARNATION

Bibliography. S. Narayanaswamy, *Gurudevi Sri Janaky Matha: A Concise Biographical Sketch of an Enlightened Disciple of Bhagawan Sri Ramana Maharishi*; Sri Ramanasramam, *Bhagavan Sri Ramana: A Pictorial Biography.*

I. Hexham

RAMANUJA. Ramanuja founded one of the most important philosophic systems in

Hinduism, a semimonotheistic view called qualified nondualism. Older and traditional biographies of Ramanuja report that he lived from AD 1017 to 1137 and died at the age of 120. However, the earliest biographies were composed one or two hundred years after his death, and modern scholars believe that a date of 1077 to 1157 is more likely, giving him a life span of eighty years.

Ramanuja was born into an aristocratic Brahmin caste in Perumdubur, Tamil Nadu, India, and was given the name Ilaya Perumal. From his childhood, he was noted as being very intelligent. Shortly after his marriage at age sixteen, his father died, and Ilaya moved his household to Karachi, where he would have the opportunity to study under some prominent teachers. He became a student under Yadava Prakash but quarreled with him, arguing against the teachings of the famed nondualist scholar Sankara (788–820). He learned that Prakash planned to kill him, so he fled to become an itinerant devotee of the god Vishnu. Around the age of thirty-two, he renounced his marriage and family life to become an ascetic *sann-yasin*. He traveled to various cities throughout India, finally settling in Sri Rangam. Ramanuja wrote a number of important treatises, which are considered foundational texts for a form of Vaishnavite devotion (devotion to Vishnu), called Vishishtadvaita (qualified nondualism).

Ramanuja's philosophy represents a sophisticated midpoint between the nondualism (*advaita*) of Sankara and the dualism (*dvaita*) of Madhva. The nondualistic view held that Brahma (ultimate reality) was distinctionless and that subject/object differences did not actually exist. What we perceive of the world is *maya*, illusion. Ramanuja held that this was a self-stultifying claim and that to even make the affirmation, one had to separate "distinction" from "distinctionless-ness." In other words, he insisted on the law of noncontradiction. In Ramanuja's view, there

was only one God, Vishnu. The polytheistic deities of the Rig Veda and the other Vedas were really gods representing Vishnu, who is omniscient, omnipresent, and omnipotent. The distinctions in the world are real, not illusory, and individuality and the universe relate to God (Vishnu) as the body relates to the self who inhabits the body. Ramanuja's view still held to some pantheistic elements, but it recognized real subject/object distinctions and affirmed the primacy of bhakti, or devotional worship, of Vishnu.

See also ADVAITA; BHAKTI YOGA; HINDU-ISM; MAYA; SANKARA; SANNYASA; VISHNU

Bibliography. J. B. Carman, "Ramanuja," in *Encyclopedia of Religion*, edited by L. Jones, 2nd ed.; S. N. Dasa, "Ramanuja Acarya (1017–1137 AD)," *Sanskrit Religions*; T. A. Forsthoefel, "Ramanuja," in *Holy People of the World: A Cross-Cultural Encyclopedia*, edited by P. G. Jestice; "Ramanjua," in *World Religions: Biographies*, edited by N. Schlager and J. Weisblatt.

E. Pement

REFORMED EGYPTIAN. "Reformed Egyptian" is a term used in the Book of Mormon (at Mormon 9:32) to denote the language of its original documents, purportedly engraved on gold plates and discovered by Mormonism's founder, Joseph Smith Jr. The Book of Mormon explains that this language "consists of the learning of the Jews and the language of the Egyptians" (1 Nephi 1:2) and that it was used because it is more compact than Hebrew for purposes of engraving (Mormon 9:33), although this efficiency also brings some "imperfection into our record" (Mormon 9:33). According to most Mormon scholars, "reformed" means that the language utilized Egyptian characters to represent Hebrew words. Some LDS scholars, however, have argued that the Book of Mormon was written in a form of Egyptian influenced by Hebrew. In short there is no consensus even among Mormons as to what kind of language was used.

Critics have noted several problems with Mormon claims regarding Reformed Egyptian. There is, for example, no evidence of such a language apart from Smith's testimony of what appeared on the golden plates, which have since disappeared. Mormon apologists respond by noting examples of such "hybrid" languages from the ancient world but are unable to identify any known language with Smith's "Reformed Egyptian." The ambiguity of the Book of Mormon's description of its original language appears to have been intended to blunt modern criticism of the book.

Another major difficulty is found in the account of Smith's follower Martin Harris, who in 1828 visited Columbia University professor of ancient languages Charles Anthon, bringing with him a sample of Reformed Egyptian. Anthon allegedly at first validated the authenticity of the language, but in later reports he indicated that he had considered the transcription to be some sort of fakery. Mormon apologists have responded by noting inconsistencies in Anthon's reports and suggesting that he engaged in a cover-up to protect himself from association with Mormonism. Adding to the confusion, Joseph Smith claimed that Anthon had pronounced Smith's translation of the ancient script to be accurate, even though the Book of Mormon itself asserts that no one would be able to understand its language. (The actual paper that Harris took to Anthon, or perhaps a copy of it, has been found, and it contains no translation at all.)

Mormon scholars also argue that certain character names in the Book of Mormon, such as Paanchi and Pahoran, find close analogues in Egyptian texts, and they claim that aspects of the Mormon scriptures accurately reflect ancient life and language. Such arguments tend to treat the evidence of the Book of Mormon selectively. For example, most of the Book of Mormon names are biblical names or variant forms of those names, and they include Greek names (e.g., Timothy) and other contextually inappropriate names (e.g., Isabel).

See also CHURCH OF JESUS CHRIST OF LATTER-DAY SAINTS; HARRIS, MARTIN; NEPHITES; SMITH, JOSEPH, JR.; STANDARD WORKS

Bibliography. T. L. Givens, *By the Hand of Mormon: The American Scripture That Launched a New World Religion*; D. Persuitte, *Joseph Smith and the Origins of the Book of Mormon*.

J. P. Holding and R. M. Bowman Jr.

REIKI. The name Reiki (Japanese, "mysterious atmosphere" or "spiritual power") refers to a form of "energy healing" that proponents believe occurs when life energy is transferred through the practitioner to the receiver by specific hand motions and symbols. Reiki traces its origins to a nineteenth-century Japanese man named Mikao Usui. Some Reiki practitioners have claimed that Usui was a Christian minister who attended the University of Chicago Divinity School and learned to read Sanskrit there. There are no records to substantiate this claim. After returning to Japan, Usui is said to have found Sanskrit texts that described the healing formulas of Jesus. In a vision, he received information about unique symbols and how to use them to activate healing. He named his discovery *rei ki*, or "universal life energy." The connection between Christianity and the origins of Reiki has since been disproven with documentary evidence.

Reiki arrived in Hawaii before World War II through the assistance of a Japanese Hawaiian woman, Hawayo Takata. Mrs. Takata trained a number of Reiki "masters" before she died in 1980.

Reiki has changed over the years, and now there are numerous forms and teachings promoting traditional Usui and modern or blended approaches. Reiki is commonly divided into three levels of initiation. The levels involve learning hand motions and symbols to release energy for a particular healing need, which can be personal, local, or distant. Each level must be passed person to person. Traditionally, information on the attunements (initiations) and symbols unique to each level was never written down or made public. In recent years, this rule has been disregarded by some for the sake of making the techniques more accessible, although this has produced conflict within the movement. Scientific studies have shown that there is no evidence supporting the effectiveness of this form of healing, and the Roman Catholic Church has classified it as superstition.

See also CHRISTIAN

Bibliography. D. Stein, *Essential Reiki.*

J. Lyons

REINCARNATION. The traditional understanding of reincarnation in major Eastern religions is outlined below.

Reincarnation in Buddhism. The Buddhist understanding of reincarnation developed in dialogue with Jainism and Hinduism but in many respects differs from the generic concept. In Buddhism, just as in Hinduism, the fundamental problem of human existence is that persons find themselves caught in a recurring cycle of death and rebirth. However, Buddhism rejects the idea of an eternal soul or the belief that there exists an enduring substance in which personal identity is grounded; there is no abiding self in Buddhism. Instead, "persons" are said to be bundles of properties in a state of continual flux. If a person fails to attain liberation during a given life, some of the psychological aggregate will survive the dissolution of the body with which it was previously associated and subsequently be reincarnated in a different body in accordance with the dictates of karma. Human life is filled with suffering, which stems from ignorance concerning the nature of reality (which most people think consists of a multiplicity of concrete objects

but actually is undifferentiated Buddha nature) and consequent attachment to things that are impermanent and ultimately unreal. This suffering is then perpetuated by means of such craving for things that exist only in the world of appearances, which in turn results in the failure to achieve enlightenment and consequent reincarnation. The solution to this predicament is following the Noble Eightfold Path, which, if done successfully, will result in nirvana: complete freedom from illusion and detachment from desire, and hence the cessation of all suffering. In Mahayana Buddhism, the attempt to escape reincarnation involves many ritual practices and efforts to help other sentient beings attain liberation. Between reincarnations "mind streams" experience an intermediate state known as *bardo*. Theravada Buddhism rejects the concept of bardo and asserts that reincarnation can be avoided primarily by means of a rigorous, self-directed program of meditation and study. At the time of death, the "mind stream" is immediately reincarnated.

Reincarnation in the Hindu Tradition. The Hindu doctrine of reincarnation cannot be adequately understood apart from the broader worldview in which it plays a role. In all of Hinduism's various forms, the fundamental problem faced by human beings is that the soul is trapped in an ongoing cycle of death and rebirth (samsara). The soul or self (Atman) is imperishable and in some sense is identical to Brahma, persisting beyond the death of the body in which it is presently incarnated. Unless the cycle of death and rebirth is broken by the attainment of liberation (*moksha*), after death the soul will travel to a new body that will serve as its next incarnation. (The type of body into which each soul is transferred after death is determined by the law of karma, which precisely and dispassionately dispenses justice by means of placing each soul in a body and set of circumstances that is fitting in light of the karma accrued in its previous

413

incarnation or incarnations.) The release of the soul from this bondage to successive embodiments (caused by the accumulation of bad karma) and from the suffering that accompanies bodily existence is difficult to achieve since many factors are at work against the person striving for liberation. The two most formidable obstacles to overcome in this regard are ignorance (*avidya*) and illusion (*maya*). Human beings are nearly incorrigible in their misapprehension of the true nature of the self, erroneously believing that the self is a real entity that is ontologically distinct from Brahma. Add to this the fact that evil actions, which result from ignorance and illusion, create bad karma, and the prospects for achieving enlightenment and liberation appear dim. This is reflected in the fact that the world is populated by untold billions of living beings still awaiting their release from the world of suffering. Those willing to undertake the rigors of the quest for liberation can travel the path of knowledge (*jnana marga*; exemplified by Advaita Vedanta) or the path of devotion (*bhakti marga*; seen in the worship of Hindu deities such as Vishnu and Shiva). In such ways people can avoid the bondage to karma and embodied existence that results from being reincarnated.

Reincarnation in Jainism. At the core of Jainism is the belief that spiritual bondage—and the endless series of reincarnations that result from this bondage—is the universal quandary of all sentient beings. Caught in the cycle of death and rebirth, the human soul (*jiva*) is embodied and covered with eight types of karma particles; the performance of evil actions causes these various particles to literally stick to the soul. The bodies in which souls are reincarnated are composed of eight types of matter (*vargana*) and have a real, substantial existence. It is because sentient beings are ignorant of their true nature as inherently perfect godhood (or, if they are aware of this fact, because they do not spend sufficient time

contemplating it) that they are confined to their bodies and must struggle to achieve liberation. Progress toward liberation from a series of otherwise unending reincarnations into bodies that prevent the experience of the supreme bliss of enlightenment involves three main components: right perception (*samyak darsana*), right knowledge (*samyak jnana*), and right conduct (*samyak charitrya*). If a person does not succeed in purifying himself of all bad karma by the time of his death, his remaining karmic matter accompanies his soul and constructs a new body for him to inhabit.

Reincarnation in Sikhism. In Sikhism the barriers that hinder persons from achieving liberation (and hence from breaking the cycle of successive reincarnations, known as *awagaun*) are primarily moral rather than epistemological, though ignorance (*tamas*) is a universal problem. Every human soul, while having within it a glimmer of divine light, is covered with a layer of infirmities and defects. These blemishes impede the spiritual journey from the world of death and rebirth to union with God (True Name) by rendering people less willing and able to pursue a life of virtue. Persons who act in ways contrary to God's decrees (*hukam*) accrue to themselves bad karma, which postpones the time of their liberation. Those who seek to attain liberation must commit themselves to working through a three-stage process: they breach the "wall of falsehood" by gradually eradicating evil from the soul, they practice meditation as a means of developing compassion for others and exalting God, and, finally, their soul is absorbed into the divine essence. Properly grasping the divine order and behaving accordingly aids in this process. Moreover, in the Sikh view of things, karma is not an immutable reality; its operation is subject to God's good pleasure (*nadar*), and thus God can choose to be gracious to his followers. Eventually, every soul will merge with the divine essence.

See also ADVAITA; ANANDA MARGA YOGA SOCIETY; ATMAN; AVIDYA; BARDO; BUDDHISM; EIGHTFOLD PATH; HINDUISM; INTERNATIONAL SOCIETY FOR KRISHNA CONSCIOUSNESS (ISK-CON); JAINISM; KARMA; MAHAYANA BUD-DHISM; MAYA; MOKSHA; SAMSARA; SHIVA; SIKHISM; THERAVADA BUDDHISM; VISHNU

Bibliography. C. Ajitsingh, *The Wisdom of Sikhism*; P. Harvey, *An Introduction to Buddhism: Teachings, History and Practices*; A. L. Herman, *A Brief Introduction to Hinduism: Religion, Philosophy, and Ways of Liberation*; H. W. House, *Charts of World Religions*; L. R. Hubbard, *What Is Scientology?*; C. Humphreys, *Karma and Rebirth*; D. Keown, *Buddhism: A Very Short Introduction*; M. S. Kumar, *The Doctrine of Liberation in Indian Religion with Special Reference to Jainism*; W. H. McLeod, *The Sikhs: History, Religion, and Society*; W. P. O'Flaherty, *Karma and Rebirth in Classical Indian Traditions*; W. G. Oxtoby, *World Religions: Eastern Traditions*; A. C. B. Swami Prabhupada, *The Science of Self-Realization*; R. H. Roberts, *India: Religion and Philosophy*; N. Shah, *Jainism: The World of Conquerors*; C. Shattuck, *Hinduism*; B. H. Streeter, *Reincarnation, Karma and Theosophy*; J. D. Walters, *Essence of Self-Realization: The Wisdom of Paramahansa Yogananda*.

H. W. House

RELIGION. Defining religion is a vexed and contentious matter, for at least two reasons. First, groups historically regarded as genuine religions vary dramatically in their essential beliefs and practices. For example, Theravada Buddhists are atheists or agnostics, Christians are trinitarian, some Hindus and New Agers are pantheistic, and (many) Mormons and all Shintoists are polytheistic. Therefore, religion cannot be defined in exclusively monotheistic terms. Nor can it be held that all religions are merely expressing the same reality in different ways. They deviate too widely on core concepts regarding ultimate reality, the human condition, and the way of spiritual liberation. Second, scholars disagree as to whether atheistic/secular

belief systems such as Marxism or secular humanism should be classified as religions or nonreligious ideologies that are pursued with "religious zeal."

Some scholars, therefore, have abandoned the attempt to find any necessary and sufficient conditions for the essence of religion and instead have adopted a Wittgensteinian "family resemblance" notion. This stipulates that religions display a cluster of related attributes, but no one religion need have any one point in common with every other religion. This is analogous to blood relations of the famous Kennedy family, who all display a noticeable resemblance to one another but without there being one "Kennedy-esque" feature they all share.

Without solving all these debates, the following definition is offered. Religions involve worldviews and social practices that lay claim to certain objective truths concerning (1) the existence of ultimate reality (the sacred or holy), which is viewed as transcendent (such as Yahweh, the Trinity, Allah, Brahman, the Tao, nirvana); (2) the human condition (as unenlightened or sinful), and (3) the means of spiritual liberation or salvation (such as faith in God, mystical experience, good works). Religions offer a wide-ranging sense of meaning to their adherents by prescribing how they ought to orient themselves toward the ultimate reality spiritually, existentially, morally, and socially. This right orientation to the transcendent is viewed as necessarily connected to proper beliefs and practices (such as prayer, meditation, ritual, rites of passage).

Some new religious movements desire the status of being officially recognized as a religion, while others shun it. Transcendental Meditation (TM), for instance, has sought to present itself as a nonreligious therapy in public schools and the military in the US but has thus far been legally barred from doing so on the grounds that TM is a form of Hinduism. Therefore, it is thought, state support would violate the US Constitution by "establishing" a religion.

The dominant view among secular thinkers is that religion began as a merely human response to the mysterious aspects of nature. Guided by evolutionary and naturalistic presuppositions, they claim that religion has progressed through various stages, each of which becomes increasingly complex intellectually. The process begins with fetishism and moves to animism, polytheism, henotheism, and finally to monotheism. The power of this model lies more in its ideological assumptions than in the historical evidence in its favor, which is thin and highly speculative. Scripture inverts the secular pyramid and reveals that monotheism was the original religion from which other forms deviated after humans fell into sin (Rom. 1:18–32). German anthropologist Wilhelm Schmidt has written in defense of original monotheism.

Many sociologists predicted the gradual demise of all religion as the world modernized and left less and less room for the supernatural. However, the "secularization thesis" has been soundly refuted by the explosion of new religious movements worldwide as well as by the resurgence of Islam and the ongoing global growth of Christianity, especially in the third world.

Some Christian thinkers, such as Karl Barth and Gordon Clark, have refused to place Christianity in the category of a religion at all since it claims to be a supernatural and divine *revelation*, not merely a human religion, which can be reduced to anthropological, psychological, and sociological phenomena. At any rate, in its supernatural attestation (particularly regarding the resurrection of its divine founder), Christianity is sufficiently different from all other religions— including other monotheistic faiths—to merit its uniqueness and supremacy.

The Bible stipulates that true religion is held only by those people who manifest in their actions and attitudes the settled convictions (saving faith) offered by God's grace in Christ for their salvation (Eph. 2:8–9; James 2:14–26).

See also ANIMISM; CHURCH OF JESUS CHRIST OF LATTER-DAY SAINTS; CHRISTIAN; HINDUISM; ISLAM, BASIC BELIEFS OF; MONOTHEISM; PANTHEISM; POLYTHEISM; SHINTO; THERAVADA BUDDHISM; TRINITY, THE

Bibliography. A. Aldridge, *Religion in the Contemporary World: A Sociological Introduction*; W. Corduan, *Neighboring Faiths: A Christian Introduction to World Religions*; P. E. Devine, "On the Definition of Religion," *Faith and Philosophy*.

D. R. Groothuis

RELIGIOUS SOCIETY OF FRIENDS (QUAKERS).

The Religious Society of Friends, better known as the Quakers, is a quietist reform movement founded in England in the seventeenth century. For the first century of their existence, Quakers were persecuted as heretical and unorthodox. In modern times, though still not evangelical, they are socially acceptable such that two US presidents have identified themselves as Quakers: Herbert Hoover and Richard Nixon.

The movement began in 1647 when George Fox (1624–91) was led to exhort the Church of England to return to primitive Christianity, often even interrupting ministers during the sermon. Fox rejected the outward or external forms of religion (baptism, confirmation, priesthood, church rituals), stressing the need for a direct, inward experience of Christ. Fox emphasized the "inner Light" or "Christ within" each person rather than the "outward Christ" of profession. Without a conversion to that Christ, one was in spiritual darkness; even a lifetime of church membership was worthless. The Friends saw themselves as a restorationist movement, recovering truth lost after centuries of apostasy and abandoning every custom not found in Scripture.

Fox's disciples dressed plainly and waited silently for the conscious moving of the Spirit before speaking, singing, or preaching.

Though they called themselves "saints," "seekers," or "children of the light," in 1650 a judge in Derby called them Quakers due to Fox's insistence that the righteous should "tremble" at God's Word (citing Isa. 66:2). The name stuck.

The new movement spread quickly. Missionaries carried it to Europe, Asia, and Africa in fewer than ten years. The established church found it blasphemous, and thousands were persecuted. In the first thirty years of the movement, over fourteen thousand suffered fines or imprisonment, thousands were tortured, and over three hundred were executed. The first Quakers in America arrived in 1656 but were forced to immediately return to England. Subsequent immigrants were imprisoned, flogged, or hanged, until King Charles II granted Quaker William Penn sovereign control of a huge tract of land, expecting most Quakers to leave England for the New World. The property was named Pennsylvania and became a centerpiece of religious liberty.

The main points of opposition to the Quakers were theological and political. Theologically, the Quakers rejected the church's authority entirely. They rejected baptism and the Lord's Supper in favor of an "inner baptism" and an "inner communion." They denied the authority of the priesthood, the need for trained or paid clergy, and clerical dress. Women were allowed to preach and teach. Quakers repudiated the use of steeples in architecture and of the church calendar. They refused to pay tithes and taught sinless perfection. They affirmed an "inner Light" within all humanity, including the pagans. They gave greater esteem to the Word in their midst than the Word in Scripture, and leading Quakers eschewed using the word "Trinity" to describe the Godhead.

Socially and politically, they did not recognize the authority of civil leaders. This meant they would not bow, kneel, or remove their hat before superiors. They did not use titles of honor, such as "sir," "lord," or even "you." (The old Quaker custom of addressing everyone as "thou" or "thee" rather than "you" stems from a provincial quirk where individuals of nobility were addressed as "you." In the King James translation of the Bible, "you" is always a second-person plural pronoun, not a pronoun of nobility.) Quakers would not take an oath in court, did not believe in the "divine right of kings," and could not participate in war, including taxation for war. They supported the abolition of slavery but could not employ violence to achieve this. They decried jewelry, wigs, decorated clothing, balls, sports, or "amusements." They adopted a distinctive and plain habit of dress, and Quakers could only marry other Quakers.

In America the Quakers generally proved to be honest, hardworking people, and many government officials in Pennsylvania were Quakers, apparently recognizing the civil authority of Quaker governmental officials, but resigned at the beginning of the French and Indian War (1754). The name Religious Society of Friends was adopted in the mid-eighteenth century, with "Friends" being the preferred nickname. Both George Whitefield and John Wesley believed that, despite their separatist ways and rejection of "externals," a number of Quaker families possessed the true Spirit of Christ.

Later Developments. Early worship was antiliturgical, as Friends silently waited for the Spirit before saying or doing anything. Frequently the worship was simply waiting on the Lord, with no one speaking at all. In later stages, influenced by Protestant preaching and worship, some Friends incorporated planned music, preaching, and exhortation into their services. Today the Friends churches can be divided into those that have programmed services and those that do not.

The Friends' corporate unity was maintained through "meetings," which were held monthly, quarterly, and annually and organized geographically. The monthly and quarterly meetings were occasions for discipline or recognition, and unity was maintained by epistles distributed from one annual meeting to the others.

By the last half of the nineteenth century, the Friends had split into four factions along issues such as participation in war, the atonement of Christ, biblical authority, education, programmed worship, and innovations such as altar calls or hiring preachers. In the first decade of the twenty-first century, there were over a dozen different factions of the Religious Society of Friends (the liberals usually omit the term Religious). Long ago they dropped their distinctive clothing and archaic forms of speech, except for a very small group called the Conservative Friends.

Today there are three main branches. Those with evangelical inclinations would prefer the Evangelical Friends International (about 24,000 members). Services are programmed, are often led by a pastor, and follow evangelical beliefs on biblical authority, salvation, and traditional marriage. Those Friends who prefer unprogrammed, silent meetings and acceptance of universalism and same-sex marriage will gravitate toward the Friends General Conference (about 32,000 members). By far the largest branch is the Friends United Meeting (about 148,000 members), where most worship is programmed, more liberal views are tolerated, and there are numerous opportunities for social action.

Bibliography. M. P. Abbott et al., *Historical Dictionary of the Friends (Quakers)*; W. J. Allinson, "Friends, Society of," in *Cyclopedia of Biblical, Theological, and Ecclesiastical Literature*, edited by J. McClintock and J. Strong; M. H. Bacon, "On the Verge: The Evolution of American Quakerism," in *America's Alternative Religions*, edited by T. Miller; H. Barbour, "Quakers," in *Encyclopedia of Religion, Second Edition*, edited by L. Jones; S. M. Janney, "Friends, Society of," in *Cyclopedia of Biblical, Theological, and Ecclesiastical Literature* (1887); F. E. Mayer, "The Quakers,"

in *Religious Bodies of America*, 4th ed.; J. G. Melton and M. Baumann, "Evangelical Friends International," "Friends General Conference," "Friends/Quakers," "Friends United Meeting," and "Friends World Committee for Consultation," in *Religions of the World: A Comprehensive Encyclopedia of Beliefs and Practices*, edited by J. G. Melton and M. Baumann; I. Sharpless, "Friends, Society of," in *The New Schaff-Herzog Encyclopedia of Religious Knowledge*, edited by S. M. Jackson (1914).

E. Pement

REN/JEN. Ren/Jen (Chinese, "human-heartedness"; "benevolence") is the most fundamental of the Confucian virtues, the moral basis for the practice of loving and humane behavior and the avoidance of impropriety. Confucius thought that human beings are essentially good; hence, *ren* was an ethical quality that resided naturally in each person. Yet ren is not viewed properly if it is taken to be a virtue possessed merely by individuals. Instead, it ought to be understood as necessarily embodied in the dynamics of socially cooperative, mutually kind, and properly respectful interpersonal relationships. Among other things, ren prevents ritual transactions—the performance of which allows for social stability—from becoming ethically and emotionally empty or merely perfunctory. Though by no means advocating lawbreaking, ren prioritizes the preservation of key social relationships over what otherwise would be the right course of action. For example, according to most traditional understandings of ren, if a son caught his father stealing, his duty to maintain loyalty to his father would outweigh his obligation to report his father to the authorities.

Ren also is an important element in the Confucian theory of government: if a ruler treats his subjects inhumanely, he forfeits his authority to rule and can be rightfully disobeyed. During the history of Confucian thought, the concept of ren has been variously elucidated as the foundation of social virtue, the primary feature that distinguishes human beings from animals, the compassion shown by rulers to their subjects, and a crucial component of the Mandate of Heaven (T'ien Ming / Tianming).

See also CONFUCIANISM; CONFUCIUS

Bibliography. J. A. Berling, "Confucianism," *Focus on Asian Studies*, vol. 2, no. 1 (Fall 1982); T. Cleary, trans., *The Essential Confucius*; A. Waley, trans., *The Analects of Confucius*, repr. ed.; X. Yao, *An Introduction to Confucianism*.

H. W. House

REORGANIZED CHURCH OF JESUS CHRIST OF LATTER DAY SAINTS. *See* COMMUNITY OF CHRIST

RESURRECTION OF JESUS. There is little dispute that the resurrection of Jesus occupies the very center of the Christian faith. I will examine briefly the nature of this event and its place in Christianity before contrasting it with other belief systems. Although I will make some comments about the historicity of the resurrection, my primary goal is not apologetic. Rather, I am describing the belief itself, its role in Christianity, and how this is distinctive vis-à-vis other faiths. Even the latter will not engender a polemical approach but will emphasize contrasting positions.

The Gospel and the Resurrection. The Gospels report that Jesus's central proclamation was the good news that the kingdom of God was at hand (Mark 1:15) and, in fact, had already arrived (Luke 11:20). Jesus's coming, preaching, and death would provide the means by which the kingdom could be appropriated (Mark 10:45; 14:24). What one did specifically with Jesus determined whether one gained entrance into God's kingdom (Matt. 10:37–38; Mark 8:34–38; 10:27–30).

Lurking behind these utterances are the incredible claims that Jesus was both the Son of Man (Mark 2:1–12; 13:26) and the Son of God (Matt. 11:27; Mark 13:32). Combining both of these titles along with the claim

that he would sit on God's right hand led to Jesus's death, due to the charge of blasphemy (Mark 14:61–64).

Following Jesus was the key. To what message, then, was one to respond? The Christian gospel is the kernel of truth that, when combined with a commitment of faith in Jesus Christ, results in salvation. When the content of this gospel is defined in the New Testament, primarily in Acts (2:29–36; 3:12–26; 10:34–43) and in the epistles (Rom. 1:1–6; 10:9–13; 1 Pet. 1:3–9, 18–21), it centers on the deity (indicated by special titles), death, and resurrection of Jesus Christ. Incidentally, each of these texts in Acts and Romans above is generally thought to be a creedal statement or tradition, a snippet of the earliest oral preaching, therefore actually predating any writing in which it appears.

The gospel message centers on the person of Jesus Christ and what he provided by his death and resurrection. He is the key to salvation. God himself provided what no human theory could offer—a sinless sacrifice for human shortcomings, an event that indicated its effectiveness through Jesus's atoning death and bodily resurrection. After all, if Jesus had not been able to conquer death, how could this path serve as the chief indication that believers would also rise from the dead and live forever?

Hence, the historical event of the resurrection took on great significance. Not only was it part of the earliest gospel proclamation, but we are told that Jesus pointed to the resurrection as the chief indicator that he was God's answer, God's path to salvation (Matt. 12:38–42; 16:1–4). According to John's Gospel, his resurrection also played a practical role in comforting believers who had lost loved ones (11:21–27). And his appearances answered the doubts and questions of his own disciples (Matt. 28:16–20; Luke 24:36–43; John 20:8–9, 19–29).

The Centrality of the Resurrection. Not only did Jesus himself make his resurrection central to his message; so did the early church in its preaching and teaching (Acts 4:1–2, 33). The resurrection grounded and evidenced the gospel message of salvation, as seen in the early creedal texts (Rom. 1:1–4; 4:25; 10:9).

In fact theology as a whole was linked to the truth of this event (1 Cor. 15:12–19); indeed, Paul's sense of its importance led him to declare that without the resurrection, even faith itself was vain (15:14, 17). It changed believers from the most miserable and pitied people in the world into those with an eternal hope (15:19–20). Almost two dozen times in the New Testament, this event was the reason for the believers' hope in their own bodily resurrection (John 14:19; 1 Cor. 6:14; 2 Cor. 4:14; 1 John 3:2) as well as their assurance of the glories of heaven (1 Pet. 1:3–4). The resurrection was well evidenced (Acts 1:3; 1 Cor. 15:3–11) and ensured the truth of the Christian message (Acts 2:22–36; 17:29–31; Rom. 1:3–4).

Further, Jesus's resurrection also undergirded the practical aspects of the Christian life. For example, it transformed lives (John 20:16–18, 28–29; Acts 4:33; 9:1–22), was the impetus for early evangelism (Matt. 28:18–20; Luke 24:47–48; Acts 1:8), and led to the birth of the church (Acts 1:21–22; 2:14–47). It comforted the doubting (Luke 24:36–42; John 20:19–20) and was the antidote to grief (John 11:21–25; 1 Thess. 4:13–14) and suffering (2 Cor. 4:7–18) alike. It evoked great joy and praise (Matt. 28:9, 17; Luke 24:52–53; 1 Pet. 1:3–9). It provided daily power (Phil. 3:10), including victory over sin (Rom. 6:6–14; 8:9–11). The resurrection also grounded the practice of Christian ethics (1 Cor. 15:32). Even the fear of death was transformed in light of Jesus's death and resurrection (Heb. 2:14–15).

For reasons such as these, we can get a small glimpse of how the event of Jesus's resurrection occupied the very center of Christian thought in the earliest church. Early Christians claimed that it corroborated Jesus's message and formed the very center of the Christian gospel. It grounded theology and made hope possible during times of rampant persecution and suffering. The resurrection teaching even inspired the everyday practice of the Christian virtues. As Paul said, without this event there is no Christianity. But with it, everything else follows.

But Did It Happen? Although this discussion is not apologetic in nature, a few things still need to be said about the historicity of the resurrection. After all, this is a major feature of the New Testament hope. And because I want to contrast Christian belief in the bodily resurrection of Jesus with other religious approaches, I should acknowledge that to do so is to assume that the resurrection actually happened. Otherwise, it could simply be dismissed. So although I will barely touch the subject, some background should be helpful, and the references below will provide more sources for historical research.

Several converging lines of testimony indicate the historical nature of Jesus's bodily resurrection. Contemporary scholarship begins with a few select writings of the apostle Paul, due to their known authorship and dates of composition. Further, the chief New Testament text here is 1 Corinthians 15:3–7, which scholars almost unanimously agree to be an oral teaching that Paul received from other authoritative leaders at a very early date. Among the many indications of this is that Paul himself explains that this is what happened (15:3a). This alone means that we have a list of resurrection appearances dating back to the earliest church, before any New Testament book was written. The text reports appearances to both individuals and groups.

How early is this creedal statement? The consensus of scholarly research is that Paul probably received either the actual list of Jesus's appearances itself or at least the report of the details from Peter and James the brother of Jesus when he visited Jerusalem just three years after his conversion (Gal. 1:18–24). This would place Paul's reception of these data around AD 35. Then, to make absolutely sure of his message, Paul went back to Jerusalem to confirm his gospel preaching with Peter, James, and John (Gal. 2:1–10). Paul explains that his explicit purpose was to receive the affirmation of his gospel from the other apostles (Gal. 2:2), which they acknowledged (Gal. 2:6, 9). This indicates that all four of these apostles agreed regarding the gospel data of the deity, death, and resurrection of Jesus.

While the emphasis is on Paul's early reception of this material from the three main apostolic witnesses, it must not be forgotten that Paul himself was an eyewitness to an appearance of the risen Jesus (1 Cor. 9:1; 15:8). Moreover, Paul states directly afterward that he was aware of the message taught by the other apostles and that they preached the same truth regarding their also having seen appearances of the resurrected Jesus (1 Cor. 15:11).

So here we have a tight, multifaceted witness to the fact of the resurrection appearances of Jesus, all from the time directly after the crucifixion of Jesus. The four most influential apostles in the early church—Paul, Peter, John, and James the brother of Jesus—all agreed that they had seen Jesus after his death, both individually and in groups. Further, as noted, the last three apostles specifically approved Paul's gospel message, just as Paul reported separately his support of their teaching. In short, these four major apostles were the right people, in the right place, at the right time, to witness these incredible events. No wonder that critical scholars realize the exceptionally good case for these events.

Intriguingly, comparatively few critical scholars try to question this appearance testimony by raising alternative scenarios. This is probably because a host of opposing arguments greets each of these natural suppositions.

Besides this tight bundle of testimony, there are still other indications that Jesus had been raised from the dead and appeared to his followers. For example, we have reports from the first century AD that at least three of these four apostles (Paul, Peter, and James) all died for their message as martyrs. While it is true that people are frequently willing to die when they are deeply committed to a religious or political message, this apostolic message is different. Since we generally conclude that a willing death indicates that the martyr truly believed his message, this is especially important in that these apostles died for the truth of their central message: the gospel, which centered on the resurrection of Jesus.

In other words, while martyrs are personally convinced that their message is true, they almost always die for the teachings of someone else who lived at an earlier time. Even in the comparatively few cases where martyrs die for their own experience, it is for something less than a resurrection. For as we will see below, Christianity is the only major religion that teaches the bodily resurrection of its founder. These apostles, then, are the chief witnesses to whether Jesus ever appeared, and their martyrdom indicates their firm conviction that they had been with the risen Jesus.

Additionally, at least two of the witnesses—Paul and James the brother of Jesus—had previously been unbelievers who were convinced against their former positions by these appearances. These events propelled them in an entirely new direction.

In addition to 1 Corinthians 15:3–7, very early creedal statements from elsewhere in the New Testament, such as the early Acts preaching and other Pauline Epistles, confirm this same message. Once again the crisscrossing of the data produces additional evidence from other perspectives.

Last, critical scholars have noted almost two dozen evidences that the tomb in which

Jesus was buried was found empty shortly afterward. True, an empty tomb does not prove a resurrection. But in light of the other evidences such as those cited above, it adds a significant amount of helpful data, especially regarding the bodily nature of this event.

Therefore, we have outstanding evidence that Jesus was raised from the dead (see especially Habermas, *Risen Jesus*, chap. 1; Habermas and Licona; and Licona). The data strongly support the bodily nature of this event as well.

Other Religious and Philosophical Positions. Here I will contrast the orthodox Christian notion of bodily resurrection with other positions.

For example, the position that Jesus was *actually* raised from the dead contrasts particularly with all philosophical naturalisms, which deny the existence of the supernatural realm, holding that nature is all that exists. Naturalism also obviously contrasts with belief in the existence of God and the deity of Jesus Christ. Still, it is intriguing that naturalistic systems of thought most often employ empirical methodologies, as do many Christian scholars. Thus the most fruitful dialogue here would probably contrast the state of the empirical evidence: who has the stronger position?

Naturalists who treat the resurrection frequently suggest natural alternative means of explaining the resurrection data. Those who do so remain a distinct minority of scholars, since as mentioned above, most do not think that these options are the best explanations of all the known historical facts, which are thought to nullify these natural hypotheses. But this does not negate the spirited conversations that sometimes ensue (see Habermas, "Mapping the Recent Trend").

Further, the predominant view today among orthodox Christians, as well as many other scholars, is that Jesus was raised in a *bodily* manner, in a form that occupied space and time. One of the chief indications

here is the meaning of the relevant Greek terms themselves, which in the ancient world virtually always referred to bodily events, whether the terms were used by pagans, Jews, or Christians. Also helpful is the predominant Jewish background of bodily resurrection at the time, as well as the New Testament contexts themselves (see especially Wright, parts 1 and 2).

The scars from Jesus's crucifixion wounds (Luke 24:39–40; John 20:20–21, 27; Rev. 1:7) indicate further that however his body may have changed, Jesus's resurrected state exhibited *continuity*—it was the same body in which he was crucified. This is taken to be a further, crucial indication that Christian believers will also be raised bodily.

This position agrees with the predominant Jewish view of the general resurrection of the body from just before and after the time of Jesus, such as that held by the Pharisees. Many Jewish and Muslim believers also hold to bodily resurrection, including continuity, although they often deny that Jesus has already been raised from the dead. Intriguingly, some Jews and many Muslims seem to hold that Jesus will be raised bodily on the last day, along with other righteous persons.

The Christian notion of Jesus's resurrection specifically in bodily form contrasts with those views that support the resurrection of Jesus but in a nonphysical body, as held by Jehovah's Witnesses, along with some Spiritists and members of the Unification Church. Others, such as many Platonists and perhaps the majority of Hindus (plus many others in the ancient world), often espouse an idealistic philosophy that accepts a more spiritual form of immortality rather than bodily resurrection.

The biblical notion of Jesus's resurrection also requires a distinct, *personal* element, as indicated chiefly by Jesus being recognized after his resurrection. Although some believers did not initially identify him (Luke 24:31–32; John 20:14–15), most did.

Several causes may account for the former: some may have been restrained supernaturally (Luke 24:16?); others may have failed to recognize him for the same reason we don't recognize friends whom we haven't seen for a while; still others, because of changes in Jesus's resurrected body. This New Testament view contrasts with those positions that dictate that the afterlife is impersonal, such as prominent forms of Buddhism and particular varieties of Hinduism.

When the conversation is extended beyond the resurrection as such to the Christian gospel as a whole, as I did above, we find that Jesus's own teaching centered on the kingdom of God, whose coming began with his preaching and would later involve a refurbished earth. Some Jews and Muslims might agree that the kingdom of God is to come literally, but many adherents of more exclusively spiritual views of reality, such as those of Buddhism and Hinduism, would deny it. For Christians one enters into gospel salvation in God's kingdom by God's grace through faith in Jesus Christ rather than by good works. This orthodox Christian position contrasts with that of most non-Christian religious adherents, as does the notion of a blood atonement by God's Messiah. These doctrines would probably be rejected by most other religious faiths.

To be sure, on some points Christianity and other faith systems agree; the chief example may be Jewish and Muslim views of general resurrection, which often involve personal continuity in a new body. However, the most important contrasts between Christianity and other religions concern Jesus's deity and atoning death and the historical event of his bodily resurrection—what we have called the gospel. Other contrasts involve appropriating this gospel message by a faith-commitment to him.

Orthodox Christians point out that, for a variety of reasons, Jesus's resurrection indicates that the Christian gospel message is true since it shows that Jesus's teachings on these matters were confirmed by God (see Habermas, *Risen Jesus*, chaps. 2–3). It seems difficult to deny that, overall, the resurrection is so momentous that, if it occurred in the manner depicted in the New Testament, it strongly challenges both entire non-Christian systems and their individual doctrines. This is probably why Jesus's resurrection is regularly denied or at least questioned by other religions and philosophies.

The Uniqueness of Jesus's Central Message. To summarize: a number of Jesus's teachings appear unique when compared to the messages of the other major religious figures. I will mention five areas of contrast.

First, among the founders of the major world religions, only Jesus placed himself in the position of Deity. It is often assumed that other founders made similar claims, but this cannot be substantiated from any reliable historical data regarding their teachings. Confucius and Lao Tzu were ethicists, while Gautama the Buddha may have been an atheist. Neither the Jewish nor the Muslim tradition deifies any of its prophets or teachers.

Second, while great religious teachers commonly claimed to help their followers discover God's path or to teach them the secrets of life, only Jesus emphasized the ontological truth that what one does specifically *with him* determines whether one will enter the eternal kingdom of God. In him his hearers were confronted with God's presence as well as God's message.

Third, Jesus is the only founder of a major world religion of whom miracles are reported within a few decades. To be sure, the Buddha is said to have performed supernatural feats, but these generally were not recorded until hundreds of years later.

Fourth, only Jesus taught that his death would provide the means by which salvation would be available. Further, although Buddhism has much to say about suffering, often teaching that it is illusory, the Christian gospel affirms the reality of evil and pain, to the point of affirming that God did not even remove his Son from the cross.

Fifth, of all the followers of major world religions, only the orthodox followers of Jesus teach that he was raised bodily from the dead and appeared in space-time history. In light of the comments by Jesus and the early church that this event indicated that his teachings were true, the resurrection is clearly a central tenet of belief.

Conclusion. People certainly can make and have made all sorts of religious claims. Whether those claims are true is the decisive issue. But this last step will not be decided here. We only made a case for the meaning of Jesus's bodily resurrection within an orthodox Christian context, including its being an indispensable part of the Christian gospel as well as the center of Christian theology and practice as a whole. We have also provided some initial reasons why many have decided in favor of the historicity of the resurrection, before contrasting it with other religious and philosophical beliefs.

See also CHRIST, NATURES AND ATTRIBUTES OF; ORTHODOXY

Bibliography. W. L. Craig, *The Son Rises: Historical Evidence for the Resurrection of Jesus*; S. T. Davis, *Risen Indeed: Making Sense of the Resurrection*; G. R. Habermas, "Mapping the Recent Trend toward the Bodily Resurrection Appearances of Jesus in Light of Other Prominent Critical Positions," in *The Resurrection of Jesus: John Dominic Crossan and N. T. Wright in Dialogue*, edited by R. B. Stewart; Habermas, *The Resurrection: Heart of New Testament Doctrine*; Habermas, *The Resurrection: Heart of the Christian Life*, vol. 2; Habermas, *The Risen Jesus and Future Hope*; G. R. Habermas and M. R. Licona, *The Case for the Resurrection of Jesus*; M. R. Licona, *The Resurrection of Jesus: A New Historiographical Approach*; N. T. Wright, *The Resurrection of the Son of God*, vol. 3 of *Christian Origins and the Question of God*.

G. R. Habermas

REVELATION. Revelation is the act whereby God, a god, or the gods reveal themselves and/or their will to humankind. In Judaism revelation comes through the Hebrew Bible; in Christianity through the Hebrew Bible and the New Testament; in Islam through the Qur'an. The Hindu tradition associates revelation with *ruti*, or "what is heard," and has increasingly seen this in connection with the Vedas, Upanishads, and other religious literature. Buddhism, in practice, treats the sayings of the Buddha as a form of revelation, which is more accurately described as "insight," and Buddhism denies the involvement of God or gods. Jainism also denies all nonhuman sources of revelation. In other religious traditions, revelation comes from ancestors and/or gods for specific purposes.

Traditionally Christians claimed that special revelation ended with the canonization of the New Testament. Claims about continuing revelation have led to the growth of new forms of Christianity that are often heretical. Recently ideas about ongoing revelation have become popular in certain branches of the charismatic movement, where prophets and prophecy are a common phenomenon.

See also REVELATION, GENERAL

Bibliography. G. C. Berkouwer, *General Revelation*; B. A. Demarest, *General Revelation*; R. C. Sproul, J. Gerstner, and A. Lindsley, *Classical Apologetics*.

I. Hexham

REVELATION, GENERAL. In Christian theology, general revelation is the self-disclosure of God in and through the natural order. General revelation is contrasted with special revelation, which is God's revelation of himself in the course of human history, especially his revelation in Scripture. General revelation is "general" in two senses. First, it is general in the sense that it is a revelation made generally to all people in all times and places. Second, it is general in the sense that it conveys only broad, general truths about the nature of God. The basic idea of general revelation is that people can know the existence of God and something of what he is like through rational reflection on the natural world. General revelation, then, is the basis for what is called natural theology—the human knowledge of God derived from nature apart from Scripture.

Biblical Data Supporting General Revelation. Many biblical texts teach that God has provided mankind with a general revelation of himself. Psalm 19:1 states, "The heavens declare the glory of God." In Acts 14:15–17, the apostle Paul speaks about "the living God, who made the heavens and the earth and the sea and everything in them. In the past, he let all nations go their own way. Yet he has not left himself without testimony: He has shown kindness by giving you rain from heaven and crops in their seasons; he provides you with plenty of food and fills your hearts with joy." Later, at Mars Hill, he preaches, "From one man [God] made all the nations, that they should inhabit the whole earth; and he marked out their appointed times in history and the boundaries of their lands. God did this so that they would seek him and perhaps reach out for him and find him, though he is not far from any one of us. 'For in him we live and move and have our being.' As some of your own poets have said, 'We are his offspring'" (Acts 17:26–28).

The most important text on general revelation is Romans 1:18–20: "The wrath of God is being revealed from heaven against all the godlessness and wickedness of people, who suppress the truth by their wickedness, since what may be known about God is plain to them, because God has made it plain to them. For since the creation of the world God's invisible qualities—his eternal power and divine nature—have been clearly seen, being understood from what has been made, so that people are without excuse."

Other texts supporting the concept of general revelation include Job 12:7–9; 36:24–37:24;

Psalms 14:1; 97:6; John 1:1–4, 9; Romans 1:30; 2:14–15. From all these texts, we learn that general revelation provides all people with the knowledge (1) that God exists, (2) that he is the creator of the universe, (3) that he constantly sustains his creation, (4) that he benevolently provides for the needs of his creatures, (5) that he is glorious, good, and wise and deserving of worship and obedience, (6) that he is all-powerful, (7) that he is righteous and holy, and (8) that he demands holiness of human beings.

The Significance of General Revelation. The fact that God provides to all people a natural knowledge of himself is important for at least two reasons. First, as Paul says, it renders all people morally culpable and "without excuse" if they fail to acknowledge the existence of God or worship him as he requires. In this connection, note that general revelation can provide no means for humanity's salvation. The Bible is clear that all human beings are sinners (Rom. 3:23), and in fact all unregenerate people reject to various degrees the light of general revelation (Rom. 1:18). Thus general revelation provides God with the just ground for condemning everyone. The knowledge of the gospel required to save human beings from God's holy wrath is available only in the special revelation of Scripture.

Second, general revelation is important for Christian apologetics. The natural theology available in general revelation is a basis for constructing arguments for God's existence that can be used to bolster the faith of doubting believers and challenge the skepticism of agnostics and atheists.

See also CHRISTIAN; REVELATION

Bibliography. G. C. Berkouwer, *General Revelation*; B. A. Demarest, *General Revelation*; R. C. Sproul, J. Gerstner, and A. Lindsley, *Classical Apologetics*.

S. B. Cowan

RITES OF PASSAGE. Rites of passage are the ritual performances in any society that mark and acknowledge the important transitional periods in a person's life. They accompany one through the life-altering changes in one's social status at times of birth, passing into adulthood, marriage, or death.

The greatest contribution to understanding rites of passage was made by Belgian anthropologist Arnold Van Gennep (1873–1957). After closely observing, recording, and analyzing the regularity and importance of such rituals, he coined the term *rite of passage* to describe this phenomenon in his book *The Rites of Passage*. He realized how significant such ceremonial proceedings were for communities when they were dealing with change or a need for renewal. Van Gennep categorized all rites of passage as having three stages, which are distinct even though sometimes one can be more prominent than the other: separation, transition, and incorporation.

When people's status or role in their society or group is changing, they first experience a distancing from their old, familiar status. This period is called rite of separation. After that they progress into what Van Gennep called a transitional period or liminality, when every participant becomes marginalized and vulnerable. Victor Turner (1969) focused on the liminal phase of rites and explored the relationships between people who are simultaneously undergoing the change in social status, and he concluded that because of lack of social structure they experienced a greater sense of what he called *communitas*, or togetherness, due to shared experience. At the end of the rite, people are finally reincorporated into their social group structure, where they are fully accepted by everyone as carrying a new social status.

Jean Holm and John Bowker's book *Rites of Passage* (1994) provides an extensive set of essays about different rites of passage from all major world religions. Among other things, they discuss Buddhist funerary rites, Christian ordination rites, Chinese birth rites, Islamic naming rites, and Jewish circumcision rites.

In Judaism boys and girls going through the physical transition from puberty to adulthood must participate in a coming-of age-ceremony, for boys, a bar mitzvah, or "son of the commandment," and for girls, a bat mitzvah, or "daughter of the commandment" (Holm and Bowker, 122). This life-changing experience can be quite trying and critical for them. The boy must stand before the whole congregation and read from the Torah, which is hard for him to do, but by overcoming his fears and performing his duty he proves that he is worthy to be accepted and treated by others as an adult and a full member of the community. The party that follows is one of reincorporation.

Christian anthropologist Victor Turner (1920–83) used rites of passage to explain membership of religious groups such as the early Franciscans and the counterculture of the 1960s in the US. Irving Hexham (b. 1943) built on Turner's work to explain conversion to New Age–type groups in Glastonbury, England. Thus the concept is very useful for understanding the phases of the conversion process and birth of new religions.

See also Bar/Bat Mitzvah; Buddhism; Christianity, Protestant; Islam, Basic Beliefs of; Judaism

Bibliography. I. Hexham, *Some Aspects of the Contemporary Search for an Alternative Society*; J. Holm and J. Bowker, eds., *Rites of Passage*; V. Turner, *The Ritual Process: Structure and Anti-Structure*; A. Van Gennep, *The Rites of Passage*, translated by M. B. Vizedom and G. L. Caffee.

D. Fatovic

RITUALS. A ritual is a sacred custom or any form of repetitive behavior that is fixed by tradition.

In different religions, people enact their beliefs and make them real by performing ceremonial rituals. These are usually socially prescribed symbolic behaviors that are formal, structured, and repetitive, such as worship, singing, recitation, manipulation of sacred objects, or dance. Rituals are often performed at regular intervals, within specialized, sacred locations.

Rituals are of many types, but common to them all is the conviction that what is being done on earth approximates the divine or supernaturally revealed order. Because of this, people can obtain certain powers through performing rituals, in order to influence the living conditions here on earth. One example of this is cyclical rituals performed to ensure a good harvest.

Victor Turner (1920–83), a British Roman Catholic and symbolic anthropological theorist, made an immense contribution to the understanding of ritual processes in his classic work *The Ritual Process: Structure and Anti-Structure* (1969). After doing fieldwork among the Ndembu people of Africa, he discussed and analyzed his findings about ritual practices in such a way as to show both symbolic structures and social implications of liminal stages of ritual. He was aware of the deeper meaning and importance of rituals for communities and therefore went beyond simply describing in detail "stylized gestures and singing the cryptic songs of ritual performance" (7). Turner also argued that during the liminal, or transitional, phase of ritual, which is defined as socially marginal, stressful, and ambiguous, the subjects of the sacred performance "tend to develop an intense comradeship and egalitarianism," which he called *communitas* (95).

Christianity is full of rich and complex rituals that enable believers to experience their relationship to God and at the same time affirm the solidarity of church membership. For instance, sacraments, or "sacred actions," such as baptism, confirmation, and the Eucharist are some of the essential rituals in Christianity, as are acts of weekly worship and special occasions like the celebration of Christmas and Easter. Baptism is an important ritual among all Christian denominations

except the Society of Friends (Quakers) and the Salvation Army, and despite some different symbolic interpretations, it can be viewed as an initiation rite. A person is either immersed in or sprinkled with water as a symbolic sign of cleansing, and through participating in this ritual act he or she becomes an official member of the church. Another Roman Catholic anthropologist, Mary Douglas (1921–2007), expanded on the meaning of rituals and explained in her book *Natural Symbols* (1970) her vision of the human body as symbolizing the social structure. She also argued that tight communities with strong social control toward conformation tend to adhere to more ritualistic religious practices. Because of the sacred meaning of ritual in those situations, followers tend to accept their reality as an unquestionable truth. This kind of worship is not individualistic or internal, as among Protestants.

Religious reformations or revitalization movements often interpret their own work as a reaction to the ritual expressions of another group—which they term "dead rituals"—and see their own activity as a total rejection of ritual, but this notion is mistaken. Thus the Plymouth Brethren reject the Roman Catholic High Mass on theological grounds, yet, in fact, their own services have many rituals, even though the participants usually do not recognize them as such.

Rituals serve to both draw people into and maintain membership in religious communities. For example, the "Christian Year" creates a calendar of events (Advent, Christmas, Lent, Easter) that shape the believers' use of time.

See also ANTHROPOLOGY OF RELIGION; RELIGION; SOCIOLOGY OF RELIGION

Bibliography. C. Bell, *Ritual Theory, Ritual Practice*; M. Douglas, *Natural Symbols: Explorations in Cosmology*; V. Turner, *The Ritual Process: Structure and Anti-Structure*.

D. Fatovic

ROMAN CATHOLICISM. The membership of the Roman Catholic Church exceeds one billion, though this number may not be completely accurate since persons generally remain on the rolls unless they are excommunicated. During the twentieth century, Roman Catholicism was found largely in Latin America, Eastern Europe, Italy, Spain, Ireland, Quebec in Canada, and portions of the US. Recently, however, the growth of the Roman Catholic Church has been in Africa and Asia.

History of the Roman Catholic Church. Although Roman Catholics claim that the Roman Catholic Church has existed from the very beginning of Christianity, many historians place the formal creation of the church in 1054, when the Roman and Eastern churches officially split. Others trace its beginning much further back, to Pope Leo I in the fifth century. Leo I was the first bishop of Rome to argue for and assert the primacy of the authority of the Roman church over all other churches. No matter which date is used, it is clear that the Western church, headed by Rome, has historically held several distinctive beliefs apart from the rest of Christianity. These include, among others, the so-called *filioque* clause, both the primacy and infallibility of the pope, the immaculate conception and bodily ascension of Mary, and indulgences.

The history of the Roman Catholic Church (RCC) can be profitably viewed from the twenty-one ecumenical councils of the Christian church that it accepts as authoritative. By contrast Eastern Orthodoxy accepts only the first seven, and most Protestants only the first four. So as time went on, the RCC moved farther and farther from its starting point and commonality with other sections of Christendom, especially in the last few centuries.

The General Councils of the Church. General church councils have played an important role in the development of Roman Catholicism. Indeed, the RCC considers the decrees of these councils infallible. The first eight councils were convened by emperors, whereas the last thirteen were convened by popes.

1. The First Council of Nicaea (AD 325) was called by the professing Christian emperor Constantine. In condemnation of the heresy of Arianism, it affirmed in the Nicene Creed on the Trinity the full deity of Christ as eternal and of the same nature as the Father. In addition, the council taught that bishops should be appointed only by other bishops (canon 4), that excommunication is to be done by a bishop (canon 5), and that the bishops have jurisdiction over their own geographical areas (canon 6). It also demanded that all who convert to the church "should profess in writing that they will observe and follow the dogmas of the Catholic and Apostolic Church" (Schaff, 14:19).

2. The First Council of Constantinople (381) was convened by Emperor Theodosius I (379–95) to unite the church. It reaffirmed the Nicene Creed, proclaimed the deity of the Holy Spirit, and united the Eastern church (divided by the Arian controversy). The emperor is said to have "founded the orthodox Christian state. Arianism and other heresies became legal offenses, sacrifice [to pagan gods] was forbidden, and paganism almost outlawed" (Cross, 1361).

The practices of Theodosius I were later codified by Emperor Theodosian II into the "Theodosian Code" (proclaimed in 438), which later was superseded by the Justinian Code (539) and was later expanded into the Corpus Juris Civilis (body of [Roman] civil law), which became the basis for Canon Law in the West (Cross, 771), which became binding on all churches under the administration of the Roman church.

3. The Council of Ephesus (431) condemned Nestorianism (which asserted there were two persons as well as two natures in Christ). Since Christ is only one person with

two natures, it concluded that "this was the sentiment of the holy Fathers; therefore they ventured to call the holy Virgin, the Mother of God, not as if the nature of the Word or his divinity had its beginning from the holy Virgin, but because of her was born that holy body with a rational soul, to which the Word being personally united is said to be born according to the flesh" (Cyril, *Epistle to Nestorius*, in Schaff, 14:198).

4. The Council of Chalcedon (451) was called by Emperor Marcian to deal with the Eutychian (Monophysite) heresy, which merged the two natures of Christ, making a logically incoherent combination of an infinite-finite nature. Of five-hundred-plus bishops present, only two were from the West, plus two papal delegates. The heretic Eutyches had said, "I confess that our Lord was of two natures before the union, but after the union I confess one nature" (Schaff, 14:258). The council agreed with Archbishop (Pope) Leo to "anathamatize" this as "absurd," "extremely foolish," "extremely blasphemous," and "impious" (Schaff, 14:258).

The council's recognition of an "archbishop" or bishop over bishops represents a new step in the long development of the Roman hierarchy, a development that culminated in the infallible authority of the bishop of bishops, the bishop of Rome (i.e., the pope), at Vatican I (1870).

Of historic importance is the statement that gives the reason any primacy was given to Rome in the first place—namely, "For the Fathers rightly granted privileges to the throne of the old Rome, because it was the royal city" (canon 28). This confirms the interpretation of Irenaeus's statement that the primacy of Rome was reflective, not authoritative. That is, Rome was given more respect, not authority, because it was the church in the capital of the empire and, therefore, more reflective of the whole church since representatives from the whole empire would naturally consort there (Schaff, 14:288).

5. The Second Council of Constantinople (553) was convoked by Emperor Justinian. It issued fourteen anathemas, the first twelve directed at Theodore of Mopsuestia. A later insert places Origen's name in the eleventh anathema, something accepted by later popes. Among the heresies condemned are Arianism, Nestorianism, Eutychianism, Monophysitism (statements 1–11), and Adoptionism (12). Two statements affirmed the perpetual virginity of Mary, calling her the "ever-virgin Mary, the Mother of God" (statements 5 and 14). The council condemned the reigning pope (Vigilius) as heretical; he later recanted and approved of the action of the council (Schaff, 14:305).

6. The Third Council of Constantinople (680) was convened by Emperor Constantine IV (Pogonatus). It affirmed the "five holy ecumenical councils" before it (Schaff, 14:345). In addition, it reaffirmed that Christ had two natures united in one person and that he had two wills, one human and one divine, which had a moral unity resulting from the complete harmony between the two natures of the God-man (as opposed to the Monothelitists, who said there was only one will in Christ). It also refers to Mary as "our Lady, the holy, immaculate, ever-virgin and glorious Mary, truly and properly the Mother of God" (Schaff, 14:340). Macarius, the archbishop of Antioch, was condemned, along with "Honorius some time Pope of Old Rome" (Schaff, 14:342–43).

This council claimed to be not only "illuminated by the Holy Spirit" (Schaff, 14:350) but also "inspired by the Holy Ghost" (Schaff, 14:347). Thus it claimed to provide "a definition, clean from all error, certain, and infallible" (Schaff, 14:350). This would later be claimed by the pope for himself at Vatican I (1870). Following the council, the emperor posted an "Imperial Edict" in the church, noting that "in no other than the orthodox faith could men be saved" (Schaff, 14:353).

7. The Second Council of Nicaea (787) was called by Emperor Constantine VI and Empress Irene and attended by legates of Pope Hadrian I. It dealt with the iconoclastic controversy. It ruled in favor of venerating images: "Receiving their holy and honorable reliques with all honour, I salute and venerate these with honour. . . . Likewise also the venerable images of the incarnation of our Lord Jesus Christ . . . and of the holy Apostles, Prophets, Martyrs, and of all the Saints—the sacred images of all these, I salute and venerate" (Schaff, 14:533). Further, it pronounced "Anathema to those who do not salute the holy and venerable images" and "Anathama to those who call the sacred images idols" (Schaff, 14:534). It zealously declared, "To those who have a doubtful mind and do not confess with their whole heart that they venerate the sacred images, anathema!" (Schaff, 14:535). It encouraged prayer to Mary and the Saints, saying, "I ask for the intercessions of our spotless Lady the Holy Mother of God, and those of the holy and heavenly powers, and those of all the Saints" (Schaff, 14:533).

The contemporary iconoclasts' objections to the council's decisions are expressed in another council claiming to be the true seventh ecumenical council. That council declared flatly that "Satan misguided men, so that they worshipped the creature instead of the Creator" (Schaff, 14:543). The council concluded: "If anyone does not accept this our Holy and Ecumenical Seventh Synod, let him be anathema" (Schaff, 14:546). They condemned Emperor Germanus of Constantinople, calling him "the double-minded, and worshipper of wood!" (Schaff, 14:546).

The Second Council of Nicaea also forbade the secular appointment of bishops, thus solidifying the independent authority of the church over against that of the state. Further, the primacy of Peter and of apostolic succession was emphasized: "For the blessed Peter himself, the chief of the Apostles, who first sat in the Apostolic See, left the chiefship of his Apostolate, and pastoral care, to his successors who are to sit in his most holy seat for ever" (Schaff, 14:537). The council further spoke of "the holy Roman Church which has a prior rank, which is the head of all the Churches of God" (Schaff, 14:537).

8. The Fourth Council of Constantinople (869) was the last council to be called by the emperor. It explicitly affirmed the Second Council of Nicaea (787) and condemned the schism of Photius, patriarch of Constantinople, who challenged the *filioque* clause in the creed (the clause that affirmed that the Holy Spirit also proceeded from the Son); this disagreement later became an important one between the Western and the Eastern churches (in 1054). The Eastern Orthodox Church rejects any council after the seventh.

9. The First Lateran Council (1123) was called by Pope Callistus. It was the first council called by a pope, which signals a further step in the development of the Roman church. It confirmed the Concordat of Worms (1122), which granted the pope, not the emperor, the sole right to invest a bishop-elect with a ring and staff and receive homage from the bishop-elect before his consecration.

10. The Second Lateran Council (1139) was convoked by Pope Innocent II for the reformation of the church. It condemned the schism of Arnold of Brescia, a reformer who spoke against confession to a priest in favor of confession of believers to one another.

11. The Third Lateran Council (1179) was convened by Pope Alexander III to counter antipope Callistus III. It affirmed that the right to elect the pope was restricted to the College of Cardinals and that a two-thirds majority was necessary for the election of a pope.

12. The Fourth Lateran Council (1215) was called by Pope Innocent III. It was another landmark council in the development from the old catholic church to the Roman Catholic Church. It affirmed the doctrine

of transubstantiation, the primacy of the bishop of Rome, and seven sacraments. It gave the Dominicans authority to institute the Office of the Inquisitors, which gave the church authority to investigate heresy and turn heretics over to the state for punishment.

13. The First Council of Lyons (1245) was convened by Pope Innocent IV to heal the "five wounds" of the church: (1) moral decadence of the clergy, (2) the danger of the Saracens (Arab Muslims against whom the crusaders fought), (3) the schism with the Eastern church, (4) the invasion of Hungary by the Tartars, and (5) the rupture between the church and Emperor Frederick II. The council condemned and formally deposed Emperor Frederick II for his imprisonment of cardinals and bishops on their way to the council. It instituted minor reforms but left the main reforms of Pope Innocent untouched.

14. The Second Council of Lyons (1274) was called by Pope Gregory X to bring about union with the Eastern church, to liberate the Holy Land, and to reform morals in the church. Noted theologians Albert the Great (1193–1280) and Bonaventure (1221–74) attended, but Thomas Aquinas (1225–74) died on the way to the council. It approved some newly founded orders, including the Dominicans and the Franciscans. It included affirmation of the procession of the Holy Spirit from the Father *and* the Son (the *filioque* clause) and did bring about union with the East, though it was short lived, ending in 1289.

15. The Council of Vienne (1311–12) was convoked by Pope Clement V to deal with the Templars (a military order of the church), who were accused of heresy and immorality. The council announced reforms, suppressed the Templars, provided assistance for the Holy Land, encouraged missions, and made decrees concerning the Inquisition, which were instituted formally in 1232 by Emperor Frederic II.

16. The Council of Constance (1414–18) was convened by Pope John XXIII in order to end the Great Schism of three simultaneous popes, to reform the church, and to combat heresy. It condemned over two hundred propositions of John Wycliffe. Reformer John Hus, who held similar doctrines, refused to recant and was burned at the stake. The council proclaimed the superiority of an ecumenical council over the pope, declaring (in a document titled *Haec Sancta*), "This Council holds its power direct from Christ; everyone, no matter his rank of office, even if it be papal, is bound to obey it in whatever pertains to faith" (Cross, 336–37). This was later contradicted by the decision of Vatican I (1870) that the pope alone has the right to make infallible pronouncements on his own (see below).

17. The Council of Basel-Ferrara-Florence (AD 1431–37) was called by Pope Martin V. It is a series of councils beginning with Basel (1431), moving to Ferrara (1438–39), then Florence (1439–43), and last to Rome (1443–45). Its chief objective was union with the Eastern church, which sought support from the West against the Turks, who were nearing Constantinople. The controversy centered on the double procession of the Holy Spirit, purgatory, and the primacy of the pope. By July 1439, there was agreement on "the Decree of Union," in which the East agreed with the West on these issues. Subsequently, many bishops recanted, and the union ceased when the Turks captured Constantinople in 1453. The Council of Basel and its members were pronounced heretical.

18. The Fifth Lateran Council (1512–17) was called by Pope Julius II to invalidate the decrees of the antipapal council of Pisa, convened by Louis XII of France. It agreed to a few minor reforms but did not treat the main issues of the Reformation. Later an Augustinian monk named Martin Luther addressed these issues by tacking up his Ninety-Five Theses on October 31, 1517, which started the great Protestant Reformation.

19. The Council of Trent (1545–63) was called to counter the Reformation. It declared

many of the characteristic doctrines of Roman Catholicism, including the equal validity of tradition with Scripture, the seven sacraments, transubstantiation, the necessity of good works for justification, purgatory, indulgences, the veneration of saints and images, prayers for the dead, prayers to the dead (saints), and the canonicity of eleven apocryphal books. Many Protestants believe Rome apostatized at Trent by a denial of the true gospel. Others see it as a significant deviation from biblical and historic orthodoxy but not a total apostasy (Geisler and McKenzie, chap. 12).

20. The First Council of the Vatican (1869–70), called by Pope Pius IX, denounced pantheism, materialism, and atheism. Pius pronounced papal infallibility. The council rejected St. Antonio of Florence's formula that the pope, "using the counsel and seeking for help of the universal Church," cannot err. Instead it ruled that the pope's definitions are "irreformable of themselves, and not from the consent of the Church," when the pope spoke ex cathedra, that is, as pastor and doctor of all Christians. This ruling directly contradicted the pronouncement of the Council of Constance (1414–18). It was during this period (1854) that the Roman church officially pronounced the immaculate conception of the Virgin Mary.

Though not at a council, in 1950 the Roman Catholic Church pronounced infallible the doctrine of the bodily assumption of the Virgin Mary.

21. The Second Council of the Vatican (1962–63) was ecumenical (with Eastern Orthodox and Protestant observers). It instituted changes in rituals (like Mass in local languages), pronounced reforms, and declared inclusivism of "separated brethren" (non-Catholic Christians) and the salvation of sincere non-Christians.

The Development of the Roman Catholic Papal Authority. The evolution of the doctrine of the infallibility of the pope, a central doctrine of Roman Catholicism, illuminates the development of the Roman church in general. It stands in contrast to the Eastern church's polity and (critics argue) to the apostolic teaching recorded in the New Testament.

Plurality of Elders in the New Testament Church. Critics of the Roman Catholic Church argue that the visible New Testament church had no hierarchy, but each church was independent and congregational in form. There was no episcopal form of government, where a bishop was distinct from and had authority over elders. The New Testament had a plurality of elders and deacons in each church (Acts 14:23; Phil. 1:1). Also, the terms *bishop* and *elder* refer to the same office (1 Tim. 3:1; Titus 1:5, 7; Acts 20:17, 28). Roman Catholics argue that the authority of the apostles extended over all churches. Individual congregations were expected to follow the teachings of the apostles. This authority was passed through apostolic succession to subsequent bishops, especially the bishop of Rome (whereas in the Eastern Orthodox tradition the authority simply resided within the episcopate as a whole). The Roman church also points to the fact that the disciples of the apostles themselves embraced a hierarchy of authority. Polycarp, disciple of John, was referred to as "Bishop of the Smyrnaeans." Ignatius, the first-century apostolic father, said, "See that ye all follow the bishop, even as Jesus Christ does the Father, and the presbytery as ye would the apostles; and reverence the deacons, as being the institution of God. Let no man do anything connected with the Church without the bishop" (*Epistle to the Smyrnaeans* 8, in *Ante-Nicene Fathers* 1:89).

The Appearance of One Bishop over a Region. This informal and local episcopate gave way eventually to regional bishops and then to one bishop who was prime among the bishops, namely, the bishop of Rome. Eusebius speaks of "Silvanus, bishop of the churches about Emesa," during the wicked reign of Emperor Diocletian (ca. 303). It is understandable that the growth of one church in an area might lead to many churches over which the bishop of the mother church would remain in charge. And Rome, being the largest and capital city of the empire, would naturally have a powerful and influential bishop.

The Inception of One Bishop over the Whole Church. Irenaeus (ca. 130–ca. 200) seems to have been a transition in this process, for he took a key step in the direction of an authoritative bishop, namely, the bishop of bishops in Rome. He stated, "That tradition derived from the apostles, of the very great, the very ancient, and universally known Church founded and organized at Rome by the two most glorious apostles, Peter and Paul; as also by pointing out the faith preached to men, which comes down to our times by means of the succession of the bishops." For "it is a matter of necessity that *every Church should agree* [Latin, *convenire*] *with this Church*, on account of its preeminent authority, that is, the faithful everywhere, inasmuch as the apostolic tradition has been preserved continuously by those [faithful men] who exist everywhere" (*Against Heresies* 3.2, in Roberts and Donaldson, 1:415–16, emphasis added). Irenaeus spoke of a single bishop over a city, for he spoke of Polycarp as "bishop of the Church in Smyrna" (*Against Heresies* 3.4, in Roberts and Donaldson, 1:416). He also acknowledged that there was a line of bishops in Rome beginning with Linus (*Against Heresies* 3.3). Likewise, he believed there was at least a reflective sense of primacy in the bishop of Rome since, as capital of the empire, Rome reflected the churches everywhere.

Certainly by the time of Cyprian (third century), a more monarchial concept of bishop had evolved. For Cyprian insisted that "there is one God, and Christ is one, and there is one Church, and one chair founded upon the rock by the word of the Lord" (*Epistle* 39:5, in Roberts and Donaldson, 5:318).

The Appearance of Papal Authority to Formulate Creeds. Another step was taken in the emergence of the doctrine of the bishop of Rome in the late Middle Ages by the time of Thomas Aquinas (d. 1274). He held that "there must be one faith for the entire Church. . . . This norm could not be followed unless every question arising out of faith were resolved by one having care over the whole Church. A new version of the creed, then, falls to the sole authority of the Pope, just as do all other matters affecting the whole church" (*Summa Theologica* 2a 2ae, q. 1, a. 10). However, Aquinas believed in the primacy of Scripture, for he affirmed that "the truth of faith is sufficiently plain in the teaching of Christ and the apostles" (2a 2ae, q. 1, a. 10). Further, "the truth of faith is contained in sacred Scripture, in diverse ways and, sometimes, darkly. . . . That is why there was a need to draw succinctly together out of the Scriptural teachings, some clear statements to be set before all for their belief. The symbol [i.e., creed] is not added to Scripture, but drawn from Scripture" (2a 2ae, q. 1, a.). Indeed, Aquinas never repudiated his earlier statement that "we believe the successors of the apostles only in so far as they tell us those things which the apostles and prophets have left in their writings" (*On Truth* 14.10–11). Likewise, the pope has the authority not to set forth new doctrines not found in Scripture but only to restate in clear form (e.g., by creeds) what the Scriptures teach.

The Pronouncement of the Infallible Authority of the Pope over the Whole Church. The final step in the evolution of the primacy of the Roman episcopacy came with the pronouncement of Pope Pius IX that the bishop of Rome is infallible when speaking from Peter's chair (ex cathedra) on matters of faith and practice. This occurred at the First Vatican Council (1870). In the words of the Roman dogma itself, the council declared:

433

We, adhering faithfully to the tradition received from the beginning of the Christian faith . . . teach and explain *that the dogma has been divinely revealed*: that the Roman Pontiff, *when he speaks ex cathedra, that is, when carrying out the duty of pastor and teacher of all Christians* in accord with his supreme apostolic authority he explains a doctrine of faith or morals to be held by the universal Church, through the divine assistance promised him in blessed Peter, operates with that *infallibility* with which the divine Redeemer wished that His church be instructed in defining a doctrine on faith and morals; and so such definitions of the Roman Pontiff *from himself, but not from the consensus of the Church, are unalterable.* (Denzinger, §1839, emphasis added)

This declaration of papal infallibility, apart from the other bishops, was the climax of centuries of increasing authority for the bishop of Rome and his successors. This represents a macro leap from the role of a bishop/elder in the New Testament as a local church leader to one God-appointed vicar of Christ over all Christian churches.

Teachings of the Roman Catholic Church. Before we look at distinctive doctrines of the Roman church, which differentiate Roman Catholics from Protestants and many other Christians, we need to focus on the many essential similarities in doctrine with all confessional sections of Christianity.

Doctrines Held in Common. Roman Catholics, Eastern Orthodox, and Protestants hold many doctrines in common. The unity of the Christian Church consists of belief in one Bible, two Testaments, three creeds, four councils, and five centuries. These three creeds (Apostles' Creed, Nicene Creed, and Chalcedonian Creed) include the following sixteen teachings: (1) human depravity, (2) Mary's virginity, (3) Christ's purity (sinlessness), (4) Christ's deity, (5) Christ's humanity, (6) God's unity, (7) God's triunity,

(8) the necessity of God's grace, (9) the necessity of our faith, (10) Christ's atoning death, (11) Christ's bodily resurrection, (12) Christ's bodily ascension, (13) Christ present priestly intercession, (14) Christ's bodily return, (15) the divine inspiration of Scripture, and (16) the literal (historical-grammatical) interpretation of Scripture. A detailed discussion of these foundational doctrines is found elsewhere (Geisler and Rhodes, part 1).

The first fourteen items of this list are essential doctrines of the Christian faith, being necessary to make our salvation possible. The last two are essential as the source and means of obtaining the fourteen salvation essentials. These doctrinal similarities are too strong to place a non-Christian label on the essential doctrines of official Roman Catholicism.

Distinctive Doctrines of Roman Catholicism. Nonetheless, significant differences in both doctrine and practice separate Roman Catholics and Protestants. Protestants reject the following teachings of Rome: (1) the bodily assumption of Mary, (2) prayers to Mary, (3) prayers to other saints, (4) regarding Mary as co-redemptrix with Jesus, (5) veneration of images of Mary and other saints, (6) veneration of Mary, (7) transubstantiation (the changing of the bread and wine into the actual body of Christ), (8) worship of the consecrated host, (9) confession of sins to a priest, (10) doing penance to gain favor with God, (11) the sale of indulgences, (12) the treasury of merit, (13) belief in purgatory, (14) adding eleven apocryphal books to the canon of Scripture, (15) the infallibility of the pope, and (16) making good works necessary for salvation. The Council of Trent infallibly pronounced that "if anyone shall say . . . that the one justified by good works . . . does not truly merit increase of grace, eternal life, and the attainment of that eternal life (if he should die in grace), and also an increase of glory; let him be anathema" (Denzinger, §842).

As can readily be seen, the differences between Protestants (evangelicals, especially) and Roman Catholics are neither few nor insignificant. Indeed, they form an unbridgeable barrier to any ecumenical unity between the two.

Distinctives of Protestants vis-à-vis Roman Catholics. What finally distinguishes Protestants from the Roman Church is the belief that salvation is derived from (1) the Bible alone (*sola Scriptura*), (2) based on the work of Christ alone (*solus Christus*), (3) achieved by grace alone (*sola gratia*), (4) received by faith alone (*sola fide*), and all for (5) the glory of God alone (*soli Deo gloria*).

While Roman Catholics believe in the necessity of grace, they do not believe in the exclusivity of grace. It is the important word *alone* that distinguishes the Protestant view on all these points.

See also EASTERN ORTHODOXY; EVANGELICALISM

Bibliography. K. Adams, *The Spirit of Catholicism*; J. Armstrong, ed., *Roman Catholicism: Evangelical Protestants Analyze What Divides and Unites Us*; Augustine, *Against the Epistle of the Manichaeans* and *On Christian Doctrine*; L. M. Bermejo, *Infallibility on Trial*; H. Bettenson, *Documents of the Christian Church*, rev. ed.; C. Castaldo, *Holy Ground*; *Catechism of the Catholic Church*; J. F. Clarkson et al., "The Vatican Council (1869–70)," in *The Church Teaches: Documents of the Church in English Translation*; F. L. Cross, ed., *Oxford Dictionary of the Christian Church*; H. Denzinger with K. Rahner, *The Sources of Catholic Dogma*; A. Dulles, "Infallibility: The Terminology," in *Teaching Authority*; A. Flannery, *Vatican Council II*; N. Geisler and J. Betancourt, *Is Rome the True Church?*; N. Geisler and R. McKenzie, *Roman Catholics and Evangelicals: Agreements and Differences*; N. Geisler and R. Rhodes, *Conviction without Compromise*; H. W. House, *Charts of World Religions*; J. N. D. Kelly, *Early Christian Doctrine*; H. Küng, *Infallible? An Inquiry*, translated by E. Quinn; J. Neuner and J. Dupuis, *The Christian Faith in the Doctrinal Documents of the Catholic Church*; *New Catholic Encyclopedia*; M. Noll and C. Nystrom, *Is the Reformation Over? An Evangelical Assessment of Contemporary Roman Catholicism*; L. Ott, *Fundamentals of Catholic Dogma*; J. Pelikan, *The Riddle of Roman Catholicism*; A. Roberts and J. Donaldson, eds., *The Ante-Nicene Fathers*, 10 vols.; G. Salmon, *The Infallibility of the Church*; P. Schaff., ed., *Nicene and Post-Nicene Fathers*, 2nd series, 14 vols.; W. Walker, *A History of the Christian Church*.

N. L. Geisler

ROSH HASHANAH (THE FEAST OF TRUMPETS). *Rosh Hashanah* (Hebrew, "the head of the year") marks the beginning of the Jewish civil year. Outside Leviticus 23:23–25, the Feast of Trumpets is mentioned in two other passages in Scripture: Numbers 29:1–6 emphasizes the various sacrifices that were obligatory for this festival, and Nehemiah 8:1–12 states that the day when Ezra read the law of Moses before the people was "the first day of the seventh month," the first day of the Feast of Trumpets.

Insofar as the biblical practice is concerned, four things should be mentioned. First, it was a one-day festival only, on the first day of the seventh month, Tishrei. Second, it was to be a day on which there was to be no labor; it was a day of rest like the Sabbath. Third, it was to be celebrated by the blowing of trumpets. Fourth, the "trumpet" was not the long silver trumpet of Numbers 10 but the horn of a ram, called the *shofar*. By Jewish law, horns of all kosher animals are permitted except for bulls, but the ram's horn has been preferred because of its symbolic link with the offering of Isaac in Genesis 22.

Within Jewish practice, on this occasion the trumpet is blown in the synagogue. Jewish theology states three reasons for blowing the trumpet. First, it is a call to remembrance and repentance. Jews are called to return to practicing their religion. Second, the trumpet reminds Israel of its covenant relationship with God. Third, the ram's horn is thought

435

to confuse Satan on the day that he accuses Israel, based on Zechariah 3:1.

Bread is dipped in honey on this occasion to symbolize hope for a sweet year, for the civil new year begins. Apples are also dipped in honey, and a hot dish known as "honey carrots" is eaten. The festive meal of this occasion includes some type of a head meat. Sometimes it is a ram's head, in memory of the sacrifice of Isaac, while other times it is a fish head, in the hope that Jews will be the "head" someday and not the "tail." The popular fruits for this occasion are apples, grapes, and pomegranates.

See also JUDAISM

Bibliography. R. Posner, *The High Holy Days*; C. Roth, "Rosh Hashanah," in *Encyclopedia Judaica*, edited by C. Roth; H. Schauss, *The Jewish Festivals: A Guide to Their History and Observance*; Rabbi N. Scherman, Rabbi H. Goldwurm, and Rabbi A. Gold, *Rosh Hashanah—Its Significance, Laws, and Prayers*; I. Singer, "Rosh Hashanah," in *The Jewish Encyclopedia*; M. Strassfeld, *The Jewish Holidays: A Guide & Commentary*; Y. Vainstein, *The Cycle of the Jewish Year: A Study of the Festivals and of Selections from the Liturgy*.

A. Fruchtenbaum

SABBATARIANISM. Sabbatarianism is the belief that the Sabbath (the seventh day of the week), derived from the fourth commandment in the Old Testament, must be observed. This is based on a literalistic understanding of the Bible and the legalistic application of biblical teachings in a Christian context. Within Christianity sabbatarianism sometimes refers to considering Sunday as the Sabbath and transferring the kinds of regulations found within the Jewish Sabbath to the Christian day of worship, Sunday (the first day of the week). In other usages within Christianity, sabbatarianism refers to the doctrine that Christians ought to observe Saturday, not Sunday, as the day of worship and rest.

The early church did not have strict regulations about Sabbath observance. Jesus Christ proclaimed that "the Sabbath was made for man, not man for the Sabbath" (Mark 2:27). Paul denounced those who made Jewish observances such as the Sabbath compulsory for Christians (Gal. 4:4–11; Col. 2:16–17). Unlike Jewish practice, in which one's activities were circumscribed on the Sabbath, for Christians no one day of the week related to "rest" since Jesus, rather than the Sabbath, gave them the rest of God (Heb. 4:8–10).

The practice of the early church, particularly under the Pauline ministry, was to meet on Sunday for worship (Acts 20:6–12; 1 Cor. 16:2). This custom probably originated due to the resurrection of Jesus on the first day of the week (John 20:1–18) and subsequent appearances by him on this day (John 20:19,

26). Paul did go to synagogue in his travels, but it was for the purpose of evangelism among Jews (Acts 13:14–15; 14:1; 17:17; 18:4), rather than the meeting of Christians.

By the fourth century, Sunday was regarded as equivalent to the Jewish Sabbath, and the prohibiting of ordinary business transactions on Sundays followed. During the Middle Ages, the fourth commandment was kept on Sundays. Yet sabbatarianism was only a minor aspect of medieval Catholicism and even invited the hostility of early reformers such as the Lollards and Martin Luther (1483–1546). The Reformers thought that sabbatarianism functioned as a part of doctrines that upheld the authority of the Catholic Church. Therefore, William Tyndale (1494–1536) and Robert Barnes (1450–1540) argued that there were no particular religious holidays at all because every day is a Sabbath for the Christian. Though Sunday was kept holy by the medieval borough and the medieval diocese and inherited by the Protestants, Sunday sports and church fairs were still permitted after the time of service, making the sabbatarian controversy less significant.

Saturday Sabbath keeping was practiced by some Socinians in Transylvania in Hungary. But its general popularity was of English origin during the sixteenth and seventeenth centuries, when sabbatarianism began to gain strength. Separatist Puritans protested against the keeping of saints' days and drew attention to the strict observation of Sunday as the Sabbath. Most Puritans regarded it not only as a holy day to be kept but also as one that ought to be spent as a holy day of rest.

During the reigns of Henry VIII (1509–47) and Edward VI (1547–53), the Anglican Church, which preserved traditions found in Catholicism, took a middle ground between the Catholic and the early Puritan position. It was not until the reign of Elisabeth I (1558–1603) that sabbatarianism was mobilized. Only after an incident in London involving bearbaiting on Sunday, January 13, 1583, when eight people were killed, did John Field (d. 1588) warn against Sabbath breaking after he equated Sunday with the Jewish Sabbath. The queen vetoed a bill for the strict observance of the Sabbath in 1585, and fairs, sports, and other secular activities were permitted and widely practiced.

Puritan magistrates tried to enforce a stricter observance of Sunday, regarding it as a Sabbath, and Lancelot Andrewes (1555–1626) wrote a comprehensive theological treatise on the fourth commandment from a moral perspective that was frequently adopted by later Puritans. Following Andrewes, Richard Greenham (1535–94) wrote a *Treatise of the Sabbath* (1592), and Nicholas Bownde (d. 1613), Greenham's son-in-law, entered the fray with his *The Doctrine of the Sabbath* (1595). Though Bownde's book was banned, it circulated widely and stirred controversy between the Stuart Crown and the Puritan-dominated Parliament. The *Book of Sports* (1618), issued by James I (r. 1603–25), intensified the Sabbath debate, regulating the playing of harmless games and maintaining sobriety on Sunday. The Saturday Sabbath movements of John Traske (1585–1636), Theophilus Brabourne (1590–1661), and Henry Jessey (d. 1660) were crucial steps in moving sabbatarianism toward developing into organized religious sects.

Sabbatarianism was later transplanted to American soil and became widespread in the nineteenth century, with both Sunday and Saturday sabbatarian movements. While the Sunday sabbatarian movement tried to secure Sunday as a holy Sabbath, Saturday sabbatarianism developed into sectarian movements. The most important of these is the Seventh-day Adventist (SDA) Church, which was influenced by the Seventh-Day Baptists.

After the Millerite "Great Disappointment" of October 22, 1844, when William Miller's prediction of the second coming of Jesus failed, Ellen G. White (1827–1915), one of Miller's followers, helped found the SDA Church, stressing the Sabbath and the "cleansing of the heavenly sanctuary." Joseph Bates (1792–1872), a retired sea captain, was instrumental in the theological articulation of the SDA views about the Sabbath. Convinced that Christians must obey God's law, particularly the seventh-day Sabbath, he made the unhistorical claim that the early church observed the seventh day as the Sabbath before Sunday was observed after the edict of Constantine.

This sabbatarian impulse influenced a new breed of religious groups around the world. Victor Houteff (1886–1955), who taught at a Sabbath school, founded the Shepherd's Rod. It was renamed the Davidian Seventh-day Adventists in 1942. From this group, Benjamin Roden (d. 1978) formed the Branch Davidians, which came under the leadership of David Koresh (1959–93), leading to the Waco tragedy.

The Church of God, another Adventist splinter group, abandoned most of White's teachings except for her seventh-day doctrine. In 1933 Herbert W. Armstrong (1892–1986) founded the Worldwide Church of God, a staunch Saturday Sabbath group.

In South Korea, the World Mission Society Church of God was founded by Ahn Sahng-hong in 1964 after he left the SDA Church. Preaching "Restore the Early Church's Truth, revive the Early Church's Faith and redeem the whole world," this church heavily focuses on the keeping of the Saturday Sabbath. It has claimed that the church ought to be the "Witness of Ahnsahnghong" since its founder came to be regarded as the true God and his teachings those of "the last Christ." In South Africa, the Church of amaNazaretha, the largest Zulu African Independent Church, founded by Isaiah Shembe (1867–1935) around 1911, like many other African Independent Churches, also observes the Old Testament Sabbath as God's holy day.

Sabbatarianism is rooted in a professedly literal interpretation of the Bible that fails to distinguish between the old and the new covenants. John Edward Carnell offers a telling biblical critique, arguing that such movements betray the hermeneutical principle by converting Old Testament ceremonies into New Testament principles and privileging Jewish tradition against the development of Christian understanding. Although evangelical Protestants continue to hold somewhat differing views of the Sabbath, the extreme, dogmatic Saturday-only sabbatarianism of many Adventist sects is clearly contrary to the Bible.

See also MILLER, WILLIAM; MILLERITE MOVEMENT; SEVENTH-DAY ADVENTISM; SHABBAT (THE SABBATH), JEWISH; SOCINIANISM

Bibliography. D. D. Barrett, *The New Believers: Sects, "Cults" and Alternative Religions*; E. J. Carnell, *The Case for Orthodox Theology*; D. A. Carson, ed., *From Sabbath to Lord's Day*; C. J. Donato, ed., *Perspectives on the Sabbath: 4 Views*; W. A. Elwell, "Lord's Day" and "Sabbath," in *Baker Encyclopedia of the Bible*, vol. 2; R. R. John, "Taking Sabbatarianism Seriously: The Postal System, the Sabbath, and the Transformation of American Political Culture," *Journal of the Early Republic*; D. S. Katz, *Sabbath and Sectarianism in Seventeenth-Century England.*

C. H. Kim

SACRAMENTS. The term *sacrament* comes from the Latin *sacramentum*, meaning "make holy," and refers to a sacred event, rite, or ritual provided to the church. Historically, Christianity has believed the sacraments were handed down from Jesus to the apostles and from the apostles to the church. Roman Catholics, Eastern Orthodox, Anglicans, Lutherans, Reformed churches, and other traditions hold at least two, and as many as seven, sacraments (though some Protestants would substitute the word *ordinance* for *sacrament*).

Roman Catholicism and Eastern Orthodoxy. Eastern Orthodoxy and the Roman Catholic Church have historically viewed the sacraments as the media through which Christ dispenses grace to the faithful. There are seven sacraments, divided into three categories: those of initiation into the church (baptism; confirmation, called *Chrismation* in the East; and Eucharist), those of healing (penance and anointing of the sick), and the sacraments of communion and of service (holy orders and matrimony). Baptism is the sacrament that washes away the stain of original sin and signifies the catechumen's entry into the life of God. All sin is forgiven through baptism, and after baptism nothing remains to inhibit the catechumen's salvation. Justification is thus given at baptism, which allows for faith and the desire to submit to the Holy Spirit's leadership.

Confirmation bestows on the neophyte the Holy Spirit's presence in him or her. It follows baptism and completes baptismal grace (in the East it is done at the time of baptism). The person who receives the sacrament of confirmation expresses the will to live a full life of discipleship, which entails living in obedience to Christ and consistently witnessing to his glory both in and out of the church. The anointing with chrism on the neophyte's forehead confers the sacrament.

The Eucharist represents the apex of the life of the church because through it the church identifies with Christ in his sacrifice. Christ himself, according to Eastern and Roman teaching, ministers the eucharistic sacrifice through the mediation of priests. While the Eastern Orthodox Church has historically affirmed the physical presence of Christ in the Eucharist, in the Roman Catholic Church, the Council of Trent emphasized that the elements of the Eucharist become the literal body, blood, soul, and divinity of Christ through the act of transubstantiation—that the wheat bread and grape wine mystically transform into the literal body and blood of Jesus. No person may receive communion unless he or she is in a state of grace and have committed no mortal sin.

Penance is the sacrament through which the forgiveness of sins committed after baptism is given. This sacrament is also known as that of conversion, confession, or reconciliation. It involves genuine regret for sins committed, repentance, confession to a priest, and the intention to perform works of reparation. Works of reparation are done so that the person may reinvigorate a will to live obediently. The effects of penance include reconciliation with the church, forgiveness of sins both eternally and temporally, the cleansing of one's conscience, and a renewal of desire to live as a Christian.

Anointing of the sick is given to those who face illness or imminent death. The sacrament is conferred in order to strengthen the person to endure suffering for Christ's sake, to restore health, and/or to prepare for passing over to the Father.

Holy orders is the sacrament bestowed on any Christian who seeks to carry out the mission of Christ and the church. It is seen as an aspect of the apostolic succession because Christ entrusted his mission to the apostles and to succeeding generations of the faithful. The episcopate, the presbyterate, and the diaconate are the three degrees of the sacrament. Thus the priesthood of ministers differs from the common priesthood of the faithful because divine power to serve the church has been conferred on ministers. This service entails teaching, worship, and pastoral governance. Holy orders are given only to baptized men.

Marriage signifies the union of Christ with the church and provides the husband and wife with the grace to love and be faithful to each other as Christ displays love and faithfulness to his bride. Remarriage after divorce is permitted, but the two spouses are not allowed to receive communion. Still, the sacrament of marriage is intended to edify the Christian home, the domestic church, where children grow in the heritage of the Lord.

Anglicanism. The Anglican Church originally held substantially the same view of the sacraments as the Roman Catholic Church, from which it broke in 1534. However, owing to the influence of the Protestant Reformation, the Anglican Church now teaches that the sacraments are "certain sure witnesses, and effectual signs of grace, and God's good will towards us" that "strengthen and confirm our Faith in Him" (Church of England, Article 25). It rejects transubstantiation in regard to the Eucharist but upholds infant baptism. Although it affirms seven sacraments, the Anglican Church only acknowledges baptism and the Eucharist as being instituted by Christ.

Lutheranism. The Lutheran Church follows Martin Luther's teachings that there are only two sacraments, baptism and the Lord's Supper, although sometimes absolution is included as a third. Further, although Luther taught the necessity of faith for salvation, he taught that the sacraments are means by which the believer secures the promise of grace. Luther also rejected transubstantiation but argued that Christ was somehow present "in, under, and through" the elements, and this presence is called "the real presence of Christ," a mystery in which the elements, though true bread and wine, nonetheless have the real presence of Christ's flesh and blood transmitted through his divine nature.

Calvinism and Reformed Churches. Calvin taught that there are only two sacraments, baptism and the Lord's Supper. The sacraments are "an external sign, by which the Lord seals on our consciences his promises of good-will toward us, in order to sustain the weakness of our faith, and we in our turn testify our piety towards him" (4.14.1).

Other Groups. Some Christian groups, such as Baptists (in general) and Pentecostals, do not practice sacraments but call baptism and Communion "ordinances" (arguing that Christ ordained them) and do not see them as having any specific spiritual benefit. Still others—generally within certain Brethren, Pentecostal, and Holiness groups—will add an ordinance called "foot washing," based on John 13:1–17 and 1 Timothy 5:10.

See also EASTERN ORTHODOXY; ROMAN CATHOLICISM

Bibliography. John Calvin, *Institutes of the Christian Religion*, translated by H. Beveridge; Church of England, *Thirty-Nine Articles*; W. Grudem, *Systematic Theology: An Introduction to Biblical Doctrine*; Libreria Editrice Vaticana, *Catechism of the Catholic Church*; G. Wainwright and K. B. Westerfield Tucker, eds., *The Oxford History of Christian Worship*.

J. D. Wilsey and H. W. House

SACRED FIRE. In Zoroastrianism a sacred fire is a ritual conflagration that symbolizes the holy light of Ahura Mazda and the cosmic struggle against the forces of evil. The prophet Zoroaster (Greek; Persian, Zarathushtra) described sacred fire as the source of all goodness, purity, and spiritual illumination and as the metaphysical ground of unity between God and human beings. There are three major types of sacred fires:

1. Atash Dadgah (fire of the appointed place) is a temporary fire intended to burn only during a particular Zoroastrian ceremony, often in the household of a devotee.
2. Atash Adaran (fire of fires) is a permanent fire that burns in a minor fire temple, monitored and kindled by a

group of Zoroastrian priests appointed to this task.
3. Atash Behram (fire of victory) is a continuous fire that represents divine kingship and burns in a major fire temple. (Starting an Atash Behram [or Bahram] poses extreme logistical problems in that one of its requirements is that it be made from the cinders of 1,001 fires, including at least one fire that was ignited by a bolt of lightning.)

Zoroastrian theology declares that Ahura Mazda created three great fires—Adur Burzen-Mihr, Adur Farnbag, and Adur Gushnasp—as a means of protecting humanity and establishing true religion and worship. Popular Zoroastrianism in modern Iran contends that this trio of fires (also known as the royal fires) have existed since the time Ahura Mazda created the world.

Sacred fire has been a defining symbol of Zoroastrianism throughout its history. According to some scholars, a proto-Zoroastrian fire cult appears to have predated Zoroastrianism by several centuries. There is archaeological evidence that Zoroastrian fire temples were built to house sacred fires as early as 500 BC and continued to be built across much of Asia for more than a thousand years. However, Islamic invasions of Persia (modern Iran) and India during the Middle Ages resulted in the destruction of many of these temples; during these assaults many Zoroastrians were forced to transport sacred fires from one location to another to avoid having them snuffed out by their Muslim conquerors. (Some historians of Zoroastrianism believe that sacred fires may still exist that have burned continuously for more than two thousand years.) As of 2017 only eight known Atash Beahrams remained in existence in India (and possibly one in Iran; there is variance among sources). However, adherents of Zoroastrianism have constructed fire temples (*atash kadeh*s) at a number of locations throughout the US, including New York City, Los Angeles, Chicago, Houston, and Washington, DC. Non-Zoroastrians are not allowed to enter most of these temples.

Ritual implements used in many sacred fire ceremonies include a metal vase in which the fire burns (*afrinagan*), a cloth mask (covering the nostrils and mouth) worn by participants to prevent the sacred fumes from being ritually contaminated by their breath, a bundle of twigs (*barsom*) held in a moon-shaped metal stand (*mah-ruy*), and ritual tongs (*chipyo*) and a ritual ladle (*chamach*) for tending the fire. During these ceremonies, the priest often recites the "litany to fire" (*Atash Nyayesh*) while worshipers place sandalwood or frankincense in the fire.

See also ZOROASTRIANISM

Bibliography. M. Boyce, "On the Zoroastrian Temple Cult of Fire," *Journal of the American Oriental Society*; Boyce, *Zoroastrians: Their Religious Beliefs and Practices*; K. E. Eduljee, "Zoroastrian Places of Worship: Atash Bahram/Behram Modern Fire Temple," http://www.heritage institute.com/zoroastrianism/temples/atashbah ram.htm; D. S. Noss and J. B. Noss, "Fire Temples," in *A History of the World's Religions*, 9th ed.; G. Sarkar, "Parsi Community, Bombay Parsi Panchayat to Take Fight against Metro III to PM," https://www.mid-day.com/articles/parsi-commun ity-bombay-parsi-panchayat-to-take-fight-against -metro-iii-to-pm/18667189; M. Stausberg, ed., *Zoroastrian Rituals in Context*; "Traditional Zoroastrianism: Tenets of the Religion," http:// tenets.zoroastrianism.com/; J. Wiesehofer, *Ancient Persia*; R. C. Zaehner, *The Dawn and Twilight of Zoroastrianism*.

H. W. House

SADHANA. Also referred to as *abhyasa*, *sadhana* (literally, "spiritual exercise") in Hinduism is the effort to fix the mind on Brahma via spiritual practices that lead to *sthitau* (a stable, undisturbed inner calmness). In Buddhism it is the repeated efforts to enter into deeper states of mind through meditation, ritual, and other such activities. Sadhana can involve meditation; chanting or invoking the name of God (*namasmarana*), Buddhas, or bodhisattvas; mortifying bodily desires; and/ or Bhakti Yoga (a type of yoga that aims to foster loving devotion to God). Along with *vairagya* (cultivating a mental state of tranquility and nonattachment), sadhana is one of the twin foundations of most types of yoga.

American Hindu cults that promote sadhana include the Ananda Marga Yoga Society, Transcendental Meditation, and the International Society for Krishna Consciousness (ISKCON). All the Tibetan sects employ sadhana, as do the Shingon and Tendai sects of Japanese Buddhism.

See also ANANDA MARGA YOGA SOCIETY; BUDDHISM; HINDUISM

Bibliography. Ananda, *Zen Buddhist Meditation and Hindu Sadhana: A Comparative and Anthological Study*; N. K. Brahma, *Philosophy of Hindu Sadhana*; S. B. P. P. Maharaja, *Art of Sadhana: A Guide to Daily Devotion*; R. Tagore, *Sadhana: The Classic of Indian Spirituality*; J. P. Vaswani, *The Way of Abhyasa: Meditation in Practice*.

M. Power

SAI BABA, SATHYA. Sathya Sai Baba (1926–2011) was a controversial Andhra-born Indian guru, the religious leader to a large number of followers and an international community reportedly numbering between six million and fifteen million. This alleged miracle worker was born Sathyanarayana Raju. In 1940, after reportedly suffering a scorpion sting that left him in a temporary coma-like state, he declared himself an incarnation of the fakir saint Sai Baba of Shirdi (ca. 1838–1918). He also repeatedly claimed that he was the incarnation of Shiva and in the future would be the incarnation of Shakti (Shiva's female consort). He claimed to be omnipresent, omniscient, and omnipotent. His disciples readily acknowledged, and some feared, his "occult powers." He had ashrams (residences) in Puttaparthi (his home town), Kadugodi,

Whitefield, and Kodaikana, as well as centers in Mumbai, Hyderabad, and Chennai. In total there are about ten thousand centers in 166 countries. His followers started a religious magazine, *Sanathana Sarathi*, in 1958.

Sai Baba's teachings include the concepts of unity of the world religions, brotherly love and love for all beings, the importance of the Vedas, and the literal interpretation of Hindu myths. He emphasizes devotion, virtue, detachment, vegetarianism, limiting desires, filial piety (especially to one's mother), meditation, good works, religious truth, and nonviolence. Throughout his teachings, he clearly emphasizes Hinduism. His religious program is encapsulated as follows: one caste—humanity; one religion—love; one language—of the heart; and one God, who is omnipresent. His followers implement these teachings by doing community service (including establishing schools and hospitals, publishing books, and teaching "human values"), singing devotional songs, studying his teachings, and following other practices like reciting his name and those of gods and other saints.

Controversies. Sai Baba claimed to be a miracle man. He was filmed making small objects like gold jewelry appear out of thin air and, most importantly, producing abundant amounts of *vibhuti*, or holy ashes. Professional magicians have debunked these "miracles" as sleight of hand. Sai Baba also reportedly cured incurable diseases (sometimes by taking on the disease himself), bilocated, levitated, manifested bright light from his body, manifested as various gods, made fruit appear on trees, controlled the weather, changed the color of his robe while wearing it, multiplied food, and more. He refused to allow investigation into his "powers" in a controlled clinical setting. Several documentary films and articles have claimed that Sai Baba was a fraud.

The suspicious killing of four people who broke into Sai Baba's apartment with knives, charges of sexual misconduct with male devotees, and rumors that he was a homosexual pedophile have been reported on TV and in the press. Some also alleged that he committed financial improprieties involving some of the charitable organizations under his direction. However, no legal charges were made. In response to these allegations, Sai Baba's organization mustered many prominent Indian politicians and other spokesmen East and West to decry the allegations and denounce those making them. He was further caught in a major political controversy on the issue of the proposed division of Andhra, which sparked street protests against him.

Sai Baba had predicted that he would be healthy and alive until the age of ninety-six. However, in his late seventies he became wheelchair bound, and in 2011 at the age of eighty-five Sai Baba died after about a month in the hospital. *Time* magazine's obituary article declared, "The man who was God is dead" (April 26, 2011).

Nonetheless, his devotees continue to worship him.

See also HINDUISM

Bibliography. V. Balu, *The Glory of Puttaparthi*; Tal Brooke, *Avatar of Night*; Brooke, *Riders of the Cosmic Circuit*.

A. W. Barber

SALVATION, EVANGELICAL VIEW OF. Soteriology is one of several divisions of systematic theology that deals specifically with the Christian doctrine of salvation. It is concerned with all aspects of God's redemptive plan by which a person is reconciled with him. One of the more specific descriptions in Scripture of God's work of redemption is found in Ephesians 1:1–14, which details the participation of the Trinity in the work in salvation. The plan of redemption begins with God the Father, who has chosen his elect before the foundation of the world (Eph. 1:4) and predestined them to be adopted as sons (Eph. 1:5). It is not any merit on our part that influences God's election but rather his good pleasure. The will of God in salvation is carried out by the obedience of Jesus Christ, who willingly took on human flesh (incarnation) and submitted himself to the will of the Father. Christ obediently gave himself up as the sacrificial lamb to die on the cross as a perfect sacrifice for the sins of humankind. The final work of salvation is accomplished by the Holy Spirit, who indwells and seals the elect and is the guarantee of our inheritance.

The Necessity of Salvation. Humanity's need for salvation originates in the garden of Eden. Humanity was created in a state of perfection, which logically follows from the fact that God, being perfect in his nature, could only create that which is in a state of perfection. However, unlike God, human beings had the capacity to be corrupted (sin) by an act of their will. Genesis 3 records the account of humanity's temptation and eventual fall. Humanity's sin, being utterly offensive to a holy God, separated human beings from God and put them at enmity with him. As a result of Adam's sin, all his posterity suffers the consequences of sin, which are spiritual and physical death. Romans 5:12 explains that because of the sin of one man (Adam), death would be passed to all, which is the imputation of Adam's sin.

The enmity that exists between God and humanity is not passive but active according to Romans 1:18, which states that humanity is the object of God's wrath. Paul uses two important terms to explain our fallen state and then proceeds to describe how that state is exhibited in human attitude and actions, thus incurring condemnation by God. First, humanity is in a state of ungodliness, which refers to our irreverence toward or total disregard for God. Our irreligious behavior is manifested in our rejection of God and ultimate demise into idolatry, the worshiping of that which is made (Rom. 1:21–25). This is an extraordinary reversal of the natural

order. In Genesis 1 and 2 humanity, as male and female, was told to subdue and have dominion over the earth. However, as a result of the fall, human beings now corrupt that mandate and subject themselves to creation.

The second term, *unrighteousness*, refers to behavior that flows from and is consistent with a state of ungodliness. In Romans 1:26–32, Paul completes his argument by describing the specific nature of human unrighteousness. Men and women engage in abominable acts, namely, homosexuality, as well as a lengthy list of other sinful acts that are irrefutable proof that humanity is truly depraved and in need of redemption.

The Provision of Salvation. God is holy and just, which means he cannot allow sin to go unpunished. However, God is also loving and merciful, and in his mercy he has made provision for the salvation of his elect. Given the fact that human beings are by nature sinful, we do not have the capacity to save ourselves. The unblemished sacrifice God righteously requires as an appeasement (propitiation) for sin is the only means by which salvation, or the work of redemption, can be accomplished (Rom. 5:1–11).

Scripture is clear that works of righteousness by human beings cannot save; they are saved exclusively by the work of Christ, who is the object of the gospel (John 14:6). Human beings appropriate saving faith in Christ (Eph. 2:8–9) by means of the Holy Spirit's convicting work (John 3:5–6; 2 Thess. 2:13; Titus 3:5).

The Elements of Salvation. The wrath of God exhibited toward humanity due to sin requires propitiation, or appeasement. *Atonement* is the payment demanded by God in order to achieve satisfaction. In the Old Testament, Israel atoned for its sins by offering an unblemished animal. However, this sacrifice was temporary, a prefiguration of the ultimate sacrifice of Christ on the cross as the once-and-for-all atonement. Salvation involves a number of particular elements.

1. *Redemption* is an act of deliverance, which in humanity's case is deliverance from the bondage of sin (Rom. 3:24; Eph. 1:7).

2. *Regeneration* is the inward transformation of the person by the power of the Holy Spirit (John 3:4–7).

3. *Justification* is a legal or penal metaphor with reference to a law court. By application it means the repentant sinner is no longer guilty before God. Justification is like a pardon in the sense that the elect of God are no longer guilty of sin but stand before God clothed in the righteousness of Christ (Rom. 4:21–24).

4. *Reconciliation* brings peace with God, a restoration to fellowship that was lost as a result of sin (Rom. 5:7–11).

5. The word *adoption* describes the relationship those who have been regenerated have with God. It is the apex of redemptive grace and privilege, denoting a legal act or transfer from the family of the world into the family of God (Rom. 8:14–23; Gal. 3:26–4:7; Eph. 1:5; Rev. 21:7).

6. *Sanctification* is the act of setting the redeemed apart from the world for the purpose of living a life of obedience to God. There is *positional* sanctification, which takes place at the moment of salvation. *Progressive* sanctification is the ongoing work of God in the believer, who, in obedience to God, continues to grow and mature spiritually (Heb. 5:11–14). Final sanctification, or *glorification*, is accomplished at the resurrection of the dead when the believer's spiritual essence is reunited with the person's glorified body (1 Cor. 15).

One of the most explicit, foundational statements regarding the gospel appears in 1 Corinthians 15:1–4. Paul reminds the Corinthians that at one time they received, stood in, and were saved by the gospel he preached. The gospel he passed on as of primary importance consisted of Christ's death (atonement) for our sins, his burial, and his resurrection. The gospel Paul preached is the proclamation of the death, burial, and resurrection of Jesus Christ, which includes the understanding that we must repent of our sins.

The Event of Salvation. The efficient cause of salvation is God, who initiates salvation internally by free grace alone (Titus 3:5), the external cause being the merit and intercession of Christ (John 17:20). The act of regeneration is solely by the power of God, who enables the mind to understand the things of God, who then moves the will to freely respond to the truth. The instrumental cause is the word of God (John 17:17; Rom. 10:17; Eph. 5:26; 2 Tim. 3:15; 1 Pet. 1:23), resulting in (final cause) salvation (justification, etc.) (2 Thess. 2:13) and the glorification of God (1 Pet. 2:9).

The logical starting point in the salvation event is the mind. In Romans 10:2, Paul expresses concern for his countrymen who seek after God, but not according to knowledge. The movement to salvation is cognitive, which proceeds to an act of the will, as moved by God, to assent to the truth of the gospel. Both the cognitive and the volitional aspects of salvation culminate in trust in Christ and a turning away (repentance) from sin in order to walk in the newness of life (2 Cor. 5:17).

Schools of Thought. There are two major Protestant schools of thought regarding the work of God on behalf of humanity. These two schools, Arminianism and Calvinism, differ on a number of issues, namely, their understanding of human depravity, election, predestination, and eternal security.

Arminianism is synergistic (from Greek, *synergos*, the idea of mutual cooperation) in its soteriology, holding to the view that human beings and God cooperate together in the process of salvation. Arminianism teaches that humans have libertarian free will and can choose to either accept or reject the free offer of salvation. Classic Arminianism is derived from the writings of Jacob Arminius and teaches that the atonement is unlimited; grace is resistible; the gospel is freely offered to all, not just the elect; one must persevere to the end; and humanity is totally depraved. It rejects Pelagianism (which claims that humanity has not been corrupted by original sin and does have the capacity, apart from prevenient grace, to live a spiritually successful life) and semi-Pelagianism (the view that humanity, though corrupted by sin, can initiate salvation). Some strains of Arminianism do embrace Pelagian or semi-Pelagian views of humanity and salvation, but these extreme views are considered heretical by classic Arminians.

Within the classic Arminian camp, more and more Christians are embracing the teachings of Luis de Molina, commonly known as Molinism. Popularized by William Lane Craig, Molinism teaches that God in his foreknowledge knows who will embrace the gospel if given the opportunity, so the elect are all individuals who freely embrace the gospel. Middle knowledge is also an important feature of Molinism. It is the view that God in his foreknowledge knows every possible choice a person will make.

Opposite Arminianism and a synergistic approach to salvation is Calvinism, which embraces monergism (Greek, *monergon*, which means a single agent, God, acts independently of any human agent), the view that God alone is the sole agent in salvation. Man does not have the capacity to initiate salvation or the free will to reject the effectual call. The acronym TULIP consists of five doctrines that epitomize classic Calvinism. Man is totally depraved (T); believers are unconditionally elect (U); the atonement is limited to the elect (L), though there are Calvinists who reject limited atonement for unlimited atonement

(Amyraldianism); the saving grace effective in the elect is irresistible (I); and the elect are eternally secure—that is, they will persevere in the faith until the end (P).

Within evangelicalism are those who believe that certain Arminian and Calvinist doctrinal views are not supported by Scripture. Moderate Arminians believe that the elect are those who freely embrace the gospel and that the ability to reject or accept salvation resides in the exercise of free will, so grace can be resisted, but they believe in eternal security. Moderate Calvinists question the extent of the atonement.

Though classical Calvinists and Arminians regard these mediating positions as illegitimate, they nevertheless continue to be a widespread view within evangelicalism.

Nature of Saving Faith. Within the evangelical community, there has been considerable debate over the nature of saving faith and specifically its relation to obedience. On one hand, there is what is popularly known as "lordship salvation," which stresses profession of faith and submission to the lordship of Jesus Christ in order to show genuine salvation. The distinguishing characteristic of this view is the believer's willing obedience to the call of Christ. Those who are truly born again will follow Christ as faithful disciples, exhibiting the evidence of faith by their good works (James 2:19–25). Opponents of lordship salvation charge that this approach is essentially works salvation, an accusation rejected by lordship adherents.

One of the better-known proponents of the lordship view is John MacArthur, pastor of Grace Community Church in Southern California. MacArthur says:

> The gospel Jesus proclaimed was a call to discipleship, a call to follow Him in submissive obedience, not just a plea to make a decision or pray a prayer. Jesus' message liberated people from the bondage of their sin while it confronted and condemned hypocrisy. It was an offer

of eternal life and forgiveness for repentant sinners, but at the same time it was a rebuke to outwardly religious people whose lives were devoid of true righteousness. It put sinners on notice that they must turn from sin and embrace God's righteousness. It was in every sense good news, yet it was anything but easy-believism. (21)

Opposite the lordship camp are those who adhere to what is commonly known as "free grace" theology. This group takes a minimalist approach to salvation, arguing that a simple profession of faith in Christ is sufficient to guarantee eternal life. While repentance is necessary for turning away from one's sins, it is not necessary for salvation, for only true faith is salvific. As for sanctification, one need not exhibit faithful obedience to Christ as evidence of salvation, so justification and sanctification are essentially stand-alone, distinct works of grace. The true believer can live a life of disobedience to Christ and suffer only the loss of rewards on the day of judgment.

Cognitive Content of Saving Faith. Another controversial question in evangelical teachings about salvation is the issue of the necessary or minimal content of the gospel message. This question concerns the extent to which one must know and accept gospel facts and doctrines in order to be saved. Unfortunately, there is no uniform agreement or consensus on this issue. Some evangelicals argue that one must clearly believe in the deity of Jesus Christ in order to be saved. Some include belief in the Trinity or Christ's substitutionary atonement as a condition for salvation. Others argue that believers can be saved without first gaining adequate understanding of such doctrines, though such understanding should follow conversion in due time.

From the time of J. Gresham Machen to the present, evangelicals continue to struggle with the question, "What is the content of the gospel that saves?" If someone fails to acknowledge Jesus as Lord, is that person saved? Is mere affirmation of the deity of Christ sufficient? If a person's Christology is flawed, is salvation possible? Is salvation belief in Christ's atoning work, repentance of sins, and trust in his resurrection? This issue poses a greater challenge to Arminians than to Calvinists, for within Arminianism there is the potential for one to embrace a false gospel, given that salvation is not exclusively the sovereign work of God but involves both the call of God and the cooperation of human beings. Since individuals are responsible for either accepting or rejecting saving faith, the responsibility is also on each person to know the content of the gospel.

In Calvinism the process of salvation is exclusively the work of God, which logically includes the content of the gospel message. So it would be impossible for the elect to embrace any variation of the gospel that is not efficacious. Just as God initiates the work of salvation and sovereignly carries it through to completion, by necessity God also enables the elect to appropriate a correct knowledge of the gospel.

Whether one is an Arminian or a Calvinist, the fact that evangelicals cannot arrive at a consensus regarding what one must believe in order to be saved poses a problem with respect to other faiths that share similar minimalist beliefs. Within the Church of Jesus Christ of Latter-day Saints, Mormon theologians such as Stephen Robinson and Robert Millet believe that Jesus Christ is God (though not in an orthodox trinitarian sense), died for the sins of humankind, and was resurrected in a literal, physical body. Millet in particular says that salvation resides in Christ, and those who want to be saved come to him by faith, repentance, and baptism; receive the Holy Spirit; and persevere to the end. For those evangelicals who embrace a minimalist view of what one must know and believe to be saved, it would be difficult to argue that

Millet and anyone else with a similar belief is not a true believer.

Salvation and Those Who Have Never Heard. This difficult issue typically involves two factors: geographical location and cultural conditioning. Geographically speaking, there are lost people in regions that have never been penetrated by the gospel. Because of the lack of physical proximity to, or potential for, sources of the gospel, it is argued that God would be unjust to consign people in such situations to eternal reprobation.

Proposed solutions to this problem are inclusivism, exclusivism, and pluralism. Inclusivism teaches that God in his mercy and grace will save people on the basis of what they are capable of knowing, particularly with respect to natural theology, or knowledge of God derived from creation (Rom. 1:19–20). Though salvation in Scripture is contingent on one's knowledge of and response to Christ, the inclusivists believe that those who have never heard can nevertheless be saved on the basis of whatever revelation they have received. Some inclusivists believe that for those who have never heard, at death God will give them the opportunity to accept or reject Christ.

Unlike inclusivism, exclusivism firmly believes that a specific knowledge of and faith in Jesus Christ is essential to salvation, thus ruling out the possibility of salvation through any other means.

The third option is pluralism, the belief that God has made himself known through many different religions and that those who are sincere in their beliefs will be saved. In other words, there are many paths to God, and no one religious system is superior to or better than another.

Inclusivism and exclusivism are typically found within the evangelical community, whereas pluralism is predominant within liberal theologies. For Arminians the salvation of those who have never heard is possible by means of either specific knowledge

of Christ or the extent of God's revelation to that person. The Molinist perspective argues that God in his foreknowledge knows who would believe if presented with the gospel. Therefore, God will make sure that those potential believers are able to encounter the gospel.

Within Calvinist theology, the salvation of those who have never heard, regardless of geographical or cultural circumstances, is exclusively the sovereign work of God. So any alleged geographical or cultural limitations or obstacles are moot.

There is no one definitive evangelical position on salvation, for within the two main schools of thought, Calvinism and Arminianism, there exist variations on such issues as eternal security, limited or unlimited atonement, what one must specifically believe in order to be saved, inclusivism or exclusivism, and so on. In spite of these particular variations, mainstream evangelicalism does embrace some level of the depravity of man, God as the efficient cause of salvation, Christ as having made atonement for sin, and salvation by grace alone.

See also CHRISTIANITY, PROTESTANT; CHURCH OF JESUS CHRIST OF LATTER-DAY SAINTS; ORTHODOXY; ROMAN CATHOLICISM

Bibliography. J. Arminius, *The Works of James Arminius*; T. Burke, *Adopted into God's Family*; J. Calvin, *Institutes of the Christian Religion*; Z. Hodges, *The Gospel under Seige;* A. Hoekema, *Saved by Grace*; M. Luther, *Bondage of the Will*; J. MacArthur, *The Gospel according to Jesus*; R. Olson, *Arminian Theology*; J. I. Packer, "The Means of Conversion," *Crux*; T. R. Schreiner and B. A. Ware, eds., *Still Sovereign*; M. Seifrid, *Christ, Our Righteousness*; J. R. W. Stott, *The Cross of Christ*.

S. J. Rost

SAMADHI. In Sanskrit *samadhi* literally means "to acquire wholeness," or "even intellect." Samadhi is a state of deep concentration achieved through meditation, in which object consciousness dissipates and finally the distinction between the subject and the object (duality) is obliterated.

Samadhi is one of the three trainings of Buddhism, along with ethics and wisdom. Buddhists seek to cultivate samadhi as exercising skillful means in all they do; hence, one can talk of the samadhi of a Zen koan or the samadhi of bodhisattva action.

The word *samadhi* also appears in late Hinduism. Samadhi is said to be the goal of yoga, when one's consciousness becomes one with reality and achieves a state of stillness. In some forms of Hinduism, it is the term used euphemistically for death, with the idea that the person has willfully departed from his physical body. It can also refer to a mausoleum for honored gurus.

See also BODHISATTVA; BUDDHISM; HINDUISM; ZEN BUDDHISM

Bibliography. B. Nyanatiloka Mahathera, *Buddhist Dictionary: Manual of Buddhist Terms & Doctrines.*

H. P. Kemp

SAMSARA. Samsara is the self-perpetuated cycle of death and rebirth in Hinduism, Jainism, Buddhism, and Sikhism. In this series of reincarnations, a person's karma (the combined spiritual effects of his ethical actions in previous lives) makes reincarnation necessary and determines what form (insect, reptile, human, hell being, god, etc.) or social caste that person is reborn into (though the details of this vary among the religions in which samsara plays a role). Sometimes *samsara* refers to the temporal, changing dimension of reality (usually identified with the physical world), the false perception of which results from ignorance regarding the true nature of existence. Release from the bondage of samsara is the highest objective of those who seek enlightenment and liberation.

See also BUDDHISM; HINDUISM; JAINISM; SIKHISM

Bibliography. M. D. Coogan, *The Illustrated Guide to World Religions*; R. H. Roberts, *India: Religion and Philosophy.*

M. Power

SANGHA. In Sanskrit and Pali, *sangha* means "assembly" or "community," referring to the community of adherents in Buddhism. Sangha is one of the "Three Jewels" in which a Buddhist "takes refuge," together with the Buddha and the dharma. In Theravada Buddhism, sangha consists of the male monastic community. In Mahayana schools, it consists in the first place of all the Buddhas, bodhisattvas, and great masters; secondarily, of the monks and nuns; and, finally, of all adherents. A sangha can be lineage specific (e.g., master-disciple relationship) and often refers to the residents or members at a Buddhist center or temple. The firstborn male is sometimes offered to the monastic sangha to be raised in some traditions. The monastic sangha is traditionally viewed by the laity as the serious practitioners of Buddhism who devote their entire lives to the pursuit of enlightenment, while the laity is resolved to minimize the accumulation of karmic debt in the Theravadan tradition. Hence the sangha is never separated from the laity since material support of the sangha is efficacious in earning karmic merit. In some cultures, it is customary for all males to join a sangha at some point in their lives, although temporarily. This may be after the death of a relative or before marrying.

With Buddhism's transcultural spread into the West, notions of sangha are changing, including a more democratized structure, a widening of the definition to any community of Buddhists who support one another in spiritual practice (including an increased role for women), and the emergence of an electronic sangha.

For the most part, those who wish to join the monastic sangha must be at least twenty years old, be healthy, be free from debts, have

449

the consent of parents, understand the rules of monastic life, and have some knowledge of Buddhist teachings.

See also BUDDHISM; PALI CANON; TIBETAN BUDDHISM; ZEN BUDDHISM

Bibliography. C. S. Prebish and K. K. Tanaka, eds., *The Faces of Buddhism in America*.

H. P. Kemp

SANKARA. Adi Sankara (also pronounced and spelled Shankara) was an Indian philosopher (AD 788–820) who founded four Hindu monasteries (*mathas*) to promote his doctrine of Advaita Vedanta (nondualism). Advaita Vedanta is the Hindu doctrine that Brahma, the one unchanging entity in the universe, is all that truly exists. Sankara's philosophy contended that there is no difference between the world and the individual (and also the Brahma). There is oneness of self with the universe and the universal spirit known as Brahma.

Sankara was a popular debater with rival Hindu teachers, was instrumental in a revival of Hinduism during his day, and was a prominent proponent and teacher in the Vedanta school of Hinduism. He also attacked Buddhism and Jainism. Some of his ideas seem to have been borrowed and modified from Mahayana Buddhism. Scholars of his life and thought argue that his views are closer to a philosophic system of nontheistic dualism. He died while trekking in the Himalayas, but his teaching has had a lasting influence in Hindu intellectual circles, and he is considered one of the "great souls" of India and Hinduism.

His life and thought came into popular Western culture through the movie *Indiana Jones and the Temple of Doom*, in which Indiana Jones is asked to retrieve a mystical stone—a Sankara Stone. In the world of the movie, it was believed that the Hindu god Shiva gave Sankara five sacred stones and charged him to go back into the world and battle evil with them.

See also ADVAITA; BRAHMA; BUDDHISM; HINDUISM; JAINISM; MAHAYANA BUDDHISM

Bibliography. A. L. Dallapicolla, *Dictionary of Hindu Lore and Legend*.

T. J. Demy

SANKIRTAN, THE HARE KRISHNA PRACTICE OF. Sankirtan is a practice of Hare Krishna devotees that involves publicly chanting of the Hare Krishna mantra ("Hare Krishna, Hare Krishna, Krishna Krishna, Hare Hare, Hare Rama, Hare Rama, Rama Rama, Hare Hare") and distributing literature published by the International Society for Krishna Consciousness (ISKCON). Adherents of Hare Krishna hand out ISKCON publications frequently since they believe that engaging in such work may result in the liberation of themselves and those to whom they give these materials. ISKCON suffered a well-publicized setback in February 1999 when the US Supreme Court let stand a lower court ruling stating that Hare Krishnas may be barred from selling their publications in airports in the states of Alabama, Georgia, and Florida. Many devotees spend several hours per day chanting, using a string of prayer beads to track their progress. Perhaps the best-known example of sankirtan in the US was the inclusion of the Hare Krishna mantra in George Harrison's 1970 tune "My Sweet Lord."

See also INTERNATIONAL SOCIETY FOR KRISHNA CONSCIOUSNESS (ISKCON); MANTRA; MOKSHA

Bibliography. E. F. Bryant and M. L. Ekstrand, *The Hare Krishna Movement: The Postcharismatic Fate of a Religious Transplant*; G. Dwyer and R. J. Cole, eds., *The Hare Krishna Movement: Forty Years of Chant and Change*; A. C. B. Swami Prabhupada, *Chant and Be Happy: The Power of Mantra Meditation*.

M. Power

SANKIRTANA. Sankirtana, from the Sanskrit *san* (together) and *kirtana* (singing the names of a deity), is the practice of singing God's name, such as Vishnu or Krishna, with divine feeling as an expression of devotion. This practice is said to remove the impurities of the mind, steady the mind, and bring the person face-to-face with the deity. Sankirtana can be found in many of the bhakti movements.

Its origin may be traced back in the Hindu Vaishnava tradition, at least to the devotional revival of the fifteenth century. Later in the sixteenth century, when the ascetic Isvara Puri met Chaitanya Mahaprabhu while on a pilgrimage to Gaya, Puri gave Chaitanya a *mahamantra* that is used by the International Society for Krishna Consciousness (ISKCON) today. Chaitanya's life was changed by singing this mantra in the village streets to proclaim his devotion to Krishna—thus, the practice of sankirtana.

Within ISKCON, sankirtana can also refer to the distribution of the group's literature and to their public preaching about Krishna consciousness.

See also BHAKTI YOGA; INTERNATIONAL SOCIETY FOR KRISHNA CONSCIOUSNESS (ISKCON); SANKIRTANA

Bibliography. N. Delmonico, "Chaitanya Vaishnavism and the Holy Names."

J. Bjornstad

SANNYASA. Meaning "renunciation," *sannyasa* is the last of the four idealized stages of life (*ashramas*) in Hinduism and Indian philosophy. It is normally accessible only to people who belong to the highest, or "twice-born," social groups (*varnas*): Brahmin, Kshatriya, and Vaishya. Though not exclusively, this stage generally comes late in an individual's life, following separated periods of celibate learning, marrying and having children as a householder, and becoming progressively detached from the world and its obligations as a forest dweller. In sannyasa, the fourth and final stage, an individual (the

sannyasin) removes attachment to the home and material goods, including all connections with family, to live the rest of life as an ascetic. The renunciation includes a search for fundamental religious truth, specifically liberation from the cycle of birth and rebirth. Usually sannyasa is also preceded by a period of instruction and initiation conveyed by a spiritual leader or religious mentor (guru). Often included in this ceremony is the acceptance of a new name and the transmission of a religious mantra.

See also BRAHMA; HINDUISM; MANTRA; RAMANUJA

Bibliography. L. Dumont, *Homo Hierarchicus: The Caste System and Its Implications*; Dumont, "World Renunciation in Indian Religions," *Contributions to Indian Sociology*; W. Doninger O'Flaherty, *Asceticism and Eroticism in the Mythology of Śiva*.

T. Aechtner

SAOSHYANT. In Zoroastrianism the term *saoshyant* (Avestan, "one who will bring benefit") refers to a coming universal savior—on some accounts the last of three such figures—who will proclaim Ahura Mazda's message to humanity and bring about a comprehensive renovation of the world. Sent by Ahura Mazda and bearing his divine authority, the saoshyant will be born following the miraculous impregnation of his virgin mother with the seed of Zoroaster (Greek name; Persian, Zarathustra). According to Zoroastrian legend, Zoroaster's seed is being preserved at the bottom of a lake. The virgin will bathe in the lake and become impregnated by this seed. The man born to this virgin will be called Astvat-ereta (He Who Embodies Righteousness). In keeping with the central role of humanity in the final struggle, the saoshyant will humanly embody righteousness (*ashoi*) and will lead an army that will defeat the forces of evil in a great, final battle. After this he will play a role in the resurrection of the dead (*ristakhiz*) and the divine judgment of wickedness. In the Gathas, Zoroaster anticipates an imminent apocalypse, writing of the saoshyant as a central figure in Zoroastrian eschatology.

See also GATHAS; ZOROASTRIANISM

Bibliography. M. Boyce, *Zoroastrians: Their Religious Beliefs and Practices*; G. W. Carter, *Zoroastrianism and Judaism*, repr. ed.; P. Clark, *Zoroastrianism: An Introduction to an Ancient Faith*; M. Moazami, "Millennialism, Eschatology, and Messianic Figures in Iranian Tradition," *Journal of Millennial Studies*.

R. L. Drouhard

SATORI. Derived from the Japanese word *satoru*, meaning "to know," this term is principally used by practitioners of Zen in Japanese Buddhism. Sometimes used interchangeably with the Japanese Buddhist term *kensho*, referring to understanding one's Buddha nature, *satori* refers roughly to the initial "enlightenment" or "awakening," and specifically to brief moments of insight and understanding concerning the nature of reality. This experience transcends any accurate description in words and conceptualization and is sometimes equated with a sense or feeling of infinite space. A Zen Buddhist may experience satori multiple times, with varying intensity; however, the first satori is often regarded as particularly important. Such experiences are generally conceived as being short but influential, though the preparation for satori may require extensive training. Traditionally, it is generally achieved through meditation, by the use of enigmatic riddles or sayings (koans), whose solution cannot be understood using analytical and conceptual thought. Within Zen Buddhism, it has been proposed that without satori there can be no Zen.

See also ZEN BUDDHISM

Bibliography. W. Barrett, ed., *Zen Buddhism: Selected Writings of D. T. Suzuki*; H. Dumoulin, *A History of Zen Buddhism*; D. T. Suzuki, *An Introduction to Zen Buddhism*.

T. Aechtner

SCRIPTURE, INTERPRETATION OF. The improper use of the Bible in the formulation of doctrines and ethical behavior is the source of many disputes among Christians. The New Testament is clear on this issue; for example, Peter warns against unstable teachers who "wrest" (KJV) or "distort" (NIV) the Scriptures "to their own destruction" (2 Pet. 3:16).

Foundational to interpreting the Bible correctly is a proper understanding of methods of Bible study and hermeneutics. Hermeneutics is a specialized discipline of study that deals with the principles and rules of biblical interpretation. If good hermeneutical skills are developed and followed, inappropriate interpretations of Scripture that contribute to doctrinal error and practices contrary to biblical truth are minimized. Good interpretive skills equip Christians to counter abuses of Scripture effectively and to handle the Bible with greater accuracy in personal study. With such skills, those who teach the Bible are able to prepare biblically sound and effective lessons. Hermeneutics helps the interpreter to know how to interpret the Bible and be confident that the interpretation is accurate. Five key areas are important to the hermeneutical endeavor. First, the interpreter approaches the text literally, to derive meaning from the text itself. Second, the interpreter sets forth the meaning of the text's words. Third, the interpreter identifies the text as referring to historical or spiritual matters, or to both. Fourth, the interpreter identifies the genre of the text and its corresponding literary style, recognizing how the features of the genre mediated meaning to the original audience. The genres of Scripture include historical narrative (Pentateuch, Acts), Wisdom literature (Proverbs, Ecclesiastes), doctrinal instruction (Romans, Ephesians), poetry (Job, Psalms, Song of Solomon), and apocalypse (portions of Isaiah and Daniel; Revelation). Fifth, the interpreter recognizes the text's theological significance, always remembering that its source is God.

Related to hermeneutics are basic Bible study procedures. That is, having committed ourselves to the principles above, we must also attend to methods. One popular and effective method approaches the Bible by means of the threefold, logical sequence of observation, interpretation, and application. In *observation* we examine every detail of a passage, listing specific words used, names of people or places, ideas stressed, grammatical structures, conjunctions, prepositions, verbs, and nouns. Thus the reader plunges into the text, gaining a thorough understanding of what the author is saying.

Next is *interpretation*, coming to a working understanding of what the passage means by considering one's observations in the light of insights derived from good study tools such as commentaries, Bible dictionaries, and works in systematic theology. Here it is essential to distinguish between meaning and application. No passage can have two conflicting interpretations that are both true. Both can be false but not mutually true. This would be a violation of the law of noncontradiction. Multiple applications are possible, but even then the application cannot conflict with interpretation. Interpretation also entails both literal and figurative approaches to the text. This is different from the allegorical method, in which historical or earthly realities set forth in the text are spiritualized, a common method of Alexandrian interpreters such as Clement and Origen. For example, interpreted literally, the Song of Solomon concerns Solomon's relationship with his wife. However, some have interpreted it allegorically, arguing it is an example of Christ's relationship to the church or of God and his love for Israel. Unless common sense or a careful reading of the text calls for interpreting words metaphorically, the literal approach is preferred. Although allegory has been used in the service of orthodox doctrine, as a method it is ripe for Scripture twisting.

Having interpreted a text, one *applies* it. When application follows good observation and interpretation, it facilitates spiritual growth. For example, James 2 appears to many readers to teach that salvation is earned by good works. However, in Ephesians 2:8–9 Paul specifically states that salvation is by faith, not works. Do Paul and James contradict each other? No, if one understands the contexts of James and Paul. James is pointing out that faith without works is questionable because works are an evidence of true faith. Paul points out that works do not save. Not only are both correct; their respective statements are compatible.

Given the importance of biblical interpretation, it is essential that Christians follow reliable methods.

Bibliography. J. S. Duvall and J. D. Hays, *Grasping God's Word*; H. W. House, *Doctrine Twisting*; E. Johnson, *Expository Hermeneutics: An Introduction*; W. Klein, C. Blomberg, and R. Hubbard, *Introduction to Biblical Interpretation*; T. Milton, *Biblical Hermeneutics*; J. Sire, *Scripture Twisting: Twenty Ways Cults Misread the Bible*.

S. J. Rost

SEER STONES. Sometimes called "peep stones," the seer stones were allegedly used by Joseph Smith Jr., the founder of the Church of Jesus Christ of Latter-day Saints (LDS Church, or Mormonism) to translate the Book of Mormon—according to the Book of Mormon itself (Alma 37:23)—from golden plates written in Reformed Egyptian hieroglyphics (1 Nephi 1:2). Smith claimed it was the "Urim and Thummim" of Exodus 28:30. Smith supposedly saw the English translation of the gold plates by using a seer stone. Witnesses said he would place the stone into a hat and peer into it to see the letters. Some who signed as witnesses testifying to the authenticity of the Book of Mormon also claimed revelation using seer stones.

See also CHURCH OF JESUS CHRIST OF LATTER-DAY SAINTS; SMITH, JOSEPH, JR.

Bibliography. R. M. Nelson, "A Treasured Testament," *Ensign.*

D. Potter

SEICHO-NO-IE. Seicho-No-Ie is a syncretistic religion combining Shinto, Buddhist, and Christian beliefs, founded in Tokyo in 1930 by Taniguchi Masaharu. Pronounced "say-cho-no-yay," its name means "house of growth." One of its mission agencies in the US provides this summary: "The *Seicho-No-Ie* Truth of Life Movement is a nondenominational New Thought movement based on the belief that all religions emanate from one universal God." One of its promoters explains, "In Seicho-No-Ie we say that the only real existence is God, or we describe this as the True Image, the real existence. . . . When we see his True Image with the eyes of our mind and worship him with our soul, his inner perfection will appear. . . . This is the power of the Seicho-No-Ie teachings" (Mallery). Masaharu's teachings are set forth in a forty-volume series titled *Truth of Life.* In brief he taught that the universe is a perfect and harmonious manifestation of divine reality. Humans perceive disease, hunger, poverty, and death due to errors in our thinking. Those errors are not absolute truth, and they can be eliminated through deep meditation (*shinsokan*) and other spiritual practices.

In 2009 the movement claimed 1.8 million adherents worldwide, served by nearly 23,000 ministers in over 440 locations. Most of its followers are in Brazil and Japan.

Bibliography. Bruce Mallery, *The Essence of Seicho-No-Ie: The Secret of the True Image and Phenomenon*; Seicho-No-Ie International home page, http://www.seicho-no-ie.org; B. Staemmler, "Seichô no Ie," in *New Religions: A Guide*, edited by C. Partridge.

E. Pement and R. L. Drouhard

SEMA. *Sema* (Persian, "listening") is a worship practice in Sufi Islam that includes such elements as ritual dancing, vocal and instrumental music, recitation from the Qur'an, the reading of devotional poetry, and elaborate ceremonies (whose particulars vary from one Sufi order to another). The best-known form of sema in Europe and North America is the elaborate dancing done by the Whirling Dervishes. Since medieval times, Sufi devotees have composed songs and poems and choreographed dancing movements for individual and communal worship. In particular the seven-stage sema practices advocated by Sufi mystic Mevlana Celaleddin-i Rumi (1207–73) are aimed at the spiritual ascent of the devotee, culminating in an ecstatic experience of God. Sema is not solely for purposes of personal liberation, however, but is intended to transform the individual into a man or a woman who loves and serves others. Almost every detail of the sema is symbolic, from the intricate movements to the colors of the clothing worn by the devotee.

See also SUFISM

Bibliography. C. Celebi, "Sema: Human Being in the Universal Movement"; L. Vaughan-Lee, *Sufism: The Transformation of the Heart.*

R. L. Drouhard

SEVENTH-DAY ADVENTISM. Seventh-day Adventism (SDA) grew out of the Millerite movement of the 1840s in the northeastern US. When Jesus failed to return in 1843 and then in 1844 as William Miller had predicted, the group of people who did not return to their churches coalesced and eventually organized the Seventh-day Adventist Church.

The group was founded by James White, a former pastor in the Christian Connexion (a Methodist breakaway group); a staunch antitrinitarian named Joseph Bates, a sea captain who was instrumental in bringing the seventh-day Sabbath to the group; and Ellen Gould White, James's wife, who received visions and was credited with having the New Testament gift of prophecy. The fledgling group organized around the investigative judgment, a doctrine that validated the 1844 date.

History. Adventism was one of the new religious movements that emerged from the Second Great Awakening of the nineteenth century. The organization grew with the help of the publishing work of James White, which begain in 1846. In 1860 the founders chose the name that defined their two prominent doctrines (namely, Saturday as the Sabbath for Christians and the second coming of Christ), establishing Battle Creek, Michigan, as their early headquarters. In 1874, following Ellen White's 1872 vision on the proper principles of education, the Adventist educational system was incorporated as the Seventh-day Adventist Educational Society. Also during the 1870s, the Adventists established their medical work, still known today as the "right arm of the message" (Land, 128).

After James White and Joseph Bates died, Ellen White was the dominant voice of the organization. In the 1880s, she visited Europe and helped establish Adventism abroad. In 1888 Adventism experienced a doctrinal crisis when Alonzo Jones and Ellet Waggoner preached "righteousness by faith" at a Bible conference in Minneapolis, Minnesota. The discussion of the relationship between law and grace has never been fully resolved within Adventism (see discussion on internal disagreements below).

Ellen White died in 1915, but as the church grew, leaders looked to her writings for guidance, and the curricula in the denominational schools and Sabbath schools continue to teach members that she is a "messenger" or "prophet" from God, an office that she said included "much more than this name [prophet] signifies" (*Selected Messages*, 35–36). This teaching continues even though extensive research by Ronald Numbers and Walter Rae, verified also by Adventist-sponsored research, has demonstrated that she plagiarized a large percentage of her work (Rae).

Today the Adventist organization is based in Silver Spring, Maryland. Because of its missionary work, Adventism is growing rapidly worldwide. In 2017 the Seventh-day Adventist Church reported 20,343,814 baptized Adventist members. According to the religious statistical website Adherents.com, as of August 2009 Adventism was the twelfth-largest religious body in the world, exceeding groups such as the Jehovah's Witnesses and the Church of Jesus Christ of Latter-day Saints. Moreover, it is the sixth-most-ubiquitous international religious body.

Typically, Adventist "evangelistic" programs do not reveal that they are Seventh-day Adventists. Their Prophecy and Revelation seminars, many of which are produced by denominationally owned It Is Written, are held around the world, and their radio program *The Voice of Prophecy* is also heard internationally. They offer multiple online and correspondence Bible courses, and they produce multiple magazines and television programs designed to introduce Adventist practices and beliefs. Many independent Adventist ministries also evangelize for the Adventist church. Among these organizations are the television program *Amazing Facts* and the satellite TV station *3ABN*.

Adventist publications include *Signs of the Times*, *Ministry Magazine*, *Liberty*, and *The Clear Word*, a Bible paraphrase with Adventist doctrines written into the text without citations. *The Clear Word* is printed and distributed by the denomination. The Andrews Study Bible, based on the New King James Version of the Bible, was released in June 2010, with study notes produced by Adventist scholars and of course reflecting SDA theology.

Beliefs in Common with Historic Christianity. Adventists agree with evangelical Christianity that God is the Creator of all things and that Jesus was born of a virgin, lived a sinless life, died, rose again, and bodily ascended into heaven. They practice baptism by immersion in the name of the Father, Son, and Holy Spirit, and this baptism is the entrance rite into Seventh-day Adventist membership. Additionally, the Adventist *28 Fundamental Beliefs* contains official statements concerning the Trinity, the three persons of the Trinity, and the Scriptures that appear to be orthodox.

Distinctive Beliefs Different from the Historic Church. Unlike the Roman Catholic Church, the Eastern Orthodox Church, and Protestant Christianity, including evangelical Christianity, Adventism teaches "soul sleep," conditional immortality, seventh-day Sabbath-keeping as the sign of the seal of God, worship on Sunday as the mark of the beast, a "great controversy" worldview that sees humanity vindicating God's character by choosing to obey him in the face of Satan's accusation to the watching universe that God is unfair, an "investigative judgment," and a nineteenth-century prophet, Ellen White.

Scripture and Revelation. While their Fundamental Belief 1 states that the word of God is "the standard of character, the test of experience, the authoritative revealer of doctrines, and the trustworthy record of God's acts in history" (General Conference of Seventh-day Adventists, *Seventh-day Adventists Believe*, 11), and their Fundamental Belief 18 states, "The Bible is the standard by which all teaching and experience must be tested," officially Adventists still consider Ellen White to be "a continuing and authoritative source of truth" (General Conference of Seventh-day Adventists, *Seventh-day Adventists Believe*, 247). As stated above, Adventists view White as a prophetess or messenger from God; they regard her writings as a light that illuminates the light of Scripture.

Doctrine of God. Critics of Seventh-day Adventism emphasize that their doctrine of God is colored by the fact that James White, one of the principal founders of the organization, was antitrinitarian and Arian or semi-Arian. *The Clear Word* (TCW),

a paraphrase of the Bible with Adventist theology written into the text without citations, demonstrates that nontrinitarian theology is still a problem in the SDA Church. John 10:30, ESV, reads, "I and the Father are one." *TCW*: "You see, my Father and I are so close, we're one." In addition, Adventism shows a strong tendency toward tritheism, seeing the persons of the Trinity as separate beings united into a God-family (Batchelor, 18–21).

Jesus, Sin, and Salvation. Two unique doctrines of Adventists cause evangelicals and other Christians to question their orthodoxy as it relates to Jesus and sin. The first is that Adventists believe that Jesus could have sinned, that his incarnation involved God risking that the Godhead and the universe might spin into "cosmic chaos" if Jesus did sin (Batchelor, 30).

The second doctrinal problem is the Adventist view of salvation based on the "great controversy" paradigm. Central to this understanding is the unique investigative judgment. The investigative judgment (or sanctuary doctrine) is based on the Adventist interpretation of Daniel 8:14 as "clarified" by a vision received by early Adventist Hiram Edson in which he saw Jesus moving from the holy place in the heavenly sanctuary to the holy of holies. The resulting doctrine, endorsed by a confirming vision received by Ellen White, teaches that Jesus's atonement was not finished on the cross. Rather, his blood provided a means of transferring the sins of those professing Christ into heaven, where they were "stored," thus defiling the heavenly sanctuary, until Jesus would complete his atonement by investigating the life records of professed believers.

When Jesus finishes investigating, probation will be over. Ellen White said, "Those who are living upon the earth when the intercession of Christ shall cease in the sanctuary above are to stand in the sight of a holy God without a mediator. Their robes must be spotless; their characters must be purified from sin by the blood of sprinkling. Through the grace of God and their own diligent effort they must be conquerors in the battle with evil" (*Great Controversy*, 425).

At the end of the investigative judgment, Jesus places the confessed sins on the scapegoat, Satan, who will bear them out of heaven into the lake of fire, where he will be punished for them. Thus the sanctuary in heaven will be cleansed.

Many Adventists focus on the aspect of the investigative judgment emphasizing that its purpose is to vindicate God's character to the watching universe. This idea is embedded in Ellen White's original writing about the investigative judgment, and Adventist theologians have focused on this facet of the doctrine and have made humanity's vindication of God's character the focal point of the judgment.

In 1980 Adventist theologian and professor Desmond Ford presented his research to a group of Adventist leaders and scholars at Glacier View, Colorado, showing conclusively that the investigative judgment is nowhere supported in the Bible (Hook, 236–56). Nevertheless, the organization continues to teach this doctrine, whose only source is the writings of Ellen White. The Adventists' Fundamental Belief 24 states in part: "The investigative judgment reveals to heavenly intelligences who among the dead are asleep in Christ and therefore, in Him, are deemed worthy to have part in the first resurrection. It also makes manifest who among the living are abiding in Christ, keeping the commandments of God and the faith of Jesus. . . . This judgment vindicates the justice of God in saving those who believe in Jesus (General Conference of Seventh-day Adventists, *Seventh-day Adventists Believe*, 347–48).

Soul Sleep. Adventists Fundamental Belief 7 states that "each [person] is an indivisible unity of body, mind, and spirit, dependent upon God for life and breath and all else" (General Conference of Seventh-day Adventists, *Seventh-day Adventists Believe*, 91). Adventists understand the phrase "an indivisible unity of body, mind, and spirit" to be teaching that no part of a human survives death except in the memory of God. They teach that the "spirit" of a human being is merely his or her breath. It is breath, not a conscious essence of a person, that they say returns to God. *Seventh-day Adventists Believe* states: "Solomon's statement that the spirit (*ruach*) returns to God who gave it indicates that what returns to God is simply the life principle that He imparted. There is no indication that the spirit, or breath, was a conscious entity separate from the body" (392). The *Amazing Facts* Bible study "Are the Dead Really Dead?" states, "God's people will know from their earnest study of His book that the dead are dead, not alive. Spirits of the dead do not exist."

Nature of Humanity and Sin. Because of Adventists' denial of a literal spirit separate from the body that can know and worship God (John 4:24), many Christian theologians believe that Adventists have no clear understanding of the new birth or of depravity. Adventists see the Holy Spirit as informing the mind and giving people the power to keep the commandments. Moreover, they believe that Jesus was exactly as we are, that he inherited fallen flesh from his mother—yet he never sinned. They perceive inherited sin to be transmitted genetically. Therefore, overcoming sin is seen as perfectly keeping the Ten Commandments by accessing enough power from the Holy Spirit to resist temptation. Adventists teach that Jesus was our example, stating in their book *Seventh-day Adventists Believe* (General Conference of Seventh-day Adventists, 58), "To set the example as to how people should live, Christ must live a sinless life as a human being. As the second Adam, He dispelled the myth that humans cannot obey God's law and have victory over sin. He demonstrated that it is possible for humanity to be faithful to God's will."

The Sabbath. Many contemporary Adventists say that the seventh-day Sabbath is not a requirement for salvation. On the other hand, Adventists believe that obedience to God's law, including the Sabbath, directly bears on their salvation, and abandoning the Sabbath would be considered blatant disobedience (Paulsen, section 4).

Ellen White established the seventh-day Sabbath as the final test that divides true believers from the lost, and she called it the "seal of God": "Too late [the enemies of God] see that *the Sabbath of the fourth commandment is the seal of the living God*" (*Great Controversy*, 640, emphasis added). Not only did White establish the Sabbath as the seal of God and the mark that identifies those who will be saved; she identified worship on Sunday as being the mark of the beast:

> The Sabbath will be the great test of loyalty . . . when the final test shall be brought to bear upon men, then the line of distinction will be drawn between those who serve God and those who serve Him not. While the *observance of the false Sabbath* in compliance with the law of the state, contrary to the fourth commandment, will be an avowal of allegiance to a power that is in opposition to God, the keeping of the true Sabbath, in obedience to God's law, is an evidence of loyalty to the Creator. While one class, by accepting the sign of submission to earthly powers, *receive the mark of the beast*, the other choosing the token of allegiance to divine authority, receive the seal of God. (*Great Controversy*, 605, emphasis added)

Adventist Fundamental Belief 20 calls the Sabbath "a sign of our sanctification, a token of our allegiance, and a foretaste of our eternal future in God's kingdom. The Sabbath is God's perpetual sign of His eternal covenant between Him and His people" (General Conference of Seventh-day Adventists, *Seventh-day Adventists Believe*, 281). White further wrote, "Then I was shown a company who were howling in agony. . . . I asked who this company were. The angel said, 'These are they who have once kept the Sabbath, and have given it up'" (*Early Writings*, 36). Thus Ellen White established the seventh-day Sabbath as the determinant of who will be saved and who will be lost.

Other Distinctive Beliefs. Adventists further believe that during the "time of trouble," there will be international Sunday laws mandating worship on Sunday and forbidding worship on Saturday. At that time, "Sunday-keepers" will hunt and kill Sabbath-keepers (White, *Great Controversy*, 615).

Additionally, Adventists officially disallow wearing jewelry, although wedding rings were approved in the 1980s. They require adherence to the Mosaic food laws and encourage veganism. Further, they officially forbid alcohol, tobacco, and caffeine.

Internal Disagreements. Individuals within Adventism vary widely in their personal theology. Growing numbers are advocating observing the Jewish feasts and holy days as well as practicing historic Adventist lifestyles as outlined by Ellen White, often including veganism, while others are seeking to align their beliefs and practices more with evangelical theology. Consequently Seventh-day Adventism is represented through a variety of perspectives, and it is difficult to know how the movement will maintain cohesion in its present structure.

The historic Adventists are classic Adventists who believe Ellen White is the messenger of God for the remnant church; who practice vegetarianism and abstain from stimulants and spicy foods, including vinegar, mustard, and black pepper; who believe the seventh-day Sabbath is the seal of God; and who believe those who are alive at Jesus's return will be perfect, standing without a mediator during the time of trouble (White, *Great Controversy,* 614).

The 1888 Message Movement has drawn on the teaching of Jones and Waggoner first presented in 1888 (see above). This movement teaches "righteousness by faith," or gratitude for God's sacrificial love that legally justified all humans. In this "anti-typical Day of Atonement," which began in 1844, the Holy Spirit is revealing all known sin, and believers will accept their justification by becoming obedient to all the commandments and overcoming all sin. They will accomplish this obedience by faith—acting in gratitude and love—not by works. Jesus will not return until his character is perfectly reflected in his people.

Progressive Adventism is theologically liberal. These Adventists are pluralistic and inclusive. Adventism, they claim, is like a large tent sheltering a wide variety of theological ideas. This movement looks for commonality with all monotheistic religions, including Islam and Judaism, and is represented by magazines such as *Spectrum* and *Adventist Today.*

Many evangelical Adventists proclaim the Pauline doctrine of salvation by grace through faith in Christ alone. These Adventists, however, remain tied to seventh-day Sabbath-keeping, soul sleep and conditional immortality, a conviction that they are helping to vindicate God, and a belief that God used Ellen White in some capacity.

Some of the better-known offshoots of Adventism include the Seventh Day Adventist Reform Movement, the Branch Davidians, and Shepherd's Rod.

Unity in the Midst of Diversity. Although diverse beliefs can be found in Adventism, the church as an organization is not changing. General Conference president Jan Paulsen said, in answer to the suggestions that the church is changing its teaching of its historic doctrines, that such a claim "is a distortion of reality, and nothing could be further from the truth." He expanded his defense by saying that the "historic sanctuary message based on Scripture and supported by the writings of Ellen White, continues to be held unequivocally." Moreover, he endorsed the Bible and the writings of Ellen White as the "hermeneutical foundation on which [they] as a church place all matters of faith and conduct. Let no one think that there has been a change of position in regard to this" (section 10).

All Adventists agree on at least four foundational beliefs: the eternal significance of the seventh-day Sabbath; a doctrine of soul sleep that denies the existence of the human spirit and has grave implications for the nature of humans, Christ, sin, and salvation; a doctrine of an ongoing judgment in which God is on trial, humans help vindicate him, and Satan is the scapegoat; and the significance of Ellen White, whom the Adventists call "a continuing and authoritative source of truth" (General Conference of Seventh-day Adventists, *Seventh-day Adventists Believe*, 247).

Critics of the Seventh-day Adventist movement charge that Adventists add to Scripture by calling Ellen White's writings a source of truth, multiply the requirements for salvation by requiring seventh-day Sabbath-keeping and old-covenant dietary laws, subtract from the atonement and person of Jesus Christ with their investigative judgment and lingering Arian influence, and divide the body of Christ by requiring worship on the seventh-day Sabbath and by seeing themselves as God's true "remnant church."

See also ADVENTIST MOVEMENT; MILLER, WILLIAM; MILLERITE MOVEMENT

Bibliography. D. Batchelor, *The Trinity*; "Are the Dead Really Dead?," *Amazing Facts*, https://www.amazingfacts.org/media-library/study-guide/e/4987/t/are-the-dead-really-dead; General Conference of Seventh-day Adventists, *Seventh-day Adventists Believe*, 2nd ed.; General Conference of Seventh-day Adventists home page, http://www.adventist.org/; M. Hook, *Desmond Ford: Reformist*

Theologian, Gospel Revivalist; G. Land, *Historical Dictionary of Seventh-day Adventists*; Life Assurance Ministries, Inc., home page, http://www.lifeassuranceministries.org/; M. J. Martin, ExAdventist Outreach home page, http://www.exadventist.com; J. Paulsen, "The Theological Landscape: Perspective on Issues facing the World Seventh-day Adventist Church," *Adventist Review*; W. Rae, *The White Lie*; D. Ratzlaff, "Are Adventists Moving to Feast-Keeping?," *Proclamation!*; Ratzlaff, *Cultic Doctrine of Seventh-day Adventists*; Ratzlaff, *Truth about Adventist "Truth"*; R. Schwartz and F. Greenleaf, *Light Bearers: A History of the Seventh-day Adventist Church*, rev. ed.; E. G. White, *Early Writings*; White, *The Great Controversy*; White, Letter 55, in *Selected Messages*, vol. 1; R. Wieland and D. K. Short, "The Righteousness by Faith Comparison," Thought Paper no. 3, repr. from *1888 Re-examined*.

C. Tinker

SHABBAT (THE SABBATH), JEWISH. The English word *Sabbath* comes from the Hebrew word *shabbat*. The root meaning is "to desist," "to cease," "to rest." The Sabbath begins at sundown on Friday and lasts until sundown of the next day. In addition to prohibited activities, a special meal accompanies the Sabbath observances.

Since the temple was destroyed in AD 70, the Sabbath has become the most important element in Judaism.

The Concepts of the Sabbath. The major concept of the Sabbath in Judaism is that of *menuchah* (rest), which includes rest of body, mind, and spirit. On this day, work is banished and replaced by rest.

Many minor concepts are involved in the Sabbath. Sabbath is a time for studying the law; it is a time for family companionship; it is a weekly protest against slavery since slaves had to work seven days a week. According to Orthodox Judaism, on the Sabbath Jews receive an additional soul. Furthermore, the Sabbath is a foundation of the faith. The Sabbath gave rise to synagogues. The day is associated with personal salvation because it is a foretaste of the bliss stored up for the righteous in the world to come.

According to Judaism, the Sabbath has three age-long functions. First, it enables one to devote oneself fully, one day a week, to becoming "a kingdom of priests and a holy nation" and, in that way, beautifying one's life. Second, it prevents one from becoming enslaved to secular activities, showing freedom from enslavement to Egypt. And third, it proves one's trust in God: that he will provide even without the material gain of working on the Sabbath.

The Laws of the Sabbath. All together the rabbis came up with about fifteen hundred rules and regulations concerning the Sabbath. These were derived from thirty-nine areas of prohibited work on the Sabbath day.

These thirty-nine areas were based on the construction of the tabernacle in the wilderness. The rabbis arrived at their deduction by juxtaposing the passages concerning the construction of the tabernacle and passages prohibiting work on the Sabbath. They interpreted these passages to mean that no work was allowed on the tabernacle on the Sabbath day. Therefore, the prohibited work for the Sabbath day was whatever area of work was required for the tabernacle. The rabbis concluded that there were thirty-nine areas of work on the tabernacle that were forbidden on the Sabbath day. From these thirty-nine areas, they developed many "offspring" or "derivatives" (Hebrew, *toledot*). They decided which other works done by human beings would fit into these areas. These were other labors of the same area that shared a purpose in common with the tabernacle works. Therefore, they were also forbidden. Through a form of rabbinic logic known as *pilpul*, they derived many new rules and regulations out of the original thirty-nine areas of work forbidden on the tabernacle on the Sabbath day. By the time all the laws were developed, there were approximately fifteen hundred rules and regulations for the

Sabbath day. These are largely still followed in Orthodox Judaism today.

The Essential Elements for Sabbath. Three basic items are essential for Sabbath meal observance: first, *challah*, an egg bread whose yellow color results from the heavy use of egg yolk; second, wine; and third, candles.

1. Sabbath Foods. Challah bread is the one essential food for the Passover, and it is prepared in a braided form for most Sabbaths. Two loaves are used to symbolize the double portion of manna that God gave for the Sabbath day. As the Sabbath begins on Friday night, the challah bread is broken with a special blessing over it, and it is then dipped in salt before it is eaten because all sacrifices were salted. The name *challah* itself means "round loaf" or "cake," and it represents the share or loaf given to the priest during the time when the tabernacle stood, and later, the temple. The Sabbath loaf subsequently retained its old Hebrew name even though it was no longer given to priests.

Traditional Sabbath foods include fish. Any kind of *kosher* meat is permitted, but according to rabbis, fish is to be preferred for several reasons. First, God promised that Israel would multiply "like the sand of the sea," and fish comes from the sea. Second, in Hebrew the word for "fish" has the numerical value of seven, which corresponds to the seventh day of the week. And third, just as God always watches over Israel, the eye of the fish is always open.

Another food for the Sabbath is *kugel*, which is a pudding or a casserole of rice or noodles with raisins.

Another specialty food is *cholent*, which comes from a word that means "warm." This was food that was kept warm from Friday into the Sabbath, so that the worshipers could enjoy a warm meal for the Sabbath day.

2. Sabbath Lights. The second essential element for Sabbath observance in Judaism is lights. In ancient times, the last act before the Sabbath began was kindling lights because it was prohibited to kindle fire on the Sabbath. Originally the intent was only to provide light for the Sabbath, but eventually the lights were associated with the Sabbath. Later the rabbis reinterpreted the lights as symbolizing the weekly refilling and rekindling of the lampstand in the temple. Today the candles are lit to symbolize the joy that fills the Jewish home on this day. The creation of light was the first work of God, and God rested from his work of creation on the Sabbath day. Furthermore, according to Judaism, when Adam and Eve sinned, the great light of creation was extinguished. The Sabbath lights manifest the Jewish longing to return to a state of sinlessness, when the first light will reappear in the world to come.

In most Jewish homes today, two candles are lit. Historically, the reason was that in the average Jewish home in talmudic times, there were just three rooms: the kitchen, the living room, and the bedroom. Before the Sabbath began, one light was lit in the kitchen, and one light in the living room, but not in the bedroom, for once the Sabbath began, one could not extinguish the light on the Sabbath day. Obviously, one did not want to have a lighted candle while sleeping. Eventually, lighting the two candles became an established religious rite. Later it was reinterpreted by the rabbis to represent the two versions of the Sabbath commandment: first, Exodus 20:8, which states: "Remember the sabbath day"; and second, Deuteronomy 5:12, which states: "Observe the sabbath day." The norm today is two candles, but some Jewish homes light seven, while others light ten.

Women kindle the Sabbath lights. It is uniquely the responsibility of the woman to light the candles because, according to the rabbis, when Adam fell, it was really the woman who caused the light to be extinguished, so it is now the woman who is responsible for bringing the light back. After kindling the lights and while saying the blessing, the woman covers her eyes with the palm

461

of her hands. Because the blessing must precede the act, she shields her eyes with the palms of her hands so as not to see or to benefit from the light until after the blessing. This also, according to Judaism, will aid in devotion during prayer.

As she lights the candles and covers her eyes, she will say the following blessing: "Blessed art You, O Lord our God, King of the universe, Who has sanctified us with Your commandments and commanded us to kindle the lights of the Holy Sabbath."

3. *Sabbath Wine.* Wine is the third essential element required for the Sabbath observance; everyone will drink a small portion of wine. This will be preceded by the recitation of a blessing: "Blessed are You, O Lord our God, King of the universe, Who created the fruit of the vine." The expression "fruit of the vine" in Judaism does not refer to grape juice. It refers to real wine that comes from the fruit of the grape. Judaism uses the expression "fruit of the vine" on special occasions.

The Meals of the Sabbath. The Sabbath is an occasion for eating. Altogether one will eat three meals on the Sabbath day. There is also a tradition of eating a fourth meal before the Sabbath actually comes to an end. The first meal is eaten on Friday night, the second meal is eaten on Saturday morning, and the third meal is eaten on Saturday afternoon following the synagogue service.

The Sabbath tablecloth is always white. The history of this custom involves the fact that tablecloths were used only on festive occasions in ancient times, and these were usually white. Eventually the Sabbath became associated with white tablecloths, and later this was reinterpreted to symbolize the manna, which was white.

See also JUDAISM

Bibliography. Rabbi S. Finkelman and Rabbi N. Scherman, *Shabbos, The Sabbath—Its Essence and Significance*; D. I. Grunfeld, *The Sabbath: A Guide to Its Understanding and Observance*; A. E. Millgram, *Sabbath: The Day of Delight*; W. G.

Plaut, *Shabbat Manual*; C. Roth, "Shabbat," in *Encyclopedia Judaica*, edited by C. Roth; I. Singer, "Shabat/Sabbath," in *The Jewish Encyclopedia*.

A. Fruchtenbaum

SHAKTI. With a name taken from the Sanskrit term for "power" or "energy," Shakti is a goddess worshiped in Hinduism. Shakti may function as an independent deity or as the consort of Shiva. In the latter case, she is worshiped under various names: Deva, Kali, Durga, or Amba. She personifies primal energy and is found in both kundalini and tantric Hinduism.

See also HINDUISM; KUNDALINI; SHIVA; TANTRA

Bibliography. K. K. Klostermaier, *A Concise Encyclopedia of Hinduism*; S. Schuhmacher and G. Woerner, eds., *The Rider Encyclopedia of Eastern Philosophy and Religion*.

E. Pement

SHANKARA, OR ADI SHANKARACHARYA. *See* SANKARA

SHARI'AH. Linguistically from a root word meaning "road, path," Shari'ah is usually glossed as "the divine law" of Islam. Shari'ah in the broadest sense includes all the legal books, discussions, polemics, and rulings by Muslim scholars. (Although the word *Shari'ah* is more closely associated with Sunnis than with Shi'ites, Shi'ites have a similar structure of law that is based on the authority of the imams, who are descendants of Muhammad.) Because the goal of Muslims is to emulate the life of Muhammad as closely as possible, the primary source of Shari'ah is the tradition (hadith) literature, which purports to relate all of Muhammad's sayings and actions on the authority of his close companions. This material, however, was early recognized to contain large numbers of forgeries, and its parts were classified by Muslim scholars as correct (*sahih*), good (*hasan*), weak (*da'if*), or forged (*mawdu'a*).

Ideally, laws should be based on traditions from the first two categories.

The Muslim scholar al-Shafi'i (d. 820), in his numerous treatises, laid down the four bases for Muslim law: the Qur'an, the hadith, analogy (*qiyas*), and consensus (*ijma'*). He specifically rejected two further categories of law, opinion (*ray*) and tribal custom (*'urf*), although non-Muslim scholars suspect that a great deal of the hadith literature consists of traditions that were originally opinions of legal scholars that have been ascribed to Muhammad. Tribal custom also has not been excised completely from Islamic societies.

From the time of al-Shafi'i, there developed four basic legal schools among Sunnis: the Maliki, the Hanafi, the Shafi'i, and the Hanbali. (Two others, the Zahiri, who were literalists and have disappeared, and the Ja'fari, who were Shi'ites, were recognized historically.) Today each of these schools predominates in one or more regions of the Muslim world: the Malikis in North and West Africa; the Hanafis throughout the Middle East, Turkey, Central Asia, Pakistan, India, and Bangladesh; the Shafi'is in parts of Egypt, East Africa, Indonesia, and Malaysia; and the Hanbalis in Saudi Arabia. From the thirteenth century onward, it was generally recognized that each legal school had Islamic legitimacy and that in theory any Sunni Muslim could belong to any school he chose.

The principal figures in the interpretation and formulation of Shari'ah were the ulama (the religious scholars), who handled and taught the hadith literature, usually in the traditional setting of the madrasa school, and the *fuqaha'* (the jurisprudents). From this latter group, the religious judges, the *qadis*, were drawn. Beginning in the thirteenth century, it became normative that there would be a separate religious court for each of the schools in the major cities.

At the beginning of the nineteenth century, the prerogatives of Shari'ah in Muslim societies began to disappear, and by the middle of the twentieth century no Muslim state other than Saudi Arabia made any pretense to being governed by the norms of Shari'ah. However, in general Muslim personal law, such as laws of marriage, divorce, and inheritance (which are delineated in the Qur'an) were influenced by Shari'ah.

With the rise of radical Islam in the 1970s and 1980s, there began to be popular calls for the implementation of Shari'ah in a number of Muslim states, and by the beginning of the twenty-first century, Libya, Pakistan, Afghanistan, Saudi Arabia, and Iran all made claims to being governed by Shari'ah norms. Additionally, since the year 2000, twelve of the Muslim-majority states in northern Nigeria have adopted Shari'ah as the law of the land. However, in each of these countries, substantial problems remain in the definition of Shari'ah because the classical meaning was not of a single legal code, whereas contemporary radicals in their calls for Shari'ah seem to imply that such a code is what they want. In addition to this conceptual problem, there is the further issue of the use of non-Islamic law because virtually every Muslim country (except Saudi Arabia) uses some form of Western law, usually dating from colonial times, as the basis for its legal system. It is not clear how Shari'ah would or could be integrated with this law.

Another serious issue is the large-scale migration of Muslims to Western countries, many of which have some of the world's most liberal law systems. Recently, in countries such as Denmark and Great Britain, Muslims have called for the implementation of Shari'ah, and even for semiautonomous ghettos and towns governed by clerics. With the unfortunate proclivity to violence exhibited by many fundamentalist Muslims, Western countries are struggling over how best to deal with these issues. For the time being, most have simply attempted to appease those calling for Shari'ah by allowing some of the less controversial aspects of Islamic law.

See also Islam, Basic Beliefs of

Bibliography. W. Hallaq, *A History of Islamic Legal Theories: An Introduction to Sunni Usul al-Fiqh*; J. Schacht, *An Introduction to Islamic Law*; B. G. Weiss, *The Search for God's Law: Islamic Jurisprudence in the Writings of Sayf al-Din al-Amidi*; Weiss, *The Spirit of Islamic Law*.

D. B. Cook

SHAVUOT (THE FEAST OF WEEKS). Because it occurs seven weeks after Passover, this feast is called Shavuot, meaning "weeks." The Feast of Weeks is mentioned in eight passages in the Bible, five of which are in the Old Testament and three in the New Testament (Exod. 23:16; 34:22; Lev. 23:15–21; Num. 28:26; Deut. 16:9–12; Acts 2:1–4; 20:16; 1 Cor. 16:8).

In the Mosaic law, two wave loaves were offered, and these loaves were to be leavened. This is the only festival where leaven was permitted, but it was not burned on the altar. Leaven is a symbol of sin, and those who are represented by this sacrifice are sinners. Also, there is no specific calendar date for the feast because it was to occur seven weeks from the Sunday following Passover.

Jewish people observe Shavuot today by reading the book of Ruth because the story took place during the time of harvest and because of a tradition that King David (a descendant of Ruth) was born during the Feast of Weeks. Another form of observance is staying up all night to study the Mosaic law, a reminder that there was thunder and lightning at the time the law was given and this kept the Jews awake all night. During Shavuot special food items are served. One is kreplach (a type of Jewish dumpling, normally consisting of chopped meat, garlic, and onions enclosed in pasta, but on this occasion filled only with cheese). Also popular are cheese blintzes, very thin pancakes, usually filled with cream cheese, folded into a rectangle and then fried or baked, usually eaten with some kind of sour cream sauce or fruit topping.

Also branches from trees and grass from the field are spread over the floor of the synagogue as a reminder that Jewish people should be praying for a bumper crop of fruit.

See also Judaism

Bibliography. A. Fruchtenbaum, *The Feasts of Israel*; C. Roth, "Shavuot," in *Encyclopedia Judaica*, edited by C. Roth; H. Schauss, *The Jewish Festivals: History & Observance*; I. Singer, "Shavuot," in *The Jewish Encyclopedia*; M. Strassfeld, *The Jewish Holidays: A Guide & Commentary*; Y. Vainstein, *The Cycle of the Jewish Year: A Study of the Festivals and of Selections from the Liturgy*.

A. Fruchtenbaum

SHAYKH/SHEIKH. *Shaykh* (Arabic, "old man"; often spelled "sheikh") is an honorific title given to elders, mainly to those who are teachers and leaders. Historically, the term described the chief of a tribe or a revered leader within the Bedouin culture of Arabia. In modern times, it has been used as a title for those who are of royal lineage (and more recently those of wealth) in most of the Persian Gulf countries. However, as Islam and Arabic culture spread, the term began to become wider in scope.

Shaykh is often used to describe a Muslim man of academic training in Islam, especially one who teaches Islamic law. In traditionally Muslim countries, the title is used for leaders of religious fraternities and orders. In the Ottoman Empire, shaykh was the title of the chief mufti of Istanbul, who was considered the religious head of the empire.

A shaykh (also known as a *pir*) is a spiritual master in Sufi Islam. A central element of Sufi practice is that every nonmaster ought to be under the oversight of a shaykh, who provides the disciple (*murid*) with authoritative counsel and insight into the doctrines and rituals of Sufism. The relationship between a shaykh and his disciple is supposed to be one in which the disciple completely trusts his shaykh and the shaykh lovingly oversees the disciple's spiritual development.

Within the Maronite Christian community of Lebanon, the term is used to describe the heads of certain Christian families who at one time ruled over parts of the area, fought against Islamic invaders, or held high offices within the Ottoman Empire.

See also ISLAM, BASIC BELIEFS OF; MARONITE CHRISTIANS; SUFISM

Bibliography. A. F. Buehler, *Sufi Heirs of the Prophet: The Indian Naqshbandiyya and the Rise of the Mediating Sufi Shaykh*; W. C. Chittick, *Sufism: A Short Introduction*; B. Lewis and B. E. Churchill, *Islam: The Religion and the People*.

H. W. House

SHIH CHING / SHIJING. Shih Ching, or the Classic of Poetry (or of odes), is one of the five classic works of Confucianism. It consists of 305 poems dated as far back as the eleventh century BC. According to tradition, it was compiled by Confucius. It is divided into four sections: popular odes, court poetry, other courtly odes, and eulogies.

See also CONFUCIANISM; CONFUCIUS

Bibliography. B. D. Kyokai, *Teachings of Confucianism*.

A. W. Barber

SHI'A ISLAM. Shi'a (or Shi'ite) Islam is the second-largest faction of Islam after Sunni Islam. Shi'as make up 14 percent of the Muslim faith, which translates into approximately one hundred million people. Although Shi'a Islam is the minority in terms of world Islamic population, it became the established religion of Persia in 1502. The majority of the population in present-day Iran and Iraq is Shi'ite.

The Shi'a faith is based on the Muslim holy book, the Qur'an, and the message of the prophet Muhammad. Shi'ism dates to a conflict that erupted soon after Muhammad's death. Because Muhammad did not appoint a successor, there was a division over who should be the new leader of this newly formed faith. Although Muhammad was followed closely by three associates whom many believed to be his successors, others thought that Ali, Muhammad's cousin and son-in-law, would be the new leader. This led to a fundamental rupture within the Muslim faith.

As the early followers of Islam attempted to discern the direction of the religion, the Shi'a followers insisted that only Ali and his descendants had a legitimate right to be caliphs. This group referred to themselves as the Shiat 'Ali (the partisans of Ali), which later came to be known simply as "Shi'a" or "Shi'ites" (see Farah, 177). At its inception, Shi'a Islam therefore differed from Sunni Islam in that the Shi'ites believed that the bloodline of Muhammad best characterized the leader of Islam, whereas the Sunnis believed that the person who best modeled Islam as did Muhammad would be most qualified to lead. Unlike divisions in many other religions, this division in Islam is not over one group being conservative and the other liberal but over the question of who should be the leader of the religion (Zepp, 105).

The first three leaders of Islam were Sunnis, and Ali became the fourth caliph, and first Sunni caliph, in 656. He gradually lost control of the Muslim world and was murdered in 661. After the death of Ali, the Umayyad Dynasty assumed leadership of the Muslim world. Ali's youngest son, Husayn, attempted to challenge the Umayyad leadership but was defeated in battle in 680. Shi'ites consider those who were defeated in this battle to be martyrs (Hopfe and Woodward, 365).

Several features distinguish Shi'a Islam from Sunni Islam. First, while Shi'ites believe that revelation ended with the prophet Muhammad and the Qur'an, they also believe that later generations of believers were given divinely inspired leaders called imams. The imam leads a community in prayer and has the ability to speak with the authority of God. Second, Shi'ites traditionally believe in the existence of a mahdi (guided one), a messiah figure who will one day lead the world into an era of justice. Third, because of the importance of the maytyrdom of Husayn, Shi'ites tend to prize martyrdom. Each year on the tenth of the month of Muharranm, Husayn's death is reenacted. The site of his death represents a special place of pilgrimage for Shi'ites. Finally, Shi'ites tend to mistrust the traditional reading and interpretation of the Qur'an. They reason that because the Qur'an does not mention Ali as Muhammad's successor, it must have been tampered with by Ali's enemies (Hopfe and Woodward, 365).

See also ISLAM, BASIC BELIEFS OF; MUHAMMAD; SUNNI ISLAM

Bibliography. C. E. Farrah, *Islam: Beliefs and Observances*, 7th ed.; M. S. Gordon, *Islam: Origins, Practices, Holy Texts, Sacred Persons, Sacred Places*; L. M. Hopfe and M. Woodward, *Religions of the World*; C. D. Malbouisson, ed., *Focus on Islamic Issues*; N. Robinson, *Islam: A Concise Introduction*; I. G. Zepp, *A Muslim Primer*, 2nd ed.

T. S. Price

SHIN BUDDHISM. Also known as Jodo Shinshu (Pure Land True Sect), Shin Buddhism is one of two main branches of Japanese "Pure Land" Buddhism. The "pure land" is a realm or world system (Buddha-land) thought to be purified by a Buddha or Buddha-to-be (bodhisattva), and subsequently ruled by the Buddha. The most popular of these bodhisattva/Buddha figures is Amitabha (Amida, Japanese for "infinite light"), also known as Amitayus (Infinite Life). According to tradition, Amida Buddha (previously the Bodhisattva Dharmakara) was originally a king who received instruction from a Buddha and, having viewed numerous Buddhalands, vowed (with forty-eight vows) to create a pure land—sometimes incorrectly termed "Western Paradise"—which humans could enter by confidence in Amida himself. Through numberless eons of time (*kalpas*) spent in meditation and the accumulation of

extraordinary merit, he attained enlightenment and fulfilled his vows.

Pure Land thought had spread to China by the fourth century (Chinese Ching-t'u/Jingtu) and to Japan by the sixth (usually with other sects), but it experienced its most marked growth under two monks, Honen (1133–1212) and his student Shinran (1173–1262), founders of Jodo Shu and Jodo Shinshu, respectively. Both schools emphasized *nembutsu*, the (repeated) ritual invocation of Amida—*Namu amida butsu* ("I trust [or 'take refuge'] in the Amida Buddha")—thought to have special efficacy, specifically as a means of purification for entrance into the Pure Land (Honen reportedly recited sixty thousand nembutsu each day). Because they taught enlightenment through the power of another (*tariki*) rather than self-power (*jiriki*), both Honen and Shinran were banished from Kyoto, the ancient capital. However, Shinran returned to teach in Kyoto, now regarded as headquarters for Jodo, which has become the largest Buddhist tradition in Japan.

Shin arrived in America with immigrants in 1869 and organized in 1914 as the Buddhist Mission of North America, later renamed (1944) the Buddhist Churches of America (BCA). Once claiming about fifty thousand members (mostly of Japanese descent), the BCA has declined precipitously in recent years. Like Jodo generally, American Shin practices nembutsu and recognizes three primary scriptures—the "Larger (Sukhavati Vyuha, 'infinite life') Sutra" (Daimuryojukyo); the "Smaller Sutra" (Amida Kyo), which summarizes the Larger Sutra and describes the Pure Land; and the "Amitayur Dhyana ['contemplation on Buddha Amitayus'] Sutra" (Kanmuryoju Kyo), which tells the story of Queen Vaidehi's rebirth in the Pure Land through trust in Amida. The Larger Sutra contains the "primal vow" (vow eighteen of Amida's forty-eight), which assures rebirth in the Pure Land to all "who sincerely and joyfully entrust themselves to"

Amida, who "desire to be born" in his land, and who "call [his] name [*nembutsu*] even ten times." American Shin has self-consciously conformed itself to mainstream Christian practice, including Sunday congregational worship, hymn singing, prayers, creeds, sermons, and the like. The Institute of Buddhist Studies, founded (1966) to train BCA ministers, affiliated with the Graduate Theological Union in Berkeley in 1985.

Jodo Shinshu lacks any teaching on sin, atonement, or judgment but accepts the Buddhist ideas of morality, karma, and rebirth. Further, despite mainstreaming efforts, the sect has not attracted a large following outside Japan.

See also BODHISATTVA; BUDDHISM; BUDDHIST CHURCHES OF AMERICA; PURE LAND BUDDHISM

Bibliography. J. Foard, M. Solomon, and R. K. Payne, eds., *The Pure Land Tradition: History and Development*; D. Hirota, ed., *Toward a Contemporary Understanding of Pure Land Buddhism: Creating a Shin Buddhist Theology*; R. H. Seager, *Buddhism in America*; D. T. Suzuki, *Shin Buddhism*; D. R. Tuck, *Buddhist Churches of America: Jodo Shinshu*; T. Unno, *River of Fire, River of Water: An Introduction to the Pure Land Tradition of Shin Buddhism*.

C. R. Wells

SHINTO. Shinto (the way of the gods) is the only indigenous Japanese religion.

History. According to mythological tradition, Shinto dates to the seventh century BC. However, many modern scholars do not believe that Shinto—which has no founder—appeared until the third century AD. In fact, some do not even consider Shinto to be a religion in the strict sense of the word. One commentator has said that Shinto is "an open-ended philosophical naturalism, and as such can speak more readily to modern seekers than the philosophies which appeal to irrational bases of authority—revealed books, church councils, or popes" (Ross, 167).

Shinto was deeply influenced by Buddhism, Taoism, and Confucianism. After the sixth century, Buddhism became the state religion of Japan and existed in a syncretic form with Shinto. Although the Shinto religion commingled with Buddhism in the Middle Ages, it began revitalizing as separate in the eighteenth century, slowly forming State Shinto in the nineteenth century. Emperor Meiji officially disenfranchised Buddhism and made Shinto the state religion in 1868. Prior to World War II, the Shinto faith was mainly responsible for the Japanese feeling of superiority, due to Shinto's teaching on the divine origins of Japan. When Emperor Hirohito surrendered to the Allied forces at the end of World War II, he was compelled not only to acknowledge defeat but also to renounce his claim to divinity as a condition of the surrender terms.

Since World War II, many in Japan have shied away from the state religion formulation but continue with more traditional Shinto practices. After the Japanese Home Ministry lost control of the country's 110,000 Shinto shrines—each of which was dedicated to a different deity—there was immediate confusion and paralysis in the nationwide religious system, and attendance at the shrines fell, although temple attendance is not compulsory or required. Presently, the shrines are organized into the Association of Shinto Shrines.

Still, Japan became a secular nation as its people searched after modernity and prosperity, and as in other nations, religions play a lesser and more private role. One University of Tokyo student poll taken just two decades after the end of World War II discovered that 97 percent of the more than six thousand students surveyed were either agnostic or atheist, with only 3 percent claiming to be Christian, Buddhist, or Shinto. However, approximately 40 percent of the general population in Japan today claim to be Shinto. Although there are no official numbers, it is estimated that there were fewer than 3.5 million Shinto adherents around the world in 2000, with fewer than a thousand of those living in North America.

Mythology. According to Shinto mythology, the Japanese people were created by a divine fiat. The male deity Izanagi and his female companion, Izanami, conceived and gave birth to the Japanese islands as well as the mountains, rivers, trees, and all other gods and goddesses. Izanami died after giving birth to fire, so Izanagi traveled to Yomi (similar to the Greek idea of Hades) to find her. Finding her maggot-infested body, Izanagi returned to the land of the living, washed himself in water and created the "three noble children": the sun goddess Amaterasu-Omikami, the moon god Tsukuyomi-no-Mikoto, and the storm god Susano-o (who was later banned from heaven to the underworld). The sun goddess later sent her grandson, Ninigi, to become the first emperor of Japan, and all future Japanese emperors were also divine.

Beliefs. There are three major sects of Shinto followers. The first emphasizes mountain or nature worship. The second stresses divination and faith healing. The third is more in line with the historic faith, with a special emphasis on yoga-like meditation techniques, purification rites, and fasting. In the modern period, minor sects have proliferated. Generally, followers of Shinto have numerous beliefs and practices. Shinto has no definite doctrines. For instance, it leaves the idea of God undeveloped and does not claim special revelation.

Shinto scriptures are not intended to be doctrinal resources. Rather, they tell the stories of the *kami* (the "gods," which can be anything from deities to people, animals, and even rocks and mountains) and Japanese history. The written scriptures are the Kojiki (Records of Ancient Matters), the Rikkokushi (six national histories), the Shoku Nihongi (continuing chronicles of Japan), and the Jinno Shotoki (a study of Shinto and Japanese politics and history).

There are four affirmations in Shinto belief:

1. *Tradition/family.* Through the family, traditions are preserved. The main celebrations in Shinto life are birth and marriage, and ancestors are highly revered. Death is considered evil in Shinto, so funerals are normally officiated by Buddhist priests.
2. *Nature.* Those who are close to nature are close to the gods, and natural objects are revered as sacred.
3. *Physical cleanliness.* Followers are constantly bathing, cleaning their mouths, and closely monitoring their personal hygiene.
4. *Matsuri.* Followers offer *matsuri*, or worship and honor, to the kami.

Honor in the home is especially important, and many Shinto families place a *kami-dana* (god shelf) in their homes to serve as a miniature temple. Flowers and food are placed on the altar in honor of the home's patron deity. The kami-dana also serves as a place for brief prayers or meditation.

In the sixteenth century, a warrior code for the samurai (knights) was well developed—it combined Shinto, Confucian, and Buddhist ideas and epitomized honorable traits. Loyalty, gratitude, courage, justice, truthfulness, politeness, reserve, and honor became the eight attitudes associated with the Bushido ethical code. Death was preferable to disgrace, and suicide (*hara-kiri*, a form of disembowelment) became the honorable way that a Bushido warrior dealt with humiliation of any kind. This code, with its strong emphasis on loyalty onto death, was used by the military government to inspire the Japanese troops in World War II.

The Japanese are also known for their colorful festivals throughout the year. Five festivals, known as the *go-sekku*, are the New Year Festival (January 1–3), the Girls' Festival

(March 3), the Boys' Festival (May 5), the Star Festival (July 7), and the Chrysanthemum Festival (September 9). There is also a Cherry Blossom Festival in the spring, a celebration of the emperor's birthday, and a fall harvest festival, along with a number of other festivals held regionally throughout Japan.

Conclusion. The Shinto religion is unlikely to expand outside the boundaries of Japan. It is at heart an indigenous religion, deeply rooted in Japanese culture. However, for the same reason it is unlikely to completely disappear. Rather than being an enforced state religion, Shinto has reverted to its ancient form of personal and familial practice. Instead of focusing on emperor worship and warrior honor, modern Shinto has reverted to home shrines honoring ancestors and securing better fortunes.

See also BUDDHISM; CONFUCIANISM; KAMI; TAOISM/DAOISM

Bibliography. J. Bowker, ed., *The Cambridge Illustrated History of Religions*; J. Breen and M. Teeuwen, eds., *Shinto in History: Ways of the Kami*; J. Herbert, *Shinto: At the Fountain-head of Japan*; G. Kato, *A Study of Shinto: The Religion of the Japanese Nation*; J. B. Noss, *Man's Religions*, 5th ed.; F. H. Ross, *Shinto: The Way of Japan*.

E. Johnson

SHIVA. In Sanskrit *Shiva* means "auspicious one." Shiva, also called Mahadeva, is one of the most complex and dynamic deities in the pan-Hindu pantheon. His name, associated myths, depictions, and modes of veneration have drastic regional and theological differences. The origins of Shiva worship are hotly contested, particularly with the discovery and the resulting genealogical claims made because of the Pashupati seal, a proto-Shiva figure found in the Mohenjo-daro excavation. Shiva is mentioned in the Mahabharata and Upanishads, where he is identified and paralleled with the destructive Vedic god Rudra. He is frequently enumerated among Hinduism's great trinities, including the Trimurti, the "divine manifestation" of Brahma the creator, Vishnu the preserver, and Shiva the destroyer. As the demolisher of the world, Shiva is venerated for his regenerative purposes, perpetuating the daily and cosmological cycle of birth, death, and rebirth. Shiva is also associated with popular forms of Hindu worship, or bhakti, which is devotion to a particular deity; as such he is commonly included in Hinduism's three major "denominations": Shaivism, devoted to Shiva; Vaishnavis, devoted to Vishnu; and Shaktism, devoted to Shakti (or Devi, the Divine Mother). Shiva is variously depicted and worshiped as white with a blue throat (the result of drinking poison), with a cobra encircling his neck, with three horizontal lines drawn across his forehead (copied by Shivites using *vibhuti*, sacred ash), with four arms, and with a third eye representing wisdom and insight. He is often seen carrying a trident and accompanied by his white bull, Nandi. Additionally, he is commonly associated with the Shivalinga, or *lingam*, a vertical, rounded column intended to represent a phallus and worshiped by Shivites.

Shiva is often portrayed using contradictory images and inconsistent characteristics. For example, he is at once described as a world-renouncing ascetic (*sannyasin*) and a domestic householder (*grihastha*). In the first instance, he is viewed as a great yogi, an image used by many yogic schools and traditions that revere Shiva as celibate and self-controlled. Yet he is also described as a householder, married to Parvati (representing Shakti, the divine feminine force), and has two sons, Kathikeya and the elephant-headed Ganesha. These paradoxical depictions of Shiva as the "erotic ascetic" (see O'Flaherty) exemplify his multiplicitous portraitures. Similarly, the ambiguity of Shiva's nature is emphasized in his representation as the androgynous Ardhanarishvara, possessing both female and male physical attributes. In this anthropomorphic form, his body is split in half, with male and female anatomy (the female half represents Shiva's consort Shakti). Shiva is perhaps best known through the Ananda Natanam, his cosmic dance, which is emulated in dance choreography and in sculptures that have become emblematic of Indian art. As Nataraja, the God of Dance, Shiva's vigorous dancing posture, called *tandava*, portrays his enigmatic nature. He is shown as dancing the universe into creation, sustaining it, and destroying it through his rhythmical movement. This image of Shiva became elaborately immortalized in South Indian bronze statues from the Chola Dynasty of the tenth century AD.

See also BRAHMA; HINDUISM; SHAKTI; UPANISHADS; VEDAS; VISHNU

Bibliography. G. Flood, *An Introduction to Hinduism*; W. D. O'Flaherty, *Shiva: The Erotic Ascetic*; S. Srinivasan, "Shiva as Cosmic Dancer: On Pallava Origins for the Nataraja Bronze," *World Archaeology*.

R. Aechtner

SHREE/SHRI/SRI. *Sri* (pronounced "shree") is a term of respect commonly prefixed to the name of a teacher or guru in Hinduism. All the spelling variants mean the same, although *Sri* is the most common transliteration. Derived from the word meaning "to flame," it has come to mean radiance and many associated notions. Well-known gurus who have used this prefix include Bhagwan Shree Rajneesh, Sri Aurobindo, Sri Chinmoy, and Shrii Shrii Anandamurti.

See also ANANDAMURTI, SHRII SHRII; AUROBINDO, SRI; CHINMOY, SRI; GURU; HINDUISM; SWAMI

Bibliography. K. K. Klostermaier, *A Concise Encyclopedia of Hinduism*; S. Schuhmacher and G. Woerner, eds., *The Rider Encyclopedia of Eastern Philosophy and Religion*.

E. Pement

SHRUTI/SRUTI. This word comes from a Sanskrit term for "that which has been

perceived through hearing." Hindu scripture falls into two categories, *shruti* (which has been heard, and thus revelation) and *smriti* (what has been remembered, or tradition). The shruti are fully authoritative for Hindus, as unmediated revelations of the Divine. Writings designated shruti are basically the Vedas, the Upanishads (commentaries on the Vedas), and sometimes the Agamas (worship manuals). Due to its enormous popularity, the Bhagavad Gita is often considered shruti, though it comes from a large body of post-Vedic literature designated as smriti.

Shruti is also a term used in Indian music, defining the smallest tonal interval that the human ear is able to discern. There are twenty-two shruti in one octave (as opposed to eight tones in a Western major or minor scale, or twelve in a Western chromatic scale).

See also HINDUISM; SMRITI; VEDAS

Bibliography. K. K. Klostermaier, *A Concise Encyclopedia of Hinduism*; S. Schuhmacher and G. Woerner, eds., *The Rider Encyclopedia of Eastern Philosophy and Religion*.

J. A. Borland and E. Pement

SHU-CHING/SHUJING. The Shu-ching (book of history) is a compilation of historical records that purport to contain royal pronouncements from the Shang Dynasty (ca. 1600–1046 BC) and afterward. Scholars think they were compiled circa the fifth century BC. The Shu-ching contains reports of both genuinely historical events and very ancient Chinese legends. Confucian tradition has it that Confucius edited these documents and produced commentaries on them, though many modern scholars doubt this. The text includes chronologies, political speeches and tributes, royal announcements, government statutes, and the pronouncements of legal councils. During most of recorded Chinese history, the Shu-ching functioned as a sourcebook of sage advice for conducting imperial rule, and many civil leaders looked to it as a model of wise government.

See also CONFUCIANISM

Bibliography. M. Nylan, *The Five "Confucian" Classics*; J. A. G. Roberts, *A Concise History of China*; C. Waltham, *Shu Ching, Book of History: A Modernized Edition of the Translations of James Legge*.

M. Power

SIDDHA YOGA. Siddha Yoga, which has its roots in Kashmir Shaivism, came to prominence through Bhagawan Nityananda (1896–1961) and his pupil Muktananda Paramahansa (1908–82). Muktananda's movement now has a quarter of a million aspirants in forty-six nations. Before he died, Muktananda nominated as joint successors Swami Chidvilasananda (now known as Gurumayi) and Swami Nityananda. A subsequent rift between them led to the ousting of Nityananda in 1985.

There are also two Western-born gurus: Swami Rudrananda (1928–73) and Da John. Rudrananda, born Albert Rudolph, was initiated by Bhagawan Nityananda in 1958. He established the Shree Gurudev Rudrananda Ashram (now known as Nityananda Institute) in 1971 after a dispute with Muktananda. Da John was one of Rudrananda's early followers and ran the Free Daist Communion.

The precepts of Siddha Yoga, as taught by Muktananda, center on devotion to the guru, who is the physical representation of Shiva. Muktananda taught that within the human body there is a female power known as Shakti. Shakti is metaphorically coiled inside like a serpent (sometimes called the kundalini). Shakti can be activated through the grace of the guru so that spiritual enlightenment is achieved. The awakening of this energy (called *shaktipat*) is often accompanied by physical phenomena: spontaneous laughter, weeping, dancing, and chanting. When Shakti is uncoiled, union with Shiva is achieved. Aspirants meditate daily, chant a devotional song called the "Guru-Gita," undertake ashram work (*seva*), and participate in satellite-linked intensive teaching seminars. Gurumayi has established a major scholarly archive for Siddha Yoga studies.

See also SHIVA; YOGA

Bibliography. P. Hayes, *The Supreme Adventure: The Experience of Siddha Yoga*; Swami Muktananda, *Siddha Meditation*, rev. ed.; D. B. S. Sharma, *The Philosophy of Sadhana*.

P. Johnson

SIKH DHARMA. Sikhism is one of the major religions of the world, originating in the sixteenth century AD through the teachings of Guru Nanak, with beliefs similar to those of Islam in some respects but also closely related to Hinduism and Buddhism in other respects. The term Sikh comes from the Sanskrit word *sisya*, meaning disciple or pupil. *Dharma* comes from a root *dhri*, "to hold or uphold," and in context refers to law or statute. As in Hinduism and Buddhism, *dharma* refers to the principles or laws that govern the universe. By following Sikh dharma, a Sikh may discover how one relates to the one deity, of which all are a part. Sikhs believe that through rituals of chanting, prayers, and singing the names of God and through following dharma, this assimilation into the one God may occur, and the mind will be liberated; one becomes part of God.

The term *Sikh Dharma* also refers to a group within Sikhism that seeks to maintain and promote the teachings of the Ten Sikh Gurus, including the late Siri Singh Sahib.

Finally, the term *Sikh Dharma* may refer to the spiritual organization of that name, founded by Yogi Bhajan in 1970. It is an alternate name for the 3HO (Holy, Happy, Healthy Organization). The late Yogi Bhajan (also known as Harbajhan Singh Yogi; 1929–2004) came to the US in the late 1960s as a master of kundalini yoga, offering kundalini training to student initiates. While Westerners generally ascribe all forms of yoga to some form of Hinduism, Yogi Bhajan was a self-described Sikh and presented his form of yoga from a Sikh perspective. The 3HO established hundreds of ashrams (dwellings of teachers) across North America. The movement later spun off the International Kundalini Yoga Teachers Association, and since the death of its founder, the 3HO has continued to serve Sikh interests to the present day.

See also BUDDHISM; DHARMA; GURU; HINDUISM; JAPA YOGA; KHALSA; SIKHISM

Bibliography. "Dictionary of Common Sanskrit Spiritual Words," Advaita Vision, http://www.advaita.org.uk/sanskrit/terms_s3.htm; "Introduction to Sikhism," SikhNet, https://www.sikhnet.com/pages/introduction-sikhism; "The Path of Sikh Dharma," Sikh Dharma International website, http://www.sikhdharma.org/content/path-sikh-dharma; "Sikh Dharma," the Hindu Universe website, http://www.hindunet.org/sikh_info/; Sikh Dharma International website, http://www.sikhdharma.org/; "Sikhism, Religion of the Sikh People," Sikhs.org, http://www.sikhs.org/topics.htm; H. Singh, ed., *Encyclopedia of Sikhism*; *The Sikh Encyclopedia*, http://www.thesikhencyclopedia.com.

H. W. House and E. Pement

SIKH FOUNDATION. Founded by Dr. Narinder Singh Kapany in the 1960s, the Sikh Foundation is headquartered in Palo Alto, California, and has trustees from major American universities. The purpose of the foundation is to propagate Sikh teachings to the Sikhs now living in the Western Hemisphere. The foundation's methods include the endowment of chairs of Sikh studies in major universities, exhibitions and galleries for Sikh art in world museums, and the infiltration of Sikh influence in Western culture. Through such venues as their magazine, *Nishaan*, their websites, and books, the Sikh Foundation has made serious inroads into the American cultural landscape. Founder Kapany, considered by *Fortune* magazine as the "Father of Fiber Optics," has written over one hundred articles on technology and Sikh culture and has used his position of entrepreneurial leadership to gain footholds in many universities, most specifically in the University of California system.

See also SIKHISM

Bibliography. N. S. Kapany, ed., *Finance and Utilization of Solar Energy.*

Ergun Caner

SIKHISM. Sikhism is a world religion founded in sixteenth-century India by Guru Nanak Dev (1469–1539). Sikhism today is one of the world's top ten religions, with 19 million of the faith's 23 million adherents living in India. An estimated 325,000 reside in North America.

Founding of the Religion. Guru Nanak was the first of ten authoritative gurus who guided Sikhism until 1708. Caring very little about material possessions, Guru Nanak, at age thirty-six, was transformed while bathing in the River Bain. Sikhs believe that he disappeared for three days while receiving God's enlightenment. This supernatural experience motivated him to teach throughout India, the Himalayas, Afghanistan, Sri Lanka, and Arabia. Although he rejected traditional Islam and his parents' Hinduism—the two predominant religions in the province of Punjab—Guru Nanak borrowed key concepts from both faiths. He focused on three main teachings concerning the way to God: hard work rather than begging or asceticism, sharing physical possessions with the needy, and remembering God at all times.

Guru Nanak convinced many followers with a practical approach to faith while minimizing religious formalities. He denounced those who went through rituals of worship but did not think about what they were doing. Before he died, he decided not to appoint his natural sons as his successors because they lacked spirituality. Instead he chose his friend Angad Dev (1504–52) to carry on the religion. The line of succession continued until the tenth and final living guru, Guru Gobind Singh (1666–1708), decided that authority should no longer be transferred to human leaders. Instead he chose to transfer ultimate authority to the Sikh scripture known as the Guru Granth Sahib. He also instituted a special baptismal rite. A new fraternity known as Khalsa, or "pure ones," was made up of followers promising to follow five aspects of a special code known as the 5 K's: *kesh* (having uncut hair under a turban or veil); *kangha* (a comb for grooming); *kara* (a metal bracelet to remind oneself of one's servanthood to God); *kacha* (short underwear for modesty); and *kirpan* (a sword to fight for the underprivileged).

Teachings. The goal in monistic and pantheistic Sikhism is for a person to merge with the impersonal God. This God, who is the "True Name," is one in being and exists throughout all creation, especially deep in people's hearts. Sikhs reject the deity of Jesus because they cannot believe that God would stoop to the low level of taking a human body. The doctrine of reincarnation is taught in Sikhism, as positive and negative actions done by a person in this life (karma) are said to have an impact on the next life. People can return as either humans or animals, depending on their actions.

Sikhism emphasizes the idea that all people can experience God, thereby rejecting the Hindu notion of the caste system. Sikhism is universalistic and considers those who belong to other religions as worshipers of truth. Social and economic equality is considered a divine principle. Men and women are considered equal despite the historical suppressing of women throughout South Asia. Economic equality is demonstrated in community kitchens known as *langars*, as the Sikhs serve free communal meals to anyone regardless of one's income. A true Sikh owes God absolute submission expressed in daily prayer, the inner repetition of God's name, detachment from the world, performing acts of service and charity, and singing devotional songs (*kirtan*). Rituals such as religious fasting and vegetarianism, pilgrimages, yoga, and idol worship are condemned. Normal family lives are encouraged as celibacy is rejected. Sikhs are admonished to extinguish the five evils: lust, anger, greed, worldly attachment, and pride. Those who have complete devotion (bhakti) can have full realization of the truth. Sikhs generally are not evangelistic in their faith, as they usually choose to focus on personal spirituality rather than debating religion. They tithe a tenth of their income. Tobacco, drugs, and alcohol are prohibited.

Recent History. Historically the Sikhs have had a difficult time finding religious liberty in their native India. In 1947 the province of Punjab was divided into Hindu India and Muslim Pakistan. Sikh separatists have unsuccessfully attempted to create an independent state called Khalistan. The situation has been tense as well as destructive. One major tragedy took place in 1984 when the Golden Temple in Amritsar, Sikhism's holiest shrine, was invaded by the Indian Army as ordered by Prime Minister Indira Gandhi. Terrible damage was inflicted on the temple site, and estimates of the dead range between 330 and 25,000. Prime Minister Gandhi was assassinated by her Sikh guards on October 31, 1984. Many Sikhs throughout India lost their lives in the wake of the assassination, with at least 8,000 dying in the city of Delhi alone.

See also BHAKTI YOGA; GOLDEN TEMPLE; GURU GRANTH SAHIB; GURU NANAK DEV; HINDUISM; ISLAM, BASIC BELIEFS OF; KHALSA; SANKIRTANA

Bibliography. M. P. Fisher, *Living Religions*; J. B. Noss, *Man's Religions*; R. Schmidt et al., *Patterns of Religion*; Sikh Missionary Center, *Sikh Religion*.

E. Johnson

SMITH, JOSEPH, III. Joseph Smith III (1832–1914) was a son of Mormon founding prophet Joseph Smith Jr. and leader of the Reorganized Church of Jesus Christ of Latter Day

Saints (RLDS Church). The oldest male child of Joseph and Emma Smith, he was recruited by Mormons dissatisfied with the leadership of Brigham Young and by others to succeed Joseph Smith Jr. as the Prophet of the Restoration. Smith reluctantly agreed to follow in his father's footsteps, but only after several years of theological investigation and spiritual reflection. At a conference meeting in Amboy, Illinois, he presented himself for ordination as the president of the High Priesthood of the RLDS Church on April 6, 1860—exactly thirty years after his father organized the first congregation of Mormons in New York. The RLDS Church distinguished itself from the Utah Mormons on the issues of polygamy and temple rites. Smith insisted that his father was not a polygamist or the originator of secret temple rites.

During his term as president, he established Sunday school for children and built Graceland College (now Graceland University) in Lamoni, Iowa. Joseph Smith III edited a publication titled *The True Latter Day Saints' Herald*, now known as the *Saints Herald*. Seventeen of his alleged revelations are recorded in the RLDS version of the Doctrine and Covenants, and he finished his *Memoirs* only a few weeks before his death in Independence, Missouri. Descendants of the Smith family would lead the RLDS Church until 1996. On April 6, 2001, the RLDS Church officially changed its name to the Community of Christ.

See also CHURCH OF JESUS CHRIST OF LATTER-DAY SAINTS; COMMUNITY OF CHRIST; SMITH, JOSEPH, JR.

Bibliography. I. S. Davis, *The Story of the Church*; R. D. Launius, *Joseph Smith III: Pragmatic Prophet*; S. Shields, *Divergent Paths of the Restoration*.

C. J. Carrigan

SMITH, JOSEPH, JR. Joseph Smith Jr. (1805–44) was the founder of the Church of Jesus Christ of Latter-day Saints (LDS Church). In his claims to be the inspired translator of the Book of Mormon and other ancient scriptures and the Prophet of the Restoration, Smith was arguably the most controversial figure in American religious history. Out of reverence for his role, faithful Mormons commonly refer to him by his first name (and almost never by his last name only).

Interpretations. So many issues pertaining to Smith's life are contested that it will be useful to begin by summarizing four main interpretations.

True Prophet. The traditional LDS interpretation accepts Smith as a prophet through whom the Lord spoke and acted from at least the late 1820s until his death in 1844. This interpretation accepts the Book of Mormon as the word of God, Smith as the founding prophet of the restored church, the priesthood system that he established as the instrumentality of God's power and authority on earth, and Smith's institution of plural marriage as divinely authorized fact. A variation of this view accepts the same interpretation of Smith but regards the LDS Church as having departed from the true path by its renunciation of plural marriage a half century after his death. A number of polygamous LDS sects adhere to this variant perspective.

False Prophet. The conventional non-Mormon interpretation regards Smith as a false prophet from beginning to end, regardless of how his actions and motivations (and those of his supporters) are explained. This interpretation regards the Book of Mormon as a modern fiction and the LDS Church as an institution predicated on Smith's false claims.

Fallen Prophet. An often overlooked interpretation maintains that Smith was a prophet of God through whom the Book of Mormon was brought to the world but that soon afterward he proved unfaithful. This was the view articulated, for example, by David Whitmer, one of the three "witnesses" to the Book of Mormon and a leader in the early LDS movement, in his booklet *An Address to All*

Believers in Christ (1887). Whitmer argued that Smith was authorized by God only to translate the Book of Mormon and bring its message to the world; the LDS priesthood system and most of Smith's revelations were, in Whitmer's view, not from God and created the conditions for the institution of polygamy.

Religious Genius. Some academics, seeking to steer clear of taking a stand on Smith's claim to speak for God, describe him as a "religious genius" or use expressions of similar import. These scholars view Smith as a revolutionary thinker and leader who was gifted with imagination, creativity, and intelligence. By his unique combination of talents, Smith reconstructed Christianity and created in effect a new world religion. Frankly, this interpretation is more or less a polite, complimentary way of saying that Smith did not really receive divine revelation. Pragmatically, there is little difference between this interpretation and the false prophet interpretation except that the religious genius model commonly assumes a noble motivation on Smith's part.

Early Life. Joseph Smith Jr. was born December 23, 1805, in Sharon, Vermont, to Joseph Smith Sr. and Lucy Mack Smith. (For the sake of simplicity, hereafter unqualified references to "Smith" refer to Joseph Jr.) Both parents were primitivists, or "seekers," followers of a movement of disaffected Protestants who regarded all denominations as having fallen away from original, true Christianity. Primitivists ran a gamut of beliefs from deism and universalism (Joseph Smith Sr. as a young adult had helped start a Universalist society) to a kind of proto-Pentecostalism that looked for miraculous manifestations of varying kinds as precursors to the second coming. Both Joseph Smith Sr. and Lucy reported having had dreams or visions portending judgment on Christendom and suggesting hope of salvation for their family. After several moves to various towns in Vermont and much hardship, the family moved to Palmyra

in upstate New York when Joseph Smith Jr. was twelve years old. In an unpublished autobiographical account he wrote in 1832, he claimed that between the ages of twelve and fifteen he had become convinced that there was no true church on the earth—a notion that he clearly could have picked up at that age from his parents.

In the winter of 1819–20, the Smith family moved into a cabin near the border of Palmyra, in an area later renamed Manchester. According to Smith's 1838 autobiographical account in what is now the LDS scripture Joseph Smith—History (part of the Pearl of Great Price), in the spring of 1820 Smith had a vision far more stupendous than those of his parents. He claimed that in answer to a prayer to know which church to join, God the Father and Jesus Christ had both appeared visibly to him and spoken to him. Christ, according to the account, told Smith to join none of the churches because all of them were wrong and their creeds were abominations. Smith's experience, commonly called the First Vision, eventually came to be regarded by Mormons as the inaugural event of a new dispensation, the most important event in history since the resurrection of Christ. Ironically, no such importance was attached to the First Vision in Smith's own day, even after the story was first published in 1842. Indeed, there is no evidence that anyone had ever heard about this vision prior to the mid-1830s. In Smith's 1832 autobiographical writing mentioned earlier, he did report a vision from his teen years, but it was a vision of "the Lord" (Jesus) alone, not of the Father and the Son. This account was never made public until it was discovered in 1965. As far as anyone knew prior to the mid-1830s, the founding event of Mormonism was Smith's encounter with the angel and the gold plates, not a vision of Jesus Christ or of Jesus Christ and the Father.

Treasure Seeking. Whatever may or may not have happened in the spring of 1820 evidently had no immediate impact on the young

Joseph Smith. A few months later that year, the family bought a property of a hundred acres, and Joseph Smith Sr. and his sons Alvin and Joseph very quickly began digging for buried treasure. There is some evidence, albeit from unfriendly sources, that Joseph Smith Sr. had also been involved in such activities in Vermont, perhaps searching for the fabled treasure of Captain Kidd. In any case, his son Joseph soon gained a special reputation in this area, particularly in 1822 after he began using a seer stone he obtained when he helped a neighbor named Willard Chase dig a well. A seer stone was a small, generally rounded stone used in divination; Smith would put it in his hat, place his face into the hat to block outside light, and report details about the treasure and its location that he claimed to see by or through the stone.

Smith was engaged in recurring efforts to locate buried treasure through the use of his seer stone during most of the years from 1822 to 1827. During most of this period, he was living in the Palmyra-Manchester area. In November 1825, Josiah Stowell hired Joseph Smith Jr. to help search for a lost Spanish silver mine near Harmony, Pennsylvania, just across the southern border of New York. The expedition was unsuccessful, but Smith remained in the area for a few months pursuing additional treasure hunts in and around nearby South Bainbridge, New York. In March 1826, Stowell's nephew Peter Bridgeman had Smith brought before a judge there named Albert Neely, accusing him, essentially, of fraud. It is disputed whether the payment the judge required from Smith was a fine (implying some guilt) or merely court costs, but what cannot be disputed is that the incident confirms Smith's heavy involvement in treasure seeking.

Although Smith found no silver mine in Harmony, he did find a wife, Emma Hale, in whose family's home the treasure seekers stayed during their expedition. Since Emma's father, Isaac, did not approve of the treasure seeker, in January 1827 Joseph Smith and Emma Hale eloped and went to live in Manchester. In August they returned to the Hale home in Harmony to collect Emma's belongings. While there Smith reportedly confessed to Isaac Hale that he had no gift of seeing and promised to abandon his activities as a seer in exchange for Isaac's help in starting a farm.

The Gold Plates and the Book of Mormon. The following month, Joseph and Emma Smith traveled back to Manchester, where Smith said a stone box was buried containing ancient gold plates. According to Smith's later accounts, he had first been told about these plates in 1823 by an angel, who allowed Smith to see them but not remove them. Each September 22 from 1823 through 1826, Smith had visited the location of the plates on a hill near his home, been visited by the angel, and viewed the plates, but each time he had not been allowed to remove them. This is the same period during which Smith was most heavily involved in the use of his seer stone to search for buried treasures. It is unclear who, if anyone, knew about the gold plates prior to September 1827. What is clear is that soon after that date others believed Smith had such plates, though it would be nearly two years before he would allow anyone else to see them.

In the spring of 1828, Smith dictated to his friend and financial supporter Martin Harris what he claimed was an inspired translation of a portion of the plates, produced supposedly using "interpreters" (described as stone spectacles), also taken from the stone box. When the handwritten manuscript of 116 pages was stolen from Harris's house, Smith was at first distraught but then issued his first "revelations"—statements of varying length in which the Lord Jesus supposedly spoke in the first person to and through Smith. These initial revelations concerning the 116 pages and other matters pertaining to the Book of Mormon (later canonized as

Doctrine and Covenants 3, 5, and 10) set the precedent for Smith to be viewed not only as the instrument for the "coming forth" of the Book of Mormon but also as a prophet of God delivering new, modern revelations.

Between September 1828 and March 1829, Smith began dictating what he said was an inspired translation of a different part of the gold plates, with his wife, Emma, as the scribe. Apparently little progress was made during this period. Then, however, a schoolteacher friend of Smith named Oliver Cowdery began serving as his scribe, and from April to June 1829 they produced a completed manuscript. According to several reports by friends who observed some of the dictation sessions, Smith never looked at the gold plates when dictating his translation. Instead he looked at his seer stone inside his hat, the same method used in his treasure-seeking ventures. On March 26, 1830, the first copies of the Book of Mormon went on sale, and on April 6 Smith and a handful of friends and family members formally established their new church, at first called simply the Church of Christ.

Revelations and Doctrinal Development. Throughout the next fourteen years, Smith produced voluminous and varied revelations. These included an inspired revision of the King James Version of the Bible (commonly known as the Joseph Smith Translation) and the Book of Abraham, purportedly an inspired translation from one of the ancient Egyptian papyri that the LDS Church purchased in 1835. Smith also delivered well over a hundred modern revelations that constitute nearly the entirety of the LDS scripture known as the Doctrine and Covenants (D&C). In effect Smith is regarded as the translator or revelator of nearly all the scriptures in the LDS "standard works," including the Bible itself.

In his early years as the leader of the LDS Church, Smith taught a view of God that roughly approximated the traditional Christian doctrine. For example, in an 1830 revelation Smith affirmed that God "is infinite and eternal, from everlasting to everlasting the same unchangeable God," and that the "Father, Son, and Holy Ghost are one God, infinite and eternal" (D&C 20:17, 28). At this point, Smith seems to have thought he was simply affirming the traditional doctrine of the Trinity. His other doctrinal views also generally corresponded to generic Protestant beliefs, though with an especially aggressive form of restorationism (the claim that his sect constituted the restoration of true Christianity).

Smith's theology changed almost constantly over the next fourteen years. That development can be charted in two periods of roughly seven years each, first in the period when the LDS Church was based in Kirtland, Ohio (1831–37), and second in the years when it was based in Far West, Missouri, and in Nauvoo, Illinois (1838–44). The changes in the early period were more modest but provided the seeds of the later dramatic changes. In 1832 Smith produced a revelation abandoning the traditional Christian view that all people will either suffer eternal punishment in hell or enjoy eternal life in the new heaven and new earth. Instead, he taught that almost all people will live as immortal beings in one of three heavenly kingdoms, the highest of which, the celestial kingdom, is for faithful saints (D&C 76). Later he taught that those who died without a chance to accept the new gospel but who would have done so had they been given the chance would be accepted into the celestial kingdom (D&C 137). In 1833 he issued a revelation stating that "man was also in the beginning with God" and that "intelligence" is uncreated (D&C 93:29). In late 1834, Smith and some associates produced the *Lectures on Faith*, which drew a clear contrast between the Father as "a personage of spirit" and the Son Jesus Christ as "a personage of tabernacle," that is, of flesh (*Lectures* 5.2). The Holy Spirit was described as the "Mind" shared by these "two personages." In effect at this point Smith had changed from a roughly trinitarian theology to a ditheistic one. The *Lectures on Faith* were part of the Doctrine and Covenants, and thus part of the LDS Church's "standard works," from early 1835 until 1921. Thus by the end of the Kirtland period, Smith was teaching a decidedly nontrinitarian theology, a somewhat vague doctrine of the preexistence of man, and a form of near-universalism.

The revelations that came in the last period of Smith's life, especially in the last two years or so, radically altered the basic worldview of the LDS religion. In 1842 he instituted baptism for the dead, which went on to become the most common ritual in Mormon temples. Instead of being saved on the basis of what they would have done given the chance, as in D&C 137, the dead who had no chance to accept the LDS gospel will have the gospel preached to them in the spirit world and have the opportunity to accept baptisms performed by Mormons for them by proxy. The Book of Abraham, published in 1843, attributed creation not to one God but to a group of Gods and reinterpreted creation as an act of organizing preexistent material: "They, the Gods, organized and formed the heavens and the earth" (Abraham 4:1). Smith taught that same year that "the Father has a body of flesh and bones as tangible as man's" (D&C 130:22) and that faithful Mormons would "be gods" with "all power" (D&C 132:20). God, then, is apparently a man, with a physical body like ours, and we can become omnipotent gods like him.

Smith brought these doctrinal ideas together in his most infamous sermon, the "King Follett Discourse" (April 7, 1844). In that sermon at the funeral of Elder King Follett, Smith denied that "God was God from all eternity," claiming instead that "God himself was once as we are now" and that he "is an exalted man," having once "dwelt on an earth, the same as Jesus Christ himself

did." Eternal life is about knowing God and learning "to be Gods yourselves . . . the same as all Gods have done before you" (*Teachings of the Prophet Joseph Smith*, 345–46, 353–54). On June 16, 1844, just eleven days before his death, Smith gave a speech known as the "Sermon at the Grove." In this sermon, he attacked the traditional Christian doctrine of the Trinity, claimed (falsely) that he had been teaching polytheism for fifteen years, and presented the idea that God the Father himself had a Father who was *his* God before him. In effect Smith proposed an endless chain of Gods, each of whom prepared the next era of spirits to become Gods. This is the doctrine that became known as *eternal progression*. This doctrine completed Smith's transformation from monotheist to polytheist and took Mormonism utterly outside the theological boundaries of historic Christianity.

Polygamy. At the same time that Smith was overhauling Christian theology, he was secretly practicing polygamy, or "plural marriage," as Mormons commonly call it. There is some dispute about when Smith initiated this practice. Some have argued that he secretly married Fannie Alger, a girl with whom he was accused of committing adultery in 1833. In any case, the historical record is quite clear that from 1841 through 1843 Smith claimed over thirty women as his plural wives. These women included at least ten whose legal husbands were still living at the time. Mormon apologists' attempts to defend Smith on this point (he was doing it to test their faith, or only for the women's celestial salvation, etc.) are unconvincing. Smith repeatedly denied in public that he was practicing polygamy, stating just a month before his death, "What a thing it is for a man to be accused of committing adultery, and having seven wives, when I can only find one" (Joseph Smith—History 6:411). Of course, Smith had only one *legal* wife since bigamy and polygamy were illegal.

Meanwhile, in 1843 (at least two years after he had begun the practice), Smith had privately issued a self-justifying "revelation" claiming divine authority for taking plural wives and even instructing Emma to accept the practice and welcome the additional wives into her home (D&C 132). This revelation became the basis for the more widespread practice of polygamy by Mormons in Utah during the second half of the nineteenth century.

Joseph Smith's Legal and Political Troubles and His Death. Smith was the object of often intense opposition for most of the fourteen years he presided over the LDS movement. Contrary to Mormon propaganda, this opposition at first had relatively little to do with Smith's religious claims (and nothing to do with the First Vision, which was unknown by most or all Mormons through most of the 1830s and largely unknown by non-Mormons even well after his death). Several factors were involved in the Kirtland period, including accusations of adultery, charges of financial wrongdoing, acquisition of land and political power, and, in Missouri, fears that the Mormon settlers there were abolitionists whose views would foment social unrest. Allegations of banking fraud led to Smith and other Mormons fleeing Kirtland in January 1838 for Missouri. Conflicts with non-Mormons in Missouri escalated and erupted in a short but violent war; Smith was arrested and nearly executed for treason, and the governor of the state ordered Mormons to leave or face extermination.

The Mormons resettled in Illinois in a new town they called Nauvoo, on the banks of the Mississippi River. There Smith sought to establish a separate, theocratic government while also running for US president. At the same time, he was advancing ever more radical doctrinal claims and secretly practicing polygamy. On June 7, 1944, dissident Mormons published the *Nauvoo Expositor*, a newspaper denouncing Smith as a fallen prophet, condemning his polytheistic teachings, his polygamy, and his pursuit of political power. The Nauvoo city council, with Smith's approval, had the newspaper office destroyed, and Smith declared martial law. Illinois authorities charged Smith and his brother Hyrum with inciting a riot and then with treason, and they were held for trial in the nearby Carthage Jail. On June 27, a mob stormed the jail and killed both Hyrum and Joseph Smith, although Joseph tried to defend against them with a pistol that had been smuggled into the jail. The mob had turned the disgraced prophet into someone whom Mormons could now hail as a martyr.

Joseph Smith's Place in Mormonism. Smith is regarded as far more than the founder of the LDS Church. Mormons regard him as the Prophet of the Restoration, easily as the most important figure in history since Jesus Christ. Joseph Smith is to Mormonism roughly what Muhammad is to Islam. Although Mormons do not worship Smith, they revere him in the same way that Muslims revere Muhammad. Smith is the subject of Mormon hymns (most famously "Praise to the Man"), and LDS leaders have taught that there is "no salvation without accepting Joseph Smith" (Joseph Fielding Smith, *Doctrines of Salvation*, 1:189). John Taylor, in a statement found in LDS scripture, claimed that "Joseph Smith, the Prophet and Seer of the Lord, has done more, save Jesus only, for the salvation of men in this world, than any other man that ever lived in it" (D&C 135:3).

See also ARTICLES OF FAITH, MORMON; BOOK OF ABRAHAM; BOOK OF MORMON; BOOK OF MOSES; CHURCH OF JESUS CHRIST OF LATTER-DAY SAINTS; DOCTRINE AND COVENANTS; FIRST VISION; HARRIS, MARTIN; JOSEPH SMITH TRANSLATION OF THE BIBLE; MASONRY (LDS); PEARL OF GREAT PRICE, THE; PLURAL MARRIAGE, MORMON TEACHING AND HISTORY OF; SMITH BIDAMON, EMMA; THEOLOGICAL METHOD OF THE CHURCH OF JESUS CHRIST OF LATTER-DAY SAINTS

Bibliography. L. F. Anderson, ed., *Lucy's Book: A Critical Edition of Lucy Mack Smith's Family Memoir*; R. D. Anderson, *Inside the Mind of Joseph Smith: Psychobiography and the Book of Mormon*; R. I. Anderson, *Joseph Smith's New York Reputation Reexamined*; R. L. Anderson, *Joseph Smith's New England Heritage: Influences of Grandfathers Solomon Mack and Asael Smith*; N. G. Bringhurst, ed., *Reconsidering "No Man Knows My History": Fawn M. Brodie and Joseph Smith in Retrospect*; F. W. Brodie, *No Man Knows My History: The Life of Joseph Smith*; R. L. Bushman, *Joseph Smith: Rough Stone Rolling*; R. N. Holzapfel and K. P. Jackson, *Joseph Smith, the Prophet and Seer*; E. D. Howe, *Mormonism Unvailed*; R. N. Hullinger, *Joseph Smith's Response to Skepticism*; D. C. Jessee et al., eds., *The Joseph Smith Papers*, multiple vols.; H. M. Marquardt, *The Rise of Mormonism: 1816–1844*; R. L. Neilson and T. L. Givens, eds., *Joseph Smith Jr.: Reappraisals after 200 Years*; H. W. Nibley, "No Ma'am, That's Not History," in *Tinkling Cymbals and Sounding Brass*; G. H. Palmer, *An Insider's View of Mormon Origins*; D. M. Quinn, *Early Mormonism and the Magic World View*, 2nd ed.; Joseph Fielding Smith, *Doctrines of Salvation*; Joseph Smith Jr., *Lectures on Faith*; Joseph Smith Jr., *Teachings of Presidents of the Church: Joseph Smith*; Joseph Smith Jr., *Teachings of the Prophet Joseph Smith*, edited by Joseph Fielding Smith; Joseph Smith Jr. et al., Doctrine and Covenants; D. Vogel, ed., *Early Mormon Documents*, 5 vols.; Vogel, *Joseph Smith: The Making of a Prophet*; Vogel, "The Locations of Joseph Smith's Early Treasure Quests," *Dialogue*; B. Waterman, ed., *The Prophet Puzzle: Interpretive Essays on Joseph Smith*; J. W. Welch, ed., *The Worlds of Joseph Smith: A Bicentennial Conference at the Library of Congress*.

R. M. Bowman Jr.

SMITH, JOSEPH F. Joseph F. Smith (not to be confused with Joseph Fielding Smith) was born November 13, 1838, the first child of Hyrum and Mary Fielding Smith. As the nephew of Joseph Smith Jr., Joseph F. Smith spent his childhood around the entire Smith family. After the death of his father and uncle, Joseph F. Smith left the Nauvoo, Illinois, area and traveled with most of the Latter-day Saints to the Wasatch Valley and the Great Salt Lake basin, in Utah. Recognizing that Joseph F. Smith had amazing leadership potential, President Brigham Young suggested that Smith be ordained a member of the Quorum of the Twelve Apostles at twenty-eight years old. After serving within the Quorum of the Twelve for some time, Smith was called as a member of the First Presidency under Presidents John Taylor, Wilford Woodruff, and Lorenzo Snow. After President Snow died, Joseph F. Smith was ordained president of the church on October 17, 1901, and served in that capacity until his death in 1918. President Joseph F. Smith was the first LDS president to visit Europe while in office, received a revelation on October 3, 1918 (now canonized as Doctrine & Covenants 138 and teaching the chance for the salvation of the dead), and saw church membership double while he was in office.

See also CHURCH OF JESUS CHRIST OF LATTER-DAY SAINTS; SMITH, JOSEPH, JR.

Bibliography. Joseph F. Smith, *Teachings of Presidents of the Church: Joseph F. Smith.*

T. S. Kerns

SMITH, JOSEPH FIELDING. Born July 19, 1876, to Joseph F. Smith and Julina Lambson Smith, Joseph Fielding Smith, like his father, grew up in the Smith family around people involved in the LDS Church from its beginnings. Because his father was heavily involved in church work, Fielding Smith spent most of his early life with his mother and thirteen siblings, and because he was the oldest son, much of his time was devoted to helping his mother with household tasks and with the care of his siblings.

Joseph Fielding Smith would eventually marry three women (each preceded him in death): Louise Emily Shurtliff (married in 1898; died in 1908), Ethel Georgina Reynolds (married in 1908; died in 1937), and Jessie Evans (married in 1937; died in 1971).

Fielding Smith served in a number of roles within LDS Church hierarchy, beginning in 1902, when he was called to serve in the Church Historian's Office. In 1910 he was ordained an apostle in the Quorum of the Twelve, and he was appointed church historian in 1921. He was set apart as president of the Quorum of the Twelve in 1951 and was ordained president of the church in 1970, at the age of ninety-three.

Under his leadership, local church leadership was restructured, and priesthood leaders at the local level were given more pastoral duties in their respective wards. One of his most significant accomplishments was the restructuring of the print publications of the church. Before Fielding Smith became president, the church produced five monthly publications. Under his leadership, those five publications were discontinued, and three new publications (*Ensign*, *New Era*, and *Friend*) were started. These three monthly publications continue to be part of the main communication network of the church.

See also CHURCH OF JESUS CHRIST OF LATTER-DAY SAINTS; SMITH, JOSEPH, JR.

Bibliography. P. Nibley, *The Presidents of the Church*, 13th ed.

T. S. Kerns

SMITH BIDAMON, EMMA. Emma Smith Bidamon (1804–79) was the wife, and later widow, of Mormonism's founder, Joseph Smith Jr. The seventh of nine children born to Isaac and Elizabeth Hale, she eloped with Joseph Smith at the age of twenty-two after her father twice refused to grant Smith permission to marry his daughter.

A staunch opponent of polygamy, Emma found herself rebuked by her husband in section 132 of the Doctrine and Covenants. Verse 54 warned that if Emma did not "abide this [polygamous] commandment," she would be destroyed. Although she refused to reverse her position on plural marriage, Emma lived a full life. Joseph Smith, on the other hand, died within a year of the prophetic announcement.

After her husband's death, she refused to follow Brigham Young when he led a majority of the Saints to the Salt Lake Valley. She remained in Nauvoo with her children and married non-Mormon Lewis C. Bidamon in December 1847. This union was seen by many as indicating a lack of loyalty to both her prophet husband and his calling.

In 1860 her eldest son, Joseph Smith III, became the first president of the Reorganized Church of Jesus Christ of Latter Day Saints. Emma Bidamon lived the rest of her life in Nauvoo and died on April 30, 1879.

See also CHURCH OF JESUS CHRIST OF LATTER-DAY SAINTS; COMMUNITY OF CHRIST; SMITH, JOSEPH, III

Bibliography. R. L. Bushman, *Joseph Smith: Rough Stone Rolling*; L. K. Newell and V. T. Avery, *Mormon Enigma: Emma Hale Smith, Prophet's Wife, "Elect Lady," Polygamy's Foe.*

W. McKeever

SMRITI. *Smriti* (Sanskrit, "what is remembered") is one of the two broad, fundamental, authoritative sources of Hindu doctrine and practice (the other being the *shruti*). Smriti is akin to the concept of tradition in religions such as Judaism; it is often said to be a recollection of formative religious experiences that shaped ancient Hinduism. Most of what is considered smriti consists of a variety of sacred Hindu texts, though many Hindu sects include their formalized systems of thought in the category of smriti as well. Various proposals for precisely classifying smriti have been submitted by various schools of Hindu thought and are not universally agreed upon, though much is held in common. Though the smriti are highly regarded, their authority is generally seen as subordinate to (and qualified by) that of the texts that are shruti. This is because the shruti are thought to be perfect transmissions of the primordial vibrations of the universe, whereas the smriti are said to suffer from the fallibility of merely human authorship.

However, in practice most Hindus treat the smriti as being equal in authority to the shruti, and in many cases devotees base their beliefs and practices primarily on the smritis because these texts are more accessible and familiar to them. The texts of the smriti include (but are not limited to) the Dharma Sutras, the Puranas, the Mahabharata (which contains the Bhagavad Gita), and the Ramayana. Arguably the most important text among the smriti is the Laws of Manu, which sets forth statutes that regulate the conduct of Hindus at the national, family, and individual levels.

See also BHAGAVAD GITA; HINDUISM; SHRUTI/SRUTI

Bibliography. Swami Bhaskarananda, *The Essentials of Hinduism: A Comprehensive Overview of the World's Oldest Religion*; M. O. Fitzgerald, *Introduction to Hindu Dharma*; K. Knott, *Hinduism: A Very Short Introduction*; V. Narayanan, *Hinduism: Origins, Beliefs, Practices, Holy Texts, Sacred Places*.

J. Bjornstad

SNOW, LORENZO. Lorenzo Snow (1814–1901) was the fifth president of the Church of Jesus Christ of Latter-day Saints (LDS Church). He was the fifth child of Oliver and Rosetta Pettibone Snow and younger brother to the famous Mormon poet Eliza Roxy Snow. Snow joined the LDS Church on June 19, 1836, and almost immediately was called to serve on several missions, including one to England in which he presented Queen Victoria with a special copy of the Book of Mormon.

On February 12, 1849, at the age of thirty-four, he was ordained as a member of the Quorum of the Twelve. He became the fifth president of the LDS Church after the death of Wilford Woodruff in 1898. An acknowledged polygamist, Snow fathered forty-two children and was arrested for unlawful cohabitation at the age of seventy-two. He was released after serving eleven months at the Utah Territorial Penitentiary.

Snow is probably best remembered for the expression, "As man now is, God once was; as God now is, man may be." This couplet, which Snow claimed was received by divine revelation, succinctly proclaims the LDS teaching that God was once a human and that human beings have the capacity to become Gods.

Snow was eighty-seven when he died in Salt Lake City on October 10, 1901.

See also ADAM-GOD THEORY; CHURCH OF JESUS CHRIST OF LATTER-DAY SAINTS; PLURAL MARRIAGE, MORMON TEACHING AND HISTORY OF

Bibliography. L. J. Arrington, ed., *The Presidents of the Church*.

W. McKeever

SOCINIANISM. Socinianism is a form of Unitarianism professed by the Polish Brethren and their Transylvanian counterparts of the sixteenth and seventeenth centuries, which takes its name from its most distinguished exponent, Faustus Socinus (1509–63). Leading characteristics of Socinianism include the following:

1. An utter denial that God has revealed anything incomprehensible to human beings

2. A corresponding penchant for construing Scripture in such a way that it contains nothing mysterious or counterintuitive to human beings

3. Implacable hostility to the doctrines of the Trinity, the hypostatic union of two natures in the person of Christ, original sin, predestination, justification by faith alone, and the necessity of supernatural regeneration

4. Psilanthropism—that is, the belief that Christ was a mere man, who did not

exist before his conception in Mary's womb

5. Abhorrence of the doctrine of Christ's substitutionary atonement

6. A Pelagian denial of human beings' moral debilitation in consequence of Adam's fall

Socinianism exerted a vast influence on the intellectual life of Europe in the sixteenth and seventeenth centuries for two principal reasons. First, the Socinian churches of Poland and Transylvania flourished in their halcyon days to an extent that no Unitarian communion has before or since that period. The Socinians, for example, were the first and only Unitarian communion ever to attain quasi-official status anywhere in Europe. As one of the three officially tolerated religions in Poland and Transylvania—alongside Roman Catholicism and conventional Protestantism—Socinianism attracted a wide following in these countries and appealed especially to intellectuals and the nobility. In the latter sixteenth and early seventeenth centuries, the Socinians of Poland and Transylvania controlled prestigious institutions of higher education, which attracted students from across Europe, and they maintained printing presses from which issued a flood of propaganda on Socinianism's behalf. For several decades, Socinianism appeared to constitute a formidable rival to Catholicism and orthodox Protestantism and thus commanded the attention of intellectuals throughout Europe.

Second, Socinianism possessed brilliant apologists in the persons of Faustus Socinus himself, Johannes Crellius (1590–1633), Jonas Schlichtingius (1592–1661), Samuel Przipcovius (1592–1670), Johannes Wolzogenius (ca. 1599–1661), Andreas Wissowatius (1608–78), and others. Especially influential was the *Bibliotheca Fratrum Polonorum*— a collection of works by Socinus, Crellius, Schlichtingius, and Wolzogenius—and the Racovian Catechism: the definitive exposition of Socinian doctrine. It is unsurprising, then, that Socinianism proved widely influential.

After the Socinians were expelled from Poland and harsh restrictions were imposed on them in Transylvania, however, Socinianism as an organized religion virtually ceased to exist. Polish exiles in the Netherlands, especially Andreas Wissowatius, continued to exert influence through their writings for several decades after the expulsion. Nevertheless, by 1700 the avant-garde of European opinion had moved beyond Socinianism to deism. Socinian writings continued to supply intellectual ammunition to opponents of the doctrines of the Trinity, Christ's deity, original sin, and so on, but by the dawn of the eighteenth century, Socinianism as a movement was almost entirely defunct. What follows is an overview of Socinian theology and then an assessment of Socinianism's legacy for the present.

Doctrine of Scripture. The Socinian doctrine of Scripture consists essentially in the following four affirmations: (1) Scripture is authentic, (2) Scripture is inspired, (3) Scripture is sufficient, and (4) Scripture is perspicuous.

The first of these tenets Socinians accept in much the same sense as conventional Protestants. On the subject of Scripture's perspicuity, however, Socinians diverge radically from orthodox Protestant belief. Socinians assert not merely that Scripture is sufficiently perspicuous that one may gain the knowledge essential to salvation by diligent study of the whole. Rather, they insist that God reveals nothing incomprehensible to the human mind, and therefore, they reject doctrines such as those of the Trinity, the incarnation, and original sin peremptorily.

Paterology. The Socinians regard the Father and only the Father as God. Unlike orthodox Protestants, who draw a conceptual distinction between the one, divine nature and the three divine persons, Socinians reject all distinctions between nature and person as spurious. Since God's nature is numerically one, the Socinians argue, the divine essence cannot contain more than one person, for a person, they assert, is nothing other than an individual, intelligent nature.

A trinitarian can answer this criticism by noting that "person," in the context of trinitarian theology, signifies something subtly different from an intelligent, individual nature as such. The word *person* signifies an intelligent, individual nature that is incommunicable, a nature that, in other words, possesses some property that really, and not merely conceptually, distinguishes it from all other persons.

The property that distinguishes the Father from the Son is his paternity. That which distinguishes the Son from the Father is his sonship; and that which distinguishes the Holy Spirit from the Father and the Son is his procession from both of them; not even a divine person can proceed from himself. One can affirm without patently contradicting oneself, therefore, (1) that there is only one divine nature; (2) that the Father, the Son, and the Spirit are identical with the same nature; and (3) that the Father, the Son, and the Spirit are, nonetheless, really and inexorably distinct from one another.

How, the Socinians ask, can the Father, the Son, and the Spirit be identical with the same nature without being identical with one another? This question Scripture does not answer. Nevertheless, it is fallacious to reason that if the Father is God and the Son is God, then the Father is the Son. For the Father is not God *simpliciter* but rather God begetting. The Son is not God *simpliciter* but God begotten; and from the premises "The Father is God begetting" and "The Son is God begotten" the identity of the Father and the Son does not follow. Even if one cannot demonstrate how the doctrine of the Trinity could be consistent, then, one can discredit the Socinians' arguments that it manifestly contradicts itself.

Naturally, the Socinians avail themselves of biblical as well as logical arguments against the doctrine of the Trinity. They argue, for example, that only the Father is God because the Son describes him as "the only true God" (John 17:3). But in this, they apparently fail to realize that Jesus's statement merely identifies the Father as identical with the only divine nature. It does not deny that Jesus is also identical with this nature. Likewise, the Socinians cite Jesus's statement, "No one is good but . . . God" as conclusive evidence that Christ is not God. Again, however, they seem not to realize that if Jesus is not God, then Jesus's statement implies that he himself is not good—a consequence evidently out of accord with the whole tenor of Scripture. As for the rest of the Socinians' scriptural arguments against the Trinity, they almost exclusively presuppose the rejection of the duality of Christ's natures and the eternal generation of the Logos, on the one hand, or the personhood and deity of the Holy Spirit, on the other hand, topics I address at length in the sections on Christology and pneumatology, respectively.

Christology. The Christology of the Socinians is simple. Regarding Christ's person, they insist that he is a mere human being, whom God, after Christ's resurrection, endowed with divine prerogatives. As to Christ's work, they believe that, although he does not suffer the penalty his people deserve for their sins on the cross, he accomplishes, in a diminished sense, the functions of prophet, priest, and king.

1. Christ's person. In order to render their psilanthropism (their belief that Christ is a mere human being) credible, the Socinians must establish at least that Christ is inferior to God. To achieve this end, they rely primarily on three classes of scriptural texts. The first includes passages in which Christ directly acknowledges his human nature's inferiority to the divine nature of God the Father. In John 14:28, for example, Jesus declares,

"The Father is greater than I." Again, in John 20:17, he asserts, "I ascend to My Father and your Father, and My God and your God" (this and all subsequent quotations in this entry are from the NASB). The second class of texts includes statements ascribing to Christ properties incompatible with deity. For example, one reads in Psalm 121:3–4: "He who keeps you will not slumber. Behold, He who keeps Israel will neither slumber nor sleep." Yet according to Mark 4:38, "Jesus . . . was in the stern, asleep on the cushion." According to Scripture, God is invisible (Col. 1:15; 1 Tim. 1:17; Heb. 11:27); yet numerous persons saw Jesus. Likewise, Scripture asserts that God is immortal (1 Tim. 1:17) but also that Jesus died an agonizing death.

The third class of texts is those in which Jesus acknowledges his dependence on the Father. In Matthew 28:18, the Socinians observe, Christ does not claim that all authority belongs to him by native right; rather, he states, "All authority . . . has been given to Me." The Socinians, then, might seem to mount a conclusive case for Christ's inferiority to God.

On closer inspection, however, the Socinian case against Christ's deity appears highly vulnerable to critique. For on at least eight occasions, Scripture refers to Jesus as God (cf. John 1:1, 18; 20:28; Acts 20:28; Rom. 9:5; Titus 2:13; Heb. 1:8; 2 Pet. 1:1). Scripture, likewise, attributes to Christ divine functions such as the creation of the universe (John 1:3, 10; Eph. 3:9 [KJV]; Col. 1:16; Heb. 1:2, 10), the preservation of all creatures (Col. 1:17; Heb. 1:3), the final judgment (Matt. 25:31–46; John 5:22, 27; Acts 10:42; 17:31; Rom. 2:16; 14:10 [KJV]; 2 Cor. 5:10; 2 Tim. 4:1, 8), the forgiveness of sins (Matt. 9:2 and parallels; Luke 7:48; Acts 5:31; Col. 3:13), and the salvation of human beings (Matt. 1:21; Acts 5:31; Phil. 3:20; 2 Tim. 1:10; Titus 1:4; 2:13; 2 Pet. 1:11; 2:20; 1 John 4:14; cf. Isa. 43:11).

Scripture ascribes to Christ, moreover, divine attributes such as omnipresence (Eph. 1:23; Col. 1:17), omniscience (John 16:30; 21:17; Col. 2:3), existence before creation (John 1:1; 17:5; Col. 1:15–17; Heb. 1:10; Rev. 1:8, 17; 2:8), equality with God (John 5:18; Phil. 2:6), and even deity itself (Col. 2:9); and the scriptural authors endorse, by precept and example, the worship of Jesus with the reverence due to God alone (John 20:28; Rom. 14:10–11; 1 Cor. 1:2; Phil. 2:10–11; Heb. 1:6; Rev. 1:5–6). The scriptural evidence for Christ's deity thus seems too strong for one reasonably to conclude, with the Socinians, that Christ is God only in the sense that the human judges of Psalm 82 are.

In order to reconcile with Christ's Godhood the first two classes of texts that the Socinians introduce—namely, those in which Christ acknowledges his inferiority to the Father and those that ascribe to Christ attributes that are incompatible with deity—one need merely establish that Christ's divine person possesses two distinct natures: one divine and the other human. Since these natures exhibit radically different, indeed incompatible, properties, Christ's simultaneous possession of the two natures would mean that he could be, at the same time, equal to the Father as God and inferior to him as a human being, incapable of sleep as God and capable of sleep as a human being, and so on.

The Socinians consider the doctrine that Christ is one divine person who possesses a human as well as a divine nature to be incoherent. It appears to them incoherent, however, only because they acknowledge no distinction between nature and person. As noted above, in order to constitute a person, an intelligent nature must possess some property, frequently referred to as its subsistence, that renders it incommunicable—that is, incapable of incorporation into another person.

That every human being, and indeed every distinct entity, possesses such a property seems evident. For a thing's nature and its existence do not suffice for it to exist as an independent entity. The sum total of a computer's parts, for example, constitutes its nature. The actually existing sum of a computer's parts, however, does not make the collection of parts a computer. In order to obtain a computer, one must bestow on the computer's existing nature a certain organization, which constitutes its subsistence.

What precisely constitutes the subsistence of human beings, admittedly, is mysterious. If, however, human beings have souls, their subsistence cannot consist merely in their organs' arrangement or in the surface of their skin. Human subsistence, rather, must be spiritual and therefore difficult, if not impossible, to apprehend.

That two spiritual natures can share a common subsistence is not self-evident; neither, however, is it demonstrably impossible. The doctrine that Christ united a human nature to his eternal person so that one person possesses a divine and a human nature is a mystery like the doctrine of the Trinity. One can refute arguments that the doctrine could not possibly be true, and although one cannot demonstrate that the doctrine is even conceivable, one possesses sufficient warrant for believing it because God affirms it in Scripture.

That God does affirm this doctrine in Scripture seems evident from the following three considerations. First, Paul teaches in Philippians 2:6–7 that "Christ Jesus . . . although He existed in the form of God, did not regard equality with God a thing to be grasped, but emptied Himself, taking the form of a bond-servant." Paul employs the word *form* (Greek *morphē*) here at least approximately in the sense of "nature" (cf. NIV: "very nature"). Otherwise, he would assert that Christ merely appeared to be human, in which case he could not have suffered "death, even the death of the cross" (Phil. 2:8).

In Philippians 2:6–7, then, Paul teaches that the eternal Son, who already possessed a divine nature, assumed the nature of a bond-servant and, in that nature, died on the cross.

The words "emptied Himself," admittedly, might tempt one to think that Christ emptied himself of his divine nature when he assumed a human nature. However, Scripture's numerous ascriptions to Christ of deity, divine attributes, divine functions, and so on, even during his period of humiliation on earth, preclude this possibility. Rightly understood, then, Philippians 2:6–7 directly teaches the doctrine that we have proposed as a solution to Socinian objections to Christ's deity, the doctrine that the Son, possessing eternally and unchangeably a divine nature, assumed into his subsistence a human nature and became thenceforth one person in two natures.

Second, passages such as Acts 20:28, "the church of God, which he purchased with his own blood," and 1 Corinthians 2:8, "they . . . crucified the Lord of glory," assert of the one Christ that, although he is God, he has blood and was crucified—which cannot be true of God but can be true of a human being. Such passages seem to suggest only slightly less directly than Philippians 2:6–7 that Christ is God and human being in one person. Third, Scripture sometimes ascribes to Jesus attributes no single nature can simultaneously possess: mutability and immutability, mortality and immortality, invisibility and visibility, and so on. If Jesus does not possess at least two natures in his one person, it seems, many of these texts must simply be false. Since Scripture clearly describes Christ as God and as human, then, it seems only reasonable for one who believes the Bible to consider Jesus one person in two natures; and one who accepts this doctrine, as we have seen, possesses an adequate answer to arguments against Christ's deity that are grounded in his possession of attributes inconceivable in the divine nature.

This doctrine, nevertheless, does not suffice to resolve the difficulties engendered by the third class of biblical texts Socinians marshal to prove Jesus inferior to the Father. In these texts, Jesus indicates that he derives not merely his humanity but his life (John 5:26), his power to act (John 5:19, 30), and his authority (Matt. 28:18) from God the Father. One may answer the charge that this implies that Jesus is not God by a twofold response. First, these texts do not invalidate the testimony of the verses cited earlier on behalf of Jesus's deity; and, second, the doctrine of the Son's eternal generation explains how the Son can be fully God, and therefore equal with the Father, and yet derive his being, in some sense, from the Father.

The doctrine of Christ's eternal generation derives its principal support from two considerations. First, a number of texts describe Jesus as "the only begotten from the Father" (John 1:14 NASB), "the only begotten God" (John 1:18 NASB), and God's "only begotten Son" (John 3:16, 18; 1 John 4:9). Second, the very names of the first two persons of the Trinity, "Father" and "Son," presuppose some relation of origination, albeit ineffable. If the Father eternally communicates his divine nature to the Son, the Son is God and, therefore, coessential and coequal with his divine Father, notwithstanding his dependence on the Father for this communication. The doctrine of Christ's eternal generation, then, appears adequate to answer the Socinian argument against Christ's deity from his dependence on the Father. The Socinians, then, fail to adequately warrant their dissent from orthodox conceptions of Christ's person and natures.

2. Christ's work. Regarding Christ's work, Socinians differ from conventional Protestants of their time primarily in that they abhor the notion of a substitutionary atonement. By his death on the cross, the Socinians maintain, Christ reconciled human beings to God in three senses. First, he sealed the covenant of salvation with his blood. Second, he demonstrated the sincerity of his preaching by suffering death on its account. Third and most importantly, Christ, by dying, occasioned his resurrection, which constitutes a pledge of

the resurrection of all and a guarantee that God will fulfill his promises. In the Socinian view, then, Christ's resurrection is more consequential than his death, and Christ's death neither satisfies God's justice nor appeases his wrath toward sinners.

The Socinians prefer this minimalistic conception of Christ's work on the cross over the notion of penal atonement for two principal reasons. First, they believe that retributive justice, the virtue that demands condign punishment for every sin, is not a divine attribute. Second, they believe that persons can be morally obligated to perform only those acts of which they are fully capable.

The first belief renders Christ's suffering of punishment on others' behalf superfluous; if God need not punish every sin condignly, he can forgive sinners without receiving a divine-human sacrifice on their behalf. And the second belief implies that the very notion of a penal atonement is absurd. The doctrine of Christ's substitutionary atonement presupposes that human beings, on account of the infinite guilt of their sins, owe God an infinitely valuable sacrifice, which they themselves cannot provide. If obligation presupposes ability, however, human beings simply cannot owe God such a sacrifice. They must be capable of pleasing him through their own resources.

The falsehood of the doctrine of substitutionary atonement follows inexorably from these two assumptions. That these assumptions are reconcilable with Scripture, however, is by no means evident. For, first, Scripture states unmistakably that God administers retributive justice (cf., e.g., Ps. 62:12; Jer. 17:10; Matt. 16:27; Rom. 2:6; Rev. 2:23), and it is difficult to imagine why he would do so if retributive justice were not among his virtues. Second, Scripture implicitly contradicts the principle that obligation presupposes ability on numerous occasions. Paul, for example, asserts, "The mind set on the flesh . . . does not subject itself to the law of God, for it is not even able to do so, and those who are in the flesh cannot please God" (Rom. 8:7–8). Likewise, Jeremiah asks, "Can the Ethiopian change his skin or the leopard his spots? Then you also can do good who are accustomed to doing evil" (Jer. 13:23; cf. also John 6:44; 8:43; 12:39; Rom. 7:18; 1 Cor. 2:14; Eph. 2:1; Col. 2:13). Each of these authors insists strenuously that God will repay the wicked fully for their evil deeds, yet each also asserts that the wicked, of their own power, cannot turn from their wickedness to God. The principle that obligation presupposes ability, therefore, runs contrary to the plain sense of Scripture. The Socinians, accordingly, succeed in overthrowing neither the doctrine of Christ's deity nor that of his substitutionary atonement.

Pneumatology. Socinians consider the Holy Spirit an impersonal power imparted by God to creatures, which, albeit of divine origin, is not itself divine and does not regenerate human beings. The Socinians deny the Spirit's personality principally because Scripture declares the Spirit to be given, poured out, and so on, and human beings are said to drink of it and be baptized into it. Such predicates, the Socinians contend, are inapplicable to persons. To refute this argument, it seems, one need merely note that Scripture applies many of the same predicates to Christ and others who are unquestionably persons. Christians, for example, are "baptized into Christ" (Rom. 6:3; Gal. 3:27). The Israelites wandering in the wilderness were "baptized into Moses" (1 Cor. 10:2) and drank of Christ (1 Cor. 10:4). Job asks God, "Did you not pour me out like milk?" (Job 10:10). David states, "I am poured out like water" (Ps. 22:14), and God declares, "I have given the Levites as a gift to Aaron and to his sons" (Num. 8:19; cf. 18:6). The Socinian case against the Spirit's personhood thus appears quite weak.

Their case against the Spirit's deity, it seems, is even weaker. The Socinians grant, for example, that in a number of instances, by the expression "Holy Spirit," Scripture means God. They explain, however, that because of the Holy Spirit's close association with God, the scriptural authors refer to God the Father as the Holy Spirit by metonymy. Inasmuch as Scripture clearly distinguishes the Spirit from the Son and the Father on multiple occasions, however, this seems hardly likely. The Socinians, naturally, object to the doctrine of the Spirit's deity on the grounds that he is not the Father and that he is received from the Father and the Son.

As we have seen, however, the doctrine of God's numerical unity does not exclude a multiplicity of divine persons. If the doctrine of the Son's eternal generation suffices to explain his dependence—even as God—on the Father, moreover, then the doctrine of the Spirit's eternal procession should suffice to reconcile his deity with his dependence on the Father and the Son.

As to the Spirit's work, the Socinians deny that the Spirit regenerates human beings in the sense of implanting supernatural capacities for faith and love because (1) such an act would be mysterious and perhaps incomprehensible and (2) they do not acknowledge the necessity of supernatural rebirth. Such a rebirth cannot be necessary for a human being to obtain salvation, in the Socinian view, because obligation presupposes ability. God, the Socinians hold, cannot require of human beings what they, of their own strength, cannot perform.

Soteriology. The just-mentioned principle constitutes the foundation of Socinian soteriology. The notion of original sin seems absurd to Socinians because if obligation presupposes ability, then even if moral disabilities were inherited from Adam, they would not increase human guilt. Rather, they would decrease human responsibility to the level of fallen humanity's modified capacities. Again, Socinians see little difficulty in the notion that human beings earn their salvation by faith and works. For if obligation presupposes ability, then human beings cannot lack the ability to do whatever God requires, and they certainly cannot require the imputed righteousness of another. The Socinians sacrifice the necessity of regeneration and the rest of what Protestants typically regard as biblical soteriology, therefore, on the altar of the principle that obligation presupposes ability.

Conclusion. The Socinians' refusal to credit any doctrine they consider unreasonable or incomprehensible thus impels them to deny key biblical doctrines about God's being and acts. They reject the doctrines of the Trinity, the hypostatic union of divine and human natures in Christ, the personality and deity of the Holy Spirit, the necessity of regeneration to salvation, original sin, and justification by faith alone. In so doing, the Socinians demonstrate that Procrustean, rationalistic exegesis can eviscerate biblical Christianity quite as easily as outright dismissal of Scripture's authority.

See also ATONEMENT; CHRIST, NATURES AND ATTRIBUTES OF; CHRISTIANITY, PROTESTANT; HOLY SPIRIT, BIBLICAL VIEW OF; ORTHODOXY; ROMAN CATHOLICISM; TRINITARIAN CONTROVERSIES; TRINITY, THE; UNITARIANISM

Bibliography. R. Dán, A. Pirnát, and M. T. Akadémia, *Antitrinitarianism in the Second Half of the Sixteenth Century*; P. Knijff and Sibbe Jan Visser, *Bibliographia Sociniana: A Bibliographical Reference Tool for the Study of Dutch Socinianism and Antitrinitarianism*; M. Muslow and J. Rohls, eds., *Socinianism and Arminianism: Antitrinitarians, Calvinists and Cultural Exchange in Seventeenth-Century Europe*; J. Owen, *Vindiciae Evangelicae: Or, the Mystery of the Gospel Vindicated and Socinianism Examined in Works of John Owen*; C. Sandius, *Bibliotheca antitrinitariorum*; F. Socinus et al., *Bibliotheca Fratrum Polonorum*; L. Szczucki, *Socinianism and Its Role in the Culture of XVIth to XVIIIth Centuries*; E. M. Wilbur, *A History of Unitarianism*, 2 vols.; G. H. Williams, trans. and ed., *The Polish Brethren: Documentation of Their History and Thought*

in the Polish-Lithuanian Commonwealth and in the Diaspora, 1601–1685, 2 vols.; A. Wissowatius et al., *Racovian Catechism*, translated by T. Rees

D. W. Jowers

SOCINUS, FAUSTUS. *See* SOCINIANISM

SOCIOLOGY OF RELIGION. Sociology is the modern, systematic, scientific study of society. The term was first used by Auguste Comte (1798–1857) in 1830, but as an academic discipline it was first developed by Herbert Spencer (1820–1903) in the late nineteenth century. It involves the application of empirical methods, such as questionnaires, survey research, and statistical analysis, to the study of society. These and other techniques are used to understand the way people act and think as members of social groups.

Other figures regarded as the founders of sociology are Alexis de Tocqueville (1805–59) and Karl Marx (1818–83), later followed by Ernst Troeltsch (1865–1923), Max Weber (1864–1920), and Emile Durkheim (1858–1917). Weber was the junior colleague of Troeltsch, and Durkheim studied the work of Weber and Troeltsch in Leipzig. All three sought to counter the arguments of Marx. The sociology of religion developed through the application of sociological methods to religion as a social reality. All the key founders of sociology were preoccupied with religion and its influence. Paradoxically today, the sociology of religion is a minor field within sociology proper.

In the latter part of the twentieth century, interest in the sociology of religion revived as a direct result of the appearance of non-Christian religions and new religious movements in Western society. Leading figures in this revival were Rodney Stark (1940–), Tom Robbins (1943–2015), Jeffery Hadden (1936–2003), Eileen Barker (1938–), and Margaret Poloma (1950–). From a Christian perspective, Ronald M. Enroth (1938–) has done much work in new religious movements.

Sociological terms are often confusing to people schooled in theology because "the same" words are used by sociologists and theologians in different ways. Thus, a term like church has a definite meaning in the New Testament and Christian discourse. For Christians a church is a community of believers. The problem arises when sociologists use the word church in a completely different manner. Most sociologists use church to identify a type of religious organization that some refer to as an ideal type. Identifying ideal types was a method developed by Troeltsch and Weber to enable comparison between different religious organizations cross-culturally. It has nothing to do with theological definitions. Thus for them a church is a religious organization that is inclusive in its scope. As such a church embraces everyone living in a given geographic area. This form of religious organization can be found in all religions and therefore compared to other forms of religious organization, such as sects, that are defined by sociologists as religious groups that are exclusive in their organization.

Rodney Stark and others have questioned this usage of ideal types, proposing instead operational definitions that allow for better use of quantitative measurement using survey research and statistical analysis. Thus for Stark and people like him a church is "a conventional religious organization," while a sect is "a deviant religious organization with traditional beliefs and practices."

This is not the place to debate these definitions or to elaborate on sociological theories but rather an occasion to note the problem of definition and remind the reader that sociologists try to understand social organizations. Therefore, the sociology of religion is very valuable for Christians wishing to understand the world they live in, but it will not (nor does it attempt to) answer theological problems. Consequently, in sociological terms many groups that Christians consider churches or parachurch organizations are technically cults or sects, while other groups that Christians see as cults are understood sociologically as churches. Recognizing this difference in usage is the key to any Christian appreciation of sociology.

Bibliography. E. Durkheim, *The Elementary Forms of Religious Life*; R. M. Enroth, *Guide to Cults and New Religions*; M. Hill, *A Sociology of Religion*; D. S. Swenson, *Society, Spirituality and the Sacred*; M. Weber, *The Sociology of Religion*.

I. Hexham

SOKA GAKKAI. Although Zen Buddhism has received the greater publicity, Soka Gakkai (Japanese, "value creation society") has been the most aggressive Buddhist movement in the Western world. A Buddhist lay movement with a worldwide following of more than seven million people, it was once affiliated with the sect called Nichiren Shoshu and still promotes Nichiren beliefs and practices.

Nichiren Daishonin (AD 1222–82) advocated a return to the teaching of the Buddha as recorded in the Lotus Sutra. Preaching that any person could achieve buddhahood by chanting this sutra's title, he inscribed the *daimoku*, an invocation of the sutra's title (*nam-myoho-renge-kyo*), on sheets of rice paper (gohonzon), which served as objects of worship. Ever since, his followers have chanted the *daimoku* in hopes of achieving personal success, world peace (*kosen-rufu*), and spiritual advancement.

Soka Gakkai originated when Tsunesaburo Makiguchi (1871–1944), advocating educational reform on the basis of values rather than conformism, resorted to Nichiren Shoshu Buddhism as a basis for his proposals. He died in prison for not recognizing the emperor as divine, but the movement was resurrected and flourished under Josei Toda (1900–1958).

Daisaku Ikeda (b. 1928) succeeded Toda as president of Soka Gakkai. He has attempted to gain worldwide respect by encouraging members to moderate their proselytizing techniques and by appearing frequently alongside celebrities promoting world peace. Even though Ikeda maintained the subordination of the Soka Gakkai to Nichiren Shoshu for many years, in 1991 the Nichiren priesthood officially expelled the group.

Soka Gakkai attracts members by promising a happy life, including material success. In the past, new members repudiated all other religions and destroyed all religious objects in their homes (e.g., crucifixes or images of *kami*, gods or forces of nature worshiped in the Shinto religion) before receiving their own gohonzon (material objects of devotion), but this position has been relaxed. Soka Gakkai presents itself to the external world by promoting the fine arts and releasing a continuous stream of messages calling for nuclear disarmament.

See also BUDDHISM; GOHONZON; LOTUS SUTRA; NICHIREN SHOSHU

Bibliography. K. Dobbelaere, *Sōka Gaikkai: From Lay Movement to Religion*; K. Murata, *Japan's New Buddhism: An Objective Account of Sōka Gakkai*; D. A. Snow, *Shakubuku: A Study of the Nichiren Shoshu Movement in America, 1960–75*.

W. Corduan

SOUL SLEEP. Soul sleep is an unconscious state that some Christians believe is the condition of a human soul between the death of the body and the resurrection. Those who hold this notion literally interpret the Old and New Testament passages that refer to death as "sleep" (Ps. 13:3; John 11:11–14; Acts 13:36; 1 Cor. 11:30; 15:6, 18, 20, 51; Eph. 5:14; 1 Thess. 4:13–15; 5:10), concluding from them that the soul is unconscious during this intermediate period prior to the resurrection. In the sixteenth century, this view was apparently held by many in the Anabaptist and Socinian traditions (Erickson, 1176). Today soul sleep is a minority position in Christianity held primarily by

the Seventh-day Adventist Church, Jehovah's Witnesses, and Christadelphians. In fact, Seventh-day Adventists list soul sleep among their "fundamental beliefs" (Erickson, 1176). In the Seventh-day Adventist tradition, the doctrine of soul sleep is closely associated with an annihilationist view of hell and eternal punishment. In this view, the righteous arise at the resurrection, and those who are not in Christ are annihilated as punishment. Those who are not in Christ never suffer a conscious awareness of their eternal state because they sleep after the death of the physical body.

The primary texts used in favor of a soul sleep position are 1 Thessalonians 4:13–14 and 1 Corinthians 15:20, 51. In the former passage, Paul comforts believers by saying that God "will bring with Jesus those who have fallen asleep in him." First Corinthians 15:20 states, "But Christ has indeed been raised from the dead, the firstfruits of those who have fallen asleep." The argument for soul sleep is built further on passages in which those who have died do not seem to have a conscious existence (Pss. 6:5; 115:17; Eccles. 9:10; Isa. 38:19; Grudem, 819). Another text that is occasionally cited in support of soul sleep is Acts 2:34, which states, "For David did not ascend to heaven."

A variety of approaches have been used to refute this belief. First, the Bible never explicitly refers to the soul when it says that a person has fallen asleep. It is usually clear in these passages that "sleep" is a metaphor used to demonstrate that death is temporary in the same manner that sleep is temporary (Grudem, 819). It is always the physical body that is in mind. For example, in the previously quoted passage of 1 Corinthians 15:20, the phrase "fallen asleep" is used directly in the context of death, as Christ has been raised from the dead. In John 11:11, Jesus says, "Our friend Lazarus has fallen asleep; but I am going there to wake him up." It is soon made clear that Lazarus has died and that

Jesus is going to raise him from the dead. Second, a literal soul sleep would be difficult to reconcile with many other passages that indicate that the souls of believers are in God's presence and fellowship immediately after death (Luke 23:43; Phil. 1:23; Heb. 12:23; Rev. 20:13).

See also ANNIHILATIONISM; SEVENTH-DAY ADVENTISM

Bibliography. B. Edgar, "Biblical Anthropology and the Intermediate State," *Evangelical Quarterly*; M. Erickson, *Christian Theology*; W. Grudem, *Systematic Theology*.

T. S. Price

SPEAKING IN TONGUES. Formally known as *glossolalia*, "speaking in tongues" typically refers to speaking in a language one has not naturally learned. It is listed as one of the gifts or manifestations of the Holy Spirit in 1 Corinthians 12:10, 28–30. Speaking in tongues and its companion practice of "interpretation" are mentioned in the New Testament only in Acts 2, 10, 19, 1 Corinthians 12–14, and Mark 16 (in a passage of disputed authenticity). The apostle Paul applied the prediction of Isaiah 28:11–12 to the glossolalic worship of the church at Corinth (1 Cor. 14:21).

In the biblical texts, this phenomenon was expressed in two forms. The Acts 2 account is an instance of xenoglossy (or *xenolalia*), where the languages were human dialects not known to the speaker but understood by some of the hearers. The accounts in 1 Corinthians 12–14 show the second form of glossolalia, where the utterance is not intelligible to anyone (14:2) and requires a spiritual gift to be interpreted (14:13), though it is recognized as an expression of prayer or thanksgiving (14:14–16).

Christians today generally take one of three positions on speaking in tongues. (1) Glossolalia was a supernatural sign given to validate the apostolic ministries and is not authentically practiced today because the sign-gifts have ceased. This perspective is known as the cessationist view. (2) Glossolalia is a valid supernatural gift for this generation but should be neither actively forbidden nor actively encouraged. This is the position of the Foursquare Gospel Church. (3) Glossolalia is a supernatural gift that should be sought and encouraged as a gift of the Holy Spirit. This view typifies charismatic and Pentecostal churches. Pentecostal views, represented by denominations such as the Assemblies of God or the Church of God in Christ, generally fall within the boundaries of orthodox Christianity and are usually deemed nonheretical (except by certain strict fundamentalists).

Bibliography. F. D. Macchia, "Glossolalia," in *Encyclopedia of Pentecostal and Charismatic Christianity*, edited by S. M. Burgess; R. P. Spittler, "Glossolalia," in *The New International Dictionary of Pentecostal and Charismatic Movements*, edited by S. M. Burgess and E. M. van der Maas, rev. ed.

E. Pement

SPIRITUALITY, CHRISTIAN. Jerome (347–420) was apparently the first to use the Latin *spiritualitas* for a quality of life imparted by the Holy Spirit (Marmion, 10), but by the twelfth century, *spiritualitas* had acquired the more expansive referent "spiritual exercises," a process of institutionalization culminating in the work of Ignatius Loyola (1491/1495–1556) and the Jesuits. The English equivalent *spirituality* still lacks adequate definition but typically denotes patterns of practices intended to foster the experience of supramundane realities in the present.

Among Christians spirituality has a venerable history from at least the second century onward. In his *Protreptikos*, Clement of Alexandria (ca. 150–215) urged believers to cultivate a yearning for truth and for their heavenly homeland and to be satisfied by the Scriptures, which are "inspired of God" and thus able to nourish the "spiritual" in humanity. The so-called desert fathers of the fourth century developed spiritual disciplines to an art form, utilizing ascetic rigor and religious exercises to die to earthly existence and thereby to experience identification with Christ. This tradition—though without the austerities of the desert fathers—may be traced through the church fathers (e.g., Athanasius, Gregory of Nazianzus, Gregory of Nyssa, Chrysostom) to medieval writers (e.g., Meister Eckhart [1260–1328], Thomas á Kempis [ca. 1380–1471]) to later Catholic mystics (e.g., St. John of the Cross [1542–91], Teresa of Ávila [1515–82]) to the Puritans to the German pietists (e.g., Philipp Spener [1635–1705]) to Holiness movements associated with John Wesley (1703–91) to the Keswick Convention to Pentecostalism. Contemporary Christian spirituality is expressed in such writers as Richard Foster (*Celebration of Discipline*, 1978), Oswald Chambers (*My Utmost for His Highest*, 1935), Henri Nouwen (*Reaching Out*, 1975), and Thomas Merton (*The Seven Storey Mountain*, 1948).

The work of Thomas Merton highlights the increasingly broad meaning of "spirituality" today. A Trappist monk, Merton nonetheless borrowed liberally from Gandhi and Zen Buddhist sources and became more and more detached from orthodox biblical truth-claims. Likewise, modern spiritualities, like numerous ancient heresies—for example, gnosticism and Manichaeism, which incorporated Greek mysticism into Christian theology—are highly eclectic and syncretistic. Their appeal lies in humankind's innate spiritual nature, in human awareness of the sacred (cf. Rudolf Otto, *The Idea of the Holy*, 1923), in the perceived contrast between Western materialism and Eastern quietude, and in the inclusivism implied by generic spirituality.

As noted, contemporary spirituality has been significantly influenced by Eastern religions and more recently by other non-Christian traditions, such as Islamic Sufism, Jewish Kabbalism, and neo-gnosticism.

It should be noted that Eastern spirituality is largely *negative* and ascetic, while Western adaptations tend to be *positive* and optimistic—the former seeking liberation through extinction of the self, the latter through realization of the self, often under the influence of humanistic psychology. Matthew Fox (an ex-Catholic Episcopal priest) has written, for example, that the essence of spirituality is to replace human identity defined by sin and redemption with identity defined by wholeness, goodness, and creative energy—"original blessing" rather than "original sin." The path to this new identity involves exercises designed to intensify awareness of one's true self and tap into the potential of that self for future growth.

See also CHRISTIANITY, PROTESTANT; EASTERN ORTHODOXY; ROMAN CATHOLICISM

Bibliography. P. N. Brooks, ed., *Christian Spirituality*; O. Chambers, *My Utmost for His Highest*; E. Cousins, ed., *World Spirituality: An Encyclopedic History of the Religious Quest*; R. Foster, *Celebration of Discipline*; M. Fox, *Original Blessing*; D. Marmion, *A Spirituality of Everyday Faith: A Theological Investigation of the Notion of Spirituality in Karl Rahner*; T. Merton, *The Asian Journal of Thomas Merton*; Merton, *The Seven Storey Mountain: An Autobiography of Faith*; H. J. M. Nouwen, *Reaching Out: Three Movements of the Spiritual Life*; R. Otto, *The Idea of the Holy*.

C. R. Wells

STANDARD WORKS. The Church of Jesus Christ of Latter-day Saints (LDS Church) recognizes four collections of scripture as its "standard works": the King James Version (KJV) of the Bible (with notes that include quotations from the Joseph Smith Translation), the Book of Mormon, the Doctrine and Covenants, and the Pearl of Great Price. The Book of Mormon and two of the books contained in the Pearl of Great Price (the Book of Moses and the Book of Abraham) were produced by Joseph Smith as translations of ancient scriptures. The other books in the Pearl of Great Price and all of the Doctrine and Covenants except for five sections and the two Official Declarations were produced by Joseph Smith as modern revelations.

The term *standard works* in LDS usage is a technical term denoting the above four collections of scripture. The closest comparable term in traditional Christian theology is *canon*, with the important difference being that in LDS doctrine the standard works remain always theoretically open to new additions. Still, other than Official Declaration 2, no new scripture has been added to the standard works in nearly a century. About 99 percent of LDS scripture other than the Bible was produced in the first fifteen years of LDS history. With the proviso that the standard works (especially the Doctrine and Covenants) are open to additions, LDS theologians can describe the standard works as "canonized scripture" (e.g., Top).

For most of the first fifty years or so of LDS history, the standard works consisted of the Bible, the Book of Mormon (published in 1830, the year the church was founded), and the Doctrine and Covenants (first published with that title in 1835 as an expansion of a collection originally produced in 1831). In sermons in 1867 and 1871, George A. Smith listed these three scriptures specifically when referring to "the standard works of the Church" (*JD* 11:364, 17:161). In 1880 the LDS Church officially adopted the Pearl of Great Price as scripture, bringing the number of the standard works to four. The shape and general contents of the standard works have remained about the same since that time with the major exception of the removal of *Lectures on Faith* from the Doctrine and Covenants in 1921.

In addition to viewing these "four books as scripture," the LDS Church teaches that "the inspired words of our living prophets are also accepted as scripture. . . . Their words come to us through conferences, the *Liahona* or *Ensign* magazine, and instructions to local priesthood leaders" (Church of Jesus Christ of Latter-day Saints, 45, 48). Brigham Young regarded his own sermons, at least after he had proofread them, to be Scripture as much as the Bible (*JD* 13:95, 264). In a broad sense, Mormons view all inspired speech as "scripture," though only scripture that has been canonized by the formal acceptance of the LDS Church is included in the standard works. "Any message, whether written or spoken, that comes from God to man by the power of the Holy Ghost is scripture. If it is written and accepted by the Church, it becomes part of the *scriptures or standard works* and ever thereafter may be read and studied with profit" (McConkie, 682).

Although the standard works may be viewed as functioning in a normative role in LDS doctrine (e.g., J. F. Smith, *Doctrines of Salvation*, 3:203–4), such an understanding must be qualified by the LDS emphasis on the essential role of the "living prophet," the current president of the LDS Church. Mormons view the teaching of the living prophet as more important and normative than the teaching of past prophets in the standard works because the former authoritatively interprets the latter. According to a story told by Wilford Woodruff, Joseph Smith once asked Brigham Young to comment on the claim someone had made that the Saints should confine their doctrine to what is found in the written word of God in the standard works. Young replied that although the standard works were "the written word of God to us . . . , when compared with the living oracles those books are nothing to me; those books do not convey the word of God direct to us now, as do the words of a Prophet or a man bearing the Holy Priesthood in our day and generation. I would rather have the living oracles than all the writing in the books." Joseph Smith commented, according to Woodruff's account, "Brother Brigham has told you the word of the Lord, and he has told you the truth" (Wilford Woodruff, in *Conference Report*, October 1897, 22–23). Woodruff argued, one could read the standard works in their entirety and any other written revelations "and they would scarcely be sufficient to guide us twenty-four hours. . . . We are to be guided by the living oracles" (*JD* 9:324).

The classic statement of the LDS view of the standard works and the living prophet is Ezra Taft Benson's 1980 lecture at Brigham Young University, "Fourteen Fundamentals in Following the Prophet." Benson's fourteen fundamentals included the following points: "Second: *The living prophet is more vital to us than the Standard Works.* . . . Third: *The living prophet is more important to us than a dead prophet.* . . . Beware of those who would set up the dead prophets against the living prophets, for the living prophets always take precedence. Fourth: *The prophet will never lead the Church astray.* . . . Sixth: *The prophet does not have to say 'Thus saith the Lord' to give us scripture.* . . . Fourteenth: *The prophet and the presidency—the living prophet and the First Presidency—follow them and be blessed—reject them and suffer.*" The lecture was published the following year in the LDS Church's official magazine *Liahona* and has been cited repeatedly in more recent conference addresses as accurately expressing the church's stance. In the October 2010 general conference, two speakers (Claudio Costa and Kevin Duncan) gave addresses in which they quoted all fourteen of Benson's points. Thus, the LDS Church definitely maintains that the teachings of its current prophet are "more vital" and "more important" than the teachings of the written scriptures in its expanded canon of the standard works.

See also ARTICLES OF FAITH, MORMON; BENSON, EZRA TAFT; BIBLE, CANON OF; BOOK OF ABRAHAM; BOOK OF MORMON; BOOK OF MOSES; CHURCH OF JESUS CHRIST OF LATTER-DAY SAINTS; DOCTRINE AND COVENANTS; JOSEPH SMITH TRANSLATION OF THE BIBLE; PEARL OF GREAT PRICE, THE; SMITH, JOSEPH, JR.; THEOLOGICAL METHOD OF THE CHURCH OF JESUS CHRIST OF LATTER-DAY SAINTS; YOUNG, BRIGHAM

Bibliography. E. T. Benson, "Fourteen Fundamentals in Following the Prophet," *Liahona*; Church of Jesus Christ of Latter-day Saints, *Gospel Principles*; C. Costa, "Obedience to the Prophets"; K. Duncan, "Our Very Survival"; B. R. McConkie, *Mormon Doctrine*; G. A. Smith, "Raising Flax and Wool [. . .]," in *JD* 11; J. F. Smith, *Doctrines of Salvation*; B. L. Top, "Standard Works," in *LDS Beliefs: A Doctrinal Reference*, by R. L. Millet et al.; D. Vogel, *The Word of God*; C. J. Williams, "Standard Works," in *Encyclopedia of Mormonism*, edited by D. H. Ludlow, 4 vols; Brigham Young, "Texts for Preaching Upon at Conference [. . .]," in *JD* 13.

R. M. Bowman Jr.

STIGMATA. *Stigmata* (Greek, "marks") is a term sometimes used to refer to a variety of bloody marks suggestive of Christ's crucifixion wounds that have allegedly been seen on the body of an individual. Stigmata are most common on the feet and/or in the palms. On rare occasions, however, stigmata appear as wheals of scourging on the back (John 19:1), lacerations on the head (as if inflicted by a crown of thorns [John 19:2]), or a bloody gash in the side (mirroring the soldier's javelin that was thrust into Christ [John 19:34]). Some Christians, on the basis of Paul's statement in Galatians 6:17, believe he was afflicted by stigmata.

More than three hundred stigmata cases have been recorded over the centuries. The first one (ca. 1224) involved St. Francis of Assisi (1182–1226), who showed wounds in his hands, feet, and side. Contemporary stigmatics include the renowned Padre Pio (1887–1968), who was canonized in 2002 by Pope John Paul II; Cloretta Robinson, a ten-year-old African American girl in the US (ca. 1972); and forty-three-year-old Episcopalian Heather Woods (1992).

Numerous stigmata studies and investigations since 1894 have yielded important information. First, non-Catholic stigmata cases are rare (nonexistent before 1972). Second, all stigmatics are intensely religious. Most of them, in fact, have come from religious orders (usually Dominican or Franciscan). Third, many stigmatics, in years prior to their stigmata, experienced physical or psychological trauma, either accidental or deliberate. Fourth, some stigmatics have a history of self-inflicted physical punishment as either a means of self-control or an act of spiritual devotion (e.g., self-flagellation). Fifth, a majority of stigmatics are obsessed with Christ's crucifixion to the point of surrounding themselves with crucifixes. Sixth, visions, ecstatic trances, and mental disturbances are common to stigmatics. Seventh, more women than men are afflicted (a 7:1 ratio). Eighth, a stigmatic's marks usually mirror the wounds (i.e., shape and location) they have seen in crucifixion pictures or on crucifixes. Ninth, the wounds of stigmatics vary greatly in size, shape, and location. Finally, most stigmatics have come from Italy, followed by France, Spain, Portugal, and other predominantly Roman Catholic or Latin American countries. Only recently (post-1908) has the phenomenon spread to other countries (e.g., UK, Australia, and the US).

Although many stigmata cases have been exposed as "pious frauds" (i.e., hoaxes motivated by misguided religious zeal), some remain a mystery. Several explanations exist. None of them can be proven. They are as follows: (1) a miracle associated with a holy person; (2) a skin disorder called dermographia (linked to persons with severe dissociative disorders), which can cause skin to grow so sensitive that the slightest touch can cause welts to appear; (3) a condition called psychogenic purpura, which is initiated by extreme stress and causes blood to leak from the skin's capillaries; and (4) self-hypnosis, by which stigmatics can induce blood to swell from specific areas.

See also ROMAN CATHOLICISM

Bibliography. M. Freze, *They Bore the Wounds of Christ: The Mystery of the Sacred Stigmata*; J. Nickell, *Looking for a Miracle: Weeping Icons, Relics, Stigmata, Visions, and Healing Cures.*

R. Abanes

SUFISM. Sufism is the mystical interpretation of Islam, common throughout both its Sunni and Shi'ite variants; in its aggregate, Sufism is the medium through which the majority of Muslims since approximately 1000 have interpreted Islam. Historically, Sufism has its roots in the vast ascetic tradition (*zuhd*) of the classical world. Through the first centuries of Islam, a number of prominent ascetics promoted self-denial, holy poverty, the life of a wandering mendicant (eventually to be called *faqir* or *dervish*), and other forms of spiritual discipline such as denying oneself sleep and food, constantly praying, and compulsively weeping. Muslim asceticism, however, does not include chastity.

These early ascetics are seen as proto-Sufis—the belief system of Sufism uses them as exemplars, but there is no indication that they thought of themselves as anything other than ascetics. Sufism as a coherent system developed during the late eighth and early ninth centuries, with two strands: one an orthodox, Sunni one, which emphasized closeness to the Shari'ah (divine law) while interpreting it mystically, and the other an antinomian one that deliberately flouted Muslim norms (e.g., drinking alcohol), following a higher law of love. Both strands, however, emphasized that the ultimate goal was union with the divine through a type of universal love.

Sufism during the tenth century began to lose its aura of rejection of and by society when the great theologian al-Ghazali (d. 1111) and others began to follow the Sufi path and harmonized it with mainstream Muslim teachings. Other prominent intellectuals such as the Spaniard Ibn al-'Arabi (d. 1240) and Jalal al-Din al-Rumi (d. 1273) enriched Sufi literature significantly and increased its social prestige. This period witnessed the foundation of Sufi brotherhoods or fraternities (*tariqa* or *turuq*) that came to dominate Muslim social and religious life. The most important of these is the Qadiriyya, which spans the entire Muslim world, but the Naqshbandiyya (common in Central and South Asia and in Indonesia), the Mevleviyya (Turkey and Central Asia), the Tijaniyya (North and West Africa), Shadhiliyya (North Africa), and Rifa'iyya (Middle East) are also important.

Today Sufism has come under strong attack by radical Muslims, who see the Sufi path as one that involves spiritual mediation (through Sufi holy men) that effectively creates a form of polytheism. Modernists and liberals today also scorn Sufis, holding them responsible for backwardness in the Muslim world. However, despite these attacks Sufism is still extremely popular and continues to gain converts to Islam throughout the world, just as it has for centuries.

See also ISLAM, BASIC BELIEFS OF; MEVLEVI ORDER; MYSTICISM; SHI'A ISLAM; SUNNI ISLAM

Bibliography. C. Ernst, *The Shambhala Guide to Sufism*; L. Lewisohn and D. Morgan, eds., *The Heritage of Sufism*; Naqshbandi-Haqqani Sufi Order of America, Naqshbandi Sufi Way home page, http://naqshbandi.org/; A. Schimmel, *Mystical Dimensions of Islam*.

D. B. Cook

SUKKOTH (THE FEAST OF TABERNACLES). The Feast of Tabernacles is mentioned in six passages: Leviticus 23:33–44; Numbers 29:12–34; Deuteronomy 16:13–15; Nehemiah 8:13–18; Zechariah 14:16–19; and John 7:1–10:2. It is called Hag Ha-Succot, the Feast of Booths or Feast of Tabernacles, because Jews were obligated to live in a *succah*, a booth or

tabernacle, on this occasion. It is a period of great rejoicing, when the Jewish people sing and dance, especially doing dances that are done in circuits.

In the Old Testament it was, first, a seven-day festival with an eighth day added to it. Second, people were to observe it by building booths or tabernacles to commemorate the forty years of wilderness wanderings. Third, it was to be celebrated with the four species, a fruit—the citron—and three types of branches: the palm branch, the myrtle branch, and the willow branch (usually tied together and called a *lulav*). Fourth, it was to be a time of rejoicing after the affliction of the Day of Atonement. Fifth, it also was a feast of firstfruits, in this case, the firstfruits of the fall harvest.

There are three key symbols in the Jewish observance of this feast. The first is the booth or tabernacle, which by Jewish practice is made of flimsy material to give the feeling of a temporary abode and provide a sense of the insecurity the Jewish people felt during the wilderness wanderings. The second is the lulav. Because the rainy season in Israel begins at this time of year, the lulav is used especially during the prayer for rain, when it is waved in every direction. The third symbol is the citron, a citrus fruit that symbolizes the fruit of the promised land.

See also JUDAISM

Bibliography. A. Fruchtenbaum, *The Feasts of Israel*; R. Posner, *Sukkot*; C. Roth, "Sukkoth," in *Encyclopedia Judaica*, edited by C. Roth; H. Schauss, *The Jewish Festivals: History & Observance*; I. Singer, "Sukkoth," in *The Jewish Encyclopedia*; M. Strassfeld, *The Jewish Holidays: A Guide & Commentary*; Y. Vainstein, *The Cycle of the Jewish Year: A Study of the Festivals and of Selections from the Liturgy*.

A. Fruchtenbaum

SULUK. In Sufi Islam, *suluk* is a prolonged and demanding process of purifying the soul. Sufis believe that practicing suluk brings peace during times of trial and gives them wisdom when they encounter challenges. The process of suluk is composed of three distinct stages: (1) The devotee strives to overcome the carnal soul (*nafs al-ammara*), a proclivity to be disobedient and to relish flouting the divine directives. Only Sufis who succeed in vanquishing the carnal soul are in a position to start stage 2 of their quest for purification. (2) The devotee takes notice of the rebukes of the reproaching soul (*nafs al-lawwama*), which chastises the devotee for his wicked actions and entreats him to be generous and compassionate. (3) The devotee works to cultivate a contented soul (*nafs al-mutma'inna*), which happens by means of severe and exacting self-discipline and perfect submission to God's will. Such persons allegedly develop the capacity to spend nearly six consecutive weeks concentrating on God.

See also SUFISM

Bibliography. A. J. Arberry, *Sufism: An Account of the Mystics of Islam.*

R. L. Drouhard

SUNNAH. In Islam *sunnah* ("trodden path" in Arabic) refers to the ways of life of the Prophet Muhammad that have been documented by trustworthy authorities and passed down to subsequent generations of Muslim believers. Customarily the sunnah is divided into those parts that are compulsory (*waajib*) and those that are merely promoted as profitable (*mustahabb*). The sunnah deals with many practical issues of Islamic ethics, ranging from prayer protocol to the allocation of time to be spent among multiple wives to the proper method of slaughtering camels. Islamic scholars and clerics have long debated which of the sunnah are required versus which are simply suggestions. Along with the Qur'an, the sunnah is used as a source from which Muslim jurists derive Islamic law. Sunni Islam considers only the deeds of Muhammad himself to be genuine sunnah, whereas

Shi'ism adds to Muhammad's example those of the twelve Holy Imams.

See also ISLAM, BASIC BELIEFS OF

Bibliography. H. Algar, *The Sunna: Its Obligatory and Exemplary Aspects*; T. W. Lippman, *Understanding Islam: An Introduction to the Muslim World*, 2nd ed.

R. L. Drouhard

SUNNI ISLAM. Sunni Islam is the largest denomination of Islam. The term *Sunni* derives from the Arabic for "people of the tradition [that is, the prophetic tradition] and the community" (Gordon, 17). The tradition to which Sunni refers is the tradition of Muhammad, who is believed to be the model for Muslim conduct. Sunnis accept the first four caliphs (leaders of the Muslim people) as having been "rightly guided," but they reject the Shi'ite belief that imams are able to speak with the authority of Allah as do the prophets in the Qur'an (Malbouisson, 14).

As much as Muhammad contributed to the faith of Islam, he failed to signify who would be the leader of this religion at his death. The Sunnis believed that leadership should be given to one who most exemplified both the spirit and the character of Muhammad. Shi'ites, on the other hand, believed Muhammad's successor should be from his family, and they thought Muhammad's cousin and son-in-law Ali should fill this leadership role. Support was voiced for a close friend of Muhammad's, Abu Bakr, who the Sunnis believed fit this role. Abu Bakr was appointed as the first caliph and led the Muslim community from 632 to 634. Sunnis consider themselves to be traditionalists of the Islamic faith who are "guardians of Islamic orthodoxy and tradition" (Hopfe and Woodward, 364). In fact, the word *Sunni* literally means "tradition" (Machatschke, 21). For Sunnis, the basis of religious and legal practice rests on the Qur'an and the hadith. Hadith is a collection of thousands of teachings that expand upon the basic teachings of the Qur'an.

There are two major schools of theology within Sunni Islam: the Mutazilites and the Asharites. These schools have historically differed in the areas they emphasized. The Mutazilites emphasized reason as the final arbiter of faith, human freedom, and responsibility; used an allegorical interpretation of the Qur'an; and believed that the Qur'an is eternal but the words that are used to convey it were created for seventh-century Islam. The Mutazilites' primary aim was to provide a rational account of the unity and justice of Allah (Robinson, 77). The Asharites emphasized revelation as the final authority, predestination as central to Islam, and belief that the Qur'an's words as well as its overall message are eternal and have eternally been with Allah; this was a retaining of orthodox Islamic theology (Zepp, 108). Another important aspect of Sunni Islam is the four schools of law within this tradition. Islamic law is known as Shari'ah law. Shari'ah law is based on the Qur'an and the sunna (a collection of deeds performed by Muhammad). Islamic law is studied at educational institutions known as madrasas. These four interpretations of law include Hanafi, Maliki, Shafi'i, and Hanbali. Despite the separation in different schools of law and theology, for the Sunni the final interpretation of the Qur'an and hadith lies with the ulama, who are a group of learned scholars. This, among other things, distinghishes Sunnis from Shi'ites, who rely on the religious leadership of the imams for definitive guidance for faith and practice (Zepp, 109).

See also ISLAM, BASIC BELIEFS OF; SHARI'AH; SHI'A ISLAM

Bibliography. C. E. Farrah, *Islam: Beliefs and Observances*, 7th ed.; M. S. Gordon, *Islam: Origins, Practices, Holy Texts, Sacred Persons, Sacred Places*; L. M. Hopfe and M. Woodward, *Religions of the World*, 11th ed.; R. Machatschke, *Islam*; C. D. Malbouisson, ed., *Focus on Islamic Issues*; N. Robinson, *Islam: A Concise Introduction*; I. G. Zepp, *A Muslim Primer*, 2nd ed.

T. S. Price

SUNYATA. In Mahayana Buddhism, *sunyata* (from *suna*, "void" in Sanskrit) refers to the "emptiness" or unreality of all things, even though they appear to exist as concrete, enduring substances. According to this doctrine, all perceived objects are merely phenomenal, are fundamentally impermanent, and lack independent existence (or even a metaphysical ground). The concept of sunyata is tightly linked to two other Buddhist doctrines: the illusory nature of personhood and dependent origination. Buddhism believes that the emptiness of the world is a corollary of the facts that (1) no true self exists and (2) nothing exists as an ontologically distinct entity. By realizing the truth of sunyata, Mahayana Buddhists believe they achieve release from *dukkha* (disquiet). Though maintaining many key features in common, various sects of Buddhism define sunyata slightly differently with respect to some of its less fundamental aspects. Many of these differences stem from competing views within Buddhist epistemology.

See also BUDDHISM; DUKKHA/DUHKHA

Bibliography. T. N. Hanh, *The Heart of the Buddha's Teaching*; C. Trungpa, *Glimpses of Shunyata*.

R. L. Drouhard

SUTRA. The word *sutra* literally means a rope or thread that holds things together. Derived from the Sanskrit verb *siv* (meaning "to sew"), the word refers to a collection of aphorisms in the form of a manual that acts as a rule of belief and/or practice. Linguistic standards for the composition of sutras were codified by the ancient grammarian Panini (ca. 400 BC). The Hindu sutras make up a set of texts that elaborate on several schools of Hindu philosophy, dealing with such varied subjects as metaphysics, cosmogony, the human condition, love, rituals, laws and customs, liberation (*moksha*) from the cycle of death and rebirth (*samsara*), dharma, karma, and reincarnation. In Buddhism the term *sutra* usually denotes those sacred texts thought to contain the authentic teachings of Gautama Buddha (563–483 BC). Adherents of Theravada Buddhism locate these teachings in the second section of the Tripitaka (Pali Canon); Mahayana Buddhists believe them to be found in a number of foundational writings, including the famous Diamond Sutra.

Several Hindu and Buddhist groups in the US look to various sutras as a basis for their doctrines and ethics. For example, the Sathya Sai Baba Society bases some of its teachings on the Brahma Sutras; Bhagwan Shree Rajneesh (1931–90), former leader of the Osho group, wrote a book eitled *The Heart Sutra: Discourses on the Prajnaparamita Hridayam Sutra*; the Lotus Sutra is a foundational text of Nichiren Shoshu Buddhism; and many American Zen practitioners look to *The Heart Sutra* for guidance.

See also BUDDHISM; DHARMA; HINDUISM; KARMA; MAHAYANA BUDDHISM; MOKSHA; REINCARNATION; THERAVADA BUDDHISM; TRIPITAKA; ZEN BUDDHISM

Bibliography. A. A. MacDonnell, *A History of Sanskrit Literature*; K. Mizuno, *Buddhist Sutras: Origin, Development, Transmission*; M. Monier-Williams, *A Sanskrit-English Dictionary*.

J. Bjornstad

SWAMI. Swami (Sanskrit, literally "sir" or "one who knows himself") is the honorific title normally prefixed to the name of a Hindu monk who belongs to an established order and is considered to have mastered the teachings of yoga. It is also used of someone who worships the gods with special devotion. In Indian usage, this term is sometimes suffixed (with the spelling -*svami*) to the name of a spiritual teacher or holy man.

In North American usage, Swami is usually prefixed to the name of a leading Hindu teacher of yoga or meditation, without the implication that that teacher belongs to a monastic order.

Many well-known figures have had the term applied to them, such as Swami Paramahansa Yogananda (the founder of Kriya Yoga), Swami Muktananda (the founder of Siddha Yoga), Swami Chinmayanda, and A. C. Bhaktivedanta Swami Prabhupada (the founder of the International Society for Krishna Consciousness [ISKCON]).

See also GURU; SHREE/SHRI/SRI

Bibliography. K. K. Klostermaier, *A Concise Encyclopedia of Hinduism*; V. Mangalwadi, *The World of Gurus*.

E. Pement and R. L. Drouhard

SYNAGOGUE. The term *synagogue* comes from the Greek term *synagogē*, which is the equivalent of the Hebrew name for *synagogue*, which is *knesset*. A synogogue is usually called *beit Knesset*, "house of gathering."

While rabbinic tradition dates the origin of the synagogue all the way back to Moses, the actual origins are obscure. The basic fact is that the concept arose in the Babylonian captivity, when the first temple was destroyed and therefore ceased to be a center of Jewish worship for seventy years. Furthermore, the Jews were in exile. The synagogue most likely simply began as a gathering place for believing Jews to study together the Scriptures of that time, and we know that Daniel had a copy of the book of Jeremiah (Dan. 9:1–3).

As a unique entity, the synagogue is not mentioned in the postexilic historical books such as Ezra, Nehemiah, or Esther, nor is it mentioned in the postexilic prophets of Haggai, Zechariah, and Malachi. Although the elements of the early synagogue would have been brought back into the land of Israel with the return of the Jews from Babylon, the synagogue did not become the center of Jewish life until AD 70, when the second temple was destroyed. Other sources suggest that the synagogue was already known to exist in the second century BC, when Jewish writings refer to public gatherings for the purpose of reading the scrolls of the Torah and singing certain hymns from the book of Psalms. As seen in the Gospels and contemporary Jewish literature, in the first century the synagogues were found throughout the land of Israel where there were Sabbath gatherings for the purpose of reading from the Law and the Prophets as well as hearing an exposition of the section that was read. Also by the first century, these synagogues were found among Jews throughout the diaspora; therefore, in most of the places to which Paul traveled, he found synagogues in which to present the gospel.

Prior to AD 70, the synagogue was viewed as having a triple function as a place for reciting the prayers, a place of instruction, and a place where communal needs could be met. The basic order of service in the synagogue prior to AD 70 included the recitation of the Ten Commandments, the *shema* (Deut. 6:4–8), and the Aaronic/priestly benediction (Num. 6:24–26). Also, the Torah (the five books of Moses) was divided into fifty-four portions, with a division read every Sabbath; thus the entire Torah was read every year (the Hebrew calendar has different year types as a result of the alignment of the lunar and solar calendars; as many as fifty-four weekly portions are needed). This was followed by the reading from the Prophets, but only segments from the Prophets were included; that division of the canon was not read in its entirety. Certain segments of the Ketuvim (Writings) would be read on a special occasions, such as the Song of Solomon being read during Passover, the book of Ruth being read during the Feast of Weeks, and so on. Furthermore, there were regular readings of the Torah on Mondays and Thursdays.

When the second temple was destroyed, the sacrificial system ceased to exist, and the Levitical priesthood ceased to function. The leading Pharisaic rabbis who survived the first Jewish revolt gathered together in the city of Yavne, and in the twenty-year period between AD 70 and 90 Judaism was totally revamped. During this time, the synagogue became the center of Jewish life, and the rabbi replaced the priest as the spiritual leader.

This is also when the format of the synagogue changed significantly. Thus many of the rituals and services performed in the temple were now transferred to the synagogue, and certain terms also changed. For example, the term *avoda* was originally applied to the sacrificial system but now was applied in the synagogue to the prayers of the synagogue. The Friday evening service and the Saturday morning service became an imitation of the evening and morning sacrifices of the temple. Five services are now held in the synagogue for Yom Kippur (Day of Atonement) to imitate the additional extra services on that day that were performed in the temple. Other services and rituals were totally excluded since they belonged to the temple only, such as the sacrificial system. Prayers and fasting replaced the sacrifices until the temple could be rebuilt.

Prior to AD 70, there was one official at the synagogue known as the *chazzan*, but after AD 70 a professional cantor was added, called the *baal keriah*. He was trained not merely to read the text of the Torah but also to chant it. The function of the chazzan was to bring out the Torah scrolls for the readings and to blow the *shofar*, or ram's-horn trumpet, to announce the inauguration of the Sabbath and the inauguration of the Jewish festivals. After AD 70, the rabbi replaced the chazzan as the head of the synagogue, though the chazzan still had a major role. Among the festivals, many rituals that were limited to the temple were also transferred to the synagogue, such as the blowing of the shofar and the carrying of the *lulav* (the branches for the Feast of Tabernacles). While architectural designs of synagogues vary from one Jewish community to another, synagogues are found both in simple forms and very elaborate forms. What is common is that they face Jerusalem and that in the front of the synagogue is what is called the ark, which contains the scrolls of the Law and the Prophets as well as other scrolls of the Writings. The bimah, or stage, is in the center or front center of the synagogue; different chosen men are called on to do the weekly readings from the bimah.

Men and women do not sit together. A one-level synagogue has a *mechitzah*, which is a screen of separation, with men on one side and women on the other. In a synagogue with a balcony, the men sit on the lower level and the women sit on the upper level behind the men, so that the men cannot see the women and be distracted from the focus of the synagogue service.

In ancient times, the synagogues were constructed near a body of water and always on the highest level of a city. But when Christianity became the state religion of the Roman Empire and churches were being built, and later on when Islam took over much of the eastern world, both churches and mosques had to be above the synagogue. To avoid unnecessary conflict, Jews built the synagogues on a lower level, and sometimes in a rather incognito style to avoid attracting unnecessary anti-Semitic attention.

In Reform Judaism, a number of changes have occurred. Orthodox Jews recognize only one temple (the one that existed in Jerusalem), and therefore they do not refer to their synagogues as "temples." Reform Judaism changed that. They rejected the sacrificial system at any future time and thus did not need a Jewish temple for that purpose. Therefore, many Reform synagogues are referred to as "Temple . . ." They also removed the mechitzah, and men and women do sit together in the Reform synagogue service. In Conservative Judaism, there are two basic attitudes. In some Conservative synagogues, men and women sit together, but in others they sit separately yet without the mechitzah between them.

In front of the ark, which is the chamber where the scrolls are kept, a light, known as the *ner tamid*, is kept burning as a reminder of the seven-branch menorah, or lampstand, that was previously in the temple.

The bimah is designed in the synagogue in such a way so that no matter where one sits one can hear the reading of the scrolls. The bimah is used only for the Torah readings. The sermon, or exposition of the day's Torah reading, is presented not from the bimah but from the *ammud*, a special lectern erected in front and to the right of the ark.

Orthodox synagogue services are always a cappella, whereas Reform synagogues have introduced musical instruments and choirs that are allowed on the Sabbath.

Sadly, throughout the centuries, as part of anti-Semitic campaigns, synagogues were continually destroyed in Muslim and so-called Christian countries. During the Holocaust, myriads of synagogues were destroyed or desecrated in Germany and other countries. On what is known as Kristallnacht (November 10, 1938), 280 synagogues were destroyed in Germany and 56 synagogues in Austria.

Today the Reform Judaism movement in the US has grown stronger, and synagogues have become not just houses of prayer and study but also Jewish community centers with elaborate facilities.

See also JUDAISM

Bibliography. R. Posner, *The Synagogue*; C. Roth, "Synagogue," *Encyclopedia Judaica*; I. Singer, "Synagogue," in *The Jewish Encyclopedia*.

A. Fruchtenbaum

SYNCRETISM. The term *syncretism* derives from the ancient political arena, where it originally referred to the Cretans, who united to face a common foe. In contemporary usage, however, it refers to the mixing of religious traditions. Modern examples would be the mix of voodoo folk-religion and Roman Catholicism in Haiti or the adoption of New Age thought and practice in American churches.

In the Old Testament, Israel's idolatrous syncretism, from the golden-calf episode at Sinai to the Baal worship of Elijah's time, is constantly punished by Yahweh and condemned by the prophets. In the New Testament, also, the apostles issue numerous warnings against syncretistic infiltration of the church (1 Cor. 8; 10; Col. 2:8–23; 1 John 5:21; Rev. 2:14, 20).

Modern missionaries labor daily to avoid syncretism while appropriately contextual-izing the gospel. This tension is not new; in Acts, on the one hand, the converted Ephesians renounce magic (19:18–19), while, on the other hand, Paul appeals to pagan philosophers to illumine his teaching of the biblical God (17:28–29; cf. Titus 1:12).

See also ROMAN CATHOLICISM

Bibliography. D. J. Hesselgrave and E. Rommen, *Contextualization: Meanings, Methods, and Models*; B. J. Nicholls, *Contextualization: A Theology of Gospel and Culture*; J. F. Shepherd, "Mission and Syncretism," in *The Church's Worldwide Mission*, edited by Harold Lindsell.

D. R. Streett

TALMAGE, JAMES. James E. Talmage (1862–1933) was a Mormon apostle, educator, and author. He was president of the University of Utah from 1894 to 1897 and an apostle of the LDS Church from 1911 until his death. Talmage was one of the most impressive intellectuals in LDS history; he was a member of several scientific societies and taught geology in addition to his more famous work as a Mormon theologian. His most important Mormon books were *The Articles of Faith* (1899) and *Jesus the Christ* (1915). In particular Talmage's *Articles of Faith*, a detailed commentary on the LDS scriptural text of the same name, functioned as a de facto systematic theology textbook for Mormons for most of the twentieth century. Talmage was also the principal author of "The Father and the Son: A Doctrinal Exposition by the First Presidency and the Twelve" (1916). This official doctrinal statement laid down what the LDS Church expected its members to believe about the names and divine statuses of the Father and the Son, issues on which Mormons had experienced significant confusion following the death of Brigham Young (especially because of his "Adam-God" teaching). To a large extent, what most Mormons believed throughout the rest of the twentieth century and still believe to this day is not the teachings of Joseph Smith or Brigham Young but the theological synthesis of their teachings with the Bible and the Mormon scriptures constructed by James Talmage.

See also ADAM-GOD THEORY; ARTICLES OF FAITH, MORMON; CHURCH OF JESUS CHRIST OF LATTER-DAY SAINTS

Bibliography. J. R. Talmage, *The Talmage Story.*

R. M. Bowman Jr. and C. J. Carrigan

TALMUD. The term *Talmud* comes from the root *lamad*, which can mean "to learn" or "to teach," depending on the grammatical form. Thus the term *Talmud* emphasizes primarily teaching and secondarily learning. The term is sometimes applied only to the Gemara section, but more often it is applied to both the Mishnah and the Gemara together. Furthermore, the term is applied to two major collections known as the Babylonian Talmud and what was historically known as the Palestinian Talmud. The preferred term now is Jerusalem Talmud or, more correctly, the Talmud of the Land of Israel, since it was produced in Galilee and not in Jerusalem. Both works underwent a long history beginning around 450 BC, with the Talmud of the Land of Israel being concluded in AD 425 and the Babylonian Talmud in 427.

First Stage: The Sopherim (450–30 BC). When the Jews returned from Babylonian captivity, their spiritual leaders who accompanied them recognized that the reason for the captivity was disobedience to the Mosaic law. Therefore, Ezra gathered these leaders into a school, called the School of the Sopherim, or the School of the Scribes. The purpose was to train them so that they could explain the law to the Jewish people. Thus the scribes would explain to the Jewish people all 613 commandments given by God through Moses: what was involved in keeping them and what was involved in breaking them. The Jewish people could keep the law and avoid further divine discipline only if they knew and kept the law (Ezra 7:10; Neh. 5:1–8). However, when the first generation of the Sopherim passed away, the next generation took the task more seriously and declared that it was not enough merely to explain the Law—the Torah—now it was essential to build a "fence" around it. The fence would consist of new rules and regulations that could be logically derived from the original 613 commandments. The thinking was that the Jews might break the laws of the fence (rabbinic law), but that might keep them from breaking *through* the fence, breaking the Mosaic law, and thus bringing on themselves further divine judgment. The goal was now to interpret individual cases of human behavior in terms of biblical precepts, to provide religious sanctions for all new institutions, and to derive from Scripture applications for any age.

The principle used was that a Sopher could disagree with a Sopher, but he could not disagree with the Torah. The Torah was given by God to Moses, and there is no basis to argue against its sanctity. But in making these new rules and regulations, the Sopherim could disagree among themselves until a decision was made by majority vote. Once the majority of the Sopherim voted on a new law, it became obligatory for all Jews everywhere in the world to follow. Furthermore, these new laws were intended not to be written down but to be passed down by memory from generation to generation; in fact would not be written down for six centuries.

The Sopherim made these new rules and regulations using a form of rabbinic logic known as *pilpul*, a Hebrew word that means "peppery" or "sharp" and refers to a form of rabbinic logic in which a rabbi states a law and then derives from it as many new laws as he can. Of course it isn't hard to see how this practice would lead to exponential growth in the number of laws.

Eventually hundreds of new laws were added to each of the 613 commandments God gave Moses. To the one commandment God gave about keeping the Sabbath, the rabbis innovated fifteen hundred additional Sabbath rules and regulations.

In the first century BC, two different schools of the Sopherim developed: the School of Shammai and the School of Hillel. Shammai was far more conservative and demanded a more stringent interpretation of the law. Hillel was more liberal and allowed for a much wider interpretation of the law. Thus Shammai limited divorce based strictly on the issue of immorality, whereas Hillel allowed divorce for any reason the husband would choose. Hillel was actually born in Babylon; he came to Israel for learning, studied in the rabbinic academies, and learned rabbinic principles of interpretation, which he perfected, thus making the development of the Talmud possible. He derived three key principles: first, each generation was not to reject previous rabbinic legislation; second, each generation must look at the Torah to arrive at new legislation; and, third, interpreters should apply general principles to particular instances.

Second Stage: The Tannaim (30 BC–AD 220). After the Sopherim came a second school of rabbis known as the Tannaim, who looked on the work of the Sopherim and determined that there were still too many holes in the fence. They would continue the process for another two and a half centuries, including the period of Jesus and the apostles.

The Tannaim updated their principle of operation. Whereas Sopherim could disagree with one another but not with the Torah, the principle of the Tannaim was that a Tanna could disagree with a Tana but not with a Sopher. Thus all the rules and regulations of the Sopherim now became sacrosanct, equal with Scripture. In order to justify that the rules of the Sopherim were equal with the rules of Moses, the Sopherim developed a theory that is still accepted in Orthodox Judaism to this day. It is taught that on Mt. Sinai, God gave Moses two separate laws. The first is the written law: the 613 commandments Moses actually penned into Exodus, Leviticus, Numbers, and Deuteronomy. But God also gave Moses the oral law, which was not written down. Moses simply memorized these additional thousands of new rules and regulations. He then passed them down by memory to Joshua, who passed them down to the judges, who passed them down to the prophets, who passed them down to the Sopherim. So the Sopherim did not innovate these new regulations and laws; they were simply passed down from Moses, who got them from God. Therefore, they were sacrosanct. Thus the Tannaim expected all Jews to submit not only to the Mosaic law but also to the rules of the Sopherim, to both the written law and the oral law. Jesus and the Pharisees contended sharply over this issue.

The two schools of Pharisaism continued until AD 70, when Jerusalem was destroyed. The key rabbi rising from that destruction was Yohanan ben Zakkai. According to rabbinic tradition, ben Zakkai opposed the revolt against Rome, and when Rome was under siege by Vespasian, ben Zakkai was able to escape from Jerusalem by being carried off in a coffin by his disciples. When he was brought before Vespasian, he predicted that Vespasian would become the next emperor, which shortly came to pass. As a result, Vespasian granted his request to set up a rabbinic school in Yavne. The school operated for twenty years, from AD 70 to 90, during which time the rabbis revamped Judaism as they sought to adapt it to the absence of the temple and the priesthood. Old national institutions had to be replaced by a new focus of loyalty, one that would at the same time perpetuate the memory of the temple. Prayer became the substitute for sacrifice, and the synagogue replaced the temple as the center of Jewish life. New rituals were adopted and adapted to reinforce the symbolic link between the synagogue and the temple, and the rabbis also attempted to establish and exercise spiritual control over the Jews of the diaspora. Thus Yavne became the new center of authority, and laws were passed to authenticate the authority of the new center.

The School of Yavne officially closed the Old Testament canon of the Hebrew Bible, or the Old Testament, as we have it today. The school collected many traditions and issued *takanot* (rabbinic enactments) as the need arose. These rabbis codified the Shmoneh Esreh (Eighteen Benedictions), which were to be recited daily.

The new Sanhedrin was now under Gamaliel, who was of the house of Hillel. He ended the conflict between the Schools of Hillel and Shammai by decreeing that the words of both Hillel and Shammai were the words of God. However, the rabbis of the School of Yavne believed that Judaism would not survive if the division continued and that the populace needed to unify the practice of Jewish law, so with a few exceptions Hillel's view became actual Jewish law and all sages had to submit to the decisions of the High Court. Thus the School of Yavne highly enhanced the authority of the rabbi.

As Judaism moved into the second century, the leading rabbi was Rabbi Akiva, who began to gather the chaotic mass of oral law and bring it into some semblance of order. He tried to find biblical justification for every rabbinic tradition and was the first to arrange the material according to subject. This key contribution introduced logical order to rabbinic law, but Rabbi Akiva also resorted to far-fetched interpretation without any consistent rules. He declared Bar Kokhba to be the Messiah, and as a result of his actions in support of Bar Kokhba, after the second Jewish revolt ended, he was executed by the Roman authorities.

After the Bar Kokhba revolt failed, disciples of Rabbi Akiva set up a new school in Usha in Galilee (since Yavne had been destroyed). The new Sanhedrin was now under the authority of Shimon ben Gamaliel, who received the title Nasi, carrying the authority of the patriarch. New rabbinic academies were founded in Galilee. Jews were forbidden to enter Jerusalem, and as the Jewish population of Judah decreased rapidly after the failure of the revolt, Galilee became the true center of Jewish life. The rabbis of the latter part of the second century continued to elaborate on the work of Akiva, without putting it into writing. They also attempted to stem the high rate of emigration by decreeing that it was better for a man to live in Israel in a city with a gentile majority than to live in an all-Jewish city in the diaspora. Living in Israel was equivalent to fulfilling all the commandments of the law, and to be buried in Israel was like being buried under the altar.

The rabbis focused on the Hebrew language, and the use of Aramaic and Greek was now forbidden in the academies of Galilee. As previously they ruled by majority vote, but the minority viewpoint was to be recorded. Another major contribution of these rabbis was the production of a unified Hebrew calendar, which is still used by the Jewish community today.

The period of the Tannaim finally ended with a key rabbi known as Judah Ha-Nasi (170–220). He was the leader of the Second Patriarchate, and his primary activity was in the Galilean city of Beth Shearim. He finally permitted all the traditions to be written down, drawing on thirteen previous collections, recording traditions handed down in the name of 115 previous rabbis going back four or five centuries. What was finally recorded in written form became known as the Mishnah, which is a Hebrew document of about fifteen hundred pages. It was divided into six specific orders:

1. Zeraim (Seeds)—dealing with agriculture problems and ritual laws associated with them
2. Moed (Feasts)—dealing with the rabbinic laws concerning the Sabbath and the festivals and holy seasons
3. Nashim (Women)—dealing with marriage and sexual relations
4. Nezikin (Damages)—dealing with civil and criminal law
5. Kodashim (Holy Things)—dealing with sacrifices and rituals of the temple
6. Tohorot (Cleanliness or Purity)—dealing with ceremonial cleanness

The six orders were divided into tractates, the tractates into chapters, and chapters into *mishnayot*, or verses. However, not every tractate necessarily deals with the biblical order it is in. For example, the Order of Seeds contains a tractate on the command to leave the corners of one's property unharvested so that the poor people can eat from these corners. This is followed by a tractate on the rules of Purim (the Feast of Lots). The logic followed here is that the yield of the soil and the enjoyment of life are associated with the gratitude due to God.

With the Mishnah now in officially recorded form, the period of the Tannaim ended.

Third Stage: The Amoraim (220–427). Now began a third school of rabbis known as the Amoraim, whose name is an Aramaic term that comes from a root meaning "to say" and carries the concept of teaching. They focused on the intensive study and interpretation of the Mishnah, yet they believed that the Mishnah did not contain all that was handed down through various generations, so they accumulated additional traditions. The task of the Amoraim was to collect and codify these traditions and give them a stamp of finality. However, they also viewed the fence as still having too many holes in it, and

507

so they began to add even more rules and regulations. Once again they changed their principle of operation: an Amora can disagree with an Amora but not with a Tanna. Thus all the work and regulations and traditions of the Tannaim also became sacrosanct, equal with Scripture. The Amoraim produced the Gemara. The term Gemara comes from the Aramaic root *gamar*, which means "to learn"; thus Gemara basically means "learning" and is the Aramaic form for the Hebrew name Talmud.

The work on the Mishnah was carried out in two localities: the land of Israel (primarily in Galilee) and Babylonia. By far the most intensive work was done in the academies of Babylonia, which superseded the work done in the land of Israel. The Babylonian work would dominate Jewish life for the next eight centuries and still dominates Orthodox Jewish life today.

There were two main Babylonian academies. The first was Neherdea, founded under Mar Samuel (d. 254), a pupil of Judah Ha-Nasi. Mar Samuel advocated the independence of the Babylonian School from the academies of Israel. Then he brought in all traditions of native Babylonian learning. The School of Neherdea was later replaced by the school of Pumbedita, founded by Rabbi Judah bar Ezekiel. The School of Pumbedita now became the main source of expertise in civil law. This school developed the principle that the law of the land is the law Jews must follow, even if it conflicts with the laws they would obey if they were independent. This principle applied only to civil law, not to religious law.

The second major academy of Babylonia was in Sura, established by Rav Abba Arika, (d. 247), also a pupil of Judah Ha-Nasi. He transplanted much of the learning of the land of Israel to Babylonia and adopted many Israeli customs. The result of these two Babylonian schools was the production of the Babylonian Gemara, which

is the Aramaic interpretation of the Mishnah; it was finally completed under Rav Ashi (352–427), the head of the Academy of Sura. The Babylonian Gemara is about the size of the *Encyclopedia Britannica*—a massive body of rabbinic work.

The Jerusalem Gemara, or the Gemara of the land of Israel, was begun by Yohanan bar Nappach (199–279), the head of the academy in Tiberias. It was completed in AD 425. The Gemara here focuses more on the conditions in the land. It lacks completeness and totality, thanks to economic and political problems as well as persecution now coming from the church. Thus the Talmud of the Land of Israel lacks the continuity of the Babylonian Talmud, and its main value is historical, providing details on the conditions of the land. The language of the Israeli Gemara is also Aramaic (sometimes called "Western Aramaic" to distinguish it from the Aramaic used in Babylonia).

What is referred to as the Talmud in most cases is the Mishnah and the Gemara put together, though sometimes the term is used more specifically of just the Gemara section, which is the larger section in both Talmuds.

The Talmud essentially contains five items. First is the halacha, which involves the actual laws that all Jews must follow. This in turn includes pilpul, a rabbinic process, described above, for generating new laws. Also included are the *tannakot*, which are rabbinic enactments claiming authority even to void some of the laws of the Torah. The key areas of concern were God, Torah, and Israel.

The second type of content is the aggadah and the haggadah. The aggadah are imaginative interpretations of the Jewish past. The haggadah covers everything else that is not halacha, which includes issues of history, folklore, medicine, biography, ethical teachings, astronomy, science, logic, and personal reminiscences of great teachers of the past. The aggadah and haggadah are narratives, not legal texts, and reflect many personal opinions of the rabbis. Passages of this type tend to digress from the starting point of the discussion into the topics described above.

The third element of the Talmud is midrash, constituting about one half of the Talmud and consisting of rabbinic interpretations and homilies of the Bible.

The fourth element is the Tosefta, additional laws from the Mishnaic period that are considered supplementary and of lesser authority.

The fifth element is baraita, an old tradition but one that does not carry the authority of a specific Tanna.

Fourth Stage: The Seboraim (Sixth and Seventh Centuries). The Hebrew term *Seboraim* means "the reasoners." The Seboraim were gathered by Rabina II of Babylonia. They came into being after a thirty-year gap in the Babylonian Jewish community, during which time the academies were closed. Up to this time, the collections of the Talmud consisted of concise notes on rabbinic discussions. The Seboraim enlarged the Talmud by adding words, phrases, and the notes to show how a discussion was to be read, which rendered the Talmud understandable for future generations. The Seboraim were responsible for completing the Talmud, especially the Babylonian Talmud in its final form.

The Talmud has often been misunderstood. For example, one tractate of the Talmud is called Beitzah, which means "egg." Critics claimed that the rabbis spent a whole tractate on the egg alone. However, the name of the tractate was based only on the first word, which was common in Jewish naming of a document.

The Talmud has also often been accused of falsehoods, often becoming a target of Christianity. Because of largely untrue assumptions, through the ages many copies of the Talmud have been burned. So many were destroyed, in fact, that very few manuscripts remain. The Talmud has tended to suffer far more abuse in so-called Christian countries than it ever suffered in Muslim countries.

See also JUDAISM

Bibliography. N. T. L. Cardozo, *The Written and Oral Torah: A Comprehensive Introduction*; A. Cohen, *Everyman's Talmud*; D. W. Halivni, *Midrash, Mishnah, and Gemara: The Jewish Predilection of Justified Law*; J. Neusner, *Invitation to the Talmud: A Teaching Book*; Neusner, ed. and trans., *Scriptures of the Oral Torah: Sanctification and Salvation in the Sacred Books of Judaism*; Neusner, *The Yerushalmi: An Introduction*; C. Roth, "Talmud," in *Encyclopedia Judaica*, edited by C. Roth; I. Singer, "Talmud," in *The Jewish Encyclopedia*; H. Strack, *Introduction to the Talmud and Midrash*.

A. Fruchtenbaum

TANACH. The term *tanach* is an acronym based on the first letter of each of the three divisions of the Hebrew Bible, what Christians refer to as "the Old Testament." The three divisions are the Torah (Law), Neviim (Prophets), and Ketuvim (Writings).

While the content of the Hebrew Bible and the Christian Old Testament is the same, the order of the books is not. The Christian Old Testament order is based primarily on the Septuagint, a Greek translation of the Old Testament done around 250 BC. The Hebrew Bible has its own order, which is as follows:

1. The Torah consists of Genesis, Exodus, Leviticus, Numbers, and Deuteronomy.

2. The Neviim consists of Joshua, Judges, 1 Samuel, 2 Samuel, 1 Kings, 2 Kings, Isaiah, Jeremiah, Ezekiel, Hosea, Joel, Amos, Obadiah, Jonah, Micah, Nahum, Habakkuk, Zephaniah, Haggai, Zechariah, and Malachi.

3. The Ketuvim consists of Psalms, Proverbs, Job, Song of Solomon, Ruth, Lamentations, Ecclesiastes, Esther, Daniel, Ezra, Nehemiah, 1 Chronicles, and 2 Chronicles.

This is the order Jesus was familiar with, as can be seen in Luke 24:44 and Matthew 23:35 (the murder of Zechariah, which Jesus mentions in the latter passage, is narrated at the end of 2 Chronicles).

Christians speak of thirty-nine books of the Old Testament, but the Jews speak of twenty-four books of the Hebrew Bible because certain books that the Christian Bible separates are counted as one book in the Hebrew Bible. Thus, in the Hebrew Bible, Samuel and Kings are one book, 1 and 2 Chronicles are one book, Ezra and Nehemiah are one book, and the twelve Minor Prophets make up one book.

See also JUDAISM

Bibliography. C. Roth, "Tanach," in *Encyclopedia Judaica*, edited by C. Roth; I. Singer, "Tanach," in *The New Jewish Encyclopedia*.

A. Fruchtenbaum

TANTRA. *Tantra* (Sanskrit, "weave," with the idea of continuity) refers to a collection of Sanskrit texts and manuals that appeared concurrently in Hinduism and Buddhism, in a pan-Indian religious movement around the sixth century AD. These texts deal with metaphysics, yoga, temple and idol construction, and esoterica. The tantra texts also outline techniques for gaining *siddhis*, or powers acquired through yogic practice: mundane or worldly siddhis include, for example, the power to fly, walk through walls, and turn metals into gold, and the supramundane or transcendent siddhi is the experience of personal empowerment.

Etymologically, the word *tantra* is derived from "loom" or "weaving" or "thread," incorporating the idea of creation, the meshing together of two items (the warp and the woof), expansion, and continuum. In tantric practice, then, the practitioner experiences an expansion of consciousness by the unification of opposites, so that one may recognize the interconnectedness of existence and experience spontaneous metaphysical

empowerment. Tantrism informs Hinduism, Jainism, Buddhism, New Age thinking, and modern sexual psychology.

Tantra in Hinduism. The earliest tantra texts emphasize the goddess Shakti as the female personification of creative power. In the Yoga tantras, Shakti is identified with kundalini, the energy coiled snakelike at the base of the spine waiting to be enticed up through the body by the yogic disciplines. These early tantric texts also explain *yantras* (ritual symbols), mandalas (ritual cosmic maps), mantras (mystical formulas), and *mudras* (ritual gestures). Other texts outline ritual copulation and magic.

Tantrism in Hinduism is viewed variously. Its "right hand" expression (*daksinacara*) is moderate and text based, while its "left hand" expression (*vamacara*) is innovative, extreme, and centered on the goddess Kali. The fundamental metaphysics of the left-hand expression is that, contrary to mainstream Hindu metaphysics, spiritual progress is achieved not by asceticism (avoiding desires) but by embracing and transforming desires (or opposites) so that they become a means of liberation.

In tantric metaphysics, man and woman are seen as expressions of the two fundamental macrocosmic energies, represented by Shiva (the male principle) and Shakti (the female principle). Hence the Hindu god Shiva and his female consort, Shakti (also known as Devi, Durga, Parvati, and Kali), predominate. These opposite principles need to be balanced; this is achieved through a variety of means, including ritual tools (yantras, mandalas, mantras, mudras) that are used variously to invite and subsequently to be empowered by the god one is invoking. More noticeably, metaphysical unity is achieved through ritual sexual intercourse. Hence sexual expression in Hinduism is not uncommon: Shiva and Shakti are depicted in sitting copulation; the *yoni-lingam* (the phallus within the womb) is venerated; the cult of Kali gives its name to

510

Kalikut, or Calcutta. The film *Indiana Jones and the Temple of Doom* (1984) played on these themes.

The balanced union of the two opposites, the female and the male, allegedly culminates in the liberation of mind and body from the endless cycle of existence (samsara). In essence, when male and female are in sexual fusion, the infinite possibilities of both are fully realized when their dormant psychosexual powers are aroused and expressed as a microcosm of the macrocosmic unity. The female aspect is energy, while the male aspect is consciousness: the perfect union of the nondual. Hence tantra claims that a harmony between sexuality and spirituality is possible. Sexual fusion becomes a sacred act through which, when it is accompanied by supplementary devotional practices (meditation, visualization, recitation of mantras), one may evolve into Supreme Absolute (in Hinduism) or achieve enlightenment (in Buddhism).

Tantra in Buddhism. The Buddhist tantric texts were translated into Tibetan and Chinese from about the eighth century AD, although we still have some in Sanskrit. The tantric master Padmasambhava took these texts along with the Buddhist canon to Tibet and translated them into Tibetan. The use of the word *vajra* (diamond/thunderbolt, also cudgel or scepter) signifies the absolutely real or the indestructible quality of humans as opposed to the delusions they entertain about themselves. Hence Tibetan Buddhist tantra—or *vajrayana*—claims to be the highest expression of Buddhism, through which humans' ultimate fictions can be expelled, and hence achievement of nirvana is possible spontaneously. This practice is now readily accessible to Westerners through the global spread of Tibetan Buddhism since the 1960s.

Like Hindu tantrism, enlightenment in Buddhist tantrism arises from the realization that seemingly opposite principles are in truth one. The sexual motif expresses more than just unity of the polarities of active-male-means and passive-female-wisdom; it also expresses the union of voidness (*sunyata*) and compassion (*karuna*), mind and body, sensory and psychic. These all merge into unity aided by the use of sound (mantra), gesture (mudra), and sight (mandalas) to focus one's mind so as to prevent it from straying into delusions. The mandala especially is a tool that one uses in an attempt to achieve this: it is a physical representation of the nature of reality (and the cosmos). Its symbolism is total: mind, deity, samsara, unity, spiritual path, nirvana—all draw the meditative practitioner into the oneness of the cosmos. Curiously, in the mandala, even the opposites of samsara and nirvana combine: contrary to orthodox Buddhist belief, where the aim is to escape from samsara, in the mandala, consciousness is expanded and one is liberated by embracing the sensory so as to transform it within samsara, the cycle of existence, all by using the energies of the body as the fuel for spiritual evolution.

This reaches its highest expression in the Kalacakra Tantra, once a well-hidden initiation but now a public spectacle, which, according to the Dalai Lama, is offered to the West to dispel misunderstandings about Tibetan Buddhism and to increase compassion and peace. Kalacakra, which means "Wheel of Time," is the name of one of the Buddhas that represent particular aspects of the enlightened mind and is said to dwell in the Kalacakra mandala. Traditionally the viewing of this laboriously constructed sand mandala forms the culmination of a twelve-day initiation ritual, but the Dalai Lama has liberally promoted the rite of the mandala construction around the world as a Tibetan cultural offering.

Practitioners use the Kalacakra mandala as a visualization tool in meditation as they symbolically progress on the path to enlightenment. In the Kalacakra mandala, 722 inhabitants reside. These are manifestations of Kalacakra—all portrayed within a two-meter-diameter circle constructed out of multicolored sand. Kalacakra—*kala* meaning "time," and *cakra*, "circle"—is the one unity: the practitioner enters the mandala meditatively from the mandala's purifying fiery external perimeter, through the symbolic four-walled castle, into the center so as to join with the Buddha, become one with him, and so experience enlightenment. If one psycho-physically joins with an enlightened being, one becomes enlightened oneself. The construction and destruction of the Kalacakra mandala was portrayed in the film *Kundun* (1997) as a metaphor for the rise of the fourteenth Dalai Lama and his subsequent escape from Tibet.

Tibetan Buddhists claim that tantric practice is the most powerful Buddhist practice. They claim that in tantra, especially in Kalacakra, the full integration of skillful means and wisdom overcomes the mundane and that the tantric path is therefore the speediest, in that it brings the very nature of the Buddha mind into one's practice spontaneously. The highest levels of this tantra utilize levels of bodily energies and consciousness that are inaccessible to the layperson and can only be known through esoteric knowledge passed down from master to initiate.

In some explanations, all prior meditative practice is preparatory for tantra's ultimate empowering. Initially in Buddhism, one wants to cultivate self-discipline, meditative concentration, and the wisdom that understands emptiness. When one achieves these, then one can commence the compassionate path of the bodhisattva, in which one aspires to achieve the highest enlightenment for the benefit of all sentient beings by training and transforming the mind. When one improves the quality of one's mind, not only does one benefit oneself, but indirectly one also benefits all other sentient beings. Training the mind is the key to achieving lasting peace and happiness. An essential part of this process is to aspire to the six perfections of generosity,

self-discipline, patience, effort, meditative stabilization, and wisdom. Only then will the tantric practice complement one's progress and empower the mind to nirvana. In other explanations, all these aspects are engaged on the tantric path.

The Dalai Lama promotes Kalacakra Tantra initiation in the West because he regards it as especially applicable for today's conditions. In a world of turmoil, the world is deemed in need of powerful medicine. The Kalacakra Tantra claims to tame the mind and increase wisdom and realize the bodhisattva ideal of compassion. When these are done, it will benefit the world by leading it toward peace.

All constructed sand mandalas are erased at their completion and dissipated into a local body of water, symbolizing variously the impermanence of existence, the release of the Buddha and deities dwelling therein, the spread of peace into the world, and/or the appeasement of *nagas* (river spirits) in the waters.

Tantra and New Age. Tantrism has a countercultural impulse: it reversed many Hindu social practices; incest became part of practice, for example, and the five purifying qualities of the cow (milk, butter, curds, urine, and feces) were changed to copulation, fish, flesh, parched grain, and wine. Widely spread throughout India until the invasion of the Moghuls in the thirteenth century, tantrism then went underground due to Muslim repression. However, this countercultural, even rebellious impulse has caused it to emerge openly within the New Age movement.

Because of the strong feminine fertility motif, tantra has comfortably combined with wicca, witchcraft, paganism, angelology, yoga, goddess movements (especially Tara), and alchemy. Common to these movements is the raising of psychosexual energy: the curled serpent (kundalini), lying at the base of the spine, is invited, by means of yogic, visualizing, and meditative techniques, upward through the body's seven successive focal points (chakras), until it reaches the highest chakra, at the top of the skull, where the practitioner experiences the union of the goddess within (Shakti) with the god from without (Shiva). This process begins with visualization of the deity, who materializes through the use of yantras (visual symbols) and the recitation of mantras (mystical syllables).

Bhagwan Shree Rajneesh promoted a socially volatile brew of amoral monism during the 1970s and 1980s, mixing Hindu tantra, Zen Buddhism, and exploitive capitalism at his Osho Commune International in Pune, India, then later at Rajneeshpuram in Oregon, for which he earned the contempt of both the US and Indian governments and the cynicism of damaged ex-devotees.

Various new movements are emerging. Neo-tantrism is an open, non-esoteric modern interpretation with democratic (rather than strict lineage) authority structures, including tantric communities of support for practitioners. Quantum Tantra aims at a deep union with nature, assisted by the insights of physics and alchemy. Rainbow Tantra aligns the seven bodily chakras with the colors of the rainbow and hence combines aurasoma, tantra, and yoga in a united path to deity.

Western Sexual Psychology. In the West, tantra is often called the "Yoga of Sex" or "Sacred Sex," where the path of ecstasy and the experience of orgasm are regarded as the gateway to a metaphysical enlightenment. This fits nicely with the sexual liberalism that has developed in Western culture since the 1960s and provides some sense of spiritual legitimacy to sexual promiscuity. It conveniently overlooks the history of tantra's priority on the union of opposites inasmuch as ritual sexual union was often done not with pretty virgins but with elderly women.

Tantra in the West claims to make sex sacred in that it uses the sexual energy to expand one's spirituality. One's lover is regarded as

a manifestation of the universal divine energy, and the sexual act can therefore be a vehicle to further intimacy, self-knowledge, spiritual evolution, and ultimately to oneness with deity. While literature now abounds with these themes, the Kama Sutra, a sexual-technique manual dating from approximately the fourth century AD and published in English in 1963, became one of the founding texts of the post-1960s sexual revolution and remains popular today.

See also BODHISATTVA; BUDDHISM; DALAI LAMA XIV (TENZIN GYATSO); HINDUISM; JAINISM; KALACAKRA; KALACAKRA TANTRA; KUNDALINI; MANDALA DIAGRAM; MANTRA; MUDRA; SHAKTI; TANTRIC YOGA; TIBETAN BUDDHISM; YOGA

Bibliography. D. Burnett, *The Spirit of Buddhism: A Christian Perspective on Buddhist Thought*; Burnett, *The Spirit of Hinduism: A Christian Perspective on Hindu Thought*; T. Gyatso, *Freedom in Exile: The Autobiography of the Dalai Lama of Tibet*; D. S. Lopez Jr., *The Story of Buddhism: A Concise Guide to Its History and Teachings*; M. Magee, "Introduction," Shiva Shakti Mandalam website, http://www.shivashakti.com; V. Mangalwadi, *The World of Gurus: A Critical Look at the Philosophies of India's Influential Gurus and Mystics*; D. G. White, *Tantra in Practice*.

H. P. Kemp

TANTRIC YOGA. Tantric Yoga claims that the universal can be experienced from the viewpoint of the individual. The individual is a microcosm of the macrocosm: if one can discipline the microcosm through tantric yoga, then one can experience macrocosmic unity and thus expand one's consciousness. When this occurs, one transcends the obstacles of ignorance, intolerance, attachment, and selfishness and can experience peace, harmony, and order.

Tantric Yoga understands the universe as a product of opposites: the male principle (Shiva) and the female principle (Shakti), a generic fertility goddess. Tantric Yoga seeks to unify these: the kundalini, the female energy coiled at the base of the spine, is enticed up through the body's seven energy centers (chakras) to the head chakra, where it unites with male shivaic energy.

Tantric Yoga assumes that one achieves empowerment not through suppressing the senses (asceticism) but by transforming the senses; hence, one embraces sensuality. Tantric Yoga therefore uses sound (mantras), gestures (*mudras*), and sight (*yantras*), within a paradigm of meditative yogic postures. The power of sexual desire is harnessed and transformed; hence ritual copulation unites the Shakti-Shiva duality into unity. Thus by combining generic breathing exercises (*pranayama*), contemplation, visualization, chanting of a mantra, and ritual copulation, Tantric Yoga claims to join one's inherent divine nature with the divine unity of the cosmos.

See also CHAKRAS; HINDUISM; KUNDALINI; MANTRA; SHAKTI; SHIVA; YOGA

Bibliography. T. Skorupski, "Sakyamuni's Enlightenment according to the Yoga Tantra," in *Buddhism: Critical Concepts in Religious Studies.*

H. P. Kemp

TAOISM/DAOISM. According to tradition, Taoism (also spelled Daoism; pronounced "Dowism"), whose name is an umbrella term, was founded by Lao Tzu (Laozi) around the seventh century BC. Most modern researchers hold that Taoism as an organized, identifiable tradition arose between about 100 BC and AD 200 with the aggregation of three streams that contain much that predates this formulation. These streams are (1) the philosophical speculations of the Lao Tzu, the Chuang Tzu (Zhuang-zi), Huang-Lao, the Lieh-tzu (Liezi), and others; (2) alchemical practices; and (3) the revelations of the gods. In addition, diverse practices and philosophies have found a home under this heading. For example, the School of Names and

Yin-Yang ideology have clearly had a notable impact. Further, the presence of Buddhism has generated both positive and reactionary developments that have been instrumental in the formation of Taoism.

At times almost everything not specifically associated with Buddhism or Confucianism was identified as Taoist. However, much of this—including some of the gods, various practices, and even rituals—is in fact general Chinese spirituality and finds no mention in the Taoist canon. These elements must be distinguished from those that are sanctioned in the canon and rightly noted as Taoist.

Doctrinal Sources. The Lao Tzu (a.k.a. Tao Te Ching / Dao de jing), allegedly composed by the founding master, was probably the work of several authors. The earliest version of the text, unearthed through excavation, can be dated to about 300 BC and is called the Guodian Chu Slips (Guodian chujian). The earliest commentaries take the text as a legalist work, and not until the first century BC was it reclassified as a Taoist work. It is a collection of aphorisms on many topics, including wisdom, returning to the Tao, vacuity, naturalness, yin values, politics, harmony, ineffability, and complementary duality. The Lao Tzu is mentioned by Ssu-ma Ch'ien (Sima Qian) in his Records of the Grand Historian (ca. second century BC), but his accounts leave little ground for establishing historical fact. The Lao Tzu became a classic and was part of the canon of well-read people in ancient times, although it usually did not have the status of a text used in the governmental examination system.

The Chuang Tzu (Zhuang-zi) was composed by Chuang Tzu (ca. 369–286 BC). One of the great compositions of the world, this work has an incredible ability to take profound points and address them with amusing stories. For example, on the topic of the relativity of identity, the writer tells of dreaming that he was a butterfly fluttering around when he suddenly woke up. Then he was not sure if he was a butterfly dreaming he was Chuang Tzu or Chuang Tzu dreaming he was a butterfly. His writings reject politics and emphasize mystic identity with the Tao and the spiritual freedom that brings. The Chuang Tzu also expresses great sympathy toward nature.

Huang-Lao, named after the alleged teachings of the Yellow Emperor (Huang-ti/Huangdi) and Lao Tzu, was philosophically a combination of legalist thought with speculations of the Lao Tzu. Silk manuscripts found in the Former Han tomb located at Mawangtui contained the Lao Tzu as well as interesting appended materials including a supposed dialogue between the Yellow Emperor and his ministers. The teachings include discussions on rewards and punishments, name and performance, the ruler and the mechanisms of state, yin-yang complementary dualism, and more. This classification also includes much of what is found in the Huai Nan Tzu (Huainanzi), a philosophical encyclopedic work of the second century BC.

Although Lieh Tzu perhaps lived in the fifth century BC, the volume that bears his name is probably the work of the third century AD. This work is also titled The Pure Classic of the Perfect Virtue of Simplicity and Vacuity (Ch'ung-hsu Chih-te Chen-Ching / Chongxu zhide zhenjing). Considered the most accessible of the Taoists' philosophical works, like the others, it is a collection of diverse writings. Skeptical in tone and presenting more fatalistic opinions than other Taoist works, it treats topics including death, heightened perceptive sensitivity, actions based on adaptability (i.e., effortless, unimpeded movement), the illusory nature of sense perceptions, the Confucian faith in knowledge (which it critiques), the futility of common sense, the decree of heaven (i.e., destiny), hedonism, and chance conjunctions of events. The chapter on the illusory nature of sense perceptions shows considerable Buddhist influence, and the chapter on hedonism is out of keeping with the rest of the work, indicating different authorship.

Alchemy. Alchemical practices include various methods of inner cultivation as well as the search for physical immortality. The techniques of inner cultivation include controlling bodily fluids (urine, breath, etc.), meditation, dietary regimens (e.g., avoiding grains), physical exercises often accompanied by breath control, sexual practices, and more. Yet even within this array of cultivated techniques, there was considerable variation. For example, meditation may include visualizations, abstract meditations (with or without specific breathing techniques), visions of the gods, ecstasy, and others. Sexual practices begin from the position that a man has a predominant amount of yang energy, and a woman, yin energy. Women's energy cannot be depleted; however, man must be reserved in his expenditures. Extremes in either yin or yang energy need to be avoided, and balance is sought. Man can obtain heightened spiritual states and even immortality by repeatedly absorbing yin energies from qualified individuals. The reverse is true for women.

The external alchemy emphasized the creation of immortality pills produced by combining various herbs and minerals in a crucible and transmuting them through heat. One of the key ingredients seems to have been cinnabar (mercury sulfate), and thus the opposite of the desired effect was often obtained. These practices were popular among those who could afford them in the early centuries of the current era but later fell out of use in favor of the inner alchemical practices.

Revelations. For the Taoists before the current era, the microcosmic world inside the body and the macrocosmic world outside are both filled with the same gods. Within the body, associated with all aspects of the mythic microcosm, there are thousands of gods. The most common number encountered is thirty-six thousand. These gods in the body have their counterparts in the macrocosm, which tends to have a structure similar to that of the imperial bureaucracy, with its palaces, departments, and bureaus. However, since many different revelations come from immortals and gods, there is a great diversity of opinions regarding these gods, their names, their functions, their titles, their costumes, their palaces, and their numbers. These works came to the human realm by way of "mediums." This diversity prevented the creation of a pan-Taoist authoritative hierarchy or even lore. On the other hand, in the current era, the Three Pure Ones— Jade Pure (not to be confused with the Jade Emperor, king of heaven), the Upper Pure, and Great Pure (deified Lao Tzu)—are most commonly encountered. There are also the eight Immortals, who play a significant role.

Taoist adepts had to cultivate a relationship with these gods according to which revelations the adepts had an affiliation with, according to destiny. To do this, they could enter into various lengthy meditational practices and thus get in touch with the inner gods in the early period or the external gods in the current era, or they could go into retreat in remote regions and hope to encounter an immortal personally. Learning this arcane lore was often a lengthy process taking many years. However, only by having a relationship with these gods could a master perform the many activities he or she was called on to undertake.

History. Although the philosophical works of Lao Tzu, Chuang Tzu, and others existed before the aggregation around the first century BC, the period of their composition and other praxis-related developments that are historically difficult to document can be termed the proto-Taoist historic period. The period from the founding of the first successful schools in the second century AD to the tenth century can be called the early classic period, when the foundation for further developments in Taoism was laid. From the eighth century to the early Ching (Qin) Dynasty (1644–1911) can be termed late classic period.

Early Classic Period. Chang Tao Ling (Zhang Daoling) received revelations from the deified Lao Tzu in about AD 142. Based on this, the philosophical texts (above) and miscellany, an organization called Five Pecks of Rice was established. Later known as the Way of the Celestial Masters, it is one of the major schools in Taoism today. Chang Tao Ling's grandson, Chang Lu (Zhang Lu), entered into open rebellion against the Han court at the time of the Yellow Turbans (Huang Jin Zhi Luan). In the fifth century, the school divided into the Northern and Southern Celestial Masters.

One of two other important movements at this time was the Yellow Turbans (founded ca. AD 170). The most influential text in this school was the Tai Ping Ching (Taiping jing), or Great Peace Classic (original now lost). This work originates with a shaman and was used by the founder Chang Chueh (Zhang Jiao, a.k.a. Zhang Jue; d. AD 184). Utopian and millenarian in nature, the school was highly critical of the existing Han government and eventually rose up in failed open rebellion trying to establish a Taoist theocracy. The other movement of significance was the "Dark Learning" (Hsuan Hsueh / Xuanxue) in the third and fourth centuries. Reacting to the fall of the Han Dynasty and philosophical in nature, the movement reinterpreted Lao-Chuang philosophy in light of Confucian norms. It also included metaphysical speculations and absorbed influences from the growing Buddhist movement.

The fourth century saw the founding of the Mao Shan sect (a.k.a. High Purity / Shang Ch'ing / Shangqing sect). Revelations received by Wei Huacun (ca. AD 251–334) were transmitted to her disciple Yang Hsi (Yang Xi). The school combined teachings from these revelations, the Way of the Celestial Masters, and other esoterica. It was influential until the fifteenth century. Also in the fourth century, the Sacred Jeweled (Ling Pao / Lingbao) sect emerged, combining new material and Mao Shan teachings with Buddhism. It was popular until the twelfth century, when it fell from grace.

Late Classic Period. Southern Taoism shows the reformation of the Celestial Master teachings under the influence of the Mao Shan and Sacred Jewel teachings. This reformulation is called the Orthodox Unity (Cheng-I/ Zhengyi) sect and dates from the thirteenth century. It is one of the major sects today (see below). Traditionally its headquarters was the Eastern Pearl Temple in Beijing.

Northern Taoism was divided into three sects: Complete Perfection (Chuan Chen P'ai / Quanzhen pai), Supreme-One (Tai-I/ Taiyi), and Perfect and Great Way (Chen Ta Tao). Founded in the twelfth century, the Complete Perfection sect combines Confucianism, Taoism, and Buddhism with emphasis on meditation and simplified rituals and decreased emphasis on texts. The sect is one of two surviving into the present. Its headquarters is the White Cloud Monastery in Beijing. Also founded in the twelfth century, the Supreme-One sect had celibate priests and was highly moralistic. It disappeared in the fourteenth century. The Perfect and Great Way was founded in the twelfth century as well. Moralistic, therapeutic, and studious, the sect discouraged reliance on magic. It lasted about 150 years.

Modern Period. The Celestial Master headquarters in China is in Louquan Temple southwest of Xian. In Taiwan, Zhang Enpu (1904–69), the sixty-third-generation grandmaster, after fleeing the Communist takeover and relocating in Taiwan, established several institutional and lay associations and established the Taiwan branch headquarters at the Enlightened Cultivation Temple (Zuexiu gong) in Taipei. His efforts along with those of many others helped reinvigorate Taoism on the island and made it one of the most important centers of Taoism in the world. He also was instrumental in preserving the tradition for future generations.

The Complete Perfection sect headquarters is located in the White Cloud Temple in Beijing. Rebuilt in 1924, the temple continued functioning until it was closed during the Culture Revolution. In the 1980s, it resumed operation. It houses the Taoists Association of China, an academy, and a cultural institute.

In the twentieth century, Taoism has spread significantly outside its homeland. Temples are found in many Western countries, Southeast Asia, and elsewhere. In North America, the Center of Traditional Taoist Studies is an affiliate of the Complete Perfection sect, and Fung Loy Kok is the largest association, with temples and centers in many American states and Canada.

See also Lao Tzu/Laozi; Lieh-tzu/Liezi; Tao Te Ching/Dao de jing

Bibliography. A. C. Graham, *The Book of Lieh-Tzu: The Wisdom of the East*; H. Maspero, *Taoism and Chinese Religion*; R. H. Van Gulik, *Sexual Life in Ancient China*; H. Welch and A. Seidel, eds., *Facets of Taoism: Essays in Chinese Religion*.

A. W. Barber

TAO TE CHING / DAO DE JING. The Tao Te Ching (Chinese, roughly "book of the way and its virtue") is the sacred text that has been the most important in forming the doctrines and practices of historic Taoism. Although traditionally the Tao Te Ching was thought to have been authored in its entirety by the ancient Chinese sage Lao Tzu (604–521 BC), more recently a number of scholars have concluded that the book probably is the combined work of several contributors whose writings were later edited and compiled. In its present form, the Tao Te Ching is arranged into two sections: Tao (chaps. 1–37) and Te (chaps. 38–81). Most of the chapters are fairly brief. The text begins with the affirmation that the Tao transcends the distinctions of human language and cannot be named. Blending theoretical and practical concerns, the remainder of the volume addresses such fundamental subjects as the nature of reality, the structure of cosmic order, the path to achieving balance and tranquility in human relationships and society, and precepts for government rulers. On one interpretation, the Tao Te Ching advocates a distinctively feminine, fluid, and "soft" approach to life, in contrast to allegedly masculine (and Confucian) qualities like solidity and rigid control. In addition to its central role in the origin and development of Taoism, the Tao Te Ching has had a significant impact on the formation and adaptation of certain schools of Chinese Buddhism. Over the past century and a half, multiple scholarly and popular editions of the Tao Te Ching have been published in Europe and North America, extending the cultural impact of the ideas set forth in the text well beyond their historical range of influence.

See also LAO TZU / LAOZI; TAOISM/DAOISM

Bibliography. J. Fowler, *An Introduction to the Philosophy and Religion of Taoism: Pathways to Immortality*; S. Mitchell, trans., *Tao Te Ching: An Illustrated Journey*; M. Roberts, trans., *Dao De Jing: The Book of the Way*; B. B. Walker, trans., *The Tao Te Ching of Lao Tzu*.

H. W. House

TAWHEED. In Islam *tawheed* is the doctrine of the absolute oneness of Allah. Tawheed declares Allah to be immutably indivisible in his divine essence, attributes, and purposes. It follows from this that Allah is utterly unique and transcendent and thus radically distinct from anything in the created universe. This view of strict divine unity distinguishes Islamic monotheism from Christian monotheism, in which God is one in substance yet also exists as three distinct persons. The antithesis of tawheed is *shirk* (division), which is primarily the sin of polytheism but includes allegedly idolatrous forms of monotheism (such as those advocated in Judaism and Christianity, with the doctrine of the incarnation being viewed as especially heinous). The first part of the Islamic proclamation, known as *shahadah* (there is no god but Allah), gives a creedal expression to tawheed that is common to all sects of Islam. Historically, Muslim scholars have relied primarily on the Qur'an as the basis for affirming tawheed but have also availed themselves of various arguments in natural theology. Sunni, Shi'ite, and Sufi Muslims concur in viewing tawheed as the most important and foundational element of Islam, though they differ concerning the precise interpretation of this doctrine. In particular Sufis affirm that the unity of God can be experienced spiritually rather than merely grasped intellectually.

See also ISLAM, BASIC BELIEFS OF

Bibliography. D. W. Brown, *A New Introduction to Islam*; C. Ernst, *Words of Ecstasy in Sufism*; J. L. Esposito, *Islam: The Straight Path*, 3rd ed.; S. Murata and W. C. Chittick, *The Vision of Islam*; D. Waines, *An Introduction to Islam*, 2nd ed.

H. W. House

TAWRAT. *Tawrat* is an Arabic word that Muslims use to describe the books revealed to Moses (Musa) and is equivalent to the Hebrew word *torah*. The Tawrat, mentioned eighteen times in the Qur'an, offers guidance (sura 32:23–25) and wisdom (3:48) and is a source by which to corroborate the gospel, as indicated in the Islamic protogospel that purports to describe the life and ministry of Jesus Christ (Injil 3:50; 5:46). Muslims believe that, unlike the Qur'an, the revelation given to Moses does not reflect its original form; therefore, they have relegated it to a lesser role within Islam.

See also INJIL; ISLAM, BASIC BELIEFS OF

Bibliography. J. L. Esposito, ed., *The Oxford Dictionary of Islam*; H. A. R. Gibb and J. H. Kramers, eds., *Shorter Encyclopedia of Islam*.

J. Holden

TAYLOR, JOHN. John Taylor (1808–87) became the third president of the Church of Jesus Christ of Latter-day Saints (LDS Church) after the death of Brigham Young. Born on November 1, 1808, to James and Agnes Taylor in Milnthorpe, England, he is the only president of the LDS Church who was born outside the US or one of its territories. He became a US citizen in 1849. A strong defender of polygamy, he married at least fifteen women and fathered thirty-five children.

Taylor converted to Mormonism in 1836 and was ordained an apostle in 1838. He was present at the Carthage jail when Joseph and Hyrum Smith were killed by a mob on June 27, 1844. In that incident, Taylor was struck several times by flying bullets, one of which remained in his body for the rest of his life.

As a result of the federal government's efforts to abolish polygamy and suspend voting rights for members of the LDS Church, Taylor spent much of his time as president hiding to avoid prosecution. He died of congestive heart failure on July 25, 1887.

See also CHURCH OF JESUS CHRIST OF LATTER-DAY SAINTS

Bibliography. R. S. Van Wagoner and S. C. Walker, *A Book of Mormons*.

W. McKeever

TELESTIAL KINGDOM. The Church of Jesus Christ of Latter-day Saints (LDS Church) teaches that there are four eternal fates of humanity. These include eternal punishment in outer darkness (what Christians commonly call hell) and three heavenly kingdoms of varying "degrees of glory": the celestial kingdom, the highest of the three kingdoms of heaven, for those who are on the path to exaltation; the terrestrial kingdom, for honorable people; and the telestial kingdom, the lowest level.

After death all persons who are not members of the LDS Church are sent to spirit prison or hell (which is *not* the place of eternal punishment) and are given a chance to repent and believe the Mormon gospel as taught by the faithful who come from paradise to bear witness. Those who fail to respond to the truth revealed to them in spirit prison will be sent to the lowest heavenly realm, known as the telestial kingdom.

The primary source of this doctrine is a vision recounted by Joseph Smith and Sidney Rigdon, at Hiram, Ohio, February 16, 1832, and recorded in the Doctrine and Covenants (D&C), section 76. The telestial kingdom is comparable to the glory of the stars. Those who will attain the telestial kingdom in the afterlife, according to the church's teachings, include the wicked and profane, unrepentant murders, thieves, those "who received not the gospel of Christ, nor the testimony of Jesus" (D&C 76:82), "liars, and sorcerers, and adulterers, and whoremongers, and whosoever loves and makes a lie" (76:103). These people will suffer in a kind of temporary hell (akin to purgatory in Roman Catholicism) before reaching the telestial kingdom. However, the telestial kingdom is not unpleasant: "The glory of the telestial . . . surpasses all understanding" (76:89). Although its inhabitants will never see God the Father or Jesus Christ, they will see the Holy Ghost and enjoy immortality.

The term *telestial* apparently did not exist prior to the 1832 revelation by Smith and Rigdon. Most likely, Smith coined the word by combining the first syllable of *terrestrial* with all but the first syllable of *celestial* (te-lestial), thus using parts of two English words that have sometimes been used to translate words Paul used in 1 Corinthians 15:40 (see, e.g., the Revised Standard Version). In support of this explanation, one may note that Smith added the term *telestial* to that verse in his "inspired" revision of the Bible to make it into a proof text for his doctrine of three levels of salvation.

See also CELESTIAL KINGDOM; CHURCH OF JESUS CHRIST OF LATTER-DAY SAINTS; TERRESTRIAL KINGDOM

Bibliography. R. M. Bowman Jr., *Gospel Principles and the Bible*; Joseph Smith Jr. et al., Doctrine and Covenants; W. J. Walsh, "Heaven and the Degrees of Glory," http://www.lightplanet.com/mormons/basic/afterlife/degrees_glory_eom.htm; C. J. Williams, "Telestial Kingdom," in *Encyclopedia of Mormonism*, edited by D. H. Ludlow, 4 vols.

R. M. Bowman Jr. and J. Easterling

TEMPLE IN JUDAISM. *Historical Overview.* The Jewish temple existed in Jerusalem on the Temple Mount (also known as Mt. Moriah) for 960 years (374 as the first temple and 586 years as the second temple). If we consider the tabernacle, the precursor to the temple, in this reckoning, we may add 485 more years. The temple was the central sanctuary of the Jewish people and was regarded by God as the pivotal institution regulating his divine covenant with the nation (Deut. 12:5–14; cf. Matt. 23:38–39). Its final destruction, by the Romans in AD 70, caused a religious crisis for Judaism since the obligation connected with the performance of the 618 (or 613) commandments depended in large measure on the existence of a functioning sanctuary. Therefore, modern Judaism has had to cope with religious life apart from the temple and, for most Jews, life outside the land of Israel. For Israeli Jews who returned to form the modern state, the capital city of Jerusalem, where the desolate Temple Mount remains a symbol of national loss, is a source of international controversy and local conflict. Yet for the Orthodox rabbis whose influence dominates in the country, the temple's restoration as announced by the biblical prophets (Isa. 2:2–3; 56:4–7; Ezek. 37:26–28; 40–48; Hag. 2:6–9) also remains a future religious goal.

After the reorganization of Judaism at Yavne in AD 90, the laws relating to the temple were recast to adapt to the reality of Jewish life without a temple. The Jewish sages therefore referred to the synagogue as *Miqdash Me'at*, "a small or minor temple" (Babylonian Talmud, *Meghilla* 29a), which, for practical purposes, replaced the temple in function, while Torah study, prayer, and those commandments that could be kept without the temple replaced the obligation of offering sacrifices. Nevertheless, the temple, if only symbolically, has remained at the center of the Jewish psyche as the focus of its principal festivals (Yom Kippur, Sukkoth, and Shavuot) as well as in its daily prayers and teaching concerning Israel's prophetic future. With the return of the Jewish people to their ancient homeland and the reestablishment of the State of Israel, the possibility of rebuilding the temple has been revived as both a national symbol of independence and a sign of the nearness of the fulfillment of the predicted age of redemption for the Jewish people. The Israeli historian David Salomon has explained this aspiration: "It [the desire for a rebuilt Temple] was the essence of our Jewish being, the unifying force of our people" (3). For this reason, Judaism's attachment to Jerusalem and the Temple Mount exceeds that of Christianity and Islam, whose histories also claim this city and site. As New Testament scholar Krister Stendahl states, "For Christians and Moslems, that term [*holy sites*] is an adequate expression of what matters. Here are sacred places hallowed by the most holy events. . . . [But Judaism] is not tied to sites, but to the land; not to what happened in Jerusalem, but to Jerusalem itself" (3).

This allegiance to Jerusalem and its Temple Mount is portrayed annually by Jews around the world in their observance of Tisha B'Av, the ninth of the Jewish month of Av (July/August on the Gregorian calendar). On this day religious Jews fast and refrain from normal pleasures as a sign of sorrow over the destruction of the first and second temples, which occurred on this date. In Israel,

Tisha B'Av has been granted the status of a national day of mourning. Movie theaters, nightclubs, and other places of entertainment are closed and strictly forbidden from being open during the entire time of the fast. However, this universal expression about the loss of the temple does not imply that there is unanimity concerning the way modern Judaism relates to the ancient concept of the temple or to the prospect of its future rebuilding. Religious Judaism must be considered in the context of national Judaism as expressed in the Zionist return to the land of Israel. The majority of contemporary Israelis are secular Jews, who resist the imposition of religious laws that affect their freedoms as a democratic culture. Nevertheless, the temple continues to define their past history (as every Israeli schoolchild learns) and to determine their future with respect to Middle Eastern politics, which presently wrestles with the competing claims of sovereignty over the Temple Mount between Judaism and Islam. Some secular Israelis consider the issue of the Temple Mount an obstacle to Middle East peace and have called for their government to abandon all claims to it. Other secularists have seen the temple as an essential part of the heritage of the Jewish people and contend that without Israeli control over the Temple Mount, national independence is incomplete. For many the basis of this contention is rooted in the Bible, which has been a part of their public school education. For this reason, the term *secular Jew* may be misleading since a significant number of secular Israelis express belief in God and keep certain laws (such as kosher laws), even though they are identified as "nonobservant" by Orthodox Jewry. In this category was David Ben-Gurion, Israel's first prime minister, who, though a secularist, studied Torah, attended weekly Talmud discussion groups, and peppered his political addresses with citations from the biblical prophets.

A survey of Jewish views concerning the temple must recognize that there is no monolithic Judaism whose beliefs characterize the religion. Since the time of the late second temple (early Roman period), Judaism has existed in a pluralistic form, with religious and political differences. In modern Judaism, these various movements may be classified as Traditional or Orthodox Judaism, Ultra-Orthodox Judaism, Conservative Judaism, and Reform or Progressive Judaism. Despite a common reverence for the concept of the temple, Jews view the temple variously as an enduring spiritual symbol, a mystical aspiration of humanity, or a future physical reality.

The View of Orthodox Judaism. Orthodox Judaism follows the traditional practice of Judaism as it was developed between AD 400 and 500, including a strict adherence to the written Torah (Bible) and to the oral Torah (contained in the Talmud and the Mishnah) as its commentary, a separated home and lifestyle marked by keeping kosher laws, religious education for children, and distinct dress (wearing *tzizit*, "fringes" on an undergarment; skullcaps, or *kippot*; and, when praying, prayer shawls and *tefillin*, or phylacteries). Orthodox Jews accept that a literal, physical temple will be rebuilt in accordance with the prophets, but they differ as to the means: divine (miraculous) or human (political). Those in the first group argue that the temple cannot be rebuilt until Elijah and the Messiah appear to resolve all discrepancies about the correct location of the temple, disclose the hiding place of the ashes of the red heifer and the ark of the covenant, and build the temple. Some who hold the miraculous view believe the restored temple will descend from heaven with fire on the Temple Mount in the age of redemption.

Those in the second group follow Rabbi Abraham Isaac Kook (1865–1935), the late chief rabbi of Israel, who taught the Jewish responsibility to obey the biblical injunction of Exodus 25:8 (NASB): "Let them construct

521

a sanctuary for Me." Since sovereignty over the Temple Mount was restored to Israel in 1967, the opportunity to rebuild has existed, and the failure of the secular government to perform this command is regarded by this group as the cause of the continuing problems experienced by the nation. However, with respect to the Temple Mount, Orthodox Judaism holds that its sanctity remains. Therefore, the rabbinate forbids Orthodox Jews to enter the Temple Mount lest they enter in an impure state and offend the divine presence by inadvertently desecrating the holy place.

The View of Ultra-Orthodox Judaism. Ultra-Orthodox Judaism, known as Hasidic (Hebrew, literally, "pious, devout ones"), or kabbalistic or mystical Judaism, refers to itself as the Chabad movement. *Chabad* is a Hebrew acrostic for the *mochin* (powers of intellect), the three *sefiroth* (or *sephirot*; emanations from God that are God himself): c = *chokmah* (wisdom), b = *binah* (understanding), and d = *da'at* (knowledge/intellect). Chabad characterizes the Ultra-Orthodox in their unique adherence to the Zohar (which contains the kabbalah and its commentary) and their attempt to attain the levels of existence revealed by the ten sefiroth. Ultra-Orthodox Judaism is distinguished by outward dress conforming to the traditional clothing of the Eastern European community from which they emigrated and by allegiance to a leading rabbi (rebbe) and his dynastic successors. The rabbi of the largest number of adherents is the late Rabbi Menachem Mendel Schneerson. His followers, known as Lubavitchers, believe that Schneerson is the Messiah and that after his resurrection from the dead he will return to Israel and initiate the rebuilding of the third temple.

However, in keeping with kabbalistic concepts, at present Jerusalem and the temple exist as spiritual, not merely material (which often conceals the spiritual) entities. Therefore, the rebuilding of the temple occurs on two levels: material and mystical. On the material level, the Messiah is coming to rebuild the temple, which will exist (as in the past) as a physical structure, complete with animal sacrifices. On the mystical level, the material temple will be constructed only after humankind has erected its own spiritual temple through study, prayer, and the mitzvah (Hebrew, "commandment") of charity. Once this level of godliness has been attained, the Messiah will arrive, the temple will be rebuilt, and God will inaugurate the age of redemption.

The View of Conservative Judaism. Conservative Judaism, a distinctly American movement, lies along the entire continuum between Reform Judaism and Orthodoxy. Based on the principles of the German Zacharias Frankel (1801–75), it advocates a theological perspective—as articulated by Jewish Theological Seminary's Solomon Schechter (1850–1915), who developed its institutions—that the legal, moral, and spiritual commandments of the Torah were placed by God in the hands of the Jewish people and may be adjusted in keeping with their own social evolution. Conservative doctrine states that the decisions of Torah and Talmud must be followed, that Zionism is a fundamental principle, and that the commandments must be practiced. However, how these commandments are to be applied is pragmatic and left open to interpretation and application by individual congregations. This separates them from the Orthodox, who permit no changes to the traditional understanding of the commandments.

Conservative Judaism views the significance of the temple and its service in light of its historic role in ordering society and strengthening national cohesion. This social-national function also serves a spiritual purpose, offering a corresponding spiritual and social ascent of the people of Israel and of all humanity, which will effectively draw all the peoples of the world closer to one another.

The View of Reform Judaism. Reform Judaism is the most progressive (liberal) of these various movements. Reform Judaism teaches that a vertical connection of humanity to God is achieved not through fulfillment of the divine commandments but through a horizontal connection (between human beings). Therefore, the spiritual standard in Reform Judaism is how people in society relate to one another. This allows for adaptation to prevailing social norms, so that whatever contemporary ethics are observed (whether or not they are the majority view) are acceptable within the broad spectrum of beliefs and practices that make up society. For this reason practices such as feminism, egalitarianism, homosexuality, Eastern meditation, New Age thinking, and so on may be fully incorporated. Despite such variance from Orthodox Judaism, the religious expression of Reform Judaism maintains the trappings of traditional Jewish life.

Reform Judaism's view of the temple is reflected in its calling its meeting places temples rather than synagogues—only, however, in the sense that the temple embodies the concept of a spiritual center that each person should erect within himself or herself. Adherents of Reform Judaism have contributed to the modern rebuilding of the land of Israel through their educational institutions, yet they have no interest in attempts to restore its historic faith and culture with a rebuilt temple. To do so would restore traditional Judaism and destroy their own movement. Nevertheless, in recent years the governing body of Reform Judaism has endorsed a return to traditional Jewish practices (keeping kosher, wearing yarmulkes, and praying in Hebrew) as a means of restoring their lost connection to Jewish history. This shift has also included a return to the study of the temple as more than a model for spiritual self-fulfillment, a move that may be taking some Reform Jews closer to orthodoxy.

Conclusion. The Jewish sages asked and answered the question of the temple's destruction: "Why was Jerusalem destroyed? The first time because of idol worship; the second time because of senseless hatred" (Babylonian Talmud, *Kallah* 5:1). This "senseless hatred" was understood by the rabbis as the rivalry and discord that existed between the various sects of Judaism at the end of the Second Temple period. For this reason, some contemporary voices within Judaism are calling for the hope that the temple might again be restored as the unifying point for world Jewry so that it, and all humanity, may obtain its promised restoration in the end of days.

See also HASIDISM; JUDAISM; KABBALAH; TALMUD; TORAH; ZOHAR

Bibliography. Y. Ariel, *The Odyssey of the Third Temple*, translated by C. Richman; J. Comay, *The Temple of Jerusalem*; S. Goren, *Sepher har-HaBayit: Meshiv malachmah Heleq Rabi'i*; R. Price, *The Temple and Bible Prophecy: A Definitive Look at Its Past, Present, and Future*; L. Reznick, *The Holy Temple Revisited*; D. Salomon, *Guide to the Treasures of the Temple Exhibition*; S. Steinberg, *The Third Beis HaMikdash: The Third Temple according to the Prophecy Yechezkel following Rashi and Tosafos Yom Tov*, translated by Rabbi M. L. Miller; K. Stendahl, "Judaism and Christianity II—after a Colloquium and a War," *Harvard Divinity Bulletin*.

R. Price

TEMPLES IN MORMONISM. Mormon sacred rites are performed in temples. As of June 2012, there were 138 LDS temples around the world and 28 more either under construction or announced. Over half of these temples are located in the US. All but 16 temples were put in service after 1980, and 49 of them were dedicated in 1999 and 2000, when the LDS Church pursued its most aggressive temple-building program to date.

The rapid expansion of temple sites since 1980 was stimulated by two alleged revelations included in Mormon writings in the late

1970s. In 1976 section 137 of the Doctrine and Covenants recorded Joseph Smith Jr.'s 1836 revelation establishing the doctrine of post-mortem salvation, and section 138 recorded Joseph F. Smith's 1918 revelation verifying postmortem proselytizing. Official Declaration 1 was also added to the Doctrine and Covenants in 1978, allowing dark-skinned people to participate in temple work. Since salvation is possible after death, and proselytizing is practiced in the realm of the dead, and since salvation in its fullest sense requires baptism and temple ordinances, there must be many people in the realm of the dead who have embraced the Mormon gospel but who lack baptism and temple ordinances. These Mormon converts in the realm of the dead, therefore, need Mormons in the realm of the living to perform temple rites on their behalf. Thus many more temples were needed to perform these works on behalf of the great multitude of the believing dead. Additionally, since dark-skinned people were permitted to participate in temple work after 1978, more temples were needed in regions with large populations of dark-skinned Mormons.

Temple Activities. Temples are not regular gathering places for Mormons. Sunday services are convened in buildings called chapels or meetinghouses. Temples are sacred places where special ordinances are performed by qualified Mormons. Temple ordinances include works for the living and works for the dead. Works for the living include washings and anointings, temple endowments, and family sealings. Works for the dead include these three together with baptisms for the dead. Washings and anointings are initiatory rites that cleanse and prepare patrons for temple endowments. Special temple undergarments are received during this ordinance. During temple endowments, solemn and secret vows are made. Groups of patrons move through a series of ordinance rooms to receive instruction given nowhere else and to reenact the drama of the plan of salvation.

Once patrons have received temple endowments, they may partake in family sealings. Couples are married and sealed for eternity during this ceremony, and children are sealed to their parents for eternity as well.

Qualifications for Temple Participation. Unbaptized children under eight years of age may take part in their own family sealing ordinance, and baptized and confirmed Mormons twelve and older may perform baptisms for the dead, but washings and anointings, temple endowments, and family sealings are limited to adults at least nineteen years old who have been baptized and confirmed and been recommended by church leaders for temple work. All men must also have been previously ordained to the Melchizedek priesthood.

See also CHURCH OF JESUS CHRIST OF LATTER-DAY SAINTS

Bibliography. R. O. Canon, *Temples to Dot the Earth*; B. K. Packer, *The Holy Temple*; J. E. Talmage, *The House of the Lord*; J. and S. Tanner, *Evolution of the Mormon Temple Ceremony (1842–1990)*.

C. J. Carrigan

TEN LOST TRIBES, ALTERNATIVE VIEWS OF. In 930 BC the northern ten tribes of Israel broke from the southern tribes of Judah and Benjamin and formed their own kingdom. In 722 the Assyrian Empire invaded the northern kingdom and carried its inhabitants off into captivity, in what is now eastern Iran and western Afghanistan.

Although there is some evidence that a few of these captives returned to the land of Israel, the vast majority disappeared from history. Until modern times, the only physical evidence for anyone who may have been part of this group is the presence of Nesranis and the Bene Israel peoples of India, whose DNA shows them to be Hebrew in origin. Many argue that these people constitute the lost tribes, but no conclusive proof has come to light. Additionally, the Samaritans in modern Israel claim they are the decendants of Manasseh and Ephraim, who were not carried off into exile. Their claims have not been proven, although there is evidence that they are at least partially descended from ethnic Israelites.

The mysterious nature of the disappearance of the so-called Ten Tribes has fueled numerous speculations, especially among alternative religions.

According to British Israelism, the lost ten tribes ended up in the British Isles, and the British people are themselves directly descended from them to this day. This view was also espoused by Herbert Armstrong and continues in the Philadelphia Church of God.

Christian Identity developed from British Israelism, but it claims the ten lost tribes are Saxons, Germanics, and Slavic peoples. They believe that these people are the rightful heirs of the promises of God to Abraham and that modern Jews are not the same people as ancient Jews but are actually descendants of the Edomites. This belief has led to virulent anti-Semitism among Christian Identity groups. Christian Identity apologists point to arguments such as the similarity between the words Dan and Danes and complicated mathematical formulations applied to historical events in England and America, though modern DNA testing has proven their claims almost entirely false.

Bibliography. W. L. Ingram, "God and Race: British-Israelism and Christian Identity," in *America's Alternative Religions*, edited by T. Miller; S. M. Lyman, "The Lost Tribes of Israel as a Problem in History and Sociology," *International Journal of Politics, Culture, and Society*.

R. L. Drouhard

TERRESTRIAL KINGDOM. The Church of Jesus Christ of Latter-day Saints (LDS Church) teaches that there are three heavenly kingdoms in which humans may spend eternity, and the second or middle level is the terrestrial kingdom.

Those Mormons who were "not as valiant in the testimony of Jesus" will go to the terrestrial kingdom. In addition, those non-Mormons who did not receive a testimony of Jesus while on earth but who could have done so except for their neglect, and honorable men who were blinded by the "craftiness of man" and did not accept the church's teaching while on earth, will be able to hear the Mormon gospel while in spirit prison, and if they accept it, they will be destined for the terrestrial kingdom (Doctrine and Covenants 76:72–74, 79).

The primary source of this doctrine is a vision recounted by Joseph Smith and Sidney Rigdon, at Hiram, Ohio, February 16, 1832, and recorded in the Doctrine and Covenants (D&C), section 76. The terrestrial kingdom has a glory comparable to that of the moon. All those in the terrestrial kingdom will not obtain "the crown over the kingdom of our God" (76:79) and will remain without exaltation in their saved condition (132:17). They "receive of the presence of the Son [Jesus], but not of the fulness of the Father," and their kingdom differs from the celestial "as the moon differs from the sun" (76:77–78).

The LDS Church presents a trifurcated Godhead in which the Father, the Son, and the Holy Ghost are three distinct "personages" and are not omnipresent—hence the Son will visit those in the terrestrial kingdom while the Father will be found only in the celestial kingdom.

See also CELESTIAL KINGDOM; CHURCH OF JESUS CHRIST OF LATTER-DAY SAINTS; TELESTIAL KINGDOM

Bibliography. S. E. Black, "Terrestrial Kingdom," in *Encyclopedia of Mormonism*, edited by D. H. Ludlow, 4 vols.; Joseph Smith Jr. et al., Doctrine and Covenants; W. J. Walsh, "Heaven and the Degrees of Glory."

R. M. Bowman Jr. and J. Easterling

TESTIMONY IN MORMONISM. Members of the Church of Jesus Christ of Latter-day

Saints (LDS Church) are encouraged to "bear their testimony"—that is, to give verbal expression to what they *know* to be true concerning the divinity of Jesus Christ, the authority of the Book of Mormon as the word of God, the restoration of the gospel through the LDS Church, and that both Joseph Smith Jr. and the current LDS president have been and are God's prophets for their generations. One's testimony relates to the spiritual knowledge that those who sincerely ask of God are promised in Moroni 10:4–5 in the Book of Mormon. Testimony bearing is thus of great importance for Mormon missionaries in carrying out their task.

The testimony serves many purposes in Mormon practice. First, it is a means of proclaiming the gospel as understood by Latter-day Saints. The Book of Mormon teaches that when one speaks by "the power of the Holy Ghost the power of the Holy Ghost carrieth it unto the hearts of the children of men" (2 Nephi 33:1). Second, it is a means of teaching one another as commanded in Doctrine and Covenants 88:118. To this end, Mormons who speak in worship services or in teaching settings are encouraged to conclude by bearing personal testimony as to the truthfulness of what they have declared. Third, testimony bearing may also be seen as a way of reclaiming wandering saints, as in Alma 4:19, where Alma sought to bring the people to remembrance by "bearing down in pure testimony against them." It is thus clear that the primary source of testimony bearing in Mormonism is Mormon scripture (see also D&C 68:4; Alma 34:8).

There are several issues with the LDS doctrine of testimony. The first is that it assumes what one sincerely believes is necessarily true. Individuals can be sincerely mistaken. The Mormon answer is that the truth claim is proven by means of a spiritual testimony from the Holy Spirit. However, there is no way to prove objectively that what is testifying to them is a spirit at all, let alone the

Holy Spirit. Second, the Mormon doctrine of testimony may lead to a kind of spiritual deception. A Mormon may have real experiences that are nevertheless not conveying truth. As is the case with postmodernism, personal experience cannot substitute for objective evidence. Finally, Mormon reliance on personal testimonies has resulted in relativism within the church. Coupled with the doctrine of "continuing revelation," this doctrine has enabled Mormon leaders to feel free to alter Mormon theology radically and to expect that church members will meekly go along. For example, at one time polygamy was considered vital to the spiritual advancement of all Mormons. However, in 1890 Mormon leaders announced that the practice was being suspended without giving any theological explanation or rationale for the change. Yet most members accepted the change on the strength of their "testimony" that the LDS Church is the true church. On the same basis, many Mormons today live with the contradictions and other problems with LDS claims by insisting that their testimonies override any such objections to their faith.

See also CHURCH OF JESUS CHRIST OF LATTER-DAY SAINTS; THEOLOGICAL METHOD OF THE CHURCH OF JESUS CHRIST OF LATTER-DAY SAINTS

Bibliography. F. Beckwith, C. Mosser, and P. Owen, *The New Mormon Challenge: Responding to the Latest Defenses of a Fast-Growing Movement*; H. W. House, *Charts of Cults, Sects, and Religious Movements*; D. H. Ludlow, ed., *Encyclopedia of Mormonism*, 4 vols.; B. McKeever and E. Johnson, *Mormonism 101: Examining the Religion of the Latter-day Saints*; R. L. Millett, *Getting at the Truth: Responding to Difficult Questions about LDS Beliefs*.

R. B. Stewart

TETRAGRAMMATON. The word *tetragrammaton* (from Greek *tetra*, "four," and *gramma*, "letter") refers to the Hebrew name of God usually transliterated as YHWH or

YHVH (German). Note that Hebrew is written from right to left. The name occurs over sixty-eight hundred times in the Hebrew Old Testament (OT).

The Greek versions of the OT used by Jews and Christians in the ancient world (somewhat loosely known as the Septuagint, or LXX) generally used the word *kurios* (Lord) or, occasionally, *theos* (God) in place of YHWH. In the King James Version (KJV), as in most English versions, YHWH is usually rendered "LORD" (note the small capital letters). It is rendered "GOD" just over three hundred times in the KJV, mostly in the expression "the Lord GOD" (more than half of which occur in Ezekiel). However, in the KJV it is also rendered as "JEHOVAH" four times (Exod. 6:3; Ps. 83:18; Isa. 12:2; 26:4). The form "Jehovah" also occurs in three place-names honoring God (Gen. 22:14; Exod. 17:15; Judg. 6:24).

The original pronunciation of YHWH is debated, though most biblical scholars accept Yahweh as most likely. It is reasonably certain that the first syllable was *Yah*, and indeed this syllable was a shortened form of the name used occasionally in liturgical material in the OT. The form occurs four times in Revelation in the expression *allēlouia*, a transliteration of the Hebrew *Hallelu-yah*, found repeatedly in Psalms 146–50 and usually translated "Praise the LORD" (Rev. 19:1–6). This is the only place in the extant Greek manuscripts of the New Testament (NT) where any form of YHWH appears. Most biblical scholars construe the full name as two syllables, Yah-weh. God gave this name to Moses as the name by which God revealed himself and by which he desired to be known for all generations (Exod. 3:14–15), though he was also known by other names. Scholars regard the form Jehovah as a mistake made by medieval Christian scribes. That form is widely believed to have been first used by Peter Galatin in the early sixteenth century, although it may have been used earlier. Be

that as it may, the form Jehovah has a venerable history in Christian hymns and Bible translations.

The practice of substituting the word meaning "lord" (*adonai*) for YHWH is usually traced to a postcaptivity rabbinical Jewish custom of avoiding all use of the Name as a safeguard against blaspheming it. When the Scriptures were being read aloud, the word *adonai* would be said instead of Yahweh. In many texts, the Masoretes (Jewish scribes of the seventh to the eleventh centuries who added vowels to the consonant-only Hebrew Bible) inserted the vowels of *adonai* under the consonants of *YHWH* to make the name of God unpronounceable, and as a reminder to say the former rather than the latter. Some believe that Christian translators, unaware of this practice, thought this hybrid word was the correct form and translated YHWH as Jehovah. Although it is possible that the use of substitutes such as Lord and God in place of YHWH originated in rabbinical Judaism, some precedent for the practice can be seen in the OT itself, notably in Psalm 53, a later form of Psalm 14 in which the word Elohim (God) has been used several times in place of YHWH. The NT authors do not attempt to use the Hebrew form of the name but follow the Septuagint in using *kurios*, Lord, in its place. In the late nineteenth century, several smaller sects in the nontrinitarian wing of the Adventist movement began teaching that God was restoring the proper use of the name YHWH in true Christianity. Most of these "Sacred Name" groups, such as the Assemblies of Yahweh, favor what they see as the only authentic Hebrew pronunciation (Yahweh or Yahvah).

The largest Sacred Name group is that known as Jehovah's Witnesses (JWs), who began emphasizing this doctrine in the 1930s. Their New World Translation (NWT) in 1950 introduced the name Jehovah into the NT 237 times, mostly but not exclusively in quotations from the OT. The rationale for this practice was that the few extant manuscripts of the Greek OT dating from the first century BC and first century AD use a form of YHWH. The JWs infer from these manuscripts that the NT writers would also have used a form of YHWH, at least when quoting from the OT. This speculative inference is contradicted by the uniform witness of the thousands of Greek NT manuscripts, a witness that the JWs' position implies was the result of a massive conspiracy during the second century (a period when the church owned no property and was subject to intense persecution).

The real reason for the use of Jehovah in the NWT is to distinguish between the Lord Jehovah (who is the Father alone, according to JW theology) and the Lord Jesus. When this unjustified translation practice is removed, the NT is found to contain numerous passages equating Jesus with the Lord Jehovah in its quotations from and allusions to the OT (e.g., compare Rom. 10:9–13 with Joel 2:32; Phil. 2:9–11 with Isa. 45:23; 1 Pet. 2:3 with Ps. 34:8; 1 Pet. 3:14–15 with Isa. 8:12–13).

See also ADVENTIST MOVEMENT; JEHOVAH'S WITNESSES (JW)

Bibliography. D. Botkin, "The Messiah's Hebrew Name: 'Yeshua' Or 'Yahshua'?," http://www.yashanet.com/library/Yeshua_or_Yahshua.htm; R. M. Bowman Jr. and J. E. Komoszewski, *Putting Jesus in His Place: The Case for the Deity of Christ*; D. B. Capes, *Old Testament Yahweh Texts in Paul's Christology*; G. D. Fee, *Pauline Christology*; I. Singer, gen. ed., *The Jewish Encyclopedia*; Watch Tower Bible and Tract Society, *The Divine Name That Will Endure Forever*.

R. M. Bowman Jr.

THEOLOGICAL METHOD OF THE CHURCH OF JESUS CHRIST OF LATTER-DAY SAINTS.

The way in which one goes about building a theological system from a scriptural foundation is of paramount importance. This is certainly true from the perspective of the Church of Jesus Christ of Latter-day Saints (LDS Church). However, as Latter-day Saint author M. Gerald Bradford noted, when considering the way in which Latter-day Saints construct theological systems, one "must acknowledge at the outset the somewhat enigmatic character of the role of theology and of the theologian in the Church" (345). Therefore, prior to any study of Latter-day Saint theological method, the role of the theologian must be studied.

Role of the Theologian. In discussing the role of the theologian in the LDS Church, Bradford observes, "On the one hand, every member of the Church is admonished to be a theologian. . . . No individuals in the Church are singled out as official theologians. On the other hand, it is obvious that there have always been certain individuals who for a variety of reasons . . . wield tremendous influence in interpreting and teaching the meaning of the gospel to others" (345). So, unlike the Roman Catholic Church and various Protestant denominations, the LDS Church has no office of "theologian." Some thinkers in the church, however, have been and continue to be looked upon as theologians, without receiving the title. Examples include James Talmage, Bruce R. McConkie, and Robert L. Millet.

The meaning of theology and the precise function of the theologian, however, are not as ill defined. Bradford argues that theology is "often defined as an exposition of religious beliefs in language which is both systematic and temporally relevant" (346). With reference to the function of the theologian, he comments, "No doubt one who undertakes to do theology ought to see his job primarily as one of exposition or description of what is taken to be the revealed word of God. His objective ought to be to portray, with as much clarity and accuracy as possible, the coherent teachings of the gospel, thereby helping himself and others to understand what they believe" (347). This statement leads to an extremely important question in the context of

Latter-day Saint theological method: In light of issues of authority, what is the revealed word of God?

Authoritative Texts. Gospel Principles, one of the standard manuals published by the LDS Church, notes, "The Church of Jesus Christ of Latter-day Saints accepts four books as scripture: the Bible, the Book of Mormon, the Doctrine and Covenants, and the Pearl of Great Price. These books are called the Standard Works of the Church. The inspired words of our living prophets are also accepted as scripture" (45). A concise explanation of these works is necessary before proceeding.

The Bible is one of the four texts accepted as scripture by the LDS Church. James Talmage has explained, "The Church of Jesus Christ of Latter-day Saints accepts the Bible as the first and foremost of her standard works, chief among the books which have been proclaimed as her written guides in faith and doctrine" (240). Latter-day Saints offer qualifications, however, when discussing the nature of the Bible. Included in the Pearl of Great Price (the fourth of the four standard works) are the Articles of Faith, a collection of belief statements composed by Joseph Smith in the spring of 1842. Article 8 reads, "We believe the Bible to be the word of God as far as it is translated correctly." Speaking of the Bible, Talmage comments, "Nevertheless, the Church announces a reservation in the case of erroneous translation. The Latter-day Saints believe the original records to be the word of God unto man, and, as far as these records have been translated correctly, the translations are regarded as equally authentic" (240). Joseph Smith has argued, "I believe the Bible as it read when it came from the pen of the original writers. Ignorant translators, careless transcribers, or designing and corrupt priests have committed many errors" (*Teachings of the Prophet Joseph Smith*, 327). When it comes to the Bible, then, Latter-day Saints argue that the Bible is a holy book and has its origin in God; however, the Bible is also a book that has been incorrectly translated and one from which many truths have been removed. Robert Millet concludes, "Having affirmed my love for the Bible, I hasten to add (as the Book of Mormon teaches) that I do not believe it has come down to us in its pristine purity, as it was written by the original writers. This perspective does not, however, weaken my faith in its essential and central messages" (*What Happened to the Cross?*, 31). The Bible, then, is an important book for Latter-day Saints, but its message has been corrupted. This corruption, though, does not negate its usefulness in the construction of theology.

The Book of Mormon is the second of the four standard works and is, as the eighth article of faith stipulates, believed by Latter-day Saints "to be the word of God." On November 8, 1841, Joseph Smith instructed the Quorum of the Twelve Apostles, saying, "The Book of Mormon was the most correct of any book on earth, and the keystone of our religion, and a man would get nearer to God by abiding by its precepts, than by any other book" (*History of the Church*, 461). Bruce McConkie, discussing the Book of Mormon, has proclaimed, "As far as learning the gospel and teaching the gospel are concerned, the Book of Mormon, by all odds, is the most important of the standard works, because in simplicity and in plainness it sets forth in a definitive manner the doctrines of the gospel" (*Foolishness of Teaching*, 6). Likewise, McConkie also writes, "Almost all of the doctrines of the gospel are taught in the Book of Mormon with much greater clarity and perfection than those same doctrines are revealed in the Bible," and goes on to argue that the Book of Mormon is superior to the Bible (*Mormon Doctrine*, 99). Former second counselor in the First Presidency Marion G. Romney notes, "One can get and keep closer to the Lord by reading the Book of Mormon than by reading any other book" ("Book of

Mormon," 66). Former president Ezra Taft Benson asked, "Is there not something deep in our hearts that longs to draw nearer to God, to be more like Him in our daily walk, to feel His presence with us constantly? If so, then the Book of Mormon will help us do so more than any other book" ("Book of Mormon," 5). Like the Bible, the Book of Mormon is an important book in the Latter-day Saint canon. The Book of Mormon is, however, more significant in the formulation of theology.

The Doctrine and Covenants is the third of the four standard works and is vitally important for the LDS Church, as Hyrum Smith and Janne Sjodahl explain: Doctrine and Covenants "contains 'doctrines,' 'covenants,' and predictions, all of the utmost importance to every nation and every individual on earth" (xiii). They continue, "As the name implies . . . this volume of Scripture contains doctrine and covenants. 'Doctrine' means 'teaching,' 'instruction.' It denotes more especially what is taught as truth, for us to believe, as distinct from precepts, by which rules, to be obeyed, are given" (xiv). Bruce McConkie declares, "Perhaps no other book is of such great worth to the saints as is the Doctrine and Covenants. It is their book, the voice of God in their day. The revelations therein are true, and men are commanded to search them" (*Mormon Doctrine*, 206). Similarly, Joseph Fielding McConkie has argued that the Doctrine and Covenants is needed because the Bible and the Book of Mormon demand another book of scripture: "Though we describe both the Bible and the Book of Mormon with superlatives— especially as they are used together—they are not in and of themselves sufficient for our generation. To so regard either book or the combination of the two would be to deny their spirit, testimony, and purpose" (105). He continues, "To attempt to study the Bible without the aid of the Doctrine and Covenants and other revelations of the

restoration would be a serious mistake in gospel scholarship" (107). The introduction in the Doctrine and Covenants concludes that the work is "of great value to the human family and of more worth than the riches of the whole earth." When theology is under consideration, then, the Doctrine and Covenants plays an extremely important role in articulating LDS theology.

The Pearl of Great Price is the fourth of the works accepted as scripture by the LDS Church. *Gospel Principles* offers the best explanation of the nature of the Pearl of Great Price:

> The Pearl of Great Price contains the book of Moses, the book of Abraham, and some inspired writings of Joseph Smith. The book of Moses contains an account of some of the visions and writings of Moses, revealed to the Prophet Joseph Smith. It clarifies doctrines and teachings that were lost from the Bible and gives added information concerning the Creation of the earth. The book of Abraham was translated by the Prophet Joseph Smith from a papyrus scroll taken from the Egyptian catacombs. This book contains valuable information about the Creation, the gospel, the nature of God, and the priesthood. The writings of Joseph Smith include part of Joseph Smith's inspired translation of the Bible, selections from his *History of the Church*, and the Articles of Faith. (48)

Joseph Fielding McConkie declares, "The Pearl of Great Price is the briefest and yet most expansive of our scriptural records. It was left to this marvelous little compilation of revelations to bind the eternities together" (114). As McConkie states, the Pearl of Great Price is viewed as one of the four standards of the written canon. Because the work is short, it is not quoted as often as the Book of Mormon or the Doctrine and Covenants, but it is still a vital piece of the Latter-day Saint canon.

These four written texts are not the only authority used by Latter-day Saints in the construction of theology. In a letter to John Wentworth, included in the Pearl of Great Price as the ninth article of faith, Joseph Smith Jr. clearly articulated the Latter-day Saint belief in continuing revelation. Smith wrote, "We believe all that God has revealed, all that He does now reveal, and we believe that He will yet reveal many great and important things pertaining to the Kingdom of God." James Talmage has defined the idea that God continues to communicate with humanity: "In a theological sense, the term *revelation* signifies the making known of Divine truth by communication from heaven" (*Articles of Faith*, 308).

Put simply, Latter-day Saints believe that God has communicated to humanity by means of the Bible, the Book of Mormon, the Doctrine and Covenants, and the Pearl of Great Price. They also believe that God continues to communicate to humanity by means of revelations given to the president of the church. Those revelations given to the president become scripture and may be added to the Latter-day Saint standard works. Functioning as a basis on which theology is constructed, the standard works and continuing revelation serve as the foundation of Latter-day Saint theology.

Challenges. Within the realm of Latter-day Saint studies, however, one faces a considerable problem when attempting to discern official church doctrine and when trying to build a Latter-day Saint systematic theology. For example, as Robert Millet has proclaimed, "One meets with great difficulty in categorizing or rubricizing Joseph Smith the Mormon Prophet, or for that matter Mormonism as a whole" ("Joseph Smith and Modern Mormonism," 65). In a lengthy but extremely helpful passage, Millet notes,

It is not so easy to determine what is "traditional" or "orthodox" Mormonism. Orthodox has to do with a straight and proper walk, with appropriate beliefs and practices. In our case, it may or may not be a course charted by Joseph Smith or Brigham Young or some Church leader of the past. Some who claim to be orthodox on the basis of following the teachings of Brother Joseph—for example, members of polygamous cults—are not in harmony with the Church's constituted authorities and are therefore not orthodox. "When the Prophet Joseph Smith was martyred," President Harold B. Lee said in 1964, "there were many saints who died spiritually with Joseph. So it was when Brigham Young died; so it was when John Taylor died. We have some today willing to believe someone who is dead and gone and to accept his words as having more authority than the words of a living authority today." ("Joseph Smith and Modern Mormonism," 65)

In attempting to determine how one might use the words of a past leader, Millet comments, "To fix ourselves too tightly to the words of a past prophet-leader—even Joseph Smith—is to approximate the mindset of certain fundamentalist Protestant groups who reject modern divine communication in the name of allegiance to the final, infallible, and complete word of God found between the covers of the Bible" ("Joseph Smith and Modern Mormonism," 65). Similarly, James Faulconer has stated, "The church neither has an official theology nor encourages theological conjecture." He continued,

As individuals, we may find a theology helpful to our understanding, but no explanation or system of ideas will be sufficient to tell us what it means to be a Latter-day Saint. For a Latter-day Saint, a theology is always in danger of becoming meaningless because it can always be undone by new revelation. Except for scripture and what the prophet reveals, there is no authoritative *logos* of the *theos* for Latter-day Saints, and given that the prophet can and does continue to reveal things, there is no *logos* of what he reveals except the record of those revelations. For LDS, the *logos* is both in principle and in practice always changing, as reflected in the open canon of LDS scripture. In principle continuing revelation precludes an account of revelation as a whole. Thus, finally our only recourse is to the revelations of the prophet since, speaking for God, he can revoke any particular belief or practice at any moment, or he can institute a new one, and he can do those things with no concern for how to make his pronouncement rationally coherent with previous pronouncements or practices.

As Millet and Faulconer have explained, determining a specific set of orthodox Latter-day Saint beliefs is incredibly difficult. From which sources, then, can Latter-day Saint beliefs be deduced?

In answering the question, "How do you decide what is your doctrine and what is not?," Robert Millet has offered one formulation helpful to answering our original question concerning source authority. Millet writes, "In determining whether something is a part of the doctrine of the Church, we might ask: Is it found within the four standard works? Within official declarations or proclamations? Is it taught or discussed in general conference or other official gatherings by general Church leaders today? Is it found in the general handbooks or approved curriculum of the Church today? If it meets at least one of these criteria, we can feel secure and appropriate about teaching it" (*What Happened to the Cross?*, 31–32). An official Latter-day Saint publication, *Gospel Principles*, agrees with Millet's assessment (45, 48). Therefore, in the assessing or building of official church doctrine, the works accredited as officially binding and declarative—as the church, its leaders, and its scholars have defined them—must be utilized.

Theologians versus Prophets within LDS Theology. With a more detailed understanding of the scriptural basis on which Latter-day Saints build theology, we must now turn to the ways in which Latter-day Saints actually construct theology. Put concisely, someone working as a theologian in the LDS Church does not have the freedom "to establish new theological truths on his own, especially for the Church at large" (Bradford, 353). Bradford offers two reasons: the role of the prophet and the nature of the religion as revealed. Concerning the role of the prophet, he notes, "The 'prophet, seer, and revelator' alone may come to know the things of God for the whole Church. Thus it is difficult to see how any Mormon theologian could mistake his role for that of the prophet. And it is doubly unfortunate if what a theologian says falls outside of what could count as meaningful discourse because not only does this render understanding difficult, if not impossible, but it also suggests that one may assume the ways of God are not reasonable. And revelation from God has always been viewed as reasonable" (356). Concerning the role of the Latter-day Saint faith as revealed, Bradford states, "My suggestions boil down to the following point: If the object or subject-matter of theology is the revealed teachings of the gospel, then the theologian must be faithful to what these teachings actually say" (357).

Conclusion. Latter-day Saint theological method is based on the revealed nature of Latter-day Saint faith. Theology within the Latter-day Saint framework may not vary from the authoritative teachings of the LDS Church. Thus the theologian is, in a sense, restricted in theological discourse to the understanding of the current gathered body of general authorities of the church. Latter-day Saint theological method is fundamentally grounded in the role and authority of the prophet, a role given to the members of the First Presidency and the Quorum of the Twelve Apostles. The utterances of the general authorities at conferences are gospel. Those sayings are the boundaries within which Latter-day Saint theologians must work.

See also CHURCH OF JESUS CHRIST OF LATTER-DAY SAINTS; STANDARD WORKS; TALMAGE, JAMES

Bibliography. E. T. Benson, "The Book of Mormon—Keystone of Our Religion," *Ensign*; C. Blomberg and S. Robinson, *How Wide the Divide?*; M. G. Bradford, "On Doing Theology," *BYU Studies*; Church of Jesus Christ of Latter-day Saints, "Explanatory Introduction," in Doctrine and Covenants; Church of Jesus Christ of Latter-day Saints, *Gospel Principles*, 2009 ed.; J. Faulconer, "Why a Mormon Won't Drink Coffee but Might Have a Coke: The Atheological Character of the Church of Jesus Christ of Latter-day Saints," Lecture, Brigham Young University; B. R. McConkie, *The Foolishness of Teaching*; McConkie, *Mormon Doctrine*, 2nd ed.; J. F. McConkie, *The Spirit of Revelation*; R. L. Millet, "Joseph Smith and Modern Mormonism: Orthodoxy, Neo Orthodoxy, Tension, and Tradition," *BYU Studies*; Millet, *What Happened to the Cross?*; S. Robinson, *Are Mormons Christians?*; M. G. Romney, "The Book of Mormon," *Ensign*; H. M. Smith and J. M. Sjodahl, *Doctrine and Covenants Commentary*, edited by J. F. Smith, H. B. Lee, and M. G. Romney; Joseph Smith Jr., *Teachings of the Prophet Joseph Smith*, edited by Joseph Fielding Smith; Joseph Smith Jr., *History of the Church of Jesus Christ of Latter-day Saints*, 7 vols.; J. Talmage, *The Articles of Faith*.

T. S. Kerns

THERAVADA BUDDHISM. Theravada Buddhism is the dominant school of Buddhism in most of Southeast Asia. There are approximately 127 million adherents worldwide. Prominent organizations in the US include the Washington Buddhist Vihara and the Buddhist Study Center of New York.

History. The school of Buddhism known today as Theravada was formulated in Sri Lanka based on earlier Indian traditions and the use the Buddhist canon in Pali.

Buddhaghosa (fifth century) was perhaps the greatest commentator on the Pali Canon and was instrumental in formulating Theravada teachings. He is said to have been born in the central kingdom (Magadha) in India and later to have moved to Sri Lanka.

King Anawrahta's eleventh-century Burmese Empire was based on Theravada Buddhism, as was Sukhothai's Thai kingdom, founded around 1260. Theravada continued to expand into Laos and Cambodia in the thirteenth century. From the fourteenth century on, however, the influence of Islam proved stronger along the coastal fringes and islands of Southeast Asia, limiting the influence of Theravada in Malaysia, Indonesia, and most of the nearby islands as far south as the Philippines. Theravada did gain some exposure in Sumatra and Java, but the small population of Buddhists there today are primarily Mahayana. Today Theravada Buddhism is established in the US.

Summary of Teachings. Theravada (meaning "teaching of the elders") is one of the eighteen to twenty Nikaya schools that formed early in the history of Buddhism. It is the only one of these schools still in existence. It is classed as Sravakayana (the vehicle of the auditor) or Nikaya Buddhism (a *nikaya* is a branch of the Pali Canon) and as Hinayana (the little vehicle). It sees the Buddha as a historical figure, is characterized by a psychological understanding of human nature, and emphasizes a meditative approach to the transformation of human consciousness. According to Theravada, the teaching of the Buddha fundamentally consists in abstaining from all kinds of evil, accumulating everything that is good, and purifying the mind. These aims can be accomplished by the "three trainings": the development of ethical conduct, meditation, and insight-wisdom. The ultimate goal of Theravada is the achievement of the state of nirvana, wherein there will be no more births or deaths and the life of holiness is fully realized.

Creation. The universe is impersonal and everlasting and undergoes endless cycles of emergence and oblivion. All worldly phenomena are subject to three characteristics: impermanence, transience, and being unsatisfactory. All nonsimple things are composed of nonmaterial and material parts. The nonmaterial aspect has the qualities of sensations, perception, mental formatives, and consciousness.

Scripture and Authority. The Tripitaka (three baskets), also known as the Pali Canon, is the collection of primary Pali-language texts that form the doctrinal foundation of Theravada Buddhism. The Tripitaka and a body of postcanonical writings together constitute the complete body of classical Theravada scriptures. The Tripitaka is divided into three parts: the Vinaya Pitaka (texts setting forth the rules of conduct for those in the *sangha,* the community of ordained monks and nuns); the Sutta Pitaka (a collection of discourses containing the central teachings of Theravada Buddhism); and the Abhidhamma Pitaka (texts in which the doctrines presented in the Sutta Pitaka are arranged in systematic form).

God. The Pali Canon generally recognizes multiple gods of Indo-European origin. However, the gods do not play a role in the gaining of nirvana. Although their life spans are extremely long, they too must die and be reborn. Thus there is always an Indra (= Zeus), but the mind stream that is Indra changes. Birth as a god requires vast amounts of positive merit. Titans are also recognized and are called *asuras.* They too are not significant for nirvana.

Buddha. Unlike in Mahayana Buddhism, only the historical (Gautama Sakyamuni) Buddha and other past Buddhas are deemed legitimate; there are no true Buddhas today. Maitreya alone is accepted as a genuine bodhisattva. A Buddha has two types of bodies, the *nirmana-kaya* (the form body) and the *dharma-kaya* (the truth/reality body). This latter body is equated with the state of buddhahood itself; it is the essential nature of mind. The state of buddhahood is timeless, permanent, lacking any characteristics, and free of duality.

Sin. Buddhism does not recognized sin as such. Transgressions against morality produce negative merit, whereas altruistic acts produce positive merit. The law of karma is understood as a universal norm. Sakyamuni Buddha did not issue commandments but advised on how to be spiritually healthy.

Salvation. This is a Christian term that distorts the Buddhist concept of liberation. There are some liberation rituals, but they are not heavily emphasized. The highest goal is to become an arhat or a Pratyeka Buddha and thus achieve nirvana; it is reached through intense study and meditation. Traditionally, this goal (and its associated techniques) has been seen as the domain of fully ordained monks, who renounce all material possessions and deny their desires. Theravadins do not distinguish between the nirvana attained by a Buddha and that of an arhat (one who has gained insight into the true nature of existence, has achieved nirvana, and will not be reborn) or a Pratyeka Buddha (an enlightened being who has achieved enlightenment without the use of teachers or guides).

Afterlife. Theravada does not postulate a period between death and rebirth; the Mahayana period of *bardo* does not exist in Theravada theory. Until such time as nirvana is attained, death is immediately followed by rebirth. This process is spoken of by the analogy of passing a flame from one lamp to another. Nirvana is the ending of the cycle of rebirths and is beyond eternalism and nihilism.

Distinctive Beliefs and Practices. *Sravaka.* A *sravaka* is a monk who follows a highly ascetic approach to attaining nirvana, one involving suppression of desire, separation from the world, and periods of solitude. Such a disciple of the Buddha understands the four dogmas and sees through the unreality of the phenomenal world.

Meditation Techniques. These include *jhana* (a Pali word for a type of meditation with four progressive states), *anapana* (mindfulness of breathing), *vipassana* (insight meditation), and *metta* (unconditional loving-kindness).

Four Levels of Spiritual Attainment. There are four kinds of disciples who correspond to four degrees of spiritual progress. (1) Stream-Enterers are those who have destroyed the three fetters (self-belief, doubt, and faith in the efficacy of rituals and observances); they will be safe from falling into the states of misery (being reborn as an animal, hungry ghost, or hell-being). At most such persons will be reborn seven more times before attaining nirvana. (2) Once-Returners have destroyed the three fetters and diminished their degree of lust, hatred, and delusion. They will attain nirvana after one more rebirth in the world. (3) Non-Returners have destroyed the five lower fetters (those that bind beings to the world of the senses); they will never return to the world of humans. After death they are reborn in the realms inhabited by deities, from where they will attain nirvana. (4) Arhats have achieved enlightenment and are free from all defilements; their ignorance, cravings, attachments, and karma are forever dispensed with.

Temporary Ordination. In most countries where Theravada Buddhism is dominant, it is a common practice for young men to be ordained as monks for a fixed time. In Thailand and Myanmar, for example, young men often are ordained specially for the three-month-long Rain Retreat, though shorter or longer periods of ordination are not uncommon.

Parittas. Chanting *parittas* (texts with protective or auspicious properties) is an important practice. The texts are portions of material derived from the Khuddaka Patha, Anguttara Nikaya, Majjhima Nikaya, and the Sutta Nipata. These protection texts serve as incantations against negative forces.

Pratyeka Buddha. A Pratyeka Buddha is a being who achieves enlightenment without the use of teachers or guides, merely by contemplating the principle of dependent arising. Such beings arise only in ages when Buddhist teachings have been lost.

See also ARHAT; BODHISATTVA; BUDDHISM; ISLAM BASIC BELIEFS OF; MAHAYANA BUDDHISM; MAITREYA; NIRVANA; PALI CANON; PRATYEKA BUDDHA; TRIPITAKA; VIPASYANA

Bibliography. T. Berry, *Buddhism*; S. Collins, *Selfless Persons: Imagery and Thought in Theravada Buddhism*; R. Gethin, *The Foundations of Buddhism*; H. W. House, *Charts of World Religions*; N. Van Gorkom, *The Buddha's Path: An Introduction to Theravada Buddhism*; P. Williams and A. Tribe, *Buddhist Thought: A Complete Introduction to the Indian Tradition*.

S. J. Rost

TIBETAN BUDDHISM. Tibetan Buddhism is literally the Buddhism of Tibet, but it is more widely defined beyond the cultural-religious ethnicity of Tibetans. Tibetan Buddhism extends through Tibet, Nepal, India (diasporan Tibetans and Ladakh), and Bhutan; the Chinese province-level divisions of Qinghai, Yunnan, Sichuan, Gansu, and Inner Mongolia; Mongolia; and the Russian provinces of Buryatia, Tuva, and Kalmykia. Since the diaspora of the Tibetans in the 1960s, Tibetan Buddhism has spread globally, especially into Europe, North America, and Australasia. It continues to be readily accessible due in large part to the globe-trotting of the Dalai Lama, the endorsement of celebrities, the active placement of lamas into Western locations, promotion by the media, and a growing internet presence.

Loosely fitting in the Mahayana stream of Buddhism (more precisely, the Vajrayana), Tibetan Buddhism was woven historically into the original underlying Bon of Tibet, shamanism of Mongolia/Siberia, and/or the animism of the host culture. Drawing strongly from Indian Buddhist tantrism and now the secularism of the West, Tibetan Buddhism has evolved into an eclectic mix of doctrines and practices. As in the rest of Buddhism, the lineage of *lama* (teacher) to student is important, and hence Tibetan Buddhism is sometimes known as "Lamaism." Devotees may take refuge in the Four Jewels: Buddha, dharma, sangha, and lama.

The Indian tantric master Padmasambhava is credited with bringing Buddhism to Tibet from India around the eighth century AD and establishing the Nyingma School. Beginnning in the tenth century, the "great translators" reformed much Tibetan Buddhism in line with current trends in India. The poet Milarepa's (ca. 1052–1135) teacher Marpa founded the Kargyu School in Tibet; the Drukpa Kargyu sect became dominant in the Ladakh region of India and in the nation of Bhutan. The Sakyas also rose about the time of Milarepa. The Kadampas, founded by the Indian Dipamkara, were reformed by Tsong Khapa (ca. 1357–1419), earning the school the new name of Gelugpa (virtuous way); the Gelugpa School then established several monasteries (Nechung, Gandan, Sera, Trashilungpo) throughout Tibet and grew to be the most influential school. The Gelugpa School is the primary affiliation of His Holiness the 14th Dalai Lama, and is resident with his government in exile in Dharmsala, in northern India.

The Tibetan Buddhist worldview is derived from a mixture of rigorous rationalistic Buddhist philosophy, the shamanism of Bon, and Indian tantrism. Rituals seek to empower participants by animating a model of the universe called a mandala, a circular picture or three-dimensional construction often made of fine colored sand. Alternatively, pilgrimages to holy sites, especially Mt. Kailash in western Tibet, are auspicious in gaining karmic merit. In the native Bon religion, it is common to appease ghosts, demons, and territorial spirits by blood sacrifices, mediated by the shaman, who is skilled in magic, ritual healings, and occasionally claiming to control the weather. The shaman enters into an ecstatic trance in which he travels to the spirit world. Buddhist Vajrayana also provides similar activities for the highly accomplished lama. All this revolves around a monastic hierarchy that originally claimed up to one-third of the male work force in pre-Chinese Tibet.

Another unique feature of Tibetan Buddhism is tantrism. Tantra seeks to break through illusion to self-realization by unifying opposites; hence, ritual sexual intercourse plays a central role. Visualization, too, is a foundation of tantra. Wrathful deities are visualized and allegedly aid in liberation: as the practitioner visualizes a liberated being, he supposedly becomes one himself.

Tibetan Buddhists have a complex worldview. Buddhas and bodhisattvas inhabit celestial spheres, and the world is in the fourth of five cosmic ages. The current age is under the bodhisattva of compassion, Avalokiteshvara, also known as Chenresig in Tibet and Kwan Yin in China. The Dalai Lama is "believed to be . . . the reincarnation of the previous thirteen Dalai Lamas, and the seventy-fourth [reincarnation of] a manifestation of Chenrezig. . . . [He is] spiritually connected both to the thirteen previous Dalai Lamas, to Chenrezig and to the Buddha himself" (Gyatso, 11–12). Thus being understood to be a reincarnation of the bodhisattva of compassion, the Dalai Lama preaches nonviolence and compassion incessantly. This doctrine is understood in Tibet mainly as benefiting animals; hence, the Tibetans' reluctance to kill, which is regarded as creating very negative merit. In Buddhism in the West, however, *compassion* is understood in the larger Mahayana framework of the bodhisattva who altruistically postpones his entrance to nirvana so as to help others through to theirs by a transfer of karmic credit, beneficial activities, and teachings. However, this compassion is understood to reach the highest level when there is no ontological difference between the subject and the object since all is one.

The West remains fascinated with Tibetan Buddhism, although it can be argued that the "Tibetan Buddhism" of the West is modifying the Buddhism of Tibet, lightening its darker shades and secularizing it. A casual browse through the BuddhaNet website's *World Buddhist Directory* reveals a large number of Tibetan Buddhist entities now located in the West: Dharma centers, publishing houses, university study groups, meditation groups, retreat centers, bookshops, and the like (BuddhaNet). The film industry continues to flirt with Tibetan Buddhism, producing *Little Buddha* (1994), *Seven Years in Tibet* (1997), *Kundun* (1997), *Himalaya* (1999), *The Cup* (2000), and *Samsara* (2001) and the International Buddhist Film Festival in Los Angeles. Celebrities in both the film and music industries boost the profile of Tibetan Buddhism: Richard Gere, Sharon Stone, Steven Seagal, Harrison Ford, Melissa Mathison (Ford's ex-wife, who wrote the screenplay for *Kundun*), Philip Glass (who wrote the musical score of *Kundun*), Herbie Hancock, Courtney Love, Goldie Hawn, Tina Turner, Oliver Stone, Adam Yauch (of the Beastie Boys), and Michael Stipe (of REM). All either explicitly or implicitly promote Tibetan Buddhism in the West.

Western literature promoting Tibetan Buddhism is proliferating. The *Bardo Thodol* (*The Tibetan Book of the Dead*) remains popular, with Sogyal Rinpoche's version, *The Tibetan Book of Living and Dying*, selling 1.5 million copies worldwide. The Dalai Lama has written forewords to over forty books published in English alone.

The Dalai Lama's globe-trotting and recent initiations using the Kalacakra Tantra are wooing a generation of Westerners into a monistic, tantric worldview.

See also BODHISATTVA; BUDDHISM; DALAI LAMA XIV (TENZIN GYATSO; DHARMA; MAHAYANA BUDDHISM; MANDALA DIAGRAM; SAMSARA; TANTRA; VAJRAYANA BUDDHISM

Bibliography. C. Bell, *Religion of Tibet*; Buddha Dharma Education Association Inc. / BuddhaNet, *World Buddhist Directory*, http://www.buddhanet.info/wbd/; G. Coleman, *A Handbook of Tibetan Culture: A Guide to Tibetan Centres and Resources throughout the World*; L. Feigon, *Demystifying Tibet: Unlocking the Secrets of the Land of the Snows*; T. Gyatso, *Freedom in Exile: The Autobiography of the Dalai Lama of Tibet*; D. S. Lopez Jr., *Buddhism: An Introduction and Guide*; Lopez, *Prisoners of Shangri-La: Tibetan Buddhism and the West*.

H. P. Kemp

T'IEN/TIAN. In Confucianism *t'ien* (Chinese, "heaven") refers to a transcendent moral order that grounds human civilization and serves as the standard of personal and corporate conduct. Prior to Confucius (551–479 BC), it was widely held that a transcendent, personal God (*ti*) ruled the universe. Confucius himself probably believed in such a sovereign deity, though in his writings he places nearly exclusive emphasis on the moral law derived from t'ien and on everyday social responsibilities; he did not concern himself with the nature of the divine or divine commands. Partly as a result of this neglect of theology and focus on ethics, Confucianism after Confucius largely abandoned the idea of God, replacing it with a view of t'ien as an impersonal (though potent) reality.

See also CONFUCIANISM; CONFUCIUS

Bibliography. D. L. Hall and R. T. Ames, *Thinking through Confucius*; D. C. Lau, trans., *Confucius: The Analects*; M. Lu, "Confucian Theory and Practice: Tradition and Transformation in the 21st Century"; T. Meng, *The Confucian Concept of God—T'ien (Heaven): An Historical and Critical Study*.

M. Power

TIRTHANKARA. In Jainism a *tirthankara* (Sanskrit, literally, "ford-maker") is a human being who has been liberated from suffering and has attained a state of omniscient enlightenment (*kevala jnana*), thus becoming a *jina* (conqueror). The absolute knowledge possessed by a tirthankara results in all his previous karma being shed and his ascension to the highest heaven, where he resides with the other tirthankaras. Tirthankaras are so named because they are thought to have been instrumental in the founding of *tirthas*, Jain communities that seek to provide a "ford across the river of human misery."

Jainism teaches that there are twenty-four tirthankaras. The first tirthankara of the present cycle of Jain time (*yuga*), Rishabhdev, is mentioned in the Rig Veda and is said to have lived billions of years ago. The last of the twenty-four tirthankaras was Mahavira (599–527 BC). Jains believe that all of them were princes, with the possible exception of Malli, the 19th tirthankara, who some Jains believe was a woman. Most historians of religion think that only the twenty-third (Parshwanath or Parshva, ca. 877 BC) and twenty-fourth tirthankaras were historical figures. Each tirthankara is associated with a particular animal, plant, object, or symbol. The teachings of these twenty-four tirthankaras are contained in the holy books of Jainism. Many Jain temples in the US contain statues of various tirthankaras.

Although in theory American Jains are committed to the soteriology of attaining *jinahood*, in practice they are less rigorous in their pursuit of becoming tirthankaras than their counterparts in India. Jainism in America is also less sectarian—and consequently more unified—than Indian Jainism. This fact has prevented Jainism from spawning large numbers of offshoot groups in the US, unlike the situation with Hinduism in that country.

See also JAINISM; MAHAVIRA

Bibliography. P. Dundas, *The Jains*; B. Kumar, *Jainism in America*; N. Shah, *Jainism: The World of Conquerors*; K. L. Wiley, *Historical Dictionary of Jainism*.

J. Bjornstad

TONGUES, SPEAKING IN. *See* SPEAKING IN TONGUES

TORAH. The Torah is the Jewish designation for the first five books of the Bible, which Christians call the Pentateuch. The term *torah* comes from the Hebrew root *yarah*, which means "to teach." Hence *torah* means "teaching," "instruction," or "doctrine." It is generally rendered as "law," which is sometimes applicable, but in Hebrew the word is used in different ways. The concept of teaching or instruction is the common meaning in all usages of it.

The term is used of commandments, laws, and instructions in general, as well as specifically the 613 commandments that make up the Mosaic law. Furthermore, it is used specifically of elements within the law of Moses, such as the offerings of Leviticus 6:7 and 7:1 and the law of the Nazirite in Numbers 6:21, among others.

In Judaism Torah is used in a technical sense to refer to the five books of Moses (Genesis through Deuteronomy) as distinguished from the other two divisions of the Hebrew Bible (Christian Old Testament), the Neviim (Prophets) and Ketuvim (Writings). Torah also came to be used to refer to the entire Hebrew Bible. Torah can also refer not only to the written Torah (the 613 commandments Moses actually wrote down in Exodus, Leviticus, Numbers, and Deuteronomy) but also to the oral law, which is composed of the rabbinic laws developed beginning in the intertestamental period. Thus the written law is called the *Torah she-bi-ktav*, and the oral law is called the *Torah she-be-al peh*. This second, broader Judaic understanding of Torah became the interpretive grid for mystical Jewish and Christian kabbalistic interpretations and the starting point for the mystical readings of the Zohar.

In the writings of Paul the apostle through the Reformers, Torah generally came to represent the Law as embodied in the Ten Commandments. The inability to keep the Torah as Law necessitated the grace of God through Christ culminating in the cross. Generally, Christians do not believe the whole Torah is applicable to them today. However, certain fringe sects and Sacred Name groups teach that Christians *are* under the Torah and that the failure to keep the laws in it are a serious sin.

See also JUDAISM; KABBALAH; TALMUD; TANACH; ZOHAR

Bibliography. N. T. Cardozo, *The Written and Oral Torah: A Comprehensive Introduction*; J. Neusner, *Invitation to the Talmud*; Neusner, *Torah from Scroll to Symbol in Formative Judaism*; C. Roth, "Torah," in *Encyclopedia Judaica*, edited by C. Roth; J. A. Sanders, *Torah and Canon*, 2nd ed.; I. Singer, "Torah," in *The Jewish Encyclopedia*.

A. Fruchtenbaum and D. Pettus

TORII. A *torii* (Japanese, possibly "where the birds reside" or "pass through and enter") is a sacred gateway often found at or near the entrance to a Shinto shrine. Toriis are thought (1) to serve as passages used by the *kami* to travel between the world of humans and their own realm and (2) to demarcate sacrosanct areas from mundane ones. As a matter of protocol, Shinto devotees bow to show their reverence for the kami (spirit-like beings or natural forces) when passing through a torii. The most common type of torii consists of two upright beams that support two crossbars; in some cases tablets engraved with Japanese characters are set between these crossbars. Today most toriis are constructed from stone, wood, or steel. Toriis are thought to be designed as bird rests because of a myth in which roosters saved the nation of Japan from unending darkness by crowing loudly enough to persuade the sun goddess Amaterasu to emerge from the cave in which she was hiding.

See also KAMI; SHINTO

Bibliography. J. Breen and M. Teeuwen, eds., *Shinto in History: Ways of the Kami*; C. S. Littleton, *Shinto and the Religions of Japan*.

R. L. Drouhard

TRIKAYA. The *trikaya* (Sanskrit, "three bodies") is an important Buddhist teaching on the nature of reality and the Buddha. Along with the rise of the Mahayana school in the first century AD, a radical reinterpretation of the Buddha developed that came to be known as the three-body doctrine. This teaching maintained that the Buddha had three distinct bodies: (1) the appearance body (*nirmana-kaya*), the one utilized by the Buddha when, out of compassion, he appeared in human form for the benefit of all sentient beings; (2) the enjoyment body (*sambhoga-kaya*), a "subtle" body that resides in pure lands for the enjoyment of bodhisattvas, who alone can perceive this body; and (3) the dharma body (*dharma-kaya*), the one that embodies the highest Buddhist Truth. The dharma body is identical with emptiness (*sunyata*), representing the Buddha's full realization of—and identification with—ultimate reality. In Vajrayana Buddhism, the trikaya was further developed to include the essential body (*svabhavikakaya*), which is the unity of the three.

See also BUDDHISM; DHARMA; MAHAYANA BUDDHISM; VAJRAYANA BUDDHISM

Bibliography. D. Keown, *Buddhism: A Very Short Introduction*; D. S. Lopez Jr., *The Story of Buddhism: A Concise Guide to Its History and Teachings*; G. Xing, *The Concept of the Buddha: Its Evolution from Early Buddhism to the Trikaya Theory*.

H. W. House

TRINITARIAN CONTROVERSIES. Disputes concerning the doctrine of the Trinity have riven the church periodically throughout its history. Four controversies, however, played decisive roles in shaping the creedal formulation of trinitarian orthodoxy, which all branches of the church have accepted as normative for the past sixteen centuries—namely, those over Adoptionism and Monarchianism in the third century and those over Arianism and Pneumatomachianism in the fourth.

Adoptionism. Adoptionism consists in the belief that Jesus is God's adopted, not his natural, son. Advocates of Adoptionist Christologies in the third century typically held at least three tenets in common. They believed, first, that Jesus's person began to exist only when the Holy Spirit conceived him in Mary's womb; second, that Jesus originally existed as a human being who possessed no divine prerogatives; and, third, that Jesus received the divine prerogatives he came subsequently to possess as a reward for upright conduct.

Theodotian Adoptionism. The Adoptionism of the third century took two primary forms. According to the first, which we shall designate Theodotian Adoptionism, the Holy Spirit conceived Christ as a mere man, and he lived an exemplary life until baptism. Then, in reward for Jesus's conduct, the divine Logos descended on him in the form of a dove and empowered him to perform miracles. Whether God promoted Jesus to fully divine status after the resurrection is a matter of dispute among Theodotian Adoptionists.

The first to advocate such views in their characteristically third-century form appears to have been Theodotus of Byzantium, a shoemaker who propagated his novel Christology in Rome near the end of the second century and suffered excommunication by Victor, then bishop of Rome, as a result. Theodotus's followers included Asclepiodotus and a banker, also named Theodotus, who rendered himself infamous by insisting that Melchizedek is superior to Christ and that he mediates between God and angels in much

the same manner as Christ mediates between God and human beings. Theodotus of Byzantium's followers appear to have engaged in a rudimentary form of textual criticism of Scripture and to have cultivated the liberal arts. It is unclear, however, (1) whether—and if so, to what extent—the sect survived after the deaths of Asclepiodotus and Theodotus the banker, and (2) whether a distinct, Melchizedekian party arose on account of Theodotus the banker's distinctive teachings.

Equally uncertain is the relation between Theodotus of Byzantium's followers and the Artemonians, an Adoptionist sect (named after its founder, Artemon) that emerged during the episcopate of Zephyrinus, Victor's successor as bishop of Rome. Although the scanty available records of the Artemonians seem to indicate that their views were at least roughly similar to those of Theodotus and his followers, the Artemonians themselves must have perceived a substantial difference. For Eusebius reports that, in the Artemonians' view, their Adoptionist Christology repristinates the teaching of the entire church before the reign of Zephyrinus. Victor, Zephyrinus's predecessor, however, excommunicated Theodotus of Byzantium, and the Artemonians presumably were aware of this. Some substantial distinction must have divided the two parties, therefore, but the nature of this distinction remains unknown.

Samosatene Adoptionism. The second school of Adoptionism prevalent in the third century was Samosatene Adoptionism, which took its name from Paul of Samosata, bishop of Antioch from 260 until 272. Paul, the sect's founder, held that Jesus was a mere man in whom the Logos dwelled in a special measure from his conception. Unlike Theodotus and his followers, who envisioned a sudden transformation of Jesus after his baptism, Paul taught that Jesus gradually became more and more godlike throughout his life until, at his resurrection, God rewarded him with the divine name. Although Paul and his followers admitted that one might therefore lawfully call Jesus God, they ascribed no ontological significance to the term.

Paul of Samosata held the episcopate of Antioch and the lucrative, secular office of *procurator ducenarius* in Antioch simultaneously, having obtained both positions through the influence of Zenobia, queen of Palmyra, whom Athanasius identifies as Paul's patron. During his tenure in Antioch, Paul rendered himself infamous for worldliness, financial malfeasance, and sexual misconduct and yet managed, by a combination of bribery and intimidation, to avoid official condemnation of his conduct. Paul's heretical Christology, however, occasioned the convocation of three synods in Antioch: one in 264, another at an unknown date between 264 and 269, and a final synod in 269. At the last of these, the presbyter Malchion, formerly a professional rhetorician, persuaded the assembled bishops to depose Paul from his ecclesiastical office and excommunicate him from the church.

Paul retained the support of his royal patron Zenobia and continued to officiate as bishop in Antioch until the Roman emperor Aurelian defeated Zenobia in battle and assumed control of the city in 272. At this point, a number of orthodox bishops appealed to Aurelian, who sympathized with Christianity, to remove Paul from his post, and Aurelian, after consulting a group of Italian bishops, granted their request. This political victory of the orthodox over Paul notwithstanding, a sect of Paulinians, who advocated the Samosatene's Christology, remained in existence until late in the fourth century. Paul of Samosata, moreover, seems indirectly to have influenced the Arianism of the fourth century through his disciple, Lucian of Antioch, whom Arius identifies as his teacher.

Conclusion. Neither of the two forms of Adoptionism prevalent in the third century possessed anything approaching the mass appeal that Arianism would exert in the fourth. The outbreaks of Adoptionism that disturbed the church of the third century, however, whether of the Theodotian or the Samosatene variety, testify to the concern of third-century Christians to reconcile their confession of Jesus Christ as the Son of God with thoroughgoing monotheism. As we shall see, this concern manifested itself in other heresies of the third century and led ultimately to the official formulation of the orthodox doctrine of the Trinity.

Monarchianism. Monarchianism consists essentially in a robust faith in Jesus Christ as God combined with a firm conviction that if there is only one God, then only one person can be divine. Acknowledging multiple persons as divine, in the Monarchian's view, was polytheism. This view proved significantly more popular than Adoptionism in the third century and frequently found advocates, especially in the West, among Adoptionism's opponents. Farsighted theologians of the third century, nevertheless, repudiated both Adoptionism and Monarchianism as heretical extremes, without, however, adequately reconciling monotheism with the full deity of Christ themselves.

Patripassianism. The earliest, and crudest, of the forms of Monarchianism that emerged in the third century is Patripassianism, the belief that the Word is fully divine and that the Word is one with the Father in such a way that the Father suffered, or at least cosuffered, on the cross. The foremost exponents of this crude Monarchianism in the third century were Noetus of Smyrna and Praxeas, a native of Asia Minor. Its foremost detractors were Tertullian of Carthage and Hippolytus of Rome.

Praxeas, who briefly suffered imprisonment on account of his faith, introduced Patripassianism into Rome during the episcopate of Eleutherus. Although he later reverted to orthodox Catholicism, Praxeas's advocacy of Patripassianism was rendered unforgettable by Tertullian, who titled a treatise written in opposition to this heresy *Against Praxeas*.

During his heretical phase, Praxeas seems to have taught that, insofar as the Son is God, he is strictly identical with the Father. He qualified this identification, however, by distinguishing between the Son, a name he reserved for Christ's flesh alone, and Christ, a name he employed when referring to the divine element in Jesus, which he equated fully with the Father. Praxeas, therefore, did not assert precisely that the Father suffered on the cross, but rather that he cosuffered in sympathizing with the passion of the flesh he had assumed.

Noetus of Smyrna, together with his disciple Cleomenes, appears to have advocated a more extreme form of Patripassianism than that of Praxeas and to have done so without recanting. Noetus introduced his form of Patripassianism at Rome during the episcopate of Zephyrinus. When first examined by Roman presbyters, it seems, Noetus denied holding Patripassian views; at his second trial, however, he openly confessed that he considered the Father to have suffered on the cross. When the presbyters duly excommunicated him for these sentiments, Noetus seems to have founded a sect, which disappeared before the end of the third century.

Sabellianism. A more sophisticated form of Monarchianism is Sabellianism, which takes its name from Sabellius, a teacher of African origin who propagated his heresy in Rome in the early third century. Sabellianism consists essentially in the belief that the divine being extends itself, as it were, for different activities, and that the names Father, Son, and Spirit refer neither to distinct divine persons nor to one and the same divine person at all times, but to the one God when he extends himself for the purposes of creation, redemption, and sanctification, respectively. The genius of this heresy is that it enables one to assert that the deity is unipersonal without implying that the Father is identical with the Son or that he suffered or cosuffered in Christ's crucifixion.

Conclusion. Monarchianism, then, in both its Patripassian and its Sabellian forms, constituted a formidable challenge to the third-century church to which it possessed no well-articulated and consistently scriptural response. The indecisive outcome of third-century debates over Monarchianism, by rendering the tension between unity and multiplicity in God more manifestly acute, set the stage for the fiercer and more consequential disputes over the relation between Father and Son that beset the church in the following century.

Arianism. Arianism consists in the belief that Christ is the first creature whom God created, who possesses numerous quasi-divine prerogatives, vastly excels all other creatures in power and dignity, and yet remains a mere creature. This conviction, famously voiced by the Alexandrian priest Arius in the early fourth century, formed the subject of a controversy that agitated all Christendom from approximately 318, when Alexander, the then-archbishop of Alexandria, excommunicated Arius, until 381, when the First Council of Constantinople decisively confirmed the anti-Arian verdict of the Council of Nicaea. The five principal parties to the Arian controversy were (1) Arius and his original sympathizers; (2) the Homoians, who advocated a mildly attenuated form of Arianism; (3) the Homoiousians, who approximated Homoousianism; (4) the neo-Arians, who carried Arianism to extremes; and (5) the Homoousians, who confessed the consubstantiality of the Father and the Son.

Arius. Of the literary works of the Alexandrian priest Arius, only three letters; fragments of another letter; and selections from the *Thalia*, an exposition of his doctrine in verse, survive. From these, one can construct a skeletal outline of Arius's teaching. The Son, Arius insists above all else, is a creature. He is the first and greatest of the Father's creatures, the greatest creature God is capable of making, and the agent by whom

God created the rest of the universe. Yet he remains, in Arius's view, only a creature: a product of creation ex nihilo.

Inasmuch as the Son is a mere creature, Arius argued, he cannot be eternal, and God was not always a Father. In Arius's view, rather, God became a Father only when he created the Son, whom he produced not out of any necessity of his nature but by the free decision of his will. God created the Son, Arius held, not because of the Son's intrinsic worthiness or dignity, but merely in order to employ him as a means of creating further creatures. The Son, according to Arius, comprehends neither his Father's nor his own nature, and the Son's nature does not preclude his falling from moral rectitude as Satan did. The Son, in short, is not God, in Arius's view, and he is one with the Father only in the sense that his will and that of his Father concur in every respect. Arius almost certainly also held, with later Arians, that Christ possesses no human soul and that Jesus's quasi-divine nature was, therefore, subject to ignorance and human emotions.

The course of Arius's career before the outbreak of the Arian controversy is uncertain. One can assert confidently, however, that he was born in Libya in the mid-third century and that he studied under Lucian of Antioch, probably in Nicomedia. After Arius, who presided in one of Alexandria's most prominent churches, began agitating on behalf of his views, Alexander, the archbishop of Alexandria, convened a synod of one hundred bishops at which he excommunicated Arius and his adherents for their doctrines. After the synod, Arius and several of his followers traveled abroad to secure episcopal support for Arianism. They succeeded in persuading a significant number of Eastern bishops, most prominently Eusebius of Nicomedia and Eusebius of Caesarea, to back Arius's cause. After small synods held in Bithynia and Palestine endorsed Arius's

position, Constantine's then-coemperor Licinius banned such meetings from 322 until 324.

After Constantine had gained sole supremacy in the empire in late 324, he addressed a letter to Alexander and Arius in which he dismissed their dispute as trivial and urged them to be reconciled to each other. After discerning that such measures would not suffice to resolve the controversy, he convoked the Council of Nicaea, which met in 325. This council condemned Arianism unequivocally, declaring the Son identical in substance (Greek, homoousios) with the Father and anathematizing all who considered the Son less than eternal, created from nothing, or even changeable. All but two of Arius's episcopal supporters present at the council subscribed to its creed when Constantine ordered them to do so.

Constantine then banished Arius and the bishops Theonas of Marmarike and Secundus of Ptolemais, who refused to endorse the Nicene Creed. Several months later, moreover, Constantine banished two Arian bishops who had signed the creed, Eusebius of Nicomedia and Theognis of Nicaea, for receiving Arians hospitably into their dioceses. Within three years, however, Constantine, who had never considered the disagreements between Alexander and Arius of great consequence, had recalled Arius, Eusebius, and Theognis from exile. Arius died in Constantinople in 336, at which time significant numbers of ecclesiastics continued to advocate Arius's views, and the outcome of the Arian controversy seemed highly uncertain.

The Homoians. The Homoians (from a Greek word meaning "like, similar to"), a party patronized by Constantine's successor, Constantius, professed a mitigated Arianism, which held sway in the Eastern church from 341 until 357. Unlike Arius, an independent thinker who outlined his views rather precisely, the Homoians were intentionally ambiguous and sought to advance a position that was sufficiently inoffensive to unite a broad range of persons suspicious of the decrees of Nicaea. The principal monuments of Homoian doctrine are four creeds: the Dedication Creed (341), the Macrostich (346), the First Sirmian Creed (351), and the Second Sirmian Creed (357), which partisans of Nicaea dubbed "the blasphemy of Sirmium." From these documents, it appears that, like Arius, the Homoians considered the Son a creature, who is essentially unlike and subordinate in every respect to the Father, and whose existence results solely from the Father's free decision. Unlike Arius, however, the Homoians denied that the Son was created ex nihilo and that he changed in the incarnation. The Homoians, moreover, refrained from affirming Arius's formula, "there was when he was not," and withheld comment on the Son's knowledge of the Father. They diverged sharply from the philosophically minded Arius, furthermore, in emphasizing the inscrutability of God and the dangers of unfettered speculation about God's inner life.

The Homoians, whose foremost leader was Acacius of Caesarea, gained Constantius's favor and prevailed in the ecclesiastical politics of the East for a time because they appeared to advocate a moderate position around which the divided church could unite. In 357, when the relatively frank Second Sirmian Creed shocked the sensibilities of the East, however, the Homoians quickly lost popular and imperial support. Homoian Arianism revived somewhat during the reign of the militantly Homoian Eastern emperor Valens (364–78) and, indeed, flourished for centuries as the religion of Germanic tribes, who would come to rule the Western Roman Empire. After the debacle of 357, however, Homoianism never again enjoyed a realistic prospect of becoming the consensus theology of the universal church.

The Homoiousians. The Homoiousians, who rose to prominence after the Second Sirmian Creed's publication, considered the Son subordinate to the Father and yet affirmed that he was "like" in substance (Greek, *homoiousios*, "similar in essence") to the Father in every respect. The most important statements of Homoiousian theology are the Epistle of the Synod of Ancyra (358) and the Dated Creed (359). This party emerged when Basil of Ancyra summoned a small synod in his city in 358 to respond to what he considered the blasphemous Second Sirmian Creed. In this synod, the Homoiousian bishops issued a statement in which they denied that the Son was *homoousios* (Greek, "the same in essence") with the Father and yet insisted that the Son's *ousia* (essence) is like that of the Father. If the Son's *ousia* were unlike the Father's, they asserted, the Son would be not a son but a mere creature alongside others. This statement in itself constitutes a radical departure from all forms of Arianism.

Basil and his Homoiousian disciples departed even more radically from Arianism, moreover, in the lost Third Creed of Sirmium (358) and the Dated Creed (359), in which they declared the Son not merely *homoiousios* to the Father but *homoiousios* to the Father in every respect. This was virtually to assert that the Father and the Son possess the same nature, which is what the Nicene Creed's authors intended to express by the term *homoousios*. In 362, then, a Homoousian synod assembled by Athanasius in Alexandria officially declared that one could truthfully acknowledge the existence of three distinct *hypostases* (Greek, "persons"), in the Godhead. Having been satisfied that the Nicene affirmation that the Son is *homoousios* with the Father does not entail Sabellianism, many of Basil's now deceased followers publicly endorsed the Nicene Creed at a synod in Tyana in 367. The vast majority of Homoiousians, accordingly, came to embrace the Homoousian position.

The Neo-Arians. The neo-Arians, under the leadership of Aetius and Eunomius, advocated an extreme, rationalistic version of Arianism. Neo-Arianism's principal literary monuments are Aetius's *Syntagmation*, Eunomius's *Apology*, his *Apology for the Apology*, and his *Confession of Faith*. These works indicate that the neo-Arians differed from all other parties to the Arian controversy in three principal respects. First, they considered the divine essence completely and, indeed, easily comprehensible. Second, they equated God's essence with his "ingenerateness." Third and finally, they rejected the practice of baptizing persons in the name of the Father, Son, and Holy Spirit. While the neo-Arians proved to be the most intellectually acute antagonists of Nicene trinitarianism, their extremism rendered them odious to all other parties and ensured that their movement did not survive the fifth century.

The Homoousians. The Homoousians, led by Athanasius of Alexandria, Hilary of Poitiers, and the three Cappadocians (Basil of Caesarea, Gregory of Nyssa, and Gregory of Nazianzus), taught, in accordance with the Nicene Creed, that the Son was *homoousios* to the Father—that is, of the same essence or nature as the Father. The principal literary monuments of fourth-century Homoousianism are Athanasius's *Orations against the Arians*, his *Tome to the Antiochians*, Hilary of Poitiers's *On the Trinity*, Basil of Caesarea's *Epistle* 38, and Gregory of Nazianzus's *Orations* 27–31.

At least four events proved critical to the Homoousians' triumph in the Arian controversy. First, the Council of Nicaea itself afforded a presumption of truth to the Homoousian position by enshrining it in the Nicene Creed. Second, the Homoian party alienated countless persons by the radicalism of its Sirmian creed. Third, Athanasius and his fellow Homoousians at the Synod of Alexandria in 362 unmistakably differentiated their position from Sabellianism, allowed that one could speak of three hypostases in the Godhead in an orthodox sense, and declared that Christ possessed a human soul. The first two steps supplied necessary reassurances to persons, such as the Homoiousians, who hitherto had suspected the pro-Nicene party of implicitly endorsing Sabellianism. The last step presented a viable means of defeating the most potent argument posed by all stripes of Arians—namely, the point that Jesus's psyche was subject to limitations that could not characterize a being consubstantial with the Father.

Fourth, the Cappadocians, by clearly distinguishing between an *ousia*, or nature, which can be shared by multiple hypostases, and a *hypostasis*, or person, which is individual in the strictest sense of the term, created a vocabulary whereby one could express coherently the consubstantiality of the divine persons and their irreducible distinctness. Fifth and finally, the emperor Theodosius convoked the Council of Constantinople, which emphatically endorsed the Homoousian position, and employed his authority to render Homoousianism the official trinitarian theology of the Roman Empire.

The Homoousians' victory in the Arian controversy was of inestimable importance to the future course of the development of Christian doctrine. The distinction between *ousia* and *hypostasis*, forged in the struggle against Arianism, supplied the Council of Chalcedon with the means to reconcile the oneness of Christ with the integrity of his two natures. The Homoousians' realization that Christ possesses a human psyche and that this is essential to the integrity of his deity, likewise, answered in advance the primary question disputed in the Monothelitist controversy of the seventh century. The essence-energies distinction, which would later become a central principle of Eastern Orthodox theology, emerged in the Cappadocians' anti-Arian polemic; and later debates over the procession of the Holy Spirit presuppose the doctrines affirmed at the First Council of Constantinople. Most significantly, this council ratified the Homoousians' reconciliation of monotheism with the worship of Christ.

Pneumatomachianism. The Pneumatomachians, also known as Macedonians, of the late fourth century seem to have been Homoiousians who reconciled themselves to the Nicene doctrine of the Son's consubstantiality with the Father but failed to acknowledge the full deity and distinct personhood of the Spirit. This party, whose only literary remnants are the *First and Second Macedonian Dialogues*, seems not to have held in common any one conception of the Spirit. Rather, the Pneumatomachians appear to have coalesced on the basis of their shared opposition to the doctrine of the Spirit's personhood and deity, a doctrine that the leading lights of Homoousianism affirmed and that the First Council of Constantinople incorporated into its creed. Eminent Homoousians such as Athanasius, Gregory of Nyssa, Gregory of Nazianzus, and Basil of Caesarea composed works against the Pneumatomachians, whose primary objection to the doctrine of the Spirit's divine personhood seems to have been that Scripture does not affirm it explicitly. In reply to this objection, the antiPneumatomachian authors demonstrated that Scripture implicitly contains the doctrines of the Spirit's deity and personality and noted that the Pneumatomachians followed the Arians in clinging to Scripture's words while denying its meaning.

Conclusion. The doctrine that the Father, the Son, and the Holy Spirit are three distinct persons who share a single substance thus emerged through two centuries of vigorous and often ferocious argument about the meaning and implications of Scripture. The history of medieval and modern struggles over the doctrine of the Trinity, regrettably, is largely a history of forgetfulness of lessons Christians ought to have learned through study of the literature produced in the controversies just surveyed. Objections and alternatives to orthodox trinitarianism, that is to say, are often, if not always, variants on ideas already advanced in the debates over Adoptionism, Monarchianism, Arianism, and Pneumatomachianism in the third and fourth centuries. By appropriating and diffusing the knowledge gained by the ancient church in these controversies, it seems, the contemporary church could suppress and/or prevent a vast amount of antitrinitarian heresy.

See also TRINITY, THE

Bibliography. L. Ayres, *Nicaea and Its Legacy: An Approach to Fourth-Century Trinitarian Theology*; J. Behr, *The Nicene Faith*; Gregory of Nyssa, *On Not Three Gods*; R. P. C. Hanson, *The Search for the Christian Doctrine of God: The Arian Controversy, 318–381*; Hilary of Poitiers, *On the Synods*; Hippolytus, *Against Noetus*; T. F. Torrance, *The Trinitarian Faith*.

D. W. Jowers

TRINITY, THE. The doctrine of the Trinity teaches that the one God exists eternally in three distinct persons: the Father, the Son, and the Holy Spirit. Although in all things that pertain to the divine essence, God is absolutely one, nevertheless, the three divine persons who share the one divine essence are truly and eternally distinct. Scripture affirms the doctrine of the Trinity indirectly by affirming the following five claims: (1) there is only one God; (2) the Father is God; (3) the Son is God; (4) the Holy Spirit is God; and (5) the Father, the Son, and the Holy Spirit are really and eternally distinct.

There Is Only One God. The first claim is manifestly biblical (cf., e.g., Deut. 4:35, 39; 6:4; 32:39; 1 Kings 8:60; Ps. 86:10; Isa. 44:6, 8; 45:5–6, 18, 21–22; 46:9; Mark 12:29, 32; John 17:3; Gal. 3:20; 1 Tim. 2:5). Scripture teaches that there is only one God, and this claim is just as fundamental to the doctrine of the Trinity as the claim that there are three divine persons.

The Father Is God. The second claim, that according to Scripture the Father is God, scarcely requires argument (cf., however, Matt. 11:25; John 6:27; Rom. 15:6; 2 Cor. 1:2–3; 11:31; Gal. 1:1, 3–4; Eph. 1:2; 4:6; Jude 1).

The Son Is God. The third claim, that Scripture affirms the deity of Christ, seems equally evident when one weighs the evidence of Scripture as a whole. On at least eight occasions, for example, Scripture explicitly refers to Jesus as God (see John 1:1, 18; 20:28; Acts 20:28; Rom. 9:5; Titus 2:13; Heb. 1:8; 2 Pet. 1:1). The biblical authors, likewise, attribute divine functions to Christ such as the creation of the universe (John 1:3, 10; Eph. 3:9 [KJV]; Col. 1:16; Heb. 1:2, 10), the preservation of all creatures (Col. 1:17; Heb. 1:3), the final judgment (Matt. 25:31–46; John 5:22, 27; Acts 10:42; 17:31; Rom. 2:16; 14:10; 2 Cor. 5:10; 2 Tim. 4:1, 8), the forgiveness of sins (Matt. 9:2 and parallels; Luke 7:48; Acts 5:31; Col. 3:13), and the salvation of human beings (Matt. 1:21; Acts 5:31; Phil. 3:20; 2 Tim. 1:10; Titus 1:4; 2:13; 2 Pet. 1:11; 2:20; 1 John 4:14; cf. Isa. 43:11). John, in fact, states that Christ performs every work whatsoever that the Father performs (John 5:19).

Scripture ascribes to Christ, moreover, divine attributes such as omnipresence (Eph. 1:23; Col. 1:17), omniscience (John 16:30; 21:17; Col. 2:3), existence before creation (John 1:1; 17:5; Col. 1:15–17; Heb. 1:10; Rev. 1:8, 17; 2:8), equality with God (John 5:18; Phil. 2:6), and even deity itself (Col. 2:9); and the scriptural authors endorse, by precept and example, the worship of Jesus with the reverence due to God alone (John 20:28; Rom. 14:10–11; 1 Cor. 1:2; Phil. 2:10–11; Heb. 1:6; Rev. 1:5–6).

Scripture, therefore, supplies ample evidence for the doctrine of the deity of Christ. Subordinationists—that is, persons who deny that Jesus is God and therefore subordinate him to the Father—typically fail to appreciate the import of this evidence, however, because they do not properly distinguish between Christ's two natures. They do not adequately distinguish, that is, between the divine nature Christ possesses eternally and necessarily and the human nature he freely assumed in the fullness of time.

Ancient and contemporary subordinationists (e.g., Arians, Jehovah's Witnesses, Christadelphians, Kenneth Copeland), therefore, (1) correctly discern that the Bible attributes immutability, aseity, eternity, and other properties incompatible with creaturehood to the divine nature; (2) discern, again correctly, that the Bible attributes to Jesus suffering, change, an origin in time, visibility, and other traits found in creatures alone; and (3) conclude, therefore, that in spite of the overwhelming scriptural evidence in favor of Jesus's deity, he cannot be of the same substance as the Father. Subordinationists thus resolve the tension between texts that attribute deity to Christ and texts that attribute humanity to him by declining to interpret the former in their full and natural sense.

Trinitarians—ones who are also orthodox in their Christology—by contrast, interpret both sets of texts literally and thus affirm both Christ's humanity and his deity without qualification. They recognize and assent to Scripture's teaching that although Christ has always possessed a divine nature, he chose in the fullness of time to assume a human nature into unity with his person so that, notwithstanding his deity, he could suffer the punishment human beings deserve for their sins (cf. Phil. 2:6–8). When orthodox trinitarians find Scripture ascribing to Christ a characteristic no human nature could possibly display (e.g., omnipresence, omniscience, or omnipotence), therefore, they recognize that Scripture is referring to Christ's divine nature. When trinitarians, however, find Scripture ascribing something manifestly incompatible with deity (e.g., sleep or ignorance) to the Son, they recognize that Scripture is speaking of Christ's human nature. Orthodox trinitarians, therefore, can affirm that Jesus possesses seemingly incompatible attributes without falling into absurdity because they distinguish Christ's divine nature, which is infinite, omnipotent, omniscient, and so on, from Christ's human nature, which is subject to human limitations.

The Holy Spirit Is God. The fourth claim, that the Holy Spirit is God, seems overwhelmingly evident from Scripture. Peter tells Ananias that in lying to the Holy Spirit, he has lied to God (Acts 5:3–4). Scripture describes Christians as temples of the Holy Spirit (1 Cor. 6:19; cf. 1 Cor. 3:16–17; 2 Cor. 6:16). The Holy Spirit stands alongside the Father and the Son in the baptismal formula (Matt. 28:19). Scripture declares that the Spirit exists eternally (Heb. 9:14) and portrays blasphemy against the Holy Spirit as an even graver offense than blasphemy against the Son (Matt. 12:31–32). If Christ is God, therefore, surely the Holy Spirit is as well.

The Father, the Son, and the Holy Spirit Are Really and Eternally Distinct. The fifth claim, that the Father, the Son, and the Holy Spirit are really and eternally distinct from one another, seems similarly difficult to dispute on the basis of Scripture. For according to Scripture, the Son is sent into the world by the Father (John 5:23, 30, 36–37; 6:39, 44, 57; 8:16, 18; 10:36; 12:49; 14:24; 20:21; 1 John 4:14), prays to the Father (Matt. 11:25–26 and parallels; John 11:41–42; 12:28; 17:1, 5, 11, 21, 24–25), and eternally proceeds from the Father (John 1:14, 18; 3:16 [KJV], 18; 5:19, 26, 30; 8:28; 1 John 4:9). The very names Father and Son, moreover, indicate the existence of a real distinction between the two. One can be neither his own Father nor his own Son. The Holy Spirit, moreover, is said to be "another advocate" besides the Son (John 14:16), to receive from the Son (John 16:14–15), and to be sent into the world by the Father and the Son (John 14:16, 26; 15:26; 16:7). The authors of Scripture, therefore, seem definitely to regard the three divine persons as really distinct; and since the same

authors teach that God is immutable (cf., e.g., Ps. 102:25–27; Mal. 3:6; Heb. 1:10–12; 6:18; 13:8; James 1:17), it seems that they must, on pain of contradiction, consider the persons' distinctness as eternal as it is real.

Modalists—that is, those who deny that the divine persons are really distinct—fail to appreciate the force of Scripture's teaching on this subject, however, largely because they do not properly distinguish between person and nature in God. Whereas the term *nature* denotes the essence whereby a thing is a certain kind of thing, the term *person* (or *suppositum* in the realm of unintelligent beings) signifies the being itself—that is, the nature conjoined with that which enables a being to exist as a coherent whole. For example, one could equate the parts of a computer, roughly speaking, with the computer's nature. Nothing of the computer's substance is quite absent from these parts, yet unless these parts are made to exist in a certain, special way, they will never exist as an individual thing.

Christian theologians refer to the additional element that enables a nature to constitute an individual thing as "subsistence." In the theology of the Trinity, therefore, when one refers to God's nature, one does not refer so much to God as to that whereby God is God. When one refers to God as a concretely existing person, however—that is, to the Father, the Son, or the Holy Spirit—one refers to the divine nature subsisting in a particular way. One refers, in other words, to the divine nature and to one of the divine subsistences considered together; and it is just this, the divine nature and one of the divine subsistences considered together, that constitutes a person in trinitarian theology.

The trinitarian persons, according to Scripture, share precisely the same nature. Insofar as their nature is concerned, they are in no way distinct. The trinitarian persons are unique, rather, inasmuch as each person possesses his own, really distinct subsistence.

When Christians say that God is three persons in one nature, therefore, they do not assert that God is like a group of three human beings, each of whom possesses his own, individual human nature. They assert, rather, that the one and only divine substance subsists in three really and eternally distinct ways.

Trinitarianism versus Tritheism. The doctrine of the Trinity differs from tritheism, therefore, as light differs from darkness. Each of the three trinitarian persons is, indeed, a person in the fullest sense of the word. Each possesses an intelligent, independent, and all-powerful nature along with a subsistence that renders him really distinct from the other persons. Each of the trinitarian persons, likewise, is fully God. For each person possesses and even consists in the entire divine substance, yet the three divine persons in no way constitute three divine substances—that is, three Gods.

Monotheistic Trinitarianism versus Absolute Monotheism. The doctrine of the Trinity, then, certainly differentiates the Christian doctrine of God from that of other monotheistic religions. Islamic theology rejects the idea that God can exist in distinct persons and accuses Christianity of polytheism. Some have sought to identify the Christian doctrine of the Trinity with the idea of triads of gods. Though Eastern religions do have these triads of gods, these triads do not represent a trinitarian God, as found within Christianity. In some schools of Eastern thought, these triads are actually similar to the teachings of modalism, in that they are manifestations of a god. This belief differs from modalism in that the Eastern concept of a god is pantheistic. In other Eastern philosophies, they are actually separate gods, existing in distinction from each other.

Groups That Deny the Orthodox Doctrine of the Trinity. Moreover, some contemporary groups embrace the ancient heresies of the nature of God. Ancient modalism, found in the heresy of Sabellianism, is expressed in Oneness Pentecostalism. This group confuses the historic doctrine of the Trinity with tritheism, revealing their own confusion and not any flaws in the doctrine of the Trinity. The heresy of Arianism is found within the teaching of Jehovah's Witnesses. Mormonism reflects in some respects the polytheism of Greco-Roman religion, with its material, finite deities.

See also CHURCH OF JESUS CHRIST OF LATTER-DAY SAINTS; GOD, MORMON VIEW OF; HINDUISM; ISLAM, BASIC BELIEFS OF; JEHOVAH'S WITNESSES (JW); ONENESS PENTECOSTALISM; TRINITARIAN CONTROVERSIES

Bibliography. T. Aquinas, *Summa Theologica*; Athanasius, *Against the Arians*; Augustine, *On the Trinity*; H. Bavinck, *Reformed Dogmatics*, vol. 2, *God and Creation*; L. Berkhof, *Systematic Theology*; Boethius, *On the Trinity*; R. M. Bowman Jr., *Why You Should Believe in the Trinity*; J. Calvin, *Institutes of the Christian Religion*; M. J. Erickson, *God in Three Persons: A Contemporary Interpretation of the Trinity*; E. J. Fortman, *The Triune God: A Historical Study of the Development of the Doctrine of the Trinity*; H. W. House, *Charts of Cults, Sects, and Religious Movements*; R. Letham, *The Holy Trinity: In Scripture, History, Theology, and Worship*; B. de Margerie, *The Christian Trinity in History*; R. A. Muller, *Post-Reformation Reformed Dogmatics*, vol. 4, *The Triunity of God*; J. L. Williams, *Identifying and Dealing with the Cults*, sound recordings, http://www.newdirections.org; B. Witherington III and L. M. Ice, *The Shadow of the Almighty: Father, Son, and Spirit in Biblical Perspective*.

D. W. Jowers

TRINITY, PATRISTIC SUPPORT FOR. The patristic era is a period of the Christian church extending from the close of the New Testament era (around 100) up to the eighth century. Patrology is the study of the lives and writings of orthodox theologians who were part of the Western church up to Gregory the Great (seventh century) as well as the Eastern church up to John Damascene (eighth century) (Quasten). Furthermore, patrology entails the study of the lives and writings of the heretics who challenged the orthodox teachings of the apostles and the fathers of the church. Prominent fathers of the church include Ambrose, Athanasius, Augustine, Basil of Caesarea, John Chrysostom, Clement of Rome, Cyprian, Cyril of Alexandria, Eusebius of Caesarea, Gregory of Nazianzus, Gregory of Nyssa, Hilary of Poitiers, Hippolytus, Ignatius of Antioch, Irenaeus, Jerome, Justin Martyr, Lactantius, Origen, Papias, Polycarp, Shepherd of Hermas, and Tertullian.

A number of the fathers of the church lived near the apostolic church, so they would have been familiar with apostolic teachings. A detailed study of the writings of the ante-Nicene, Nicene, and post-Nicene fathers shows considerable agreement with New Testament apostolic Christianity. The fathers of the church developed extensive theological treatises articulating in detail such crucial doctrines as the Trinity and the deity of Jesus Christ, as well as defending the Christian faith against the errors propagated by heretical teachers and the misrepresentations of Christianity by pagan philosophers, who in turn influenced Roman emperors to persecute Christians.

The development of the doctrine of the Trinity in the patristic period entailed a long process. Church historian John Hannah describes it as follows: "One of the serious attacks upon the church [by pagan scholars] was relative to the doctrine of God. The attempt to formulate an adequate defense led some Christian teachers to inadequately state the deity of Christ. The attacks outside the church and the error perpetuated within it by those who explained it inappropriately provided the context for intense reflection and finally a clear explanation of the orthodox position in creedal form" (75). It took several centuries for the church to finally overcome the heretical teachings that either denied or compromised the deity of Christ and the

Holy Spirit and to establish the Trinity as the only orthodox view of God the Father, God the Son, and God the Holy Spirit.

Jaroslav Pelikan states:

The climax of the doctrinal development of the early church was the dogma of the Trinity. In this dogma the church vindicated the monotheism that had been at issue in its conflicts with Judaism, and it came to terms with the concept of Logos, over which it had disputed with paganism. The bond between creation and redemption, which the church had defended against Marcion and other gnostics, was given creedal status in the confession concerning the relation of the Father to the Son; and the doctrine of the Holy Spirit, whose vagueness had been accentuated by the conflict with Montanism, was incorporated into this confession. The doctrine believed, taught, and confessed by the church catholic of the second and third centuries also led to the Trinity, for in this dogma Christianity drew the line that separated it from pagan supernaturalism and it reaffirmed its character as a religion of salvation. (172)

The doctrine of the Trinity was both implicitly and explicitly articulated by the fathers. John 1:1, an important passage stating the full deity of Jesus Christ with trinitarian overtones, is cited by the fathers without alteration. Irenaeus writes,

In the beginning was the Word, and the Word was with God, and the Word was God; the same was in the beginning with God. . . . For "the beginning" is in the Father, and of the Father, while "the Word" is in the beginning, and of the beginning. Very properly, then, did he [John] say, "In the beginning was the Word," for He was in the Son; "and the Word was with God," for He was in the beginning, "and the Word was God," of course, for that which is begotten of God is God. (*Against Heresies*, in Roberts and Donaldson, 1:328)

According to the *Epistle of Mathetes to Diognetus*, "As a king sends his Son, who is also a king, so sent He Him; as God He sent Him; as to men He sent Him; as a Savior He sent Him, and as seeking to persuade, not to compel us; for violence has no place in the character of God" (Roberts and Donaldson, 1:27).

In Ignatius of Antioch's epistle *To the Ephesians*, Jesus Christ is addressed as God (Roberts and Donaldson, 1:49), is said to have been God in the flesh (Roberts and Donaldson, 1:52, short version), and is identified as "a Physician the Lord our God" (Roberts and Donaldson, 1:52, long version). In *To the Magnesians*, Ignatius calls Jesus "God the Word, the only-begotten son" (Roberts and Donaldson, 1:61, long version). In *To the Trallians*, he calls Jesus God (Roberts and Donaldson, 1:68, short version). In *To the Romans*, Jesus is identified as God numerous times (Roberts and Donaldson, 1:73, 76, long and short versions), and in *To the Philadelphians* Ignatius candidly states that "there is but one unbegotten Being, God, even the Father; and one only-begotten Son, God, the Word and man, and one Comforter, the Spirit of truth" (Roberts and Donaldson, 1:81, long version).

In his treatise *Against the Heresy of One Noetus*, Hippolytus refutes the modalistic heresy, arguing for a distinction in the persons of the Trinity. "For who will not say that there is one God? Yet he will not on that account deny the economy (i.e., the number and disposition of persons in the Trinity)" (Roberts and Donaldson, 5:224); "God, subsisting alone, and having nothing contemporaneous with Himself, determined to create the world. And conceiving the world in mind, and willing and uttering the word, He made it; and straightway it appeared, formed as it had pleased Him. For us, then, it is sufficient simply to know that there was nothing contemporaneous with God. Beside Him there was nothing; but He, while existing alone, yet existed in plurality" (Roberts and Donaldson, 5:227); "We accordingly see the Word incarnate, and we know the Father by Him, and we believe in the Son, (and) we worship the Holy Spirit" (Roberts and Donaldson, 5:228).

Marcellus of Ancyra writes, "We have learned from the holy Scriptures that the Godhead of the Father and the Son is indivisible" (quoted in McGuckin, 2:45). Concerning the eternality (aseity) of Jesus Christ, Cyril of Jerusalem states he is "God begotten of God" and "did not begin his existence in time" (quoted in McGuckin, 2:45). Athanasius writes that Jesus Christ, being uncreated, "exists eternally with the Father" (quoted in McGuckin, 2:46).

Gregory of Nazianzus, in his treatise *On Holy Baptism*, is explicitly trinitarian, writing, "I give you this profession of faith as a life-long guide and protector: One sole divinity and one power, found in the Three in Unity, and comprising the Three separately, not unequal in substances or natures, neither increased nor diminished by addition or subtraction, in every respect equal, in every respect one and the same. . . . Three Infinite Ones, each being God as considered apart, as the Father so the Son, as the Son so the Holy Ghost, each being distinct in his personal property, the Three one God when contemplated together" (Quasten, 3:249).

Johannas Quasten, commenting on the theology of Gregory of Nyssa, reveals that Nyssa had a more sophisticated trinitarianism than Gregory of Nazianzus, given Nyssa's use of Platonic philosophy in his treatise *That There Are Not Three Gods* (Quasten, 3:285–86).

St. Augustine, considered the most influential theologian of the church, wrote an extensive work titled *The Trinity*, in which he expounds the orthodox doctrine of the Trinity. His treatise was a profound achievement in setting forth the doctrine of the Trinity with rigorous theological and philosophical precision, influencing the trinitarian theology of both Roman Catholicism and evangelical Protestantism.

See also JEHOVAH'S WITNESSES (JW)

Bibliography. A. Grillmeier, *Christ in Christian Tradition*, 2 vols.; J. Hannah, *Our Legacy: The History of Christian Doctrine*; R. P. C. Hanson, *The Search for the Christian Doctrine of God*; L. Hurtado, *Lord Jesus Christ: Devotion to Jesus in Earliest Christianity*; J. B. Lightfoot and J. R. Harmer, eds., *The Apostolic Fathers*; J. McGuckin, *Ancient Christian Doctrine: We Believe in One Lord Jesus Christ*; Thomas Oden, series ed., *Ancient Christian Doctrine*, 5 vols.; J. Pelikan, *The Emergence of the Catholic Tradition*; J. Quasten, *Patrology*, 4 vols.; A. Roberts and J. Donaldson, eds., *The Ante-Nicene Fathers*, 10 vols.; P. Schaff, ed., *The Nicene and Post-Nicene Fathers*, series 1 and 2, 28 vols.

S. J. Rost

TRIPITAKA. In the Pali language, *tripitaka* means literally "three baskets" and refers to the three sections of the Buddhist canon. The Vinaya Pitaka outlines the rules of the monastic order; the Sutra Pitaka is a collection of sermons and general discussions of Sakyamuni Buddha (a.k.a. Siddhartha Gautama Buddha) and his monks; and the Abhidharma Pitaka is a philosophical development and interpretation of Buddha's teaching. The Abhidharma Pitaka is the most complex section, describing "reality" and how "reality" appears. It also discusses causation of reality, how the world "hangs together." Finally, the Abhidharma Pitaka describes how behavior affects humanity's liberation. All Buddhist schools consider this collection to be the word of the Buddha (or approved by him).

See also BUDDHISM; PALI CANON

Bibliography. D. S. Lopez Jr., *Buddhism: An Introduction and Guide*; P. Williams and A. Tribe, *Buddhist Thought: A Complete Introduction to the Indian Tradition*.

H. P. Kemp

TWELVE TRIBES. Alternately known as Messianic Communities, Twelve Tribes is a Judaizing sect of Christianity whose members live communally at various locations around the globe. The movement was founded in the 1970s by Elbert Eugene Spriggs (b. 1937), who now goes by the name Yoneq. The movement's origins can be traced to a youth outreach Spriggs started in Chattanooga, Tennessee, called the Yellow Deli. Over time his teachings became more sectarian and organized around Old Testament law, although the members of his community are gentiles and not of Jewish heritage.

The group moved to Vermont, where they became known as the "Northeast Kingdom Community Church of Island Pond, Vermont," or more simply as the Community at Island Pond. A police raid spurred by a disaffected member in 1984 resulted in 112 children being removed from the sect by authorities, due to suspicion of abusive child discipline. The children were returned to the group after the accusations proved to be unfounded. Although the community is probably not guilty of abusive corporal punishment, it does practice disciplinary spanking whenever children play or fantasize, which is not permitted by the group. Yoneq took his disciples to Massachusetts, where they became known as Messianic Communities and later as the Twelve Tribes.

Members believe "Jesus" is a false name and insist on the name Yahshua. They deny the Trinity and believe that the gospel preached by virtually all other churches is false. Members commit to the organization for life, and leaving it is considered apostasy. They teach that "every human being is born into the category of the Righteous, because each one is created in the image of the Creator with an inborn, instinctive knowledge of Him." God gave human beings consciences to guide them even in the absence of the gospel message. They teach that all who obey their conscience and choose a life of "honesty, fairness, and kindness" will be given eternal life in the "kingdom of the Nations" because they "earned it" and deserve it, even if they have not heard the gospel. Those who violate their conscience and choose "selfishness, greed, lust, betrayal . . . murder . . ." will be condemned. Thus it is entirely up to each person where he or she will spend eternity.

Those who "obey the gospel" (i.e., follow the tenets of the Twelve Tribes) will inherit eternal life and are granted citizenship into the "commonwealth of Israel" as "a united twelve-tribed Holy nation" and will live in the "Holy City" for eternity ("Eternal Destinies").

See also UNITARIANISM

Bibliography. A. Kreiner, "Twelve Tribes," http://web.archive.org/web/20060829151659/religiousmovements.lib.virginia.edu/nrms/tribes.html; R. Pardon, "Twelve Tribes," http://www.neirr.org/mcconclu.html; The Twelve Tribes, "Introduction to the Three Eternal Destinies of Man," https://www.twelvetribes.com/articles/introduction-three-eternal-destinies-man.

E. Pement and R. L. Drouhard

TZADDIK. In Hasidic Judaism, a *tzaddik* ("righteous one" in Hebrew) is a learned and virtuous man who serves as an intercessor or mediator between God and the community of Jews he represents. Many sects of Hasidism teach that rank-and-file Jews must regularly confer with and submit to the judgment of their tzaddik in order to achieve lasting restoration and holiness (*tikkun*). This is thought to be the case for several reasons. The tzaddik is considered uniquely competent to direct devotees in their religious activities. It is through the tzaddik that one may participate in the devekuth (attachment to God) the tzaddik achieves. Only the tzaddik has the ability to maximize the effectiveness of prayers. Also, devotees cannot receive forgiveness from God apart from the mediating work of the tzaddik. The degree to which the tzaddik exerts control over those under his authority can vary from one Hasidic community to the next.

See also DEVEKUTH; HASIDISM; JUDAISM

Bibliography. S. Boteach, *Wisdom, Understanding, and Knowledge: Basic Concepts of Hasidic Thought*; M. Shapiro, *The Rebbe's Daughter: Memoir of a Hasidic Childhood*.

R. L. Drouhard

U

UNITARIANISM. This is a long-standing heresy of the church, appearing in a variety of different groups and movements through church history. Generally speaking, Unitarianism is nontrinitarian and affirms a very strict monotheism. Various explanations are given regarding the supernatural abilities of Christ, but all advocates of Unitarianism deny that the Son and the Spirit are of the same substance as the Father.

Arius. Perhaps Arius is the clearest example of this view in the early church, as he emphasized the "begottenness" of the Son and famously argued that "there was a time when the Son was not." Despite the condemnation of his doctrine at the Council of Nicaea in 325, the doctrine continued to endure. Examples are numerous, but include people like King Theodoric, who had Boethius condemned to death in 524; Michael Servetus in the sixteenth century; Joseph Priestley in the eighteenth century; and many Congregational churches in New England during the eighteenth century.

Unitarian Universalists. Unitarian Universalists (UU) are a conglomeration of Unitarians and Universalists who joined together in the nineteenth century and who also deny the Trinity. They claim descent from the earliest Christians, arguing that certain church fathers like Origen taught universalism and that trinitarianism is an addition to Christianity rather than a foundational belief. Although UUs have held other Christian beliefs throughout history, today most UUs embrace Eastern religious teachings. Even as they undermine or deny the deity of Christ, most Unitarians do not teach universalism.

Oneness Pentecostalism. Another group that might be classified as Unitarian is the United Pentecostal movement. Historically we think of Unitarians as denying the deity of Christ and affirming the Father as God alone (called Dynamic Monarchianism in historic Christianity). United Pentecostals do not commit this error, but are Unitarian nonetheless since they deny the Trinity of three divine persons. Instead, they maintain one divine person who manifests himself in various forms at different times (called Modalistic Monarchianism in historic Christianity). This is distinct from the orthodox trinitarian view, in which all three persons of the one divine being exist at the same time, sharing the same substance indivisibly and distinct from one another.

Other Pentecostal groups that may be categorized as Unitarian are the Apostolic Movement and the United Church of Jesus Christ (Apostolic). Like the United Pentecostal Movement, the United Church of Jesus Christ takes a modalistic view of the Godhead in which the one God reveals himself in three different persons on various occasions.

See also ONENESS PENTECOSTALISM

Bibliography. H. W. House, *Charts of Cults, Sects & Religious Movements*; W. Martin, *The Kingdom of Cults*; M. Noll, *A History of Christianity in the United States and Canada*; R. Tucker, *Another Gospel.*

J. K. Dew

UPANISHADS. The Upanishads are sacred texts of Hinduism that constitute the central teachings of the Vedanta, a body of philosophy based on the end or conclusion of the Vedas (the *-anta* means "end") and used for the traditions relating to self-realization that help one understand ultimate reality or Brahma. The term *Upanishads* is from a Sanskrit word that refers to sitting near a teacher in order to receive instruction (Macdonell, 53).

The Upanishads date to the late Brahmana period, between 800 and 300 BC, but some were written in the modern period and are very important for understanding the Hindu religion. The Upanishads teach important Vedic doctrines such as self-realization, yoga, meditation, karma, and reincarnation. A major personage of the Upanishads is Yajnavalkya. His philosophy informs later Hindu scriptures such as the Bhagavad Gita.

The underlying philosophy of the Upanishads is the combination of mysticism and speculation and the acceptance of the belief in an absolute reality called Brahma, the monistic force from which the universe extends. The highest goal for a person's life is to achieve enlightenment by means of three avenues: karma *marga*, the way of action and ritual; *jnana marga*, the way of knowledge and meditation; and bhakti *marga*, the way of devotion. Interpretation of the Upanishads has given rise to three major schools of Vedanta: *dvaita* (dualism), *advaita* (nondualism), and *vishishtadvaita* (qualified nondualism). The Dvaita School, espoused by teacher Madhvacharya, considers Brahma a personal deity. The Advaita School, promoted by Sankara, does *not* understand Brahma in a personalistic sense, and the third school shares elements of both.

See also BHAGAVAD GITA; HINDUISM; VEDAS

Bibliography. The Hindu Universe, "Upanishads," http://www.hindunet.org/upanishads/;

A. A. Macdonell, *A Practical Sanskrit Dictionary*; Max Müller, trans., *The Upanishads*.

H. W. House

URIM AND THUMMIM, MORMON USE OF. In a biblical context, the Urim and Thummim are thought to be gems or stones that were somehow associated with the breastplate used by Israel's high priest (Exod. 28:30). Numerous biblical passages suggest it was used in decision making, although how exactly this was done remains a mystery (Num. 27:21). Some scholars believe they were used to give yes-no or true-false answers.

In the context of Mormonism, it is believed that the Urim and Thummim were a set of stones fastened like "spectacles." These stones were allegedly buried with the "gold plates" and would enable Joseph Smith to translate the plates' "Reformed Egyptian" characters into English. This translation would come to be known as the Book of Mormon. Even within Mormonism, the use of Urim and Thummim is somewhat nebulous. Depictions of Smith translating the plates rarely, if ever, show him wearing any such spectacles. Martin Harris, one of Smith's scribes, claimed in 1829 that Smith placed "the spectacles in a hat" and that by looking into the hat Smith could translate the characters into English. According to most eyewitness reports, Smith did most of the translation using a "seer stone" in his hat, not the stone spectacles.

See also CHURCH OF JESUS CHRIST OF LATTER-DAY SAINTS; REFORMED EGYPTIAN; SMITH, JOSEPH, JR.

Bibliography. G. W. Bromiley, *International Standard Bible Encyclopedia*; B. R. McConkie, *Mormon Doctrine*; C. Van Dam, *The Urim and Thummim: A Means of Revelation in Ancient Israel*; R. S. Van Wagoner and S. C. Walker, *Joseph Smith: The Gift of Seeing*.

W. McKeever

VAJRAYANA BUDDHISM. Vajrayana is a tradition within Buddhism whose most distinctive element is the accelerated process toward enlightenment that it offers its practitioners (relative to the time frame for attaining enlightenment typical of other Buddhist sects). The word *vajrayana* (which is translated variously as "diamond vehicle" and "thunderbolt vehicle") is suggestive of both the indestructibility of enlightenment and the fact that enlightenment comes very suddenly and powerfully. Sometimes the term *Tibetan Buddhism* is used interchangeably with *Vajrayana Buddhism*, although, strictly speaking, the former term refers to that form of Vajrayana that took root in Tibet during the eighth century and whose various lineages, until the last fifty years or so, proceeded largely within the geographical confines of Tibet. (By contrast, Shingon Buddhism is a form of Vajrayana practiced largely in Japan.) Moreover, though Vajrayana usually is distinguished from Mahayana Buddhism, the former is a species of the latter, having branched out from it while retaining many of its fundamental characteristics. Nearly universal among adherents of Vajrayana is the belief that their tradition is the culmination of doctrinal and methodological development.

History. Scholars who work in the area of Vajrayana Buddhism are divided in their view of where geographically Vajrayana Buddhism originated. Some scholars think Vajrayana began in what was once a region of northwestern India, which is now a part of Pakistan. Another school of thought holds that Vajrayana started in southern India. Regardless of which viewpoint is supported by the preponderance of the evidence, modern historians of Buddhism agree that the first texts propounding distinctively Vajrayana ideas date from the early fourth century. In India Vajrayana Buddhism developed both in the monasteries and among the lay population, with wandering masters who frequented towns, caves, forests, and charnel grounds. In its mature form, Vajrayana studies have been pursued in monastic universities such as Nalanda, Odantapuri, and Vikramashila. As the popularity of Vajrayana grew, many traveling masters spread the teachings across India and beyond.

Some of them traveled to China and reached the capital city of Chang'an, where they presented their novel ideas to the Tang emperor Taizong (r. 627–49). In other cases, Vajrayana monks were summoned by foreign rulers to appear before them. The Tibetan monarch Trisong Detsen (r. 742–97) requested that the Swat Valley scholar-yogi Padmasambhava (ca. eighth century) travel to his palace and teach Vajrayana and, more importantly, subdue the negative spirits of Tibet. Late in his reign, Emperor Kammu (r. 781–806) of Japan dispatched Kukai (774–835), a prominent Buddhist monk, to China, where he was to gain a thorough knowledge of Vajrayana before returning with a report on it. (Kukai later founded the Shingon sect of Japanese Buddhism.) By the ninth century, Vajrayana Buddhism had been established on the Indonesian islands of Java and Bali. However, the fortunes of Vajrayana Buddhism (along with those of every other form of Buddhism in India) began to change dramatically just before the turn of the eleventh century, when a series of invasions by Muslim conquerors from the north resulted in the massacre of thousands of Indian Buddhists and the destruction of their temples and monasteries. Three hundred years after the first wave of these attacks, Vajrayana and the rest of Buddhism had been nearly wiped out in India. During this attempt to expunge Buddhism from India, however, the Vajrayana tradition was able to continue in Nepal; Tibet, where many refugees of the Islamic invasions had fled; and East Asia and parts of Southeast Asia. The three renowned Buddhist masters Drakpa Gyaltsen (1147–1216), Sakya Pandita (1182–1251), and Chogyal Phakpa (1235–80) each journeyed from Tibet to present Vajrayana teachings to Prince Godan of Mongolia, who subsequently became an adherent of Vajrayana. In 1279, not long after this last visit, by Chogyal Phakpa, the Mongol ruler Kublai Khan (1215–94) defeated the military forces of the Song Dynasty of China and supported the Tibetan form of Vajrayana Buddhism in China. Over the centuries, many great Tibetan Vajrayana masters toured China and received support from the emperors. After the end of the Mongolian dynasty, in the late fourteenth century, the influence of Vajrayana waned in China, eventually being nearly eclipsed by a combination of Pure Land Buddhism, Confucianism, and Taoism. During the seventeenth century, Tibetan lamas routinely advised the emperors of Mongolia. When the Chinese Communist Revolution broke out in 1950, China's army invaded Tibet in an attempt to force Tibet to submit to Communist rule. Many Vajrayana Buddhists had little choice but to flee the country. In November of that year, fifteen-year-old Tenzin Gyatso (1935–) was installed as the supreme ruler of Tibet (the 14th Dalai Lama) in the midst of Chinese

occupation of his nation. In 1959 Gyatso escaped from Tibet and began his work (which continues today) as the spiritual head of world Tibetan Buddhism and the political head of the government of Tibet, all of which he has accomplished while in exile. During the last several decades a number of prominent institutes and other organizations committed to the dissemination and promotion of Vajrayana Buddhism have been founded in North America. These include the Nyingma Institute (Berkeley, California), the Shambhala Meditation Center (Halifax, Nova Scotia), the Dzogchen Foundation (Garrison, New York), the Tibetan Buddhist Learning Center (Washington, New Jersey), and Karma Triyana Dharmachakra (Woodstock, New York). It is estimated that presently there are between fifteen and thirty million adherents worldwide, mostly concentrated in Tibet, Mongolia, Bhutan, and Nepal.

Canon and Authority. The Tibetan canon is divided into two major sections: the Kangjur (Translation of the Words) and the Tanjur (Translation of the Teachings). The Tanjur is generally deemed less authoritative than the Kangjur because the latter consists entirely of the Buddha's utterances, whereas the former includes the teachings of Buddhist spiritual guides other than Siddhartha Gautama. The canon of Tibetan Buddhism is not closed, however. Reportedly, Padmasambhava hid a number of Buddhist scriptures (called *termas*) throughout Tibet so that they would be found at various future times when they were especially needed for the continuing development of the Vajrayana tradition. When discovered, these previously concealed texts become part of the Tibetan canon. Although the scriptures of Vajrayana Buddhism in one sense are viewed as authoritative in themselves, it is also the case that they can be properly interpreted only by an authorized spiritual master. Within the Gelug sect of Tibetan Buddhism, the Dalai Lama—currently Tenzin Gyatso—is considered the most important and reliable interpreter of Vajrayana, though the Panchen Lama also is a significant authority on matters of Vajrayana doctrine and practice. (The identity of the individual currently holding the latter title is disputed.) It is believed that the persons who hold these two eminent positions within Tibetan Buddhism (*tulku*s) are successively reincarnated into new bodies over time, so that supreme spiritual authority is possessed by the same person throughout history. Vajrayana Buddhism maintains a highly secretive process of transmitting the wisdom that is to be used for attaining enlightenment (*bodhi*) quickly. This information is handed down during clandestine rituals and is never revealed to the public. According to Vajrayana devotees, such secrecy is necessary because if not performed within a community of practitioners, Vajrayana methods are not only ineffective but quite possibly harmful.

Ultimate Reality and Humanity. Unlike the monotheistic religions such as Islam, Christianity, and Judaism, in which a transcendent God creates the universe ex nihilo, or polytheistic systems that believe God fashioned eternally existing matter into an orderly cosmos (a view found in Mormon cosmology), in Vajrayana Buddhism the totality of phenomena originate interdependently in a reality known as the Primordial Buddha (*samantabhadra*), the source and ground of existence. This Primordial Buddha does not exist as an independent, objective reality from which other entities proceed. Instead, the Buddhist doctrine of "dependent arising" maintains that the Primordial Buddha and the subjective consciousness of each person are inextricably intertwined, such that in the final analysis they are seen to be one and the same fundamental reality. In this view, the reality body (or truth body; *dharmakaya*) of Vajrayana devotees who have become enlightened contains within itself the Primordial Buddha. This means that whereas the minds of those who are

not Buddhas ("awakened ones"; those who have reached enlightenment) remain cluttered with worldly phenomena, those who have achieved buddhahood have rid themselves of such transient and illusory appearances. The true nature of a Buddha—and, by extension, the nature of reality as a whole—is described by the doctrine of *trikaya* (three bodies). This doctrine maintains that each Buddha has three different bodies, each of which possesses unique properties: a created body (*nirmanakaya*) whose attributes are exhibited in the world of appearances; a "mutual enjoyment" body (*sambhogakaya*) that is experienced when a person is fast approaching enlightenment; and a reality body (*dharmakaya*) that is a vehicle of enlightenment itself.

Though more often in popular Vajrayana than in its intellectually sophisticated forms, devotees venerate a number of Buddhas and bodhisattvas (enlightened beings who have devoted themselves to helping others attain buddhahood). The most popular of these quasi-divine beings include Amitabha, Vairocana, Akshobhya, Ratnasambhava, and Amogasiddhi (the five Dhyani Buddhas); Avalokiteshvara (a.k.a. Chenrezig), Manjusri, Maitreya, Tara, and Vajrapani (all prominent bodhisattvas); and sixteen reincarnated lamas known as arhats who will eventually become bodhisattvas. Some, usually wrathful bodhisattvas are known as *dharmapalas*; these fearsome defenders of Buddhist teaching assist wavering devotees in their quest for enlightenment. Prominent among the wrathful manifestations of Buddhas are Mahakala, Vajrakilaya, Guhyasamaja, Kalacakra, Yamantaka, and Cakrasamvara. Countless other beings, though lesser in stature than the Buddhas, bodhisattvas, and arhats, are objects of high esteem in that they are enjoyment bodies of the Buddha.

Ignorance and Enlightenment. According to Vajrayana teaching, the true nature of all people is that of "pure emptiness," otherwise known as the ubiquitous Buddha nature or the Primordial Buddha. However, nearly all people are ignorant of their true nature, and thus they continue in bondage to the illusions and desires of this-worldly existence. This, in turn, has the unfortunate consequence of perpetuating the cycle of death and rebirth, which can be broken only by achieving enlightenment. The path to enlightenment consists of two interrelated sets of practices, ethical and ritual. The former consists primarily of cultivating virtues that promote (and, secondarily, eliminating vices that inhibit) the successful living-out of the Buddhist worldview. Compassion is the key virtue in this regard. Although vices like theft, lying, drunkenness, and dissolute behavior are frowned upon, one of the most serious transgressions in Vajrayana is the breaking of religious vows. The latter set of practices on the path to enlightenment involves a plethora of esoteric tantric practices including meditation techniques, the visualization of symbols, ceremonial offerings, mantras, and in some cases the performance of sex rituals between males and females. Some practitioners focus their thoughts during meditation on a particular *yidam*, an enlightened being with whom they identify. (Popular yidams include Cakrasamvara, Guhyasamaja, Hayagriva, Hevajra, Kalacakra, Kurukulle, Yamantaka, Vajrakilaya, and Vajrayogini, as well as the Buddhas and bodhisattvas mentioned above). Each of these practices is a heuristic designed to assist devotees in realizing their present identity with the Primordial Buddha.

The Vajrayana tradition especially emphasizes the use of particular ritual objects as a means of hastening the attainment of enlightenment. Included among these are the *ghanta*, a bell symbolizing wisdom; the *dorje*, a representation of a thunderbolt that symbolizes creativity and skillful means; and the *damaru*, a small hand drum with two skins in the shape of twin wheels. Another such ritual object is the mandala diagram, an elaborate, multicolored atlas of the cosmos depicting methods of attaining enlightenment and signifying the ephemeral nature of life. In the construction of these diagrams, Vajrayana monks employ exact measurements and a variety of complex geometric configurations. The best known of these diagrams is the Kalacakra mandala, which portrays over seven hundred members of the Vajrayana pantheon.

Postmortem Existence. After death persons who have achieved enlightenment during their life will be immediately liberated from the cycle of reincarnation and enter into complete nirvana, a spiritual state described variously as the extinction of all desire and indescribable bliss. The exceptions to this rule are those exceptionally compassionate persons who have decided to become bodhisattvas, delaying their own liberation and reentering the world of phenomenal things so as to help greater numbers of sentient beings attain enlightenment. The mind streams of those who did not reach enlightenment prior to their demise will pass through an intermediate state (*bardo*)—consisting of three stages and lasting forty-nine days in all—that precedes their reincarnation or (in the case of those who become enlightened while in bardo) entry into nirvana. Being reborn from the bardo, the mind stream may experience a series of hells; heavens; birth as an animal, ghost, human, or titan; or rebirth in one of the Pure Lands, depending on one's practice.

Major Tibetan Lineages. 1. Nyingma. Nyingma (Tibetan, the ancient ones), the earliest form of Tibetan Buddhism, was established during the eighth and ninth centuries when the intrepid Indian masters Padmasambhava and Shantarakshita introduced Vajrayana ideas, Buddhist philosophy, and the *vinaya* to the rulers of the Tubo kingdom in Tibet. These two scholars also were instrumental in translating Sanskrit Buddhist texts into Tibetan and in founding the first

Tibetan Buddhist monastery. Nyingma faced no rival schools until the eleventh century, although much of the three centuries during which it stood alone witnessed substantial maltreatment of its members by various Tibetan kings. Beginning in the eleventh and twelfth centuries and continuing until the Chinese Communist invasion of 1950, the Nyingma sect and a number of emerging Tibetan Buddhist schools thrived and coexisted peacefully. Several of its most significant scholars during this time were Rongzom Mahapandita (1012–88), Kunkhyen Longchen Rabjam (1308–63), Jigme Lingpa (1730–98), and Mipham Jamyang Namgyal Gyamtso (1846–1912). Traditionally, the most important tulku in the school was the head abbot of the Mingdrolling monastery, who upheld certain ritual functions representing the Nyingma in Lhasa. Kyabje Dudjom Rinpoche (ca. 1904–87) was installed, while in exile in India, as the official acting head of the Nyingma lineage. Since then he has been succeeded by three others, the most recent of whom (installed in 2003) was Penor Rinpoche (ca. 1932–2009). Unique features of the Nyingma lineage include its eschewal of political power, its deemphasis on the monastic life, its contention that there are six levels of tantric instruction rather than the usual four, and the great importance it places on finding previously undiscovered Vajrayana texts.

2. *Kagyu*. The Kagyu sect (in Tibetan *kagyu* means "whispered transmission") was founded in the eleventh century primarily through the efforts of two industrious scholar-practitioners: Khyungpo Nyaljor (978–1079), who founded the Shangpa Kagyu, and Marpa Choekyi Lodoe (1012–99), who founded the more important Drakpo Kagyu. Both were heavily influenced in their thinking by the teachings of the Indian tantric practitioners Tilopa (988–1069) and Naropa (1016–1100). It was Marpa who did the bulk of the translation work that made the writings of Tilopa and Naropa available to Tibetan monks in their native language. Marpa's most influential pupils, Milarepa (1052–1135) and his student Gampopa (1079–1153), were instrumental in the early period; the latter's teaching gave rise to the development of four major subschools of Kagyu: Barom, Pagdru, Karma, and Tsalpa. Kalu Rinpoche (1905–89), perhaps the most highly regarded proponent of Kagyu in the twentieth century, belonged to the Shangpa. The analogue of the Dalai Lama in Kagyu is the Karmapa Lama, a position currently held by Trinlay Thaye Dorje (1983–). The most distinctive mark of Kagyu is its claim that it provides its adherents with instructors who have not only mastered its doctrines but also retain no flaws relating to the practice of Buddhism. The pinnacle of Kagyu spirituality is the reception of the Great Seal teachings of Gampopa, which expound four critical stages of Buddhist meditation.

3. *Sakya*. The Sakya sect was founded by Khon Konchog Gyalpo (1034–1102) in the middle of the eleventh century when he established the school's first monastery on the gray terrain of the Ponpori Hills in southern Tibet (in Tibetan, *sakya* means "pale or gray earth"). Konchog Gyalpo had been greatly influenced by the teachings of Drokmi Lotsawa (992–1072), his guru. Following Konchog Gyalpo were five successive leaders of the sect whose work led to its continued flourishing in later centuries: Sachen Kunga Nyingpo (1092–1158), Sonam Tsemo (1142–82), Drakpa Gyaltsen (1147–1216), Sakya Pandita (1182–1251), and Chogyal Pakpa (1235–80). From the late thirteenth to the mid-fourteenth centuries, Sakya lamas served as rulers of Tibet under the graces of the emperors of Mongolia. During the fifteenth and sixteenth centuries, two prominent subsects emerged within Sakya: Ngor and Tshar. In the nineteenth century, three highly esteemed Sakya devotees, Jamyang Khyentse Wangpo (1820–92), Jamgon Kongtrul Lodro Thaye

(1813–99), and Orgyen Chokyur Lingpa (1829–70), began the Rime Movement, a non-sectarian Tibetan Buddhist tradition whose goal was to integrate the disparate doctrines of the various schools of Vajrayana. Hailing from the Khon family lineage, the present (and forty-first) Sakya Trizin (spiritual head of the Sakya sect), Ngawang Kunga Tegchen Palbar Samphel Wanggi Gyalpo (1945–), performs the duties of his office from exile in the city of Rajpur, India. Teachings that have had a substantial formative influence on the Sakya tradition include the Mahamudra system of Siddha Virupa (ninth century), the esoteric Vajrayogini doctrine of Mal Lotsawa (eleventh century), and the tantric practices of Bari Lotsawa (1040–1112).

4. Gelug. Founded by the scholar-monk Je Tsongkhapa (1357–1419), the Gelug (way of virtue) sect traces its roots back to the Kadampa tradition of the legendary Indian Buddhist master Dipankara. One of Tsongkhapa's brightest students, Gyalwa Gedun Drupa (1391–1474), was installed as the first Ganden Tripa (this title now is referred to as "Dalai Lama") of Tibetan Buddhism. This position conferred on its holder both temporal and spiritual authority over Tibet. The most important subsequent Dalai Lamas have included Gendun Gyatso (1475–1542), Lozang Gyatso (1617–82), Thupten Gyatso (1876–1933), and the present Dalai Lama, Tenzin Gyatso, who was awarded the Nobel Peace Prize in 1989. Gelug is arguably the most eclectic of the Tibetan Buddhist lineages. It has attempted to synthesize the doctrines and practices of the Indian tantra and sutra teachings and the philosophical systems of Nagarjuna (ca. 150–250) and Asanga (ca. 300–375). The Gelug School emphasizes the Vinaya, a set of 253 rules for monastic discipline.

See also ARHAT; BARDO; BODHISATTVA; BUDDHA, THREE BODIES OF; BUDDHISM; CHRISTIAN; DALAI LAMA XIV (TENZIN GYATSO); DHARMAKAYA; ISLAM, BASIC BELIEFS OF; JUDAISM; KALACAKRA; MAHAYANA BUDDHISM; MANDALA DIAGRAM; NIRVANA; POLYTHEISM; THERAVADA BUDDHISM; TIBETAN BUDDHISM

Bibliography. Diamond Way Buddhism home page, http://www.diamondway-buddhism.org/; K. Dowman, *Masters of Mahamudra: Songs and Histories of the Eighty-Four Buddhist Siddhas*; G. K. Gyatso, *Tantric Grounds and Paths: How to Enter, Progress on, and Complete the Vajrayana Path*; T. Gyatso, *The Way to Freedom: Core Teachings of Tibetan Buddhism*; V. Huckenpahler, ed., *Great Kagyu Masters: The Golden Lineage Treasury*; J. Kongtrul, *The Treasury of Knowledge*, book 1, *Myriad Worlds*; R. M. Novick, *Fundamentals of Tibetan Buddhism*; J. Powers, introduction to *Tibetan Buddhism*; D. Rinpoche, *The Nyingma School of Tibetan Buddhism: Its Fundamentals and History*; H. E. K. Rinpoche, *Secret Buddhism: Vajrayana Practices*; C. Trichen, *The History of the Sakya Tradition*; Tsongkhapa, *Tantric Ethics: An Explanation of the Precepts for Buddhist Vajrayana Practice*; G. Tucci, *The Religions of Tibet*, repr. ed.

S. J. Rost

VEDANTA. The term *Vedanta* is formed from *Veda* (Sanskrit, "book of knowledge") and *anta* (Sanskirt, "at the end"). At the end of each of four Vedas are the Upanishads, from which the philosophy of Vedanta has been derived. The Hindu philosophical system of Vedanta has been a significant component of Indian religious history for more than twelve hundred years.

Within Vedanta are three schools, each with its own philosophy regarding Brahma. Advaita (nondualism) teaches that Brahma is the ultimate reality. The world and everything in it are but illusion. Vishishtadvaita (qualified nondualism) has a philosophy similar to Advaita but ascribes attributes and personality to Brahma. Dvaita (dualism) teaches that Brahma is God (including all the manifestations, such as Krishna and Vishnu), that Brahma has personality, and that all individuals possess their own souls. Souls and matter are entities separate from Brahma. Dvaita also teaches that bhakti (benevolent devotion) is the way to enlightenment.

Included among the early proponents of Advaita are Adi Sankara (788–820), Gaudapada (ca. eighth century), and Govinda Bhagavatpada (ca. eighth century). During the nineteenth century, Guru Ramakrishna Paramahamsa (1836–86) was a leading proponent of this philosophy.

More recently, the teachings of Advaita have become the dominant school within Vedanta, and Advaita has been adopted (though in many cases modified) by a number of American groups whose doctrinal roots are found within historic Hinduism. Some of its contemporary adherents contend that modern physics has provided evidence for the unity of the cosmos taught in Advaita.

Featuring a sophisticated metaphysics and epistemology, Vedanta stems from the fundamental conviction that human beings suffer from a deep and systemic illusion (*maya*) regarding the nature of reality and thus are trapped in an endless cycle of death and rebirth (samsara). Central to Vedanta is the pursuit of a decisive freedom from this spiritual bondage, wherein the cycle of death and rebirth is brought to an end and the enlightened practitioner attains liberation (*moksha*). It is held that knowledge (*jnana*) of the true nature of humanity brings about this liberation, whereas bondage is the result of ignorance (*avidya*) concerning this matter. Enlightenment, then, consists in understanding one's real nature (Atman), which in turn is (in the final analysis) identical with ultimate reality (Brahma). One who achieves this realization escapes from the cycle of death and rebirth (thus attaining liberation); such a person is known as a *jivanmukta*. Those who fail to overcome their erroneous perception of themselves as an abiding, truly existing self must undergo rebirth and try again.

According to Advaita Vedanta, eternal Brahma is the material and instrumental cause of the universe, and hence the world does not exist independently of Brahma. However, adherents of Advaita Vedanta understand the world in three primary ways: (1) Ajati Vada, which states that the world is not a real event, (2) Srshti-drshti Vada, which asserts that the world is merely perceived, and (3) Drshti-srshti Vada, which contends that the world is created simultaneously with the human perception of it. Moreover, Brahma is said to be beyond all action, causality, or change, and is devoid of diversity, parts, or attributes (*nirguna*). Brahma, then, cannot be equated with the universe of appearances (which was not created ex nihilo but rather proceeds out of Brahma, although Brahma remains unchanged). Adherents to Advaita Vedanta admit that the Upanishads attribute properties to Brahma but also maintain that a proper interpretation of these texts precludes the predication of genuine attributes to Brahma. (The Vedas are said to contain faultless, authoritative information concerning Brahma that cannot be inferred from anything else, and Advaitans consult the Brahma Sutras for additional help in grasping the nature of Brahma.) In fact, Advaita Vedanta alleges that the reality of Brahma cannot be captured in words and thus that human descriptions of Brahma invariably fail to convey the true nature of Brahma, amounting to little more than flawed mental constructs. This, in turn, has implications for the ontological status of the human self (*jiva*), which ultimately is identical with Brahma: once the "individual" sees the unreality of his own existence, he realizes that all is Brahma. A person's quest for liberation is thus impeded by his unreflective habit of making false distinctions between the self and Brahma.

See also ADVAITA; ATMAN; AVIDYA; BRAHMA; ENLIGHTENMENT; HINDUISM; MAYA; MOKSHA; SAMSARA

Bibliography. E. Deutsch, *Advaita Vedanta: A Philosophical Reconstruction*; S. H. Phillips,

"Vedanta," in *Routledge Encyclopedia of Philosophy*, vol. 9; K. H. Potter, A. B. Creel, and E. Gerow, *Guide to Indian Philosophy*; S. Satchidanandendra, *The Method of the Vedanta: A Critical Account of the Advaita Tradition*; V. Vidyasankar, Advaita Vedānta home page, http://www.advaita-vedanta.org/.

H. W. House

VEDAS. The Vedas are a collection of the oldest Hindu scriptures, which are dated as an oral tradition to about 1500–300 BC, although actual textual sources do not appear until between AD 1000 and 1500. It is generally thought that the Vedas (Sanskrit, "knowledge") were gathered and evolved over roughly nine hundred to twelve hundred years.

The Vedic works stem from four primary scriptures, called the Samhitas ("collections"). The four Samhitas are the Rig Veda (composed ca. 1500 BC), the Sama Veda (ca. 1200 BC), the Yajur Veda (ca. 1000 BC), and the Atharva Veda (ca. 1000 BC). Note that these centuries are very approximate.

The Rig Veda consists of ten books and 1,028 "hymns" praising the older Hindu gods and giving instructions on the proper forms of sacrifice or service to scores of different deities. The hymns are not to be sung by a group but are to be chanted by a priest; most are about ten verses long.

The Sama Veda, the Veda of sacrificial formulas, largely praises the god Soma (of the hallucinogenic soma plant); 95 percent of its hymns are copied from Rig Veda.

The Yajur Veda, the Veda of sung chants, also contains hymns from the Rig Veda, but adds speculations and interpretations of their meaning. There are two versions, and each branch of Hinduism tends to prefer one or the other: the Black Yajur Veda (of which there are four recensions) and the White Yajur Veda (two recensions). The Black and the White incorporate significantly different texts.

The Atharva Veda contains mantras, spells, and incantations for health, prosperity, success, and other benefits. The Atharva Veda is also called the Brahma Veda, receiving its name from an earlier age when Brahma referred to cosmic power or magic.

Associated with each Samhita are three additional groups of writings: the Brahmanas, the Aranyakas, and the Upanishads. In other words, there are Brahmanas, Aranyakas, and Upanishads for each Veda.

Between eight and nineteen Brahmanas are distributed among the four Samhitas, ranging in length from five volumes to a single page. The Brahmanas are prose works commenting on the hymns and interpreting the meaning of the sacrifices. They give attention to Brahma (a creator deity who displaces two earlier gods of the Samhitas) and to the priestly Brahmin caste, seen as essential to regulating accurate worship. The Brahmanas and the Aranyakas originate in a later period, circa 1000–600 BC.

The Aranyakas (forest texts) originated sometime after the Brahmanas. They received their name from their emphasis on retreating into the woods for meditation, and they question the value of sacrifices, suggesting that a symbolic or spiritual sacrifice will do just as well.

The Upanishads are the most recent texts (major Upanishads were composed ca. 600–300 BC), representing a distillation of the meaning of the Samhitas, the Brahmanas, and the Aranyakas. Their literary genre takes the form of dialogues between guru and disciple, from which comes the term Upanishad, "to sit under." The Upanishads attend to the nature of Brahma, the undifferentiated substrate of the cosmos, and Atman, the individual self or identity. They introduce and develop concepts not stated in the Samhitas, such as reincarnation and the law of karma. The number of Upanishads ranges widely; it is often given as 108, but some authorities say there are as few as 10 essential Upanishads.

Note that the term *Vedas* is multivalent, meaning different things depending on the context. Normally the term refers specifically to the four Samhitas (whose titles all end in Veda). Sometimes Vedas refers to the Samhitas, the Brahmanas, and the Aranyakas; other times it includes the Upanishads as well. Occasionally, the term incorporates two additional bodies of writing, the Sutras and the Vedangas.

Devout Hindus believe the Vedic scriptures (including the Upanishads) are inspired in a sense surpassing the strictest inerrantist sense given to the word *inspired* by Christian fundamentalism. The Vedas are believed to be infallible and eternal, not discovered or composed by human authors. They are *shruti*, revelations that were heard and recorded by the *rishi*, divine-human seers of ancient times.

No single version of the Vedas, even in Sanskrit, is accepted by all Hindus as authoritative. The true Vedas existed only in oral form and were not committed to manuscript for hundreds of years. And paradoxically, despite the concept of inerrant revelation, there is no universally fixed canon or approved list of Vedic texts because there are different branches of Hinduism. There are different recensions of each major text; sometimes the Atharva Veda is omitted from the list; and the number of Upanishads varies depending on the Vedic tradition or school of thought. The oldest extant manuscripts of the Vedas date from the eleventh and fourteenth centuries AD.

Although printed versions and translations from the Vedas exist, tradition stands against copying or printing the Vedic scriptures. According to the Mahabharata, "Those who sell the Veda, those who defile the Veda, and those who write the Veda, they shall go to hell" (13.23). Vedic writings often appear in anthologies or abridged editions for English readers, while unabridged and scholarly translations are very rare. The most authoritative, unabridged translations of the Rig Veda were produced in the nineteenth century by H. H. Wilson and Ralph T. H. Griffith (separate works).

See also HINDUISM; MANTRA; SHRUTI/ SRUTI; UPANISHADS

Bibliography. A. C. Clayton, *The Rig-Veda and Vedic Religion, with Readings from the Vedas*; R. N. Dandekar, "Vedas," in *Encyclopedia of Religion*, edited by L. Jones, 2nd ed.; W. Doniger O'Flaherty, ed. and trans., *Textual Sources for the Study of Hinduism*; C. A. Jones and J. D. Ryan, "Veda(s)," in *Encyclopedia of Hinduism*, edited by D. Cush, C. Robinson, and M. York; D. Killingley, "Veda," in *Encyclopedia of Hinduism*, edited by D. Cush, C. Robinson, and M. York; J. F. Lewis and W. G. Travis, *Religious Traditions of the World*; S. Schuhmacher and G. Woerner, eds., *The Rider Encyclopedia of Eastern Philosophy and Religion*; M. E. Snodgrass, *Encyclopedia of World Scriptures*; B. Walker, "Vedas" and "Vedism," in *The Hindu World: An Encyclopedic Survey of Hinduism*, 2 vols.

E. Pement

VIPASYANA. *Vipasyana* (Pali, *vipassana*; both mean "insight" or "clear seeing") denotes the intuitive cognition that recognizes the Buddhist truth about impermanence, suffering, and egolessness. This cognition does not arise through intellectual assent but rather occurs in the process of meditation. Vipasyana is a crucial component in the attainment of enlightenment. "Insight meditation" is a core practice in the Theravadan Buddhist tradition, as found in Thailand and Burma. In the Mahayana tradition, *vipasyana* is defined as the experience of the cosmos that yields the true insight about emptiness.

Vipasyana meditation has been transplanted from its Theravadan Southeast Asian context into the West and is particularly popular in the US. Dhiravamsa, a Thai monk, brought vipasyana meditation to the US in 1969. He pioneered the Vipassana Fellowship of America (now called the Dhiravamsa Foundation). Another prominent Asian teacher of Theravada vipasyana whose work has been popularized in the West is S. N. Goenka. In addition, many Tibetan monks have taught vipasyana according to their traditions in the West as well.

The most obvious adaptation of vipasyana in the West is seen in the Insight Meditation Society in Barre, Massachusetts. Joseph Goldstein, Jack Kornfield, and Sharon Salzberg, each of whom had studied in Southeast Asia, established the society in 1976. Both Goldstein and Kornfield have been prolific writers, popularizing the tenets of vipasyana or insight meditation. In their adaptation, vipasyana is presented as a breath meditation or mindfulness meditation for individuals who live in a fast-paced consumer culture. Aspirants may attend a weekend intensive seminar to be inducted into the precepts and practices, which after that event may be applied according to the dictates of Western lifestyles. The Four Noble Truths are expounded, but the stringent requirements in an ordered monastic community in Asia are absent in this Westernized adaptation. In 1958 Geshe Ngawang Wangyal established the first Tibetan (Gelugpa) monastery in the US, where he taught Tibetan practices and philosophy, including vipasyana.

See also BUDDHISM; ENLIGHTENMENT; MEDITATION; THERAVADA BUDDHISM

Bibliography. J. Goldstein, *Insight Meditation: The Practice of Freedom*; J. Kornfield, *A Path with Heart*; A. S. S. Namto, *Insight Meditation: Practical Steps to Ultimate Truth*.

P. Johnson

VIRGIN BIRTH. The virgin birth of Jesus is one of the signature doctrines of the Christian faith. It is the belief that Mary as a virgin, and without the instrumentality of human sexual intercourse, conceived and gave birth to Jesus Christ. The virginal conception of Jesus with Mary as his mother was believed, according to the witness of Christian Scripture (the Bible), to have been accomplished by the miraculous activity of God the Holy Spirit.

Two New Testament texts clearly assert the fact of the virgin birth: Matthew 1:18–25 and Luke 1:26–38. Other texts are referred to as supporting the virgin birth, such as Mark 6:3; John 1:13; and Galatians 4:4. Additionally, Isaiah 7:14 includes the prophecy that a "virgin shall conceive and bear a Son, and shall call His name Immanuel" (NKJV). The Hebrew text uses the term *'almah*, meaning a young woman of marriageable age, probably implying that she would be a virgin, although not specifically stating so. The Septuagint (Greek) version of Isaiah does expressly use the term for "virgin" (*parthenos*). The Septuagint possibly correctly reflected the pre-Christian Jewish interpretation of the word by using a Greek term that refers specifically to one who is a virgin.

Although some argue that the lack of other biblical verses explicitly stating the fact of the virgin birth militates against its importance, it is notable that Matthew's and Luke's infancy narratives, though very different in many respects and clearly independent of each other, both agree on the virgin birth, "a clear indication that it is based on an earlier common tradition" (Ferguson et al., 709).

Given the unmarried status of Mary, the only other possible explanation of her pregnant state, apart from the virginal conception, would be an illegitimate pregnancy outside wedlock. The Talmud claims that Jesus's birth occurred outside wedlock, a claim repugnant and reprehensible to Christians.

In addition to the Bible itself, the early church fathers wrote often about the virgin birth. They affirmed its historicity and reflected on its theological significance. Additionally, two widely utilized and early Christian creeds, the Apostles' and the Nicene, contain clear affirmations of the virgin birth, an indication of its early and substantial acceptance.

The virgin birth of Christ is not to be confused with either the immaculate conception of Mary or her perpetual virginity, two much later Roman Catholic dogmas. The first maintains that Mary was born without the influence and essence of original sin, and the latter declares that she remained a virgin even during the birth process of Jesus, without a broken hymen, and lived as such having borne no children through her marriage with Joseph. The first is rejected by evangelicals because there is no scriptural witness for it, and the second because there are passages that speak of the brothers and sisters of Jesus. In their scriptural context, references to brothers and sisters of Jesus clearly referred to a physical, familial relationship, and not a spiritual relationship (Matt. 13:55–56; Mark 3:31–35).

Other misinterpretations of the virgin birth include liberal nineteenth- and twentieth-century theologies that generally interpreted the virgin birth as a spiritual metaphor. They said, that is, that in the primitive, prescientific worldview of early Christianity, the virgin birth was a legendary accretion to the story of Jesus reflecting the Christian movement's devotion, admiration, and reverence for Jesus but not the literal, historical truth of his human experience.

Other aberrations of the virgin birth among religions and heterodox groups include Islam's perspective. The Qur'an, in sura 19:16–21, maintains that Jesus indeed was born of a virgin. His birth without a human father was a sign to the world of Jesus's prophetic status. The Qur'an does not develop the idea theologically, and while Islam affirms this miraculous occurrence, the religion denigrates the notion of Allah having a son. The breathing of Gabriel on Mary is generally believed to be the means whereby God's spirit entered Mary in order for Jesus to be conceived. Notably, Islam does not attempt to define or elucidate what or who this spirit is.

The Jehovah's Witnesses accept that Mary was a virgin at the conception of Jesus but do not accept his eternal divine nature as God the Word. Rather, they believe that the virgin birth was a transitional phase of the process by which Michael the archangel became God's son Jesus. In the parlance of the Watch Tower movement, God transferred the life force of Michael from heaven into Mary's womb: "He willingly submitted as God transferred his life from heaven to the womb" (Watch Tower Bible and Tract Society, *Knowledge That Leads*). Jesus was not, therefore, God in the flesh—the divine Son of God—but "the glorified spirit Son of God" (Watch Tower Bible and Tract Society, *Reasoning from the Scriptures*).

The Church of Jesus Christ of Latter-day Saints (LDS Church) also reconstructs the virgin birth. While the Book of Mormon texts highlight the teaching that Mary "did conceive by the power of the Holy Ghost and bring forth a son" (Alma 7:10), and contemporary spokesmen reaffirm this concept, other interpretations emerged within Mormonism. One is the notion that Jesus was conceived in the first instance as a premortal spirit son of God in the premortal realm (Doctrine and Covenants 93:21; Church of Jesus Christ of Latter-day Saints, 9). Then he was conceived again in this world, as a mortal human, by and through the person of Mary. Brigham Young, an early leader of the LDS Church (1801–77), denied that the "Holy Ghost" was the instrument of conception. Bruce McConkie, a Mormon apostle and theologian, commented, "Christ was begotten by an Immortal Father in the same way that mortal men are begotten by mortal fathers" (546–47). Others have similarly suggested a literal sexual union between God and Mary: "The body [Jesus's] . . . was sired by the same Holy Being we worship as God, our Eternal Father" (Benson, 6–7). *Gospel Principles*, the catechetical manual of the LDS Church, maintains that "God the Father became the literal father of Jesus Christ" (53).

The virgin birth is a revealed truth of the Holy Scripture. It explicates the mode whereby God the Word became fully human and was born in the flesh while retaining all his divine nature.

See also CHRISTIANITY, PROTESTANT; CHURCH OF JESUS CHRIST OF LATTER-DAY SAINTS; ISLAM, BASIC BELIEFS OF; JEHOVAH'S WITNESSES (JW)

Bibliography. E. T. Benson, *The Teachings of Ezra Taft Benson*; Church of Jesus Christ of Latter-day Saints, *Gospel Principles*; S. B. Ferguson et al., eds., *New Dictionary of Theology*; B. R. McConkie, *Mormon Doctrine*; Joseph Smith Jr. et al., Doctrine and Covenants; Watch Tower Bible and Tract Society, *Knowledge That Leads to Everlasting Life*; Watch Tower Bible and Tract Society of Pennsylvania, *Reasoning from the Scriptures*.

R. P. Roberts

VISHNU. In Vedic literature, Vishnu is the god who sustains the universe. He is one of the three main gods of Hinduism along with Brahma, regarded as the creator of the universe, and Shiva, regarded as the destroyer of the universe. Vishnu is said to be involved in ensuring that a proper balance between good and evil exists at all times on the earth. When the balance between these two forces is unsettled, Vishnu appears among human beings to correct the imbalance and restore harmony. When compared to Brahma and Shiva, Vishnu is shown to be the most active among the Hindu Vedic gods. Brahma is rarely worshiped individually among the Hindus since the cosmos is seen as an emanation of him, and Shiva has no recorded manifestations in the Hindu literature.

Worshipers of Vishnu. Those who worship Vishnu among the Hindu faithful are called Vaishnavites. Images of Vishnu in Hindu art take the form of blue- or black-skinned figures with four arms. Hinduism teaches that Vishnu has over one thousand names, and the repetitious pronouncement of them is a form of worship. Vishnu is said to have appeared on earth in nine different avatars, or manifestations, to assist in overcoming evil, with one avatar still to come.

Manifestations of Vishnu. In Indian mythology, Vishnu appears in numerous incarnations. As Matsya, Vishnu appeared in the form of a fish to rescue the first man, Manu. As Kurma, Vishnu was a turtle that saved the cosmos from destruction from the churning of the oceans, which was caused by the gods and demons who were working together to mine the ocean bottoms. As Varaha, he appeared as a boar and killed the titan Hiranyaksh, who had stolen the sacred Vedas; this act by Vishnu resulted in releasing the earth from its imprisonment at the bottom of the ocean. Vishnu's fourth avatar was a half lion and half man who battled and killed the titan Hiranyashasipu, brother of the titan Niranyaksha. Vishnu appeared as Vamana the dwarf, to deliver the earth from Bali the titan, who had forced the gods to flee from the heavens. Parasurama was Vishnu's sixth manifestation; he appeared to kill power-drunk King Kartavirya, who had stolen the holy cow Kamadhenu, said to grant the wishes of its owner. As Rama he appeared in order to kill the demon King Ravana, who had kidnapped Rama's wife, Sita.

The last two manifestations of Vishnu are perhaps the two most recognizable.

As Krishna, Vishnu appeared in order to kill the tyrannical king of Mathura, Kansa. It is this avatar that the Mahabharata epic captures in story. Vishnu as Krishna visits Arjuna, one of five Pandava brothers, who is fighting to regain rule of the kingdom. Krishna-Vishnu discusses with Arjuna the responsibility that he has to perform his duty (dharma) and tells him about the three paths to a better life: devotion (Bhakti Yoga), action (Karma Yoga), and knowledge (Jnana Yoga). This conversation became known as the Bhagavad Gita.

Vishnu's final avatar was in the form of Buddha. In this appearance, Vishnu is said to have come to alleviate the suffering of humankind. Buddhism as a formal religion does not view Buddha in the same way as Hinduism views him. Within Buddhism, Buddha was an enlightened one who came to teach others the path of enlightenment. Vishnu's final appearance is anticipated within Hinduism as Kalki, seated on a white horse at the end of the present age, referred to as Kaliyuga.

See also AVATAR; BHAKTI YOGA; BRAHMA; DHARMA; HINDUISM; KARMA; SHIVA; VEDAS; YOGA

Bibliography. A. Michaels and B. Harshav, *Hinduism: Past and Present*; H. W. Tull, *The Vedic Origins of Karma: Cosmos as Man in Ancient Indian Myth and Ritual*; M. B. Wangu, *Hinduism*.

M. Spaulding

WAHHABIYYA ISLAM. Wahhabiyya Islam is an Islamic renewal and reform movement founded in the Nejd province of the central Arabian peninsula in the eighteenth century. Adherents of this Islamic group are often referred to as Wahhabis, though they refer to themselves as Muwahhidun, an Arabic term meaning "those who champion the unity and oneness of God."

Its founder, Muhammad Ibn Abd al-Wahhab, received training as a Hanbali scholar of Sunni Islamic religious law in Basra and Medina. Like other Islamic revivalists of the eighteenth century, al-Wahhab identified an apparent corrosion of Islam through the continued acceptance of rituals and beliefs from other religions. The adoption of other religious praxis was thought to contradict the unconditional monotheism of Islam (*tawheed*), while leading to the perceived moral decline of Arabic Muslim communities. Thus al-Wahhab advocated the elimination of what he considered foreign, non-Islamic practices and beliefs from the Muslim religion in favor of a disciplinary adherence to tawheed. Essentially, these teachings culminated in three significant conceptions: (1) consideration of motivation and intent is encouraged over mere ritual perfection, (2) any reverence for the dead is impermissible, and (3) all intercessory prayer is forbidden and contradictory to the constitutive beliefs of Islam. These points were to be conjoined with the implementation of Islamic Shari'ah law and with a singular focus on religious scripture. Al-Wahhab

emphasized a primary role for the Qur'an and the hadith, promoting a relatively literalistic reading of these texts and the dismissal of medieval commentaries of Islam and its laws. This movement claimed that adherence to such literal interpretations would assist in ushering in a fundamental sociopolitical and moral transformation of society.

As a result of these propositions, a severe antipathy developed toward the popular cult of saints, the associated shrine and temple pilgrimages, and all the use of rosaries or wearing of religious charms. This is demonstrated in Ibn Abd al-Wahhab's rejection of Sufism as idolatrous and his attacks on Shi'ite shrines, emphasized in the 1802 offensive against the Najaf and Karbala holy sites. In this vein, the movement limited Muslim festivals and denounced the popular celebration of Muhammad's birthday, formulating what is often considered a type of puritanical Islam. Luxurious attire and habits were censured, and strict prohibitions against alcohol, tobacco, and gambling came into effect. From this perspective al-Wahhab even associated the general population of Muslims with polytheists (*musrik*) and condemned as unbelievers those who did not practice the established times of prayer. This antagonism extended to other religions, which contrasted with Islam's conception of tawheed. As a result, both Muslims and non-Muslims may deserve judgment.

The Wahhabiyya movement formed a strategic alliance with Muhammad Ibn Saud in 1747, which led to the consolidation of contemporary Saudi Arabia. In affiliation with the Saud family, Wahhabi forces initiated significant military campaigns into the Hejaz, Iraq, and Syria, including the successful 1806 capture of Mecca. Despite serious opposition and defeat at the hands of Ottoman forces, Wahhabis maintained their presence across the peninsula.

Since World War II the movement has developed in conjunction with the contemporary growth of Islamic fundamentalism, playing a significant role in the Afghan civil war and being associated with modern terrorist fronts. Osama bin Laden's al-Qaeda and the Taliban proclaim they are upholding the virtues of Wahhabi Islam, and many in the West are concerned about the spread of Wahhabi clerics and schools into Europe and America (including those supported by the Saudi royal family).

See also BIN LADEN, OSAMA BIN MUHAMMAD BIN 'AWAD; ISLAM, BASIC BELIEFS OF; QUR'AN; SHARI'AH; SHI'A ISLAM; SUFISM; SUNNI ISLAM; TAWHEED

Bibliography. N. J. DeLong-Bas, *Wahhabi Islam: From Revival and Reform to Global Jihad*; S. Schwartz, *The Two Faces of Islam: The House of Sa'ud from Tradition to Terror*.

T. Aechtner

WAR AND PEACE IN WORLD RELIGIONS. No religion eschews war in all circumstances, and no faith tradition (especially Christianity) is monolithic in its dogma and practice regarding war and peace.

Zoroastrianism. Dating to around 1300 BC in Persia, Zoroastrianism has a long history of nationalism and militarism. The idea of conflict and battle, spiritual and physical, is central in its thought, which views life as a battleground between good and evil, light and darkness, that will culminate in an eschatological conflict between the powers of light and darkness.

Hinduism. Hinduism has a strong teaching of nonviolence, or *ahimsa*, a concept shared in Jainism and Buddhism. But the social structure of the caste system also has a place for a warrior class (Kshatriyas). One's religious and social obligations are tied to one's role in the caste system; therefore performing one's duty appropriately does not attach the penalty of evil karma for such actions. Thus nonviolence as a virtue may not be appropriate for everyone. In the Hindu epic the Bhagavad Gita, there is strong fatalism, indifference toward the physical world, and ambivalence toward war. There are, however, strict rules of war, similar to just war doctrine.

Jainism. Tracing its roots to the eighth century BC, Jainism has a strong sense of nonviolence, asceticism, and renunciation of the desire to kill or do harm to any living creature, human or otherwise (although in the twelfth century there were famous Jain military commanders).

Buddhism. Since its founding in northern India by Siddhartha Gautama (ca. 563–ca. 483 BC), Buddhism has fostered both pacifistic and militaristic strands in both of its main traditions—Theravada and Mahayana Buddhism—but today it is understood primarily as a religion of peace. Both schools emphasize self-improvement through meditation and gaining a compassionate attitude to oneself and others through recognition of the Four Noble Truths and practice of the Five Precepts (among them, abstaining from killing) and the Eightfold Path. Buddhist belief in reincarnation fosters the sense of compassion for all living creatures and the renunciation of violence. Concurrently, militaristic strands of Buddhism arose historically, due in part to the coexistence of Buddhism with Taoism, Shinto, and Confucianism in a geographic region where one of the accepted traits of personal greatness was skill in the martial arts. As with many other religions, the monks and religious leaders were often educated, and literate members of a society were sought out by warlords, rulers, and political figures in matters of war and peace.

Sikhism. Though known as a religion of peace, Sikhism is not a pacifistic religion, and there is a militant tradition within it. It stresses on human dignity, freedom, and justice that permits self-defense and resistance when necessary, especially to protect the rights of Sikhs. This concept is idealized in the *kirpan*, a dagger carried by all Sikhs as a matter of religious devotion.

Bahá'í. Bahá'ís are not pacifists but rather stress the unity of all people and believe that world peace is possible and inevitable. They argue that humankind is experiencing an "adolescence" and must move to adulthood to arrive at peace. World peace, according to Bahá'ís, will be achieved through the cessation of racism, the disappearance of extreme wealth and poverty, the achievement of equality between men and women, the end of nationalism, and the elimination of religious strife.

Judaism. Drawing on the Old Testament and centuries of rabbinic literature, Judaism understands peace as part of God's original purpose for humanity and therefore individuals. Jews are to pursue peace wherever possible and also to work in partnership with God in repairing a broken world, practicing a principle known as *tikkun olam.* The idea of holy war as found in the Old Testament conquest of Canaan, the Maccabbean wars, and the revolt against Rome is not the same as later Jewish understanding of war, represented by thinkers such as Maimonides (1135–1204). There are times when war may be an unfortunate necessity. Rabbinic literature distinguishes between two kinds of war: optional war (*milchemet reshut*) and obligatory war (*milchemet chovah*). The latter is also called religious war (*milchemet mitzvah*). An example of an obligatory war is when the survival of the nation of Israel is at stake. Verses in the Torah, such as Deuteronomy 20, provide guidelines for waging war that seek to minimize destruction and protect noncombatants. Centuries of persecution

and pogroms, culminating in the Holocaust during World War II (and continued conflict in the Middle East), have also significantly affected Jewish perspectives.

Islam. In both of its main traditions—Sunni and Shi'a—Islam has a long history of war and peace most often associated with the concept of jihad, which literally means "struggle" but is often translated "holy war" and understood to include war against unbelievers and enemies of the faith. Jihad has always been a strong force in Islam, and it has connotations of internal struggles against one's evil inclinations (known as the "greater jihad") as well as external struggles that may include armed violence (the "lesser jihad"). Jihad is both a personal and a corporate commitment within Islam to spread the faith. The greater jihad is the personal struggle that a Muslim wages against sin and all that is against Allah. It is a personal battle for righteousness. The lesser jihad is the struggle against the enemies of Islam. It is a holy war waged in the name of Allah and according to the will of Allah. The divinely mandated defense and expansion of Islamic power through physical confrontation is understood through the division of two realms, which are ideological, political, and theological. The first is *dar al-Islam* (the house of Islam), in which Muslim law and rule prevail, and the second is *dar al-harb* (the house of war), in which resides the rest of the world, including unbelievers, infidels, and apostates. According to Islamic belief, a perpetual state of conflict will exist between the two houses, until the house of Islam prevails.

Islamic jurists through the centuries have established certain rules of war, some of which parallel ideas in the just war doctrine. Only a caliph or imam has the legitimate authority to declare jihad. Additionally, the war must be waged with good intentions, and there should always be an invitation to accede to Islam before attack. Further, noncombatant immunity must be observed, as well as concerns for property and the environment. In the twentieth century, many Muslims believed that there had been a suspension of jihad—a view that coincided with the rise of nationalism (a view popular in Sufi Islam, wherein self-mastery and purification are stressed over violence). Toward the end of the century, however, Islamic militant thought revived and reinvoked the idea of jihad against secular governments that had been "corrupted" by Western influences and values.

Christianity. Throughout its two millennia, Christianity has justified, rationalized, restrained, and informed war and the conduct of warfare. It has, in various times and by diverse means, both upheld and departed from biblical standards, and both ecclesiastical and secular leaders have appealed to its teachings for personal and national guidance and support. At the foundation of the Christian understanding of war is a belief in the fallen and broken nature of humanity—a belief that all humanity and every aspect of personal and corporate life are marred by sin and original sin. War is ultimately a reflection and consequence of sin.

Christians throughout history have recognized that the formulation of a doctrine of war or approach to war is a theological and biblical deduction based on the interpretation of numerous passages in the Bible (see Eccles. 3:1, 8; Matt. 5:44; 24:6–7; Acts 10:1–23; Rom. 13:1–7; 1 Tim. 2:1–2; 1 Pet. 2:13–17). How those passages are interpreted determines the position that one holds. There is no "red letter" biblical doctrine of war. Thus the issue is not "What is the Bible's view of war?" but "What view best interprets and reflects fully the biblical passages regarding war?"

The Christian response to war has been a spectrum ranging from absolute rejection of war and of participation in war to full participation with the proclamation of divine blessing and authority. The spectrum has ranged from the pacifist words of the American folk hymn "Gonna lay down my sword and shield, down by the riverside . . . ain't gonna study war no more" to the cry of the crusaders of the Middle Ages, "Deus lo volt! [God wills it!]"

Several Christian perspectives on war have emerged over the centuries. The spectrum of Christian participation in war runs as follows: pacifism, nonresistance, just war, preventive war, and crusade. Each of these views has secular as well as religious counterparts—namely, pacifism and Christian pacifism, just war and Christian just war. Each view also has strengths and weaknesses as well as variations.

At the two ends of the spectrum are pacifism and the crusade. The "just war" position ideologically is the moderating position in the spectrum, and historically, it is the view that has been most prevalent throughout church history. It is also a view that was developed largely by Christians (especially Ambrose, Augustine, Thomas Aquinas, and Hugo Grotius).

The strongest and most well-defined position (whether religious or secular) regarding war and peace is that of the just war tradition. Some aspects of the just war tradition predate Christianity, extending back to classical Rome and Athens. Others are firmly grounded in Christian history and theology stemming from Christian theologians such as Ambrose and Augustine. Yet other parts of the tradition can be found in events of twentieth- and twenty-first-century human rights and legal theories. The tradition has always been multidisciplinary and far reaching in the social, political, theological, legal, and philosophical net cast by its proponents. The just war tradition has developed over hundreds of years. It has been and continues to be heavily influenced by Christianity but also continues to draw on Roman law and Greek philosophy.

Four presuppositions undergird the just war tradition: (1) Some evil in the world cannot be avoided. (2) The principles of a just war are normative for all people, both Christian and non-Christian. The tradition describes not how people act but how they should act, and it applies to all people, whether they accept the tradition or not, whether they are Christian or not. (3) People should not seek to justify war. Rather, war must be brought within the limits of justice, so that if everyone were guided by these principles, many wars would be eliminated. (4) Individuals or private citizens do not have the right to use military force. Only governments have such a right. Thus, the key issue is not whether an individual can fight in war but whether a government has the right to engage in armed conflict and whether a citizen, Christian or not, should participate as an agent of that government. All aggression is condemned in the just war tradition. Participation in the war in question must be prompted by a just cause or defensive cause. No war of unprovoked aggression can ever be justified. Only defensive war is legitimate.

There are seven principles or criteria for the just war. The first five principles apply as a nation is "on the way to war" (*jus ad bellum*), and the final two apply to military forces "in the midst of war" (*jus in bello*). They are, consequently, just cause, just intention (right intention), last reasonable resort, formal declaration, limited objectives, proportionate means, and noncombatant immunity. The just war tradition has three important functions: it seeks to limit the devastation and outbreak of war; it offers a common moral framework and language with which to discuss issues of war in the public arena; it gives moral guidance to individuals in developing their conscience, responsibilities, and response to issues of war and peace.

See also AHIMSA; BAHÁ'Í; BUDDHISM; CHRISTIAN; HINDUISM; JAINISM; JUDAISM; SHI'A ISLAM; SIKHISM; SUNNI ISLAM; ZORO-ASTRIANISM

Bibliography. R. G. Clouse, ed., *War: Four Christian Views*; J. Ferguson, *War and Peace in the World's Religions*; J. Kelsay, *Arguing the Just War in Islam*; V. Popovski, ed., *World Religions and Norms of War*; H. O. Thompson, *World Religions in War and Peace*.

T. J. Demy

WARD. *Ward* is the term used to designate the "basic ecclesiastical unit" of the Church of Jesus Christ of Latter-day Saints (Mormons). Its membership range is from three hundred to six hundred members, and its structure and purpose are comparable to those of a Protestant congregation. The structure includes three principal church-appointed leaders: a bishop and two counselors. Along with weekly sacrament meetings, the ward provides for education and member discipline.

See also CHURCH OF JESUS CHRIST OF LATTER-DAY SAINTS

Bibliography. D. J. Davies, *An Introduction to Mormonism*.

R. P. Roberts

WATCHTOWER, THE. The principal semimonthly publication of the Watch Tower Bible and Tract Society (WT, or Jehovah's Witnesses [JW]) is *The Watchtower announcing Jehovah's Kingdom* (known simply as the *Watchtower*). The magazine was begun in 1879 by Charles Taze Russell as *Zion's Watch Tower and Herald of Christ's Presence*. In 1920 *Zion's* was dropped from the title. In January 1939 *Presence* was changed to *Kingdom*, and in March of that year the present title was adopted. Until 1990 the *Watchtower* was available for a fee, but in that year the Supreme Court ruled that religious literature which is only available for sale was subject to taxation. Since that time the *Watchtower* has been free, although the society asks for a donation to support the printing and distribution of the magazine.

The WT communicates to its members four times each month through two publications, the *Watchtower* magazine and *Awake!* These publications are also distributed to the general public as a means of introducing people to the WT and recruiting them into the organization. Witnesses often leave them in waiting rooms and other public places and distribute them door-to-door and on street corners.

The *Watchtower* claims average printing of nearly forty-six million copies, and it is currently published in 214 languages. *Awake!* and the *Watchtower* have different emphases. While the former focuses on the WT's view of current events, scientific discoveries, and interesting topics, the latter is devoted more to the study of WT doctrine. The *Watchtower*'s masthead announces that it "comforts people with the good news that God's heavenly Kingdom will soon end all wickedness and transform the earth into a paradise." This earthly paradise is where, according to the WT, most of God's faithful will live since, in their view, heaven's human population will be limited to 144,000 (however, see Rev. 7:9; 19:1–6).

The *Watchtower* contains articles on doctrinal issues, studies on religious themes, background information on other religious groups, and a number of other themes. But whatever the topic, the point is to convey the official WT perspective, and many of the articles stress the importance of following WT leaders and avoiding independent thinking and independent Bible study. Major doctrinal changes are announced through this publication.

One major controversy erupted over a change announced in the November 1, 1995, issue. For many years, the WT had told followers that the generation that saw the events of 1914 would not die but rather live to see the beginning of God's kingdom on earth, based on Matthew 24:34. In 1995 the WT said that its understanding of the word *generation* no longer meant a physical generation of people but could mean a longer period of uncertain duration. This change was necessary because so few of the 1914 generation were still alive.

On May 1, 2007, the society reversed a long-standing teaching that the 144,000 "anointed class" had been full since 1931. The new teaching is that the 144,000 total is not known to be filled, and Witnesses who feel they have a "heavenly hope" should not be presumed to be in error. WT observers note that for years the members of the society's Governing Body have been part of the Great Crowd. The new ruling allows board members to now identify themselves with the "anointed class," which they formerly could not do.

On July 15, 2013, another major reversal occurred. Formerly, it was taught that the "faithful and discreet slave" who was put in charge over Jesus's "domestics" (household servants) began with the apostles in AD 33 and included all "anointed" Christians. Now, the society teaches that the "faithful and discreet slave" is the Governing Body alone, not all anointed Christians, and that it was not put in charge of Jesus's servants until 1919. Formerly, it was taught that Jesus's prediction of the "faithful slave" being put in charge of all the Master's "belongings" (see Matt. 24:47) was fulfilled by the Watch Tower Society in 1918; now, it is taught that this will be fulfilled by the Governing Body *in the future*. The effect of this new teaching is to restict the "faithful slave" to the Governing Body alone and to remove Charles Russell from any activity as part of that "slave."

See also JEHOVAH'S WITNESSES (JW)

Bibliography. D. Reed, ed., *Index of Watchtower Errors.*

E. Shropshire and E. Pement

WISDOM, BIBLICAL VIEW OF. In Hebrew thought and the Bible generally, wisdom is seen as a great virtue consisting of knowledge based on the experience of life and God's creation order. It is practical insight rather than theory and involves good judgment and prudent action. The Wisdom literature of the Bible instructs believers in how to act in a wise way and includes the books of Job, Ecclesiastes, and Proverbs.

I. Hexham

WORD OF WISDOM. The "Word of Wisdom" is the common designation for section 89 of the Doctrine and Covenants, a scripture of the Church of Jesus Christ of Latter-day Saints (LDS Church, or Mormonism); it is also the title of a related, compulsory health regulation advocated by the LDS Church. Mormon founder Joseph Smith Jr. (1805–44) alleged that the Word of Wisdom was revealed to him by God on February 27, 1833. The text of section 89 lists all of those substances whose use by Mormons is subject to various restrictions or discouraged altogether. Specifically, it promotes abstinence from using tobacco and from consuming wine and strong or hot drinks, suggests limitations on eating meat, and encourages the consumption of herbs, grains, and fruit. It also promises health and wisdom to those who obey its pronouncements.

At the time it was given, the Word of Wisdom was viewed as a revelation whose observance was not obligatory. However, in September 1851 LDS president Brigham Young (1801–77) transformed the Word of Wisdom into a moral mandate for all Mormons. Today, Mormons cannot be baptized or allowed to enter LDS temples if they violate the Word of Wisdom (as it is presently understood by the LDS leadership).

The interpretation and application of the Word of Wisdom has changed in significant ways during the history of Mormonism. One was a shift away from prohibiting the particular items enumerated in the text of section 89 of Doctrine and Covenants and toward the banning of all potentially addictive substances. This eventually resulted in the prohibition of all alcoholic beverages,

even though using Mormon-made wine during Communion services and drinking beer are permitted in the text. More recently the LDS Church has banned the use of narcotics except as prescribed by a physician. Another change is the official LDS interpretation of the "hot drinks" statement in section 89, so that it now requires only the prohibition of coffee and nonherbal tea, regardless of their temperature; the drinking of hot chocolate, for example, is allowed. Although the LDS Church does not officially forbid the consumption of caffeinated beverages, it advises Mormons to eschew caffeinated soft drinks and iced tea. Some Mormons go so far as to refrain from drinking even decaffeinated coffee, tea, or soda and from eating chocolate. Yet most Mormons ignore the recommendations concerning meat found in section 89.

Much of the reason for confusion among LDS Church members regarding the specifics of the Word of Wisdom can be traced to conflicting statements of LDS authorities over time. Mormon apostle George Q. Cannon (1827–1901) stated that Mormons should not consume hot soups or chocolate drinks. LDS president Joseph Fielding Smith (1876–1972) declared that persons who drink tea may be barred from the celestial kingdom. Mormon theologian Bruce R. McConkie (1915–85) asserted that the Word of Wisdom revelation forbids the use of tobacco, coffee, tea, and liquor. Yet each of these famous statements conflicts in some way with the current, official stance of the LDS Church.

See also CHURCH OF JESUS CHRIST OF LATTER-DAY SAINTS

Bibliography. T. G. Alexander, *Mormonism in Transition: A History of the Latter-day Saints, 1890–1930*, repr. ed.; L. J. Arrington and D. Bitton, *The Mormon Experience: A History of the Latter-day Saints*, 2nd ed.; W. F. W. Johanson, *What Is Mormonism All About? Answers to the 150 Most Commonly Asked Questions about the Church of Jesus Christ of Latter-day Saints*; B. R. McConkie, *Mormon Doctrine*, 2nd ed.;

J. Shipps, *Mormonism: The Story of a New Religious Tradition*; Joseph Smith Jr. et al., Doctrine and Covenants, section 89; J. Tanner and S. Tanner, *Mormonism: Shadow or Reality?*

H. W. House

WORLD COUNCIL OF CHURCHES. The World Council of Churches is an ecumenical organization bringing together a wide variety of Christian denominations, including Anglicans, Eastern Orthodox, and Protestants of various types. It was founded in Amsterdam in 1948 and has become increasingly liberal and politically radical over time, with the result that it is distrusted by many fundamentalist and evangelical Christians.

I. Hexham

WORLD'S PARLIAMENT OF RELIGIONS (1893 AND 1993). In 1893 the city of Chicago hosted the World's Columbian Exposition, and under the umbrella of that six-month fair the World's Parliament of Religions was convened. The principal organizers were Charles Bonney, a lawyer and follower of Swedenborg, and John Henry Barrows, a Presbyterian minister in Chicago. A steering committee was formed that included Chicago's Roman Catholic archbishop Feehan, Rabbi Emil Hirsch, the Unitarian Jenkin Jones, and fourteen Protestant ministers. The purpose of this parliament was to demonstrate a humanitarian unity of religions in their good deeds—a brotherhood among the world's diverse religious traditions. It was infused with optimism about the moral evolution of humanity in the coming century.

Delegates included representatives from the Roman Catholic, Eastern Orthodox, and Protestant churches, as well as Unitarians, Theosophists, Universalists, Jews, and a small number of Muslims, Buddhists, Jains, and Hindus. Some of the Christian delegates who spoke were the apologist Alexander Bruce, South Pacific missionary John G. Paton, church historian Philip Schaff, and biblical scholar Charles Briggs. Mary Baker Eddy gave a presentation about Christian Science, Swami Vivekananda of the Ramakrishna Math spoke on Hinduism, and Anagarika Dharmapala of the Maha Bodhi Society gave three presentations concerning the Buddha. A few scholars of comparative religion, such as Max Müller and Estlin Carpenter, sent papers that were delivered on their behalf.

The delegates expressed at least three broad viewpoints: exclusion, inclusion, and plurality. The exclusionist view was that Christianity is the only true religion and is destined to supplant all other faiths. Some, such as the Baptist Reverend William Wilkinson, maintained that Christianity alone had the truth, while others, such as Milton Valentine, admitted there was some good in other faiths but Christianity was superior. The inclusionist view was that there is one true religion, but it had yet to evolve in human history and would partake of the best elements of several faiths or comprise those things that the world's religions held in common. This view was expressed by Rabbi Hirsch, Reverend Merwin Snell, and Reverend E. L. Rexford. The pluralist view was that no one religion could claim exclusive truth and that in their essentials all religions hold to a belief in a supreme being and common ethical beliefs. External differences between the religions were not considered fundamental. Charles Bonney, John Barrows, and Hirai Kinzo took this position.

In 1993 the centenary of the parliament was observed in Chicago with the Second World's Parliament of Religions. It included representatives from the major religions, as well as indigenous tribes, neo-pagans, New Agers, and various new religious movements. Delegates included the Dalai Lama, Louis Farrakhan (Nation of Islam), Hans Küng, Barbara Marx Hubbard, and Robert Muller. The global nature of interfaith dialogue and religious tolerance was meant to be reflected, but some Jewish delegates objected to Farrakhan, and Eastern Orthodox delegates left because of neo-pagan ceremonies. A document proclaiming a global ethic was issued by the parliament. Another outcome was a further parliamentary assembly convened in South Africa in 1999.

See also DALAI LAMA XIV (TENZIN GYATSO); EASTERN ORTHODOXY; HINDUISM; ISLAM, BASIC BELIEFS OF; JAINISM; JUDAISM; ROMAN CATHOLICISM; UNITARIANISM

Bibliography. R. H. Seager, ed., *The Dawn of Religious Pluralism: Voices from the World's Parliament of Religions*; Seager, *The World's Parliament of Religions: The East/West Encounter, Chicago, 1893*; W. Teasdale and G. F. Cairns, eds., *The Community of Religions: Voices and Images of the Parliament of the World's Religions*.

P. Johnson

WU-WEI. In Taoism *wu-wei* (Chinese, "no deliberative action" or "effortless performance") refers to the engagement of a person in non-self-conscious feats of skill as a result of his inner harmony with the Tao; it presupposes that the person in question is not striving against the Tao in any way. These highly adept actions are performed in a state of deep tranquility and flow from their doer in such a way that the doer is not mindful of exertion. The concept of wu-wei was first set forth in the writings of the ancient Chinese philosopher Lao Tzu (or Laozi; ca. fourth century BC). It is a paradoxical concept in that it involves "trying not to try" (in a certain sense). Many practitioners of Taoism and some Confucians hold to wu-wei as a defining ethical standard.

See also LAO TZU/LAOZI; TAOISM/DAOISM

Bibliography. R. Kirkland, *Taoism: The Enduring Tradition*; E. Slingerland, *Effortless Action: Wu-wei as Conceptual Metaphor and Spiritual Ideal in Early China*.

M. Power

XIAO/HSIAO. In Confucianism *xiao* (Chinese, "filial piety") denotes the attitude of deference and its accompanying attentive care displayed by those occupying lower social stations toward those in more highly esteemed positions. Most prominently this involves the love and honor sons show their parents and the respect and humane treatment older people receive from younger people. However, xiao encompasses a broad range of social relationships, among which are those between father and son, ruler and subject, husband and wife, older brother and younger brother, and one friend and another. In particular Confucianism deems it critical that children render unquestioning obedience to their parents, that subjects demonstrate loyalty to their rulers (*zhong*), and that wives obey their husbands. Some of the obligations involved in xiao continue even after the death of the one to whom these duties are rendered (i.e., the veneration of ancestors). More generally, xiao is thought to provide the moral basis for family harmony, political stability, and the flourishing of culture. The authoritative source on xiao is the Xiao Jing, or Classic of Xiao, apparently written in 470 BC, which records a conversation between Confucius and Zeng Shen, his student.

See also CONFUCIANISM

Bibliography. A. K. L. Chan and S. Tan, eds., *Filial Piety in Chinese Thought and History*; N. Kutcher, *Mourning in Late Imperial China: Filial Piety and the State*; L. G. Thompson, *Chinese Religion: An Introduction*, 5th ed.

H. W. House

Y

YAHWEHISM. The term *Yahwehism* refers to two unrelated forms of worship.

In studies of the Old Testament and the history of Israel, Yahwehism refers to the worship of God under the name Yahweh, as distinguished from the worship of God under the name El, Elohim, other divine names, or the syncretistic worship of Ba'al and other deities. When the term *cult* or *cultus* occurs in these contexts, it is an academic synonym for particular ritual forms, routines, or distinguishing traits; it is not a pejorative word for social control.

The term *Yahwehism* is also used to designate the aspect of the Sacred Name movement that insists on frequent use of the covenant name of the God of Israel (the Tetragrammaton) or some English transliteration or pronunciation of the name, as essential to true worship. Various Sacred Name groups differ on how the name should be pronounced, but virtually all discourage the use of "God" or "Lord," even if capitalized as GOD and LORD. It is common for Yahwehism to occur in conjunction with sabbatarianism, legalism, Jewish dietary laws, renewal of Old Testament festivals, and other aspects of the Sacred Name movement. The Hebrew Israelite movement is one manifestation of Yahwehism, but there are others as well.

See also SABBATARIANISM; TETRAGRAMMATON

Bibliography. J. R. Lewis, *Cults: A Reference Handbook*; J. Walker, *Concise Guide to Today's Religions and Spirituality*.

E. Pement

YAWM AL-QIYAMAH. *See* DAY OF JUDGMENT, ISLAMIC

YIDAM. In Tibetan Buddhism, a *yidam* ("tutelary deity"; sometimes referred to as an *ishtadevata*) is an enlightened being (Buddha, bodhisattva, etc.) who, during meditation, is the focus of intense concentration on the part of his or her devotee. Each yidam possesses unique characteristics such that their devotees are able to closely identify with that particular yidam and thereby come to recognize the inherent purity of their mind and their ontological unity with the Primordial Buddha. A yidam, then, is not viewed as a dispenser of favors or a personal savior whose work takes place independently of the devotee, but is seen as a refuge from the distractions of the world of illusion and a powerful aid in the quest for enlightenment and liberation from the cycle of death and rebirth. Some devotees take yidams to be literal "deities" within the Vajrayana pantheon—tantric gods, Buddhas, or bodhisattvas—while others understand them as extensions of their own consciousness. Practitioners desiring to identify with a yidam engage in *sadhana* (means of accomplishment), a set of meditation rituals that facilitate the transformation of their false self-understanding into a state of awakened wisdom wherein they grasp the truth of the emptiness of all phenomena. Popular yidams include Avalokiteshvara, Cakrasamvara, Guhyasamaja, Hayagriva, Hevajra, Kalacakra, Kurukulla, Manjusri, Marici, Surata, Vajrakilaya, Vajrayogini, and Yamantaka.

See also KALACAKRA; TANTRA; TIBETAN BUDDHISM; VAJRAYANA BUDDHISM

Bibliography. A. T. Palmo, *Reflections on a Mountain Lake: Teachings on Practical Buddhism*; S. Rinpoche, *The Tibetan Book of Living and Dying: A New Spiritual Classic from One of the Foremost Interpreters of Tibetan Buddhism to the West*; Sangharakshita, *A Guide to the Buddhist Path*; B. A. Wallace, *Tibetan Buddhism from the Ground Up: A Practical Approach for Modern Life*.

H. W. House

YIN AND YANG. In Chinese philosophy, Yin and Yang are the impersonal, oscillating energy force that transcends time and space and permeates the entire universe. Lao Tzu, the founder of Taoism, conceived the universe to be dualistic in nature. This dualistic principle eventually became known as yin/yang. Yin represents dark, female, negative, passive, wet, earth, and the inward side. Yang represents its polar opposite: light, male, positive, active, dry, sun, and outward aspects of nature. As these two principles constantly interact with each other and saturate all that exists, one or the other may dominate. This imbalance causes chaos of all sorts, ranging from disease in the body to war among nations. For example, if there is a disproportionate amount of yin or yang within a human body, sickness results. To bring things back into balance, one may seek help from an acupuncturist who inserts needles into the skin at certain key points to disrupt the flow of yin/yang and rebalance whichever one is in excess. Another ailing person may visit a mesmerist who will use magnetism to restore balance. Others may seek help from a New Age chiropractor who will manipulate the spine to release the unwanted energy force.

Yin/Yang is called by various names in different cultures and by different religions, but all refer to the same thing. The Japanese Buddhists refer to this vital energy as *ki*. In Confucianism it is labeled *chi*. In Hinduism

it is *prana*; Franz Mesmer called it the "heavenly tides"; the Nazis touted it as the "odic force"; Buckminster Fuller described it as "orgone"; the Kalahari Kung bushmen dub it *num*; Maharaji identifies it as *élan vital*; Czech touch therapist Zdenek Rejdak named it "bioenergy"; and New Age practitioners merely call it "life force."

The idea of a pervasive universal energy, however identified, is the basis of a pantheistic worldview.

See also BUDDHISM; PANTHEISM; TAOISM/DAOISM

Bibliography. Robin R. Wang, *Yinyang: The Way of Heaven and Earth in Chinese Thought and Culture*.

R. A. Streett

YOGA. Some claim the word *yoga* derives from *yujir*, "to yoke"; others, from *yuj*, "to contemplate." Broadly speaking, yoga is a system of psycho-physical exercises aimed at enabling a spiritual seeker, step-by-step, to attain eternal perfection and freedom. Although lesser goals are sometimes sought—paranormal powers, perfect health—orthodox teachers of yoga (gurus) usually direct their students' attention toward its highest goal: liberation (*mukti* or *moksha*). The best way to understand yoga is to become familiar with its principles, basic terminology, and varied applications.

Following the orthodoxy of today, a serious yogi (also, *yogin*, male, or *yogini*, female) is instructed in certain disciplines. The yogi receives instruction on how to control nature (*prakriti*), especially human nature; overcome desire; and transcend the ego sense (*ahamkara*). Detachment from the senses and self-mastery are regarded as essential in preparing the individual soul (*jiva*-atman) for union with the transcendental soul (*purusha*, Atman, Brahma) or for identification with it, in superconscious ecstasy (*nirvikalpa samadhi*), according to Hinduism, but Buddhists would explain this differently. The result for the individual, say gurus, is eternal liberation from ignorance (*avidya*) and from the endless cycles of births and deaths (samsara). This liberated soul (*jivanmukta*) is said to possess self-knowledge (*atmajnana* or *atmabodha*).

The practice of yoga, however, is difficult to define precisely because of the diverse approaches within the yoga tradition. Students of "classical yoga" insist that it must be understood through the teachings of Patanjali, who compiled and systematized its principles and practices in his *Yoga Aphorisms* (*Yoga Sutras*, AD 150–200). But because Patanjali was influenced by Samkhya philosophy, one of the six main philosophical systems of Hinduism, his instructions on yoga are grounded in that system's dualism. In Samkhya everything is either nature (*prakriti*) or spirit (*purusha*). Patanjali did not define the end of yoga as the union of the individual soul and the transcendental soul. For him yoga involves the restraining of mental modifications (*chitta-vritti-nirodha*) so that the yogi can attain self-mastery and liberation from *prakriti*. Also critical to the practice of yoga are his teachings on the eight limbs of yoga (*ashtanga*): an eightfold method of moral discipline (*yama*), self-control (*niyama*), steady posture (*asana*), breath control (*pranayama*), withdrawal of the senses (*pratyahara*), fixity of attention (*dharana*), unbroken meditation (*dhyana*), and liberation (*samadhi*). The first two limbs, say the best authorities, represent the ethical prerequisites for the practice of yoga.

The history of yoga further complicates the search for a definition. The word *yoga* appears as early as the Rig Veda (ca. 2500–600 BC). Evidence of the practice appears in the Upanishads (1500–500 BC), which declare that self-realization is the goal of life and that asceticism and meditation are the way to it. Further evidence appears in the Bhagavad Gita (ca. 500–400 BC). Describing yoga as "equanimity," it advises seekers to make their lives a continuous yoga and to

practice "control of the self by the self." It also synthesizes three main yogas: Karma Yoga (work), Bhakti Yoga (devotion), and Jnana Yoga (knowledge). This book, as its colophon suggests, teaches *brahmavidya* (knowledge of God) and *yoga-shastra* (knowledge of yoga).

In the centuries after Patanjali, many commentaries on his Yoga Sutras and other adaptations of yoga appeared. In the fourth century AD appeared Vyasa's Yoga Bhashya, the oldest extant commentary, in which Vyasa defines yoga as "ecstasy" (samadhi). Later commentaries derived new meanings from Patanjali's aphorisms. After the seventh century, many sought to explain the practice of yoga in light of Hindu systems other than Samkhya. After the tenth century, the system known as tantra began to leave its indelible mark on yoga. It introduced elaborations on the life force (*prana*) and seven energy centers in the body (chakras), the latter having only been hinted at in the Yoga Sutras (3.28–33). It developed the idea of the *kundalini-shakti*, the "coiled serpent power" located at the base of the spine, which the yogi learns to control through yogic disciplines. Out of tantra has arisen Hatha Yoga as it is known today. By postures and breath control, the hatha yogi strives to develop an "adamantine" or divine body. He struggles to raise the kundalini-shakti up his spinal column, awakening each chakra along the way, to the last at the crown of the head (*sahasrara*), whereupon he achieves liberation. Thereafter he lives a long life in a body made fit to bear the force of illumination. The Buddhist tantras have similar teachings, with "psychic heat" similar to kundalini, chakras, and various postures.

In the last few centuries, yoga has become dominated by Vedanta, and especially by Advaita Vedanta (nondualism), which holds that all yogas and paths lead to God. In the West, those who follow an orthodox Indian guru tend to remain closer to the Eastern traditions. Those who do not, or who follow

Western-born teachers, tend to practice less-demanding forms of yoga, ones that are more compatible with their interests in the New Age movement, modern science (e.g., quantum mechanics), holistic health, ecology, and so on.

Meanwhile, a hunger for spiritual experiences has resulted in a proliferation of yogas, some orthodox, others not. The traditionally recognized big-four yogas are Karma, Bhakti, Raja, and Jnana. Other types—one authority estimates more than forty—are Mantra Yoga (meditating on sound), Laya Yoga (intellectually dissolving the universe), Kriya Yoga (practicing asceticism, study, and devotion), and the integral yoga of Sri Aurobindo (seeking synthesis). Then there are also Kundalini Yoga, Tantric Yoga, and Maha Yoga, to name a few others. The Buddhists have such specializations as Anuyoga and Atiyoga. Despite such variety, all applications of yoga share in common an insistence on one-pointed concentration on something other than the ego-self as the one thing needful for enlightenment.

Yoga, then, is a path that requires willpower and strenuous self-exertion. Without striving to master mind and body, say gurus, seekers cannot be yogis. Nor can they expect to achieve liberation as long as they remain attached to the ego-self and its desires. According to yoga tradition, such souls remain bound by karma and ignorance, repeating endlessly the cycle of births and deaths, until they awaken and embark on the path of yoga.

See also ADVAITA; ATMAN; BHAGAVAD GITA; BHAKTI YOGA; BRAHMA; CHAKRAS; KARMA; KUNDALINI; MOKSHA; PRANA; PRANAYAMA; SAMADHI; SAMSARA; SWAMI; TANTRA; TANTRIC YOGA; UPANISHADS; VEDANTA

Bibliography. G. Feuerstein, *The Yoga Tradition: Its History, Literature, Philosophy and Practice*; Swami Prabhavananda and C. Isherwood, *How to Know God: The Yoga Aphorisms of Patanjali*; S. Radhakrishnan and C. A. Moore,

A Sourcebook in Indian Philosophy; Swami Vivekananda, *Raja Yoga*; Swami Yogananda, *The Autobiography of a Yogi*.

B. Scott

YOGANANDA, SWAMI PARAMAHANSA. Swami Paramahansa Yogananda (1893–1952) was born Mukunda Lal Ghosh in Gorakhpur, India. The name Yogananda refers to "one who has attained bliss through yoga," and in his lifetime he taught the benefits of Kriya Yoga in India and the US. In 1920 he was the Indian delegate to the International Congress of Free Christians and Other Religious Liberals held in Boston, where he spoke on the "science of religion." Later that year he established the Self-Realization Fellowship, based in Los Angeles. His most famous book, *Autobiography of a Yogi*, a perennial best seller, recounts his childhood, quest for enlightenment, and yogic practices.

See also YOGA

Bibliography. P. Yogananda, *Autobiography of a Yogi*.

R. Aechtner

YOGI. *Yogi* (feminine, *yogini*) is the term for one who practices Hindu or Buddhist meditative and ascetic techniques. The meaning of the word itself does not demand practice of the bodily postures (*asanas*) and breathing exercises (*pranayamas*) typically associated with yoga but is most commonly used in that connection.

The goal of a yogi's practice is to liberate the spirit from the restrictions of the body. This effort has been associated with a number of different religious schools, but they all seek a way to the release (*moksha*) of one's true nature from the physical world.

The following generalizations tend to apply to the life of a yogi. A yogi (1) needs to be solitary, if not reclusive; (2) must focus on spiritual attainment; (3) must observe requirements of personal righteousness (dharma); (4) must practice regularly; (5) must not call attention to himself or herself or his or her supernatural powers.

In the West, many people claim to "do" yoga as physical recreation, a highly dubious application of the term, as Mark Singleton has shown in various books, particularly his *Yoga Body: The Origins of Modern Yoga Practice*, in which he shows that what most Westerners regard as yoga originated as British Indian Army exercises that were appropriated by Indian gurus in the late nineteenth century as a way of promoting the Hindu tradition in the modern world. Yoga is far more than a simple exercise technique. In order to achieve the true goal of yoga, one must subdue one's body *and* mind, not simply learn the positions.

See also DHARMA; HINDUISM; MOKSHA; PRANAYAMA; YOGA

Bibliography. C. F. Haanel, *The Amazing Secrets of the Yogi*; Y. Ramacharaka, *Fourteen Lessons in Yogi Philosophy*; M. M. Yogi, *Science of Being and Art of Living: Transcendental Meditation*.

W. Corduan

YOGI, MAHARISHI MAHESH. *See* MAHA-RISHI MAHESH YOGI

YOGINI. *See* YOGI

YOM KIPPUR (DAY OF ATONEMENT). The name Yom Kippur means "the day of atonement." Yom Kippur is the tenth day of the Jewish month of Tishri (Tishri falls between September and October). Because the Day of Atonement is not a festival and actually extends over several days, the expression "holy season" is a better way to describe it. This holy season is also mentioned in six passages in the Bible (Lev. 16:1–34; 23:26–32; 25:8–12; Num. 29:7–11; Heb. 9:11–10:18; 13:10–16).

The Biblical Practice. In biblical practice, the Day of Atonement was to be a time of the affliction of the soul, a day of individual atonement. On this day one goat was sacrificed as a sin offering on behalf of the whole nation, and one goat was sent alive into the wilderness to remove sins. Thus the *provision* of the atonement was for all Israel. However, the *application* of the atonement was only to those who afflicted their souls.

The Jewish Observance. In the absence of a temple in which to make sacrifices, the basic tenet in modern Judaism is that human beings can achieve atonement for their sins by their own efforts. However, to enable them to do so, substitutions have been made for the biblical practices. Instead of the affliction of the soul (or in addition to it), modern Judaism practices the affliction of the body. Modern Yom Kippur is a day of fasting. In keeping with the motif of the affliction of the body, Jews practice five self-denials. First, in order to enhance spirituality, there is to be no eating or drinking. Second, because one is not to be comfortable on this day, there is to be no washing and bathing. Third, there is to be no anointing of oil, including modern-day hand and face creams. Fourth, there is to be no spousal intimacy. Fifth, because one is not to enjoy luxury on this occasion, items such as leather shoes or sandals cannot be worn. Furthermore, the rabbis taught that all the earth is holy on the Day of Atonement, so Jews must wear shoes made of rubber or canvas so they can feel that holy ground.

In the synagogue service, the book of Jonah is read because it teaches that a person cannot run away from God and also teaches the efficacy of repentance. Just as God heard the repentance of Nineveh and spared its people, he will again spare those who repent.

The rabbis teach that repentance, prayer, and charity are valid substitutes for sacrifice. However, Ultra-Orthodox Jews still practice a form of blood sacrifice. Instead of the goat, they sacrifice a chicken: a rooster for a man and a hen for a woman. Before the fowl is sacrificed, it is raised over the head and the following prayer is recited: "This is my substitute. This is my exchange. This is my atonement. This fowl will go to its death, and I shall enter into a good and long life and peace."

To this day in Israel, Yom Kippur is almost universally celebrated. Schools and shops are closed, and even the military is granted leave for the day. Because of this last practice, on Yom Kippur (October 6) in 1973, Egypt, Syria, and Iraq launched a simultaneous attack on Israel to start what was later called the Yom Kippur War.

See also JUDAISM

Bibliography. R. Posner, *The High Holy Days*; C. Roth, "Yom Kippur," in *Encyclopedia Judaica*, edited by C. Roth; H. Schauss, *The Jewish Festivals: History & Observance*; Rabbi N. Scherman, Rabbi H. Goldwurm, and Rabbi A. Gold, *Yom Kippur—Its Significance, Laws, and Prayers*; I. Singer, "Yom Kippur," in *The Jewish Encyclopedia*; M. Strassfeld, *The Jewish Holidays: A Guide & Commentary*; Y. Vainstein, *The Cycle of the Jewish Year: A Study of the Festivals and of Selections from the Liturgy*.

A. Fruchtenbaum

YONI. Yoni (literally, "source" or "origin" of life, thought of as a womb) in Hinduism is the depiction of the goddess as a female sexual organ and symbol of fertility. It usually has a "keyhole" or triangular shape and is frequently joined with Shiva's cone-shaped phallus (*lingam*). The yoni declares that, just as the female awakens the sexual energy of the male biologically, so does the goddess activate the spiritual powers of the universe. When depicted together, the yoni and the lingam represent the symbol of awakening knowledge and the union of matter and energy.

See also HINDUISM; LINGAM; SHAKTI; SHIVA

Bibliography. U. Becker and L. W. Garmer, *The Continuum Encyclopedia of Symbols*.

W. Corduan

YOUNG, BRIGHAM. Nicknamed "The Lion of the Lord," Brigham Young (1801–77) was the second president of the Church of Jesus Christ of Latter-day Saints (LDS Church or Mormon Church). This dynamic leader is probably best known for leading the Mormons to the Salt Lake Valley in 1847 and then shaping much of the doctrine in the early LDS Church.

Early Life. Born in Whittingham, Vermont, Young was the ninth of eleven children. His parents were poor farmers who moved frequently throughout upstate New York. After his mother died while he was a teenager, Young—whose formal education was limited—became a carpenter and handyman at the age of fourteen. In 1824 he joined the Methodist Church. That same year, he married Miriam Works, with whom he had two daughters before she died eight years later. Young moved to Mendon, New York, in 1829, a year before LDS founder Joseph Smith Jr. published the Book of Mormon. After two years of hearing about this book, Young was baptized and ordained an elder in the LDS Church on April 14, 1832.

When Young first met Smith in November 1832, he told the Mormon prophet that he, Young, had no purpose in life until he read the Book of Mormon. That night Smith told Young to pray, and Young began to speak in tongues. Young quickly became a stalwart in the church, desiring, as he said, to "thunder and roar out the Gospel to the nations. It burned in my bones like fire pent up. . . . Nothing would satisfy me but to cry abroad in the world, what the Lord was doing in the latter days" (*JD* 1:313).

He married Mary Ann Angell on February 18, 1834. Young was appointed a captain of two hundred men in the Zion's Camp expedition, a forty-eight-day trip in the spring of 1834 organized by Smith. The party traveled from Kirtland, Ohio, to Clay County, Missouri, to assist church members who were being threatened by the non-Mormon "Gentiles." Young's fierce loyalty to Smith in this expedition earned him the right to be ordained on February 14, 1835, as an original

Mormon apostle by the Three Witnesses to the Book of Mormon.

While Joseph Smith was imprisoned in 1838, Young took on the important role of leading the Mormons out of Missouri because of problems with the state government. They traveled to a swampland off the Mississippi River known as Commerce City, Illinois (later renamed "Nauvoo" by Smith, which supposedly meant "beautiful"). Young did not stay very long to participate in the transformation of Nauvoo. Instead, he traveled overseas to England from 1839 to 1841 to supervise the dramatic growth of Mormonism there.

When he returned to Illinois, Young was introduced to the doctrine of polygamy, or plural marriage, as revealed to him by Smith. This teaching was later recorded on July 12, 1843, in section 132 of the LDS scripture Doctrine and Covenants. Although it appears that Young may have initially been reluctant to accept the teaching—he wrote, "I could hardly get over it for a long time"—he ended up embracing the principle and eventually had at least twenty-seven wives (some scholars document as many as fifty-six) and, with sixteen of them, fifty-seven children (forty-six who lived past infancy). This teaching became important to him, as he later promised that those who denied polygamy would be "damned" (*JD* 3:266; 11:269).

Young's devotion to Smith's teachings gave him the right in 1841 to become the president of the Quorum of the Twelve Apostles and second in authority after Smith himself. Smith and Young were alike in many ways. Both were strong leaders with firm wills. Like his predecessor, Young was deeply interested in folk magic and superstition. According to historian D. Michael Quinn, Young believed in astrology and planned his early polygamous marriages "according to the moon's transit through the Zodiac" (77).

The Trek to Utah. Young was on the East Coast looking for new converts and raising money for the Nauvoo temple when Smith was killed by a mob on June 27, 1844. Although several others were attempting to become the new Mormon leader, Young was able to convince the majority of the Saints that he was the best choice.

With federal authorities after Young for counterfeiting money, it became apparent in 1845 that the Latter-day Saints would have to leave Illinois. In February 1846, Young led some twenty thousand Mormons westward in the "Mormon migration." He was able to secure promises from the US government in exchange for help in fighting the Mexican War. Young sent more than five hundred of his members westward in July. (When the group, known as the "Mormon Battalion," the only overtly religious military unit in American history, arrived in California in 1847, the war had already ended.)

In September the Mormons established winter quarters near Omaha, Nebraska. That winter, starvation and disease along with the brutally cold weather killed more than six hundred Mormons. Young continued the journey in the spring of 1847, and on July 24, the ill leader saw the Great Salt Lake Valley for the first time. He is quoted as exclaiming, "It is enough, this is the right place, drive on." He laid claim to Utah, Nevada, and sections of Idaho, Oregon, Colorado, Wyoming, New Mexico, and much of Arizona and California, totaling more than a quarter of a million square miles of land. At the time, this represented about one-sixth of America's geography. During the next three decades, Mormons—including emigrants from European nations—descended on Utah via covered wagons and handcarts and by railroad when that became possible in 1869.

Conflicts in the West. Utah became a US territory in 1850, and Young became the governor of this territory in 1851. The Mormon leader and the federal government were quite suspicious of each other, especially when authorities discovered in 1852 that the

Mormons were openly practicing polygamy. Young was suspicious of any outsiders who did not belong to his church. For instance, alarmed at the number of "Gentiles" who were being drawn west in 1849 thanks to the discovery of gold at Sutter's Mill, Young put together the Perpetual Emigrating Fund Company to financially help converts travel to the Utah territory.

By 1857 US president James Buchanan had sent twenty-five hundred troops to the territory to release Young and commission a new governor. The troops were dispatched because Buchanan believed that Young would not peacefully step down. This move, historically known as "Buchanan's Blunder," angered Young, and he declared martial law. Among other things, he had the Mormon militia, known as the Nauvoo Legion, harass the American troops by burning three supply trains. An additional three thousand US troops were then called to Utah, and Young rallied his followers by reminding them of the persecution that the Mormon people had suffered over the previous two decades. The Utah War ended in late June 1858.

The air of hostility during that time is believed to have caused the demise of the California-bound Baker-Fancher wagon train, which was made up of emigrants from Missouri and Arkansas. Young had declared martial law on August 5, 1857, forbidding anyone to travel through the Utah territory without written permission. The Mormons were also forbidden to sell food to the emigrants. On September 7, Mormons who disguised themselves as Indians, along with their local Paiute Indian accomplices, surrounded the forty-wagon train in a place called Mountain Meadows in southwestern Utah. Having run out of supplies by September 11, the emigrant leaders agreed to abandon their wagons and weapons in exchange for their freedom (they were told that the Mormons could safely rescue them from the local Indians). However, with the exception of 17 children,

the entire party, estimated to be more than 120 people, was brutally massacred by their armed Mormon escorts. Although LDS leader John D. Lee became the scapegoat and was the only one executed for the murders of what is known as the "Mountain Meadows Massacre," there has been much speculation about Young's involvement. Mormon historian Will Bagley has stated, "Claiming that Brigham Young had nothing to do with Mountain Meadows is akin to arguing that Abraham Lincoln had nothing to do with the Civil War" (379).

There is no doubt that Young lacked tolerance for those who were unfaithful to him and his leadership. He had at his disposal a group of men called the Danites who would perform bloody deeds. One of the most notorious Danites was a man named "Wild" Bill Hickman, who wrote in his book *Brigham's Destroying Angel* about thirteen murders, many of which he claimed Young ordered.

Clearly, Young was a skilled businessman and leader who had a take-charge attitude. He had barely discovered the Salt Lake Valley when he was already mapping out the structure of the city streets. On April 6, 1853, Young laid the cornerstone for the Salt Lake temple (which opened forty years later); he later dedicated three other Utah temple sites. Among his business ventures were supervising the establishment of Zion's Cooperative Mercantile Institution (ZCMI); establishing businesses involving wagon express, ferryboats, and railroads; manufacturing lumber, wool, and iron; processing sugar beets; and even operating a distillery.

Although his members were not allowed to own their land, Young had numerous real estate holdings, including two spacious homes located a block away from the Salt Lake City temple. The Beehive House (built in 1854) served as the executive mansion that Young used as territorial governor, while the Lion House (built in 1856) was home to a dozen of Young's wives. By the time he died, Young was worth at least $600,000, an unheard-of sum in those days.

Young also attempted to create an alphabet. In 1854 George D. Watt of the University of Deseret (the predecessor to the University of Utah) established the Deseret Alphabet, which was made up of thirty-eight symbols utilizing the basic sounds in English. Young pushed the exclusive alphabet on his less-than-excited followers in the hopes that this would further separate Mormons from the rest of the American society and help immigrants in their language abilities. The Book of Mormon and sections of the 1859 LDS Church–owned *Deseret News* were printed using this alphabet. However, it soon proved to be a dismal failure.

Doctrinal Teachings. Young and other LDS general authorities gave numerous sermons that were recorded from 1852 until his death and were compiled in the twenty-six-volume work called *Journal of Discourses.* Young was most prolific in his teaching, speaking with authority and even declaring, "I have never yet preached a sermon and sent it out to the children of men, that they may not call scripture. Let me have the privilege of correcting a sermon, and it is as good Scripture as they deserve. The people have the oracles of God continually" (*JD* 13:95). He also declared, "I have never given counsel that is wrong" (*JD* 16:161).

Some of his interesting doctrines as recorded in the *Journal of Discourses* include the following:

- Adam was God the Father, and Jesus was begotten not by the Holy Ghost but rather by Adam (1:50–51; 4:218; 8:115).
- God the Father was once a mortal child (1:123).
- God the Father progresses in his knowledge (6:120) and can attain greater heights of perfection (1:93).

- Blacks are inferior to whites (2:172; 7:290; 10:110).
- A person's shed blood can atone for his or her sins (3:247; 4:53–54, 219–20).
- A person who hopes to make it to the highest level of heaven needs Joseph Smith's approval (7:289).

Conclusion. Brigham Young kept an active schedule as late as June 1877. However, on August 23, he suddenly began to experience nausea, vomiting, and a high temperature. He died six days later in Salt Lake City at the age of seventy-six, reportedly with the words "Joseph, Joseph, Joseph" on his lips. A total of twenty-three of his wives survived him, with seventeen receiving a share of his estate. Today most of the world only knows the name Brigham Young because the LDS Church operates the well-respected Brigham Young University in Provo, Utah, and Rexburg, Idaho. Yet there can be little doubt that, with the exception of Mormon founder Joseph Smith Jr., nobody has had as great an influence on the Mormon religion as Brigham Young.

See also ADAM-GOD THEORY; BOOK OF MORMON; CHURCH OF JESUS CHRIST OF LATTER-DAY SAINTS; *JOURNAL OF DISCOURSES*; SMITH, JOSEPH, JR.

Bibliography. R. Abanes, *One Nation under Gods: A History of the Mormon Church*; L. Arrington, *Brigham Young: American Moses*; W. Bagley, *Blood of the Prophets: Brigham Young and the Massacre at Mountain Meadows*; F. Brodie, *No Man Knows My History*; The Church of Jesus Christ of Latter-day Saints, *Teachings of the Prophet Brigham Young*; W. A. Hickman, *Brigham's Destroying Angel*: D. M. Quinn, *Early Mormonism and the Magic World View*.

E. Johnson

ZABUR. An Arabic word from the pre-Islamic period, *zabur* referred to "writ" or "writings." Eventually, Muslims employed the term in the Qur'an to identify the revealed heavenly books (sura 3:184; 26:196) and, with its more common use, to refer in particular to the Psalms of David (4:163; 17:55; 21:105). The term is used twice in the hadith to refer to the Psalms of David (Al-Bukhari, 4.628; Al-Tirmidhi, 654). Though the Tawrat (Torah), Zabur (Psalms), Injil (Gospel), and Qur'an compose 4 of the 104 divisions of the "eternal tablet" revealed by Allah throughout history, according to Muslims the only uncorrupted revelation, which possesses highest authority, is the Qur'an.

See also ISLAM, BASIC BELIEFS OF; MUHAMMAD; QUR'AN

Bibliography. J. L. Esposito, ed., *The Oxford Dictionary of Islam*; H. A. R. Gibb and J. H. Kramers, eds., *Shorter Encyclopedia of Islam*.

J. Holden

ZARATHUSTRA (NIETZSCHE). Friedrich Nietzsche (1844–1900) appropriated the name of the sixth-century-BC Persian prophet Zarathustra (Zoroaster) for his own literary creation. *Also Sprach Zarathustra* (*Thus Spake Zarathustra*) was published in four separate parts: the first two in 1883, the second in 1884, and the fourth (after Nietzsche's mental breakdown) in 1892. This use of the name is highly ironic insofar as the historical Zarathustra (hereafter, Zoroaster) and Nietzsche's figure (hereafter Zarathustra) are antithetical to each other in many significant respects.

1. Zoroaster taught a religion that chose light over dark, and his followers extolled the sun deity Mithra. When Zarathustra decided to return to society, he said farewell to the sun and set his face to enter darkness.

2. Zoroaster asserted the reality of Ahura Mazda, the one true God. Zarathustra's message to the world was that God is dead.

3. According to Zoroaster, God, who is the truth, is opposed by the devil, who is the lie. Zarathustra believed that sometimes the devil had some truth on his side.

4. Zoroaster taught that there is an absolute distinction between good and evil, and that the destiny of human beings depends on their siding with good over evil. Zarathustra attempted to convince his listeners that they must go beyond both good and evil.

5. Zoroaster predicted a cataclysmic end to time, at which point there would be a final judgment and a final redemption for all. Zarathustra declared that time is a never-ending repetition of all events.

At the core of Nietzsche's thought is the affirmation of one's life. "My happiness ought to justify existence itself," proclaims Zarathustra to the crowd (Kaufmann, 125), and all aspects of his philosophy, including those specifically associated with Zarathustra, need to be understood along this line:

1. The death of God. When Zarathustra came down from his mountain, he was surprised to learn that not everyone had yet heard that God was dead. God, for Nietzsche, is a concept that has to be shoved aside in order for human beings to come to full realization of their humanity. As long as there is a God inflicting his standards, not to mention his cloying love and pity on human beings, they will never become what they could by themselves.

2. The transcendence of good and evil. It is not that Zarathustra wants people to do evil things or deliberately violate proper behavior. His goal is much further; he wants them to wean themselves off there being standards of good and evil altogether. Zarathustra sees human beings as trying to achieve total conformity with one another. "No shepherd and one herd! Everybody wants the same, everybody is the same: whoever feels different goes voluntarily into a madhouse" (Kaufmann, 130). Nietzsche's prophet proclaims that, instead, all people ought to choose their actions on the basis of their personal preference alone.

3. The Overman. The goal of Zarathustra's message is that human beings should eventually attain a higher stage of life, called the "Overman" (*Übermensch*, often also translated as "superman"). He declares that "man is a rope, tied between beast and Overman—a rope over an abyss" (Kaufmann, 126). Just as the human being is superior to animals, so Overman will be superior to human beings. He will have greater knowledge, greater power, and greater happiness than any present human being.

However, we need to be clear about several important items concerning Overman. First, Nietzsche is not here (or anywhere else, for that matter) talking about a "race" or "nation" of superior beings. Even though Nietzsche has sometimes been accused of being a proto-Nazi, the fact is that the only thing he detested more than nationalism in general was German nationalism. If an Overman will arise, his first distinctive will be that he is an individual, not affiliated with any "herd." Second, the Overman is not the product of biological evolution. Darwinism explains the development of races and groups through factors beyond their control, but the Overman becomes what he will be on the basis of his personal decision to assert himself and his life, in flagrant disregard of all others if necessary. Zarathustra himself is not the Overman; he points the way, but he also shows in his personal struggles how difficult it will be for anyone to become Overman.

4. Eternal recurrence. As a metaphysical doctrine, the idea of the infinite repetition of all events is highly problematic, but it would be silly to take it that way for Nietzsche. Zarathustra does present an argument on its behalf— namely, that, given an infinite amount of time, any configuration of items in the universe must be repeated an infinite number of times; but Nietzsche's point is hardly to advocate such a dubious cosmology for its own sake. Instead, he is saying that Zarathustra and all other human beings must be willing to affirm all of their lives, even the minutest and most trivial parts, to the point of being willing to live them over and over again. Think of the most

mediocre person you know or the most annoying day you have ever had, and accept that they will come around again and again an infinite number of times. Zarathustra's reaction to this idea at first is nausea, but he slowly learns to accept it.

Zarathustra is an interesting literary creation, representing both the struggles and the arrogance of Nietzsche's thought. It is hard not to get caught up in the humor of the parodies or the exaggerated pathos of this prophet. However, if one steps back and looks at Zarathustra's message with discernment, one should wonder why anyone should accept his ideas. There is neither rational grounding nor hope, only a desperate attempt at self-assertion, which ultimately can be nothing more than an empty cry into an empty void.

See also ZOROASTER; ZOROASTRIANISM

Bibliography. W. Kaufmann, ed., *The Portable Nietzsche*.

W. Corduan

ZEN BUDDHISM. Zen claims to contain the essence of Buddhism, that enlightenment is achievable not merely in this lifetime but here and now. Derived from Chinese Ch'an, and etymologically from the Sanskrit *dhyana* ("mind training" / meditation), *Zen* (as a noun) refers to a rigorous, disciplined meditation system, but it is routinely used adjectivally to mean spontaneous yet disciplined, tranquil yet rigorous, engaged yet detached, and overall spiritually uplifting— amazon.com lists books on everything from Zen golf to Zen cooking, from Zen motorcycling to Zen sex.

Ch'an Buddhism came to China through the introduction of dhyana by the Indian Buddhist monk Bodhidharma in AD 520, joining Taoism and Confucianism in spiritual dialogue and becoming associated with the martial arts. It had taken root as Zen in Japan

by the twelfth century. The characteristics of the enlightened mind—namely, peacefulness, fearlessness, and spontaneity—have had a lasting influence on Japanese culture.

Zen is based on the Perfection of Wisdom sutras, the Diamond Cutter Sutra, and other Mahayana texts. Zen has in common with Mahayana Buddhism the belief that everyone has the potential to achieve enlightenment, but this lies dormant because of ignorance. However, Zen uniquely proposes that this Buddha potential is awakened not so much by the accumulation of merit, the study of scripture, paying homage to images, or the practice of rites and ceremonies but rather by a sudden breaking through the boundaries of logical thought. Thus enlightenment (satori) is an individual intuitive experience that is indescribable, as it is beyond the constructs of reason, logic, or language. It is claimed that this is what Gautama Buddha experienced under the Bodhi tree in Bodhgaya. Zen practice is usually done in the *zendo* (meditation hall) under the guidance of a Zen master (*roshi*), but the precise path to satori varies among the three schools of Zen.

Rinzai Zen, introduced from China to Japan by Eisai in AD 1191, emphasizes meditation on paradoxical statements called koans. Originally the utterances of Chinese Ch'an masters, koans have been compiled into a number of volumes but also shortened into pithy, nonlogical statements. One does not so much study the koan as experience its nonlogic and hence transcend conceptualization in the mind—thus one breaks down the duality of subject-object, good-bad, I-you/it. In shattering duality, one realizes one's own Buddha mind and achieves satori. "The sound of one hand clapping" is a well-known koan.

Soto Zen, introduced from China to Japan by Dogen in 1227, prefers "silent illumination" or mere sitting (*zazen*), usually in the lotus position, with eyes cast down and counting one's breathing. No mental effort should be made toward enlightenment, so as to purge the mind, through silence, of all conceptualization and fantasy. The aim is to become aware of the mind's incessant activity without being drawn into it or identifying with it. There is no object on which to meditate (like a koan)—it is assumed that the mind in and of itself is pure. Therefore, the meditator's aim is to get out of the way, so that this innate Buddha-mind can manifest. Zazen claims to open the practitioner to wisdom and compassion by returning constantly to the present moment.

Obaku Zen, a later arrival in Japan (1654) combines the Rinzai practice of koan with the Pure Land Buddhist practice of recitation of the *nembutsu*, that is, the continuous invocation of Amitabha Buddha.

Zen priests have been influential in the history and culture of Japan, serving as diplomats and administrators. Zen is patriotic, encouraging prayers for the emperor, and hence was influential among the samurai and informs the martial arts today. Zen monastic centers are usually self-sufficient due to the belief that a monk shouldn't eat if he doesn't work: as with other aspects of life, the work ethic comes from spontaneity and naturalness, and hence a harmonious aesthetic dominates life. Japanese art, literature, theater, poetry, flower arrangement, calligraphy, and the tea ceremony all have their roots in Zen. Formal Zen practitioners and adherents number around ten million in Japan today.

Zen became popular in the West from the 1960s onward, due to the influence of D. T. Suzuki (1870–1966), who, in being the first to attempt to repackage Zen for the West, promoted Zen as the pure experience of unmediated encounter with reality and the spontaneous living in harmony with that reality—in essence, the mystical experience he believed was common to all the world's religions. New lineages (master-disciple relationships) have been established since then—the Diamond Sangha being a notable one, established in 1959 by Robert Aitken and based in Hawaii. Strong Zen centers in the US have been influential (for example, the San Francisco Zen Center), although these have not been without their scandals.

The strongest school in the US is Soto, although the first established was Rinzai. Western Zen is marginalizing the Japanese cultural elements of Zen, deemphasizing the doctrinal, philosophical, and ritualistic elements, while the Western roshis are steering Zen toward meditation practice alone, consistent with Suzuki's initial agenda. As with most Buddhist lineages in the West, there is a significant degree of cross-pollination between Zen schools, but also with *vipassana* (insight meditation from within Theravada Buddhism), due to their common practice of meditation. Zen practitioners may often embrace other non-Zen practices, including elements of Western psychology, hence becoming syncretistic and eclectic. Most Zen practitioners are Caucasian, affluent, and university educated, and remain lay, fitting their practice into hectic schedules, often punctuating the year with longer *sesshins*, or retreats.

A new generation of Western Zen teachers is emerging, who show charismatic leadership and a serious commitment to transmission of the dharma. Some have had extensive training in Japan and are fluent in several Asian languages. Some have been initiated into a number of Buddhist traditions. Teaching is often formalized in popular retreats that are supported by a plethora of commodities, specifically *zafus* (meditation cushions) and books. Some teachers have specialized; for example, Roshi Bernard Glassman is a proponent of Engaged Buddhism, promoting a proactive involvement in social issues. A Zen *sangha* has struggled to form in the West due to issues of work, child raising, and authority. Practitioners are experimenting with innovations, notably the possibility of hybridizing with the Unitarian Universalist churches of America.

See also BUDDHISM; DHARMA; KOAN; MA-HAYANA BUDDHISM; SANGHA; SATORI; TAOISM/DAOISM

Bibliography. C. Humphreys, *Zen Buddhism*; C. S. Prebish and M. Baumann, *Westward Dharma: Buddhism beyond Asia*; C. S. Prebish and K. K. Tanaka, *The Faces of Buddhism in America*; D. T. Suzuki, *An Introduction to Zen Buddhism*.

H. P. Kemp

ZEND-AVESTA. *See* AVESTA

ZHUANG-ZI/CHUANG-TZU. The Taoist holy book Zhuang-zi ("Master Zhuang"; also spelled Chuang-tzu) has been an integral part of Chinese religion and philosophy since it was written more than two millennia ago. Though traditionally the entire volume (consisting of thirty-three chapters) was ascribed to Zhuang-zi (ca. fourth century BC), most contemporary scholars of ancient Chinese history think it more likely that Zhuang-zi authored only the first seven chapters and that various of his students and other thinkers influenced by his teachings wrote the remainder of the book. Broadly speaking, Zhuang-zi's thought can be characterized as skeptical and pluralistic. One of his main arguments is that since human perceiving and knowing are both severely limited and heavily influenced by linguistic and cultural factors, people should refrain from making universal value judgments and be cautious in drawing sweeping conclusions about most matters. He also contends that each person's innate behavioral dispositions, in conjunction with that individual's unique life experiences, create proclivities to interpret and evaluate the world that must not be accepted or employed uncritically. This approach to epistemology is exemplified in the second chapter of the text in a section often referred to as the Butterfly Dream.

Here it says that Zhuang-zi had a dream in which he was a butterfly and did not realize his personal identity. After waking, he was unsure whether he was Zhuang-zi (and merely had dreamed of being a butterfly) or was actually a butterfly having a dream of being Zhuang-zi.

See also TAOISM/DAOISM

Bibliography. T. C. Chung, *The Dao of Zhuangzi: The Harmony of Nature*; S. Coutinho, *Zhuangzi and Early Chinese Philosophy: Vagueness, Transformation and Paradox*; C. Hansen, "Zhuangzi," in *The Stanford Encyclopedia of Philosophy*, https://plato.stanford.edu/archives/spr2017/entries/zhuangzi/; H. D. Roth, "Who Compiled the Chuang-tzu," in *Chinese Texts and Philosophical Contexts*, edited by H. Rosemont; Roth, ed., *A Companion to Angus C. Graham's Chuang Tzu*; B. Watson, trans., *Zhuangzi: Basic Writings*.

H. W. House

ZION, MORMON BELIEFS ABOUT. According to Mormon teaching, Zion is primarily the name that God gives to his people, but it has other definitions as well. In the period that is called the "latter days" as commenced by LDS founder Joseph Smith Jr., Zion refers to the Church of Jesus Christ of Latter-day Saints; all of North and South America is said to make up the land of Zion. Smith specifically declared that Jackson County, Missouri—a place where Adam lived on the American continent, according to LDS teaching—would become the site of the New Jerusalem, or the City of Zion. This New Jerusalem is distinct from the city of Jerusalem in Palestine. Together these two cities will become capitals for the kingdom of God during the millennial reign of Jesus (Doctrine and Covenants 45:66–67; 57:2; 58:7). A special temple location in Independence, Missouri, was specified by Smith in 1832 as he declared that "this generation shall not all pass away until an house shall be built unto the Lord" (Doctrine and Covenants 84:4–5).

Mormon leaders, including apostle Orson Pratt in 1870, believed that this temple would be completed in that generation. However, it was never built. Today a small splinter group called the Church of Christ (Temple Lot), also known as Hedrickites, owns the land designated for the temple.

See also CHURCH OF JESUS CHRIST OF LATTER-DAY SAINTS; PRATT, ORSON; SMITH, JOSEPH, JR.

Bibliography. B. R. McConkie, *Mormon Doctrine*; Joseph Fielding Smith, *Doctrines of Salvation*.

E. Johnson

ZIONISM. Zionism was and still is an international movement advocating the return of the Jewish people to their ancestral homeland in Israel, together with the consequent restoration of Jewish sovereignty in Palestine. Zionism derives from the Hebrew word *Tsion*, the name of the hill in Jerusalem where the third Jewish monarch, King Solomon, constructed the Jewish temple, though the location of Zion changed to various locations in Jerusalem during the centuries. For many Jews, Zion came to represent the entire political and religious existence of Israel itself and encapsulated the desire of Jews—conquered and dispersed first by the Babylonians in 586 BC and later by the Romans in AD 68—to return to their homeland.

Theodor Herzl and Early Zionism. Like the term *Zion*, modern Zionism from the beginning included both political and religious elements. Though there were many antecedent figures, the father of modern Zionism was Theodor Herzl. Born in 1860, Herzl moved with his family to Vienna, where he ultimately earned a doctorate in law. A talented writer and journalist, Herzl encountered anti-Semitism, both personally at the university and in the surrounding culture in Paris, where he worked as a journalist. Though at first Herzl believed anti-Semitism could be addressed through Jewish-gentile dialogue, the pogroms in Russia and events such as the Dreyfus case (in which a French military officer was falsely accused and convicted of a crime because he was Jewish) convinced him that anti-Semitism was endemic to all humankind, and thus a more radical solution was needed. Herzl's political answer came in his book *The Jewish State* in 1896, wherein he argued that Jews must unite as one people and establish a Jewish state with the help and consent of the world powers. He proposed a Zionist organization to work toward the practical realization of this goal. Though many leaders were less than enthusiastic, the Jewish masses in Eastern Europe responded favorably, and the first of six Zionist Congresses was convened in Basel, Switzerland, in 1897. Herzl attempted to obtain a charter for an Israeli state in Palestine but was blocked by Turkey, which ruled Palestine at the time. However, the Zionist movement led a number of Jews who had suffered persecution in Eastern Europe to emigratine to Palestine in the late nineteenth and early twentieth centuries.

After the defeat of the Ottoman Turks in World War I, Great Britain supported the establishment of a Jewish homeland in Palestine, and the League of Nations approved a British mandate over Palestine in 1922. Members of the Zionist movement advised the British and Jewish settlers, who continued to pour into the land, farming and building up the cities.

After World War II. The horrifying nature of the Nazi persecution of European Jews and the consequent Holocaust convinced many Jews that only the Zionist realization of a homeland could provide them with security. They flooded into Israel despite the efforts of Britain and the surrounding Arab countries to contain them. The Holocaust also made nations more sympathetic to the Jewish plight, resulting in the United Nations' partitioning of Palestine into Jewish and Arab states in 1947. When Britain gave up its mandate in May 1948 and Zionists proclaimed an Israeli state, the Arab League nations attacked unsuccessfully, and warfare ceased in 1949 under UN mediation. Despite several wars between Israel and its Arab neighbors and constant terrorism, the Zionist movement has realized its primary goal of establishing a nation state for the Jewish people. Zionism, with its doctrine of a self-determining Jewish state where all Jews are welcome, continues to be a force that unites secular and religious, conservative and liberal Jews in Israel and around the world to the present day.

See also JUDAISM

Bibliography. The American-Israeli Cooperative Enterprise, "Israel: Zionism," Jewish Virtual Library, http://www.jewishvirtuallibrary.org/zionism; I. Epstein, *Judaism*; J. Phillips, *Exploring the World of the Jew*.

H. W. House

ZOHAR. The Zohar (whose full title, Sefer ha-Zohar, means literally "book of splendor") is the best-known and most influential text of kabbalah, the Jewish mystical tradition. Its main body was most likely written by a Spanish Jew named Moses de León and distributed by him around AD 1285.

Kabbalah has two main strands: the speculative, which involves the contemplation of God and of the emanation of beings from him, and the methodical, which teaches the techniques for achieving a vision of God. The Zohar falls mainly into the first category, providing an insider's knowledge into the state of the universe. The life of the mystical adept is essentially an outworking of the truths about God and the world, not an implementation of techniques.

The Zohar is written in Aramaic. It includes more than twenty treatises of varying subject matter, length, and style. However, Gershom G. Scholem, undoubtedly the most respected scholar of kabbalah of the twentieth century, argued that almost all of them bear the direct imprint of de León's hand. Most of the treatises are either commentaries on the Bible or cosmological speculations. What unites them is that they purport to have been disclosed by Rabbi Simeon ben Yohai, who lived in Palestine in the second century AD, a claim that is undoubtedly spurious.

As indicated above, the Zohar covers a number of subjects, but it does maintain a fairly consistent understanding of God and the universe, which serves as esoteric knowledge for the truly pious person. The most important features are the following:

1. *En sof*. This term refers to God as he is in himself. God is one. He is all. There can be no other being beside himself.

2. The *sefiroth*. God has disclosed himself by way of a set of emanations, called the *sefiroth* (or *sephirot*). These are not creatures or angels or just manifestations of God; they are God. Their translated names are supreme crown, understanding, knowledge, judgment, beauty, love, splendor, foundation, endurance, kingdom. They do not appear in one long string but follow a more complex, double pattern, in which beauty connects with most elements on both sides.

3. Creation. Creation does not constitute a second kind of being alongside God. Despite appearances to the contrary, creation is also ultimately a direct self-giving of God. Consequently, as the pious Jew obeys the Torah in all respects, even without mystical pursuits, he makes contact with God in all phases of his life. Perhaps this "democratic" aspect of the Zohar contributed to its exceptional acclaim over the centuries.

4. *Sitra ahra*. This is "the other side," the reality of evil. A part of the Zohar's surprising teaching is that evil is not completely external to God but arose when the side of God manifesting

wrath and judgment severed itself from the side of love and grace.

5. *Devekuth*. The person who understands all the requisite mysteries and lives by them may eventually achieve a direct union (but not identity) with God, called *devekuth*.

See also DEVEKUTH; KABBALAH; MYSTICISM

Bibliography. G. Scholem, *Major Trends in Jewish Mysticism*.

W. Corduan

ZOROASTER. Zoroaster (Greek; Persian: Zarathustra) was a poet and philosopher, born in northeastern Persia (Iran) as part of the Spitama family. Very little is known about his life, except from his writings, specifically his Divine Songs, the Gathas. When he lived is debated by scholars, as the Gathas give no clue. The range of possible times for his birth spans nearly a thousand years, from 1500 to 550 BC. Although his birthplace is often said to be in eastern Persia/Iran, it may also have been in Afghanistan (farther east) or Turkmenistan (farther north).

In his poetry, Zoroaster wrote that he was a spiritual seeker during his teens and young adulthood, but at age thirty he received the "revelation" about the god Ahura Mazda and how to attain salvation that would become known as Zoroastrianism. Zoroaster's converts were at first few, the first being his cousin, Maidhyoimanha. His new offer of salvation to anyone who would follow his teachings angered the established religious hierarchy and caused suspicion among the general populace. Because of his controversial new faith, he faced major persecution in virtually every country to which he traveled, causing his family and disciples to move often.

At age forty-two, Zoroaster received an audience with King Vishtaspa, in a region of northeastern Persia, near the Aral Sea. The king, along with his wife, Queen Hutaosa, and their children, converted to Zoroaster's philosophical religion of "good words, good thoughts, and good deeds." The king then urged his subjects to convert as well, and Zoroaster and his system came into favor. Tradition states that Zoroaster lived to old age, dying at seventy-seven, peacefully, in his sleep.

His philosophy predated so-called positive mental attitudes by thousands of years. He believed that goodness and evil were not innate but the freewill direction of the thoughts of the individual. To become a morally correct being, a person must create goodness in his mind, and the transfer from thought to deed comes naturally.

Zoroaster is not to be confused with the fictional character Zarathustra in *Thus Spake Zarathustra*, by Friedrich Nietzsche, in which Nietzsche develops his personal philosophy through his literary figure.

See also AHURA MAZDA; AVESTA; DUALISM; GATHAS; ZARATHUSTRA (NIETZSCHE); ZOROASTRIANISM

Bibliography. M. Boyce, *Zoroastrians: Their Religious Beliefs and Practices*; A. Jafarey, *Good Conscience: The Rational Religion of Zarathushtra*; M. L. West, *The Hymns of Zoroaster: A New Translation of the Most Ancient Sacred Texts of Iran*; Zoroastrian Association of Greater New York, *The Good Life: An Introduction to the Religion of Zarathushtra*.

Ergun Caner

ZOROASTRIANISM. Zoroastrianism is an ancient monotheistic religion centered in Persia (modern Iran) and is named for its founder, Zoroaster (Persian: Zarathustra). It centers on the ancient dualistic struggle of the good creator god Ahura Mazda and the evil spirit Angra Mainyu. Humans participate in this struggle by remaining pure and following the teachings of the religion's founding prophet, Zoroaster.

History. No one is sure when Zoroaster lived and taught. Tradition and ancient sources put it as early as 6000 BC. This is most likely an exaggeration. Some argue for a date as late as 600 BC, based on a Pahlavi text saying Zoroaster lived 258 years before Alexander's invasion. However, these texts were written in the first century AD, possibly as much as five hundred years after Alexander. Based on internal linguistic and external archaeological and sociological evidence, most scholars today date Zoroaster to between 1500 and 1200 BC. The language of the sacred writings of Zoroastrianism strongly resembles other writings from the same period and shows an intimate familiarity with the social conditions and practices of the period.

Zoroastrianism has both enjoyed official support and suffered intense persecutions throughout its history. Zoroastrians fled to northern Afghanistan and India to escape Muslim persecution, and in modern times they have sought refuge in Australia, South America, and the US. Probably due to persecution, Zoroastrianism has become a very insular religion. Zoroastrians do not proselytize, and they almost never allow those outside the religion to convert. There are approximately 145,000 to 200,000 Zoroastrians today, but due to falling birth rates, the number of Zoroastrians is expected to dramatically decrease in the next fifty years.

Beliefs. Ahura Mazda is the god of Zoroastrianism. He is the eternal and uncreated creator of the universe. He is inherently and totally good and will ultimately prevail over Angra Mainyu and his evil forces. Everything he created was good and free from evil before Angra Mainyu began to attack it. Ahura Mazda has six "emanations," called Amesha Spentas (Persian, "holy immortals") that assist him; each represents an aspect of Ahura Mazda and an element of the universe: good purpose / animals (especially cattle), truth and righteousness / fire, desirable rule / minerals, holy devotion / earth, wholeness/water, and immortality/plants. Fire and water are especially important in Zoroastrianism. Adherents normally pray in the presence of fire

(or any source of light) because they see it as a medium through which spiritual wisdom flows. As Zoroastrianism developed, fire temples began to be used to preserve sacred fires and serve as gathering places for Zoroastrians to worship. Although all the elements should be kept pure, water, as the source of wisdom, is carefully protected from defilement.

In Ahura Mazda's continual struggle against the forces of evil, his principal antagonist is Angra Mainyu, who constantly seeks to bring disorder and destruction to Ahura Mazda's creation. It is not an eternal battle, for Ahura Mazda will eventually prevail and evil will end.

Humankind is the chief creation of Ahura Mazda, and as such its chief goal according to Zoroastrianism is keeping evil at bay through good thoughts, good words, and good deeds. Good thoughts and words consist of worshiping Ahura Mazda and venerating the Amesha Spentas. Good deeds consist of keeping oneself from becoming defiled through a highly organized and detailed set of purity laws. Some of these include destroying "impure" or harmful creatures (like toads and wasps), avoiding the flow of blood, performing cleansing rituals involving washing with increasingly pure substances (starting with cattle urine, then sand, then water), and avoiding contact with dead things (especially the bodies of the righteous because it is thought that evil spirits concentrate around the righteous in an effort to hamper them). Because of their belief in the impurity of dead things, Zoroastrians do not bury their dead. Rather, they construct towers of stone and allow the bones to bleach in the sun at the top of the tower. The bones are then placed inside the tower and dissolved with acid.

Zoroastrians are also expected to pray at appointed times during the day, and especially at midnight, when it is believed the forces of evil are at the height of their power. The most important prayer, akin to the Lord's Prayer in Christianity, is the Ahunvar. It is the first prayer a Zoroastrian child learns, saying, "He [Ahura Mazda] is as much the desired Master as the Judge according to asha. [He is] the doer of the acts of good purpose, of life. To Ahura Mazda [is] the kingdom, whom they have established as pastor for the poor" (Boyce, 34–35).

There are seven festivals celebrating Ahura Mazda and the six Amesha Spentas. They are spread through the year and generally correspond to agricultural and celestial events (e.g., the equinoxes, planting, harvest).

Zoroastrians believe that a person's good and evil will be weighed at death. If the person's good outweighs the bad, that person is escorted across a bridge by a beautiful maiden into paradise. If the bad outweighs the good, the bridge becomes as narrow as a knife edge, and the person is dragged by a horrible hag into hell. Hell is a place not of suffering but of nonfeeling, lacking both joy and sorrow. Paradise is not perfect, however,

for happiness can be achieved only with the reunion of the spirit and the body.

At the end of time (called *frashegird*, meaning "renovation" or "healing"), when evil has been totally overcome and the universe is returned to its original perfection, Ahura Mazda will resurrect all people. He will melt all the gold in the world and with it purge the world of evil. Zoroastrian teaching says, "The righteous will wade as if through warm milk, and the evil will be scalded." Once again people will be judged, but this time those whose deeds were more evil than good will be punished, then forgiven. All people will be made immortal and will no longer suffer hunger, sickness, or death, but will live in the presence of Ahura Mazda for eternity.

See also AMESHA SPENTAS; AVESTA; DUALISM; SACRED FIRE; ZOROASTER

Bibliography. M. A. Boyce, *Zoroastrians: Their Religious Beliefs and Practices*; G. W. Carter, *Zoroastrianism and Judaism*.

R. L. Drouhard

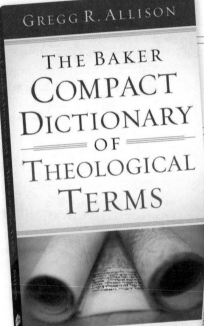
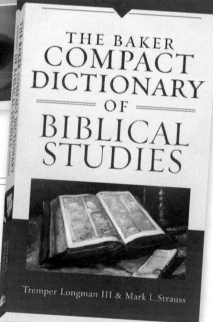